Movie Characters of Leading Performers of the Sound Era

Movie Characters of Leading Performers of the Sound Era

ROBERT A. NOWLAN

and

GWENDOLYN WRIGHT NOWLAN

American Library Association

Chicago and London / 1990

Cover designed by Jim Lange

Text designed by ALA Books staff

Type prepared by ALA Books using a BestInfo Wave 4 pre-press system and an NEC 890 laser printer

Printed on 50-pound Glatfelter,
a pH-neutral stock, and bound in
10-point Carolina cover stock by
Malloy Lithographing, Inc.

The paper used in this publication meets the minimum requirements of American National Standard for Information Sciences—Permanence of Paper for Printed Library Materials, ANSI Z39.48-1984. ♾

Library of Congress Cataloging-in-Publication Data

Nowlan, Robert A.
Movie characters of leading performers of the sound era / by Robert A. Nowlan and Gwendolyn Wright Nowlan.
p. cm.
ISBN 0-8389-0480-7
1. Characters and characteristics in motion pictures—Dictionaries. 2. Film adaptations—Dictionaries. 3. Motion picture actors and actresses—Biography—Dictionaries. I. Nowlan, Gwendolyn Wright, 1945– II. Title.
PN1995.9.C36N69 1989
791.43′09′0927—dc19 88-37686
CIP

Printed in the United States of America.

93 92 91 90 5 4 3 2 1

For our fathers,

Robert Anthony Nowlan, Sr.

and

Ray Newton Lawson, M.D.

Contents

For our fathers,

Robert Anthony Nowlan, Sr.

and

Ray Newton Lawson, M.D.

Contents

Preface

Mention Scarlett O'Hara, Quasimodo, Fletcher Christian, or Longfellow Deeds, and most movie fans will picture Vivien Leigh at Tara in **Gone with the Wind**, Charles Laughton or perhaps Lon Chaney, Sr., as the deaf, grotesque bell-ringer in **The Hunchback of Notre Dame**, dashing Clark Gable swearing that Captain Bligh will give no more orders in **Mutiny on the Bounty**, or Gary Cooper proving that he's not crazy in **Mr. Deeds Goes to Town**.

No doubt the actors and actresses whose careers are detailed in this book were all interesting people, but we suspect we would be somewhat disappointed if we had actually met them. It is the characters they portrayed that have come to mean so much to us, rivaling our parents and teachers in educating us about ourselves and about life. Whereas early in our lives we chose movies strictly for their entertainment value, later we found many which informed and forced us to view things in new and revealing ways. While some films taught us to hate and stereotype, others demanded that we reassess our beliefs and question our prejudices. We laughed, we cried, we got angry. We were delighted, incensed, shocked, appalled, titillated, touched, and inspired. We came to see the motion picture as an important art form and the performers as artists who made us believe they were who they seemed to be.

We acknowledge that in one way or another, each of the following has contributed to the way we are and therefore to the way the book is: Marion Nowlan, Gertrude Lawson, Katie Nowlan, Maggie Shields, Paul and Marilyn Montlick, Robert Andrew Nowlan, Ruth Kindersley, Andrew Wright, Elnora Potter, Pam and Marty Anisman, Annabel Lee, Esther Anderson, Gennaro and Miss Tina, Milko Jeglic, Daddy Mac, Poke, Georgie and Jimmy McGoon, Ed and Amy Nowlan, John and Gay Evans, Evan Wright, Dan and Sharon Ort, Mackay Barron, Rod and Sarah Lane, Philip Nowlan, Laura DeMartino, Leonard Goss, Watson and Jean Evans, Marion and Howard Wright, Mary and Bill Corcoran, Jennifer Nowlan, Bud Stone, Marty and Steve Johnson, Andy and Polly Fiddler, Ann Demsky, James Stasheff, Frank and Marge Lawson, Ted Sands, Mary Nowlan, Grace Kelly, Bob Thomas, Ray and Mollie Lawson, Sandy and Kerry Grant, Manson and Debbie Jennings, Helen Bass, Tom and Miggsie Lawson, Roland Chamblee, Rae and Rocco Orlando, Mike and Kitty Nowlan, Claire Bennett, Anne, Peter and Joe Lawson, Theodore Hesburgh, Ellen Tillotson, Dan and Lynn Nowlan, Ross and Gail Anderson, Ron Malooley, Steve Nowlan, Mariellen Black, Dorothy Schrader, Ann Farncomb, Sonny Detherage, the Chicago Cubs, Mary Gale, Shirley Nowlan, Phyllis and Lloyd Hisey, Jack Morante, Chris Melz, Jim Countryman, Hattie, Rachel and Ansel Garcia, Walter Petroskey, Gwennie and Don Sutherland, the Dominican nuns at St. Laurence Parochial School, and the Carmelite priests at Mt. Carmel High School. There are many others who might also be mentioned but, as is the case with our entries for the performers in the book, the list must be restricted to a manageable number.

We have researched our entries as carefully as possible, using the *New York Times* movie reviews and *Variety* as our main sources, although hundreds of other books and periodicals have proved very helpful in locating the names of the more than 20,000 characters portrayed by our featured performers. Still, we realize that we may have missed a film or character now and then, and would appreciate having these unintentional exclusions pointed out to us along with the authoritative sources where the missing information can be found. Amazingly, we have found many discrepancies in reputable sources as to whether a performer did or did not appear in a particular film. We have chosen not to list such an actor or actress as part of the cast of the movie if we could not find definitive evidence that he or she did work in the picture. In the case of a movie released under more than one title, the original title is listed first, followed by the subsequent release title.

By ''leading performers'' we do not mean merely those who have attained ''star'' status or those who have been considered romantic leads for most of their careers. The chosen actors and actresses are those who, for most of their careers, have played an important part in carrying the story of the movies in which they appeared. Some have had careers of such length that they began as extras, moved up to bit parts, became second leads and finally leads.

We recognize that many of our readers will disagree with some of our choices, believing that a particular actor or actress is more deserving of inclusion than some that do appear. While we feel confident that we can defend about 85 percent of our selections, we admit that the other 15 percent could easily be replaced by other performers of equal or perhaps even superior credentials. Readers may also disagree with our choices of key roles, insisting that a film and character relegated to the ''other role'' category would be more appropriately included with those that are more fully described. Anticipating these disagreements, we will be delighted to hear from our readers with their suggestions and arguments for performers and key roles to appear in the next edition of this work. As many of the performers included in this volume are still active, revisions will be necessary a few years down the road to reflect the new films these and other performers have made. At such time, other actors and actresses can be added to our roster and new key roles can be described.

Some 450 actors and actresses have been selected, and for each there is a brief biographical sketch followed by a list of *key roles* including descriptions of the characters played by the performer. *Key roles* is not meant to be synonymous with best roles. In some cases they include examples of the worst work of the performer. Instead, these represent the film milestones of the artist, his or her typical performances, changes of pace, award-winning roles, critically acclaimed appearances, disastrous performances—in short, a sampling of the actor's or actress's career in films. Following the key roles is a list of *other roles* of the performer, listing the character names of his or her remaining film appearances in chronological order.

As there are so many performers to choose from, we have been forced to set some limitations on this volume, including only ''leading performers of the sound era.'' This requires the exclusion of actors and actresses who spent the greatest part of their film careers making silent movies. However, several of those included in the book started with silents and continued to be successful in talkies. Regrettably, the many marvelous character actors, who often made the difference in the quality of a movie, are excluded by this criterion. We hope to feature these wonderful performers in another work, a volume dedicated to the supporting players and star character actors.

We wish to thank Herbert Bloom, Bettina MacAyeal, and the staff of ALA Books for their expert, thoughtful, and enthusiastic participation in the planning and production of the work. This project has been a labor of love and we hope that our readers will find the results interesting and useful.

We will never forget Harold Hill, Otis B. Driftwood, Margo Channing, Will Kane, Kay Miniver, Dorothy Gale, and many other memorable characters from the movies. This book is a tribute to those marvelous characters portrayed by the leading performers of the sound era.

Movie Characters of Leading Performers of the Sound Era

ABBOTT, BUD

(William Abbott, 1895–1974)

COSTELLO, LOU

(Louis Cristillo, 1906–1959)

Vaudeville comedians Bud Abbott and Lou Costello were famous for their fast-paced routines in which Abbott was speaking figuratively and Costello was taking it literally. Their film debut was in ONE NIGHT IN THE TROPICS (1940). The general premise of their comedy never changed over the years. Neither was very bright, but Abbott was able to manipulate simpleton Costello into some crazy and often—for Costello—dangerous escapades. As the years wore on, their act continued beyond their friendship and in the latter part of their career it was apparent that they didn't want to work together anymore.

KEY ROLES

Slicker Smith and Herbie Brown / BUCK PRIVATES, 1941, Universal, d-Arthur Lubin.

The boys enlist in the army by mistake. Abbott is a classic goldbrick and Costello has two left feet and still they become heroes.

Smokey Adams and Pomeroy Watson / IN THE NAVY, 1941, Universal, d-Arthur Lubin.

Having almost ruined the army, the boys do the same for the navy. In this one, Costello proves to Abbott that 28 divided by 7 is 13. In a later movie, Abbott demonstrates this little known fact of arithmetic to Costello.

Chuck Murray and Ferdinand Jones / HOLD THAT GHOST, 1941, Universal, d-Arthur Lubin.

When the boys find themselves stranded in an apparently haunted house, Costello and Joan Davis scare themselves silly in a hilarious sequence featuring a moving candle.

Eddie Harrington and Albert Mansfield / IN SOCIETY, 1944, Universal, d-Jean Yarborough.

Abbott and Costello do their "Bagel Street" routine, and poor Costello gets pummelled each time he mentions the street, in this story about plumbers who ruin a mansion.

Dexter Broadhurst and Sebastian Dinwiddle / THE NAUGHTY NINETIES, 1945, Universal, d-Jean Yarborough.

Abbott and Costello foil a gang of card sharks who have won a showboat in a crooked game. They also run through their classic "Who's on First" routine. For the benefit of those not familiar with the St. Louis team: Who's on first, What's at second, I Don't Know holds down the hot corner, I Don't Care (aka I Don't Give a Damn) is at short, the catcher is Today, Tomorrow is pitching, Why roams left field, and Because is in center. No right fielder is mentioned.

Cuthbert / Dr. Greenway and Horatio Prim / THE TIME OF THEIR LIVES, 1946, Universal, d-Charles Barton.

Costello and Marjorie Reynolds are revolutionary ghosts cursed to be confined to an estate until someone proves that they weren't British spies. Back in Revolutionary times they were mistakenly thought to be spies so they were shot, their bodies were thrown in a well, and they were cursed to spend eternity there. Abbott is the descendent of the one responsible for their deaths.

Chick Young and Wilbur Grey / ABBOTT AND COSTELLO MEET FRANKENSTEIN, 1948, Universal-International, d-Charles Barton.

In this one they meet the Baron's monster, not the Baron. But their titles are often misleading; in ABBOTT AND COSTELLO GO TO MARS, they end up on Venus.

Slim and Tubby / ABBOTT AND COSTELLO MEET DR. JEKYLL AND MR. HYDE, 1953, Universal-International, d-Charles Lamont.

The boys are dumb "bobbies" who run into a monster. Costello gets some of the infamous serum and becomes a pint-size Mr. Hyde who scares only himself.

OTHER ROLES

1940: *themselves* / ONE NIGHT IN THE TROPICS. **1941:** *Blackie Benson and Heathcliffe* / KEEP 'EM FLYING. **1942:** *Duke and Willoughby* / RIDE 'EM COWBOY; *Doc and Wishy* / RIO RITA; *Algey Shaw and Wellington Phlug* / PARDON MY SARONG; *Chick Larkin and Mervyn Melgrim* / WHO DONE IT? **1943:** *Grover Mockridge and Wilbur Hoolihan* / IT AIN'T HAY; *Flash Fulton and Weejis "Tubby" McCoy* / HIT THE ICE. **1944:** *Peter Johnson and Harvey Garvey* / LOST IN A HAREM. **1945:** *Slats and Oliver Quackenbush* / HERE COME THE CO-EDS; *Buzz Kurtis and Abercrombie* / ABBOTT AND COSTELLO IN HOLLYWOOD. **1946:** *John Morrison* / *Tom Chandler and Benny Miller* / LITTLE GIANT. **1947:** *Slicker Smith and Herbie Brown* / BUCK PRIVATES COME HOME; *Duke Eagan and Chester Wooley* / THE WISTFUL WIDOW OF WAGON GAP. **1948:** *Ted Higgins and Homer Hinchcliffe* / THE NOOSE HANGS HIGH; *Harry Lambert and Joe Bascom* / MEXICAN HAYRIDE. **1949:** *Buzz Johnson and Stanley Livingston* / AFRICA SCREAMS; *Casey Edwards and Freddie Phillips* / ABBOTT AND COSTELLO MEET THE KILLER, BORIS KARLOFF. **1950:** *Bud Jones and Lou Hotchkiss* / ABBOTT AND COSTELLO IN THE FOREIGN LEGION. **1951:** *Bud Alexander and Lou Francis* / ABBOTT AND COSTELLO MEET THE INVISIBLE MAN; *Al Stewart and Wilbert McCoy* / COMIN' ROUND THE MOUNTAIN. **1952:** *Dinklepuss and Jack* / JACK AND THE BEANSTALK; *Tom Watson and George Bell* / ABBOTT AND COSTELLO LOST IN ALASKA; *Rocky Stonebridge and Oliver Johnson* / ABBOTT AND COSTELLO MEET CAPTAIN KIDD. **1953:** *Lester and Orville* / ABBOTT AND COSTELLO GO TO MARS. **1954:** *Harry Pierce and Willie Piper* / ABBOTT AND COSTELLO MEET THE KEYSTONE KOPS. **1955:** *Pete Patterson and Freddie Franklin* / ABBOTT AND COSTELLO MEET THE MUMMY. **1956:** *Bud Flick and Lou Henry* / DANCE WITH ME HENRY.

AHERNE, BRIAN

(William Brian de Lacy Aherne, 1902–1986)

Born in England and an actor from the age of eight, Brian Aherne was known for his charm. He appeared in a number of English silent films, then was called to Hollywood after receiving rave reviews for his stage work in "The Barretts of Wimpole Street" with Katherine Cornell. Handsome, moustached Aherne played a series of urbane, sophisticated gentlemen. While never a major star, he was an accomplished actor who could be counted on to add some class to the proceedings and was simply marvelous in movies like JUAREZ.

KEY ROLES

Richard Waldrow / SONG OF SONGS, 1933, Paramount, d-Rouben Mamoulian.

Aherne is a sculptor in love with German peasant girl Marlene Dietrich, but she marries Lionel Atwill, a lecherous aristocrat.

Lewis Dodd / THE CONSTANT NYMPH, 1934, Great Britain, Gaumont, d-Basil Dean.

Aherne is a composer loved by a school-girl named Tessa. He marries her cousin, but discovers that life is unbearable without the delicate Tessa. He leaves his wife to be with her, but it's too late, she has died from a heart condition. It was typical of Aherne's career that he seldom got the girl, right or wrong for him.

Dennis Riordan / BELOVED ENEMY, 1936, Goldwyn, d-H. C. Potter.

In this story about a young Irish rebel, Aherne falls in love with the enemy: the daughter of a British conciliator (Merle Oberon). According to the film, this resulted in peace between the British and the Irish.

David Garrick / THE GREAT GARRICK, 1937, Warners, d-James Whale.

The members of the Comédie Française take light-hearted revenge on the famous English actor, stylishly played by Aherne, when he announces that the reason for his trip to Paris is to give them all an acting lesson. His impersonation of the great actor is extremely well done.

Captain Fury / CAPTAIN FURY, 1939, United Artists, d-Hal Roach.

Aherne is an Irish patriot sent to Australia to serve a prison sentence. He escapes with five other prisoners and becomes a down-under Robin Hood who dashes through danger with nonchalance and abandon. It's a wonderfully old-fashioned adventure story with Aherne, Victor McLaglen, and John Carradine in great form.

Emperor Maximilian / JUAREZ, 1939, Warners, d-William Dieterle.

Aherne was nominated for an Academy Award for his superb portrayal of the masterful but tragic puppet of Napoleon III, who was made emperor of Mexico and then abandoned. The emperor bravely went to his execution when the Mexican president, Juarez, regained command of his country. Aherne is so noble and his concern for Mexico so pure that it's hard not to wish that Juarez (Paul Muni) will accept a constitutional monarchy.

Andre Moresian / THE LADY IN QUESTION, 1940, Columbia, d-Charles Vidor.

Aherne plays a kindly, Parisian shop-keeper who sits on a jury that acquits Rita Hayworth of murder. He takes her into his home without telling his family of her background but begins to worry when his son (Glenn Ford) falls for her.

William Essex / MY SON, MY SON, 1940, United Artists, d-Charles Vidor.

Aherne struggles to escape the Manchester slums, and succeeds to become a famous writer. Wanting to provide his son with the things he had to do without, he coddles the boy and lives to regret it. When the son is a man, he believes the world owes him a living.

Willy Robertson / I CONFESS, 1953, Warners, d-Alfred Hitchcock.

Aherne is the prosecutor in the murder trial of an innocent Quebec priest (Montgomery Clift) who knows the real murderer but can't say anything because he would break the seal of confession.

Father Hyacinth / THE SWAN, 1956, MGM, d-Charles Vidor.

In a rare comedy role, Aherne is a monk and the uncle of a noblewoman (Grace Kelly) whom the family hopes to marry to the crown prince. As he dashes down a corridor in his bloomers, he makes the aside to a startled servant, "Now you know."

King Arthur / LANCELOT AND GUINEVERE, 1963, Great Britain, Emblem, d-Cornel Wilde.

Aherne loves his wife Guinevere (Jean Wallace), but he also has deep affection for Lancelot (Cornel Wilde), the knight who covets her.

OTHER ROLES

1924: *Norman Barchester* / THE ELEVENTH COMMANDMENT. **1925:** *Colin O'Farrell* / KING OF THE CASTLE; *Jim Luttrele* / THE SQUIRE OF LONG HADLEY. **1926:** *Hippocrates Rayne* / SAFETY FIRST. **1927:** *Geoffrey Maynefleet* / A WOMAN REDEEMED. **1928:** *Julian Gordon* / SHOOTING STARS. **1929:** *Bill* / UNDERGROUND. **1930:** *Col. Duncan Grant* / THE W PLAN. **1931:** *Louis Dubois* / MADAME GUILLOTINE. **1934:** *John Shand* / WHAT EVERY WOMAN KNOWS; *Lewis Allison* / THE FOUNTAIN. **1935:** *Michael Fane* / SYLVIA SCARLETT; *Terry* / I LIVE MY LIFE. **1938:** *Wade Rawlins* / MERRILY WE LIVE. **1940:** *Dr. Prescott* / VIGIL IN THE NIGHT; *Stephen Dexter* / HIRED WIFE. **1941:** *John Evans* / *Malcolm Scott* / THE MAN WHO LOST HIMSELF; *Jim Blake* / SKYLARK; *Sir John Carteret* / SMILIN' THROUGH. **1942:** *Robert Baker* / MY SISTER EILEEN. **1943:** *Jim Trimble* / FOREVER AND A DAY; *Jeff Troy* / A NIGHT TO REMEMBER; *Capt. Allan Lowell* / FIRST COMES COURAGE; *Henry Pepper* / WHAT A WOMAN! **1946:** *Dr. Blair* / THE LOCKET. **1948:** *Robert Larrimore* / SMART WOMAN; *Anthony Ridgeway* / ANGEL ON THE AMAZON. **1953:** *Captain Smith* / TITANIC. **1954:** *King Arthur* / PRINCE VALIANT; *David Canham* / A BULLET IS WAITING. **1959:** *Mr. Shalimar* / THE BEST OF EVERYTHING. **1961:** *Stanton Corbett* / SUSAN SLADE. **1964:** *Johann Strauss, Sr.* / THE WALTZ KING. **1965:** *General Braithwaite* / THE CAVERN. **1967:** *Oliver Stevenson* / ROSIE!

ALDA, ALAN

(1936–)

Son of actor Robert Alda, Alan's biggest success has been the TV series "M*A*S*H." The big-screen roles for this clever, articulate actor have rarely been memorable, but for the last several years he has been writing, directing, and starring in his own films.

KEY ROLES

George Plimpton / PAPER LION, 1968, United Artists, d-Alex March.

Alda plays author George Plimpton who, in order to collect material for a book on football, joins the training camp of the Detroit Lions. Although performing with enthusiasm for the part, Alda sometimes shows less acting ability than his pro teammates.

Myles Clarkson / THE MEPHISTO WALTZ, 1971, 20th Century-Fox, d-Paul Wendkos.

Journalist Alda inherits the soul of satanic concert pianist Curt Jurgens on the latter's death. He is also left with Jurgens's daughter (Barbara Parkins), which doesn't sit well with Alda's wife (Jacqueline Bisset), who does some fancy switching herself. It's hokum and not very good hokum at that.

George / SAME TIME, NEXT YEAR, 1978, Universal, d-Robert Mulligan.

This is a delightful two-person show, with Alda and Ellen Burstyn playing lovers who meet once a year at the same time, same place. They go through many changes but their affection for each other remains constant.

Joe Tynan / THE SEDUCTION OF JOE TYNAN, 1979, Universal, d-Jerry Schatzberg.

Alda is unfaithful to his wife (Barbara Harris) when he has an affair with Meryl Streep, but it's the sacrifice of his principles to advance his career in politics to which the title refers.

Jack Burroughs / THE FOUR SEASONS, 1981, Universal, d-Alan Alda.

Alda is one-sixth of a group of three married couples who spend a great deal of time together. When one of the men dumps his wife and replaces her with an attractive, younger woman, tension and jealousy build and threaten to ruin the enjoyable seasonal vacations the couples have taken together for so long.

OTHER ROLES

1963: *Charley Cotchipee* / GONE ARE THE DAYS. **1968:** *Lt. (jg) Morton Krim* / THE EXTRAORDINARY SEAMAN. **1970:** *Delano* / JENNY. **1972:** *Major Ritchie* / TO KILL A CLOWN. **1974:** *Martin* / THE MOONSHINE WAR. **1978:** *Bill Warren* / CALIFORNIA SUITE. **1986:** *Michael Burgess* / SWEET LIBERTY. **1988:** *Steve* / A NEW LIFE.

ALLBRITTON, LOUISE

(1920–1979)

A beautiful, sophisticated blonde, Louise Allbritton was most adept at screwball comedy, although she starred mostly in "B" movies and was assigned only second leads in big-budget films. Poised and intelligent, she quit movies shortly after marrying CBS foreign correspondent Charles Collingwood in 1946.

KEY ROLES

Elizabeth Christine Smith / GOOD MORNING, JUDGE, 1943, Universal, d-Jean Yarborough.

A music publisher slips Allbritton a Mickey Finn when he realizes that she is the attorney for a lady suing him for plagiarism.

Katherine Caldwell / SON OF DRACULA, 1943, Universal, d-Robert Siodmak.

Allbritton is an occult worshipper who marries Lon Chaney, believing him to be a Hungarian count of a very old family. Her former fiancé kills the pair for their antisocial behavior as Mr. and Mrs. Vampire.

Lillian Russell / BOWERY TO BROADWAY, 1944, Universal, d-Charles Lamont.

Allbritton is excellent as the famous 1890s star, singing "Under The Bamboo Tree" by Robert Cole and J. Rosamond Johnson. Her figure is not quite Miss Russell's famed hourglass shape but no one complains.

Dr. Toni Neva / WALK A CROOKED MILE, 1948, Columbia, d-Gordon Douglas.

Allbritton is a scientist working in a plant that is losing atomic secrets. Government agents Dennis O'Keefe and Louis Hayward suspect that she's part of the spy ring.

Rose of Cimarron / THE DOOLINS OF OKLAHOMA, 1949, Columbia, d-Gordon Douglas.

Allbritton is the operator of the dance hall and hotel where the Doolin gang hangs out when not holding up trains, banks, and stagecoaches.

OTHER ROLES

1942: *bit* / NOT A LADIES' MAN; *Helen Ames* / PARACHUTE NURSE; *Jane Claymore* / DANGER IN THE PACIFIC; *Jane Little* / WHO DONE IT?; *Shannon Prentiss* / PITTSBURGH. **1943:** *Edo Ives* / IT COMES UP LOVE; *Tig Callahan* / FIRED WIFE. **1944:** *guest* / FOLLOW THE BOYS; *Harriet* / THIS IS THE LIFE; *Sheila Winthrop* / HER PRIMITIVE MAN; *Virginia McCooley* / SAN DIEGO, I LOVE YOU. **1945:** *Isabel Glenning* / MEN IN HER DIARY; *Sheila Morgan* / THAT NIGHT WITH YOU. **1946:** *Dolores* / TANGIER. **1947:** *Harriet Putnam* / THE EGG AND I. **1948:** *Edna Philby* / SITTING PRETTY; *Margot Fraser* / DON'T TRUST YOUR HUSBAND. **1964:** *Felicia* / FELICIA.

ALLEN, WOODY

(Allen Stewart Konigsberg, 1935–   )

Woody Allen's comical genius is seen more and more in his screenplays and directing, and less and less in his acting as he appears less frequently in his films. He began as a comedy writer, along with Neil Simon and Mel Brooks, on TV's "The Sid Caesar Show" before deciding to deliver his own lines. His film work has always received mixed reviews, with some critics believing that his work is derivative. Others deplore it when he deviates from comedy and makes a serious film. Those who have enjoyed and proclaimed some of his films to be masterpieces are surely going to expect whatever he does, whatever the theme, to be first rate.

KEY ROLES

Jimmy Bond / CASINO ROYALE, 1967, Columbia, d-John Huston et al.

Allen is the nephew of retired Agent 007 in this madcap self-parodying spoof of the Bond movies, and is such a bungler that he escapes from one firing squad by jumping over a wall, only to face another one.

Virgil Starkwell / TAKE THE MONEY AND RUN, 1969, Palomar, d-Woody Allen.

In this farce, Allen is a social misfit who opts for a life of crime and, in the process, pays tribute to many of the finest gangster movies of the past including I AM A FUGITIVE FROM A CHAIN GANG. When last seen Allen is whittling a gun from a piece of soap à la John Dillinger.

Fielding Mellish / BANANAS, 1971, United Artists, d-Woody Allen.

Allen is a meek, New York failure who by accident becomes the hero of a Central American revolution and the president of that Cuba-like country.

Allan Felix / PLAY IT AGAIN, SAM, 1972, Paramount, d-Herbert Ross.

With the help of the spirit of Humphrey Bogart, neurotic film critic Allen sees Diane Keaton as his Ingrid Bergman and plays the farewell scene from CASABLANCA with her.

Alvy Singer / ANNIE HALL, 1977, United Artists, d-Woody Allen.

This film won the Academy Award for Best Picture; Allen won for his screenplay and direction but lost out as Best Actor; and Diane Keaton won for Best Actress. The story involves a neurotic, Jewish comedian who falls in love with a non-Jewish midwestern girl. They live together and he gives her a lot of books with the word "death" in the title, but she moves to Hollywood to pursue a singing career and he remains in his beloved, dreary New York.

Isaac Davis / MANHATTAN, 1979, United Artists, d-Woody Allen.

Although it is sometimes hard to distinguish Allen the actor, Allen the director, and Allen the writer, it is unnecessary to do so in this masterpiece. Allen, whose ex-wife Meryl Streep has written a best-seller about their failed marriage and her lesbian lover, is having an affair with seventeen-year-old Mariel Hemingway. Not realizing how much the girl means to him, he breaks off their relationship to be with Diane Keaton, who had been having an affair with Allen's best friend, a married professor. When Keaton decides to go back to the professor, Allen begins to understand that he really loves Hemingway, but now he must wait.

OTHER ROLES

1965: *Victor Shakapopulis* / WHAT'S NEW PUSSYCAT? **1967:** *on-screen narrator* / WHAT'S UP, TIGER LILY? **1972:** *Victor / Fabiziro / Fool / Sperm* / EVERYTHING YOU ALWAYS WANTED TO KNOW ABOUT SEX (BUT WERE AFRAID TO ASK). **1973:** *Miles Monroe* / SLEEPER. **1976:** *Boris Dimitrovitch Grushenko* / LOVE AND DEATH; *Howard Prince* / THE FRONT. **1980:** *Sandy Bates* / STARDUST MEMORIES. **1982:** *Andrew* / A MIDSUMMER NIGHT'S SEX COMEDY. **1983:** *Leonard Zelig* / ZELIG. **1984:** *Danny Rose* / BROADWAY DANNY ROSE. **1986:** *Mickey* / HANNAH AND HER SISTERS. **1987:** *narrator* / RADIO DAYS.

ALLYSON, JUNE

(Ella Geisman, 1917–)

Husky voiced and petite, June Allyson enjoyed some of her greatest box-office hits in movies with James Stewart. The hard-working actress had mainly light roles, but her goal was to be a movie star, not a great actress. Her thoughts on the matter were: "I always wanted to be a movie star. I thought it meant being famous and having breakfast in bed. I didn't know you had to be up at 4:00 a.m." Her TV movies include SEE THE MAN RUN (1972), LETTERS FROM THREE LOVERS (1973), and the pilot for VEGAS (1978).

KEY ROLES

Patsy Deyo / TWO GIRLS AND A SAILOR, 1944, MGM, d-Richard Thorpe.

Allyson and her sister (Gloria De Haven) are entertainers who turn their home into a private USO for servicemen. They are helped by donations from a young sailor (Van Johnson), loved by both, who just happens to be a millionaire.

Barbara Ainsworth / MUSIC FOR MILLIONS, 1944, MGM, d-John G. Blystone.

Allyson plays a cellist with the Jose Iturbi orchestra who is about to have a baby, but she has not heard from her serviceman husband in the longest time. She is comforted by Jimmy Durante and Margaret O'Brien in this lightweight musical.

Connie Lane / GOOD NEWS, 1947, MGM, d-Charles Walters.

Allyson isn't the flashiest girl at Tait College, but when she tutors a football star (Peter Lawford), he discovers that brains and French can be fun. Her songs include "The Varsity Drag" and "The Best Things in Life Are Free."

Jo March / LITTLE WOMEN, 1949, MGM, d-Mervyn LeRoy.

Allyson plays the oldest and most sensible of the four March sisters in the familiar Louisa May Alcott story of an ordinary family in Civil War America. Allyson couldn't compete with Katharine Hepburn, who earlier played the role, but her gumption and courage did win the praise of audiences.

Lt. Ruth McCara / BATTLE CIRCUS, 1953, MGM, d-Richard Brooks.

This movie answers the trivia question, "Which motion picture first featured a Mobile Army Surgical Hospital in Korea?" No, the answer is not M*A*S*H, but this fairly serious piece featuring Humphrey Bogart as a doctor on the make for nurse Allyson.

Helen Burger Miller / THE GLENN MILLER STORY, 1954, Universal-International, d-Anthony Mann.

Allyson has little to do in this film except look admiringly at her man, Jimmy Stewart, who portrays the great bandleader.

Ann Downs / THE SHRIKE, 1955, Universal-International, d-Jose Ferrer.

In this, her most serious role, Allyson plays a vindictive harpy who all but ruins her husband. Allyson wasn't often called on to demonstrate acting ability, but in this film she demonstrates that she was capable of giving a strong emotional performance if someone had only asked.

OTHER ROLES

1943: *Ethel* / BEST FOOT FORWARD; *herself* / THOUSANDS CHEER; *specialty number* / GIRL CRAZY. **1944:** *Annie* / MEET THE PEOPLE. **1945:** *Leslie Odell* / HER HIGHNESS AND THE BELLBOY; *Mary* / THE SAILOR TAKES A WIFE. **1946:** *Martha Canford Chandler* / TWO SISTERS FROM BOSTON; *Penny Addams* / THE SECRET HEART; *guest* / TILL THE CLOUDS ROLL BY. **1947:** *Nancy Fraser* / HIGH BARBAREE. **1948:** *Martha Terryton* / THE BRIDE GOES WILD; *Constance Bonacieux* / THE THREE MUSKETEERS; *guest* / WORDS AND MUSIC. **1949:** *Ethel Stratton* / THE STRATTON STORY. **1950:** *Kathleen Maguire* / THE REFORMER AND THE REDHEAD; *Pat O'Malley* / RIGHT CROSS. **1951:** *Cynthia Potter* / TOO YOUNG TO KISS. **1952:** *Dr. Emily Dunning* / THE GIRL IN WHITE. **1953:** *Jody Revere* / REMAINS TO BE SEEN. **1954:** *Mary Belmond Walling* / EXECUTIVE SUITE; *Katie* / WOMEN'S WORLD. **1955:** *Sally Holland* / STRATEGIC AIR COMMAND; *Pearl "Butch" Brown* / THE MCCONNELL STORY. **1956:** *Kay Hilliard* / THE OPPOSITE SEX; *Ellen Andrews* / YOU CAN'T RUN AWAY FROM IT. **1957:** *Helen Banning* / INTERLUDE; *Irene Bullock* / MY MAN GODFREY. **1959:** *Christine Beasley* / STRANGER IN MY ARMS. **1972:** *Mrs. Watkins* / THEY ONLY KILL THEIR MASTERS.

AMECHE, DON

(Dominic Felix Amici, 1908–)

Don Ameche has had a 50-year film career, and received an Academy Award for COCOON at the age of 78. When he started his career he was particularly suited to play good-natured heroes in lighthearted romances and biopics. Ameche has always been known more for his personality than his acting ability and after the war years his career in movies seemed to come to an end. But, as he explained when brought back in 1983 to appear in TRADING PLACES, he had never retired. His made-for-TV movies include RINGS AROUND THE WORLD (1966), SHADOW OVER ELVERON (1968), and GIDGET GETS MARRIED (1971).

KEY ROLES

Allessandro / RAMONA, 1936, 20th Century-Fox, d-Henry King.

Ameche is an Indian chief's son who marries a half-breed (Loretta Young) and suffers the prejudice of white homesteaders. He is killed by John Carradine when he "borrows" a horse to seek help for his sick daughter.

Jack O'Leary / IN OLD CHICAGO, 1938, 20th Century-Fox, d-Henry King.

In this deliberate attempt to one-up SAN FRANCISCO, Ameche is a lawyer who becomes mayor of Chicago, and dies in a heroic attempt to control the great fire that leveled large parts of the city caused by his mother's cow kicking over a lantern.

Charlie Dwyer / ALEXANDER'S RAGTIME BAND, 1938, 20th Century-Fox, d-Henry King.

Ameche plays a pianist who marries Alice Faye, a singer who really loves Tyrone Power. After a few years Ameche and Faye realize it can't work, and they split as friends. That's two in a row in which Ameche loses Faye to Power.

D'Artagnan / THE THREE MUSKETEERS, 1939, 20th Century-Fox, d-Allan Dwan.

Ameche is a dashing, singing D'Artagnan with the Ritz Brothers as his lackeys, taking the place of Athos, Porthos, and Aramis. A strange film, indeed.

Tibor Czerny / MIDNIGHT, 1939, Paramount, d-Mitchell Leisen.

Ameche is a taxi-driver and friend of Claudette Colbert. Colbert is hired by a jealous husband to distract a gigolo after his wife. Ameche, who loves Colbert, pretends to be her husband in this crazy adult comedy.

Alexander Graham Bell / THE STORY OF ALEXANDER GRAHAM BELL, 1939, 20th Century-Fox, d-Irving Cummings.

Ameche is the great teacher and inventive genius who comes up with the idea of the telephone after marrying a deaf woman (Loretta Young). Henry Fonda plays Mr. Watson, the inventor's assistant, to whom Ameche yells through the instrument when he burns himself with acid, "Mr. Watson, come here, I need you."

Stephen Foster / SWANEE RIVER, 1939, 20th Century-Fox, d-Sidney Lanfield.

This is an attractive, rich, early color picture, but not much is learned about the life and loves of America's great folk song composer. Ameche is quite charming in his suffering as he creates the likes of "Old Folks at Home," "I Dream of Jeannie with the Light Brown Hair," and "Old Black Joe."

Chris Bernie / FOUR SONS, 1940, 20th Century-Fox, d-Archie Mayo.

Ameche is a Czech patriot, one of four sons of Eugenie Leontovich. One brother sides with the Germans, one goes to America, and the other is a German soldier killed in the war. Mama goes to stay with her son in America.

Larry Martin / Baron Duarte / THAT NIGHT IN RIO, 1941, 20th Century-Fox, d-Irving Cummings.

As an entertainer, Ameche is paid to impersonate a count to whom he bears a remarkable resemblance. This causes some complications for the countess, Alice Faye.

Henry Van Cleve / HEAVEN CAN WAIT, 1943, 20th Century-Fox, d-Ernst Lubitsch.

In what is arguably Ameche's best film, he portrays an elderly playboy who arrives in Hades and tells his satanic majesty (Laird Cregar) of his "sins." It's as charming a movie as ever made with Ameche just perfect as the innocent roué who would like to be naughty with the ladies, but is too well-mannered to be really bad.

Lew Marsh / HAPPY LAND, 1943, 20th Century-Fox, d-Roy Del Ruth.

When Ameche's beloved only son is killed in World War II, his deceased grandfather (Harry Carey) comes back to prove that Ameche has something to live for. It's a morale-builder but a bit too sentimental.

Mortimer Duke / TRADING PLACES, 1983, Paramount, d-John Landis.

Ameche plays one of two brothers who wager on the effects of heredity versus environment, and test it by trading the places of stockbroker Dan Aykroyd with street con man Eddie Murphy. They get their comeuppance when Aykroyd and Murphy join forces and ruin them in the commodities market.

Art Selwyn / COCOON, 1985, 20th Century-Fox, d-Ron Howard.

Ameche is one of several lovable old coots who are regenerated by swimming in a pool prepared as a recovery space for aliens who had been left behind by Brian Dennehy centuries before. After demonstrating his break-dancing prowess to new bride Gwen Verdon, he and his friends leave with the aliens.

OTHER ROLES

1936: *Karl Freyman / Mario Singarelli* / SINS OF MAN; *Bob Harris* / ONE IN A MILLION. **1937:** *Dr. Rudi Imre* / LADIES IN LOVE; *Peter Nostrand* / FIFTY ROADS TO TOWN; *George MacRoe* / YOU CAN'T HAVE EVERYTHING; *Tracy Egan* / LOVE UNDER FIRE; *Marty Canavan* / LOVE IS NEWS. **1938:** *Jimmy Hall* / HAPPY LANDING; *David Brossard, Jr.* / JOSETTE; *Dick* / GATEWAY. **1939:** *Michael Linnett Connors* / HOLLYWOOD CAVALCADE. **1940:** *Edward Solomon* / LILLIAN RUSSELL; *Ricardo Quintana* / DOWN ARGENTINE WAY. **1941:** *Phil O'Neal* / MOON OVER MIAMI; *Lloyd Lloyd* / KISS THE BOYS GOODBYE; *John Hathaway* / THE FEMININE TOUCH;*Mitch* / CONFIRM OR DENY; *cameo* / LAND OF LIBERTY. **1942:** *Dwight Dawson* / THE MAGNIFICENT DOPE; *Pedro Sullivan* / GIRL TROUBLE. **1943:** *Ken Douglas* / SOMETHING TO SHOUT ABOUT. **1944:** *Bingo Harper* / A WING AND A PRAYER; *Kenneth Harvey* / GREENWICH VILLAGE. **1945:** *Joe* / GUEST WIFE; *guest* / IT'S IN THE BAG. **1946:** *Hiram Stephen Maxim* / SO GOES MY LOVE. **1947:** *Joe Grange* / THAT'S MY MAN. **1948:** *Richard Courtland* / SLEEP MY LOVE. **1949:** *John Gayle* / SLIGHTLY FRENCH. **1961:** *Sen. A. S. Simon* / A FEVER IN THE BLOOD. **1966:** *Edward Shelley* / PICTURE MOMMY DEAD. **1970:** *Colonel Flanders* / SUPPOSE THEY GAVE A WAR AND NOBODY CAME?; *Cmdr. Taylor* / THE BOATNIKS. **1987:** *Dr. Wallace Wrightwood* / HARRY AND THE HENDERSONS.

ANDREWS, DANA

(Carver Daniel Andrews, 1909–)

A leading man of the 1940s and 1950s, Dana Andrews was handed a number of roles that might ordinarily have gone to Henry Fonda or Tyrone Power, who were in the service. No actor as good as Andrews ever appeared in so many "B" or otherwise inferior movies. He established himself as a star with NORTH STAR, PURPLE HEART, and WING AND A PRAYER, and then cemented it with LAURA and THE BEST YEARS OF OUR LIVES. By the late 1940s and early 1950s the really great roles were drying up, but Andrews kept busy making movies into the 1980s. His TV movies include THE FAILING OF RAYMOND (1971), THE FIRST 36 HOURS OF DR. DURANT (1975), SHADOW IN THE STREETS (1976), and IKE (1979).

KEY ROLES

Donald Martin / THE OX-BOW INCIDENT, 1943, 20th Century-Fox, d-William Wellman.

Andrews, one of three innocent men who are lynched for a murder they did not commit, gives a masterful performance as a man trying to cope first with the injustice that fate has dealt him and then with the fact that he can do nothing to change it.

Capt. Harvey Ross / THE PURPLE HEART, 1944, 20th Century-Fox, d-Lewis Milestone.

Andrews is the ranking American officer in a group of flyers captured and put on trial as war criminals for the Jimmy Doolittle raid on Tokyo early in World War II. They are mere pawns in a struggle between the Japanese army and the Japanese navy. Andrews and his men refuse to give their captors any information, even though they are tortured. Their sentence is death.

Mark McPherson / LAURA, 1944, 20th Century-Fox, d-Otto Preminger.

Andrews is a police detective who falls in love with the portrait of Gene Tierney, a woman whose murder he's investigating. When she shows up alive, Andrews is delighted. Yet he must find out who the corpse is, who the murderer is, and whether he or she may make a second attempt on Tierney's life.

Sergeant Tyne / A WALK IN THE SUN, 1945, 20th Century-Fox, d-Lewis Milestone.

Andrews gives one of his forthright performances as a sergeant with a platoon of American foot soldiers who hit the beach at Salerno and are given the mission of wiping out a farmhouse filled with Germans. It shows the drudgery of war as well as the horror.

Fred Derry / THE BEST YEARS OF OUR LIVES, 1946, Goldwyn, d-William Wyler.

As a representative of many GIs returning from World War II, Andrews plays an air force officer who discovers that bombing raids didn't prepare him for civilian life and that his wife (Virginia Mayo) doesn't see him as dashing and handsome in civilian clothes. Feeling bitter and sorry for himself, he tells Teresa Wright, who has fallen for him despite his marital status, "I'm really in the junk business—an occupation for which many people feel I'm well qualified by temperament and training. It's fascinating work."

Henry L. Harvey / BOOMERANG, 1947, 20th Century-Fox, d-Elia Kazan.

Andrews plays a D.A. in a New England town who won't allow an innocent man to be convicted of the murder of a clergyman. But he can't find the real killer in this true-life thriller.

Walt Dreiser / MY FOOLISH HEART, 1950, Goldwyn, d-Mark Robson.

Wife Susan Hayward deceives Andrews into believing that he is the father of the child she is expecting.

Dick Carver / ELEPHANT WALK, 1954, Paramount, d-William Dieterle.

Andrews is the friendly overseer of a tea plantation in Ceylon to whom Elizabeth Taylor turns for comfort when her husband (Peter Finch), owner of the plantation, makes no time for her.

Dr. John Holden / NIGHT OF THE DEMON, 1957, Columbia, d-Jacques Tourneur.

Andrews is an American psychologist who turns the tables on an occultist (Niall MacGinnis) who dispatches his enemies by calling on a giant, medieval devil. It's good, gory fun, and at least Andrews will be remembered for being in one of the better horror cheapies of the period.

OTHER ROLES

1940: *Bart Cobble* / THE WESTERNER; *Sergeant Dunn* / LUCKY CISCO KID; *Scrappy Wilson* / SAILOR'S LADY; *Capt. John C. Fremont* / KIT CARSON. **1941:** *Dr. Tim* / TOBACCO ROAD; *Maj. Thomas Grail* / BELLE STARR; *Ben* / SWAMP WATER; *Joe Lilac* / BALL OF FIRE. **1942:** *Bill Roberts* / BERLIN CORRESPONDENT. **1943:** *Lt. Cmdr. Dewey Connors* / CRASH DIVE; *Kolya* / THE NORTH STAR. **1944:** *Sqdn. Cmdr. Edward Moulton* / WING AND A PRAYER; *Joe Nelson* / UP IN ARMS. **1945:** *Pat Gilbert* / STATE FAIR; *Eric Stanton* / FALLEN ANGEL. **1946:** *Logan Stuart* / CANYON PASSAGE. **1947:** *Dan* / NIGHT SONG; *Dan O'Mara* / DAISY KENYON. **1948:** *Igor Gouzenko* / THE IRON CURTAIN; *Hod Stillwell* / DEEP WATERS; *Perry Aswell* / NO MINOR VICES; *Gilbert Lauderdale* / *Herbert Lambert* / BRITANNIA MEWS. **1949:** *Mike Dillon* / SWORD IN THE DESERT. **1950:** *Mark Dixon* / WHERE THE SIDEWALK ENDS; *Father Roth* / EDGE OF DOOM; *Flannigan* / THE FROGMEN. **1951:** *Pat Bannon* / SEALED CARGO; *Martin Greer* / I WANT YOU. **1952:** *Jimmy Race* / ASSIGNMENT—PARIS. **1954:** *Scott Walters* / DUEL IN THE JUNGLE; *Jim Guthrie* / THREE HOURS TO KILL. **1955:** *Brett Halliday* / SMOKE SIGNAL; *Rork O'Brien* / STRANGE LADY IN TOWN. **1956:** *Read* / COMANCHE; *Edward Mobley* / WHILE THE CITY SLEEPS; *Tom Garrett* / BEYOND A REASONABLE DOUBT. **1957:** *Fred Davis* / SPRING REUNION; *Ted Stryker* / ZERO HOUR. **1958:** *Alan Eaton* / THE FEARMAKERS; *Abner Bedford* / ENCHANTED ISLAND. **1960:** *Dick Barnett* / THE CROWDED SKY. **1962:** *Clint Lorimer* / MADISON AVENUE. **1965:** *Stephen Sorenson* / CRACK IN THE WORLD; *the general* / THE SATAN BUG; *Admiral Broderick* / IN HARM'S WAY; *Cort Benson* / BRAINSTORM; *Tom Rosser* / TOWN TAMER; *General Brinkson* / THE LOVED ONE; *Colonel Pritchard* / BATTLE OF THE BULGE. **1966:** *Johnny Reno* / JOHNNY RENO; *Colonel Lancaster* / SPY IN YOUR EYE. **1967:** *Tom Phillips* / HOT RODS TO HELL; *Dr. Norberg* / THE FROZEN DEAD; *Kelly* / THE COBRA. **1968:** *Gen. Walter Naylor* / THE DEVIL'S BRIGADE. **1972:** *Blake* / INNOCENT BYSTANDERS. **1975:** *Scott Freeman* / AIRPORT 1975; *Morgan* / TAKE A HARD RIDE. **1976:** *Red Ridingwood* / THE LAST TYCOON. **1978:** *government man* / GOOD GUYS WEAR BLACK. **1979:** *Tom Phillips* / BORN AGAIN. **1981:** *pilot's employer* / THE PILOT. **1986:** *The Cardinal* / PRINCE JACK.

ANDREWS, JULIE

(Julia Wells, 1934–)

Julie Andrews's first success was on TV with Bing Crosby in HIGH TOR. She became a Broadway star with "My Fair Lady" but was denied the right to re-create the role of Eliza Doolittle on the screen because the studio wrongly felt she wasn't a big enough name to carry the picture. Instead, she won an Oscar the same year for her screen debut in MARY POPPINS. After that she was typecast in sticky-sweet roles like Maria in THE SOUND OF MUSIC. To rid herself of the wholesome image she bared her breasts in a movie directed by her husband, Blake Edwards. Her own thoughts on her stardom include: "How does it feel to be a star? I suck my thumb a lot."

KEY ROLES

Mary Poppins / MARY POPPINS, 1964, Walt Disney, d-Robert Stevenson.

Andrews is a magical nanny in Edwardian England who not only teaches her slightly naughty charges to make life enjoyable for others, but helps their parents learn what's really important in life.

Emily Barham / THE AMERICANIZATION OF EMILY, 1964, MGM, d-Arthur Hiller.

Andrews is a British war widow who falls in love with an American commander (James Garner), a self-confessed coward, just before the Normandy invasion. She's not so sweet in this one, but it doesn't seem to help her escape the typecasting her next big hit will condemn her to forever.

Maria Von Trapp / THE SOUND OF MUSIC, 1965, 20th Century-Fox, d-Robert Wise.

Andrews is so downright wholesome here it's almost sickening, but look at all the money it made for Fox. Andrews is a novice nun who doesn't seem to have a calling, and when she becomes governess to the Von Trapp family she falls in love with the seven children and their father (Christopher Plummer). She was nominated for an Academy Award for her performance.

Millie Dillmount / THOROUGHLY MODERN MILLIE, 1967, Universal, d-George Roy Hill.

The film was a box-office dud, but Andrews's performance as the twenties girl who moves to New York, falls for her boss, and unmasks a white slavery racket is not the problem.

Gertrude Lawrence / STAR! 1968, 20th Century-Fox, d-Robert Wise.

It's not that the life of revue artist Gertrude Lawrence was boring, nor was Andrews miscast. It's just that the time for such a biopic had passed.

Samantha / 10, 1979, Warners, d-Blake Edwards.

Andrews starts looking more appealing to lover Dudley Moore and to male members of the audience the more that perfect "10" Bo Derek is allowed to speak.

Victor / Victoria / VICTOR / VICTORIA, 1982, MGM, d-Blake Edwards.

To survive in Paris in 1934, Andrews poses as a Polish homosexual female impersonator who lives with gay Robert Preston and loves macho James Garner.

OTHER ROLES

1952: *voice only* / ROSE OF BAGDAD. **1966:** *Sarah Sherman* / TORN CURTAIN; *Jerusha Bromley Hale* / HAWAII. **1967:** *voice only* / THE SINGING PRINCESS. **1970:** *Lili Smith* / DARLING LILI. **1974:** *Judith Farrow* / THE TAMARIND SEED. **1980:** *Amanda* / LITTLE MISS MARKER. **1981:** *Sally Miles* / S.O.B. **1983:** *Marianna* / THE MAN WHO LOVED WOMEN. **1986:** *Gillian Fairchild* / THAT'S LIFE; *Stephanie Anderson* / DUET FOR ONE.

ANKERS, EVELYN

(1918–1985)

This fair-haired, Chilean-born actress began her career in Great Britain but is most remembered for being the beautiful screamer in many U.S. "B" horror movies. "The Poor Man's Fay Wray" and "Ankers Aweigh," as she was known, stopped appearing in movies in order to boost the acting career of her husband, Richard Denning. It's a shame that this stunning beauty's acting ability didn't match her remarkable good looks, or perhaps she didn't possess the ambition to be a major star. She is nevertheless saluted for those wonderful appearances that made all the young boys at her horror movies wish to grow up quickly.

KEY ROLES

Norma Lind / HOLD THAT GHOST, 1941, Universal, d-Arthur Lubin.

Ankers is stranded with Abbott and Costello, Joan Davis, and Richard Carlson in an apparently haunted house. She and Carlson supply the love interest in one of Abbott and Costello's best comedies. Ankers said that it wasn't safe to be near the boys unless she was with her back to a wall or sitting down.

Gwen Conliffe / THE WOLF MAN, 1941, Universal, d-George Waggner.

This is one of the movies that helped Ankers earn the title of "The Screamer." She's the girl Lon Chaney, Jr., rescues from a werewolf, getting bit in the process, and as Maria Ouspenskaya would say: "Even the man who is pure in heart and says his prayers by night, may become a wolf when the wolf bane blooms and the moon is pure and bright...."

Elsa Frankenstein / THE GHOST OF FRANKENSTEIN, 1942, Universal, d-Eric C. Keaton.

Ankers is fine in support of Cedric Hardwicke as the second son of Baron Frankenstein who plans to remove his father's monster's murderous brain and replace it with that of hunchback Igor.

Kitty / SHERLOCK HOLMES AND THE VOICE OF TERROR, 1942, Universal, d-John Rawlins.

Holmes (Basil Rathbone) hires Ankers to spy on Nazi agent Thomas Gomez, but the latter kills her when he catches on.

Isabel Lewis / THE MAD GHOUL, 1943, Universal, d-James Hogan.

Ankers is a singer menaced by George Zucco who has isolated a noxious gas of ancient Egyptian origin so horrible that its effects can be neutralized only by heart fluid from a recently deceased individual.

Moura Daniel / THE FROZEN GHOST, 1945, Universal, d-Harold Young.

Ankers is the assistant and love of mentalist Lon Chaney, Jr., who comes to fear his own power when a member of his audience dies while under his hypnotic spell.

OTHER ROLES

1936: *bit* / LAND WITHOUT MUSIC; *girl* / REMBRANDT; *Joan* / VILLIERS DIAMOND, THE; *Molly* / SECOND THOUGHTS. **1937:** *bit* / FIRE OVER ENGLAND; *bit* / KNIGHT WITHOUT ARMOUR; *bit* / WINGS OF THE MORNING; *girl* / OVER THE MOON. **1938:** *Christine Squire* / COMING OF AGE; *Dorothy Osborne* / MURDER IN THE FAMILY; *Rosemary Claydon* / THE CLAYDON TREASURE MYSTERY. **1941:** *Patience Ryan* / HIT THE ROAD; *Beth Chase* / BACHELOR DADDY; *Ann McBragel* / BURMA CONVOY. **1942:** *Mary Sloan* / NORTH TO THE KLONDIKE; *Nancy Mitchell* / EAGLE SQUADRON; *Celia Wellsby* / PIERRE OF THE PLAINS; *Muriel* / THE GREAT IMPERSONATION. **1943:** *Sheila* / KEEP 'EM SLUGGING; *Lynn Smith* / YOU'RE A LUCKY FELLOW, MR. SMITH; *Jean Wells* / ALL BY MYSELF; *Flo Simpson* / HERS TO HOLD; *Beth Colman* / CAPTIVE WILD WOMAN; *Claire Caldwell* / SON OF DRACULA; *Elizabeth Campbell* / HIS BUTLER'S SISTER. **1944:** *guest* / FOLLOW THE BOYS; *Wilhelmina Van Kronk* / LADIES COURAGEOUS; *Julia Munson* / PARDON MY RHYTHM; *Julie Herrick* / INVISIBLE MAN'S REVENGE; *Beth Mason* / JUNGLE WOMAN; *Naomi Drake* / THE PEARL OF DEATH; *Ilona Carr* / WEIRD WOMAN; *Bonnie Latour* / BOWERY TO BROADWAY. **1945:** *Priscilla Ames* / THE FATAL WITNESS. **1946:** *Crystal McCoy* / QUEEN OF BURLESQUE; *Janet Morgan* / THE FRENCH KEY; *Evelyn Carrington* / BLACK BEAUTY. **1947:** *Laura Reed* / SPOILERS OF THE NORTH; *Alice Monroe* / THE LAST OF THE REDMEN; *Iris Chatham* / THE LONE WOLF IN LONDON. **1949:** *Gloria James* / TARZAN'S MAGIC FOUNTAIN; *Jojo Dumont* / PAROLE, INC. **1950:** *Calamity Jane* / THE TEXAN MEETS CALAMITY JANE.

ANN-MARGRET

(Ann-Margaret Olsson, 1941–)

This Swedish-born redhead began her film career playing quiet, refined young women, but she soon took on a sexier image. During the late 1960s her film career was in such decline that she took roles in Italian cheapies. After sustaining serious injury when she fell from the stage in her nightclub act, she went back to Hollywood, still playing sexy women but now ones with more substance and maturity. Her roles today are earth-mother types, but a little bit of the sex kitten is still present. At least she seems to meet her own definition of the kind of woman men want: "A man who is honest with himself wants a woman to be soft and feminine, careful of what she's saying, and to talk like a man."

KEY ROLES

Emily Porter / STATE FAIR, 1962, 20th Century-Fox, d-Jose Ferrer.

Ann-Margret is a sexy show girl at the Texas State Fair, where she meets clean-cut young farm lad Pat Boone. Certain that his family will think her a tramp she walks out on Boone at the close of the fair. She sings the Rodgers and Hammerstein song "Isn't it Kind of Fun."

Kim McAfee / BYE BYE BIRDIE, 1963, Columbia, d-George Sidney.

Ann-Margret plays the Sweet Apple, Ohio teenager who is to be given a symbolic farewell kiss by rock star Conrad Birdie on the Ed Sullivan Show, just prior to Birdie leaving for the Army. The event turns her family, friends, and town upside down. She's very much a voluptuous Lolita, dancing and singing songs by Lee Adams and Charles Strouse such as "How Lovely to Be a Woman," "A Lot of Living to Do," and the title number.

Melba / THE CINCINNATI KID, 1965, MGM, d-Norman Jewison.

Ann-Margret plays the wife of Rip Torn, one of several players in a big-time poker game in New Orleans. Other players include national champion Edward G. Robinson, Joan Blondell, and Steve McQueen, a contender for Robinson's crown. She has a brief affair with McQueen during a break in the game while his main squeeze (Tuesday Weld) is absent.

Bobbie / CARNAL KNOWLEDGE, 1971, Avco Embassy, d-Mike Nichols.

Ann-Margret gives a fine performance as the sex object Jack Nicholson uses, enjoys, and abandons in this story of a man who never seems to outgrow his adolescent notions of sex and love. She received an Academy Award nomination for her performance.

Nora Walker Hobbs / TOMMY, 1975, Great Britain, Columbia, d-Ken Russell.

Ann-Margret earned another Academy Award nomination for her portrayal of the mother of Tommy, the deaf, dumb, and blind kid who is eventually cured and becomes a rock star.

Sue Ann / MIDDLE AGE CRAZY, 1980, Canada, Tormont, d-John Trent.

When Ann-Margret's 40-year-old husband (Bruce Dern) begins to feel his age, he buys himself a Porsche and leaves her for cheerleader Deborah Wakeham.

Audrey Minelli / TWICE IN A LIFETIME, 1985, Yorkin, d-Bud Yorkin.

In this film, Gene Hackman reaches a mid-life crisis and leaves his wife (Ellen Burstyn) for barmaid Ann-Margret.

OTHER ROLES

1961: *Louise* / POCKETFUL OF MIRACLES. **1964:** *Rusty Martin* / VIVA LAS VEGAS; *Jody Dvorak* / KITTEN WITH A WHIP; *Fran Hobson* / THE PLEASURE SEEKERS. **1965:** *Laurel* / BUS RILEY'S BACK IN TOWN; *Kristine Pedak* / ONCE A THIEF. **1966:** *Maggie Scott* / MADE IN PARIS; *Kelly Olsson* / THE SWINGER; *Dallas* / STAGECOACH; *Suzie Solaris* / MURDERER'S ROW. **1967:** *Carolina* / THE TIGER AND THE PUSSYCAT. **1970:** *Ann McCalley* / C.C. AND CO.; *Rhoda* / R.P.M. **1973:** *Mrs. Lily Lowe* / THE TRAIN ROBBERS; *Nancy* / THE OUTSIDE MAN. **1976:** *Charley* / THE TWIST. **1977:** *Lady Booby* / JOSEPH ANDREWS; *Lady Flavina Geste* / THE LAST REMAKE OF BEAU GESTE. **1978:** *Jezebel Dezire* / THE CHEAP DETECTIVE; *Peggy Ann Snow* / MAGIC. **1979:** *Charming Jones* / THE VILLAIN. **1982:** *Stephanie* / I OUGHT TO BE IN PICTURES; *Patti Warner* / LOOKIN' TO GET OUT; *Jenny Baldry* / THE RETURN OF THE SOLDIER. **1986:** *Barbara Mitchell* / 52 PICK-UP. **1987:** *Rose* / A TIGER'S TALE. **1988:** *Jackie* / A NEW LIFE.

ARDEN, EVE

(Eunice Quedens, 1912–)

Eve Arden often had the best lines in the movies she appeared in and was known as "The Queen of the Caustic Crack," a tribute to her droll, fast-talking talents. She often appeared as the man-chasing best friend of the heroine, and she gained even greater fame as Our Miss Brooks on radio starting in 1948 and then on television from 1952-57. Her first two film appearances as Mazie in SONG OF LOVE (1929) and as Marcia in DANCING LADY (1933) were made using her real name, Eunice Quedens. Her TV movies include A VERY MISSING PERSON (1972) and FOR THE LOVE OF IT (1980).

KEY ROLES

Eve / STAGE DOOR, 1937, RKO, d-Gregory La Cava.

With this film Arden established her screen persona as a worldly, wise, warmhearted, slightly daffy lady. She's one of a group of girls living in a theatrical boarding house. To prove her sophistication she wears a live cat as a fur stole.

Cornelia "Stonewall" Jackson / COVER GIRL, 1944, Columbia, d-Charles Vidor.

Arden plays a wise-cracking, high-powered executive on the lookout for the perfect cover girl, who turns out to be Rita Hayworth.

Natalia Moskeroff / THE DOUGHGIRLS, 1944, Warners, d-James V. Kern.

Arden steals the picture as a Russian guerrilla who moves into a Washington hotel suite with a group of unmarried girls. Arden practices her marksmanship by shooting at pigeons from the terrace and spends the rest of her free time attending double features and extricating her roommates from their troubles.

Ida / MILDRED PIERCE, 1945, Warners, d-Michael Curtiz.

Arden plays Joan Crawford's friend and is the one person who sees the latter's unthankful daughter (Ann Blyth) as the cold, uncaring person she really is, noting, "Personally, Veda's convinced me that alligators have the right idea. They eat their young."

Olive Lashbrooke / THE VOICE OF THE TURTLE, 1947, Warners, d-Irving Rapper.

Arden plays the promiscuous, wise-cracking friend of Eleanor Parker. The latter shares her apartment with soldier Ronald Reagan.

Lucille McCabe / THREE HUSBANDS, 1950, United Artists, d-Irving Reis.

Arden is one of three wives whose husbands receive letters from a recently dead bachelor friend who claims to have had an affair with their respective spouses. It's clearly an attempt to show the other side of the successful A LETTER TO THREE WIVES (1948) but isn't nearly as interesting.

Katie Woodruff / WE'RE NOT MARRIED, 1952, 20th Century-Fox, d-Edmund Goulding.

Arden is married to Paul Douglas and they seldom communicate. Then, along with four other couples, they learn that the justice of the peace who married them did so before the authorized date of his appointment—so they're not married after all. Now they have a lot to talk about.

Connie Brooks / OUR MISS BROOKS, 1955, Warners, d-Al Lewis.

Despite all of her best efforts, Arden wasn't able to bring her radio and TV comedy series successfully to the big screen. In the story she's a teacher engaged to a colleague who is still mommy's little boy.

Maida / ANATOMY OF A MURDER, 1959, Columbia, d-Otto Preminger.

Arden plays lawyer Jimmy Stewart's very efficient secretary as he takes on the case of an army officer who has killed a man he claims has raped his wife.

Lottie / DARK AT THE TOP OF THE STAIRS, 1960, Warners, d-Delbert Mann.

Arden is Dorothy McGuire's big-mouth, bigoted sister in this charming story of the adjustments a 1920s small town family must make as the father loses his job, a daughter befriends a Jewish boy, and the mother tries to cut her son free from her apron strings.

OTHER ROLES

1937: *Shirley Truman* / OH, DOCTOR. **1938:** *Sophie de Lemma* / COCOANUT GROVE; *Cora* / LETTER OF INTRODUCTION; *Henrietta* / HAVING WONDERFUL TIME. **1939:** *Kit Campbell* / WOMEN IN THE WIND; *Susan Warren* / BIG TOWN CZAR; *Carrie Ashburn* / THE FORGOTTEN WOMAN; *Gloria* / ETERNALLY YOURS; *Peerless Pauline* / AT THE CIRCUS. **1940:** *Miss Pinty* / A CHILD IS BORN; *Miss Alter* / SLIGHTLY HONORABLE; *Jane Wilson* / COMRADE X; *Winnie* / NO, NO, NANETTE. **1941:** *Patsy Dixon* / ZIEGFELD GIRL; *Sally* / THAT UNCERTAIN FEELING; *Alice Hinsdale* / SHE COULDN'T SAY NO; *Sally Long* / SHE KNEW ALL THE ANSWERS; *Gabby Trent* / SAN ANTONIO ROSE; *Barbara Stevens* / SING FOR YOUR SUPPER. **1942:** *Dolly* / MANPOWER; *Buzz Baker* / WHISTLING IN THE DARK; *Kate* / THE LAST OF THE DUANES; *Space O'Shea* / OBLIGING YOUNG LADY; *Virginia Cole* / BEDTIME STORY. **1943:** *Belinda Wright* / HIT PARADE OF 1943; *Maggie Watson* / LET'S FACE IT. **1945:** *Hoppy* / PAN-AMERICANA; *Jean Mathews* / PATRICK THE GREAT; *Tex Donnolly* / EARL CARROLL VANITIES. **1946:** *Ginna Abbott* / MY REPUTATION; *Ann Westley* / THE KID FROM BROOKLYN; *Gabrielle* / NIGHT AND DAY. **1947:** *Madame de Talavera* / SONG OF SCHEHERAZADE; *Vivian Delwyn* / THE ARNELO AFFAIR; *Paula* / THE UNFAITHFUL. **1948:** *Molly Grant* / ONE TOUCH OF VENUS; *Chris* / WHIPLASH. **1949:** *Vivian Martin* / MY DREAM IS YOURS; *Susan Wayne* / THE LADY TAKES A SAILOR. **1950:** *Tommy Thompson* / PAID IN FULL; *Lily Martin* / CURTAIN CALL AT CACTUS CREEK; *Pauline Hastings* / TEA FOR TWO. **1951:** *Woody* / GOODBYE, MY FANCY. **1953:** *Gladys Jones* / THE LADY WANTS MINK. **1965:** *Lt. Charlotte Kinsey* / SERGEANT DEADHEAD. **1975:** *Harriet* / THE STRONGEST MAN IN THE WORLD. **1978:** *Principal McGee* / GREASE. **1981:** *Duchess* / UNDER THE RAINBOW. **1982:** *Principal McGee* / GREASE 2.

ARLISS, GEORGE

(George A. Andrews, 1868–1946)

A distinguished English stage actor, George Arliss made his debut with a walk-on in "Vidocq" in London in 1886. His London stage career lasted twenty years followed by twenty more successful years on Broadway in which he created a series of historical characters who proved to be unforgettable. In the 1920s he recreated many of these stage triumphs on the screen, although he was 53 when he made his first movie appearance in 1921. He was in his 60s when he had his greatest film successes, winning an Oscar for DISRAELI and being nominated for THE GREEN GODDESS.

KEY ROLES

Benjamin Disraeli / DISRAELI, 1929, Warners, d-Alfred Green.

Arliss won an Academy Award for his portrayal of the Victorian English Prime Minister, repeating a role in which he appeared in the 1921 silent. Seen today, most would find the acting a trifle forced and unrealistic, but the power of the actor's performance still is evident.

Rajah of Rukh / THE GREEN GODDESS, 1930, Warners, d-Alfred Green.

Arliss is an Indian potentate who threatens to execute his British prisoners if the English carry through with the execution of his brothers. Arliss was nominated for an Academy Award for this role which he had also played as a silent in 1923.

Montgomery Royale / THE MAN WHO PLAYED GOD, 1932, Warners, d-John Adolfi.

Arliss plays a musician who has gone deaf but who takes some satisfaction in helping a young student and others whom he notices through his window looking onto the street. His lip-reading ability provides him with much news of what's going on around him—some of which he'd just as soon not learn. Liberace massacred this role in 1955 in SINCERELY YOURS.

Voltaire / VOLTAIRE, 1933, Warners, d-John Adolfi.

Perhaps Arliss's best role is as the French philosopher. At least his stagey performance matches the story, which is not quite as faithful to the facts as one might expect from Hollywood. Even with the life of one of the greatest wits and activists of the 18th century, the studio couldn't resist tampering with the truth to make it more dramatic.

Mayer Rothschild / Nathan Rothschild / THE HOUSE OF ROTHSCHILD, 1934, 20th Century-Fox, d-Alfred Werker.

Arliss plays the dual role of the patriarch of a German / Jewish ghetto family who on his deathbed urges his five sons (the eldest also played by Arliss) to travel to the five capitals of Europe and establish a banking empire. They do precisely that, slowly becoming the most powerful banking conglomerate in Europe. They become involved in all the important historical events of the time and play a major part in the Napoleonic Wars but are ever persecuted for being Jewish by the same people who come to them for money.

Cardinal Richelieu / CARDINAL RICHELIEU, 1935, 20th Century-Fox, d-Rowland V. Lee.

Arliss is masterful as the grey eminence behind the throne of Louis XIII. The unscrupulous cardinal is less a scoundrel in this film than in the Dumas stories.

OTHER ROLES

1921: *Dr. Muller* / THE DEVIL; *Benjamin Disraeli* / DISRAELI. **1922:** *John Arden* / THE MAN WHO PLAYED GOD. **1923:** *Rajah of Rukh* / THE GREEN GODDESS; *James Alden* / THE RULING PASSION. **1924:** *John Reeves* / $20 A WEEK. **1930:** *Sylvanus Heythrop* / OLD ENGLISH. **1931:** *James Alden* / THE MILLIONAIRE. **1932:** *Henry Wilton* / A SUCCESSFUL CALAMITY. **1933:** *King Philip* / THE KING'S VACATION. **1934:** *Cabot Barr* / THE LAST GENTLEMAN. **1935:** *Duke of Wellington* / THE IRON DUKE; *Francis Rothschild* / *Spike* / *The Guv'nor* / THE GUV'NOR; *British Prime Minister* / THE TUNNEL. **1936:** *Sultan, The Rajah of Rungay* / EAST MEETS WEST. **1937:** *Richard* / *Lord Dunchester* / MAN OF AFFAIRS; *Christopher Syn* / DR. SYN. **1941:** *cameo* / LAND OF LIBERTY.

ARTHUR, JEAN

(Gladys Greene, 1905–   )

Jean Arthur appeared in over two dozen silent films and serials, mostly for minor production companies that specialized in westerns. In 1931, she left Hollywood for two years to work on the New York stage and in summer stock. On her return, she starred in a series of sophisticated comedies and Frank Capra populist movies, appearing as sentimental, wistful, and urbane heroines. With her husky, cracked voice and tomboyish good looks, she was more than a match for any of her leading men. But she never really enjoyed the Hollywood life, and made only two more films after 1944 before retiring for good.

KEY ROLES

Ada Greene / THE GREENE MURDER CASE, 1929, Paramount, d-Frank Tuttle.

It didn't take the audience as long as detective Philo Vance to spot Arthur as the hidden killer. The climactic scenes show her trying to escape across snowy rooftops, only to fall into the Hudson River.

Wilhelmina "Bill" Clark / THE WHOLE TOWN'S TALKING, 1935, Columbia, d-John Ford.

Arthur created the good-natured, sentimental girl-next-door who finds herself involved with Edward G. Robinson, who plays both a meek little clerk and his gangster double.

Jane Matthews / Emma / DIAMOND JIM, 1935, Universal, d-Edward Sutherland.

In this highly fictionalized account of the life and appetites of multimillionaire Diamond Jim Brady, Arthur is loved by Brady (Edward Arnold), but she in turn loves Cesar Romero who loves Lillian Russell (Binnie Barnes).

Joan Hawthorne / IF YOU COULD ONLY COOK, 1936, Columbia, d-William Seiter.

In this whimsical comedy, Arthur plays a poor girl who meets a young millionaire and together they go into service as a cook and butler.

Babe Bennett / MR. DEEDS GOES TO TOWN, 1936, Columbia, d-Frank Capra.

Director Capra called Arthur his favorite actress. Here she is a hard-boiled reporter who writes a series of unflattering articles about naive Mr. Deeds (Gary Cooper) before falling in love with the man who wishes to give his millions away.

Calamity Jane / THE PLAINSMAN, 1936, Paramount, d-Cecil B. DeMille.

Arthur is the hard-riding woman in this western epic. She loves Wild Bill Hickok (Gary Cooper) and that buys them both a heap of trouble with Indians and gunrunners.

Irene Vail / HISTORY IS MADE AT NIGHT, 1937, United Artists, d-Frank Borzage.

Colin Clive plots to frame his wife (Arthur) by planting their chauffeur in her room and then bursting in on them with his lawyer in tow. Charles Boyer, who just happens to be climbing down her balcony, sees Arthur struggling with the chauffeur. He knocks out the man and takes Arthur to safety. Clive, thinking Boyer is her lover, kills the chauffeur hoping Boyer will be blamed. Unaware that he is suspected of murder, Boyer and Arthur fall in love, but she leaves with her husband on one of his ships with Boyer slipping aboard. Clive orders his captain to go full speed ahead through an iceberg field and the ship crashes. Clive, believing that Boyer and Arthur have been killed, confesses that he killed the chauffeur and then takes his own life. But, surprise, Boyer and Arthur are just fine.

Mary Smith / EASY LIVING, 1937, Paramount, d-Mitchell Leisen.

In this delightful slapstick farce Edward Arnold throws his wife's fur coat out a window and it lands on typist Arthur—and then the fun begins. Arnold, trying to teach his spouse a lesson, insists that Arthur keep the coat and he buys her a hat to match. She is fired from her job because of suspicion over how she acquired the fur and before long it's all over town that she's Arnold's mistress. But she falls for her benefactor's son, Ray Milland.

Alice Sycamore / YOU CAN'T TAKE IT WITH YOU, 1938, Columbia, d-Frank Capra.

Arthur is one daughter of a very eccentric family. When she falls in love with Jimmy Stewart, scion of a conservative rich family, her family teaches his what's really important in life.

Clarissa Saunders / MR. SMITH GOES TO WASHINGTON, 1939, Columbia, d-Frank Capra.

The corrupt senior senator of a mid-western state employs Arthur to babysit Jimmy Stewart, the newly appointed junior senator, to make certain he doesn't stick his nose into anything important. Having been around for awhile she seems just the girl for the job, admitting, "Look, when I came here, my eyes were big question marks. Now they're big green dollar marks." Instead she falls in love with Stewart and helps him expose the dishonest political bosses of his state.

Mary Jones / THE DEVIL AND MISS JONES, 1941, RKO, d-Sam Wood.

Arthur works in a department store owned by Charles Coburn, the world's richest man. Hoping to learn who the union leaders causing all the aggravation are, he poses as a clerk in his own store and is subjected to the same miserable treatment as the other employees. Thinking him destitute, fellow clerk Arthur takes pity on him and shows him how things work in the shoe department. It's a sparkling comedy and, although the lion's share of credit goes to Coburn, Arthur's contribution is first-rate.

Nora Shelley / THE TALK OF THE TOWN, 1941, Columbia, d-George Stevens.

Arthur is in love with both a murder suspect (Cary Grant) and a law school dean awaiting nomination to the Supreme Court (Ronald Colman). The one she settles on in this zany comedy isn't revealed until the last moment in the picture.

Connie Milligan / THE MORE THE MERRIER, 1943, Columbia, d-George Stevens.

Conned by Charles Coburn into sharing her apartment with him in crowded wartime Washington, Arthur next finds that the old codger has given Joel McCrea squatter's rights as well. It works out okay as she falls in love with the newcomer and gets an Academy Award nomination to boot.

Phoebe Frost / A FOREIGN AFFAIR, 1948, Paramount, d-Billy Wilder.

Arthur is a congresswoman on a junket to post-World War II Berlin who finds herself part of a triangle involving an American captain (John Lund) and his German mistress (Marlene Dietrich).

Marion Starrett / SHANE, 1953, Paramount, d-George Stevens.

In her final film, Arthur is the wife of a farmer (Van Heflin) who is having a tough time with cattlemen. When gunman Shane (Alan Ladd) joins their side, she is shyly attracted to the stranger though she remains faithful to her very good man.

OTHER ROLES

1923: *Ann Playdell* / CAMEO KIRBY. **1924:** *Mary Brown* / FAST AND FEARLESS; *Bonnie Norton* / BIFF BANG BUDDY; *Nancy Norton*

/ BRINGIN' HOME THE BACON. **1925:** *Betty Conway* / TRAVELIN' FAST; *Jean* / THE DRUG STORE COWBOY; *Loria Gatlin* / A MAN OF NERVE; *Sally Harris* / TEARING LOOSE; *Mary Watkins* / THUNDERING ROMANCE; *cameo* / SEVEN CHANCES; *Rose Craddock* / THE FIGHTING SMILE. **1926:** *Marie Denton* / LIGHTNIN' BILL; *Ruth Burroughs* / THUNDERING THROUGH; *Eunice Morgan* / BORN TO BATTLE; *June Mathews* / THE HURRICANE HORSEMAN; *Ruth Wells* / THE FIGHTING CHEAT; *Marie Wells* / DOUBLE DARING; *Margaret Cranston* / UNDER FIRE; *Virginia Selby* / THE COWBOY COP; *Ruth Regan* / TWISTED TRIGGERS; *Angela Boothby* / THE COLLEGE BOOB; *Grace Ryan* / THE BLOCK SIGNAL. **1927:** *Lettie Crane* / HUSBAND HUNTERS; *Ruth Hale* / THE BROKEN GATE; *Miss Baker* / HORSE SHOES; *Margie* / THE POOR NUT; *the girl* / FLYING LUCK. **1928:** *Sandra* / WALLFLOWERS; *Mary Post* / WARMING UP; *Mary* / BROTHERLY LOVE. **1929:** *Mary Spengler* / SINS OF THE FATHER; *Alys La Fosse* / THE CANARY MURDER CASE; *Ruth Hutt* / STAIRS OF SAND; *Lia Eltham* / THE MYSTERIOUS DR. FU MANCHU; *Janie* / THE SATURDAY NIGHT KID; *Greta Nelson* / HALF WAY TO HEAVEN. **1930:** *Babe Mardsen* / STREET OF CHANCE; *Mary Gordon* / YOUNG EAGLES; *guest* / PARAMOUNT ON PARADE; *Lia Eltham* / THE RETURN OF DR. FU MANCHU; *Mary Ryan* / DANGER LIGHTS; *Mildred Wayland* / THE SILVER HORDE; *Sylvia Martine* / THE GANG BUSTER. **1931:** *Barbara Olwell* / VIRTUOUS HUSBAND; *Beatrice Stevens* / THE LAWYER'S SECRET; *Ethel Simmons* / EX-BAD BOY. **1933:** *Joan Hoyt* / THE PAST OF MARY HOLMES. **1934:** *Sandra Morrison* / WHIRLPOOL; *Joan Hayes* / THE DEFENSE RESTS; *waitress / mother* / THE MOST PRECIOUS THING. **1935:** *Theresa O'Reilly* / PUBLIC HERO NO. 1; *Marge Oliver* / PARTY WIRE. **1936:** *Paula Bradford* / THE EX-MRS. BRADFORD; *Claire Peyton* / ADVENTURE IN MANHATTAN; *Carol Baldwin* / MORE THAN A SECRETARY. **1939:** *Bonnie Lee* / ONLY ANGELS HAVE WINGS. **1940:** *Vicky Lowndes* / TOO MANY HUSBANDS; *Phoebe Titus* / ARIZONA. **1943:** *Molly Truesdale* / A LADY TAKES A CHANCE. **1944:** *Janice Anderson* / THE IMPATIENT YEARS.

ASTAIRE, FRED

(Frederick Austerlitz, 1899–1987)

"Can't act. Can't sing. Slightly bald. Can dance a little." This was reportedly the evaluation of Fred Astaire by a Universal agent scouting him on Broadway. His own evaluation of his talents was the overly modest, "I don't understand what people see in me. I don't look like a movie star and I don't act like a movie star. I'm just an old so and so from Omaha." RKO benefited from ignoring these judgments when they teamed him with Ginger Rogers in a series of 1930s musical masterpieces. Astaire began dancing professionally in 1906 with his sister Adele, working vaudeville circuits then moving on to a string of Broadway musical hits between 1918 and 1931. His partnership with his sister ended that year when she married. Astaire is recognized as being in a class by himself when it comes to the art of the dance. He was always a charming performer, a more-than-adequate singer, and a better-than-average actor. His first straight dramatic role was in ON THE BEACH in 1959. In 1949 he was given an honorary Academy Award for his contribution to films. In 1974 he was nominated for a Best Supporting Actor Oscar for his work in THE TOWERING INFERNO, and in 1975 he received a Life Achievement Award from the American Film Institute.

KEY ROLES

Fred Ayres / FLYING DOWN TO RIO, 1933, RKO, d-Thorton Freeland.

With this film RKO made movie history, uniting for the first time Astaire and Ginger Rogers. The teaming was magic. Astaire is cast as a dancer with an American dance band which becomes a big hit in Rio de Janeiro. He and Rogers dance to the captivating "Carioca."

Guy Holden / THE GAY DIVORCEE, 1934, RKO, d-Mark Sandrich.

Ginger Rogers mistakes Astaire for a professional correspondent hired by her lawyer so that she can secure a divorce. As for the more important aspects of the movie, the two thrilled audiences dancing to "The Continental."

Huckleberry "Huck" Haines / ROBERTA, 1935, RKO, d-William A. Seiter.

Astaire plays the buddy of Randolph Scott, who has inherited a dress salon in Paris. He runs into old flame Ginger Rogers who is posing as a Polish countess. The best of their five numbers together is Jerome Kern and Otto Harbach's "I'll Be Hard To Handle."

Jerry Travers / TOP HAT, 1935, RKO, d-Mark Sandrich.

Astaire falls in love with Rogers, but she believes he is married to her friend (Helen Broderick). He ends up chasing her all over Europe to correct the misunderstanding. He delighted audiences with Irving Berlin's "Top Hat, White Tie and Tails," and was forever after associated with formal wear, even though he wasn't thrilled by such foppery.

"Bake" Baker / FOLLOW THE FLEET, 1936, RKO, d-Mark Sandrich.

Astaire takes off his usual tuxedo and puts on a sailor's suit while he and Rogers quarrel, make up, and dance to the sublime "Let's Face the Music and Dance" by Irving Berlin. Their other numbers include "Let Yourself Go" and "I'm Putting All My Eggs in One Basket."

John "Lucky" Garnett / SWING TIME, 1936, RKO, d-George Stevens.

Astaire dances with his shadow in the production of "Bojangles of Harlem," and with Rogers to the dazzling "Never Gonna Dance." Early in the movie Astaire pretends to have two left feet and takes dancing lessons from Rogers—but he proves that she's the world's best teacher. Other Jerome Kern / Betty Fields numbers include "Pick Yourself Up" and "The Way You Look Tonight."

Peter P. "Pete" Peters / Petrov / SHALL WE DANCE, 1937, RKO, d-Mark Sandrich.

In this one Astaire is a world-famous ballet artist and Rogers is a revue star. They're both phonies and they soon catch on to each other's act. The plot is silly, as usual, but it doesn't really matter with numbers like "They Can't Take that Away from Me" and "Slap that Bass" by Ira and George Gershwin. The pair also do "Let's Call the Whole Thing Off" on roller skates.

Tony Flagg / CAREFREE, 1938, RKO, d-Mark Sandrich.

Astaire is a psychiatrist who agrees to analyze Rogers to find out why she's broken her engagement to Ralph Bellamy three times. The reason is he's the wrong man, and Astaire's the right one. The score by Irving Berlin includes "Since They Turned Loch Lomond into Swing" and "Change Partners." By this time Astaire and Rogers didn't want to continue the partnership and it shows.

Vernon Castle / THE STORY OF VERNON AND IRENE CASTLE, 1939, RKO, d-H. C. Potter.

Astaire is one half of the famous husband-and-wife ballroom team. He joins the British Royal Flying Corps in World War I and is killed in a plane crash. "Only When You're in My Arms" by Con Conrad, Harry Ruby, and Bert Kalmar was the only song written especially for the show. The other numbers are standards of the era such as "Glow, Little Glow Worm," "By the Light of the Silvery Moon," "Way Down Yonder in New Orleans," and "Oh, You Beautiful Doll."

Robert Curtis / YOU'LL NEVER GET RICH, 1941, Columbia, d-Sidney Lanfield.

Astaire is a play producer who gets drafted just before his big show. He finds time to serve his country, put on the show, and win Rita Hayworth as well. The two team up on "So Near and Yet So Far" and "Boogie Barcarolle."

Ted Hanover / HOLIDAY INN, 1942, Paramount, d-Mark Sandrich.

Astaire is (what else?) a song and dance man who tries to steal his ex-partner's (Bing Crosby) girl (Marjorie Reynolds). Astaire is not given enough to do in this picture, but he does team up with others for "I'll Capture Your Heart Singing," "You're Easy to Dance With," and "Be Careful It's My Heart."

Jed Potter / BLUE SKIES, 1946, Paramount, d-Stuart Heisler.

Astaire is back in competition with Bing Crosby, his ex-partner again, for the affection of Joan Caulfield. Astaire is outstanding in "Puttin' on the Ritz." His other Irving Berlin numbers include "A Pretty Girl Is Like a Melody" and, with Bing, "A Couple of Song and Dance Men."

Don Hewes / EASTER PARADE, 1948, MGM, d-Charles Walters.

Astaire made something of a comeback when he replaced Gene Kelly, who had broken his leg, in this Irving Berlin musical about a dancer who grooms young Judy Garland to take the place of his partner (Ann Miller), who walked out on him when a better opportunity came along. Astaire and Garland team up for "A Couple of Swells" and the title song. Alone, Astaire does justice to "Drum Crazy" and "Steppin' Out with My Baby."

Tony Hunter / THE BAND WAGON, 1953, MGM, d-Vincente Minnelli.

Many consider this the best of Astaire's pictures. He plays a movie song-and-dance man who can't find work. He is talked into starring in a Broadway show written by two old friends (Nanette Fabray and Oscar Levant) and directed by a genius (Jack Buchanan). The show bombs but Astaire takes over and turns it into a smash hit. His dance routines with Cyd Charisse and his clowning with Buchanan, Fabray, and Levant are priceless. Astaire dances alone to "A Shine on Your Shoes" and joins the others for "That's Entertainment." He and Charisse dance superbly to "Dancing in the Dark" and in the "Girl Hunt" ballet.

Dick Avery / FUNNY FACE, 1957, Paramount, d-Stanley Donen.

Astaire is a fashion photographer who turns drab Audrey Hepburn into a top model while falling in love with her. They collaborate on the title number and "S'Wonderful" by the Gershwins.

Julian Osborn / ON THE BEACH, 1959, United Artists, d-Stanley Kramer.

In his first straight dramatic role, Astaire is one of the last survivors of Atomic War, facing certain death through radioactive poisoning. It's a depressing movie and Astaire's performance is properly gloomy.

Harlee Claiborne / THE TOWERING INFERNO, 1974, 20th Century-Fox / Warners, d-John Guillermin and Irwin Allen.

Astaire is an aging con man who crashes the gala celebration for the opening of a 138-story skyscraper. He falls for Jennifer Jones, who doesn't survive a disastrous fire in the glass and steel building.

OTHER ROLES

1933: *himself* / DANCING LADY. **1937:** *Jerry Halliday* / A DAMSEL IN DISTRESS. **1940:** *Johnny Brett* / BROADWAY MELODY OF 1940; *Danny O'Neill* / SECOND CHORUS. **1942:** *Robert Davis* / YOU WERE NEVER LOVELIER. **1943:** *Fred Atwell (Fred Burton)* / THE SKY'S THE LIMIT. **1945:** *Johnny Riggs* / YOLANDA AND THE THIEF. **1946:** *guest* / ZIEGFELD FOLLIES. **1949:** *Josh Barkley* / THE BARKLEYS OF BROADWAY. **1950:** *Bert Kalmar* / THREE LITTLE WORDS; *Donald Elwood* / LET'S DANCE. **1951:** *Tom Bowen* / ROYAL WEDDING. **1952:** *Charles Hill* / THE BELLE OF NEW YORK. **1955:** *Jervis Pendleton* / DADDY LONG LEGS. **1957:** *Steve Canfield* / SILK STOCKINGS. **1961:** *Biddeford "Pogo" Poole* / THE PLEASURE OF HIS COMPANY. **1962:** *Franklin Armbruster* / THE NOTORIOUS LANDLADY. **1968:** *Finian McLonergan* / FINIAN'S RAINBOW. **1969:** *John Pedley* / MIDAS RUN. **1974:** *host* / THAT'S ENTERTAINMENT! **1976:** *host* / THAT'S ENTERTAINMENT, PART 2; *Daniel Hughes* / THE AMAZING DOBERMANS. **1977:** *Dr. Scully* / THE PURPLE TAXI. **1981:** *Ricky Hawthorne* / GHOST STORY.

ASTOR, MARY

(Lucille Langhanke, 1906–1987)

A beauty queen at 15, Mary Astor was pushed into acting by her father. After bit appearances she became a star when she appeared with John Barrymore in BEAU BRUMMELL. Her major silent roles were as innocent heroines in costume dramas. In talkies she played devious seductresses and demure women, finishing her career as mother to all of MGM's ingenues. Her career survived a scandalous divorce in 1936 in which excerpts from her "purple" diary were read in court detailing her affair with George S. Kaufman. She always maintained that it was a clever forgery. This intelligent, dark-haired woman published five novels and two autobiographies. Speaking of herself, she observed, "I was neither a peacock nor the girl next door, and heads turning in my direction always gave me sweaty palms."

KEY ROLES

Adriana Della Varnese / DON JUAN, 1926, Silent, Warners, d-Alan Crosland.

Astor, who had an affair off screen with John Barrymore when she was 17, portrays Don Juan's main romantic interest, much to the distress of Lucretia Borgia (Estelle Taylor), who plans her usual way of getting rid of adversaries.

Barbara Willis / RED DUST, 1932, MGM, d-Victor Fleming.

Astor is the wife of an engineer on a rubber plantation in Indochina, who pursues the overseer (Clark Gable). Her passion for the macho Gable is more than she can handle and it almost drives her mad. Fortunately for Gable, Astor's competition (Jean Harlow) can take care of things when they get too hot.

Edith Cortright / DODSWORTH, 1936, Goldwyn, d-William Wyler.

Although suffering notoriety because of her divorce case, the charming Astor delighted audiences as the expatriate widow who helps Walter Huston find solace when his unfaithful wife (Ruth Chatterton) abandons him. She introduces herself to Huston when he asks the steward to bring him a drink to steady his nerves, and she answers, "Why don't you try stout, Mister Dodsworth?"

Antoinette de Mauban / THE PRISONER OF ZENDA, 1937, David O. Selznick, d-John Cromwell.

Because of her love for Black Michael (Raymond Massey), commoner Astor, who could only be his mistress if he came to the throne, helps thwart his plans to usurp the throne of his brother Rudolph, who is Massey's prisoner at Zenda. Loyalists have gotten a look-alike British cousin to impersonate the king until the coronation is over. Both the king and his cousin are played by Ronald Colman. Astor must also fend off the advances of Massey's lecherous aide, played by Douglas Fairbanks, Jr.

Helen Flammarion / MIDNIGHT, 1939, Paramount, d-Mitchell Leisen.

John Barrymore hires Claudette Colbert to distract a gigolo who is paying too much attention to Barrymore's wife (Astor). It's a charming comedy with Astor creating one of her best characterizations.

Sandra Kovak / THE GREAT LIE, 1941, Warners, d-Edmund Goulding.

Astor won the Best Supporting Actress Oscar for her performance as a nasty concert pianist who accepts money from Bette Davis in exchange for her baby, whose father is George Brent. Astor wars with Davis, yelling, "There's only one thing holding him to you, Maggie, and that's my baby. Why, I'd be too proud to hold a man with another woman's child."

Brigid O'Shaughnessy / THE MALTESE FALCON, 1941, Warners, d-John Huston.

Astor is perfect as the pathological liar who drags Sam Spade (Humphrey Bogart) into a quest for the fabulously valuable, jewel-encrusted Maltese Falcon. Her deceptive talents and scene-stealing abilities were never more in evidence than in this film. She begs Bogie, "Be generous, Mr. Spade," but the only time she tells the truth is when she admits "I've always been a liar."

Alberta Marlow / ACROSS THE PACIFIC, 1942, Warners, d-John Huston.

Astor helps Bogart thwart the Japanese attempt to destroy the Panama Canal just prior to the attack at Pearl Harbor.

Princess Centimillia / THE PALM BEACH STORY, 1942, Paramount, d-Preston Sturges.

Astor plays the man-hungry sister of Rudy Vallee, who sets her cap for Joel McCrea when her millionaire brother proposes to his ex-wife (Claudette Colbert) in this crazy but delightful comedy. McCrea is just her meat as she stakes her claim: "How wonderful to meet a silent American again! All my husbands were foreigners—and such chatterboxes."

Mrs. Anne Smith / MEET ME IN ST. LOUIS, 1944, MGM, d-Vincente Minnelli.

Astor plays the mother of a loving family at the turn of the century faced with a possible move from St. Louis to New York at the time of the World's Fair. The film, and all who perform in it, bring to the audience a very delectable slice of life.

Marmee March / LITTLE WOMEN, 1949, MGM, d-Mervyn LeRoy.

Astor once again demonstrates her maternal instincts as she plays the mother of the four March sisters in this story of growing up in pre-Civil War America.

Roberta Carter / RETURN TO PEYTON PLACE, 1961, 20th Century-Fox, d-Jose Ferrer.

In this movie all the sweetness is gone from Astor as she plays a mean and selfish mother, for a change.

Irene Perry / YOUNGBLOOD HAWKE, 1964, Warners, d-Delmer Daves.

Astor is an aging stage star for whom the title character accepts a commission to dramatize his best-selling novel.

OTHER ROLES

Two-reelers

1921: THE BEGGAR MAID; BROTHER OF THE BEAR; LADY OF THE PINES; THE BASHFUL SUITOR; THE YOUNG PAINTER. **1922:** THE SCARECROW; THE ANGELUS; THE RAPIDS.

Feature films

1922: *bit* / HOPE; *bit* / BALLOTS OR BULLETS; *young woman* / THE MAN WHO PLAYED GOD; *Irene Mason* / JOHN SMITH. **1923:** *bit* / HOLLYWOOD; *bit* / TO THE LADIES; *Vivian Hope-Clarke* / THE MARRIAGE MAKER; *Narcissa Escobar* / THE BRIGHT SHAWL; *Rachel* / PURITAN PASSIONS; *Rose Randolph* / SUCCESS; *Polly Crawford* / SECOND FIDDLE; *Violet Lynwood* / WOMAN-PROOF. **1924:** *Lady Margery Alvanley* / BEAU BRUMMELL; *Helen Castle* / UNGUARDED WOMEN; *Mary O'Mallory* / THE FIGHTING AMERICAN; *Lucy* / THE FIGHTING COWARD; *Fay Bartholdi* / INEZ FROM HOLLYWOOD; *Alice Barrows* / THE PRICE OF A PARTY. **1925:** *Dolores de Muro* / DON Q, SON OF ZORRO; *Leonore Bewlay* / ENTICEMENT; *Doris* / THE PACE THAT THRILLS; *Margo* / PLAYING WITH SOULS; *Dolores Hicks* / OH, DOCTOR!; *Fidele Tridon* / SCARLET SAINT. **1926:** *Mary* / THE WISE GUY; *Jennie Clayton* / FOREVER AFTER; *Audrey Nye* / HIGH STEPPERS. **1927:** *Elena (Rosita)* / ROSE OF THE GOLDEN WEST; *Anis Bin Adham* / TWO ARABIAN NIGHTS; *Dolly* / THE ROUGH RIDERS; *Amy Cortissos* / THE SEA TIGER; *Molly Gibson* / THE SUNSET DERBY; *Sally Montgomery* / NO PLACE TO GO. **1928:** *Princess Delatorre / Ellen Gutherie* / HEART TO HEART; *Anna* / THREE-RING MARRIAGE; *Carol Trent* / SAILORS' WIVES; *Elizabeth Quimby* / DRY MARTINI; *Jeanne* / DRESSED TO KILL. **1929:** *Judith Andrews* / ROMANCE OF THE UNDERWORLD; *Marjorie Ware* / NEW YEAR'S EVE; *Dee Renaud* / THE WOMAN FROM HELL. **1930:** *Mimi Howell* / LADIES LOVE BRUTES; *Mary Gray* / THE RUNAWAY BRIDE; *Julia Seton* / HOLIDAY; *Rosita Garcia* / THE LASH; *Kitty Marsden* / THE SIN SHIP; *Princess Anne* / THE ROYAL BED. **1931:** *Lily* / OTHER MEN'S WOMEN; *Mary Linden* / BEHIND OFFICE DOORS; *Norma Selbee* / WHITE SHOULDERS; *Nancy Gibson* / SMART WOMAN; *Martha Silk* / MEN OF CHANCE. **1932:** *Follette March* / THE LOST SQUADRON; *Emmie Wilton* / A SUCCESSFUL CALAMITY; *May* / THOSE WE LOVE. **1933:** *Ruth Wayburn* / THE LITTLE GIANT; *Letty Pace* / JENNIE GERHARDT; *Hilda Lake* / THE KENNEL MURDER CASE; *Arlene Dale* / CONVENTION CITY; *Virginia Clafin Nordholm* / THE WORLD CHANGES. **1934:** *Charlotte* / EASY TO LOVE; *Jessica Wells* / THE MAN WITH TWO FACES; *Olga Morgan* / RETURN OF THE TERROR; *Mrs. Hettie Stream* / UPPER WORLD; *Bessie Foley* / THE CASE OF THE HOWLING DOG; *Odette Mauclair* / I AM A THIEF. **1935:** *Vida* / MAN OF IRON; *Patricia Sanford* / RED HOT TIRES; *Marian Henshaw* / STRAIGHT FROM THE HEART; *Mrs. Daniels* / DINKY; *Gladys Russell* / PAGE MISS GLORY; *Lilian Ash* / THE MURDER OF DR. HARRIGAN. **1936:** *Polly* / LADY FROM NOWHERE; *Edith Farnham* / AND SO THEY WERE MARRIED; *Bobby Blake* / TRAPPED BY TELEVISION. **1937:** *Madame Germaine De Laage* / THE HURRICANE. **1938:** *Mrs. Mallebre* / PARADISE FOR THREE; *Kay McGowan* / NO TIME TO MARRY; *Lola Fraser* / THERE'S ALWAYS A WOMAN; *Cynthia Holland* / WOMAN AGAINST WOMAN. **1939:** *Dottie Wingate* / LISTEN DARLING. **1940:** *Mary Ann Young* / BRIGHAM YOUNG. **1943:** *Jo Evans* / YOUNG IDEAS; *Hyllary Jones* / THOUSANDS CHEER. **1944:** *Delilah Donay* / BLONDE FEVER. **1946:** *Elizabeth Van Doren* / CLAUDIA AND DAVID. **1947:** *Fritzi Haller* / DESERT FURY; *Louise Bishop* / CYNTHIA; *Senora Morales* / FIESTA; *Queenie Havock* / CASS TIMBERLANE. **1948:** *Pat* / ACT OF VIOLENCE. **1949:** *Ada* / ANY NUMBER CAN PLAY. **1956:** *Mrs. Corliss* / A KISS BEFORE DYING; *Mrs. George Salt* / THE POWER AND THE PRIZE. **1957:** *Mrs. Jargin* / THE DEVIL'S HAIRPIN. **1958:** *Mrs. Tremaine* / THIS HAPPY FEELING. **1959:** *Mrs. Beasley* / STRANGER IN MY ARMS. **1964:** *Mrs. Jewel Mayhew* / HUSH...HUSH, SWEET CHARLOTTE.

AYRES, LEW

(Lewis Frederick Ayres, 1908–)

The soft-spoken Lew Ayres became an international star with his portrayal of a disillusioned German soldier in ALL QUIET ON THE WESTERN FRONT (1930). Years later, the deeply religious actor declared himself a conscientious objector in World War II. His career, then at a high point with his Dr. Kildare portrayals, was all but destroyed, even though he served with honor as a medical corpsman and assistant chaplain. Ayres said, "To me war was the greatest sin. I couldn't bring myself to kill other men." He was nominated for a Best Actor Oscar in 1948 for JOHNNY BELINDA, and was married to actresses Lola Lane and Ginger Rogers. In the early 1950s he began producing religious documentaries. His made-for-TV films include HAWAII FIVE-O (1968), MARCUS WELBY (1968), THE BISCUIT EATER (1972), FRANCIS GARY POWERS (1976), and GREATEST HEROES OF THE BIBLE (1978).

KEY ROLES

Pierre / THE KISS, 1929, Silent, MGM, d-Jacques Feyder.

Greta Garbo personally chose Ayres to appear as her leading man in her last silent film. He plays the son of her husband's business partner, and is in love with the great Garbo. She is forced to kill her jealous husband to protect Ayres.

Paul Baumer / ALL QUIET ON THE WESTERN FRONT, 1930, Universal, d-Lewis Milestone.

Ayres is one of a group of German schoolboys who enthusiastically enlist in the army in World War I, and are killed one by one. Ayres lives long enough to learn that there's no glory in war, only insanity. As he says to other students when back home on leave: "We live in the trenches out there. We fight. We try not to be killed, but sometimes we are. That's all." He also expresses the very sane observation: "When it comes to dying for your country, it's better not to die at all."

Pat Gilbert / STATE FAIR, 1933, Fox Films, d-Henry King.

Ayres is the rather flippant man Janet Gaynor meets at the state fair she attends with her farm family. Despite a few complications, they fall in love in this pleasant family story.

Bill Dexter / LAST TRAIN FROM MADRID, 1937, Paramount, d-James Hogan.

Ayres is a journalist covering the Spanish Civil War. Although the movie was roundly panned, his performance was singled out for praise.

Ned Seaton / HOLIDAY, 1938, Columbia, d-George Cukor.

This was Ayres's favorite role. He plays the alcoholic playboy brother of Katharine Hepburn, who helps her steal her sister's fiancé (Cary Grant) so at least one of the three children of wealth can escape it's burden.

Dr. James Kildare / YOUNG DR. KILDARE, 1938, MGM, d-Harold S. Bucquet.

Ayres didn't originate the role of Dr. Kildare; that honor went to Joel McCrea over at Paramount in the 1937 feature INTERNS CAN'T TAKE MONEY. However, Ayres made the character his own and was extremely popular as the new doctor matching wits with cranky but lovable old Dr. Gillespie, played by Lionel Barrymore. Ayres made nine movies in the series but was dropped when he declared himself a conscientious objector during World War II.

Dr. Scott Elliott / THE DARK MIRROR, 1946, International, d-Robert Siodmak.

Ayres is a psychiatrist brought into a criminal case to determine which of two identical twins is a murderer. It is an unconvincing but highly interesting example of the film noir genre of movies.

Dr. Robert Richardson / JOHNNY BELINDA, 1948, Warners, d-Jean Negulesco.

Ayres was nominated for an Oscar for his touching portrayal of a kindly doctor in a Nova Scotia village who befriends a deaf-mute girl (Jane Wyman) who is raped. Ayres is suspected of being the father of the child that is a consequence of the brutal attack by Stephen McNally. In the end, the child and Wyman become his in bonds stronger than blood.

Vice President Harley Hudson / ADVISE AND CONSENT, 1962, Columbia, d-Otto Preminger.

Ayres, the seemingly incompetent and unheeded vice president of the United States, is all set to cast the tie-breaking vote in a Senate hearing on the appointment of a controversial nominee for secretary of state, when the president dies, and Ayres decides he will name his own man.

"Mac" McAllister / THE CARPETBAGGERS, 1964, Paramount, d-Edward Dmytryk.

Ayres has the unenviable task of serving as head accountant for a Howard Hughes-like character (George Peppard) until the latter summarily fires him after years of faithful service.

OTHER ROLES

1927: *bit* / FLIGHT COMMANDER. **1928:** *bit* / MEN WITHOUT FEAR. **1929:** *bit* / THE SOPHOMORE; *bit* / THE SHAKEDOWN. **1930:** *Jerry Brooks* / MANY A SLIP; *Hugh Fullerton* / COMMON CLAY; *Billy Benson* / EAST IS WEST; *Louis Ricardo* / DOORWAY TO HELL. **1931:** *Young Mason* / IRON MAN; *Robert Marshall* / UP FOR MURDER; *Bucky O'Brien* / THE SPIRIT OF NOTRE DAME; *States* / HEAVEN ON EARTH. **1932:** *Dr. Myron Brown* / IMPATIENT MAIDEN; *Michael Rand* / NIGHT WORLD; *Larry Wayne* / OKAY AMERICA. **1933:** *Bill McCaffery* / DON'T BET ON LOVE; *Ronnie Gregory* / MY WEAKNESS. **1934:** *Norman* / CROSS COUNTRY CRUISE; *Larry Wilson* / SHE LEARNED ABOUT SAILORS; *Erik Landstrom* / SERVANTS' ENTRANCE; *Jimmie* / LET'S BE RITZY. **1935:** *Frank Harrington* / LOTTERY LOVER; *Eddie Howard* / SILK HAT KID; *Caleb Enix* / SPRING TONIC. **1936:** *Woody Davis* / THE LEATHERNECKS HAVE LANDED; *Jerry* / PANIC ON THE AIR; *Bob Sanderson* / SHAKEDOWN; *Dud "Dynamite"* / LADY BE CAREFUL; *Kent Murdock* / MURDER WITH PICTURES; *Nicholas Carter* / THE CRIME NOBODY SAW. **1937:** *Tommy Graham* / HOLD 'EM NAVY. **1938:** *Joe McKnight* / SCANDAL STREET; *Jerry Flynn* / KING OF NEWS BOYS; *Henry Thayer* / RICH MAN, POOR GIRL; *Sam Thatcher* / SPRING MADNESS. **1939:** *Eddie Burgess* / ICE FOLLIES OF 1939; *James Godfrey Seymour* / BROADWAY SERENADE; *Dr. James Kildare* / CALLING DR. KILDARE; *Phillip S. Griswold* / THESE GLAMOUR GIRLS; *Dr. James Kildare* / THE SECRET OF DR. KILDARE; *Sky Ames* / REMEMBER? **1940:** *Dr. James Kildare* / DR. KILDARE'S STRANGE CASE; *Dr. James Kildare* / DR. KILDARE GOES HOME; *Henry Twinkle* / THE GOLDEN FLEECING; *Dr. James Kildare* / DR. KILDARE'S CRISIS. **1941:** *Bob Rawlston* / MAISIE WAS A LADY; *Dr. James Kildare* / THE PEOPLE VS. DR. KILDARE; *Dr. James Kildare* / DR. KILDARE'S VICTORY; *Dr. James Kildare* / DR. KILDARE'S WEDDING DAY. **1942:** *Oliver Duffy* / FINGERS AT THE WINDOW. **1947:** *Larry Hannaford* / THE UNFAITHFUL. **1950:** *Vanner* / THE CAPTURE. **1951:** *Captain Hunt* / NEW MEXICO. **1953:** *John Tracy* / NO ESCAPE; *Dr. Patrick J. Cory* / DONOVAN'S BRAIN. **1972:** *Noah Calvin* / THE MAN. **1973:** *Mandemus* / BATTLE FOR THE PLANET OF THE APES. **1977:** *alien* / END OF THE WORLD. **1978:** *Bill Atherton* / DAMIEN—OMEN II. **1979:** *Adar* / BATTLESTAR GALACTICA; *Jason Burke* / SALEM'S LOT.

BACALL, LAUREN

(Betty Jean Perske, 1924–)

Lauren Bacall was a model for *Harper's Bazaar* when she was spotted by Howard Hawks, who offered her a part in TO HAVE AND HAVE NOT (1944). The film made a star of the 19-year-old beauty and won her a husband in co-star Humphrey Bogart. Her deep, sexy voice and sophisticated toughness gave this tall, slim blonde with the almond-shaped eyes what then was called the 1940s "look." Also married to Jason Robards, Jr., Bacall has long been associated with liberal causes. In 1947, she and Bogart joined other actors and actresses in protesting the House Un-American Activities Committee in Washington. Starting at the top as she did, she had no place to go but down in the movies, and when roles appropriate for her dried up in the 1960s, she moved on to Broadway where she scored great successes in "Cactus Flower" and "Applause." She has made a number of very forgettable movie appearances since, but now seems best suited to the stage in works such as her 1981 hit "Woman of the Year."

KEY ROLES

Marie Browning / TO HAVE AND HAVE NOT, 1944, Warners, d-Howard Hawks.

"You know you don't have to act with me, Steve. You don't have to say anything, and you don't have to do anything. Not a thing. Oh, maybe just whistle. You know how to whistle, don't you Steve? You just put your lips together and blow." With this little speech, Bacall makes it perfectly clear that she wants Humphrey Bogart, and if this isn't enough her body language is equally as sultry. Bacall is stranded on Martinique during World War II and helps him save some French resistance leaders from the Nazis. She captures the great Bogart in the process.

Vivian Sternwood Rutledge / THE BIG SLEEP, 1946, Warners, d-Howard Hawks.

General Sternwood hires Philip Marlowe (Humphrey Bogart) to save his younger daughter from her own wild indiscretions. But it seems that Bacall, the general's older daughter, is caught up in murder and blackmail herself. Her crack to Bogart, "So you're a private detective. I didn't know they existed, except in books—or else they were greasy little men snooping around hotel corridors. My, you're a mess, aren't you?" didn't prevent them from falling for each other.

Nora Temple / KEY LARGO, 1948, Warners, d-John Huston.

Bacall lives at a run-down Key Largo hotel that is visited by Humphrey Bogart, an officer who knew her late husband; a mobster (Edward G. Robinson) and his henchmen; and a hurricane. She falls for Bogart and helps him dispose of Robinson and the other baddies and looks just fine at the end of the storm.

Amy North / YOUNG MAN WITH A HORN, 1950, Warners, d-Michael Curtiz.

Bacall marries a jazz trumpet player (Kirk Douglas) she doesn't love and her selfishness almost ruins him. This thinly disguised biopic of cornet great Bix Beiderbecke fails to address the problems of the famed jazz musician, but is still interesting.

Schatze Page / HOW TO MARRY A MILLIONAIRE, 1953, 20th Century-Fox, d-Jean Negulesco.

Betty Grable, Marilyn Monroe, and Bacall are out to catch millionaire husbands. Bacall gets one in Cameron Mitchell but when she says yes to his proposal of marriage she believes he is a car mechanic.

Lucy Moore Hadley / WRITTEN ON THE WIND, 1957, Universal-International, d-Douglas Sirk.

In this movie, Bacall is a secretary who marries Robert Stack and finds herself as the steadying force for his dissolute Texas oil family.

Mrs. Sampson / HARPER, 1966, Warners, d-Jack Smight.

Bacall plays a wealthy woman who hires a private detective (Paul Newman) to locate her missing husband. This movie has some aspects of THE BIG SLEEP, but is not nearly as good.

OTHER ROLES

1945: *Rose Cullen* / CONFIDENTIAL AGENT. **1946:** *guest* / TWO GUYS FROM MILWAUKEE. **1947:** *Irene Jansen* / DARK PASSAGE. **1950:** *Sonia Kovac* / BRIGHT LEAF. **1954:** *Elizabeth* / WOMAN'S WORLD. **1955:** *Meg Faversen Rinehart* / THE COBWEB; *Cathy* / BLOOD ALLEY. **1957:** *Marilla Hagen* / DESIGNING WOMAN. **1958:** *Julie Beck* / THE GIFT OF LOVE. **1959:** *Catherine Wyatt* / NORTH WEST FRONTIER. **1964:** *Dr. Edwina Beighley* / SHOCK TREATMENT; *Sylvia Broderick* / SEX AND THE SINGLE GIRL. **1974:** *Mrs. Hubbard* / MURDER ON THE ORIENT EXPRESS. **1976:** *Bond Rogers* / THE SHOOTIST. **1980:** *Esther Brill* / HEALTH. **1981:** *Sally Ross* / THE FAN; *herself* / THE GREAT MUPPET CAPER.

BAKER, CARROLL

(1931–)

Carroll Baker's first important movie roles were as a sensible and sweet young woman in GIANT and a nymphet in BABY DOLL. She saw the possibilities of the latter and made a deliberate decision to become a sex symbol, at which she was only partially successful. Hers was not the wholesome sexuality of a Marilyn Monroe, but rather a tawdry vulgarity meant to appeal to prurient interests, and even at this she was less than a smash. As her career developed she became increasingly more difficult to cast, so she moved to Europe to appear in cheap exploitation films, many of which were just short of being pornographic. These included ORGASMO (1968), SO SWEET...SO PERVERSE (1969), THE SPIDER and AT THE BOTTOM OF THE POOL (1971), THE DEVIL HAS SEVEN FACES, BEHIND THE SILENCE, and BLOODY MARY (1972), THE FLOWER WITH THE DEADLY STING and THE MADNESS OF LOVE (1973), TAKE THIS MY BODY (1974), THE PRIVATE LESSON, THE LURE, THE SKY IS FALLING, and VIRGIN WIFE (1975), THE BODY, CONFESSIONS OF A FRUSTRATED HOUSEWIFE, and ZERSCHOSSENE TRAUME (1976), CYCLONE (1977), RICH AND RESPECTABLE (1978), and THE SECRET DIARY OF SIGMUND FREUD (1983).

KEY ROLES

Luz Benedict II / GIANT, 1956, Warners, d-George Stevens.

Named for her late, revered maiden aunt (Mercedes McCambridge) Baker has more of the gumption admired by her cattle baron father (Rock Hudson) than does his wimpy son (Dennis Hopper).

Baby Doll / BABY DOLL, 1956, Warners, d-Elia Kazan.

Playing the chaste, thumb-sucking child-wife of Karl Malden, Baker was carnally suggestive enough to get the movie condemned by the Legion of Decency and to make baby doll pajamas popular.

Rina Marlowe Cord / THE CARPETBAGGERS, 1964, Paramount, d-Edward Dmytryk.

First Baker is George Peppard's girl, but when she discovers that his dad (Leif Erickson) has all the money, she marries him. When he dies and Peppard inherits everything, she makes another play for him. Her end comes in a plunge to her death from a large chandelier from which she is dancing.

Deborah Wright / CHEYENNE AUTUMN, 1964, Warners, d-John Ford.

Baker plays a Quaker schoolteacher who is sympathetic to the plight of the Cheyenne. After years of waiting for promised federal aid and seeing their numbers decimated, the Cheyenne decide to make the 1,500 mile journey from their Oklahoma reservation to their former Yellowstone hunting grounds. Baker makes the trek with them.

Jean Harlow / HARLOW, 1965, Paramount, d-Gordon Douglas.

This is one of two films made that year on the life of the platinum blonde sex symbol. Though Baker could show off her body as well as Harlow, she didn't have the latter's talent for comedy.

OTHER ROLES

1953: *Clarice* / EASY TO LOVE. **1958:** *Patricia Terrill* / THE BIG COUNTRY. **1959:** *Teresa* / THE MIRACLE; *Eleanor Brown* / BUT NOT FOR ME. **1961:** *Mary Ann Gates* / SOMETHING WILD; *Gwen Terasaki* / BRIDGE TO THE SUN. **1963:** *Eve Prescott* / HOW THE WEST WAS WON. **1964:** *Catherine* / STATION SIX-SAHARA. **1965:** *Veronica* / THE GREATEST STORY EVER TOLD; *Sylvia West* / SYLVIA; *Julie Anderson* / MR. MOSES. **1967:** *herself* / JACK OF DIAMONDS. **1968:** *Deborah* / THE SWEET BODY OF DEBORAH; *Kathryn West* / PARANOIA; *woman* / THE HAREM. **1971:** *Mrs. Anderson* / THE FOURTH MRS. ANDERSON; *Maude* / CAPTAIN APACHE. **1972:** *Mary* / BLOODY MARY. **1974:** *black-clad woman* / BAGA YAGA DEVIL WITCH. **1977:** *Mrs. Aiken* / ANDY WARHOL'S BAD. **1979:** *Linda Cooper* / THE WORLD IS FULL OF MARRIED MEN. **1980:** *Helen Curtis* / THE WATCHER IN THE WOODS. **1983:** *Mrs. Stratton* / STAR 80; *Brown* / RED MONARCH. **1985:** *Gerda Hoffman* / HITLER'S S.S.: PORTRAIT IN EVIL. **1986:** *Mrs. Dalton* / NATIVE SON. **1987:** *Annie Phelan* / IRONWEED.

BAKER, SIR STANLEY

(1928–1976)

This forceful, Welsh-born actor progressed from lovable villains to tough and uncompromising working-class roles. A mature and talented performer, he co-produced several of his films including ZULU, ROBBERY, and WHERE'S JACK? He was knighted shortly before he died from pneumonia after an operation.

KEY ROLES

First Officer Bennett / THE CRUEL SEA, 1953, Great Britain, Ealing, d-Charles Frend.

Baker's unsympathetic role as a gluttonous petty officer on an Atlantic corvette during World War II established him as a screen actor. Shot in harsh black and white, the film faithfully recreates the mood of the often harsh life on a ship trailed by German U-boats.

Erik Bland / HELL BELOW ZERO, 1954, Columbia, d-Mark Robson.

Suspicion points toward Baker as the man responsible for the death of Joan Tetzel's father, especially as he tries to ram the ship in which she and Alan Ladd are sailing.

Henry Tudor / RICHARD III, 1955, Great Britain, London Films, d-Laurence Olivier.

Baker makes regal the role of the future king of England who defeats Richard III (Olivier) at Bosworth.

Tom Yatley / HELL DRIVERS, 1957, Great Britain, Rank, d-C. Raker Endfield.

In this violent, thrilling, funny, and generally absurd film, Baker is one of a group of truck drivers who must drive at breakneck speed on unfit roads to make their deliveries for a two-bit trucking firm.

Owen Morgan / CAMPBELL'S KINGDOM, 1957, Great Britain, Rank, d-Ralph Thomas.

Baker is a crooked contractor who wants to flood the land inherited by Dirk Bogarde to benefit his hydroelectric dam. He's willing to kill to get what he wants, but Bogarde fights back with a motley bunch of volunteers.

Johnny Bannion / THE CRIMINAL, 1960, Great Britain, Merton Park, d-Joseph Losey.

Sentenced to fifteen years in prison for a racetrack robbery, Baker plans to do his time, figuring that when he is released he will be a rich man. On the outside his old friends think that his silence about where the loot is hidden shows a lack of trust in them. They arrange for a prison riot which allows Baker to escape and he leads them right to the money. They kill him and, at the end of the film, are frantically digging for the hidden dough.

Lt. John Chard / ZULU, 1964, Great Britain, Paramount, d-Cy Endfield.

Baker is an engineering officer who, in 1879, commands an undermanned group of British soldiers at Rorke's Drift against 3,000 Zulus. He, the other officer (Michael Caine), and his small group of men demonstrate extreme bravery. When the Zulus break off the fighting, they salute their adversaries.

Paul Clifton / ROBBERY, 1967, Great Britain, Joseph E. Levine, d-Peter Yates.

Baker leads a group of crooks who rob the night mail train from Glasgow. It's an exciting cops-and-robbers film.

OTHER ROLES

1943: *Peter* / UNDERCOVER. **1948:** *bit* / OBSESSION. **1949:** *Barnes* / ALL OVER TOWN. **1950:** *Sergeant Bannoch* / YOUR WITNESS; *Evans* / LILI MARLENE. **1951:** *Joe* / THE ROSSITER CASE; *milkman* / CLOUDBURST; *Willie Dougan* / HOME TO DANGER; *Mr. Harrison* / CAPTAIN HORATIO HORNBLOWER. **1952:** *reporter* / WHISPERING SMITH VS. SCOTLAND YARD. **1953:** *Breton* / THE RED BERET; *Edgar Allen Poe* / THE TELL-TALE HEART. **1954:** *Mike* / THE GOOD DIE YOUNG; *Louis Galt* / BEAUTIFUL STRANGER; *Mordred* / KNIGHTS OF THE ROUND TABLE. **1955:** *Achilles* / HELEN OF TROY. **1956:** *Attalus* / ALEXANDER THE GREAT; *Stephen Lorimer* / CHILD IN THE HOUSE; *Corporal Ryker* / HELL IN KOREA; *O'Donovan* / CHECKPOINT. **1957:** *Sergeant Truman* / VIOLENT PLAYGROUND. **1958:** *Abel Hewson* / SEA FURY. **1959:** *Konrad Heisler* / THE ANGRY HILLS; *Captain Langford* / YESTERDAY'S ENEMY; *Captain Bardow* / JET STORM; *Inspector Morgan* / BLIND DATE. **1960:** *Inspector Martineau* / HELL IS A CITY. **1961:** *CPO Brown* / THE GUNS OF NAVARONE. **1962:** *Astaroth* / SODOM AND GOMORRAH; *Tyvian Jones* / EVA; *Walter Beddoes* / IN THE FRENCH STYLE; *Turpin* / A PRIZE OF ARMS; *Joe Newman* / THE MAN WHO FINALLY DIED. **1965:** *Tom Davis* / DINGAKA; *Bain* / SANDS OF THE KALAHARI; *narrator* / ONE OF THEM IS NAMED BRETT. **1967:** *Charley* / ACCIDENT. **1968:** *Dr. Osborne* / THE GIRL WITH THE PISTOL. **1969:** *Jonathan Wild* / WHERE'S JACK?; *Bill Oliver* / THE GAMES. **1970:** *Mr. Graham* / PERFECT FRIDAY; *Maj. Harry Grigsby* / THE LAST GRENADE; *Inspector Silva* / POPSY POP. **1971:** *Inspector Corvin* / A LIZARD WITH A WOMAN'S SKIN. **1972:** *John Craig* / INNOCENT BYSTANDERS. **1975:** *Huerta* / ZORRO. **1976:** *Pedro de Vargas* / PETITA JIMINEZ.

BALL, LUCILLE

(1910–1989)

In 1933 an MGM talent scout took Lucille Ball to Hollywood, where she became a decorative bit player in literally dozens of movies. In 1935 she got her first billed role as Nurse in CARNIVAL. By 1936 she had roles with names, but her parts, and the movies she appeared in, weren't very important. Many of these small roles were made for RKO studios, which she bought twenty years later as a home for Desilu, her personal production company. Although she is best remembered as the zany TV comedienne who during the 1950s practically owned the medium, Ball did make several very fine movies.

KEY ROLES

Judy Canfield / STAGE DOOR, 1937, RKO, d-Gregory La Cava.

Ball plays one of the hopeful actresses living in a theatrical boarding house in this sterling comedy-drama. Her name is far down the credits but she makes her presence known.

Annabel / THE AFFAIRS OF ANNABEL, 1938, RKO, d-Ben Stoloff.

Ball is an actress whose press agent (Jack Oakie) arranges for her to be sent to jail for a crime she didn't commit. The publicity stunt backfires when Ball is kidnapped by real crooks and forced to be part of a crime. But in the end she is vindicated and Hollywood sits up and takes notice. Getting herself into a series of wild straits is of course just what she did so well on her TV show.

Peggy / FIVE CAME BACK, 1939, RKO, d-John Farrow.

Ball is one of the passengers on a plane downed in a jungle full of headhunters. The plane can be repaired but will only hold five. Who's to go and who's to stay is the drama in this excellent "B" film that has attained cult status.

Gloria / THE BIG STREET, 1942, RKO, d-Irving Reis.

Ball is a nasty nightclub entertainer, adored by a Mindy's busboy (Henry Fonda). When she runs afoul of a gangster he knocks her down some stairs, permanently crippling her. Ball loses everything but her mean disposition, which she takes out on Fonda, the only one to take care of her. She insists on going to Florida where she's sure she will attract a rich man and she and Fonda hitchhike south with him pushing her in the wheelchair most of the way and Ball continuously complaining. Once in Florida, Fonda rounds up as many Broadway types as he can find and holds a grand party in a nightclub for her. She has no idea that Fonda has taken all of this on himself and she expires in his arms while he is dancing her around the ballroom, her feet never touching the floor.

May Daly / Madame Du Barry / DU BARRY WAS A LADY, 1943, MGM, d-Roy Del Ruth.

Red Skelton works in a nightclub, wins a sweepstake, drinks a Mickey Finn, and dreams that he is Louis XV. Ball is his Madame Du Barry as well as the nightclub singer that he loves from a distance. These two redheads try hard to salvage this disappointing rendition of the Broadway hit, but they are up against too many obstacles with the script.

Kitty Trimble / WITHOUT LOVE, 1945, MGM, d-Harold S. Bucquet.

This is a Tracy and Hepburn pairing, with the addition of Ball as a real estate agent always on the lookout for male properties as she lets her tongue wag through a series of wisecracks. Unfortunately this story of a Washington widow who allows a scientist to move in with her is missing some sparks.

Guest / ZIEGFELD FOLLIES, 1945, MGM, d-Vincente Minnelli.

William Powell plays Florenz Ziegfeld reminiscing in heaven about his career and the acts he would include if he could just put on one more show. He sees Ball dressed to the tees, taming a group of sexy girls posing as panthers. The music is "Bring on the Beautiful Girls."

Gladys Benton / EASY TO WED, 1946, MGM, d-Edward Buzzell.

The stars of this remake of LIBELED LADY are Van Johnson and Esther Williams, but the plaudits go to Ball for her smash comedy performance. The story is about a newspaper editor who postpones his own wedding in order to find someone to compromise a socialite who is threatening to sue him for libel.

Margaret Weldon / HER HUSBAND'S AFFAIRS, 1947, Columbia, d-S. Sylvan Simon.

Ball is half of a husband-and-wife team advertising a hair remover for women which does just the opposite. She works well with Franchot Tone as her husband in this very funny film.

Gladys O'Neill / SORROWFUL JONES, 1948, Paramount, d-Sidney Lanfield.

In this Damon Runyon story, when Bob Hope, in the title role as a racehorse bookie, is left with a little girl as a marker, Ball, who until that point had loathed him, falls for him as she exercises her maternal instincts with the child.

Agatha Floud / FANCY PANTS, 1950, Paramount, d-George Marshall.

In this remake of RUGGLES OF RED GAP, Ball is the daughter of a western family that has hired an actor posing as an English butler to lord it over their friends. It's a pretty good Bob Hope and Ball romp.

Tracy Collini / THE LONG, LONG TRAILER, 1954, MGM, d-Vincente Minnelli.

Trying to take advantage of the TV success of Ball and husband Desi Arnaz, MGM cast them as a newlywed couple traveling in an extra large trailer—and learning that this is no way to start a marriage.

Kitty Weaver / THE FACTS OF LIFE, 1960, United Artists, d-Melvin Frank.

Ball and Bob Hope are two middle-aged suburbanites who have a brief, unsuccessful affair. The laughs are there but they're so predictable.

Helen North / YOURS, MINE AND OURS, 1968, United Artists / Desilu, d-Melville Shavelson.

Ball is a widow with eight kids who marries a widower with nine. They all settle in an old San Francisco house and she has another baby.

Mame Dennis / MAME, 1974, Warners, d-Gene Saks.

While this might have been the sort of thing Ball would have handled with ease in her earlier days, she was just too old for the zany Mame Dennis role and she looks it.

OTHER ROLES

1929: *bit* / BULLDOG DRUMMOND. **1933:** *bit* / BROADWAY THROUGH A KEYHOLE; *bit* / BLOOD MONEY; *bit* / ROMAN SCANDALS; *bit* / THE BOWERY; *slave girl* / MOULIN ROUGE. **1934:** *bit* / NANA; *bit* / BOTTOMS UP; *bit* / HOLD THAT GIRL; *bit* / JEALOUSY; *bit* / MEN OF THE

NIGHT; *bit* / THE FUGITIVE LADY; *bit* / BULLDOG DRUMMOND STRIKES BACK; *bit* / THE AFFAIRS OF CELLINI; *bit* / KID MILLIONS; *bit* / BROADWAY BILL. **1935:** *bit* / ROBERTA; *bit* / OLD MAN RHYTHM; *bit* / TOP HAT; *nurse* / CARNIVAL; *bit* / THE THREE MUSKETEERS; *Gwendolyn Dilley* / I DREAM TOO MUCH. **1936:** *Kitty Collins* / FOLLOW THE FLEET; *Gloria* / THE FARMER IN THE DELL; *Miss Kelly* / BUNKER BEAN; *Claire Williams* / THAT GIRL FROM PARIS; *girl* / WINTERSET. **1937:** *Ann Howell* / DON'T TELL THE WIFE. **1938:** *Salina* / JOY OF LIVING; *Carol Meely* / GO CHASE YOURSELF; *Miriam* / HAVING WONDERFUL TIME; *Christine* / ROOM SERVICE; *Nancy Fleming* / NEXT TIME I MARRY; *Annabel* / ANNABEL TAKES A TOUR. **1939:** *Jean Russell* / BEAUTY FOR THE ASKING; *Paula Sanders* / TWELVE CROWDED HOURS; *Lucy* / PANAMA LADY; *Sandra Sand* / THAT'S RIGHT—YOU'RE WRONG. **1940:** *Joan Grant* / THE MARINES FLY HIGH; *Clara Hinklin* / *Mercedes Vasquez* / YOU CAN'T FOOL YOUR WIFE; *Bubbles* / *Tiger Lily White* / DANCE, GIRL, DANCE; *Connie Casey* / TOO MANY GIRLS. **1941:** *Dot Duncan* / A GIRL, A GUY AND A GOB; *Julie Patterson* / LOOK WHO'S LAUGHING. **1942:** *Christine Larson* / VALLEY OF THE SUN; *Terry* / SEVEN DAYS' LEAVE. **1943:** *herself* / BEST FOOT FORWARD; *specialty number* / THOUSANDS CHEER. **1944:** *Julie Hampton* / MEET THE PEOPLE. **1945:** *guest* / ABBOTT AND COSTELLO IN HOLLYWOOD. **1946:** *Kathleen* / THE DARK CORNER; *Ricki Woodner* / TWO SMART PEOPLE; *Kay Williams* / LOVER COME BACK. **1947:** *Sandra Carpenter* / LURED. **1949:** *Anne* / EASY LIVING; *Ellen Grant* / MISS GRANT TAKES RICHMOND. **1950:** *Sally Elliot* / THE FULLER BRUSH GIRL. **1951:** *Narah* / THE MAGIC CARPET. **1956:** *Susan Vega* / FOREVER DARLING. **1963:** *Angela Ballantine* / CRITIC'S CHOICE. **1967:** *cameo* / A GUIDE FOR THE MARRIED MAN.

BANCROFT, ANNE

(Anna Maria Italiano, 1931–)

Trained at the American Academy of Dramatic Arts, Anne Bancroft did a lot of TV work early in her career. She became a starlet in 1951 when given a contract with 20th Century-Fox. She chose the name Anne Bancroft from a list supplied by Darryl Zanuck and made her screen debut in 1952 in DON'T BOTHER TO KNOCK. When that appearance was followed by inconsequential roles Bancroft reassessed her situation and declared, "I'm going back to New York, where an over-sized bosom doesn't take priority over reading your lines." Starting in 1957 she spent five years on Broadway, triumphing in "The Miracle Worker." She returned to Hollywood to make the film version and won an Oscar for her brilliant performance. Since then she has appeared in many memorable dramatic and comical films, the latter mostly with her second husband, Mel Brooks. She has been nominated for Oscars for THE PUMPKIN EATER, THE GRADUATE, THE TURNING POINT, and AGNES OF GOD. Her made-for-TV films include SO SOON TO DIE (1957) and JESUS OF NAZARETH (1977).

KEY ROLES

Annie Sullivan / THE MIRACLE WORKER, 1962, United Artists, d-Arthur Penn.

Bancroft is magnificent as the dedicated and strong-willed teacher of the blind, deaf, and dumb Helen Keller. Her work with Patty Duke as the young Helen is very physical, as the two fight and struggle to get or keep the upper hand in the relationship. Tears come to all when at last Bancroft gets through to Duke and the younger woman understands that they can really communicate.

Jo Armitage / THE PUMPKIN EATER, 1964, Columbia, d-Jack Clayton.

Bancroft won an Academy Award nomination for her portrayal of a compulsive mother who finds her third marriage rocky when she gets evidence of her husband's affairs.

Inge Dyson / THE SLENDER THREAD, 1965, Paramount, d-Sydney Pollack.

Bancroft plays a desperate woman who calls a Seattle crisis center to announce that she has taken an overdose of pills. She won't give her address, so police must track her down from clues received by the social worker who keeps her on the phone. It's an effectively taut picture.

Mrs. Robinson / THE GRADUATE, 1967, United Artists, d-Mike Nichols.

Bancroft received an Oscar nomination for her role as the married woman who seduces a recent college graduate (Dustin Hoffman). When Hoffman begins dating Bancroft's daughter (Katharine Ross), he learns what it is to deal with a woman scorned.

Lady Jenny Churchill / YOUNG WINSTON, 1972, Columbia, d-Richard Attenborough.

Bancroft is effective in the role of the bright and intelligent American-born mother of the young Winston Churchill.

Emma Jacklin / THE TURNING POINT, 1977, 20th Century-Fox, d-Herbert Ross.

When the American Ballet Theater visits Oklahoma City, its aging star (Bancroft) visits an ex-colleague who quit dancing to get married many years earlier. Bancroft received yet another Oscar nomination.

Mrs. Kendal / THE ELEPHANT MAN, 1980, EMI / Brooksfilms, d-David Lynch.

Bancroft is the British society woman who befriends the hideously deformed "elephant man" (John Hurt) and introduces him to fashionable society.

Maria Bronski / TO BE OR NOT TO BE, 1983, 20th Century-Fox, d-Alan Johnson.

Bancroft does a fine job as the Polish actress in this remake of the 1940s comedy about how a troupe of actors outsmart the Nazis and escape to England.

Mother Miriam / AGNES OF GOD, 1985, Columbia, d-Norman Jewison.

Bancroft gives a somewhat uncontrolled portrayal of the mother superior who must deal with a young nun who apparently has killed her baby, but seems to have no knowledge of how she came to have a child or, for that matter, how children are made.

OTHER ROLES

1952: *Lyn Leslie* / DON'T BOTHER TO KNOCK. **1953:** *Emma Hurok* / TONIGHT WE SING; *Marie* / TREASURE OF THE GOLDEN CONDOR; *Marian* / THE KID FROM LEFT FIELD. **1954:** *Paula* / DEMETRIUS AND THE GLADIATORS; *Katy Bishop* / THE RAID; *Laverne Miller* / GORILLA AT LARGE. **1955:** *Maria Ibinia* / A LIFE IN THE BALANCE; *Kathy Lupo* / NEW YORK CONFIDENTIAL; *Rosalie Regalzyk* / THE NAKED STREET; *Corinna Marston* / THE LAST FRONTIER. **1956:** *Tianay* / WALK THE PROUD LAND; *Marie Gardner* / NIGHTFALL. **1957:** *Angelita* / THE RESTLESS BREED; *Beth Dixon* / THE GIRL IN BLACK STOCKINGS. **1965:** *Dr. D. R. Cartwright* / SEVEN WOMEN. **1974:** *Edna* / THE PRISONER OF SECOND AVENUE. **1975:** *the countess* / THE HINDENBERG. **1976:** *Carla Bondi* / LIPSTICK. **1980:** *Antoinette* / FATSO. **1984:** *Estelle Rolf* / GARBO TALKS. **1987:** *Thelma Cates* / 'NIGHT, MOTHER; *Helene Hanff* / 84 CHARING CROSS ROAD.

BANKHEAD, TALLULAH

(1902–1968)

Hollywood could only rarely find the right material for this talented daughter of the South with all of her theatrical airs and her husky voice. Still, when she was in a picture her presence could not be ignored. She played a maneater in most of her pictures, but might have been more successful in movies had she sought comical rather than dramatic roles. But, then, she spent a lifetime playing herself and observed, "Nobody can be exactly like me. Sometimes even I have trouble doing it." A considerably gifted stage actress in the plays "The Dancers," "The Little Foxes," and "The Skin of Our Teeth," she is believed to have been the inspiration for Margo Channing in ALL ABOUT EVE. But Bette Davis, who played Margo, disputed the claim saying, "Miss Bankhead isn't well enough known nationally to warrant my imitating her."

KEY ROLES

Nancy Courtney / TARNISHED LADY, 1931, Paramount, d-George Cukor.

Bankhead's acting in this drama didn't excite audiences nearly as much as reports of her numerous affairs while starring on the London stage. Bankhead portrays a Park Avenue woman who marries for money, gets bored with her hubby, leaves him for a job and freedom, and returns to him when he is wiped out by the stock market crash.

Elsa Carlyle / THE CHEAT, 1931, Paramount, d-George Abbott.

Audiences familiar with Bankhead's reputation for affairs snickered a bit when she was cast as an innocent, put-upon wife in this film. After all, her position on sin was well known: "The only thing I regret about my past is the length of it. If I had to live my life again, I'd make all the same mistakes—only sooner."

Pauline Sturm / DEVIL AND THE DEEP, 1932, Paramount, d-Marion Gering.

Bankhead is the wife of a very jealous submarine commander (Charles Laughton) who becomes wild if any of his men even look at her. Gary Cooper does more than look and Laughton sinks the sub with the guilty parties aboard. This film fits Bankhead's clever remark on refusing a part: "There is less in this than meets the eye."

Connie Porter / LIFEBOAT, 1944, 20th Century-Fox, d-Alfred Hitchcock.

Bankhead is among the survivors of a torpedoed passenger ship. She is a rich woman who takes time to fall for ordinary seaman John Hodiak and play poker with Henry Hull while sitting in her mink in a leaking lifeboat. She also matches wits with the commander of the U-boat that sunk them, whom they fish from the water.

Catherine II / A ROYAL SCANDAL, 1945, 20th Century-Fox, d-Otto Preminger.

Bankhead is Russia's Catherine the Great who takes a fancy to a young officer and discovers that he's a leader of a revolt against her. She orders his execution but commutes it when she discovers he is loved by her ever-faithful lady-in-waiting (Anne Baxter). It is a showcase for Bankhead's flamboyant acting.

OTHER ROLES

1918: *bit* / WHEN MEN BETRAY; *bit* / THIRTY A WEEK; *bit* / THE TRAP. **1928:** *Nina Graham* / HIS HOUSE IN ORDER. **1931:** *Carlotta* / *Ann Trevor* / MY SIN. **1932:** *Susan* / THUNDER BELOW; *Carol Morgan* / FAITHLESS; *guest* / MAKE ME A STAR. **1943:** *guest* / STAGE DOOR CANTEEN. **1965:** *Mrs. Trefoile* / FANATIC (DIE! DIE! MY DARLING). **1966:** *voice only* / THE DAYDREAMER.

BANKS, LESLIE

(1890–1952)

Taciturn British stage actor Leslie Banks began his film career in middle age in the United States with THE MOST DANGEROUS GAME, then returned to Great Britain. Badly wounded in World War II, his once classic good looks were disfigured, giving him a more rugged appearance. With his distinctive, well-bred voice and underplayed style he was always a strong, reliable actor.

KEY ROLES

Count Zardoff / THE MOST DANGEROUS GAME, 1932, RKO, d-Ernest B. Schoedsack.

Banks is a mad hunter, bored with tracking down animals. So he lures guests to his island so that they can become his prey. When he takes on Joel McCrea and Fay Wray he meets his match.

Bob Lawrence / THE MAN WHO KNEW TOO MUCH, 1934, Great Britain, GFD / Gaumont, d-Alfred Hitchcock.

Banks's daughter is kidnapped so that Banks and his wife won't tell what they know about plans to assassinate a diplomat in Albert Hall. At the risk of being accused of always preferring an original to a remake, we must insist that this version is superior to the 1956 production.

B. G. Sanders / SANDERS OF THE RIVER, 1935, Great Britain, London Films, d-Zoltan Korda.

In this very old-school movie, Banks is a British civil servant in colonial Africa, charged with keeping the natives in line. It's very much a "white man's burden" story with even Paul Robeson dancing to the white man's tune.

Keith Darrant / TWENTY-ONE DAYS TOGETHER, 1939, Great Britain, London Films, d-Basil Dean.

When Laurence Olivier kills the husband of his girlfriend (Vivien Leigh) by accident, his barrister brother (Banks), fearing for his own career, begs Olivier not to go to the police. A mentally unbalanced ex-clergyman is accused of the crime and it's only his death from heart failure in court which saves the lot from confessing the crime.

Chorus / HENRY V, 1944, Great Britain, Eagle-Lion, d-Laurence Olivier.

As narrator, Banks introduces and comments on the play-within-a-play in this Shakespeare story of a young king's coming of age.

OTHER ROLES

1933: *Francis Relf* / STRANGE EVIDENCE; *Jim Bronson* / THE FIRE RAISERS; *Baron* / I AM SUZANNE; *Sir John Holland* / NIGHT OF THE PARTY. **1934:** *David Barr* / THE RED ENSIGN; *Robbie* / THE TUNNEL. **1936:** *Maj. Jimmy Stanton* / DEBT OF HONOR; *Mac* / THE THREE MAXIMS; *Earl of Leicester* / FIRE OVER ENGLAND. **1937:** *Col. Harry Blair* / FAREWELL AGAIN; *Lord Clontarf* / WINGS OF THE MORNING. **1939:** *Joss Merlyn* / JAMAICA INN; *Roger de Vetheuil* / DEAD MAN'S SHOES; *Insp. Roger Slade* / THE ARSENAL STADIUM MYSTERY; *Captain Hyde* / SONS OF THE SEA. **1940:** *Inspector Kirk* / BUSMAN'S HONEYMOON; *Dr. Manetta* / THE DOOR WITH SEVEN LOCKS; *George Carter* / NEUTRAL PORT. **1941:** *Vice Admiral Wetherby* / SHIPS WITH WINGS; *John Barrington* / COTTAGE TO LET. **1942:** *Taylor* / BIG BLOCKADE. **1944:** *Oliver Wilsford* / WENT THE DAY WELL? **1947:** *Charles Fox* / MRS. FITZHERBERT. **1948:**

Colonel Holland / THE SMALL BACK ROOM. **1949:** *James Smith* / MADELEINE. **1950:** *Colonel Summerfield* / EYE WITNESS.

BARNES, BINNIE

(Gitelle Barnes, 1905–1983)

Binnie Barnes was a sophisticated blonde who moved from England to Hollywood in 1934 and was often cast as the "other woman," a role she handled splendidly. Her good looks and slightly superior manner tagged her as someone not quite to be trusted, especially when men were involved. She starred in many two-reel comedies and a dozen features before her big break in 1933 as Katherine Howard in THE PRIVATE LIFE OF HENRY VIII. The film also provided the first push in successful careers of three other actresses who played wives of Henry: Merle Oberon, Wendy Barrie, and Elsa Lanchester.

KEY ROLES

Katherine Howard / THE PRIVATE LIFE OF HENRY VIII, 1933, Great Britain, London Films, d-Alexander Korda.

Barnes is Henry's (Charles Laughton) fifth wife who commits adultery with Robert Donat and is beheaded for her crime.

Alice Munro / THE LAST OF THE MOHICANS, 1936, United Artists, d-George B. Seitz.

Barnes and Heather Angel play the two English girls who are captured by the treacherous Huron (Bruce Cabot) and rescued by the great frontier scout Hawkeye (Randolph Scott) and his Indian companions, Chingachgook and his son Uncas, the last of the Mohicans.

Donna Lyons / THREE SMART GIRLS, 1937, Universal, d-Henry Koster.

Barnes is the gold digger that Deanna Durbin and her sisters (Barbara Read and Nan Grey) are trying to pry their father (Charles Winninger) from.

Milady de Winter / THE THREE MUSKETEERS, 1939, 20th Century-Fox, d-Allan Dwan.

Barnes plays the evil foil of Cardinal Richelieu in this song and dance burlesque of the classic Dumas adventure story. She hides state secrets in her ample bosom.

Barbara / GETTING GERTIE'S GARTER, 1945, United Artists, d-Allan Dwan.

Barnes has a small but very amusing role in this dim comedy about a sappy husband (Dennis O'Keefe) who must retrieve a garter he has given to Marie "The Body" McDonald before she can show it to his jealous wife.

Eve Floogle / IT'S IN THE BAG, 1945, United Artists, d-Richard Wallace.

Fred Allen and his wife (Barnes) own a flea market. When they inherit money sewn into the seat of one of five antique chairs, they must track the chairs down and get them away from the people who bought them.

Sister Celestine / THE TROUBLE WITH ANGELS, 1966, Columbia, d-Ida Lupino.

Together with the mother superior (Rosalind Russell), nun Barnes must cope with the chaos that two new students (Hayley Mills and June Harding) cause at a school for girls.

OTHER ROLES

1931: *Junetta* / LOVE LIES; *girl* / MURDER AT COVENT GARDEN; *Therese* / NIGHT IN MONTMARTE; *Spanish lady* / STRIP, STRIP, HOORAY! *Billie* / PARTNERS PLEASE; *Rosa Wopp* / DR. JOSSER KC; *Rosa* / OUT OF THE BLUE; *Tessie Bernstein* / DOWN OUR STREET. **1932:** *Peg Guinan* / INNOCENTS OF CHICAGO; *Mrs. Meredith* / THE LAST COUPON; *Carmen* / OLD SPANISH CUSTOMERS. **1933:** *Valerie Petrovna* / FORBIDDEN TERRITORY; *Joan Melhuish* / TAXI TO PARADISE; *Lil Pickering* / CHARMING DECEIVER; *Lady Perivale* / THE SILVER SPOON; *Leslie* / COUNSEL'S OPINION; *Lola* / THEIR NIGHT OUT. **1934:** *Rosita* / THE PRIVATE LIFE OF DON JUAN; *guest* / GIFT OF GAB; *Alice White* / THERE'S ALWAYS TOMORROW; *Rena Sorel* / ONE EXCITING ADVENTURE; *Helene Dupont* / THE LADY IS WILLING; *Ruth Jordan* / NINE FORTY-FIVE. **1935:** *Lillian Russell* / DIAMOND JIM; *Olivia Karloff* / RENDEZVOUS. **1936:** *Della Lane* / THE MAGNIFICENT BRUTE; *Countess Elizabeth Bartoffski* / SUTTER'S GOLD; *Priscilla* / SMALL TOWN GIRL. **1937:** *Henrietta Fairfax* / BREEZING HOME; *Caroline Whipple* / BROADWAY MELODY OF 1938. **1938:** *Nazama* / THE ADVENTURES OF MARCO POLO; *Miriam* / THREE BLIND MICE; *Lady Mere* / THE DIVORCE OF LADY X; *Marilyn Joyce* / TROPIC HOLIDAY; *Claudia Weston* / THE FIRST HUNDRED YEARS; *Harriet Martin* / ALWAYS GOODBYE; *Mrs. Simms* / GATEWAY; *Kay Swift* / THANKS FOR EVERYTHING; *Laura Cram* / HOLIDAY. **1939:** *Cecil Carver* / WIFE, HUSBAND AND FRIEND; *Jerry* / FRONTIER MARSHAL; *Blanche* / DAY-TIME WIFE; *Lady Arlington* / MAN ABOUT TOWN. **1940:** *Contesse de Vaubert* / TIL' WE MEET AGAIN. **1941:** *Sybil Ash* / TIGHT SHOES; *Myrtle Vantine* / SKYLARK; *Faith Banner* / THREE GIRLS ABOUT TOWN; *Charlotte Campbell* / THIS THING CALLED LOVE; *Sybil Barton* / ANGELS WITH BROKEN WINGS; *cameo* / LAND OF LIBERTY; *the countess* / NEW WINE. **1942:** *Vi* / CALL OUT THE MARINES; *Peggy* / I MARRIED AN ANGEL; *Lacey Miller* / IN OLD CALIFORNIA. **1943:** *Aggie Dawlins* / THE MAN FROM DOWN UNDER. **1944:** *Lil Damish* / BARBARY COAST GENT; *Alicia Larchment* / UP IN MABEL'S ROOM; *May Heatherton* / THE HOUR BEFORE DAWN. **1945:** *Anne Bonney* / THE SPANISH MAIN. **1946:** *Mildred Prescott* / THE TIME OF THEIR LIVES. **1947:** *Natalie Bagshaw* / IF WINTER COMES; *Kiki Kelly* / THE DUDE GOES WEST. **1948:** *Geraldine* / MY OWN TRUE LOVE. **1949:** *Queen Carolina* / THE PIRATES OF CAPRI. **1950:** *Catherine the Great* / SHADOW OF THE EAGLE. **1951:** *Esther Clementi* / FUGITIVE LADY. **1953:** *Countess of Florence* / *Nerina* / *Old Witch* / DECAMERON NIGHTS. **1954:** *Frisco* / FIRE OVER AFRICA. **1968:** *Sister Celestine* / WHERE ANGELS GO, TROUBLE FOLLOWS. **1972:** *Maud Ericson* / FORTY CARATS.

BARRYMORE, JOHN

(John Blythe, 1882–1942)

Son of stage actors Maurice Barrymore (Herbert Blythe) and Georgianna Drew, and brother of Ethel and Lionel, John Barrymore made his stage debut in "Magda" in 1903 and in 1913 began making movies because he had become bored with the stage. He immediately became a major box-office attraction. His career continued on into the sound era, but his drinking and wild living resulted in failing memory to the point that he could no longer recall the soliloquy for a part in his last movie, MIDNIGHT, even with the help of the ever-present giant cue cards. If he lost his memory and his looks, "The Great Profile" never lost his style, so that even in his hammy self-parodies he could make audiences forget whoever else was on the screen. About himself, he observed, "My head is buried in the sands of tomorrow, while my tail-feathers are singed by the hot sun of today." When he died in 1942, he was penniless, having lost his constant struggle for much-needed money.

KEY ROLES

Henry Jekyll / Mr. Hyde / DR. JEKYLL AND MR. HYDE, 1920, Silent, Paramount, d-John S. Robertson.

Barrymore was able to complete some transformations from Jekyll to Hyde in full view of the audience by masterful facial distortions. His appearance as the respected London physician's alter ego truly showed the evil part of his soul.

Sherlock Holmes / SHERLOCK HOLMES, 1922, Silent, Goldwyn, d-Albert Parker.
The "Great Profile" portrays the great detective. He is asked by his friend Dr. Watson to help Prince Alexis to clear himself of an alleged theft. He traps the real culprit, Professor Moriarty, and finds love with Miss Alice Faulkner.

Gordon Bryon "Beau" Brummel / BEAU BRUMMEL, 1924, Silent, Warners, d-Harry Beaumont.
Barrymore plays the European trend-setter and friend of the Prince of Wales with great style and disdain. The arrogance and insolent living of his character matches that of the handsome actor.

Ahab Ceeley / THE SEA BEAST, 1926, Silent, Warners, d-Millard Webb.
In this version of Melville's *Moby Dick*, Ahab (Barrymore) competes with brother Derek for the hand of Esther Harper (played by Dolores Costello who in 1928 married Barrymore). To get Ahab out of the way, Derek pushes him overboard where Moby Dick takes his leg. A bitter man, Ahab first seeks out the whale to kill, then brother Derek, before settling down with Esther.

Don Juan / DON JUAN, 1926, Silent, Warners, d-Alan Crosland.
In this the first feature to be released with a synchronized musical score, Barrymore scored a huge success as the man who takes all from women and yields nothing. Mary Astor was not his choice for his leading lady—his affair with her had long been over and he wanted his current lady-fair, Dolores Costello, opposite him.

François Villon / BELOVED ROGUE, 1927, Silent, United Artists, d-Alan Crosland.
The role of the adventurer poet, who charms King Louis XI of France, inspires a Paris mob to fight against Burgundy, and wins the love of the King's ward Charlotte, is just right for Barrymore and he plays it with great gusto.

Sgt. Ivan Markov / TEMPEST, 1928, Silent, United Artists, d-Sam Taylor.
Barrymore is a Russian peasant soldier who loves Princess Tamara but she scorns him because of his low birth. When the Revolution begins, Barrymore becomes an important Red official, saves Tamara from execution, and escapes with her to a new beginning.

Guest / SHOW OF SHOWS, 1929, Warners, d-John G. Adolfi.
Barrymore makes his talkie debut in this all-star revue, acting in a scene from "Richard III."

Captain Ahab / MOBY DICK, 1930, Warners, d-Lloyd Bacon.
The plot to this talkie is similar to that of Barrymore's 1926 silent film, THE SEA BEAST.

Svengali / SVENGALI, 1931, Warners, d-Archie Mayo.
Barrymore is an 1890s Parisian hypnotist who can turn Marian Marsh into a great opera star but can't control who she loves. Once again Barrymore demonstrates his genius for becoming his character, showing all the suffering of a victim of unrequited love who must blank out the mind of his beloved to keep her.

Duke of Chermerace (Arsene Lupin) / ARSENE LUPIN, 1932, MGM, d-Jack Conway.
Barrymore is a Parisian gentleman thief who almost gets away with the Mona Lisa. Lionel Barrymore, in the first film where John and Lionel appear together, is the detective who is determined to capture the infamous thief.

Baron Felix von Geigern / GRAND HOTEL, 1932, MGM, d-Edmund Goulding.
Barrymore is an adventurer who comes to the Berlin Grand Hotel to steal the jewels of a famous ballet star (Greta Garbo). Instead he prevents her from committing suicide and they fall in love. But he is killed by Wallace Beery when he attempts to rob him.

Hillary Fairchild / A BILL OF DIVORCEMENT, 1932, RKO, d-George Cukor.
In this tearjerker, Barrymore has just been released from a mental institution and comes home to meet his strong-willed daughter (Katharine Hepburn) for the first time. When she realizes where he has been, she sends her fiancé away, fearing insanity to be hereditary, and pledges to stay and care for the father she has never known.

Prince Paul Chegodieff / RASPUTIN AND THE EMPRESS, 1932, MGM, d-Richard Boleslawsky.
In the only film that John ever made with his sister Ethel and brother Lionel, he portrays the Russian aristocrat who kills the evil monk Rasputin. The real prince and princess sued MGM and won considerable damages on the libel charge that the prince's rape of the princess was fiction.

Auguste Topaze / TOPAZE, 1933, RKO, d-Harry d'Abbabie d'Arrast.
Barrymore is a mousy, French schoolmaster who learns the wicked ways of the business world and turns them to his advantage.

Larry Renault / DINNER AT EIGHT, 1933, MGM, d-George Cukor.
In this superb all-star drama, Barrymore is excellent as an alcoholic, fading matinee idol. Producer Jean Hersholt tells him "You sag, Renault, like an old woman...You're a corpse...go get yourself buried!" Barrymore takes his advice and kills himself in his cheap room.

Oscar Jaffe / TWENTIETH CENTURY, 1934, Columbia, d-Howard Hawks.
This is the marvelously hilarious comedy about a temperamental Broadway producer (Barrymore) and the unknown actress (Carole Lombard) he turns into a star. When she fails to show the proper amount of appreciation, he rages, "I'll tell the world who's a fake! You are! I taught you everything you know. Even your name, Lily Garland—I gave you that. If there is a justice in heaven, Mildred Plotka, you will end up where you belong—in the burlesque house."

Mercutio / ROMEO AND JULIET, 1936, MGM, d-George Cukor.
In this cast of senior citizens, Barrymore begins his slide into self-parody, playing Mercutio as a somewhat portly, lecherous, aging man.

Colonel Nielson / BULLDOG DRUMMOND COMES BACK, 1937, Paramount, d-Louis King.
Although nominally in a supporting role, Barrymore, donning and doffing disguises, is clearly the star of this story about villains who want revenge on the gentleman adventurer of the title.

Windy Turlon / SPAWN OF THE NORTH, 1938, Paramount, d-Henry Hathaway.

Barrymore, once again very much the ham, gives a flamboyant portrayal of a grizzled, guzzling Alaskan newspaperman.

Vance / THE GREAT MAN VOTES, 1938, RKO, d-Garson Kanin.

Still displaying his proud theatrical manner and marvelous voice, Barrymore, the longtime matinee idol, gives one last excellent performance playing a drunken professor who turns out to have the deciding vote in a local election.

George Flammarion / MIDNIGHT, 1939, Paramount, d-Mitchell Leisen.

Barrymore is amusing as the Parisian husband who hires Claudette Colbert to seduce the gigolo who is putting the rush on his wife (Mary Astor). Barrymore couldn't remember his lines for this film even though he worked from cue cards. Astor, who had been his lover twenty years earlier, remarked later that Barrymore had been old and sick while making the movie.

OTHER ROLES

1913: *Frank Perry* / ARE YOU A MASON?; *Beresford Kruger* / AMERICAN CITIZEN. **1914:** *Fitzhew* / THE MAN FROM MEXICO. **1915:** *Brooke Travers* / THE DICTATOR. **1916:** *James Dukane* / THE INCORRIGIBLE DUKANE; *Bertie Joyce* / THE LOST BRIDEGROOM; *Cicero Hannibal Butts* / THE RED WIDOW; *Jack Merriwell, Prince of Bulwana* / NEARLY A KING. **1917:** *A. J. Raffles* / RAFFLES, THE AMATEUR CRACKSMAN. **1918:** *Robert Ridgeway* / ON THE QUIET. **1919:** *Frederick Tile* / HERE COMES THE BRIDE; *Martin Wingrave* / THE TEST OF HONOR. **1921:** *Jacques Leroi* / THE LOTUS EATER. **1927:** *Chevalier des Grieux* / WHEN A MAN LOVES. **1929:** *Marcus Poltran* / ETERNAL LOVE; *Duke of Kurland* / *Prince Christian (General Crack)* / GENERAL CRACK. **1930:** *Lord Strathpeffer* / THE MAN FROM BLANKLEY'S. **1931:** *Ivan Tsarakov* / THE MAD GENIUS. **1932:** *Tom Cardigan* / STATE'S ATTORNEY. **1933:** *Rudolf* / REUNION IN VIENNA; *Riviere* / NIGHT FLIGHT; *George Simon* / COUNSELOR AT LAW. **1934:** *Carl Bellaire* / LONG LOST FATHER. **1937:** *Nicolai Nazaroff* / MAYTIME; *Dr. Ernest Tindal* / NIGHT CLUB SCANDAL; *Colonel Neilson* / BULLDOG DRUMMOND'S REVENGE; *Colonel Neilson* / BULLDOG DRUMMOND'S PERIL. **1938:** *Charley* / TRUE CONFESSION; *Zoltan Jason* / ROMANCE IN THE DARK; *King Louis XV* / MARIE ANTOINETTE; *Governor* / HOLD THAT CO-ED. **1940:** *Evans Garrick* / THE GREAT PROFILE. **1941:** *Professor Gibbs* / THE INVISIBLE WOMAN; *Duncan de Grasse* / WORLD PREMIERE. **1942:** *himself* / PLAYMATES.

BARTHELMESS, RICHARD

(1895–1963)

Described by Lillian Gish as having "the most beautiful face of any man who went before the camera," this spaniel-eyed son of an actress was discovered at Trinity College in Connecticut by Nazimova. He became a star in BROKEN BLOSSOMS with Gish in 1919. He is most remembered for his sweet, country-boy roles during the silent era and, though he found it difficult to adapt to the fast-talking style of the early talkies, he remained popular into the thirties. He continued to make films in the late 1930s but his days as a big star were over. He quit the movies in 1942 to join the naval reserve and he never returned.

KEY ROLES

Cheng Haun / BROKEN BLOSSOMS, 1919, Silent, United Artists, d-D. W. Griffith.

This film has been proclaimed a silent masterpiece and in it Barthelmess is a Chinese boy who has a pure and holy love for Lillian Gish. But she lives with her brute of a father (Donald Crisp) who flies into a rage and beats the poor, innocent Gish to death when he learns that his daughter is living under the protection of a Chinaman. Heartbroken, Barthelmess empties his pistol into Crisp, carries the lifeless body of Gish to his home, lays her out in a silken gown, and commits suicide.

David Kinemon / TOL'ABLE DAVID, 1921, Silent, First National, d-Henry King.

In what was probably his best role, Barthelmess plays the youngest son of a Virginia mountain family who, after being branded a coward, finally engages three marauding convicts in an unequal fight.

Oliver Bashforth / THE ENCHANTED COTTAGE, 1924, Silent, First National, d-John S. Robertson.

Left disfigured by World War I, Barthelmess moves into a secluded cottage to escape other people. He meets and marries plain-looking May McAvoy and their mutual admiration grows into love as they find beauty within each other that no one else can see or share.

Patent Leather Kid / THE PATENT LEATHER KID, 1927, Silent, First National, d-Alfred Santell.

As an East Side boxer, Barthelmess has little affection for his country now at war with Germany. After he and his trainer are drafted, the latter is shot in action. The loss spurs Barthelmess to acts of heroism and pride in his country. Barthelmess was nominated for an Academy Award for this film and THE NOOSE for 1927–1928.

Dick Courtney / THE DAWN PATROL, 1930, First National, d-Howard Hawks.

Barthelmess is a fearless World War II British aviator who discovers that the responsibility of sending young flyers to their certain death is worse than taking the risk one's self.

Cary Lockwood / THE LAST FLIGHT, 1931, Warners, d-William Dieterle.

Barthelmess is one of four veteran Yank flyers who stay on in Paris after World War I in the hope of calming their physical and emotional states.

Marvin / CABIN IN THE COTTON, 1932, Warners, d-Michael Curtiz.

Barthelmess is an indignant sharecropper who gets the runaround from southern belle Bette Davis, an evil, wealthy woman who almost ruins him. An indication of her character is in the line she delivers to our hero: "Ah'd love to kiss yuh, but ah just washed mah hair."

Pierre Radler / A MODERN HERO, 1934, Warners, d-G. W. Pabst.

In the only American film ever directed by Pabst, Barthelmess gives one of his best performances playing a ruthless circus rider who reveals his business ambitions, only to find his dreams turning into nightmares with the stock market crash.

Bat McPherson / ONLY ANGELS HAVE WINGS, 1939, Columbia, d-Howard Hawks.

Barthelmess is a disgraced aviator whose wife (Rita Hayworth) is the cause of pilot Cary Grant's negative attitude toward women. Barthelmess wins respect back with some very dangerous flying—he has nitroglycerine as his cargo.

Bronco Kid Farrell / THE SPOILERS, 1942, Universal, d-Ray Enright.

In his final film role Barthelmess is a gambler who works for and loves Marlene Dietrich, who fancies John Wayne.

OTHER ROLES

1916: *Arno* / WAR BRIDES; *George Turner* / JUST A SONG AT TWILIGHT. **1917:** *bit* / CAMILLE; *Gennaro* / THE ETERNAL SIN; *bit* / THE MORAL CODE; *Prince Charming* / THE SEVEN SWANS; *Tommy Gray* / BAB'S BURGLAR. **1919:** *Tom Ballantyne* / THE HOPE CHEST; *Everett White* / BOOTS; *Ralph Grey* / THE GIRL WHO STAYED AT HOME; *Dr. James Merritt* / PEPPY POPPY; *Scoop McCready* / I'LL GET HIM YET; *Alvarez* / SCARLET DAYS. **1920:** *Dan McGuire* / THE IDOL DANCER; *Bruce Sanders* / THE LOVE FLOWER; *David Bartlett* / WAY DOWN EAST. **1921:** *youth* / EXPERIENCE. **1922:** *John Alden, Jr.* / THE SEVENTH DAY; *Sonny* / *Joe* / SONNY; *Peter Newbolt* / *Joe Newbolt* / THE BOND BOY. **1923:** *Charles Abbott* / THE BRIGHT SHAWL; *Karl Van Kerstenbroock* / THE FIGHTING BLADE. **1924:** *Julian McCullough* / TWENTY-ONE; *Duncan Irving, Jr.* / CLASSMATES. **1925:** *Will Webb* / NEW TOYS; *Eric Fane* / SOUL-FIRE; *Bilge Smith* / SHORE LEAVE; *Tony Gillardi* / THE BEAUTIFUL CITY. **1926:** *Prince Rupert of Koronia* / JUST SUPPOSE; *Lieutenant Ranson* / RANSON'S FOLLY; *Barnabas Barty* / THE AMATEUR GENTLEMAN; *Robert Kincarin* / THE WHITE BLACK SHEEP. **1927:** *Jack Hamill* / THE DROPKICK. **1928:** *Nickie Elkins* / THE NOOSE; *Chad Buford* / KENTUCKY COURAGE; *Nickolai* / *Schumulka* / WHEEL OF CHANCE; *Lt. Pierre Dumont* / OUT OF THE RUINS; *Steven Dunkin* / SCARLET SEAS. **1929:** *Jerry Larrabee* / WEARY RIVER; *David Carroll* / DRAG; *Albert "Binky" Whalen* / YOUNG NOWHERES; *guest* / THE SHOW OF SHOWS. **1930:** *Sam Lee* / SON OF THE GODS; *Francisco Delfina* / THE LASH. **1931:** *Breckenridge Lee* / THE FINGER POINTS. **1932:** *Karl Miller* / ALIAS THE DOCTOR. **1933:** *Jim* / CENTRAL AIRPORT; *Tom* / HEROES FOR SALE. **1934:** *Joe Thunderhorse* / MASSACRE; *Lance McGowan* / MIDNIGHT ALIBI. **1935:** *Tony* / FOUR HOURS TO KILL. **1936:** *Gerard de Lancy* / SPY OF NAPOLEON. **1940:** *J. B. Roscoe* / THE MAN WHO TALKED TOO MUCH. **1942:** *Ed Kirby* / THE MAYOR OF 44TH STREET.

BARTHOLOMEW, FREDDIE

(Frederick Llewellyn, 1924–)

This dark-haired, British-born lad was a great favorite with moms who wished their boys had his good manners. To the boys he was a big sissy, and it was in sissified roles that he was most successful. In real life he was victimized by adults, spending a great deal of his young life in courtrooms as relatives fought over his earnings. His success as a child actor did not follow him into adulthood and in the 1950s he moved into an advertising career.

KEY ROLES

David Copperfield / DAVID COPPERFIELD, 1935, MGM, d-George Cukor.

Bartholomew is the Dickens lad who is disliked by his cruel stepfather, helped by his eccentric aunt, and grows up to become an author who marries his childhood sweetheart.

Cedric "Ceddie" Erroll / LITTLE LORD FAUNTLEROY, 1936, David O. Selznick, d-John Cromwell.

Bartholomew is a well-refined but poor American boy living with his widowed mother, when he learns that he is heir to an English dukedom. In his most sissified role he had his biggest hit.

Harvey Cheyne / CAPTAINS COURAGEOUS, 1937, MGM, d-Victor Fleming.

Spoiled rotten by his wealthy, often absent father, Bartholomew learns important lessons about life and helping others from a Portuguese fisherman (Spencer Tracy) when Bartholomew falls from an oceanliner and is rescued by Tracy. Before he changes, though, there is some sentiment to throw him back to the fishes.

David Balfour / KIDNAPPED, 1938, 20th Century-Fox, d-Alfred L. Werker.

During the Jacobite rebellion in 18th-century Scotland, young Bartholomew is sold by his wicked uncle to be a slave, but is helped by a rebel outlaw (Warner Baxter) to reclaim his rightful position. This is a much altered version of the Robert Louis Stevenson story.

Jack Robinson / THE SWISS FAMILY ROBINSON, 1940, RKO, d-Edward Ludwig.

Bartholomew and his parents (Thomas Mitchell and Edna Best) build a new home on a deserted island when the ship on which they are traveling is sunk. It's mildly interesting with too little adventure.

East / TOM BROWN'S SCHOOL DAYS, 1940, RKO, d-Robert Stevenson.

Bartholomew is one of Tom Brown's classmates and closest friends until he comes to believe that Brown has squealed on an upperclassman who got him sent down.

OTHER ROLES

1935: *Sergei Karenin* / ANNA KARENINA. **1936:** *Claude* / THE DEVIL IS A SISSY; *Young Jonathan Blake* / LLOYDS OF LONDON; *King Peter* / PROFESSIONAL SOLDIER. **1938:** *Geoffrey Braemer* / LORD JEFF; *Buzz Mitchell* / LISTEN DARLING; *Bob Randolph* / SPIRIT OF CULVER. **1939:** *David Harrington* / TWO BRIGHT BOYS. **1941:** *Steve Kendall* / NAVAL ACADEMY. **1942:** *Freddie Hewlett* / CADETS ON PARADE; *Peter Carlton* / A YANK AT ETON. **1944:** *David Conway* / THE TOWN WENT WILD. **1947:** *himself* / SEPIA CINDERELLA. **1951:** *Reverend Wilbur* / ST. BENNY THE DIP.

BASEHART, RICHARD

(1915–1984)

Richard Basehart never attained top stardom but he was a strong leading man adept at portraying characters with psychological problems or suffering mental anguish. He made many films abroad which did not enjoy wide circulation in the United States. Besides his successful TV series "Voyage to the Bottom of the Sea," his TV movies include SO SOON TO DIE (1957), THE DEATH OF ME YET (1971), MANEATER (1973), MARILYN, THE UNTOLD STORY (1980), and KNIGHT RIDER (1982).

KEY ROLES

Davis Morgan / HE WALKED BY NIGHT, 1948, Eagle-Lion, d-Alfred Werker (and uncredited Anthony Mann).

Basehart is a psychotic but brilliant cop-killer who robs electronics stores. The police are thwarted by the successful burglar because he listens in on their radio network and knows their plans concerning him. He is tracked down through dogged detective work by Scott Brady and Roy Roberts.

Robespierre / THE BLACK BOOK, (REIGN OF TERROR), 1949, Eagle-Lion, d-Anthony Mann.

Basehart is the French leader whose plans to establish a one-man dictatorship are thwarted by Robert Cummings, who secures the black book that contains the names of future guillotine victims.

Robert Cosick / FOURTEEN HOURS, 1951, 20th Century-Fox, d-Henry Hathaway.

The title of the movie refers to the time Basehart spends on a ledge of a Manhattan building before deciding to jump. Policeman Paul Douglas tries to talk him out of it. It's a tightly drawn film with Basehart's intensity almost physically felt by the audience.

Il Matto / LA STRADA, 1954, Italy, Ponti / de Laurentiis, d-Frederico Fellini.

Basehart plays a dim-witted clown and trapeze artist whom Anthony Quinn accidentally kills in a fight when the former becomes too friendly with the girl Quinn has "bought."

Ishmael / MOBY DICK, 1956, Warners, d-John Huston.

Basehart portrays Melville's narrator and only survivor of the ill-fated quest for the great white whale. Besides delivering the perfect opening line, "Call me Ishmael," he describes the call of the sea: "Choose any path you please and tend to one that carries you down to water. There is a magic in water that draws all men away from the land, that leads them over the hills down creeks and streams and rivers to the sea—the sea where each man, as in a mirror, finds himself."

Maj. Harry Cargill / TIME LIMIT, 1957, United Artists, d-Karl Malden.

Basehart is a major charged with collaboration with the enemy while a POW in a North Korean prison camp. He admits his guilt, but investigator Richard Widmark keeps finding inconsistencies in his story and proves that Basehart collaborated to prevent his men from being shot.

Ivan Karamazov / THE BROTHERS KARAMAZOV, 1958, MGM, d-Richard Brooks.

Basehart glows with hatred for his lecherous buffoon of a father (Lee J. Cobb) in this decent, but not commercially successful, adaptation of the Dostoyevsky novel. He yearns for Claire Bloom, but she has pledged herself to his brother (Yul Brynner). He is the intellectual of the four sons, but all his learning prevents him from ever involving himself in life.

OTHER ROLES

1947: *James Demarest* / CRY WOLF; *William Williams* / REPEAT PERFORMANCE. **1949:** *Mounts Hatfield* / ROSEANNA MCCOY; *Warren Quimby* / TENSION. **1950:** *Larry Nelson* / OUTSIDE THE WALL. **1951:** *Alan Spender* / THE HOUSE ON TELEGRAPH HILL; *Corporal Denno* / FIXED BAYONETS; *Lieutenant Rennick* / DECISION BEFORE DAWN. **1953:** *Joe Hamstringer* / THE STRANGER'S HAND; *George Headley* / TITANIC. **1954:** *Joe* / THE GOOD DIE YOUNG. **1955:** *Larry Kendall* / CARTOUCHE; *Picasso* / THE SWINDLE. **1956:** *Reggie Wilson* / THE INTIMATE STRANGER; *Joe Blake* / THE EXTRA DAY. **1959:** *Georges* / THE RESTLESS AND THE DAMNED. **1960:** *Captain Reinhardt* / FIVE BRANDED WOMEN; *Father Phelan* / NONE BUT THE BRAVE; *Howard Mason* / PORTRAIT IN BLACK. **1961:** *Don Benton* / PASSPORT TO CHINA; *Steve Fallon* / THE SAVAGE GUNS. **1963:** *Adolf Hitler* / HITLER; *Ah Min* / KINGS OF THE SUN; *narrator* / FOUR DAYS IN NOVEMBER. **1965:** *Dr. Hoffman* / THE SATAN BUG. **1972:** *Nye Buell* / CHATO'S LAND; *Dr. Caldwell* / RAGE. **1973:** *narrator* / DRIVE TO DANGER; *narrator* / AND MILLIONS WILL DIE. **1976:** *Dr. Leonard Chaney* / MANSION OF THE DOOMED. **1977:** *sayer of the law* / THE ISLAND OF DR. MOREAU. **1979:** *Vladimir Skrapinov* / BEING THERE.

BATES, ALAN

(1934–)

Dark-haired, British stage actor Alan Bates came to prominence in films portraying angry young men of the 1960s. These were followed by impressive appearances as British literary heroes. In the 1970s he mostly concentrated his flexible talents on the theater and his most recent movie appearances have been disappointing. His TV movies have included THE STORY OF JACOB AND JOSEPH (1974), A VOYAGE ROUND MY FATHER (1982), AN ENGLISHMAN ABROAD (1983), and DR. FISCHER OF GENEVA (1984).

KEY ROLES

Arthur Blakey / WHISTLE DOWN THE WIND, 1961, Great Britain, Rank, d-Bryan Forbes.

Three north country children believe murderer Bates to be Jesus Christ and offer him shelter from the police.

Vic Brown / A KIND OF LOVING, 1962, Great Britain, Anglo-Amalgamated, d-John Schlesinger.

Bates, a north country draftsman, is forced into marriage. Later he and his unhappy wife are able to come to some kind of understanding about their relationship despite living with her battle-ax of a mother.

Jimmy Brewster / NOTHING BUT THE BEST, 1964, Great Britain, Anglo-Amalgamated, d-Clive Donner.

Bates is an ambitious clerk who claws his way to success through gall, sham, and one-upsmanship. He even marries the boss's daughter and then kills the boss.

Basil / ZORBA THE GREEK, 1964, Great Britain, 20th Century-Fox, d-Michael Cacoyannis.

Bates is a young English writer visiting Crete who is befriended by a gregarious Greek (Anthony Quinn) who soon dominates the younger man's life.

Jos / GEORGY GIRL, 1966, Great Britain, Columbia, d-Silvio Narizzano.

In this frantic black farce, Bates is the father of the baby expected by dumpy Lynn Redgrave's selfish roommate. Bates and Redgrave prepare for the child as if they are the parents until the mother has an abortion without telling them.

Gabriel Oak / FAR FROM THE MADDING CROWD, 1967, Great Britain, EMI / Appia, d-John Schlesinger.

Bates is a shepherd and one of three men on whom Julie Christie has a profound effect in this underrated adaptation of the Thomas Hardy novel. When relationships with her landowning neighbor and an army officer don't work out she decides that Bates is the man for her.

Yakov Bok / THE FIXER, 1968, MGM, d-John Frankenheimer.

Bates plays a Jew in Czarist Russia who is framed for various crimes, put in prison without trial, and becomes a cause célèbre. Bates was nominated for an Academy Award for his performance.

Rupert Birkin / WOMEN IN LOVE, 1969, Great Britain, United Artists, d-Ken Russell.

Bates and Oliver Reed have a nude wrestling sequence in this story about the sexual encounters of two men with two working girls (Glenda Jackson and Jennie Linden) in the Midlands during the 1920s.

Ted Burgess / THE GO-BETWEEN, 1971, Great Britain, Columbia, d-Joseph Losey.

Bates is a farmer and the secret lover of the daughter of a wealthy family living on a nearby estate. Played by Julie Christie, the daughter uses the services of a young boy infatuated with her to take messages back and forth between her and Bates. The carryings-on of Bates and Christie ultimately cause a scandal.

Ben Butley / BUTLEY, 1974, Great Britain, American Film Theatre, d-Harold Pinter.

Bates is an English lecturer at a university who must deal with his personal problems in this adequate adaptation of the successful play.

Saul Keplan / AN UNMARRIED WOMAN, 1978, 20th Century-Fox, d-Paul Mazursky.

Bates plays an artist who is the first real man Jill Clayburgh meets after her divorce. Unfortunately, he's married and plans to stay that way, but he does want to maintain their affair.

OTHER ROLES

1959: *Frank Rice* / THE ENTERTAINER. **1963:** *Mick* / THE CARETAKER; *Stephen Maddox* / THE RUNNING MAN. **1965:** *narrator* / INSH' ALLAH. **1967:** *Pvt. Charles Plumpick* / KING OF HEARTS. **1970:** *Col. Vershinin* / THREE SISTERS. **1971:** *Bri* / A DAY IN THE DEATH OF JOE EGG. **1973:** *Harry* / IMPOSSIBLE OBJECT. **1974:** *narrator* / MIKIS THEODORAKIS: A PROFILE OF GREATNESS. **1975:** *Andrew Shaw* / IN CELEBRATION; *Rudi von Sternberg* / ROYAL FLASH. **1978:** *Charley Crossley* / THE SHOUT. **1979:** *Rudge* / THE ROSE. **1980:** *Sergei Diaghilev* / NIJINSKY. **1981:** *H. J. Heidler* / QUARTET. **1982:** *Capt. Chris Baldry* / THE RETURN OF THE SOLDIER; *guest* / BRITANNIA HOSPITAL. **1983:** *Capt. Jerry Jackson* / THE WICKED LADY. **1986:** *David Cornwallis* / DUET FOR ONE; **1987:** *Jack Meehan* / A PRAYER FOR THE DYING.

BAXTER, ANNE

(1923–1985)

Dark and attractive, Anne Baxter was a stage actress from her teen years. Although she never reached superstar status, she did perfect the role of the deceptively sweet young woman who hid the fact that she was really a nasty schemer. She maintained, "I'm an actress first and last. I don't want any of this whole schmeer about being a movie star." This granddaughter of architect Frank Lloyd Wright had her best roles early in her career, with more routine assignments coming when she should have been at her peak. In her later years she made many TV movies including STRANGER ON THE RUN (1968), MARCUS WELBY (1969), and THE MONEYCHANGERS (1976).

KEY ROLES

Lucy Morgan / THE MAGNIFICENT AMBERSONS, 1942, RKO, d-Orson Welles.

Baxter is Joseph Cotton's lovely daughter who attracts Tim Holt, the spoiled son of Dolores Costello, the woman whom Cotton loved and lost years before.

Mouche / FIVE GRAVES TO CAIRO, 1943, Paramount, d-Billy Wilder.

Baxter is the innkeeper of a Sahara hotel during World War II's North African campaign. Her star guest is Field Marshall Rommel, from whom a British agent (Franchot Tone) is trying to learn the location of the former's ammunition dumps.

Katherine Mary Sullivan / THE SULLIVANS, 1944, 20th Century-Fox, d-Lloyd Bacon.

In this sentimental but true story of one family's loss of five brothers in the sinking of the cruiser Juneau off Guadalcanal, Baxter portrays the sweetheart and wife of the youngest brother (Edward Ryan).

Evelyn Heath / GUEST IN THE HOUSE, 1944, United Artists, d-John Brahm.

Baxter is a seemingly pleasant young woman who is invited to stay with an artist and his family. She repays the artist's kindness by driving his model away, turning his daughter against him, exploiting the love of his brother, and making her own play for the artist. The only one to see through this viper is an aunt who plays on Baxter's fear of birds to drive her to suicide.

Sophie Nelson / THE RAZOR'S EDGE, 1946, 20th Century-Fox, d-Edmund Goulding.

Baxter won an Academy Award as Best Supporting Actress in her role as Tyrone Power's alcoholic fiancée who commits suicide after Gene Tierney breaks up the engagement.

Eve Harrington / ALL ABOUT EVE, 1950, 20th Century-Fox, d-Joseph L. Mankiewicz.

Baxter received an Oscar nomination for her portrayal of an overly ingratiating and humble schemer, intent on usurping the roles, loves, and friends of aging stage star Bette Davis. In 1971 Baxter appeared in the Davis role in the Broadway musical version of the story, APPLAUSE. Applause is the one thing that seems to motivate Baxter, as she insists, "So little, did you say? Why, if there's nothing else there's applause. I've listened, from backstage, to people applaud. It's like—like waves of love coming over the footlights and wrapping you up. Imagine, to know every night that different hundreds of people love you. They smile. Their eyes shine. You've pleased them. They want you. You belong. Just that alone is worth anything."

Joanna / O. HENRY'S FULL HOUSE, 1952, 20th Century-Fox, d-Jean Negulesco.

In the "Last Leaf" segment of this quintet of O. Henry stories, Baxter plays a sick girl who is convinced that her death will coincide with the falling of the last leaf on the tree outside her window.

Ruth Grandfort / I CONFESS, 1953, Warners, d-Alfred Hitchcock.

The details of Baxter's innocent affair with Montgomery Clift, before he became a priest, become admissible evidence in Clift's trial. He is accused of a murder he did not commit but he cannot reveal the identity of the real murderer as the latter told him of the crime in the confessional.

Nefretiri / THE TEN COMMANDMENTS, 1956, Paramount, d-Cecil B. DeMille.

Baxter is the frequently furious queen who is in love with Moses (Charlton Heston). Not that she isn't beautiful, but Baxter was not meant to portray a sex goddess.

Kimberley / CHASE A CROOKED SHADOW, 1958, Associated Dragon Films, d-Michael Anderson.

Baxter is an heiress who finds her home invaded by a man posing as her deceased brother. It's a superbly crafted thriller with Baxter realizing that the impostor is trying to drive her mad, kill her, and steal her diamonds.

Teresina Vidaverri / A WALK ON THE WILD SIDE, 1962, Columbia, d-Edward Dmytryk.

Baxter is a sex-starved Mexican widow who operates a cafe in which she encounters Laurence Harvey, a Texas farmer on his way to New Orleans to locate his true love.

OTHER ROLES

1940: *Joan Johnson* / 20 MULE TEAM; *Mary Maxwell* / THE GREAT PROFILE. **1941:** *Amy Spettigue* / CHARLEY'S AUNT; *Julie* / SWAMP WATER. **1942:** *Nicole Rougeron* / THE PIED PIPER. **1943:** *Jean Hewlett* / CRASH DIVE; *Marina* / THE NORTH STAR. **1944:** *Janet Feller* / THE EVE OF ST. MARK; *Tessa Osborne* / SUNDAY DINNER FOR A SOLDIER. **1945:** *Countess Anna Jaschikoff* / A ROYAL SCAN-

DAL. **1946:** *Julie Richards* / SMOKY; *Barbara Foster* / ANGEL ON MY SHOULDER. **1947:** *narrator* / MOTHER WORE TIGHTS; *Lucille Stewart* / BLAZE OF NOON. **1948:** *Penny Johnson* / HOMECOMING; *Julia Norman* / THE WALLS OF JERICHO; *Nora* / THE LUCK OF THE IRISH; *Mike* / YELLOW SKY. **1949:** *Hannah Adams* / YOU'RE MY EVERYTHING; *Kit Dodge, Jr.* / A TICKET TO TOMAHAWK. **1951:** *Valerie Hogan* / FOLLOW THE SUN. **1952:** *Cal* / THE OUTCASTS OF POKER FLAT; *Virginia Mason* / MY WIFE'S BEST FRIEND. **1953:** *Norah Larkin* / THE BLUE GARDENIA. **1954:** *Willie* / CARNIVAL STORY. **1955:** *Monica Johnson* / BEDEVILED; *Tacey Cromwell* / ONE DESIRE; *Cherry Malotte* / THE SPOILERS. **1956:** *Rita Kendrick* / THE COME ON; *Lorna Hunter Saunders* / THREE VIOLENT PEOPLE. **1960:** *Dixie Lee* / CIMARRON. **1961:** *Olive* / SUMMER OF THE SEVENTEENTH DOLL; *Dr. Anne Dyson* / MIX ME A PERSON. **1965:** *Star of "Sustenance"* / THE FAMILY JEWELS. **1967:** *Margo Foster* / THE BUSY BODY. **1968:** *Mary Ann* / THE TALL WOMEN. **1971:** *Cleo* / FOOL'S PARADE; *Liz Addams Hatch* / THE LATE LIZ. **1980:** *Lilianna Zorska* / JANE AUSTEN IN MANHATTAN.

BAXTER, WARNER

(1889–1951)

Warner Baxter, who guarded his privacy as if he were a male Greta Garbo, was reported to be the highest paid male actor in Hollywood at the end of the 1930s. From then on, he quickly faded into "B" movie productions, mostly as the Crime Doctor in a series of unexceptional mysteries. During the silent era, this dashing and handsome actor with a resonant voice became Fox's biggest star, alternating between sophisticated romances and exotic adventures. Long celebrated as one of the industry's greatest worriers, he was known as stubborn, competent, quarrelsome, versatile, and responsible. In 1941 he suffered a nervous breakdown due to his extensive work schedule and was inactive until 1943. His self-composed epitaph was "Did you hear about my operation?"

KEY ROLES

Jay Gatsby / THE GREAT GATSBY, 1926, Silent, Paramount, d-Herbert Brenon.

Baxter is the young World War I army officer who swears to society belle Daisy (Lois Wilson) that he will raise himself to her social status. But by the time he does raise himself through criminal associations, she's married to another man and their renewed affair leads to tragedy.

Alessandro / RAMONA, 1928, Silent, United Artists, d-Edwin Carewe.

Baxter is a young Indian chief who elopes with the half-breed Romona (Dolores Del Rio). Their pastoral happiness is ruined by the death of their daughter and by his being accused of stealing horses.

The Cisco Kid / IN OLD ARIZONA, 1929, Fox Films, d-Raoul Walsh.

Director Walsh was set to play the Cisco Kid but he lost an eye in an accident and Baxter was brought in. Baxter made the most of the opportunity, winning an Oscar for his portrayal of the happy-go-lucky caballero whose flair for dramatic thievery and penchant for dangerous meetings with the ladies keeps him just one step ahead of the authorities.

Jim Carston / THE SQUAW MAN, 1931, MGM, d-Cecil B. DeMille.

Baxter is a British aristocrat whose life is saved by an Indian maiden (Lupe Velez). She bears his child, but commits suicide when society will not allow them to find happiness together.

Jervis Pendleton / DADDY LONG LEGS, 1931, Fox Films, d-Alfred Santell.

In this Cinderella-like story Baxter is Janet Gaynor's mysterious benefactor whom she grows up to love. Baxter, a man of wealth and influence, has been besieged by people begging for his money, so he is charmed to find that Gaynor loves him for himself.

Paul Onslow / SIX HOURS TO LIVE, 1932, Fox Films, d-William Dieterle.

Baxter is a political emissary from an unnamed country, holding his own against others at a world treaty meeting despite threats on his life. When he is strangled, a scientist revives him for six hours so he may complete his mission. He not only casts the deciding vote on the treaty, but also kills the man who killed him before curling up for good, at peace with the world.

Julian Marsh / 42ND STREET, 1933, Warners, d-Lloyd Bacon.

Baxter is the worried producer of a new Broadway show opening in the midst of the Depression. He finds he must send unknown Ruby Keeler on stage when his star (Bebe Daniels) is injured. He also delivers the immortal cliche, "...you're going out a youngster, but you've got to come back a star."

Dan Brooks / BROADWAY BILL, 1934, Columbia, d-Frank Capra.

Baxter is the broke owner of racehorse Broadway Bill. The horse proves to be a winner but at the expense of its own life.

Jaret Otkar / ONE MORE SPRING, 1935, Fox Films, d-Henry King.

Baxter is a failed antiques dealer who, together with Janet Gaynor and others, sets up camp in New York's Central Park during the Depression. The people in the group help each other find the will to go on and succeed once again in the world.

Dr. Samuel Mudd / THE PRISONER OF SHARK ISLAND, 1936, 20th Century-Fox, d-John Ford.

Baxter plays the doctor who treats John Wilkes Booth as he tries to escape after assassinating Abraham Lincoln. The doctor is convicted as a co-conspirator and sentenced to imprisonment at Shark Island, where he performs heroically, containing a yellow fever epidemic. Eventually he is exonerated and released.

Capt. Paul La Roche / THE ROAD TO GLORY, 1936, 20th Century-Fox, d-Howard Hawks.

Baxter is a French captain in the trenches in World War I whose men are constantly being killed. As replacements are sent to the front, he tells them of the regiment's proud history and later sacrifices his life in combat.

Leonard Borland / WIFE, HUSBAND AND FRIEND, 1939, 20th Century-Fox, d-Gregory Ratoff.

When Baxter's wife (Loretta Young) has delusions about becoming a great singer, Baxter takes lessons with the encouragement of Binnie Barnes but flops when he tries his hand at opera. He and Young come to their senses and decide to sing only at home.

Robert Ordway / CRIME DOCTOR, 1943, Columbia, d-Michael Gordon.

Baxter plays the former brains of a burglary gang who loses his memory as a result of a blow to the head and becomes a successful psychiatrist and head of the state parole board. He gets hit on the head again and realizes who he is, but is given a suspended sentence because of his reformed ways.

OTHER ROLES

1914: *Lewalden* / HER OWN MONEY. **1918:** *bit* / ALL WOMAN. **1919:** *bit* / LOMBARDI LTD. **1921:** *Tom Gordon* / CHEATED HEARTS; *Donald Halliday* / FIRST LOVE; *Thomas Morgan* / THE LOVE CHARM. **1922:** *Pep Mullins* / SHELTERED DAUGHTERS; *Vlademir* / IF I WERE QUEEN; *King Waring* / THE GIRL IN HIS ROOM; *Jones* / *Lord Dysart* / A GIRL'S DESIRE; *Tom Silverton* / *Phil Bradbury* / THE NINETY AND NINE; *Lew Alden* / HER OWN MONEY. **1923:** *Jack Dunbar* / BLOW YOUR OWN HORN; *Adrian Torrens* / IN SEARCH OF A THRILL; *Murray Hammond* / ST. ELMO; *Jimmy Mason* / ALIMONY. **1924:** *Stuart Knight* / CHRISTINE OF THE HUNGRY HEART; *Colonel Valentia* / THE FEMALE; *Douglas Crawford* / THE GARDEN OF WEEDS; *John Rolfe* / HIS FORGOTTEN WIFE; *Bob Kane* / THOSE WHO DANCE. **1925:** *Bunny O'Neill* / THE GOLDEN BED; *Russ Kane* / THE AIR MAIL; *Norman Slatterley* / THE AWFUL TRUTH; *Henry Morgan* / THE BEST PEOPLE; *Calvin Homer* / RUGGED WATER; *Big Boy Morgan* / A SON OF HIS FATHER; *Fred Prouty* / WELCOME HOME. **1926:** *John Herrick* / MANNEQUIN; *Thomas B. Hancock, Jr.* / MISS BREWSTER'S MILLIONS; *Nuitane* / ALOMA OF THE SOUTH SEAS; *Wade Murrell* / THE RUNAWAY; *Ted Carroll* / MISMATES. **1927:** *Matthew Standish* / THE TELEPHONE GIRL; *Clinton Philbrook* / THE COWARD; *John Curry* / DRUMS OF THE DESERT; *Royce Wingate* / SINGED. **1928:** *Rolly Sigsby* / DANGER STREET; *Walter Craig* / CRAIG'S WIFE; *Frank Gordon* / THE TRAGEDY OF YOUTH; *Tony* / A WOMAN'S WAY. **1929:** *Dr. Paul Randall* / LINDA; *Jack Winfield* / THRU DIFFERENT EYES; *John Boetham* / BEHIND THAT CURTAIN; *Pablo Wharton Cameron* / ROMANCE OF THE RIO GRANDE; *Doc* / WEST OF ZANZIBAR; *himself* / HAPPY DAYS; *James Harris* / THREE SINNERS. **1930:** *Deucalion* / RENEGADES; *Ludwig Kranz* / SUCH MEN ARE DANGEROUS. **1931:** *The Cisco Kid* / THE CISCO KID; *Dr. Judson Penning* / DOCTORS' WIVES; *Sergeant Dumaine* / SURRENDER. **1932:** *Stephen Morrow* / MAN ABOUT TOWN; *Jim Gladden* / AMATEUR DADDY. **1933:** *Lawrence Blake* / PADDY, THE NEXT BEST THING; *Phillip Fletcher* / I LOVED YOU WEDNESDAY; *Jackson Durant* / PENTHOUSE. **1934:** *Andrew Burke* / DANGEROUSLY YOURS; *Laurence Cromwell* / STAND UP AND CHEER; *Charles Lingard* / AS HUSBANDS GO; *Michael Shawn* / SUCH WOMEN ARE DANGEROUS. **1935:** *Dr. Harvey Leith* / GRAND CANARY; *Lt. Steve Warner* / HELL IN THE HEAVENS; *Cesar Campo* / UNDER THE PAMPAS MOON; *Kerry Bolton* / KING OF BURLESQUE. **1936:** *Jack Wallace* / TO MARY—WITH LOVE; *Capt. Clark Rutledge* / WHITE HUNTER; *Joaquin Murrieta* / ROBIN HOOD OF EL DORADO. **1937:** *Jim Lovett* / SLAVE SHIP; *George Curson* / VOGUES OF 1938; *Dr. Judd Lewis* / WIFE, DOCTOR, AND NURSE. **1938:** *Alan Breck* / KIDNAPPED; *Tony Newlander* / I'LL GIVE A MILLION. **1939:** *Hank Topping* / BARRICADE; *The Cisco Kid* / THE RETURN OF THE CISCO KID. **1940:** *Nick Desborough* / EARTHBOUND. **1941:** *Adam Stoddard* / ADAM HAD FOUR SONS; *cameo* / LAND OF LIBERTY. **1943:** *Robert Ordway* / THE CRIME DOCTOR'S STRANGEST CASE. **1944:** *Kendall Nesbitt* / LADY IN THE DARK; *Robert Ordway* / SHADOWS IN THE NIGHT. **1945:** *Robert Ordway* / THE CRIME DOCTOR'S COURAGE; *Robert Ordway* / THE CRIME DOCTOR'S WARNING. **1946:** *Robert Ordway* / JUST BEFORE DAWN; *Robert Ordway* / THE CRIME DOCTOR'S MAN HUNT. **1947:** *Robert Ordway* / THE MILLERSON CASE; *Robert Ordway* / THE CRIME DOCTOR'S GAMBLE. **1948:** *Earl Donovan* / A GENTLEMAN FROM NOWHERE. **1949:** *Victor Burnell* / PRISON WARDEN; *Jess Arno* / THE DEVIL'S HENCHMAN; *Robert Ordway* / THE CRIME DOCTOR'S DIARY. **1950:** *Roger Manners* / STATE PENITENTIARY.

BEATTY, WARREN

(Warren Beaty, 1937–)

Shirley MacLaine's younger brother, Warren Beatty appears in movies only when he is satisfied that he has a project that interests him as a producer, director, writer, or actor. Sometimes what interests this popular playboy also strikes the fancy of audiences, sometimes it does not. With BONNIE AND CLYDE, Beatty became a cult figure. He is almost better known for his many romances than for his creative movie efforts. A true hedonist where women are concerned, he prides himself on being honest about his limited attention span to the women in his life. "Marriage is a lie. How can you stand up and vow you'll stay together for life, when all the time you know you'll stick it out only while it's good?"

KEY ROLES

Bud Stamper / SPLENDOR IN THE GRASS, 1961, Warners, d-Elia Kazan.

Beatty and Natalie Wood play two high school students in a small Kansas town during the 1920s. They are frightened by their sexual desires and resist having a physical relationship, but their confusion is not aided by their well-meaning but insensitive parents.

Berry-Berry Willart / ALL FALL DOWN, 1962, MGM, d-John Frankenheimer.

Beatty is a selfish, shallow womanizer whose affair with Eva Marie Saint results in her pregnancy, his abandonment of her, and her suicide.

Vincent Bruce / LILITH, 1964, Columbia, d-Robert Rossen.

Working as an occupational therapist in a mental institution, Beatty has an affair with patient Jean Seberg, whom he discovers pursues love in a limitless and dangerous way. Events lead to the suicide of another patient, Seberg's complete retreat into madness, and Beatty's decision that he himself needs help.

The Comic / Mickey One / MICKEY ONE, 1965, Columbia, d-Arthur Penn.

Beatty is a nightclub comedian who's in trouble with the mob because of his gambling debts. He goes on the run, meets and falls in love with Alexandra Stewart, and tries to find a way to stay alive and resume his career.

Clyde Barrow / BONNIE AND CLYDE, 1967, Warners / Seven Arts, d-Arthur Penn.

Beatty plays the notorious bank robber of the 1920s who, with Bonnie Parker (Faye Dunaway), terrorizes the Southwest as they race toward an expected appointment with death. He proudly announces to all he meets, "We rob banks." It's an extraordinary movie and Beatty portrays the impotent Barrow with a combination of boyish charm and murderous intent. Beatty was nominated for an Oscar and the film, which he produced, was up for the Best Picture Award.

John Q. McCabe / MCCABE AND MRS. MILLER, 1971, Warners, d-Robert Altman.

Beatty is a gambling gunfighter at the turn of the century who sets up a lavish brothel in a northwest mining town. His madam is Julie Christie (then Beatty's main love off screen) and their success attracts the attention of mobsters who wish to cut themselves in.

George Roundy / SHAMPOO, 1975, Columbia, d-Hal Ashby.

In this sex farce, Beatty is a Beverly Hills hairdresser who seduces Jack Warden's wife, mistress, and daughter. These are only three of the conquests of this modern Casanova with a hairblower.

Joe Pendleton / Leo Farnsworth / Tom Jarrett / HEAVEN CAN WAIT, 1978, Paramount, d-Warren Beatty and Buck Henry.

In this delightful remake of HERE COMES MR. JORDAN, Beatty is a pro-football quarterback with the L.A. Rams who is killed before his time and must return to earth to find a new body as his was cremated. Beatty was up for a Best Actor Oscar for this film.

John Reed / REDS, 1981, Paramount, d-Warren Beatty.

Beatty was nominated for Oscars for his writing, acting, and directing and won for directing. In the movie he portrays the American radical writer and newspaperman who went to Russia at the time of the Revolution and wrote *Ten Days that Shook the World*.

OTHER ROLES

1961: *Paolo di Leo* / THE ROMAN SPRING OF MRS. STONE. **1966:** *Harley Rummel* / PROMISE HER ANYTHING; *Barney Lincoln* / KALEIDOSCOPE. **1970:** *Joe Grady* / THE ONLY GAME IN TOWN. **1971:** *Joe Collins* / $ (DOLLARS). **1973:** *guest* / YEAR OF THE WOMAN. **1974:** *Joseph Frady* / THE PARALLAX VIEW. **1975:** *Nicky* / THE FORTUNE. **1987:** *Lyle Rogers* / ISHTAR.

BEERY, WALLACE

(1885–1949)

An unusual candidate for stardom, Wallace Beery started his career as a hulky, female Swedish maid in silent shorts, played a series of beastly Huns raping stars such as Blanche Sweet in the 1917–19 period, and moved into lovable, old rogue roles in the sound era. This rubbery-faced, crooked-mouthed, big lummox with a mischievous twinkle in his eye became one of the most popular performers of his time. He correctly observed, "Like my dear old friend, Marie Dressler, my mug has been my fortune." But his strange, gargley voice had a lot to do with it as well. Beery was nominated for an Academy Award for his work in THE BIG HOUSE and won for THE CHAMP.

KEY ROLES

Richard the Lion-Hearted / ROBIN HOOD, 1922, Silent, United Artists, d-Allan Dwan.

Beery plays King Richard who makes a timely return to England to help Robin Hood foil the plans of Richard's brother, Prince John.

Professor Challenger / THE LOST WORLD, 1925, Silent, First National, d-Harry O. Hoyt.

While delivering a paper to a scientific society, Beery claims to have discovered a world in South America filled with prehistoric animals. Scorned by his peers, he forms an expedition to the Amazon and reaches the lost world. After encounters with ape-men and dinosaurs, he returns to civilization with a brontosaurus to substantiate his claim.

Butch Schmidt / THE BIG HOUSE, 1930, MGM, d-George Hill.

Beery leads a riot in a prison but the plan is thwarted when Robert Montgomery warns the warden and Chester Morris, who intervenes in the battle between Beery and the guards. His performance as the tough con with nothing to lose gained him an Oscar nomination.

Bill / MIN AND BILL, 1930, MGM, d-George Hill.

Beery is a boozy old waterfront character who helps his wife (Marie Dressler) work to keep a child who was deserted in infancy. The truant officer insists that they are unfit to raise the child.

Andy Purcell / THE CHAMP, 1931, MGM, d-King Vidor.

Beery is a washed-up prize-fighter who is adored by his son (Jackie Cooper); but the boy's mother wants Cooper back. Beery won the Academy Award for Best Actor for his role in this weepy movie.

General Director Preysing / GRAND HOTEL, 1932, MGM, d-Edmund Goulding.

Beery is a German industrialist who goes to Berlin's Grand Hotel to negotiate a business deal. When the deal backfires, so that things won't be a total loss, he arranges to buy Joan Crawford's favors, and kills John Barrymore when the latter is found in Beery's room.

Terry Brennan / TUGBOAT ANNIE, 1933, MGM, d-Mervyn LeRoy.

In this bit of hokum, Beery plays the captain of a tugboat who must be replaced by his wife (Marie Dressler) because of his drinking problems.

Dan Packard / DINNER AT EIGHT, 1933, MGM, d-George Cukor.

Beery's bickering with his wife (Jean Harlow) is among the highlights of this all-star comedy-drama about the lives of the guests invited to a society dinner party.

Chuck Connors / THE BOWERY, 1933, 20th Century-Fox, d-Raoul Walsh.

Beery and George Raft are rivals over everything, from gals to fighting ability, in this San Francisco-based burlesque about Steve Brodie, the man who survived a leap from the Golden Gate Bridge.

Pancho Villa / VIVA VILLA! 1934, MGM, d-Jack Conway.

In this violent horse opera, Beery is the Mexican bandit and revolutionary leader who is eventually gunned down away from fields of battle. His dying words are ad-libbed by his war correspondent buddy (Stuart Erwin) who composes the noble thought, "Goodbye, my Mexico. Forgive me for my crimes. Remember if I sinned against you, it was because I loved you too much." Beery, mystified, adds his real dying words, "Forgive me? Johnny, what I done wrong?"

Long John Silver / TREASURE ISLAND, 1934, MGM, d-Victor Fleming.

In one of the year's biggest hits Beery is perfect as the man who jumps back and forth between being Jackie Cooper's friend and leading the pirates who are out to kill the lad.

P. T. Barnum / THE MIGHTY BARNUM, 1934, 20th Century-Fox, d-Walter Lang.

Beery is enjoyable in his portrayal of the great showman of the 1890s who believed that "there's a sucker born every minute."

Sid Miller / AH, WILDERNESS, 1935, MGM, d-Clarence Brown.

In Eugene O'Neill's only comedy, Beery plays the alcoholic uncle who is able to commiserate with his nephew when the lad has his first encounter with demon rum and a scarlet woman.

Jack Thompson / SLAVE SHIP, 1937, 20th Century-Fox, d-Tay Garnett.

When Beery marries, he vows to end his career as a slave trader. But his first mate (Warner Baxter) and others in the crew mutiny to show their disagreement with his career decision.

Capt. Boss Starkey / STAND UP AND FIGHT, 1939, MGM, d-W. S. Van Dyke II.

Beery comes into conflict with Robert Taylor over the former's use of Taylor's stagecoach operation to transport stolen slaves.

Honest Plush Brannon / BARBARY COAST GENT, 1944, MGM, d-Roy Del Ruth.

Beery is a bandit in the California goldfields who tries to go straight in San Francisco. It's an attractive star vehicle for Beery late in his career.

OTHER ROLES

1919: *bit* / THE UNPARDONABLE SIN; *bit* / LIFE LINE; *Mendoza* / SOLDIERS OF FORTUNE; *Schomberg* / VICTORY. **1920:** *Lieutenant Brandt* / BEHIND THE DOOR; *Achmed Hamid* / THE VIRGIN OF STAMBOUL; *Henry Von Holkar* / THE MOLLYCODDLE; *Magua* / THE LAST OF THE MOHICANS; *Buck McKee* / THE ROUND UP; *Maj. Parbury* / *Ribiera* / EIGHT THIRTEEN. **1921:** *Ling Jo* / A TALE OF TWO WORLDS; *Bram Johnson* / THE GOLDEN SNARE; *Lt. Col. von Richthoffen* / THE FOUR HORSEMEN OF THE APOCALYPSE; *William Kirk* / THE LAST TRAIL; *Francois Dupont* / THE ROOKIE'S RETURN. **1922:** *"Buck" Roper* / WILD HONEY; *Chris Borg* / HURRICANE'S GAL; *Fu Chang* / I AM THE LAW; *Kenwood Wright* / THE ROSARY; *Gaspard* / THE MAN FROM HELL'S RIVER; *Ed Lee* / TROUBLE; *Jim Brennan* / ONLY A SHOP GIRL; *Jose Fagaro* / THE SAGEBRUSH TRAIL. **1923:** *Felix Bavu* / BAVU; *Gregor Karlov* / THE DRUMS OF JEOPARDY; *Don Lowrie* / THE FLAME OF LIFE; *William McCabe* / STORMSWEPT; *the villain* / THE THREE AGES; *Count Donelli* / *Hawkes* / WHITE TIGER; *Duc de Tours* / ASHES OF VENGEANCE; *Jules Repin* / DRIFTING; *King Philip IV* / THE SPANISH DANCER; *Barode Dukane* / THE ETERNAL STRUGGLE. **1924:** *Jean Scholast* / UNSEEN HANDS; *Captain Wolf* / ANOTHER MAN'S WIFE; *Jasper Leigh* / THE SEA HAWK; *"Slugger" Rourke* / DYNAMITE SMITH; *Joe Standish* / THE SIGNAL TOWER; *Bill Smythe* / MADONNA OF THE STREETS; *Bobo* / THE RED LILY; *Klaus Poole* / SO BIG. **1925:** *Joe Lawler* / COMING THROUGH; *Ben* / THE DEVIL'S CARGO; *M. Glavis* / IN THE NAME OF LOVE; *Cap Bullwinkle* / LET WOMEN ALONE; *Dutch* / THE GREAT DIVIDE; *Morgan* / ADVENTURE; *"Rhode Island" Red* / THE PONY EXPRESS; *Captain Bartlett* / RUGGED WATER. **1926:** *Pharis* / THE WANDERER; *Riff Swanson* / BEHIND THE FRONT; *Quembo* / VOLCANO; *Knockout Hansen* / WE'RE IN THE NAVY NOW; *Bos'n* / OLD IRONSIDES. **1927:** *Casey* / CASEY AT THE BAT; *Elmer* / FIREMAN, SAVE MY CHILD; *Wally* / NOW WE'RE IN THE AIR. **1928:** *Louis Hozenozzle* / WIFE SAVERS; *Mike Doolan, the dectective* / PARTNERS IN CRIME; *Powder-Horn Pete* / THE BIG KILLING; *Oklahoma Red* / BEGGARS OF LIFE. **1929:** *Chuck Riley* / CHINATOWN NIGHTS; *Gen. Orlando Jackson* / THE RIVER OF ROMANCE; *Guard Larey* / STAIRS OF SAND. **1930:** *Pat Garrett* / BILLY THE KID; *P. T. Barnum* / A LADY'S MORALS; *Tripod McMasters* / WAY FOR A SAILOR. **1931:** *Louis Scorpio* / THE SECRET SIX; *Windy* / HELL DIVERS. **1932:** *Polikai* / FLESH. **1935:** *Big Mike* / WEST POINT OF THE AIR; *Jamesy MacArdle* / CHINA SEAS; *Windy* / O'SHAUGHNESSY'S BOY. **1936:** *Sergeant Dory* / A MESSAGE TO GARCIA; *Hutch* / OLD HUTCH. **1937:** *Clem Hawley* / THE GOOD OLD SOAK. **1938:** *"Trigger" Bill* / BAD MAN OF BRIMSTONE; *Cesar* / PORT OF SEVEN SEAS; *Tom Terry* / STABLEMATES. **1939:** *John Thorson* / THUNDER AFLOAT. **1940:** *Sergeant Barstow* / THE MAN FROM DAKOTA; *Skinner Bill Bragg* / 20 MULE TEAM; *Reb Harkness* / WYOMING. **1941:** *Pancho Lopez* / THE BAD MAN; *Bill Johansen* / BARNACLE BILL. **1942:** *Hap Doan* / THE BUGLE SOUNDS; *Marmaduke "Just" Baggott* / JACKASS MAIL. **1943:** *Sgt. Maj. William Bailey* / SALUTE TO THE MARINES. **1944:** *Ben Barton* / RATIONING. **1945:** *Ned Trumpet* / THIS MAN'S NAVY. **1946:** *Zed Bascomb* / BAD BASCOMB. **1947:** *Roy "Slag" McGurk* / THE MIGHTY MCGURK. **1948:** *Jim Breedin* / ALIAS A GENTLEMAN; *Melvin R. Foster* / A DATE WITH JUDY. **1949:** *Big Jack Horner* / BIG JACK.

BELLAMY, RALPH

(1904–)

Ralph Bellamy, who began his career on the stage, was best known in the movies as the nice, dependable man who didn't get the girl. In fact, when given an honorary career Oscar in 1987, he promised that he would continue making movies until he did get the girl. His only Academy Award nomination was in 1937 for THE AWFUL TRUTH. In later years Bellamy turned in many fine performances as craggy and crusty characters, with his biggest success being his various portrayals on stage, in the movies, and on TV of Franklin D. Roosevelt. His many made-for-TV movies include WINGS OF FIRE (1968), SOMETHING EVIL (1972), THE BOY IN THE PLASTIC BUBBLE (1976), and THE WINDS OF WAR (1983).

KEY ROLES

Bill / THE MAGNIFICENT LIE, 1931, Paramount, d-Berthold Viertel.

Bellamy is an ex-doughboy who has lost his eyesight to the war and his heart to French singing star Ruth Chatterton. The latter arranges for a cafe entertainer (also Ruth Chatterton) to pose as her, and this incarnation falls in love with Bellamy.

Dr. Barclay / ONCE TO EVERY WOMAN, 1934, Columbia, d-Lambert Hillyer.

In his second feature Bellamy is the young, idealistic doctor who, at the critical moment in a delicate brain operation, pushes aside old-fashioned Dr. Walter Connelly to save the day.

Inspector Trent / ONE IS GUILTY, 1934, Columbia, d-Lambert Hillyer.

In this unpretentious detective mystery, Bellamy solves a murder involving a millionaire, his wife, and a double-crossing boxer.

Daniel Leeson / THE AWFUL TRUTH, 1937, Columbia, d-Leo McCarey.

In this film about a divorcing couple (Irene Dunne and Cary Grant), Bellamy plays the dependable but dull Texas oil man whom Dunne uses to make Grant jealous.

Dr. Shelby / BLIND ALLEY, 1939, Columbia, d-Charles Vidor.

Bellamy is a psychiatrist who tames escaped killer Chester Morris by exploring his subconscious when the latter invades Bellamy's home. Both Bellamy and Morris are superb in this taut psychological drama.

Bruce Baldwin / HIS GIRL FRIDAY, 1940, Columbia, d-Howard Hawks.

Bellamy is a sea of calm and dull reflection in this fast-paced, madcap comedy about a newspaper reporter (Rosalind Russell) being conned by her editor and ex-husband (Cary Grant) into covering one final story before marrying the patient and none too bright Bellamy.

Ellery Queen / ELLERY QUEEN, MASTER DETECTIVE, 1940, Columbia, d-Kurt Neumann.

In a story with too many plots, Bellamy plays the author of mystery stories who decides to solve one of his father's cases about a missing heiress. It was not an auspicious start for the brief series.

Franklin D. Roosevelt / SUNRISE AT CAMPOBELLO, 1960, Warners, d-Vincent J. Donehue.

After having made only one film in 15 years, Bellamy returned to movies to recreate his stage portrayal of the young Roosevelt, including his struggle with polio and return to politics.

Dr. Abe Sapirstein / ROSEMARY'S BABY, 1968, Paramount, d-Roman Polanski.

Bellamy portrays a member of a devil-worshipping cult who prescribes evil concoctions for Mia Farrow to take while she is pregnant with the son of the Prince of Darkness.

Randolph Duke / TRADING PLACES, 1983, Paramount, d-John Landis.

Bellamy is one of a pair of brothers who are crooked commodities traders. They experiment with the lives of two men from different environments (Dan Aykroyd and Eddie Murphy) to see what happens when their lives and fortunes are interchanged.

OTHER ROLES

1931: *Johnny Franks* / THE SECRET SIX; *Captain Ebbing* / SURRENDER. **1932:** *Al Holland* / FORBIDDEN; *Mac* / WEST OF BROADWAY; *Tom Manning* / DISORDERLY CONDUCT; *Judge Blake* / YOUNG AMERICA; *Dr. Ladd* / REBECCA OF SUNNYBROOK FARM; *John Bruce* / THE WOMAN IN ROOM 13; *Mike Miller* / AIR MAIL; *Denee Maxwell* / ALMOST MARRIED; *Carter Cavendish* / SECOND HAND WIFE. **1933:** *Joe Smith* / PAROLE GIRL; *the stowaway* / DESTINATION UNKNOWN; *McLean* / PICTURE SNATCHER; *Eric* / THE NARROW CORNER; *Steve McCreary* / BELOW THE SEA; *Hal Caldwell* / HEADLINE SHOOTER; *Speed Hardy* / FLYING DEVILS; *Jim Steel* / BLIND ADVENTURE; *Major Blake* / ACE OF ACES; *Jeff* / EVER IN MY HEART. **1934:** *George Fleetwood* / SPITFIRE; *Jim Dunlap* / THIS MAN IS MINE; *Inspector Trent* / BEFORE MIDNIGHT; *Inspector Trent* / THE CRIME OF HELEN STANLEY; *Inspector Trent* / GIRL IN DANGER; *Bradley* / WOMAN IN THE DARK. **1935:** *J. F. Van Avery* / HELLDORADO; *Fredrik Sobieski* / THE WEDDING NIGHT; *Bob Edmonds* / RENDEZVOUS AT MIDNIGHT; *Barry* / AIR HAWKS; *Steve Andrews* / EIGHT BELLS; *Terry Gallagher* / GIGOLETTE; *Dr. Quentin Harden* / NAVY WIFE; *Allen Macklyn* / HANDS ACROSS THE TABLE; *the doctor* / THE HEALER. **1936:** *Tony* / DANGEROUS INTRIGUE; *John Vickery* / THE FINAL HOURS; *Dan* / ROAMING LADY; *Curt Hayden* / STRAIGHT FROM THE SHOULDER; *Brian Kent* / WILD BRIAN KENT. **1937:** *Russ Matthews* / IT CAN'T LAST FOREVER; *Johnny* / COUNTERFEIT LADY; *James Blake* / *Slick Rawley* / THE MAN WHO LIVED TWICE; *Kirk Duncan* / LET'S GET MARRIED. **1938:** *Dr. Paul Hallet* / THE CRIME OF DR. HALLET; *Phillip Chester* / FOOLS FOR SCANDAL; *C. Elliott Friday* / BOY MEETS GIRL; *Stephen Arden* / CAREFREE; *Michael Hendragin* / GIRL'S SCHOOL; *Ben Blodgett* / TRADE WINDS; *Lieutenant Everett* / LET US LIVE. **1939:** *John Baxter* / SMASHING THE SPY RING; *Lt. Raymond Dower* / COAST GUARD. **1940:** *Graves* / FLIGHT ANGELS; *Clarence Fletcher* / BROTHER ORCHID; *Scott Langham* / QUEEN OF THE MOB; *Steve Adams* / DANCE, GIRL, DANCE; *Bruce Fairchild* / PUBLIC DEB NUMBER ONE; *Brad Williams* / MEET THE WILDCAT. **1941:** *Ellery Queen* / ELLERY QUEEN'S PENTHOUSE MYSTERY; *Dr. Davis* / FOOTSTEPS IN THE DARK; *Owen Wright* / AFFECTIONATELY YOURS; *Ellery Queen* / ELLERY QUEEN AND THE PERFECT CRIME; *Dr. Lance Rogers* / DIVE BOMBER; *Ellery Queen* / ELLERY QUEEN AND THE MURDER RING; *Capt. Paul Montford* / THE WOLF MAN. **1942:** *Erik Ernst* / THE GHOST OF FRANKENSTEIN; *Stanley* / LADY IN A JAM; *Major Lamphere* / MEN OF TEXAS; *Sir Edward Domney* / *Baron von Ragenstein* / THE GREAT IMPERSONATION. **1943:** *guest* / STAGE DOOR CANTEEN. **1944:** *Douglas Proctor* / GUEST IN THE HOUSE. **1945:** *Arthur Hale* / DELIGHTFULLY DANGEROUS; *Jonathan* / LADY ON A TRAIN. **1955:** *Congressman Frank Reid* / THE COURT-MARTIAL OF BILLY MITCHELL. **1966:** *J. W. Grant* / THE PROFESSIONALS. **1971:** *Jake Porter* / DOCTORS' WIVES. **1972:** *John Ed* / CANCEL MY RESERVATION. **1977:** *Sam Raven* / OH, GOD! **1987:** *Albert Dennison* / THE DISORDERLIES; *Mr. Gower* / AMAZON WOMEN ON THE MOON.

BENNETT, CONSTANCE

(1904–1965)

Constance Bennett, older sister of Joan Bennett, played leads in silents while still in her teens. The cool, worldly-wise, slender blonde—daughter of stage-screen idol Richard Bennett—was a major movie star before she reached 25, and at one time was the highest paid actress in Hollywood. Her most popular films were made in the 1930s. After that her decline was swift and by the age of 35 she was playing supporting roles. She was never considered a great actress but her deadpan expression and beauty were perfect for a series of amusing, if not outstanding, comedies. She did have her standards, however, as she declined to pose too provocatively, saying, "No! Five years from now, when I am married and have a family, I don't want pictures of me in underwear staring at me from the Police Gazette."

KEY ROLES

Lois Ingals / THE GOOSE HANGS HIGH, 1925, Silent, Paramount, d-James Cruze.

Bennett is one of three selfish children of George Irving who take their father for granted until his wise, old mother shows them that their father needs help for a change.

Hazel Woods / THE GOOSE WOMAN, 1925, Silent, Universal, d-Clarence Brown.

Bennett is the fiancée of Jack Pickford, son of the Goose Woman (Louise Dresser). Dresser's desire to bask in the spotlight almost gets her son convicted of murder.

Frances Hawtree / THREE FACES EAST, 1930, Warners, d-Roy Del Ruth.

Bennett is a British double spy who is responsible for eliminating a major German agent during World War I.

Mary Evans / WHAT PRICE HOLLYWOOD? 1932, RKO, d-George Cukor.

In this precursor of A STAR IS BORN, Bennett is a waitress who becomes a movie star with the help of an alcoholic director who later commits suicide.

Helen Hall / Raquel / MOULIN ROUGE, 1933, 20th Century-Fox, d-Sidney Lanfield.

When the magic goes out of her marriage, Bennett impersonates her own more glamorous sister to revitalize the union.

Marian Kirby / TOPPER, 1937, MGM, d-Norman Z. McLeod.

Bennett and husband Cary Grant play two wealthy party animals who are killed in a car crash. Their ghosts complicate the life of their stuffy banker (Roland Young), the only one who can see or hear them.

Jerry Kilbourne / MERRILY WE LIVE, 1938, Hal Roach, d-Norman Z. McLeod.

Bennett is the daughter in a zany family that hires Brian Aherne as a chauffeur and later learns that he is a famous writer posing as a tramp.

Christine Blaine / ESCAPE TO GLORY, 1940, Columbia, d-Jon Brahm.

In this minor sea-going version of GRAND HOTEL, Bennett is one of the passengers aboard a merchant ship being stalked by a German submarine.

Griselda Vaughn / TWO-FACED WOMAN, 1941, MGM, d-George Cukor.

Bennett portrays the glamorous woman that Greta Garbo, in her final film appearance, fears will steal her husband (Melvyn Douglas).

Jayne Moynihan / THE UNSUSPECTED, 1947, Warners, d-Michael Curtiz.

Bennett gives a nice, easy-going performance as the radio producer of a crime show whose star (Claude Rains) commits what he considers to be a perfect murder and then is forced to recreate it on the air.

Estelle Anderson / MADAME X, 1965, Universal, d-David Lowell Rich.

In this film Bennett plays Lana Turner's mother-in-law. When Turner seeks comfort with another man because she is neglected by her husband, Bennett is able to break up the marriage and take custody of her grandson. Years later the boy, now a lawyer, unknowingly defends his mother against a murder charge.

OTHER ROLES

1916: *bit* / THE VALLEY OF DECISION. **1922:** *chorus girl* / RECKLESS YOUTH; *Elise Bascom* / WHAT'S WRONG WITH WOMEN?; *Edith* / EVIDENCE. **1924:** *Annette Sherman* / CYTHEREA. **1925:** *Aileen Alton* / MY WIFE AND I; *Sally* / SALLY, IRENE AND MARY; *Abby Nettleton* / THE PINCH HITTER; *Georgie May* / CODE OF THE WEST; *Betty Smith* / MY SON. **1926:** *Marcia Livingston* / MARRIED?. **1929:** *Ann Marvin* / THIS THING CALLED LOVE. **1930:** *Ellen Neal* / COMMON CLAY; *Sylvia* / SIN TAKES A HOLIDAY; *Allana* / SON OF THE GODS. **1931:** *Valerie West* / THE COMMON LAW; *Laura Murdock* / THE EASIEST WAY; *Doris Kendall* / BORN TO LOVE; *Stephany Dale* / BOUGHT. **1932:** *Venice Muir* / LADY WITH A PAST; *Dell Hamilton* / TWO AGAINST THE WORLD; *Judy Carroll* / ROCKABYE. **1933:** *Lady Pearl Grayston* / OUR BETTERS; *Lorry Evans* / BED OF ROSES; *Carla* / AFTER TONIGHT. **1934:** *Duchess of Florence* / AFFAIRS OF CELLINI; *Iris March* / OUTCAST LADY. **1935:** *Sharon Norwood* / AFTER OFFICE HOURS. **1936:** *Anna von Stucknadel* / EVERYTHING IS THUNDER. **1938:** *Helen Murphy* / SERVICE DE LUXE; *Marian Kirby* / TOPPER TAKES A TRIP. **1939:** *Gerry Lester* / TAIL SPIN. **1941:** *Joan Madison* / LAW OF THE TROPICS; *Belle Andrews* / WILD BILL HICKOK RIDES. **1942:** *Kye Allen* / SIN TOWN; *Joan Bannister* / MADAME SPY. **1945:** *Kitty de Mornay* / MADAME PIMPERNEL. **1946:** *Zenia Lascalles* / CENTENNIAL SUMMER. **1948:** *Paula Rogers* / SMART WOMAN; *Dr. Karen Lawrence* / ANGEL ON THE AMAZON. **1951:** *Lucille McKinley* / AS YOUNG AS YOU FEEL. **1953:** *guest* / IT SHOULD HAPPEN TO YOU.

BENNETT, JOAN

(1910–)

This exquisitely beautiful actress's career seemed to take off just as her sister Constance's was in decline. When she was 16 she ran away with a millionaire, had a child, and was divorced by 18. Like her sister, she began her career as a blonde, but is probably better remembered for her lovely dark hair. She made her stage debut in Chicago in 1914 in "Damaged Goods" which also starred her father, Richard Bennett. She made her film debut the next year with her sister and father in THE VALLEY OF DECISION. Bennett was able to shift her style to fit whatever type of acting was popular. But she was not able to save her career after her husband, Walter Wanger, shot her agent, Jennings Lang, whom Wanger felt was looking for more than his ten percent. Lang recovered and Wanger went to prison for awhile, and though Bennett stood by her husband she never had a truly good role again. Her TV movies include GIDGET GETS MARRIED (1971), THE EYES OF CHARLIE SAND (1972), and SUDDENLY, LOVE (1978).

KEY ROLES

Lady Clarissa Pevensey / DISRAELI, 1929, Warners, d-Alfred E. Green.

As George Arliss, who played the title character, was too old to be a romantic lead, his films usually had a secondary story about the love of a young couple. In this film, Bennett is a young woman in love with Anthony Bushnell.

Amy March / LITTLE WOMEN, 1933, RKO, d-George Cukor.

Those who recall this lovely, simple movie of the four March sisters growing up in pre-Civil War America will no doubt also recall Bennett's excellent performance.

Sally MacGregor / PRIVATE WORLDS, 1935, Paramount, d-Gregory La Cava.

Bennett is the wife of Joel McCrea, a psychiatrist in a sanitarium, in this film about a subject that, at the time, was a new region to mine for dramatic possibilities. The excellent cast also includes Claudette Colbert and Charles Boyer.

Hilda / THE HOUSEKEEPER'S DAUGHTER, 1939, United Artists, d-Hal Roach.

Bennett appears in the title role of this comedy playing a tough cookie who helps a young, aspiring professor (John Hubbard) solve the case of a murdered showgirl. Clues seem to point to Marc Lawrence, a mobster who had once been involved with Bennett.

Jerry / MAN HUNT, 1941, 20th Century-Fox, d-Fritz Lang.

Bennett is the love interest in this thriller about a big-game hunter (Walter Pidgeon) who takes a shot at Hitler, misses, and is chased back to England by the Gestapo.

Alice Reed / THE WOMAN IN THE WINDOW, 1944, International, d-Fritz Lang.

In this film noir, Edward G. Robinson admires a portrait of Bennett in an art shop's window. When he meets her he wishes he hadn't, as she gets him involved in a murder.

Kitty March / SCARLET STREET, 1945, Universal, d-Fritz Lang.

Once again Bennett is bad news for Edward G. Robinson who saves her from her pimp (Dan Duryea), falls in love with her, then kills her when he discovers that she is selling his paintings as her own. He also allows Duryea to go to the chair for her murder.

Margaret Macomber / THE MACOMBER AFFAIR, 1947, United Artists, d-Zoltan Korda.

Bennett makes a play for hunter Gregory Peck whom she finds preferable to her cowardly husband (Robert Preston). She kills Preston while trying to save him from a buffalo stampede. The question is was she a good shot or a bad one? Her own thoughts on the matter are inconclusive but damning: "I hated Francis. I wanted him dead. Maybe I killed him. If there's such a thing as murder in the heart, there's your certain answer."

Lucia Harper / THE RECKLESS MOMENT, 1949, Columbia, d-Max Ophuls.

After accidentally killing her daughter's would-be seducer, Bennett is trailed by blackmailer James Mason.

Ellie Banks / FATHER OF THE BRIDE, 1950, MGM, d-Vincente Minnelli.

Bennett is the mother of Elizabeth Taylor, whose wedding plans are a costly and chaotic problem for her and her husband (Spencer Tracy).

Amelie Ducotel / WE'RE NO ANGELS, 1955, Paramount, d-Michael Curtiz.

Bennett—whose acting career was revived after the scandal caused by her husband shooting her agent—is the wife of Leo G. Carroll who is helped by three convicts (Humphrey Bogart, Peter Ustinov, and Aldo Ray) in dealing with Basil Rathbone, who's about to take away their livelihood on Devil's Island.

OTHER ROLES

1916: *an "unborn soul"* / THE VALLEY OF DECISION. **1928:** *a dame* / POWER. **1929:** *extra* / THE DIVINE LADY; *Phyllis* / BULLDOG DRUM-

MOND; *Lucy Blackburn* / MISSISSIPPI GAMBLER; *Rose Gordon* / THREE LIVE GHOSTS. **1930:** *Dolores Fenton* / PUTTIN' ON THE RITZ; *Ann Jordan* / CRAZY THAT WAY; *Faith Creely* / MOBY DICK; *Nan Sheffield* / MAYBE IT'S LOVE; *Lady Lasher* / SCOTLAND YARD. **1931:** *Pat Coster* / MANY A SLIP; *Nina Wyndram* / DOCTORS' WIVES; *Janet Gordon* / HUSH MONEY; *Marie* / OTHER MEN'S WOMEN. **1932:** *Jane Miller* / SHE WANTED A MILLIONAIRE; *Sally Brown* / CARELESS LADY; *Vivienne Ware* / THE TRIAL OF VIVIENNE WARE; *Venetia Carr* / WEEK-ENDS ONLY; *Salomy Jane* / WILD GIRL; *Helen Riley* / ME AND MY GAL; *Lynn Martin* / ARIZONA TO BROADWAY. **1934:** *Prudence Kirkland* / THE PURSUIT OF HAPPINESS; *Adele Verin* / THE MAN WHO RECLAIMED HIS HEAD. **1935:** *Lucy Rumford* / MISSISSIPPI; *Bobbie Lockwood* / TWO FOR TONIGHT; *Helen Berkeley* / THE MAN WHO BROKE THE BANK AT MONTE CARLO; *Carol Van Dyke* / SHE COULDN'T TAKE IT. **1936:** *Felice Rollins* / THIRTEEN HOURS BY AIR; *Eve Fallon* / BIG BROWN EYES; *Julia Wayne* / TWO IN A CROWD; *Monica "Rusty" Fleming* / WEDDING PRESENT. **1937:** *Wendy van Klettering* / VOGUES OF 1938. **1938:** *Julie* / I MET MY LOVE AGAIN; *Ivy Preston* / THE TEXANS; *Patricia Harper* / ARTISTS AND MODELS ABROAD. **1939:** *Kay Kerrigan* / TRADE WINDS; *Maria Theresa* / THE MAN IN THE IRON MASK. **1940:** *Stephanie Richardson* / GREEN HELL; *Brenda Bentley* / THE HOUSE ACROSS THE BAY; *Carol Hoffman* / THE MAN I MARRIED; *Grand Duchess Zona* / SON OF MONTE CRISTO. **1941:** *Gloria Winters* / SHE KNEW ALL THE ANSWERS; *Sally Murdock* / WILD GEESE CALLING; *Jennifer Carson* / CONFIRM OR DENY. **1942:** *Julie Abbott* / TWIN BEDS; *Anita Woverman* / THE WIFE TAKES A FLYER; *June Delaney* / GIRL TROUBLE. **1943:** *Sophie Baumer* / MARGIN FOR ERROR. **1945:** *Harriet Carruthers* / NOB HILL; *Ella Sue Dozier* / COLONEL EFFINGHAM'S RAID. **1947:** *Celia Lamphere* / THE SECRET BEYOND THE DOOR; *Peggy Butler* / THE WOMAN ON THE BEACH; *Evelyn Hahn* / THE SCAR. **1950:** *Lydia Bolton* / FOR HEAVEN'S SAKE. **1951:** *Ellie Banks* / FATHER'S LITTLE DIVIDEND; *Kath Joplin* / THE GUY WHO CAME BACK. **1954:** *Mrs. Cummings* / HIGHWAY DRAGNET. **1956:** *Marion Groves* / THERE'S ALWAYS TOMORROW; *Peg Blain* / NAVY WIFE. **1960:** *Mrs. Marquand* / DESIRE IN THE DUST. **1970:** *Elizabeth Stoddard* / HOUSE OF DARK SHADOWS. **1977:** *Madame Blank* / SUSPIRIA.

BENNY, JACK

(Benjamin Kubelsky, 1894–1974)

Jack Benny was a child prodigy on the violin, but made fun of his playing as part of his comedy persona of a miserly, boastful, and inept man who was forever 39. Speaking of his violin, he said, "If it isn't a Stradivarius, I've been robbed of $110." In reality he was a kind man of great comical timing, always willing to act the fall guy for others so that they might deliver the punch line. Movies were not his major area of success, as he was much more at home on radio and television, but his films weren't as bad as he kidded. He died before being able to appear in THE SUNSHINE BOYS and was replaced by his dear friend George Burns, who won an Oscar and started a new career.

KEY ROLES

M.C. / HOLLYWOOD REVUE OF 1929, 1929, MGM, d-Charles Reisner.

Besides taking a turn with his own routine, Benny introduces and comments on the acts in this musical without a story.

Babbs Babberley (Lord Fancourt) / CHARLEY'S AUNT, 1941, 20th Century-Fox, d-Archie Mayo.

Benny is an Oxford undergraduate who is forced to impersonate his roommate's rich aunt from Brazil (where the nuts come from), when they need a chaperone for two young women invited for the weekend.

Josef Tura / TO BE OR NOT TO BE, 1942, United Artists, d-Ernst Lubitsch.

In surely his best movie role Benny is an egotistical Polish actor who outsmarts the Nazis in Warsaw, and leads his entire troupe to freedom. It's not only a thrilling comedy, it's also an exciting thriller. Speaking of his director, Benny enthused, "Lubitsch's method of direction was perfect for me. He would act out the whole scene—and then he'd say, 'Now let's see how you'd do it.'"

Athanael / THE HORN BLOWS AT MIDNIGHT, 1945, Warners, d-Raoul Walsh.

Benny always claimed this was the movie that ended his film career. But that was just more of his self-deprecating routine. The story, about a musician who dreams he is sent to earth to destroy it with Gabriel's horn, is not the most plausible but it's much better than the critics believed or Mr. Benny pretended.

OTHER ROLES

1930: *Eddie* / CHASING RAINBOWS; *Dr. John Harvey* / THE MEDICINE MAN. **1933:** *guest* / MR. BROADWAY. **1935:** *Bert Keeler* / BROADWAY MELODY OF 1936; *Calvin Churchill* / IT'S IN THE AIR. **1936:** *Jack Carson* / BIG BROADCAST OF 1937; *J. Davis Bowster* / COLLEGE HOLIDAY. **1937:** *Mac Brewster* / ARTISTS AND MODELS. **1938:** *Buck Boswell* / ARTISTS AND MODELS ABROAD. **1939:** *Bob Temple* / MAN ABOUT TOWN. **1940:** *himself* / LOVE THY NEIGHBOR; *Buck Benny* / BUCK BENNY RIDES AGAIN. **1942:** *Bill Fuller* / GEORGE WASHINGTON SLEPT HERE. **1943:** *Richard Clark* / THE MEANEST MAN IN THE WORLD. **1944:** *guest* / HOLLYWOOD CANTEEN. **1945:** *himself* / IT'S IN THE BAG. **1946:** *cameo* / WITHOUT RESERVATIONS. **1952:** *cameo* / SOMEBODY LOVES ME. **1954:** *guest* / SUSAN SLEPT HERE. **1957:** *guest* / BEAU JAMES. **1962:** *guest* / GYPSY. **1963:** *cameo* / IT'S A MAD, MAD, MAD, MAD WORLD. **1967:** *cameo* / A GUIDE FOR THE MARRIED MAN.

BERGMAN, INGRID

(1915–1982)

Like her predecessor, Greta Garbo, Swedish actress Ingrid Bergman was known for her beauty and her acting ability. When brought to Hollywood by David Selznick, Bergman resisted his attempts to change her name, face, or teeth. So he sold her as the great natural beauty and it hit the proper chord with men and women alike. Bergman also refused to hide her affair with director Roberto Rossellini, which made her persona non grata in Hollywood for years. She commented, "In America people think, if they buy their tickets, they own you." All seemed to be forgiven when she made ANASTASIA in 1956 and won her second Oscar. Her first was for GASLIGHT in 1944, and her third was for Best Supporting Actress in MURDER ON THE ORIENT EXPRESS in 1974. Her other Oscar nominations were for FOR WHOM THE BELL TOLLS, THE BELLS OF ST. MARY'S, JOAN OF ARC, and AUTUMN SONATA. Bergman—tall, beautiful, versatile, intelligent, and honest—never gave the same performance twice. She was one of the most idolized and most notorious actresses in the history of motion pictures. Her last portrayal, as Golda Meir in the TV movie A WOMAN CALLED GOLDA (1982), won her an Emmy as Outstanding Lead Actress in a Drama Special.

KEY ROLES

Anita Hoffman / INTERMEZZO, 1936, Sweden, Svenskfilmindustri, d-Gustaf Molander.

Bergman has a special quality as the talented pianist who becomes the accompanist and lover of a world-famous (but married) violinist. In the end, she unselfishly gives him up so he may return to his wife and children.

Anna Holm / A WOMAN'S FACE, 1938, Sweden, Svenskfilmindustri, d-Gustaf Molander.

Bergman is a scarred and bitter woman who turns to crime until a plastic surgeon restores her beauty and she undergoes a spiritual and moral rejuvenation.

Anita Hoffman / INTERMEZZO, A LOVE STORY, 1939, Selznick / United Artists, d-Gregory Ratoff.
Bergman recreates her Swedish triumph in this almost perfect sentimental movie.

Ivy Peterson / DR. JEKYLL AND MR. HYDE, 1941, MGM, d-Victor Fleming.
Bergman convinced the producers to let her switch roles with Lana Turner and play the more interesting prostitute rather than Dr. Jekyll's goody-goody fiancée. She makes a very fetching victim for the barbaric Mr. Hyde.

Ilsa Lund Laszlo / CASABLANCA, 1942, Warners, d-Michael Curtiz.
Was ever an actress more lovely than Bergman in her slouch hat and her black and white closeups? She plays the wife of a Resistance leader (Paul Henreid) trying to escape the Nazis and hoping for help from her ex-lover, Humphrey Bogart. She's the one who says to Dooley Wilson, "Play it, Sam. Play 'As Time Goes By'."

Maria / FOR WHOM THE BELL TOLLS, 1943, Paramount, d-Sam Wood.
Bergman received her first Academy Award nomination for her performance as the Spanish peasant girl who falls in love with an American (Gary Cooper) during the Spanish Civil War.

Paula Alquist / GASLIGHT, 1944, MGM, d-George Cukor.
Bergman won an Academy Award for her performance as the young wife who is slowly being driven out of her mind by her murderous husband (Charles Boyer). Her vulnerability is heartbreakingly effective. When she finally understands Boyer's plot against her, she rages at him as he is tied in a chair awaiting the coming of the police, "If I were not mad, I could have helped you. Whatever you had done, I could have pitied you. But, because I am mad, I have betrayed you. And because I am mad, I'm rejoicing in my heart without a shred of regret, watching you go with glory in my heart."

Sister Benedict / THE BELLS OF ST. MARY'S, 1945, RKO, d-Leo McCarey.
Proving her versatility, Bergman demonstrates that it is okay for a nun to be beautiful, even if it only shows in her expressive and intelligent face. She is the principal of a grade school who has her friendly differences with the parish priest (Bing Crosby). But she handles them tactfully, asking, "Did anyone ever tell you that you have a dishonest face—for a priest, I mean?" The role brought her another Oscar nomination.

Dr. Constance Peterson / SPELLBOUND, 1945, United Artists, d-Alfred Hitchcock.
Bergman is a psychiatrist who must probe the mind of the man she loves so he will remember whether he's a murderer or not.

Alicia Huberman / NOTORIOUS, 1946, RKO, d-Alfred Hitchcock.
The daughter of a Nazi sympathizer, Bergman is recruited by the United States to infiltrate a group of post-war Nazis in Rio de Janeiro. She goes so far as to marry one of the Nazis (Claude Rains). When he discovers her plot he sets about to poison her slowly, but she is rescued by her American lover (Cary Grant).

Joan of Arc / JOAN OF ARC, 1948, RKO, d-Victor Fleming.
Bergman received another Academy Award nomination for her appearance as the Maid of Orleans, although most critics were not impressed by her performance.

Anastasia / ANASTASIA, 1956, 20th Century-Fox, d-Anatole Litvak.
After six years of exile from the American screen Bergman came back in triumph, winning an Oscar for her portrayal of the pretender who is trained by a White Russian general to pass for the Grand Duchess Anastasia, reputedly the sole survivor of the execution of Russia's last Imperial Family. Her training is so effective that she despairs, "I don't know who I am anymore. I don't know what I remember and what I've been told I remember. What is real? Am I?"

Ann Kalman / INDISCREET, 1958, Warners, d-Stanley Donen.
Bergman is an internationally renowned actress who has an affair with an American diplomat (Cary Grant) and is furious when she discovers he was lying when he told her he was married.

Gladys Aylward / THE INN OF THE SIXTH HAPPINESS, 1958, 20th Century-Fox, d-Mark Robson.
Bergman plays an English servant girl who becomes a missionary and spends many difficult years in China. At one point she leads 100 orphans to safety on a dangerous journey through Japanese-held territory.

Stephanie Dickinson / CACTUS FLOWER, 1969, Columbia, d-Gene Saks.
Bergman is dentist Walter Matthau's nurse, whom he gets to pose as his wife in order to deceive his mistress (Goldie Hawn). She's so good at the impersonation, that they make it permanent.

Greta Ohlsson / MURDER ON THE ORIENT EXPRESS, 1974, Paramount, d-Sidney Lumet.
Winning an Academy Award for Best Supporting Actress for this film must have amused Bergman. Her performance as a missionary and one of the suspects in the murder of Richard Widmark is hardly outstanding.

Charlotte / AUTUMN SONATA, 1978, New World Pictures, d-Ingmar Bergman.
In her farewell appearance on the big screen, Bergman plays a concert pianist who, after her lover dies, visits the daughter she has not seen for years. The performance won her yet one more Academy Award nomination.

OTHER ROLES

1934: *Elsa* / THE COUNT OF THE MONK'S BRIDGE. **1935:** *Karin Ingman* / OCEAN BREAKERS; *Astrid* / SWEDENHIELMS; *Lena Bergstrom* / WALPURGIS NIGHT. **1936:** *Eva Bergh* / ON THE SUNNY SIDE. **1938:** *Marianne* / THE FOUR COMPANIONS; *Julia Balzar* / DOLLAR. **1939:** *Eva* / ONLY ONE NIGHT. **1940:** *Kerstin Nordback* / A NIGHT IN JUNE. **1941:** *Emilie Gallatin* / ADAM HAD FOUR SONS; *Stella Bergen* / RAGE IN HEAVEN. **1945:** *Clio Dulaine* / SARATOGA TRUNK. **1948:** *Joan Madou* / ARCH OF TRIUMPH. **1949:** *Lady Henrietta Considine* / UNDER CAPRICORN. **1950:** *Karin Bjiorsen* / STROMBOLI. **1951:** *Irene Girard* / EUROPA '51, (THE GREATEST LOVE). **1953:** *actress* / WE, THE WOMEN. **1954:** *Katherine Joyce* / JOURNEY TO ITALY; *Joan of Arc* / JOAN AT THE STAKE. **1955:** *Irene Wagner* / FEAR. **1957:** *Princess Elena Sorokowska* / PARIS DOES STRANGE THINGS. **1961:** *Paula Tessier* / GOODBYE AGAIN. **1964:**

Karla Zachanassian / THE VISIT. **1965:** *Mrs. Gerda Millett* / THE YELLOW ROLLS-ROYCE. **1967:** *government clerk's wife* / STIMULANTIA. **1970:** *Libby Meredith* / A WALK IN THE SPRING RAIN. **1973:** *Mrs. Frankweiler* / FROM THE MIXED-UP FILES OF MRS. BASIL E. FRANKWEILER. **1976:** *the contessa* / A MATTER OF TIME.

BEST, EDNA

(1900–1974)

Soft-spoken, ladylike Edna Best was very much the British actress, with most of her major successes on the stage. She is perhaps best remembered in the United States for her role in Hitchcock's THE MAN WHO KNEW TOO MUCH (1934) as her British films had very limited distribution here. Her first U.S. movie was THE KEY with William Powell in 1934. She finally got some recognition in the states portraying the wife of Leslie Howard in the 1939 remake of INTERMEZZO.

KEY ROLES

Mary Rowe / MICHAEL AND MARY, 1932, Great Britain, Ideal / Gainsborough, d-Victor Saville.

When her husband deserts her during the Boer War, Best marries aspiring author Herbert Marshall (first of her three real-life husbands). Many years later her real husband returns, threatening to blackmail the pair, but he is killed in a fall. They confess everything to their son and find that their love is only stronger.

Jill Lawrence / THE MAN WHO KNEW TOO MUCH, 1934, Great Britain, Gaumont-British, d-Alfred Hitchcock.

Before he dies, a secret agent tells Best and her husband (Leslie Banks) about an assassination plot against the life of a diplomat. To ensure that the couple does not tell what they know, the plotters kidnap their daughter. The parents must then find their child before the time of the assassination.

Sarah Burton / SOUTH RIDING, 1938, Great Britain, London Films, d-Victor Saville.

Best is a school headmistress who is loved by a country squire (Ralph Richardson) in this story about civic responsibility and dishonest political officials.

Margit Brandt / INTERMEZZO, 1939, Selznick, d-Gregory Ratoff.

Best is the wife of Leslie Howard, a renowned violinist who has an affair with his young accompanist (Ingrid Bergman). In the end, the lovers break off the relationship so Howard will be reconciled with Best.

Elizabeth Robinson / THE SWISS FAMILY ROBINSON, 1940, RKO, d-Edward Ludwig.

In this pleasant low-budgeter, Best, husband Thomas Mitchell, and their children create a new life on a deserted island after their ship sinks.

OTHER ROLES

1921: *Tilly Welwyn* / TILLY OF BLOOMSBURY. **1923:** *Molly Roarke* / A COUPLE OF DOWN AND OUTS. **1930:** *Nina Grant* / LOOSE ENDS; *Shingled Lady* / ESCAPE; *Mary Hayes* / BEYOND THE CITIES; *she* / SLEEPING PARTNERS. **1931:** *Jill Panniford* / THE CALENDAR. **1932:** *Blackie Anderway* / *Blackie's daughter* / THE FAITHFUL HEART. **1934:** *Norah Kerr* / THE KEY. **1939:** *Yvonne Chanel* / PRISON WITHOUT BARS. **1940:** *Ida Magnus* / A DISPATCH FROM REUTERS. **1946:** *Catherine Apley* / THE LATE GEORGE APLEY. **1947:** *Martha* / THE GHOST AND MRS. MUIR. **1948:** *Mrs. Foster* / THE IRON CURTAIN.

BLAINE, VIVIAN

(Vivian S. Stapleton, 1921–)

This vivacious blonde band singer had her greatest successes on Broadway, with the highlight of her film career being the recreation of her marvelous Miss Adelaide from "Guys and Dolls." Dubbed "The Cherry Blonde" by studio publicists, Blaine got her movie break in GREENWICH VILLAGE because both Alice Faye and Betty Grable got pregnant.

KEY ROLES

Emily Joyce / STATE FAIR, 1945, 20th Century-Fox, d-Walter Lang.

Blaine appears as a dance-band singer to whom Dick Haymes croons a tune or two. Everyone, including Blaine, gets in on singing "It's a Grand Night for Singing" at the Iowa State Fair.

Liz / THREE LITTLE GIRLS IN BLUE, 1946, 20th Century-Fox, d-H. Bruce Humberstone.

Together with June Haver and Vera-Ellen, Blaine pretends to be wealthy in order to ensnare a millionaire husband in Atlantic City. She wins wealthy aristocrat Frank Latimore after a series of musical numbers.

Miss Adelaide / GUYS AND DOLLS, 1955, Samuel Goldwyn, d-Joseph L. Mankiewicz.

Blaine is the best thing in this delightful Damon Runyon tale about several New York characters. Showgirl Blaine has long been engaged to gambler Frank Sinatra but can never get him to the altar. She finally succeeds when he and a fellow gambler (Marlon Brando) get involved with a Salvation Army-like operation. She scores with her songs "Adelaide's Lament," "Sue Me," "Take Back Your Mink," and "Pet Me, Poppa."

OTHER ROLES

1942: *Sue Boardman* / THRU DIFFERENT EYES; *Barbara* / GIRL TROUBLE. **1943:** *Sally Conway* / HE HIRED THE BOSS; *Susan Cowan* / JITTERBUGS. **1944:** *Bonnie Watson* / GREENWICH VILLAGE; *Blossom Hart* / SOMETHING FOR THE BOYS. **1945:** *Sally Templeton* / NOB HILL; *Doll Face* / DOLL FACE. **1946:** *Linda* / IF I'M LUCKY. **1952:** *Una Yancy* / SKIRTS AHOY. **1957:** *Rita DeLacey* / PUBLIC PIGEON NO. ONE.

BLONDELL, JOAN

(1909–1979)

Joan Blondell was the cheerful, wisecracking blonde of the 1930s so often cast as the pert gold digger, free-spirited chorus girl, eager secretary, dumb waitress, or flippant reporter. She served as a wonderful foil for James Cagney and was a snappy example of what Yul Brynner must have had in mind when he complained, "Girls have an unfair advantage over men. If they can't get what they want by being smart, they can get it by being dumb." As she matured, her roles as cynical, wisecracking women with hearts of gold became rather cheap-looking, middle-aged women with hearts of gold. Like many aging actresses, she took roles in drive-in cheapies such as the trashy BIG DADDY with Victor Buono. Her TV movies included WINNER TAKE ALL and THE DEAD DON'T SCREAM (1975), DEATH AT LOVE HOUSE (1976), BATTERED (1978), and THE REBELS (1978).

KEY ROLES

Mamie / PUBLIC ENEMY, 1931, Warners, d-William Wellman.

Blondell is perfect doing one her tough but loyal dame bits in this story of two slum kids who move into the rackets and are rubbed out when they mix it up with the big boys.

Miss Adams / Miss Pinkerton / MISS PINKERTON, 1932, Warners, d-Lloyd Bacon.

As a private nurse, Blondell helps the police solve a murder case. Along the way she has a wisecrack for every situation.

Carol King / GOLD DIGGERS OF 1933, 1933, Warners, d-Mervyn LeRoy.

Blondell is one of three chorus girls seeking rich husbands in this cheerful and somewhat vulgar musical comedy. She is memorable singing "My Forgotten Man." The Busby Berkeley staged numbers are "a mad geometry of patterned chorines."

Nan Prescott / FOOTLIGHT PARADE, 1933, Warners, d-Lloyd Bacon.

Blondell is Jimmy Cagney's assistant as he stages prologues—the live musical numbers that precede feature films in theaters. She's in love with the guy and stands by him even when he gets ideas about other girls. Her wisecracks include the fine put-down of Claire Dodd, "As long as they've got sidewalks, you've got a job."

Nancy Lorraine / CONVENTION CITY, 1933, Warners, d-Archie Mayo.

Blondell is just the kind of good-hearted gold-digging girl that wife-avoiding men like Guy Kibbee are looking for when they hold their annual salesmen convention in the big city.

Mabel Anderson / DAMES, 1934, Warners, d-Ray Enright.

In this familiar formula piece, Dick Powell is an ambitious songwriter who needs a backer for a show. The film is another of Busby Berkeley's inventive masterpieces and Blondell is a hoofer who sings the simple but effective "The Girl at the Ironing Board."

Peggy Revere / STAGE STRUCK, 1936, First National, d-Busby Berkeley.

Blondell appears as a no-talent star performer who finances her own Broadway show, hiring then husband Dick Powell to direct it. Their temperaments clash but suave Warren William is able to put things right.

Mabel / THREE MEN ON A HORSE, 1936, Warners, d-Mervyn LeRoy.

Blondell provides the romantic interest for the greeting card verse writer (Sam Levene) who sure knows how to pick horses in this enjoyable version of the successful Broadway farce.

Lester Plum / STAND-IN, 1937, United Artists, d-Tay Garnett.

In this burlesque of the movie industry, Blondell is the character who takes efficiency expert Leslie Howard in hand when he is sent to save a studio from bankruptcy. She rescues him from a vamp and gets him to stand up to the studio head.

Gail Richards / TOPPER RETURNS, 1941, United Artists, d-Roy del Ruth.

In perhaps the most inventive "Topper" film, Blondell is a ghost who helps Roland Young solve her murder.

Hope Banner / THREE GIRLS ABOUT TOWN, 1941, Columbia, d-Leigh Jason.

This comedy-mystery about three sisters who discover a corpse in their hotel room is only a "B" programmer, but Blondell makes it lively and fun.

Aunt Sissy / A TREE GROWS IN BROOKLYN, 1945, 20th Century-Fox, d-Elia Kazan.

Blondell gives her best dramatic performance as the flashy aunt in a poor, struggling Irish family at the turn of the century.

Lady Fingers / THE CINCINNATI KID, 1965, MGM, d-Norman Jewison.

Blondell is a blowzy-looking poker player in a big-stakes game in New Orleans involving Edward G. Robinson and Steve McQueen.

OTHER ROLES

1930: *Catherine Murdock* / THE OFFICE WIFE; *Myrtle* / SINNER'S HOLIDAY. **1931:** *Duckie Childers* / ILLICIT; *Angie* / MILLIE; *Marion Moore* / MY PAST; *Pearl* / BIG BUSINESS GIRL; *Fifi* / GOD'S GIFT TO WOMEN; *Marie* / OTHER MEN'S WOMEN; *Myrtle Nichols* / THE RECKLESS HOUR; *Maloney* / NIGHT NURSE; *Ann Roberts* / BLONDE CRAZY. **1932:** *Schatze* / THE GREEKS HAD A WORD FOR THEM; *Ruth* / UNION DEPOT; *Anne* / THE CROWD ROARS; *Maizie Dickson* / THE FAMOUS FERGUSON CASE; *Flips Montague* / MAKE ME A STAR; *Vida* / BIG CITY BLUES; *Mary Keaton* / THREE ON A MATCH; *Dot* / CENTRAL PARK; *Olga* / LAWYER MAN. **1933:** *Tony Landers* / BROADWAY BAD; *Blondie Johnson* / BLONDIE JOHNSON; *Anne* / GOODBYE AGAIN; *Mae Wright* / HAVANA WIDOWS. **1934:** *Marie Lawson* / I GOT YOUR NUMBER; *Vicki Wallace Thorpe* / SMARTY; *Rose Lawrence* / HE WAS HER MAN; *Rosy* / KANSAS CITY PRINCESS. **1935:** *Angela Twitchell* / TRAVELING SALESLADY; *Alice Hughes* / BROADWAY GONDOLIER; *Ginger Stewart* / WE'RE IN THE MONEY; *Gloria Fay* / MISS PACIFIC FLEET. **1936:** *Minnie Hawkins* / COLLEEN; *Yvonne* / SONS O' GUNS; *Lee Morgan* / BULLETS OR BALLOTS; *Norma Perry* / GOLD DIGGERS OF 1937. **1937:** *Dorothy* / THE KING AND THE CHORUS GIRL; *Timmy Blake* / BACK IN CIRCULATION; *Mona Carter* / PERFECT SPECIMEN. **1938:** *Sally Reardon* / THERE'S ALWAYS A WOMAN. **1939:** *Jane Morgan* / OFF THE RECORD; *Mary Wilson* / EAST SIDE OF HEAVEN; *Doris Harvey* / THE KID FROM KOKOMO; *Jenny Swanson* / GOOD GIRLS GO TO PARIS; *Maxine Carroll* / AMAZING MR. WILLIAMS. **1940:** *Molly Mahoney* / TWO GIRLS ON BROADWAY; *Geraldine (Jerry) Brokaw* / I WANT A DIVORCE. **1941:** *Joan Chambers* / MODEL WIFE; *Jenny Blake* / LADY FOR A NIGHT. **1943:** *Grace* / CRY HAVOC. **1945:** *Marjorie Mossrock* / DON JUAN QUILLIGAN; *Helen Melohn* / ADVENTURE. **1947:** *Rosemary Durant* / THE CORPSE CAME C.O.D.; *Zeena* / NIGHTMARE ALLEY; *Ann Nelson* / CHRISTMAS EVE. **1950:** *Lydia* / FOR HEAVEN'S SAKE. **1951:** *Annie Rawlings* / THE BLUE VEIL. **1956:** *Edith Potter* / THE OPPOSITE SEX. **1957:** *Aunt Morgan* / LIZZIE; *Peg Costello* / DESK SET; *Violet* / WILL SUCCESS SPOIL ROCK HUNTER? *Crystal St. Clair* / THIS COULD BE THE NIGHT. **1961:** *Mollie Hays* / ANGEL BABY. **1964:** *Easy Jenny* / ADVANCE TO THE REAR. **1966:** *Mrs. Lavender* / RIDE BEYOND VENGEANCE. **1967:** *Lavinia* / WATERHOLE NO. 3. **1968:** *Kittibelle Lightfoot* / KONA COAST. **1970:** *Ruby* / THE PHYNX. **1971:** *Jenny* / SUPPORT YOUR LOCAL GUNFIGHTER. **1976:** *landlady* / WON TON TON, THE DOG WHO SAVED HOLLYWOOD. **1977:** *Sarah Goode* / OPENING NIGHT. **1979:** *Vi* / GREASE; *Dolly Kenyon* / THE CHAMP. **1981:** *Mrs. Fitzgerald* / THE GLOVE; *Aunt Coll* / THE WOMAN INSIDE.

BLOOM, CLAIRE

(1931–)

A beautiful, dark-haired, English actress, Claire Bloom was given her first big film break in 1952 in Charles Chaplin's LIMELIGHT. She became a professional actress when, at 15, she appeared with the Oxford Repertory Theatre, moving on a little later to the Shakespeare company at Stratford-on-Avon. During her stage career she has played in many of the classics with the Old Vic. Once married to Rod Steiger, Bloom is still active in films and still beautiful, although she has acknowledged the effects of aging: "The problem of fading beauty in a woman is one of the powerful themes not only of drama but life itself." In addition to her big screen films, she has appeared in made-for-TV movies including THE GOING UP OF DAVID LEV (1971) and BRIDESHEAD REVISITED (1981).

KEY ROLES

Terry / LIMELIGHT, 1952, Chaplin, d-Charles Chaplin.
Bloom is a suicidal young ballerina who inspires a broken-down music hall comedian to have one final triumph. The musical theme of the film received an Academy Award for Chaplin, who wrote it.

Lady Anne / RICHARD III, 1956, Great Britain, London Films, d-Laurence Olivier.
When Bloom spits in Olivier's face as he tries to woo her at her husband's coffin, she wishes that the spit had been mortal poison. Audiences agreed with Olivier's rejoinder, "Never came poison from so sweet a place."

Helena Charles / LOOK BACK IN ANGER, 1959, Great Britain, ABP / Woodfall, d-Tony Richardson.
Variety said Bloom played the other woman in this version of John Osborne's play "with a neat variation of bite and comehitherness." She has an affair with her best friend's husband (Richard Burton).

Naomi Shields / THE CHAPMAN REPORT, 1962, Warners, d-George Cukor.
In a boring attempt to exploit the "Kinsey Report," Bloom is sultry and sad as the nymphomaniac who commits suicide rather than give in further to the depravity she so craves.

Theodora / THE HAUNTING, 1963, MGM, d-Robert Wise.
Bloom is a lesbian medium who spends a weekend in a haunted Boston mansion with repressed Julie Harris, who experiences extrasensory occurrences, a professor of anthropology (Richard Johnson), his wife (Lois Maxwell), and the heir to the house (Russ Tamblyn). It's a truly frightening chiller.

Nan Perry / THE SPY WHO CAME IN FROM THE COLD, 1966, Great Britain, Paramount, d-Martin Ritt.
Bloom is part of an elaborate plot to strengthen the hand of an agent planted by the British in East Germany, using intelligence officer Richard Burton as an unknowing conduit. She and Burton prove expendable and are killed.

Felicia / THE ILLUSTRATED MAN, 1969, Warners, d-Jack Smight.
Bloom is (perhaps) a witch from another planet who, through her sexual offerings, entices Rod Steiger (at the time her real-life husband) to let her cover his body with tattoos. Years later he searches for her to have his revenge.

Nora Helmer / A DOLL'S HOUSE, 1973, Great Britain, Elkins / Freeward, d-Patrick Garland.
Bloom performs well as Henrik Ibsen's heroine, a wife who begins to resist her husband's will as she begins to see herself as an independent person.

OTHER ROLES

1948: *Mary Dearing* / THE BLIND GODDESS. **1952:** *Susan Robbins* / INNOCENTS IN PARIS. **1953:** *Susan Mallinson* / THE MAN BETWEEN. **1956:** *Barzine* / ALEXANDER THE GREAT. **1958:** *Katya* / THE BROTHERS KARAMAZOV. **1959:** *Bonnie Brown* / THE BUCCANEER. **1960:** *Irene Andreny* / BRAINWASHED. **1963:** *Dorothea Grimm* / THE WONDERFUL WORLD OF THE BROTHERS GRIMM; *Julie Monks* / 80,000 SUSPECTS. **1964:** *Ada* / IL MAESTRO DI VIGEVANO; *the wife* / THE OUTRAGE; *Laura* / HIGH INFIDELITY. **1968:** *Alice Kinian* / CHARLY. **1969:** *Frances Howard* / THREE INTO TWO WON'T GO. **1970:** *Honor Klein* / A SEVERED HEAD. **1971:** *Ann Arnold* / RED SKY AT MORNING. **1977:** *Audrey* / ISLANDS IN THE STREAM. **1981:** *Hera* / CLASH OF THE TITANS. **1985:** *Eleanor Harvey* / DÉJA VU. **1987:** *Alice* / SAMMY AND ROSIE GET LAID.

BLYTH, ANN

(1928–)

Ann Blyth, a diminutive, dark-haired actress with slightly oriental eyes, had a pleasant soprano voice that was featured in a number of MGM operettas. Her most memorable role, however, was as the movies' best spoiled brat, Veda Pierce in MILDRED PIERCE, for which she received a Best Supporting Actress Academy Award nomination. After a disastrous miscasting as 1920s torch singer Helen Morgan (singing dubbed by Gogi Grant), Blyth retired from movies at age 29 to devote herself to her family and appearances in light operas and stage musicals.

KEY ROLES

Veda Pierce / MILDRED PIERCE, 1945, Warners, d-Michael Curtiz.
Sixteen-year-old Blyth is terrific in her portrayal of the most ungrateful daughter ever to appear on the screen. She takes what her mother's earnings can buy but is ashamed that her mother (Joan Crawford) has to work for a living. The contempt in her voice drips when she learns how her mother earns the money that gives her the luxuries she takes for granted: "My mother—a waitress!" Not content with all the luxuries showered upon her, she also goes after Mom's useless husband (Zachary Scott), and when she can't get him, she shoots him to death.

Regina Hubbard / ANOTHER PART OF THE FOREST, 1948, Universal, d-Michael Gordon.
In this prequel to Lillian Hellman's "The Little Foxes," we learn how the nasty Hubbards got that way. Blyth is Regina, the role Bette Davis played as a mature, hard-hearted woman.

The Mermaid / MR. PEABODY AND THE MERMAID, 1948, Universal, d-Irving Pichel.
Meant to cash in on the success of the British film MIRANDA, this story about a middle-aged man (William Powell) who fantasizes about having an affair with a mermaid (Blyth) didn't quite make it.

Dorothy Benjamin / THE GREAT CARUSO, 1951, MGM, d-Richard Thorpe.
Although this is meant as a biopic of Enrico Caruso, Blyth, not Mario Lanza, sings the best new song in the movie, "The Loveliest Night of the Year."

Rose Marie Lemaitre / ROSE MARIE, 1954, MGM, d-Mervyn LeRoy.
Even though this film has the songs that thrilled the public, Blyth, Howard Keel, and Fernando Lamas could not make it as successful as the 1936 version starring Jeanette MacDonald and Nelson Eddy.

Kathie / THE STUDENT PRINCE, 1954, MGM, d-Richard Thorpe.
Looking more like Jane Powell than herself, Blyth sings to Edmund Purdom (standing in for Mario Lanza who dubbed the songs but had grown too heavy for a romantic lead). Despite all the strikes against it,

the Sigmund Romberg music and Lanza's voice save the film.

Marsinah / KISMET, 1955, MGM, d-Vincente Minnelli. Blyth is the daughter of the Baghdad poet and thief (Howard Keel) who outwits the Grand Vizier. Meanwhile, Blyth wins the heart of the young Caliph, Vic Damone. Her best singing comes in "And this Is My Beloved" with Keel and Damone.

OTHER ROLES

1944: *Glory Marlow III* / CHIP OFF THE OLD BLOCK; *Sheila De Royce* / THE MERRY MONAHANS; *Carol Curtis* / BABES ON SWING STREET; *Bessie Jo Kirby* / BOWERY TO BROADWAY. **1946:** *Marian Tyler* / SWELL GUY. **1947:** *Ruth* / BRUTE FORCE; *Sheila Carrson* / KILLER MCCOY; *Doris* / A WOMAN'S VENGEANCE. **1949:** *Lucy Bostel* / RED CANYON; *Marita Connell* / ONCE MORE, MY DARLING; *Conn McNaughton* / TOP O' THE MORNING; *Ann Abbott* / FREE FOR ALL. **1950:** *Gail Macaulay* / OUR VERY OWN. **1951:** *Katherine Standish* / KATIE DID IT; *Valerie Carns* / THUNDER ON THE HILL; *Helen Pettigrew* / *Martha Forsyth* / I'LL NEVER FORGET YOU; *Princess Shalimar* / THE GOLDEN HORDE. **1952:** *Countess Marina Selanova* / THE WORLD IN HIS ARMS; *Linda Day* / ONE MINUTE TO ZERO; *Sally O'Moyne* / SALLY AND SAINT ANNE. **1953:** *Priscilla Hunt* / ALL THE BROTHERS WERE VALIANT. **1955:** *Lady Mary* / THE KING'S THIEF. **1956:** *Connie Martin* / SLANDER. **1957:** *Peggy Courtney* / THE BUSTER KEATON STORY; *Helen Morgan* / THE HELEN MORGAN STORY.

BOGARDE, DIRK

(Derek van den Bogaerde, 1921–)

Dirk Bogarde, the son of a Dutch-born art editor for the London *Times*, began his movie career as a J. Arthur Rank contract star and British matinee idol. He later won international acclaim for his more serious and demanding roles, often calling for him to play neurotic, complex, and gloomy characters. His work in VICTIM, the first British film to deal seriously with the issue of homosexuality in public life, was justifiably praised. He amusingly observed about his career: "According to American critics, I don't make 'great' movies. I make 'art' films in which I'm great." Bogarde has written three bestselling autobiographies and two novels and sold a drawing to the British Museum. He has appeared in such TV movies as LITTLE MOON FOR ALBAN (1965), BLITHE SPIRIT (1966), UPON THIS RISK (1969), and THE PATRICIA NEAL STORY (1981).

KEY ROLES

George Bland / QUARTET, 1948, Great Britain, Gainsborough, d-Harold French.

Bogarde appears in "The Alien Corn" segment of this film made up of four stories written and introduced by Somerset Maugham. When Bogarde, who has trained to become a concert pianist, is told he will never make the grade, he commits suicide.

Tom Riley / THE BLUE LAMP, 1950, Great Britain, Ealing, d-Basil Dearden.

The blue lamp of the title is the one that shines above the entrance to every British police station. In the film, a neurotic, small-time crook (Bogarde) has killed a constable in a hold-up and is tracked down by other policemen.

Dr. Simon Sparrow / DOCTOR IN THE HOUSE, 1953, Great Britain, General Films, d-Ralph Thomas.

In this very amusing film, Bogarde is a medical student who, with his chums, gets into an assortment of scrapes, including several with the hospital's chief surgeon (James Robertson Justice) before passing his course of studies.

Frank Clements / THE SLEEPING TIGER, 1954, Great Britain, Anglo-Amalgamated, d-Joseph Losey.

Bogarde is a petty criminal who tries to rob a psychiatrist, and the latter tries to probe his mind to learn why he is so antisocial. Bogarde seduces the doctor's wife but she pretends he attacked her, so her husband pretends to shoot him. Bogarde flees but is picked up by the wife in her car, which she promptly drives over a cliff.

Edward Bare / CAST A DARK SHADOW, 1955, Great Britain, Frobisher, d-Lewis Gilbert.

Bogarde plays a man who makes his living by murdering his rich elderly wives. He meets his match though, in a widow who learns of his plans for her, and he dies in a car with which he had tampered.

Jose / THE SPANISH GARDENER, 1956, Great Britain, Rank, d-Philip Leacock.

Jon Whiteley, son of a diplomat, becomes friends with Bogarde, the gardener at a nearby Spanish consulate. Whiteley's father resents the relationship and has Bogarde framed for theft. When Whiteley runs away to help the escaping Bogarde, his father sees the error of his ways and puts things right.

Sydney Carton / A TALE OF TWO CITIES, 1958, Great Britain, Rank, d-Ralph Thomas.

Bogarde's portrayal of the man who does the "far, far better thing" by sacrificing his life to save the husband of the woman he loves, compares most favorably with that of Ronald Colman's in the 1930s.

Franz Liszt / SONG WITHOUT END, 1960, Columbia, d-Charles Vidor and George Cukor.

Bogarde tries very hard as Liszt but this biopic of the great pianist is a dud.

Melville Farr / VICTIM, 1961, Great Britain, Rank, d-Basil Dearden.

Bogarde is a homosexual lawyer who exposes a blackmailer despite the risk to his career. The film is as tautly drawn as the finest murder thriller.

Hugo Barrett / THE SERVANT, 1963, Great Britain, Elstree, d-Joseph Losey.

Slowly, but surely, manservant Bogarde and his sexy "sister" (Sarah Miles) take control of his rich, ineffectual master (James Fox). Bogarde's insinuating evil is superbly subtle.

Captain Hargreaves / KING AND COUNTRY, 1964, Great Britain, BHE, d-Joseph Losey.

Bogarde serves as the defense lawyer for Tom Courtenay in the latter's trial for desertion. He loses the case and, when his client's execution is botched by a drunken firing squad, is forced to put a bullet through the boy's head.

Robert Gold / DARLING, 1965, Great Britain, Vic-Appia, d-John Schlesinger.

Bogarde is a married television journalist who becomes involved with Julie Christie. For a time he believes there is hope for them as they look forward to her having their baby, but without consulting him she has an abortion because she can't stand the alteration in her lifestyle. She's soon on her way to the next in a long string of men in her life.

Frederick Bruckman / THE DAMNED, 1969, West Germany, Praesidens / Pegaso, d-Luchino Visconti.

This is an X-rated film with Bogarde as a member of a family of German industrialists at the time of the Nazi takeover.

Gustav von Aschenbach / DEATH IN VENICE, 1971, Italy, Warners / Alfa, d-Luchino Visconti.
Bogarde is a dying, middle-aged, German composer staying at a plush Lido hotel in the early part of this century. He develops an obsessive love for a radiant 15-year-old boy (Bjorn Andersen) and stays in the city too long to escape the plague.

OTHER ROLES

1947: *policeman* / DANCING WITH CRIME. **1948:** *William Latch* / ESTHER WATERS; *Bill Fox* / ONCE A JOLLY SWAGMAN. **1949:** *Charles Prohack* / DEAR MR. PROHACK; *Alfie Rawlins* / BOYS IN BROWN; *George Hathaway* / SO LONG AT THE FAIR. **1950:** *Bob Baker* / THE WOMAN IN QUESTION. **1951:** *Stephen Mundy* / BLACKMAILED; *Tony Craig* / PENNY PRINCESS. **1952:** *Matt Sullivan* / THE GENTLE GUNMAN; *Chris Lloyd* / HUNTED. **1953:** *Wing Comdr. Tim Mason* / APPOINTMENT IN LONDON; *Lieutenant Graham* / THEY WHO DARE; *Simon Von Halder* / DESPERATE MOMENT. **1954:** *Alan Howard* / SIMBA; *Flight Sergeant MacKay* / THE SEA SHALL NOT HAVE THEM; *Tony Howard* / FOR BETTER FOR WORSE. **1955:** *Dr. Simon Sparrow* / DOCTOR AT SEA. **1956:** *Dr. Simon Sparrow* / DOCTOR AT LARGE. **1957:** *Maj. Paddy Leigh-Fermor, "Phildem"* / ILL MET BY MOONLIGHT. **1959:** *Bruce Campbell* / CAMPBELL'S KINGDOM; *Louis Dubedat* / THE DOCTOR'S DILEMMA; *Sir Mark Loddon* / *Number 15* / *Frank Welney* / LIBEL. **1960:** *Arturo Carrera* / THE ANGEL WORE RED; *Anacleto* / THE SINGER NOT THE SONG. **1962:** *First Lieutenant Scott-Padget* / H.M.S. DEFIANT. **1963:** *Sgt. Maj. Charles Coward* / THE PASSWORD IS COURAGE; *David Donne* / I COULD GO ON SINGING; *Dr. Henry Longman* / THE MIND BENDERS. **1964:** *Nicholas Whistler* / HOT ENOUGH FOR JUNE; *Dr. Simon Sparrow* / DOCTOR IN DISTRESS. **1965:** *Major McGuire* / THE HIGH BRIGHT SUN. **1966:** *Gabriel* / MODESTY BLAISE. **1967:** *Stephen* / ACCIDENT; *Charlie Hook* / OUR MOTHER'S HOUSE; *Sebastian* / MR. SEBASTIAN. **1968:** *Bibikov* / THE FIXER. **1969:** *Stephen* / OH! WHAT A LOVELY WAR; *Pursewarden* / JUSTINE. **1972:** *Philip Boyle* / THE SERPENT. **1974:** *Max* / THE NIGHT PORTER. **1975:** *Alan Curtis* / PERMISSION TO KILL. **1977:** *David Langham* / PROVIDENCE; *Lt. Gen. Frederich "Boy" Browning* / A BRIDGE TOO FAR. **1978:** *Hermann Karlovich* / DESPAIR.

BOGART, HUMPHREY

(1899–1957)

Thirty years after his death, Humphrey Bogart is as popular as ever. He was not one of the truly handsome leading men, his voice was handicapped by something of a lisp, and he certainly wasn't bigger than life. No, his appeal is that he was an average guy thrust into extraordinary circumstances who, in most cases, could be counted on to rise to the occasion and do precisely what was necessary—though reluctantly. His popularity is based on his being the kind of guy you'd have out to the house and never have to worry about trying to impress. The son of a noted physician and an artist, Bogart led a privileged life. He served in the navy in World War I and was wounded in the shelling of the Leviathan, which gave him a partially paralyzed lip, causing his characteristic snarl. In 1922 he began acting regularly on the New York stage. He made his film debut in 1930 in a short, BROADWAY'S LIKE THAT, followed by minor film roles until, in 1936, Leslie Howard insisted that Bogart recreate his stage role of Duke Mantee in the screen version of "The Petrified Forest." Yet Bogart didn't become a real star until his appearance as Sam Spade in THE MALTESE FALCON in 1941. He was nominated for Academy Awards for CASABLANCA (1942) and THE CAINE MUTINY (1954), winning for THE AFRICAN QUEEN (1951). He had some difficulty separating his tough guy roles from his real person, though. As Dave Chasen once noted, "Bogey's a helluva nice guy until 11:30 p.m. After that he thinks he's Bogart."

KEY ROLES

Duke Mantee / THE PETRIFIED FOREST, 1936, Warners, d-Archie Mayo.
Leslie Howard insisted that Bogart recreate his stage role as the killer who holes up in a cafe in Arizona's Petrified Forest. He obliges when Howard requests that Bogart kill him so Bette Davis can collect his insurance to pay for a trip to France.

Frank Taylor / BLACK LEGION, 1937, Warners, d-Archie Mayo.
Bogart is a factory worker who joins a Ku Klux Klan-like group when he loses a promotion to a foreign-born fellow worker.

David Graham / MARKED WOMAN, 1937, Warners, d-Lloyd Bacon.
Bogart is the district attorney who uses the testimony of nightclub hostesses (prostitutes) to convict a Lucky Luciano-like mobster.

Baby Face Martin / DEAD END, 1937, United Artists, d-William Wyler.
Visiting his old New York slum neighborhood isn't a good idea for gangster Bogart. The cops are searching for him, his mother (Marjorie Main) won't have anything to do with him, his old girlfriend (Claire Trevor) has become a prostitute, and a childhood friend (Joel McCrea) is forced to kill him.

James Frazier / ANGELS WITH DIRTY FACES, 1938, Warners, d-Michael Curtiz.
Bogart is the bad guy with no redeeming qualities, while James Cagney is the bad guy with some goodness in him. As a crooked lawyer Bogart makes the mistake of crossing Cagney and is gunned down for his trouble.

George Hally / THE ROARING TWENTIES, 1939, Warners, d-Raoul Walsh.
Bogart is an ex-World War I soldier who becomes a big shot New York bootlegger and engages in a gang war with ex-buddy James Cagney. He takes great pleasure in gunning down his former sergeant (Joe Sawyer), saying, "I told you we'd meet up sometime when you didn't have no stripes on your sleeve, and here we are."

Roy "Mad Dog" Earle / HIGH SIERRA, 1941, Warners, d-Raoul Walsh.
Just out of prison, Bogart is planning one last heist before retirement. But things get complicated by two women—one a crippled girl (Joan Leslie) for whom he pays for a corrective operation, and the other (Ida Lupino) is the only one to mourn him when he is hunted down and killed like a wild animal.

Sam Spade / THE MALTESE FALCON, 1941, Warners, d-John Huston.
In the definitive private eye movie, Bogart is the definitive private eye. He's hired by Mary Astor and meets several unsavory characters including Sydney Greenstreet, Peter Lorre, and Elisha Cook, Jr., who are all seeking a priceless jeweled bird which Bogart describes as "the, er, stuff that dreams are made of." In this marvelous classic Bogart perfects the style that will fire his legend for all time. His explanation of his obligation to his deceased partner (Jerome Cowan) very much demonstrates the character's

reluctant taking on of responsibility: "When a man's partner's killed, he's supposed to do something about it. It doesn't make any difference what you thought of him. He was your partner, and you're supposed to do something about it. As it happens, we're in the detective business. Well, when one of your organization gets killed, it's bad business to let the killer get away with it. Bad all around. Bad for every detective everywhere."

Rick Leland / ACROSS THE PACIFIC, 1942, Warners, d-John Huston.

Bogart is an army intelligence officer who poses as a cashiered soldier in order to infiltrate a pro-Japanese spy ring with plans of blowing up the Panama Canal.

Rick Blaine / CASABLANCA, 1942, Warners, d-Michael Curtiz.

In this most famous and memorable movie Bogart plays a Casablanca saloon keeper who sees the woman he once loved (Ingrid Bergman) walk into his place with her husband (Paul Henreid), a Resistance leader attempting to escape the Nazis. The following exchange between Claude Rains as Captain Renault and Bogart best illustrates Bogart's character: Bogart: "I came to Casablanca for the waters." Rains: "The waters? What waters? We're in the desert." Bogart: "I was misinformed." His farewell to Bergman at the airport when she must leave with her husband is a classic: "Ilsa, I'm no good at being noble, but it doesn't take much to see that the problems of three little people don't amount to a hill of beans in this crazy world. Someday you'll understand that. Now, now. Here's looking at you, kid."

Sgt. Joe Gunn / SAHARA, 1943, Columbia, d-Zoltan Korda.

Bogart is a tank commander who, with his crew, is cut off from the British Eighth Army by a German battalion in the Libyan desert. He tricks the thirst-crazed enemy into surrendering by making them think he and his men have water.

Harry Morgan / TO HAVE AND HAVE NOT, 1945, Warners, d-Howard Hawks.

Bogart is an American skipper of a fishing boat out of Martinique who is hired to smuggle a French underground leader to safety. The excitement of the yarn is almost overshadowed by the suggestive interplay between Bogart and newcomer Lauren Bacall. She criticizes his kissing, "It's even better when you help," but he gets the hang of it.

Philip Marlowe / THE BIG SLEEP, 1946, Warners, d-Howard Hawks.

No one could seem to make heads or tails out of the strange screenplay fashioned by William Faulkner, Leigh Brackett, and Jules Furthman for this interpretation of the Raymond Chandler novel. Somehow or other it doesn't really matter, because of the stylish performances of Bogart and Lauren Bacall (now Mrs. Bogart). Bogart plays a private eye who finds himself up to his ears in murders, blackmail, and the two wacky but lovely daughters of his employer. It's uncertain if the case is solved in the end, but most agree it is an enjoyable romp.

Fred C. Dobbs / THE TREASURE OF THE SIERRA MADRE, 1948, Warners, d-John Huston.

Bogart goes gold prospecting with Walter Huston and Tim Holt in Mexico's Sierra Madre mountains. They find the gold but the fever is too much for Bogart, who imagines the others wish to steal his "goods." In the end he is murdered by bandits who don't realize the value of the ore carried by his burros.

Frank McCloud / KEY LARGO, 1948, Warners, d-John Huston.

Two of Bogart's speeches sum up this story of his conflict with mobster Edward G. Robinson in the Florida Keys: "One Rocco more or less isn't worth dying for"; and, when he realizes that he must confront the mobster, "You were right. If your head says one thing and your whole life says another, your head always loses."

Martin Ferguson / THE ENFORCER, 1951, Warners, d-Bretaigne Windust.

Bogart is a crusading assistant D.A. who has until morning to find a way to convict Everett Sloane, the head of Murder, Inc., an organization of killers for hire. Bogart pores over the evidence and finally realizes that there is one witness against Sloane still living. But the killer realizes this too and sends word to his boys to rub out this last obstacle to his freedom.

Charlie Allnut / THE AFRICAN QUEEN, 1951, United Artists, d-John Huston.

Bogart won an Academy Award for his portrayal of an alcoholic riverboat captain who, during World War I, heads down an African river with a puritanical spinster (Katharine Hepburn), falls in love, and encounters a German gunboat. Just before he and Hepburn are about to be hanged, Bogart convinces the German captain to marry them.

Billy Dannreuther / BEAT THE DEVIL, 1954, United Artists, d-John Huston.

Bogart is the frontman for a group of international crooks who plan to acquire land known to contain uranium deposits. It's a strange, comical story without a well-defined plot, but nevertheless enjoyable.

Lt. Philip Francis Queeg / THE CAINE MUTINY, 1954, Columbia, d-Edward Dmytryk.

Bogart plays the war-weary captain of the destroyer Caine who, during World War II in the Pacific, loses control during a storm and is relieved of command by his first officer (Van Johnson). When Johnson is subsequently tried for mutiny, it's the unpleasant task of his defense lawyer (José Ferrer) to demonstrate Bogart's deteriorated mental condition. Bogart blows his cool on the witness stand, insisting, "Ah, but the strawberries! That's—that's where I had them. They laughed and made jokes, but I proved beyond a shadow of a doubt, and with geometric logic, that a duplicate key to the wardroom icebox did exist. And I'd have produced that key if they hadn't have pulled the Caine out of action. I know now they were out to protect some fellow officer."

Harry Dawes / THE BAREFOOT CONTESSA, 1954, United Artists, d-Joseph L. Mankiewicz.

Bogart is a has-been movie director who gets another chance when boorish millionaire Warren Stevens discovers barefoot dancer Ava Gardner. The sexual problems of the fiery, Spanish girl cause her death.

Eddie Willis / THE HARDER THEY FALL, 1956, Columbia, d-Mark Robson.

In his final screen appearance, Bogart is a press agent for a South American boxer being pushed towards oblivion by a crooked promoter (Rod Steiger) who plans to clean up when the glass-jawed giant is pulverized in the championship match.

OTHER ROLES

1930: *Tom Standish* / A DEVIL WITH WOMEN; *Steve* / UP THE RIVER. **1931:** *Jim Watson* / BODY AND SOUL; *Valentine Corliss* / BAD SISTER; *Stone* / WOMEN OF ALL NATIONS; *Steve Nash* / A HOLY TERROR. **1932:** *Jim Leonard* / LOVE AFFAIR; *Adkins* / BIG CITY BLUES; *"The Mug"* / THREE ON A MATCH. **1934:** *Garboni* / MIDNIGHT. **1936:** *Nick "Bugs" Fenner* / BULLETS OR BALLOTS; *Sherry Scott* / TWO AGAINST THE WORLD; *Hap Stuart* / CHINA CLIPPER; *Val Stevens* / ISLE OF FURY. **1937:** *John Phillips* / THE GREAT O'MALLEY; *Turkey Morgan* / KID GALAHAD; *Joe "Red" Kennedy* / SAN QUENTIN; *Douglas Quintain* / STAND-IN. **1938:** *Ed Hatch* / SWING YOUR LADY; *Mark Braden* / CRIME SCHOOL; *Harry Galleon* / MEN ARE SUCH FOOLS; *Rocks Valentine* / THE AMAZING DR. CLITTERHOUSE; *Pete Martin* / RACKET BUSTERS. **1939:** *Joe Gurney* / KING OF THE UNDERWORLD; *Whip McCord* / THE OKLAHOMA KID; *Michael O'Leary* / DARK VICTORY; *Frank Wilson* / YOU CAN'T GET AWAY WITH MURDER; *Marshall Quesne* / THE RETURN OF DOCTOR X. *Chuck Martin* / INVISIBLE STRIPES. **1940:** *John Murrell* / VIRGINIA CITY; *Chips Maguire* / IT ALL CAME TRUE; *Jack Buck* / BROTHER ORCHID; *Paul Fabrini* / THEY DRIVE BY NIGHT. **1941:** *Nick Coster* / THE WAGONS ROLL AT NIGHT. **1942:** *Gloves Donahue* / ALL THROUGH THE NIGHT; *Duke Berne* / THE BIG SHOT. **1943:** *Joe Rossi* / ACTION IN THE NORTH ATLANTIC; *guest* / THANK YOUR LUCKY STARS. **1944:** *Matrac* / PASSAGE TO MARSEILLES. **1945:** *Richard Mason* / CONFLICT. **1946:** *guest* / TWO GUYS FROM MILWAUKEE. **1947:** *Rip Murdock* / DEAD RECKONING; *Geoffrey Carroll* / THE TWO MRS. CARROLLS; *Vincent Parry* / DARK PASSAGE. **1948:** *guest* / ALWAYS TOGETHER. **1949:** *Andrew Morton* / KNOCK ON ANY DOOR; *Joe Barrett* / TOKYO JOE. **1950:** *Matt Brennan* / CHAIN LIGHTNING; *Dixon Steele* / IN A LONELY PLACE. **1951:** *Harry Smith* / SIROCCO. **1952:** *Ed Hutchinson* / DEADLINE U.S.A. **1953:** *Maj. Jed Webbe* / BATTLE CIRCUS; *guest* / LOVE LOTTERY. **1954:** *Linus Larrabee* / SABRINA. **1955:** *Joseph* / WE'RE NO ANGELS; *Jim Carmody* / THE LEFT HAND OF GOD; *Glenn Griffin* / THE DESPERATE HOURS.

BOLES, JOHN

(1895–1969)

John Boles was a handsome and affable leading man with a trim moustache and cleft chin, who was at his most popular singing in films like THE DESERT SONG. Gloria Swanson gave him his first movie break casting him opposite her in the 1927 silent THE LOVE OF SUNYA. In the 1930s he provided an attentive and non-threatening leading man for Ann Harding, Irene Dunne, and Rosalind Russell in some notable tearjerkers. He handled himself so well in these pictures that the women who flocked to them for a good cry didn't seem to mind that he usually was a married man in love with some other woman, whom he didn't treat particularly well. He retired from the movies in 1943 to concentrate on the stage.

KEY ROLES

Paul Judson / THE LOVE OF SUNYA, 1927, Silent, United Artists, d-Albert Parker.

Boles is a mining engineer and one of three men vying for Gloria Swanson's hand. The latter ultimately listens to her heart and marries Boles.

The Red Shadow / Pierre Birbeau / THE DESERT SONG, 1929, Warners, d-Roy Del Ruth.

Boles plays the Red Shadow—the leader of a tribe of Riff horsemen—but is actually Pierre Birbeau, the seemingly simple-minded son of the commandant of French forces in the Moroccan desert. As the Red Shadow he kidnaps the girl he loves (Carlotta King) and takes her into the desert where he sings the title song. Other Hammerstein and Romberg songs include "Riff Song," "Love's Dear Yearning," and "Romance."

Capt. Jim Stewart / RIO RITA, 1929, RKO, d-Luther Reed.

Boles is a Texas Ranger assigned to bring in the mysterious bandit called the Kinkajou. In a small, Mexican border town he encounters and falls in love with Rita Ferguson. Rascally General Ravinoff convinces Ferguson that Boles is out to arrest her brother, rumored to be the bandit, but Boles discovers that Ravinoff is the Kinkajou. Songs by Harry Tierney and Joe McCarthy include the title song, "You're Always in My Arms," and "Sweetheart, We Need Each Other."

Victor Moritz / FRANKENSTEIN, 1931, Universal, d-James Whale.

Boles is the close friend of Dr. Frankenstein (Colin Clive). He is also in love with Clive's fiancée, Mae Clarke.

Walter Saxel / BACK STREET, 1932, Universal, d-John M. Stahl.

Doris Lloyd is Boles's wife, but Irene Dunne is the one he loves. She's a self-effacing mistress whom he keeps for over twenty years, though the film doesn't give much evidence of any benefits to her. Boles must have something going for him more than his sleek good looks.

James Stanton Emerson / ONLY YESTERDAY, 1933, Universal, d-John M. Stahl.

Boles is a caddish World War I lieutenant who has an affair with Margaret Sullavan. But when he comes back from the war he has no recollection of the one-night stand that resulted in a child, and he seduces her once again.

John Shadwell / THE LIFE OF VERGIE WINTERS, 1934, RKO, d-Alfred Santell.

Boles is a rising politician who maintains his marriage for the position it gives him but really cares more for his mistress (Ann Harding) and their child.

Walter Craig / CRAIG'S WIFE, 1936, Columbia, d-Dorothy Arzner.

Boles's wife (Rosalind Russell) has more love for her house and its possessions than she does for Boles. Ultimately he leaves her to her first love.

Stephen Dallas / STELLA DALLAS, 1937, Samuel Goldwyn, d-King Vidor.

Boles's marriage to the uncouth and slatternly Stella (Barbara Stanwyck) is a mistake, but she does right when she gives their daughter to him, believing he can provide a better future for the girl. By this time he's also found a more suitable wife.

OTHER ROLES

1924: *Uriah* / SO THIS IS MARRIAGE. **1925:** *Lieutenant Shaw* / EXCUSE ME. **1928:** *Young Matt* / THE SHEPHERD OF THE HILLS; *Hugh Bradleigh* / WE AMERICANS; *John Clavering* / FAZIL; *Bert Durland* / THE WATER HOLE; *Barry* / VIRGIN LIPS; *John Payson* / MAN-MADE WOMAN; *Stephen Ransome* / ROMANCE OF THE UNDERWORLD. **1929:** *Qualie* / THE LAST WARNING; *Maurice* / SCANDAL. **1930:** *Captain Stanton* / SONG OF THE WEST; *guest* / KING OF JAZZ; *Rouget de Lisle* / CAPTAIN OF THE GUARD; *Count Mirko Tibor* / ONE HEAVENLY NIGHT. **1931:** *Prince Dmitri Nekhlyudoff* / RESURRECTION; *Bart Carter* / SEED; *Boyce Cameron* / GOOD SPORT. **1932:** *Stephen Illington* / CARELESS LADY; *Karl Kranz* / SIX HOURS TO LIVE. **1933:** *Paul Vanderkill* / CHILD OF MANHATTAN; *King Rupert* / MY LIPS BETRAY. **1934:** *Michael Harrison* / I BELIEVED IN YOU; *Carl Hausmann* / BELOVED; *Hal Reede* / BOTTOMS UP; *himself* / STAND UP AND CHEER; *Steve Miller* / WILD GOLD; *Newland Archer* / AGE OF INNOCENCE; *Ronald Hall* / THE WHITE PARADE; *Bruno Mahler* / MUSIC IN THE AIR. **1935:** *Thomas Bentley* / ORCHIDS TO YOU; *Edward Morgan* / CURLY TOP; *John Bruce*

/ REDHEADS ON PARADE; *Capt. Herbert Cary* / THE LITTLEST REBEL. **1936:** *Jim Kearney* / ROSE OF THE RANCHO; *Lt. Andrew Rowan* / A MESSAGE TO GARCIA. **1937:** *Alexander Drew* / AS GOOD AS MARRIED; *Robert Densmore* / FIGHT FOR YOUR LADY. **1938:** *Lee Thorwood* / SHE MARRIED AN ARTIST; *Antal Kovach* / ROMANCE IN THE DARK; *Jim Taylor* / SINNERS IN PARADISE. **1942:** *Steven Forbes* / BETWEEN US GIRLS. **1943:** *Colonel Jones* / THOUSANDS CHEER. **1952:** *Hassan* / BABES IN BAGDAD.

BOOTH, SHIRLEY

(Thelma Booth Ford, 1907–)

Stage star Shirley Booth had a brief but impressive film career, although today most will probably remember her for her TV role of Hazel the maid. Her views on her profession are nicely summed up as follows: "Acting is a way to overcome your own inhibitions and shyness. The writer creates a strong, confident personality, and that's what you become—unfortunately, only for the moment."

KEY ROLES

Lola Delaney / COME BACK, LITTLE SHEBA, 1952, Paramount, d-Daniel Mann.

Booth won an Academy Award for Best Actress for her recreation of her Broadway role as the well-meaning but exasperating wife of an ex-alcoholic (Burt Lancaster). Other actresses might have made this housewife overly sentimental but Booth and the role were made for each other and her performance is truly moving. Very few could get away with her line about her missing dog, Little Sheba: "I don't think Little Sheba's ever coming back, Doc, I ain't going to call her anymore."

Dolly Levi / THE MATCHMAKER, 1958, Paramount, d-Joseph Anthony.

Booth is wonderful in the role of the Yonkers matchmaker who sets her own cap for Paul Ford, a widower merchant looking to marry again.

OTHER ROLES

1953: *guest* / MAIN STREET TO BROADWAY. **1954:** *Mrs. Vivien Leslie* / ABOUT MRS. LESLIE. **1958:** *Alma Duvall* / HOT SPELL.

BOYER, CHARLES

(1899–1978)

Charles Boyer, the "great lover" of the screen, was a devoted husband in real life as he remained married to actress Pat Paterson for 44 years. Four days after her death and two days before his 79th birthday he committed suicide. He began his film career in supporting roles in French films. By the mid-1920s he was established as a French star with the title role in LE CAPITAIN FRACASSE (1927). He signed with UFA to make French versions of German movies in Berlin, making only LA BARCAROLLE D'AMOUR (1930) before having his contract bought by MGM so that he could make French versions of U.S. films. He did a French version of BIG HOUSE called REVOLTE DANS LA PRISON, recreating the Chester Morris role, and he was Jimmy Dugan in LE PROCES DE MARY DUGAN. Throughout the years, Boyer returned to France from time to time to make movies. His cultured voice with the French accent and his soulful eyes were the characteristics that so endeared him to female fans. And as his bedroom eyes grew older, he happily played charming roués.

KEY ROLES

Latzi / CARAVAN, 1934, Fox Films, d-Erik Charell.

In his first Hollywood starring role, Boyer plays a gypsy who falls in love with and marries a Hungarian countess (Loretta Young). After the hastily arranged marriage, Young meets and falls in love with Phillips Holmes, and Boyer bows out so she may marry her true love.

Boris Androvsky / THE GARDEN OF ALLAH, 1936, United Artists, d-Richard Boleslawski.

Boyer is a disillusioned monk who flees a Trappist monastery to yield to carnal temptations. At an Algerian desert oasis he meets Marlene Dietrich, who is seeking God. They fall in love, marry, and he experiences the pleasures of the flesh. But in the end he returns to the monastery. It's a silly movie with both leads way over the top in their acting, but still somehow entertaining.

Archduke Rudolph / MAYERLING, 1937, France, Nero Film, d-Anatole Litvak.

The heir to the Hapsburg Empire, Boyer uses his deep brown eyes and soulful looks to convince his mistress (Danielle Darrieux) to join him in a suicide pact at his hunting lodge in 1889.

Prince Mikail Alexandrovitch Ouratieff / TOVARICH, 1937, Warners, d-Anatole Litvak.

In this lively comedy, Boyer and his wife (Claudette Colbert) are Russian aristocrats who have fled to Paris with letters of credit worth millions at the time of the Revolution. They do not spend the money belonging to the Imperial family and instead take positions as maid and butler in a wealthy family's home.

Napoleon Bonaparte / CONQUEST, 1937, MGM, d-Clarence Brown.

In this dignified and sometimes dull costume piece, Boyer plays Napoleon to Greta Garbo's Countess Marie Walewska, the Emperor's most enduring mistress. Boyer was nominated for an Academy Award for his performance.

Paul Dumond / HISTORY IS MADE AT NIGHT, 1937, United Artists, d-Frank Borzage.

Boyer, the "finest head waiter in all Europe," is in love with wealthy Jean Arthur. But her ex-husband (Colin Clive) sets Boyer up on a phony murder charge which he eventually beats.

Pepe Le Moko / ALGIERS, 1938, United Artists, d-John Cromwell.

This is the movie in which Boyer does not say to Hedy Lamarr, "Come with me to the Casbah." That's where they meet and his mistake is leaving the safety of the native quarter of Algiers to follow her. A native police inspector (Joseph Calleia) who likes his criminal adversary says after Boyer has been fatally wounded: "I'm sorry, Pepe. He thought you were going to escape." Boyer, who no longer must be confined to the Casbah, replies, "And so I have, my friend."

Michel Marnet / LOVE AFFAIR, 1939, RKO, d-Leo McCarey.

In this romance, which is one of Hollywood's most fondly remembered films, Boyer and Irene Dunne meet on a ship bound for New York, fall hopelessly in love, and agree to meet at the top of the Empire State Building in six months to see if they still feel the same about each other. She is prevented from making the meeting because of an accident and he believes she no longer cares. But they are ultimately reunited.

Andre Praslin / ALL THIS AND HEAVEN TOO, 1940, Warners, d-Anatole Litvak.
Boyer is a 19th-century nobleman who falls in love with Bette Davis, his children's governess, for whom he murders his wife.

Walter Saxel / BACK STREET, 1941, Universal, d-Robert Stevenson.
In all the film versions of this Fannie Hurst weeper, Boyer is clearly the best actor to appear as the married man who maintains the same mistress for over twenty years.

Georges Iscovescu / HOLD BACK THE DAWN, 1941, Paramount, d-Mitchell Leisen.
In order to get into the United States, Boyer marries schoolteacher Olivia de Havilland, whom he does not love. She learns of his deception from Paulette Goddard who reveals, "Yes, he married you. He married you to get past that gate—for the same reason that I married my little American and with the same ring. Just look inside at the engraving: 'To Toots, For Keeps.'"

Lewis Dodd / THE CONSTANT NYMPH, 1943, Warners, d-Edmund Goulding.
Composer Boyer discovers too late that the perfect mate for him is the fragile, sickly schoolgirl (Joan Fontaine) with whom he wrote his best composition.

Gregory Anton / GASLIGHT, 1944, MGM, d-George Cukor.
In this classic psychological thriller, Boyer plays a man deliberately attempting to drive his wife (Ingrid Bergman) mad so he will be undisturbed in seeking the jewels his previous murder victim had hidden in the house years earlier. When he is finally caught, he tries to explain why he undertook such a dastardly plot, but his eyes betray his madness: "Between us all the time were those jewels, like a fire—a fire in my brain that separated us—those jewels which I wanted all my life."

Jacques Bonnard / THE HAPPY TIME, 1952, Columbia, d-Richard Fleischer.
Boyer is a most understanding father, son, and brother in this perfectly delightful story of a French-Canadian family during the 1920s, and the coming of age of Boyer's adolescent son (Bobby Driscoll).

General Andre de / THE EARRINGS OF MADAME DE..., 1953, Indus / Rizzoli, d-Max Ophuls.
In this elegant movie, tragedy occurs when Danielle Darrieux sells her earrings and tells Boyer that she has lost them.

Cesar / FANNY, 1961, Warners, d-Joshua Logan.
Boyer is the proprietor of a waterfront bar in Marseilles and the father of a son (Horst Buchholz) who ships out leaving Leslie Caron pregnant. Boyer and Maurice Chevalier are wonderful in this otherwise dull version of Marcel Pagnol's "Marseilles Trilogy."

Michel Boullard / A VERY SPECIAL FAVOR, 1965, Universal, d-Michael Gordon.
In this tasteless but amusing film, Boyer asks Rock Hudson to initiate his spinster daughter (Leslie Caron) into the world of "love."

Victor Velasco / BAREFOOT IN THE PARK, 1968, Paramount, d-Gene Saks.
Boyer is the eccentric neighbor who lives in a loft above a newly married couple (Jane Fonda and Robert Redford). He puts a spark of romance back into the life of Fonda's mother, Mildred Natwick.

OTHER ROLES

1931: *Jacques* / THE MAGNIFICENT LIE. **1932:** *Albert* / RED-HEADED WOMAN; *Gene Gaudin* / THE MAN FROM YESTERDAY. **1933:** *Duke* / THE ONLY GIRL; *Marquis Yurisaka* / THE BATTLE. **1934:** *Liliom* / LILIOM. **1935:** *Charles Monet* / PRIVATE WORLDS; *Roberti* / BREAK OF HEARTS; *Dimitri Koslov* / SHANGHAI. **1936:** *Phillippe* / LE BONHEUR. **1938:** *Andre Pascand* / L'ORAGE. **1939:** *Philip Andre Durand* / WHEN TOMORROW COMES. **1940:** *Count George Dasetta* / LES AMOUREX. **1941:** *Andre Cassil* / APPOINTMENT FOR LOVE. **1942:** *Paul Orman* / TALES OF MANHATTAN. **1943:** *The Great Gaspar* / FLESH AND FANTASY; *narrator* / THE HEART OF A NATION. **1944:** *George Corday* / TOGETHER AGAIN. **1945:** *Denard* / CONFIDENTIAL AGENT. **1946:** *Adam Belinski* / CLUNY BROWN. **1948:** *Dr. Ravic* / ARCH OF TRIUMPH; *Henry Maurier* / A WOMAN'S VENGEANCE. **1949:** *narrator* / LA BATAILLE DU RAIL. **1951:** *Dr. Paul Laurent* / THE 13TH LETTER. **1952:** *Fr. Marc Arnoux* / THE FIRST LEGION. **1953:** *Singh* / THUNDER IN THE EAST. **1955:** *Dr. Douglas N. Devanal* / THE COBWEB; *Count Muffat* / NANA; *Count Gregorio* / LUCKY TO BE A WOMAN. **1956:** *Delomel* / PARIS PALACE HOTEL; *Monsieur Gasse* / AROUND THE WORLD IN 80 DAYS. **1958:** *Prince Charles* / UNE PARISIENNE; *Dominique You* / THE BUCCANEER; *Maxime* / MAXIME. **1961:** *Pierre* / LES DEMONS DE MINUIT. **1962:** *Marcello Desnoyers* / THE FOUR HORSEMEN OF THE APOCALYPSE; *Michael Gosselyn* / ADORABLE JULIA. **1963:** *M. Etienne Pimm* / LOVE IS A BALL. **1966:** *De Solnay* / HOW TO STEAL A MILLION; *Monod* / IS PARIS BURNING? **1967:** *LeGrand* / CASINO ROYALE. **1969:** *Andre Greenlaw* / THE APRIL FOOLS; *the broker* / THE MADWOMAN OF CHAILLOT; *Vostov* / THE DAY THE HOT LINE GOT HOT. **1973:** *High Lama* / LOST HORIZON. **1974:** *Baron Raoul* / STAVISKY. **1976:** *Count Sanziani* / A MATTER OF TIME.

BRACKEN, EDDIE

(Edward V. Bracken, 1920–)
Never a great actor, never a great comedian, Eddie Bracken nevertheless pleased audiences in two of Preston Sturges's best movies. His on-screen personality as a shy, bumbling, naive schnook made him a favorite during the war years, but his limited appeal soon faded in the early 1950s. His work in the stage musical "Too Many Girls," in which he introduced the hit song "I Didn't Know What Time It Was," got him called to Hollywood in 1940 to recreate his stage role in the movie version. He boasts that he has made over ten thousand performances on the legitimate stage.

KEY ROLES

JoJo Jordan / TOO MANY GIRLS, 1940, RKO, d-George Abbott.
Bracken reprises his original stage role in his movie debut as a featured actor, playing one of four football players hired by the wealthy father of coed Lucille Ball to protect her when she attends college. Bracken introduced Ball to his pal Desi Arnaz.

Bert / CAUGHT IN THE DRAFT, 1941, Paramount, d-David Butler.
When film star Bob Hope is drafted, his silly chauffeur (Bracken) goes along and shares in the antics.

Norval Jones / THE MIRACLE OF MORGAN'S CREEK, 1943, Paramount, d-Preston Sturges.
When Betty Hutton can't recall which soldier got her pregnant, 4-F Bracken is tapped as a likely husband and father. It's a weird and wonderful assault on the Hays Office and Bracken is perfect. He has no illusions about his appeal as he explains to Hutton, "The older I got the uglier I got. When I was a kid, they said, 'He'll grow out of it.' But I guess a face like mine you just can't grow out of so easy. It's like it's cast in iron."

Woodrow Truesmith / HAIL THE CONQUERING HERO, 1944, Paramount, d-Preston Sturges.

Bracken is an army reject who is mistakenly believed to be a hero by the folks in his home town. He meets some tough marines who help him keep up the pretense since it's good for the morale of the home front. When he finally confesses, the people still love him and elect him mayor of the town, and he gets the girl (Ella Raines). It's Bracken's best role.

Roy Walley / NATIONAL LAMPOON'S VACATION, 1983, Warners, d-Harold Ramis.

In something of a cameo role, Bracken appears as the Walt Disney-like owner of the west coast theme and amusement park that Chevy Chase and his family have driven from Chicago to visit.

OTHER ROLES

1938: *bit* / BROTHER RAT. **1941:** *Dizzy Stevens* / LIFE WITH HENRY; *Benny Morgan* / REACHING FOR THE SUN. **1942:** *Jack Mitchell* / SWEATER GIRL; *Barney Walters* / THE FLEET'S IN; *Jimmy Webster* / STAR SPANGLED RHYTHM. **1943:** *Wally Case* / HAPPY GO LUCKY; *George Bodell* / YOUNG AND WILLING. **1944:** *Toby Smith* / RAINBOW ISLAND. **1945:** *Herbie Fenton* / OUT OF THIS WORLD; *J. Newport Bates* / BRING ON THE GIRLS; *guest* / DUFFY'S TAVERN; *Ogden Spencer Trulow III* / HOLD THAT BLONDE. **1947:** *Henry Haskell* / LADIES' MAN; *P. P. Porterhouse III* / FUN ON A WEEKEND. **1949:** *Chuck Donovan* / THE GIRL FROM JONES BEACH. **1950:** *Orville Wingait* / SUMMER STOCK. **1951:** *Lew Conway* / TWO TICKETS TO BROADWAY. **1952:** *Willie Fisher* / WE'RE NOT MARRIED; *Boff Roberts* / ABOUT FACE. **1953:** *Frederick Winthrop Clopp* / A SLIGHT CASE OF LARCENY. **1961:** *cameo* / WILD WILD WORLD. **1962:** *cameo* / A SUMMER SUNDAY. **1971:** *Voice* / SHINBONE ALLEY.

BRANDO, MARLON

(1924–)

Initially identified with the mumbling, brooding, raw sexuality school of acting, Marlon Brando has brought intelligence and intensity to a broad range of roles, playing a variety of characters from different sections of life and different periods of time. He was once the symbol of rebellion and unconventionality, but now has become a recluse willing to appear in a movie only now and then in a role that takes a minimum amount of time to film for an exorbitant amount of money. Even though he may believe that he is conning the production companies and public into paying for a reputation rather than a performance, he is too much of an original not to bring to even the most unworthy projects his special electrifying personality. He studied acting with Stella Adler at the New School for Social Research, then made his New York stage debut in "I Remember Mama," with his stardom achieved in "A Streetcar Named Desire." His Oscar nominations have been for A STREETCAR NAMED DESIRE, VIVA ZAPATA!, JULIUS CAESAR, SAYONARA, and LAST TANGO IN PARIS. He won Academy Awards for ON THE WATERFRONT and THE GODFATHER; the latter award he turned down.

KEY ROLES

Ken Wilozek / THE MEN, 1950, United Artists, d-Fred Zinnemann.

In his first film role, Brando plays a bitter ex-GI paralyzed from the waist down. Before filming began he spent several weeks with actual paraplegics to get the proper feeling for their plight.

Stanley Kowalski / A STREETCAR NAMED DESIRE, 1951, Warners, d-Elia Kazan.

Brando received his first Academy Award nomination for this recreation of his stage role as the crude, illiterate, New Orleans workingman who brutalizes his neurotic sister-in-law both mentally and physically, pushing her over the brink into insanity.

Emiliano Zapata / VIVA ZAPATA! 1952, 20th Century-Fox, d-Elia Kazan.

Brando received an Oscar nomination for his portrayal of the Mexican revolutionary of the 1920s, who becomes president of his country but later abandons the office and is killed in an ambush by soldiers following a rival political leader. When he walks away from the presidency, he explains to his wife (Jean Peters): "A strong man needs a weak people. A strong people don't need a strong man."

Marc Antony / JULIUS CAESAR, 1953, MGM, d-Joseph L. Mankiewicz.

Brando's "Friends, Romans, Countrymen" speech is one of the better things about this all-star adaptation of the Shakespeare play.

Johnny / THE WILD ONE, 1953, Columbia, d-Laslo Benedek.

Brando is very "cool" as a motorcycle punk who leads one of two rival gangs into a small California town, which they terrorize until the state police are called in.

Terry Malloy / ON THE WATERFRONT, 1954, Columbia, d-Elia Kazan.

Brando won an Academy Award for his performance as a longshoreman who fingers his crooked union boss and suffers greatly for his good deed. Brando testifies before the crime commission, giving the facts they need to shut down at least one crooked union official, but he suffers a shunning from other dock workers and a tremendous beating for his reward. One can still hear the special pain in his accusation that his brother (Rod Steiger) had sold him out in his boxing career: "I coulda had class! I coulda been a contender! I coulda been somebody! Instead of a bum which is what I am! Let's face it. It was you, Charley!"

Sky Masterson / GUYS AND DOLLS, 1955, Samuel Goldwyn, d-Joseph L. Mankiewicz.

Brando tries his hand at musical comedy in this story of a Damon Runyon gambler who bets he can get a Salvation Army lass to go away with him to Havana. He handles the singing and dancing with ease.

Sakini / THE TEAHOUSE OF THE AUGUST MOON, 1956, MGM, d-Daniel Mann.

As an Okinawan interpreter, Brando teaches army captain Glenn Ford a thing or two about democracy when the latter is assigned to pacification of Brando's village after World War II. The film ends with Brando wrapping things up for the audience: "Little story now concluded but history of world unfinished. Lovely ladies, kind gentlemen: go home to ponder. What was true at beginning remains true. Play make man think. Thought make man wise. And wisdom make life endurable."

Christian Diestl / THE YOUNG LIONS, 1958, 20th Century-Fox, d-Edward Dmytryk.

Brando is an ex-ski instructor who, as a German lieutenant near the end of World War II, becomes disillusioned with the Nazis and is killed by American GIs.

Fletcher Christian / MUTINY ON THE BOUNTY, 1962, MGM, d-Lewis Milestone.

In sharp contrast to the macho interpretation given by Clark Gable in the 1930s, Brando plays Christian as something of a lisping fop whose problems with

Captain Bligh are as much due to class differences as to the latter's cruelty to the men of the ship. Reportedly, Trevor Howard, who plays Bligh, would have liked to keel-haul the impossible Brando.

Don Vito Corleone / THE GODFATHER, 1972, Paramount, d-Francis Ford Coppola.
Brando won and turned down the Oscar for his brilliant portrayal of the head of a crime family of Italian-American heritage who made the public "an offer they couldn't refuse."

Paul / LAST TANGO IN PARIS, 1972, United Artists, d-Bernardo Bertolucci.
Brando's sixth Academy Award nomination was for the role of an American in Paris who, after the death of his wife, has a three-day sexual orgy with Maria Schneider when they both arrive at the same time to rent an apartment.

Jor-El / SUPERMAN, 1978, Warners, d-Richard Donner.
Brando got top billing and $3 million for a ten-minute appearance as the father who sends Superman to Earth when their home planet Krypton is doomed.

Col. Walter E. Kurtz / APOCALYPSE NOW, 1979, United Artists, d-Francis Ford Coppola.
Brando got top billing but only appeared in about the last 15 minutes of this two-and-a-half-hour film. The story is about an army Special Services officer (Martin Sheen) who is sent to kill Brando, an insane, renegade Green Berets officer who has taken refuge in the Cambodian jungles where he commands a group of fierce fighting Montagnard tribesmen. Aware of Sheen's mission, Brando informs him, "You got no right to call me a murderer. You have a right to kill me and you have the right to do that—but you have no right to judge me."

OTHER ROLES

1954: *Napoleon Bonaparte* / DESIREE. **1957:** *Maj. Lloyd Gruver* / SAYONARA. **1960:** *Rio* / ONE-EYED JACKS. **1961:** *Val Xavier* / FUGITIVE KIND. **1962:** *Harrison Carter MacWhite* / THE UGLY AMERICAN. **1964:** *Freddy Benson* / BEDTIME STORY. **1965:** *Robert Crain* / THE SABOTEUR, CODE NAME MORITURI. **1966:** *Sheriff Calder* / THE CHASE; *Matt Fletcher* / THE APPALOOSA. **1967:** *Ogden Mears* / A COUNTESS FROM HONG KONG; *Maj. Weldon Penderton* / REFLECTIONS IN A GOLDEN EYE. **1968:** *Grindl* / CANDY; *Bud the chauffeur* / THE NIGHT OF THE FOLLOWING DAY. **1970:** *Sir William Walker* / BURN! **1972:** *Peter Quint* / THE NIGHTCOMERS. **1976:** *Robert E. Lee Clayton* / THE MISSOURI BREAKS. **1980:** *Adam Steiffel* / THE FORMULA.

BRENT, GEORGE

(George Brent Nolan, 1904–1979)
George Brent claimed that he served as a dispatch rider for Michael Collins—the IRA leader during the 1922 "troubles"—and had to flee Ireland with a price on his head. Whatever the truth was, he did not pose any threat to the strong-willed actresses he appeared opposite in numerous "women's pictures" of the 1930s and 1940s. He was the ideal prop for Bette Davis in seven films as he was a gallant, romantic, dependable leading man who was willing to take second billing. For most of his career he had to carefully dye his hair jet black as he had grayed early in life and his true color was white as snow.

KEY ROLES

Pat Denning / 42ND STREET, 1933, Warners, d-Lloyd Bacon.
Brent loves Bebe Daniels, his former vaudeville partner, but stands in the background as she plays up to Guy Kibbee, the angel for her Broadway show. Brent takes a half-hearted interest in chorus girl Ruby Keeler, who later replaces Daniels as the star of the show.

Jack Townsend / THE PAINTED VEIL, 1934, MGM, d-Richard Boleslawski.
Brent is a diplomatic attaché with whom Greta Garbo has an affair before she returns to her doctor husband, who is fighting a cholera epidemic in China.

Curt Devlin / FRONT PAGE WOMAN, 1935, Warners, d-Michael Curtiz.
Brent and Bette Davis are rival reporters who try to outscoop each other. He's a chauvinist who doesn't believe there's any room for women in serious reporting. They are in love, but his attitude stands in the way of marriage. When they compete on a murder story, he uses some very dirty tricks to make her look bad. But in the end she traps the real killer and proves her worth, forcing Brent to admit that some women actually make "good newspapermen."

Buck Cantrell / JEZEBEL, 1938, Warners, d-William Wyler.
According to the ads for the picture Bette Davis is "half-angel, half-siren, all woman," and George Brent is one of her rejected suitors. Davis so outrages her fiancée (Henry Fonda) that he breaks with her and moves to Philadelphia. When he returns three years later, he is married and Davis tells Brent that her honor has been besmirched. Brent calls Fonda out but Fonda has better things to do and Brent finds himself facing Fonda's younger brother (Richard Cromwell) on the field of honor, where Brent is killed.

Dr. Frederick Steele / DARK VICTORY, 1939, Warners, d-Edmund Goulding.
Brent is a neurosurgeon who cannot save Bette Davis from going blind and dying from a brain tumor; but he can give her a few months of happiness as his wife.

Tom Ransome / THE RAINS CAME, 1939, 20th Century-Fox, d-Clarence Brown.
Brent is an alcoholic artist who, along with some other parasitic individuals, proves his mettle when a disastrous flood strikes India during the Raj.

Dan Hardesty / 'TIL WE MEET AGAIN, 1940, Warners, d-Edmund Goulding.
Brent is a crook being taken back to San Francisco to be executed and Merle Oberon is a dying woman aboard the same oceanliner from Hong Kong. They fall in love and don't let on that future meetings are unlikely in this world.

Peter Van Allen / THE GREAT LIE, 1941, Warners, d-Edmund Goulding.
Bette Davis's passion for Brent is so great that when he is reported killed in a plane crash, she pays Mary Astor for the right to adopt the baby Astor is carrying—a baby fathered by Brent.

Roger Berton / THE AFFAIRS OF SUSAN, 1945, Paramount, d-William A. Seiter.
Brent is one of four men who each see Joan Fontaine in a different light. Walter Abel proposes and is accepted by Fontaine; Brent, a movie producer, was once married to her; Dennis O'Keefe, a novelist, believes Fontaine to be an intellectual; and Don DeFore, a lumber king, has enjoyed endless nightclubbing with her. Told mostly in flashback, it's a witty film.

Professor Warren / THE SPIRAL STAIRCASE, 1946, RKO, d-Robert Siodmak.

Someone is killing deformed girls in a small 1906 New England town. Dorothy McGuire looks like the next victim. Could Brent be the psychopath?

OTHER ROLES

1930: *Inspector Turner* / UNDER SUSPICION. **1931:** *Jimmy* / HOMICIDE SQUAD; *Alan Scott* / LIGHTNING WARRIOR; *James Brent* / ONCE A SINNER; *Les Haines* / FAIR WARNING; *Capt. Ronald Keane* / CHARLIE CHAN CARRIES ON; *Donald Swift* / EX-BAD BOY. **1932:** *Roelf Pool* / SO BIG; *Julian Tierney* / THE RICH ARE ALWAYS WITH US; *Percy Acton* / WEEK-END MARRIAGE; *Inspector Patten* / MISS PINKERTON; *Jim Gibson* / THE PURCHASE PRICE; *Geoffrey Gault* / THE CRASH; *Dr. Tony Travers* / THEY CALL IT SIN. **1933:** *Dr. Thomas Bernard* / LUXURY LINER; *Neil Davis* / THE KEYHOLE; *Bob Chandler* / LILLY TURNER; *Mr. Trenholm* / BABY FACE; *Jim Thorne* / FEMALE; *Lt. J. Stevens* / FROM HEADQUARTERS. **1934:** *Beall* / STAMBOUL QUEST; *William Reynolds* / HOUSEWIFE; *Stuart McAllister* / DESIRABLE. **1935:** *Terry Parker* / LIVING ON VELVET; *Mack Hale* / STRANDED; *Bob McNear* / THE GOOSE AND THE GANDER; *Bill Bradford* / SPECIAL AGENT; *Emory Muir* / IN PERSON; *Colin Trent* / THE RIGHT TO LIVE. **1936:** *Alan Tanner* / SNOWED UNDER; *Johnny Jones* / THE GOLDEN ARROW; *Matt Logan* / THE CASE AGAINST MRS. AMES; *Jim Baker* / GIVE ME YOUR HEART; *Fred Gilbert* / MORE THAN A SECRETARY. **1937:** *Steve Russell* / GOD'S COUNTRY AND THE WOMAN; *Bill Austin* / THE GO-GETTER; *Paul Cameron* / MOUNTAIN JUSTICE; *Jared Whitney* / GOLD IS WHERE YOU FIND IT; *Lieutenant Commander Matthews* / SUBMARINE D-1. **1938:** *Denny Jordan* / RACKET BUSTERS; *Dick Orr* / SECRETS OF AN ACTRESS. **1939:** *Cass Harrington* / WINGS OF THE NAVY; *Clem Spender* / THE OLD MAID. **1940:** *Stephen Forbes* / THE MAN WHO TALKED TOO MUCH; *Wild Bill Donovan* / THE FIGHTING 69TH; *John Gamble / Bradley* / SOUTH OF SUEZ; *Capt. Stephen Dennett* / ADVENTURE IN DIAMONDS. **1941:** *Kenneth Bixby* / HONEYMOON FOR THREE; *cameo* / LAND OF LIBERTY; *Prince Kurt von Rotenberg* / THEY DARE NOT LOVE; *Tim Hanley* / INTERNATIONAL LADY. **1942:** *Mike Abbott* / TWIN BEDS; *Charles Barclay* / THE GAY SISTERS; *Craig Fleming* / IN THIS OUR LIFE; *Steve "Mitch" Mitchell* / YOU CAN'T ESCAPE FOREVER; *James Kincaid* / SILVER QUEEN. **1944:** *Dr. Huntington Bailey* / EXPERIMENT PERILOUS. **1945:** *Maj. Scott Landis* / MY REPUTATION. **1946:** *Larry Hamilton* / TOMORROW IS FOREVER; *Bill Williams* / LOVER COME BACK; *Nigel* / TEMPTATION. **1947:** *Matt Claibourne* / SLAVE GIRL; *Arthur Earthleigh* / OUT OF THE BLUE; *Joe Medford* / THE CORPSE CAME C.O.D. *Michael Brooks* / CHRISTMAS EVE. **1948:** *Capt. Jeremy Bradford* / LUXURY LINER; *Jim Warburton* / ANGEL ON THE AMAZON. **1949:** *Mathew Bostel* / RED CANYON; *Dan Collins* / ILLEGAL ENTRY; *Mike Jackson* / THE KID FROM CLEVELAND; *Paul Martin* / BRIDGE FOR SALE. **1950:** *John Harman* / THE LAST PAGE. **1951:** *Jeff Donley* / FBI GIRL. **1952:** *Tom Bradfield* / MONTANA BELLE. **1953:** *Steve* / TANGIER INCIDENT. **1978:** *Judge Gerhard Gesell* / BORN AGAIN.

BRONSON, CHARLES

(Charles Buchinsky, 1921–)

Rugged, mean-looking Charles Bronson is an unlikely candidate for stardom, but his roles as men of violence strike a chord with those frustrated with criminals who seem to get away with everything. Apparently there are millions who, at least vicariously, enjoy vigilante methods for dealing with scum who prey on the weak. Bronson has created only one film persona and he keeps repeating it over and over, but fans of his brand of violence don't seem to mind and his movies are box-office successes. His first seventeen films were made under the names of Charles Buchinski (or Buchinsky). Candidly, he has admitted, "I'm not one of my favorite actors." His wife, actress Jill Ireland, has appeared in a number of his films.

KEY ROLES

George "Machine Gun" Kelly / MACHINE GUN KELLY, 1958, American International, d-Roger Corman.

In this routine crime melodrama, Bronson plays one of the most wanted public enemies of the 1930s. After dishing it out for most of the film, he gets his expected reward.

Bernardo O'Reilly / THE MAGNIFICENT SEVEN, 1960, United Artists, d-John Sturges.

As an Irish-Mexican gunfighter who joins six others in defending a Mexican village from bandits, Bronson portrays a sensitive man who knows what he has missed because of his choice of occupations.

Danny Velinski / THE GREAT ESCAPE, 1963, United Artists, d-John Sturges.

Even though he suffers from claustrophobia, Bronson does most of the work in building the tunnels that will be used by Allied POWs escaping from a German prison camp.

Joseph Wladislaw / THE DIRTY DOZEN, 1967, MGM, d-Robert Aldrich.

Bronson is the only one of twelve World War II American soldier-convicts to survive an attack on a French chateau filled with high-ranking Nazi officers.

The Man (Harmonica) / ONCE UPON A TIME IN THE WEST, 1969, Paramount, d-Sergio Leone.

In this violent and remarkable western, Bronson is on the trail of Henry Fonda, who years earlier had forced Bronson to play the harmonica while his older brother was tortured and hanged.

Pardon Chato / CHATO'S LAND, 1972, United Artists, d-Michael Winner.

Bronson is an Apache half-breed who kills a man in self-defense and then destroys the posse chasing him in this exhaustingly violent western.

Joseph Valachi / THE VALACHI PAPERS, 1972, Columbia, d-Terence Young.

Bronson is quite effective portraying the Brooklyn-born mobster who is persuaded by the FBI to testify before the Senate committee investigating organized crime.

Paul Kersey / DEATH WISH, 1974, Paramount, d-Michael Winner.

When his home is invaded by muggers who kill his wife and rape his daughter, Bronson becomes a vigilante who roams the streets looking for muggers and other criminals to kill. He is so good as the stoical avenger that he has appeared in three sequels of this film.

Chaney / HARD TIMES, 1975, Columbia, d-Walter Hill.

Bronson is a Depression-era drifter who becomes a bare-knuckles street fighter in matches arranged by gambler James Coburn.

Leo Kessler / TEN TO MIDNIGHT, 1983, Cannon, d-J. Lee Thompson.

In this violent and nasty film, Bronson is a cop and the father of a girl threatened by a sexual deficient who kills girls who reject him. In the end, daddy makes certain that the deviant killer doesn't get off on some plea of insanity.

OTHER ROLES

As Charles Buchinski (Buchinsky)

1951: *Wascylewski* / YOU'RE IN THE NAVY NOW; *Angelo Korvac* / THE PEOPLE AGAINST O'HARA; *Jack* / THE MOB. **1952:** *Eddie* / THE MARRYING KIND; *Neff* / RED SKIES OF MONTANA; *Jocko* / MY SIX CONVICTS; *the Russian* / DIPLOMATIC COURIER; *Hank Tasling* / PAT AND MIKE; *Pittsburgh Philo* / BLOODHOUNDS OF BROADWAY. **1953:** *Eddie* / THE CLOWN; *Igor* / HOUSE OF WAX; *Edwards* / MISS

SADIE THOMPSON; *Ben Hastings* / CRIME WAVE; *Sixty Jubel* / TENNESSEE CHAMP.

As Charles Bronson

1954: *Pinto* / RIDING SHOTGUN; *Hondo* / APACHE; *Pittsburgh* / VERA CRUZ; *Captain Jack* / DRUM BEAT. **1955:** *Benny Kelly* / BIG HOUSE, U.S.A.; *Vince Gaspari* / TARGET ZERO. **1956:** *Reb Haislipp* / JUBAL. **1957:** *Blue Buffalo* / RUN OF THE ARROW. **1958:** *Luke Welsh* / SHOWDOWN AT BOOT HILL; *Alan Avery* / GANG WAR; *Steve Boland* / WHEN HELL BROKE LOOSE. **1959:** *John Danforth* / NEVER SO FEW. **1961:** *Strock* / MASTER OF THE WORLD; *Trooper Hanna* / A THUNDER OF DRUMS. **1962:** *Lt. Col. Lee Brandon* / X-15; *Lew Nyack* / KID GALAHAD; *Paul Moreno* / THIS RUGGED LAND. **1963:** *Matson* / FOUR FOR TEXAS. **1964:** *Linc Murdock* / GUNS OF DIABLO. **1965:** *Cos Erickson* / THE SANDPIPER; *Wolenski* / BATTLE OF THE BULGE. **1966:** *J. J. Nichols* / THIS PROPERTY IS CONDEMNED. **1967:** *Teclo* / GUNS FOR SAN SEBASTIAN. **1968:** *Franz Propp* / FAREWELL, FRIEND. **1969:** *Scott Wardman* / TWINKY. **1970:** *Col. Harry Dobbs* / RIDER ON THE RAIN; *Josh Corey* / YOU CAN'T WIN 'EM ALL; *Jeff* / VIOLENT CITY. **1971:** *Joe Martin* / COLD SWEAT; *the stranger* / SOMEONE BEHIND THE DOOR; *Link* / RED SUN. **1972:** *Arthur Bishop* / THE MECHANIC. **1973:** *Det. Lou Torrey* / THE STONE KILLER. **1974:** *Chino Valdez* / CHINO; *Vince Majestyk* / MR. MAJESTYK. **1975:** *Nick Colton* / BREAKOUT. **1976:** *John Deakin* / BREAKHEART PASS; *Raymond St. Ives* / ST. IVES; *Graham Dorsey* / FROM NOON TILL THREE. **1977:** *Wild Bill Hickok (James Otis)* / THE WHITE BUFFALO; *Grigori Borzov* / TELEFON. **1979:** *Charles Congers* / LOVE AND BULLETS. **1980:** *Giff Hoyt* / CABOBLANCO; *Jeb Maynard* / BORDERLINE. **1981:** *Albert Johnson* / DEATH HUNT. **1982:** *Paul Kersey* / DEATH WISH II. **1984:** *Holland* / THE EVIL THAT MEN DO. **1985:** *Paul Kersey* / DEATH WISH 3. **1986:** *Jack Murphy* / MURPHY'S LAW. **1987:** *Paul Kersey* / DEATH WISH 4: THE CRACKDOWN; *Jay Killion* / ASSASSINATION.

BRUCE, VIRGINIA

(Helen Virginia Briggs, 1910–1982)

Blonde Virginia Bruce with the big, blue eyes and the milky, white complexion was lured from UCLA to play innumerable bit parts in Paramount productions of the early 1930s. When she moved to MGM she got better roles and many leads but usually not in the studio's major pictures. She continued to make movie appearances in increasingly smaller roles until 1960. She was once married to silent idol John Gilbert, but at a time when she was a bigger name than he.

KEY ROLES

Jane Eyre / JANE EYRE, 1934, Monogram, d-Christy Cabanne.

Monogram was one of the poverty row studios of the time, therefore very little should be expected of this rendition of the Charlotte Brontë romantic novel, but Bruce gives it her best shot.

Jenny Lind / THE MIGHTY BARNUM, 1934, 20th Century-Fox, d-Walter Lang.

Bruce gives a lively, if not inspired, portrayal of the Swedish Nightingale.

Eleanor Spencer / LET 'EM HAVE IT, 1935, United Artists, d-Sam Wood.

Bruce is a Washington society girl whose chauffeur (Bruce Cabot) robs a bank and is tracked down by the FBI.

Audrey Dane / THE GREAT ZIEGFELD, 1936, MGM, d-Robert Z. Leonard.

Bruce is glorified in two spectacular production numbers: "You Never Looked So Beautiful Before" and the more memorable "A Pretty Girl Is Like a Melody." She was also one of a number of pretty girls who caught the eye (and a bit more) of the great impresario between and during his marriages to Anna Held and Billie Burke.

Lucy James / BORN TO DANCE, 1936, MGM, d-Roy Del Ruth.

Bruce is the temperamental revue star who is replaced by Eleanor Powell just before the show goes on. No one seemed to notice or care that Bruce was a singer and Powell a dancer.

Wanda Werner / WHEN LOVE IS YOUNG, 1937, Universal, d-Hal Mohr.

This modest, second-programme comedy is fairly typical of the movies made with Bruce in the lead. Here she plays a Broadway stage star who returns to her hometown in hopes of marrying her old boyfriend.

Steve / WIFE, DOCTOR AND NURSE, 1937, 20th Century-Fox, d-Walter Lang.

Bruce is Park Avenue doctor Warner Baxter's nurse, and she's in love with him. His wife (Loretta Young) insists Bruce be sent away. But when Bruce is gone, Baxter's practice suffers and he neglects his wife. The solution for Young is to call Bruce back and agree to share Baxter with her.

Joan Butterfield / THERE GOES MY HEART, 1938, United Artists, d-Norman Z. McLeod.

Bruce is an heiress who gets a job as a salesgirl, under an assumed name, in her family's department store. Tough and cynical reporter Fredric March threatens to expose her but falls for her instead.

Kitty Carroll / THE INVISIBLE WOMAN, 1941, Universal, d-A. Edward Sutherland.

Mad scientist John Barrymore turns a model (Bruce) invisible in this screwball comedy. She gets involved with a nutty group of crooks intent on stealing the scientist's machine for their own criminal uses.

OTHER ROLES

1929: *bit* / FUGITIVES; *bit* / BLUE SKIES; *nurse* / WOMAN TRAP; *bit* / ILLUSION; *bit* / WHY BRING THAT UP?; *bit* / THE LOVE PARADE. **1930:** *bit* / FOLLOW THRU; *bit* / WHOOPEE!; *bit* / RAFFLES; *bit* / SOCIAL LION; *Doris* / LILIES OF THE FIELD; *Elizabeth* / ONLY THE BRAVE; *Enid Corbett* / SLIGHTLY SCARLET; *guest* / PARAMOUNT ON PARADE; *Florence Welford* / YOUNG EAGLES; *Alma McGregor* / SAFETY IN NUMBERS. **1931:** *girl* / HELL DIVERS; *bit* / ARE YOU LISTENING?; *bit* / THE WET PARADE. **1932:** *Margaret Thornton* / THE MIRACLE MAN; *Ruth Dunning* / SKY BRIDE; *Joan Gibson* / WINNER TAKE ALL; *Anna* / DOWNSTAIRS; *Ann* / KONGO. **1934:** *Olwen* / DANGEROUS CORNER. **1935:** *Toni Bradley* / TIMES SQUARE LADY; *Madge* / SOCIETY DOCTOR; *Trenna* / SHADOW OF A DOUBT; *Gerta* / ESCAPADE; *Margaret* / HERE COMES THE BAND; *Mary Shannon* / THE MURDER MAN; *Anne Merrill* / METROPOLITAN. **1936:** *Zalia Graem* / THE GARDEN MURDER CASE. **1937:** *Gloria Hudson* / WOMEN OF GLAMOUR; *Patricia Sloan* / BETWEEN TWO WOMEN. **1938:** *Lynn Conway* / THE FIRST HUNDRED YEARS; *Lorraine de Crissac* / ARSENE LUPIN RETURNS; *Loretta Douglas* / BAD MAN OF BRIMSTONE; *Frances Blake* / YELLOW JACK; *Maris Kent* / WOMAN AGAINST WOMAN; *Sally Reardon* / THERE'S THAT WOMAN AGAIN. **1939:** *Maggie Adams* / LET FREEDOM RING; *Pat Abbott* / SOCIETY LAWYER; *Elizabeth Flagg* / STRONGER THAN DESIRE. **1940:** *Mary* / FLIGHT ANGELS; *Joan Reed* / THE MAN WHO TALKED TOO MUCH; *Phyllis Walden* / HIRED WIFE. **1941:** *Jane Scott* / ADVENTURE IN WASHINGTON. **1942:** *Susie O'Neill* / BUTCH MINDS THE BABY; *Joan Marshall* / PARDON MY SARONG; *Connie Mathers* / CAREFUL, SOFT SHOULDERS. **1944:** *Nicky Henderson* / BRAZIL; *Yvonne* / ACTION IN ARABIA. **1945:** *Roberta Baxter* / LOVE, HONOR AND GOODBYE. **1948:** *Jenny Courtland* / NIGHT HAS A THOUSAND EYES. **1949:** *Marge* / STATE DEPARTMENT—FILE 649. **1955:** *Laura Weeks* / RELUCTANT BRIDE. **1960:** *Mrs. Wagner* / STRANGERS WHEN WE MEET.

BRYNNER, YUL

(Taidje Kahn, 1915–1984)

Yul Brynner's real name is also given as Youl Bryner, but this is just one of many inconsistencies in the "facts" of his early life. Brynner fabricated several versions of his early life for various publications, telling of his days playing the balalaika with gypsy groups in nightclubs, his work as a trapeze artist, his Sorbonne philosophy studies, etc. What of this is true hardly matters as Brynner will be identified forever with his bald-headed role as the king of Siam in "The King and I" which he played on the stage, in the movie, and on TV. While this stands out as his most memorable role, Brynner was also entertaining in numerous historical pieces and westerns. His exotic personality and the sexiness of his bald head did not come across as well, though, in contemporary pictures.

KEY ROLES

The King of Siam / THE KING AND I, 1956, 20th Century-Fox, d-Walter Lang.

Brynner's celebrated portrayal of the king of Siam, who introduces western ways to his kingdom even though he himself isn't ready for them, won him a much deserved Academy Award. Brynner brings humor, dignity, warmth, and credibility to his role in this lavish Rodgers and Hammerstein musical.

Rameses / THE TEN COMMANDMENTS, 1956, Paramount, d-Cecil B. DeMille.

Playing the pharaoh allows Brynner to show off his bald head as he proves to be one of the best things in this picture stuffed with star performers.

Prince Bounine / ANASTASIA, 1956, 20th Century-Fox, d-Anatole Litvak.

Brynner makes a convincing and commanding White Russian general who coaches an amnesiac (Ingrid Bergman) to play the role of the Czar's daughter who supposedly survived the execution of her family at the time of the Revolution. He is pretty much sized up by Bergman when she says, "You never did anything for the sake of anybody but yourself. You enjoy playing with people, making fools of them. That's why you're doing it, as a joke—to prove that you are great and alive and the others are small and dead. Yes, and for the money."

Dmitri Karamazov / THE BROTHERS KARAMAZOV, 1958, MGM, d-Richard Brooks.

Brynner portrays one of the three legitimate sons of a Russian man (Lee J. Cobb) who is killed by one of his boys. Brynner fits in quite nicely in this emotional production of the Fyodor Dostoyevski novel, and his lovemaking with Maria Schell is wildly romantic and sensual.

Jean Lafitte / THE BUCCANEER, 1958, Paramount, d-Anthony Quinn.

This is the first film in which Brynner appears with hair. He should have left the wig at home. This remake of the story of the pirate who helps Andrew Jackson defend New Orleans after the War of 1812 is officially over, is a routine action film with more talk than action.

Chris Adams / THE MAGNIFICENT SEVEN, 1960, United Artists, d-John Sturges.

This classic western is an American version of the Japanese film THE SEVEN SAMURAI. Brynner is the leader of seven gunfighters who are hired by Mexican farmers to protect their village from marauding bandits. Brynner was at the peak of his film popularity in this exciting and violent film.

Taras Bulba / TARAS BULBA, 1962, United Artists, d-Lee Thompson.

Brynner portrays a Cossack leader who not only has to fight the accursed Poles but also has to kill his rebellious son (Tony Curtis) because he has betrayed his people by falling in love with a Polish girl.

Jules Gaspard D'Estaing / INVITATION TO A GUNFIGHTER, 1964, United Artists, d-Richard Wilson.

Pat Hingle hires gunfighter Brynner to keep the farmers in line, a task that Brynner does all too well as far as Hingle is concerned. Before sending someone to his maker in a gunfight, Brynner politely explains the proper pronunciation of his name.

Catlow / CATLOW, 1971, MGM, d-Sam Wanamaker.

Brynner is a likable outlaw just trying to recover his hidden gold without starting any trouble. But he is hunted by a friend and lawman (Richard Crenna) and by a killer (Leonard Nimoy).

The Gunslinger / WESTWORLD, 1973, MGM, d-Michael Crichton.

Brynner is a mechanical robot in a plush fantasy resort. As a western badman he goes berserk and relentlessly tracks down guests Richard Benjamin and James Brolin.

OTHER ROLES

1949: *Paul Vicola* / PORT OF NEW YORK. **1959:** *Major Surov* / THE JOURNEY; *Jason* / THE SOUND AND THE FURY; *Solomon* / SOLOMON AND SHEBA. **1960:** *Victor Fabian* / ONCE MORE WITH FEELING; *Nico March* / SURPRISE PACKAGE. **1962:** *Sharif* / ESCAPE FROM ZAHRAIN. **1963:** *Chief Black Eagle* / KINGS OF THE SUN. **1964:** *Sgt. Mike Takashima* / FLIGHT FROM ASHIYA. **1965:** *Captain Muller* / THE SABOTEUR, CODE NAME MORITURI. **1966:** *Asher Gonen* / CAST A GIANT SHADOW; *Chris Adams* / RETURN OF THE SEVEN; *Colonel Salem* / THE POPPY IS ALSO A FLOWER. **1967:** *Baron von Grunen* / TRIPLE CROSS; *Dan Slater / Kalmar* / THE DOUBLE MAN; *Sultan* / THE LONG DUEL. **1968:** *Pancho Villa* / VILLA RIDES. **1969:** *the chairman* / THE MADWOMAN OF CHAILLOT; *Peter Novak* / THE FILE OF THE GOLDEN GOOSE; *transvestite* / THE MAGIC CHRISTIAN. **1970:** *Viado* / THE BATTLE OF NERETVA; *Sabata* / ADIOS SABATA. **1971:** *Jonathan Kongre* / THE LIGHT AT THE EDGE OF THE WORLD; *Captain Stoloff* / ROMANCE OF A HORSETHIEF. **1972:** *the deaf man* / FUZZ; *Vlassov* / THE SERPENT. **1974:** *Carson* / THE ULTIMATE WARRIOR. **1976:** *gunslinger* / FUTUREWORLD; *American hit man* / DEATH RAGE.

BUJOLD, GENEVIEVE

(1942–)

Baby-faced, Canadian actress Genevieve Bujold began her film career in France, becoming an international star when she appeared opposite Richard Burton in ANNE OF THE THOUSAND DAYS (1969). She is able to portray women who are both tough and vulnerable at the same time, and her views on her craft include, "As soon as they say 'Action' I can smell in the first two seconds whether I am going to get on the wave or not. And if you don't get on, you have this disastrous feeling. I can tell you—it's like love without climax." She has also starred in a number of inferior French-Canadian films not much seen anywhere else.

KEY ROLES

Nadine Sallanches / LA GUERRE EST FINIE, (THE WAR IS OVER), 1966, France / Sweden, Sofracima / Europa Film, d-Alain Resnais.

Bujold is the romantic interest of Spanish revolutionary Yves Montand in this dreary story of idealism and betrayal.

Coquelicot / KING OF HEARTS, 1966, United Artists, d-Phillipe de Broca.

Bujold is an inhabitant of a war-torn town occupied only by lunatics who wish to make a Scottish soldier (Alan Bates) their king.

Anne Boleyn / ANNE OF THE THOUSAND DAYS, 1969, Great Britain, Universal, d-Charles Jarrott.

Bujold was nominated for an Academy Award for her brilliant portrayal of the woman who could not give Henry VIII the son he sought, and paid for this with her head. She did give him a daughter, though, who became England's greatest queen, Elizabeth I.

Cassandra / THE TROJAN WOMEN, 1971, Shaftel Production, d-Michael Cacoyannis.

Bujold is quite impressive in this all-star filming of Euripides's tragedy about the women of Troy bemoaning their fate after Troy has fallen to the Greeks.

Dr. Susan Wheeler / COMA, 1978, MGM, d-Michael Crichton.

Physician Bujold comes to suspect that patients are being deliberately put into comas at a Boston hospital so that their organs can be sold to the highest bidders.

Beryl Thibodeaux / TIGHTROPE, 1984, Warners, d-Richard Tuggle.

Bujold is a psychologist who works with New Orleans cop Clint Eastwood in trying to anticipate the moves of a murdering sex maniac.

OTHER ROLES

1963: *bit* / AMANITA PESTILENS. **1964:** *Genevieve* / THE ADOLESCENTS. **1967:** *Charlotte* / THE THIEF OF PARIS. **1968:** *Isabel* / ISABEL. **1970:** *Martha Hayes* / ACT OF THE HEART. **1973:** *Elizabeth* / KAMOURASKA. **1974:** *Denise* / EARTHQUAKE. **1976:** *Jane Barnet* / SWASHBUCKLER; *Elizabeth Courtland* / OBSESSION; *Maritza* / ALEX AND THE GYPSY. **1977:** *Jeanne Leroy* / ANOTHER MAN, ANOTHER CHANCE; *Saguenay* / JOURNEY. **1979:** *Annie Crook* / MURDER BY DECREE; *Nicole Thompson* / FINAL ASSIGNMENT. **1980:** *Marie-Charlotte* / THE INCORRIGIBLE; *Bernadette Lafleur* / THE LAST FLIGHT OF NOAH'S ARK. **1982:** *Clara* / MONSIGNOR. **1984:** *Dr. Nancy Love* / CHOOSE ME. **1985:** *Wanda* / TROUBLE IN MIND.

BURSTYN, ELLEN

(Edna Rae Gillooly, 1932–)

Ellen Burstyn, a graduate of Lee Strasberg's Actor Studio, has been described as an actress's actress. Her success has come because of her hard work, talent, dedication, and years of apprenticeship. Age 38 when she made her first major mark on the screen in THE LAST PICTURE SHOW (1971), this determined pro moves back and forth between Broadway and the movies, excelling in roles about women who have had to face tough times, but who will probably make it. Nominated for Academy Awards for THE LAST PICTURE SHOW; THE EXORCIST; SAME TIME, NEXT YEAR; RESURRECTION; and ALICE DOESN'T LIVE HERE ANYMORE, she won for the last of these.

KEY ROLES

Lois Farrow / THE LAST PICTURE SHOW, 1971, Columbia, d-Peter Bogdanovich.

Burstyn is the very sexy mother of Cybil Shepherd in this slice-of-life drama examining the inhabitants of a small Texas town during the 1950s. Her performance gained her the first of her five Academy Award nominations.

Sally / THE KING OF MARVIN GARDENS, 1972, Columbia, d-Bob Rafelson.

Burstyn superbly portrays an aging beauty in this story of disc-jockey Jack Nicholson's attempts to keep his boisterous gambler brother (Bruce Dern) out of trouble.

Chris MacNeil / THE EXORCIST, 1973, Warners, d-William Friedkin.

Burstyn has to deal with a daughter (Linda Blair) who is possessed by a demon (as if normal teenagers aren't enough of a problem). Burstyn's sensible performance earned her another Oscar nomination.

Alice Hyatt / ALICE DOESN'T LIVE HERE ANYMORE, 1975, Warners, d-Martin Scorsese.

Burstyn won the Best Actress Oscar for her portrayal of a recently widowed woman who hits the road with her teenage son in search of something not altogether clear. Coming in the midst of the feminist movement the picture may have won more praise than it deserved, but Burstyn's performance will stand the test of time.

Doris / SAME TIME, NEXT YEAR, 1978, Universal, d-Robert Mulligan.

Burstyn's excellent performance in this two-character play about a man and woman who meet once a year for twenty-five years resulted in her fourth Oscar nomination. She was recreating a role that she had originated on Broadway.

Edna McCauley / RESURRECTION, 1980, Universal, d-Daniel Petrie.

Burstyn's fifth Academy Award nomination was for her portrayal of a woman who, after surviving a car crash, finds herself able to cure others. Her performance is excellent, but the movie is difficult to take.

OTHER ROLES

As Ellen McRae

1964: *Franny* / GOODBYE CHARLIE. **1965:** *Dr. Pauline Thayer* / FOR THOSE WHO THINK YOUNG. **1969:** *Ellen McLeod* / PIT STOP; *Mona* / TROPIC OF CANCER.

As Ellen Burstyn

1970: *Beth* / ALEX IN WONDERLAND. **1974:** *Shirley* / HARRY AND TONTO. **1977:** *Sonia Langham* / PROVIDENCE. **1978:** *Brenda* / A DREAM OF PASSION. **1982:** *Olive Fredrickson* / SILENCE OF THE NORTH. **1984:** *Alex Hacker* / THE AMBASSADOR; *guest* / IN OUR HANDS. **1985:** *Kate MacKenzie* / TWICE IN A LIFETIME.

BURTON, RICHARD

(Richard Walter Jenkins, 1925–1984)

The twelfth of a Welsh coalminer's thirteen children, Richard Burton's greatest influence was Philip Burton, his high school English teacher, who in 1943 became the young man's legal guardian thus giving him his surname. Burton's majestic, rich speaking voice and his intelligent performances led to eight Oscar nominations, but he came away empty-handed every time. Some critics felt that in later years he chose film properties unwisely, more with an eye on money than on quality. For some he is more remembered for his two marriages to Elizabeth Taylor. Yet, despite the shortcomings in his personal life and the poor movies he appeared in, the number of his film triumphs is enough to be the envy of most actors.

KEY ROLES

Philip Ashley / MY COUSIN RACHEL, 1952, 20th Century-Fox, d-Henry Koster.

When Burton's foster-father dies in Italy shortly after marrying mysterious Olivia de Havilland, Burton suspects the worst about her. He received his first Academy Award nomination for this film.

Marcellus Gallio / THE ROBE, 1953, 20th Century-Fox, d-Henry Koster.

Burton plays the centurion who carries out the crucifixion of Christ, leading him to die with his love (Jean Simmons) as a believer. He received a Best Actor nomination for this role.

Edwin Booth / PRINCE OF PLAYERS, 1954, 20th Century-Fox, d-Philip Dunne.

Burton portrays the famous actor and brother of Abraham Lincoln's assassin.

Alexander / ALEXANDER THE GREAT, 1956, United Artists, d-Robert Rossen.

Burton gives an excellent performance as the Macedonian warrior who conquers the known world by the time he is 33 and dies because there is nothing more to conquer. He is much better than audiences had come to expect in epics.

Jimmy Porter / LOOK BACK IN ANGER, 1959, Great Britain, ASP / Woodfall, d-Tony Richardson.

Burton plays a bad-tempered young man with a grudge against the world in this film version of the realistic John Osborne play.

Marc Antony / CLEOPATRA, 1962, 20th Century-Fox, d-Joseph L. Mankiewicz.

This film is as dull as it is spectacular. The interest in what went on between Burton and Elizabeth Taylor off the screen exceeded that generated on the screen.

Paul Andros / THE V.I.P.S, 1963, MGM, d-Anthony Asquith.

The producers of this multi-story film were exploiting the interest in the Burton-Taylor romance, but did so in a very competent picture. Elizabeth Taylor is running away with Louis Jourdan to get away from Burton, but a delay in the departure of her plane gives Burton a chance to change her mind.

Thomas à Becket / BECKET, 1964, Paramount, d-Peter Glenville.

Burton received an Oscar nomination for his portrayal of the archbishop and chancellor of England who refuses to give his old friend Henry II his way in running the church.

Rev. T. Lawrence Shannon / THE NIGHT OF THE IGUANA, 1965, MGM, d-John Huston.

Three women in this film—itinerant artist Deborah Kerr, teenage nymphomaniac Sue Lyon, and middle-aged hotel owner Ava Gardner—sexually desire defrocked clergyman Burton, who is acting as a guide in Mexico. Elizabeth Taylor was on location with Burton to make certain he didn't confuse fact with fiction.

Alec Leaman / THE SPY WHO CAME IN FROM THE COLD, 1966, Paramount, d-Martin Ritt.

Burton is excellent as an embittered agent at the end of his career who is used one last time to serve the needs of espionage. Chalk up another Oscar nomination.

George / WHO'S AFRAID OF VIRGINIA WOOLF? 1966, Warners, d-Mike Nichols.

Burton probably should have won an Oscar for his brilliant portrayal of a college professor who spends an emotionally draining evening with his harpy of a wife (Elizabeth Taylor) and another academic couple (George Segal and Sandy Dennis) raking each other over the coals. One of his shots to Taylor and his guests is: "Now that we're through with Humiliate the Host, we're through with that one for this round anyway, and we don't want to play Hump the Hostess yet, not yet—so I know what we do: how about a little round of Get the Guests? How about that? How about a little game of Get the Guests?"

Harry Leeds / STAIRCASE, 1969, 20th Century-Fox, d-Stanley Donen.

Burton and Rex Harrison are effective as two aging homosexual hairdressers. It was a new experience for Burton and he proved effective.

Henry VIII / ANNE OF THE THOUSAND DAYS, 1970, Universal, d-Charles Jarrott.

As long as Anne Boleyn (Genevieve Bujold) could promise Burton that she could give him sons, she had the upper hand. When she couldn't deliver, though, he started looking for Jane Seymour. It was another Oscar nomination and loss for Burton.

Martin Dysert / EQUUS, 1977, United Artists, d-Sidney Lumet.

In his last Oscar-nominated role, Burton is a middle-aged psychiatrist who tries to find out why a 17-year-old boy has blinded six horses.

OTHER ROLES

1948: *Gareth* / THE LAST DAYS OF DOLWYN. **1949:** *Paddy* / NOW BARABBAS WAS A ROBBER. **1950:** *Ben Satterthwaite* / WATERFRONT; *Nick Chamerd* / THE WOMAN WITH NO NAME. **1951:** *Hammond* / GREEN GROW THE RUSHES. **1953:** *Captain McRoberts* / THE DESERT RATS. **1955:** *Dr. Safti* / THE RAINS OF RANCHIPUR. **1957:** *Biscuit* / SEA WIFE; *Captain Leigh* / BITTER VICTORY. **1959:** *Guy* / THE BRAMBLE BUSH. **1960:** *Zeb Kennedy* / ICE PALACE. **1962:** *RAF Pilot* / THE LONGEST DAY. **1964:** *Hamlet* / HAMLET. **1965:** *Dr. Edward Hewitt* / THE SANDPIPER; *cameo* / WHAT'S NEW, PUSSYCAT? **1967:** *Petruchio* / THE TAMING OF THE SHREW; *Faustus* / DR. FAUSTUS; *Brown* / THE COMEDIANS; *cameo* / CASINO ROYALE. **1968:** *Chris Flanders* / BOOM; *John Smith* / WHERE EAGLES DARE; *McPhisto* / CANDY. **1971:** *Capt. Alec Foster* / RAID ON ROMMEL; *Vic Dakin* / VILLAIN; *first voice* / UNDER MILK WOOD. **1972:** *Leon Trotsky* / THE ASSASSINATION OF TROTSKY; *Hammersmith* / HAMMERSMITH IS OUT; *Bluebeard* / *Baron Von Sepper* / BLUEBEARD. **1973:** *Sutjeska* / TITO. **1974:** *Colonel Kappler* / MASSACRE IN ROME; *Breck Stancill* / THE KLANSMAN; *Cesar Braggi* / THE VOYAGE. **1977:** *Father Lamont* / EXORCIST II: THE HERETIC; *John Morlar* / THE MEDUSA TOUCH. **1978:** *Allen Faulkner* / THE WILD GEESE. **1979:** *Sergeant Steiner* / BREAKTHROUGH; *Father Goddard* / ABSOLUTION. **1980:** *King Mark* / TRISTAN AND ISOLDE. **1983:** *Richard Wagner* / WAGNER. **1984:** *O'Brien* / 1984.

CAGNEY, JAMES

(James F. Cagney, Jr., 1899–1986)

This short, jaunty, aggressive redhead was most at home playing cocksure, trigger-tempered, pugnacious characters. Winner of the American Film Institute's Life Achievement Award in 1974, he won an Oscar for his portrayal of George M. Cohan in YANKEE DOODLE DANDY in 1942 and received nominations for his work in ANGELS WITH DIRTY FACES and LOVE ME OR LEAVE ME. He retired from films in 1961, but came back in 1981 to appear as the police chief in RAGTIME. On the screen he was confident with the ladies and just as likely to slug one as any man who got in his way. He will always be remembered for his swaggering bad guys, moving on the balls of their feet, fists at the ready. He began his career as a hoofer in Broadway shows and was always willing to demonstrate that he really could dance. He had charisma and vitality and was one of the best natural screen actors around. Noel Coward observed, "James Cagney rolled through the film like a very belligerent barrel." As for himself, Cagney advised: "Walk in, plant yourself, look the other fellow in the eye, and tell the truth."

KEY ROLES

Tom Powers / THE PUBLIC ENEMY, 1931, Warners, d-William Wellman.

Cagney plays a cop's son who is bumped off and delivered to his mother's home wrapped like a mummy when his rum-running ways annoy the big shots of crime. He is remembered just as much for the fact that he pushes a grapefruit into the complaining puss of Mae Clark.

Chester Kent / FOOTLIGHT PARADE, 1933, Warners, d-Lloyd Bacon and Busby Berkeley.

In this classic putting-on-a-show movie, Cagney produces live prologues to be shown in movie theaters but finds the going pretty rough. He dances in the "Shanghai Lil" number about a sailor looking for a girl he finally finds in a waterfront dive; he tap dances with her and returns to his ship but not before hundreds of others join him in a variety of Berkeley dance formations.

Dan Quigley / LADY KILLER, 1933, Warners, d-Roy Del Ruth.

Cagney is a movie usher who turns to crime. When things get too hot, he flees to Hollywood where he becomes a movie star, though his former associates pressure him to join a plot to burgle movie stars' homes.

Timmy O'Toole / DEVIL DOGS OF THE AIR, 1935, Warners, d-Lloyd Bacon.

Cagney is a cocky stunt flyer who joins the U.S. Marine Flying Corps and refuses to do things the marine way. It's not much of a story but there is some good aerial footage.

James "Brick" Davis / G-MEN, 1935, Warners, d-William Keighley.

In this film Cagney is on the side of the law as an attorney who becomes a government man when a close friend is killed. He learns that another old friend is the responsible party.

Bottom / A MIDSUMMER NIGHT'S DREAM, 1935, Warners, d-Max Reinhardt and William Dieterle.

The jury is still out as to whether Cagney's performance as the weaver who ends up with the head of an ass was a highlight of his career or a serious casting error. The picture itself has undergone revisionist evaluations several times. As in all cases, Cagney did not shortchange. He made the most of the part he was given.

Robert Law / BOY MEETS GIRL, 1938, Warners, d-Lloyd Bacon.

Cagney and Pat O'Brien play two crazy Hollywood screenwriters who make a star of Marie Wilson's unborn child. Along the way, Cagney demonstrates his great flair for comedy.

Rocky Sullivan / ANGELS WITH DIRTY FACES, 1938, Warners, d-Michael Curtiz.

Cagney plays a convicted criminal who is asked by a priest (Pat O'Brien) to go to the hot seat as a coward in order to kill the hero-worship of some slum kids. Cagney says no. But, in the end he has to be dragged to the electric chair screaming and crying. Whether this is in response to O'Brien's request or out of fear is left for the viewer to decide. One of his best lines in the film is: "You know, Jerry, I think in order to be afraid, you got to have a heart. I don't think I got one. I had that cut out of me a long time ago."

Jim Kincaid / THE OKLAHOMA KID, 1939, Warners, d-Lloyd Bacon.

This movie is worth seeing if only because it's the only western in which Cagney and Humphrey Bogart appear together. In the title role, Cagney even sings when he's not hunting down the outlaw leader who framed his father.

Frank Ross / EACH DAWN I DIE, 1939, Warners, d-William Keighley.

Cagney is a reporter who is sent to prison on a phony manslaughter charge when his investigation of crooked politicians gets too hot. In jail he is almost turned into a hardened con by the brutal conditions but, with the help of habitual criminal George Raft, he's able to prove his innocence.

Eddie Bartlett / THE ROARING TWENTIES, 1939, Warners, d-Raoul Walsh.

When grieving Gladys George is asked about Cagney's bullet-riddled body, she says, "He used to be a big shot." Before this inglorious end, Cagney was an ex-World War I doughboy who turned to bootlegging and clashed with an old army buddy and rival racketeer (Humphrey Bogart).

Biff Grimes / THE STRAWBERRY BLONDE, 1941, Warners, d-Raoul Walsh.

Cagney is a dentist who loves strawberry blonde Rita Hayworth, loses her to contractor Jack Carson, and marries Hayworth's best friend (Olivia De Havilland) on the rebound. Bitter because he once served an unjust prison term, he comes to learn that he married the right girl after all.

George M. Cohan / YANKEE DOODLE DANDY, 1942, Warners, d-Michael Curtiz.

There are other performers in this schmaltzy, flag-waving movie but with Cagney's performance one may not notice them. George M. Cohan was a celebrated actor, dancer, singer, dramatist, and composer. But as long as this film is around he will be remembered as looking and dancing like Jimmy Cagney. His famous curtain speech was, "My mother thanks you. My father thanks you. My sister thanks you. And I thank you."

Nick Condon / BLOOD ON THE SUN, 1945, United Artists, d-Frank Lloyd.

Cagney is the editor of an American newspaper in Japan prior to World War II. One of his reporters is killed because he has gotten hold of the secret Tanaka Plan for world domination and Cagney tries to get it out of the country as the Japanese Secret Police try to get him.

Bob Sharkey / 13 RUE MADELEINE, 1946, 20th Century-Fox, d-Henry Hathaway.

The title refers to the Gestapo headquarters where OSS agent Cagney is tortured by Richard Conte. Cagney had been captured while on a mission to locate a Nazi rocket site in France during World War II.

Cody Jarrett / WHITE HEAT, 1949, Warners, d-Raoul Walsh.

In one of his best roles, Cagney is a psychotic killer with a mother fixation. When Ma Cody, marvelously portrayed by Margaret Wycherly, is killed by a former gang member Cagney goes completely berserk in prison and escapes to avenge his ma, not knowing that he has taken an undercover agent with him. Trapped at the top of a burning oil tank, the raving Cagney yells, "Made it, Ma. Top of the world!" just before being blown up.

Lew Marsh / COME FILL THE CUP, 1951, Warners, d-Gordon Douglas.

Newspaper editor Cagney blows his career and loses his girl because of his alcoholism. After drying out he pieces his life together again, rehabilitating others along the way. Raymond Massey, his publisher, gives him the assignment of reforming a drunken nephew who just happens to be married to Cagney's ex-girl. In the film Cagney gives an excellent account of why people drink: "A lush can always find a reason, if he's thirsty. Listen. If he's happy, he takes a couple of shots to celebrate his happiness. Sad, he needs 'em to drown his sorrow. Low, to pick him up. Excited, to calm him down. Sick, for his health. And healthy, it can't hurt him. So you see, Al, a lush can't lose."

Martin "The Gimp" Snyder / LOVE ME OR LEAVE ME, 1955, MGM, d-Charles Vidor.

Cagney is the cruel, club-footed Chicago racketeer who discovers, manages, and marries 1920s singer Ruth Etting. He drives her to drink and shoots her accompanist in a jealous rage.

The Captain / MISTER ROBERTS, 1955, Warners, d-John Ford.

Cagney is the tyrannical skipper of a cargo ship in the Pacific Ocean during World War II. He has a constant battle with his well-liked executive officer (Henry Fonda) over Cagney's mistreatment of the men and Fonda's desire to transfer to a ship that's really in the war.

Lon Chaney / MAN OF A THOUSAND FACES, 1957, Universal, d-Joseph Pevney.

Cagney gives an excellent portrayal of the great silent film character actor. Too bad the plot isn't as good as Cagney's performance.

C. R. MacNamara / ONE, TWO, THREE, 1961, United Artists, d-Billy Wilder.

Cagney is the head of Coca-Cola in Berlin, looking for a little hanky-panky with his well-built, German secretary (Lilo Pulver). While Cagney plays host to the big boss's daughter, she meets and marries a Communist and becomes pregnant. When her daddy announces his arrival, Cagney must convert the husband (Horst Buchholz) into a good capitalist, posthaste.

Rheinlander Waldo / RAGTIME, 1981, Paramount, d-Milos Forman.

Cagney is the shrewd New York police chief who, in 1906, is faced with removing a group of black urban guerrillas from the J. P. Morgan Library.

OTHER ROLES

1930: *Harry Delano* / SINNER'S HOLIDAY; *Steve Mileway* / DOORWAY TO HELL. **1931:** *Ed* / OTHER MEN'S WOMEN; *Schofield* / THE MILLIONAIRE; *Jack* / SMART MONEY; *Bert Harris* / BLONDE CRAZY. **1932:** *Matt Nolan* / TAXI; *Joe Greer* / THE CROWD ROARS; *Jim Kane* / WINNER TAKE ALL. **1933:** *Lefty Merrill* / HARD TO HANDLE; *Danny Kean* / PICTURE SNATCHER; *Patsy Gargan* / THE MAYOR OF HELL. **1934:** *Jimmy Corrigan* / JIMMY THE GENT; *Flicker Hayes* / HE WAS HER MAN; *Chesty O'Connor* / HERE COMES THE NAVY; *Eddie Kennedy* / THE ST. LOUIS KID. **1935:** *Danny O'Hara* / THE IRISH IN US; *Bat Morgan* / FRISCO KID; *Dizzy Davis* / CEILING ZERO. **1936:** *Johnny Cave* / GREAT GUY. **1937:** *Terry Rooney* / SOMETHING TO SING ABOUT. **1940:** *Pvt. Jerry Plunkett* / THE FIGHTING 69TH; *Nick Butler* / TORRID ZONE. **1941:** *Danny Kenny* / CITY FOR CONQUEST; *Steve Collins* / THE BRIDE CAME C.O.D. **1942:** *Brian MacLean* / CAPTAINS OF THE CLOUDS. **1943:** *Tom Richards* / JOHNNY COME LATELY. **1948:** *Joe* / THE TIME OF YOUR LIFE. **1950:** *Elwin Bixby* / THE WEST POINT STORY; *Ralph Cotter* / KISS TOMORROW GOODBYE. **1951:** *cameo* / STARLIFT. **1952:** *Captain Flagg* / WHAT PRICE GLORY? **1953:** *Hank Martin* / A LION IS IN THE STREETS. **1955:** *Matt Dow* / RUN FOR COVER; *George M. Cohan* / THE SEVEN LITTLE FOYS. **1956:** *Jeremy Rodock* / TRIBUTE TO A BAD MAN; *Steve Bradford* / THESE WILDER YEARS. **1958:** *Jake MacIllaney* / NEVER STEAL ANYTHING SMALL. **1959:** *Sean Lenihan* / SHAKE HANDS WITH THE DEVIL. **1960:** *Adm. William F. "Bull" Halsey* / THE GALLANT HOURS.

CAINE, MICHAEL

(Maurice Micklewhite, 1933–)

Michael Caine, who took his surname from *The Caine Mutiny*, has portrayed a number of antiheroes in a succession of entertaining films. This tall, blond, not especially handsome, working-class star was nominated for Academy Awards for ALFIE, SLEUTH, and EDUCATING RITA, and won for HANNAH AND HER SISTERS. Caine served in Korea with the Royal Fusiliers in the early 1950s. He played small roles in provincial theaters and frequently appeared on television between 1954 and 1956, and in 1956 began appearing in bit roles in movies. He first won critical notice for ZULU in 1964, followed by his successful role in THE IPCRESS FILE and an Academy Award nomination for ALFIE in 1966. Speaking of this pivotal role in his career, he has said: "You know the thing that surprises people about me is that they expect to meet Alfie—and when they talk to me, they find a gardener."

KEY ROLES

Lt. Gronville Bromhead / ZULU, 1964, Great Britain, Paramount / Diamond, d-Cy Endfield.

Surprisingly, Caine with his working-class accent made his first major impression in the movies portraying an upper-class British officer at the defense of Rorkesdrift in 1879.

Harry Palmer / THE IPCRESS FILE, 1965, Great Britain, Rank, d-Sidney J. Furie.

Intelligence agent Caine traces a missing scientist and discovers that one of his superiors is a spy. He's an unsophisticated James Bond.

Alfie Elkins / ALFIE, 1966, Great Britain, Paramount, d-Lewis Gilbert.

In his Academy Award-nominated portrayal of a cockney Don Juan, Caine has success with women but is unable or unwilling to develop relationships with them.

Jack Carter / GET CARTER, 1971, Great Britain, MGM, d-Mike Hodges.

Caine is a small-time hood who searches out those responsible for his brother's death. He takes revenge but is shot by a sniper.

Milo Tindle / SLEUTH, 1972, Great Britain, Palomar, d-Joseph L. Mankiewicz.

In this two-person adaptation of the successful stage play, Caine and Laurence Olivier spar very nicely before the comical aspects take on a serious and deadly turn. Both Caine and Olivier were nominated for Oscars.

Peachy Carnehan / THE MAN WHO WOULD BE KING, 1976, Columbia, d-John Huston.

Caine and Sean Connery are given the royal treatment in a remote region of India until they become too greedy and the natives decide to eliminate the monarchy.

Sidney Cochran / CALIFORNIA SUITE, 1978, Columbia, d-Herbert Ross.

In this story about four sets of guests at the Beverly Hills Hotel, Caine is a witty bisexual married to an actress (Maggie Smith) who is in town because she is up for an Academy Award.

Sidney Bruhl / DEATHTRAP, 1982, Warners, d-Sidney Lumet.

Playwrights Christopher Reeve and Caine devise a plot to scare Caine's wife (Dyan Cannon) to death. But Reeve hasn't seen the final act. Once again, Caine is bisexual.

Dr. Frank Bryant / EDUCATING RITA, 1983, Great Britain, Rank, d-Lewis Gilbert.

In this film Caine tutors a hairdresser (Julie Walters) who has enrolled in an Open University course to satisfy her desire to improve herself by studying English literature. Caine is first-rate as the alcoholic poet who has given up on himself. It won him another Oscar nomination.

Elliott / HANNAH AND HER SISTERS, 1986, Orion, d-Woody Allen.

Caine won an Oscar for his portrayal of a husband who has an affair with his wife's sister (Barbara Hershey) in this marvelous study of a strange family held together by the strength of one woman (Mia Farrow).

OTHER ROLES

1956: *Private Lockyer* / A HILL IN KOREA. **1957:** *Gilrony* / HOW TO MURDER A RICH UNCLE. **1958:** *bit* / THE KEY; *Gestapo agent* / THE TWO-HEADED SPY; *bit* / CARVE HER NAME WITH PRIDE; *Johnny Brent* / BLIND SPOT. **1959:** *bit* / PASSPORT TO SHAME; *bit* / DANGER WITHIN. **1960:** *Weber* / FOXHOLE IN CAIRO; *sailor* / THE BULLDOG BREED. **1961:** *bit* / THE DAY THE EARTH CAUGHT FIRE. **1962:** *Paddy Mooney* / SOLO FOR SPARROW; *bit* / THE WRONG ARM OF THE LAW. **1966:** *Michael Finsbury* / THE WRONG BOX; *Harry Dean* / GAMBIT; *Harry Palmer* / FUNERAL IN BERLIN; *handsome stranger* / WOMAN TIMES SEVEN. **1967:** *Henry Warren* / HURRY SUNDOWN; *Harry Palmer* / BILLION DOLLAR BRAIN. **1968:** *Henry Clarke* / DEADFALL; *Nicholas Urfe* / THE MAGUS; *Captain Douglas* / PLAY DIRTY. **1969:** *Charlie Croker* / THE ITALIAN JOB; *Squadron Leader Canfield* / THE BATTLE OF BRITAIN; *Pvt. Tosh Hearne* / TOO LATE THE HERO. **1970:** *Captain* / THE LAST VALLEY. **1971:** *Robert Blakely* / X, Y AND ZEE. **1972:** *Alan Breck* / KIDNAPPED; *Mickey King* / PULP. **1973:** *Maj. John Tarrant* / THE BLACK WINDMILL. **1974:** *Deray* / THE MARSEILLES CONTRACT. **1975:** *Jim Keogh* / THE WILBY CONSPIRACY; *Leslie Tucker* / PEEPER. **1976:** *Adam Worth* / HARRY AND WALTER GO TO NEW YORK; *Col. Kurt Steiner* / THE EAGLE HAS LANDED. **1977:** *Lt. Col. Joe Vandeleur* / A BRIDGE TOO FAR; *Doc Fletcher* / SILVER BEARS. **1978:** *Brad Crane* / THE SWARM; *Dr. David Lenderby* / ASHANTI. **1979:** *Mike Turner* / BEYOND THE POSEIDON ADVENTURE; **1980:** *Dr. Robert Elliott* / DRESSED TO KILL; *Maynard* / THE ISLAND. **1981:** *Jon Lansdale* / THE HAND; *John Colby* / VICTORY. **1983:** *Charles Fortnum* / BEYOND THE LIMIT. **1984:** *Matthew Hollis* / BLAME IT ON RIO; *Sir Philip Kimberly* / *Sergi Kuzminsky* / THE JIGSAW MAN. **1985:** *Noel Holcroft* / THE HOLCROFT COVENANT. **1986:** *Elliott James* / SWEET LIBERTY; *Baxter* / WATER; *Mortwell* / MONA LISA; *Lord Bulbeck* / HALF MOON STREET. **1987:** *Hoagie* / JAWS, THE REVENGE; *Frank Jones* / THE WHISTLE BLOWER; *John Preston* / THE FOURTH PROTOCOL; *Sean Stein* / SURRENDER.

CANTOR, EDDIE

(Edward I. Iskowitz, 1892–1964)

Old "Banjo Eyes" had a pretty fair run at the movies during the early 1930s, recreating some of his Broadway successes. He usually played a put-upon young man who somehow got the better of the bullies, but his film career faded when the public grew tired of straight film versions of stage productions. Cantor was the first big radio star and followed this long association with a successful TV run. In addition to his feature-length films, Cantor appeared in shorts such as THE SPEED HOUND (1927), THAT PARTY IN PERSON (1929), INSURANCE (1930), HOLLYWOOD CAVALCADE, and SCREEN SNAPSHOTS NO. 11 (1934).

KEY ROLES

Kid Boots / KID BOOTS, 1926, Silent, Paramount, d-Frank Tuttle.

Cantor scored in his first film role by recreating his stage character, a tailor's helper who becomes a caddy-master at a golf course. He helps his friend, a professional golfer, get a divorce from an heiress.

Henry Williams / WHOOPEE! 1930, United Artists, d-Thornton Freeland.

Cantor is a hypochondriac living on a western dude ranch. He helps Eleanor Hunt marry her true love (Paul Gregory). He also sings one of his all-time big hits, the title number.

Eddie Williams / THE KID FROM SPAIN, 1932, United Artists, d-Leo McCarey.

Simpleton Cantor is mistaken for a famous bullfighter from Spain. He throws a lot of suggestive bull at the likes of Lyda Roberti and Ruth Hall, while fending off villain Noah Beery.

Eddie / ROMAN SCANDALS, 1933, United Artists, d-Frank Tuttle.

In his best film appearance, Cantor dreams that he is back in ancient Rome, and has some sexy dance numbers with the Goldwyn Girls, including Lucille Ball and Betty Grable.

Himself / Joe Sampson / THANK YOUR LUCKY STARS, 1943, Warners, d-David Butler.

Cantor is one of the best things in this loud, all-star, wartime musical, appearing as himself and his double working together to put on a patriotic show.

Eddie Martin / SHOW BUSINESS, 1944, RKO, d-Edwin L. Marin.

Together with Joan Davis, George Murphy, and Constance Moore, Cantor demonstrates how life in old-time vaudeville really was.

OTHER ROLES

1927: *Eddie, the mail carrier* / SPECIAL DELIVERY. **1929:** *himself in revue scenes* / GLORIFYING THE AMERICAN GIRL. **1931:** *Eddie Simpson* / PALMY DAYS. **1934:** *Eddie Wilson, Jr.* / KID MILLIONS. **1935:** *Eddie Pink* / STRIKE ME PINK. **1937:** *Ali Baba* / ALI BABA GOES TO TOWN. **1940:** *Gilbert J. Thompson* / FORTY LITTLE MOTHERS. **1944:** *guest* / HOLLYWOOD CANTEEN. **1948:** *guest* / RHAPSODY IN BLUE. **1952:** *guest* / THE STORY OF WILL ROGERS. **1953:** *bit* / THE EDDIE CANTOR STORY.

CARON, LESLIE

(1931–)

The word cute could have been coined to describe Leslie Caron, although as she aged, her gamine-like appeal matured into a subtle beauty. Her most successful film roles were as innocent girls who became wise to the ways of love. When she began her movie career she was valued more for her ballet training than her looks or acting ability. Since her early roles, her work has been patchy, including films with limited distribution and modest budgets such as PURPLE NIGHT (1971), L'HOMME QUI AIMENT CES FEMMES (1977), TOUS VEDETTES (1980), CHANEL SOLITAIRE (1981), IMPERATIVE (1982), and REEL HORROR (1985). She observed, probably accurately, "I don't think Hollywood is an appropriate place for an actress of forty."

KEY ROLES

Lise Bouvier / AN AMERICAN IN PARIS, 1951, MGM, d-Vincente Minnelli.

In this delightful musical, which won the year's Best Picture Academy Award, Caron is a young French girl who falls in love with an American artist (Gene Kelly) who is working in Paris. Their dancing together, particularly in the lengthy title ballet, is spectacular.

Lili Dauvier / LILI, 1953, MGM, d-Charles Walters.

Caron was nominated for an Academy Award for her work as a naive orphan who joins a small carnival, falls in love with a married magician, and ultimately finds her true love—the mean puppeteer with whose puppets she works so believably.

Gigi / GIGI, 1958, MGM, d-Vincente Minnelli.

In her most delightful role, Caron is a young girl in Paris in the 1890s, trained by her aunt to follow the family tradition of becoming a cocotte. Instead she so charms wealthy Louis Jourdan that he offers marriage instead of just an arrangement. Caron is convincing both as a gawky adolescent and as a beautiful young woman and the musical won eleven Oscars, including Best Picture.

Fanny / FANNY, 1960, Warners, d-Joshua Logan.

The fact that this film is an overly ambitious attempt to tell in one movie what was told in the 1930s in three, takes nothing away from the fine performances by Caron, Charles Boyer, and Maurice Chevalier. However, this story about a girl from the Marseilles waterfront who finds herself pregnant and unmarried does not hold together well.

Jane Fosset / THE L-SHAPED ROOM, 1962, Great Britain, British Lion, d-Bryan Forbes.

Caron discovers she is pregnant after having spent a weekend with an unemployed actor. She moves into a squalid l-shaped room in a London boardinghouse and arranges to have an abortion. The rest of the movie is about her affair with another tenant and her unsuccessful attempt to kill her baby. She received an Oscar nomination for her performance.

Catherine Freneau / FATHER GOOSE, 1964, Universal, d-Ralph Nelson.

Schoolteacher Caron and six children are stranded on a small South Seas island during World War II with ne'er-do-well Cary Grant. Grant is less than thrilled by the association and makes it clear that he wants nothing to do with Caron and her charges: "Let me tell you something. I am not a father figure. I am not an uncle figure or a brother figure or a cousin figure. In fact, the only figure I intend being is a total stranger figure." But he mellows.

OTHER ROLES

1951: *Madeline Minot* / THE MAN WITH A CLOAK. **1952:** *Angela* / GLORY ALLEY. **1953:** *Mademoiselle* / THE STORY OF THREE LOVES. **1954:** *Ella* / THE GLASS SLIPPER. **1955:** *Julie* / DADDY LONG LEGS. **1956:** *Gaby* / GABY. **1958:** *Jennifer Dubedat* / DOCTOR'S DILEMMA. **1959:** *Ann Garantier* / THE MAN WHO UNDERSTOOD WOMEN. **1960:** *Mardou Fox* / THE SUBTERRANEANS; *Mlle. de Vaudey* / AUSTERLITZ. **1963:** *Claire Jordan* / GUNS OF DARKNESS; *Annie* / THREE FABLES OF LOVE. **1965:** *Lauren Boullard* / A VERY SPECIAL FAVOR. **1966:** *Michelle O'Brien* / PROMISE HER ANYTHING; *Françoise Labe* / IS PARIS BURNING? **1968:** *Paola* / HEAD OF THE FAMILY. **1969:** *Sister Mary* / MADRON. **1972:** *Katherine* / CHANDLER. **1976:** *Celeste* / SERAIL. **1977:** *Vera* / THE MAN WHO LOVED WOMEN; *Nazimova* / VALENTINO; *herself* / *narrator* / JAMES DEAN—THE FIRST AMERICAN TEENAGER. **1979:** *Dr. Lee* / GOLDENGIRL. **1980:** *Penelope* / CONTRACT. **1984:** *Henia Liebskind* / DANGEROUS MOVES.

CARROLL, MADELEINE

(Marie Madeleine Bernadette O'Carroll, 1906–1987)

Madeleine Carroll's glamorous, cool, fragile-looking beauty was so spectacular that one can enjoy a movie in which she appears just by looking at her. From her point of view, this fact was not quite a compliment, as she noted, "Producers don't look at you as a man looks at a woman; they look at you as if they were judging a horse." But there was a great deal more to this British, blonde actress than her exquisite looks. Her studied lack of animation added class to many a movie, whether it be a romance, comedy, or drama. Carroll became an American citizen in 1943 and after her film career worked for UNESCO and made documentary films for the United Nations. She was awarded the French Legion of Honor and the United States Medal of Freedom.

KEY ROLES

Diana Cheswick / THE GUNS OF LOOS, 1928, Silent, Great Britain, Stoll / New Era, d-Sinclair Hill.

In one of the better British silents, Carroll weds the blind war hero who comes home to settle a strike in his family's industrial empire.

Laura Simmons / YOUNG WOODLEY, 1930, Great Britain, Regal / Wardour, d-Thomas Bentley.

Carroll is the young wife of an elderly, pompous schoolmaster. One of her husband's teenage students falls in love with her and she is very understanding of his feelings.

Martha Cnockhaert / I WAS A SPY, 1933, Great Britain, Gaumont-British, d-Victor Saville.

In this film based on a true story, Carroll portrays the Belgian nurse who spies for the Allies in World War I. Working with a secret service agent she survives blowing up an arms dump and prevents a German gas attack.

Pamela / THE 39 STEPS, 1935, Great Britain, Gaumont-British, d-Alfred Hitchcock.

Carroll is the girl who finds herself handcuffed to Robert Donat, who is fleeing both the police and spies. She has no choice but to go along with him until she discovers that he's telling the truth.

Judy Perrie / THE GENERAL DIED AT DAWN, 1936, Paramount, d-Lewis Milestone.

Carroll is a beautiful spy with whom mercenary Gary Cooper falls in love while thwarting an evil Chinese warlord (Akim Tamiroff).

Mimi Caraway / ON THE AVENUE, 1937, 20th Century-Fox, d-Roy Del Ruth.

Carroll is an heiress who is more than a little annoyed at being satirized in a revue. But she falls in love with the star, Dick Powell.

Princess Flavia / THE PRISONER OF ZENDA, 1937, Selznick, d-John Cromwell.

Carroll notices a change for the better in her intended husband (Ronald Colman) when he poses as the king-to-be of Ruritania. She is so beautiful that it is easy to believe Colman's concern when he tells her, "If I see your eyes I might forget to be a king."

Karen Bentley / MY FAVORITE BLONDE, 1942, Paramount, d-Sidney Lanfield.

Carroll is a spy who enlists the reluctant help of Bob Hope, a burlesque clown who gets second billing to a penguin. They have plenty of trouble with George Zucco and Gale Sondergaard.

Mrs. Erlynne / THE FAN, 1949, 20th Century-Fox, d-Otto Preminger.

In this questionable Hollywood version of Oscar Wilde's "Lady Windermere's Fan," Carroll is an attractive widow who inveigles her way into London society through her contact with Lord Windermere, whose wife is having an affair with Lord Darlington, in whose apartment she leaves her fan. Carroll claims the fan as her own and must leave London in disgrace, but she does so willingly because Lady Windermere is her long-lost daughter.

OTHER ROLES

1928: *Lady Madeleine Boycott* / THE FIRST BORN. **1929:** *Rhoda Pearson* / WHAT MONEY CAN BUY; *Grace Malherb* / THE AMERICAN PRISONER; *Joan Easton* / THE CROOKED BILLET. **1930:** *Monica* / ATLANTIC; *Dora* / ESCAPE; *Rosa Hartmann* / THE W PLAN; *Lady Molly Adair* / THE KISSING CUP RACE. **1931:** *Lucille de Choisigne* / MADAME GUILLOTINE; *Lady Margaret Rochester* / THE WRITTEN LAW. **1932:** *Gwenda Farrell* / FASCINATION. **1933:** *Lady Teazle* / SCHOOL FOR SCANDAL; *Anne* / SLEEPING CAR. **1934:** *Mrs. Warburton* / *Mary Warburton* / THE WORLD MOVES ON. **1935:** *Queen Caroline Struensee* / LOVES OF A DICTATOR. **1936:** *Hope Ames* / THE CASE AGAINST MRS. AMES; *Elsa Carrington* / SECRET AGENT; *Lady Elizabeth Stacy* / LLOYDS OF LONDON; *guest* / THE STORY OF PAPWORTH. **1938:** *Linda Gray* / IT'S ALL YOURS; *Norma* / BLOCKADE. **1939:** *Gail Allen* / HONEYMOON IN BALI; *Christopher West* / CAFE SOCIETY. **1940:** *Livia Vaynol* / MY SON, MY SON; *Linda Stuart* / SAFARI; *April Logan* / NORTHWEST MOUNTED POLICE. **1941:** *Charlotte Dunterry* / VIRGINIA; *Leonora Perrycoate* / ONE NIGHT IN LISBON; *Carol Delbridge* / BAHAMA PASSAGE. **1946:** *Magda* / WHITE CRADLE INN. **1948:** *Paula Doane* / DON'T TRUST YOUR HUSBAND.

CARROLL, NANCY

(Ann La Hiff, 1905–1965)

Petite, redheaded Nancy Carroll was one of the first talking picture stars. She started as a dancer and made her stage mark opposite Buddy Rogers in Broadway's "Abie's Irish Rose" in 1928. This vivacious, bubbly star with the cupid-bow mouth had a great following in the early 1930s, but poor movie assignments and changing tastes, combined with her spectacular tantrums on the set, eventually finished her career before the end of the decade. She was nominated for an Oscar for her work in THE DEVIL'S HOLIDAY.

KEY ROLES

Rosemary Murphy / ABIE'S IRISH ROSE, 1928, Paramount, d-Victor Fleming.

During World War I, Jewish soldier Abie Levy (Charles Rogers) meets and falls in love with Irish Catholic entertainer Rosemary Murphy (Carroll). They marry and then must withstand all their families' prejudices.

Daisy Heath / THE SHOPWORN ANGEL, 1929, Paramount, d-Richard Wallace.

A sophisticated New York chorus girl (Carroll) falls in love with a naive soldier from Texas (Gary Cooper) who goes A.W.O.L. so they can be together. They decide to marry but he's arrested halfway through the ceremony and taken off to join his overseas-bound regiment. She abandons her former life and, although she has a vision of his death in battle, she plans to wait for him.

Hallie Hobart / THE DEVIL'S HOLIDAY, 1930, Paramount, d-Edmund Goulding.

Carroll is a man-hating manicurist who has made a small fortune taking advantage of salesmen. She meets the unsophisticated son (Phillips Holmes) of a wealthy farmer and marries him, even though she's not in love with him. She exacts a payment from the farmer to be rid of her, but eventually regrets her decision and is reconciled with her husband.

Lora Moore / FOLLOW THRU, 1930, Paramount, d-Laurence Schwab.

In this musical comedy, Carroll and Thelma Todd are both out to get the same golf pro (Charles Rogers). Songs by De Sylva, Brown, and Henderson include "Button Up Your Overcoat" and "A Peach of a Pair."

Peggy Gibson / LAUGHTER, 1930, Paramount, d-Harry d'Abbabie.

Ex-Follies girl Carroll marries a millionaire but then goes on a spree with her former lover.

Elsa / THE MAN I KILLED, (BROKEN LULLABY), 1931, Paramount, d-Ernst Lubitsch.

In an atypical Lubitsch film, Carroll is the girlfriend of a German soldier killed during World War I. The young Frenchman who killed the German comes to confess his deed to the slain man's family and is accepted by them as a friend. It's a strong story but was not well received by viewers.

Yula Martini / THE NIGHT ANGEL, 1931, Paramount, d-Edmund Goulding.

Prague lawyer Fredric March falls in love with Carroll, the daughter of a madam he had sent to jail. Audiences didn't think much of the film, the story, or the acting, and Carroll's career took a turn for the worse.

Glenda O'Brien / THE WOMAN ACCUSED, 1933, Paramount, d-Paul Sloane.

Luckless Nancy Carroll is the star of this story written for a magazine by ten well-known authors, without any joint consultation. In it she plays an actress having an affair with Cary Grant and, when her ex-lover shows up and gets killed, she is naturally suspected of murder and has to endure a mock shipboard trial.

OTHER ROLES

1927: *Mazie* / LADIES MUST DRESS. **1928:** *Barbara Quayle* / EASY COME, EASY GO; *Maisie Devoe* / CHICKEN A LA KING; *Judith Endicott* / THE WATER HOLE; *Babs* / MANHATTAN COCKTAIL. **1929:** *Gert the maid* / THE WOLF OF WALL STREET; *Pearl* / THE SIN SISTER; *Marjorie Merwin* / CLOSE HARMONY; *Bonnie Lee King* / THE DANCE OF LIFE; *Claire Jernigan* / ILLUSION; *Barbara Pell* / SWEETIE. **1930:** *Alma* / DANGEROUS PARADISE; *Olivia Dangerfield* / HONEY; *guest* / PARAMOUNT ON PARADE. **1931:** *Mary* / STOLEN HEAVEN; *Nora Ryan* / PERSONAL MAID. **1932:** *Daisy Frost* / WAYWARD; *Tanyusha* / SCARLET DAWN; *Ruth Brock* / HOT SATURDAY; *Lora Madigan* / UNDER-COVER MAN. **1933:** *Madeleine McGonegal* / CHILD OF MANHATTAN; *Maria Held* / THE KISS BEFORE THE MIRROR; *Grace Clark* / I LOVE THAT MAN. **1934:** *Julia*

Jelliwell / SPRINGTIME FOR HENRY; *herself* / TRANSATLANTIC MERRY-GO-ROUND; *Jo Douglas* / JEALOUSY. **1935:** *Nora Clegg* / I'LL LOVE YOU ALWAYS; *Anne Taylor* / AFTER THE DANCE; *Helen* / ATLANTIC ADVENTURE. **1938:** *Dorothy Moore* / THERE GOES MY HEART; *Grace Bristow* / THAT CERTAIN AGE.

CAULFIELD, JOAN

(1922–)

Joan Caulfield was first a model, then Paramount's top female star for several years in the 1940s. When her career bottomed out in the early 1950s, this winsome, demure blonde was forced to end her big-screen days by appearing in some low-budget westerns. Later she had two successful TV series: "My Favorite Husband" and "Sally." Speaking of the time when she was a star, she said, "I miss the glamour, the beauty, the gaiety—the mystique that movie people had in those days."

KEY ROLES

Mimi / MONSIEUR BEAUCAIRE, 1946, Paramount, d-George Marshall.

Caulfield dresses up this costume piece in which Bob Hope plays a bumbling barber in the court of France's King Louis XV, who is forced to impersonate a dandy and goes to Spain as an ambassador.

Mary O'Hara / BLUE SKIES, 1946, Paramount, d-Mark Sandrich.

In this meandering musical yarn, Caulfield marries singer Bing Crosby and later leaves him for his ex-partner (Fred Astaire), whom she dumps later as well.

Ruth Wilkins / DEAR RUTH, 1947, Paramount, d-William Russell.

Caulfield's younger sister (Mona Freeman) is a pen-pal with airman William Holden. Her letters, each more passionate than the last, go out with Caulfield's name and, when Holden wants a picture, Freeman sends Caulfield's. When Holden shows up at the old homestead the fun begins and, though Joan is cool to him at first, things eventually heat up.

Victoria Braymore / THE PETTY GIRL, 1950, Columbia, d-Henry Levin.

When calendar artist Robert Cummings makes staid college professor Caulfield his newest model, it causes a big scandal.

OTHER ROLES

1945: *Margaretta Howe* / MISS SUSIE SLAGLE'S; *guest* / DUFFY'S TAVERN. **1947:** *Trudy Mason* / WELCOME STRANGER; *Matilda Frazier* / THE UNSUSPECTED; *guest* / VARIETY GIRL. **1948:** *Jane Stanton* / THE SAINTED SISTERS; *Deborah Owen Clark* / LARCENY. **1949:** *Ruth Seacroft* / DEAR WIFE. **1951:** *Dorinda* / THE LADY SAYS NO. **1955:** *Fern Simon* / THE RAINS OF RANCHIPUR. **1963:** *Sharleen* / CATTLE KING. **1967:** *Dakota Lil* / RED TOMAHAWK. **1968:** *Nora Johnson* / BUCKSKIN.

CHANDLER, JEFF

(Ira Grossel, 1918–1961)

Curly-haired, square-jawed, 6-foot-4 Jeff Chandler was most at home in action pieces or period films; he seemed out of place any time he wore a suit in a contemporary picture. He was nominated for an Oscar for his portrayal of BROKEN ARROW's Cochise, but in fact he wasn't much of an actor. This was overlooked in films where his scowling good looks were more essential than histrionics. He died at age 42 after an injury suffered making a film in the Philippines.

KEY ROLES

Cochise / BROKEN ARROW, 1950, 20th Century-Fox, d-Delmer Daves.

Chandler's portrayal of the great Apache Indian chief as a man of intelligence, good sense, patience, and refinement makes all the white men look like barbarians—and perhaps they are.

Lt. Chick Campbell / RED BALL EXPRESS, 1952, Universal, d-Budd Boetticher.

In this standard war adventure, Chandler heads up a U.S. Army Transportation Corps trucking unit whose function it is to transport gasoline and ammunition during Patton's push to Paris.

Jason / YANKEE PASHA, 1954, Universal, d-Joseph Pevney.

Chandler is just the man to rescue a New England lass (Rhonda Fleming) who has been kidnapped by Barbary pirates and sold into a Moroccan harem.

Marcian / SIGN OF THE PAGAN, 1954, Universal, d-Douglas Sirk.

This film about a Roman centurion (Chandler) and his run-ins with Attila the Hun (Jack Palance) allows audiences to compare extremes in acting. Chandler underacts to the point of looking like he's asleep, and Palance overacts at the top of his lungs, heaving with emotion all the time.

Drummond Hall / FEMALE ON THE BEACH, 1955, Universal, d-Joseph Pevney.

Chandler is a beach bum who lives next door to a beach house rented by Joan Crawford. The previous tenant of the house had fallen, or been pushed, to her death from a balcony. After a short courtship Chandler and Crawford get married and she discovers she also is marked for murder—not by Chandler, but by a real estate agent (Jan Sterling) who wants Chandler for herself.

Sal Satori / JEANNE EAGELS, 1957, Columbia, d-George Sidney.

Chandler is the carnival operator who discovers and falls in love with a tragic sideshow dancer who becomes a Broadway star, but is done in by drugs. Kim Novak plays the title role in this dreary biopic.

Brig. Gen. Frank D. Merrill / MERRILL'S MARAUDERS, 1961, Warners, d-Samuel Fuller.

Completed shortly before he died mysteriously of complications from a minor operation, this film has Chandler climbing back into uniform to head up a crack U.S. army unit in Burma in World War II.

OTHER ROLES

1947: *Turk* / JOHNNY O'CLOCK; *Al Conway* / THE INVISIBLE WALL; *Knuckles* / ROSES ARE RED. **1949:** *Pratt* / MR. BELVEDERE GOES TO COLLEGE; *Kurta* / SWORD IN THE DESERT; *Chief McRae* / ABANDONED. **1950:** *Kenniston* / TWO FLAGS WEST; *Vic Smith* / DEPORTED. **1951:** *Tenga* / BIRD OF PARADISE; *Steve Kent* / SMUGGLER'S ISLAND; *Coke Mason* / IRON MAN; *Tamerlane* / FLAME OF ARABY. **1952:** *Cochise* / THE BATTLE AT APACHE PASS; *Cmdr. David Porter* / YANKEE BUCCANEER; *Steve Kimberly* / BECAUSE OF YOU. **1953:** *Jonathan Westgate* / THE GREAT SIOUX UPRISING; *Duke Mullane* / EAST OF SUMATRA. **1954:** *Maj. Howell Brady* / WAR ARROW; *Cochise* / TAZA, SON OF COCHISE. **1955:** *Jonathan Dartland* / FOXFIRE; *Roy Glennister* / THE SPOILERS; *Rick Todd* / TOY TIGER. **1956:** *Capt. Jedediah Hawks* / AWAY ALL BOATS; *1st Sgt. Emmett Bell* / PILLARS OF THE SKY. **1957:** *Drango* / DRANGO; *James Gordon Blaine* / THE TATTERED DRESS; *Ben Sadler* / MAN

IN THE SHADOW. **1958:** *Mike Dandridge* / THE LADY TAKES A FLYER; *Mark Moore* / *Scott Moorehouse* / RAW WIND IN EDEN. **1959:** *Pike Yarnell* / STRANGER IN MY ARMS; *Lon Bennett* / THUNDER IN THE SUN; *Karl Wirtz* / TEN SECONDS TO HELL; *Luke Darcy* / THE JAYHAWKERS. **1960:** *Sam Christy* / THE PLUNDERERS. **1961:** *Lewis Jackman* / RETURN TO PEYTON PLACE.

CHARISSE, CYD

(Tula Ellice Finklea, 1921–)

Cyd Charisse was not a very good actress and she couldn't sing at all, but the movies have seen no better female dancer. Tall, stately, dark, and beautiful, Charisse was most wonderful when going through one of her ballet routines; she came alive in a remarkable way when she danced. She was sensual and elegant and the possessor of the greatest legs of all time (and we take note of Betty Grable and Ann Miller in making the claim). She had bit roles in 1943 under the name Lily Norwood and her first appearance in a movie as Cyd Charisse was in a specialty dance number in ZIEGFELD FOLLIES (1946). Her made-for-TV movies include CALL HER MOM (1972) and PORTRAIT OF AN ESCORT (1980). In addition, she appeared in the little seen Italian film, IL SEGRETO DEL VESTITO ROSSO (1963).

KEY ROLES

Mlle. Ariane Bouchet / THE UNFINISHED DANCE, 1947, MGM, d-Henry Koster.

In this tearjerker Charisse is a ballerina. Margaret O'Brien adores Charisse, and when she feels Charisse's success is in danger because of a foreign star, O'Brien cripples the competition. But the ending is happy when the two become friends. Charisse is lovely in the ballet numbers, particularly the "Holiday for Strings" finale.

Guest artist / SINGIN' IN THE RAIN, 1952, MGM, d-Gene Kelly and Stanley Donen.

Charisse dances superbly with Gene Kelly in the exciting film-within-a-film final production number.

Gaby Gerard / THE BAND WAGON, 1953, MGM, d-Vincente Minnelli.

Charisse is a ballerina chosen to appear in a Broadway musical with fading Hollywood song-and-dance man Fred Astaire. Their initial dislike of each other eventually turns to love, and their best scene together is in a Central Park setting where they flow together perfectly in the lovely number "Dancing in the Dark."

Fiona Campbell / BRIGADOON, 1954, MGM, d-Vincente Minnelli.

Charisse resides in a Scottish village that only awakens for one day in each century. In the 20th century Gene Kelly wanders in and falls in love with Charisse and must decide if he will join her and her disappearing town.

Jackie Leighton / IT'S ALWAYS FAIR WEATHER, 1955, MGM, d-Gene Kelly and Stanley Donen.

Charisse becomes involved with Gene Kelly, one of three GI buddies who vow to meet ten years after the war. When they do meet they find they don't like each other, but with the help of Charisse and other women, the guys recreate what they had before.

Guest / INVITATION TO THE DANCE, 1957, MGM, d-Gene Kelly.

Charisse is more at home with the European ballet styles than is Kelly in this very enjoyable film.

Ninotchka / SILK STOCKINGS, 1957, MGM, d-Rouben Mamoulian.

When she's dancing, Charisse is more beautiful in the role than was Greta Garbo. However, her donning a pair of silk stockings in a sort of reverse striptease is about the only other thing well done in this loud, musical remake of NINOTCHKA.

Carlotta / TWO WEEKS IN ANOTHER TOWN, 1962, MGM, d-Vincente Minnelli.

Charisse is part of the nostalgic past that pops up as an ex-alcoholic film director (Kirk Douglas) tries to make the most of a comeback chance in Rome.

OTHER ROLES

As Lily Norwood

1943: *Lily* / SOMETHING TO SHOUT ABOUT; *specialty dancer* / MISSION TO MOSCOW; *bit* / THOUSANDS CHEER.

As Cyd Charisse

1946: *chicken* / ZIEGFELD FOLLIES; *Deborah* / THE HARVEY GIRLS; *Rena Fairchild* / THREE WISE FOOLS; *dance specialty* / TILL THE CLOUDS ROLL BY. **1947:** *Conchita* / FIESTA. **1948:** *Yvonne Torro* / ON AN ISLAND WITH YOU; *herself* / WORDS AND MUSIC. **1949:** *fiesta dancer* / THE KISSING BANDIT; *Rosa Senta* / EAST SIDE, WEST SIDE; *Mary Chanler* / TENSION. **1951:** *Manuella* / MARK OF THE RENEGADE. **1952:** *Indian girl* / THE WILD NORTH. **1953:** *Lola de Torrano* / SOMBRERO; *guest* / EASY TO LOVE; **1954:** *guest* / DEEP IN MY HEART. **1956:** *Maria Corvier* / MEET ME IN LAS VEGAS. **1958:** *Charlotte King* / TWILIGHT FOR THE GODS; *Vicki Gaye* / PARTY GIRL. **1961:** *Baronessa Sandra* / FIVE GOLDEN HOURS. **1962:** *the widow* / BLACK TIGHTS. **1966:** *Sarita* / THE SILENCERS. **1967:** *Louise Henderson* / MAROC 7. **1976:** *President's girl 4* / WON TON TON, THE DOG WHO SAVED HOLLYWOOD. **1978:** *Atsil* / WARLORDS OF ATLANTIS.

CHATTERTON, RUTH

(1893–1961)

Dark-haired Ruth Chatterton was a successful stage star when she came to movies at a rather late age. She found success on the screen playing brittle, tense, and overwrought women who invariably adopted a mechanical smile and struggled on. In her roles she was liked by male characters because she was "experienced." In 1931 she was voted "Finest Actress on the Screen" and was frequently referred to as "The First Lady of the Screen." She received Academy Award nominations for MADAME X and SARAH AND SON. She couldn't win against Hollywood's preoccupation with youth, though, and her movie career petered out in the late 1930s, forcing her to return to the stage.

KEY ROLES

Jacqueline Floriot / MADAME X, 1929, MGM, d-Lionel Barrymore.

Chatterton leaves her husband for another man, and when her son becomes ill, her husband won't let her go to him. This starts her on a path to degradation. Years later she gets involved with a cad who, when learning her story, decides to blackmail her ex-husband. In a rage she shoots and kills him and is defended in court by her grown son who doesn't know her.

Sarah Storm / SARAH AND SON, 1930, Paramount, d-Dorothy Arzner.

In this soggy mother-love story, Chatterton, an impoverished widow, searches for the baby her husband (Fuller Melish, Jr.) took from her. *Variety* called it "Madame X with a slightly varied theme."

Poll / French actress / MAGNIFICENT LIE, 1931, Paramount, d-Berthold Viertel.

Chatterton appears in the dual roles of an aging French actress who has dominated the dreams of a blind ex-doughboy (Ralph Bellamy) for 13 years, and a cafe singer who is talked into impersonating the star to appease the stricken man.

Anna Keremazoff / ONCE A LADY, 1931, Paramount, d-Guthrie McClintic.

Chatterton is a loose woman who abandons her husband and daughter, letting them believe she is dead, until twenty years later. It's a weeper remade from a Pola Negri silent called THREE SINNERS in 1928.

Prof. Anna Mathe / GIRLS' DORMITORY, 1936, 20th Century-Fox, d-Irving Cummings.

When Simone Simon, a young student at a girl's private school in Europe, learns that Chatterton also loves headmaster Herbert Marshall, she stands aside for the older woman.

Fran Dodsworth / DODSWORTH, 1936, United Artists, d-William Wyler.

In the role for which she is probably best remembered today, Chatterton is the empty, vulgar wife of a self-made man (Walter Huston) who finds new values on a trip they take to Europe. Chatterton and Huston reach a parting of the ways when she tells him, "Remember, I-I did make a home for you, and I'll do it again—only you've got to let me have my fling now! Because you're simply rushing at old age, Sam, and I'm not ready for that yet."

OTHER ROLES

1928: *Greta* / SINS OF THE FATHERS. **1929:** *Lillian Garson* / THE DOCTOR'S SECRET; *Agnes Meredith* / THE DUMMY; *Kathryn Miles* / CHARMING SINNERS; *Marjorie Lee* / THE LAUGHING LADY. **1930:** *guest* / PARAMOUNT ON PARADE; *Elsie* / THE LADY OF SCANDAL; *Pansy Gray* / ANYBODY'S WOMAN; *Brooks & Naomi Evans* / THE RIGHT TO LOVE. **1931:** *Fay Kilkerry* / UNFAITHFUL. **1932:** *Eve Redman* / TOMORROW AND TOMORROW; *Caroline Grannard* / THE RICH ARE ALWAYS WITH US; *Linda Gault* / THE CRASH. **1933:** *Frisco Jenny* / FRISCO JENNY; *Lilly Turner* / LILLY TURNER; *Allison Drake* / FEMALE. **1934:** *Francoise Moliet* / JOURNAL OF A CRIME. **1936:** *Celia Whittaker* / LADY OF SECRETS. **1938:** *Zelia de Chaumont* / THE RAT; *Josephine de Beauharnais* / A ROYAL DIVORCE.

CHRISTIE, JULIE

(1940–)

Blonde Julie Christie was featured as the free-spirited girl of the 1960s in several movies including her Academy Award-winning role in DARLING (1964). But by the early 1970s critics and fans alike had grown tired of her eccentric roles and, although she has attempted to broaden her range, her appeal remains limited to "Julie Christie" types—beautiful but off-beat women. Born in India, she studied art in France before beginning a stage career with the Frinton Repertory Company in Essex in 1957. In 1962 she made her film debut in a small part in CROOKS ANONYMOUS. Besides DARLING, she was nominated for an Academy Award for MCCABE AND MRS. MILLER. She is now active in the anti-nuclear movement and involved herself in the making of the 1983 TV feature, TAKING ON THE BOMB.

KEY ROLES

Liz / BILLY LIAR, 1963, Great Britain, Vic Films, d-John Schlesinger.

Newsweek described Christie as "beautiful, dark, graceful, sweet and would even make a television commercial worth watching." She's the third woman in the life of Billy Liar (Tom Courtenay) in this story about a British Walter Mitty. She tries to get him to go away with her, but he prefers his make-believe world.

Diana Scott / DARLING, 1964, Great Britain, Vic Films, d-John Schlesinger.

Christie is an ambitious, amoral, young woman who deserts her journalist lover for a company director, a gay photographer, and finally an Italian prince. It's all very fashionable and mod, but it's hard to tell if there is any point to it. One of her lovers (Dirk Bogarde) observes, "Your idea of fidelity is not having more than one man in the bed at the same time." The fact of the matter is she doesn't enjoy sex at all.

Lara / DOCTOR ZHIVAGO, 1965, MGM, d-David Lean.

Christie is the true love of a Moscow doctor (Omar Sharif) who is exiled for writing poetry and is forced into service with the partisans. She's lovely as the man's beloved who is almost always just out of reach.

Bathsheba Everdene / FAR FROM THE MADDING CROWD, 1967, Great Britain, Vic Films, d-John Schlesinger.

In this production of the Hardy novel, headstrong Christie causes unhappiness and tragedy for landowner Peter Finch and husband Terence Stamp before realizing that shepherd Alan Bates has been the right man for her all along. It's a beautifully photographed, scenic, slow-moving but enjoyable romance.

Constance Miller / MCCABE AND MRS. MILLER, 1971, Warners, d-Robert Altman.

Small-time gambler Warren Beatty sets up hard-nosed madam Christie in the brothel business in the zinc-mining town of Presbyterian Church at the turn of the century. "The Company" attracts the attention of local mobsters who wish to be cut in. This film has been praised and damned just about equally. It has more style than content, but Christie is very credible in her part.

Marian Maudsley / THE GO-BETWEEN, 1971, Great Britain, EMI, d-Joseph Losey.

This is a rather tiresome story about a 12-year-old boy on holiday who carries love letters between his friend's sister (Christie) and a young farmer (Alan Bates). The film is not as good as the first line promises: "The past is foreign country. They do things differently there."

Laura Baxter / DON'T LOOK NOW, 1974, Great Britain, BL / Eldorado, d-Nicholas Roeg.

In this macabre story, Christie and husband Donald Sutherland are in Venice shortly after the death of their daughter. When they meet two old women who claim to be in contact with the child, Sutherland scoffs at the idea. But they repeatedly see a little red-coated figure in shadowy passages of the canals.

Jackie Shawn / SHAMPOO, 1975, Columbia, d-Hal Ashby.

Christie is one of a string of women that Beverly Hills hairdresser Warren Beatty keeps and loses. Yet, she is perhaps the one he most misses when she gets away. The scene when she goes under the table at a political banquet is the most shocking in the film.

Susan Harris / DEMON SEED, 1977, MGM, d-Donald Cammell.

Christie's husband invents a computer that's just too human. It locks her up, rapes her, and leaves her with child.

OTHER ROLES

1962: *Babette* / CROOKS ANONYMOUS. **1963:** *Claire Chingford* / THE FAST LADY. **1964:** *Daisy Butler* / YOUNG CASSIDY. **1966:** *Linda* / *Clarisse* / FAHRENHEIT 451. **1968:** *Petulia Danner* / PETULIA. **1969:** *Catherine* / IN SEARCH OF GREGORY. **1978:** *Betty Logan* / HEAVEN CAN WAIT. **1981:** *narrator* / THE ANIMALS FILM. **1982:** *'D'* / MEMOIRS OF A SURVIVOR. **1983:** *Ruby* / THE GOLD DIGGERS; *Anne* / HEAT AND DUST. **1985:** *Ellen Freeman* / POWER. **1986:** *Maggie* / MISS MAGGIE.

CLAYBURGH, JILL

(1945–)

This tawny-haired actress with the distinctive, honey-toned voice received an Academy Award nomination in 1978 for her tour de force performance in AN UNMARRIED WOMAN. A graduate of Sarah Lawrence College, Clayburgh married playwright David Rabe in 1979. Her Broadway appearances in the 1970s included the shows "Pippin," "The Rothschilds," and "Jumpers." Her made-for-TV movie HUSTLING (1974) led to more important movie roles.

KEY ROLES

Carole Lombard / GABLE AND LOMBARD, 1976, Universal, d-Sidney J. Furie.

Clayburgh is the best thing in this insipid, rather vulgar, inaccurate, and overly sentimental recollection of the love affair of Carole Lombard and Clark Gable (James Brolin) up to the time of her death in an air crash in 1942.

Barbara Jane Bookman / SEMI-TOUGH, 1977, United Artists, d-Michael Ritchie.

Clayburgh is the daughter of the owner of a professional football team. She lives with two of the team's stars (Kris Kristofferson and Burt Reynolds) but must finally decide between them.

Erica Benton / AN UNMARRIED WOMAN, 1978, 20th Century-Fox, d-Paul Mazursky.

A sophisticated New York woman (Clayburgh) is shocked when her husband announces he is leaving her for a younger woman. Being single once again after so many years, she finds she no longer knows the rules of courtship. She meets a series of creeps who use her, and some she uses, before meeting a married artist (Alan Bates) with whom she can have a meaningful relationship. The messages in the movie were appreciated by many women at the time including the one stated to Clayburgh by Penelope Russianoff: "Well, guilt is something that I get livid about because it's kind of a man-made emotion. And I would like to see you take a vacation from guilt. Stop feeling guilty for one week. Just, just say, 'Erica, turn off the guilt. Just turn it off. Don't feel guilty.' It doesn't get you anywhere. It really prolongs the agony."

Marilyn Holmberg / STARTING OVER, 1979, Paramount, d-Alan J. Pakula.

In this rather touching story, Clayburgh is a nursery school teacher who takes up with divorced Burt Reynolds and almost loses him to his ex-wife (Candice Bergen). Both Clayburgh and Reynolds are appealing as they show the suffering of learning to live again after divorce.

Ruth Loomis / FIRST MONDAY IN OCTOBER, 1981, Paramount, d-Ronald Neame.

In this comedy released just about the same time that Ronald Reagan appointed Sandra Day O'Connor as the first female Supreme Court Justice, Clayburgh has the same distinction and wins over her most severe critic, fellow Justice Walter Matthau.

OTHER ROLES

1969: *Josephine Fish* / THE WEDDING PARTY. **1971:** *bit* / THE TELEPHONE BOOK. **1972:** *Naomi* / PORTNOY'S COMPLAINT. **1973:** *Jackie* / THE THIEF WHO CAME TO DINNER. **1974:** *Angela Black* / THE TERMINAL MAN. **1976:** *Hilly Burns* / SILVER STREAK. **1979:** *Caterina Silveri* / LA LUNA. **1980:** *Kate Gunzinger* / IT'S MY TURN. **1982:** *Barbara Gordon* / I'M DANCING AS FAST AS I CAN. **1983:** *Hanna Kaufman* / HANNA K. **1986:** *Nancy Eldridge* / WHERE ARE THE CHILDREN? **1987:** *Diana Sullivan* / SHY PEOPLE.

CLEMENTS, SIR JOHN

(1910–)

A distinguished stage actor and director since 1930, Sir John Clements has appeared sporadically in films since 1935 with his best roles being in pictures for Alexander Korda. Married to actress Kay Hammond, he was knighted in 1968.

KEY ROLES

Gavaert Flink / REMBRANDT, 1936, Great Britain, London Films, d-Alexander Korda.

Although this film about a period in the life of the Dutch painter almost completely belongs to Charles Laughton, Clements is excellent in a supporting role.

Poushkroff / KNIGHT WITHOUT ARMOUR, 1936, Great Britain, London Films, d-Jacques Feyder.

Once again Clements is rather far down the list of credits in this story about a British secret service agent (Robert Donat) posing as a Russian revolutionary in 1917. Clements plays a Russian official with great credibility.

Harry Faversham / THE FOUR FEATHERS, 1939, Great Britain, London Films, d-Zoltan Korda.

In his best film role, Clements resigns his commission just as his regiment is ordered to the Sudan to fight the Arabs. Despite his belief that war is absurd, he is believed to be a coward by his friends and fiancée, each of whom present him with the symbol of cowardice, a white feather. To redeem himself he goes to Egypt, disguises as a native, and saves the lives of his three friends, returning to each their white feather. Back in England, his fiancée takes back the last white feather.

Julius Ikon / CALL OF THE BLOOD, 1947, Great Britain, Pendennis, d-John Clements and Ladislas Vajda.

Playing opposite his real-life wife Kay Hammond, Clements is a man on his honeymoon in Sicily in 1900. He seduces a villager and is killed by her fisherman father.

Major Hall / THE MIND BENDERS, 1963, Great Britain, Novus / Allied Artists, d-Basil Dearden.

Clements is a security officer at Oxford who brainwashes a physiologist (Dirk Bogarde) into mistrusting his pregnant wife and then finds he can't undo the damage.

OTHER ROLES

1934: *Edward Teale* / ONCE IN A NEW MOON. **1935:** *Lucky Fisher* / TICKET OF LEAVE; *Florino* / CASTA DIVA. **1936:** *the airman* / THINGS TO COME. **1938:** *Joe Astell* / SOUTH RIDING. **1940:** *Lt. David Cranford* / CONVOY. **1941:** *John Rookeby* / THIS ENGLAND; *Lt. Dick Stacey* / SHIPS WITH WINGS. **1942:** *Jean Baptiste* / TOMORROW WE LIVE; *Milosh Petrovich* / UNDERCOVER. **1944:** *Joe Dinmore* / THEY CAME TO A CITY. **1949:** *Raymond Hillary* / TRAIN OF EVENTS. **1957:** *the admiral* / THE SILENT ENEMY. **1969:** *General von Moltke* / OH! WHAT A LOVELY WAR. **1982:** *advocate general* / GANDHI. **1984:** *cameo* / THE JIGSAW MAN.

CLIFT, MONTGOMERY

(1920–1966)

Montgomery Clift was an intense actor most popular in the early 1950s. A twin, Clift as a child was so dominated by his mother that he was never allowed any normal life away from her and his family. As a child performer he made his Broadway debut in "Fly Away Home" in 1935, then starred in "Foxhole in the Parlor" in 1945. He made his screen debut in THE SEARCH in 1948 and was nominated for four Academy Awards for THE SEARCH, A PLACE IN THE SUN, FROM HERE TO ETERNITY, and JUDGMENT AT NUREMBERG. When he refused the lead role in SUNSET BOULEVARD, Paramount canceled his contract. Clift's ability to portray the inner struggles of his characters was no doubt influenced by his own struggle with his homosexuality, which he at various times attempted to resist through relations with women, including Elizabeth Taylor, whom he almost married. Taylor noted, "Montgomery Clift is the only person I know who is in worse shape than I am." In 1956 he experienced a horrible automobile accident which altered his personality as well as his physical appearance. Clift was always considered "unusual," but after his accident his reputation as an alcoholic and drug addict grew, as did his erratic behavior both on and off the set. The tragedy of his life is that Clift may have been the best actor of his generation, but this was demonstrated on far too few occasions.

KEY ROLES

Ralph Stevenson / THE SEARCH, 1948, MGM, d-Fred Zinnemann.

In his film debut, Clift, a GI in occupied Germany, rescues and cares for a war orphan. It's a splendid tearjerker with Clift underacting and changing moods by slight alterations in his face and eyes—a revelation to audiences.

Matthew Garth / RED RIVER, 1948, United Artists, d-Howard Hawks.

In a story reminiscent of MUTINY ON THE BOUNTY, Clift takes over command of a cattle drive from the man (John Wayne) who has raised him as his son since he was orphaned in an Indian attack. Despite something of a cop-out at the final showdown, this epic about the opening of the Chisholm Trail is a western classic.

Morris Townsend / THE HEIRESS, 1949, Paramount, d-William Wyler.

Clift, a charming fortune hunter, convinces plain Olivia de Havilland that he loves her. Her father discourages the young cad and, years later when he realizes that he really wants her, she takes her sweet revenge. Some critics complained that Clift's performance was too modern for the Henry James period piece.

George Eastman / A PLACE IN THE SUN, 1951, Paramount, d-George Stevens.

Clift falls in love with beautiful Elizabeth Taylor, but is saddled with a pregnant girlfriend (Shelley Winters). He plans to drown the latter but it happens accidentally and at his trial prosecutor Raymond Burr gets to him with: "Eastman, that night when you left that dinner party at the house at Bride's Lake to meet Alice Tripp in the bus station, do you remember leaving anything behind you? I'm referring to your heart, Eastman. Did you leave that behind you? Did you, Eastman?" Recognizing his guilt, Clift goes to his execution knowing he did not wish to save Winters.

Robert E. Lee Prewitt / FROM HERE TO ETERNITY, 1953, d-Fred Zinnemann.

Clift, a moody army bugler, gets "the treatment" from the guys on the base for his refusal to join the boxing team. (He had blinded a friend in a match and doesn't ever want to fight again.) However, when his buddy (Frank Sinatra) is killed by Ernest Borgnine, Clift takes Borgnine on and kills him. Then he goes A.W.O.L. to be with Donna Reed, a prostitute he loves, but is killed in the Japanese raid on Pearl Harbor, trying to get back to his unit. He had tried to explain his feeling about the army to Reed earlier: "I love the army. A man loves a thing, that don't mean it's got to love him back....You love a thing, you gotta be grateful. See, I left home when I was 17. Both my folks is dead, and I don't belong no place—till I entered the army. If it weren't for the army, I wouldn't have learned how to bugle....I play the bugle well."

Noah Ackerman / THE YOUNG LIONS, 1958, 20th Century-Fox, d-Edward Dmytryk.

Clift gives a stoic performance as a GI in World War II in this adaptation of Irwin Shaw's novel that falls just short of being a great movie about the absurdity of war.

Sigmund Freud / FREUD, 1963, Universal-International, d-John Huston.

Clift, who had plenty of mental suffering himself, earnestly portrays the great neurologist and father of psychiatry in this competent and frank film.

OTHER ROLES

1950: *Danny McCullough* / THE BIG LIFT. **1953:** *Fr. Michael William Logan* / I CONFESS. **1954:** *Giovanni Doria* / INDISCRETION OF AN AMERICAN WIFE. **1957:** *John Wickliff Shawnessy* / RAINTREE COUNTY. **1958:** *Adam White* / LONELYHEARTS. **1959:** *Dr. John Cukrowicz* / SUDDENLY, LAST SUMMER. **1960:** *Chuck Glover* / WILD RIVER; *Perce Howland* / THE MISFITS. **1961:** *Rudolph Petersen* / JUDGMENT AT NUREMBERG. **1966:** *Prof. James Bower* / THE DEFECTOR.

CLIVE, COLIN

(Clive Greig, 1898–1937)

Colin Clive's tortured roles were not unlike his own life. He died rather mysteriously in 1937 from a "pulmonary and intestinal ailment." He is best known for his two appearances as Dr. Henry Frankenstein in FRANKENSTEIN and THE BRIDE OF FRANKENSTEIN. Educated at Sandhurst, Clive was on the London stage from 1919 and went to Hollywood in 1930 to appear in the film version of his theatrical hit "Journey's End." His dark, brooding looks made him ideal to play jealous suitors and husbands, but he was at his best when tormented to a point of near hysteria.

KEY ROLES

Captain Denis Stanhope / JOURNEY'S END, 1930, Tiffany / Gainsborough, d-James Whale.
The action takes place in the trenches on the western front during World War I. Clive, shattered after three years of battle, survives on alcohol. He is afraid to be a coward, and resents the bravery of a boy whose sister he loves. One after one, men around him are mortally wounded, but he survives to face yet another battle.

Dr. Henry Frankenstein / FRANKENSTEIN, 1931, Universal, d-James Whale.
Clive plays the research scientist who creates a monster from parts of corpses, including an insane brain. Clive's acting in this film is so over the edge that he often appears more mad than his monster. It's a seminal film and no one has done it better than Clive, though many have tried.

Edward Rochester / JANE EYRE, 1934, Monogram, d-Christy Cabanne.
This is a poverty row version of the Charlotte Brontë novel of a mysterious Yorkshire lord who wishes to marry the governess at his manor, but can't because he has a living, insane wife whom he keeps locked away. The way Clive acts makes it seem that you can catch insanity by marriage.

Dr. Henry Frankenstein / THE BRIDE OF FRANKENSTEIN, 1935, Universal, d-James Whale.
Baron Frankenstein is blackmailed by Dr. Praetorious into reviving his monster and making a mate for it. Clive is just as maniacal-looking as in the earlier film, yelling "It's alive! It's alive!" in a voice totally out of control.

Stephen Orlac / MAD LOVE, 1935, MGM, d-Karl Freund.
Clive is a pianist who loses his hands in a train accident and has the hands of an executed murderer grafted on by a mad surgeon (Peter Lorre) who is in love with Clive's wife (Frances Drake). The hands have this thing about throwing knives.

Bruce Vail / HISTORY IS MADE AT NIGHT, 1937, United Artists, d-Frank Borzage.
Clive is Jean Arthur's ex-husband who does his best to ruin her love affair with Charles Boyer, including framing Boyer for murder.

OTHER ROLES

1931: *Warren Barrington* / THE STRONGER SEX. **1932:** *Rupert Harvey* / LILY CHRISTINE. **1933:** *Christopher Strong* / CHRISTOPHER STRONG; *Geoffrey Fielding* / LOOKING FORWARD. **1934:** *Andrew Kerr* / THE KEY; *Sir Gerald Corven* / ONE MORE RIVER. **1935:** *Captain Johnstone* / CLIVE OF INDIA; *Maurice Trent* / THE RIGHT TO LIVE; *John Marland* / THE GIRL FROM 10TH AVENUE; *Bertrand Berkeley* / THE MAN WHO BROKE THE BANK AT MONTE CARLO. **1936:** *Eric* / THE WIDOW FROM MONTE CARLO. **1937:** *Captain Thelius* / THE WOMAN I LOVE.

CLOSE, GLENN

(1947–)
This short blonde with the blue-grey eyes was named after her godmother, another Glenn. The daughter of a wealthy Connecticut surgeon, she spent her time in her father's clinic in Zaire, boarding schools in Switzerland, and her family's 500-acre Greenwich estate. After graduating Phi Beta Kappa from William and Mary, she performed in regional theaters and starred on Broadway in the hit musical "Barnum" before making her movie debut in THE WORLD ACCORDING TO GARP, for which she received her first Academy Award nomination. She has also received nominations for THE BIG CHILL, THE NATURAL, and FATAL ATTRACTION.

KEY ROLES

Jenny Fields / THE WORLD ACCORDING TO GARP, 1982, Warners, d-George Roy Hill.
Close is an eccentric nurse who employs the unconscious body of a brain-damaged soldier to father her son, known only as Garp. As Garp (Robin Williams) grows to manhood and has a family of his own, he is overshadowed by Close, whose rather bizarre views makes her a heroine to feminists.

Sarah / THE BIG CHILL, 1983, RCA / Columbia, d-Lawrence Kasdan.
In this story about a group of former college radicals gathering for the funeral of their one-time leader, Close is married to Kevin Kline whom she generously lends to Mary Kay Place—whose biological clock is running out—so the latter may become pregnant. The friends talk well, eat a lot, and wonder why they have changed.

Iris Gaines / THE NATURAL, 1984, Tri-Star Pictures, d-Barry Levinson.
Close portrays the childhood sweetheart of a man (Robert Redford) who leaves her to become a professional baseball player. He gets detoured along the way, though, by another woman and a shooting. Years later he gets his chance to play and is inspired by Close to hit the homer that gets his team into the world series. Her revelation that her child is his son gives him herculean strength.

Teddy Barnes / JAGGED EDGE, 1985, RCA / Columbia, d-Richard Marquand.
Close portrays the attorney who is defending a successful newspaper editor (Jeff Bridges) accused of the grisly murder of his wife. To complicate matters, she's having an affair with him.

Alex Forrest / FATAL ATTRACTION, 1987, Paramount, d-Adrian Lyne.
Close plays an attractive editor who has a weekend affair with a happily-married lawyer (Michael Douglas) and then doesn't wish to give him up. When he leaves her she slashes her wrists, and then directs her rage toward Douglas and his family. It's a remarkable performance by a remarkable actress. Once again she was nominated for an Academy Award.

OTHER ROLES

1985: *Jan* / *Maxie* / MAXIE; *Ruth Hillerman* / THE STONE BOY.

COLBERT, CLAUDETTE

(Lily Claudette Chauchoin, 1905–)
This sparkling, French-born actress had an almost uninterrupted string of successes in a wide range of parts, including spirited comedies, tasteful weepies, and costume pieces. She was brought to the United States when she was age six, made her stage debut at 18, and made her first film appearance in 1927 in FOR THE LOVE OF MIKE. She was best portraying well-dressed, modern women with natural glamour and good instincts. She won an Oscar for IT HAPPENED ONE NIGHT and nominations for SINCE YOU WENT AWAY and PRIVATE WORLDS. After twenty years of stardom as pert, impish, intelligent women, she retired from the

screen and now lives in Barbados, accepting work once in a while in TV or the theater.

KEY ROLES

Franzi / THE SMILING LIEUTENANT, 1931, Paramount, d-Ernst Lubitsch.

A beautiful violinist (Colbert) has a romance with officer Maurice Chevalier which is interrupted when he is assigned as an escort to a dowdy princess. The princess falls for him and he is ordered to marry her. Colbert takes pity on the princess (Miriam Hopkins), shows her how to improve her looks, and leaves her to the lieutenant.

Poppaea / THE SIGN OF THE CROSS, 1932, Paramount, d-Cecil B. DeMille.

As Nero's lustful empress, Colbert wants Roman centurion Fredric March, but he has eyes only for a virginal Christian girl (Elissa Landi). Colbert doesn't get her man but she gets most of the lascivious attention, showing a bit and suggesting a great deal more in her famous bath in asses' milk scene.

Elizabeth Rimplegar / THREE-CORNERED MOON, 1933, Paramount, d-Elliott Nugent.

Colbert is at the center of a daft family that finds it hard to adjust to the need to find employment after their assets are wiped out in the stock market crash of 1929.

Ellie Andrews / IT HAPPENED ONE NIGHT, 1934, Columbia, d-Frank Capra.

In an almost flawless comedy, Colbert plays a runaway heiress who is abetted by Clark Gable, a reporter with whom she falls in love. Although over 50 years old, the film is not dated and scenes such as the one showing Colbert's successful technique for hitching a ride will always remain fresh. When she successfully gets a car to stop by adjusting the stockings on her shapely legs, she observes, "I proved once and for all the limb is mightier than the thumb." Colbert won a deserved Oscar for her performance.

Cleopatra / CLEOPATRA, 1934, Paramount, d-Cecil B. DeMille.

Colbert is the queen of the Nile who uses both her slender body and her intelligence to capture first tired and aging Julius Caesar and then stuffy Marc Antony. It's not a good film but it's a good epic.

Beatrice "Bea" Pullman / IMITATION OF LIFE, 1934, Universal, d-John Stahl.

Colbert becomes wealthy when she markets the pancake recipe of her black friend and maid (Louise Beavers). But she is unable to help when the maid's daughter tries to pass for white and cuts off all contact with her mother.

Dr. Jane Everest / PRIVATE WORLDS, 1935, Paramount, d-Gregory La Cava.

Colbert was nominated for an Oscar but this film about the romances of doctors at a mental hospital is not even a good tearjerker.

Barbara Clarke / MAID OF SALEM, 1937, Paramount, d-Frank Lloyd.

Can anyone really believe that Colbert is a witch? In this film the people of Salem do and, without the last-moment heroics of Fred MacMurray, they will burn her at the stake.

Eve Peabody / MIDNIGHT, 1939, Paramount, d-Mitchell Leisen.

How can a tale about adultery among the rich miss? This one certainly doesn't. It is a delightful movie with plenty of marvelous verbal sparring in which John Barrymore hires Colbert to divert the attentions of a gigolo from his wife. The wife (Mary Astor) is given a compliment of sorts by Colbert regarding her hat: "Oh, I think it's a dream on you. You know, it—it does something to your face. It—it gives you a chin."

Augusta Nash / ARISE MY LOVE, 1940, Paramount, d-Mitchell Leisen.

Colbert is a Paris-based fashion reporter who decides to come up with a war story, travels to Spain to locate noted rebel Ray Milland, and ends up helping him escape by posing as his wife. This is just the beginning of the dangerous adventures they share in Europe at the outbreak of World War II.

Gerry Jeffers / THE PALM BEACH STORY, 1942, Paramount, d-Preston Sturges.

This seldom-seen comedy is among Preston Sturges's best works. Colbert is married to an unsuccessful architect and, although she loves him, she leaves him to go to Palm Beach looking for a rich man to take care of her. Her prey is Rudy Vallee, who has a sister who finds that Colbert's husband (Joel McCrea) meets her specifications precisely. Fortunately for all, both Colbert and McCrea have exact twins and everyone gets what they want. One of the most delightful characters in the film is Robert Dudley as the very deaf "Wiener King," who gives Colbert some money and philosophy: "Anyway, I'd be too old for you. 'Cold are the hands of time that creep along relentlessly, destroying slowly but without pity that which yesterday was young. Alone our memories resist the disintegration and grow more lovely with the passing years.' That's hard to say with false teeth."

Anne Hilton / SINCE YOU WENT AWAY, 1944, United Artists, d-John Cromwell.

Colbert received an Oscar nomination for her portrayal of a wife and mother faithfully coping while her husband is away at war. In this sentimental but enjoyable flag-raiser, Colbert is somewhat comforted in her loneliness by the tempting attentions of Joseph Cotten.

Betty MacDonald / THE EGG AND I, 1947, Universal-International, d-Chester Erskine.

In this pleasant comedy, Colbert and husband Fred MacMurray buy a poultry farm and must cope with the problems of adjusting to a new lifestyle. They are "aided" by Ma and Pa Kettle and their brood of children.

Agnes Keith / THREE CAME HOME, 1950, 20th Century-Fox, d-Jean Negulesco.

In 1941, when writer Agnes Keith (Colbert) attempts to leave Borneo, she is interned and badly treated by the Japanese, one of whom has romantic designs on her.

OTHER ROLES

1927: *Mary* / FOR THE LOVE OF MIKE. **1929:** *Jean Oliver* / THE HOLE IN THE WALL; *Joyce Roamer* / THE LADY LIES. **1930:** *Barbara Billings* / THE BIG POND; *Ann Vaughn* / YOUNG MAN OF MANHATTAN; *Lydia Thorne* / MANSLAUGHTER. **1931:** *Julia Traynor* / HONOR AMONG LOVERS; *Helen Blake* / SECRETS OF A SECRETARY; *Sally Clark* / HIS WOMAN. **1932:** *Margaret Hughes* / THE WISER SEX; *Helen Steele* / THE MISLEADING LADY; *Sylvia Suffolk* / THE MAN FROM YESTERDAY; *Felicia Hammond* / THE PHANTOM PRESIDENT; *guest* / MAKE ME A STAR. **1933:** *Nadya* / TONIGHT IS OURS; *Julie Kirk* / I COVER THE WATERFRONT; *Sally Trent* / *Mimi Benton* / TORCH SINGER. **1934:** *Judy Cavendish* / FOUR FRIGHTENED

PEOPLE. **1935:** *Lillian David* / THE GILDED LILY; *Julia Scott* / SHE MARRIED HER BOSS; *Jeanette Desmereau* / THE BRIDE COMES HOME. **1936:** *Cigarette* / UNDER TWO FLAGS. **1937:** *Kay Denham* / I MET HIM IN PARIS; *Grand Duchess Tatiana Petrovna* / TOVARICH. **1938:** *Nicole de Loiselle* / BLUEBEARD'S EIGHTH WIFE. **1939:** *Zaza* / ZAZA; *Edwina Corday* / IT'S A WONDERFUL WORLD; *Lana Martin* / DRUMS ALONG THE MOHAWK. **1940:** *Betsy Bartlett* / BOOM TOWN. **1941:** *Lydia Kenyon* / SKYLARK; *Nora Trinell* / REMEMBER THE DAY. **1943:** *Lt. Janet Davidson* / SO PROUDLY WE HAIL; *Katherine Grant* / NO TIME FOR LOVE. **1945:** *Peggy Martin* / PRACTICALLY YOURS; *Mary* / GUEST WIFE. **1946:** *Elizabeth Hamilton* / TOMORROW IS FOREVER; *Christopher "Kit" Madden* / WITHOUT RESERVATIONS; *Lee Adams* / THE SECRET HEART. **1948:** *Alison Courtland* / SLEEP MY LOVE. **1949:** *Katie Armstrong Jordan* / FAMILY HONEYMOON; *Nora Shelley* / BRIDE FOR SALE. **1950:** *Ellen* / THE SECRET FURY. **1951:** *Sister Mary* / THUNDER ON THE HILL; *Miriam Denham* / LET'S MAKE IT LEGAL. **1952:** *Liz Fraser* / THE PLANTER'S WIFE. **1954:** *Elizabeth* / DAUGHTERS OF DESTINY; *Madame de Montespan* / ROYAL AFFAIRS IN VERSAILLES. **1955:** *Prudence Webb* / TEXAS LADY. **1960:** *Ellen McLean* / PARRISH.

COLMAN, RONALD

(1891–1958)

Ronald Colman was a handsome, mustached, dark-haired actor with a very cultured, very English voice and perfect delivery. He was among the limited number of actors who were stars in both the silent and sound eras. While he may be now most remembered for the "important" pictures of the 1930s when he portrayed mature, romantic heroes, in his youth he was as athletic as Douglas Fairbanks and formed a winning partnership with Vilma Banky in a series of adventurous romances. He won an Academy Award for his performance in A DOUBLE LIFE and received nominations for BULLDOG DRUMMOND, CONDEMNED, and RANDOM HARVEST. Words that come to mind to describe Colman's movie characters include: droll, urbane, distinguished, suave, gentle, aristocratic, idealistic, and sympathetic.

KEY ROLES

Capt. Giovanni Severini / THE WHITE SISTER, 1923, Silent, Metro, d-Henry King.

Colman is the fiancé of Lillian Gish, a woman left penniless when her half-sister destroys their father's will. Colman goes to war in Africa, promising to return and marry Gish. But when he is reported killed, she joins a convent. He had only been a prisoner, though, and when he works his way back to her, he is unable to convince her to renounce her vows. He is killed helping the townspeople escape the erupting Vesuvius.

Capt. Alan Trent / THE DARK ANGEL, 1925, Silent, First National, d-George Fitzmaurice.

Colman is blinded during World War I. Not wishing to be a burden to his fiancée (Vilma Banky), he tries to persuade her to marry a willing fellow officer without letting either know of his infirmity. Later he innocently gives himself away and they are reunited.

Beau Geste / BEAU GESTE, 1926, Silent, Paramount, d-Herbert Brenon.

The Gary Cooper version of the story about three brothers who join the French Foreign Legion after Beau steals a fake sapphire from their benefactor is probably better known, but except for sound it follows this silent version very closely. It's ironic that Cooper's western twang is heard and Colman's cultured, British accent is not.

Bulldog Drummond / BULLDOG DRUMMOND, 1929, United Artists, d-Richard Jones.

Colman admirably impersonates the bored, young British officer who after World War I advertises for adventures and is hired to save a wealthy man from the torture and imprisonment of a sadistic physician.

A. J. Raffles / RAFFLES, 1930, United Artists, d-Harry D'Abbadie D'Arrast.

Colman is a clever, suave safecracker who falls in love with Kay Francis and decides to go straight. Circumstances cause him to try one last job, though, the theft of a fabulous diamond necklace owned by Alison Skipworth. Despite the presence of a Scotland Yard inspector who knows a robbery is planned, Colman succeeds and gets away.

Dr. Martin Arrowsmith / ARROWSMITH, 1931, United Artists, d-John Ford.

The story about a self-sacrificing doctor throughout the life of his medical career isn't great drama, but Colman's performance is exemplary.

Sydney Carton / A TALE OF TWO CITIES, 1935, MGM, d-Jack Conway.

Colman is a British lawyer who takes the place of the husband of the woman he loves and goes to the guillotine, believing "it is a far, far better thing I do than I have ever done. It is a far, far better rest I go to than I have ever known."

Robert Conway / LOST HORIZON, 1937, Columbia, d-Frank Capra.

When seen in its entirety, this film about visitors to the utopian Shangri-la is one of the most satisfying films ever made. Colman, as the world-weary diplomat brought to the hidden Tibetan valley to replace the aged and dying head Lama, could not be more perfect. At the end of the film audiences rejoice with the toast of Hugh Buckler, "Here is my hope that Robert Conway will find his Shangri-la. Here is my hope that we all find our Shangri-la."

Rudolph Rassendy / King Rudolf V / THE PRISONER OF ZENDA, 1937, United Artists, d-John Cromwell.

While on holiday in Ruritania, Colman is prevailed upon to impersonate his distant cousin who, before his coronation, is kidnapped by his half-brother who wants the throne. Colman is twice as good playing dual roles.

François Villon / IF I WERE KING, 1938, Paramount, d-Frank Lloyd.

Colman portrays the 14th-century poet and rascal Villon and matches wits with Basil Rathbone as King Louis XI of France. He also leads the people of Paris in a defense of the city against the Burgundians.

Dick Heldor / THE LIGHT THAT FAILED, 1939, Paramount, d-William A. Wellman.

Colman is a London artist who must complete the portrait of his love, cockney Ida Lupino, before he goes totally blind. In a fit of rage, Lupino splashes his masterpiece with turpentine and ruins it.

Michael Lightcap / THE TALK OF THE TOWN, 1942, Columbia, d-George Stevens.

Colman is a law school dean who defends Cary Grant against a murder charge. The two men are both in love with Jean Arthur in this nice blend of comedy and drama.

Charles Ranier / RANDOM HARVEST, 1942, MGM, d-Mervyn LeRoy.

Colman was nominated for an Academy Award for his portrayal of a shell-shocked World War I officer who marries singer Greer Garson and is blissfully happy until another shock makes him remember he's the head of a noble family. Garson becomes his loyal secretary until years later another shock completely restores his memory. Reviewing the movie, James Agee commented, "I would like to recommend this film to those who can stay interested in Ronald Colman's amnesia for two hours and who could with pleasure eat a bowl of Yardley's shaving soap for breakfast."

Anthony John / A DOUBLE LIFE, 1947, Universal, d-George Cukor.

Colman won an Oscar for his role as a stage actor playing Othello who is so obsessed with the character that he strangles a woman (Shelley Winters) he imagines is Desdemona. The police plan to arrest him after he comes off the stage in a performance of Othello. He almost strangles his ex-wife (Signe Hasso) appearing opposite him, but he stops in time and plunges a knife in his own chest.

OTHER ROLES

1919: *Bob* / THE TOILERS; *Maurice Phillips* / A SON OF DAVID; *Rupert Sylvester* / THE SNOW IN THE DESERT. **1920:** *Vicomte de Beaurais* / THE BLACK SPIDER; *Brendan* / ANNA THE ADVENTURESS. **1921:** *Lodyard* / HANDCUFFS OR KISSES. **1924:** *Emmet Carr* / TARNISH; *Chester Reeves* / TWENTY DOLLARS A WEEK; *Carlo Buccellini* / ROMOLA; *Paul Menford* / HER NIGHT OF ROMANCE; *Maurice Blake* / A THIEF IN PARADISE. **1925:** *John Douglas* / HIS SUPREME MOMENT; *Donald MacAllan* / THE SPORTING VENUS; *Joseph Weyringer* / HER SISTER FROM PARIS; *Stephen Dallas* / STELLA DALLAS; *Lord Darlington* / LADY WINDERMERE'S FAN. **1926:** *Victor Renal* / KIKI; *Willard Holmes* / THE WINNING OF BARBARA WORTH. **1927:** *Montero* / THE NIGHT OF LOVE; *Tito the Clown* / *the count* / THE MAGIC FLAME. **1928:** *Mack van Rycke* / THE LOVERS. **1929:** *Tom Lingard* / THE RESCUE; *Michel* / CONDEMNED. **1930:** *Willie Leeland* / THE DEVIL TO PAY. **1931:** *Barrington Hunt* / THE UNHOLY GARDEN. **1932:** *Jim Warlock* / CYNARA. **1933:** *Sir John Chilcote* / *his cousin* / THE MASQUERADER. **1934:** *Bulldog Drummond* / BULLDOG DRUMMOND STRIKES BACK. **1935:** *Robert Clive* / CLIVE OF INDIA; *Paul Gailard* / THE MAN WHO BROKE THE BANK AT MONTE CARLO. **1936:** *Sergeant Victor* / UNDER TWO FLAGS. **1940:** *David Grant* / LUCKY PARTNERS. **1941:** *Anthony Mason* / MY LIFE WITH CAROLINE. **1944:** *Hafiz* / KISMET. **1947:** *George Apley* / THE LATE GEORGE APLEY. **1950:** *Beauregard Bottomley* / CHAMPAGNE FOR CAESAR. **1956:** *railroad official* / AROUND THE WORLD IN 80 DAYS. **1957:** *spirit of man* / THE STORY OF MANKIND.

CONNERY, SEAN

(Thomas Connery, 1929–)

As hard as Sean Connery tries to show his versatility, this tall, dark, handsome, Scottish-born actor will always be remembered mainly as having created the screen role of Ian Fleming's "James Bond" character. (Pat Hingle beat him to the part, appearing as 007 on television.) Even Connery admitted the futility of fighting it when he returned to the role in 1983, twelve years after "retiring" from it. He has also played a number of rugged roles in action films and, on occasion, these have been most enjoyable romps. In 1987 he won an Oscar for THE UNTOUCHABLES.

KEY ROLES

James Bond / DR. NO, 1962, Great Britain, United Artists / Eon, d-Terence Young.

In the first Bond film, Connery creates the persona of a handsome supercilious agent licensed to kill, but just as likely to bed down with a beautiful woman as shoot someone. The evil enemy who threatens the world is a Chinese menace operating out of the West Indies.

James Bond / FROM RUSSIA WITH LOVE, 1963, Great Britain, United Artists / Eon, d-Terence Young.

In probably the best of the Bond movies, a beautiful Russian spy is innocently drawn into the plot of an international crime organization to kill Bond. The backgrounds for the shenanigans are Istanbul and Venice. Robert Shaw and Lotte Lenya are great villains, Pedro Armendariz is a staunch and lustful supporter of 007, and Daniela Bianchi is lovely wearing a blue ribbon around her neck—and nothing else.

Mark Rutland / MARNIE, 1964, Universal, d-Alfred Hitchcock.

Connery is a rich businessman who forces thief Tippi Hedren to marry him and employs rape as part of his treatment of her sexual frigidity.

James Bond / GOLDFINGER, 1964, Great Britain, United Artists / Eon, d-Guy Hamilton.

Before foiling a plot to loot Fort Knox, Connery beds Shirley Eaton, cheats a cheater at golf, converts a lesbian pilot, and electrocutes an oriental whose weapon is a deadly derby. By this time Connery was getting bored with Bond, and said, "...remove the exotic touches and what have you got? A dull, prosaic English policeman."

Joe Roberts / THE HILL, 1965, Great Britain, MGM, d-Sidney Lumet.

Connery is one of a group of prisoners who rebel against the harsh discipline of a British military detention center in North Africa during World War II. They are punished by being forced to run up and down a hill of sand and stone under the hot sun. When Connery tries to file a formal complaint he is given a brutal beating. And before a kindly doctor (Michael Redgrave) can do anything to change the treatment, Connery and the others mutiny and kill a sadistic sergeant.

John Anderson / THE ANDERSON TAPES, 1971, Columbia, d-Sidney Lumet.

Connery is an ex-con and habitual criminal who puts together a gang to rob a building, unaware that the police and others are recording his phone conversations. He and his gang are gunned down as they invade the apartments of the target building.

Daniel Dravot / THE MAN WHO WOULD BE KING, 1975, Columbia, d-John Huston.

In probably his best non-Bond role, Connery stars with Michael Caine as British non-coms who march into a remote part of India and are mistaken for gods whose coming had been long foretold. When the natives discover that they are just mercenary men, they force Connery onto a rope bridge over a deep chasm, hack away the lines, and send him singing to his death far below. Caine is allowed to live to bring back Connery's severed head.

Robin Hood / ROBIN AND MARIAN, 1976, Columbia, d-Richard Lester.

Someone got the great idea: "What would happen if, after Robin Hood returns from the Crusades, he looks up his old flame Maid Marian who all these years has been living in a convent?" The answer is: apparently not very much that's interesting or exciting.

O'Neil / OUTLAND, 1981, Columbia / EMI / Warners, d-Peter Hyams.

In a futuristic fantasy reminiscent of HIGH NOON, Connery is the marshal of a mining base on the third moon of Jupiter who waits for hired guns from Earth to come and kill him, because he has unmasked the one behind a series of drug-induced suicides.

James Bond / NEVER SAY NEVER AGAIN, 1983, Columbia / EMI / Warners, d-Irvin Kershner.

An aging Connery returns to the role that made him famous and demonstrates that he hasn't lost his touch by bedding down three or four passionate women including the evil Klaus Maria Brandauer's voluptuous and violent assassin, Barbara Carrera.

OTHER ROLES

1955: *Spike* / NO ROAD BACK. **1956:** *Welder* / TIME LOCK. **1957:** *Johnny* / HELL DRIVERS; *Mike* / ACTION OF THE TIGER. **1958:** *Mark Trevor* / ANOTHER TIME, ANOTHER PLACE. **1959:** *Michael McBride* / DARBY O'GILL AND THE LITTLE PEOPLE; *O'Bannion* / TARZAN'S GREATEST ADVENTURE. **1960:** *Paddy Damion* / THE FRIGHTENED CITY. **1961:** *Pedlar Pascoe* / ON THE FIDDLE. **1962:** *Private Flanagan* / THE LONGEST DAY. **1964:** *Anthony Richmond* / WOMAN OF STRAW. **1965:** *James Bond* / THUNDERBALL. **1966:** *Samson Shillitoe* / A FINE MADNESS. **1967:** *James Bond* / YOU ONLY LIVE TWICE. **1968:** *Shalako* / SHALAKO. **1969:** *Jack Kehoe* / THE MOLLY MAGUIRES; *Roald Amundsen* / THE RED TENT. **1971:** *James Bond* / DIAMONDS ARE FOREVER. **1972:** *Detective Sergeant Johnson* / THE OFFENCE. **1974:** *Zed* / ZARDOZ; *Nils Tahlvik* / RANSOM; *Colonel Arbuthnot* / MURDER ON THE ORIENT EXPRESS. **1975:** *Mulay el Raisuli* / THE WIND AND THE LION. **1976:** *Kahil Abdul-Muhsen* / THE NEXT MAN. **1977:** *Major General Urquhart* / A BRIDGE TOO FAR. **1978:** *Edward Pierce* / THE FIRST GREAT TRAIN ROBBERY. **1979:** *Dr. Paul Bradley* / METEOR; *Robert Drapes* / CUBA. **1981:** *King Agamemnon* / TIME BANDITS. **1982:** *Douglas* / FIVE DAYS ONE SUMMER; *Patrick Hale* / WRONG IS RIGHT. **1985:** *Green Knight* / SWORD OF THE VALIANT; *Ramirez* / HIGHLANDER. **1986:** *William of Baskerville* / THE NAME OF THE ROSE. **1987:** *Malone* / THE UNTOUCHABLES.

COOPER, GARY

(Frank James Cooper, 1901–1961)

Carl Sandburg called Gary Cooper "one of the most beloved illiterates the country has ever known." Cooper was admired all right, because audiences saw in him what they rightly or wrongly believed were American values: dependability, decency, integrity, gallantry, honor, and simplicity. He was a major western star for over 30 years, but he also scored in Frank Capra's populist comedies, in dramas where he had only his native wit and determination to see him through, and in believable biopics. He won Oscars for SERGEANT YORK and HIGH NOON, and was nominated for his roles in MR. DEEDS GOES TO TOWN, PRIDE OF THE YANKEES, and FOR WHOM THE BELL TOLLS. He could say more than "yep" and "nope" if there was a reason to, but being taciturn only added to his image as the ideal model of a sincere American. Away from the screen he had no trouble communicating with beautiful women without gulping, as was his frequent onscreen reaction. This gentle-mannered, soft-spoken actor with the piercing blue eyes had a face one could trust. He most certainly deserved the title of superstar. Speaking on his longevity, Cooper allowed, "Everybody asks me 'How come you're around so long?' Well, I always attribute it to playing the part of Mr. Average Joe American. Just an average guy from the middle of the U.S.A. And then I guess I got to believe it...Gary Cooper, an Average Charlie, who became a movie actor."

KEY ROLES

Cadet White / WINGS, 1927, Silent, Paramount, d-William A. Wellman.

Cooper has only one significant scene in this epic of American World War I pilots, but it made quite an impression on audiences. Taking a bite from a candy bar he says, "When your time comes, you're going to get it." Then he sets down the candy bar and leaves for his plane. Later, as the audience learns that his plane has been shot down, the camera pans to the candy bar.

The Virginian / THE VIRGINIAN, 1929, Paramount, d-Victor Fleming.

It's in this film that Cooper delivers the often misquoted line, "If you want to call me that, smile." Walter Huston is the villain who receives the gentle warning. After being forced to hang his best friend for cattle rustling, Cooper goes looking for Huston.

Tom Brown / MOROCCO, 1930, Paramount, d-Josef von Sternberg.

In a role that contradicts the idea that Cooper was always nervous around women, he plays a devil-may-care American in the French Foreign Legion who is ruthless with women. This includes sultry Marlene Dietrich who gives up a millionaire and becomes a camp follower to be near Cooper.

Lt. Frederick Henry / A FAREWELL TO ARMS, 1932, Paramount, d-Frank Borzage.

Cooper is an American ambulance driver during World War I who falls in love with an English nurse (Helen Hayes). They have a brief, blissful time together in Milan then he must return to the front and she goes to Switzerland to await the birth of their child. Cooper locates her later, arriving just after the baby is born dead and Hayes is near death. They hold each other as they hear that the war is over.

Lieutenant McGregor / THE LIVES OF A BENGAL LANCER, 1935, Paramount, d-Henry Hathaway.

Cooper enjoys a hero's death as he is able, with the help of Franchot Tone and the cowardly Richard Cromwell, to thwart the plans of evil Mohammed Khan.

Longfellow Deeds / MR. DEEDS GOES TO TOWN, 1936, Columbia, d-Frank Capra.

As a quiet, tuba-playing, young poet from Mandrake Falls, Cooper inherits twenty million dollars. Jean Arthur, a reporter, gains his confidence so that she can get an exclusive story about the reclusive millionaire. In her articles she ridicules Cooper as a dumb hick and when he discovers that the woman with whom he is falling in love is the reporter who has dubbed him "Cinderella Man," his disappointment with the phonies and con-artists he has encountered in New York convinces him that he should give his money away. This decision gets him hauled into a sanity hearing where Arthur's help proves that he's not crazy.

Wild Bill Hickok / THE PLAINSMAN, 1936, Paramount, d-Cecil B. DeMille.

This is an episodic telling of the life of the famed Old West character from the time he leaves service after the Civil War until he is shot in the back by Jack McCall. When he is shot he is holding what ever after has been referred to as the "dead man's hand"—aces and eights.

Michael "Beau" Geste / BEAU GESTE, 1939, Paramount, d-William A. Wellman.

Cooper is the oldest of the three Geste brothers who join the French Foreign Legion and come under the command of the beastly Brian Donlevy. When Cooper is killed, Robert Preston (as his brother Digby) remembers a childhood promise and gives Cooper a Viking funeral. The prologue to the movie quotes the Arabian proverb: "The love of a man for a woman waxes and wanes like the moon, but the love of a brother is steadfast as the stars and endures like the word of the prophet."

Cole Hardin / THE WESTERNER, 1940, United Artists, d-William Wyler.

Cooper is a drifter who escapes hanging by convincing his honor Judge Roy Bean that he can arrange a meeting with actress Lily Langtry. The judge rules: "I've talked with the prisoner. He's a friend of Lily Langtry's. It stands to reason no friend of Lily Langtry goes around stealing horses and leastways, there's a reasonable doubt."

Long John Willoughby / MEET JOHN DOE, 1940, Warners, d-Frank Capra.

Cooper is a down-on-his-luck bush league baseball pitcher who poses as "John Doe," a man who claims he will symbolically commit suicide on Christmas Eve to protest world conditions. In the end he almost has to go through with it.

Alvin C. York / SERGEANT YORK, 1941, Warners, d-Howard Hawks.

Cooper won an Oscar for his compelling portrayal of a simple hill man who is taken into the army in World War I despite his religious beliefs against fighting and killing. He says, "What kind of law is it that says a man's gotta go against the Book and its teachings?" In a turnaround he becomes the most decorated doughboy in the war.

Prof. Bertram Potts / BALL OF FIRE, 1941, RKO, d-Howard Hawks.

In a takeoff on SNOW WHITE AND THE SEVEN DWARFS, Cooper is one of seven professors compiling an encyclopedia of slang. In the interests of research they take in Barbara Stanwyck, a burlesque stripper hiding out from the law. Of course, Cooper and Stanwyck learn to communicate on a very personal level.

Lou Gehrig / PRIDE OF THE YANKEES, 1942, RKO, d-Sam Wood.

Cooper makes a very convincing Lou Gehrig, the Yankee player who took over at first base and did not relinquish the position, even for a day, until he could no longer play because of a rare neurological disease. Cooper is touching when he says, "I consider myself the luckiest man on the face of the earth."

Robert Jordan / FOR WHOM THE BELL TOLLS, 1943, Paramount, d-Sam Wood.

Cooper makes an excellent Hemingway hero in this story about a man who knows how to die well, as he blows up a bridge after joining a group of Loyalist guerrilla fighters during the Spanish Civil War. His new-found love for peasant girl Ingrid Bergman makes doing his duty and dying a bit more difficult.

Capt. Christopher Holden / UNCONQUERED, 1947, Paramount, d-Cecil B. DeMille.

Cooper is a Virginia militiaman who buys bondswoman Paulette Goddard to anger Howard da Silva. Cooper must later rescue her again as they find themselves in the middle of an Indian war arranged by da Silva.

Howard Roark / THE FOUNTAINHEAD, 1948, Warners, d-King Vidor.

Cooper is an idealistic architect who blows up his own buildings whenever unauthorized changes are made.

Will Kane / HIGH NOON, 1952, United Artists, d-Raoul Walsh.

On the day Cooper weds Quaker girl Grace Kelly, he resigns as marshal of Hadleyville and learns that Frank Miller, a man who has promised to kill Cooper, is arriving on the noon train to be met by three members of his gang. Cooper finds that no one in the town will help him face Miller and, because of her views on violence, Kelly walks out on him. In the end, though, she helps her man as he faces the four and kills them all.

Benjamin Trane / VERA CRUZ, 1954, United Artists, d-Robert Aldrich.

Cooper is one of a group of gunmen who are hired by Maximilian of Mexico to escort a countess from Mexico City to Vera Cruz, unaware that she is transporting a load of gold. Ultimately Cooper sides with the rebels and must face his erstwhile friend (Burt Lancaster) in a gunfight.

Jess Birdwell / FRIENDLY PERSUASION, 1956, Allied Artists, d-William Wyler.

Cooper is a Quaker who finds his southern Indiana farm is a battlefield and that his son has taken up arms against the Confederates, despite his religious convictions.

Joe Chapin / TEN NORTH FREDERICK, 1958, 20th Century-Fox, d-Philip Dunne.

Cooper is a middle-aged millionaire who thinks he'd like to be the president of the United States, but he can't even manage his own family. He has a brief affair with Suzy Parker but gives her up when the difference in their ages is painfully brought home to him.

Link Jones / MAN OF THE WEST, 1958, United Artists, d-Anthony Mann.

Cooper is a reformed outlaw who is forced to kill the uncle (Lee J. Cobb) who wants him to rejoin the gang of robbers.

OTHER ROLES

1925–1926: *extra* / DICK TURPIN; *extra* / THE THUNDERING HERD; *extra* / WILD HORSE MESA; *extra* / THE LUCKY HORSESHOE; *extra* / THE VANISHING AMERICAN; *extra* / THE EAGLE; *extra* / THE ENCHANTED HILL; *extra* / WATCH YOUR WIFE. **1926:** *bit* / TRICKS; *bit* / THREE PALS; *bit* / LIGHTNIN' WINS; *Abe Lee* / THE WINNING OF BARBARA WORTH. **1927:** *reporter* / IT; *Ted Larrabee* / CHILDREN OF DIVORCE; *Dave Saulter* / ARIZONA BOUND; *Nevada* / NEVADA; *Sheriff Buddy Hale* / THE LAST OUTLAW. **1928:** *Maj. Henri de Beaujolais* / BEAU SABREUR; *Gale Price* / THE LEGION OF THE CONDEMNED; *Arnold Furze* / DOOMSDAY; *Captain Edmunds* / HALF A BRIDE; *Capt. Philip Blythe* / LILAC TIME; *Mulligan Talbot* / THE FIRST KISS; *William Tyler* / THE SHOPWORN ANGEL. **1929:** *Sam Lash* / WOLF SONG; *Andre Frey* / BETRAYAL. **1930:** *Capt. James Braydon* / ONLY THE BRAVE; *Enrique, "Quico" the Llano Kid* / THE TEXAN; *Kenneth Dowey* / SEVEN DAYS LEAVE; *Jim Baker* / A MAN FROM WYOMING; *Roy Glenister* / THE SPOILERS; *guest* / PARAMOUNT ON PARADE. **1931:** *Clint Belmet* / FIGHTING CARAVANS; *The Kid* / CITY STREETS; *Tom McNair* / I TAKE THIS WOMAN; *Capt. Sam Whalan* / HIS WOMAN. **1932:** *guest* / MAKE ME A STAR; *Lieutenant Sempter* / DEVIL AND THE DEEP; *Gallagher* / IF I HAD A MILLION. **1933:** *Richard Bogard* / TODAY WE LIVE; *Biff Grimes* / ONE SUNDAY AFTERNOON; *George Curtis* / DESIGN FOR LIVING; *the White Knight* / ALICE IN WONDERLAND; *Capt. Jack Gailliard* / OPERATOR 13. **1934:** *Jerry Day* / NOW AND FOREVER. **1935:** *Tony Barrett* / THE WEDDING NIGHT; *Peter Ibbetson* / PETER IBBETSON. **1936:** *guest* / HOLLYWOOD BOULEVARD; *Tom Bradley* / DESIRE; *O'Hara* / THE GENERAL DIED AT DAWN. **1937:** *Michael "Nuggin" Taylor* / SOULS AT SEA. **1938:** *Marco Polo* / THE ADVENTURES OF MARCO POLO; *Michael Brandon* / BLUEBEARD'S EIGHTH WIFE; *Stretch Willoughby* / THE COWBOY AND THE LADY. **1939:** *Dr. Bill Canavan* / THE REAL GLORY. **1940:** *Dusty Rivers* / NORTHWEST

MOUNTED POLICE. **1944:** *Dr. Corydon M. Wassell* / THE STORY OF DR. WASSELL. *Casanova Brown* / CASANOVA BROWN. **1945:** *Melody Jones* / ALONG CAME JONES; *Col. Clint Maroon* / SARATOGA TRUNK. **1946:** *Prof. Alvah Jasper* / CLOAK AND DAGGER. **1947:** *guest* / VARIETY GIRL. **1948:** *Sam Clayton* / GOOD SAM. **1949:** *guest* / IT'S A GREAT FEELING; *Jonathan L. Scott* / TASK FORCE. **1950:** *Brant Royle* / BRIGHT LEAF; *Blayde "Reb" Hollister* / DALLAS. **1951:** *Lt. John Harkness* / YOU'RE IN THE NAVY NOW; *"Texas"* / IT'S A BIG COUNTRY; *cameo* / STARLIFT; *Capt. Quincy Wyatt* / DISTANT DRUMS. **1952:** *Maj. Alex Kearney* / SPRINGFIELD RIFLE. **1953:** *Mr. Morgan* / RETURN TO PARADISE; *Jeff Dawson* / BLOWING WILD. **1955:** *Gen. Billy Mitchell* / THE COURT-MARTIAL OF BILLY MITCHELL. **1957:** *Frank Flannagan* / LOVE IN THE AFTERNOON. **1959:** *cameo* / ALIAS JESSE JAMES; *Doc Joseph Trail* / THE HANGING TREE; *Maj. Thomas Thorn* / THEY CAME TO CORDURA; *Gideon Patch* / THE WRECK OF THE MARY DEARE. **1961:** *George Radcliffe* / THE NAKED EDGE.

COOPER, JACKIE

(1921–)

Jackie Cooper was one of Hollywood's most popular child stars. He began his film career in Bobby Clark comedies at the age of three. From there he starred in "Our Gang" shorts before moving into a long string of popular tearjerkers. He was nominated for an Academy Award for his performance in SKIPPY. As he grew older his acting became less natural and parts were harder to come by. He fell to "B" movies after his World War II service, before moving on to two successful TV series, "Hennessy" and "The People's Choice." Cooper has found that having been a child star has been hard to live beyond: "My whole life I've been trying to prove I'm not just yesterday. The whole child-star situation can become a demon walking along with you." His made-for-TV movies include SHADOW ON THE LAND (1968), THE ASTRONAUT and MAYBE I'LL COME HOME IN THE SPRING (1971), THE DAY THE EARTH MOVED (1974), and MOBILE TWO (1975).

KEY ROLES

Skippy Skinner / SKIPPY, 1931, Paramount, d-Norman Taurog.

Surprisingly, this film was not only a box-office hit but received a slew of Oscar nominations including one for Cooper as the young son of a health inspector who makes friends with a boy from the slums and tries to raise enough money to buy back the friend's dog from the local dog catcher.

Dink Purcell / THE CHAMP, 1931, MGM, d-King Vidor.

In MGM's biggest hit of the year, Wallace Beery, a broken-down boxer, is attempting a comeback for the sake of his adoring son (Cooper). To make matters more tearful, Cooper's mother wants him to leave Beery and live with her and her new husband. Cooper really could turn on the tear works.

Swipes McGurk / THE BOWERY, 1933, Fox Films, d-Raoul Walsh.

Cooper gives good support to Wallace Beery and George Raft as two boisterous rivals in the New York of the 1890s. It's a rowdy, enjoyable film.

Jim Hawkins / TREASURE ISLAND, 1934, MGM, d-Victor Fleming.

Cooper makes the most of a role that child actors would kill for. He comes into possession of an old pirate map and accompanies a group of treasure hunters on a long sea voyage to an island where the buccaneer booty is buried. Also on the ship are other pirate cutthroats including Wallace Beery as Long John Silver.

Jackie Peck / PECK'S BAD BOY, 1934, Fox Films, d-Eddie Cline.

Cooper at age 12 gives a restrained performance as a mischievous, but not really bad, boy. It's just that when an idea comes to him he acts without considering the consequences. Sometimes his curiosity leads him astray but his heart is in the right place.

Henry Aldrich / WHAT A LIFE, 1939, Paramount, d-Theodore Reed.

In the first of a series of films dealing with the trials and tribulations of teenager Henry Aldrich, Cooper plays the role straight. It became a farce only when the role passed on to Jimmy Lydon.

William Sylvanus Baxter / SEVENTEEN, 1940, Paramount, d-Louis King.

Once again Cooper portrays what many felt was the typical American boy. Only now he's growing up and faces problems both of romance and finance.

Perry White / SUPERMAN, 1978, Warners, d-Richard Donner.

Stocky, snub-nosed Cooper, still tough and defiant, plays the editor of the *Daily Planet*, the Metropolis newspaper for which Clark Kent, aka Superman, works.

OTHER ROLES

1929: *tenement boy* / SUNNY SIDE UP. **1931:** *Midge Murray* / YOUNG DONOVAN'S KID; *Skippy Skinner* / SOOKY. **1932:** *Eddie Randall* / WHEN A FELLER NEEDS A FRIEND; *Terry Parker* / DIVORCE IN THE FAMILY. **1933:** *Ted Hackett, Jr.* / BROADWAY TO HOLLYWOOD. **1934:** *Scooter O'Neal* / LONE COWBOY. **1935:** *Dinky Daniels* / DINKY; *Stubby O'Shaughnessy* / O'SHAUGHNESSY'S BOY. **1936:** *Freddie* / TOUGH GUY; *Buck Murphy* / THE DEVIL IS A SISSY. **1937:** *Chuck* / BOY OF THE STREETS. **1938:** *Ken* / THAT CERTAIN AGE; *Larry Kelly* / GANGSTER'S BOY; *Peter Trimble* / WHITE BANNERS. **1939:** *"Rie" Edwards* / NEWSBOYS' HOME; *Bruce Scott* / SCOUTS TO THE RESCUE; *Tom Allen* / SPIRIT OF CULVER; *Jimmy* / STREETS OF NEW YORK; *Rory O'Donnell* / TWO BRIGHT BOYS; *Jimmy Hutchins* / THE BIG GUY. **1940:** *Clem* / *Tom Grayson* / THE RETURN OF FRANK JAMES; *Byron "By" Newbold* / GALLANT SONS. **1941:** *Henry Aldrich* / LIFE WITH HENRY; *Jerry Regan* / ZIEGFELD GIRL; *Chuck Harris* / HER FIRST BEAU; *Tiny Barlow* / GLAMOUR BOY. **1942:** *Johnnie* / SYNCOPATION; *Robert Houston Scott* / MEN OF TEXAS; *Babe* / THE NAVY COMES THROUGH. **1943:** *Danny* / WHERE ARE YOUR CHILDREN? **1947:** *Ernie* / STORK BITES MAN; *John S. Kilroy* / KILROY WAS HERE. **1948:** *Skitch* / FRENCH LEAVE. **1961:** *Lieutenant Parmell* / EVERYTHING'S DUCKY. **1971:** *Danton Miller* / THE LOVE MACHINE. **1974:** *Raymond Couzins* / CHOSEN SURVIVORS. **1980:** *Perry White* / SUPERMAN II. **1983:** *Perry White* / SUPERMAN III. **1987:** *Perry White* / SUPERMAN IV; *Ace Morgan* / SURRENDER.

COSTELLO, DOLORES

(1905–1979)

This fragile-looking blonde (originally dark-haired) began her film career in the silent movies of her father Maurice Costello, one of the foremost leading men of the period. These shorts and features included THE MEETING OF THE WAYS, THE CHILD CRUSOES, HER SISTER'S CHILDREN, and THE GERANIUM (1911); A JUVENILE LOVE AFFAIR, WANTED, A GRANDMOTHER, VULTURES AND DOVES, IDA'S CHRISTMAS, and A REFORMED SANTA CLAUS (1912); THE HINDOO CHARM (1913); SOME STEAMER SCOOPING, ETTA OF THE FOOTLIGHTS, THE EVIL MEN DO, and TOO MUCH BURGLAR (1914). She was the wife of John Barrymore from 1928 to 1935, during which time she worked infrequently and, when she did, her billing was Dolores Costello Barrymore. The slender, delicate beauty was a charming and talented star, no more evidently so than in her memorable performances in LITTLE LORD FAUNTLEROY and THE MAGNIFICENT AMBERSONS.

KEY ROLES

Esther Harper / THE SEA BEAST, 1926, Silent, Warners, d-Millard Webb.

Calling Costello "the most beautiful woman in the world," John Barrymore insisted that his new love play opposite his Captain Ahab in this adaptation of *Moby Dick*. Costello is the minister's beautiful daughter whom both Barrymore and his brother (George O'Hara) seek for their wife.

Manon Lescaut / WHEN A MAN LOVES, 1927, Silent, Warners, d-Alan Crosland.

Costello is a beautiful French girl at the time of King Louis XV. She is sought and eventually won by John Barrymore, who forsakes his plans to enter the priesthood, but not before having to fight off the plans of both a lustful count and the king.

Jane Witherspoon / THE COLLEGE WIDOW, 1927, Silent, Warners, d-Archie Mayo.

In order to save her father's job as president of Atwater College, whose football team loses all its games, Costello uses her charm and beauty to persuade star players from other schools to transfer to Atwater. This scheme backfires when the boy she really loves gets wind of her activities and questions her virtue. But all ends well when he leads the team to victory in the big game and realizes that Costello's actions were completely innocent.

Mary / Miriam / NOAH'S ARK, 1929, Warners, d-Michael Curtiz.

In this film Costello plays dual roles. As Mary she is in the modern setting of 1914, caught up in the intrigues of World War I, almost being executed as a spy when she repulses the advances of a Russian officer. As Miriam in the biblical setting, she barely escapes becoming a human sacrifice at the Festival of Jaghut when she is rescued by Japheth, the youngest son of Noah, to whom she is betrothed.

"Dearest" Erroll / LITTLE LORD FAUNTLEROY, 1936, United Artists, d-John Cromwell.

Costello portrays the loving, widowed mother of Freddie Bartholomew, an American boy who discovers that he is heir to an English title. Their affection for each other is so great that their endearments almost sound like those of lovers rather than a mother and son.

Isabel Amberson Minafer / THE MAGNIFICENT AMBERSONS, 1942, RKO, d-Orson Welles.

In what some consider one of the finest movies ever made, Costello is the lovely mother of Tim Holt, a spoiled and selfish man who resents the attention an old suitor (Joseph Cotten) is paying Costello. Costello's performance is elegant and poised, and displays an exquisite and mature beauty.

OTHER ROLES

1923: *Nora* / LAWFUL LARCENY; *bit* / THE GLIMPSES OF THE MOON. **1925:** *bit* / BOBBED HAIR; *Isabel Frances / Princess of Lividia* / GREATER THAN A CROWN. **1926:** *Faith Fitzhugh* / BRIDE OF THE STORM; *Joan Herrick* / MANNEQUIN; *Dot Walker* / THE LITTLE IRISH GIRL. **1927:** *Dolores Vasquez* / OLD SAN FRANCISCO; *Annie Daly* / THE THIRD DEGREE; *Maryland Calvert* / THE HEART OF MARYLAND. **1928:** *Betsy Patterson* / GLORIOUS BETSY; *Rose Shannon* / TENDERLOIN. **1929:** *Joan Billaire* / THE REDEEMING SIN; *herself* / SHOW OF SHOWS; *Annabel Lee* / GLAD RAG DOLL; *Maria Morton* / MADONNA OF AVENUE A; *Vera Zuanova* / HEARTS IN EXILE. **1930:** *Vallery Grove* / SECOND CHOICE. **1931:** *Constance Newton* / EXPENSIVE WOMEN. **1936:** *Lucille Sutton* / YOURS FOR THE ASKING. **1938:** *Helen Cosgrove* / THE BELOVED BRAT; *Martha Martin* / BREAKING THE ICE. **1939:** *Mrs. Barnes* / KING OF THE TURF; *Laura Crandall* / WHISPERING ENEMIES; *Margaret Bronson* / OUTSIDE THESE WALLS. **1943:** *Mrs. Davidson* / THIS IS THE ARMY.

COTTEN, JOSEPH

(1905–)

Joseph Cotten was most at home playing characters who are decent but not very effective. His distinctive rasping voice and intelligent face were welcome additions to many extraordinary and ordinary films. He made his screen debut late in life, appearing in Orson Welles's CITIZEN KANE, after having made his mark on Broadway playing opposite Katharine Hepburn in "The Philadelphia Story." His thoughts on his craft include, "Movies and the theater aren't life. They're only a part of it. We make a living out of acting and pray we don't get associated with too much junk...but, in the end, all we hope to reach is a high standard of compromise." Cotten's career declined in the 1950s, and he worked in many vehicles unworthy of his talents. His made-for-TV movies include CUTTER'S TRAIL (1969), DO YOU TAKE THIS STRANGER? (1970), CITY BENEATH THE SEA (1971), THE DEVIL'S DAUGHTER (1972), THE LINDBERGH KIDNAPPING CASE (1976), and CHURCHILL AND THE GENERALS (1979). His quickie European films with limited distribution in this country include DAYS OF FIRE (1968), GANGSTER '70 (1968), KEENE (1969), E VENNE L'ORA DELLA VENDETTA (1970), GLI ORRORI DEL CASTELLO DI NORIMBERGA (1972), TIMBER TRAMPS (1973), IL GIUSTIZIERE SFIDA CA CITTA (1975), UN SUSSURRO NEL BUIO (1976), and L'ISOLA DEGLI UOMINI PESCI (1979).

KEY ROLES

Jedediah Leland / CITIZEN KANE, 1941, RKO, d-Orson Welles.

In what may be the greatest movie ever made, Welles cast Cotten as a drama critic. Cotten is Kane's closest friend until he tries to tell the truth about the talent of Dorothy Comingore, the great man's mistress. In answer to Cotten's question about whether they are still on speaking terms, Welles replies, "Sure we're speaking, Jedediah. You're fired."

Eugene Morgan / THE MAGNIFICENT AMBERSONS, 1942, RKO, d-Orson Welles.

Cotten plays an automobile inventor who had been a suitor of Isabel Amberson (Dolores Costello), but she chose to marry a more socially prominent man. When Cotten returns to town with his daughter, he's a widower and Costello is a widow. But her selfish son does not approve of her renewed friendship with Cotten, and when she suffers a heart attack he denies her dying wish to see him. Cotten had earlier written Costello about her son, "At 21 or 22 so many things appear solid, permanent, untenable, which at 40 seems nothing but disappearing mire. Forty can't tell 20 about this. Twenty can find that only by getting to be 40."

Howard Graham / JOURNEY INTO FEAR, 1942, RKO, d-Norman Foster and Orson Welles.

Cotten is an American naval ordinance engineer returning to the United States from Istanbul. When an attempt is made on his life, he has to be smuggled home in order to escape the Nazi agents trailing him.

Charlie Oakley / SHADOW OF A DOUBT, 1943, Universal, d-Alfred Hitchcock.

Cotten, the favorite uncle of Teresa Wright, is the infamous Merry Widow murderer. As his niece begins to realize that he is a madman, Cotten plots her death.

Zachary Morgan / I'LL BE SEEING YOU, 1945, United Artists, d-William Dieterle.

In this sentimental wartime romance, Cotten is an ex-soldier suffering from shell shock. He is invited to stay during the Christmas holidays at a farm owned by the uncle of paroled prisoner Ginger Rogers. In the peaceful setting they fall in love, but he has to wait for her to complete her sentence.

Jesse McCandless / DUEL IN THE SUN, 1946, Selznick, d-King Vidor and others.

In this film Cotten is the modern, sensible son who opposes his cattle baron father (Lionel Barrymore). He is no match, however, for his wild brother (Gregory Peck), as he competes for the love of passionate half-breed Jennifer Jones.

Glenn Morley / THE FARMER'S DAUGHTER, 1947, Selznick, d-H. C. Potter.

Here Cotten is a U.S. congressman from a politically prominent family headed by his mother, Ethel Barrymore. The family's Swedish maid (Loretta Young) teaches him a thing or two about democracy.

Eben Adams / PORTRAIT OF JENNIE, 1948, Selznick, d-William Dieterle.

An unsuccessful artist meets a strange child in New York's Central Park. Each time he sees her she seems to have grown older. When she becomes a lovely young woman with whom he has fallen in love, he paints her portrait then discovers that she has been long dead. Although he tries, he is unable to change that fact.

Holly Martins / THE THIRD MAN, 1949, Great Britain, British Lion, d-Carol Reed.

Cotten, a writer of western novels, arrives in post-World War II Vienna to meet his friend Harry Lime (Orson Welles), only to be told by a British colonel (Trevor Howard) that his friend has been killed and that he was a black market drug pusher. Cotten won't believe it. He meets and falls in love with Lime's mistress, Alida Valli, and finds that Welles was just as bad as advertised.

George Loomis / NIAGARA, 1952, 20th Century-Fox, d-Henry Hathaway.

While visiting Niagara Falls, Cotten's cheating wife (Marilyn Monroe) plans to do away with him. But Cotten turns the tables on her.

Dr. Drew Bayliss / HUSH...HUSH, SWEET CHARLOTTE, 1965, 20th Century-Fox, d-Robert Aldrich.

Cotten and Olivia de Havilland plot to drive recluse Bette Davis insane in order to get her money.

Dr. Vesalius / THE ABOMINABLE DR. PHIBES, 1971, AIP, d-Robert Fuest.

Here Cotten is one of the doctors blamed by horribly disfigured Vincent Price for not saving the life of his wife. Price plots a biblical-style death for each doctor he blames.

The Reverend Doctor / HEAVEN'S GATE, 1980, United Artists, d-Michael Cimino.

Cotten's liberal exhortation in a graduation speech to the Harvard class of 1870 couldn't save this film from being an epic failure, both financially and aesthetically.

OTHER ROLES

1941: *Michael Fitzpatrick* / LYDIA. **1943:** *Bill Morley* / HERS TO HOLD. **1944:** *Brian Cameron* / GASLIGHT; *Lt. Tony Willett* / SINCE YOU WENT AWAY. **1945:** *Alan Quinton* / LOVE LETTERS. **1949:** *Dr. Lewis Moline* / BEYOND THE FOREST; *Sam Flusky* / UNDER CAPRICORN. **1950:** *Col. Clay Tucker* / TWO FLAGS WEST; *Chris Hale* / WALK SOFTLY, STRANGER; *David Lawrence* / SEPTEMBER AFFAIR. **1951:** *John Raymond* / HALF ANGEL; *Dupin* / THE MAN WITH A CLOAK. **1952:** *Michael Bachlin* / PEKING EXPRESS; *Kirk Denbow* / UNTAMED FRONTIER; *Jim Osborne* / THE STEEL TRAP. **1953:** *Whitney Cameron* / A BLUEPRINT FOR MURDER. **1954:** *John Adams* / SPECIAL DELIVERY. **1955:** *P. M.* / THE BOTTOM OF THE BOTTLE. **1956:** *Sam Wagner* / THE KILLER IS LOOSE; *Daniel* / THE HALLIDAY BRAND. **1958:** *Victor Barbicane* / FROM THE EARTH TO THE MOON; *cameo* / TOUCH OF EVIL. **1961:** *John Breckenridge* / THE LAST SUNSET. **1965:** *Dr. Horace Van Tilden* / THE MONEY TRAP; *Major Reno* / THE GREAT SIOUX MASSACRE. **1966:** *Temple Cordeen* / THE TRAMPLERS; *Kenneth H. Regan* / THE OSCAR; *Jonas* / THE HELLBENDERS. **1967:** *Ace of Diamonds* / JACK OF DIAMONDS; *Jim Owen* / BRIGHTY OF THE GRAND CANYON. **1968:** *Mr. Danner* / PETULIA. **1969:** *Capt. Craig McKenzie* / LATITUDE ZERO. **1970:** *Richard Morgan* / THE GRASSHOPPER. **1971:** *Henry Stimson* / TORA! TORA! TORA!; *Baron Frankenstein* / LADY FRANKENSTEIN. **1972:** *Alfred Becker* / BARON BLOOD; *Captain Jason* / DOOMSDAY VOYAGE. **1973:** *William Simonson* / SOYLENT GREEN; *Harry* / A DELICATE BALANCE. **1975:** *guest* / F FOR FAKE. **1976:** *Arthur Renfrew* / TWILIGHT'S LAST GLEAMING. **1977:** *Nicholas St. Downs III* / AIRPORT '77. **1978:** *Crandall* / CARAVANS; *Johnson* / THE FISH MEN. **1980:** *Walter Pritchard* / THE HEARSE; *Richard Gable* / GUYANA, CULT OF THE DAMNED. **1981:** *the priest* / THE SURVIVOR. **1982:** *Ivar* / THE HOUSE WHERE EVIL DWELLS.

COURTENAY, TOM

(1937–)

After training at the Royal Academy of Dramatic Art, Tom Courtenay made his stage debut in the Old Vic production of "The Sea Gull" in 1960. Later he took over for Albert Finney in "Billy Liar," a role he later repeated on the screen. Courtenay has mostly played misunderstood, nonconforming youths. He has been nominated for Academy Awards for DOCTOR ZHIVAGO and THE DRESSER. Despite his occasional triumphs in films, he has dedicated most of his acting career to, and found his greatest successes in, the theater.

KEY ROLES

Colin Smith / THE LONELINESS OF THE LONG DISTANCE RUNNER, 1962, Great Britain, Woodfall Films, d-Tony Richardson.

Socially deprived Courtenay is arrested for robbery and sent to an English reform school. His long distance running ability leads the institution's governor to train him for a race with a local public school. However, Courtenay deliberately loses the race because he doesn't want to be seen as the governor's boy, and is sent back to manual labor for the rest of his term.

Billy Fisher / BILLY LIAR, 1963, Great Britain, Vic Films, d-John Schlesinger.

Courtenay, an employee of a North Country mortician, lives in a fantasy world so as to escape his grim, ordinary life. Others believe him lazy and touched, and so he is. When Julie Christie visits his town she persuades him to come to London with her. He deliberately misses the train, though, and returns to the world of his daydreams.

Lieutenant Grey / KING RAT, 1965, Columbia, d-Bryan Forbes.

Courtenay is a self-righteous English soldier and prisoner of the Japanese who deeply resents the fact that enterprising George Segal has found ways to make the best of his interment.

Pasha / Strelnikoff / DOCTOR ZHIVAGO, 1965, MGM, d-David Lean.

In this film Courtenay is an idealistic revolutionary married to Julie Christie, the love of Omar Sharif's life. Courtenay is unconcerned with his wife's unfaithfulness as he is much too busy fighting in the Russian Revolution.

Gerald Arthur Otley / OTLEY, 1969, Great Britain, Columbia, d-Dick Clement.

In this spy spoof Courtenay is a petty thief who falls for Romy Schneider and finds himself involved with spies and murderers.

Norman / THE DRESSER, 1983, Great Britain, Columbia, d-Peter Yates.

Here Courtenay is the homosexual dresser of an exhausted Shakespearean actor (Albert Finney). The story takes place on the last day of a tour.

OTHER ROLES

1962: *Private Potter* / PRIVATE POTTER. **1964:** *Pvt. Arthur Hamp* / KING AND COUNTRY. **1965:** *Robert Henshaw* / OPERATION CROSSBOW. **1966:** *Corporal Hartmann* / THE NIGHT OF THE GENERALS. **1967:** *navigator* / THE DAY THE FISH CAME OUT. **1968:** *Gatiss* / A DANDY IN ASPIC. **1971:** *Ivan Denisovitch* / ONE DAY IN THE LIFE OF IVAN DENISOVITCH; *Baxter Clarke* / CATCH ME A SPY. **1987:** *jewelry store owner* / HAPPY NEW YEAR; *Frayn* / LEONARD PART 6.

CRAIN, JEANNE

(1925–)

This green-eyed, fresh-faced beauty-contest winner and model was quickly established as the girl-next-door type, a role she played with considerable charm for several years during the 1940s and early 1950s. When she tried to follow these successes with more dramatic roles the results were not generally distinctive, although she was nominated for an Academy Award for her portrayal in PINKY. Her trim figure and excellent features were her main assets and when she tried to change her wholesome look to a more glamorous one, she proved that a woman who had had seven children could still be quite beautiful. Later in her career, however, she found herself cast in more and more forgettable westerns and even lower quality European movies.

KEY ROLES

Margy Frake / STATE FAIR, 1945, 20th Century-Fox, d-Walter Lang.

Although Lorraine Hogan sings "It Might as Well Be Spring" for Crain, it is Crain who looks so scrubbed and wholesome sitting at her window. Crain is delightful in this amiable story of the romances and adventures one family finds at the Iowa State Fair.

Margie McDuff / MARGIE, 1946, 20th Century-Fox, d-Henry King.

Married and with children, Crain reminisces about her school days, her crush on her French teacher, and her embarrassing habit of losing her bloomers at the darndest times. It's a bright and refreshing story with Crain just about perfect in the part.

Peggy / APARTMENT FOR PEGGY, 1948, 20th Century-Fox, d-George Seaton.

Crain plays the young wife of William Holden, a veteran attending college under the GI Bill. They move into the home of a professor of philosophy (Edmund Gwenn), and Crain injects her winning personality into everyone's life, and also changes Gwenn's plans about suicide.

Patricia "Pinky" Johnson / PINKY, 1949, 20th Century-Fox, d-Elia Kazan.

In her most dramatic role to this point, Crain plays a black girl in the South who passes for white. Crain was good enough to receive an Oscar nomination, but the picture isn't much, although at the time it was considered quite daring.

Della / O. HENRY'S FULL HOUSE, 1952, 20th Century-Fox, d-Henry King.

Here Crain appears with Farley Granger in the sweet and touching story "The Gift of the Magi." She plays a wife who cuts off her long, beautiful hair so that she can sell it and buy her husband a fob for his watch. At the same time, he pawns the watch to buy her combs to wear in her hair.

Mitzi Jones / GENTLEMEN MARRY BRUNETTES, 1955, United Artists, d-Richard Sale.

In a rather jaded sequel to GENTLEMEN PREFER BLONDES, Crain more than holds her own with Jane Russell in this story of two American shopgirls seeking rich husbands in Paris.

Letty Page / THE JOKER IS WILD, 1957, Paramount, d-Charles Vidor.

Here Crain portrays comedian Joe E. Lewis's first wife—a quiet, loyal woman who loses him to the more flamboyant Mitzi Gaynor.

OTHER ROLES

1943: *girl by the pool* / THE GANG'S ALL HERE. **1944:** *Char* / HOME IN INDIANA; *Maggie Preston* / IN THE MEANTIME, DARLING; *Helen* / WINGED VICTORY. **1945:** *Ruth Berent* / LEAVE HER TO HEAVEN. **1946:** *Julia Rogers* / CENTENNIAL SUMMER. **1948:** *Peggy Mayhew* / YOU WERE MEANT FOR ME. **1949:** *Deborah Bishop* / A LETTER TO THREE WIVES; *Lady Windermere* / THE FAN. **1950:** *Ann Gilbreth* / CHEAPER BY THE DOZEN; *guest* / I'LL GET BY. **1951:** *Liz Erickson* / TAKE CARE OF MY LITTLE GIRL; *Annabel Higgins* / PEOPLE WILL TALK. **1952:** *Kitty Bennett* / THE MODEL AND THE MARRIAGE BROKER; *Ann Gilbreth* / BELLES ON THEIR TOES. **1953:** *Ruth Bowman* / DANGEROUS CROSSING; *Linda Culligan* / CITY OF BAD MEN; *Jill Lynn* / VICKI. **1954:** *Marian* / DUEL IN THE JUNGLE. **1955:** *Reed Bowman* / MAN WITHOUT A STAR; *Liza McClure* / THE SECOND GREATEST SEX. **1956:** *Dora Temple* / THE FASTEST GUN ALIVE. **1957:** *Diane Blane* / THE TATTERED DRESS. **1960:** *Laura Riley* / GUNS OF THE TIMBERLAND. **1961:** *Linda Foster* / TWENTY PLUS TWO; *Nefertiti* / QUEEN OF THE NILE; *Elena* / WITH FIRE AND SWORD; *Claudia Procula* / PONTIUS PILATE. **1962:** *Peggy Shannon* / MADISON AVENUE. **1967:** *Peg Phillips* / HOT RODS TO HELL. **1972:** *Mrs. Clara Shaw* / SKYJACKED. **1973:** *preacher's widow* / THE NIGHT GOD SCREAMED.

CRAWFORD, JOAN

(Lucille Fay Le Sueur, 1908–1977)

Joan Crawford had a long, rich career over five decades playing leading ladies well into her fifties. Less than a classical beauty, she changed her image as often as necessary to keep her star shining. Early on she was a devil-may-care flapper, followed over the years by fallen women that men found irresistible, career women quite capable of taking charge, women born to suffer, androgynous women who were selfish and neurotic, wives and mothers too hard on their men and too easy on the kids, society queens, a westerner who wore a gun and knew how to use it, and a star in a modern gothic horror film. One type of film she did not master and correctly avoided was the costume picture; Crawford was always of today, not the past. This somber-faced, broad-shouldered, wide-mouthed woman, best when playing a bitch-goddess, rivaled Bette Davis for the title of most dominant female movie actress of her time. She won an Oscar for MILDRED PIERCE and received nominations for POSSESSED and SUDDEN FEAR.

KEY ROLES

"Dangerous Diana" / OUR DANCING DAUGHTERS, 1928, Silent, MGM, d-Harry Beaumont.

In this silent picture, Crawford portrays a wild, young socialite who loves parties. Despite appearances to the contrary, she is virtuous and idealistic but loses the man she wants (Johnny Mack Brown) to a girl who plays the innocent (Anita Page). Once married, Page shows her true self and makes Brown realize that it is Crawford he has loved all along. When Page conveniently and drunkenly falls down some stairs to her death, Crawford and Brown get another chance.

Flaemmchen / GRAND HOTEL, 1932, MGM, d-Edmund Goulding.

Here Crawford is a stenographer at the Grand Hotel, and one who is not too particular about how she picks up extra money. When obnoxious industrialist Wallace Beery suggests a liaison, she's agreeable. But Lionel Barrymore, a dying bookkeeper, is also interested in Crawford and takes her away with him, at the same time saving her from being implicated in a murder.

Sadie Thompson / RAIN, 1932, United Artists, d-Lewis Milestone.

Prostitute Crawford runs afoul of fanatical missionary Walter Huston when they are forced to share the same hotel in Pago Pago. Huston is adamant that he will "reform and purify" Crawford. He finally succeeds in getting her to repent her sins and accept religion, but she reverts to her old ways when she discovers that the preacher is just like all other men as he gives into his passions, rapes her, and then kills himself.

Janie Barlow / DANCING LADY, 1933, MGM, d-Robert Z. Leonard.

In this film Crawford, a burlesque dancer, is given a part in a Broadway show by its wealthy backer (Franchot Tone), and agrees to marry him if she and the show flop. Tone works toward that end but is frustrated by Crawford's talent and the work of the dance director (Clark Gable) whom Crawford comes to love.

Peggy O'Neal / THE GORGEOUS HUSSEY, 1936, MGM, d-Clarence Brown.

Crawford, the much courted daughter of a Washington innkeeper, becomes a friend and confidante to Andrew Jackson (Lionel Barrymore). She marries Franchot Tone, who later becomes one of the president's cabinet members. As she is much admired by important men in the nation's capital, the other cabinet members' wives become jealous and impugn her loyalty to the Union. The president, angry at their slander, dismisses his cabinet members.

Crystal Allen / THE WOMEN, 1939, MGM, d-George Cukor.

Here Crawford is an ambitious showgirl who manages to steal Norma Shearer's husband, marry him, and then lose him when Shearer decides to fight fire with fire in this all-female film. Crawford gets in a fine parting shot in this catty movie: "There's a name for you ladies, but it isn't used in high society—outside of a kennel."

Anna Holm / A WOMAN'S FACE, 1941, MGM, d-George Cukor.

In this one Crawford is a lonely and bitter woman, hideously scarred on one side of her face by a childhood accident. In her unhappiness she turns to crime, leading a gang of blackmailers. One of her intended victims (Melvyn Douglas) is a plastic surgeon who offers to operate on her. The surgery is a success, turning Crawford into a striking beauty and causing a gradual change in her attitude toward her occupation.

Mildred Pierce / MILDRED PIERCE, 1945, Warners, d-Michael Curtiz.

Here Crawford leaves her husband (Bruce Bennett) after the death of one daughter, becomes a waitress to support and spoil her other child (Ann Blyth), and ultimately works until she owns a chain of restaurants. She meets and marries socially prominent but impoverished Zachary Scott, then finds her selfish, ungrateful daughter making a play for him. When Blyth kills him, Crawford is at first suspected of the crime, but a clever detective soon figures out what has happened. Crawford tells Blyth, "I can't get you out of this, Veda."

Helen Wright / HUMORESQUE, 1946, Warners, d-Jean Negulesco.

Crawford is a neurotic, dissolute, wealthy woman bogged down in a loveless marriage with an elderly man who is tolerant of her use of men as sexual toys. She fosters the career of violinist John Garfield and, though they love each other, she is aware of how unsuited they are. In the end she commits suicide by walking into the ocean while listening to his concert on the radio.

Louise Howell / POSSESSED, 1947, Warners, d-Curtis Bernhardt.

Emotionally unstable Crawford marries the widower (Raymond Massey) of a woman she had been nursing, even though she loves an engineer (Van Heflin) who does not feel the same about her. When Heflin begins courting Crawford's stepchild, Crawford goes off the deep end, kills him, and ends up in a mental institution.

Lane Bellamy / FLAMINGO ROAD, 1949, Warners, d-Michael Curtiz.

As a stranded carnival dancer, Crawford gets involved with the local deputy sheriff (Zachary Scott), which doesn't fit in with the political boss's plans for his protégé. Crawford moves on to marry David Brian, a power in state politics.

Harriet Craig / HARRIET CRAIG, 1950, Columbia, d-Vincent Sherman.

Crawford is a domineering woman who loves her meticulously kept house and its well-appointed furnishings more than she does her hard-working husband. He finally can stand it no longer and walks out on her, leaving her with what really matters to her—material possessions.

Myra Hudson / SUDDEN FEAR, 1952, RKO, d-David Miller.

In this film noir Crawford is a playwright who learns of her husband and his mistress's plan to murder her. Proving that she is both a good playwright and an actress, Crawford designs a scheme to turn the tables on them.

Vienna / JOHNNY GUITAR, 1954, Republic, d-Nicholas Ray.

Crawford builds a gambling saloon in Arizona on a site near where a railroad will soon be passing. Her enemy in the story is Mercedes McCambridge, a bitter, sexually frustrated woman who resents Crawford's affair with Scott Brady. Into this picture rides Sterling Hayden with whom Crawford falls in love. In the end Crawford must face McCambridge in a gun fight.

Blanche Hudson / WHAT EVER HAPPENED TO BABY JANE? 1962, Warners, d-Robert Aldrich.

Crawford portrays a once-famous film star, now crippled and sharing a house with her nutty sister (Bette Davis) who was once a child star. When Davis learns that Crawford plans to sell the house and put her in a sanitarium, she holds Crawford prisoner, mentally and physically tortures her, and plans to kill her when the time is ripe. Crawford and Davis were bitter rivals in real life and Davis once said, "The best time I ever had with Joan Crawford was when I pushed her down the stairs in WHAT EVER HAPPENED TO BABY JANE?"

OTHER ROLES

1925: *Bobby* / PRETTY LADIES; *Mary Riley* / OLD CLOTHES; *young Lady Catherine* / THE ONLY THING; *Irene* / SALLY, IRENE AND MARY. **1926:** *Jane* / THE BOOB; *Betty Burton* / TRAMP, TRAMP, TRAMP; *"the girl"* / PARIS. **1927:** *Joselyn Poe* / THE TAXI DANCER; *Rene Contrecoeur* / WINNERS OF THE WILDERNESS; *Monica Dale* / THE UNDERSTANDING HEART; *Estellita* / THE UNKNOWN; *Jane* / TWELVE MILES OUT; *Allie Monte* / SPRING FEVER. **1928:** *Betty Channing* / WEST POINT; *Rose-Marie* / ROSE-MARIE; *Priscilla Crowninshield* / ACROSS TO SINGAPORE; *Betty Dallas* / THE LAW OF THE RANGE; *Frieda* / FOUR WALLS; *Adrienne Lecouvreur* / DREAM OF LOVE. **1929:** *Susie* / THE DUKE STEPS OUT; *herself* / HOLLYWOOD REVUE OF 1929; *Billie Brown* / OUR MODERN MAIDENS; *"Bingo"* / UNTAMED. **1930:** *Joan Prescott* / MONTANA MOON; *Jerry Marsh* / OUR BLUSHING BRIDES; *Mary Turner* / PAID. **1931:** *Bonnie Jordan* / DANCE, FOOLS, DANCE; *Ivy Stevens* / LAUGHING SINNERS; *Valentine Winters* / THIS MODERN AGE; *Marian Martin* / POSSESSED. **1932:** *Letty Lyndon* / LETTY LYNDON. **1933:** *Diana Boyce-Smith* / TODAY WE LIVE. **1934:** *Sadie McKee* / SADIE MCKEE; *Diane Lovering* / CHAINED; *Mary Clay* / FORSAKING ALL OTHERS. **1935:** *Marcia Townsend* / NO MORE LADIES; *Kay* / I LIVE MY LIFE. **1936:** *Sally Parker* / LOVE ON THE RUN. **1937:** *Fay Cheyney* / THE LAST OF MRS. CHEYNEY; *Anni* / THE BRIDE WORE RED. **1938:** *Jessica Cassidy* / MANNEQUIN; *Olivia Riley* / THE SHINING HOUR. **1939:** *Mary McKay* / ICE FOLLIES OF 1939. **1940:** *Julie* / STRANGE CARGO; *Susan Trexel* / SUSAN AND GOD. **1941:** *Mary Howard* / WHEN LADIES MEET. **1942:** *Margaret J. Drew* / THEY ALL KISSED THE BRIDE; *Michelle De La Becque* / REUNION IN FRANCE. **1943:** *Frances Myles* / ABOVE SUSPICION. **1944:** *guest* / HOLLYWOOD CANTEEN. **1947:** *Daisy Kenyon* / DAISY KENYON. **1949:** *cameo* / IT'S A GREAT FEELING. **1950:** *Ethel Whitehead* / THE DAMNED DON'T CRY. **1951:** *Agatha Reed* / GOODBYE, MY FANCY. **1952:** *Beth Austin* / THIS WOMAN IS DANGEROUS. **1953:** *Jenny Stewart* / TORCH SONG. **1955:** *Lynn Markham* / FEMALE ON THE BEACH; *Eva Phillips* / QUEEN BEE. **1956:** *Millicent Wetherby* / AUTUMN LEAVES. **1957:** *Margaret Landi* / THE STORY OF ESTHER COSTELLO. **1959:** *Amanda Farrow* / THE BEST OF EVERYTHING. **1963:** *Lucretia Terry* / THE CARETAKERS. **1964:** *Lucy Harbin* / STRAIT-JACKET. **1965:** *Amy Nelson* / I SAW WHAT YOU DID. **1967:** *Monica Rivers* / BERSERK. **1970:** *Dr. Brockton* / TROG.

CROMWELL, RICHARD

(Roy Radebaugh, 1910–1960)

Fresh-faced, sensitive-looking Richard Cromwell has been likened in appearance to today's Richard Chamberlain. He was boyish and mild-mannered, most at home in youthful roles or as soft-spoken neurotics. After a bit role in THE KING OF JAZZ, he scored with audiences in his most memorable movie—TOL'ABLE DAVID. His career playing headstrong youths continued throughout the 1930s but went nowhere after World War II.

KEY ROLES

David Kinemon / TOL'ABLE DAVID, 1930, First National, d-Henry King.

In this film Cromwell worships his older brother, driver of the stagecoach carrying U.S. mail in the Virginia mountains. Their quiet community is invaded by three fugitives from justice who cripple the older brother in an uneven fight. About the same time the boys' father suffers a fatal stroke and Cromwell must assume the role of head of the family. At his mother's insistence, he puts aside thoughts of vengeance and is branded a coward, but the day comes when he faces his brother's cripplers and defeats them. He later becomes the stagedriver and wins the girl he loves.

Lieutenant Stone / LIVES OF A BENGAL LANCER, 1935, Paramount, d-Henry Hathaway.

When Cromwell arrives at an outpost on India's Northwest Frontier, he is treated contemptuously by his stern father, commander of the post. Later Cromwell and fellow officers Franchot Tone and Gary Cooper are captured by a rebel leader, and Cromwell responds to torture by giving the information sought. When the trio escapes, however, Cromwell redeems himself and is decorated by his father.

Billy Farnsworth / POPPY, 1936, Paramount, d-A. Edward Sutherland.

In a role fairly typical for Cromwell, he is a small-town mayor's son who falls in love with the daughter of an itinerant patent medicine salesman (W. C. Fields).

Ted Dillard / JEZEBEL, 1938, Warners, d-William Wyler.

In one of his headstrong roles, Cromwell is a proud, young son of the South who accepts the challenge of George Brent, and kills Brent in a duel fought over Bette Davis.

Matt Clay / YOUNG MR. LINCOLN, 1939, 20th Century-Fox, d-John Ford.

Here Cromwell is one of the two backwoods brothers who are accused of murder. Henry Fonda, in the title role, saves the brothers, first from a lynching and then in court.

OTHER ROLES

1930: *bit* / KING OF JAZZ. **1931:** *Pinky Caldwell* / FIFTY FATHOMS DEEP; *the boy* / SHANGHAIED LOVE; *Bob Dudley* / MAKER OF MEN. **1932:** *Tommy* / THAT'S MY BOY; *Ronnie Smith* / EMMA; *Jimmy* / THE STRANGE LOVE OF MOLLY LOUVAIN; *Michael* / AGE OF CONSENT; *Bob Randolph* / TOM BROWN OF CULVER. **1933:** *Steve Smith* / THIS DAY AND AGE; *Chris* / HOOPLA. **1934:** *Dick Robinson* / ABOVE THE CLOUDS; *Allen* / CAROLINA; *the kid* / AMONG THE MISSING; *cub reporter* / NAME THE WOMAN; *Paul Tarman* / WHEN STRANGERS MEET; *college boy* / MOST PRECIOUS THING IN LIFE. **1935:** *Sandy McTavish* / MCFADDEN'S FLATS; *Lee Austin* / LIFE BEGINS AT FORTY; *Dave Durkin* / MEN OF THE HOUR; *Larry Condon* / UNKNOWN WOMAN; *Boyce Avery* / ANNAPOLIS FAREWELL. **1937:** *Jimmy Caldwell* / THE WRONG ROAD; *Bill Armstrong* / OUR FIGHTING NAVY; *Ludwig* / THE ROAD BACK. **1938:** *Jimmy* / COME ON, LEATHERNECKS; *Neil Allison* / STORM OVER BENGAL. **1940:** *Jimmy Saunders* / ENEMY AGENT; *Edward the Hero* / THE VILLAIN STILL PURSUED HER; *Dan* / VILLAGE BARN DANCE. **1941:** *Spence* / PARACHUTE BATTALION. **1942:** *Dr. Tom* / RIOT SQUAD; *Baby Face Morgan* / BABY FACE MORGAN. **1948:** *Patrick Macy* / BUNGALOW 13.

CROSBY, BING

(Harry Lillis Crosby, 1903–1977)

Certainly not one of the most talented of entertainers, Bing Crosby was nevertheless one of the best liked. As a crooner he sold millions of records and enjoyed success and popularity both on radio and television. In the movies he was at his best in light comedies or misty, sentimental melodramas. Although he won an Oscar for GOING MY WAY and was nominated for others in THE BELLS OF ST. MARY'S and THE COUNTRY GIRL, it is for the "road pictures" with Bob Hope and Dorothy Lamour that Crosby will be best remembered. In these he played a delightful con man ready to sell his none-too-bright partner down the road at a moment's notice. Perhaps the greatest compliment that can be paid to Crosby is that he made many second-rate movies enjoyable. His relaxed manner carried over to his own preference for his movies: "My favorite kind of picture would be one that opened with me sitting in a rocking chair on a front porch. The rest of the picture would be what I saw."

KEY ROLES

Tom Grayson / MISSISSIPPI, 1935, Paramount, d-A. Edward Sutherland.

In this musical version of Booth Tarkington's "Magnolia," Crosby is an outcast in the Old South because he won't fight duels. He gets a job on a riverboat as a singer, redeems his reputation, wins Joan Bennett, and sings Rogers and Hart songs such as "Down By the River" and "It's Easy to Remember (But So Hard to Forget)."

Billy Crocker / ANYTHING GOES, 1936, Paramount, d-Lewis Milestone.

Crosby woos English heiress Ida Lupino, stowing away on an oceanliner to be near her in this Cole Porter musical. Unfortunately for Crosby, Ethel Merman got the Porter songs and he had to settle for tunes by other composers.

Joe Beebe / SING, YOU SINNERS, 1938, Paramount, d-Wesley Ruggles.

In his first semi-serious role, Crosby is the feckless brother of hard-working Fred MacMurray. An unsuccessful gambler, Crosby keeps the two broke until he scrapes enough money together to buy a racehorse who wins a big race. Crosby also sings the unforgettable "Small Fry" to 13-year-old Donald O'Connor.

Josh Mallon / ROAD TO SINGAPORE, 1940, Paramount, d-Victor Schertzinger.

In the first and most controlled film in the Road Pictures series, Crosby is a rich young man who runs away from his father and fiancée to take a footloose trip to Singapore with Bob Hope. There they compete for native girl Dorothy Lamour, and Crosby sings "Too Romantic."

Jeff Lambert / BIRTH OF THE BLUES, 1941, Paramount, d-Victor Schertzinger.

When Crosby bails out trumpet player Brian Donlevy from jail, they put together the hottest Dixieland band in New Orleans. The songs include the title number, Johnny Mercer's "The Waiter, the Porter and the Upstairs Maid," and classics like "St. Louis Blues" and "St. James Infirmary."

Jim Hardy / HOLIDAY INN, 1942, Paramount, d-Mark Sandrich.

After breaking up with his partner (Fred Astaire), Crosby buys a Connecticut farmhouse and converts it into a nightclub open only on holidays. Irving Berlin wrote 13 songs for the film, including "White Christmas" (Crosby's biggest seller) and "Be Careful, It's My Heart."

Jeff Peters / ROAD TO MOROCCO, 1942, Paramount, d-David Butler.

Crosby and Hope were at the peak of their ad-libbing abilities in this story about finding a captive princess (Lamour) in an Arabian palace. Crosby warbles "Moonlight Becomes You."

Father Chuck O'Malley / GOING MY WAY, 1944, Paramount, d-Leo McCarey.

Crosby is a laid-back priest sent to a financially troubled parish to replace its crusty old pastor (Barry Fitzgerald). It's a sloppy, sentimental piece but it sat well with audiences during the war years. Crosby sings "Swinging on a Star," which won an Academy Award for Best Song for Johnny Burke and James Van Heusen.

Father Chuck O'Malley / THE BELLS OF ST. MARY'S, 1945, RKO, d-Leo McCarey.

The affable priest is back, gently dueling with Ingrid Bergman, the mother superior of his new parish's parochial school. Together they get stingy Henry Travers to donate his new building to replace the crumbling school. Crosby sings the Oscar-nominated song by Burke and Van Heusen, "Aren't You Glad You're You?"

Johnny Adams / BLUE SKIES, 1946, Paramount, d-Stuart Heisler.

In this Irving Berlin musical, Crosby and Fred Astaire are occasional partners who both want the same girl (Joan Caulfield). Crosby sings "You Keep Coming Back Like a Song" and, with Astaire, "A Couple of Song and Dance Men."

Hank Martin / "Sir Boss" / A CONNECTICUT YANKEE IN KING ARTHUR'S COURT, 1949, Paramount, d-Tay Garnett.

When Connecticut blacksmith Crosby is accidentally knocked out, he wakes up at the time of King Arthur, where his modern knowledge earns him the title of Sir Boss, the love of Rhonda Fleming, and the hatred of Merlin and others. His tunes include "Busy Doing Nothing."

Bob Wallace / WHITE CHRISTMAS, 1954, Paramount, d-Michael Curtiz.

Crosby and Danny Kaye bring together all the ex-soldiers who served with them in World War II under the command of Dean Jagger to hold a benefit show to save Jagger's mountain resort from foreclosure. Yes, Crosby sings the title song.

Frank Elgin / THE COUNTRY GIRL, 1954, Paramount, d-George Seaton.

In a story that in some ways parallels his own, Crosby is a washed-up, alcoholic singer who, with the help of his wife (Grace Kelly) and a Broadway director (William Holden), tries to make a comeback. He's scared. "You don't know what it's like to stand out there on the stage all alone, with the whole show on your shoulders. If I'm no good, the show's no good! I've got the future of one hundred people in my hand—this hand! This hand!" Having once had something of a drinking problem himself, Crosby may have really known the feeling.

C. K. Dexter-Haven / HIGH SOCIETY, 1956, MGM, d-Charles Walters.

In this musical remake of THE PHILADELPHIA STORY, Crosby comes back to Newport, Rhode Island, on the weekend of his ex-wife's (Grace Kelly) second marriage. After clowning around with Frank Sinatra and Louis Armstrong, he wins her back and walks away with another hit, "True Love" by Cole Porter.

OTHER ROLES

1930: *band singer* / KING OF JAZZ; *band singer* / REACHING FOR THE MOON. **1931:** *band singer* / CONFESSIONS OF A CO-ED. **1932:** *Bing Hornsby* / THE BIG BROADCAST. **1933:** *Prof. Frederick Danvers* / COLLEGE HUMOR; *Eddie Bronson* / TOO MUCH HARMONY; *Bill Williams* / GOING HOLLYWOOD. **1934:** *Steve Jones* / WE'RE NOT DRESSING; *Paul Lawton* / SHE LOVES ME NOT; *J. Paul Jones* / HERE IS MY HEART. **1935:** *Gilbert Gordon* / TWO FOR TONIGHT. **1936:** *Jeff Larrabee* / RHYTHM ON THE RANGE; *Larry* / PENNIES FROM HEAVEN; *guest* / THE BIG BROADCAST OF 1936. **1937:** *Tony Martin* / WAIKIKI WEDDING; *Lefty Boylan* / DOUBLE OR NOTHING. **1938:** *Dr. Bill Remsen* / DR. RHYTHM. **1939:** *Lucky Lawton* / PARIS HONEYMOON; *Denny Martin* / EAST SIDE OF HEAVEN; *Larry Earl* / THE STAR MAKER. **1940:** *Buzz Blackwell* / IF I HAD MY WAY; *Bob Sommers* / RHYTHM ON THE RIVER. **1941:** *Chuck Reardon* / ROAD TO ZANZIBAR. **1942:** *cameo* / MY FAVORITE BLONDE; *guest* / STAR-SPANGLED RHYTHM. **1943:** *Dan Emmett* / DIXIE. **1944:** *Johnny Cabot* / HERE COME THE WAVES; *cameo* / THE PRINCESS AND THE PIRATE. **1945:** *Duke Johnson* / ROAD TO UTOPIA; *guest* / DUFFY'S TAVERN; *voice* / OUT OF THIS WORLD. **1947:** *guest* / VARIETY GIRL; *cameo* / MY FAVORITE BRUNETTE; *Dr. James Pearson* / WELCOME STRANGER; *Scat Sweeney* / ROAD TO RIO. **1948:** *Virgil Smith* / THE EMPEROR WALTZ. **1949:** *Joe Mulqueen* / TOP O' THE MORNING. **1950:** *Dan Brooks* / RIDING HIGH; *Paul Merrick* / MR. MUSIC. **1951:** *Pete Garvey* / HERE COMES THE GROOM. **1952:** *Jordan Blake* / JUST FOR YOU; *George Cochran* / ROAD TO BALI; *cameo* / THE GREATEST SHOW ON EARTH; *cameo* / SON OF PALEFACE. **1953:** *Bill Wainwright* / LITTLE BOY LOST; *cameo* / SCARED STIFF. **1956:** *Bill Benson* / ANYTHING GOES. **1957:** *Earl Carleton* / MAN ON FIRE. **1959:** *Father Conroy* / SAY ONE FOR ME; *cameo* / ALIAS JESSE JAMES. **1960:** *Harvey Howard* / HIGH TIME; *guest* / LET'S MAKE LOVE; *guest* / PEPE. **1962:** *Harry Turner* / THE ROAD TO HONG KONG. **1964:** *Allen A. Dale* / ROBIN AND THE SEVEN HOODS. **1966:** *Doc Boone* / STAGECOACH. **1971:** *Dr. Cook* / DR. COOK'S GARDEN. **1972:** *cameo* / CANCEL MY RESERVATION. **1974:** *host* / *narrator* / THAT'S ENTERTAINMENT!

CUMMINGS, ROBERT

(Charles Clarence Robert Orville Cummings, 1909–)
Perennially young-looking, he's been Bob Cummings in comedies and Robert Cummings in more serious movies. He started his career on Broadway by posing as an Englishman. A couple of years later he pulled a similar trick to get a break in the movies when he presented himself as a Texan with a drawl. This health food and vitamin devotee was one of the earliest Hollywood actors to make his mark on television. Not an outstanding performer, Cummings nevertheless has never failed to be entertaining and charming.

KEY ROLES

George Martin / LAST TRAIN FROM MADRID, 1937, Paramount, d-James Hogan.
In what Graham Greene described as "probably the worst film of the decade...it should have been the funniest," Cummings is one of many people attempting to escape the Spanish Civil War.

Dan Trimball / WELLS FARGO, 1937, Paramount, d-Frank Lloyd.
Cummings is well spotted in support of Joel McCrea, as they blaze a trail for the famous cross-country express company.

Harry Loren / THREE SMART GIRLS GROW UP, 1939, Universal, d-Henry Koster.
Helpful Deanna Durbin finds beaus for her two older sisters, including Cummings for Nan Grey.

Jeff Bolton / MOON OVER MIAMI, 1941, 20th Century-Fox, d-Walter Lang.
When Betty Grable and sister Carole Landis go to Miami in search of wealthy husbands, Cummings meets their specifications. Grable lands Cummings, but really prefers his friend Don Ameche. But that's okay, Landis is just fine for Cummings.

Jonathan Reynolds, Jr. / IT STARTED WITH EVE, 1941, Universal, d-Henry Koster.
Charles Laughton is Cummings's cantankerous millionaire father whose deathbed wish is to meet his son's future bride. Since she's not readily available and the end seems near for Laughton, Cummings gets Deanna Durbin to pinch-hit. The old man is delighted with the bride-to-be—so much so that he recovers. This leaves Cummings with a problem or two.

Parris Mitchell / KINGS ROW, 1941, Warners, d-Sam Wood.
In surely his best dramatic role, Cummings is a young medical student in love with Betty Field, daughter of Claude Rains, the doctor who teaches Cummings about medicine. Field's mother is mad and confined to the house, and when Rains realizes that his daughter is also doomed to insanity, he kills her and commits suicide. This leads Cummings to specialize in psychiatry and there is enough madness left in Kings Row to keep him busy.

Barry Kane / SABOTEUR, 1942, Universal, d-Alfred Hitchcock.
Cummings is a defense plant worker believed to be a saboteur. He flees across the country to unmask the real villain and exposes a spy ring in the process. The climax of the film is a fight in the torch of the Statue of Liberty.

George Petty / THE PETTY GIRL, 1950, Columbia, d-Henry Levin.
Cummings is the famous calendar cheesecake artist who causes a scandal when he chooses beautiful college professor Joan Caulfield as his newest model.

Mark Halliday / DIAL M FOR MURDER, 1954, Warners, d-Alfred Hitchcock.
Cummings is an American mystery writer who is Grace Kelly's lover. Her husband (Ray Milland) plots to have her killed, using Cummings as his alibi. When she manages to kill her attacker, Milland tries to make it appear that it was premeditated murder. Cummings and Inspector John Williams both figure out what really happened just before Kelly is to be executed.

Dan Pierce / THE CARPETBAGGERS, 1964, Paramount, d-Edward Dmytryk.
Cummings is a treacherous public relations man hired by George Peppard in this thinly disguised story of the life of Howard Hughes. Peppard is determined to own the studio that has as its only asset a Jean Harlow-like blonde (Carroll Baker). Cummings keeps Peppard from learning of her death in a car accident until the sale goes through, a service for which he receives a huge bonus.

OTHER ROLES

1935: *Jim Preston* / THE VIRGINIA JUDGE; *George Pendleton* / SO RED THE ROSE; *Jimmy* / MILLIONS IN THE AIR. **1936:** *Clinton Faraday* / FORGOTTEN FACES; *Fordyce Mortimer* / DESERT GOLD; *Randall* / ARIZONA MAHONEY; *Lt. Box Dixon* / BORDER FLIGHT; *Jimmy Tuttle* / THREE CHEERS FOR LOVE; *Jay Wallace* / HOLLYWOOD BOULEVARD; *Jimmy Ellis* / THE ACCUSING FINGER. **1937:** *Mike Winslow* / HIDEAWAY GIRL; *George Martin* / SOULS AT SEA.

1938: *radio announcer* / COLLEGE SWING; *Jim* / YOU AND ME; *Alan Sanford* / THE TEXANS; *Jimmy Howell* / TOUCHDOWN ARMY; *Fred* / I STAND ACCUSED. **1939:** *Dennis Lane* / THE UNDER-PUP; *Bill Gregory* / RIO; *Ken Morgan* / EVERYTHING HAPPENS AT NIGHT; *Scotty Hamilton* / CHARLIE MCCARTHY, DETECTIVE. **1940:** *Ridley Crane* / AND ONE WAS BEAUTIFUL; *Jimmy Nolan* / PRIVATE AFFAIRS; *Harry Marten* / SPRING PARADE. **1941:** *Steve Harper* / ONE NIGHT IN THE TROPICS; *Max Clemington* / FREE AND EASY; *Joe O'Brien* / THE DEVIL AND MISS JONES. **1942:** *Jimmy Blake* / BETWEEN US GIRLS. **1943:** *guest* / FOREVER AND A DAY; *Eddie O'Rourke* / PRINCESS O'ROURKE; *Michael* / FLESH AND FANTASY. **1945:** *Bob Collins* / YOU CAME ALONG. **1946:** *Jeff Warren* / THE BRIDE WORE BOOTS; *Chuck Scott* / THE CHASE. **1947:** *Mike* / HEAVEN ONLY KNOWS; *Lewis Venable* / THE LOST MOMENT. **1948:** *Duke Crawford* / LET'S LIVE A LITTLE; *Warren Ford* / THE ACCUSED; *Bruce Elicott* / SLEEP MY LOVE. **1949:** *Christopher Parker* / FREE FOR ALL; *Pete Webb* / TELL IT TO THE JUDGE. **1950:** *Bill Prentice* / PAID IN FULL; *Jeff Bolton* / FOR HEAVEN'S SAKE. **1951:** *Sylvanus Hasley* / THE BAREFOOT MAILMAN. **1952:** *Joe Bennett* / THE FIRST TIME. **1953:** *Bill* / MARRY ME AGAIN. **1954:** *Dick Carson* / LUCKY ME. **1955:** *Wedgewood* / HOW TO BE VERY, VERY POPULAR. **1962:** *Bob Moore* / MY GEISHA. **1963:** *Professor Sutwell* / BEACH PARTY. **1964:** *Dr. Stephanson* / WHAT A WAY TO GO! **1966:** *Dr. Peter Brook* / PROMISE HER ANYTHING; *Mr. Gatewood* / STAGECOACH. **1967:** *Bob Mitchell* / FIVE GOLDEN DRAGONS.

CURTIS, TONY

(Bernard Schwartz, 1925-)

In the 1950s Tony Curtis was badly miscast in numerous films but survived to become a teenage rage by baring his chest and giving his all in several low-budget swashbucklers. He later proved himself an actor, being nominated for an Oscar in THE DEFIANT ONES. Today he may be most famous with the younger set for being Jamie Lee Curtis's father. All in all, his film appearances were entertaining if not always great theater. He didn't take his acting ability too seriously, although he did insist, "I educated my fans. They began to say to themselves, 'Well Burt Lancaster don't play scenes with bums.' " Curtis showed considerable talent for comedy, as in SOME LIKE IT HOT, but after THE BOSTON STRANGLER in 1968 his roles and movies have been highly forgettable.

KEY ROLES

Julna / THE PRINCE WHO WAS A THIEF, 1951, Universal-International, d-Rudolph Mate.

In this Arabian Nights story, Curtis is a prince who as a child was stolen and raised by thieves. With the help of Piper Laurie he wins back his rightful place on the throne.

Harry Houdini / HOUDINI, 1953, Paramount, d-George Marshall.

Curtis is quite entertaining as the great escape artist who tries to discover if communication with the dead is possible. Later he joins the deceased when he fails to perform a spectacular escape.

Jerry Florea / SIX BRIDGES TO CROSS, 1955, Universal-International, d-Joseph Pevney.

In this modern version of PUBLIC ENEMY, Curtis is a young Boston hoodlum in the 1930s. His Bronx accent is not completely out of place for those who feel that all big-city criminals sound alike.

Tino Orsini / TRAPEZE, 1956, United Artists, d-Carol Reed.

Curtis is a young trapeze artist who asks crippled Burt Lancaster to teach him to perform a triple somersault. Both men get involved with Gina Lollobrigida; Curtis gets the triple, and Lancaster gets Lollobrigida.

Sidney Falco / SWEET SMELL OF SUCCESS, 1957, United Artists, d-Alexander Mackendrick.

In his best performance to this point, Curtis plays a crooked press agent who helps megalomaniac New York columnist Burt Lancaster break up his sister's romance with a drummer. There are no heroes here, but the villains are excellent.

Eric / THE VIKINGS, 1958, United Artists, d-Richard Fleischer.

Curtis is a slave who doesn't know that the Viking king is his father (the king raped Curtis's mother years before), and Kirk Douglas is his half-brother. He and Douglas fight over British princess Janet Leigh until they learn of their relationship.

John "Joker" Jackson / THE DEFIANT ONES, 1958, United Artists, d-Stanley Kramer.

Curtis plays a bigoted white convict chained to a black convict (Sidney Poitier), who slowly learns about brotherhood after the two sworn enemies escape together. Curtis gives a very fine performance as a man who finally discovers that the color of a man's skin is no test of his worth.

Joe / Josephine / SOME LIKE IT HOT, 1959, United Artists, d-Billy Wilder.

Together with Jack Lemmon, Curtis witnesses the St. Valentine's Day Massacre and, to escape the pursuing mobsters, poses as a female saxophone player with an all-girl band. He falls in love with the band's singer (Marilyn Monroe) and wins her after he and Lemmon survive the gangsters. Curtis, posing as a rich oil man with a Cary Grant accent, tells Monroe, "With the unrest in the world, I don't think anybody should have a yacht that sleeps more than 12."

Antoninus / SPARTACUS, 1960, Universal-International, d-Stanley Kubrick.

Curtis is a slave of a Roman general (Laurence Olivier) who becomes a trusted aid to Spartacus (Kirk Douglas), the leader of an unsuccessful slave revolt. In the climax, he and Douglas are forced to fight to the death with the winner being crucified.

Ferdinand Waldo Demara, Jr. / THE GREAT IMPOSTER, 1960, Universal-International, d-Robert Mulligan.

In this story based on fact, Curtis is refreshingly eager as an AWOL soldier who, without benefit of education or training, successfully poses as a Trappist monk, a penologist in a redneck southern prison, a Harvard research fellow, and a surgeon aboard a Canadian fighting ship.

Leslie Gallant III / THE GREAT RACE, 1965, Warners, d-Blake Edwards.

Curtis is pure, he's clean, he's a real Boy Scout, and he's one of the leading contenders in the first New York-to-Paris car race. Dastardly Professor Fate (Jack Lemmon) is his main competition, and Natalie Wood is the only female contestant.

Albert De Salvo / THE BOSTON STRANGLER, 1968, 20th Century-Fox, d-Richard Fleischer.

In this semi-documentary film about the rapist / murderer of Boston women during the mid-1960s, Curtis is spectacular in the lead role. He plays a man who apparently does not know what he is doing; a man who can put the crimes completely out of his mind when he's with his wife and children, until the urge to kill becomes too overpowering to resist.

OTHER ROLES

1949: *gigolo* / CRISS CROSS; *Mitch* / CITY ACROSS THE RIVER; *bell-boy* / THE LADY GAMBLES; *Joey Hyatt* / JOHNNY STOOL PIGEON; *Captain Jones* / FRANCIS. **1950:** *Pepe* / I WAS A SHOPLIFTER; *Brent Coulter* / SIERRA; *Kit Dalton* / KANSAS RAIDERS; *Doan* / WINCHESTER '73. **1952:** *Paul Callan* / FLESH AND FURY; *Alvah Morrell* / NO ROOM FOR THE GROOM; *Kashma Baba* / SON OF ALI BABA. **1953:** *Nick Bonelli* / THE ALL AMERICAN; *Eddie Darrow* / FORBIDDEN. **1954:** *Burke* / BEACHHEAD; *Myles Falworth* / THE BLACK SHIELD OF FALWORTH; *Johnny Dark* / JOHNNY DARK; *Joe Maxwell* / SO THIS IS PARIS; *Rene* / THE PURPLE MASK. **1955:** *Eddie Quaid* / *Packy Gennon* / THE SQUARE JUNGLE. **1956:** *Ben Matthews* / THE RAWHIDE YEARS. **1957:** *Mister Cory* / MISTER CORY; *Joe Martini* / THE MIDNIGHT STORY. **1958:** *Britt Harris* / KINGS GO FORTH; *Paul Hodges* / THE PERFECT FURLOUGH. **1959:** *Lt. Nick Holden* / OPERATION PETTICOAT. **1960:** *guest* / PEPE; *David Wilson* / WHO WAS THAT LADY?; *Pete Hammond, Jr.* / THE RAT RACE. **1961:** *Ira Hamilton Hayes* / THE OUTSIDER. **1962:** *Steve McCluskey* / FORTY POUNDS OF TROUBLE; *Andrei Bulba* / TARAS BULBA. **1963:** *cameo* / THE LIST OF ADRIAN MESSENGER; *Cpl. Jackson Leibowitz* / CAPTAIN NEWMAN, M.D. **1964:** *Terry Williams* / WILD AND WONDERFUL; *George Tracy* / GOODBYE CHARLIE; *Bob Weston* / SEX AND THE SINGLE GIRL. **1965:** *Bernard Lawrence* / BOEING BOEING. **1966:** *Tom Ferris* / NOT WITH MY WIFE YOU DON'T! **1967:** *Nick Johnson* / ARRIVEDERCI, BABY; *Carlo Cofield* / DON'T MAKE WAVES. **1968:** *Guerrando* / THE CHASTITY BELT. **1969:** *Chester Schofield* / THOSE DARING YOUNG MEN IN THEIR JAUNTY JALOPIES. **1970:** *Adam Dyer* / YOU CAN'T WIN 'EM ALL. **1971:** *Shannon Gambroni* / SUPPOSE THEY GAVE A WAR AND NOBODY CAME? **1975:** *Louis "Lepke" Buchalter* / LEPKE. **1976:** *Casanova Giovanni* / CASANOVA; *Rodriguez* / THE LAST TYCOON. **1978:** *Harry Erskine* / THE MANITOU. **1980:** *Blackie* / LITTLE MISS MARKER; *Marty N. Fenn* / THE MIRROR CRACK'D. **1983:** *Dr. Clavius* / BRAIN WAVES. **1984:** *Parsifal Katzenellenbogen* / WHERE IS PARSIFAL? **1985:** *The Senator* / INSIGNIFICANCE.

CUSHING, PETER

(1913–)

This refined gentleman with the quiet, authoritative manner will be remembered as a mainstay of the British horror film series of Hammer Productions. Often seen with Christopher Lee, he appeared in modern versions of most of the standard horror movies. He played Frankenstein six times and Dr. Van Helsing five. He started his film career in bit or exceedingly minor roles in American pictures such as THE MAN IN THE IRON MASK (1939) and A CHUMP AT OXFORD (1940). Essentially his film career began eight years later with HAMLET.

KEY ROLES

Osric / HAMLET, 1948, Great Britain, Two Cities, d-Laurence Olivier.

Cushing's role is not large in Olivier's HAMLET but the gaunt-faced actor gives a distinctive performance.

Baron Victor Frankenstein / THE CURSE OF FRANKENSTEIN, 1957, Hammer / Warners, d-Terence Fisher.

Dr. Frankenstein, the brilliant scientist (Cushing), uses sections of stolen corpses to make a creature of his own (Christopher Lee). Cushing murders a scientist to get a good brain for his creation, but it is damaged and the creature develops homicidal tendencies. Cushing goes to the guillotine for the crimes committed by the creature.

Dr. Van Helsing / DRACULA, 1958, Great Britain, Hammer / Rank / U-I, d-Terence Fisher.

Dracula (Christopher Lee) finishes off Cushing's friend and lures both the latter's fiancée and sister into his trap. Later Cushing saves his sister, battles with Lee, and finally catches him in a shaft of sunlight that destroys the evil one.

Sherlock Holmes / THE HOUND OF THE BASKERVILLES, 1959, Great Britain, Hammer / United Artists, d-Terence Fisher.

As the famous detective, Cushing sends his colleague Dr. Watson to Baskerville Hall to look after Sir Henry who is in danger of being the latest of a long line of Baskervilles killed by a ghostly hound that roams the moors. Using many disguises, Cushing is able to prove that Sir Henry's danger comes from a deadly woman, not a devil dog.

Fordyce / CASH ON DEMAND, 1962, Great Britain, Hammer / Columbia, d-Quentin Lawrence.

Cushing is a fussy and unpopular bank manager whose staff helps him outwit a bank robber who is holding Cushing's wife and child as hostages.

Dr. Who / DR. WHO AND THE DALEKS, 1965, Great Britain, British Lion, d-Gordon Flemyng.

Absent-minded Cushing shows his grandchildren his latest invention—a time machine. They are swept away to a planet where they are captured by villainous Daleks—robot-like creatures who rule the planet. Dr. Who and the children are able to prevent the Daleks from destroying the peaceful Thals and they ultimately return to earth.

Mr. Grimsdyke / TALES FROM THE CRYPT, 1972, Great Britain, Amicus / Metromedia, d-Freddie Francis.

In "Poetic Justice," a segment of this omnibus movie, Cushing is a kindly old widower driven to suicide by a heartless neighbor.

Grand Moff Tarkin / STAR WARS, 1976, 20th Century-Fox, d-George Lucas.

As one of the villains from the Empire, Cushing can't rival Darth Vader in evil-doing. But as the one who gives the orders, he is cold, sinister, and obviously bad in this grand fairy tale.

OTHER ROLES

1939: *bit* / THE MAN IN THE IRON MASK. **1940:** *bit* / LADDIE; *bit* / WOMEN IN WAR; *bit* / A CHUMP AT OXFORD; *bit* / VIGIL IN THE NIGHT. **1941:** *bit* / THEY DARE NOT LOVE. **1952:** *Marcel de la Voisier* / MOULIN ROUGE. **1954:** *Sir Palamides* / THE BLACK KNIGHT. **1955:** *Henry Miles* / THE END OF THE AFFAIR. **1956:** *Otto Wesendonk* / MAGIC FIRE; *Memnon* / ALEXANDER THE GREAT; *Jerry Clayton* / TIME WITHOUT PITY. **1957:** *Dr. John Rollason* / THE ABOMINABLE SNOWMAN OF THE HIMALAYAS. **1958:** *the priest* / VIOLENT PLAYGROUND. **1959:** *John Banning* / THE MUMMY; *Captain Pearson* / JOHN PAUL JONES. **1960:** *Dr. Robert Knox* / THE FLESH AND THE FIENDS; *Capt. Clive Judd* / CODE OF SILENCE; *Professor Sewell* / SUSPECT; *Dr. Van Helsing* / BRIDES OF DRACULA; *Sheriff of Nottingham* / SWORD OF SHERWOOD FOREST. **1961:** *Squire Trevenyan* / FURY AT SMUGGLER'S BAY; *Mr. Wrack* / THE NAKED EDGE; *Merryweather* / THE HELLFIRE CLUB. **1962:** *Dr. Blyss* / CAPTAIN CLEGG; *Dr. Von Brecht* / THE MAN WHO FINALLY DIED. **1964:** *Baron Frankenstein* / THE EVIL OF FRANKENSTEIN; *Dr. Sandor Schreck* / DR. TERROR'S HOUSE OF HORRORS; *Dr. Namaroff* / THE GORGON. **1965:** *Maj. Horace Holly* / SHE; *Dr. Christopher Maitland* / THE SKULL. **1966:** *Dr. Brian Stanley* / ISLAND OF TERROR; *Dr. Who* / DALEKS—INVASION EARTH 2150 A.D. **1967:** *Baron Frankenstein* / FRANKENSTEIN CREATED WOMAN; *Lancelot Canning* / TORTURE GARDEN; *narrator* / THE MUMMY'S SHROUD; *Dr. Stone* / NIGHT OF THE BIG HEAT. **1968:** *Inspector Quennell* / BLOOD BEAST TERROR; *Sir John Brown* / CORRUPTION. **1969:** *Baron Frankenstein* / FRANKENSTEIN MUST BE DESTROYED; *Maj. Benedek Heinrich* / SCREAM AND SCREAM AGAIN; *Baron Frankenstein* / ONE MORE TIME. **1970:** *General Spielsdorf* / THE VAMPIRE LOVERS; *Philip Grayson* / THE HOUSE THAT DRIPPED BLOOD; *Dr. Goodrich* / INCENSE FOR THE DAMNED. **1971:** *Gustav Weil* / TWINS OF EVIL. **1972:** *Utterson* / I, MONSTER; *Sir Mark Ashley* / NOTHING BUT THE NIGHT; *Michael Carmichael* / FEAR IN

THE NIGHT; *Smith* / ASYLUM; *captain* / DR. PHIBES RIDES AGAIN; *Dr. Van Helsing* / DRACULA A.D. 1972; *Dr. Wells* / HORROR EXPRESS. **1973:** *Dr. Van Helsing* / THE SATANIC RITES OF DRACULA; *Baron Frankenstein* / FRANKENSTEIN AND THE MONSTER FROM HELL; *Emmanuel Hildern* / THE CREEPING FLESH; *Dr. Pope* / AND NOW THE SCREAMING STARTS; *shopkeeper* / FROM BEYOND THE GRAVE. **1974:** *Paul Catflangue* / LEGEND OF THE WEREWOLF; *Dr. Van Helsing* / THE LEGEND OF THE SEVEN GOLDEN VAMPIRES; *Herbert Flay* / MADHOUSE; *voice only* / LA GRANDE TROUILLE; *Dr. Lundgren* / THE BEAST MUST DIE. **1975:** *Mr. Shatter* / CALL HIM MR. SHATTER; *Dr. Lawrence* / THE GHOUL; *SS commander* / SHOCK WAVES. **1976:** *Baron Corofax* / THE DEVIL'S MEN; *Sir Edward Gifford* / TRIAL BY COMBAT; *Dr. Abner Perry* / AT THE EARTH'S CORE. **1977:** *Wilbur Gray* / THE UNCANNY; *Maj. Von Hackenberg* / DIE STANDARTE. **1978:** *Heinrich Hussner* / HITLER'S SON; *narrator* / THE DETOUR: COUNT DRACULA AND HIS VAMPIRE BRIDE. **1979:** *Commissioner Potts* / TOUCH OF THE SUN; *Wazir Al Wuzara* / ARABIAN ADVENTURE. **1980:** *Dr. Manette* / A TALE OF TWO CITIES; **1981:** *Kolderup* / MONSTER ISLAND. **1982:** *Sebastian* / HOUSE OF LONG SHADOWS. **1983:** *Seneschal* / SWORD OF THE VALIANT. **1984:** *Sven Jorgeson* / TOP SECRET!

DAHL, ARLENE

(1924–)

This ravishing redhead was the Rheingold beer girl in 1946. From there she moved on to Broadway and then to a series of roles as luscious women too beautiful to get the hero or schemers too nasty to keep the man of their choice. Dahl was born to appear before a Technicolor camera in lavish gowns that showed off her excellent figure as well as her piercing eyes and flaming red hair. After a number of roles in which she was more decoration than actress, she became a beauty columnist, writing about something she knew a great deal more about than acting.

KEY ROLES

Rose Donovan / MY WILD IRISH ROSE, 1947, Warners, d-David Butler.

As a gorgeous newcomer to the screen, Dahl was given good marks for her role as the girl who inspired Chauncey Olcott, a singer-actor, to compose the title tune. But other than looking good, the demands made on her in the film were minor.

Eileen Percy / THREE LITTLE WORDS, 1950, MGM, d-Richard Thorpe.

It wasn't Dahl's fault that this movie biopic of songwriters Bert Kalmar and Harry Ruby was so deadly dull. She plays the silent movie star who marries Ruby.

Nancy Darby / SANGAREE, 1953, Paramount, d-Edward Ludwig.

Dahl gets the opportunity to play opposite Fernando Lamas (who became her real-life husband) in this dullish adventure story of a plantation owner who wills his wealth to the son of a slave.

Carol / WOMAN'S WORLD, 1954, 20th Century-Fox, d-Jean Negulesco.

In possibly the best acting of her career, Dahl is the wife of Van Heflin, one of three men being considered to become the new head of a company. She will do just about anything to get him the job—just about anything.

Carla / JOURNEY TO THE CENTER OF THE EARTH, 1959, 20th Century-Fox, d-Henry Levin.

Dahl is one of a group of people taking an explorer's trail down an extinct Icelandic volcano to the earth's center. She doesn't look appropriately dressed for the trek, but "looking good" was always her major talent.

OTHER ROLES

1947: *girl in Delmonic's* / LIFE WITH FATHER. **1948:** *Tillie Smith* / THE BRIDE GOES WILD; *Sallyann Weatharby* / A SOUTHERN YANKEE. **1949:** *Madelon* / REIGN OF TERROR; *Gloria Conovan* / SCENE OF THE CRIME; *Ann Duverall* / AMBUSH. **1950:** *Jen Gort* / THE OUTRIDERS; *Lucia Corlane* / WATCH THE BIRDIE. **1951:** *Lily Douvane* / INSIDE STRAIGHT; *Ellen Sayburn* / NO QUESTIONS ASKED. **1952:** *Christine McAllister* / CARIBBEAN. **1953:** *Ena Dacey* / JAMAICA RUN; *Morjana* / DESERT LEGION; *Maya* / THE DIAMOND QUEEN; *Irene Bailey* / HERE COME THE GIRLS. **1954:** *Vivian Morrow* / BENGAL BRIGADE. **1956:** *Dorothy Lyons* / SLIGHTLY SCARLET; *Kathy Allen* / WICKED AS THEY COME. **1957:** *Sarah Moreton* / FORTUNE IS A WOMAN. **1964:** *Doris Reid* / KISSES FOR MY PRESIDENT. **1969:** *Martha Carden* / THE LAND RAIDERS.

DAILEY, DAN

(1914–1978)

Dan Dailey, a lanky song-and-dance man, came from a family of vaudevillians, worked in a minstrel show as a boy, appeared in Minsky's burlesque troupe, and made his Broadway debut in 1937. He appeared in some nonmusical movies but it wasn't until after World War II that he was given starring roles. He was nominated for an Academy Award for WHEN MY BABY SMILES AT ME (1948), but this cheerful actor enjoyed only a ten-year period of success in mostly Fox musicals. With the death of the Hollywood musical, the decline of his movie career was swift. Later, though, he enjoyed some success in TV situation comedies.

KEY ROLES

Frank Burt / MOTHER WORE TIGHTS, 1947, 20th Century-Fox, d-Walter Lang.

In a film with almost no plot Dailey and Betty Grable play a vaudeville couple who marry, raise their family, and never leave show business. Most of the action takes place on the boards with just enough of a story to fill in between the acts. Dailey and Grable are charming together. A hit song from the movie is "You Do" by Mack Gordon and Joseph Myrow.

Chuck Arnold / YOU WERE MEANT FOR ME, 1948, 20th Century-Fox, d-Lloyd Bacon.

Dailey is a bandleader married to small-town girl Jeanne Crain. They tour midwest towns during the Depression, hoping for a break. When the jobs run out, they go to live with her folks, but he can't stand small-town living and takes off. When he lands a job with a hotel band in New York, he sends for Crain. Songs and musical numbers include "Crazy Rhythm" and the title song.

Skid / WHEN MY BABY SMILES AT ME, 1948, 20th Century-Fox, d-Walter Lang.

Dailey is a putty-nosed burlesque comic who winds up in Bellevue Hospital when his once successful career hits the skids. Two new songs in the production are "By the Way" and "What Did I Do?" by Mack Gordon and Joseph Myrow.

Bill Kluggs / WHEN WILLIE COMES MARCHING HOME, 1950, 20th Century-Fox, d-John Ford.

Dailey is the first in his home town to enlist in World War II, but finds himself assigned locally as an instructor, while everyone else goes off to the shooting war. He continues to seek a transfer but is turned down until he replaces a gunner who is sick. Dailey is forced to bail out over France where he meets beautiful Corinne Calvet. With her help he locates German rocket emplacements, escapes, and back in the

United States, is sworn to secrecy. As far as people in his home town are concerned, he's never been away.

Jay Hanna "Dizzy" Dean / THE PRIDE OF ST. LOUIS, 1952, 20th Century-Fox, d-Harmon Jones.
In another of Hollywood's gee-whiz biopics of baseball players, Dailey portrays "immortal" Dizzy Dean, a pitcher for the St. Louis Cardinals and Chicago Cubs in the 1930s. The only resemblance to persons, living or dead, takes place on the baseball diamond. The homelife with Joanne Dru is all soap opera.

Tim Donahue / THERE'S NO BUSINESS LIKE SHOW BUSINESS, 1954, 20th Century-Fox, d-Walter Lang.
Dailey is the head of a family of vaudevillians that includes his wife (Ethel Merman) and children (Donald O'Connor, Mitzi Gaynor, and Johnnie Ray). The story is merely an excuse to catalog a long list of Irving Berlin songs, including the title number.

Ray Henderson / THE BEST THINGS IN LIFE ARE FREE, 1956, 20th Century-Fox, d-Michael Curtiz.
Dailey is Henderson of the team of songwriters, DeSylva, Brown, and Henderson in this fairly typical show business biopic. As one of the composers, Dailey gets a chance to spotlight some of the trio's best-known numbers including "Button Up Your Overcoat," "Birth of the Blues," and the title song.

OTHER ROLES

1940: *Holl* / THE MORTAL STORM; *Bill Ward* / DULCY; *Perth Nickerson* / THE CAPTAIN IS A LADY; *Bob Strong* / HULLABALOO; *Homer* / SUSAN AND GOD. **1941:** *Jim Reynolds* / KEEPING COMPANY; *Sonny Black* / THE GETAWAY; *Jimmy Walters* / ZIEGFELD GIRL; *Whitney King* / WASHINGTON MELODRAMA; *Bill Pattison* / LADY BE GOOD; *Al Haines* / DOWN IN SAN DIEGO; *Rex* / MOON OVER HER SHOULDER. **1942:** *Olaf Jensen* / THE SUNDAY PUNCH; *Herbert Delano* / MOKEY; *Dick Bulliett* / PANAMA HATTIE; *Kansas* / TIMBER; *Bob Edwards* / GIVE OUT, SISTER. **1948:** *Bert* / GIVE MY REGARDS TO BROADWAY; *Jim Hefferen* / CHICKEN EVERY SUNDAY. **1949:** *Timothy O'Connor* / YOU'RE MY EVERYTHING. **1950:** *guest* / I'LL GET BY; *Johnny Behind-the-Deuces* / TICKET TO TOMAHAWK; *Jack Moran* / MY BLUE HEAVEN. **1951:** *Teddy Sherman* / I CAN GET IT FOR YOU WHOLESALE; *Shep Dooley* / CALL ME MISTER. **1952:** *Sgt. Quirt* / WHAT PRICE GLORY? **1953:** *Doc Tilbee* / MEET ME AT THE FAIR; *Ed Nielson* / TAXI; *Bill Carter* / THE GIRL FROM NEXT DOOR; *Larry "Pop" Cooper* / THE KID FROM LEFT FIELD. **1955:** *Doug Hallerton* / IT'S ALWAYS FAIR WEATHER. **1956:** *"Jughead" Carson* / THE WINGS OF EAGLES; *Chuck Rodwell* / MEET ME IN LAS VEGAS. **1957:** *Arthur Turner* / OH MEN! OH WOMEN!; *Ernest Horton* / THE WAYWARD BUS. **1958:** *Cmdr. David Forest* / UNDERWATER WARRIOR. **1960:** *Ted Holt* / PEPE. **1962:** *Billy Campbell* / HEMINGWAY'S ADVENTURES OF A YOUNG MAN. **1977:** *Clyde Tolson* / THE PRIVATE FILES OF J. EDGAR HOOVER.

DARNELL, LINDA

(Monetta E. Darnell, 1921-1965)
Linda Darnell, who was once described as "the girl with the perfect face," began her movie career at age 15 with bit parts and was groomed for stardom by 20th Century-Fox. First featured as virginal heroines and demure young girls, her beauty and smoldering sexuality soon opened up more interesting roles as loose women and seductresses. She was never a great performer but she was a sultry, lightweight, dark-haired sex goddess. When roles for her became scarce, she took the usual route of playing in some foreign cheapies such as DONNE PROBITE (1953) and EL VALLE DE LOS ESPADOS (1963). She never had an opportunity to test the truth of her statement: "I am told when surface beauty is gone, the real woman emerges." She died in a fire at her home when only 44, reportedly while watching one of her old movies on television.

KEY ROLES

Zina Webb / BRIGHAM YOUNG—FRONTIERSMAN, 1940, 20th Century-Fox, d-Henry Hathaway.
Darnell is the only wife in evidence of polygamist Tyrone Power in this story of pioneering Mormons and their cross-country trek to the great Salt Lake in their quest for a home where they might practice their religion.

Lolita Quintero / THE MARK OF ZORRO, 1940, 20th Century-Fox, d-Rouben Mamoulian.
As the niece of the cruel tyrant ruling a district of Spanish California circa 1820, virginal Darnell is excited by the derring-do of Zorro, but put off by the foppish young Don (Tyrone Power) paying her court, without realizing that they are one and the same.

Sylvia / IT HAPPENED TOMORROW, 1944, United Artists, d-Rene Clair.
Darnell plays the girlfriend of Dick Powell, a reporter who is given the power to see tomorrow's newspaper headlines today so that he always gets the scoops. One headline he sees foretells his own death.

Tuptim / ANNA AND THE KING OF SIAM, 1946, 20th Century-Fox, d-John Cromwell.
Darnell is very unhappy as another wife of the king (Rex Harrison). She is befriended by Anna (Irene Dunne), the English woman who spends five years as secretary-tutor-confidante to the king in the 1860s.

Chihuahua / MY DARLING CLEMENTINE, 1946, 20th Century-Fox, d-John Ford.
Here Darnell is the fiery mistress of Doc Holliday (Victor Mature). She can't understand the indifferent way he treats her, and dies because of her love for him.

Amber St. Clair / FOREVER AMBER, 1947, 20th Century-Fox, d-Otto Preminger.
Darnell lightens her hair and sheds her inhibitions in this story of the time of Charles II of England. She becomes a London courtesan, having affairs with many men, and eventually becoming a favorite of the king. By today's standards it's pretty tame stuff, and playing a spicy wench proved almost too much for Darnell.

Lora May Hollingsway / A LETTER TO THREE WIVES, 1949, 20th Century-Fox, d-Joseph L. Mankiewicz.
In what may be her best performance, Darnell plays a girl from the wrong side of the tracks who lands her boss (Paul Douglas) as a husband. Later she is one of three wives to receive a letter from a mutual "friend" informing them that she has run off with one of their husbands.

OTHER ROLES

1939: *Marcia Bromely* / HOTEL FOR WOMEN; *Jane Norton* / DAYTIME WIFE. **1940:** *Carolyn Sayres* / STAR DUST; *Caroline* / CHAD HANNA. **1941:** *Carmen Espinosa* / BLOOD AND SAND; *Louise Murray* / RISE AND SHINE. **1942:** *Virginia Clemm* / THE LOVES OF EDGAR ALLAN POE. **1943:** *con's wife* / CITY WITHOUT MEN; *Virgin Mary* / THE SONG OF BERNADETTE. **1944:** *Dawn Starlight* / BUFFALO BILL; *Olga Urbenin* / SUMMER STORM; *Trudy Wilson* / SWEET AND LOWDOWN. **1945:** *Anne Livingstone* / THE GREAT JOHN L; *Stella* / FALLEN ANGEL; *Netta Longdon* / HANGOVER SQUARE. **1946:** *Edith Rogers* / CENTENNIAL SUMMER. **1948:** *Algeria Wedge* / THE WALLS OF JERICHO; *Daphne de Carter* / UNFAITHFULLY YOURS. **1949:** *Aggie Slattery* / SLATTERY'S HURRICANE; *Cecil Carver* / EVERYBODY DOES IT. **1950:** *Edie* / NO WAY OUT; *Elena Kenniston* / TWO FLAGS WEST. **1951:** *Denise Tourneur* / THE 13TH LETTER; *Evelyn Warren* / THE LADY PAYS OFF; *Dee* / THE GUY WHO CAME BACK. **1952:** *Elizabeth Smythe* / SATURDAY ISLAND; *Julie Bannon* / NIGHT WITHOUT SLEEP; *Edwina* / BLACKBEARD, THE PI-

RATE. **1953:** *Clare Shepperd* / SECOND CHANCE. **1956:** *Renata* / THE LAST FIVE MINUTES; *Amy Clarke* / DAKOTA INCIDENT. **1957:** *Ellen Stryker* / ZERO HOUR. **1965:** *Sadie* / BLACK SPURS.

DAVIES, MARION

(Marion Douras, 1897–1961)

Featured in the Ziegfeld Follies of 1916, this bright blonde was discovered by William Randolph Hearst, who made her his mistress. Seeing Davies as a new Lillian Gish, Hearst formed Cosmopolitan Pictures for the sole purpose of producing her movies. Pretty, and with a natural air for comedy, Davies played fragile and innocent girls. Hearst's overbearing attentions probably robbed her of a career in which her true talents could be used. Yet Davies was not overly ambitious and her honesty about herself is reflected in her observation: "With me it was 5% talent and 95% publicity." Still, she was unjustly caricatured in CITIZEN KANE, leaving many who had not seen her movies to believe that she was a no-talent creation of a rich man. Viewing her films today reveals that the fun-loving girl with a delightful stutter had a fine comedic sense and a pleasing film personality.

KEY ROLES

Mary Tudor / WHEN KNIGHTHOOD WAS IN FLOWER, 1922, Silent, Cosmopolitan / Paramount, d-Robert G. Vignola.

In this film Davies loves a commoner but agrees to marry Louis XII of France on the condition that she may choose her second husband. Shortly after the wedding Louis dies and Davies takes the commoner for her husband.

Patricia O'Day / LITTLE OLD NEW YORK, 1923, Silent, Cosmopolitan, d-Sidney Olcott.

Davies and her brother are en route from Ireland to America to claim a fortune left to the brother. But he dies during the trip and under those circumstances the fortune should go to another relative. In order to collect the inheritance, Davies poses as her brother and becomes quite close to the new true heir. When she reveals her true identity, they marry.

Janice Meredith / JANICE MEREDITH, 1924, Silent, Cosmopolitan / MGM, d-Mason Hopper.

Davies plays a coquettish daughter of a New Jersey family, caught up in the historical events of the Revolutionary War.

Phoebe Throssel / QUALITY STREET, 1927, Silent, Cosmopolitan / MGM, d-Sidney Franklin.

Davies's long-standing courtship with a doctor is further interrupted when he goes off to the Napoleonic Wars for ten years. Fearing that when he returns he will be disappointed in her aged appearance, she spruces herself up, passes herself off as her imaginary niece, and flirts with the doctor. But she has misjudged him, as he is happy when she reverts to her true self.

Peggy Pepper / SHOW PEOPLE, 1928, Silent, MGM, d-King Vidor.

Davies is a Georgia girl who goes to Hollywood to become a dramatic actress. At first she can find only roles in slapstick comedies, but the star of these shows falls for her and helps her achieve her goals. Initially she snubs her old benefactor but later comes to realize that she loves him.

Tony Flagg / THE BACHELOR FATHER, 1931, MGM, d-Robert Z. Leonard.

Davies is one of several illegitimate children of C. Aubrey Smith who gather together once before their father dies. For the times, it was a risqué comedy.

Polly Fisher / POLLY OF THE CIRCUS, 1932, MGM, d-Alfred Santell.

Davies is a trapeze artist who falls for local minister Clark Gable. They marry but he loses his church when the marriage becomes public knowledge.

Peg O'Connell / PEG O' MY HEART, 1933, MGM, d-Robert Z. Leonard.

Davies is excellent as an Irish colleen with whom an English nobleman falls in love. She's excellent in this old chestnut well past its prime in appeal.

Loretta Dalrymple / PAGE MISS GLORY, 1935, Cosmopolitan / Warners, d-Mervyn LeRoy.

Pat O'Brien plays a con man who wins a beauty contest with a composite picture of a nonexistent girl. He needs to find someone who looks like the photo and Davies fits the bill.

Mabel O'Dare / CAIN AND MABEL, 1936, Warners, d-Lloyd Bacon.

In this interesting but not totally successful comedy-drama, Davies plays a showgirl in love with prize-fighter Clark Gable.

OTHER ROLES

1917: *Romany* / RUNAWAY ROMANY; *Cecilia* / CECILIA OF THE PINK ROSES; *Elaine Brooks* / THE BURDEN OF PROOF. **1919:** *Violet Gray* / THE BELLE OF NEW YORK; *Mary* / GETTING MARY MARRIED; *Rue Carew* / THE DARK STAR; *Elizabeth Dalston* / THE CINEMA MURDER. **1920:** *April Poole* / APRIL FOLLY; *Stephanie Cleland* / THE RESTLESS SEX. **1921:** *Pauline Vandermuellen* / BURIED TREASURE; *Ethyl Hoyt* / ENCHANTMENT. **1922:** *Prudence Cole* / BEAUTY'S WORTH; *Aileen Barrett* / THE BRIDE'S PLAY; *Diana May* / THE YOUNG DIANA; *Eva King* / ADAM AND EVA. **1924:** *Princess Mary* / *Yolanda* / YOLANDA. **1925:** *Fely* / *Anne* / LIGHTS OF OLD BROADWAY; *Mamie Smith* / ZANDER THE GREAT. **1926:** *Beverly Calhoun* / BEVERLY OF GRAUSTARK. **1927:** *Tina* / THE RED MILL; *Tillie Jones* / TILLIE THE TOILER; *Marion* / THE FAIR CO-ED. **1928:** *Patricia Harrington* / THE PATSY; *Sally* / HER CARDBOARD LOVER. **1929:** *guest* / HOLLYWOOD REVUE OF 1929; *Marianne* / MARIANNE. **1930:** *Dulcy* / NOT SO DUMB; *Daisy* / THE FLORADORA GIRL. **1931:** *Joyce* / IT'S A WISE CHILD; *Jennifer Rarick* / FIVE AND TEN; *guest* / THE CHRISTMAS PARTY. **1932:** *Blondie McClune* / BLONDIE OF THE FOLLIES. **1933:** *Sylvia Bruce* / GOING HOLLYWOOD. **1934:** *Gale Loveless* / OPERATOR 13. **1936:** *Betsy Patterson* / HEARTS DIVIDED. **1937:** *Marge Winton* / EVER SINCE EVE.

DAVIS, BETTE

(Ruth Elizabeth Davis, 1908–1989)

Bette Davis was magnificent on the screen portraying spitfires who took no guff, and in real life she was every bit as independent and sure of herself. Her habit of spitting out venom at whoever crossed her made her a favorite of impersonators, but so far no one has come along who can match her contributions to the motion picture industry. Davis won Oscars for DANGEROUS and JEZEBEL, and nominations for DARK VICTORY; THE LETTER; THE LITTLE FOXES; NOW, VOYAGER; MR. SKEFFINGTON; ALL ABOUT EVE; THE STAR; and WHAT EVER HAPPENED TO BABY JANE? She was not even nominated for OF HUMAN BONDAGE, what may have been her best performance, because of her conflicts with Warner Brothers over her demands for more say in the roles she was given. She has been justifiably described as "First Lady of the American Screen," having time and time again fooled those who felt her career as a star was over. When Davis was first signed to a movie contract, producer Carl Laemmle complained she had "as much sex appeal as Slim Summerville," but she proved over the next 50 years that the public could recognize more than just the most obvious beauty. Her intensity and hard work rescued many an otherwise dismal movie because she made the audience believe in her character. This fighter and survivor, on and off the screen, has been America's most influential screen actress—tough, ambitious, vulnerable, and feminine. The secret of her success? "I learn the lines and pray to God."

KEY ROLES

Grace Blair / THE MAN WHO PLAYED GOD, 1932, Warners, d-John Adolphi.

George Arliss personally picked Davis to appear with him in this sound remake of his silent hit about a famous musician who loses his hearing, becomes bitter, but then finds comfort in helping others. Davis is willing to forsake her happiness with the man she loves to stay with and help Arliss. He learns of this by lip reading and sends her on to her lover.

Madge Norwood / CABIN IN THE COTTON, 1932, Warners, d-Michael Curtiz.

Davis is both sexy and nasty as the southern belle who gives a poor sharecropper's son (Richard Barthelmess) a royal runaround. The picture is worth seeing just to hear Davis's line, "Ah's love to kiss yuh, but ah jes' washed mah hay-uh."

Fay / 20,000 YEARS IN SING SING, 1933, Warners, d-Michael Curtiz.

When Davis, as Spencer Tracy's moll, kills a mobster while being visited by Tracy on a furlough from the penitentiary, he takes the blame and goes to the chair in her place.

Mildred Rogers / OF HUMAN BONDAGE, 1934, RKO, d-John Cromwell.

Davis is masterful as Somerset Maugham's slatternly English waitress and prostitute who nearly ruins the man who is obsessed with her, club-footed Leslie Howard. When she didn't earn an Academy Award nomination for this role, Hollywood was scandalized. The slight made it painfully clear that the awarding of Oscars was based on the political clout of the major studio heads and not on strength of performance. Her berating of Howard is truly a tirade to be appreciated: "You cad! You dirty swine! I never cared for you, not once. I was always making a fool of you. You bored me stiff. I hated you. It made me sick when I had to let you kiss me. I only did it because you begged me. You hounded me. You drove me crazy. And after you kissed me, I always used to wipe my mouth—wipe my mouth. But I made up for it. For every kiss, I had to laugh."

Ellen Garfield / FRONT PAGE WOMAN, 1935, Warners, d-Michael Curtiz.

In this film Davis is out to prove that she's just as good a reporter as her sweetheart George Brent—and she succeeds. As one might suspect, he doesn't even play fair.

Joyce Heath / DANGEROUS, 1935, Warners, d-Alfred E. Green.

Trying to make up for the affront of not nominating Davis for an Oscar the previous year, the Academy gave her one for a far inferior performance as a jinxed alcoholic actress who is saved from herself by an architect (Franchot Tone) who helps her make a comeback.

Gabrielle "Gabby" Maple / THE PETRIFIED FOREST, 1936, Warners, d-Archie Mayo.

Davis is a waitress working at a cafe / gas station in Arizona, who wants to travel to Paris to become an artist. Itinerant poet Leslie Howard makes her dream come true when he makes her beneficiary of his insurance policy and convinces killer Humphrey Bogart to shoot him so he may die for love.

Julie Marston / JEZEBEL, 1938, Warners, d-William Wyler.

Davis credits William Wyler for making a true actress of her while working with her on this film. He is credited with converting her mannerisms into adaptable techniques. Davis plays a willful southern belle who loses her fiancé (Henry Fonda) after making him jealous. She shows her true colors, however, when he is stricken with the plague.

Judith Traherne / DARK VICTORY, 1939, Warners, d-Edmund Goulding.

Davis portrays a spoiled Long Island society girl who develops a brain tumor. The operation performed by George Brent appears to be successful, but when Davis learns that the tumor will recur and take her life, she opts for a few months of happiness as Brent's wife. Her death scene is deeply moving. Her dying words are to her maid: "That you, Martha?...I don't want to be disturbed."

Charlotte Lovell / THE OLD MAID, 1939, Warners, d-Edmund Goulding.

In the course of the film Davis, then 31, ages from a sparkling youth in love with George Brent to a tight-lipped woman of 60 who has never forgotten him, even though she has let her scheming cousin (Miriam Hopkins) raise her illegitimate daughter as her own.

Queen Elizabeth / THE PRIVATE LIFE OF ELIZABETH AND ESSEX, 1939, Warners, d-Michael Curtiz.

Davis wanted Laurence Olivier as her co-star but ended up with Errol Flynn, an actor whose work habits offended her. Davis is splendid, but the film itself is neither historically or dramatically up to snuff.

Leslie Crosbie / THE LETTER, 1940, Warners, d-William Wyler.

Davis is remarkable as a woman who kills her lover when he attempts to break off the affair. She calmly lets her husband (Herbert Marshall) and their friends assume that it was done in self-defense. Unfortunately, she had written an incriminating letter to the man she killed which his Malayan wife is willing to sell. Davis is acquitted when her lawyer buys the letter, but she is later killed by the man's revenge-seeking wife. Before the end, Davis passionately confesses, "With all my heart, I still love the man I killed."

Maggie Patterson / THE GREAT LIE, 1941, Warners, d-Edmund Goulding.

Davis is a wealthy woman with a grand passion for George Brent. When he is reported killed in a plane crash, Davis offers a cash settlement to her rival (Mary Astor) if Astor will allow her to adopt the baby (Brent's) that Astor is carrying.

Regina Giddens / THE LITTLE FOXES, 1941, RKO, d-William Wyler.

In this film Davis plays a heartless woman whose husband (Herbert Marshall) refuses to give her money for her brothers' crooked scheme. When Marshall has a coronary, she stands back and allows him to die instead of fetching the medicine that will save his life.

Maggie Cutler / THE MAN WHO CAME TO DINNER, 1941, Warners, d-William Keighley.

Davis's role is secondary to that of Monte Woolley appearing as the acid-tongued author of the title. But she succeeds in the part, playing the only person who can handle the great man.

Charlotte Vale / NOW, VOYAGER, 1942, Warners, d-Irving Rapper.

Here Davis plays a repressed spinster who is helped out of her shell by psychiatrist Claude Rains. While on a cruise she meets and falls in love with a married man (Paul Henreid) whom she realizes she can never have completely. When at the end of the movie he asks if she will be happy, she replies, "Oh, Jerry, don't let's ask for the moon. We have the stars."

Sara Muller / WATCH ON THE RHINE, 1943, Warners, d-Herman Shumlin.

Davis's role in the Lillian Hellman story is minor but was intended to add distinction to a film for which the studio could expect only prestige and not much in the way of receipts. She is the American-born wife of German anti-Nazi leader Paul Lukas, who finds himself still pursued by fascists in Washington, D.C. She does deliver this inspiring speech: "Papa wrote it years ago. Papa said the only men on earth worth their time on earth were the men who would fight for other men. Papa said: 'We have struggled through from darkness. But man moves forward with each day and each hour to a better, freer life. That desire to go forward—that willingness to fight for it—cannot be put in a man. But when it is there—!' "

Kit Marlowe / OLD ACQUAINTANCE, 1943, Warners, d-Vincent Sherman.

Audiences cheered when Davis almost throttled her childhood friend (Miriam Hopkins) in this story of the jealousy between two authors. Apparently, Hopkins was an s.o.b. on the set as well.

Fanny Trellis / MR. SKEFFINGTON, 1944, Warners, d-Vincent Sherman.

Davis plays a vain, irresponsible society woman who marries Claude Rains because he lent $25,000 to her beloved brother. She believes that because she does not love her husband, she may have affairs whenever she wants. When she loses her looks in a bout with diphtheria, Rains, who has been blinded in a Nazi concentration camp, cannot see how grotesque she has become, and she ends up unselfishly caring for him.

Lilly Moffat / THE CORN IS GREEN, 1945, Warners, d-Irving Rapper.

Davis is a dedicated turn-of-the-century Welsh schoolteacher who devotes herself to transforming belligerent young miner John Dall (who works under the ground where the corn is green) into a successful student who wins a scholarship to Oxford.

Margo Channing / ALL ABOUT EVE, 1950, 20th Century-Fox, d-Joseph L. Mankiewicz.

Those who felt Davis had reached the end of her career as a star at age 40 had not reckoned with the tenacity of this remarkable woman and actress. In a truly marvelous performance, Davis is the fortyish stage actress who is used by the young, ambitious Anne Baxter in her own quest for stardom. Davis's line, "Fasten your seatbelts. It's going to be a bumpy night," is one of the best in the film.

Jane Hudson / WHAT EVER HAPPENED TO BABY JANE? 1962, Warners, d-Robert Aldrich.

As there was no love lost between the two screen queens, Davis must have enjoyed torturing Joan Crawford, both mentally and physically, in this modern gothic horror. The fact that Davis got an Oscar nomination and Crawford did not probably was enjoyed as well.

Charlotte Hollis / HUSH...HUSH, SWEET CHARLOTTE, 1965, 20th Century-Fox, d-Robert Aldrich.

In order to control Davis's fortune, her cousin (Olivia de Havilland) and doctor (Joseph Cotten) plot to drive the southern recluse mad.

Mrs. Taggart / THE ANNIVERSARY, 1968, 20th Century-Fox, d-Roy Ward Baker.

In this one Davis wears an eye patch to emphasize her evil nature. She plays a widow who keeps her three sons by a despised husband under her domination.

OTHER ROLES

1931: *Laura Madison* / BAD SISTER; *Margaret Carter* / SEED; *Janet Wetherby* / WATERLOO BRIDGE. **1932:** *Mary Lucy* / WAY BACK HOME; *Peggy* / THE MENACE; *Peggy Gardner* / HELL'S HOUSE; *Dallas O'Mara* / SO BIG; *Malbro* / THE RICH ARE ALWAYS WITH US; *Kay Russell* / THE DARK HORSE; *Ruth Wescott* / THREE ON A MATCH. **1933:** *Alabama* / PARACHUTE JUMPER; *Jenny Hartland* / THE WORKING MAN; *Helen Bauer* / EX-LADY; *Norma Phillips* / BUREAU OF MISSING PERSONS. **1934:** *Lynn Mason* / FASHIONS OF 1934; *Norma Frank* / THE BIG SHAKEDOWN; *Joan Martin* / JIMMY THE GENT; *Arlene Bradford* / FOG OVER FRISCO; *Patricia Berkeley* / HOUSEWIFE. **1935:** *Marie Roark* / BORDERTOWN; *Miriam Brady* / THE GIRL FROM TENTH AVENUE; *Julie Gardner* / SPECIAL AGENT. **1936:** *Daisy Appleby* / THE GOLDEN ARROW; *Valerie Purvis* / SATAN MET A LADY. **1937:** *Mary Dwight* / MARKED WOMAN; *Fluff Phillips* / KID GALAHAD; *Mary Donnell* / THAT CERTAIN WOMAN; *Joyce Arden* / IT'S LOVE I'M AFTER. **1938:** *Louise Elliott* / THE SISTERS. **1939:** *Empress Carlotta von Habsburg* / JUAREZ. **1940:** *Henriette Deluzy Desportes* / ALL THIS AND HEAVEN TOO. **1941:** *Joan Winfield* / THE BRIDE CAME C.O.D. **1942:** *Stanley Timberlake* / IN THIS OUR LIFE. **1943:** *guest* / THANK YOUR LUCKY STARS. **1944:** *guest* / HOLLYWOOD CANTEEN. **1946:** *Kate and Patricia Bosworth* / A STOLEN LIFE; *Christine Radcliffe* / DECEPTION. **1948:** *Susan Grieve* / WINTER MEETING; *Linda Gilman* / JUNE BRIDE. **1949:** *Rosa Moline* / BEYOND THE FOREST. **1951:** *Joyce Ramsey* / PAYMENT ON DEMAND. **1952:** *Janet Frobisher* / ANOTHER MAN'S POISON; *Marie Hoke* / PHONE CALL FROM A STRANGER; *Margaret Elliot* / THE STAR. **1955:** *Queen Elizabeth* / THE VIRGIN QUEEN. **1956:** *Alicia Hull* / STORM CENTER; *Agnes Hurley* / THE CATERED AFFAIR. **1959:** *Empress Catherine* / JOHN PAUL JONES; *Countess de Gue* / THE SCAPEGOAT. **1961:** *Apple Annie* / *"Mrs. E. Worthington Manville"* / POCKETFUL OF MIRACLES. **1964:** *Edith Phillips and Margaret De Lorca* / DEAD RINGER; *the countess* / THE EMPTY CANVAS; *Mrs. Gerald Hayden* / WHERE LOVE HAS GONE. **1965:** *Nanny* / THE NANNY. **1970:** *Wanda Fleming* / CONNECTING ROOMS. **1971:** *Bunny O'Hare* / BUNNY O'HARE. **1976:** *Aunt Elizabeth* / BURNT OFFERINGS. **1978:** *Letha* / RETURN FROM WITCH MOUNTAIN. **1980:** *Mrs. Aylwood* / THE WATCHER IN THE WOODS. **1986:** *herself* / DIRECTED BY WILLIAM WYLER. **1987:** *Libby Strong* / THE WHALES OF AUGUST.

DAY, DORIS

(Doris Kappelhoff, 1924–)

Day began her career as a band singer in the early 1930s, taking her professional surname from the pop song "Day by Day." In the movies she demonstrated her comedy talent, proving that she was more than just a girl next door with a pleasant singing voice. She received an Oscar nomination for PILLOW TALK. Before that the freckle-faced blonde with the very good figure poured herself into pure and wholesome roles. Her singing was always something special and her speaking voice was vivacious but her laughter, more a nervous twitter than anything else, never sounded true. When her movie career ended she went on to some TV success. She had many personal problems, though: two unhappy early marriages and the mismanagement of her life's savings by her husband of 17 years.

KEY ROLES

Georgia Garrett / ROMANCE ON THE HIGH SEAS, 1948, Warners, d-Michael Curtiz.

Given fourth billing in her debut, breezy Day stole the show singing "It's Magic." Day, then a club singer, got the part when Betty Hutton got pregnant. The movie is a lightweight story of assorted romances on an early day "Love Boat."

Jo Jordan / YOUNG MAN WITH A HORN, 1950, Warners, d-Michael Curtiz.

Band singer Day is the girl that jazz musician Kirk Douglas should have married rather than cold, selfish Lauren Bacall in this story inspired by the life of Bix Beiderbecke.

Judy Rice / STORM WARNING, 1950, Warners, d-Stuart Heisler.

Day is excellent in her first non-musical as a southern wife visited by her New York model sister (Ginger Rogers). They both get involved with the Ku Klux Klan, persecution, and violence.

Marjorie Winfield / ON MOONLIGHT BAY, 1951, Warners, d-Roy Del Ruth.

Based on the Booth Tarkington Penrod stories, this simple tale of a pretty girl falling in love with the boy next door is a fine nostalgia piece. Day sings the title song with Gordon MacRae, as well as the standards "Till We Meet Again," "Cuddle Up a Little Closer," "I'm Forever Blowing Bubbles," and "Pack Up Your Troubles."

Calamity Jane / CALAMITY JANE, 1953, Warners, d-David Butler.

Day is terrific as the gun-toting, buckskin-wearing stage driver who has a hankering for a cavalry officer, but has an off-again, on-again romance with Wild Bill Hickok (Howard Keel). Her songs include the Oscar-winning "Secret Love," "The Deadwood Stage," and "Just Blew in from the Windy City."

Laurie Tuttle / YOUNG AT HEART, 1955, Warners, d-Gordon Douglas.

In this slick remake of FOUR DAUGHTERS, Day is a respectable girl from a respectable New England home who marries an itinerant piano player (Frank Sinatra). She sings "Someone to Watch Over Me" by the Gershwins.

Ruth Etting / LOVE ME OR LEAVE ME, 1955, MGM, d-Charles Vidor.

No innocent girl next door is Day as twenties blues singer Ruth Etting. She marries racketeer James Cagney who pushes her to the top but also to a dependency on alcohol before she finally escapes him. The song "I'll Never Stop Loving You" earned an Oscar nomination but Day was more spectacular singing the title song and "Ten Cents a Dance."

Jo McKenna / THE MAN WHO KNEW TOO MUCH, 1956, Paramount, d-Alfred Hitchcock.

Day seems an odd choice for a Hitchcock heroine, having only blonde hair to recommend her, but she does not embarrass herself as the mother whose child has been kidnapped to ensure that she and husband Jimmy Stewart won't spill what they know about an assassination plot. She sings the Academy Award winning "Que Sera Sera."

Katie "Babe" Williams / THE PAJAMA GAME, 1957, Warners, d-Stanley Donen.

Playing against type, Day is a hard-boiled, been-around factory girl and union leader who fights with pajama factory manager John Raitt over a 7 cent per hour raise. Day is enchanting as she looks both sexy and wholesome in the title number finale.

Jan Morrow / PILLOW TALK, 1959, Universal, d-Michael Gordon.

Day shares a party line with amorous bachelor Rock Hudson and every time she attempts to make a call she hears him crooning some love song to one of his many girlfriends. Her interjections on the line convince Hudson that she is a repressed, sex-starved old maid. When he sees her, he changes his tune and, posing as a mild-mannered, wealthy Texan, he sets out to seduce her. It all works out delightfully in the end.

Cathy Timberlake / THAT TOUCH OF MINK, 1962, Universal, d-Delbert Mann.

Philandering Cary Grant sets his lecherous sights on thirtyish Day, but anytime he gets near the big moment she breaks out in a mysterious rash. This enables her to hold out for a wedding ring, but then he gets the rash.

OTHER ROLES

1949: *Martha Gibson* / MY DREAM IS YOURS; *Judy Adams* / IT'S A GREAT FEELING. **1950:** *Nanette Carter* / TEA FOR TWO; *Jan Wilson* / WEST POINT STORY. **1951:** *Melinda Howard* / LULLABY OF BROADWAY; *Grace LeBoy Khan* / I'LL SEE YOU IN MY DREAMS; *herself* / STARLIFT. **1952:** *Aimee Alexander* / THE WINNING TEAM; *Dynamite Jackson* / APRIL IN PARIS. **1953:** *Marjorie Winfield* / BY THE LIGHT OF THE SILVERY MOON. **1954:** *Candy Williams* / LUCKY ME. **1956:** *Julie Benston* / JULIE. **1958:** *Erica Stone* / TEACHER'S PET; *Isolde Poole* / THE TUNNEL OF LOVE. **1959:** *Jane Osgood* / IT HAPPENED TO JANE. **1960:** *Kate MacKay* / PLEASE DON'T EAT THE DAISIES; *Kit Preston* / MIDNIGHT LACE. **1962:** *Carol Templeton* / LOVER COME BACK; *Kitty Wonder* / JUMBO. **1963:** *Beverly Boyer* / THE THRILL OF IT ALL; *Ellen Wagstaff Arden* / MOVE OVER, DARLING. **1964:** *Judy Kimball* / SEND ME NO FLOWERS. **1965:** *Janet Harper* / DO NOT DISTURB. **1966:** *Jennifer Nelson* / THE GLASS BOTTOM BOAT. **1967:** *Patricia Fowler* / CAPRICE. **1968:** *Josie Minick* / THE BALLAD OF JOSIE; *Margaret Garrison* / WHERE WERE YOU WHEN THE LIGHTS WENT OUT?; *Abby McClure* / WITH SIX YOU GET EGG ROLL.

DAY, LARAINE

(Laraine Johnson, 1917–)

Laraine Day was best known for her role as nurse Mary Lamont in the Dr. Kildare movies, and for her marriage to baseball's Leo Durocher, when she was given the title "first lady of baseball" because of the interest she took in the game. Fresh-faced Day began her career with a bit role in STELLA DALLAS and then appeared in George O'Brien westerns at RKO under her real name. This middle-range star with the demure features left films in the 1950s to concentrate on her work within the Mormon church.

KEY ROLES

Mary Lamont / YOUNG DR. KILDARE, 1938, MGM, d-Harold S. Bucquet.

Day provided the love interest for Dr. Kildare (Lew Ayres) in eight films and did it so well that audiences prized the loyal nurse as much as the dedicated doctor.

Carol Fisher / FOREIGN CORRESPONDENT, 1940, United Artists, d-Alfred Hitchcock.

Herbert Marshall plays Day's dear old dad, who appears to be a man of peace at the beginning of World War II. Things get pretty rough for Joel McCrea, with whom Day has fallen in love, before all of the misdeeds have been exposed.

Maeve O'Riorden / MY SON, MY SON, 1940, United Artists, d-Charles Vidor.

Brian Aherne plays a father who bestows all of his riches on his son (Louis Hayward). The latter then becomes a spoiled, vicious person who destroys Day, the daughter of the father's best friend.

Mary Dugan / THE TRIAL OF MARY DUGAN, 1941, MGM, d-Norman Z. McLeod.

Voted 1940's most promising newcomer, Day is a girl on trial for murder, with both prosecution and defense counsels changing their feelings toward her before the case is resolved.

Nora Davis / JOURNEY FOR MARGARET, 1942, MGM, d-W. S. Van Dyke.

In this heart-tugger about wartime Europe, Day and her husband (Robert Young), a London-based reporter, adopt blitz orphan Margaret O'Brien. It was always tough to be matched with the moppet with the exceptional emotional range, but Day held her own.

Dorothy Bryant / MR. LUCKY, 1943, RKO, d-H. C. Potter.

Day is the main reason Cary Grant doesn't carry through with his plans to use a "Bundles for Britain" operation as a front for his gambling schemes.

Helen / THOSE ENDEARING YOUNG CHARMS, 1945, RKO, d-Lewis Allen.

Bill Williams makes the mistake of introducing his girl, Day, to pilot Robert Young, over whom she flips. At first it looks like Young is just out for a quick score before shipping out, but he gets a change of heart and becomes the marrying kind.

Nancy Blair / THE LOCKET, 1946, RKO, d-John Brahm.

Playing against type, Day is believable in the role of a girl with an obsession which leads her to kill one man, let another die for the crime, drive a third to suicide, and ruin the happiness of two others who dearly love her. All of this seems to be the result of some childhood misunderstanding about a missing locket.

Lydia Rice / THE HIGH AND THE MIGHTY, 1954, Warners, d-William A. Wellman.

Day is one of many cast members who give laudatory performances in this pre-AIRPORT, near-tragedy-in-the-sky movie.

OTHER ROLES

1937: *girl at soda fountain* / STELLA DALLAS. **1938:** *Betty Holden* / BORDER G-MEN; *Peg Smith* / SCANDAL STREET; *Carol Banning* / PAINTED DESERT; *Letty Meade* / THE ARIZONA LEGION; *Eileen Daly* / SERGEANT MADDEN. **1939:** *Mary Lamont* / CALLING DR. KILDARE; *Mrs. Richard Lancing* / TARZAN FINDS A SON; *Mary Lamont* / SECRET OF DR. KILDARE. **1940:** *Linda Rogers* / I TAKE THIS WOMAN; *Kate Lattimer* / AND ONE WAS BEAUTIFUL; *Mary Lamont* / DR. KILDARE'S STRANGE CASE; *Mary Lamont* / DR. KILDARE COMES HOME; *Mary Lamont* / DR. KILDARE'S CRISIS. **1941:** *Lucia Pell* / THE BAD MAN; *Mary Lamont* / THE PEOPLE VS. DR. KILDARE; *Mary Lamont* / DR. KILDARE'S WEDDING DAY; *Miss Cronin* / UNHOLY PARTNERS; *Dr. A. Martha Kent* / KATHLEEN. **1942:** *Edwina Brown* / FINGERS AT THE WINDOW; *Gail Farwood* / A YANK ON THE BURMA ROAD. **1944:** *Madeleine* / THE STORY OF DR. WASSELL; *Norah* / BRIDE BY MISTAKE. **1945:** *Leigh Rand* / KEEP YOUR POWDER DRY. **1947:** *Maura Alexander* / TYCOON. **1948:** *Stephanie Gaylord* / MY DEAR SECRETARY. **1949:** *Nan Collins* / I MARRIED A COMMUNIST; *Jane Bandle* / WITHOUT HONOR. **1956:** *Sue* / THREE FOR JAMIE DAWN; *Gwen Taylor* / THE TOY TIGER. **1960:** *Marian Forbes* / THE THIRD VOICE.

DEAN, JAMES

(1931–1955)

James Dean was already dead when his second feature film was shown in theaters. He was killed in a car crash at the age of 24. To many, though, his legend was already ensured and he became the personification of cool for young men and women of the 1950s. Speaking of his reason for acting, Dean explained, "I act for the same reason most actors act, to express the fantasies in which I have involved myself." After his death, many of his intended roles were given to Paul Newman.

KEY ROLES

Jim "Jimbo" / REBEL WITHOUT A CAUSE, 1955, Warners, d-Nicholas Ray.

Dean's performance in this film was the inspiration for a whole series of actors, including Paul Newman. As the vulnerable adolescent son of a well-to-do family, Dean gets into constant trouble with both his peers and his elders. The title of the film really tells it all. Dean is rebelling but it is not clear what he is rebelling against. At the time, though, a lot of young people seemed to know just how he felt.

Cal Trask / EAST OF EDEN, 1955, Warners, d-Elia Kazan.

Dean is a rebellious adolescent growing up in a California farming valley in 1917. His father is a stern Bible-reading man who is unable to show love. His mother is believed dead but runs a brothel in a nearby community. It's John Steinbeck's interpretation of the Cain and Abel story.

Jett Rink / GIANT, 1956, Warners, d-George Stevens.

In this Edna Ferber story, Dean plays the brooding, angry cowhand who becomes an oil baron, richer than the cattle king (Rock Hudson) whom he hates. In his own mind, Dean believes himself worthy of the love of Hudson's wife (Elizabeth Taylor).

OTHER ROLES

1951: *youth* / HAS ANYBODY SEEN MY GAL?; *sailor* / SAILOR BEWARE. **1952:** *GI* / FIXED BAYONETS. **1953:** *bit* / TROUBLE ALONG THE WAY.

DE CARLO, YVONNE

(Peggy Yvonne Middleton, 1922–)

Born in Vancouver, Canada, dancer Yvonne de Carlo became a star playing exotic women wearing bangles, baubles, and yashmaks in a series of "easterns." This dark-haired, dark-skinned actress played Arabs, mulattos, Mexicans, Polynesians, and Native Americans. After her film career as a leading lady was essentially over, she became a favorite of the young set as Lily on TV's "The Munsters."

KEY ROLES

Salome / SALOME, WHERE SHE DANCED, 1945, Universal, d-Charles Lamont.

This stinker was de Carlo's big break, and in some places it has achieved cult status. In it she plays a Viennese dancer who is suspected of being a spy and flees to Drinkman's Wells, Arizona, where the unlawful citizens change its name to that of the heroine.

Cara de Talavera / SONG OF SCHEHERAZADE, 1947, Universal, d-Walter Reisch.

In this campy biopic of Russian composer Rimsky-Korsakov, de Carlo is the inspiration for the famous "Scheherazade," and she dances the title role in its premier at the St. Petersburg Opera House.

Inez / CASBAH, 1948, Universal, d-John Berry.

The story of Pepe Le Moko had been told twice before; once with Jean Gabin and once with Charles Boyer. This is the musical version, and the thief of Algeria (Tony Martin) has the voice for the part. De Carlo is the native girl whom Martin rejects in favor of Marta Toren.

Anna / CRISS CROSS, 1949, Universal, d-Robert Siodmak.

In this film noir, de Carlo is married to gangster Dan Duryea, and is the former wife of Burt Lancaster. When she and Lancaster meet some time later, they discover the spark is still there. This leads to tragic consequences as Lancaster turns to crime for her.

Nita St. James / THE CAPTAIN'S PARADISE, 1953, Great Britain, British Lion, d-Anthony Kimmins.

Steamer captain Alec Guinness travels back and forth between his wife in Tangier and his wife in Gibraltar. De Carlo and Celia Johnson are the two wives, each suited to different aspects of the captain's personality. De Carlo satisfies his wild side; Johnson provides the quiet peace of a stay-at-home type. His problems come when the two women's paths cross and each wants the life of the other.

Minna / MAGIC FIRE, 1954, Republic, d-William Dieterle.

De Carlo is the love of composer Richard Wagner in this boring biopic with a lot of music but little story or character development.

Sephora / THE TEN COMMANDMENTS, 1956, Paramount, d-Cecil B. DeMille.

De Carlo is the wife that Moses (Charlton Heston) finds in the desert after he is driven from Egypt. She's the oldest of seven daughters, and the one with the most intelligence and spirit.

Bridget Kelly / DEATH OF A SCOUNDREL, 1956, RKO, d-Charles Martin.

De Carlo is one of the stepping stones used by Czech scoundrel George Sanders in this film about the notorious financial manipulator Serge Rubenstein.

Lily Munster / MUNSTER, GO HOME, 1966, Universal, d-Earl Bellamy.

De Carlo recreates her TV hit on the big screen in this story of the Munsters' sea voyage to England where they have inherited a large manor.

OTHER ROLES

1942: *show girl* / THIS GUN FOR HIRE; *bathing beauty* / HARVARD, HERE I COME; *handmaiden* / ROAD TO MOROCCO; *girl* / LUCKY JORDAN; *student* / YOUTH ON PARADE. **1943:** *chorus girl* / LET'S FACE IT; *secretary* / THE CRYSTAL BALL; *singer in quartet* / SALUTE FOR THREE; *girl in cafe* / FOR WHOM THE BELL TOLLS; *girl* / TRUE TO LIFE; *girl* / SO PROUDLY WE HAIL!; *Wah-Tah* / THE DEERSLAYER. **1944:** *office worker* / PRACTICALLY YOURS; *native girl* / THE STORY OF DR. WASSELL; *secretary* / STANDING ROOM ONLY; *girl* / HERE COME THE WAVES; *girl in queen's retinue* / KISMET; **1945:** *Lorena Dumont* / FRONTIER GAL. **1947:** *Gina* / BRUTE FORCE; *Francesca* / SLAVE GIRL. **1948:** *Lola Montez* / BLACK BART; *Sequin* / RIVER LADY. **1949:** *Calamity Jane* / CALAMITY JANE AND SAM BASS; *Linda Marlowe* / THE GAL WHO TOOK THE WEST. **1950:** *Deborah McCoy* / BUCCANEER'S GIRL; *Princess Scheherazade* / THE DESERT HAWK. **1951:** *Yasmin Pallas* / HOTEL SAHARA; *Julie Madden* / TOMAHAWK; *Candace Surrency* / SILVER CITY. **1952:** *Adelaide McCall* / THE SAN FRANCISCO STORY; *Roxy McClanahan* / SCARLET ANGEL; *Luana* / HURRICANE SMITH. **1953:** *Maria* / SOMBRERO; *Drouette* / SEA DEVILS; *Yvette* / FORT ALGIERS. **1954:** *Virginia* / THE CONTESSA'S SECRET; *Carmelita Carjas* / BORDER RIVER; *Rosa and Tonya Melo* / PASSION; *Serena McGluskey* / TONIGHT'S THE NIGHT. **1955:** *Abby* / SHOTGUN; *Rosalind Dee* / FLAME OF THE ISLANDS. **1956:** *Hannah Montgomery* / RAW EDGE. **1957:** *Amantha Starr* / BAND OF ANGELS. **1958:** *Mary Magdalene* / MARY MAGDALENE. **1959:** *Natalie DuFort* / TIMBUKTU. **1963:** *Louise Warren* / MCLINTOCK! **1964:** *Dolores* / A GLOBAL AFFAIR; *Ellie Irish* / LAW OF THE LAWLESS. **1967:** *Laura Mannon* / HOSTILE GUNS. **1968:** *Jill Wyler* / ARIZONA BUSHWHACKERS; *Sally Hallson* / THE POWER. **1970:** *Valerie* / THE DELTA FACTOR. **1971:** *Constance Cumberland* / THE SEVEN MINUTES. **1974:** *female rustler* / BLAZING STEWARDESSES. **1975:** *Julia* / IT SEEMED LIKE A GOOD IDEA AT THE TIME. **1976:** *cleaning woman* / WON TON TON, THE DOG WHO SAVED HOLLYWOOD. **1977:** *Emma Bub / sheriff's wife / high priestess* / SATAN'S CHEERLEADERS. **1979:** *Jugula* / GRANDDAUGHTER OF DRACULA, (NOCTURNA). **1980:** *Mrs. Engels* / SILENT SCREAM; *Susan Ames* / GUYANA, CULT OF THE DAMNED; *Teresa Anastas* / THE MAN WITH BOGART'S FACE. **1982:** *mother* / LIAR'S MOON.

DEE, SANDRA

(Alexandra Zuck, 1942–)

At the peak of her popularity, Sandra Dee was petite, cute, and curvy. She usually played sexy nymphets in roles that might be described as early Doris Day. The boys were after her but she always kept her virginity—well, almost always. She was everyone's notion of what a high school prom queen should look like but while very popular in the 1960s, she wasn't able to make a career of merely being cute.

KEY ROLES

Susie Meredith / IMITATION OF LIFE, 1959, Universal-International, d-Douglas Sirk.

Dee plays Lana Turner's daughter in this story of a woman who becomes wealthy because of her maid's pancake recipe. The maid's life, though, is laced with tragedy when her daughter passes for white.

Gidget Lawrence / GIDGET, 1959, Columbia, d-Paul Wendkos.

Dee is a teenager who falls for an older surfer of whom her parents disapprove until they discover that he's the son of their best friends.

Molly Jorgenson / A SUMMER PLACE, 1959, Warners, d-Delmer Daves.

In her best role Dee plays a youngster who falls in love with the son of her father's mistress. When the father and mistress marry, the adjustment period for the two youngsters, Dee and Troy Donahue, is complicated by the behavior of the other two parents.

Tammy Tyree / TAMMY TELL ME TRUE, 1961, Universal-International, d-Harry Keller.

Dee takes over for Debbie Reynolds in the sequel to the very popular movie about a backwoods tomboy. In this production she goes to college and charms everyone she meets.

OTHER ROLES

1957: *Evelyn Leslie* / UNTIL THEY SAIL. **1958:** *Jane Broadbent* / THE RELUCTANT DEBUTANTE; *Melinda Grant* / THE RESTLESS

YEARS. **1959:** *Pat Beasley* / STRANGER IN MY ARMS; *voice only* / SNOW QUEEN; *Rosalie Stocker* / THE WILD AND THE INNOCENT. **1960:** *Catherine Cabot* / PORTRAIT IN BLACK. **1961:** *Juliet Moulsworth* / ROMANOFF AND JULIET; *Sandy Stevens* / COME SEPTEMBER. **1962:** *Chantel Stacy Wright* / IF A MAN ANSWERS. **1963:** *Tammy Tyree* / TAMMY AND THE DOCTOR; *Mollie Michaelson* / TAKE HER, SHE'S MINE. **1964:** *Cynthia Dulaine* / I'D RATHER BE RICH. **1965:** *Joan Howell* / THAT FUNNY FEELING. **1966:** *Amy Franklin* / A MAN COULD GET KILLED. **1967:** *Heather Halloran* / DOCTOR, YOU'VE GOT TO BE KIDDING; *Daphne Shaw* / ROSIE!

DE HAVEN, GLORIA

(1924–)

Gloria De Haven, singer, dancer, and lightweight actress, came from a vaudevillian family, her father and mother being the popular entertainers Carter De Haven and Flora Parker. Her film career as the heroine's sister or best friend lasted as long as the Hollywood musical had an audience. After that there were no roles for the peppy strawberry blonde.

KEY ROLES

Minerva / BEST FOOT FORWARD, 1943, MGM, d-Edward Buzzell.

De Haven's is a minor supporting role in this story of a glamorous film star (Lucille Ball) accepting an invitation to a military school ball. Reviewers, though, gave De Haven special mention as a comer.

Jean Deyo / TWO GIRLS AND A SAILOR, 1944, MGM, d-Richard Thorpe.

De Haven and her sister (June Allyson) are a singing team with the Henry James and Xavier Cugat bands, who turn their home into a place to entertain servicemen. One sailor (Van Johnson) arranges for a warehouse to be given to the girls so they can expand their operations. He keeps his gift a secret as he falls first for De Haven and then for Allyson.

Muriel McComber / SUMMER HOLIDAY, 1948, MGM, d-Rouben Mamoulian.

In this musical remake of "Ah, Wilderness," De Haven is the girl to whom Mickey Rooney recites poetry that her father considers scandalous. Denied De Haven's company, Rooney seeks comfort in alcohol and a "scarlet" woman.

Mrs. Carter De Haven / THREE LITTLE WORDS, 1950, MGM, d-Richard Thorpe.

De Haven has the pleasure of portraying her mother on the screen in this ordinary biopic of the careers of songwriters Harry Ruby and Bert Kalmar.

Abigail Falbury / SUMMER STOCK, 1950, MGM, d-Charles Walters.

De Haven convinces sister Judy Garland to allow a theater troupe, led by her latest love (Gene Kelly), to use the old family barn to rehearse for a show. When it's just about time to take the show on the road, Garland steps in, saves the show, and gets Kelly.

Colette d'Avril (Janie Mitchell) / SO THIS IS PARIS, 1954, Universal, d-Richard Quine.

De Haven is one of three girls who meet three American sailors on leave in Paris and, instead of making love, they stage a benefit to help war orphans. De Haven does her best work in a hot rendition of "I Can't Give You Anything But Love."

OTHER ROLES

1936: *bit* / MODERN TIMES. **1940:** *bit* / THE GREAT DICTATOR; *Enid* / SUSAN AND GOD. **1941:** *debutante* / TWO-FACED WOMAN; *Evelyn Thomas* / KEEPING COMPANY; *Anne Logan* / THE PENALTY. **1943:** *guest* / THOUSANDS CHEER. **1944:** *Patsy Demming* / BROADWAY RHYTHM; *Christine* / STEP LIVELY; *Laura Ronson* / THE THIN MAN COMES HOME. **1945:** *Edna* / BETWEEN TWO WOMEN. **1949:** *Lili* / SCENE OF THE CRIME; *Fabienne Corday* / THE DOCTOR AND THE GIRL; *Sarah Jane Winfield* / YES, SIR, THAT'S MY BABY. **1950:** *Ellen Goodrich* / THE YELLOW CAB MAN; *Terry Martin* / I'LL GET BY. **1951:** *Hannah Holbrook* / TWO TICKETS TO BROADWAY. **1953:** *Angela Toland* / DOWN AMONG THE SHELTERING PALMS. **1955:** *Taffy Tremaine* / THE GIRL RUSH. **1976:** *president's girl* / WON TON TON, THE DOG WHO SAVED HOLLYWOOD.

DE HAVILLAND, OLIVIA

(1916–)

This remarkably talented and attractive woman added a special elegance to movies that otherwise would be mere action pictures. At the peak of her career she portrayed simple women who were able to call upon hidden strengths to survive extreme emotional upheavals. Seemingly warm and gentle, de Havilland nevertheless was a battler who grew tired of being handed insubstantial roles. Her fight for better roles paid off when she won a lawsuit to end her contractual obligations to Warner Brothers. Although the litigation kept her away from the cameras for nearly three years, in the next five years she received Academy Award nominations for four films: TO EACH HER OWN and THE HEIRESS, for which she won the award, and THE SNAKE PIT and HOLD BACK THE DAWN. Earlier she had won the Best Supporting Actress Award for her role in GONE WITH THE WIND. After her victory in the courts and her demonstration of her remarkable acting talents, de Havilland seemed to lose interest in her career, moving to France to live with her husband and working only sporadically in the 1960s and 1970s. In addition to her movie work, de Havilland made several TV movies including THE SCREAMING WOMAN (1972), ROOTS: THE NEXT GENERATION (1979), MURDER IS EASY (1982), and CHARLES AND DIANA: A ROYAL ROMANCE (1982).

KEY ROLES

Hermia / A MIDSUMMER NIGHT'S DREAM, 1935, Warners, d-Max Reinhardt and William Dieterle.

De Havilland was chosen to make her film debut playing the role she had done in college, where she was seen by producer Max Reinhardt. For an actress of such limited experience, she was a delight as one of the star-crossed lovers.

Arabella Bishop / CAPTAIN BLOOD, 1935, Warners, d-Michael Curtiz.

In the first of many appearances with Errol Flynn, de Havilland is the niece of a cruel Caribbean planter (Lionel Atwill) to whom Flynn and other convicted British rebels and criminals are sent to become slaves. Flynn escapes and takes up pirating, is appointed governor of the island, and wins de Havilland's love.

Angela Guisseppi / ANTHONY ADVERSE, 1936, Warners, d-Mervyn LeRoy.

De Havilland is the heroine in this rather lengthy tale of the adventures of young Anthony Adverse (Fredric March) in 19th-century America and Mexico. Even here she must have wondered why all she was asked to do was look attractive and play a foil for the male lead.

Maid Marian / THE ADVENTURES OF ROBIN HOOD, 1938, Warners, d-William Keighley and Michael Curtiz.

De Havilland is charming, brave, and demure as the noblewoman who comes to love the bandit Robin Hood, who is trying to save England's throne for Richard the Lion Hearted and put an end to Norman persecution of the Saxons.

Melanie Hamilton / GONE WITH THE WIND, 1939, MGM, d-Victor Fleming and others.

Melanie Hamilton is so sweetly good, caring, and understanding—in contrast to wild and selfish Scarlett O'Hara—that with another actress in the part audiences might find her goodness cloying. But de Havilland, whose role is more demanding than that of Vivien Leigh, makes the character believable and beloved.

Emmy Brown / HOLD BACK THE DAWN, 1941, Paramount, d-Mitchell Leisen.

De Havilland is an American schoolteacher in Mexico whom Charles Boyer woos and weds even though he does not love her, so he can get into the United States. The romantic pairing of Boyer and de Havilland is quite effective.

Charlotte Brontë / DEVOTION, 1946 (completed in 1943), Warners, d-Curtis Bernhardt.

Because of her outspoken criticism of the studio's policies, de Havilland was given third billing after Ida Lupino and Paul Henreid in this romantically absurd story about the Brontë sisters. De Havilland's sister Joan Fontaine had been planned for the role taken by Lupino, but the sisters' feud had reached a point where the teaming was impossible. The feud appears to have been over the fact that Fontaine received an Academy Award for Best Actress before de Havilland did, and flaunted the fact.

Terry and Ruth Collins / THE DARK MIRROR, 1946, International, d-Robert Siodmak.

De Havilland plays identical twins—one sweet and demure, the other wild and free-spirited. One may have killed a suitor, but which one?

Josephine Norris / TO EACH HIS OWN, 1946, Paramount, d-Mitchell Leisen.

De Havilland gives a moving performance as an unwed mother who gives her son up for adoption and lives to regret it. Years later, as a middle-aged woman in wartime London, she meets her grown-up son (John Lund) and they are brought together at last. With the last line of the picture, Lund (who had also played his father) acknowledges de Havilland by asking, "May I have this dance, Mother?"

Virginia Stuart Cunningham / THE SNAKE PIT, 1947, 20th Century-Fox, d-Anatole Litvak.

The subject matter of a mental institution makes it difficult to describe this film as enjoyable, but de Havilland's performance as a mentally deranged housewife who lives through the horrifying experiences of an asylum is top notch and extremely sympathetic. The film's title comes from de Havilland's line, "I remembered once reading in a book that long ago they used to put insane people into pits full of snakes. I think they figured that something which might drive a normal person insane might shock an insane person back into sanity."

Catherine Sloper / THE HEIRESS, 1949, Paramount, d-William Wyler.

In what must rank as one of the finest performances ever seen on the screen, de Havilland is a plain and shy spinster, daughter of a prominent Washington Square physician (Ralph Richardson). Handsome Montgomery Clift pays her court and she is thrilled, but Richardson suspects Clift of being a fortune hunter, believing no one could actually care for his talentless daughter. He proves that Clift is a cad by offering him a large sum of money to go away from her. She is not thankful for her father's interference or for his opinion of her and in a neat change of character she "who has been taught by masters" cruelly speaks no more to her father as he dies and she has her revenge on Clift as well.

Rachel Ashley / MY COUSIN RACHEL, 1952, 20th Century-Fox, d-Henry Koster.

Richard Burton comes to believe that de Havilland has poisoned her husband (his foster father). He swears revenge, but when she arrives in Cornwall, he finds himself falling in love with her. She refuses to marry him, but does nurse him through an illness apparently caused by poison. When it seems she is about to leave him, he confronts her on a cliff, causing her to accidentally fall to her death.

Miriam Deering / HUSH...HUSH, SWEET CHARLOTTE, 1965, 20th Century-Fox, d-Robert Aldrich.

De Havilland and physician Joseph Cotten conspire to drive her cousin (Bette Davis), an ex-southern belle and recluse, mad so they may control her fortune.

OTHER ROLES

1935: *Lucille Jackson* / THE IRISH IN US; *Dolly* / ALIBI IKE. **1936:** *Elsa Campbell* / THE CHARGE OF THE LIGHT BRIGADE. **1937:** *Catherine Hilton* / CALL IT A DAY; *Germaine de la Corbe* / THE GREAT GARRICK; *Marcia West* / IT'S LOVE I'M AFTER; *Serena Ferris* / GOLD IS WHERE YOU FIND IT. **1938:** *Lorri Dillingwell* / FOUR'S A CROWD; *Margaret Richards* / HARD TO GET. **1939:** *Irene Dale* / WINGS OF THE NAVY; *Abbie Irving* / DODGE CITY; *Lady Penelope Gray* / THE PRIVATE LIVES OF ELIZABETH AND ESSEX; *Gwen Manders* / RAFFLES. **1940:** *Amelia Cullen* / MY LOVE CAME BACK; *Kit Carson Halliday* / SANTA FE TRAIL. **1941:** *Amy Lind* / STRAWBERRY BLONDE; *Elizabeth Bacon Custer* / THEY DIED WITH THEIR BOOTS ON. **1942:** *Ellen Turner* / THE MALE ANIMAL; *Roy Timberlake* / IN THIS OUR LIFE. **1943:** *Smokey* / GOVERNMENT GIRL; *guest* / THANK YOUR LUCKY STARS; *Maria O'Rourke* / PRINCESS O'ROURKE. **1945:** *Margie Dawson* / THE WELL-GROOMED BRIDE. **1955:** *Ava de Mendoza* / THAT LADY. **1956:** *Kristina Hedvigson* / NOT AS A STRANGER; *Joan Fiske* / THE AMBASSADOR'S DAUGHTER. **1958:** *Linnett Moore* / THE PROUD REBEL. **1960:** *Lady Maggie Loddon* / LIBEL. **1962:** *Margaret Johnson* / THE LIGHT IN THE PIAZZA. **1964:** *Mrs. Hilyard* / LADY IN A CAGE. **1969:** *Deborah Hadley* / THE ADVENTURERS. **1972:** *mother superior* / POPE JOAN. **1977:** *Queen Anne* / THE FIFTH MUSKETEER; *Emily Livingston* / AIRPORT '77. **1978:** *Maureen Schuster* / THE SWARM.

DEL RIO, DOLORES

(Dolores Asunsolo, 1905–1983)

Among the most beautiful women to ever appear on the screen, Mexican actress Delores Del Rio played many exotic roles in silent movies of the late 1920s and early 1930s. With the coming of sound, her charming accent typecast her in ethnic roles—not as a fiery Mexican like Lupe Velez but as a dignified lady. Later in her career she made most of her films in Mexico, winning four Arieles, the equivalent of the U.S. Oscar. As Mexico's foremost actress, she made several impressive movies directed by Emilio Fernandez and co-starring Pedro Armendariz. Her secret for maintaining exquisite beauty, which kept her as lovely in her sixties as she was in her twenties, was: "Sleep 16 hours a day, do not smoke and do not drink." She also correctly noted, "So long as a woman has twinkles in her eyes, no man notices whether she has wrinkles under them."

KEY ROLES

Carmen / THE LOVES OF CARMEN, 1927, Silent, Fox Films, d-Raoul Walsh.

This is the familiar story of Carmen, the gypsy who works in a cigar factory, and who seduces both a soldier and a bullfighter. When she tires of the soldier, he kills her at a bull ring.

Ramona / RAMONA, 1928, Silent, United Artists, d-Edwin Carewe.

Del Rio plays a half-breed adopted by a wealthy sheep rancher. She is treated cruelly, and when she discovers her ancestry, she defies her guardian and weds a young Indian chief. Their bliss is marred by the death of their daughter and his being accused of stealing horses. When he is killed, she suffers a nervous collapse, becoming a wandering outcast until the care of an old friend brings her back to the present.

Lucana / BIRD OF PARADISE, 1932, RKO, d-King Vidor.

When director King Vidor told David O. Selznick that the play "Bird of Paradise" was hopelessly outdated, the producer roared, "I don't care what story you use as long as we call it BIRD OF PARADISE and Del Rio jumps into a flaming volcano at the finish." And so it was done. Del Rio is a Polynesian girl who falls in love with sailor Joel McCrea and, after some incredibly happy times together, she sacrifices herself to the gods to save her people.

Belinha de Rezende / FLYING DOWN TO RIO, 1933, RKO, d-Thornton Freeland.

With the success of the first teaming of Fred Astaire and Ginger Rogers, people sometimes forget that the nominal leads of this movie are Del Rio and Gene Raymond. The story deals with Del Rio as an engaged Brazilian heiress who falls in love with bandleader Raymond.

Josette Martel / JOURNEY INTO FEAR, 1942, RKO, d-Norman Foster and Orson Welles.

Del Rio is a world-wise dancer who helps an American gunnery engineer (Joseph Cotten) who is being pursued by Gestapo agents. They share a ship with an interesting assortment of passengers as Cotten is smuggled home.

Maria Candelaria / MARIA CANDELARIA, 1943, Mexico, Clasa / Films Mundiales, d-Emilio Fernandez.

Del Rio won international acclaim for her portrayal of a tragic Indian peasant girl who, together with the man she loves, is hounded by the people of her primitive community. Her mother had once posed nude for an artist, and had been stoned to death.

Esperanza / FLOR SYLVESTRE, 1944, Mexico, Clasa / Films Mundiales, d-Emilio Fernandez.

Del Rio is a laborer's daughter who marries a landowner's son. When the son's father disowns him, he joins the revolutionary forces, and later is executed for killing his father in battle.

Mexican Woman / THE FUGITIVE, 1947, Argosy / RKO, d-John Ford.

Del Rio is a victim of the law in this story about a priest on the run in an anti-clerical country.

Spanish Woman / CHEYENNE AUTUMN, 1964, Warners, d-John Ford.

Del Rio's role is not large in this story about the ill treatment of the American Indians. It is the 1860s, and the Cheyennes are moved to a new reservation 1,500 miles away without being given the promised means of survival. When they begin the long trek back home, they are forced to fight the white man along the way.

OTHER ROLES

1925: *Carlotta de Silva* / JOANNA. **1926:** *Evelyn Iffield* / HIGH STEPPERS; *Jeanne Lamont* / PALS FIRST; *Rita Renault* / THE WHOLE TOWN'S TALKING. **1927:** *Charmaine* / WHAT PRICE GLORY? **1928:** *Katusha Maslova* / RESURRECTION; *Chela (Toni)* / THE GATEWAY OF THE MOON; *Berna* / THE TRAIL OF '98; *Carmelita de Granados* / NO OTHER WOMAN; *Tasia* / THE RED DANCE; *Rascha* / REVENGE. **1929:** *Evangeline* / EVANGELINE. **1930:** *Lita* / THE BAD ONE. **1932:** *Dolores* / GIRL OF THE RIO. **1934:** *Inez* / WONDER BAR; *Madame Dubarry* / MADAME DUBARRY. **1935:** *Rita Gomez* / IN CALIENTE; *Donna Alvares* / I LIVE FOR LOVE; *Inez, Duchess of Rye* / WIDOW FROM MONTE CARLO. **1936:** *Gaby Seymour* / ACCUSED. **1937:** *Carmen* / DEVIL'S PLAYGROUND; *Dolores Daria Sunnell* / LANCER SPY; *herself* / ALI BABA GOES TO TOWN. **1938:** *Leonore Dixon* / INTERNATIONAL SETTLEMENT. **1940:** *Eugenia "Jenny"* / THE MAN FROM DAKOTA. **1944:** *Margarita Perez* / LOS ABANDONODOS; *Amalita de Losrobles* / BUGAMBILIA. **1945:** *Estrella* / LA SELVA DE FUEGO. **1946:** *Magdalena and Maria Mendez* / LA ORTA. **1948:** *Mrs. Erlynne* / HISTORIA DE UNA MALA MUJER. **1949:** *Raimunda* / LA MALQUERIDA; *Amalia Estrada* / LA CASA CHICA. **1950:** *Dona Perfecta* / DONA PERFECTA. **1951:** *Deseda* / DESEDA. **1953:** *Maria Enriquetta* / REPARTAJE; *Marta* / EL NINO Y LA NIEBLA. **1954:** *Dominica* / SENORA AMA. **1956:** *herself* / TORERO! **1958:** *Chabela* / LA CUCARACHA; *Rosa* / A DONDE VAN NUESTROS HIJOS. **1960:** *Neddy Burton* / FLAMING STAR; *Mother* / EL PECADO DE UNA MADRE. **1966:** *Lady of the Dawn* / LA DAME DEL ALBA. **1967:** *Princess Mother* / MORE THAN A MIRACLE; *a revolutionary* / RIO BLANCO. **1978:** *Grandma* / THE CHILDREN OF SANCHEZ.

DE NIRO, ROBERT

(1943–)

Robert De Niro is a method actor with great drive and the ability to really "get into" his roles. He studies each part carefully months in advance so that during shooting he may spontaneously act as he imagines the character would act. He explains, "You have to earn the right to play a character." By all appearances his methods have proven successful. His intensity and dedication are sensed in each portrayal, and at times are overpowering. It is fair to say that he was among the finest leading men of the 1970s, and in the 1980s he seems intent on becoming one of the best character actors. De Niro won an Oscar for Best Actor for RAGING BULL in 1980 and Best Supporting Actor for THE GODFATHER, PART II in 1974. He was nominated as Best Actor for TAXI DRIVER and THE DEER HUNTER.

KEY ROLES

Bruce Pearson / BANG THE DRUM SLOWLY, 1973, Paramount, d-John Hancock.

De Niro's role as a baseball catcher dying of leukemia is a touching portrait of a dumb but sympathetic jock who doesn't understand why things have never gone well for him. He is consoled by his friend, pitcher Michael Moriarty, who sadly notes, "Everybody knows everybody is dying. That's why people are as good as they are."

Johnny Boy / MEAN STREETS, 1973, Taplin / Perry / Scorsese, d-Martin Scorsese.

De Niro, who grew up in New York's Little Italy, the film's setting, brilliantly portrays one of four young Italian-American hustlers who hang out at Tony's Bar. His notions of right and wrong make us shudder.

Don Vito Corleone / THE GODFATHER, PART II, 1974, Paramount, d-Francis Ford Coppola.

De Niro demonstrates perfectly the workings of a man's mind in this story about an orphaned child who comes alone to America after seeing his Sicilian mother and brother killed by a local "Don." Eventually he becomes a man who commands respect and fear as he builds his criminal empire.

Travis Bickle / TAXI DRIVER, 1976, Columbia, d-Martin Scorsese.

This is the terrifyingly violent but compelling story of a lonely New York Vietnam vet who drives a taxi and makes the saving of a pre-teen streetwalker his crusade. It's a film of sordid realism with De Niro frighteningly effective.

Michael / THE DEER HUNTER, 1978, Universal, d-Michael Cimino.

De Niro plays one of three steelworker buddies from Pennsylvania who enlist to fight in Vietnam. After their capture by the Viet Cong, one (John Savage) returns home crippled for life, and another (Christopher Walken) becomes a willing puppet in a Russian roulette game in Vietnam. De Niro is the only one who seems unscathed by the experience. In the end, he and those he comes home to still patriotically believe their involvement in the war was right and just. The point of this long but fascinating film is not clear, but De Niro's acting is achingly superb.

Jake LaMotta / RAGING BULL, 1980, United Artists, d-Martin Scorsese.

For his Academy Award-winning portrayal of middleweight boxer Jake LaMotta, De Niro put on 50 pounds to have the realistic appearance of an athlete gone to pot. De Niro is excellent, but his character is one of the least likable of any in the movies.

Mendoza / THE MISSION, 1986, Warners, d-Roland Joffe.

De Niro is a murdering Indian slave trader in South America who turns Christian and becomes a Jesuit priest.

OTHER ROLES

1968: *Jon Rubin* / GREETINGS. **1969:** *Cecil* / THE WEDDING PARTY. **1970:** *Jon Rubin* / HI, MOM! *Lloyd Barker* / BLOODY MAMA. **1971:** *Danny* / BORN TO WIN; *Marlo* / THE GANG THAT COULDN'T SHOOT STRAIGHT; *gypsy cab driver* / JENNIFER ON MY MIND. **1976:** *Monroe Stahr* / THE LAST TYCOON; *Alfredo Berlinghieri* / 1900. **1977:** *Jimmy Doyle* / NEW YORK, NEW YORK. **1981:** *Fr. Desmond Spellacy* / TRUE CONFESSIONS. **1983:** *Rupert Pupkin* / THE KING OF COMEDY. **1984:** *Frank Raftis* / FALLING IN LOVE; *Noodles Aaronson* / ONCE UPON A TIME IN AMERICA. **1985:** *Tuttle* / BRAZIL. **1987:** *Louis Cyphre* / ANGEL HEART; *Al Capone* / THE UNTOUCHABLES.

DENNIS, SANDY

(Sandra Dale Dennis, 1937–)

Sandy Dennis, the honey-blonde actress with an intense, nervous look, studied at the Actors Studio and went on to win consecutive Tony Awards for "A Thousand Clowns" and "Any Wednesday." She won an Academy Award for WHO'S AFRAID OF VIRGINIA WOOLF? her first substantial role. Her whiney voice and nervous mannerisms make her appearances overly intense, though she is a very talented actress. Her best film roles were in the 1960s and nothing since has been worthy of her talents.

KEY ROLES

Honey / WHO'S AFRAID OF VIRGINIA WOOLF? 1966, Warners, d-Mike Nichols.

Dennis and husband George Segal become part of an all-night yelling match between their hosts, Richard Burton and Elizabeth Taylor. Dennis is superb as the shy wife who admits more than she should during the embarrassing evening. But she can't get the upper hand in the Taylor / Burton home even when confessing a minor compulsion: "I—I peel labels." "We all peel labels," says Burton.

Sylvia Barrett / UP THE DOWN STAIRCASE, 1967, Warners, d-Robert Mulligan.

Dennis gives an earnest performance as a new teacher in a tough New York high school that has more Mickey Mouse rules than serious students. In the last scene of the movie, she flouts the rules by deliberately going up the down staircase.

Jill Banford / THE FOX, 1967, Warners, d-Mark Rydell.

Dennis and Anne Heywood play a pair of lesbians living on an isolated farm who find their lives disturbed by the arrival of a wandering seaman (Keir Dullea).

Gwen Kellerman / THE OUT-OF-TOWNERS, 1970, Paramount, d-Arthur Hiller.

Dennis and husband Jack Lemmon survive their trip to New York City even though everything that can go wrong does. It's meant to be a comedy but it's hard to laugh at some of their many disasters.

Anne Callan / THE FOUR SEASONS, 1981, Universal, d-Alan Alda.

When Len Cariou shocks his friends by leaving his wife (Dennis) for Bess Armstrong, the camaraderie of the three couples is gone forever.

OTHER ROLES

1961: *Kay* / SPLENDOR IN THE GRASS. **1966:** *Antonia* / THREE SISTERS. **1968:** *Sara Deever* / SWEET NOVEMBER. **1969:** *Frances Austen* / THAT COLD DAY IN THE PARK; *Rosamund Stacey* / A TOUCH OF LOVE. **1975:** *Jane Gwilt* / MR. SYCAMORE. **1976:** *Winifred* / NASTY HABITS; *Martha Nicholas* / GOD TOLD ME TO. **1983:** *Mona* / COME BACK TO THE FIVE AND DIME, JIMMY DEAN, JIMMY DEAN.

DE WILDE, BRANDON

(1942–1972)

No one will ever know if Brandon De Wilde could have made the transition from outstanding child actor to a successful adult performer. His death in a car accident at age 29 left him with only a little more than a dozen films, four of them triumphs. While trying to find his place as he aged, he was forced to appear in a couple of cheapies that hardly anyone saw: THE DAY THEY GAVE BABIES AWAY (1956) and GOD BLESS YOU UNCLE SAM (1969).

KEY ROLES

John Henry / THE MEMBER OF THE WEDDING, 1952, Columbia, d-Fred Zinnemann.

De Wilde beautifully recreates his Broadway role as a boy whose death is just one of the lessons of growing up a 12-year-old girl (Julie Harris) must learn. His sensitive performance is remarkable for one so young.

Joey Starret / SHANE, 1953, Paramount, d-George Stevens.

De Wilde plays a boy who idolizes the mysterious cowboy (Alan Ladd) who helps his family. Trying to imagine the movie without De Wilde, one is forced to conclude that it would only be an ordinary western, not the classic it has become.

Arthur Bartley / BLUE DENIM, 1959, 20th Century-Fox, d-Philip Dunne.
This is a well-meaning tale of two youngsters who are old enough to have children, but not old enough to know how to handle the responsibility. Both De Wilde and Carol Lynley are effective as the troubled teenagers who eventually opt for marriage, perhaps not the best solution.

Lon Bannon / HUD, 1963, Paramount, d-Martin Ritt.
De Wilde is the nephew of Hud (Paul Newman), a hard-drinking, skirt-chasing rancher whom De Wilde admires. But his grandfather (Melvyn Douglas) dislikes Hud and, in the end, De Wilde walks out on his amoral uncle, who by now disgusts him.

OTHER ROLES

1956: *Skeeter* / GOODBYE, MY LADY. **1957:** *Joey Adams* / NIGHT PASSAGE. **1958:** *Brian Turner* / THE MISSOURI TRAVELER. **1962:** *Clinton Willart* / ALL FALL DOWN. **1965:** *Ensign Jeremiah Torrey* / IN HARM'S WAY; *Bucky Calloway* / THOSE CALLOWAYS. **1970:** *Ferguson* / THE DESERTER. **1972:** *Josh* / WILD IN THE SKY.

DICKINSON, ANGIE

(Angeline Brown, 1931–)
This lovely woman is probably best known for her TV show "Police Woman." In films, she has often been cast as tarts with hearts of gold who can hold their own with any man. Dickinson is one of those women who seem to become more attractive with age, and her popularity should assure her many roles as mature women for years to come. In addition to the features listed below, she has appeared in the following foreign language exploitation films: THE SCORPIO SCARAB (1972), LABYRINTHS (1978), and L'HOMME EN COLERE (1979). Her made-for-TV movies include A CASE OF LIBEL (1968), THE LOVE WAR (1969), THE NORLISS TAPES (1973), PRAY FOR THE WILDCATS (1974), A SENSITIVE, PASSIONATE MAN (1977), OVERBOARD (1978), THE SUICIDE'S WIFE (1979), DIAL M FOR MURDER (1981), ONE SHOE MAKES IT MURDER (1982), JEALOUSY (1982), and A TOUCH OF SCANDAL (1984).

KEY ROLES

Feathers / RIO BRAVO, 1959, Warners, d-Howard Hawks.
Dickinson gets a chance to display her talent as she helps sheriff John Wayne and his drunken deputy hold a killer in jail until the U.S. Marshal arrives. She is much too young for the Duke, but her role is more than mere decoration in this enjoyable western.

Rachel Cade / THE SINS OF RACHEL CADE, 1961, Warners, d-Gordon Douglas.
Dickinson is an American missionary nurse in the Belgian Congo who falls in love with a downed pilot (Roger Moore), and bears his child. As a result of her indiscretion she decides to stay in Africa with her agnostic doctor friend (Peter Finch) rather than return to America.

Jessica / JESSICA, 1962, France / Italy, United Artists / Ariane / Dear Film, d-Jean Negulesco.
Dickinson plays an attractive midwife in a Sicilian village who is so desired by all of the men that their wives go on a sex strike.

Lt. Francie Corum / CAPTAIN NEWMAN, M.D., 1963, Universal, d-David Miller.
Dickinson is an army nurse who works closely with Gregory Peck in the psychiatric ward of a World War II army hospital. She does fine work in this rather curious comedy-drama.

Sheila Farr / THE KILLERS, 1964, Universal-International, d-Don Siegel.
Dickinson plays the no-good girl that John Cassavetes falls for in this remake of the Ernest Hemingway story of a man who patiently and resignedly waits for two hired killers to come and rub him out. The film was intended for TV but was released in theaters because it was considered too violent for the small screen.

Chris / POINT BLANK, 1967, MGM, d-John Boorman.
In this violent screenplay, Dickinson becomes involved with Lee Marvin, a brutal escaped convict who is searching for his loot.

Miss Smith / PRETTY MAIDS ALL IN A ROW, 1971, MGM, d-Roger Vadim.
Dickinson is a high school teacher who follows the suggestion of the school's guidance counselor (Rock Hudson) to help overcome the shyness of a male student by taking him to bed. After all, Hudson is sleeping with every female student he can find, and when they get pushy he kills them.

Wilma McClatchie / BIG BAD MAMA, 1974, Santa Cruz / Corman, d-Steve Carver.
In this film Dickinson plays a 1930s Texas widow who turns to bank robberies to make ends meet. It's violent nonsense, but Dickinson looks good.

OTHER ROLES

1954: *party guest* / LUCKY ME. **1955:** *Kitty* / MAN WITH THE GUN; *girl* / TENNESSEE'S PARTNER; *Polly Logan* / THE RETURN OF JACK SLADE. **1956:** *Becky Carter* / HIDDEN GUNS; *Janice* / GUN THE MAN DOWN; *Cathy* / TENSION AT TABLE ROCK. **1957:** *Sally* / THE BLACK WHIP; *Priscilla* / SHOOT-OUT AT MEDICINE BEND; *airline stewardess* / CALYPSO JOE; *Lucky Legs* / CHINA GATE. **1958:** *Kelly* / CRY TERROR. **1960:** *Fran* / THE BRAMBLE BUSH; *Beatrice Ocean* / OCEAN'S ELEVEN. **1961:** *Cathy Simon* / A FEVER IN THE BLOOD. **1962:** *Lyda* / ROME ADVENTURE. **1965:** *Laurie* / THE ART OF LOVE. **1966:** *Ruby Calder* / THE CHASE; *Emma Marcus* / CAST A GIANT SHADOW. **1967:** *Lisa Denton* / THE LAST CHALLENGE. **1969:** *Laura Breckenridge* / SAM WHISKEY; *Lily Beloit* / YOUNG BILLY YOUNG; *Rachel Amidon* / SOME KIND OF A NUT. **1971:** *Dr. Johnson* / THE RESURRECTION OF ZACHARY WHEELER. **1973:** *Jackie* / THE OUTSIDE MAN. **1980:** *Kate Miller* / DRESSED TO KILL; *Vanessa* / DEATH HUNT; *Belinda McNair* / KLONDIKE FEVER. **1982:** *Dragon Queen* / CHARLIE CHAN AND THE CURSE OF THE DRAGON QUEEN.

DIETRICH, MARLENE

(Maria Magdalene Dietrich, 1901–)
Marlene Dietrich was the creation of director Josef von Sternberg and, next to Greta Garbo, the actress with the most sensuous face and voice of the early sound era. Possessor of one of the best pair of legs to appear on the screen, and a successful nightclub entertainer, Dietrich was not so much an actress as she was a happening. She was a seductively androgynous woman of tawdry glamour; a shimmering blonde goddess who enslaved males with her mocking eyes and breathy voice. Her best film roles occurred while working with von Sternberg. After that period her work was often little more than a parody of her earlier screen persona. Even when she was no longer box office, her screen appearances, while no great acting achievements, were of interest because of her

peculiar charisma and intriguing femme fatale mystery. Her views on men and women include: "The average man is more interested in a woman who is interested in him than he is in a woman with beautiful legs," and "A man would prefer to come home to an unmade bed and a happy woman than to a neatly made bed and an angry woman." Dietrich was decorated with the Medal of Freedom and Chevalier de la Legion d'Honneur for her wartime anti-Nazi broadcasts, and received an Oscar nomination for MOROCCO in 1930.

KEY ROLES

Lola Lola / THE BLUE ANGEL, 1930, UFA, d-Josef von Sternberg.

In the role that brought her international stardom as a sex symbol, Dietrich portrays a tawdry Berlin cabaret singer who causes the ruin of a German teacher she enslaves. She gives a languorous and erotic rendition of "Falling in Love Again."

Amy Jolly / MOROCCO, 1930, Paramount, d-Josef von Sternberg.

Dietrich is an absolute sensation as a mysterious cabaret singer torn between a French Foreign Legionnaire (Gary Cooper) and wealthy Adolphe Menjou. It's hard to believe she'd choose to become a camp follower to be with Cooper.

Madeline (alias Shanghai Lily) / SHANGHAI EXPRESS, 1932, Paramount, d-Josef von Sternberg.

"It took more than one man to change my name to Shanghai Lily." So Dietrich informs Clive Brook and the audience that she is not as pure as the driven snow in this story of a glorified prostitute who saves an ex-lover and other passengers on a train that has been taken over by Chinese rebels.

Helen Faraday / BLONDE VENUS, 1932, Paramount, d-Josef von Sternberg.

Dietrich plays a cabaret singer (what else?) who emerges from a gorilla suit to render "Hot Voodoo." Her poor but honest husband (Herbert Marshall) requires expensive medical treatment. She knows only one way to get money, so she employs her charms to win wealthy Cary Grant's assistance. Cured, Marshall is not understanding and he banishes her. She wanders into prostitution until Marshall takes her child from her. Then, without any explanation, she becomes the rage of Paris, where Grant catches her act and takes her back to her husband and child.

Sophia Frederica (Catherine the Great) / THE SCARLET EMPRESS, 1934, Paramount, d-Josef von Sternberg.

Dietrich portrays the German princess brought to Russia by the Empress Elizabeth to marry her imbecilic son, Grand Duke Peter, played maniacally by Sam Jaffe. When the latter inherits the throne, Dietrich has him killed before he can dispose of her.

Madeleine de Beaupre / DESIRE, 1936, Paramount, d-Ernst Lubitsch.

Dietrich plays a jewel thief who drops some pearls in the pocket of a stranger (Gary Cooper) in order to get past customs. While trying to reclaim the jewels, she develops a romantic interest in Cooper, then returns the jewels to their rightful owner.

Frenchy / DESTRY RIDES AGAIN, 1939, Universal, d-George Marshall.

Dietrich plays a hard-boiled saloon singer in cahoots with a crooked land-grabber (Brian Donlevy). She has a change of heart when she meets the new deputy (Jimmy Stewart) who has been called in by the sheriff to clean up the town. She dies taking a bullet meant for him.

Erika von Schluetow / A FOREIGN AFFAIR, 1948, Paramount, d-Billy Wilder.

Dietrich, a German nightclub singer in post-World War II Berlin, has been involved with a handsome American army captain (John Lund) and finds she has some serious competition from a junketing U.S. congresswoman (Jean Arthur).

Altar Keane / RANCHO NOTORIOUS, 1952, RKO, d-Fritz Lang.

Dietrich is a former dance hall girl who operates a hideout for outlaws called "Chuck-a-Luck." It's a nice place to visit until Arthur Kennedy, trailing the man who raped and killed his sweetheart, arrives. He gets a yen for Dietrich and has a run in with Mel Ferrer, whom Dietrich favors.

Christine Vole / WITNESS FOR THE PROSECUTION, 1957, United Artists, d-Billy Wilder.

Dietrich plays a nightclub singer who first insists that her husband (Tyrone Power) is innocent of killing a woman infatuated with him. At the trial, though, she appears for the prosecution, until her husband's barrister (Charles Laughton) proves her testimony had been a lie. Then the surprises begin.

Madame Bertholt / JUDGMENT AT NUREMBERG, 1961, United Artists, d-Stanley Kramer.

Dietrich plays a German general's widow playing hostess to Spencer Tracy, one of the judges sent to Nuremberg to preside over the trials of former Nazis. Their conversations allow the director and screenwriter to make some points about the propriety, legality, and morality of the trials.

OTHER ROLES

1923: *Kathrin* / THE LITTLE NAPOLEON; *Lucie* / TRAGEDY OF LOVE; *peasant girl* / MAN BY THE ROADSIDE. **1924:** *girl* / THE LEAP INTO LIFE. **1925:** *girl in a queue* / THE JOYLESS STREET. **1926:** *Micheline* / MANON LESCAUT; *Coquette* / A MODERN DU BARRY; *extra* / MADAME WANTS NO CHILDREN; *Edmee Marchand* / HEADS UP, CHARLY! **1927:** *Sophie* / THE IMAGINARY BARON; *Yvette* / HIS GREATEST BLUFF; *Erni* / CAFE ELECTRIC. **1928:** *Chichotte de Gastone* / PRINCESS OLALA. **1929:** *Laurence Gerard* / I KISS YOUR HAND, MADAME; *Miss Ethel* / THE SHIP OF LOST MEN; *Evelyne* / DANGERS OF THE ENGAGEMENT PERIOD. **1931:** *"X-27"* / DISHONORED. **1933:** *Lily Czepanek* / SONG OF SONGS. **1935:** *Concha Perez* / THE DEVIL IS A WOMAN. **1936:** *Domini Enfilden* / THE GARDEN OF ALLAH. **1937:** *Countess Alexandra Vladinoff* / KNIGHT WITHOUT ARMOUR; *Maria Barker* / ANGEL. **1940:** *Bijou Blanche* / SEVEN SINNERS. **1941:** *Claire Ledeux* / THE FLAME OF NEW ORLEANS; *Fay Duval* / MANPOWER. **1942:** *Elizabeth Madden* / THE LADY IS WILLING; *Cherry Malotte* / THE SPOILERS; *Josie Winters* / PITTSBURGH. **1944:** *Jamilla* / KISMET; *guest* / FOLLOW THE BOYS. **1946:** *Blanche Ferrand* / MARTIN ROUMAGNAC. **1947:** *Lydia* / GOLDEN EARRINGS. **1949:** *guest* / JIGSAW. **1950:** *Charlotte Inwood* / STAGE FRIGHT. **1951:** *Monica Teasdale* / NO HIGHWAY IN THE SKY. **1956:** *cameo* / AROUND THE WORLD IN 80 DAYS. **1957:** *Marquise Maria de Crevecoeur* / THE MONTE CARLO STORY. **1958:** *Tanya* / TOUCH OF EVIL. **1964:** *guest* / PARIS WHEN IT SIZZLES. **1978:** *Baroness Von Semering* / JUST A GIGOLO.

DONAT, ROBERT

(1905–1958)

Plagued by ill health and self-doubt, Robert Donat made only 19 films in a 25-year movie career. Among those, however, are several well-remembered classics. Tall and distinguished looking, Donat possessed a rich, mellifluous speaking voice, a sensitive expression, and an open acting style that critics and fans adored, but which did not always meet his own high standards. He refused a Hollywood career, turning down both CAPTAIN BLOOD and THE ADVENTURES OF ROBIN HOOD. He preferred to work in England in movies, on the stage, and on radio, and in making poetry recordings. He won an Academy Award for GOODBYE, MR. CHIPS and a nomination for THE CITADEL.

KEY ROLES

Edmond Dantes / THE COUNT OF MONTE CRISTO, 1934, Reliance, d-Rowland V. Lee.

In his only Hollywood picture, Donat appeared as the young sailor who is arrested, charged with being a supporter of the deported Napoleon, and thrown into prison at the Chateau d'If without trial and with no hope of release. A fellow prisoner, the Abbe Faria, fills him with dreams of a great treasure on the island of Monte Cristo. Years later Donat escapes, makes his way to Monte Cristo, and claims the great fortune, making him the richest man in Europe. Then he prepares to take revenge on the three men responsible for his unjust imprisonment.

Richard Hannay / THE 39 STEPS, 1935, Great Britain, Gaumont-British, d-Alfred Hitchcock.

Donat encounters a woman who, before she is murdered, tells him about a ring of spies. Suspected of her murder, he flees the police in order to uncover the real culprits. Later he finds himself handcuffed to the unwilling Madeleine Carroll, who eventually believes his story and helps him expose the spy ring in the music hall where everything began.

Murdoch and Donald Glourie / THE GHOST GOES WEST, 1936, Great Britain, London Films, d-Rene Clair.

In this delightfully whimsical comedy Donat plays a dual role: a 17th-century Scottish ghost who cannot rest in peace until his clan's supremacy has been conceded by a member of a rival clan, and his 20th-century descendant who sells the castle together with his ancestor to an American who moves it stone by stone to the United States. Here the older Donat finds the man he needs, and the younger finds a wife.

Dr. Andrew Manson / THE CITADEL, 1938, Great Britain, MGM British, d-King Vidor.

A dedicated and idealistic young doctor (Donat) fights conditions in a Welsh mining community, marries schoolteacher Rosalind Russell, and then moves to London where he nearly loses his ideals while caring for rich society patients. He comes to his senses in time to save his career.

Charles Chipping / GOODBYE, MR. CHIPS, 1939, Great Britain, MGM British, d-Sam Wood.

As the aged Mr. Chips, Donat reminisces about his years at Brookfield, a boys' public school. His early difficulties were overcome when his beloved wife (Greer Garson) humanized him to such a point that he became headmaster. In a year of great competition for the Oscar, Donat walked off with the honor by beautifully creating a character more realistic than sentimental.

William Pitt / Earl of Charton / THE YOUNG MR. PITT, 1941, Great Britain, 20th Century-Fox, d-Carol Reed.

Made prime minister of Britain at only 24, Donat gradually overcomes the bitter opposition of C. J. Fox (Robert Morley). His career is jeopardized when France declares war on England in 1793. He is compelled to resign in 1801 because of poor health, but is recalled to the post in 1804 and lives to see Napoleon defeated at Trafalgar, before dying the next year.

Sir Robert Morton / THE WINSLOW BOY, 1948, Great Britain, London Films, d-Anthony Asquith.

Demanding "Let justice be done" in the House of Commons, Donat proves that a young boy who has been expelled from a naval college is innocent of stealing a postal order. He thus justifies the lad's father (Cedric Hardwicke) who has risked his own health and wealth and his family's reputation to arrive at the verdict.

The Mandarin / INN OF THE SIXTH HAPPINESS, 1958, Great Britain, 20th Century-Fox, d-Mark Robson.

"Stay here for a time. It will comfort me as I leave to know it. We shall not see each other again I think. Farewell." The dying words of the Mandarin to Ingrid Bergman might have been those of Donat himself as he would succumb to his unending battle with asthma soon after. The story is that of a serving girl who realizes her burning desire to become a missionary. Donat, as the local official who befriends her, gives a fitting final performance.

OTHER ROLES

1932: *Julian Angell* / MEN OF TOMORROW; *Dick Warren* / THAT NIGHT IN LONDON; *Paul Martin* / CASH. **1933:** *Thomas Culpepper* / THE PRIVATE LIFE OF HENRY VIII. **1937:** *A. J. Fothergill* / KNIGHT WITHOUT ARMOUR. **1943:** *Terence Stevenson* / THE ADVENTURES OF TARTU. **1945:** *Robert Wilson* / PERFECT STRANGERS. **1947:** *Charles Stewart Parnell* / CAPTAIN BOYCOTT. **1950:** *Jack Hardacre* / THE CURE FOR LOVE; *William Friese-Greene* / THE MAGIC BOX. **1955:** *Rev. William Thorne* / LEASE OF LIFE.

DOUGLAS, KIRK

(Issur Danielovitch, 1916–)

The son of Russian immigrants, Kirk Douglas studied at the American Academy of Dramatic Arts, and began his career on Broadway. He returned to the stage after naval service in World War II and was brought to Hollywood to appear as the weak lawyer husband of Barbara Stanwyck in THE STRANGE LOVE OF MARTHA IVERS. After appearing in a few minor league roles, he burst onto the silver screen with his role as the selfish boxer in CHAMPION. After that he played driven men, resolute and intense, with eyes ablaze and cleft chin stuck firmly out. He made his most impressive films in the 1950s but continued to play leading men into his 60s. He has been most convincing playing outrageous, cocky, rugged, and often selfish individuals. He has been nominated for Academy Awards for CHAMPION, THE BAD AND THE BEAUTIFUL, and LUST FOR LIFE. His oldest son, Michael, has been successful in following his dad into a career in the movies. About himself, Douglas has said: "My life is a 'B' movie...the typical American success story is a 'B' movie."

KEY ROLES

Walter O'Neil / THE STRANGE LOVE OF MARTHA IVERS, 1946, Paramount, d-Lewis Milestone.

Douglas plays the alcoholic district attorney husband of Barbara Stanwyck, and they are a couple with a dark secret. One person who knows about their secret is Van Heflin, whom they try to get rid of in various ways, but end up shooting themselves because they are sure their guilty secret is about to become known.

Midge Kelly / CHAMPION, 1949, United Artists, d-Mark Robson.

Boxer Douglas alienates his friends and family, doublecrosses his manager, leaves his wife for a blonde singer whom he dumps for another woman, and slugs his crippled brother. He's a heel who, in the end, gets his comeuppance as he goes mad and dies in his dressing room after his last fight. Brother Arthur Kennedy then tells the press what they want to hear: "He was a champion. He went out like a champion. He was a credit to the fight game to the very end."

Rick Martin / YOUNG MAN WITH A HORN, 1950, Warners, d-Michael Curtiz.

In this film loosely based on the life of Bix Beiderbecke, Douglas is a coronet player who wants to play jazz, though the bands he plays with expect him to be part of a group. He marries a cold and heartless woman (Lauren Bacall) who almost ruins him, until he comes to his senses and sees that Doris Day was always the right woman for him. It might have been more effective at the end if he had died for his musical principles rather than compromising and living.

Charles Tatum / THE BIG CARNIVAL, (ACE IN THE HOLE), 1951, Paramount, d-Billy Wilder.

Douglas demonstrates his ability to play a totally selfish, cynical, and despicable individual in this film about a reporter who deliberately delays the rescue of a man trapped in a cave, just so that he will have a big scoop for his paper. The man dies and so does Douglas, who earlier told his former editor, "How'd you like to make a thousand dollars a day, Mr. Boot? I'm a thousand-dollar-a-day newspaperman. You can have me for nothing."

Det. James McLeod / DETECTIVE STORY, 1951, Paramount, d-William Wyler.

Douglas has an almost psychopathic hatred of criminals in this film about a detective who is unable to distinguish between a career criminal and a first offender. When he learns that his wife was once pregnant by a small-time crook and had an abortion at the hands of a butcher that Douglas arrested, he cannot forgive her. He berates her, "What's there to understand? You went with him, a pig like that. You had a child by him. Then you went to that butcher Schneider—everything I hate. What's left to understand?" Shortly thereafter he is killed by a drug addicted burglar who has grabbed a gun from a rookie cop.

Jonathan Shields / THE BAD AND THE BEAUTIFUL, 1952, MGM, d-Vincente Minnelli.

Douglas plays a ruthless Hollywood David O. Selznick-like producer who victimizes Lana Turner, Barry Sullivan, and Dick Powell, among others, in his quest to make the movies he wants. When his career is in ashes, he seeks help from the very people he used and discarded, but whose careers he advanced, to get back on top.

Vincent Van Gogh / LUST FOR LIFE, 1956, MGM, d-Vincente Minnelli.

Douglas deserved the Best Actor Award for his powerful portrayal of Vincent Van Gogh, the artist who never sold a painting. He didn't win an Oscar though his work was better than Laurence Olivier's as Richard III and certainly as good as that of Yul Brynner who won for THE KING AND I.

Doc Holliday / GUNFIGHT AT THE O.K. CORRAL, 1957, Paramount, d-John Sturges.

Douglas plays the consumptive dentist turned gambler and gunfighter who befriends Wyatt Earp (Burt Lancaster), and joins him in the shoot-out with the Clanton gang at the O.K. Corral. Douglas's gambling confidence is explained like this: "I never lose. You see, poker is played by desperate men who cherish money. I don't lose because I have nothing to lose, including my life."

Colonel Dax / PATHS OF GLORY, 1957, United Artists, d-Stanley Kubrick.

Douglas strives unsuccessfully to prevent the execution of three French World War I soldiers, chosen at random to die as punishment for the supposed cowardice of the troops under Douglas's command. It's based on a true incident.

Einar / THE VIKINGS, 1958, United Artists, d-Richard Fleischer.

Douglas is the savage Viking son of a barbaric chief (Ernest Borgnine). He kidnaps a Welsh princess (Janet Leigh) whom he intends for his bride, but is foiled by his father's bastard son (Tony Curtis). The two meet in mortal combat, not knowing of their blood tie until it is too late.

Dick Dudgeon / THE DEVIL'S DISCIPLE, 1959, United Artists, d-Guy Hamilton.

Douglas is delightful in this adaptation of a George Bernard Shaw story about an American rogue. Douglas is almost hanged by British general "Gentleman Johnny" Burgoyne (Laurence Olivier) when he is mistaken for an American rebel pastor (Burt Lancaster).

Spartacus / SPARTACUS, 1960, Universal, d-Stanley Kubrick.

In this epic film, Douglas is a slave trained to become a gladiator who leads an army of Roman slaves in a revolt ultimately put down by Laurence Olivier, who has all, including Douglas, crucified.

Jack Burns / LONELY ARE THE BRAVE, 1962, Universal, d-David Miller.

Douglas plays a rebellious cowboy who finds the new West too civilized for his tastes. He ends up in trouble, the object of an all-out man hunt by a posse, using jeeps and helicopters. He is hit and killed by a truck on a highway when his horse becomes spooked.

George Brougham / THE LIST OF ADRIAN MESSENGER, 1963, Universal, d-John Huston.

Douglas plays a master of disguises who systematically kills a long list of people so that he will be able to inherit a title and estate.

Col. Martin Casey / SEVEN DAYS IN MAY, 1964, Paramount, d-John Franckenheimer.

In this film, Douglas has the thankless job of spying on his boss, the highly respected but right-wing head of the Joint Chiefs of Staff (Burt Lancaster). Douglas suspects the latter is planning a military takeover of the United States government.

Col. David "Mickey" Marcus / CAST A GIANT SHADOW, 1966, United Artists, d-Melville Shavelson.

Douglas is an American colonel who is persuaded to train and command Israeli troops in the 1947 fight with the Arabs, after the British withdrawal from Palestine. He gets help from John Wayne, Yul Brynner, and Frank Sinatra in cameo roles.

Paris Pittman, Jr. / THERE WAS A CROOKED MAN, 1970, Warners / Seven Arts, d-Joseph L. Mankiewicz.

Douglas plays a mean-spirited, recalcitrant outlaw who escapes from an 1880s Arizona prison to retrieve a half-million dollars that he has stashed away. But he is killed by a rattler that is nesting with the loot.

Peg / SCALAWAG, 1973, Paramount, d-Kirk Douglas.
Douglas plays a roguish, one-legged pirate who encounters hostile Indians and cutthroats as he seeks a buried treasure.

OTHER ROLES

1947: *Whit Sterling* / OUT OF THE PAST; *Peter Niles* / MOURNING BECOMES ELECTRA. **1948:** *Noll Turner* / I WALK ALONE; *Tucker Wedge* / THE WALLS OF JERICHO; *Owen Waterbury* / MY DEAR SECRETARY; *George Phipps* / A LETTER TO THREE WIVES. **1950:** *Jim O'Connor* / THE GLASS MENAGERIE. **1951:** *Len Merrick* / ALONG THE GREAT DIVIDE. **1952:** *Jim Fallon* / THE BIG TREES; *Deakins* / THE BIG SKY. **1953:** *Pierre Narval* / THE STORY OF THREE LOVES; *Hans Muller* / THE JUGGLER; *Robert Teller* / ACT OF LOVE. **1954:** *Ulysses* / ULYSSES; *Ned Land* / 20,000 LEAGUES UNDER THE SEA. **1955:** *Gino* / THE RACERS; *Dempsey Rae* / MAN WITHOUT A STAR; *Johnny Hawks* / THE INDIAN FIGHTER. **1957:** *Maj. Gen. Melville Goodwin* / TOP SECRET AFFAIR. **1959:** *Matt Morgan* / LAST TRAIN FROM GUN HILL. **1960:** *Larry Coe* / STRANGERS WHEN WE MEET. **1961:** *Brendon O'Malley* / THE LAST SUNSET; *Maj. Steve Garrett* / TOWN WITHOUT PITY. **1962:** *Jack Andrus* / TWO WEEKS IN ANOTHER TOWN. **1963:** *Sgt. P. J. Briscoe* / THE HOOK; *Deke Gentry* / FOR LOVE OR MONEY. **1965:** *Cmdr. Paul Eddington* / IN HARM'S WAY; *Dr. Rolf Pedersen* / THE HEROES OF TELEMARK. **1966:** *Gen. George S. Patton* / IS PARIS BURNING? **1967:** *Sen. William J. Tadlock* / THE WAY WEST; *Lomax* / THE WAR WAGON. **1968:** *Jim Schuyler* / A LOVELY WAY TO DIE. **1969:** *Frank Ginetta* / THE BROTHERHOOD; *Eddie Anderson* / THE ARRANGEMENT. **1971:** *Will Tenneray* / A GUNFIGHT; *Will Denton* / THE LIGHT AT THE EDGD OF THE WORLD; *Andrej* / CATCH ME A SPY. **1975:** *Mike Wayne* / JACQUELINE SUSANN'S ONCE IS NOT ENOUGH; *Howard Nightingale* / POSSE. **1977:** *Robert Caine* / THE CHOSEN. **1978:** *Peter Sanza* / THE FURY; *Cactus Jack* / THE VILLAIN. **1979:** *Adam* / SATURN 3. **1980:** *Dr. Tuttle "The Maestro"* / HOME MOVIES; *Capt. Matthew Yelland* / THE FINAL COUNTDOWN. **1983:** *Harrison and Spur* / THE MAN FROM SNOWY RIVER; *Carl "Buster" Marzack* / EDDIE MACON'S RUN. **1986:** *Archie Long* / TOUGH GUYS.

DOUGLAS, MELVYN

(Melvyn Hesselberg, 1901–1981)
Elegant, witty, and charming, Melvyn Douglas had careers both as suave leading men and later as crotchety, old gentlemen. It was in these later roles that his acting caught the attention of the Academy Awards, as he won Oscars for HUD in 1963 and BEING THERE in 1979. He was also nominated for the Award in 1969 for I NEVER SANG FOR MY FATHER. In his earlier days he was both a romantic lead and an indispensable mainstay of several screwball comedies of the 1930s. This tall, dapper, and intelligent man with the pencil-thin moustache and splendid voice distinguished himself on the stage as well, winning a Tony for his performance in "The Best Man." He also received an Emmy for his TV work in "Do Not Go Gentle into that Good Night."

KEY ROLES

Roger Penderel / THE OLD DARK HOUSE, 1932, Universal, d-James Whale.
In this film Douglas is one of several stranded travelers forced to take refuge in the home of a family of very inhospitable eccentrics. It's an eerie tale with fine performances all around.

Charles / DANGEROUS CORNER, 1934, RKO, d-Phil Rosen.
Douglas gets top billing in this story of a group of people revealing their suppressed passions and guilty secrets as they learn what might have been if they had spoken the truth about a friend's suicide.

Michael Lanyard / THE LONE WOLF RETURNS, 1936, Columbia, d-Roy William Neill.
Douglas stars as a jewel thief turned private sleuth. He did not play the role in the other pictures in the series.

John Randolph / THE GORGEOUS HUSSEY, 1936, MGM, d-Clarence Brown.
A foreword for this movie reads: "This story of Peggy Eaton and her times is not presented as a precise account of either, rather as fiction founded upon historical fact." Thus warned, one should not imagine that Douglas portrays anything factual in the life of the Virginia congressman who was a fervent defender of states' rights.

Michael Grant / THEODORA GOES WILD, 1936, Columbia, d-Richard Boleslawski.
Douglas is consistently intelligent as Irene Dunne's romantic interest in this screwball comedy about a small-town girl who writes a titillating bestseller and hits Manhattan like a bombshell.

George Potter / I MET HIM IN PARIS, 1937, Paramount, d-Wesley Ruggles.
Douglas is one of two philanderers who pursue Claudette Colbert as she spends her savings on a fling in Paris and Switzerland.

Vincent Bullitt / THAT CERTAIN AGE, 1938, Universal, d-Edward Ludwig.
Douglas is the "older" man on whom Deanna Durbin has a crush in this pleasant musical.

Count Leon Dalga / NINOTCHKA, 1939, MGM, d-Ernst Lubitsch.
Greta Garbo, in the title role, usually gets most of the praise when this sparkling comedy is discussed, but Douglas is delightful as the debonair playboy who thaws the cold Russian emissary and helps her loveliness bloom. Douglas makes viewers glad that the role wasn't given to William Powell or Robert Montgomery as originally planned.

Dr. Gustaf Segert / A WOMAN'S FACE, 1941, MGM, d-George Cukor.
Douglas is the plastic surgeon whose magic with a scalpel not only turns hideously scarred Joan Crawford into a beautiful woman but cleanses her embittered soul and turns her away from her life of crime.

Michael Holmes / THEY ALL KISSED THE BRIDE, 1942, Columbia, d-Alexander Hall.
Douglas is a crusading writer out to expose the working conditions in a company owned by Joan Crawford. As one might expect, they fall in love in this romantic comedy.

Bill Cole / MR. BLANDINGS BUILDS HIS DREAM HOUSE, 1948, RKO, d-H. C. Potter.
Douglas is the best friend and attorney of Cary Grant, the title character in this still funny film about a New York advertising man who learns the joys and pains of house-building in Connecticut. Douglas is also an ex-suitor of Grant's wife (Myrna Loy), whom he still deeply admires.

The Dansker / BILLY BUDD, 1962, Great Britain, Anglo-Allied, d-Peter Ustinov.

After an eleven-year absence and a series of Broadway successes, Douglas returns to the screen as a character actor in Melville's allegory of good and evil. Terrence Stamp plays the innocent young British sailor who must hang for the accidental killing of the sadistic master at arms (Robert Ryan).

Homer Bannon / HUD, 1963, Paramount, d-Martin Ritt.

Douglas is excellent as the aging Texas rancher who must raise his parentless grandson (Brandon De Wilde) and deal with his ne'er-do-well son (Paul Newman). His Oscar for Best Supporting Actor seemed entirely justified.

Tony Garrison / I NEVER SANG FOR MY FATHER, 1969, Columbia, d-Gilbert Cates.

When the cantankerous Douglas's wife dies, the old man interferes with his middle-aged widower son's (Gene Hackman) plans to remarry.

Ben Rand / BEING THERE, 1979, Lorimar / North Star / CIP, d-Hal Ashby.

Douglas is a wealthy, dying businessman who takes in Peter Sellers, an illiterate gardener, because he believes him to be a homespun philosopher. Douglas even bequeaths his wife (Shirley MacLaine) to Sellers, who has become a national celebrity.

OTHER ROLES

1931: *Fletcher, the unknown gentleman* / TONIGHT OR NEVER. **1932:** *Lt. Andre Verlaine* / PRESTIGE; *David Rolfe* / THE WISER SEX; *Philip Marvin* / BROKEN WING; *Bruno Varelli* / AS YOU DESIRE ME. **1933:** *Dr. Walter Tradnor* / NAGANA; *Karl Brettschneider* / THE VAMPIRE BAT; *Roy Darwin* / COUNSELLOR-AT-LAW. **1934:** *Robson* / WOMAN IN THE DARK. **1935:** *Traps* / PEOPLE'S ENEMY; *Richard Barclay* / SHE MARRIED HER BOSS; *Martin Powell* / MARY BURNS, FUGITIVE; *Jeff Hogarth* / ANNIE OAKLEY. **1936:** *Stephen Blake* / AND SO THEY WERE MARRIED. **1937:** *Dick Stark* / WOMEN OF GLAMOUR; *Mr. Cheyne* / CAPTAINS COURAGEOUS; *Anthony Halton* / ANGEL; *James Guthrie* / I'LL TAKE ROMANCE. **1938:** *William Reardon* / THERE'S ALWAYS A WOMAN; *Rene Farrand (Lupin)* / ARSENE LUPIN RETURNS; *George Sartoris* / THE TOY WIFE; *Joel Sloane* / FAST COMPANY; *William Reardon* / THERE'S THAT WOMAN AGAIN. **1939:** *Michael Cassidy* / TELL NO TALES; *Ronald Brooke* / GOOD GIRLS GO TO PARIS; *Kenny Williams* / THE AMAZING MR. WILLIAMS. **1940:** *Henry Lowndes* / TOO MANY HUSBANDS; *Paul Boliet* / HE STAYED FOR BREAKFAST; *Jeff Thompson* / THIRD FINGER, LEFT HAND. **1941:** *Tice Collins* / THIS THING CALLED LOVE; *Larry Baker* / THAT UNCERTAIN FEELING; *Jerry Marvin* / OUR WIFE. **1942:** *Nicki Prax* / WE WERE DANCING. **1943:** *Jeff Seabrook* / THREE HEARTS FOR JULIA. **1947:** *Bruce Chamberlain* / THE SEA OF GRASS. **1948:** *Clive Heath* / MY OWN TRUE LOVE. **1949:** *Luke Jordan* / A WOMAN'S SECRET; *Armand De Grasse* / THE GREAT SINNER. **1951:** *Paul Beaurevel* / MY FORBIDDEN PAST; *Frank Bradley* / ON THE LOOSE. **1964:** *Colonel Brackenbury* / ADVANCE TO THE REAR; *Adm. William Jessup* / THE AMERICANIZATION OF EMILY. **1965:** *Frederick Larbaud* / RAPTURE. **1967:** *Warren Trent* / HOTEL. **1972:** *Joseph Provo* / ONE IS A LONELY NUMBER; *John J. McKay* / THE CANDIDATE. **1976:** *Monsieur Zy* / THE TENANT. **1979:** *Senator Birney* / THE SEDUCTION OF JOE TYNAN; *David* / TELL ME A RIDDLE. **1981:** *Sen. Joseph Carmichael* / THE CHANGELING; *John Kaffrey* / GHOST STORY.

DOUGLAS, PAUL

(1907–1959)

This affable, burly, big-hearted ex-football player and radio sportscaster was nearly 40 when he was chosen to play the loud-mouthed, crooked tycoon in Broadway's "Born Yesterday." Paul Douglas made over 1,000 appearances as Harry Brock before making his film debut in 1948 in A LETTER TO THREE WIVES. In his movie roles he usually played middle-aged, cynical men in both comedies and melodramas. Despite his cantankerous nature in films, he also showed an appealing vulnerability.

KEY ROLES

Porter Hollingsway / A LETTER TO THREE WIVES, 1948, 20th Century-Fox, d-Joseph L. Mankiewicz.

In his screen debut, Douglas is the best thing in this story about three wives who each receive a letter from a "friend" who claims to have run off with one of their husbands. Douglas, married to Linda Darnell, a girl from the wrong side of the tracks, seems like the leading candidate for the missing husband because of the many fights he and Darnell have.

Police Capt. Tom Warren / PANIC IN THE STREETS, 1950, 20th Century-Fox, d-Elia Kazan.

Working with a public health doctor (Richard Widmark), Douglas must track down Jack Palance, a small-time New Orleans crook who is a carrier of bubonic plague.

Dunnigan / 14 HOURS, 1951, 20th Century-Fox, d-Henry Hathaway.

Douglas is a likable policeman who wins the confidence of a man who stands on a ledge, high above a Manhattan street, threatening to jump.

Josiah Dudley / EXECUTIVE SUITE, 1954, MGM, d-Robert Wise.

When the president of a big furniture company dies, Douglas is one of several candidates to replace him in this story about struggles in a boardroom.

Joe MacBeth / JOE MACBETH, 1955, Columbia, d-Ken Hughes.

In this effort to update MacBeth, Douglas is a gangster whose wife urges him to rub out his boss. Shakespeare can rest easy.

Edward L. McKeever / THE SOLID GOLD CADILLAC, 1956, Columbia, d-Richard Quine.

When Judy Holliday, a minor stockholder, takes on the crooked board of a large corporation, she is aided by Douglas, the former president of the company. These two make a great comedy team. Too bad their early deaths didn't allow them to work together in other vehicles.

OTHER ROLES

1949: *Monk Lanigan* / IT HAPPENS EVERY SPRING; *Leonard Borland* / EVERYBODY DOES IT. **1950:** *Hank* / THE BIG LIFT; *Big Ed Hanley* / LOVE THAT BRUTE. **1951:** *Harry Joplin* / THE GUY WHO CAME BACK; *guest* / RHUBARB; *Guffy McGovern* / ANGELS IN THE OUTFIELD. **1952:** *Joe Brewster* / WHEN IN ROME; *Jerry D'Amato* / CLASH BY NIGHT; *Hector Woodruff* / WE'RE NOT MARRIED; *Andrew McBain* / NEVER WAVE AT A WAC. **1953:** *E. Harry Phillips* / FOREVER FEMALE. **1954:** *Marshall* / THE MAGGIE; *Vic Leonard* / GREEN FIRE. **1956:** *Mike Wilson* / THE GAMMA PEOPLE; *Gus MacAuliffe* / THE LEATHER SAINT. **1957:** *Rocco* / THIS COULD BE THE NIGHT; *Chris Nolan* / BEAU JAMES. **1959:** *Pop Larkin* / THE MATING GAME.

DREYFUSS, RICHARD

(1949–)

An unusual leading man, Richard Dreyfuss has proven himself capable of a wide range of roles, though he is best as aggressive, cocky, comedic characters. He won an Academy Award for THE GOODBYE GIRL in 1977. Dreyfuss, who seemed to age overnight, had a several year hiatus from the movies, but is once again finding roles that allow him to stand out as an actor.

KEY ROLES

Curt Henderson / AMERICAN GRAFFITI, 1973, Universal, d-George Lucas.

Looking very much like a chubby Paul Newman, Dreyfuss spends the last night before he's to go away to college seeking a very sexy blonde who has given him a come-on from her convertible.

Duddy Kravitz / THE APPRENTICESHIP OF DUDDY KRAVITZ, 1974, Canada, Kravitz Syndicate, d-Ted Kotcheff.

Dreyfuss, an ambitious Jewish anti-hero, discovers that it is best to be well-liked if one wants to become rich. Dreyfuss portrays his character as loathsome, funny, and vulnerable. There were some complaints that the film is anti-Semitic, but that surely wasn't the intent of the film.

Matt Hooper / JAWS, 1975, Universal, d-Steven Spielberg.

Scientist Dreyfuss, fisherman Robert Shaw, and sheriff Roy Scheider set out to destroy a great white shark who has made a habit of attacking residents of an East Coast resort area. If producers had let the story go with this film, things would have been just fine, but three poor sequels have taken away from the original.

Roy Neary / CLOSE ENCOUNTERS OF THE THIRD KIND, 1977, Columbia, d-Steven Spielberg.

Dreyfuss is a workman who is led by intuition and detection to the concealed Wyoming landing site of a group of UFOs.

Elliott Garfield / THE GOODBYE GIRL, 1977, Warners, d-Herbert Ross.

Due to a misunderstanding, aspiring actor Dreyfuss has to share the apartment he is subletting with a dancer (Marsha Mason) and her daughter (Quinn Cummings). The three principals handle Neil Simon's one-liners with great skill.

Bill "B.B." Babowsky / TIN MEN, 1987, Touchstone, d-Barry Levinson.

Dreyfuss is an aluminum siding salesman in Baltimore in the 1960s. While he is backing his new Cadillac out of a dealer's lot, he is hit by the car driven by Danny DeVito, a tin man (aluminum siding salesman) for another company. This begins a series of stunts as the two take revenge on each other. Dreyfuss steals DeVito's wife, but the catch is DeVito's glad she's gone.

OTHER ROLES

1967: *bit* / VALLEY OF THE DOLLS; *Berkeley student* / THE GRADUATE. **1968:** *Harold Webster* / HELLO DOWN THERE; *Terry* / THE YOUNG RUNAWAYS. **1973:** *Baby Face Nelson* / DILLINGER; *Clavius* / THE SECOND COMING OF SUZANNE. **1975:** *Boy Wonder* / INSERTS. **1978:** *Moses Wine* / THE BIG FIX. **1980:** *Paul Dietrich* / THE COMPETITION. **1981:** *Ken Harrison* / WHOSE LIFE IS IT ANYWAY? **1984:** *Joe* / THE BUDDY SYSTEM. **1986:** *narrator* / STAND BY ME; *Dave Whiteman* / DOWN AND OUT IN BEVERLY HILLS. **1987:** *Chris Lecce* / STAKEOUT; *Aaron Levinsky* / NUTS.

DRU, JOANNE

(Joanne Laycock, 1923–)

Fetching, green-eyed Joanne Dru played several resolute heroines in a number of western classics after coming to films via her husband, Dick Haymes. She later married John Ireland who appeared with her in RED RIVER. The former model with a sparkling smile did not live up to her early promise and moved into more wholesome matronly roles by the late 1950s.

KEY ROLES

Rosemary Murphy / ABIE'S IRISH ROSE, 1946, United Artists, d-Edward A. Sutherland.

In her film debut, Dru plays the part of the Irish Catholic girl who marries a Jewish boy, which leads to clashes between the two very prejudiced families.

Tess Millay / RED RIVER, 1948, United Artists, d-Howard Hawks.

Dru is the girl who tries to prevent John Wayne from killing his foster son (Montgomery Clift) for taking over command of the cattle drive.

Olivia Dandridge / SHE WORE A YELLOW RIBBON, 1949, RKO, d-John Ford.

Dru fends off the attentions of two young army lieutenants (John Agar and Harry Carey, Jr.) while she sizes up her feelings for retiring cavalry captain John Wayne.

Anne Stanton / ALL THE KING'S MEN, 1949, Columbia, d-Robert Rossen.

Dru plays a girl from a prominent Louisiana family who becomes fascinated with a once simple, honest lawyer (Broderick Crawford) who has become the most powerful politician in the state.

Stella Rigaud / THUNDER BAY, 1953, Universal-International, d-Tony Mann.

Dru provides the romantic interest for James Stewart, an engineer convinced that oil can be raised from the Louisiana seabed.

Marion Moore / SINCERELY YOURS, 1955, Warners, d-Gordon Douglas.

Dru appears as an ever-faithful secretary in this disappointing remake of THE MAN WHO PLAYED GOD, the story of a concert pianist (Liberace) who has gone deaf.

OTHER ROLES

1950: *Denver* / WAGONMASTER; *Gail Mason* / 711 OCEAN DRIVE. **1951:** *Jen Stroble* / VENGEANCE VALLEY; *Miss Tripp* / MR. BELVEDERE RINGS THE BELL. **1952:** *Ann Marshall* / RETURN OF THE TEXAN; *Patricia Nash Dean* / PRIDE OF ST. LOUIS; *Lydia Marble* / MY PAL GUS. **1953:** *Hallie* / HANNAH LEE; *Christine Lawrence* / FORBIDDEN; *Linda Culligan* / CITY OF BAD MEN. **1954:** *Anne Halsey* / DUFFY OF SAN QUENTIN; *Nora Curtis* / THE SIEGE AT RED RIVER; *Lilly* / SOUTHWEST PASSAGE; *Jill Brent* / THREE RING CIRCUS; *Mary Magdalene* / DAY OF TRIUMPH. **1955:** *Lady Joan Holland* / WARRIORS; *Marcia Rollins* / HELL ON FRISCO BAY. **1957:** *Kate* / DRANGO. **1958:** *Milly Elden* / THE LIGHT IN THE FOREST. **1959:** *Marcy Howard* / THE WILD AND THE INNOCENT. **1960:** *Anne Traymore* / SEPTEMBER STORM. **1965:** *Jane Phillips* / SYLVIA. **1981:** *Rosy* / SUPERSNOOPER.

DUNAWAY, FAYE

(1941–)

The films of this blonde with the horsey smile have been mixed. She has had a tendency to overplay her parts. In some cases this has resulted in sterling performances but in others it is extremely unappealing. Determined to become an actress, Faye Dunaway successfully auditioned for the Lincoln Center Repertory Company and in 1962 appeared in "A Man for All Seasons," and in 1964 starred in "After the Fall." Dunaway, who made her film debut in 1966 in THE HAPPENING, won an Oscar for her aggressive career woman in NETWORK, and was nominated for BONNIE

AND CLYDE and CHINATOWN. Sadly, for every outstanding role and performance, Dunaway has had two or three forgettable ones. It will be interesting to see what roles will come to this assuredly talented actress in her middle age.

KEY ROLES

Bonnie Parker / BONNIE AND CLYDE, 1967, Warners, d-Arthur Penn.

Dunaway demonstrates what can happen to a sexually frustrated country girl when she teams up with an impotent bank robber. From the very first scene, when Dunaway looks out from her bedroom window and spies handsome Warren Beatty messing with her mother's car, audiences knew they had walked in on something special. Dunaway was brilliant as the pretty girl racing towards her doom.

Vicky Anderson / THE THOMAS CROWN AFFAIR, 1968, United Artists, d-Norman Jewison.

Dunaway is a glamorous insurance investigator called in to have a sexy chess match with Steve McQueen, who everyone is sure masterminded a major robbery merely to relieve his boredom.

Gwen / THE ARRANGEMENT, 1969, Warners, d-Elia Kazan.

Dunaway is the mistress of a man (Kirk Douglas) who makes an unsuccessful suicide attempt in the opening of the film. The remainder of the film deals with his convalescence and reflection on how materialism is destroying people's emotional lives.

Milady De Winter / THE THREE MUSKETEERS, 1973, Film Trust, d-Richard Lester.

Dunaway is the beautiful, seductive, and deadly agent of Cardinal Richelieu, who plots with His Eminence to prevent D'Artagnan and his friends Athos, Porthos, and Aramis from rescuing the Queen of France from an indiscretion with England's Lord Buckingham. She pays with her head in the sequel.

Evelyn Cross Mulray / CHINATOWN, 1974, Paramount, d-Roman Polanski.

It is 1937 and private eye Jack Nicholson takes it on himself to investigate the murder of Dunaway's husband. Among other things, he discovers that the father of Dunaway's daughter is her own father (John Huston). It's a pretentious piece but Dunaway is excellent as the tragic beauty.

Diana Christensen / NETWORK, 1976, MGM, d-Sidney Lumet.

Dunaway's character in her Oscar-winning role is an obsessed TV executive determined to use the rantings of a mad news anchorman (Peter Finch) to increase ratings. Co-star William Holden gives the best description of her character: "You're television incarnate, Diana, indifferent to suffering, insensitive to joy. All of life is reduced to the common rubble of banality. War, murder, death are all the same to you as bottles of beer, and the daily business of life is a corrupt comedy. You even shatter the sensations of time and space into split seconds and instant replays. You're madness, Diana."

Joan Crawford / MOMMIE DEAREST, 1981, Paramount, d-Frank Perry.

Dunaway looks quite like the great actress in this unflattering view of Crawford based on the recollections of her adopted daughter, Christina. Crawford may have mistreated her children, but she seldom mistreated her audiences with such a hammy performance.

OTHER ROLES

1967: *Sandy* / THE HAPPENING; *Lou McDowell* / HURRY SUNDOWN. **1969:** *Jennifer Winslow* / THE EXTRAORDINARY SEAMAN. **1970:** *Louise Pendrake (Lulu Kane)* / LITTLE BIG MAN. **1971:** *Lou Andreas Sand* / PUZZLE OF A DOWNFALL CHILD; *Kate Elder* / DOC; *Jill* / THE DEADLY TRAP. **1973:** *Lena Doyle* / OKLAHOMA CRUDE. **1974:** *Milady De Winter* / THE FOUR MUSKETEERS; *Susan Franklin* / THE TOWERING INFERNO. **1975:** *Kathy Hale* / THREE DAYS OF THE CONDOR. **1976:** *Denise Kreisler* / VOYAGE OF THE DAMNED. **1978:** *Laura Mars* / THE EYES OF LAURA MARS. **1979:** *Annie* / THE CHAMP. **1980:** *Barbara Delaney* / THE FIRST DEADLY SIN. **1983:** *Lady Barbara Skelton* / THE WICKED LADY. **1984:** *Selena* / SUPERGIRL; *Rachel* / ORDEAL BY INNOCENCE. **1987:** *Wanda Wilcox* / BARFLY.

DUNNE, IRENE

(1901–)

Trained as a singer, Irene Dunne was one of Hollywood's biggest stars during the 1930s and early 1940s as queen of the melodramas, a comedienne in a number of classic comedies, and a fine singer in many musicals. A versatile actress, Dunne received Oscar nominations for CIMARRON (1931), THEODORA GOES WILD (1936), THE AWFUL TRUTH (1937), LOVE AFFAIR (1939), and I REMEMBER MAMA (1948), but came away empty-handed each time. This spunky lady was cast as modern, independent, witty, and imaginative ladies in Hollywood's Golden Era. She was a durable and delightful true beauty. Retiring from the screen in 1952, Dunne hosted the Schlitz Playhouse of Stars on TV and made numerous television appearances on dramatic series. From 1957–58 she was the alternate delegate to the 12th General Assembly of the United Nations.

KEY ROLES

Sabra Cravat / CIMARRON, 1931, RKO, d-Wesley Ruggles.

Dunne is the patient wife of a restless, wandering do-gooder. When he disappears for years at a time she carries on his fight for justice and runs his newspaper. Her spirit and fortitude are remarkable to see, but she makes her character's acceptance of her man's ways credible.

Ray Schmidt / BACK STREET, 1932, Universal, d-John M. Stahl.

Dunne suffers like a saint as the sinner who spends over twenty years as the mistress of a man. Dunne's characters were quite forgiving of the men they loved. Others might have grown weary of a "back street" love with no future.

Ann Vickers / ANN VICKERS, 1933, RKO, d-John Cromwell.

Dunne plays the head of a detention home for women whose damaging relationship with an army officer years earlier has turned her against all men. Later she meets a judge (Walter Huston) who changes her attitude.

Stephanie / ROBERTA, 1935, RKO, d-William Seiter.

Dunne is a Parisian dress designer who pretends to be a Russian princess. The musical highlight is her beautiful rendition of Jerome Kern and Otto Harbach's "Smoke Gets in Your Eyes."

Magnolia Hawks / SHOWBOAT, 1936, Universal, d-James Whale.

Dunne makes a charming Nolia in this stylish musical production of the Edna Ferber story. Raised by her adoring parents on a river showboat, Dunne falls in love with and marries gambler Allan Jones. When he deserts her and their child when his luck runs out, mother and daughter go on to become musical stars. Her songs include "Make Believe," "You Are Love," and "Can't Help Lovin' Dat Man," to which she does a cakewalk as she sings the song with Helen Morgan and Hattie McDaniel.

Theodora Lynn / THEODORA GOES WILD, 1936, Columbia, d-Richard Boleslawski.

Dunne sets the literary world on its ear with a titillating novel which many misinterpret as being autobiographical. She gets things straightened out only after some hilarious episodes.

Lucy Warriner / THE AWFUL TRUTH, 1937, Columbia, d-Leo McCarey.

While waiting for their divorce to become final, Dunne and husband Cary Grant try to make each other jealous and cause a reconciliation. She doesn't really mean it when she tells Grant, "I wouldn't go on living with you if you were dipped in platinum."

Terry McKay / LOVE AFFAIR, 1939, RKO, d-Leo McCarey.

Dunne gives a sensitive and poignant performance as a jaded woman who meets equally world-weary Charles Boyer on an oceanliner and they fall in love. When they reach New York, they agree to test their love by not seeing each other for six months. But as the appointed time for their reunion comes, Dunne is crippled in an accident as she hurries to him. He thinks she has changed her mind; she won't contact him because of her condition. But they do meet again. It's in this movie that Dunne asks the question about sex which has long been on everyone's mind: "Do you think it will ever take the place of night baseball?" The two stars and the rest of the very fine cast make this familiar material seem fresh and charming.

Ellen Arden / MY FAVORITE WIFE, 1940, RKO, d-Garson Kanin.

In a switch on the "Enoch Arden" story, Dunne has just been declared legally dead after having been missing for seven years. Her husband (Cary Grant) takes the occasion to remarry, and Dunne shows up from her shipwreck experience in time for the honeymoon. Although there is little doubt that Grant will choose to be reunited with Dunne, getting to that point takes some funny turns.

Anna Leonowens / ANNA AND THE KING OF SIAM, 1946, 20th Century-Fox, d-John Cromwell.

Dunne plays the English governess who arrives in Bangkok in 1862 to teach the 67 children of the king (Rex Harrison). She later becomes one of his most trusted advisers and helps with his plans to bring his country into the modern world.

Vinnie Day / LIFE WITH FATHER, 1947, Warners, d-Michael Curtiz.

Dunne is the loyal wife of an irascible family tyrant who resists her urgings to become baptized. It's lovely to look at, but there's nothing much to it.

Mama Hanson / I REMEMBER MAMA, 1948, RKO, d-George Stevens.

Dunne is the heart and soul of a Norwegian-American family, who is as sweet, understanding, and loving as the ideal mother should be.

Queen Victoria / THE MUDLARK, 1950, 20th Century-Fox, d-Jean Negulesco.

Dunne is splendid as Queen Victoria who, after years of seclusion, begins to reenter public life when she makes friends with an agreeable boy who breaks into Windsor Castle to see her.

OTHER ROLES

1930: *Delphine* / LEATHERNECKING. **1931:** *Helene Andrews* / BACHELOR APARTMENT; *Diana Page* / THE GREAT LOVER; *Mary* / CONSOLATION MARRIAGE. **1932:** *Jessica* / SYMPHONY OF SIX MILLION; *Laura Stanhope* / THIRTEEN WOMEN. **1933:** *Sally St. John* / THE SECRET OF MADAME BLANCHE; *Anna Stanley* / NO OTHER WOMAN; *Christina Phelps* / THE SILVER CORD; *Sarah Cazenove* / IF I WERE FREE. **1934:** *Toni Dunlap* / THIS MAN IS MINE; *Hilda Bouverie* / STINGAREE; *Countess Ellen Olenska* / AGE OF INNOCENCE. **1935:** *Adeline Schmidt* / SWEET ADELINE; *Helen Hudson* / MAGNIFICENT OBSESSION. **1937:** *Sally Walterson* / HIGH, WIDE AND HANDSOME. **1938:** *Margaret "Maggie" Garret* / JOY OF LIVING. **1939:** *Eleanor Wayne* / INVITATION TO HAPPINESS; *Helen* / WHEN TOMORROW COMES. **1941:** *Julie Gardner* / PENNY SERENADE; *Nancy Andrews* / UNFINISHED BUSINESS; *cameo* / LAND OF LIBERTY. **1942:** *Jane Palmer* / LADY IN A JAM. **1943:** *Dorinda Durston* / A GUY NAMED JOE. **1944:** *Susan Dunn Ashwood* / THE WHITE CLIFFS OF DOVER; *Anne Crandall* / TOGETHER AGAIN. **1945:** *Paula Wharton* / OVER 21. **1950:** *Kay* / NEVER A DULL MOMENT. **1952:** *Polly Baxter* / IT GROWS ON TREES.

DURBIN, DEANNA

(Edna Mae Durbin, 1921–)

Dark-haired teenager Deanna Durbin is said to have single-handedly saved Universal Studios from bankruptcy with her series of wholesome 1930s musicals. When she retired to live in France in 1950, she was the highest paid female actress in Hollywood. She suffered none of the emotional trauma that haunted her singing partner in the 1936 short EVERY SUNDAY, Judy Garland, and spoke of the girl she was in the 1930s as "a fairytale character." She also correctly recognized the basis of her success: "Just as the Hollywood pinup represents sex to dissatisfied erotics, so I represented the ideal daughter millions of fathers and mothers wished they had."

KEY ROLES

Penny Craig / THREE SMART GIRLS, 1936, Universal, d-Henry Koster.

Durbin and her two sisters (Nan Grey and Barbara Read) save their father from a gold digger and reunite him with their mother. Durbin's versions of "My Heart Is Singing" and "Someone to Care for Me" became instant hits.

Patricia Cardwell / 100 MEN AND A GIRL, 1937, Universal, d-Henry Koster.

Durbin persuades Leopold Stokowski to form an orchestra of out-of-work musicians. She pleased fans of her voice with "It's Raining Sunbeams," "A Heart that's Free," and excerpts from "La Traviata."

Gloria Harkinson / MAD ABOUT MUSIC, 1938, Universal, d-Norman Taurog.

In her third feature, Durbin gets top billing as a schoolgirl who invents a father and, when her friends insist on meeting him, she prevails on Herbert Marshall to fill the role. She sings "I Love to Whistle" and "Ave Maria."

Alice Fullerton / THAT CERTAIN AGE, 1938, Universal, d-Edward Ludwig.

Now growing up, Durbin develops a crush on charming Melvyn Douglas but settles for Jackie Cooper. Her songs include "Juliet's Waltz Song" and "You're as Pretty as a Picture."

Anne Terry / IT STARTED WITH EVE, 1941, Universal, d-Henry Koster.

To please a dying millionaire (Charles Laughton) Durbin becomes his grandson's fiancée. But the old fella recovers, and love develops between Durbin and the lad (Bob Cummings). She sings "Clavelitos" and Dvorak's "Going Home."

Caroline Frost / CAN'T HELP SINGING, 1944, Universal, d-Frank Ryan.

While chasing an army officer (Robert Paige) across the country, heiress Durbin sings "More and More," "Any Moment Now," and "Finale Ultimo."

OTHER ROLES

1939: *Penny Craig* / THREE SMART GIRLS GROW UP; *Connie Harding* / FIRST LOVE. **1940:** *Pamela Drake* / IT'S A DATE; *Ilonka Tolnay* / SPRING PARADE. **1941:** *Jane Dana* / NICE GIRL? **1943:** *Ruth Kirke* / THE AMAZING MRS. HOLLIDAY; *Penny Craig* / HERS TO HOLD; *Ann Carter* / HIS BUTLER'S SISTER. **1944:** *Jackie Lamont (Abigail Martin)* / CHRISTMAS HOLIDAY. **1945:** *Nikki Collins* / LADY ON A TRAIN; *Kim Walker* / BECAUSE OF HIM. **1947:** *Louise Ginglebusher* / I'LL BE YOURS; *Mary Collins* / SOMETHING IN THE WIND. **1948:** *Rosie Moore* / UP IN CENTRAL PARK; *Mary Poppertree* / FOR THE LOVE OF MARY.

DUVALL, ROBERT

(1931–)

Robert Duvall has the uncanny ability to look completely different with each character he plays. His versatility is admirable and he doesn't allow his audiences to catch him acting. He blends in perfectly with whatever the atmosphere of the movie is, although he generally portrays ordinary men who have trouble dealing with their ordinary lives. Even in his first film, TO KILL A MOCKINGBIRD, where he is only briefly seen, one has the feeling that here is someone who will be heard from in the future. Duvall was nominated for Oscars for THE GODFATHER (1972), APOCALYPSE NOW (1979), and THE GREAT SANTINI (1980); he won in 1983 for TENDER MERCIES. He has appeared in the TV movies IKE (1979) and THE TERRY FOX STORY (1983).

KEY ROLES

Ned Pepper / TRUE GRIT, 1969, Paramount, d-Henry Hathaway.

Duvall heads the outlaw gang that includes the man that John Wayne, Glen Campbell, and Kim Darby are seeking for killing Darby's father. His last apparent words to Wayne are, "I call that bold talk for a one-eyed fat man;" to which the Duke replies, "Fill your hands, you son of a bitch."

Col. Frank Burns / M*A*S*H, 1970, 20th Century-Fox, d-Robert Altman.

Duvall is the puritanical hypocrite that Hawkeye, Trapper John, and other staffers drive over the brink at a mobile army surgical unit during the Korean War.

Tom Hagen / THE GODFATHER, 1972, Paramount, d-Francis Ford Coppola.

Duvall plays the almost adopted son and lawyer of Marlon Brando in this story about the end of a Mafia Don and the ascendency of his youngest son to that position. In the sequel, Al Pacino as the new Don, eases Duvall out because he's not a blood relative.

Frank Hackett / NETWORK, 1976, MGM, d-Sidney Lumet.

Duvall is a TV executive who doesn't like the way the news division is run because it has low ratings and loses money. He supports the lunatic schemes of Faye Dunaway for making the news both profitable and entertaining.

Lieutenant Colonel Kilgore / APOCALYPSE NOW, 1979, Omni Zoetrope, d-Francis Ford Coppola.

Duvall is the gung-ho commander of a helicopter unit during the Vietnam War. His character is summed up nicely as he swaggeringly says, "I love the smell of napalm in the morning...It smells like victory."

Bull Meechum / THE GREAT SANTINI, 1980, Warners, d-Lewis John Carlino.

Crack fighter pilot Duvall has trouble adjusting to peacetime domestic life. His family has even more difficulty adjusting to him and his expectations.

Mac Sledge / TENDER MERCIES, 1982, EMI / Anton, d-Bruce Beresford.

Duvall wrote and sang his own songs to accompany his Oscar-winning performance as an ex-alcoholic country and western singer who, through the love of a good woman, gains enough confidence to resume his career.

OTHER ROLES

1962: *Boo Radley* / TO KILL A MOCKINGBIRD. **1963:** *motorcyclist* / NIGHTMARE IN THE SUN; *Captain Winston* / CAPTAIN NEWMAN, M.D. **1965:** *Edwin Stewart* / THE CHASE. **1968:** *Weissberg* / BULLITT. **1969:** *Gordon* / THE RAIN PEOPLE. **1971:** *Vernon Adams* / LAWMAN; *THX 1138* / THX 1138. **1972:** *Jesse James* / THE GREAT NORTHFIELD MINNESOTA RAID; *Jackson Fentry* / TOMORROW. **1973:** *Earl Macklin* / THE OUTFIT; *Eddie Ryan* / BADGE 373; *Ford Pierce* / LADY ICE. **1974:** *The Director* / THE CONVERSATION. **1975:** *Jay Wagner* / BREAKOUT; *George Hansen* / THE KILLER ELITE. **1976:** *Dr. John Watson* / THE SEVEN PERCENT SOLUTION. **1977:** *Bill McDonald* / THE GREATEST; *Col. Max Radl* / THE EAGLE HAS LANDED. **1978:** *Loren Hardeman, III* / THE BETSY; *guest* / INVASION OF THE BODY SNATCHERS. **1981:** *Tom Spellacy* / TRUE CONFESSIONS; *Gruen* / THE PURSUIT OF D. B. COOPER. **1984:** *Joe Hillerman* / THE STONE BOY; *Mac Mercy* / THE NATURAL. **1986:** *Caspary* / THE LIGHTSHIP; *preacher* / BELIZAIRE THE CAJUN. **1987:** *Carrasco* / HOTEL COLONIAL.

DVORAK, ANN

(Ann McKim, 1912–)

Daughter of silent-film actress Anna Lehr, Ann Dvorak made her first movie appearance at age three in RAMONA (1916), billed as Baby Ann Lehr. She returned to the screen some 16 years later, but the studios did not always find it easy to cast this lithe and leggy former chorus girl. Having more talent than her bosses recognized, Dvorak fought for better roles, but this did not help her cause. She was often cast in sluttish or spiteful roles. Away from the camera, though, she was very likable and continued making pictures into the 1950s.

KEY ROLES

Mary / SKY DEVILS, 1931, United Artists, d-Edward Sutherland.

Dvorak was taken out of the chorus by Howard Hughes to provide the love interest for Spencer Tracy in this story of two draft dodgers who become World War I heroes.

Cesca Camonte / SCARFACE, 1932, United Artists, d-Howard Hawks.
Dvorak is the sister of the title character (Paul Muni), and there is a strong suggestion of an incestuous relationship between the siblings.

Jean Morgan / G-MEN, 1935, Warners, d-William Keighley.
Dvorak provides the appropriate feminine interest for James Cagney in this rat-a-tat-tat story of a young attorney who becomes a G-man in order to avenge the death of a friend.

Josephine Gray / DR. SOCRATES, 1935, Warners, d-William Dieterle.
Dvorak is a gun moll for mobsters who force small-town doctor Paul Muni to tend to their wounds. He does so and ends the mobsters' careers by injecting them with morphine.

Sally Mason / THANKS A MILLION, 1935, 20th Century-Fox, d-Roy Del Ruth.
Dvorak walks out of the life of crooner Dick Powell when he is elected governor and walks right back in when he resigns. Not wishing to lose the man they elected, the voters insist that he return to office, which he does, this time with Dvorak's approval.

Ann Rogers / MANHATTAN MERRY-GO-ROUND, 1937, Republic, d-Charles F. Reisner.
Dvorak is just one of a very large cast in this musical revue held together by the lame story of a gang of racketeers taking over a sound recording studio.

Barbara Lucas / SQUADRON LEADER X, 1942, Great Britain, RKO, d-Lance Comfort.
Dvorak is the ex-fiancée of ace Luftwaffe pilot Eric Portman who poses as an RAF pilot and bombs Belgian civilian targets. He is picked up by the underground and sent to England where he blackmails Dvorak into helping him steal a plane.

OTHER ROLES

1916: *bit* / RAMONA. **1929:** *chorus girl* / THE HOLLYWOOD REVUE OF 1929. **1930:** *dance hall girl* / WAY OUT WEST; *bit* / FREE AND EASY. **1931:** *a fan* / THE GUARDSMAN; *bit* / THIS MODERN AGE. **1932:** *Lee* / THE CROWD ROARS; *Molly Louvain* / THE STRANGE LOVE OF MOLLY LOUVAIN; *Sally* / LOVE IS A RACKET; *Judy* / CROONER; *Marian* / STRANGER IN TOWN; *Vivian Revere* / THREE ON A MATCH. **1933:** *Madeleine* / THE WAY TO LOVE; *Claire Gore* / COLLEGE COACH. **1934:** *Lydia* / MASSACRE; *Myra* / HEAT LIGHTNING; *Joan Morley* / MIDNIGHT ALIBI; *Beulah* / FRIENDS OF MR. SWEENEY; *Nan Wilson Reynolds* / HOUSEWIFE; *Marguerite Gilbert* / SIDE STREETS; *Susan Merrill* / GENTLEMEN ARE BORN; *Barbara* / I SELL ANYTHING; *Judy Wagner* / MURDER IN THE CLOUDS. **1935:** *Bonnie Haydon* / SWEET MUSIC. **1936:** *Connie* / WE WHO ARE ABOUT TO DIE. **1937:** *Ruth Martin* / RACING LADY; *Carol O'Neil* / MIDNIGHT COURT; *Jerry* / SHE'S NO LADY; *Della Street* / THE CASE OF THE STUTTERING BISHOP. **1938:** *Minerva Harlan* / MERRILY WE LIVE; *Connie* / GANGS OF NEW YORK. **1939:** *Mary* / BLIND ALLEY; *Eva McLain* / STRONGER THAN DESIRE. **1940:** *Jo* / CAFE HOSTESS; *Kay Warren* / GIRLS OF THE ROAD. **1942:** *Anne Morgan* / THIS WAS PARIS. **1944:** *Joan Grahame* / ESCAPE TO DANGER. **1945:** *Flaxen Tarry* / FLAME OF THE BARBARY COAST; *Helen Grant* / MASQUERADE IN MEXICO. **1946:** *Terry* / THE BACHELOR'S DAUGHTERS; *Rita* / ABILENE TOWN. **1947:** *Madeleine Forester* / THE PRIVATE AFFAIRS OF BEL AMI; *Charlene* / THE LONG NIGHT; *Olive Jensen* / OUT OF THE BLUE. **1948:** *Belle Connors* / THE WALLS OF JERICHO. **1950:** *Mary Ashlon* / A LIFE OF HER OWN; *Mrs. Lynch* / OUR VERY OWN; *Sue Younger* / THE RETURN OF JESSE JAMES; *Connie Kepplar* / MRS. O'MALLEY AND MR. MALONE. **1951:** *Claire Phillips* / I WAS AN AMERICAN SPY; *Rachel* / THE SECRET OF CONVICT LAKE.

EASTWOOD, CLINT

(Clinton Eastwood, Jr., 1930–)
Clint Eastwood has come a long way since his name appeared lower in the credits than that of Francis the mule in FRANCIS IN THE NAVY in 1955. He enjoyed some success as the second lead on TV's "Rawhide" (1958–1965), but he became an international star when he appeared in spaghetti westerns as "the Man with No Name." Eastwood's fascist heroes have come under fire from critics. On the other hand, it seems, his lonely characters vicariously appeal to the many who can't put things right in their own lives, and for whom taking the law in one's own hands seems the preferable option. Tall, lean, and blue-eyed, Eastwood is a soft-spoken avenging angel with a gaze that puts the fear of God in any wrongdoer. Eastwood has also shown talent directing films for his own production company, bringing projects in on time and under budget.

KEY ROLES

The man with no name / A FISTFUL OF DOLLARS, 1964, Italy, United Artists, d-Sergio Leone.
Eastwood is a violent and mysterious cigar-smoking, gunslinging stranger who disposes of two rival gangs that are battling for control of a Mexican border town.

The stranger (Blondy) / THE GOOD, THE BAD, AND THE UGLY, 1966, Italy, PEA, d-Sergio Leone.
Eastwood, Eli Wallach, and Lee Van Cleef are the three mentioned in the title who, during the U.S. Civil War, are roaming the West seeking hidden loot.

Walt Coogan / COOGAN'S BLUFF, 1968, Universal, d-Don Siegel.
Eastwood is a deputy sheriff from Arizona who escorts a murder suspect to New York City. When he loses his prisoner, he tracks him down in the canyons of New York.

"Pardner" (Sylvester Newel) / PAINT YOUR WAGON, 1969, Paramount, d-Joshua Logan.
Eastwood sings "I Talk to the Trees" in this musical very short on singers. He and his gold-mining partner (Lee Marvin) share a wife (Jean Seberg) until civilization reaches No Name City.

John McBurney / THE BEGUILED, 1971, Universal, d-Don Siegel.
Eastwood is a wounded Yankee soldier hiding out in a southern girls' school during the Civil War. His presence causes many sexual problems for both the students and teachers who ultimately kill him.

Dave Garver / PLAY MISTY FOR ME, 1971, Universal, d-Clint Eastwood.
Eastwood is a late-night disc jockey on a California radio station who is pestered by a woman who turns out to be homicidal.

Harry Callahan / DIRTY HARRY, 1971, Warners, d-Don Siegel.
Eastwood plays a cop who brings in a sniper but, since he didn't read the suspect his constitutional rights, the murderer is released. Later the murderer kidnaps a girl, buries her alive, and taunts Eastwood to come after him, which the violence-inclined cop does. In the opening scenes Eastwood gives a good indication of his character when, after a shoot-out with some

crooks, he comes across one still alive and quietly says, "I know what you're thinking. Did he fire six shots or only five? Well, to tell you the truth, in all the excitement I've kinda lost track myself. But being this is a .44 magnum, the most powerful handgun in the world, and would blow your head clean off, you've got to ask yourself one question: Do I feel lucky? Well, do ya, punk?"

Josey Wales / THE OUTLAW JOSEY WALES, 1976, Warners, d-Clint Eastwood.
In this bloodthirsty film, farmer Eastwood avenges the murders of his wife and son by renegade Union soldiers.

Philo Beddoe / EVERY WHICH WAY BUT LOOSE, 1978, Warners, d-James Fargo.
Eastwood is a bare-knuckles fighter who travels around the country in the company of an orangutan called Clyde. It's an unusual comedy showing another side of the laconic loner.

Bronco Billy / BRONCO BILLY, 1980, Warners, d-Clint Eastwood.
Eastwood is the owner and star of a small traveling Wild West show, who persuades a spoiled runaway heiress (Sondra Locke) to be his assistant in a knife-throwing act.

Harry Callahan / SUDDEN IMPACT, 1983, Warners, d-Clint Eastwood.
This DIRTY HARRY sequel contains the classic line, "Go ahead, make my day." The story is about Eastwood going after a woman (Sondra Locke) who is methodically killing those who raped her and her sister. He lets her go when the last of the scum is taken care of.

Wes Block / TIGHTROPE, 1984, Warners, d-Richard Tuggle.
New Orleans police detective Eastwood finds that he has much in common with the sex murderer that he is tracking. The murderer is equally interested in playing mind games with Eastwood, using Eastwood's children and girlfriend (Genevieve Bujold) as pawns.

OTHER ROLES

1955: *lab technician* / REVENGE OF THE CREATURE; *Jonesy* / FRANCIS IN THE NAVY; *First Saxon* / LADY GODIVA; *air force pilot* / TARANTULA. **1956:** *Will* / NEVER SAY GOODBYE; *Jack Rice* / THE FIRST TRAVELING SALESLADY; *ranch hand* / STAR IN THE DUST. **1957:** *Dumbo* / ESCAPADE IN JAPAN. **1958:** *George Moseley* / LAFAYETTE ESCADRILLE; *Keith Williams* / AMBUSH AT CIMARRON PASS. **1965:** *the stranger* / FOR A FEW DOLLARS MORE. **1967:** *husband* / THE WITCHES. **1968:** *Jed Cooper* / HANG 'EM HIGH. **1969:** *Lt. Morris Schaffer* / WHERE EAGLES DARE. **1970:** *Kelly* / KELLY'S HEROES; *Hogan* / TWO MULES FOR SISTER SARA. **1972:** *Joe Kidd* / JOE KIDD. **1973:** *the stranger* / HIGH PLAINS DRIFTER; *Harry Callahan* / MAGNUM FORCE. **1974:** *John "Thunderbolt" Doherty* / THUNDERBOLT AND LIGHTFOOT. **1975:** *Jonathan Hemlock* / THE EIGER SANCTION. **1976:** *Harry Callahan* / THE ENFORCER. **1977:** *Ben Shockley* / THE GAUNTLET. **1979:** *Frank Morris* / ESCAPE FROM ALCATRAZ. **1980:** *Philo Beddoe* / ANY WHICH WAY YOU CAN. **1982:** *Mitchell Gant* / FIREFOX; *Red Stovall* / HONKYTONK MAN. **1984:** *Lieutenant Speer* / CITY HEAT. **1985:** *preacher* / PALE RIDER. **1986:** *Gunnery Sgt. Tom Highway* / HEARTBREAK RIDGE.

EDDY, NELSON

(1901–1967)

Jeanette MacDonald and Nelson Eddy formed one of the most successful film singing teams in movie history in a series of 1930s musicals. It must be confessed that Eddy had no idea at all how to act, but this blond, square-shouldered baritone had a schmaltzy voice that was quite attractive. He made his debut with the Philadelphia Civic Opera in 1924 and in 1931 appeared at the Metropolitan Opera in Berg's "Wozzeck." In 1933 he signed a film contract with MGM and teamed for the first time with MacDonald in the 1935 film NAUGHTY MARIETTA. After his last film in 1947 he continued to work in radio, concerts, and nightclubs. He died of a heart attack while on stage in 1967.

KEY ROLES

Capt. Richard Warrington / NAUGHTY MARIETTA, 1935, MGM, d-W. S. Van Dyke.
Eddy is a dashing mercenary who comes to the rescue of a ship carrying a French princess (Jeanette MacDonald) when it is attacked by pirates off the coast of Louisiana. His songs are Victor Herbert's "Tramp, Tramp, Tramp" and "Ah, Sweet Mystery of Life."

Sergeant Bruce / ROSE MARIE, 1936, MGM, d-W. S. Van Dyke.
Eddy is the Mountie who always gets his man. This time, though, he must bring in James Stewart, the brother of his love (Jeanette MacDonald). His songs include the title number as well as a duet of "Indian Love Call" with MacDonald.

Paul Allison / MAYTIME, 1937, MGM, d-Robert Z. Leonard.
Opera star, Jeanette MacDonald falls in love with penniless singer Eddy, but her impresario (John Barrymore) shoots him. Eddy's Sigmund Romberg songs include "Will You Remember" and "Love's Old Sweet Song."

Ernest Lane / SWEETHEARTS, 1938, MGM, d-W. S. Van Dyke.
This was MGM's first three-color movie and it stars Eddy and Jeanette MacDonald as a musical comedy team in the sixth year of their hit Broadway show. When they are coaxed to Hollywood it almost ruins their private lives. The best number is, of course, the title song by Victor Herbert.

Charles, Duc de Villiers / NEW MOON, 1940, MGM, d-Robert Z. Leonard.
Eddy is a pirate chief who falls for French aristocrat Jeanette MacDonald who once again is forced to flee to Louisiana. His Romberg songs include "Softly as in a Morning Sunrise" and "Stout-Hearted Men."

Anatole Carron / PHANTOM OF THE OPERA, 1943, Universal, d-Arthur Lubin.
Eddy is a singer at the Paris Opera House where phantom Claude Rains hides out. He tries to help a young singer (Susanna Foster) who interests him both personally and professionally.

Brom Broeck / KNICKERBOCKER HOLIDAY, 1944, United Artists, d-Harry Joe Brown.
Eddy is a printer of subversive literature in New Amsterdam at the time of Peter Stuyvesant. He doesn't get to sing the only hit song in the show. The honor of singing "September Song" goes to Walter Huston.

OTHER ROLES

1933: *cameo* / BROADWAY TO HOLLYWOOD; *himself* / DANCING LADY. **1934:** *himself* / STUDENT TOUR. **1937:** *Dick Thorpe* / ROSALIE. **1938:** *Ramerez (Lieutenant Johnson)* / THE GIRL OF THE GOLDEN WEST. **1939:** *Steve Logan* / LET FREEDOM RING; *Peter* / BALALAIKA. **1940:** *Carl Linden* / BITTER SWEET. **1941:** *Karl Lang* / THE CHOCOLATE SOLDIER. **1942:** *Count Willi Palaffi* / I MARRIED

AN ANGEL. **1946:** *voice* / MAKE MINE MUSIC. **1947:** *James Lawrence* / NORTHWEST OUTPOST.

FAIRBANKS, DOUGLAS, JR.

(1909–)

Douglas Fairbanks, Jr. received no encouragement from his father, who took little interest in Jr.'s career. The lad followed in his father's footsteps, nevertheless, appearing in several swashbuckling roles. He was more versatile than dad but never a star of the same magnitude. Good looking, urbane, and pleasant, he graced many movies without ever being truly outstanding. Later he grew tired of acting, moved to England, and took up production. His first wife, from 1929 to 1933, was Joan Crawford of whom he said, "She is a ten-year-old girl who has put on her mother's dress—and has done it convincingly."

KEY ROLES

Steve Maxwell / THE JAZZ AGE, 1929, FBO Pictures, d-Lynn Shores.

When Fairbanks and his girl wreck one of her father's streetcars while on a careless spree, her father uses this incident to prevent Fairbanks's father from opposing his shady dealings with the city. But Fairbanks and his girl appear before the city council and admit their culpability.

Douglas Scott / THE DAWN PATROL, 1930, First National, d-Howard Hawks.

The strain of seeing young pilots being sent to almost certain death during World War I severs the friendship between Fairbanks and his squadron commander (Richard Barthelmess) when the latter sends Fairbanks's younger brother on a mission from which he may not return.

Henry / OUTWARD BOUND, 1930, Warners, d-Robert Milton.

Fairbanks and his lover (Helen Chandler) find themselves on a strange oceanliner with an odd assortment of passengers and only one crewman. It is slowly revealed to the audience that everyone aboard the ship is dead, and all are making their final trip to a place of judgment.

Joe Massara / LITTLE CAESAR, 1931, First National, d-Mervyn LeRoy.

Fairbanks is a close friend of the title character (Edward G. Robinson). He is not a hood like Little Caesar, but he finds himself in the middle of the hoodlum wars because of his questionable choice of friends.

Joseph Sheridan / MORNING GLORY, 1933, RKO, d-Lowell Sherman.

Fairbanks is a young playwright who falls in love with a stagestruck girl (Katharine Hepburn) who has come to New York from Vermont to become an actress. When his temperamental star walks out on opening night, Fairbanks sends on Hepburn who, of course, is a smash.

Grand Duke Peter / CATHERINE THE GREAT, 1934, Great Britain, Korda / United Artists, d-Paul Czinner.

In this version of the life and rule of Russia's Catherine, Grand Duke Peter (Fairbanks) doesn't lose his wits until after his marriage to the future czarina. But then he also forfeits his life.

Rupert of Hentzau / THE PRISONER OF ZENDA, 1937, Selznick / United Artists, d-John Cromwell.

In what may be his best role, Fairbanks is a dashing villain in league with Raymond Massey to usurp the Ruritanian throne from the latter's brother (Ronald Colman). Both are thwarted by a look-alike English cousin. When Fairbanks sees how things are, he flees to fight another day, but always for causes that will serve his own best interests.

Richard Carleton / THE YOUNG IN HEART, 1938, Selznick / United Artists, d-Richard Wallace.

Fairbanks is the son in a family of con artists who eventually are shown the error of their ways by sweet old Minnie Dupree. Fairbanks is even willing to get a job to please his lady love, Paulette Goddard.

Sergeant Ballantine / GUNGA DIN, 1939, RKO, d-George Stevens.

When Fairbanks announces his intention to leave military service and marry Joan Fontaine, his two friends (Cary Grant and Victor McLaglen) involve him in a rousing adventure with Indian thuggees.

Mario and Lucien / THE CORSICAN BROTHERS, 1942, United Artists, d-Gregory Ratoff.

Fairbanks plays both Siamese twins who were miraculously separated at birth. Brought up apart, they maintain a physical bond—when one is hurt, the other also feels the pain. They also develop a love for the same woman as they unite to take vengeance on the villain who stole their family home.

Sinbad / SINBAD THE SAILOR, 1947, RKO, d-Richard Wallace.

In a performance that reminds one of his father, Fairbanks sets off on Sinbad's eighth voyage to find Alexander the Great's lost treasure.

Dr. John Marlowe / STATE SECRET, 1950, Great Britain, British Lion, d-Sidney Gilliat.

Fairbanks is a surgeon invited to the country of Vosnia to care for the critically ill dictator who must be kept alive until after the elections. When his patient dies, Fairbanks realizes that it's time to make tracks. He flees, is chased by the State police, and is caught at the border. Later he escapes execution because of a political change in the country brought on by the news of the dictator's death.

OTHER ROLES

1920: *Jay Rountree* / PARTY GIRL. **1923:** *Stephen Harlow, Jr.* / STEPHEN STEPS OUT. **1925:** *Sandy* / THE AIR MAIL; *Chess Weymer* / WILD HORSE MESA; *Richard Grovesnor* / STELLA DALLAS; *Triton* / THE AMERICAN VENUS. **1926:** *Sonny Galloway* / PADLOCKED; *Jeff Sanford* / MAN BAIT; *Hal Terwilliger* / BROKEN HEARTS OF HOLLYWOOD. **1927:** *G. Clifton Blackburn* / IS ZAT SO? *Farleigh Bright* / A TEXAS STEER. **1928:** *Chris Miller* / THE BARKER; *Geoffrey Merrick* / A WOMAN OF AFFAIRS; *Steve* / THE TOILERS. **1929:** *Douglas Stratton* / FAST LIFE; Gil / OUR MODERN MAIDENS; *Wyn* / THE CARELESS AGE; *Marty Reid* / THE FORWARD PASS; *himself* / THE SHOW OF SHOWS. **1930:** *Gil Hayden* / LOOSE ANKLES; *Norman Overbeck* / LITTLE ACCIDENT; *Billy Bear* / THE WAY OF ALL MEN; *Dick* / ONE NIGHT AT SUSIE'S. **1931:** *Jack Ingleside* / CHANCES; *Larry O'Brien* / I LIKE YOUR NERVE. **1932:** *Chic Miller* / UNION DEPOT; *Scotty McClenahan* / IT'S TOUGH TO BE FAMOUS; *Jimmy Russell* / LOVE IS A RACKET; *Bill Keller* / PARACHUTE JUMPER. **1933:** *Fred Blake* / THE NARROW CORNER; *Digby* / CAPTURED; *Jimmy Dolan* / THE LIFE OF JIMMY DOLAN. **1934:** *Joe Martin* / SUCCESS AT ANY PRICE. **1935:** *Rodolphe* / MIMI; *Barnabas Barty* / THE AMATEUR GENTLEMAN; *Tony* / MAN OF THE MOMENT. **1936:** *Tony Seymour* / ACCUSED; *Ricky Morgan* / WHEN THIEF MEETS THIEF. **1938:** *Dan Webster* / JOY OF LIVING; *James Trevor* / THE RAGE OF PARIS; *Chick Kirkland* / HAVING WONDERFUL TIME. **1939:** *John Randolph* / THE SUN NEVER SETS; *David Gillespie* / RULERS OF THE SEA. **1940:** *Keith Brandon* / GREEN HELL; *Jim Logan* / SAFARI; *Bill O'Brien* / ANGELS OVER BROADWAY. **1947:** *Charles*

Stuart / THE EXILE. **1948:** *Col. Ladislas Karolyi Teglash / the duke* / THAT LADY IN ERMINE. **1949:** *the O'Flynn* / THE FIGHTING O'FLYNN. **1951:** *Don Drake* / MR. DRAKE'S DUCK. **1981:** *Edward Wanderly* / GHOST STORY.

FARMER, FRANCES

(1913–1970)

More known for the movie made about her life (starring look-alike Jessica Lange), Frances Farmer was a determined and troubled woman who lost her screen popularity when her alcoholism and mental problems put an end to her career. She had started as an actress with the Group Theatre in New York, playing the female lead in "Golden Boy." Talented, bright, and beautiful, she was frequently in conflict with her studio over her movie assignments in unimportant second features.

KEY ROLES

Doris Halliday / RHYTHM ON THE RANGE, 1936, Paramount, d-Norman Taurog.

Farmer is a footloose heiress that the old "cowboy" Bing Crosby would like to corral. She is fine in the film, but the picture is mainly Crosby's singing.

Lotta Bostrom / Lotta Morgan / COME AND GET IT, 1936, United Artists, d-Howard Hawks and William Wyler.

In a dual role Farmer is the lost love of a self-made lumber tycoon (Edward Arnold) and the woman's daughter who prefers Arnold's son (Joel McCrea) to him, when Arnold becomes infatuated with the second generation Farmer. This is usually recognized as her best performance.

Josie Mansfield / THE TOAST OF NEW YORK, 1937, RKO, d-Rowland V. Lee.

Financier Jim Fisk (Edward Arnold) and one of his close friends (Cary Grant) conspire to control Wall Street and win the lovely Farmer in this box-office failure about the greed of business magnates after the Civil War.

Ruby Taylor / SOUTH OF PAGO PAGO, 1940, United Artists, d-Alfred E. Green.

Farmer is a barroom queen who lures the son of the chief of a South Sea island away from his native sweetheart so her crooked associates can steal some pearls. She dies at the end protecting him from her gang.

Calamity Jane / BADLANDS OF DAKOTA, 1941, Universal, d-Alfred E. Green.

Farmer looks fetching in buckskin as the Wild West's number one female scout, but this third-rate story about a sheriff cleaning up a corrupt town doesn't give her much else to do.

OTHER ROLES

1936: *Sally Colman* / TOO MANY PARENTS; *Ann Blane* / BORDER FLIGHT. **1937:** *Vina Swain* / EXCLUSIVE; *Faith Wishart* / EBB TIDE. **1938:** *Trina* / RIDE A CROOKED MILE. **1940:** *Linda Chalmers* / FLOWING GOLD. **1941:** *Kitty Carr* / WORLD PREMIERE; *Elaine Raden* / AMONG THE LIVING. **1942:** *Isobel Blake* / SON OF FURY. **1958:** *Mrs. Bickford* / THE PARTY CRASHERS.

FARRELL, CHARLES

(1902–)

Recognizing both his good fortune and his limitations, Charles Farrell noted, "Success came too soon for me. I hadn't had the experience to go with the star status I suddenly acquired." Fans of the team of Farrell and Janet Gaynor didn't seem to mind that he wasn't much of an actor; he was handsome and the twelve lyrical love stories in which they co-starred required little else from him. Later he would acquire a new generation of admirers with the hit TV show "My Little Margie."

KEY ROLES

Chico / SEVENTH HEAVEN, 1927, Silent, Fox Films, d-Frank Borzage.

Farrell is a Paris sewer worker who gives shelter to street waif Janet Gaynor, falls in love with her, marries her, and shares some idyllic time with her in their "seventh heaven"—his seventh-floor flat—until he must go to war.

Gino / STREET ANGEL, 1928, Silent, Fox Films, d-Frank Borzage.

Farrell is a struggling painter who asks girl-of-the-streets Janet Gaynor to pose for a Madonna portrait. The police arrest her and she is sent to prison. He loves her but is disillusioned and loses interest in painting. On her release she finds him and convinces him that they belong together.

Timothy Osborn / LUCKY STAR, 1929, Fox Films, d-Frank Borzage.

Farrell returns from World War I a cripple, but regains enough strength to thrash his rival for the hand of Janet Gaynor.

Jack Cromwell / SUNNY SIDE UP, 1929, Fox Films, d-David Butler.

In the team's first all-talking film, they joined everyone else in the movie business and not only talked but sang and danced as well. Farrell is a society man spending his summer at a Long Island resort where he gives tenement girl Janet Gaynor a taste of the good life.

Liliom / LILIOM, 1930, Fox Films, d-Frank Borzage.

Farrell's co-star in this story of a carousel barker in Budapest is Rose Hobart, a servant girl he marries and mistreats until he learns she is pregnant. He tries to get money to provide for his growing family through a robbery, but is killed. Later he is given a chance to come back to earth, but this doesn't work out well.

Stephen Randolph / THE MAN WHO CAME BACK, 1931, Fox Films, d-Raoul Walsh.

Farrell is a reckless, wild, and wealthy young man who reforms when he discovers that his erstwhile sweetheart (Janet Gaynor) is a drug-addicted floozy in a Shanghai opium den. Together the two lovers reclaim their lives.

Frederick Garfield, Jr. / TESS OF THE STORM COUNTRY, 1932, Fox Films, d-Alfred Santell.

Although Farrell loves Tess (Janet Gaynor), he leaves her when he finds her with what he believes is her illegitimate child. The baby has been born out of wedlock, but the mother is Farrell's own sister, for whom Tess is caring. Things get straightened out over the baptismal font.

OTHER ROLES

1923: *bit* / THE CHEAT; *bit* / ROSITA. **1925:** *Ted Spaulding* / WINGS OF YOUTH; *Kid Lewis* / THE LOVE HOUR; *Dave Weston* / CLASH OF THE WOLVES. **1926:** *Timmy* / SANDY; *Gayne Wilder* / A TRIP TO CHINATOWN; *the commodore* / OLD IRONSIDES. **1927:**

Stewart Van Brunt / THE ROUGH RIDERS. **1928:** *The Grand Duke Eugen* / THE RED DANCE; *Allen John Spender* / THE RIVER. **1930:** *himself* / HAPPY DAYS; *the son* / CITY GIRL; *Eddie Granger* / HIGH SOCIETY BLUES; *Charlie Peters* / THE PRINCESS AND THE PLUMBER. **1931:** *Mal Andrews* / BODY AND SOUL; *John Lonsdale* / MERELY MARY ANN; *Larry Beaumont* / DELICIOUS. **1932:** *Peter Piper* / AFTER TOMORROW; *Tommy Tucker* / THE FIRST YEAR; *Billy, the stranger* / WILD GIRL. **1933:** *Adoniram Schlump* / AGGIE APPLEBY, MAKER OF MEN; *Tom Duncan* / GIRL WITHOUT A ROOM. **1934:** *Jimmy Morrell* / THE BIG SHAKEDOWN; *Chris Thring* / CHANGE OF HEART. **1935:** *Larry Davis* / FIGHTING YOUTH. **1936:** *Niba* / FORBIDDEN HEAVEN; *Howard Elliott* / FALLING IN LOVE; *Sandy Nelson* / THE FLYING DOCTOR; *Logan* / NOT WANTED ON VOYAGE. **1937:** *Eric Molander* / MOONLIGHT SONATA; *Brian Gaunt* / MIDNIGHT MENACE. **1938:** *Jeff Hale* / JUST AROUND THE CORNER; *Captain Lawrence* / FLIGHT TO FAME. **1939:** *Bud* / TAIL SPIN; *Spike Nelson* / JAILBIRDS. **1941:** *Walker* / THE DEADLY GAME.

FARRELL, GLENDA

(1904–1971)

Glenda Farrell found her niche as a tough, uncompromising, wisecracking woman of the world. It was a movie type of her own invention but, as enjoyable as it was for audiences of the 1930s, it became a trap for her. She was forever destined to appear as a hard-driving, tough-talking, soft-hearted blonde, snapping both her gum and her lines. No matter how good she was—and she was very good—her caustic roles grew wearisome after a while. Fortunately for movie buffs, we can be selective and review those films in which she was delightful as a cocky reporter or a saucy gold digger and once again savor her specialty.

KEY ROLES

Marie Woods / I AM A FUGITIVE FROM A CHAIN GANG, 1932, Warners, d-Mervyn LeRoy.

Farrell blackmails Paul Muni, an escaped chain gang convict, into marrying her. When he tries to leave her for a woman he really loves, she turns him in to the authorities.

Florence Dempsey / MYSTERY OF THE WAX MUSEUM, 1933, Warners, d-Michael Curtiz.

Farrell is a wisecracking reporter who helps bring to justice a mad sculptor (Lionel Atwill) who uses real bodies in his wax museum creations. Typical of Farrell's character is her response when asked to marry her editor, Frank McHugh: "I'm going to get even with you, you dirty stiff, I'll do it."

Missouri Martin / LADY FOR A DAY, 1933, Columbia, d-Frank Capra.

Farrell is one of the characters who help turn Apple Annie into a society lady when Annie's daughter decides to pay a visit before she marries a rich aristocrat from South America.

Betty Hawes / GOLD DIGGERS OF 1935, 1935, Warners, d-Busby Berkeley.

Farrell is cast as a sharp-tongued chorus girl willing to go to the highest bidder in this story about putting on a Broadway show at a socialite's country home.

Torchy Blane / SMART BLONDE, 1936, Warners, d-Frank McDonald.

In this first of the Torchy Blane series, Farrell is a tough reporter who scoops the other papers and beats the cops when she solves a murder case.

Torchy Blane / TORCHY BLANE IN CHINATOWN, 1939, Warners, d-William Beaudine.

Farrell had Torchy down pat by this sixth film in the series. Once again she is the sharp reporter who is many steps ahead of her cop boyfriend Barton MacLane. Interestingly enough, Chinatown has nothing to do with the story, although the villains are Oriental.

Maude / SUSAN SLEPT HERE, 1954, RKO, d-Frank Tashin.

Farrell's tongue is as acid as ever as she plays screenwriter Dick Powell's secretary and helps him cope with a runaway teenager (Debbie Reynolds) dropped off by a friendly cop to give the writer some research material for a new movie.

OTHER ROLES

1929: *bit* / LUCKY BOY. **1930:** *Olga Strassoff* / LITTLE CAESAR. **1932:** *Stella* / SCANDAL FOR SALE; *Florette* / LIFE BEGINS; *reformatory girl* / THREE ON A MATCH; *Babe* / THE MATCH KING. **1933:** *Blondie* / GRAND SLAM; *Kay Curtis* / GIRL MISSING; *Dot* / THE KEYHOLE; *Jeanne Sands* / GAMBLING SHIP; *Glenda* / MARY STEVENS, M.D.; *Belle* / BUREAU OF MISSING PERSONS; *Sadie Appleby* / HAVANA WIDOWS; *Fay La Rue* / MAN'S CASTLE. **1934:** *Lil* / THE BIG SHAKEDOWN; *Gerry* / HI NELLIE; *Valerie* / DARK HAZARD; *Bunny* / THE MERRY WIVES OF RENO; *Bonnie* / I'VE GOT YOUR NUMBER; *Mrs. Tifton* / HEAT LIGHTNING; *Joan McCarthy* / THE PERSONALITY KID; *Marie* / KANSAS CITY PRINCESS. **1935:** *Hazel Normandie* / THE SECRET BRIDE; *Claudette Ruggles* / TRAVELING SALESLADY; *Sadie Howard* / GO INTO YOUR DANCE; *Clara* / IN CALIENTE; *Dixie Tilton* / WE'RE IN THE MONEY; *Jean* / LITTLE BIG SHOT; *Mae O'Brien* / MISS PACIFIC FLEET. **1936:** *Daisy Lowell* / SNOWED UNDER; *Dorothy Davis* / THE LAW IN HER HANDS; *Ruby Miller* / NOBODY'S FOOL; *Edith McNeil* / HIGH TENSION; *Genevieve Larkin* / GOLD DIGGERS OF 1937; *Verna Kennedy* / HERE COMES CARTER. **1937:** *Torchy Blane* / FLY-AWAY BABY; *Fanny Morgan* / DANCE, CHARLIE, DANCE; *Mamie Wallis* / YOU LIVE AND LEARN; *Carol Wallace* / BREAKFAST FOR TWO; *Torchy Blane* / THE ADVENTUROUS BLONDE; *Jonesey* / HOLLYWOOD HOTEL. **1938:** *Torchy Blane* / BLONDES AT WORK; *Rita* / STOLEN HEAVEN; *Sylvia Shane* / THE ROAD TO RENO; *Jean Fenderson* / PRISON BREAK; *Torchy Blane* / TORCHY GETS HER MAN; *Click Stewart* / EXPOSED. **1940:** *Torchy Blane* / TORCHY RUNS FOR MAYOR. **1941:** *Mae Blythe* / JOHNNY EAGER. **1942:** *Sonya Cherupin* / TWIN BEDS; *Regina Bush* / THE TALK OF THE TOWN. **1943:** *Susan* / A NIGHT FOR CRIME; *Molly* / KLONDIKE KATE; *con's wife* / CITY WITHOUT MEN. **1944:** *Babs Cartwright* / EVER SINCE VENUS. **1947:** *Nora* / HEADING FOR HEAVEN; *Winnie Winford* / MARY LOU; *Hazel Bixby* / I LOVE TROUBLE. **1948:** *Molly Benson* / LULU BELLE. **1952:** *Fanny Webson* / APACHE WAR SMOKE. **1953:** *Alice Haynes* / GIRLS IN THE NIGHT. **1954:** *Mrs. Winston* / SECRET OF THE INCAS. **1955:** *Mrs. Nesbit* / THE GIRL IN THE RED VELVET SWING. **1959:** *Mrs. Preisser* / MIDDLE OF THE NIGHT. **1964:** *Ma Tatum* / KISSIN' COUSINS; *Dr. Jean Howard* / THE DISORDERLY ORDERLY. **1968:** *Sarah Harvey* / TIGER BY THE TAIL.

FARROW, MIA

(Maria Farrow, 1945–)

Farrow, the daughter of actress Maureen O'Sullivan and director John Farrow, contracted polio at age nine and was left with the fragile looks that are part of her appeal. She has proudly boasted, though, "I can match bottoms with anyone in Hollywood." This diminutive actress got her start on TV's "Peyton Place" portraying Allison MacKenzie. In most of her movie roles she has seemed a virginal child-woman who, with her almost boyish charm and luminous eyes, is the essence of vulnerability. In recent years, she has been part of Woody Allen's group of performers and recently gave birth to Allen's first child.

KEY ROLES

Rosemary Woodhouse / ROSEMARY'S BABY, 1968, Paramount, d-Roman Polanski.
Farrow unwittingly becomes the mother of a demonic infant when her ambitious actor husband and her Satan-worshipping New York neighbors conspire to have her impregnated by the devil.

Mary / JOHN AND MARY, 1969, 20th Century-Fox, d-Peter Yates.
Farrow is an art gallery assistant who meets a furniture designer (Dustin Hoffman) at a New York single's bar. Without exchanging names, they go to his apartment to make love. The next day they have off-and-on feelings about continuing the affair.

Daisy Buchanan / THE GREAT GATSBY, 1973, Paramount, d-Jack Clayton.
Farrow is the southern belle for whom Jay Gatsby (Robert Redford) succeeds in keeping his pledge to acquire enough wealth to be worthy of her. The duo are rather strange. She seems to love just looking at his elaborate home and fancy clothes, and he seems delighted with her reaction.

Jacqueline de Bellefort / DEATH ON THE NILE, 1978, Great Britain, EMI, d-John Guillermin.
When Hercule Poirot deduces that Farrow is behind the death of a spoiled heiress on a steamer cruising down the Nile, Farrow kills her accomplice husband and commits suicide before the detective can prevent the double tragedy.

Cecilia / THE PURPLE ROSE OF CAIRO, 1985, Orion, d-Woody Allen.
Farrow is a Depression-era housewife whose only escape from the harshness of her life is the movies. At one matinee, a dashing romantic hero leaves the screen and sweeps her off her feet.

Hannah / HANNAH AND HER SISTERS, 1986, Orion, d-Woody Allen.
Farrow is the competent, nurturing sister in a family that includes her mother, father, two sisters, their assorted lovers, her former husband (Woody Allen), and her present husband (Michael Caine), both of whom have fallen for her two sisters.

OTHER ROLES

1959: *bit* / JOHN PAUL JONES. **1964:** *Karen Ericksson* / GUNS AT BATASI. **1967:** *Caroline* / A DANDY IN ASPIC. **1968:** *Cenci* / SECRET CEREMONY. **1971:** *Sarah* / SEE NO EVIL. **1972:** *Belinda Sidley* / FOLLOW ME; *Christine* / SCOUNDREL IN WHITE, (DOCTOR POPAUL). **1977:** *Julia* / FULL CIRCLE. **1978:** *Buffy Brenner* / A WEDDING; *Caroline Brace* / AVALANCHE. **1979:** *Charlotte Bruckner* / THE HURRICANE; *Julia* / THE HAUNTING OF JULIA. **1982:** *Ariel* / A MIDSUMMER NIGHT'S SEX COMEDY; *Last Unicorn* / *Lady Amalthea* / THE LAST UNICORN. **1983:** *Dr. Eudora Fletcher* / ZELIG. **1984:** *voice* / SARAH AND THE SQUIRREL; *Alivia* / SUPERGIRL; *Tina Vitale* / BROADWAY DANNY ROSE. **1987:** *Sally White* / RADIO DAYS; *Lane* / SEPTEMBER.

FAYE, ALICE

(Alice Jeanne Leppert, 1912–)
Alice Faye started her singing career with Rudy Vallee's band and was a big hit in movie musicals of the 1930s and early 1940s. Her singing voice was excellent, but her acting was nothing special. She mainly played herself, a wholesome but sexy blonde who never provided any real trouble for the men in her life. Hollywood had ideas of making her another Jean Harlow, but being a sex queen was too much work for this basically unambitious actress. When her popularity started to wane and Faye saw Betty Grable getting the roles that once would have been hers, she took the transition without rancor and retired to spend more time with her new husband, Phil Harris. The secret of her success? Faye wasn't too sure: "What did I have? I don't know. Maybe it was the girl-next-door, the one you left behind. It was wartime."

KEY ROLES

Belle Fawcett / IN OLD CHICAGO, 1938, 20th Century-Fox, d-Henry King.
Faye is a Chicago show girl who stands between two of the O'Leary brothers just before their mother's cow starts the Great Chicago Fire. Faye's songs include "I've Taken a Fancy to You" and "I'll Never Let You Cry" by Lew Pollack and Sidney Mitchell, and the title song by Mack Gordon and Harry Revel.

Stella Kirby / ALEXANDER'S RAGTIME BAND, 1938, 20th Century-Fox, d-Henry King.
What little plot there is in this salute to the songs of Irving Berlin deals with the on-again, off-again love affair between singer Faye and songwriter / bandleader Tyrone Power. Faye sings the title number, plus "What'll I Do," "All Alone," "Remember," and "Blue Skies."

Rose Sargent / ROSE OF WASHINGTON SQUARE, 1939, 20th Century-Fox, d-Gregory Ratoff.
Faye plays a singer whose love and devotion for no-good Tyrone Power, even when he's sent to prison, is very similar to that of Fanny Brice for Nicky Arnstein. Brice also must have felt so, because she sued and got an out-of-court settlement. Faye sings Brice's great song, "My Man" by Channing Pollock and Maurice Yvain.

Molly Adair / HOLLYWOOD CAVALCADE, 1939, 20th Century-Fox, d-Irving Cummings.
Faye is talked into a movie contract by director Don Ameche and together they build their fortunes as they go from comedy shorts to features and Faye becomes a major star. Although she loves Ameche, he's always too busy to notice her that way. Her star continues to ascend while his burns out. But when sound comes in, she picks him as the director of her first talkie and it's a big hit.

Lillian Russell / LILLIAN RUSSELL, 1940, 20th Century-Fox, d-Irving Cummings.
Faye portrays the famous musical star of the gay nineties, detailing her career from the time she was discovered in 1880 by bandleader Tony Pastor to her retirement in 1912. Her songs include "After the Ball" by Charles K. Harris and "The Band Played On" by John E. Palmer and Charles B. Ward.

Katie Blane / TIN PAN ALLEY, 1940, 20th Century-Fox, d-Walter Lang.
Faye and newcomer Betty Grable are sisters in this story of two songwriters who get Faye and Grable to introduce their new song "You Say the Sweetest Things, Baby" (actually written by Mack Gordon). Other numbers for Faye include "I'll Get By," "The Sheik of Araby," "Moonlight and Roses," "Honeysuckle Rose," and "Moonlight Bay."

Judy Evans / HELLO FRISCO, HELLO, 1943, 20th Century-Fox, d-H. Bruce Humberstone.
Faye sings the Oscar-winning "You'll Never Know" by Mack Gordon and Harry Warren in this story about the Barbary Coast, a sharp operator (John Payne),

and a musical star (Faye). Faye sings "By the Light of the Silvery Moon," "Sweet Cider Time," and—with Payne, Jack Oakie, and June Havoc—the title number.

Melissa Drake / STATE FAIR, 1962, 20th Century-Fox, d-José Ferrer.
Proving that she is still an attractive woman, Faye appears as Pat Boone's mother in this remake of the story of a farm family's adventures at a state fair. Faye gives a pleasant rendition of "Never Say No" by Richard Rodgers.

OTHER ROLES

1934: *Happy McGillicuddy* / GEORGE WHITE'S SCANDALS; *Peggy Warren* / NOW I'LL TELL; *Jean Legoi* / SHE LEARNED ABOUT SAILORS; *Alice Perkins* / 365 NIGHTS IN HOLLYWOOD. **1935:** *Honey Walters* / GEORGE WHITE'S 1935 SCANDALS; *Dixie Dean* / EVERY NIGHT AT EIGHT; *Peggy Harper* / MUSIC IS MAGIC. **1936:** *Pat Doran* / KING OF BURLESQUE; *Jerry Dolan* / POOR LITTLE RICH GIRL; *Jean Warren* / SING, BABY, SING; *Susan Parker* / STOWAWAY. **1937:** *Mona Merrick* / ON THE AVENUE; *Alice Huntley* / WAKE UP AND LIVE; *Judith Poe Wells* / YOU CAN'T HAVE EVERYTHING; *Betty Bradley* / YOU'RE A SWEETHEART. **1938:** *Sally Day* / SALLY, IRENE AND MARY. **1939:** *Trixie Lee* / TAIL SPIN; *Emmy Jordan* / BARRICADE. **1940:** *Pat O'Day* / LITTLE OLD NEW YORK. **1941:** *Cecilia Duarte* / THAT NIGHT IN RIO; *Vicki Adams* / THE GREAT AMERICAN BROADCAST; *Nan Spencer* / WEEKEND IN HAVANA. **1943:** *Eadie Allen* / THE GANG'S ALL HERE. **1944:** *guest* / FOUR JILLS IN A JEEP. **1945:** *June Mills* / FALLEN ANGEL. **1976:** *secretary at gate* / WON TON TON, THE DOG WHO SAVED HOLLYWOOD. **1978:** *waitress* / THE MAGIC OF LASSIE.

FERRER, JOSÉ

(José Ferrer y Cintron, 1909–)
Said to be the model for the character Jeffery Cordova in the movie THE BANDWAGON, Puerto Rican José Ferrer was a versatile and acclaimed Broadway actor when he entered films. He received an Academy Award nomination in 1948 for his first movie, JOAN OF ARC. He won the Best Actor Award for his third film, CYRANO DE BERGERAC, and was also nominated for MOULIN ROUGE. Ferrer has played a broad range of characters, usually of sensitive souls and often with some physical defect. In addition to his big-screen roles, he has appeared in many made-for-TV movies or mini-series, such as BANYON (1971), THE MARCUS-NELSON MURDERS (1973), THE FRENCH ATLANTIC AFFAIR (1979), EVITA PERON (1982), and SEDUCED (1985).

KEY ROLES

Dauphin / JOAN OF ARC, 1948, RKO, d-Victor Fleming.
Ferrer made an impressive debut as the dauphin of France who was made king by Joan of Arc, even though he was reluctant and afraid to make the move. He later deserted his champion.

Cyrano de Bergerac / CYRANO DE BERGERAC, 1950, United Artists, d-Michael Gordon.
Ferrer reprises his bravura Broadway performance as the famous 17th-century swordsman and poet with the tremendously long nose. Because of his deformity he keeps his love for Roxanne to himself for years, only letting her know the truth and the depth of his feelings when he is dying.

Toulouse-Lautrec / the Comte de Toulouse-Lautrec / MOULIN ROUGE, 1952, Great Britain, Romulus, d-John Huston.
Ferrer is magnificent as the dwarfish French painter in 19th-century Montmartre. This fictitious account of the artist's loves is beautifully photographed and captures a genuine feeling for the period.

Alfred Davidson / MISS SADIE THOMPSON, 1953, Columbia, d-Curtis Bernhardt.
Ferrer portrays the puritanical reformer in this remake of Somerset Maugham's "Rain." He commits suicide after raping prostitute Sadie Thompson, whom he had first convinced to give up her unsavory life.

Lt. Barney Greenwald / THE CAINE MUTINY, 1954, Columbia, d-Edward Dmytryk.
Ferrer is the reluctant defense attorney for Van Johnson and Robert Francis, two naval officers accused of mutiny when they take over their ship from the captain (Humphrey Bogart) when the captain can't handle a storm at sea. Ferrer gets an acquittal by leading Bogart into his paranoid behavior before the court.

Sigmund Romberg / DEEP IN MY HEART, 1954, MGM, d-Stanley Donen.
Ferrer portrays composer Romberg in a fictitious biopic with just enough story to get from one familiar song to the next.

Jim Downs / THE SHRIKE, 1955, Universal-International, d-José Ferrer.
In his directorial debut, Ferrer appears as a brilliant theater man who suffers a nervous breakdown because of his vindictive wife (June Allyson).

Joe Harris / THE GREAT MAN, 1956, Universal-International, d-José Ferrer.
Ferrer is given the assignment of developing a memorial program for a much-loved TV personality who has just died. In gathering material, Ferrer discovers what a rotten man the honoree was.

Capt. Alfred Dreyfus / I ACCUSE! 1958, Great Britain, MGM, d-José Ferrer.
Ferrer is a very stiff Dreyfus, the French Jewish officer who in 1894 was wrongly tried, convicted, and sentenced to Devil's Island for treason. His case became a cause célèbre, and his defense was led by novelist Émile Zola.

Rieber / SHIP OF FOOLS, 1965, Columbia, d-Stanley Kramer.
Ferrer's character is an anti-Semitic, crude German passenger on a German ocean liner that in 1933 leaves Vera Cruz for Bremerhaven with a mixed lot of travelers.

Professor Siletski / TO BE OR NOT TO BE, 1982, 20th Century-Fox, d-Alan Johnson.
Ferrer is a Polish traitor acting as a spy for the Germans when the Nazis overrun Poland. He meets his end comically when he gets mixed up with a troupe of actors headed by Mel Brooks.

OTHER ROLES

1949: *David Korvo* / WHIRLPOOL. **1950:** *cameo* / THE SECRET FURY; *Raoul Farrago* / CRISIS. **1952:** *Giorgi* / ANYTHING CAN HAPPEN. **1955:** *Major Stringer* / THE COCKLESHELL HEROES. **1958:** *Jim Fry* / THE HIGH COST OF LOVING. **1961:** *narrator* / FORGET THEM NOT. **1962:** *the Bey of Deraa* / LAWRENCE OF ARABIA. **1963:** *Supt. Gopal Das* / NINE HOURS TO RAMA; *Cyrano de Bergerac* / CYRANO ET D'ARTAGNAN. **1964:** *Cowan, the reporter* / STOP TRAIN 349. **1965:** *Herod Antipas* / THE GREATEST STORY EVER TOLD. **1967:** *Mr. Marlowe* / ENTER LAUGHING. **1968:** *Hassam Bey* / CERVANTES. **1975:** *Inspector Reed* / ORDER TO KILL; *Uncle* / PACO; *Father Alberto* / FOREVER YOUNG, FOREVER FREE. **1976:** *Ironman* / THE BIG BUS; *Benitez* / VOYAGE OF THE DAMNED; *Mark* / CRASH. **1977:** *robed figure* / THE SENTINEL. **1978:** *Lionel McCoy* / THE

PRIVATE FILES OF J. EDGAR HOOVER; *Inspector Branco* / DRACULA'S DOG; *Dr. Andrews* / THE SWARM; *Captain Nemo* / THE AMAZING CAPTAIN NEMO. **1979:** *Harry Rosenthal* / NATURAL ENEMIES; *Athos* / THE FIFTH MUSKETEER; *Dr. Vando* / FEDORA. **1980:** *Dominici* / THE BIG BRAWL; *Ben* / WHO HAS SEEN THE WIND. **1982:** *Nereus* / BLOOD TIDE; *Leopold* / A MIDSUMMER NIGHT'S SEX COMEDY. **1983:** *Mayor* / THE BEING. **1984:** *Padishah Emperor Shaddam IV* / DUNE; *Lomelin* / THE EVIL THAT MEN DO.

FERRER, MEL

(1917–)

Gaunt, sensitive, and cold-looking, Mel Ferrer had his best movie roles during the 1950s. Since then this former Broadway chorus boy has worked mostly in Europe acting, producing, screenwriting, and directing films. He was a producer-director before taking up acting in movies. He has always been difficult to cast, and has been at his best in his spotty career portraying angry or melancholy men. His third wife (1954–1968) was actress Audrey Hepburn.

KEY ROLES

Scott Carter / LOST BOUNDARIES, 1949, Film Classics, d-Alfred Werker.

Ferrer is a black doctor who, with his wife, passes for white in a New Hampshire town for twenty years until their secret, kept even from their children, comes out.

Luis Bello / THE BRAVE BULLS, 1951, Columbia, d-Robert Rossen.

Ferrer is a Mexican bullfighter who first loses and then regains his courage, but his sweetheart is killed in an automobile accident.

Noel, Marquis de Maynes / SCARAMOUCHE, 1952, MGM, d-George Sidney.

Ferrer is a wicked marquis and master swordsman who almost meets his maker after a long duel with Stewart Granger. But Granger learns later why he can't bring himself to kill Ferrer: he is his half-brother.

Frenchy Fairmont / RANCHO NOTORIOUS, 1952, RKO, d-Fritz Lang.

In this bizarre and unique western, Marlene Dietrich operates a hideout for outlaws, and Ferrer is one of her lovers. Their unusual happiness is upset with the arrival of Arthur Kennedy, who has trailed the man who raped and killed his wife to Dietrich's ranch.

Paul Berthalet / LILI, 1953, MGM, d-Charles Walters.

Ferrer is a bitter, lame puppeteer with a small French carnival, who can show kindness and his love for a 16-year-old orphan (Leslie Caron) only through his puppets.

Prince Andrei Bolkonsky / WAR AND PEACE, 1956, Pontii / de Laurentis / Paramount, d-King Vidor and Mario Soldati.

Ferrer is a confident Russian military officer battling the invasion of Napoleon's troops and competing with Henry Fonda for the love of Audrey Hepburn in this three-hour production of Leo Tolstoy's gargantuan epic.

Robert Cohn / THE SUN ALSO RISES, 1957, 20th Century-Fox, d-Henry King.

Ferrer's character in this film version of the Hemingway classic is a passive participant in the activities of an odd group of expatriates looking for something to do in Europe between the world wars. He is tolerated by the likes of Tyrone Power and Errol Flynn only because he pays for some drinks.

El Greco / EL GRECO, 1965, Italy / France, 20th Century-Fox, d-Luciano Salce.

Ferrer portrays the 16th-century Greek-Italian painter who finds favor in Spain and the love of an aristocratic woman.

OTHER ROLES

1950: *Gobby* / BORN TO BE BAD. **1953:** *Henrik* / SAADIA. **1954:** *King Arthur* / KNIGHTS OF THE ROUND TABLE. **1955:** *Capt. Alfred Westerman* / OH, ROSALINDA. **1957:** *Giancarlo Barandero* / THE VINTAGE. **1958:** *Foster MacLain* / FRAULEIN. **1959:** *Benson Thacker* / THE WORLD, THE FLESH, AND THE DEVIL. **1960:** *Stephen Orlac* / THE HANDS OF ORLAC. **1961:** *Leopoldo De Karnstein* / BLOOD AND ROSES. **1962:** *Gen. Robert Haines* / THE LONGEST DAY. **1963:** *Philip Allan* / THE DEVIL AND THE TEN COMMANDMENTS. **1964:** *Cleander* / THE FALL OF THE ROMAN EMPIRE; *Rudy DeMeyer* / SEX AND THE SINGLE GIRL. **1971:** *Dr. Harrison* / A TIME FOR LOVING. **1975:** *Mel Fields* / BRANNIGAN. **1977:** *alligator's victim* / EATEN ALIVE; *Van Gould* / THE BLACK PIRATE. **1978:** *King Eurich* / THE NORSEMAN; *Massimo* / THE TEMPTER; *Colonel Stone* / YESTERDAY'S TOMORROW. **1979:** *guest* / THE GREAT ALLIGATOR. **1980:** *Dr. Coleman* / THE FIFTH FLOOR.

FIELD, BETTY

(1918–1973)

A versatile actress, but never a great beauty, Betty Field began her career on Broadway in the 1930s playing ingenues. She recreated her stage role in WHAT A LIFE in her film debut in 1939, and moved on to play a series of young women with some kind of mental or physical defect. She was excellent as neurotic characters, but when she was unable to find more of them she moved on to character parts while still in her 30s, frequently playing slovenly but concerned moms.

KEY ROLES

Mae / OF MICE AND MEN, 1939, Hal Roach / United Artists, d-Lewis Milestone.

Field is the coquettish wife of a ranch foreman's son, who is strangled by half-witted Lenny who really meant her no harm but was frightened by her. Field is excellent as the sultry tramp.

Lola Pratt / SEVENTEEN, 1940, Paramount, d-Louis King.

Field is the semi-sophisticated flapper whom Booth Tarkington's coming-of-age hero (Jackie Cooper) thinks is the cat's pajamas.

Cassandra Tower / KINGS ROW, 1942, Warners, d-Sam Wood.

As a child, Robert Cummings falls in love with Field, but her father takes her out of school and keeps her locked away at home. He fears she will go mad as her mother did earlier. On one occasion, when Field sees her old friends, she hysterically cries, "Why do any of us have to cry? You or me? What have we done? Oh, I hate it! I hate everything! I'd hate God if I could, but there's nothing you can reach." Whether being removed from society and friends causes her mental deterioration or not, the father's worst fears are realized and he kills her and then takes his own life.

Nona Tucker / THE SOUTHERNER, 1945, United Artists, d-Jean Renoir.

Field and husband Zachary Scott are penniless sharecroppers in the deep South during the Depression years. Her strength sees them through many struggles.

Daisy Buchanan / THE GREAT GATSBY, 1949, Paramount, d-Elliot Nugent.
Field's portrayal of the neurotic southern belle who indirectly causes the death of wealthy, retired Long Island gangster Jay Gatsby (Alan Ladd) is far superior to that of Mia Farrow years later.

Flo Owens / PICNIC, 1955, Columbia, d-Joshua Logan.
Field's hopes that her beautiful but none-too-bright daughter (Kim Novak) will marry the son of the town's richest family are dashed when brawny wanderer William Holden arrives in town one 4th of July. Field warns Novak: "A pretty girl doesn't have long—just a few years. Then she's the equal of kings. She can walk out of a shanty like this and live in a palace. If she loses her chance when she's young, she might as well throw all her prettiness away."

OTHER ROLES

1939: *Barbara Pearson* / WHAT A LIFE. **1940:** *Alma* / VICTORY. **1941:** *Sammy Lane* / THE SHEPHERD OF THE HILLS; *Kay Grant* / BLUES IN THE NIGHT. **1942:** *Mary Elizabeth Cugat* / ARE HUSBANDS NECESSARY? **1943:** *Henrietta* / FLESH AND FANTASY. **1944:** *Elizabeth Morton* / THE GREAT MOMENT; *Leona Richards* / TOMORROW THE WORLD. **1956:** *Grace* / BUS STOP. **1957:** *Nellie Cross* / PEYTON PLACE. **1959:** *Cora* / HOUND-DOG MAN. **1960:** *Mrs. Fanny Thurber* / BUTTERFIELD 8. **1962:** *Stella Johnson* / BIRDMAN OF ALCATRAZ. **1965:** *Florrie Pether* / SEVEN WOMEN. **1968:** *Thelma* / HOW TO SAVE A MARRIAGE (AND RUIN YOUR LIFE); *Ellen Ringerman* / COOGAN'S BLUFF.

FIELD, SALLY

(1946–)
Tiny, pug-nosed Sally Field, with the sexy little figure, is one of only a small number of actresses who got their start in TV series and then went on to stardom in movies. The ex-Flying Nun has won two Academy Awards, one for NORMA RAE in 1979 and one for PLACES IN THE HEART in 1985. Some, perhaps even Sally herself, are not convinced that Field is a quality actress, but she has been fortunate enough to land at least two parts perfectly suited to her perhaps limited talents. Only time will tell what the truth is, but as long as she is assigned roles in which she can show her sensuality, determination, and vulnerability, she should do just fine.

KEY ROLES

Carrie / SMOKEY AND THE BANDIT, 1977, Universal, d-Hal Needham.
Field is a runaway bride who is picked up by Georgia bootlegger Burt Reynolds and shares with him the thrills of a cross-country chase with sheriff Jackie Gleason in hot pursuit.

Norma Rae / NORMA RAE, 1979, 20th Century-Fox, d-Martin Ritt.
Field is a poor, white, southern factory girl who helps a northern Jewish organizer (Ron Liebman) bring a union to her plant, despite strong opposition from management and fear and indifference from other workers, including her parents.

Megan Carter / ABSENCE OF MALICE, 1981, Columbia, d-Sidney Pollack.
Field is a newspaper reporter whose stories make it appear that honest businessman Paul Newman, tarred by having relatives in the rackets, may have something to do with the disappearance of a Hispanic labor leader. Her journalistic abuses hurt Newman further when they meet and develop romantic feelings for each other.

Edna Spaulding / PLACES IN THE HEART, 1985, Tri-Star Pictures, d-Robert Benton.
Field is a young Texas widow during the Depression who bands together with her extended family to raise a cotton crop so she can save her farm. When she won her second Oscar for this work, she yelled, "You really like me! You really like me!" That is perhaps too great an assumption to make about Hollywood people.

OTHER ROLES

1967: *Mercy McBee* / THE WAY WEST. **1976:** *Mary Tate* / STAY HUNGRY. **1977:** *Carol Bell* / HEROES. **1978:** *Gwen* / HOOPER; *Mary Ellen* / THE END. **1979:** *Celeste Whitman* / BEYOND THE POSEIDON ADVENTURE. **1980:** *Carrie* / SMOKEY AND THE BANDIT II. **1981:** *Amy Post* / BACK ROADS. **1982:** *Kay Villano* / KISS ME GOODBYE. **1985:** *Emma Moriarty* / MURPHY'S ROMANCE. **1987:** *Daisy Morgan* / SURRENDER.

FIELDS, DAME GRACIE

(Gracie Stansfield, 1898–1979)
Although she did not debut in films until she was in her 30s, music hall star Gracie Fields became Britain's highest paid screen personality. Her homey comedy and plain looks made her ideal for her usual role of a girl from London's slums or the north country who rises above adversity. This show business phenomenon was particularly appealing in her teaming with Monty Woolley. Audiences loved her for representing the ordinary English working woman.

KEY ROLES

Sally Winch / SALLY IN OUR ALLEY, 1931, Great Britain, Associated Talking Pictures, d-Maurice Elvey.
Fields is a London coffee shop singer who believes her lover has been killed in World War I. But he returns and Fields has to fight off some competition from a vamp for her man, but all ends well.

Gracie Platt / SING AS WE GO, 1934, Great Britain, ATP / Associated British, d-Basil Dean.
When Fields's mill closes down, she takes on various jobs at Blackpool as an entertainer and, through a chance meeting with an industrialist, is able to get the mill going again.

Alice Challice / HOLY MATRIMONY, 1943, 20th Century-Fox, d-John M. Stahl.
Fields claims a marriage proposal she received through the mail from the valet of a famous painter who has died. In fact it is the valet who has died, with the publicity-shy painter (Monty Woolley) having taken his place. Rather than reveal himself he marries Fields and, after a series of comical complications, settles down to wedded bliss.

Molly Barry / MOLLY AND ME, 1945, 20th Century-Fox, d-Lewis Seiler.
Fields is an out-of-work singer who, with others in her troupe in similar straits, takes employment in the home of a grumpy old gentleman (Monty Woolley). They help him reconcile with his son and save him from the schemes of his ex-wife.

OTHER ROLES

1932: *Gracie* / LOOKING ON THE BRIGHT SIDE. **1933:** *Grace Milroy* / THIS WEEK OF GRACE. **1934:** *Nellie Gwynn* / LOVE, LIFE AND LAUGHTER. **1935:** *Gracie Pearson* / LOOK UP AND LAUGH. **1936:** *Grace Perkins* / QUEEN OF HEARTS. **1937:** *Sally Lee* / THE SHOW GOES ON. **1938:** *Kit Dobson* / WE'RE GOING TO BE RICH; *Gracie Gray* / KEEP SMILING. **1939:** *Sally Fitzgerald* / SHIPYARD SALLY. **1943:** *guest* / STAGE DOOR CANTEEN. **1945:** *Emmeline Quayle* / PARIS UNDERGROUND, (MADAME PIMPERNEL).

FIELDS, W. C.

(William Claude Dukenfield, 1879–1946)

Burly, red-nosed, child-hating, and relentlessly misogynistic, W. C. Fields was a comical genius who made the best of usually rotten times in his portrayals of men not above bending the law. His rasping voice, resulting from his two-quart-a-day alcohol habit, routinely snarled belligerence at all authority. His humor was at war with stupidity, convention, and most especially children and female relatives. Among his familiar lines on these subjects are: "Women are like elephants to me. I like to look at them, but I wouldn't want to own one"; "If at first you don't succeed, try again. Then quit—no use being a damn fool about it"; "Anyone who hates small dogs and children can't be all bad"; and "Somebody left the cork out of my lunch." The first film appearance of the master juggler was in the 1915 one-reeler, POOL SHARKS, in which he repeated his famous stage act. Other shorts featuring Fields include THE GOLF SPECIALIST, THE DENTIST, THE FATAL GLASS OF BEER, THE PHARMACIST, and THE BARBER SHOP.

KEY ROLES

Augustus Winterbottom / TILLIE AND GUS, 1933, Paramount, d-Francis Martin.

Fields is a professional card shark who, together with his wife Alison Skipworth, is able to save the inheritance of their niece from a crooked lawyer by winning a boat race.

Humpty Dumpty / ALICE IN WONDERLAND, 1933, Paramount, d-Norman McLeod.

In this cameo role, Fields's head is made up to be the egg-like nursery rhyme character who "eggages" Alice in conversation before experiencing his destiny.

The Great Mark Anthony McGonigle / THE OLD-FASHIONED WAY, 1934, Paramount, d-William Beaudine.

Fields and his troupe of actors are touring the cheap circuit during the gaslight days, always just ahead of some sheriff. Despite the problems and his daughter's romantic troubles, he always sees that the show goes on.

Mr. C. Ensworth Stubbins / MRS. WIGGS OF THE CABBAGE PATCH, 1934, Paramount, d-Norman Taurog.

In a secondary story to the tear-jerker comedy of the Wiggs family and their ever-hopeful mother, Fields is the traveler the family sets its cap for as a husband to neighbor Zasu Pitts. The interchanges between these two are hilarious.

Harold Bissonette / IT'S A GIFT, 1934, Paramount, d-Norman McLeod.

Fields is the bumbling owner of a small-town general store who is henpecked by a shrewish wife. He purchases an orange grove sight unseen and, with his family, sets off across the country for California where he finds his land is in the desert. Fortunately a promoter wants the land for a racetrack and our hero makes a big profit.

Mr. Wilkins Micawber / DAVID COPPERFIELD, 1934, MGM, d-George Cukor.

When Charles Laughton abruptly quit the role, Cukor had the inspired idea of replacing him with Fields. It is the only role in which Fields did not tinker with the script because he had such great respect for Dickens. He plays the flamboyant head of a large family who takes David as a boarder until Fields is sent to debtor's prison. Later he helps the adult Copperfield deal with oily Uriah Heep.

Prof. Eustace McGargle / POPPY, 1936, Paramount, d-A. Edward Sutherland.

Fields is a patent medicine salesman usually just one step ahead of the law, whose arrival with his daughter into a new town is complicated by her falling in love with the mayor's son. Fields makes a claim for his daughter to an estate, and it turns out that she really is the heir, having been adopted by Fields years earlier.

Larson E. Whipsnade / YOU CAN'T CHEAT AN HONEST MAN, 1939, Universal, d-George Marshall.

Having financial difficulties with his circus and facing constant wisecracks from Edgar Bergen's dummy Charlie McCarthy, Fields still isn't willing to let his daughter go through with her plans to wed a wealthy suitor in order to help him.

Cuthbert J. Twillie / MY LITTLE CHICKADEE, 1940, Universal, d-Edward Cline.

Fields is a card shark Mae West marries because she mistakenly believes he has money. When she learns the truth she leaves a goat in bed with him and runs back to her masked lover. West later rescues Fields from hanging when he is caught cheating at cards.

Egbert Souse / THE BANK DICK, 1940, Universal, d-Edward Cline.

When Fields accidentally foils a bank robbery, he is rewarded with the job of special officer. He becomes involved with a fast-talking stock salesman and gets his daughter's fiancé to borrow some of the bank's money to buy shares in a beefstake mine. Then the bank examiner shows up and Fields must go into high gear to put things right.

The Great Man / NEVER GIVE A SUCKER AN EVEN BREAK, 1941, Universal, d-Edward Cline.

Fields is a washed-up movie actor who acts out the plot of a way-out story he is trying to sell to a producer at Esoteric Studios.

OTHER ROLES

1924: *British sergeant* / JANICE MEREDITH. **1925:** *Prof. Eustace McGargle* / SALLY OF THE SAWDUST. **1926:** *Mr. Royle* / THAT ROYLE GIRL; *Elmer Prettywillie* / IT'S THE OLD ARMY GAME; *Samuel Bisbee* / SO'S YOUR OLD MAN. **1927:** *Pa Potter* / THE POTTERS; *Elmer Finch* / RUNNING WILD; *Gabby Gilfoil* / TWO FLAMING YOUTHS. **1928:** *the ringmaster* / TILLIE'S PUNCTURED ROMANCE; *Richard Whitehead* / FOOLS FOR LUCK. **1931:** *Mr. Torrek* / HER MAJESTY LOVE. **1932:** *The President* / MILLION DOLLAR LEGS; *Rollo* / IF I HAD A MILLION. **1933:** *Professor Quail* / INTERNATIONAL HOUSE. **1934:** *Sheriff John Hoxley* / SIX OF A KIND; *Sam Bisbee* / YOU'RE TELLING ME. **1935:** *Comm. Orlando Jackson* / MISSISSIPPI; *Ambrose Wolfinger* / THE MAN ON THE FLYING TRAPEZE. **1938:** *T. Frothingell Bellows* / *S. B. Bellows* / THE BIG BROADCAST OF 1938. **1942:** *himself* / TALES OF MANHATTAN (his 20-minute sequence was cut before release of the film). **1944:** *guest* / FOLLOW THE BOYS; *himself* / SONG OF THE OPEN ROAD. **1945:** *himself* / SENSATIONS OF 1945.

FINCH, PETER

(William Mitchell, 1916–1977)

Born in London, Finch spent his youth in Australia and made a name for himself there in radio, theater, and bit parts in movies. After World War II he returned to England, then briefly appeared on the British stage before settling into films, with an early involvement in American movies. He became a leading performer in the 1950s, winning British Film Academy Awards as Best Actor for A TOWN LIKE ALICE, THE TRIALS OF OSCAR WILDE, NO LOVE FOR JOHNNIE, and SUNDAY, BLOODY SUNDAY, being nominated for an Oscar for this last film. In 1976 he was awarded an Oscar posthumously for his brilliant work in his last film, NETWORK. Speaking of himself, he noted: "I've grown accustomed to my face, as the song goes, and, I gather, so have film producers. Others call it sex appeal. I call it a character-filled face that has lived."

KEY ROLES

De Lacy, Sheriff of Nottingham / THE STORY OF ROBIN HOOD, 1951, Great Britain, Disney / RKO, d-Ken Annakin.

Finch brings a bit more wit to the role than did Melville Cooper in the 1938 ADVENTURES OF ROBIN HOOD, but he's still frustrated by the bandits of Sherwood.

Richard D'Oyley Carte / THE STORY OF GILBERT AND SULLIVAN, 1953, Great Britain, British Lion, d-Sidney Gilliat.

Finch is the theatrical manager who builds a theater to accommodate composer Arthur Sullivan's more serious ambitions, resulting in a breakup with librettist W. S. Gilbert.

John Wiley / ELEPHANT WALK, 1954, Paramount, d-William Dieterle.

Finch is the owner of a Ceylon tea plantation who ignores his British bride (Elizabeth Taylor). Later she proves her worth when the elephants go on a rampage through the plantation because the manor house is right in the path of their traditional walk.

Simon Foster / SIMON AND LAURA, 1955, Great Britain, GFD / Group Films, d-Muriel Box.

Finch plays an actor married to an actress; they hate each other and are on the brink of bankruptcy as well as divorce. They stay together for the sake of what becomes a successful TV series. When the program starts losing ratings, their dislike for each other surfaces on the show, saving it from cancellation.

Capt. Hans Langsdorff / THE BATTLE OF THE RIVER PLATE, 1956, Great Britain, Rank / Arcturus, d-Michael Powell and Emeric Pressburger.

Finch is the captain of the German pocket battleship Admiral Graf Spee which is scuttled off Montevideo, Uruguay, during World War II.

Joe Harmon / A TOWN LIKE ALICE, 1956, Great Britain, Vic / Rank, d-Jack Lee.

Finch is an Aussie who steals food for a group of British women and children captured by the Japanese in Malaya, but is brutally tortured for his efforts. After the war he is reunited with one of the women whom he had come to love.

Dr. Fortunati / THE NUN'S STORY, 1959, Warners, d-Fred Zinnemann.

Finch is the attractive but agnostic physician whose irreverent views upset Belgian Congo nursing nun Audrey Hepburn and lead her to reassess her values and leave the order.

Oscar Wilde / THE TRIALS OF OSCAR WILDE, 1960, Great Britain, Warwick / Viceroy, d-Ken Hughes.

When the great wit and writer (Finch) sues the Marquis of Queensberry, he finds himself prosecuted on charges of sodomy.

Johnnie Byrne / NO LOVE FOR JOHNNIE, 1961, Great Britain, Rank / Five Star, d-Ralph Thomas.

When Finch is reelected to the House of Commons, he suffers two disappointments: he's not offered a cabinet post, and his wife, an ardent Communist, leaves him. He joins a splinter group of the party intent on harassing the prime minister and eventually gets his cabinet post, but by this time he is alone with neither friends nor love.

William Boldwood / FAR FROM THE MADDING CROWD, 1967, Great Britain, Vic / Appia Films, d-John Schlesinger.

When gentleman farmer Finch receives an impulsively sent valentine from neighbor Julie Christie, he proposes to her. She marries another, who later disappears, presumably a suicide, and Finch and Christie become engaged on the very day that her husband returns. Finch kills the latter and is sent to prison, leaving Christie to marry the shepherd (Alan Bates) she has loved all along.

Dr. Daniel Hirsch / SUNDAY, BLOODY SUNDAY, 1971, Great Britain, United Artists / Vectia, d-John Schlesinger.

Finch is a homosexual, Jewish doctor who shares the sexual favors of his lover with a lady executive.

Richard Conway / LOST HORIZON, 1973, Columbia, d-Charles Jarrott.

It's not Finch's fault that this tepid musical remake of the 1937 classic was a box-office and critical disaster. He's about the best thing in the film, appearing in the role of the British statesman brought to Shangri-la to replace the dying High Lama.

Howard Beale / NETWORK, 1976, MGM, d-Sidney Lumet.

Finch is a network news anchorman who, when his ratings slip, announces that he plans to commit suicide on the air. Rather than taking this as a call for medical help, certain elements of the network hierarchy decide that he can be promoted as a messiah. At last the same people arrange for him to be murdered on camera. Of course he's mad as a hatter, but now and then he makes some sense, as when he rages: "I don't know what to do about the depression and the inflation and the Russians and the crime in the street. All I know is that first you've got to get mad. You've got to say, 'I'm a human being, goddammit! My life has value!' So I want you to get up now. I want all of you to get up out of your chairs. I want you to get up right now and go to the window, open it and stick your head out and yell, 'I'm mad as hell, and I'm not going to take this anymore.'"

OTHER ROLES

1938: *Bill Ryan* / DAD AND DAVE COME TO TOWN. **1939:** *bit* / MR. CHEDWORTH STEPS OUT; *bit* / ANTS IN HIS PANTS. **1941:** *bit* / THE POWER AND THE GLORY. **1944:** *Englishman* / RATS OF TOBRUK. **1945:** *Michael* / RED SKY AT MORNING. **1946:** *Paul Graham* / A SON IS BORN; *narrator* / INDONESIA CALLING. **1947:** *John Humffray* / EUREKA STOCKADE. **1949:** *Philip Mason* / TRAIN OF EVENTS. **1950:** *the Australian* / THE WOODEN HORSE; *Polish officer* / THE MINIVER STORY. **1953:** *Father Rank* / THE HEART OF THE

MATTER. **1954:** *Flambeau* / FATHER BROWN; *Charlie* / MAKE ME AN OFFER. **1955:** *Count DeVille* / THE DARK AVENGER; *Capt. Lucky Ryland* / PASSAGE HOME; *David Hewes* / JOSEPHINE AND MEN; *narrator* / PRIMITIVE PEOPLE: AUSTRALIAN ABORIGINES. **1956:** *Jim Macauley* / THE SHIRALEE. **1957:** *Captain Starlight* / ROBBERY UNDER ARMS; *Alec Windom* / WINDOM'S WAY. **1958:** *Jan Smit* / OPERATION AMSTERDAM. **1959:** *Alan Breck Stewart* / KIDNAPPED; *narrator* / MELBOURNE—OLYMPIC CITY; *narrator* / A FAR CRY. **1960:** *Col. Henry Derode* / THE SINS OF RACHEL CADE. **1962:** *Stephen Dane* / I THANK A FOOL. **1963:** *Murray Logan* / IN THE COOL OF THE DAY. **1964:** *Eugene Gaillard* / THE GIRL WITH GREEN EYES; *Jake Armitage* / THE PUMPKIN EATER; *guest* / FIRST MEN IN THE MOON. **1965:** *Aaron Stein* / JUDITH; *Captain Harris* / THE FLIGHT OF THE PHOENIX. **1967:** *Paul* / 10:30 P.M. SUMMER. **1968:** *Lewis Zarkin* / THE LEGEND OF LYLAH CLARE. **1969:** *Gen. Umberto Nobile* / THE RED TENT. **1972:** *Harry Field* / SOMETHING TO HIDE; *Erik Krogh* / ENGLAND MADE ME. **1973:** *Horatio Nelson* / BEQUEST TO THE NATION; *Cardinal Azzolino* / THE ABDICATION.

FINNEY, ALBERT

(1936–)

Trained classically at the Royal Academy of Dramatic Art, Albert Finney collaborated with playwright John Osborne and director Tony Richardson as part of the "angry young men" brigade of the 1960s that made films and plays featuring lower-class characters. Finney's star status was assured with SATURDAY NIGHT AND SUNDAY MORNING in 1960 and enhanced with his enjoyable performance in TOM JONES in 1963. Some of Finney's film appearances have been so impressive that his other screen roles have seemed disappointing by comparison. Hailed as a "second Olivier" by many fans and critics, he has not yet earned the mantle of Sir Laurence. Finney has been nominated for Academy Awards for TOM JONES and MURDER ON THE ORIENT EXPRESS.

KEY ROLES

Arthur Seaton / SATURDAY NIGHT AND SUNDAY MORNING, 1960, Great Britain, Bryanston / Woodfall, d-Karel Reisz.

Finney is a Nottingham factory worker who is unhappy with his lot. He slaves away at his lathe during the week but cuts loose on the weekend in rounds of drinking, brawling, and chasing women. Of the many girls he encounters, Shirley Anne Field is the one who holds out for marriage, but Finney gets plain, married Rachel Roberts pregnant. When he fails to arrange an abortion, he offers to marry her, but she realizes their affair is over. After her brother-in-law beats up Finney, he decides to marry Field and settle down.

Tom Jones / TOM JONES, 1963, Great Britain, United Artists / Woodfall, d-Tony Richardson.

Finney exploded onto the world scene as the 18th-century foundling who grows up to be a lusty young man. He has many adventures with women before being saved from hanging and marrying the neighboring squire's daughter. While the best lines in the film go to the unseen but often heard narrator (Michael MacLiammoir), Finney gets away with the fine pun for the benefit of raunchy Diane Cilento: "It's a good night to be abroad looking for game."

Mark Wallace / TWO FOR THE ROAD, 1967, Great Britain, 20th Century-Fox, d-Stanley Donen.

In this fractured, light comedy, successful architect Finney and his wife of twelve years (Audrey Hepburn) recall the ups and downs of their relationship. The film jumps back and forth between four different periods in their lives, and although a bit confusing, the device is not offensive.

Charlie Bubbles / CHARLIE BUBBLES, 1968, Great Britain, Universal / Memorial, d-Albert Finney.

Finney is a successful novelist who loathes the pointlessness of his life and tries to recapture his innocence by returning to his North Country working-class background. What did Thomas Wolfe say?

Ebenezer Scrooge / SCROOGE, 1970, Great Britain, Cinema Center / Waterbury, d-Ronald Neame.

Finney has his moments in this musical version of Dickens's *A Christmas Carol*. Unfortunately there aren't enough of them. For many, the only Scrooges are Alastair Sim on film and Lionel Barrymore on radio.

Hercule Poirot / MURDER ON THE ORIENT EXPRESS, 1974, Great Britain, EMI / GW Films, d-Sidney Lumet.

Finney's makeup effectively disguises his usual stocky build, but his affected accent makes the Belgian detective hard to understand as he unravels the murder of Richard Widmark aboard a sleeping car on the fabled Orient Express.

Daddy Warbucks / ANNIE, 1982, Columbia, d-John Huston.

At least in one respect Finney is the "new Olivier" in that he will seemingly take any kind of role, even if it is a bald-headed tycoon from the comic strips who plays second fiddle to a little red-headed moppet. Unfortunately, he doesn't even have any good songs.

Sir / THE DRESSER, 1983, Columbia, d-Peter Yates.

Finney is an exhausted Shakespearean actor who is comforted by his homosexual dresser on the last day of his tour.

OTHER ROLES

1959: *Mick Rice* / THE ENTERTAINER. **1963:** *Russian soldier* / THE VICTORS; *Danny* / NIGHT MUST FALL. **1969:** THE PICASSO SUMMER. **1971:** *Eddie Ginley* / GUMSHOE. **1975:** *guest* / THE ADVENTURES OF SHERLOCK HOLMES' SMARTER BROTHER. **1977:** *Fouche* / THE DUELLISTS. **1980:** *Dewey Wilson* / WOLFEN; *Dr. Larry Rogers* / LOOKER. **1981:** *Mike Daniels* / LOOPHOLE. **1982:** *George Dunlap* / SHOOT THE MOON. **1984:** *Geoffrey Firmin* / UNDER THE VOLCANO. **1987:** *Harold* / ORPHANS.

FITZGERALD, GERALDINE

(1912–)

While never a major star this talented, gracious, and attractive Irish actress maintained her high ideals and was suspended a number of times by Warners for refusing roles she felt were wrong for her. She recalled: "We were like pawns in a game of chess; we were permitted to move in only one direction. Only queens could move in all directions." She received a nomination for Best Supporting Actress for her performance in WUTHERING HEIGHTS in 1939, but, unlike her friend Bette Davis, she did not win her fight to have more say about choosing her roles and never advanced beyond second female leads. Later she distinguished herself in several fine character roles and in work on the stage.

KEY ROLES

Ruth Fosdyck / TURN OF THE TIDE, 1935, Great Britain, British National, d-Norman Walker.

In this story about a Yorkshire fishing village, Fitzgerald plays the daughter of a fisherman who resents the introduction of a modern motorboat for deep-sea fishing. But all ends well when she marries the owner of the new contraption.

Ann King / DARK VICTORY, 1939, Warners, d-Edmund Goulding.

Fitzgerald is the best friend of a woman (Bette Davis) who is dying of a brain tumor. The final sequences in the film between the two fine actresses are most impressive as they both handle Davis's death with great dignity.

Isabella Linton / WUTHERING HEIGHTS, 1939, United Artists, d-William Wyler.

Fitzgerald is the sister of the man (David Niven) who marries Cathy, the love of the gypsy lad Heathcliffe. When the latter (Laurence Olivier) returns wealthy, he marries Fitzgerald and makes her miserable because he still loves Cathy (Merle Oberon). She grieves: "If Cathy died, I might begin to live."

Marthe de Brancovis / WATCH ON THE RHINE, 1943, Warners, d-Herman Schumlin.

Fitzgerald is a countess married to a fascist (George Coulouris) who is a menacing threat to a German anti-fascist refugee (Paul Lukas) and his wife (Bette Davis) who have escaped to the United States to stay with her mother.

Edith Wilson / WILSON, 1944, 20th Century-Fox, d-Henry King.

Fitzgerald is the second wife of President Woodrow Wilson. When he suffers a crippling stroke after being defeated on the League of Nations, she acts in her husband's behalf, almost as if she were the first female president of the United States.

Crystal / THREE STRANGERS, 1946, Warners, d-Jean Negulesco.

Fitzgerald shares a winning sweepstake ticket with Sidney Greenstreet and Peter Lorre, whom she had never met before. These three excellent character performers make the simple story quite enjoyable.

Edith Chapin / TEN NORTH FREDERICK, 1958, 20th Century-Fox, d-Philip Dunne.

Fitzgerald handles with great style and authority the thankless role of the shrewish, unfaithful wife of a businessman with ambitions of becoming president of the United States. No one can accuse her of being a straw woman in this John O'Hara story.

Marilyn Birchfield / THE PAWNBROKER, 1965, Landau-Unger, d-Sidney Lumet.

Fitzgerald is the middle-aged mistress of a Jewish pawnbroker (Rod Steiger) who is haunted by his memories of Nazi concentration camps.

OTHER ROLES

1935: *Diane Morton* / THREE WITNESSES; *Peggy Summers* / BLIND JUSTICE; *window cleaner* / RADIO PARADE OF 1935; *Jane Grey* / DEPARTMENT STORE. **1936:** *Maggie Tulliver* / THE MILL ON THE FLOSS; *Peggy Mayhew* / DEBT OF HONOR. **1940:** *Bonny Coburn* / TIL WE MEET AGAIN; *Grace Sutton* / A CHILD IS BORN. **1941:** *Betty Farroway* / FLIGHT FROM DESTINY; *Dr. Mary Murray* / SHINING VICTORY. **1942:** *Evelyn Gaylord* / THE GAY SISTERS. **1944:** *Vinnie Alford* / LADIES COURAGEOUS. **1945:** *Lettie Quincy* / THE STRANGE CASE OF UNCLE HARRY. **1946:** *Elle Rogers* / O.S.S.; *Gladys Halvorsen* / NOBODY LIVES FOREVER. **1948:** *Susan Courtney* / SO EVIL MY LOVE. **1951:** *Elizabeth* / THE LATE EDWINA BLACK. **1961:** *Tante Maria* / THE FIERCEST HEART. **1968:** *Reverend Wood* / RACHEL, RACHEL. **1973:** *Mrs. Jackson* / THE LAST AMERICAN HERO. **1974:** *Jessie* / HARRY AND TONTO. **1976:** *Sara* / ECHOES OF A SUMMER. **1981:** *Martha Bach* / ARTHUR. **1982:** *Grandma Carr* / THE MANGO TREE. **1983:** *Mrs. Monahan* / EASY MONEY. **1986:** *Granna Jess* / POLTERGEIST II.

FLEMING, RHONDA

(Marilyn Louis, 1923–)

As a high school student this stunning, green-eyed, auburn-haired beauty reached the finals of a radio talent show and appeared on the cover of a magazine. Had she won the contest she would have become "Gale Storm"—the name given to winner Josephine Cottle. After a series of bit roles in movies she was cast in her first color film, A CONNECTICUT YANKEE IN KING ARTHUR'S COURT, and soon after became known as the "Queen of Technicolor." At her best when called on to be a femme fatale, Fleming was never mistaken for a great actress, but she was wonderful to look at, and she never disgraced herself with her performances.

KEY ROLES

Meta Carson / OUT OF THE PAST, 1947, RKO, d-Jacques Tourneur.

Fleming is a homicidal secretary who frames a private detective for murder.

Alisande La Carteloise / A CONNECTICUT YANKEE IN KING ARTHUR'S COURT, 1949, Paramount, d-Tay Garnett.

Fleming is Bing Crosby's lady fair, whom he calls Sandy, when the crooner is transformed from 19th-century Connecticut to King Arthur's court. When Crosby comes back to the present he runs into a descendant of Sandy, also played by Fleming.

Nancy / CRY DANGER, 1951, RKO, d-Robert Parrish.

Fleming is the wife of a man in prison who turns out to be one of the heavies in this tale about a con out on parole who is trying to clear his name of a robbery conviction and get Fleming's husband freed as well.

Izora / LITTLE EGYPT, 1951, Universal, d-Frederick de Cordova.

Fleming is an American girl who poses as an Egyptian princess and belly dancer at the Chicago World's Fair.

Roxana / YANKEE PASHA, 1954, Universal-International, d-Joseph Pevney.

In this 19th-century hokum, Fleming needs to be saved from pirates out of Marseilles. Jeff Chandler rushes to the rescue.

Dorothy Kyne / WHILE THE CITY SLEEPS, 1956, RKO, d-Fritz Lang.

Fleming is the wife of Vincent Price, an obnoxious playboy who has inherited a newspaper and has triggered a vicious competition among his employees to discover the identity of a psychopathic killer who is terrorizing the women of the city. Fleming is having an affair with her husband's photo bureau chief who plans to use the relationship to feather his own nest.

Laura Denbow / GUNFIGHT AT THE O.K. CORRAL, 1957, Paramount, d-John Sturgis.

Fleming is a professional gambler who gets under the skin of Wyatt Earp (Burt Lancaster), almost making him forget his destiny with the Clanton gang at the O.K. Corral.

OTHER ROLES

1943: *bit* / IN OLD OKLAHOMA. **1944:** *girl* / SINCE YOU WENT AWAY; *girl on train* / WHEN STRANGERS MARRY. **1945:** *Miss Carmichael* / SPELLBOUND; *Blanche* / THE SPIRAL STAIRCASE. **1946:** *Sherry Balder* / ABILENE TOWN. **1947:** *Faith Wishart* / ADVENTURE ISLAND. **1949:** *Duchess Alexandria* / THE GREAT LOVER. **1950:** *Madeline Danzeeger* / THE EAGLE AND THE HAWK; *Candace Bronson* / THE REDHEAD AND THE COWBOY. **1951:** *Julie McCloud* / THE LAST OUTPOST; *Katherine Shelley* / CROSSWINDS; *Victoria Evans*

/ HONG KONG. **1952:** *Rouge* / THE GOLDEN HAWK; *Flanders White* / TROPIC ZONE. **1953:** *Evelyn* / PONY EXPRESS; *Cleopatra* / SERPENT OF THE NILE; *Geraldine Carson* / INFERNO; *Kathie Edmonds* / THOSE REDHEADS FROM SEATTLE. **1954:** *Alice Parker* / JIVARO. **1955:** *Elizabeth "Duchess" Farnham* / TENNESSEE'S PARTNER. **1956:** *Lila Wagner* / THE KILLER IS LOOSE; *June Lyons* / SLIGHTLY SCARLET; *Pamela Muir* / ODONGO. **1957:** *Peggy Courtney* / THE BUSTER KEATON STORY; *Jo* / GUN GLORY. **1958:** *Cheyenne* / BULLWHIP; *Joan Carlisle* / HOME BEFORE DARK. **1959:** *the duchess* / ALIAS JESSE JAMES; *Helen Harrison* / THE BIG CIRCUS. **1960:** *Cheryl Heath* / THE CROWDED SKY. **1964:** *guest* / THE PATSY. **1965:** *oil heiress* / AN AMERICAN WIFE. **1966:** *Nita* / RUN FOR YOUR WIFE. **1976:** *Rhoda Flaming* / WON TON TON, THE DOG WHO SAVED HOLLYWOOD. **1980:** *Edith von Secondberg* / THE NUDE BOMB.

FLYNN, ERROL

(1909–1959)

Born in Tasmania, Australia, Errol Flynn was a mixture of legend and myth as he was the movies' greatest swashbuckler who did the best job he knew how to ensure that he would die young. Always a heavy drinker, he also developed a drug problem and, with his youth gone, was reduced to roles as middle-aged drunks. It didn't help that he had a reputation as a lecher and was accused of being a rapist. The phrase "in like Flynn" was first coined to suggest someone who had succeeded sexually with a woman. Early in his career he could joke about his exploits and how they were received, saying: "Son, it isn't what they say about you—it's what they whisper...." Flynn's life is a good example of why some movie buffs prefer to remember the wonderful screen personalities rather than the weaknesses and failures of the actors who portrayed them. In Flynn's case, at least in the early years, he was delightfully athletic, carefree, heroic, and amusingly charming. Those who came to admire this personality don't wish to be reminded of the sad truth about the man.

KEY ROLES

Peter Blood / CAPTAIN BLOOD, 1935, Warners, d-Michael Curtiz.

When the daughter of one of your authors was only nine months old she bounced with joy, cooing loudly, while sitting in her jump seat watching the handsome and dashing Errol Flynn in this film. He plays the young physician who, in the reign of James II of England, is convicted of treason for treating a rebel and is sent as a bond slave to Jamaica. Later he escapes, becomes a pirate, and eventually is appointed governor of the island. The kid could pick a winner.

Maj. Geoffrey Vickers / THE CHARGE OF THE LIGHT BRIGADE, 1936, Warners, d-Michael Curtiz.

This fictitious story gives an implausible explanation for the charge of the Light Brigade at Balaklava in 1854 by the 27th Lancers, led by a dashing British major (Flynn). It has been reported that many horses were killed in the filming of the charge and that Flynn, who disliked director Curtiz, reported this to the ASPCA.

Robin Hood / Sir Robin of Locksley / THE ADVENTURES OF ROBIN HOOD, 1938, Warners, d-Michael Curtiz and William Keighley.

Flynn is the perfect Robin Hood, the swordsman and archer who commands the respect of the "merry men" of Sherwood Forest and wins the love of Maid Marian as he thwarts the plans of Claude Rains and Basil Rathbone to usurp the throne of Richard the Lion-Hearted. Audiences cheer when Flynn challenges his men: "Kneel and swear this oath: That you, the free men of the forest, swear to despoil the rich only to give to the poor, to shelter the old and the helpless, and to protect all women, rich or poor, Norman or Saxon."

Capt. Richard Courtney / THE DAWN PATROL, 1938, Warners, d-Edmund Goulding.

Flynn, a pilot with Britain's Royal Flying Corps in France during World War I, calls the squadron's commander a butcher for sending young, inexperienced pilots into combat where they are easy prey for the veteran German flyers. When Flynn is made commander he discovers that it is only bravado that makes the boys sing: "So stand by your glasses steady, this world is a world of lies. Here's to the dead already—Hurrah for the next man who dies."

Wade Hatton / DODGE CITY, 1939, Warners, d-Michael Curtiz.

Flynn is an Irish soldier of fortune transplanted to the West who becomes sheriff of Dodge City and eventually brings law and order to the wide-open cattle town.

Capt. Geoffrey Thorpe / THE SEA HAWK, 1940, Warners, d-Michael Curtiz.

This movie contains one of the most exciting sword fights in the history of motion pictures. Flynn is a privateer who, with others of his ilk, keeps the Spanish from taking England from Elizabeth. Nasty villain Henry Daniell, Flynn's dueling partner, is a despicable traitor.

Jeb Stuart / SANTA FE TRAIL, 1940, Warners, d-Michael Curtiz.

This movie has nothing to do with the caravan route from Missouri to New Mexico. Rather it has Jeb Stuart (Flynn) and other famous men—Custer, Sheridan, Longstreet, Pickett, and Hood—in conflict with radical abolitionist John Brown.

George Armstrong Custer / THEY DIED WITH THEIR BOOTS ON, 1942, Warners, d-Raoul Walsh.

Once again Flynn appears in a revision of history. If one buys this exciting plot, Custer and his men went to their deaths at Little Big Horn because Custer wanted to prevent the exploitation of Indian land by greedy white men. It's nonsense but a lot of fun because of the way Flynn plays the egotistical soldier.

James J. Corbett / GENTLEMAN JIM, 1942, Warners, d-Raoul Walsh.

Flynn portrays the brash Irishman who incorporated scientific boxing to take the heavyweight championship away from John L. Sullivan.

Jean Picard / UNCERTAIN GLORY, 1944, Warners, d-Raoul Walsh.

Now in the downswing of his career, Flynn plays a man facing the guillotine who escapes during a World War II air raid of Paris. He is recaptured by a detective and, on the way back to Paris, the two are forced to spend some time in a village from which the Nazis have chosen 100 hostages they plan to execute if a saboteur is not surrendered. Flynn goes to his death posing as the saboteur, dying a hero rather than a common criminal.

Soames Forsyte / THAT FORSYTE WOMAN, 1949, MGM, d-Compton Bennett.

Flynn plays a stuffy, pompous, Victorian society gentleman who loses his free-spirited wife to the family's black sheep, an artist.

Mike Campbell / THE SUN ALSO RISES, 1957, 20th Century-Fox, d-Henry King.

With his starring days long over and not even a decent part for years, the physically deteriorating Flynn scored a triumph as one of the quintet of "lost generation" expatriates in Europe after World War I, who drink constantly and talk incessantly as they try to run away from themselves.

John Barrymore / TOO MUCH, TOO SOON, 1958, Warners, d-Art Napoleon.

Flynn was a perfect choice to portray "the Great Profile"—the actor who had literally drunk himself to death. Flynn is impressive in the sordid tale about the troubled life of Diana Barrymore, John's child by his first wife.

Major Forsythe / THE ROOTS OF HEAVEN, 1958, 20th Century-Fox, d-John Huston.

In what should have been Flynn's final screen appearance, he portrays a cashiered British officer who is trying to find forgiveness in a bottle for having betrayed fellow officers to the Nazis. He is one of a small band of men that joins with Trevor Howard in an attempt to save the African elephant from extinction.

OTHER ROLES

1933: *Fletcher Christian* / IN THE WAKE OF THE BOUNTY. **1935:** *Dyter, newspaper reporter* / MURDER AT MONTE CARLO; *Gregory Moxley* / THE CASE OF THE CURIOUS BRIDE; *David Van Dusen* / DON'T BET ON BLONDES. **1937:** *Dr. Newell Paige* / GREEN LIGHT; *Miles Hendon* / THE PRINCE AND THE PAUPER; *Capt. Denny Roark* / ANOTHER DAWN; *Gerald Beresford Wicks* / THE PERFECT SPECIMEN. **1938:** *Robert Kensington Lansford* / FOUR'S A CROWD; *Frank Medlin* / THE SISTERS. **1939:** *Earl of Essex* / THE PRIVATE LIVES OF ELIZABETH AND ESSEX. **1940:** *Kerry Bradford* / VIRGINIA CITY. **1941:** *Francis Warren* / FOOTSTEPS IN THE DARK; *Lt. Douglas Lee* / DIVE BOMBER. **1942:** *Fl. Lt. Terence Forbes* / DESPERATE JOURNEY. **1943:** *Gunnar Brogge* / EDGE OF DARKNESS; *himself* / THANK YOUR LUCKY STARS; *Steve Wagner* / NORTHERN PURSUIT. **1945:** *Major Nelson* / OBJECTIVE, BURMA!; *Clay Hardin* / SAN ANTONIO. **1946:** *Phil Gayley* / NEVER SAY GOODBYE. **1947:** *Mark Caldwell* / CRY WOLF; *Sebastian Dubrok* / ESCAPE ME NEVER. **1948:** *Mike McComb* / SILVER RIVER. **1949:** *Don Juan de Marana* / ADVENTURES OF DON JUAN; *Jeffrey Bushfinkle* / IT'S A GREAT FEELING. **1950:** *Morgan Lane* / MONTANA; *Lafe Barstow* / ROCKY MOUNTAIN. **1951:** *Mahbub Ali, the Red Beard* / KIM; *man on Anzio Beach* / HELLO GOD; *Capt. Michael Fabian* / THE ADVENTURES OF CAPTAIN FABIAN. **1952:** *Gregory Mason* / MARA MARU; *Brian Hawke* / AGAINST ALL FLAGS. **1953:** *Jamie Durrisdeer* / THE MASTER OF BALLANTRAE. **1954:** *Renzo* / CROSSED SWORDS; *William Tell* / WILLIAM TELL (not completed). **1955:** *John Beaumont* / LET'S MAKE UP; *Prince Edward* / THE WARRIORS; *King Richard* / KING'S RHAPSODY. **1956:** *James Brennan* / ISTANBUL. **1957:** *Ned Sherwood* / THE BIG BOODLE. **1959:** *himself* / CUBAN REBEL GIRLS.

FOCH, NINA

(Nina Consuelo Maud Fock, 1924–)

Versatile Nina Foch, who had a brief early career as a concert pianist, didn't fit the usual studio patterns and found herself cast in lesser movies or second female leads. Despite that, the chic, cool blonde demonstrated a fine stage presence, and was most effective playing sophisticated ladies, usually a bit on the neurotic side. She has often appeared on the Broadway stage and in several Shakespearean productions. Although not allowed to demonstrate it very often in her movies, she had a deft sense of humor, as in her comment about making housework more interesting: "When I'm cleaning around the house I wear an apron, but nothing else. It makes my activities—dusting, washing—more interesting to my husband."

KEY ROLES

Julia Ross / MY NAME IS JULIA ROSS, 1945, Columbia, d-Joseph H. Lewis.

In this rather short film noir, Foch takes a job as a secretary for wealthy Dame May Whitty. On her first day she meets Whitty's son (George Macready) who shows her to her room and brings her dinner. The next day she wakes up in a different house wearing someone else's clothes, and Macready informs her that she is his wife and she has just been sent home from a mental institution. She cannot escape and later overhears a plan to kill her and make it look like a suicide. She is saved in the nick of time by her boyfriend and the police.

Betty / THE DARK PAST, 1948, Columbia, d-Rudolph Mate.

Foch is tough and smoldering as William Holden's moll in this story about convicts who break into the home of a psychiatrist (Lee J. Cobb) who turns the tables on them when he spots Holden's mental weakness, and uses it to save all the hostages.

Judith Warren / THE UNDERCOVER MAN, 1949, Columbia, d-Joseph H. Lewis.

Foch is effective as the demure wife of Glenn Ford, a U.S. Treasury agent out to get evidence of tax evasion by an Al Capone-like gangleader.

Milo Roberts / AN AMERICAN IN PARIS, 1951, MGM, d-Vincente Minnelli.

Foch is a wealthy woman in Paris who, among other things, wishes to sponsor and promote artist Gene Kelly. Despite his compliment on her sexy, one-shouldered gown—"That's quite a dress you almost have on"—he prefers innocent, unsophisticated Leslie Caron.

Erica Martin / EXECUTIVE SUITE, 1954, MGM, d-Robert Wise.

Foch is a super-efficient executive secretary in a large furniture manufacturing company when the president of the company dies, setting off a scramble among company executives to replace him. The deceased may have meant more to Foch than she will let on.

Bithiah / THE TEN COMMANDMENTS, 1956, Paramount, d-Cecil B. DeMille.

Foch is the Pharaoh's sister who finds a Jewish baby in the bullrushes and raises the child as her own. He grows to be Prince Moses who, when his true heritage is discovered, is banished from Egypt. Later Moses returns to get Pharaoh to set his people free and takes both his real and adopted mothers with him.

OTHER ROLES

1943: *Nicki Saunders* / THE RETURN OF THE VAMPIRE. **1944:** *Alice Blake* / NINE GIRLS; *Celeste* / CRY OF THE WEREWOLF; *cabbie* / SHE'S A SOLDIER TOO; *Lois Garland* / SHADOWS IN THE NIGHT; *Jeanne* / SHE'S A SWEETHEART; *Freda Brenner* / STRANGE AFFAIR. **1945:** *Constantia* / A SONG TO REMEMBER; *Ellen Monk* / I LOVE A MYSTERY; *Sally Brown* / BOSTON BLACKIE'S RENDEZVOUS; *Anne Graham* / PRISON SHIP. **1947:** *Harriet Hobbs* / JOHNNY O'CLOCK; *Susie Pierson* / THE GUILT OF JANET AMES. **1949:** *Glenda Chapman* / JOHNNY ALLEGRO. **1951:** *Linda Kovacs* / ST. BENNY THE DIP. **1952:** *Marie Antoinette* / SCARAMOUCHE; *Joyce Laramie* / YOUNG MAN WITH IDEAS. **1953:** *Elena Cantu* / SOMBRERO; *Mercedes Bellway* / FAST COMPANY. **1954:** *Maggie Flannery* / FOUR GUNS

TO THE BORDER. **1955:** *Gretchen Brendan* / YOU'RE NEVER TOO YOUNG; *Ellen Miles* / ILLEGAL. **1957:** *Lieutenant McCoy* / THREE BRAVE MEN. **1959:** *Maud Kennard* / CASH MCCALL. **1960:** *Helena Glabrus* / SPARTACUS. **1971:** *Mrs. Wallman* / SUCH GOOD FRIENDS. **1975:** *Miss Evans* / MAHOGANY.

FONDA, HENRY

(1905-1982)

Winner of an Academy Award for his final role in ON GOLDEN POND, Henry Fonda was the movies' dreamy idealist and liberal who tried to change minds with reason rather than fists. He was also nominated for an Oscar for THE GRAPES OF WRATH, a performance that deserved the award if any ever did, but he lost to his good friend James Stewart who scored with THE PHILADELPHIA STORY. Fonda's movie characters were honest men of sympathetic natures who met any problems, whether serious or comical, with good grace and shy charm. He was on occasion effectively cast against type, as in FORT APACHE where he played a hopeless martinet and in ONCE UPON A TIME IN THE WEST in which he was a brutally cruel villain. Winner of a Lifetime Achievement Award in 1978, Fonda brought great dignity to his roles and remained an audience favorite even when good roles for the aging actor became scarce. Having made his Broadway debut in 1929, he returned to the Great White Way after World War II for seven years before going back to films with MISTER ROBERTS in 1955. His acting children, Jane and Peter, were born to his second wife, Frances Seymour Brokaw, who died in 1950. His first wife was actress Margaret Sullavan whom he had worked with at Falmouth, Massachusetts, in a company called the University Players. Other members included Joshua Logan, James Stewart, Kent Smith, Myron McCormick, and Mildred Natwick. Speaking of his craft, Fonda noted: "The best actors do not let the wheels show. This is the hardest kind of acting, and it works only if you look as if you are not acting at all." No one saw the wheels turning when Fonda worked.

KEY ROLES

Dan Harrow / THE FARMER TAKES A WIFE, 1935, Fox Films, d-Victor Fleming.

Fonda was a star in his first picture, repeating his stage role of a conscientious young man who works on the Erie Canal in order to earn enough money to buy a farm and marry his sweetheart (Janet Gaynor).

Anthony Amberton / THE MOON'S OUR HOME, 1936, Paramount, d-William A. Seiter.

Celebrated writer Fonda meets and falls in love with a tempestuous movie star (Margaret Sullavan). They marry impulsively without knowing anything about each other. It's a fine screwball comedy, well worth a late-night recording on your VCR.

Eddie Taylor / YOU ONLY LIVE ONCE, 1937, United Artists, d-Fritz Lang.

Fonda is a young ex-convict, hounded and persecuted even after trying to go straight. He's sentenced to death for a murder he didn't commit, breaks out of jail and, with his wife (Sylvia Sidney), tries to escape to Canada.

Preston Dillard / JEZEBEL, 1938, Warners, d-William Wyler.

Despite this being a "woman's picture," Fonda won applause for his portrayal of Bette Davis's fiancé who breaks his engagement with the fiery southern belle when she goes too far to make him jealous, wearing a red dress to a cotillion where unmarried ladies wear white.

Abraham Lincoln / YOUNG MR. LINCOLN, 1939, 20th Century-Fox, d-John Ford.

Fonda portrays Lincoln as the struggling young lawyer who defends two innocent backwoods lads against a charge of murder, using his horse sense and humor to get them off. "If these boys had more than one life, I'd say, 'Go ahead. Maybe a little hanging mighn't do 'em any harm.' But the sort of hanging you boys'd give 'em would be so—so permanent. Trouble is, when men start taking the law into their own hands, they're just as apt to—in all the confusion and fun—to start hanging somebody who's not a murderer as somebody who is. Then the next thing you know, they're hanging one another just for fun till it gets to a place a man can't pass a tree or look at a rope without feeling uneasy."

Gil Martin / DRUMS ALONG THE MOHAWK, 1939, 20th Century-Fox, d-John Ford.

Fonda plays a farmer who takes his young bride (Claudette Colbert) to the Mohawk Valley at the time of the American Revolution. The Indians destroy his family's cabin, burn his crop, and cause his wife to have a miscarriage. He's able to save the settlement by outrunning Indians to bring help.

Tom Joad / THE GRAPES OF WRATH, 1940, 20th Century-Fox, d-John Ford.

In one of the most impressive movies ever made, Fonda is a bitter ex-convict who comes home to his Oklahoma family during the Depression, only to find that erosion and wind have made the area a dust bowl. He, his family, and countless others pile their meager belongings on run-down old vehicles and make the long trek from Oklahoma to California in hope of finding a better life. Forced to kill a man, Fonda must leave his family, but he tells his ma (Jane Darwell): "I'll be all around in the dark. I'll be ever'where and wherever you can look. Wherever there's a fight so hungry people can eat, I'll be there. Wherever there's a cop beatin' up a guy, I'll be there. I'll be in the way guys yell when they're mad—an' I'll be in the way a kid laughs when they're hungry an' they know supper's ready. An' when the people are eatin' the stuff they raise, livin' in the houses they build—I'll be there, too."

Frank James / THE RETURN OF FRANK JAMES, 1940, 20th Century-Fox, d-Fritz Lang.

In this sequel to JESSE JAMES, Fonda avenges the killing of his brother Jesse by Bob Ford and is acquitted when tried for murder.

Charles Pike / THE LADY EVE, 1941, Paramount, d-Preston Sturges.

In this delightful comedy, Fonda is a wealthy simp who is singled out as the latest mark of Barbara Stanwyck and her card shark father. The fish gets away but Stanwyck shows up at his mansion claiming to be another girl and the dumb innocent falls for her and marries her before putting two and two together. It's a witty and wacky picture with a lot of suggestive dialogue.

"Little Pinks" / THE BIG STREET, 1942, RKO, d-Irving Reis.

Fonda is a Mindy's busboy who idolizes selfish New York nightclub singer Lucille Ball. He totally devotes himself to caring for her when she is knocked down a set of stairs by a gangster and crippled. She never shows any appreciation, her nasty disposition staying with her right up until her death.

Gil Carter / THE OX-BOW INCIDENT, 1943, 20th Century-Fox, d-William A. Wellman.

In this grim, uncompromising movie, Fonda is a cowboy who rides into a western town where a rancher is reported killed by cattle rustlers. He joins a posse that comes across three strangers and the leader decides they are the guilty parties. Fonda isn't so sure, but he can't prevent the three men, who will later be proven innocent, from being hanged.

Wyatt Earp / MY DARLING CLEMENTINE, 1946, 20th Century-Fox, d-John Ford.

This is the story of the marshal of Tombstone in which Fonda and his brothers, with the help of Doc Holliday (Victor Mature), take on the Clanton gang. It is a beautifully photographed black-and-white film; colorization of this movie would be a sin. Fonda plays the lawman as a laid-back individual, slow to anger but a bad man to cross. The film also contains J. Farrell MacDonald's classic non-sequitur answer to Fonda's question, "Mack, you ever been in love?": "No. I been a bartender all my life."

Col. Owen Thursday / FORT APACHE, 1948, RKO, d-John Ford.

Fonda is the inflexible new Fort Apache commander who ignores the warnings of his more experienced second-in-command (John Wayne) and leads his outnumbered troops against Cochise's Apaches.

Lt. (jg) Douglas Roberts / MISTER ROBERTS, 1955, Warners, d-John Ford and Mervyn LeRoy.

Repeating the role he played in a long run on Broadway, Fonda is the well-liked and respected executive officer on a World War II cargo ship in the Pacific who, despite opposition from his tyrannical captain (James Cagney), keeps asking for a transfer to the shooting war. Old friends Fonda and Ford are reported to have come to actual blows over their interpretations of the film, with Ford being replaced.

Juror No. 8 (Davis) / 12 ANGRY MEN, 1957, United Artists, d-Sidney Lumet.

Fonda produced this movie himself. In it he appears as the lone juror to vote not guilty on the first ballot in the murder trial of a young man accused of killing his father. One by one Fonda convinces the other eleven jurors that the prosecutor has not proven his case. He offers a reasonable alternate explanation for the evidence that convinced each of them of the defendant's guilt. It's an absorbing film with a marvelous cast.

William Russell / THE BEST MAN, 1964, United Artists, d-Franklin Schaffner.

Fonda is a former secretary of state who is running for his party's nomination as its presidential candidate. He's an intelligent liberal whose main rival is amoral, conservative Cliff Robertson, of whom Fonda observes: "He has every characteristic of a dog except loyalty."

The President / FAIL-SAFE, 1964, Columbia, d-Sidney Lumet.

When a mechanical error sends American bombers on their way to drop atomic bombs on Moscow, the United States president (Fonda) tries to come up with a way to halt the planes and, failing that, to prevent an all-out nuclear war that will destroy the world. To prove to the Russians that the destruction of Moscow was not planned, he has New York City nuked.

Frank / ONCE UPON A TIME IN THE WEST, 1969, Paramount, d-Sergio Leone.

Italian director Leone planned to make the definitive western, casting Fonda as an icy-eyed villain who orders the slaughter of an entire family and calmly guns down a nine-year-old boy. It's an interesting experimental film, but does not live up to Leone's hopes.

Woodward Lopeman / THERE WAS A CROOKED MAN, 1970, Warners, d-Joseph L. Mankiewicz.

In 1883 Fonda, an ex-lawman who is now a prison warden, trails escaped convict Kirk Douglas to where the latter has hidden half a million dollars in loot. When Douglas is killed by a rattlesnake, Fonda takes off for Mexico with the money.

Norman Thayer, Jr. / ON GOLDEN POND, 1981, Universal, d-Mark Rydell.

Fonda is a retired 80-year-old professor who spends a holiday with his wife (Katharine Hepburn) and his daughter (Jane Fonda)—from whom he is alienated—at their New Hampshire lakeside cottage. He won an Oscar supposedly for his performance but, in reality, the Academy was making up for overlooking him throughout the years.

OTHER ROLES

1935: *David Bartlett* / WAY DOWN EAST; *Jonathan Street* / I DREAM TOO MUCH. **1936:** *Dave Tolliver* / THE TRAIL OF THE LONESOME PINE; *Townsend Middleton* / SPENDTHRIFT. **1937:** *Kerry* / WINGS OF THE MORNING; *Eddie Taylor* / YOU ONLY LIVE ONCE; *Slim* / SLIM; *Jack Merrick* / THAT CERTAIN WOMAN. **1938:** *Ives Towner* / I MET MY LOVE AGAIN; *Marco* / BLOCKADE; *Jim Kimmerlee* / SPAWN OF THE NORTH; *Peter Ames* / THE MAD MISS MANTON. **1939:** *Frank James* / JESSE JAMES; *Brick Tennant* / LET US LIVE; *Thomas Watson* / THE STORY OF ALEXANDER GRAHAM BELL. **1940:** *Alexander Moore* / LILLIAN RUSSELL; *Chad Hanna* / CHAD HANNA. **1941:** *John Murdock* / WILD GEESE CALLING; *Peter Kirk* / YOU BELONG TO ME. **1942:** *Tommy Turner* / THE MALE ANIMAL; *John Wheeler* / RINGS ON HER FINGERS; *Tad Page* / THE MAGNIFICENT DOPE; *George* / TALES OF MANHATTAN. **1943:** *Cpl. Colin Spence* / THE IMMORTAL SERGEANT. **1947:** *Joe Adams* / THE LONG NIGHT; *fugitive* / THE FUGITIVE; *Peter Laphan* / DAISY KENYON. **1948:** *Lank* / ON OUR MERRY WAY. **1949:** *himself* / JIGSAW. **1956:** *Pierre Bezukhov* / WAR AND PEACE. **1957:** *Manny Balestrero* / THE WRONG MAN; *Morg Hickman* / THE TIN STAR. **1959:** *Clay Blaisdell* / WARLOCK; *Willie Bauche* / THE MAN WHO UNDERSTOOD WOMEN. **1962:** *Robert Leffingwell* / ADVISE AND CONSENT; *Gen. Theodore Roosevelt, Jr.* / THE LONGEST DAY. **1963:** *Jethro Stuart* / HOW THE WEST WAS WON; *Clay Spencer* / SPENCER'S MOUNTAIN. **1964:** *Frank Broderick* / SEX AND THE SINGLE GIRL. **1965:** *Howdy Lewis* / THE ROUNDERS; *CINCPAC II Admiral* / IN HARM'S WAY; *Lieutenant Colonel Kiley* / BATTLE OF THE BULGE. **1966:** *Meredith* / A BIG HAND FOR THE LITTLE LADY; *Kourlov* / THE DIRTY GAME. **1967:** *Will Blue* / WELCOME TO HARD TIMES; *the stranger* / STRANGER ON THE RUN. **1968:** *Larkin* / FIRECREEK; *Frank Beardsley* / YOURS, MINE AND OURS; *Anthony X. Russell* / MADIGAN; *John S. Bottomley* / THE BOSTON STRANGLER. **1970:** *Capt. John G. Nolan* / TOO LATE THE HERO; *Harley Sullivan* / THE CHEYENNE SOCIAL CLUB. **1971:** *Henry Stamper* / SOMETIMES A GREAT NOTION. **1973:** *Allan Davies* / THE SERPENT; *Mark Sawyer* / ASH WEDNESDAY; *Jack Beauregard* / MY NAME IS NOBODY. **1974:** *Cardinal Schuster* / LAST DAYS OF MUSSOLINI. **1976:** *Adm. Chester W. Nimitz* / MIDWAY. **1977:** *Simon Davenport* / ROLLERCOASTER; *Mr. Whitehead* / TENTACLES; *Elegant John* / THE GREAT SMOKEY ROADBLOCK. **1978:** *Dr. Krim* / THE SWARM; *himself* / FEDORA. **1979:** *The President of the United States* / METEOR; *Chief Albert Risley* / CITY ON FIRE; *old prospector* / WANDA NEVADA; *General Foster* / THE GREATEST BATTLE.

FONDA, JANE

(1937–)

The beautiful and talented daughter of Henry Fonda, Jane follows the beat of her own drummer at all times, risking her career and popularity by speaking out for many causes, most notably her opposition to the U.S. involvement in Vietnam and her public support of the Viet Cong. Politics aside, this committed former high-fashion model has had a rich film career, being nominated for Academy Awards for THEY SHOOT HORSES, DON'T THEY?; JULIA; THE CHINA SYNDROME; and ON GOLDEN POND, and winning Oscars for KLUTE and COMING HOME. Always controversial and always a knockout, exercise-conscious Fonda has mellowed somewhat in recent years, although she is still very active in feminist and environmental causes. More and more, though, she allows her movies to make her political and social statements.

KEY ROLES

June Ryder / TALL STORY, 1960, Warners, d-Joshua Logan.

Fonda plays a coed who grabs basketball player Tony Perkins and then helps him deal with a tempting offer from gamblers to throw a game.

Kitty Twist / WALK ON THE WILD SIDE, 1962, Columbia, d-Edward Dmytryk.

In 1930 Fonda leaves the farm and moves to New Orleans, where she becomes a popular whore and the beloved of the bordello's lesbian madam. There's not much social commentary in this lurid movie, but Fonda was singled out for praise by critics.

Catherine "Cat" Ballou / CAT BALLOU, 1965, Columbia, d-Elliot Silverstein.

In this wild spoof of westerns, Fonda is just home from school in the East when she discovers that her widowed father is very unpopular in town because he refuses to sell his land. The people hire a gunfighter to kill her dad, after which Fonda and a motley crew of followers, including a drunken ex-gunman (Lee Marvin), start on a career of robbing trains which almost gets her hanged.

Corie Bratter / BAREFOOT IN THE PARK, 1967, Paramount, d-Gene Saks.

In this film version of Neil Simon's successful Broadway play, Fonda is the enthusiastic and childlike bride of somewhat stuffy Robert Redford. They rent a cold-water, walk-up, fifth-floor apartment in Greenwich Village and then happily resolve some marital problems while entertaining audiences with pleasant comedy.

Barbarella / BARBARELLA, 1968, Paramount, d-Roger Vadim.

Director Vadim casts his then-wife Fonda as the sexy, futuristic, French comic strip heroine whose costumes are a voyeur's delight. It's all nonsensical high camp.

Gloria Beatty / THEY SHOOT HORSES, DON'T THEY? 1969, Cinerama, d-Sydney Pollack.

In the Depression era of the 1930s, Fonda is a desperate girl from Texas who enters a dance marathon with aimless partner Michael Sarrazin. Although Fonda didn't win her Oscar, she did earn the New York Film Critics' Award as Best Actress.

Bree Daniels / KLUTE, 1971, Warners, d-Alan Pakula.

Fonda is an unsuccessful model but an in-demand call girl who becomes involved in a small-town detective's investigation of a missing businessman. The Oscar she won was very much deserved for her flawless performance. When Donald Sutherland (as the detective) is reluctant to take a bit of comfort with her, she scolds him: "Men have paid $200 for me, and here you are, turning down a freebie. You could get a perfectly good dishwasher for that."

Lillian Hellman / JULIA, 1977, 20th Century-Fox, d-Fred Zinnemann.

Fonda portrays the American playwright who, because of her childhood friend Julia (Vanessa Redgrave), becomes involved with the anti-Nazi movement in Europe in the 1930s, just at the time when she is writing her classic "The Little Foxes."

Sally Hyde / COMING HOME, 1978, United Artists, d-Hal Ashby.

Married to a gung-ho marine captain, Fonda volunteers to work in a veteran's hospital while her husband is in Vietnam. There she falls in love with embittered paraplegic Jon Voight. Both Fonda and Voight won Best Actor Oscars, but the film is too preachy and self-indulgent to be good drama.

Kimberly Wells / THE CHINA SYNDROME, 1979, Columbia, d-James Bridges.

This movie is about a TV reporter (Fonda) who exposes the plot of a nuclear power plant to cover up an accident that resulted in a potentially dangerous radiation leak. In a bit of good luck for the producers, the film was released at about the time of the Three Mile Island nuclear accident.

Judy Bernly / 9 TO 5, 1980, 20th Century-Fox, d-Colin Higgins.

Lily Tomlin, Dolly Parton, and Fonda are secretaries fed up with their sexist boss (Dabney Coleman). They devise a plan to get him out of the way and make life more pleasant on the job.

Chelsea Thayer Wayne / ON GOLDEN POND, 1981, Universal, d-Mark Rydell.

Alienated from her 80-year-old father, played by Henry Fonda, her real father, resentful Jane makes some headway toward reconciliation during a summer holiday with her parents in their New Hampshire lakeside summer home.

OTHER ROLES

1962: *Kathleen Barclay* / THE CHAPMAN REPORT; *Isabel Haverstick* / A PERIOD OF ADJUSTMENT. **1963:** *Christine Bonner* / IN THE COOL OF THE DAY. **1964:** *Eileen Tyler* / SUNDAY IN NEW YORK; *Melinda* / JOY HOUSE. **1965:** *married woman* / CIRCLE OF LOVE. **1966:** *Anna Reeves* / THE CHASE; *Ellen Gordon* / ANY WEDNESDAY; *Renee Saccard* / THE GAME IS OVER. **1967:** *Julie Ann Warren* / HURRY SUNDOWN. **1969:** *Countess Frederica* / SPIRITS OF THE DEAD. **1972:** *Iris Caine* / STEELYARD BLUES; *Susan De Witt* / TOUT VA BIEN. **1973:** *Nora Helmer* / A DOLL'S HOUSE. **1976:** *Night* / THE BLUE BIRD; *Jane Harper* / FUN WITH DICK AND JANE. **1978:** *Ella Connors* / COMES A HORSEMAN; *Hannah Warren* / CALIFORNIA SUITE. **1979:** *Hallie Martin* / THE ELECTRIC HORSEMAN. **1981:** *Lee Winters* / ROLLOVER. **1985:** *Dr. Martha Livingston* / AGNES OF GOD. **1987:** *Alex Sternbergen* / THE MORNING AFTER; *herself* / LEONARD PART 6.

FONTAINE, JOAN

(Joan De Havilland, 1917–)

Sister of actress Olivia De Havilland, Joan Fontaine took the surname of her stepfather. She made both her stage and film debuts in 1935, but it wasn't until her role in REBECCA in 1940 that she became a leading lady. She won the Best Actress Academy Award in

1941 for her work in SUSPICION. The award came before De Haviland won her Oscar, which contributed to the bad feelings that existed between the siblings for years. Fontaine also received an Academy Award nomination for THE CONSTANT NYMPH. Viewers remember Fontaine most fondly for her roles as awkward but lovely women, none too sure of their sweethearts' love. By the 1950s, though, there was little need for Fontaine's particular type of character, as all movie women then were played either as virgins fighting to keep it that way or sexpots who weren't as easy as they seemed. Fontaine moved into more mature characters, often with unpleasant natures.

KEY ROLES

Emmy Stebbins / GUNGA DIN, 1939, RKO, d-George Stevens.

British sergeants Cary Grant and Victor McLaglen in India do not look kindly on Fontaine's plans to marry their buddy Douglas Fairbanks, Jr., so they trick him into re-enlisting while fighting rebels at the Northwest Frontier.

the second Mrs. De Winter / REBECCA, 1940, David O. Selznick, d-Alfred Hitchcock.

Fontaine isn't given a name in this tale of a shy, young girl who marries a wealthy Cornish landowner (Laurence Olivier) who is haunted by the memory of his glamorous and sophisticated first wife, but not for the reasons Fontaine believes. Not Olivier's choice for the part—he wanted his current love Vivien Leigh—Fontaine was harassed by Sir Laurence on the set as he whispered obscenities in her ear during love scenes. Director Hitchcock allowed this because it caused Fontaine to get the startled and frightened looks he wanted from her.

Lina McLaidlaw Aysgarth / SUSPICION, 1941, RKO, d-Alfred Hitchcock.

Sedate Fontaine falls in love with and marries playboy Cary Grant and comes to suspect he is trying to murder her. In the novel by Frances Iles the heroine was right, but the plot was changed for the movie to have a surprise ending.

Tessa Sanger / THE CONSTANT NYMPH, 1943, Warners, d-Edmund Goulding.

Composer Charles Boyer finally realizes that the fragile Fontaine, suffering from a heart condition, is his true soul mate. But it's too late; she dies before Boyer can leave his wife for her.

Jane Eyre / JANE EYRE, 1944, 20th Century-Fox, d-Robert Stevenson.

Orphaned Fontaine becomes a governess in the Yorkshire mansion of brooding Orson Welles, whom she falls in love with. Their wedding is interrupted by the news that Welles already has a wife, a madwoman he keeps locked up. This wife is eventually out of the picture, but not before many tragic occurrences.

Lady Dona St. Columb / FRENCHMAN'S CREEK, 1944, Paramount, d-Mitchell Leisen.

In a change of pace for her, Fontaine plays an assertive lady of Restoration England who falls in love with a French pirate.

Susan Darell / THE AFFAIRS OF SUSAN, 1945, Paramount, d-William A. Seiter.

In this comedy, four men love Fontaine, but they all know a different woman as she changes her personality to suit the man.

Susan / FROM THIS DAY FORWARD, 1946, RKO, d-John Berry.

Fontaine and her husband (Mark Stevens) think back to happier times when they were courting and first married in the 1930s.

Lisa Berndl / LETTER FROM AN UNKNOWN WOMAN, 1948, Universal, d-Max Ophuls.

In surely Fontaine's best performance, she is a young girl who falls in love with a rakish concert pianist (Louis Jourdan). She follows his career from a distance until one night before he is to leave on a tour they meet and have a beautiful night of love. He promises to return but promptly forgets her and she marries another man to give the son conceived that night a name. Years later she meets Jourdan again, but he does not remember her. She goes to him again and shortly thereafter both she and her son die of typhus, but not before she has sent a letter to Jourdan telling him of her love. He remembers just as he is to go face her husband in a duel, a match he cannot win.

Lady Rowena / IVANHOE, 1952, MGM, d-Richard Thorpe.

In this tale of the derring-do of knights in medieval England, Fontaine gets Robert Taylor but has a lot of competition from lovely Elizabeth Taylor.

Mavis Norman / ISLAND IN THE SUN, 1957, Great Britain, 20th Century-Fox, d-Robert Rossen.

In this multi-level story set in the Caribbean, Fontaine almost has an affair with Harry Belafonte, a sensitive, young, black attorney. But he rejects her in the end.

François Ferrand / A CERTAIN SMILE, 1958, 20th Century-Fox, d-Jean Negulesco.

Fontaine plays the understanding but hurt wife of a middle-aged lothario who preys on young girls. This Françoise Sagan comedy of sexual errors among the rich on the French Riviera is competently produced but not very exciting.

OTHER ROLES

1935: *bit* / NO MORE LADIES. **1937:** *bit* / MUSIC FOR MADAME; *Charlotte Parratt* / QUALITY STREET; *Trudy Olson* / YOU CAN'T BEAT LOVE; *Lady Alyce* / A DAMSEL IN DISTRESS. **1938:** *Ann* / BLOND CHEAT; *Joan Stevens* / A MILLION TO ONE; *Sheila Harrison* / MAID'S NIGHT OUT; *Doris King* / THE MAN WHO FOUND HIMSELF; *Meg* / SKY GIANT; *Ann Porter* / THE DUKE OF WEST POINT. **1939:** *Eliza Allen* / MAN OF CONQUEST; *Peggy Day* / THE WOMEN. **1942:** *Prudence Cathaway* / THIS ABOVE ALL. **1947:** *Ivy Lexton* / IVY. **1948:** *Johanna Augusta Franziska* / THE EMPEROR WALTZ; *Jane Wharton* / KISS THE BLOOD OFF MY HANDS; *Dee Dee Dillwood* / YOU GOTTA STAY HAPPY. **1950:** *Christabel* / BORN TO BE BAD; *Manina Stuart* / SEPTEMBER AFFAIR. **1951:** *Alice Grey* / DARLING, HOW COULD YOU. **1952:** *Jenny Carey* / SOMETHING TO LIVE FOR. **1953:** *Fiametta* / *Bartolomea* / *Ginevra* / *Isabella* / DECAMERON NIGHTS; *Susan* / FLIGHT TO TANGIER; *Eve Graham* / THE BIGAMIST. **1954:** *Francesca Bruni* / CASANOVA'S BIG NIGHT. **1955:** *unbilled guest* / OTHELLO. **1956:** *Kendall Hale* / SERENADE; *Susan Spencer* / BEYOND A REASONABLE DOUBT. **1957:** *Anne Leslie* / UNTIL THEY SAIL. **1961:** *Dr. Susan Hiller* / VOYAGE TO THE BOTTOM OF THE SEA; *Baby Warren* / TENDER IS THE NIGHT. **1967:** *Gwen Mayfield* / THE DEVIL'S OWN.

FORD, GLENN

(Gwyllyn Ford, 1916–)

Born in Quebec, Glenn Ford grew up in California, making his stage debut in 1935 in a production of "The Children's Hour." He made his first film in 1939, but didn't click until after World War II with his electrifying performance in GILDA. His star status never reached the level of those male actors who could allow their emotions to smolder, though; in his serious roles he was usually a man in control of himself, cool, and calculating. His work in comedies, while amusing on occasion, was not all that funny. We laughed at him only when he played incompetents who were always in there trying. Ford remained popular for a longer period than many might have predicted for the serious-looking actor. Besides his two TV series—"Cade's County" and "The Family Holvak"—he made several TV movies and mini-series including BROTHERHOOD OF THE BELL (1970), THE GREATEST GIFT (1975), EVENING IN BYZANTIUM (1978), and BEGGERMAN, THIEF (1980).

KEY ROLES

Johnny Farrell / GILDA, 1946, Columbia, d-Charles Vidor.

In this archetypal film noir, Ford is a gambler in South America who renews a romance with an old flame (Rita Hayworth) now married to Ford's dangerous new boss (George Macready). Some audiences were shocked when Ford slapped Hayworth to stop her attempted striptease, others were just sorry he stopped her.

Ben Hogan / FOLLOW THE SUN, 1951, 20th Century-Fox, d-Sidney Lanfield.

For the duffers who wonder why Hollywood has not made more biopics of famous golfers, seeing this very ordinary movie may supply the answer.

Dave Bannion / THE BIG HEAT, 1953, Columbia, d-Fritz Lang.

Ford could have used some more roles like the one in this excellent film noir about a police detective who goes undercover to track down those responsible for the death of his wife by a bomb meant for him.

Richard Dadier / THE BLACKBOARD JUNGLE, 1955, MGM, d-Richard Brooks.

At the time of this film's release many people in their safe suburbs or small towns couldn't believe that high schools with conditions like the ones endured by Ford and his fellow teachers—as they tried unsuccessfully to educate students in a slum school—existed. Tragically, it doesn't seem so rough and tough compared to what one finds in all too many schools today. The film also introduced what many consider to be the first rock'n'roll hit: "Rock Around the Clock."

David Blake / TRIAL, 1955, MGM, d-Mark Robson.

Ford is a young lawyer hired to defend a Mexican boy against charges of murder and rape. His job is made all the more difficult by local bigots, Communists, and McCarthyites.

George Temple / THE FASTEST GUN ALIVE, 1956, MGM, d-Russell Rouse.

Ford is a mild-mannered western storekeeper who is revealed to be the son of a famous gunfighter. There are those such as gunslinger Broderick Crawford who want to test him to see if he inherited any of his father's talents. Well, yes and no. He's fast, perhaps the fastest ever, but he's never faced another man before and he's scared.

Captain Fisby / THE TEAHOUSE OF THE AUGUST MOON, 1956, MGM, d-Daniel Mann.

Ford is an army officer who doesn't fit in anywhere. When assigned to teach democracy to inhabitants of an Okinawan village in 1944, he is instead converted to their oriental ways and uses the wood intended for a schoolhouse to build a teahouse for the local geisha girl.

Ben Wade / 3:10 TO YUMA, 1957, Columbia, d-Delmer Daves.

Farmer Van Heflin has agreed to get a desperate outlaw (Ford) on a train bound for a Yuma prison because he needs the reward money to save his land. Ford's friends are intent on rescuing him. This is a taut western with suspense to rival HIGH NOON.

Lt. Max Seigel / DON'T GO NEAR THE WATER, 1957, MGM, d-Charles Walters.

Ford is one of a company of incompetent public relations officers stationed on a Pacific island during World War II. The story is rambling and the farce only ends because the war does. Nothing much is resolved, but there are some very funny sequences.

Jason Sweet / THE SHEEPMAN, 1958, MGM, d-George Marshall.

Anyone who has seen a lot of westerns knows how much cattlemen hate sheep. Well, Ford knows this too. So, before bringing his flock into the territory, he moves into town and proves that he's tougher and meaner and more dangerous than anyone working for the cattlemen.

Dave the Dude Conway / POCKETFUL OF MIRACLES, 1961, United Artists, d-Frank Capra.

This remake of LADY FOR A DAY proves that even Capra didn't always have his magic working for him. Ford is too straight for the role of the Damon Runyon character who helps an old apple seller (Bette Davis) become a lady of means long enough to fool her long-absent daughter.

Tom Corbett / THE COURTSHIP OF EDDIE'S FATHER, 1963, MGM, d-Vincente Minnelli.

Ronny Howard, widower Ford's young son, tries to fix up dear old dad with prospective new mothers. His schemes don't work until he comes up with Shirley Jones.

Jonathan Kent / SUPERMAN, 1978, Warners, d-Richard Donner.

Ford portrays Superman's foster father on Earth. His part wasn't big and it rather amazed fans to see how old Ford had become.

OTHER ROLES

1939: *Joe* / HEAVEN WITH A BARBED WIRE FENCE; *Barney* / MY SON IS GUILTY. **1940:** *Jim Brent* / CONVICTED WOMAN; *Johnny Adams* / MEN WITHOUT SOULS; *Steve Burton* / BABIES FOR SALE; *Charlie* / BLONDIE PLAYS CUPID; *Pierre Moresian* / THE LADY IN QUESTION. **1941:** *Ludwig Kern* / SO ENDS OUR NIGHT; *Tod Ramsey* / TEXAS; *Tex Miller* / GO WEST, YOUNG LADY. **1942:** *Martin Eden* / THE ADVENTURES OF MARTIN EDEN; *Danny Doyle* / FLIGHT LIEUTENANT. **1943:** *Cheyenne Rogers* / THE DESPERADOES; *Mickey Donahue* / DESTROYER. **1946:** *Bill Emerson* / A STOLEN LIFE. **1947:** *Mike Lambert* / FRAMED. **1948:** *Doug Andrews* / THE MATING OF MILLIE; *Don Jose* / THE LOVES OF CARMEN; *Professor Bassett* / THE RETURN OF OCTOBER; *Col. Owen Devereaux* / THE MAN FROM COLORADO. **1949:** *Frank Warren* / THE UNDERCOVER MAN; *Joe Miracle* / MR. SOFT TOUCH; *Jacob Walz* / LUST FOR GOLD; *Dr. Michael Corday* / THE DOCTOR AND THE GIRL. **1950:** *Martin Ordway* / THE WHITE TOWER; *Joe Hufford* / CONVICTED; *Gil Kyle* / THE REDHEAD AND THE COWBOY; *Comdr. Bill Talbot* / THE FLYING MISSILE. **1951:** *Canfield* / THE SECRET OF CONVICT LAKE. **1952:** *Michael Blake* / THE GREEN GLOVE; *Steve Emery* / AFFAIR IN TRINIDAD; *Maxwell Webster* / YOUNG MAN WITH IDEAS. **1953:** *Peter Lyncort* / TIME BOMB; *John Stroud* / THE MAN FROM THE ALAMO; *Al Colby* / PLUNDER OF THE SUN; *Steve Corbett* / APPOINTMENT IN HONDURAS. **1954:** *Jeff Warren* / HUMAN DESIRE; *Sam Dent* / THE AMERICANO. **1955:** *John Parrish* / THE VIOLENT MEN; *Dr. Thomas King* / INTERRUPTED MELODY. **1956:** *David G. Stannard* / RAN-

SOM; *Jubal Troop* / JUBAL. **1958:** *Tom Reece* / COWBOY; *M / Sgt. Murphy Savage* / IMITATION GENERAL; *Lt. Comdr. Barney Doyle* / TORPEDO RUN. **1959:** *Sgt. Joe Fitzpatrick* / IT STARTED WITH A KISS; *Elliott Nash* / THE GAZEBO. **1960:** *Yancey Cravet* / CIMARRON. **1961:** *Andy Cyphers* / CRY FOR HAPPY. **1962:** *Julio Desnoyers* / THE FOUR HORSEMEN OF THE APOCALYPSE; *John "Rip" Ripley* / EXPERIMENT IN TERROR. **1963:** *John Davis* / LOVE IS A BALL. **1964:** *Capt. Jared Heath* / ADVANCE TO THE REAR; *Sam McBane* / FATE IS THE HUNTER; *Harry Mork* / DEAR HEART. **1965:** *Ben Jones* / THE ROUNDERS. **1966:** *Joe Baron* / THE MONEY TRAP; *Gen. Omar N. Bradley* / IS PARIS BURNING? **1967:** *Reuben* / RAGE; *Marshal Dan Blaine* / THE LAST CHALLENGE; *Maj. Charles Walcott* / A TIME FOR KILLING. **1968:** *Lorn Warfield* / DAY OF THE EVIL GUN. **1969:** *Jim Killian* / HEAVEN WITH A GUN; *Smith* / SMITH! **1973:** *Santee* / SANTEE. **1976:** *Admiral Spruance* / MIDWAY. **1981:** *Dr. Faraday* / HAPPY BIRTHDAY TO ME.

FORD, HARRISON

(1942–)

This aggressive-looking, rugged, and handsome actor never seems to smile. It appears that, for his characters, life is much too serious to even crack a grin. Ford had numerous small roles in films before hitting the big time in STAR WARS in 1977. This success was followed by immediate camp and cult fame as Indiana Jones in RAIDERS OF THE LOST ARK. Whether he can adapt to less dangerous roles remains to be seen. In WITNESS he appeared to be acting at the top of his voice even in his love scenes.

KEY ROLES

Han Solo / STAR WARS, 1977, 20th Century-Fox, d-George Lucas.

Ford is a hot rod spaceship pilot who helps Mark Hamill fight Darth Vader and the Empire as he attempts to help rebel princess Carrie Fisher. Ford has romantic interest in Fisher, but has a great deal of difficulty expressing it in a way that will get her approval.

Indiana Jones / RAIDERS OF THE LOST ARK, 1981, Paramount, d-Steven Spielberg.

In the 1930s, American archaeologist Ford competes with the Nazis in a search for the sacred lost Ark of the Covenant. He's in constant peril from one source or another, but accepts these dangers as almost nothing more than annoyances he must put up with. The movie was very successful, but the sequel, INDIANA JONES AND THE TEMPLE OF DOOM, lacked the charm and humor of the original. A third installment, INDIANA JONES AND THE LAST CRUSADE, was released in 1989.

Rick Deckard / BLADE RUNNER, 1982, Warners, d-Ridley Scott.

In Los Angeles circa 2019, Ford is a licensed-to-kill policeman who tracks down and wipes out a gang of intelligent robots that have returned to Earth on a hijacked space shuttle.

John Book / WITNESS, 1985, Paramount, d-Peter Weir.

When a little Amish boy witnesses a murder, police detective Ford is assigned to the case. After looking at mug shots without any luck, the boy sees the killer and he's a policeman. Ford reports what he's found to his superior, but this one is in on the crime as well, so Ford, the boy, and the boy's widowed mother hit the road to Amish country where, in the peace before the storm, Ford and the mother (Kelly McGillis) fall in love.

OTHER ROLES

1966: *bit* / DEAD HEAT ON A MERRY-GO-ROUND. **1967:** *Lieutenant Shaffer* / A TIME FOR KILLING; *bit* / LUV. **1968:** *Willie Bill Rearden* / JOURNEY TO SHILOH. **1970:** *Jake* / GETTING STRAIGHT; *bit* / ZABRISKIE POINT. **1973:** *Bob Flafa* / AMERICAN GRAFFITI. **1974:** *Martin Street* / THE CONVERSATION. **1977:** *Ken Boyd* / HEROES. **1978:** *Barnsby* / FORCE 10 FROM NAVARONE. **1979:** *Colonel* / APOCALYPSE NOW; *Tommy* / THE FRISCO KID; *David Halloran* / HANOVER STREET. **1980:** *Han Solo* / THE EMPIRE STRIKES BACK. **1983:** *Han Solo* / RETURN OF THE JEDI. **1984:** *Indiana Jones* / INDIANA JONES AND THE TEMPLE OF DOOM. **1986:** *Allie Fox* / THE MOSQUITO COAST.

FOSTER, PRESTON

(1901–1970)

This tall, burly, rugged actor proved himself capable of giving sensitive performances as heroes and also as a few fine, menacing villains. His best work was in the 1930s; after that he mostly worked in lesser films or in character roles. But in 1932 THE LAST MILE established the curly-haired, two-fisted actor as a top star. Although originally under contract with Warners, Foster ultimately worked with just about every studio in Hollywood. Originally a singer with the Grand Opera Company of Philadelphia, this star of TV's "Waterfront" series didn't get opportunities to demonstrate his fine baritone voice in his movies. After leaving films, though, he and his wife Sheila D'Arcy formed a singing act which they took on the road.

KEY ROLES

Killer John Mears / THE LAST MILE, 1932, World Wide, d-Sam Bischoff.

Foster is a killer on death row who garrotes a contemptible guard, gets possession of his keys and gun, and takes command of the prison. He allows his anger and hate to boil over into many forms of violence, until he realizes that he can't escape and walks into a hail of bullets.

Dan Gallagher / THE INFORMER, 1935, RKO, d-John Ford.

Foster is the IRA leader who orders Victor McLaglen's death after the latter turns in his friend Wallace Ford to the British in order to get money to emigrate to the United States. This was Foster's favorite movie role.

Marcus / THE LAST DAYS OF POMPEII, 1935, RKO, d-Ernest B. Schoedsack.

Foster is a blacksmith who becomes obsessed with making money after his wife and child die. His adopted son is cured by Jesus while the two are on a trip to Judea, but he refuses to act when Christ is crucified. He finally undergoes a spiritual awakening when Vesuvius spews out the lava that buries Pompeii.

Toby Walker / ANNIE OAKLEY, 1935, RKO, d-George Stevens.

Foster is the sharpshooter who claims to be the world's best marksman, a claim challenged by Annie Oakley. Their rivalry turns to love.

John Clitheroe / THE PLOUGH AND THE STARS, 1937, RKO, d-John Ford.

Sean O'Casey's comment on the futility of Irish national politics doesn't come off very well in this ordinary movie. Foster is a rebel officer whose wife (Barbara Stanwyck) is determined to keep him from fighting.

John Oakhurst / THE OUTCASTS OF POKER FLAT, 1937, RKO, d-Christy Cabanne.

In this saga of love, conflict, and sacrifice against the backdrop of a California gold rush, Foster plays a picturesque gambler whom a teacher (Jean Muir) tries to reform.

Captain Starrett / GERONIMO, 1939, Paramount, d-P. H. Sloane.

Foster has the Gary Cooper role in this adaptation of THE LIVES OF A BENGAL LANCER, as he unsuccessfully attempts to prevent an Indian war.

Sgt. Jim Brett / NORTHWEST MOUNTED POLICE, 1940, Paramount, d-Cecil B. DeMille.

Foster might have been the Mountie who started the claim "they always get their man." This redcoat is in love with a nurse (Madeleine Carroll) but gets some stiff competition from a Texas Ranger (Gary Cooper) who has crossed the border seeking a fugitive.

Rob McLaughlin / MY FRIEND FLICKA, 1943, 20th Century-Fox, d-Harold Schuster.

In this story about Roddy McDowall and his pet colt, Foster is the lad's father, a pretty understanding guy.

Father Donnelly / GUADALCANAL DIARY, 1943, 20th Century-Fox, d-Lewis Seiler.

As there are no atheists in foxholes, an Irish priest (Foster) is a good man to have around.

Roger Touhy / ROGER TOUHY, GANGSTER, 1944, 20th Century-Fox, d-Robert Florey.

A contemporary of Al Capone, Roger Touhy (Foster) is finally cornered by the FBI. Not part of the movie, but of interest anyway: when Touhy was released from prison years later he was gunned down shortly thereafter just as he had expected.

Judge Sam Purvis / THE HARVEY GIRLS, 1946, MGM, d-George Sidney.

Foster and John Hodiak compete for the affection of Judy Garland in a western town served by waitresses at a Harvey restaurant. Foster is a respectable suitor and Hodiak, a gambler.

Capt. Pat Chambers / I, THE JURY, 1953, United Artists, d-Harry Essex.

Foster is a New York police detective who warns his friend, private eye Mike Hammer, not to use illegal tactics in investigating the murder of one of his friends.

OTHER ROLES

1930: *bit* / NOTHING BUT THE TRUTH; *Blake* / HEADS UP. **1932:** *Bud Clark* / TWO SECONDS; *Dr. Wells* / DOCTOR X; *Pete* / I AM A FUGITIVE FROM A CHAIN GANG; *Ed Dover* / YOU SAID A MOUTHFUL; *Steve Kelly* / THE ALL-AMERICAN. **1933:** *David Slade* / LADIES THEY TALK ABOUT; *Walker* / ELMER THE GREAT; *Tim Butler* / CORRUPTION; *Jan Novak* / THE MAN WHO DARED; *Inspector O'Brien* / DEVIL'S MATE; *Nifty* / HOOPLA; *sailor* / SENSATION HUNTERS. **1934:** *Como* / WHARF ANGEL; *George* / HEAT LIGHTNING; *Jason Everett* / SLEEPERS EAST; *Howdy* / THE BAND PLAYS ON. **1935:** *Vince* / PEOPLE'S ENEMY; *Tex Randolph* / THE ARIZONIAN; *Murray Carter* / STRANGERS ALL. **1936:** *Pete McCaffrey* / WE'RE ONLY HUMAN; *Tip O'Neil* / MUSS 'EM UP; *Scott Miller* / LOVE BEFORE BREAKFAST; *Mathews* / WE WHO ARE ABOUT TO DIE. **1937:** *Mike O'Shay* / SEA DEVILS; *Jimmy Hughes* / YOU CAN'T BEAT LOVE; *Stephen Wayne* / FIRST LADY; *Det. Bill Crane* / THE WESTLAND CASE. **1938:** *Robert Crane* / DOUBLE DANGER; *Bruce* / EVERYBODY'S DOING IT; *Det. Bill Crane* / LADY IN THE MORGUE; *Dike Conger* / ARMY GIRL; *Det. Bill Crane* / THE LAST WARNING; *Chipper Morgan* / UP THE RIVER; *Jack Stacey* / THE STORM; *Lt. J. G. Drake* / SUBMARINE PATROL. **1939:** *Sully* / SOCIETY SMUGGLERS; *Steve Mitchell* / CHASING DANGER; *Steve Drum* / NEWS IS MADE AT NIGHT; *Bill Collins* / MISSING EVIDENCE; *Jim Howell* / 20,000 MEN A YEAR. **1940:** *Don Walters* / CAFE HOSTESS; *Bill Gordon* / MOON OVER BURMA. **1941:** *Greg* / THE ROUNDUP; *Steve Duncan* / UNFINISHED BUSINESS. **1942:** *Tom Gaynor* / A GENTLEMAN AFTER DARK; *Roy Bonnell* / SECRET AGENT OF JAPAN; *Steve Abbott* / A NIGHT IN NEW ORLEANS; *Michael Steele* / LITTLE TOKYO U.S.A.; *Steve Britt* / THUNDER BIRDS; *Paxton Bryce* / AMERICAN EMPIRE. **1944:** *Steve Carromond* / BERMUDA MYSTERY. **1945:** *Rob McLaughlin* / THUNDERHEAD—SON OF FLICKA; *guest* / ABBOTT AND COSTELLO IN HOLLYWOOD; *Jim Brennan* / THE VALLEY OF DECISION; *Jeff Turner* / TWICE BLESSED. **1946:** *Col. Jose Artiego* / TANGIER; *Bart Madden* / INSIDE JOB; *Sam Crane* / STRANGE TRIANGLE. **1947:** *Frank Ivey* / RAMROD; *Boyd Fielding* / KING OF THE WILD HORSES. **1948:** *Scotty Mason* / THUNDERHOOF. **1949:** *John Kelley* / I SHOT JESSE JAMES; *Tom Eggers* / THE BIG CAT. **1950:** *Joe McKinely* / THE TOUGHER THEY COME. **1951:** *Colonel Carrington* / TOMAHAWK; *Tom Denton* / THREE DESPERATE MEN; *Andy La Main* / THE BIG NIGHT; *Hank Mason* / THE BIG GUSHER. **1952:** *Sheriff Plummer* / MONTANA TERRITORY; *Timothy Foster* / KANSAS CITY CONFIDENTIAL. **1953:** *Kurt Durling* / LAW AND ORDER. **1957:** *Col. Ed Buckley* / DESTINATION 60,000. **1964:** *General Bateman* / ADVANCE TO THE REAR; *Judge Homer Black* / THE MAN FROM GALVESTON; *Dr. Erik von Steiner* / THE TIME TRAVELERS. **1967:** *Nick* / CHUBASCO. **1968:** *D. A. Griggs* / YOU'VE GOT TO BE SMART.

FOSTER, SUSANNA

(Susanna DeLee Larson, 1924–)

This strawberry blonde's film career was brief. She appeared in a few films of the 1940s featuring her operatic soprano voice but, clearly not interested in a movie career, she walked out on her contract in 1945 to star on stage in operettas with Wilbur Evans, whom she later married and divorced. By the mid-1950s she discovered there was no demand for her either in the theater or the movies, and was forced to take a wide assortment of menial jobs to support herself and her two sons. The once golden songbird of Universal studios, who also had a reputation for being a terrible brat, found that show business had finished with her.

KEY ROLES

Peggy / THE GREAT VICTOR HERBERT, 1939, Paramount, d-Andrew L. Stone.

Fifteen-year-old child coloratura Foster gives a stunning rendition of operetta composer Victor Herbert's "Kiss Me Again," as she portrays the daughter of Mary Martin in this very popular biopic.

Christine Dubois / THE PHANTOM OF THE OPERA, 1943, Universal, d-Arthur Lubin.

A disfigured composer who makes his home in the sewers below the Paris Opera House intends to make Foster a famous prima donna because he loves her. She also receives quite a bit of attention from singer Nelson Eddy and police inspector Edgar Barrier. She looks and sounds great.

Angela / THIS IS THE LIFE, 1944, Universal, d-Felix Feist.

Foster develops a crush on an older army officer (Patric Knowles) and boyfriend Donald O'Connor conspires to keep the two apart. Foster's songs include "L'Amour Toujours, L'Amour" and "All or Nothing at All."

OTHER ROLES

1941: *Toodles LaVerne* / THERE'S MAGIC IN MUSIC, (THE HARDBOILED CANARY); *Jan Winslow* / GLAMOUR BOY. **1942:** *guest* / STAR SPANGLED RHYTHM. **1944:** *cameo* / FOLLOW THE BOYS; *Angela* / THE CLIMAX; *Peggy Fleming* / BOWERY TO BROADWAY. **1945:** *Sally* / FRISCO SAL; *Penny* / THAT NIGHT WITH YOU.

FRANCIS, KAY

(Katherine Gibbs, 1899–1968)

An elegant beauty with jet-black hair, Kay Francis excelled at playing suffering women in many tear-jerkers of the 1930s. Wags made fun of her trouble pronouncing Rs which usually came out as Ws, but fans overlooked this minor speech defect and enjoyed the work of the actress given the title "best dressed woman." Her act soon became dated, however, and by the late 1930s her once great appeal was no more. This "clothes horse," married four times—twice to millionaires—left the bulk of her million-dollar estate to the Seeing Eye Dog Foundation. She once observed, "A dog has kindliness in his heart and dignity in his demeanor, the finest qualities anyone can have."

KEY ROLES

Alma Mardsen / STREET OF CHANCE, 1930, Paramount, d-John Cromwell.

Francis plays the wife of William Powell, a notorious gambler very like New York's Arnold Rothstein. She is a stunning beauty in this story about the dangerous life of those on the edge of the law, always willing to make a deal to make their way by whatever means available.

Joan Ames / ONE WAY PASSAGE, 1932, Warners, d-Tay Garnett.

With William Powell again, Francis is a dying girl on an ocean voyage who meets and falls in love with a man being returned to the states to face a life sentence in prison. It is her best work and, despite the story line, is really very moving and beautiful.

Mariette Colet / TROUBLE IN PARADISE, 1932, Paramount, d-Ernst Lubitsch.

In one of the most sophisticated comedies ever made, Francis is a wealthy charmer whom jewel thieves Herbert Marshall and Miriam Hopkins have chosen as their next mark. Things become complicated when Marshall falls for Francis.

Clemency Warlock / CYNARA, 1932, United Artists, d-King Vidor.

The title of this film about adultery comes from the poem by Ernest Dawson containing the line, "I have been faithful to thee, Cynara; in my fashion." Francis is the nobly suffering wife who leaves her husband (Ronald Colman) alone in London while she holidays in Venice. He has an affair with shopgirl Phyllis Barry, who kills herself when Colman goes back to his wife.

Tanya Borisoff / MANDALAY, 1934, Warners, d-Michael Curtiz.

Francis is a world-weary lady of the tropics who murders her lover and pushes his body out a porthole. That's about all there is to the plot, but audiences of the time found the steamy story absorbing.

Florence Nightingale / THE WHITE ANGEL, 1936, Warners, d-William Dieterle.

In this sketchy biopic of the battlefield nurse, Francis seems miscast, but she almost pulls it off despite the false Victorian atmosphere.

Lucy Chase Wayne / FIRST LADY, 1937, Warners, d-Stanley Logan.

This is basically a two-person catfight between Francis and Veree Teasdale, Francis being the wife of the secretary of state while Teasdale's husband is a member of the Supreme Court. The George S. Kaufman and Katherine Dayton play has plenty of sharp lines, but Francis can't match Teasdale in this regard.

Donna Lucia / CHARLEY'S AUNT, 1941, 20th Century-Fox, d-Archie Mayo.

Francis is an Oxford undergraduate's aunt from Brazil, "where the nuts come from," whose delay in arrival causes the student to impersonate her so that his chums will have a chaperone for two female guests visiting them.

OTHER ROLES

1929: *Myra May* / GENTLEMEN OF THE PRESS; *Penelope* / THE COCOANUTS; *Zara Flynn* / DANGEROUS CURVES; *Zelda Paxton* / ILLUSION; *Zinnie la Crosse* / THE MARRIAGE PLAYGROUND. **1930:** *Kitty Parker* / BEHIND THE MAKEUP; *guest* / PARAMOUNT ON PARADE; *Countess Balakireff* / A NOTORIOUS AFFAIR; *Lady Gwen Manders* / RAFFLES; *Irene Manners* / FOR THE DEFENSE; *Constance Cook* / LET'S GO NATIVE; *Marya Ivanovna* / THE VIRTUOUS SIN; *Dulce Morado* / PASSION FLOWER. **1931:** *Mrs. Flint* / SCANDAL SHEET; *Norma Page* / LADIES' MAN; *Alice Morrison* / THE VICE SQUAD; *Elsie Maury* / TRANSGRESSION; *Marjorie West* / GUILTY HANDS; *Fanny Towner* / TWENTY-FOUR HOURS; *Wanda Howard* / GIRLS ABOUT TOWN. **1932:** *Tina* / THE FALSE MADONNA; *Diana Merrow* / STRANGERS IN LOVE; *Lois Ames* / MAN WANTED; *Natalie Upton* / STREET OF WOMEN; *Baroness Teri von Horhenfels* / JEWEL ROBBERY. **1933:** *Anne Brooks* / THE KEYHOLE; *Irina Dushan* / STORM AT DAYBREAK; *Dr. Mary Stevens* / MARY STEVENS, M.D.; *Laura McDonald* / I LOVED A WOMAN; *Peggy Van Tyle* / THE HOUSE ON 56TH STREET. **1934:** *Liane Renaud* / WONDER BAR; *Dr. Monica Braden* / DOCTOR MONICA; *Elena* / BRITISH AGENT; *Lynn Palmer* / STRANDED. **1935:** *Georgiana Summers* / THE GOOSE AND THE GANDER; *Amy Prentiss* / LIVING ON VELVET; *Stella Parrish* / I FOUND STELLA PARRISH. **1936:** *Belinda Warren* / GIVE ME YOUR HEART. **1937:** *Nicole Picot* / STOLEN HOLIDAY; *Vera* / CONFESSION; *Julie Ashton* / ANOTHER DAWN. **1938:** *Claire Landin* / WOMEN ARE LIKE THAT; *Mary Colbrook* / MY BILL; *Fay Carter* / SECRETS OF AN ACTRESS; *Eve Appleton* / COMET OVER BROADWAY. **1939:** *Carole Nelson* / KING OF THE UNDERWORLD; *Janet Steele* / WOMEN IN THE WIND; *Malda Walker* / IN NAME ONLY. **1940:** *Georgia Drake* / IT'S A DATE; *Jo Marsh* / LITTLE MEN; *Julie King* / WHEN THE DALTONS RODE; *Grace Herbert* / PLAY GIRL; *Adrienne Scott* / THE MAN WHO LOST HIMSELF. **1941:** *Nellie Woods* / THE FEMININE TOUCH. **1942:** *Marjorie Scott* / ALWAYS IN MY HEART; *Chris Bishop* / BETWEEN US GIRLS. **1944:** *herself* / FOUR JILLS IN A JEEP. **1945:** *Diane Carter* / DIVORCE; *Sheila Seymour* / ALLOTMENT WIVES. **1946:** *Carole Raymond* / WIFE WANTED.

GABLE, CLARK

(William Clark Gable, 1901–1960)

The man who one day would be called "The King" began his film career in a bit part in FORBIDDEN PARADISE (1924), followed by stage work and his sound debut in THE PAINTED DESERT (1931). Clark Gable's impressive size, charmingly naughty smile, and self-confidence came to represent the ultimate in masculinity for millions of women and the envy and admiration of a like number of men. Despite Gable's own assessment, "I'm no actor and I never have been. What people see on the screen is me," critics and fans alike admired not only his handsome physique and face, but his acting talents as well. He was nominated for Academy Awards for MUTINY ON THE BOUNTY and GONE WITH THE WIND, winning the Oscar for his performance in IT HAPPENED ONE NIGHT. Shortly after his third wife, Carole Lombard, was killed in a plane crash, Gable joined the air force, rising to the rank of major and receiving the Distinguished Flying Cross and Air Medal for flying several bombing missions over Germany. After the war, MGM trumpeted his return to films in ADVENTURE with the slogan, "Gable's back and Garson's got him!" which Gable found as distasteful as the movie itself. But as Gable said, "I am paid not to think." His post-war films couldn't hold a candle to his earlier adventure and romantic yarns, but several showed that the man with the pencil-thin moustache hadn't lost his sheer animal magic. Fittingly enough, his last film (THE MISFITS) was also the end of the trail for America's biggest sex queen, Marilyn Monroe. Gable, of course, will always be remembered best for his Rhett Butler in GONE WITH THE WIND, but his mark doesn't rest on this one admittedly great role. The man with the protruding ears seldom disappointed.

KEY ROLES

Rodney Spencer / SUSAN LENOX: HER FALL AND RISE, 1931, MGM, d-Robert Z. Leonard.

Gable is the one true love of a woman (Greta Garbo) who keeps seeking him often in other men's beds. She finally catches up to engineer Gable in South America where her past affairs are finally forgiven and perhaps even forgotten.

Mark Whitney / POSSESSED, 1931, MGM, d-Clarence Brown.

Gable, a wealthy lawyer with a political future, secretly marries a factory girl (Joan Crawford) who is prepared to give him up rather than harm his political future. He refuses to allow her to make the sacrifice.

Dennis Carson / RED DUST, 1932, MGM, d-Victor Fleming.

Gable, the overseer of a large rubber plantation in Indochina, finds himself with two women on his hands: Jean Harlow, a stranded prostitute, and Mary Astor, the wife of an engineer who has been stricken with fever, giving Astor some time to consider the passion she is feeling for Gable. They become lovers, but eventually Gable sends Astor back to her unsuspecting husband, realizing that Harlow is more the woman for him.

Dr. Ned Darrell / STRANGE INTERLUDE, 1932, MGM, d-Robert Z. Leonard.

When Norma Shearer's father prevents her from marrying the man she loves, who is killed in World War I, she marries an impotent man who is all but repulsed by sex. She takes her husband's physician (Gable) as her lover and conceives his child, with her husband believing the boy to be his own. Gable and Shearer keep their secret even when the lad grows up and Shearer almost prevents him from marrying the girl of his choice.

Peter Warne / IT HAPPENED ONE NIGHT, 1934, Columbia, d-Frank Capra.

Gable was lent to a poverty-row studio for this film and saw it as punishment, but it turned out to be a happy chastisement, as the story of a reporter who helps a runaway heiress and then falls in love with her is still fresh, funny, and delightful all these years later. It is one of the very few films to win all four major Academy Awards: Best Actor, Best Actress, Best Director, and Best Picture. Gable just about put the undershirt manufacturers out of business when he undressed for bed and revealed only a massive, bare chest under his shirt.

Blackie Gallagher / MANHATTAN MELODRAMA, 1934, MGM, d-W. S. Van Dyke.

Gable is prosecuted and sent to the chair by his lifelong friend, D.A. William Powell, for a murder that gambler Gable committed to stop the efforts of a man trying to ruin Powell's chances of being elected governor. Gable's ex-girl (Myrna Loy), now Powell's wife, begs Powell to commute Gable's sentence, but Gable refuses the offer insisting: "If I can't live the way I want, let me die the way I want." This was the film that John Dillinger attended at the Biograph Theater in Chicago with the "Lady in Red" just prior to being gunned down by FBI agents.

Jack Thornton / CALL OF THE WILD, 1935, 20th Century-Fox, d-William Wellman.

Gable, an adventurous prospector, makes a gold strike in the Klondike and saves a seemingly unmanageable dog, Buck, and trains him to become his sled dog. Gable falls in love with Loretta Young, who believes her husband to be dead, but Buck locates the man and she gives up Gable, whom she loves, to return to her husband.

Capt. Alan Gaskell / CHINA SEAS, 1935, MGM, d-Tay Garnett.

Gable, the captain of a ship on its way to Hong Kong with a valuable cargo, is annoyed to find both his fiancée (Rosalind Russell) and his mistress (Jean Harlow) aboard. Before long he has to worry about other matters such as crooked Wallace Beery and Chinese pirates.

Fletcher Christian / MUTINY ON THE BOUNTY, 1935, MGM, d-Frank Lloyd.

"From now on, they'll spell mutiny with my name." Thus Gable accepts his place in history after taking control of the H.M.S. Bounty and setting its cruel captain, William Bligh (Charles Laughton), adrift in a long boat thousands of miles from land. It's a stirring adventure yarn, with Gable as a man who finds that things have gone too far and feels compelled to act, even though he knows that he will never see England again and will remain a hunted man the rest of his life.

Blackie Norton / SAN FRANCISCO, 1936, MGM, d-W. S. Van Dyke.

Gable is the ruthless proprietor of a Barbary Coast saloon who hires singer Jeanette MacDonald and then refuses to release her from her contract when a Nob Hill society man wishes to put her in the San Francisco opera. Their on-again, off-again love affair is interrupted by the 1906 earthquake but, bloody and bruised, they are brought together by their friend, priest Spencer Tracy.

Charles Parnell / PARNELL, 1937, MGM, d-John M. Stahl.

Gable's portrayal of the champion of Irish Home Rule is arguably his worst performance and is often used as evidence that Gable, despite his talent, was not a good judge of what roles were right for him.

Rhett Butler / GONE WITH THE WIND, 1939, Selznick International / MGM, d-Victor Fleming, George Cukor, and Sam Wood.

Gable is a disreputable gambler and cynic who takes a fancy to strong-willed, southern beauty Scarlett O'Hara (Vivien Leigh) shortly before the Civil War. Attracted to him, Scarlett nevertheless maintains a lifelong infatuation for Leslie Howard who instead loves and marries Olivia De Havilland. After the war and two marriages to men who have gone to their rewards, Scarlett deigns to marry Gable. After their child is killed in an accident, Gable leaves her, and answers her query as to what she is to do with the classic reply, "Frankly, my dear, I don't give a damn."

"Big John" McMasters / BOOM TOWN, 1940, MGM, d-Jack Conway.

When Gable meets Claudette Colbert, without realizing that she is the back-home girlfriend of his oil prospecting partner (Spencer Tracy), it's love at first sight. Tracy accepts his loss but later, when he believes that Gable is being unfaithful to Colbert with Hedy Lamarr, they gamble for their oil company and Gable loses. The two men subsequently make and lose fortunes several times, and Gable is reunited with Colbert through the efforts of Tracy who, despite all of his differences with Gable, still likes the big lug.

Candy Johnson / HONKY TONK, 1941, MGM, d-Jack Conway.

Gable is a con man who gains control of a western town shortly after having been ridden out of another following a tarring and feathering ceremony in his honor. He earns the enmity of fellow con man Frank Morgan when he marries Morgan's lovely and innocent young daughter (Lana Turner).

Vic Norman / THE HUCKSTERS, 1947, MGM, d-Jack Conway.

Returning home after World War II, Gable takes a position with a swank advertising agency and is given the difficult account of Beautee Soap, manufactured by crude Sydney Greenstreet. Gable plans to get a beautiful British lady (Deborah Kerr) to endorse the soap, but soon grows weary of being a yes-man to the disgusting and never pleased Greenstreet. So he gives up his career as a huckster and goes off with Kerr.

Brig. Gen. K. C. "Casey" Dennis / COMMAND DECISION, 1948, MGM, d-Sam Wood.

Gable continues to order daytime bombing raids over Germany despite heavy losses. When he is relieved of command his successor decides Gable had been correct and continues the practice, wiping out strategic German airplane factories.

Vic Marswell / MOGAMBO, 1953, MGM, d-John Ford.

In this updated version of RED DUST, Gable is a celebrated white hunter in Africa who finds his hands full on a safari when both a show girl (Ava Gardner) and (Grace Kelly) the wife of a wimpy anthropologist decide they want a piece of him. As his affair with Kelly progresses, Gardner's wisecracks and the trust of Kelly's husband bother Gable, so he sends Kelly packing and resumes his affair with Gardner.

Jim Gannon / TEACHER'S PET, 1958, Paramount, d-George Seaton.

Gable is a self-taught newspaper editor who believes that journalism courses are a waste of time. He becomes involved with journalism professor Doris Day after he enrolls in her class without revealing his true identity in order to show her up. But, of course, he falls in love with her.

Gay Langland / THE MISFITS, 1961, United Artists, d-John Huston.

Gable is a rugged, aging cowboy who meets recently divorced Marilyn Monroe in Reno. Gable and a couple of other wranglers come up with a plan to round up some wild mustangs (called "misfits") to sell. When Monroe learns that the horses are to be used for dog food, she tries to stop Gable, but he captures the horses and, having proven his point, lets them go. Some believe that doing some of his own strenuous stunts led to Gable's death shortly after the completion of the movie.

OTHER ROLES

1931: *Brett* / THE PAINTED DESERT; *Nick Felici* / THE EASIEST WAY; *Jake Luva* / DANCE, FOOLS, DANCE; *Carl Luckner* / THE SECRET SIX; *Louis Blanco* / THE FINGER POINTS; *Carl Loomis* / LAUGHING SINNERS; *Ace Wilfong* / A FREE SOUL; *Nick* / NIGHT NURSE; *Tip Scanlon* / SPORTING BLOOD; *Steve* / HELL DIVERS. **1932:** *Rev. John Hartley* / POLLY OF THE CIRCUS; *Jerry "Babe" Stewart* / NO MAN OF HER OWN. **1933:** *Giovanni Severi* / THE WHITE SISTER; *Eddie Nugent* / HOLD YOUR MAN; *Jules Fabian* / NIGHT FLIGHT; *Patch Gallagher* / DANCING LADY. **1934:** *Dr. George Ferguson* / MEN IN WHITE; *Mike Bradley* / CHAINED; *Jeff Williams* / FORSAKING ALL OTHERS. **1935:** *Jim Branch* / AFTER OFFICE HOURS. **1936:** *Dan Sanford* / WIFE VS. SECRETARY; *Larry Cain* / CAIN AND MABEL; *Michael Anthony* / LOVE ON THE RUN. **1937:** *Duke Bradley* / SARATOGA. **1938:** *Jim Lane* / TEST PILOT; *Chris Hunter* / TOO HOT TO HANDLE. **1939:** *Harry Van* / IDIOT'S DELIGHT. **1940:** *Andre Verne* / STRANGE CARGO; *McKinley B. Thompson* / COMRADE X. **1941:** *Gerald Meldrick* / THEY MET IN BOMBAY. **1942:** *Johnny Davis* / SOMEWHERE I'LL FIND YOU. **1945:** *Harry Patterson* / ADVENTURE. **1948:** *Ulysses Johnson* / HOMECOMING. **1949:** *Charley King* / ANY NUMBER CAN PLAY. **1950:** *Steve Fisk* / KEY TO THE CITY; *Mike Brannon* / TO PLEASE A LADY. **1951:** *Flint Mitchell* / ACROSS THE WIDE MISSOURI; *himself* / CALLAWAY WENT THATAWAY. **1952:** *Devereaux Burke* / LONE STAR. **1953:** *Philip Sutherland* / NEVER LET ME GO. **1954:** *Col. Pieter Deventer* / BETRAYED. **1955:** *Hank Lee* / SOLDIER OF FORTUNE; *Ben Allison* / THE TALL MEN. **1956:** *Dan Kehoe* / THE KING AND FOUR QUEENS. **1957:** *Hamish Bond* / BAND OF ANGELS. **1958:** *Cmdr. "Rich" Richardson* / RUN SILENT, RUN DEEP. **1959:** *Russell Ward* / BUT NOT FOR ME. **1960:** *Michael Hamilton* / IT STARTED IN NAPLES.

GARBO, GRETA

(Greta Lovisa Gustafsson, 1905–)

Swedish-born Greta Garbo was the epitome of film glamour. She made her screen debut in 1922 in PETER THE TRAMP, playing a bathing beauty. She studied acting at the Royal Dramatic Theatre in Stockholm where she met Mauritz Stiller, the foremost Swedish director, who changed her name to Greta Garbo and gave her an important role in THE STORY OF GOSTA BERLING. When Stiller went to the United States to work for MGM, he insisted that Garbo also be given a contract, describing her as "an actress who will be the greatest in the world." There are many, critics and fans alike, who insist that Garbo made Stiller's prediction come true with the 24 films she made in 16 years. She was twice nominated for an Academy Award: in 1930 for ANNA CHRISTIE and in 1939 for NINOTCHKA. At the age of 36 she retired from films and nothing induced her to return. Considered a recluse by many, she feels she is merely protecting her privacy. She is quoted as having said, "I never said 'I want to be alone.' I only said 'I want to be left alone.' There is all the difference." In a 1950 *Variety* poll, Garbo was named the best actress of the half-century, and if her films remain available, she may be named the best actress of the century in 2000.

KEY ROLES

Countess Elisabeth Dohna / THE LEGEND OF GÖSTA BERLING, 1924, Silent, Sweden, Svensk Filmindustri, d-Mauritz Stiller.

Garbo helps redeem a minister who has lost his position in the church because of his problems with alcohol.

Leonora Moreno / THE TORRENT, 1926, Silent, MGM, d-Monta Bell.

In her first Hollywood film, Garbo portrays a Spanish girl in love with an aristocrat whose mother prevents their marriage. They encounter each other on several occasions during their lifetimes as she becomes a famous prima donna.

Felicitas von Rhaden / FLESH AND THE DEVIL, 1927, Silent, MGM, d-Clarence Brown.

Garbo's lover (John Gilbert) kills her husband in a duel and then flees from Austria to America. His best friend (Lars Hanson) marries Garbo, unaware of her affair with Gilbert. A few years later, Gilbert is able to return and Garbo once again lures him into an affair. When Hanson finds out, Garbo blames Gilbert for tempting her. Then the two friends have a duel, and as Garbo hurries to prevent it, she falls through the ice and drowns. Hanson is wounded but Gilbert nurses him back to health and they become friends again.

Diana Merrick / A WOMAN OF AFFAIRS, 1929, Silent, MGM, d-Clarence Brown.

Aristocratic English girl Garbo loves John Gilbert, but his father prevents their marriage because he disapproves of her family's way of life. She goes through a series of affairs and then marries John Mack Brown without knowing that he is a thief. When he is caught he commits suicide, and she sets out to pay back what he's stolen.

Irene Guarry / THE KISS, 1929, Silent, MGM, d-Jacques Feyder.

When Garbo's jealous French husband tries to kill a man (Lew Ayres) who has a crush on her, she shoots her husband and is put on trial. She is acquitted, though, when a former lover (Conrad Nagel) defends her.

Anna Christie / ANNA CHRISTIE, 1930, MGM, d-Clarence Brown.

"Gimme a viskey. Ginger ale on the side. And don't be stingy, ba-bee." With this line Garbo enters the sound era. In this old chestnut, she is a prostitute who is disgusted with her life. Completely broke, she looks up the father who had deserted her when she was a child and moves in with him and his mistress aboard his fishing barge. Then she falls in love with rugged seaman Charles Bickford.

Rita Cavallini / ROMANCE, 1930, MGM, d-Clarence Brown.

Italian prima donna Garbo is a rich man's mistress when she falls in love with a young minister. When he discovers her relationship with the other man he denounces her in one breath and tries to get her to go to bed with him in another. She begs him not to treat her as other men have. He comes to his senses and leaves—never to see her again.

Mata Hari / MATA HARI, 1932, MGM, d-George Fitzmaurice.

Garbo is the infamous World War I German spy who is discovered and executed by the French. In the film she is caught because of her love for a French officer Ramon Novarro.

Grusinskaya / GRAND HOTEL, 1932, MGM, d-Edmund Goulding.

Garbo is a famous ballet star appearing in Berlin and staying at the Grand Hotel. There she meets John Barrymore who has come to steal her jewels. She is dejected about her career and plans suicide, but is stopped by Barrymore. They fall in love but, when she happily departs the hotel planning a new life with Barrymore, she is unaware that he has been killed in a robbery attempt in the room of Wallace Beery. Just for the record, her character does say "I want to be alone."

Queen Christina / QUEEN CHRISTINA, 1933, MGM, d-Rouben Mamoulian.

The 17th-century queen is to marry for political reasons a man she does not love. She declines and dons boys' clothes, meets an ambassador from Spain (John Gilbert), and shares a room with him. When he discovers her sex, they fall in love. She abdicates her throne to be with him, but a former lover kills Gilbert. She leaves for Spain with his body—never to return. Before leaving she had visited the room where she and Gilbert made love, saying: "I have been memorizing this room. In the future, in my memory, I shall live a great deal in this room."

Anna Karenina / ANNA KARENINA, 1935, MGM, d-Clarence Brown.

Garbo had appeared in a silent version of the Tolstoy novel in 1927, then titled LOVE. She is the wife of a wealthy Russian aristocrat whom she deserts to become the mistress of an officer (Fredric March). When he grows tired of her, she throws herself under the wheels of a train.

Marguerite Gautier (Camille) / CAMILLE, 1937, MGM, d-George Cukor.

Garbo is a fancy Parisian courtesan who meets Robert Taylor and falls deeply in love with him. He feels the same about her, but his father warns him that marrying Garbo will ruin his career. To save her lover, she pretends that her love is not as deep as his and that she prefers being kept by rich men. Later she contracts tuberculosis and is forced to sell her possessions. When Taylor learns of her condition, he goes to her, and she dies in his arms. Her last words are, "Perhaps it's better if I live in your heart where the world can't see me. If I am dead, there'll be no strain on our love."

Ninotchka / NINOTCHKA, 1939, MGM, d-Ernst Lubitsch.

Garbo is a delight as the beautiful but icy special Russian emissary sent to Paris to check up on three Russian agents who were sent there to sell jewels and use the money to buy farm equipment. She finds that they have fallen sway to capitalistic luxuries, a fate that happens to her as well when she falls in love with Melvyn Douglas, the ex-lover of the grand duchess who originally owned the jewels everyone is trying to sell. In this film, Garbo dismisses Melvyn Douglas's butler with the line, "Go to bed, little father. We want to be alone."

OTHER ROLES

1922: *Greta* / PETER THE TRAMP. **1925:** *Greta Rumfort* / THE JOYLESS STREET. **1926:** *Elena Fontenoy* / THE TEMPTRESS. **1927:** *Anna Karenina* / LOVE. **1928:** *Marianne* / THE DIVINE WOMAN; *Tania* / THE MYSTERIOUS LADY. **1929:** *Lillie Sterling* / WILD ORCHIDS; *Arden Stuart* / THE SINGLE STANDARD. **1931:** *Yvonne* / INSPIRATION; *Helga Ohlin (Susan Lenox)* / SUSAN LENOX: HER FALL AND RISE. **1932:** *Maria / Zara* / AS YOU DESIRE ME. **1934:** *Katrin Fane* / THE PAINTED VEIL. **1937:** *Countess Marie Walewska* / CONQUEST. **1941:** *Karin Blake* / TWO-FACED WOMAN.

GARDNER, AVA

(Lucy Johnson, 1922–)

Green-eyed, dark-haired Ava Gardner, with the animal-like sexuality, was one of several starlets hired by MGM in the early 1940s to pose for cheesecake pictures and, if they were lucky enough, to appear fleetingly in a movie or two as decoration. Gardner's name became known first not for her performances in films, but because she had become the bride of one of America's biggest stars, Mickey Rooney. Seventeen months later, the marriage was finished and she became one of bandleader Artie Shaw's many wives. This lasted another seven months. A celebrity by marriage first, Gardner was built into a sex symbol by MGM and in the late 1940s and 1950s she enjoyed considerable popularity and even surprised people when she showed on occasion that she could also act. The glamorous star made another celebrity marriage when she wed Frank Sinatra, a tempestuous pairing that has been detailed in the various biographies of the two stars. Never fooled about her own talents she self-deprecatingly noted: "Deep down, I'm pretty superficial."

KEY ROLES

Kitty Collins / THE KILLERS, 1946, Universal-International, d-Robert Siodmak.

Looking perfectly gorgeous in her one-strap evening gown, Gardner double-crosses Burt Lancaster in this film noir about a man who waits unprotestingly in a small hotel room for the men he knows have been sent to kill him.

Jean Ogilvie / THE HUCKSTERS, 1947, MGM, d-Jack Conway.

Gardner loses out to Deborah Kerr in the love sweepstakes for advertising man Clark Gable. But she had a lot of men who would have been more than happy to settle for Gable's discard.

Venus / Venus Jones / ONE TOUCH OF VENUS, 1948, Universal, d-William A. Seiter.

Not many movie love goddesses can say they portrayed the real love goddess. In this whimsical story, when window dresser Robert Walker impulsively kisses a statue of Venus, it comes to life in the person of Gardner.

Isabel Lorrison / EAST SIDE, WEST SIDE, 1949, MGM, d-Mervyn LeRoy.

Alluring Gardner almost breaks up the marriage of New York businessman James Mason and his wife Barbara Stanwyck.

Julie Laverne / SHOWBOAT, 1951, MGM, d-George Sidney.

Judy Garland was supposed to portray the showboat actress who is revealed to have Black blood in this remake of the musical version of Edna Ferber's story about life on a Mississippi showboat. But, as happened too often, Garland wasn't up to the task and Gardner got her chance, although her singing was dubbed by Annette Warren.

Pandora Reynolds / PANDORA AND THE FLYING DUTCHMAN, 1951, Great Britain, Romulus, d-Albert Lewin.

Gardner is a cold but beautiful American heartbreaker who meets the Flying Dutchman (James Mason) who is doomed to roam the seas. But he is granted six months of every seven years to search for a woman willing to die for him and thus end his eternal suffering. Gardner's just the woman.

Eloise Kelly / MOGAMBO, 1953, MGM, d-John Ford.

Gardner is an American showgirl stranded in Kenya who has an affair with great white hunter Clark Gable and then has to wait around until he gets over his dalliance with the wife (Grace Kelly) of an anthropologist.

Maria Vargas / THE BAREFOOT CONTESSA, 1954, United Artists, d-Joseph L. Mankiewicz.

In a story said to be inspired by certain aspects of the life of Rita Hayworth, Gardner is a glamorous, barefoot, Spanish dancer whom a Howard Hughes-like producer turns into a major star. Then she marries an impotent, Italian aristocrat who kills her when she seeks sexual relief elsewhere.

Lady Brett Ashley / THE SUN ALSO RISES, 1957, 20th Century-Fox, d-Henry King.

Once again Gardner's man is sexually dysfunctional. Tyrone Power was hurt in World War I and although the expatriate feels passionately for his lady, he's no good to her.

Duchess of Alba / THE NAKED MAJA, 1959, Italy / U.S., MGM / Titanus, d-Henry Koster.

Francisco Goya, portrayed by Anthony Franciosa, becomes a famous painter through the sponsorship of Gardner. Her posing for him, both clothed and undraped, also helps.

Baroness Natalie Ivanoff / 55 DAYS AT PEKING, 1962, U.S. / Spain, Bronston, d-Nicholas Ray.

When the Boxer fanatics, encouraged by China's last empress, attack the foreign compound at Peking, the multi-national force holds out for 55 days and Gardner is killed trading her jewels for medicine.

Maxine Faulk / THE NIGHT OF THE IGUANA, 1964, MGM, d-John Huston.

Gardner is the bawdy owner of a run-down Mexican hotel where a defrocked clergyman turned tourist guide (Richard Burton) brings his traveling flock. The sexual heat is blistering as every female in sight has her flame turned all the way up for the fallen cleric.

OTHER ROLES

1942: *bit* / WE WERE DANCING; *bit* / JOE SMITH, AMERICAN; *bit* / SUNDAY PUNCH; *bit* / THIS TIME FOR KEEPS; *bit* / CALLING DR. GILLESPIE; *car hop* / KID GLOVE KILLER. **1943:** *bit* / PILOT NO. 5; *bit* / REUNION IN FRANCE; *girl* / DUBARRY WAS A LADY; *girl* / YOUNG IDEAS; *hat check girl* / LOST ANGEL; *Katy Chotnik* / HITLER'S MADMAN; *Betty* / GHOSTS ON THE LOOSE. **1944:** *girl* / SWING FEVER; *bit* / MUSIC FOR MILLIONS; *Jean Brown* / THREE MEN IN WHITE; *bit* / BLONDE FEVER; *Gloria Fullerton* / MAISIE GOES TO RENO; *Rockette girl* / TWO GIRLS AND A SAILOR. **1945:** *Hilda Spotts* / SHE WENT TO THE RACES. **1946:** *Mary* / WHISTLE STOP. **1947:** *Linda Gordon Van Leyden* / SINGAPORE. **1949:** *Pauline Ostrovski* / THE GREAT SINNER; *Elizabeth Hintten* / THE BRIBE. **1951:** *Barbara Beaurevel* / MY FORBIDDEN PAST. **1952:** *Martha Ronda* / LONE STAR; *Cynthia* / THE SNOWS OF KILIMANJARO. **1953:** *Cordelia Cameron* / RIDE VAQUERO!; *herself* / THE BAND WAGON; *Queen Guinevere* / KNIGHTS OF THE ROUND TABLE. **1956:** *Victoria Jones* / BHOWANI JUNCTION. **1957:** *Lady Susan Ashlow* / THE LITTLE HUT. **1959:** *Moira Davidson* / ON THE BEACH. **1960:** *Soledad* / THE ANGEL WORE RED. **1964:** *Eleanor Holbrook* / SEVEN DAYS IN MAY. **1966:** *Sarah* / THE BIBLE. **1968:** *Empress Elizabeth* / MAYERLING. **1970:** *Michaela* / TAM-LIN. **1972:** *Lily Langtry* / THE LIFE AND TIMES OF JUDGE ROY BEAN. **1974:** *Remy Graff* / EARTHQUAKE. **1975:** *Katina Petersen* / PERMISSION TO KILL. **1976:** *Luxury* / THE BLUE BIRD. **1977:** *Miss Logan* / THE SENTINEL. **1979:** *guest* / CITY ON FIRE. **1980:** *Beth Richards* / THE KIDNAPPING OF THE PRESIDENT. **1981:** *Mabel Dodge Luhan* / PRIEST OF LOVE. **1982:** *Regina* / ROMA REGINA.

GARFIELD, JOHN

(Julius Garfinkle, 1913–1952)

Garfield studied acting at the American Laboratory School under Maria Ouspenskaya. He became a member of the Group Theater and acted on the stage in "Waiting for Lefty" (1935), "Awake and Sing" (1935), and "Golden Boy" (1937). He made his movie debut in

FOOTLIGHT PARADE (1933) with his first billed part being in 1938 in FOUR DAUGHTERS. Garfield was an actor of great intensity, the likes of which audiences had never seen before. He was the forerunner of James Dean, Marlon Brando, and Paul Newman. His rebellious, antihero roles excited audiences when he was on the screen, but his liberal causes and left-wing friends bothered others. He was subpoenaed by the House Un-American Activities Committee and answered all questions pertaining to him, but did not give the congressmen any other names. This resulted in his unofficial blacklisting in Hollywood. He died before he could secure any additional roles. Nominated for Academy Awards for his work in FOUR DAUGHTERS and BODY AND SOUL, Garfield will long be remembered for his searing portrayals of good guys who got bad breaks and had to fight their way back. Unfortunately, he was unable to do that in his own life.

KEY ROLES

Mickey Borden (Bolgar) / FOUR DAUGHTERS, 1938, Warners, d-Michael Curtiz.

Garfield was a sensation in his first real movie role as an indolent and caustic young man who comes into the lives of four girls in a small-town American family. He's a disillusioned, fatalistic, world-weary man from the city slums. He marries Priscilla Lane but, when he realizes that he will not be able to make her happy, he kills himself (a shocking turn for audiences used to happy endings in romantic melodramas). Earlier, he laid out his sad life for Lane, saying: "The fates, the destinies—whoever they are that decide what we do or don't get—they've been at me now nearly a quarter of a century. No letup. First they said, 'Let him do without parents. He'll get along.' Then they decided, 'He doesn't need any education—that's for sissies.' And, right at the beginning, they tossed a coin. Heads, he's poor; tails, he's rich. So they tossed a coin—with two heads. And when you put all this together you got Michael Bolgar."

Johnny Bradfield / THEY MADE ME A CRIMINAL, 1939, Warners, d-Busby Berkeley.

In this remake of THE LIFE OF JIMMY DOLAN, Garfield plays a boxer falsely accused of murder who flees west and hides out at a ranch run by two women and the six New York slum delinquents they are trying to reform. Garfield risks being discovered by the authorities by entering a prize-fight contest in order to raise money for the women, one of whom (Gloria Dickson) he has come to love.

George Leach / THE SEA WOLF, 1941, Warners, d-Michael Curtiz.

Garfield's character did not appear in the Jack London novel, but was created by screenwriter Robert Rossen. He plays the crew member who leads a revolt against the mentally disturbed skipper (Edward G. Robinson) of the doomed ship Ghost, after it picks up passengers from a San Francisco ferry that sank in the fog. They are then kept as virtual prisoners by the sick captain.

Danny / TORTILLA FLAT, 1942, MGM, d-Victor Fleming.

Garfield is one of a group of ignorant, indolent, irresponsible, and generally worthless descendants of Spanish settlers of Monterey in northern California. He inherits two houses and a gold watch and is joined in a celebration by several other shiftless paisanos, which results in one of the houses burning to the ground. No matter, they just move into the other. When Garfield meets a Portuguese girl (Hedy Lamarr) he actually contemplates marriage and a job.

Tom Prior / BETWEEN TWO WORLDS, 1944, Warners, d-Edward A. Blatt.

In this remake of OUTWARD BOUND, Garfield is among a group of dead people who are on a cruise to a place where their ultimate fate will be decided by the Examiner. Garfield is the first to realize that all aboard the ship are beyond the veil.

Al Schmid / THE PRIDE OF THE MARINES, 1945, Warners, d-Delmer Daves.

In this film based on a true story, Garfield appears as a young marine who loses his sight in the battle of Guadalcanal and returns home to his wife (Eleanor Parker) to face adjustment to his affliction.

Frank Chambers / THE POSTMAN ALWAYS RINGS TWICE, 1946, MGM, d-Tay Garnett.

Wanderer Garfield is hired by Cecil Kellaway to help out at the latter's cafe and motel. When Garfield sees Kellaway's beautiful, young wife (Lana Turner) it's not too long before she has him thinking of murdering the older man. After a couple of false starts which don't make Kellaway any wiser, they kill him, are tried for the crime, and, due to a sharp lawyer's trick, they get off. Then in a neat twist of fate, Turner is killed in an accident and Garfield is sent to the chair for her death.

Paul Boray / HUMORESQUE, 1946, Warners, d-Jean Negulesco.

Fire meets fire when Garfield, as a budding violinist, meets a wealthy woman (Joan Crawford) willing to be his sponsor. That she has more in mind than being a patron of the arts is betrayed in her complaint, "I'm tired of playing second fiddle to the ghost of Beethoven." Eventually Garfield chooses Beethoven and the other musical boys over the charms of Crawford.

Charlie Davis / BODY AND SOUL, 1947, Enterprise / United Artists, d-Robert Rossen.

Garfield is an unemployed Jewish kid from New York who finds he can make a lot of money in the fight game and save his widowed mother from poverty. He loses his artist girlfriend (Lilli Palmer) when he gets involved with a crooked promoter and a showgirl. He comes to his moral senses, however, when he refuses to take a dive.

Dave / GENTLEMAN'S AGREEMENT, 1947, 20th Century-Fox, d-Elia Kazan.

Writer Gregory Peck is posing as a Jew to collect material for a series on anti-Semitism and Garfield is eloquent as his Jewish friend. When he talks with Peck's girl (Dorothy McGuire) about her passive disapproval of "nice" anti-Semites Garfield is admirable in his restraint.

Joe Morse / FORCE OF EVIL, 1949, MGM, d-Abraham Polansky.

In the last film by director Abraham Polansky, Garfield is embroiled in the numbers racket for 20 years because of the Red Scare. It's a moody film, brilliantly photographed on location in New York City.

OTHER ROLES

1933: *sailor* / FOOTLIGHT PARADE. **1938:** *Tim Hayden* / BLACKWELL'S ISLAND. **1939:** *Porfirio Diaz* / JUAREZ; *Mickey Borden* / FOUR WIVES; *Gabriel Lopez* / DAUGHTERS COURAGEOUS; *Joe Bell* / DUST BE MY DESTINY. **1940:** *Rims O'Neill* / SATURDAY'S CHILDREN; *Joe Lorenzo* / EAST OF THE RIVER; *Tommy Gordon* /

CASTLE ON THE HUDSON; *Johnny Blake* / FLOWING GOLD. **1941:** *Harold Goff* / OUT OF THE FOG. **1942:** *Dr. Michael Lewis* / DANGEROUSLY THEY LIVE. **1943:** *Sgt. Joe Winocki* / AIR FORCE; *Kit* / THE FALLEN SPARROW; *guest* / THANK YOUR LUCKY STARS. **1944:** *himself* / HOLLYWOOD CANTEEN; *Wolf* / DESTINATION TOKYO. **1946:** *Nick Blake* / NOBODY LIVES FOREVER. **1948:** *Tony Ferrer* / WE WERE STRANGERS. **1949:** *cameo* / JIGSAW. **1950:** *narrator* / THE DIFFICULT YEARS; *Dan Butler* / UNDER MY SKIN; *Harry Morgan* / THE BREAKING POINT. **1951:** *Nick Robey* / HE RAN ALL THE WAY.

GARLAND, JUDY

(Frances Ethel Gumm, 1922–1969)

First teamed with her two older sisters, Judy Garland signed with MGM at age 13. She made a short with Deanna Durbin called EVERY SUNDAY in 1936, but nothing came of it. Then she made a definite impression singing a special arrangement of "You Made Me Love You" to a picture of Clark Gable in BROADWAY MELODY OF 1938 and became a star with her portrayal of Dorothy in THE WIZARD OF OZ in 1939. With BABES IN ARMS and STRIKE UP THE BAND, co-starring Mickey Rooney, she consolidated her stardom. What her millions of fans didn't know at the time was the price she was paying for her success. Being slim was a continuing battle for this five-footer and the diet drugs she was given were addictive. Over the years Garland was often unable to keep commitments and this was laid at the steps of temperament, but it was usually a result of illness, both physical and mental. Those who loved the lady with the marvelous voice and gift for comedy only wish she had been allowed to be what she was—a delightful musical-comedy star—instead of being forced into being some kind of sex princess also. Her performances in movies and on the concert stage, even after she was long past her prime, were frequently inspirational. She won a special Academy Award for her performance in THE WIZARD OF OZ and was nominated for the real thing for A STAR IS BORN and JUDGMENT AT NUREMBERG.

KEY ROLES

Betsy Booth / LOVE FINDS ANDY HARDY, 1938, MGM, d-George B. Seitz.

To advance Garland's career, MGM featured her with its then biggest star, Mickey Rooney, as a new girl in Carvel who falls for Andy Hardy.

Dorothy Gale / THE WIZARD OF OZ, 1939, MGM, d-Victor Fleming.

When a Kansas tornado transports Garland and her little dog Toto "Over the Rainbow," she is sent on her way to the Emerald City to see the Wizard who she hopes will show her how to get home. On the way she runs into the Scarecrow (Ray Bolger), the Tin Man (Jack Haley), and the Cowardly Lion (Bert Lahr). They are in constant danger from the Wicked Witch of the West, marvelously played by Margaret Hamilton. The Wizard (Ralph Morgan) proves to be a phony, but Dorothy returns home nevertheless.

Patsy Barton / BABES IN ARMS, 1939, MGM, d-Busby Berkeley.

This is the first of many films in which someone—in this case Mickey Rooney—exclaims: "Hey kids, let's put on a show." They do so and Garland sings and dances to "I Cried for You," "I'm Just Wild about Harry," and "Broadway Rhythm."

Mary Holden / STRIKE UP THE BAND, 1940, MGM, d-Busby Berkeley.

Garland and Rooney are teamed again, transforming a high school band into a swing group that competes in a national radio show contest sponsored by Paul Whiteman. Besides collaborating with Rooney on the title song, Garland sings "Nobody" and "Heaven Will Help the Working Girl."

Penny Morris / BABES ON BROADWAY, 1942, MGM, d-Busby Berkeley.

Garland and Rooney get together to put on a settlement-house show in order to raise enough money to send some underprivileged kids to the country. Some of the numbers performed by the talented duo are "How about You" and "Chin Up Cheerio."

Jo Hayden / FOR ME AND MY GAL, 1942, MGM, d-Busby Berkeley.

This patriotic film introduced Gene Kelly to movies. He plays a fast-talking heel who competes with nice guy George Murphy for the affection of vaudeville star Garland. Her songs include "Smiles" and "After You've Gone."

Esther Smith / MEET ME IN ST. LOUIS, 1944, MGM, d-Vincente Minnelli.

Garland is the second daughter in an ordinary St. Louis family the year before the World's Fair. Nothing really happens in the film and isn't it wonderful? Garland's songs include "The Trolley Song," "The Boy Next Door," and the title number.

Alice Mayberry / THE CLOCK, 1945, MGM, d-Vincente Minnelli.

This is a beautiful little story about Garland meeting, falling in love with, and marrying soldier Robert Walker while he's on a 48-hour furlough in New York during World War II.

Susan Bradley / THE HARVEY GIRLS, 1946, MGM, d-George Sidney.

In this fictional account of Fred Harvey's railroad restaurants and his traveling waitresses, Garland sings "On the Atchison, Topeka and the Santa Fe." She's a rather straight-laced girl who declares a private war on the manager of a local gambling house (John Hodiak).

Manuela / THE PIRATE, 1948, MGM, d-Vincente Minnelli.

Garland is a Caribbean maiden who yearns for excitement, expressing her fascination with a notorious pirate, Mack the Black. Gene Kelly lets her believe that he is Mack, but actually Mack is Walter Slezak, her family's choice for her spouse. Songs include "Be a Clown" and "Love of My Life."

Hannah Brown / EASTER PARADE, 1948, MGM, d-Charles Walters.

When Ann Miller walks out on Fred Astaire, he chooses Garland as his new partner. Besides the title song, Garland sings "I Want to Go Back to Michigan" and "Everybody's Doin' It."

Veronica Fisher / IN THE GOOD OLD SUMMERTIME, 1949, MGM, d-Robert Z. Leonard.

In this remake of THE SHOP AROUND THE CORNER, Garland and fellow employee Van Johnson exchange letters of friendship without knowing each other's identity. Her songs include "I Don't Care" and "Play that Barber Shop Chord." Of course she and others in the splendid cast sing the title song.

Esther Blodgett / Vicki Lester / A STAR IS BORN, 1954, Warners, d-George Cukor.

In this musical remake of the 1937 Janet Gaynor story about the rising star of a new Hollywood actress corresponding with the decline of her drunken actor husband's career, Garland sings the marvelous "The Man Who Got Away" as well as an 18-minute musical sequence called "Born in a Trunk." When her husband (James Mason) commits suicide rather than be a burden to her, she meets her public for the first time after his death as a widow rather than a star, giving the picture's last line: "Hello, everybody. This is Mrs. Norman Maine."

Irene Hoffman / JUDGMENT AT NUREMBERG, 1961, United Artists, d-Stanley Kramer.

Garland is a German hausfrau who testifies at the Nuremberg Nazi trials that a former friend, an elderly Jew, was falsely accused of being intimate with her—a crime for which he was executed.

OTHER ROLES

1936: *Sairy Dodd* / PIGSKIN PARADE. **1937:** *Betty Clayton* / BROADWAY MELODY OF 1938; *Cricket West* / THOROUGHBREDS DON'T CRY. **1938:** *Judy Bellaire* / EVERYBODY SING; *Pinky Wingate* / LISTEN, DARLING. **1940:** *Betsy Booth* / ANDY HARDY MEETS DEBUTANTE; *Nellie Kelly* / LITTLE NELLIE KELLY. **1941:** *Susan Gallagher* / ZIEGFELD GIRL; *Betsy Booth* / LIFE BEGINS FOR ANDY HARDY. **1943:** *Lily Mars* / PRESENTING LILY MARS; *Ginger Gray* / GIRL CRAZY; *guest* / THOUSANDS CHEER. **1946:** *Marilyn Miller* / TILL THE CLOUDS ROLL BY; *herself* / ZIEGFELD FOLLIES. **1948:** *herself* / WORDS AND MUSIC. **1950:** *Jane Falbury* / SUMMER STOCK. 1962 : *voice of Mewsette* / GAY PURR-EE. **1963:** *Jean Hansen* / A CHILD IS WAITING; *Jenny Bowman* / I COULD GO ON SINGING.

GARNER, JAMES

(James Baumgarner, 1928–)

Tall, happy-looking James Garner has found success both in movies and on TV, although his two TV series "Maverick" and "The Rockford Files" probably are better and more fondly remembered than his big-screen roles. He's at his best playing a charming rascal who isn't looking for trouble but won't duck it if it comes looking for him. His movie roles have been pleasant enough and provided entertaining diversion, but none will ever be mistaken for great theater, nor will his acting be recalled as of high dramatic quality.

KEY ROLES

Capt. Mike Bailey / SAYONARA, 1957, Goetz Pictures / Pennebaker, d-Joshua Logan.

Garner is stationed in Japan and fights the racism of the U.S. military that opposes Americans marrying Japanese girls. He gets southern air force Major Marlon Brando interested in a Japanese actress.

Cash McCall / CASH MCCALL, 1960, Warners, d-Joseph Pevney.

Garner plays a corporate raider who merges sick companies with healthy ones, thereby finding tax relief for the healthy concern. One of his ventures almost destroys his romance with Natalie Wood.

Dr. Joe Cardin / THE CHILDREN'S HOUR, 1961, United Artists, d-William Wyler.

Garner is the fiancé of Audrey Hepburn, one of two schoolmistresses accused by a horrible child of being lesbians in this second filming of Lillian Hellman's classic play.

"The Scrounger" Hendley / THE GREAT ESCAPE, 1963, United Artists, d-John Sturges.

Garner's nickname tells his specialty as he and others prepare for a mass breakout of Allied prisoners from a German camp during World War II. He's also among the very few who actually get away and are not recaptured or killed.

Dr. Gerald Boyer / THE THRILL OF IT ALL, 1963, Universal-International, d-Norman Jewison.

Garner is a gynecologist whose wife (Doris Day) becomes an advertising model, which places extreme pressures on their marriage.

Lt. Cmdr. Charles Madison / THE AMERICANIZATION OF EMILY, 1964, MGM, d-Arthur Hiller.

Just prior to the Normandy invasion, self-confessed coward Garner is set up by a crazy admiral to be the victim of his plot to have the first casualty of the landings be a naval officer.

Maj. Jefferson Pike / 36 HOURS, 1964, MGM, d-George Seaton.

In 1944, Garner has all the information about the coming invasion of Europe by the Allies and he is kidnapped by the Germans and made to believe that he is in an American hospital years after the Allies have won the war. They almost get away with it.

Jason McCullough / SUPPORT YOUR LOCAL SHERIFF, 1969, United Artists, d-Burt Kennedy.

Garner is a stranger who rides into a western town and is appointed sheriff. He cleans up the town using his brains more than his brawn in this spoof of the genre.

Quincy Drew / THE SKIN GAME, 1971, Warners, d-Paul Bogart.

In this good-humored comedy Garner and Lou Gossett are a couple of con men. Their sting features Gossett posing as Garner's slave, being auctioned to the highest bidder, and later being set free by Garner in order to repeat the scam in the next town.

King Marchant / VICTOR / VICTORIA, 1982, Great Britain, MGM, d-Blake Edwards.

Garner is a Chicago nightclub owner and semi-gangster who is in Paris in 1934. He falls in love with Julie Andrews who poses as a man posing as a woman. He knows she's a woman, but everyone else thinks Garner has come out of the closet and he's mad as hell about it.

OTHER ROLES

1956: *Maj. Joe Craven* / TOWARD THE UNKNOWN; *Preston* / THE GIRL HE LEFT BEHIND. **1957:** *Maitland* / SHOOT OUT AT MEDICINE BEND. **1958:** *Maj. William Darby* / DARBY'S RANGERS. **1959:** *Bret Maverick* / ALIAS JESSE JAMES; *Ken* / UP PERISCOPE. **1962:** *Fred Williams* / BOYS' NIGHT OUT. **1963:** *Henry Tyroon* / THE WHEELER DEALERS; *Nick Arden* / MOVE OVER, DARLING. **1965:** *Casey Barnett* / THE ART OF LOVE. **1966:** *Jess Remsberg* / DUEL AT DIABLO; *William Beddoes* / A MAN COULD GET KILLED; *Mr. Buddwing* / MISTER BUDDWING; *Pete Aron* / GRAND PRIX. **1967:** *Wyatt Earp* / HOUR OF THE GUN. **1968:** *Ben Morris* / THE PINK JUNGLE; *Grif Henderson* / HOW SWEET IT IS. **1969:** *Philip Marlowe* / MARLOWE. **1970:** *Luther Sledge* / A MAN CALLED SLEDGE. **1971:** *Latigo Smith* / SUPPORT YOUR LOCAL GUNFIGHTER. **1972:** *Police Chief Abel Marsh* / THEY ONLY KILL THEIR MASTERS. **1973:** *Cpl. Clint Keyes* / ONE LITTLE INDIAN. **1974:** *Lincoln Costain* / THE CASTAWAY COWBOY. **1980:** *Harry Wolff* / HEALTH. **1981:** *Jake Berman* / THE FAN. **1984:** *Zack* / TANK. **1985:** *Murphy Jones* / MURPHY'S ROMANCE. **1987:** *Wyatt Earp* / SUNSET.

GARSON, GREER

(1908–)

It must be remembered that Greer Garson made movies other than MRS. MINIVER, but for many she was so fine in the role of the nobly suffering, wartime British wife and mother that it's hard for them to remember her in anything else. This Irish-born redhead was spotted on the London stage in 1938 by Louis B. Mayer who quickly put her under contract. She made her debut as the schoolmaster's wife in GOODBYE, MR. CHIPS (1939), gaining an Oscar nomination for her work. Garson holds the distinction of six Academy Award nominations in a seven-year period, and for three successive performances. Other nominations were for BLOSSOMS IN THE DUST (1941), MRS. MINIVER (1942)—for which she won the Oscar—MADAME CURIE (1943), MRS. PARKINGTON (1944), and THE VALLEY OF DECISION (1945). Her seventh nomination came in 1960 for SUNRISE AT CAMPOBELLO. Despite all this acclaim, Garson became too identified with the same sentimental type of character and her popularity quickly waned after World War II. Today's film fans seem a bit cool to her performances and there is little interest in holding festivals of her movies. But she was a lovely, refined lady with a warm, cultured, and distinctive voice.

KEY ROLES

Katherine Chipping / GOODBYE, MR. CHIPS, 1939, MGM, d-Sam Wood.
Garson's character (Mr. Chips's wife) single-handedly turns Robert Donat's distant and unpopular teacher into the beloved Mr. Chips. When she dies, he is almost destroyed by the loss of this marvelously alive and loving creature.

Elizabeth Bennet / PRIDE AND PREJUDICE, 1940, MGM, d-Robert Z. Leonard.
In this splendid version of Jane Austen's romantic comedy, Garson is an opinionated, young woman of the early 19th century who comes to love wealthy Laurence Olivier, though she had at first despised him because she felt him too prideful. The title of Jane Austen's novel and that of the movie comes from this exchange between Garson and Olivier: "You're very puzzling, Mr. Darcy. At this moment, it's difficult to believe that you're so proud." His response is: "At this moment, it's difficult to believe that you're so prejudiced. Shall we not call it quits and start again?"

Kay Miniver / MRS. MINIVER, 1942, MGM, d-William Wyler.
Revisionist movie historians and critics have tried valiantly to explain the popularity of not only Garson but this movie about the struggles of an English housewife during World War II. Their message is always the same: the movie is sentimental claptrap and Garson is just too noble to be believed. An interesting bit of trivia: a year after the movie, Garson took as her second husband Richard Ney, who had appeared as her son in MRS. MINIVER.

Paula Ranier / RANDOM HARVEST, 1942, MGM, d-Mervyn LeRoy.
Garson is a music-hall girl who meets and marries a shell-shocked soldier (Ronald Colman) with no memory of his identity. Later another shock leaves him with no recollection of Garson. It will require one more shock before everything is put right.

Marie Curie / MADAME CURIE, 1943, MGM, d-Mervyn LeRoy.
Once again Garson teams with her co-star of MRS. MINIVER (Walter Pidgeon) as the scientific husband and wife, Pierre and Marie Curie.

Susie Parkington / MRS. PARKINGTON, 1944, MGM, d-Tay Garnett.
Garson is a lady's maid who marries a miner and, when he becomes rich, pushes herself into society. It's a three-generation melodrama that really has very little to say.

Irene Forsyte / THAT FORSYTE WOMAN, 1949, MGM, d-Compton Bennett.
Garson is married to a prig (Errol Flynn) and falls in love with her niece's fiancé in this film version of John Galsworthy's novel of Edwardian England.

Jan Stewart / HER TWELVE MEN, 1954, MGM, d-Robert Z. Leonard.
Garson plays a pedagogue in a boys' school who reforms an unruly class. Many teachers would like to know how she could afford her fabulous wardrobe on a teacher's salary.

Eleanor Roosevelt / SUNRISE AT CAMPOBELLO, 1960, Warners, d-Vincent J. Donehue.
Garson sheds her glamorous image to appear as the wife of the future president of the United States. She helps him when he develops polio, and won't allow him to resign himself to a life as a useless cripple.

OTHER ROLES

1939: *Linda Bronson* / REMEMBER? **1941:** *Claire Woodruff* / WHEN LADIES MEET. **1943:** *guest* / THE YOUNGEST PROFESSION. **1945:** *Mary Rafferty* / THE VALLEY OF DECISION; *Emily Sears* / ADVENTURE. **1947:** *Marise Aubert* / DESIRE ME. **1948:** *Julia Packett* / JULIA MISBEHAVES. **1950:** *Kay Miniver* / THE MINIVER STORY. **1951:** *Jane Hoskins* / THE LAW AND THE LADY. **1952:** *Mrs. Patrick McChesney* / SCANDAL AT SCOURIE. **1953:** *Calpurnia* / JULIUS CAESAR. **1954:** *Dr. Julia Winslow Garth* / STRANGE LADY IN TOWN. **1960:** *guest* / PEPE. **1966:** *Mother Prioress* / THE SINGING NUN. **1967:** *Mrs. Cordelia Biddle* / THE HAPPIEST MILLIONAIRE.

GAYNOR, JANET

(Laura Gainor, 1906–1985)
While it's not possible to think of Janet Gaynor without thinking of matinee idol Charles Farrell, it happens that Gaynor had a reputation for quality acting independent of her twelve-time co-star. Although Gaynor's career in talking pictures was slightly longer than her silent period, she seemed more a product of the earlier era. She won an Academy Award for her work in 1927–28—SEVENTH HEAVEN, STREET ANGEL, and SUNRISE—a time when the award was not given for a particular role but for the year's output. She received an Oscar nomination for A STAR IS BORN in 1937. Oddly, this movie was her last great role, that of an actress whose star is at its highest just as her husband's is burning out. Child-woman Gaynor was adored by her fans. A worthy successor to Mary Pickford, she was often called on to grow from a frightened, weak girl to a woman with inner strength, and she did it with great style. Speaking of her career, she said, "I enjoyed it all and have no sad tales to tell you."

KEY ROLES

Diane / SEVENTH HEAVEN, 1927, Silent, Fox Films, d-Frank Borzage.
Waifish Gaynor is rescued by a Paris street cleaner (Charles Farrell) from her cruel sister who denounces her to the police. Farrell claims that Gaynor is his wife and takes her to his seventh-floor walk-up which they blissfully call their seventh heaven. World War I breaks out, postponing their wedding plans, and after

having been reported killed in action, Farrell returns home blinded, but still able to share Gaynor's love.

The Wife / SUNRISE, 1927, Silent, Fox Films, d-F. W. Murnau.
Subtitled "A Song of Two Humans," the story deals with a woman from the city who so enslaves a farmer (George O'Brien) that he is driven to murder his wife (Gaynor). His attempt to drown her is a failure—he can't go through with it. Later, during a day in the city, they renew their vows, but on the way home she is lost in a storm on the river. He rushes to the city woman and is about to strangle her when word comes that his wife has been found alive. At Gaynor's sickbed they watch the sunrise together.

Eleanor Divine / HIGH SOCIETY BLUES, 1930, Fox Films, d-David Butler.
The nouveau riche Grangers move from Iowa to Scarsdale, New York, settling next door to Mr. Granger's rival on Wall Street. Mrs. Granger is planning to have her daughter (Gaynor) marry a rich lad, but instead she falls in love with the boy next door (Charles Farrell) when he gives her ukelele lessons. They elope and the rift between the two families is healed.

Judy Abbott / DADDY LONG LEGS, 1931, Fox Films, d-Alfred Santell.
In this Cinderella-like romance Gaynor is an orphan girl who grows up and falls in love with her mysterious benefactor (Warner Baxter). It became the classic May and September love story.

Mary Ann / MERELY MARY ANN, 1931, Fox Films, d-Henry King.
Gaynor is a charwoman in a rooming house where composer Charles Farrell lives and works. She falls in love with him, even though at first he is rude to her because he feels she is below him. Just when he comes to love her she inherits a fortune and, rather than seem to be marrying her for her money, he departs. Later, one of the compositions he wrote for her proves very popular and she is present at its first performance. Successful but unhappy, Farrell returns to the inn where they first met, and she follows him. All ends as it should.

Margy Frake / STATE FAIR, 1933, Fox Films, d-Henry King.
In this pleasant family piece, the Frake farm family makes its annual excursion to the state fair, with Gaynor finding romance with Lew Ayres along the midway.

Kay Brannan / SMALL TOWN GIRL, 1936, MGM, d-William Wellman.
Wealthy Robert Taylor stops off in a small town and leaves with Gaynor as his new bride after a whirlwind courtship. Whether the marriage will survive his former fiancée and his snobbish family is the basis of this simple story.

Esther Blodgett / Vicki Lester / A STAR IS BORN, 1937, Selznick / United Artists, d-William Wellman.
Even though the movie won an Oscar for Best Original Story for William Wellman and Robert Carson, the story was derived from WHAT PRICE HOLLYWOOD? (1932). Gaynor is a stagestruck farm girl who is discovered by alcoholic actor Fredric March. They marry and her career takes off while his sinks. She wins an Oscar and he kills himself, delivering his pet expression for her just before his suicidal swim in the ocean: "Hey—do you mind if I take just one more look?"

George-Ann Carleton / THE YOUNG IN HEART, 1938, Selznick / United Artists, d-Richard Wallace.
Gaynor and Douglas Fairbanks, Jr., are the supposedly thick-skinned children of Roland Young and Billie Burke, a family of con artists out to take wealthy Minnie Dupree. But it is the crooked family that is robbed of its wicked ways by the "young in heart" Dupree whose endearing ways would melt the most hardened heart.

OTHER ROLES

1926: *Anna Burger* / THE JOHNSTOWN FLOOD; *Sheila Gaffney* / THE SHAMROCK HANDICAP; *Mildred Hastings* / THE MIDNIGHT KISS; *Rose Cooper* / THE BLUE EAGLE; *Catherine* / THE RETURN OF PETER GRIMM. **1927:** *Marianna Wright* / TWO GIRLS WANTED. **1928:** *Angela* / STREET ANGEL. **1929:** *Marion* / FOUR DEVILS; *Christina* / CHRISTINA; *Mary Tucker* / LUCKY STAR; *Molly Carr* / SUNNY SIDE UP. **1930:** *interlocutor* / HAPPY DAYS; *Angie Randolph* / THE MAN WHO CAME BACK. **1931:** *Heather Gordon* / DELICIOUS. **1932:** *Grace Livingston* / THE FIRST YEAR; *Tess Howland* / TESS OF THE STORM COUNTRY. **1933:** *the girl* / ADORABLE; *Paddy Adair* / PADDY, THE NEXT BEST THING. **1934:** *Joanna* / CAROLINA; *Catherine Furness* / CHANGE OF HEART; *Heddie Nisson* / SERVANTS' ENTRANCE. **1935:** *Elizabeth Cheney* / ONE MORE SPRING; *Molly Larkins* / THE FARMER TAKES A WIFE. **1936:** *Martha Kerenye* / LADIES IN LOVE. **1938:** *Nancy Briggs* / THREE LOVES HAS NANCY. **1941:** *cameo* / LAND OF LIBERTY. **1957:** *Mrs. Wilson* / BERNARDINE.

GAYNOR, MITZI

(Franceska Mitzi Gerber, 1930–)

A vivacious bundle of energy, Mitzi Gaynor never quite made it to the top rung of stardom in the movies despite her peppy personality and lovely long legs. She will be best remembered for singing and dancing in SOUTH PACIFIC, but her acting in the same is better forgotten. It has been reported that Gaynor was the compromise made by Richard Rodgers and Joshua Logan; Rodgers had Doris Day in mind and Logan saw Elizabeth Taylor in the role of Nellie. Now that we think on the subject, Gaynor seems the best choice of the three. Later, when it became clear that her film career would go no further, she took her dancing feet to nightclubs and TV.

KEY ROLES

Lotta Crabtree / GOLDEN GIRL, 1951, 20th Century-Fox, d-Lloyd Bacon.
Gaynor portrays the entertainer from Rabbit Creek, California, who, during the Civil War, becomes a musical star and falls for a handsome Confederate spy. Her best scene is singing "Dixie" to a booing New York audience.

Eva Tanguay / THE I DON'T CARE GIRL, 1953, 20th Century-Fox, d-Lloyd Bacon.
In another musical star biopic, Gaynor portrays tempestuous vaudeville star Eva Tanguay, who's theme song was the title number. This is an easily forgettable musical and, although Gaynor tries very hard to entertain, she breathes very little life into her subject.

Joy Henderson / LES GIRLS, 1957, MGM, d-George Cukor.
Despite three beautiful girls—Gaynor, Kay Kendall, and Taina Elg—Gene Kelly's last film for MGM doesn't work. Each of the three former showgirls has a different version of her relationship with Kelly when the four worked together as an act called "Les Girls." Gaynor is the one that ultimately winds up with him.

Nellie Forbush / SOUTH PACIFIC, 1958, 20th Century-Fox, d-Joshua Logan.

Gaynor is the navy nurse from Arkansas on a South Pacific island during World War II who falls in love with a handsome French planter (Rossano Brazzi). She almost gives him up, though, because of her ingrained prejudices when she learns that he has two children by his dead first wife, a native woman. Her songs include Rodgers and Hammerstein's "A Cockeyed Optimist," "I'm Gonna Wash that Man Right out of My Hair," "I'm in Love with a Wonderful Guy," and with Brazzi (dubbed by Giorgio Tozzi) "Some Enchanted Evening."

OTHER ROLES

1950: *Gloria Adams* / MY BLUE HEAVEN. **1951:** *Adelaide* / TAKE CARE OF MY LITTLE GIRL; *Emily Ann Stackerlee* / BLOODHOUNDS OF BROADWAY. **1952:** *Patsy Fisher* / WE'RE NOT MARRIED. **1953:** *Rozouila* / DOWN AMONG THE SHELTERING PALMS. **1954:** *Rusty Blair* / THREE YOUNG TEXANS; *Kathy Donahue* / THERE'S NO BUSINESS LIKE SHOW BUSINESS. **1956:** *Patsy Blair* / ANYTHING GOES; *Jean Harris* / THE BIRDS AND THE BEES. **1957:** *Martha Stewart* / THE JOKER IS WILD. **1959:** *Alice Walters* / HAPPY ANNIVERSARY. **1960:** *Gabby Rogers* / SURPRISE PACKAGE. **1963:** *Kate Brasher* / FOR LOVE OR MONEY.

GERE, RICHARD

(1949–)

A mournful-looking, intensely sexual, and macho star of the late 1970s and 1980s, Richard Gere has been most effective as working-class men who aspire to something better and are seen as rebels with causes. Gere started out to become a musician and has mastered several instruments, including the coronet he plays in THE COTTON CLUB. Though he is now very popular, it's too early in his career to judge if his potential as an actor and star will be fully realized.

KEY ROLES

Tony Lopanto / LOOKING FOR MR. GOODBAR, 1977, Paramount, d-Richard Brooks.

Gere is a sadistic stud who gives a teacher of deaf children (Diane Keaton) the rough treatment she enjoys, but at least he's not the psychopath who ends her life.

Bill / DAYS OF HEAVEN, 1978, Paramount, d-Terrence Malick.

In one of the most beautifully photographed color pictures ever made, Gere encourages his girl to marry a wealthy wheat farmer who supposedly has only a short time to live. But it's Gere who finally takes the farmer's life, and it costs him his.

Julian / AMERICAN GIGOLO, 1980, Paramount, d-Paul Schraeder.

Gere is a male prostitute catering only to women, who is set up to take the rap for the murder of one of his clients.

Zack Mayo / AN OFFICER AND A GENTLEMAN, 1982, Paramount, d-Taylor Hackford.

Gere is an officer candidate who suffers through thirteen weeks of intensive training and abuse at the hands of instructor Lou Gossett, Jr., at the Naval Aviation Officer School. He also has some pleasure in bed with a local gal (Debra Winger).

Dixie Dwyer / THE COTTON CLUB, 1984, Orion / Zoetrope, d-Francis Coppola.

Gere's a coronet player who takes up with gangster Dutch Schultz's mistress (Diane Lane) during the 1920s. Later he becomes a movie star, playing gangsters based on those he had known while hanging around the Cotton Club in Harlem.

OTHER ROLES

1975: *Billy* / REPORT TO THE COMMISSIONER. **1976:** *marine raider* / BABY BLUE MARINE. **1978:** *Stony DeCoco* / BLOODBROTHERS. **1979:** *Matt* / YANKS. **1982:** *guest* / REPORTERS. **1983:** *Dr. Eduardo Plarr* / BEYOND THE LIMIT; *Jesse Lujack* / BREATHLESS. **1985:** *King David* / KING DAVID; *Pete St. John* / POWER. **1986:** *Eddie Jilette* / NO MERCY.

GIBSON, MEL

(1956–)

While the history of motion pictures has had many young actors who looked like they'd become longtime favorites who then all but disappeared, it's hard to resist the urge to make a claim for Mel Gibson as one who will prevail. He's a handsome lad in a way that is appealing to the ladies, but not so much so that men will be envious. Although forced to repeat his success as Mad Max in two sequels, his few pictures demonstrate that he is versatile. Born in New York, but raised in Australia, Gibson has charisma that will probably last even when he outgrows his boyish looks.

KEY ROLES

Mad Max Rockatansky / MAD MAX, 1979, Australia, Mad Max Pty, d-George Miller.

Gibson is a cop living sometime in the near future—when violence has become the norm—who turns vigilante to track down the marauding motorcycle gang that killed his wife.

Frank Dunne / GALLIPOLI, 1981, Australia, Associated R and R, d-Peter Weir.

During World War I two Australian friends (Gibson and Mark Lee) make the trek from Perth across the desert to sign up for the army. They meet their fate at Gallipoli in the Dardanelles. The freeze-frame shot at the finish when they go over the top is similar to the shot of the Spanish Civil War soldier at the moment of his death taken by Robert Capa for *Life* magazine.

Guy Hamilton / THE YEAR OF LIVING DANGEROUSLY, 1983, Australia, MGM / Weir, d-Peter Weir.

Gibson is an Australian journalist whose first international assignment drops him into strife-torn Indonesia just before Sukarno's fall in 1965. He's helped by diminutive Linda Hunt who plays a man (for which she won a deserved Academy Award). His romantic interest is Sigourney Weaver who looks good but seems almost superfluous.

Tom Garvey / THE RIVER, 1984, Universal, d-Mark Rydell.

To save the family farm Gibson and wife Sissy Spacek fight floods, foreclosures, and government efforts to construct a hydroelectric plant in this old-fashioned rural drama which was surprisingly popular. Gibson's perennial unsmiling face is completely appropriate in this picture.

OTHER ROLES

1977: *bit* / SUMMER CITY. **1980:** *bit* / ATTACK FORCE Z. **1981:** *Tim* / TIM. **1982:** *Mad Max* / THE ROAD WARRIOR, (MAD MAX 2). **1984:** *Fletcher Christian* / THE BOUNTY; *Mad Max* / MAD MAX BEYOND THUNDERDOME. **1985:** *Ed Biddle* / MRS. SOFFEL. **1987:** *Martin Riggs* / LETHAL WEAPON.

GIELGUD, SIR JOHN

(Arthur John Gielgud, 1904–)

A tall, mellifluous-voiced actor, John Gielgud's greatest success has been in Shakespearean roles on the stage, but he has been making movies for over 60 years with mixed success. Before World War II he appeared as a leading man in a few films, but afterwards his roles ran to cameos and leading character parts. He was nominated for an Academy Award for his portrayal of King Louis VII of France in BECKETT (1964) and won an Oscar for his perfectly sarcastic valet in ARTHUR (1981). Since that time, like fellow great Sir Laurence Olivier, he seems quite willing to appear in anything movie and TV producers propose as long as they are willing to make it worth his while, which they are happy to do as he brings a touch of class to their pictures. His made-for-TV movies include LES MISERABLES (1978), THE HUNCHBACK OF NOTRE DAME and INSIDE THE THIRD REICH (1981), and BUDDENBROOKS (1984). He was knighted in 1953.

KEY ROLES

Inigo Jolifant / THE GOOD COMPANIONS, 1933, Great Britain, Gaumont / Ideal, d-Victor Saville.

Gielgud is a disillusioned music teacher who, together with a Yorkshire joiner and a middle-aged spinster, backs a failing concert party and, with a lot of hard work, makes a star of its leading lady (Jessie Matthews).

Benjamin Disraeli / THE PRIME MINISTER, 1941, Great Britain, Warners, d-Thorold Dickinson.

Gielgud is adequate in this biopic of the British prime minister who brings England back from the brink of war in 1878.

Cassius / JULIUS CAESAR, 1953, MGM, d-Joseph L. Mankiewicz.

Gielgud hadn't appeared in a movie for over a decade, but he was the best thing in this production of Shakespeare's story about the Roman general who would be king, and the assassination plot led by Cassius and Brutus (James Mason).

Duke of Clarence / RICHARD III, 1955, Great Britain, London Films, d-Laurence Olivier.

Gielgud stands in the way of his brother's (Olivier) plans to become king of England. He is eliminated along with other superfluous relatives in the way of Crookback.

Edward Moulton-Barrett / THE BARRETTS OF WIMPOLE STREET, 1956, Great Britain, MGM-British, d-Sidney Franklin.

Gielgud rules his six sons and seven daughters with fear. He has more than a parental interest in his daughter Elizabeth (Jennifer Jones) and is outraged by her romance with poet Robert Browning, but is unable to prevent her from fleeing to him and becoming his wife. It can't compare to the 1934 film with Charles Laughton in the role of the tyrannical and perhaps incestuous father.

Louis VII / BECKET, 1964, Great Britain, Paramount, d-Peter Glenville.

Gielgud's king of France tries to exploit the rift between Henry II of England and his former friend Thomas à Becket, once chancellor of England and now Archbishop of Canterbury.

Julius Caesar / JULIUS CAESAR, 1970, Great Britain, Commonwealth United, d-Stuart Burge.

Gielgud moves up from Cassius to the title character in this perfectly awful production of the Shakespeare play. British stage actors apparently do not find it necessary to maintain their star image by carefully choosing not only their parts, but the producers and directors of their films as well.

Chang / LOST HORIZON, 1972, Columbia, d-Charles Jarrott.

No doubt everyone had high hopes for this musical remake of Frank Capra's 1937 masterpiece, but it only makes one yearn for another showing of the earlier picture. Gielgud doesn't shame himself, but H. B. Warner handled the assignment better.

Hobson / ARTHUR, 1981, Warners / Orion, d-Steve Gordon.

This film was one of the biggest hits of the year and Gielgud deserves most of the credit for his performance as the gentleman's gentleman to a rich, useless alcoholic (Dudley Moore) who falls in love with a strange girl (Liza Minnelli). Gielgud dies and, despite its success, so does the movie when he leaves it.

Cornelius Cardew / THE SHOOTING PARTY, 1984, Great Britain, Thorn / EMI, d-Alan Bridges.

Gielgud is a one-man protest of the slaughter of birds at the estate of aristocrat James Mason on the eve of World War I. The interplay between Gielgud and Mason in the latter's final movie role is touching and lovely.

OTHER ROLES

1924: *Daniel* / WHO IS THE MAN? **1929:** *Rex Trasmere* / THE CLUE OF THE NEW PIN. **1932:** *Henri Dubois* / INSULT. **1936:** *Edgar Brodie* / SECRET AGENT. **1939:** *Hamlet* / HAMLET. **1941:** *voice* / AN AIRMAN'S LETTER TO HIS MOTHER. **1954:** *narrator of prologue* / ROMEO AND JULIET. **1956:** *Foster* / AROUND THE WORLD IN 80 DAYS. **1957:** *Warwick* / SAINT JOAN. **1958:** *narrator* / THE IMMORTAL LAND. **1964:** *voice of ghost* / HAMLET. **1965:** *Sir Francis Hinsley* / THE LOVED ONE. **1966:** *Henry IV* / CHIMES AT MIDNIGHT. **1967:** *head of British intelligence* / MR. SEBASTIAN; *Curt Valayan* / ASSIGNMENT TO KILL; *narrator* / TO DIE IN MADRID; *narrator* / OCTOBER REVOLUTION. **1968:** *Lord Raglan* / THE CHARGE OF THE LIGHT BRIGADE; *the elder pope* / THE SHOES OF THE FISHERMAN. **1969:** *Count Berchtold* / OH! WHAT A LOVELY WAR. **1970:** *Lord Sissal* / EAGLE IN A CAGE. **1974:** *Meecham* / 11 HARROWHOUSE; *Farrell* / GOLD; *Beddoes* / MURDER ON THE ORIENT EXPRESS; *old cardinal* / GALILEO. **1976:** *headmaster* / ACES HIGH; *doctor* / JOSEPH ANDREWS. **1977:** *preacher* / A PORTRAIT OF THE ARTIST AS A YOUNG MAN; *Clive Langham* / PROVIDENCE. **1978:** *Lord Salisbury* / MURDER BY DECREE; *Nerva* / CALIGULA. **1979:** *the conductor* / THE CONDUCTOR; *Sharif El Gariani* / LION OF THE DESERT; *Brigadier Tomlinson* / THE HUMAN FACTOR. **1980:** *Carr Gomm* / THE ELEPHANT MAN; *Dr. Esau* / THE FORMULA; *Herbert G. Muskett* / PRIEST OF LOVE. **1981:** *Abdu Hamdi* / SPHINX; *master of Trinity* / CHARIOTS OF FIRE. **1982:** *Lord Irwin* / GANDHI; *Pope Pacelli* / THE VATICAN PIMPERNEL; *Texas evangelist* / INVITATION TO A WEDDING. **1983:** *Hogarth* / THE WICKED LADY. **1984:** *Uncle Willie* / SCANDALOUS. **1985:** *Jasper Swift* / TIME AFTER TIME; *Sir Leonard Darwin* / PLENTY; *John Middleton Murray* / LEAVE ALL FAIR. **1987:** *Sir Adrian Chapple* / THE WHISTLE BLOWER.

GODDARD, PAULETTE

(Pauline G. Levee, 1911–)

Paulette Goddard, the vivacious brunette, was a Ziegfeld showgirl when only 14. In the mid-1930s she secretly married Charlie Chaplin, her second of four husbands. Her first was a millionaire who reportedly settled half a million dollars in alimony when they split. Goddard co-starred with Chaplin in two films, MODERN TIMES (1936) and THE GREAT DICTATOR (1941). She later married Burgess Meredith and author Erich Maria Remarque. Her cute grin, lively spirit, and svelte figure established her as one of Paramount's biggest stars in the late 1930s and 1940s. She received an Oscar nomination for SO PROUDLY WE HAIL, but she made more enjoyable pictures, especially her costume pieces for Cecil B. DeMille and her comedies with Bob Hope. Her best role was as the coquettish title character in A DIARY OF A CHAMBERMAID. In the 1950s the roles offered her were of no importance, so Goddard chose luxurious retirement instead. Responding to charges that she was difficult, Goddard said, "I am not temperamental. I just know what I want, and if I don't have it, I try to get it."

KEY ROLES

A gamin / MODERN TIMES, 1936, Silent, Chaplin, d-Charles Chaplin.

Goddard holds her own with genius real-life husband Charles Chaplin in this tale of an assembly-line worker who goes berserk and can't get another job. She plays the beautiful waif befriended by Chaplin during his adventures.

Joyce Norman / THE CAT AND THE CANARY, 1939, Paramount, d-Elliott Nugent.

Twice earlier filmed as a straight thriller, this version of the old stage melodrama is played for laughs with Bob Hope as a chicken-hearted hero who helps Goddard maintain her sanity in a sinister family mansion, a prerequisite if she is to get a vast inheritance. If she goes mad or dies, it's divided among other relatives. Her sanity and her life are very much in danger.

Mary Carter / THE GHOST BREAKERS, 1940, Paramount, d-George Marshall.

The teaming of Bob Hope and Goddard in the previous picture was so successful that they came right back with this one in which Goddard inherits a West Indian castle complete with zombies, ghosts, and a hidden treasure. Goddard in her torn clothes is sexier than all the young actresses today who are required to take everything off.

Hannah / THE GREAT DICTATOR, 1940, Chaplin, d-Charles Chaplin.

By the time this film was released Goddard and Charles Chaplin were divorced. She plays the love of the Jewish barber who is mistaken for dictator Adenoid Hynkel. Seeing the picture today, one notices that Goddard's performance stands up better than most in the film.

Loxi Claiborne / REAP THE WILD WIND, 1942, Paramount, d-Cecil B. DeMille.

Ray Milland and John Wayne fight over sunken treasure and Goddard in this adventure yarn set on and off the coast of Georgia in the 19th century. Someone is deliberately sinking ships in order to claim salvage and, for different reasons, neither Milland nor Wayne is very happy about it.

Lt. Joan O'Doul / SO PROUDLY WE HAIL, 1943, Paramount, d-Mark Sandrich.

Goddard gives her most dramatic performance in this patriotic salute to the sacrifices of American nurses in the Pacific during World War II. Even in this unglamorous setting Goddard and co-stars Claudette Colbert and Veronica Lake look great.

Kitty / KITTY, 1945, Paramount, d-Mitchell Leisen.

Beginning as an 18th-century guttersnipe, Goddard is transformed into a duchess by fop Ray Milland and a dowager who intend to collect when their protégée marries rich nobleman Reginald Owen.

Celestine / THE DIARY OF A CHAMBERMAID, 1946, Bogeaus / Meredith / Goddard, d-Jean Renoir.

Goddard goes back to being a blonde in this tale of an outspoken 19th-century maid who causes sexual frustration in two households. It doesn't seem so shocking seen today, but Goddard gives a superior performance to that of Jean Moreau in the 1964 remake.

Abby Hale / UNCONQUERED, 1947, Paramount, d-Cecil B. DeMille.

Set in 18th-century America, the film features Goddard as an indentured bondslave whom Gary Cooper believes he has bought and set free to spite evil Howard da Silva. But Cooper must win her from da Silva again as the two find themselves in the middle of an Indian war near Fort Pitt.

OTHER ROLES

1931: *lingerie salesgirl* / THE GIRL HABIT. **1932:** *girl at party* / THE MOUTHPIECE; *Goldwyn girl* / THE KID FROM SPAIN. **1938:** *Leslie Saunders* / THE YOUNG IN HEART; *Nana* / DRAMATIC SCHOOL. **1939:** *Miriam Aarons* / THE WOMEN. **1940:** *Louvette Corbeau* / NORTHWEST MOUNTED POLICE; *Ellen Muller* / SECOND CHORUS. **1941:** *Molly McCorkle* / POT O' GOLD; *Gwen Saunders* / NOTHING BUT THE TRUTH; *Anita Dixon* / HOLD BACK THE DAWN. **1942:** *Sidney Royce* / THE LADY HAS PLANS; *Celia Huston* / THE FOREST RANGERS. **1943:** *cameo* / STAR SPANGLED RHYTHM; *Toni Gerard* / THE CRYSTAL BALL. **1944:** *Jane Rogers* / STANDING ROOM ONLY; *Eva Morgan* / I LOVE A SOLDIER. **1945:** *guest* / DUFFY'S TAVERN. **1947:** *Mary Morley* / SUDDENLY IT'S SPRING; *Mrs. Cheveley* / AN IDEAL HUSBAND; *guest* / VARIETY GIRL. **1948:** *Martha Pease* / ON OUR MERRY WAY; *Ellen Crane* / HAZARD. **1949:** *Lucrezia Borgia* / BRIDE OF VENGEANCE; *Anna Lucasta* / ANNA LUCASTA. **1950:** *Maria Dolores* / THE TORCH. **1952:** *Kyra* / BABES IN BAGDAD. **1953:** *Mona* / VICE SQUAD; *Betty Barnes* / PARIS MODEL; *Jezebel* / SINS OF JEZEBEL. **1954:** *Tanya* / CHARGE OF THE LANCERS; *Angie Vickers* / THE STRANGER CAME HOME, (THE UNHOLY FOUR). **1966:** *Maria Grazia Ardengo* / TIME OF INDIFFERENCE.

GOULD, ELLIOTT

(Elliot Goldstein, 1938–)

This former Broadway chorus boy and husband of Barbra Streisand experienced great success with his first few movies, being nominated for an Academy Award for his second starring movie, BOB AND CAROL AND TED AND ALICE. His soulful looks and sincere cynicism stood him in good stead until 1971 when a nervous breakdown kept him away from films for two years. Since then he has had more modest success, appearing in pictures of far less quality than his earlier pieces.

KEY ROLES

Billy Minsky / THE NIGHT THEY RAIDED MINSKY'S, 1968, United Artists, d-William Friedkin.

In this lightweight, disorganized movie, Gould plays the owner of a burlesque house where Amish girl Britt Ekland accidentally invents the striptease. The picture evokes some lovely images of another time but these are only fragments, not a whole.

Ted Henderson / BOB AND CAROL AND TED AND ALICE, 1969, Columbia, d-Paul Mazursky.

Gould is a lawyer married to Dyan Cannon. Their best friends (Robert Culp and Natalie Wood) attempt to turn them on to open marriage and it almost ends in a foursome in a large bed. But the participants find that they can't go through with it. Adultery it would seem cannot be shared with the ones you love.

Trapper John McIntyre / M*A*S*H, 1970, 20th Century-Fox, d-Robert Altman.

Gould is a "chest cutter," i.e., a surgeon with a Mobile Army Surgical Hospital during the Korean War. Together with other doctors and nurses he assumes an irreverent attitude toward life, death, sex, men, women, the American way, and football.

Albert Chamberlain / LITTLE MURDERS, 1971, 20th Century-Fox, d-Alan Arkin.

In this ultra-black comedy written by Jules Feiffer, Gould is a New York photographer who deals with the horrors of modern urban life until his wife is killed by a sniper and he turns to violence himself.

Charlie Waters / CALIFORNIA SPLIT, 1974, Columbia, d-Robert Altman.

Gould and George Segal are two cheerful compulsive gamblers who get drunk, pick up a couple of one night stands, are cheated, and are relatively happy with the emptiness of their lives.

Harry Lewis / FALLING IN LOVE AGAIN, 1980, International Picture Show of Atlanta, d-Steven Paul.

Middle-aged New Yorker Gould reminisces about his romances in his youth and tries desperately to recapture some of the magic in his relationship with wife Susannah York.

OTHER ROLES

1966: *the mute* / THE CONFESSION. **1970:** *Harry Bailey* / GETTING STRAIGHT; *Hiram Jaffe* / MOVE; *Dr. Richard Burrows* / I LOVE MY WIFE; *David Kovac* / THE TOUCH. **1973:** *Philip Marlowe* / THE LONG GOODBYE; *Michael Keneely* / BUSTING. **1974:** *Griff* / S*P*Y*S; *Sean Rogers* / WHO? **1975:** *himself* / NASHVILLE; *Dudley Frapper* / WHIFFS; *Les Bingham* / I WILL, I WILL...FOR NOW; *Johnny Barrows* / MEAN JOHNNY BARROWS. **1976:** *Walter Hill* / HARRY AND WALTER GO TO NEW YORK. **1977:** *Col. Bobby Stout* / A BRIDGE TOO FAR. **1978:** *Bernie Bonnelli* / MATILDA; *Miles Cullen* / THE SILENT PARTNER; *Robert Caulfield* / CAPRICORN ONE. **1979:** *Charlie* / ESCAPE TO ATHENA; *Robert Condon* / THE LADY VANISHES; *guest* / THE MUPPET MOVIE. **1980:** *Noah Dugan* / THE LAST FLIGHT OF NOAH'S ARK. **1981:** *Colin Chandler* / DIRTY TRICKS; *Max Devlin* / THE DEVIL AND MAX DEVLIN. **1987:** *Jimmy Morgan* / INSIDE OUT.

GRABLE, BETTY

(1916–1973)

Betty Grable was singing and dancing in the chorus lines of Hollywood musicals before she was 14. It took ten years of such anonymity before she received the break (Alice Faye's illness) which set her on the way to top stardom: the female lead in DOWN ARGENTINE WAY. Her million-dollar legs so superbly displayed in the GIs' favorite World War II pinup kept her on top until the 1950s when the popularity of film musicals went into sharp decline and a new blonde bombshell, Marilyn Monroe, pushed her aside. Grable never deceived herself about her acting ability. She knew as well as anyone that her assets were her peaches and cream complexion, her smile, and her great figure. She labeled herself "a truck driver's delight." She had a pleasant singing voice and introduced a number of hits in her movies, but was not allowed to profit from their success as her contract didn't allow her to make outside recordings. Her husbands were Jackie Cooper and bandleader Harry James. She died of lung cancer at the age of 56.

KEY ROLES

Carol Parker / MILLION DOLLAR LEGS, 1939, Paramount, d-Nick Grinde.

Yes, Grable had them, the legs that is, in this modest 59-minute "B" picture about college students and a horse race.

Glenda Crawford / DOWN ARGENTINE WAY, 1940, 20th Century-Fox, d-Irving Cummings.

Alice Faye's appendectomy gave Grable her chance to star as an American heiress who falls in love with an Argentinian horse breeder (Don Ameche). Grable is good but Carmen Miranda, whose character has nothing to do with the plot, steals the show with Al Dubin and Jimmy McHugh's "South American Way."

Lily Blane / TIN PAN ALLEY, 1940, 20th Century-Fox, d-Walter Lang.

Grable had been brought in by the studio to keep Alice Faye in line, and the latter knew it. Still, she good-naturedly accepted the fact that Grable was given second billing to herself in this story about two dancing sisters and a song composer (John Payne). Together the rivals sing a number of standards including "The Sheik of Araby," which the Hays Office objected to, claiming that too much skin showed.

Kay Latimer / MOON OVER MIAMI, 1941, 20th Century-Fox, d-Walter Lang.

The grooming to have Grable replace Alice Faye was in full swing. In this lightweight but enjoyable piece, Grable, her sister (Carole Landis), and their aunt (Charlotte Greenwood) descend on Miami looking to land some rich husbands. Robert Cummings and Don Ameche fill the bill, but not before resolving the mandatory complications. Grable's songs include Leo Robin and Ralph Rainger's "You Started Something" and "Oh Me Oh Mi-A-Mi."

Jill Lynn / I WAKE UP SCREAMING, 1941, 20th Century-Fox, d-H. Bruce Humberstone.

When beautiful Carole Landis is murdered, her sister (Grable) demands action from the police. The amicable detective (Laird Cregar) assigned to the case is actually the murderer, not main suspect Victor Mature.

Kate Farley / CONEY ISLAND, 1943, 20th Century-Fox, d-Walter Lang.

Set in New York's Coney Island at the turn of the century, two rival saloon keepers (George Montgomery and Cesar Romero) both want a flashy entertainer (Grable). Montgomery gets her in this lush Technicolor feature with Grable memorable for singing Robin and Rainger's "Cuddle Up a Little Closer."

Madeleine Marlowe / Rosie O'Grady / SWEET ROSIE O'GRADY, 1943, 20th Century-Fox, d-Irving Cummings.

In the 1880s Grable is hoping to marry a duke but her chances are ruined when a reporter for the *Police Gazette* (Robert Young), who wants her for himself, exposes her as a singer named Rosie O'Grady from a Bowery beer hall. Naturally this is the beginning of what will lead to their marriage. Grable's numbers include "My Heart Tells Me" sung with Grable in a bathtub, and "Going to the County Fair" by Mack Gordon and Harry Warren.

Lorry Jones / PIN-UP GIRL, 1944, 20th Century-Fox, d-H. Bruce Humberstone.
More than two million of Grable's pinups showing her in a white bathing suit looking seductively over her shoulder toward her perfect legs adorned the lockers of servicemen; on this historic note, an idea for a movie was born. The plot has something to do with a navy hero who pretends to be a Broadway star in order to meet Grable. Seven months pregnant at the end, trouper Grable does her best with very little.

Jenny Dolly / THE DOLLY SISTERS, 1945, 20th Century-Fox, d-Irving Cummings.
Unable to coax Alice Faye out of retirement to co-star with Grable as one of two Hungarian sister singers at the turn of the century, the studio settled for pretty June Haver. This fictionalized account of the brunette Dolly Sisters played by two lovely blondes is a typically lavish Fox production. Hit songs from the film are "I Can't Begin to Tell You" by Mack Gordon and James V. Monaco, and "I'm Always Chasing Rainbows" by Harry Carroll and Joseph McCarthy, and a Chopin melody.

Myrtle McKinley Burt / MOTHER WORE TIGHTS, 1947, 20th Century-Fox, d-Walter Lang.
Grable and co-star Dan Dailey are a happily married vaudeville team who are hurt when daughter Mona Freeman, away at a finishing school, is ashamed of how they earn their living. As to be expected in such lightweight musicals, all ends well. The hit song of the movie is "You Do" by Mack Gordon and Joseph Myrow.

Freddie Jones / THE BEAUTIFUL BLONDE FROM BASHFUL BEND, 1949, 20th Century-Fox, d-Preston Sturges.
Pistol-packing saloon girl Grable accidentally shoots a judge in the rear and must flee to a new community where she is mistaken for a school marm. It is a fun western farce with some very forgettable songs.

Loco / HOW TO MARRY A MILLIONAIRE, 1953, 20th Century-Fox, d-Jean Negulesco.
Grable gets first billing but Marilyn Monroe gets all the attention and Lauren Bacall does most of the work in this tale of three dim-witted beauties united in pursuit of rich husbands. Grable settles for handsome forest ranger Rory Calhoun.

OTHER ROLES

1930: *chorus girl* / LET'S GO PLACES; *bit* / NEW MOVIETONE FOLLIES OF 1930; *chorus girl* / WHOOPEE! **1931:** *bit* / KIKI; *chorus girl* / PALMY DAYS. **1932:** *bit* / THE GREEKS HAD A WORD FOR THEM; *chorus girl* / THE KID FROM SPAIN; *bit* / CHILD OF MANHATTAN; *bit* / PROBATION; *bit* / HOLD 'EM JAIL. **1933:** *bit* / CAVALCADE; *Beverly Bennett* / WHAT PRICE INNOCENCE? **1934:** *bit* / STUDENT TOUR; *dancer* / THE GAY DIVORCEE. **1935:** *Mary Roberts* / THE NITWITS; *Sylvia* / OLD MAN RHYTHM; *Dorothy* / COLLEGIATE; *Frances Gretchell* / BY YOUR LEAVE. **1936:** *part of a trio* / FOLLOW THE FLEET; *Laura Watson* / PIGSKIN PARADE; *Mildred* / DON'T TURN 'EM LOOSE. **1937:** *Jane Morrow* / THIS WAY PLEASE; *Gwen* / THRILL OF A LIFETIME. **1938:** *Betty* / COLLEGE SWING; *Nancy Larkin* / GIVE ME A SAILOR; *Joyce Gilmore* / CAMPUS CONFESSIONS. **1939:** *Susan* / MAN ABOUT TOWN; *Ina Firpo* / THE DAY THE BOOKIES WEPT. **1941:** *Carol Brown* / A YANK IN THE RAF. **1942:** *Pat Lambert* / FOOTLIGHT SERENADE; *Eileen O'Brien* / SONG OF THE ISLANDS; *Vicky* / SPRINGTIME IN THE ROCKIES. **1944:** *herself* / FOUR JILLS IN A JEEP. **1945:** *Bonnie Collins* / BILLY ROSE'S DIAMOND HORSESHOE. **1946:** *guest* / DO YOU LOVE ME? **1947:** *Cynthia Pilgrim* / THE SHOCKING MISS PILGRIM. **1948:** *Angelica* / *Francesca* / THAT LADY IN ERMINE. **1950:** *Ruby Summers* / WABASH AVENUE; *Molly Moran* / MY BLUE HEAVEN. **1951:** *Kay Hudson* / CALL ME MISTER; *Delilah* / MEET ME AFTER THE SHOW. **1953:** *Molly Larkin* / THE FARMER TAKES A WIFE. **1954:** *Julie Lowndes* / THREE FOR THE SHOW. **1955:** *Stormy* / HOW TO BE VERY, VERY POPULAR.

GRAHAME, GLORIA

(Gloria Grahame Hallward, 1924–1982)
Gloria Grahame was Hollywood's stereotyped bad girl. With her seductive stance and pouting lips she was best as some kind of tramp. Nominated for a Best Supporting Actress Award for CROSSFIRE, she won an Oscar for THE BAD AND THE BEAUTIFUL. Her best work, though, was in THE BIG HEAT and IN A LONELY PLACE. In both she plays sexual outlaws who can't quite help themselves but know what they are doing. In a sense Grahame came along at the wrong time. Females of the 1950s were more plastic than real and Grahame's sultry looks and behavior proved a dubious asset. There weren't enough suitable vehicles for her unique talent. Some of today's actresses, such as Kathleen Turner, are provided with roles as sexually active and aware women who still carry the lead of the film and are not targets to be properly punished before the fadeout. From 1959 on Grahame was forced to accept increasingly cheap horror films and thrillers, the worst of which were the three-day wonders, TAROT and MAMA'S DIRTY GIRLS. But she was able to end her career with a couple of fine performances in the critically acclaimed films, CHILLY SCENES OF WINTER and MELVIN AND HOWARD.

KEY ROLES

Violet Bick / IT'S A WONDERFUL LIFE, 1946, RKO, d-Frank Capra.
Grahame is delightful as the small-town flirt who is among the people Jimmy Stewart's life positively affects. When he gets his wish to have never been born, he discovers that Grahame is a shady woman of the evening.

Ginny Tremaine / CROSSFIRE, 1947, RKO, d-Edward Dmytryk.
Grahame appears as a pathetic, disillusioned dance hall girl who lives on mean streets in a world of casual pickups. The story is about a soldier who kills a man merely because he is a Jew.

Laurel Gray / IN A LONELY PLACE, 1950, Columbia, d-Nicholas Ray.
Grahame is brilliant as Humphrey Bogart's passionate, paranoid neighbor who takes up with him even though he is strongly suspected of having murdered a young woman. The sexual tension between Bogart and Grahame is as hot as movies could get away with at the time.

Rosemary Bartlow / THE BAD AND THE BEAUTIFUL, 1952, MGM, d-Vincente Minnelli.
Grahame is the southern belle wife of a writer (Dick Powell) who is brought to Hollywood by producer Kirk Douglas to write the screenplay for his very sexy and popular novel. Grahame gets in the way of Powell's work so Douglas arranges for her to be "entertained" by movie star Gilbert Roland. She is killed in an

accident with her new sexual partner but the screenplay is completed first.

Angel / THE GREATEST SHOW ON EARTH, 1952, Paramount, d-Cecil B. DeMille.
In this all-star circus epic, Grahame works with elephants and a nasty partner (Lyle Bettger) who constantly conspires to take liberties with her. She holds her own with the skunk.

Debby Marsh / THE BIG HEAT, 1954, Columbia, d-Fritz Lang.
In this exceptional film noir, Grahame is a vain call girl who is horribly scarred by Lee Marvin when he throws hot coffee in her face. Realizing that she no longer has a place in society, she turns informer and helps a man (Glenn Ford) who is trying to get those responsible for the death of his wife by a bomb meant for him.

Harriet Lang / NOT AS A STRANGER, 1955, United Artists, d-Stanley Kramer.
In this rambling medical movie, Grahame plays a bored, wealthy woman who has an affair with the new doctor in town (Robert Mitchum) who had only married wife Olivia De Havilland so she could pay for his medical school expenses.

Ado Annie Carnes / OKLAHOMA! 1956, Magna / Rodgers and Hammerstein, d-Fred Zinnemann.
In a brilliant casting decision Grahame plays the farmer's daughter who falls in love with whoever happens to be around at the time. As she sings in "Ay Cain't Say No," she's a wholesome girl who enjoys kissing and at age 17 almost aches with sexual awakening.

OTHER ROLES

1944: *Sally Murfin* / BLONDE FEVER. **1945:** *flower girl* / WITHOUT LOVE. **1947:** *nurse* / IT HAPPENED IN BROOKLYN; *Beulah Baxter* / MERTON OF THE MOVIES; *Fran Page* / SONG OF THE THIN MAN. **1948:** *Mary* / ROUGHSHOD; *Susan Caldwell* / A WOMAN'S SECRET. **1952:** *Margie* / MACAO; *Irene Neves* / SUDDEN FEAR. **1953:** *Maggie* / THE GLASS WALL; *Zama Cernik* / MAN ON A TIGHTROPE; *Princess Nadja* / PRISONERS OF THE CASBAH. **1954:** *Marianna* / NAKED ALIBI; *Denise* / THE GOOD DIE YOUNG. **1955:** *Vicki Buckley* / HUMAN DESIRE; *Lucy* / THE MAN WHO NEVER WAS; *Karen McIver* / THE COBWEB. **1957:** *Amy Porter* / RIDE OUT FOR REVENGE. **1959:** *Helen* / ODDS AGAINST TOMORROW. **1966:** *Bonnie Shelley* / RIDE BEYOND VENGEANCE. **1970:** *Mrs. Roy* / THE TODD KILLINGS. **1972:** *Selma* / CHANDLER; *Annabelle* / THE LONERS; *Mrs. Deere* / BLOOD AND LACE. **1973:** *Angela* / TAROT. **1974:** *Mama* / MAMA'S DIRTY GIRLS. **1975:** *Nurse Katherine* / THE TERROR OF DR. CHANEY, (MANSION OF THE DOOMED). **1979:** *Clara* / CHILLY SCENES OF WINTER, (HEAD OVER HEELS). **1980:** *Mrs. Sisk* / MELVIN AND HOWARD; *Ma Fox* / A NIGHTINGALE SANG IN BERKELEY SQUARE, (THE BIGGEST BANK ROBBERY). **1981:** *Florinda* / THE NESTING.

GRANGER, FARLEY

(1925–)

Farley Granger started as a juvenile lead with Goldwyn and, after the war, gave some interesting performances as brooding, complex young men in movies such as Hitchcock's ROPE and STRANGERS ON A TRAIN, and Nicholas Ray's THEY LIVE BY NIGHT. In the mid-1950s, he left movies for the stage and television. When he returned to the big screen it was in cheap Italian exploitation films not generally released in the United States. He also made cheapies that have seldom been seen outside drive-ins, including X-rated trash like CONFESSIONS OF A SEX MANIAC and MANIAC MANSION (1972), PENETRATION (1974), ROSEMARY'S KILLER (1981), and THE WHOOPEE BOYS (1986). There must be an explanation beyond the obvious monetary one why an actor who once knew decent roles would appear in such garbage, but we can't think of any.

KEY ROLES

Sgt. Howard Clinton / THE PURPLE HEART, 1944, 20th Century-Fox, d-Lewis Milestone.
Granger is one of eight American prisoners of the Japanese who are tried as criminals following their capture in China after taking part in Jimmy Doolittle's bombing raid of Tokyo early in 1942. He is tortured and strangled to the point that his ability to speak is destroyed. But, in the end, he has another person read his elegant words to the court that will sentence him and his comrades to death.

Philip / ROPE, 1948, Transatlantic, d-Alfred Hitchcock.
Granger and John Dall are two homosexuals who murder a friend for the thrill of it and conceal his body in a trunk which they use as a cocktail table for a party whose guests include the deceased's father and girlfriend. The movie's main interest is that Hitchcock filmed it as a continuous shot.

Guy Haines / STRANGERS ON A TRAIN, 1951, Warners, d-Alfred Hitchcock.
Granger is a tennis player who has a conversation with a strange man (Robert Walker) on a train who believes that they have an agreement to perform each other's murder. Walker proceeds to kill Granger's faithless wife and then insists that Granger should carry through with his part of the bargain and kill Walker's father.

Niels / HANS CHRISTIAN ANDERSEN, 1952, Goldwyn, d-Charles Vidor.
Granger is the director of a ballet and his wife Jeanmarie is his prima ballerina. Danny Kaye, as the great fairy tale creator, has made special slippers for the dancer on whom he has developed a major crush. He feels that she can't love Granger when he treats her so cruelly at rehearsals of Kaye's ballet which Jeanmarie will dance.

Harry K. Thaw / THE GIRL IN THE RED VELVET SWING, 1955, 20th Century-Fox, d-Richard Fleischer.
When his beautiful showgirl wife Evelyn Nesbitt (Joan Collins) becomes a playboy architect's (Stanford White) mistress, Granger, a spoiled, erratic millionaire, kills White. His wife saves him from the gallows when she testifies that White was a great scoundrel and seducer.

OTHER ROLES

1943: *Damian* / THE NORTH STAR. **1948:** *Bowie* / THEY LIVE BY NIGHT; *Pat Masterson* / ENCHANTMENT. **1949:** *Joe Norson* / SIDE STREET. **1950:** *Martin Lynn* / EDGE OF DOOM; *Chuck* / OUR VERY OWN. **1951:** *Jack Greer* / I WANT YOU; *Bill Denny* / BEHAVE YOURSELF. **1952:** *Jim* / O. HENRY'S FULL HOUSE. **1953:** *Thomas Campbell, Jr.* / THE STORY OF THREE LOVES; *Lt. Franz Mahler* / SENSO; *Rick Belrow Livingston* / SMALL TOWN GIRL. **1955:** *Nicky Bradna* / THE NAKED STREET. **1970:** *Major Harriman* / THEY CALL ME TRINITY. **1972:** *computer programming chief* / THE SERPENT. **1973:** *Judge Niland* / THE MAN CALLED NOON; *Evan Lyons* / ARNOLD. **1981:** *Sheriff George Fraser* / THE PROWLER.

GRANGER, STEWART

(James Stewart, 1913–)

Stewart Granger was a worthy claimant to the swashbuckling crown of Errol Flynn, starring in a series of lavish costume pieces in the 1950s for MGM after having spent several years in romantic leads for Rank in films such as THE MAN IN GREY and MADONNA OF THE SEVEN MOONS. His first role in the United States was as Alan Quartermain in KING SOLOMON'S MINES (1950). He followed this with nearly 20 such costume-adventure movies. After his seven-year MGM contract expired, Granger was reduced to appearing in a series of forgettable European adventure epics. On television in 1971 he tried his hand as Sherlock Holmes in THE HOUND OF THE BASKERVILLES and did not disappoint. While neither a major star nor a great actor, six-foot-three Granger, with his virile good looks and ironic sense of humor, always could be counted on for an entertaining performance.

KEY ROLES

Peter Rokeby / Swinton Rokeby / THE MAN IN GREY, 1943, Great Britain, Gainsborough, d-Leslie Arliss.
Granger is a dashing actor in Regency times to whom Phyllis Calvert, the wife of a rakish dandy (James Mason), is attracted. Her childhood friend (Margaret Lockwood) encourages the "friendship," hoping to snatch Mason for herself. When Calvert becomes ill, Lockwood lets her die and Mason horsewhips her to death. At the end of the film, Granger and Calvert appear as descendants of the illicit lovers of the past.

Ted Purvis / WATERLOO ROAD, 1944, Great Britain, Gainsborough, d-Sidney Gilliat.
In London of 1940, Granger is a local Romeo who has ducked military service through a forged medical certificate. He romances Joy Shelton whose husband (John Mills) is in the army. When Mills learns of it, he goes A.W.O.L. to give Granger a beating (rather a ludicrous notion considering the size difference of the two men), then sorts things out with Shelton.

Kit Firth / LOVE STORY, 1944, Great Britain, Eagle-Lion / Gainsborough, d-Leslie Arliss.
Granger is an RAF pilot going blind who falls in love with Margaret Lockwood, a dying pianist. It was a gold mine at the box office, being one of England's better entries into the "woman's weeper" category.

Nino Barucci / MADONNA OF THE SEVEN MOONS, 1944, Great Britain, Gainsborough, d-Arthur Crabtree.
In this lurid melodrama, the wife of an Italian merchant has a split personality which causes her to periodically flee to the "Seven Moons" in Florence as the mistress of a notorious jewel thief (Granger).

Apollodorus / CAESAR AND CLEOPATRA, 1945, Great Britain, Eagle-Lion, d-Gabriel Pascal.
In this film Cleopatra (Vivian Leigh) is a naive child and Caesar (Claude Rains) is "a nice old gentleman." Granger is by contrast a handsome hunk, slim of torso, with flashing eyes, a dazzling smile, and just what a young maid, even a queen, might lick her lips for. Yet Cleopatra shows no interest in Granger, at least not according to George Bernard Shaw's words.

Hugh Davin / CAPTAIN BOYCOTT, 1947, Great Britain, General Film Distributors, d-Frank Launder.
This historical piece explains the origin of the word "boycott" as Granger plays the leader of Irish villagers and farmers who are rebelling against harsh landlord Captain Boycott.

Alan Quartermain / KING SOLOMON'S MINES, 1950, MGM, d-Compton Bennett.
This film was nominated for the Best Picture Award and, although not quite that good, Granger's performance as the heroic explorer is as exciting as any romantic could hope for.

André Moreau / "Scaramouche" / SCARAMOUCHE, 1952, MGM, d-George Sidney.
Granger clowns as a long-nosed, comical actor and duels like a devil in this cheerful swashbuckler set in pre-Revolution France. Granger is in a quandary over the identity of his father. When he finally discovers it, he is relieved to find that he is not Janet Leigh's brother as he feared and he also understands why he could not kill a cruel marquis (Mel Ferrer)—the man is his half-brother.

George Bryan "Beau" Brummel / BEAU BRUMMEL, 1954, MGM, d-Curtis Bernhardt.
With skill and panache Granger plays the part of the Regency dandy who becomes a close friend of the Prince of Wales and a taste-maker of Europe. It's a good thing, because the story of his rise and fall isn't too exciting.

Col. Rodney Savage / BHOWANI JUNCTION, 1956, Great Britain, MGM, d-George Cukor.
Ava Gardner is half British and half Indian and the conflict shows. Granger is a British officer wishing for her to fall in love with him.

Sir Philip Ashlow / THE LITTLE HUT, 1957, MGM, d-Mark Robson.
Granger, his wife (Ava Gardner), and his best friend (David Niven) are shipwrecked on a deserted island. Being all very sophisticated and civilized, they agree to Niven's demand that Gardner be shared by the two men. How this doesn't happen is the subject of the farce.

Lot / SODOM AND GOMORRAH, 1962, Italy / France, Titanus / Pathé, d-Robert Aldrich.
Granger hadn't changed but the U.S. public's interest in his adventure pieces had, so he was happy to find work in this Biblical piece as the man whose wife turns to salt when she disobeys God's command and turns to look at his destruction of the evil city.

OTHER ROLES

1933: *bit* / A SOUTHERN MAID. **1934:** *a diner* / GIVE HER A RING. **1938:** *Lawrence* / SO THIS IS LONDON. **1940:** *Sutton* / CONVOY. **1942:** *Sub-Lieutenant Jackson* / SECRET MISSION. **1943:** *David Penley* / THURSDAY'S CHILD; *Larry Rains* / THE LAMP STILL BURNS; *Harry Somerford* / FANNY BY GASLIGHT. **1946:** *Richard Darrel* / CARAVAN; *Niccolo Paganini* / THE MAGIC BOW. **1948:** *Philip Thorn* / BLANCHE FURY; *Count Philip Koenigsmark* / SARABAND FOR DEAD LOVERS. **1949:** *Lord Terence Datchett* / WOMAN HATER; *Adam Black* / ADAM AND EVELYNE. **1951:** *Sam Conride* / THE LIGHT TOUCH; *Pvt. Archibald Ackroyd* / SOLDIERS THREE. **1952:** *Jules Vincent* / THE WILD NORTH; *Rudolf Rassendyl / King Rudolf V* / THE PRISONER OF ZENDA. **1953:** *Thomas Seymour* / YOUNG BESS; *Commander Claudius* / SALOME. **1954:** *Mark Shore* / ALL THE BROTHERS WERE VALIANT. **1955:** *Rian X. Mitchell* / GREEN FIRE; *Jeremy Fox* / MOONFLEET. **1956:** *Sandy McKenzie* / THE LAST HUNT. **1957:** *Tom Earley* / GUN GLORY. **1958:** *Max Poulton* / THE WHOLE TRUTH; *Harry Black* / HARRY BLACK AND THE TIGER. **1960:** *George Pratt* / NORTH TO ALASKA. **1961:** *John Brent* / THE SECRET PARTNER. **1962:** *Thomas Stanswood* / THE SWORDSMAN OF SIENA. **1963:** *Captain Le Blanc* / THE LEGION'S LAST PATROL. **1964:** *Maj. Richard Mace* / THE SECRET INVASION. **1965:** *Duke of Orgagna* / THE CROOKED ROAD; *Old Surehand* / RAMPAGE AT APACHE WELLS; *Old Surehand* / FRONTIER HELLCAT; *Michael Scott* / MISSION HONG KONG. **1966:** *John "Bingo" Merrill* / REQUIEM FOR A SECRET AGENT. **1967:** *Superintendent Cooper-Smith* / THE TRYGON FACTOR; *Miles Gilchrist* / THE LAST SAFARI. **1968:** *Old Surehand* / THE FLAMING FRONTIER. **1977:** *Sir Edward Malherson* / THE WILD GEESE.

GRANT, CARY

(Archibald Leach, 1904–1986)

Debonair they called him, and debonair he was. Cary Grant was not a versatile actor, but what he did, the public just loved. He was a romantic ideal for millions of women, while men admired his casualness and sense of humor. Born in England, at age 15 he joined a company of acrobats with whom he sang, danced, and juggled, traveling with them to the United States and staying when they returned to England. He worked the vaudeville circuit and by the late 1920s was appearing regularly on Broadway. Paramount, which made films on both coasts, hired Grant to appear in a 1931 short. He made quite an impression, was put under contract, moved west, and made seven films in his first year in Hollywood. He really began to be noticed when he appeared with Mae West in SHE DONE HIM WRONG and I'M NO ANGEL in 1933. By 1937 he had become one of the top male stars and a sure box-office draw, a position he maintained throughout his career which ended with his retirement in 1966. A master of timing, Grant was at his best in screwball or sophisticated comedies, in which he co-starred with the cream of female actresses. He was seldom given the opportunity to be less than totally charming because the public wouldn't hear of it. Grant, a failure in five marriages, saw himself somewhat differently, observing, "Everyone tells me I've had such an interesting life, but sometimes I think it's been nothing but stomach disturbances and self-concern."

KEY ROLES

Nick Townsend / BLONDE VENUS, 1932, Paramount, d-Josef von Sternberg.

Grant is the wealthy playboy who becomes Marlene Dietrich's lover but ultimately brings her together again with her husband (Herbert Marshall) for whom he had provided the money to recover from radiation poisoning.

Lt. B. F. Pinkerton / MADAME BUTTERFLY, 1932, Paramount, d-Marion Gering.

In this version of Puccini's opera (sans his beautiful music), Grant is a U.S. naval officer who lives with a Japanese maiden (Sylvia Sidney) who bears their child. Grant sails back to America and returns for the child three years later with a wife.

Captain Cummings / SHE DONE HIM WRONG, 1933, Paramount, d-Lowell Sherman.

Grant is a federal undercover agent posing as a Salvation Army worker so he can keep tabs on Mae West. He arrests her but not before falling for her.

Jack Clayton / I'M NO ANGEL, 1933, Paramount, d-Wesley Ruggles.

Mae West, a shady show woman who has been known to shake down a sucker or two, sues wealthy Grant for breach of promise but finally confesses her true love for him and gets him as a bridegroom.

Porter Madison III / THIRTY-DAY PRINCESS, 1934, Paramount, d-Marion Gering.

Grant is a newspaper publisher and foreigner-baiter who falls for a foreign princess. Actually he falls for a New York girl posing as a princess—the real one has the mumps.

Jimmy Monkley / SYLVIA SCARLETT, 1936, RKO, d-George Cukor.

Grant is a raffish cockney swindler who hitches up with Katharine Hepburn, who is disguised as a boy, and her father on their way to London.

George Kerby / TOPPER, 1937, MGM, d-Norman Z. McLeod.

Along with his kooky wife (Constance Bennett) Grant is killed in an automobile accident and, as ghosts, they help their banker friend Roland Young assert himself.

Jerry Warriner / THE AWFUL TRUTH, 1937, Columbia, d-Leo McCarey.

Grant and wife Irene Dunne take each other for granted and decide that divorce is the only answer. When it doesn't work out, they get together again after trying to make each other jealous.

David Huxley / BRINGING UP BABY, 1938, RKO, d-Howard Hawks.

Grant is an absent-minded paleontologist who gets involved with kooky Katharine Hepburn and her pet leopard Baby, whose favorite song is "I Can't Give You Anything But Love." He reluctantly falls in love with Hepburn and explains, "Now it isn't that I don't like you, Susan. After all, in moments of quiet, I'm strangely drawn toward you. But, well, there haven't been any quiet moments."

Johnny Case / HOLIDAY, 1938, Columbia, d-George Cukor.

Grant is a lawyer with little ambition who becomes the fiancé of wealthy Doris Nolan, but by the film's end he finds her sister (Katharine Hepburn) more to his liking.

Sergeant Cutter / GUNGA DIN, 1939, RKO, d-George Stevens.

Grant and his two sergeant buddies (Victor McLaglen and Douglas Fairbanks, Jr.) along with Sam Jaffe thwart the plans of Indian guru Eduardo Cianelli to ambush a British regiment. Grant is a fun-loving cockney, full of bravado and charm.

Walter Burns / HIS GIRL FRIDAY, 1940, Columbia, d-Howard Hawks.

Newspaper editor Grant cons ex-wife and ace reporter Rosalind Russell into covering one last story before she marries wimpy Ralph Bellamy. Grant takes exception to her choice of a new husband, telling Bellamy, "I'm more or less particular about whom my wife marries."

Nick Arden / MY FAVORITE WIFE, 1940, RKO, d-Garson Kanin.

Grant appears in court to have his wife (Irene Dunne), who disappeared several years earlier in a shipwreck, proclaimed legally dead. This accomplished, he marries Gail Patrick. Almost immediately Dunne shows up, having been rescued from an island where her only companion was Randolph Scott. It takes a string of highly comical scenes to get everything resolved and Grant back with Dunne.

C. K. Dexter Haven / THE PHILADELPHIA STORY, 1940, MGM, d-George Cukor.

Grant is able to sabotage his ex-wife's (Katharine Hepburn) plans to remarry. He is helped by the appearance of a writer (James Stewart) and a photographer (Ruth Hussey) sent to cover the society wedding by the scandal sheet they work for. At one point Grant tells Hepburn, "You're slipping, Red. I used to be frightened of that look—the withering glance of the goddess." In the end the two make the same mistake twice and remarry.

Mortimer Brewster / ARSENIC AND OLD LACE, 1944, Warners, d-Frank Capra.

Filmed in 1942 but released in 1944 when its Broadway run ended, this movie has Grant as a newly married man who discovers that his sweet old aunts have killed a dozen men, as has his brother (Raymond Massey). It's a wonderful black comedy with Grant at his hammiest. He tries to get rid of his bride (Priscilla Lane) by telling her, "Insanity runs in my family. It practically gallops."

Devlin / NOTORIOUS, 1946, RKO, d-Alfred Hitchcock.

Grant is Ingrid Bergman's U.S. contact as she infiltrates a group of South American Nazis, going so far as to marry one (Claude Rains) even though she loves Grant.

Dudley / THE BISHOP'S WIFE, 1947, RKO, d-Henry Koster.

Grant is a very human angel sent to earth to answer the prayer of an Episcopalian bishop (David Niven) who is trying to raise funds to build a cathedral. Grant seems to spend more time giving Loretta Young the attention her husband has lately denied her. He compliments her, saying, "There are few people who know the secret of making a heaven here on earth. You are one of those rare people."

Jim Blandings / MR. BLANDINGS BUILDS HIS DREAM HOUSE, 1948, RKO, d-H. C. Potter.

When advertising man Grant and wife Myrna Loy decide to build a house in Connecticut, they find out all about hidden expenses as they attempt to make their "dream house a reality."

Capt. Henri Rochard / I WAS A MALE WAR BRIDE, 1949, 20th Century-Fox, d-Howard Hawks.

Grant is a French army officer who marries WAC Ann Sheridan and then poses as a war bride to escape all the red tape involved in accompanying his wife to the United States.

John Robie / TO CATCH A THIEF, 1955, Paramount, d-Alfred Hitchcock.

Grant is an infamous, retired jewel thief whose technique is being imitated by someone on the French Riviera. Grace Kelly helps him clear himself and find the new "Cat."

Nickie Ferrante / AN AFFAIR TO REMEMBER, 1957, 20th Century-Fox, d-Leo McCarey.

Grant and Deborah Kerr meet on an ocean liner. Both are on their way to others, but they enjoy each other's company. They part when they land, planning to meet again later, but Kerr is hurt in an accident and it takes a lot of effort on Grant's part to find her.

Philip Adams / INDISCREET, 1958, Warners, d-Stanley Donen.

Grant, who has never been married, tells Ingrid Bergman that he has a wife and can never get a divorce. He feels he can play the field better this way. This makes Bergman mad: "How dare he make love to me and not be a married man."

Roger Thornhill / NORTH BY NORTHWEST, 1959, MGM, d-Alfred Hitchcock.

Advertising executive Grant is mistaken for a nonexistent U.S. agent by some foreign bad guys. He is kidnapped, appears to kill a U.N. delegate, and is chased across the country, often in the arms of beautiful Eva Marie Saint, before thwarting villain James Mason at Mount Rushmore.

Sir William Rutland / WALK, DON'T RUN, 1966, Columbia, d-Charles Walters.

Grant makes his farewell appearance in movies in a repeat of the role played by Charles Coburn in THE MORE THE MERRIER (1943). Grant fast-talks Samantha Eggar into sharing an apartment in crowded Japan during the Olympic Games. He in turn takes in Jim Hutton, a participating athlete, then plays Cupid to the youngsters.

OTHER ROLES

1932: *Stepan (Stephen) Mendanich* / THIS IS THE NIGHT; *Ridgeway* / SINNERS IN THE SUN; *Charles Exeter* / MERRILY WE GO TO HELL; *Lieutenant Jaeckel* / DEVIL AND THE DEEP; *Romer Sheffield* / HOT SATURDAY. **1933:** *Jeffrey Baxter* / WOMAN ACCUSED; *Henry Crocker* / THE EAGLE AND THE HAWK; *Ace Corbin* / GAMBLING SHIP; *the Mock Turtle* / ALICE IN WONDERLAND. **1934:** *Malcolm Trevor* / BORN TO BE BAD; *Dr. Maurice Lamar* / KISS AND MAKE UP; *Julian de Lussac* / LADIES SHOULD LISTEN. **1935:** *Gerald Fitzgerald* / ENTER MADAME; *Ken Gordon* / WINGS IN THE DARK; *Michael Andrews* / THE LAST OUTPOST. **1936:** *Danny Barr* / BIG BROWN EYES; *Andre Charville* / SUZY; *Charlie Mason* / WEDDING PRESENT. **1937:** *Jimmy Hudson* / WHEN YOU'RE IN LOVE; *Ernest Bliss* / ROMANCE AND RICHES; *Nick Boyd* / THE TOAST OF NEW YORK. **1939:** *Jeff Carter* / ONLY ANGELS HAVE WINGS; *Alec Walker* / IN NAME ONLY; *cameo* / TOPPER TAKES A TRIP. **1940:** *Matt Howard* / THE HOWARDS OF VIRGINIA. **1941:** *Roger Adams* / PENNY SERENADE; *Johnnie Aysgarth* / SUSPICION. **1942:** *Leopold Dilg* / THE TALK OF THE TOWN. **1943:** *Joe Adams* / MR. LUCKY. **1944:** *Captain Cassidy* / DESTINATION TOKYO; *Jerry Flynn* / ONCE UPON A TIME; *Ernie Mott* / NONE BUT THE LONELY HEART. **1946:** *Cole Porter* / NIGHT AND DAY; *cameo* / WITHOUT RESERVATIONS. **1947:** *Richard Nugent* / THE BACHELOR AND THE BOBBY-SOXER. **1948:** *Dr. Madison Brown* / EVERY GIRL SHOULD BE MARRIED. **1950:** *Dr. Eugene Ferguson* / CRISIS. **1951:** *Dr. Noah Praetorius* / PEOPLE WILL TALK. **1952:** *"Poppy" Rose* / ROOM FOR ONE MORE; *Prof. Barnaby Fulton* / MONKEY BUSINESS. **1953:** *Clemson Reade* / DREAM WIFE. **1957:** *Capt. Anthony Trumbull* / THE PRIDE AND THE PASSION; *Commander Crewson* / KISS THEM FOR ME. **1958:** *Tom Winston* / HOUSEBOAT. **1959:** *Lt. Cmdr. M. T. Sherman* / OPERATION PETTICOAT. **1961:** *Victor Rhyall* / THE GRASS IS GREENER. **1962:** *Philip Shayne* / THAT TOUCH OF MINK. **1963:** *Peter Joshua* / CHARADE. **1964:** *Walter Eckland* / FATHER GOOSE.

GRANVILLE, BONITA

(1923–1988)

Bonita Granville went on stage when she was only three and in the 1930s she became very popular playing cruel and naughty children, with her meanest performance as the little horror in THESE THREE. To prove she wasn't a one-movie brat she played the leader of the girls who told tales about women in Salem, Massachusetts, leading to their execution as witches, in the movie MAID OF SALEM. A little later she made a mark as Nancy Drew in a series of films. In the 1940s she appeared in a number of routine "B" movies as a leading lady, then she retired to marry a Texas oilman. She has maintained control over the production of several lucrative TV series, including "Lassie."

KEY ROLES

Mildred Miller / AH, WILDERNESS, 1935, MGM, d-Clarence Brown.

Granville plays a bratty sister to Eric Linden in this screen adaptation of the Eugene O'Neill play about an adolescent's coming of age in Connecticut in 1906.

Mary Tilford / THESE THREE, 1936, United Artists, d-William Wyler.

The power of Granville's performance as a malevolent and spiteful child who slanders her two teachers (Miriam Hopkins and Merle Oberon), forcing them to close their school, is still amazing when seen today. This is no mixed-up youngster in need of love and understanding. She is just plain mean and bad.

Ann Goode / MAID OF SALEM, 1937, Paramount, d-Frank Lloyd.
Granville, Virginia Weidler, and Bennie Bartlett play three children who start witchcraft hysteria in Salem in 1692. Granville, as in THESE THREE, is the ringleader, a girl who can easily sway other girls to her cruel will.

Roberta Morgan / BELOVED BRAT, 1938, Warners, d-Arthur Lubin.
Now firmly established as the little brat everyone loves to hate, Granville portrays the neglected child of wealthy parents Donald Crisp and Natalie Moorehead. It takes the compassionate understanding of teacher Dolores Costello to put things right.

Nancy Drew / NANCY DREW, DETECTIVE, 1938, Warners, d-William Clemens.
Growing up now, Granville plays a girl with a bent for solving mysteries who proves that an old woman thought to be eccentric is not. Granville sees to it that the old lady is rescued from a gang of kidnappers who are after her money, which then goes to Granville's school.

Elsa / THE MORTAL STORM, 1940, MGM, d-Frank Borzage.
Granville is part of the extended family of non-Aryan, German professor Frank Morgan who finds his happy life and that of his children and their friends being destroyed by the rise of Nazism.

Opal Madvig / THE GLASS KEY, 1942, Paramount, d-Stuart Heisler.
In this lively crime melodrama, Granville plays slightly corrupt but good-natured politician Brian Donlevy's sister. She is somewhat of a problem for him to protect and keep away from some of his more questionable associates.

Anna Muller / HITLER'S CHILDREN, 1943, RKO, d-Edward Dmytryk.
In this account of Germany's indoctrination of its youth, Tim Holt is a thoroughly Nazified youngster and Granville remains unconvinced. They are in love but she is marked for sterilization because she's deemed unfit to bear children for the Fatherland. Ultimately she converts Holt to her way of thinking and they die together defiantly.

Kay Wilson / LOVE LAUGHS AT ANDY HARDY, 1946, MGM, d-Willis Goldbeck.
Granville, as the campus siren, is Mickey Rooney's love interest in this second to last of the Andy Hardy films for 12 years. The thinness of the series is really beginning to show.

OTHER ROLES

1932: *bit* / WESTWARD PASSAGE; *little girl* / SILVER DOLLAR. **1933:** *Fanny, age 7* / CAVALCADE; *bit* / CRADLE SONG. **1934:** *Joan Winters as a girl* / THE LIFE OF VERGIE WINTERS; *bit* / A WICKED WOMAN. **1936:** *Little Jen* / SONG OF THE SADDLE; *Mollser Cogan* / THE PLOUGH AND THE STARS; *child in convent* / THE GARDEN OF ALLAH. **1937:** *Ann Helton* / CALL IT A DAY; *Isabella* / QUALITY STREET; *Gracie Kane* / IT'S LOVE I'M AFTER. **1938:** *Marion Kilbourne* / MERRILY WE LIVE; *Sally Ward* / WHITE BANNERS; *Gwen Colbrook* / MY BILL; *Connie Richards* / HARD TO GET. **1939:** *Peggy Finnegan* / ANGELS WASH THEIR FACES; *Nancy Drew* / NANCY DREW—REPORTER; *Nancy Drew* / NANCY DREW—TROUBLE-SHOOTER; *Nancy Drew* / NANCY DREW AND THE HIDDEN STAIRCASE. **1940:** *Doris* / FORTY LITTLE MOTHERS; *Martha Scroggs* / THOSE WERE THE DAYS; *Vicky Sherwood* / THIRD FINGER, LEFT HAND; *Ursula* / ESCAPE; *Kate Pendleton* / GALLANT SONS. **1941:** *Frances Marlowe* / THE PEOPLE VS. DR. KILDARE; *Francine Diamond* / THE WILD MAN OF BORNEO; *Betty Haines* / DOWN IN SAN DIEGO; *Mary Pulham* / H. M. PULHAM, ESQ.; *cameo* / LAND OF LIBERTY. **1942:** *Kit Lodimer* / SYNCOPATION; *June Vale* / NOW, VOYAGER. **1943:** *Anne Porter* / SEVEN MILES FROM ALCATRAZ. **1944:** *Bonnie* / SONG OF THE OPEN ROAD; *Kay Wilson* / ANDY HARDY'S BLONDE TROUBLE; *Toddy* / YOUTH RUNS WILD. **1945:** *Alice* / THE BEAUTIFUL CHEAT; *Jeanne Blake* / SENORITA FROM THE WEST. **1946:** *Chris Allen* / THE TRUTH ABOUT MURDER; *Dorothy Larson* / BREAKFAST IN HOLLYWOOD; *Ronnie* / SUSPENSE. **1947:** *Estelle and Linda Mitchell* / THE GUILTY. **1948:** *Julie Brady* / STRIKE IT RICH. **1950:** *Stephanie Varna* / GUILTY OF TREASON. **1956:** *Welcome Kilgore* / THE LONE RANGER.

GRAYSON, KATHRYN

(Zelma Hedrick, 1922–)
Blessed with a fine soprano voice, Kathryn Grayson charmed audiences in a number of Hollywood musicals in the late 1940s and early 1950s. By the mid-1950s, however, interests had changed and Grayson's career as the movies' reigning prima donna was at an end. She was discovered by MGM on Eddie Cantor's radio show in 1940 and in her first real film she was a cutie in the title role of ANDY HARDY'S PRIVATE SECRETARY. Her singing co-stars included Frank Sinatra, Mario Lanza (whom she found boorish), and her best partner, Howard Keel. Since her last film she has sung in nightclubs and on the stage.

KEY ROLES

Kathryn Land / ANDY HARDY'S PRIVATE SECRETARY, 1940, MGM, d-George B. Seitz.
Grayson is Andy Hardy's latest romantic interest, but off the screen she wasn't interested in dating the diminutive star.

Patricia Rawnsley / THOUSANDS CHEER, 1943, MGM, d-George Sidney.
In this all-star extravaganza, Grayson is Mary Astor's daughter. Astor has been long separated from John Boles, an army major, and Grayson tries to play Cupid and bring her parents together again. But she has her own troubles with soldier Gene Kelly. Her songs include Verdi's "Sempre Libera" and "Let There Be Music" by E. Y. Harburg and Earl Brent.

Susan Abbott / ANCHORS AWEIGH, 1945, MGM, d-George Sidney.
Grayson is a would-be singer for whom sailor Gene Kelly promises to arrange an audition with Jose Iturbi. The fact that he doesn't know Iturbi doesn't matter to the brash young man. Grayson sings "Jealousy" by Vera Bloom and Jacob Gade, "My Heart Sings" by Harold Rome and Henri Herpin, and Brahms's "Waltz from Serenade in C, Opus 48."

Prudence Budell / THAT MIDNIGHT KISS, 1949, MGM, d-Norman Taurog.
Philadelphia heiress Grayson, determined to become an opera star, is swept off her feet by the singing talent and good looks of truck driver Mario Lanza. The plot is paper thin, but it allows for much fine singing by the two stars separately and together. In the latter category is "They Didn't Believe Me" by Jerome Kern and Herbert Reynolds. Grayson also sings Verdi's "Caro Nome."

Suzette Micheline / THE TOAST OF NEW ORLEANS, 1950, MGM, d-Norman Taurog.
Although Mario Lanza and Grayson beautifully sing numerous operatic extracts, the hit song from the

picture is their duet of "Be My Love" by Nicholas Brodsky and Sammy Cahn. Grayson plays a famous soprano and Lanza a New Orleans fisherman groomed by David Niven for an operatic career. Reportedly Grayson and Lanza almost came to blows during the filming.

Magnolia Hawks / SHOW BOAT, 1951, MGM, d-George Sidney.

In this Technicolor remake of the Edna Ferber, Jerome Kern, and Oscar Hammerstein stage musical, Grayson makes a very pretty Nolia, daughter of a Mississippi showboat captain, who falls in love with a gambler who, when his luck runs out, abandons her and their daughter. Grayson nicely handles the musical numbers sung with Howard Keel. They include "Make Believe" and "You Are Love."

Grace Moore / SO THIS IS LOVE, 1953, Warners, d-Gordon Douglas.

This biopic traces the rise of soprano Moore (Grayson) from her childhood in Tennessee to her acclaimed debut at New York's Metropolitan Opera House. It leaves out her tragic death in a plane crash. Songs sung by Grayson include extracts from Mozart's "The Marriage of Figaro," Gounod's "Faust," and Puccini's "La Bohème."

Lilli Vanessi / Katherine / KISS ME KATE! 1953, MGM, d-George Sidney.

In probably her best role, Grayson plays a musical star cast with her ex-husband (Howard Keel) in a musical version of "The Taming of the Shrew." The movie details the conflict of these two people who are still in love both on and off the stage. Grayson spits out Cole Porter's "I Hate Men" and sings "So in Love" and "Wunderbar" with Keel.

OTHER ROLES

1939: *bit* / ANDY HARDY GETS SPRING FEVER. **1941:** *Rebecca Yancey* / THE VANISHING VIRGINIAN. **1942:** *Rita Winslow* / RIO RITA; *Billie Van Maaster* / SEVEN SWEETHEARTS. **1946:** *Abigail Chandler* / TWO SISTERS FROM BOSTON; *specialty number* / ZIEGFELD FOLLIES; *Magnolia Hanks speciality* / TILL THE CLOUDS ROLL BY. **1947:** *Amy Fielding* / IT HAPPENED IN BROOKLYN. **1948:** *Teresa* / THE KISSING BANDIT. **1950:** *Ina Massine* / GROUNDS FOR MARRIAGE. **1952:** *Stephanie* / LOVELY TO LOOK AT. **1953:** *Margot Birabeau* / THE DESERT SONG. **1956:** *Catherine de Vaucelles* / THE VAGABOND KING. **1976:** *guest* / THAT'S ENTERTAINMENT, PART 2.

GREENWOOD, JOAN

(1921–1987)

With a breathily husky voice, Joan Greenwood specialized in playing delicate, witty British sexpots too seldom seen by U.S. audiences. She trained at the Royal Academy of Dramatic Arts, making her stage debut in 1938 and her first movie in 1940. Unfortunately she was not always properly used in films and devoted herself mostly to the stage. But she did leave a few memorable performances which teasingly suggest what might have been.

KEY ROLES

Betty Miller / THE GENTLE SEX, 1943, Great Britain, Two-Cities, d-Leslie Howard and Adrian Brunel.

Greenwood is one of seven girls from various backgrounds who join the British Women's Military Unit in World War II. Trained for different jobs, they separate but come together again to ward off an enemy bombing of an anti-aircraft station.

Jennie Carden / THE OCTOBER MAN, 1947, Great Britain, Eagle-Lion, d-Roy Baker.

Greenwood portrays a woman who helps brain-injured John Mills prove that he isn't guilty of strangling model Kay Walsh. She prevents him from throwing himself under a train.

Sophie Dorothea / SARABAND FOR DEAD LOVERS, 1948, Great Britain, Ealing, d-Basil Dearden.

Greenwood is unhappily married to the dissolute George Louis of Hanover, later George I of England. She falls in love with a count (Stewart Granger) but when they plan to flee, his ex-mistress has him killed and Greenwood is sent to a remote castle where she spends the rest of her life.

Lady Caroline Lamb / BAD LORD BYRON, 1949, Great Britain, Triton, d-David Macdonald.

As Lady Caroline Lamb, Greenwood is one of several women whose relationships with the poet Byron are recounted in detail before a heavenly tribunal judging him.

Peggy MacCroon / WHISKY GALORE! (TIGHT LITTLE ISLAND), 1949, Great Britain, Ealing, d-Alexander Mackendrick.

In 1941, off the Isle of Eriskay in the Outer Hebrides, a ship carrying 50,000 cases of Scotch whisky flounders. This is the story of how the islanders, including Greenwood, risk life and limb to rescue the "water of life" from the doomed ship.

Sibella / KIND HEARTS AND CORONETS, 1949, Great Britain, Ealing, d-Robert Hamer.

Petite and delicately sexy, Greenwood plays Dennis Price's mistress in this brilliant black comedy. She is playfully erotic as she breathes sexual innuendo into the role that is one of her finest performances.

Gwendolyn Fairfax / THE IMPORTANCE OF BEING EARNEST, 1951, Great Britain, Two-Cities, d-Anthony Asquith.

Greenwood and Dorothy Tutin are two charming society ladies who feel they can only love a man named Ernest. The two men-about-town who yearn for them (Michael Redgrave and Michael Denison) are only too happy to be rechristened Ernest, but it proves to be unnecessary for Redgrave.

Lady Warren / FATHER BROWN, 1954, Great Britain, Facet / Columbia, d-Robert Hamer.

Father Brown (Alec Guinness), as an amateur detective, gets Greenwood to put up her valuable chess set as bait to capture master of disguise crook Flambeau (Peter Finch).

Lady Bellaston / TOM JONES, 1963, Great Britain, Woodfall, d-Tony Richardson.

While dallying with foundling Albert Finney, fashionable Lady Greenwood endeavors to teach him the manners of a gentleman. But she finds that he learns other things more quickly. She encourages David Tomlinson in his pursuit of Susannah York, so as to have Finney for herself, saying: "Fie upon it, have more resolution. Are you frightened by the word rape? All women love a man of spirit. Remember the story of the Sabine ladies. I believe they made tolerably good wives afterwards."

OTHER ROLES

1941: *Irma Bagshott* / MY WIFE'S FAMILY; *Babe Cavour* / HE FOUND A STAR. **1945:** *Ruth Blake* / THEY KNEW MR. KNIGHT; *Christine Minetti* / LATIN QUARTER. **1946:** *Gay Sultzman* / A GIRL IN A MILLION. **1947:** *Elizabeth* / THE MAN WITHIN; *Lottie Smith* / THE

WHITE UNICORN, (BAD SISTER). **1950:** *Susan* / MR. PEEK-A-BOO. **1951:** *Wilhelmina Cameron* / FLESH AND BLOOD; *Sabina Pennant* / YOUNG WIVES' TALE; *Daphne Birnley* / THE MAN IN THE WHITE SUIT. **1954:** *Norah* / KNAVE OF HEARTS. **1955:** *Lady Ashwood* / MOONFLEET. **1958:** *Rita Vernon* / STAGE STRUCK. **1959:** *voice only* / HORSE ON HOLIDAY. **1962:** *Lady Mary Fairchild* / MYSTERIOUS ISLAND; *Lady Fitzadam* / THE AMOROUS MR. PRAWN. **1964:** *Frances Ferris* / THE MOON-SPINNERS. **1971:** *Lettice Mason* / GIRL STROKE BOY. **1977:** *Miss Malkin* / THE UNCANNY; *Beryl Stapleton* / THE HOUND OF THE BASKERVILLES. **1978:** *Lady Harriet* / THE WATER BABIES.

GREER, JANE

(Bettejane Greer, 1924–)

Jane Greer overcame facial paralysis as a child and as a young woman she sang with a Latin-American band. Her husband of the time, Rudy Vallee, helped her secure a contract with RKO where she appeared in various "B" features as girls who came to bad ends. She later moved on to MGM and better roles, but her general lack of ambition and her preference for raising a family prevented her from becoming a big star. Never officially retired, she made movie appearances sporadically throughout the years.

KEY ROLES

Judith Owens / DICK TRACY, DETECTIVE, 1945, RKO, d-William Berke.

Greer doesn't get the role of Tess Trueheart in this feature about the jut-jawed police detective. That honor goes to Anne Jeffreys. Instead Greer plays the daughter of an intended victim of a crazy killer named Splitface (Mike Mazurki).

Janice Bell / THEY WON'T BELIEVE ME, 1947, RKO, d-Irving Pichel.

Robert Young is a heel who sponges off his wife (Rita Johnson), loves and deserts Greer, and runs off with Susan Hayward. He kills the latter in a car accident and is arrested for murdering his wife, who had actually committed suicide. At least Greer's character survives.

Kathie Moffatt / OUT OF THE PAST, 1947, RKO, d-Jacques Tourneur.

In this under-appreciated film noir, almond-eyed Greer is a marvelous homicidal femme fatale in a small mountain community where Robert Mitchum and Kirk Douglas are caught in the web of this "black widow." Looking into those huge, trusting eyes, it's hard to believe how amoral she really is. When the film was remade in 1984 as AGAINST ALL ODDS with Rachel Ward in Greer's part, Greer played the girl's mother, another one not to be trusted.

Joan "Chiquita" Graham / THE BIG STEAL, 1949, RKO, d-Don Seigel.

Reunited, Greer and Robert Mitchum are hot on the trail of a man (Patrick Knowles) who has framed Mitchum for the theft of an army payroll. This enjoyable, tension-filled comedy-melodrama is full of twists and is a pleasant surprise.

Katy Connors / RUN FOR THE SUN, 1956, United Artists, d-Roy Boulting.

When their plane crashes in a Mexican jungle, journalist Greer and disillusioned author Richard Widmark find themselves at the mercy of renegade Nazis.

Hazel Bennett / MAN OF A THOUSAND FACES, 1957, Universal-International, d-Joseph Pevney.

Greer portrays Lon Chaney's second wife in this sudsy biopic. Greer brings Chaney (James Cagney) and his alienated son (Roger Smith) by his hated first wife together before the great silent-screen actor dies.

OTHER ROLES

1945: *Miss Downing* / PAN-AMERICANA; *Helen* / TWO O'CLOCK COURAGE; *Billie Randall* / GEORGE WHITE'S SCANDALS. **1946:** *Lola Carpenter* / THE FALCON'S ALIBI; *Eileen Sawyer* / THE BAMBOO BLONDE; *Helen* / SUNSET PASS; *Pirouze* / SINBAD THE SAILOR. **1948:** *Charlie* / STATION WEST. **1951:** *Ellie Harkness* / YOU'RE IN THE NAVY NOW; *Diane* / THE COMPANY SHE KEEPS. **1952:** *Antoinette de Mauban* / THE PRISONER OF ZENDA; *Julie Heldon* / DESPERATE SEARCH; *Katie McDermad* / YOU FOR ME. **1953:** *Paula Henderson* / THE CLOWN; *Diane Forrester* / DOWN AMONG THE SHELTERING PALMS. **1964:** *Marian Spicer* / WHERE LOVE HAS GONE. **1965:** *Agnes Carol* / BILLIE. **1974:** *Alma* / THE OUTFIT. **1984:** *Mrs. Wyler* / AGAINST ALL ODDS.

GUINNESS, SIR ALEC

(1914–)

Alec Guinness has been described as a chameleon for the way he loses himself in his roles. He even says, "I don't really know who I am. Quite possibly, I do not exist." Guinness was dismissed from Martita Hunt's acting school because she felt he would never become an actor. After working as an extra in EVENSONG, he appeared in GREAT EXPECTATIONS, which also featured his old teacher, Hunt. He won international acclaim with OLIVER TWIST and KIND HEARTS AND CORONETS. Next, he appeared in a series of Ealing comedies that included THE LAVENDER HILL MOB, for which he received an Academy Award nomination. He won an Oscar for his eccentric British commander in THE BRIDGE ON THE RIVER KWAI. Later he was nominated again for STAR WARS. Knighted in 1959, Guinness played roles as diverse as Adolf Hitler, Fagin, Disraeli, a timid bank clerk who steals a fortune, a happy bigamist, an almost-mad painter, a tortured Cardinal, Jacob Marley's ghost, a vacuum cleaner salesman turned spy in Cuba, and an Arab prince. In all these roles and others besides, Guinness has distinguished himself as one of the finest actors ever to appear on a screen.

KEY ROLES

Fagin / OLIVER TWIST, 1948, Great Britain, Cineguild, d-David Lean.

Guinness is so convincing as the mentor of juvenile thieves that the film was not shown in the United States until 1970 because it was believed that his character is anti-Semitic.

Lord D'Ascoyne / Henry D'Ascoyne / Canon D'Ascoyne / General D'Ascoyne / Admiral D'Ascoyne / Ascoyne D'Ascoyne / Duke of Chalfont / Lady Agatha D'Ascoyne / KIND HEARTS AND CORONETS, 1949, Great Britain, Ealing, d-Robert Hamer.

Guinness plays each of the eight relatives that Dennis Price kills in order to inherit a dukedom. Guinness is flawless in briefly bringing to life these stuffy aristocrats.

Benjamin Disraeli / THE MUDLARK, 1950, Great Britain, 20th Century-Fox, d-Jean Negulesco.

Guinness portrays the great British prime minister in this tale of how a street urchin (Andrew Ray) breaks into Windsor Castle, meets and charms Queen Victoria, and helps bring her out of self-imposed retirement.

Henry Holland / THE LAVENDER HILL MOB, 1951, Great Britain, Ealing, d-Charles Crichton.

After 20 years serving as a prissy bank clerk, Guinness plans the perfect robbery. He will steal a million pounds in gold bars, melt them down into statuettes of the Eiffel Tower, and smuggle them out of the country. His plans go astray in this delightful, inventive comedy, but unlike his accomplices, he is able to escape to Brazil where he lives the high life until he is extradited.

Sidney Stratton / THE MAN IN THE WHITE SUIT, 1951, Great Britain, Ealing, d-Alexander Mackendrick.

Shy textile research chemist Guinness develops a soil-resistant fabric that will never wear out. However, the wondrous fabric will not absorb dyes and so only white clothes may be made from it. Both management and labor see the new fabric as an economic threat, but not to worry, the material comes apart like cotton candy.

Edward Henry "Denry" Machin / THE CARD, 1952, Great Britain, British Film Makers, d-Ronald Neame.

Guinness is an engagingly cheeky fellow who lives by his wits quite well in the 1890s, becoming a moneylender, rent-collector, and youngest mayor of Bursley. He dallies with a gold digger and a countess but marries local girl Petula Clark.

Father Brown / FATHER BROWN, 1954, Great Britain, Facet / Columbia, d-Robert Hamer.

Guinness is a priest-detective tricked by master-of-disguise thief Flambeau (Peter Finch) who steals a priceless cross the clergyman was to take to Rome. Guinness traps the crook but, more importantly to his way of thinking, he redeems the man's immortal soul.

Professor Marcus / THE LADYKILLERS, 1955, Great Britain, Ealing, d-Alexander Mackendrick.

Guinness, the leader of a string quintet, rents a room from sweet old Katie Johnson. Actually the men plan and pull off a big robbery, but Johnson discovers the loot. They plan to kill her but can't decide who is to carry out the deed and bump off each other, one by one, instead.

Colonel Nicholson / THE BRIDGE ON THE RIVER KWAI, 1957, Great Britain, Horizon / Columbia, d-David Lean.

In Burma in 1943, Guinness is the commanding officer of a group of British prisoners who are ordered to surrender to the Japanese. He and his officers suffer great torture and deprivation before he convinces the Japanese commander to let his officers direct the work on a bridge to be built across the River Kwai. To rub salt in the wounds of the POW camp commandant (Sessue Hayakawa), Guinness vows to build the best possible bridge to show the supremacy of British know-how, losing sight of the fact that in doing so he is aiding the enemy. Later, guerrillas arrive to blow up the bridge.

Gulley Jimson / THE HORSE'S MOUTH, 1958, Great Britain, Knightsbridge / United Artists, d-Ronald Neame.

Guinness portrays an eccentric artist who loves to paint murals—the larger, the better. The fact that the walls he uses belong to others who do not share his obsession bothers him not a whit in this offbeat black comedy.

Lt. Col. Jock Sinclair / TUNES OF GLORY, 1960, Great Britain, Knightsbridge, d-Ronald Neame.

Guinness plays a crude Scottish colonel who is a lax disciplinarian and a lover of hard drink. Still he has the respect of his men. When he is replaced by strict martinet John Mills, the conflict between the two men results in Guinness cracking up and Mills committing suicide.

Prince Feisal / LAWRENCE OF ARABIA, 1962, Great Britain, Horizon / Columbia, d-David Lean.

Guinness portrays the great Arab prince who knows the English are as treacherous as the Turks, but for the present needs their help in this biopic of adventurer T. E. Lawrence. Speaking of the English officer, the prince describes how they differ: "With Major Lawrence, mercy is a passion. With me, it is merely good manners. You may judge which motive is more reliable."

King Charles I / CROMWELL, 1969, Great Britain, Columbia, d-Ken Hughes.

Guinness invests King Charles I of England with considerable dignity when Oliver Cromwell (Richard Harris) comes to power and orders the monarch's execution.

Adolf Hitler / HITLER: THE LAST TEN DAYS, 1973, Great Britain / Italy, MGM / Westfilm, d-Ennio de Concini.

Guinness appears uncomfortable in the role of the Führer and one wonders why he accepted the assignment to portray him in this poorly produced picture.

Ben (Obi-Wan) Kenobi / STAR WARS, 1977, 20th Century-Fox, d-George Lucas.

In this fairy tale, Guinness is the wise old Jedi knight who acts as Mark Hamill's instructor as the latter comes to the aid of a rebel princess (Carrie Fisher) and duels with Darth Vader.

OTHER ROLES

1933: *extra* / EVENSONG. **1946:** *Herbert Pocket* / GREAT EXPECTATIONS. **1949:** *Whimple* / A RUN FOR YOUR MONEY. **1950:** *George Bird* / LAST HOLIDAY. **1952:** *Henry St. James* / THE CAPTAIN'S PARADISE. **1953:** *Flight Lt. Peter Ross* / THE MALTA STORY. **1954:** *Col. Sir Edgar Fraser* / TO PARIS WITH LOVE. **1955:** *the Cardinal* / THE PRISONER. **1956:** *Prince Albert* / THE SWAN. **1957:** *William Horatio Ambrose* / ALL AT SEA, (BARNACLE BILL). **1958:** *John Barrett* / *Jacques de Gue* / THE SCAPEGOAT. **1959:** *Jim Wormold* / OUR MAN IN HAVANA. **1961:** *Koichi Asano* / A MAJORITY OF ONE. **1962:** *Captain Crawford* / H.M.S. DEFIANT. **1964:** *Marcus Aurelius* / THE FALL OF THE ROMAN EMPIRE; *Herr Frick* / SITUATION HOPELESS—BUT NOT SERIOUS. **1966:** *Gen. Yevgraf Zhivago* / DOCTOR ZHIVAGO; *Benedict Boniface* / HOTEL PARADISO; *Pol* / THE QUILLER MEMORANDUM. **1967:** *Major Jones* / THE COMEDIANS. **1970:** *Jacob Marley* / SCROOGE. **1973:** *Pope Innocent III* / BROTHER SUN, SISTER MOON. **1976:** *Butler Bensonumum* / MURDER BY DEATH. **1980:** *Ben (Obi-Wan) Kenobi* / THE EMPIRE STRIKES BACK. **1983:** *Ben (Obi-Wan) Kenobi* / RETURN OF THE JEDI; *Sigmund Freud* / LOVESICK. **1984:** *Professor Godbole* / A PASSAGE TO INDIA.

HACKMAN, GENE

(1930–)

Before his appearance in THE FRENCH CONNECTION, Gene Hackman had established himself as a competent character actor. Afterwards he was an unlikely star, and it has not always been easy for him to maintain this identification. Hackman has been nominated for Academy Awards for his roles in BONNIE AND CLYDE and I NEVER SANG FOR MY FATHER, winning for his "Popeye" Doyle in THE FRENCH CONNECTION. Not a handsome man, he's at his best playing average men, probing their emotional depths and showing them to be just as interesting as the beautiful people. In his own opinion, "Seventy-five percent of being successful as an actor is pure luck—the rest is just endurance."

KEY ROLES

Buck Barrow / BONNIE AND CLYDE, 1967, Warners, d-Arthur Penn.

Hackman was nominated for an Oscar for his impressive performance as Clyde Barrow's (Warren Beatty) older brother who joins with him and Bonnie Parker (Faye Dunaway) to form a gang of ruthless bank robbers. In the end he is rewarded by being riddled with bullets.

Gene Garrison / I NEVER SANG FOR MY FATHER, 1969, Columbia, d-Gilbert Cates.

When his mother dies, Hackman, a widower, must contend with his ill-tempered father (Melvyn Douglas), who doesn't want his son to remarry. He eulogizes Douglas as follows: "Death ends a life, but it does not end a relationship, which struggles on in the survivor's mind toward some resolution which it may never find."

Jimmy "Popeye" Doyle / THE FRENCH CONNECTION, 1971, 20th Century-Fox, d-William Freidkin.

Hackman finally got his Academy Award for his portrayal of a New York police detective who tracks down a consignment of drugs smuggled into the Big Apple from France. As good as his performance is, one wonders how well it will stand the test of time.

Rev. Frank Scott / THE POSEIDON ADVENTURE, 1972, 20th Century-Fox, d-Ronald Neame.

Hackman is a clergyman who leads a band of survivors of a capsized luxury liner to the bottom of the ship, which of course is the top, in an effort to escape a watery grave. He doesn't see the promised land.

Harry Caul / THE CONVERSATION, 1973, Paramount, d-Francis Ford Coppola.

A professional bugging expert (Hackman) develops a conscience when he feels that he is being used as an accomplice in a murder plot. Hackman is outstanding but the movie is difficult to follow.

Blind Hermit / YOUNG FRANKENSTEIN, 1974, 20th Century-Fox, d-Mel Brooks.

In this spoof of the classic monster movie, Hackman plays the blind hermit who entertains a strange visitor, offering him food, drink, and smoke, but the monster is not allowed to enjoy any of them.

Kibby / LUCKY LADY, 1975, 20th Century-Fox, d-Stanley Donen.

In a great cinematic failure Hackman, Burt Reynolds, and Liza Minnelli combine to waste their talents in a movie whose intentions could not be agreed upon by the producers, writers, and director.

Lex Luthor / SUPERMAN, 1978, Warners, d-Richard Donner.

Hackman appears as the self-proclaimed greatest criminal genius in the world who poses quite a challenge for the Man of Steel. It pays the rent but it's not Hackman at his best.

OTHER ROLES

1961: *a cop* / MAD DOG COLL. **1964:** *Norman* / LILITH. **1966:** *Rev. John Whipple* / HAWAII. **1967:** *Sergeant Tweed* / FIRST TO FIGHT; *Harmsworth* / A COVENANT WITH DEATH; *Tommy Del Gaddio* / BANNING. **1968:** *Detective Brille* / THE SPLIT; *Red Fletcher* / RIOT. **1969:** *Eugene Claire* / DOWNHILL RACER; *Joe Browdy* / THE GYPSY MOTHS. **1970:** *Buzz Lloyd* / MAROONED. **1971:** *Dr. David Randolph* / DOCTORS' WIVES; *Brandt Ruger* / THE HUNTING PARTY. **1972:** *Officer Leo Holland* / CISCO PIKE; *"Mary Ann"* / PRIME CUT. **1973:** *Max* / SCARECROW. **1974:** *Zandy Allan* / ZANDY'S BRIDE. **1975:** *Sam Clayton* / BITE THE BULLET; *Jimmy "Popeye" Doyle* / THE FRENCH CONNECTION II. **1976:** *Harry Moseby* / NIGHT MOVES. **1977:** *Roy Tucker* / THE DOMINO PRINCIPLE; *Maj. Gen. Stanislaw Sosabowski* / A BRIDGE TOO FAR; *guest* / A LOOK AT LIV; *Maj. William Sherman Foster* / MARCH OR DIE. **1980:** *Lex Luthor* / SUPERMAN II. **1981:** *George Dupler* / ALL NIGHT LONG; *Pete Van Wherry* / REDS. **1983:** *Jack McCann* / EUREKA; *Cal Rhodes* / UNCOMMON VALOR; *Alex Grazies* / UNDER FIRE. **1984:** *Ned* / MISUNDERSTOOD. **1985:** *Wilfred Buckley* / POWER; *Walter Lloyd* / TARGET; *Harry Mackenzie* / TWICE IN A LIFETIME. **1987:** *David Brice* / NO WAY OUT.

HAGEN, JEAN

(Jean Verhagen, 1924–1977)

Most famous for her role as the beautiful silent-screen star with a horrible speaking voice in SINGING IN THE RAIN, Jean Hagen had a short but impressive movie career before moving on to TV where she played Danny Thomas's wife in "Make Room for Daddy." Sadly, the motion picture industry didn't seem to know what to do with this talented comedienne and dramatic actress. She died of throat cancer at 54.

KEY ROLES

Beryl Caighn / ADAM'S RIB, 1949, MGM, d-George Cukor.

Hagen is the lady friend of Tom Ewell. The two become a target for his wife (Judy Holliday) when she wildly shoots a gun in their general direction after finding them in an embrace in Hagen's apartment. Katharine Hepburn is able to get Holliday acquitted by having the jury imagine Hagen as a slick gigolo and Ewell as a faithless wife.

Doll Conovan / THE ASPHALT JUNGLE, 1950, MGM, d-John Huston.

In this crime caper, Hagen is hooligan Sterling Hayden's girlfriend who tries to run away with him when his jewelry heist goes wrong.

Maggie Williams / CARBINE WILLIAMS, 1952, MGM, d-Richard Thorpe.

Hagen portrays the wife of the imprisoned bootlegger (Jimmy Stewart) who perfects a new gun, the carbine. It results in his pardon.

Lina Lamont / SINGING IN THE RAIN, 1952, MGM, d-Gene Kelly and Stanley Donen.

Hagen and Gene Kelly, a star silent-screen team, are faced with adjusting to talking movies. It's no big problem for Kelly, but Hagen has such a horrible voice that they are forced to have her speaking dubbed by Kelly's sweetheart (Debbie Reynolds). The jig is up when Hagen insists on addressing her fans after her latest movie: "If we bring a little joy into your humdrum lives, it makes us feel our work ain't been in vain for nothin'." She is so unlikable in this film that one realizes that this is the work of a truly remarkable actress.

Connie Bliss / THE BIG KNIFE, 1955, United Artists, d-Robert Aldrich.

A depressed Hollywood star (Jack Palance) has an affair with the wife (Hagen) of an associate before being blackmailed into signing a new contract.

OTHER ROLES

1949: *Harriett Sinton* / SIDE STREET; *Martha Conovan* / AMBUSH. **1950:** *Maggie Collins* / A LIFE OF HER OWN. **1951:** *girl next door* / NIGHT INTO MORNING; *Joan Brenson* / NO QUESTIONS ASKED; *Stella* / SHADOW IN THE SKY. **1953:** *Meg Hutchins* / ARENA; *Martha Dobson* / HALF A HERO; *Anne Kellwood* / LATIN LOVERS. **1957:** *Barna Forrest* / SPRING REUNION. **1959:** *Freida Daniels* /

THE SHAGGY DOG. **1960:** *Missy Lehand* / SUNRISE AT CAMPOBELLO. **1962:** *Ann Baldwin* / PANIC IN YEAR ZERO. **1964:** *Dede Marshall* / DEAD RINGER.

HALL, JON

(Charles Locher, 1913–1979)

Hall began his movie career using the name Charles Locher, then changed it to Lloyd Crane in 1936 before settling on Jon Hall in 1937. He specialized in adventure films where his muscles and athletic prowess could be seen to best advantage, preferably in a loin cloth or the burnoose of a Bedouin chieftain. He was all right until he could no longer control his waistline. Never much of an actor, Hall nevertheless excited youngsters who sought vicarious thrills at Saturday matinees.

KEY ROLES

Terangi / THE HURRICANE, 1937, Goldwyn, d-John Ford and Stuart Heisler.

Hall is a native of a South Seas island who loves Dorothy Lamour, gets in trouble with the authorities, is jailed, escapes, is jailed again, escapes again, and so on until he kills a cruel guard and the orders are to bring him in dead or alive. He is saved from this fate by a typhoon, after which he and Lamour canoe away to another island and a new life.

Kit Carson / KIT CARSON, 1940, United Artists, d-George B. Seitz.

Hall portrays the legendary Indian scout, wagon-train guide, soldier, and plainsman in a fairly accurate account of his life. It's a long-winded tale with the romance provided by a three-way love affair involving Hall, Dana Andrews as John C. Frémont, and Lynn Bari as a California beauty.

Haroun al Raschid / ARABIAN NIGHTS, 1942, Universal, d-John Rawlins.

In this spectacular Technicolor fairy tale, Hall is the Caliph of Bagdad deposed by his half-brother, who wins back his throne with the help of a dancer (Maria Montez) and an acrobat (Sabu).

Ali Baba / ALI BABA AND THE FORTY THIEVES, 1944, Universal, d-Arthur Lubin.

In this absurd but likable yarn, a young prince deposed and raised by bandits grows into the strapping Hall who regains his rightful place at the side of Maria Montez.

Ramu / COBRA WOMAN, 1944, Universal, d-Robert Siodmak.

Hall is the main squeeze of both a South Seas beauty and her evil twin sister who leads a band of snake worshipers. Both lovelies are played by (who else?) Maria Montez.

Robin Hood / THE PRINCE OF THIEVES, 1948, Columbia, d-Howard Bretherton.

This minor entry into the films on the life and adventures of the leader of the Merry Men has Hall saving a nobleman's intended from an evil baron. It's a forgettable second feature that doesn't even have Maria Montez going for it.

Martin Viking / LAST TRAIN FROM BOMBAY, 1952, Columbia, d-Fred F. Sears.

Cheap melodramas like this, with Hall as a diplomat in Bombay falsely accused of murdering an old friend, at least paid the rent, but they are strictly drive-in features.

OTHER ROLES

1935: *Philip Nash* / CHARLIE CHAN IN SHANGHAI; *bit* / WOMEN MUST DRESS. **1936:** *bit* / MIND YOUR OWN BUSINESS; *bit* / THE LION MAN; *Lafe* / THE MYSTERIOUS AVENGER. **1937:** *Bertie* / THE GIRL FROM SCOTLAND YARD. **1940:** *Kehane* / SOUTH OF PAGO PAGO; *Danny Malone* / SAILOR'S LADY. **1941:** *Tanoa* / ALOMA OF THE SOUTH SEAS. **1942:** *Chester Tuttle* / THE TUTTLES OF TAHITI; *Hank Starr* / EAGLE SQUADRON; *Frank Raymond* / THE INVISIBLE AGENT. **1943:** *Kaloe* / WHITE SAVAGE. **1944:** *Robert Griffin* / THE INVISIBLE MAN'S REVENGE; *John Caldwell* / SAN DIEGO, I LOVE YOU; *Randy Curtis* / LADY IN THE DARK; *Michael* / GYPSY WILDCAT. **1945:** *Merab* / SUDAN; *Randolph Glenning* / MEN IN HER DIARY. **1947:** *Michigan Kid* / THE MICHIGAN KID; *Major Heyward* / LAST OF THE REDMEN; *Johnnie Taggart* / THE VIGILANTES RETURN. **1949:** *Ed Garry* / DEPUTY MARSHAL; *Nick Shaw* / THE MUTINEERS; *Steve* / ZAMBA. **1950:** *Kenneth Crandall* / ON THE ISLE OF SAMOA. **1951:** *McMillen* / CHINA CORSAIR; *Capt. Carlos Montalvo* / HURRICANE ISLAND. **1952:** *Steve Ruddell* / BRAVE WARRIOR. **1953:** *Ramar* / WHITE GODDESS; *Ramar* / EYES OF THE JUNGLE. **1955:** *Ramar* / PHANTOM OF THE JUNGLE; *Ramar* / THUNDER OVER SANGOLAND. **1957:** *Captain Knight* / HELL SHIP MUTINY. **1959:** *Dave Courtney* / FORBIDDEN ISLAND. **1965:** *Otto Lindsay* / THE BEACH GIRLS AND THE MONSTER.

HARDING, ANN

(Dorothy Gatley, 1902–1981)

Ann Harding was perfect as the gallant, self-sacrificing, and understanding wife or mistress in a series of wonderful "women's movies" during the 1930s. A pale and graceful beauty, her typecasting as a woman who suffered for her love became more than most moviegoers could stand. Fortunately, in the 1940s she was able to move into more mature roles as dignified ladies, mothers, and older wives with husbands a bit too elderly to stray. She was nominated for an Oscar in 1930 for her work in HOLIDAY. Of her acting style, she said, "I don't want to look like an actress, I want to look like a person."

KEY ROLES

Linda Seton / HOLIDAY, 1930, Pathe, d-Edward H. Griffith.

Harding received an Academy Award nomination for her performance as a bright, wealthy girl who steals her sister's fiancé. It is a very competent version of a hit stage comedy.

Minnie / GIRL OF THE GOLDEN WEST, 1930, Warners, d-John Francis Dillon.

In this straight word-for-word, scene-for-scene transcription of the 1905 stage piece, Harding is a saloon owner who wins the life of her bandit lover in a poker game played with the sheriff who seeks him and loves her.

Lady Isabella / EAST LYNNE, 1931, Fox Films, d-Frank Lloyd.

Through no fault of her own, Harding is divorced by her husband, and later loses both her lover and her sight. It's a solid Victorian melodrama with Harding in her most familiar role, a suffering woman.

Daisy Sage / THE ANIMAL KINGDOM, 1932, RKO, d-Edward H. Griffith.

When amicable Leslie Howard finds that his marriage to Myrna Loy is a mistake, he returns to the arms of Harding, an artist who understands him. It's a smart comedy-drama based on a hit play by Philip Barry.

Sally / GALLANT LADY, 1933, United Artists, d-Gregory La Cava.

Harding is an unmarried mother forced to give up her son. Five years later she meets her son again and he takes to her, even though he doesn't know her identity. The boy's adoptive father, who has just become a widower, also takes to Harding and before you know it they're a nice family unit.

Vergie Winters / THE LIFE OF VERGIE WINTERS, 1934, RKO, d-Alfred Santell.
Harding was adept at playing noble women who sacrificed all for their men. Here she philosophically accepts her fate as John Boles's mistress, even giving up their daughter so the child can be raised in the lap of luxury while Harding herself remains ostracized.

Marion / BIOGRAPHY OF A BACHELOR GIRL, 1935, MGM, d-Edward H. Griffith.
Harding is an artist who lives by her wits and has done quite well. She causes quite a fuss when she publishes her memoirs and names names.

Carol Howard / LOVE FROM A STRANGER, 1936, Great Britain, Trafalgar, d-Rowland V. Lee.
In what would be her last role as the female lead, Harding marries Basil Rathbone and then comes to suspect that he is a maniac. It is a fine, suspenseful film and Harding's last for six years.

Mary O'Connor / IT HAPPENED ON 5TH AVENUE, 1947, Allied Artists, d-Roy Del Ruth.
In this cheerful, sentimental comedy, Harding is the estranged wife of a millionaire who sees her family reunited and put straight about what's important and what's not by an amicable bum (Victor Moore) who winters in their New York mansion, while the family is off to warmer climates.

Fanny Bowditch Holmes / THE MAGNIFICENT YANKEE, 1950, MGM, d-John Sturges.
Harding is the very sensible and loving wife of Judge Oliver Wendell Holmes in this story of his later life.

OTHER ROLES

1929: *Mary Hutton* / PARIS BOUND; *Vera Kessler* / HER PRIVATE AFFAIRS; *Madame Vidal* / CONDEMNED. **1931:** *Shirley Mortimer* / DEVOTION; *Therese Du Flos* / PRESTIGE. **1932:** *Olivia Van Tyne* / WESTWARD PASSAGE; *Caroline Ogden Standish* / THE CONQUERORS. **1933:** *Claire Woodruff* / WHEN LADIES MEET; *Joan Colby* / DOUBLE HARNESS; *Dr. Margaret Simmons* / RIGHT TO ROMANCE. **1934:** *Julie von Narwitz* / THE FOUNTAIN. **1935:** *Lotty Wilkins* / ENCHANTED APRIL; *Mary White* / THE FLAME WITHIN; *Mary, Duchess of Towers* / PETER IBBETSON. **1936:** *Anne Talbot* / THE LADY CONSENTS; *Paula Young* / THE WITNESS CHAIR. **1942:** *Norma Lawry* / EYES IN THE NIGHT. **1943:** *Mrs. Davies* / MISSION TO MOSCOW; *Sophia* / THE NORTH STAR. **1944:** *Lucille Conway* / JANIE; *Gracie Thornton* / NINE GIRLS. **1945:** *Mrs. Brandt* / THOSE ENDEARING YOUNG CHARMS. **1946:** *Lucille Conway* / JANIE GETS MARRIED. **1947:** *Matilda Reid* / CHRISTMAS EVE. **1950:** *Katherine Robinson* / TWO WEEKS WITH LOVE. **1951:** *Stella Mason* / THE UNKNOWN MAN. **1956:** *Mrs. Hopkins* / THE MAN IN THE GRAY FLANNEL SUIT; *Jane Stone* / I'VE LIVED BEFORE; *Mary Carmichael* / STRANGE INTRUDER.

HARLOW, JEAN

(Harlean Carpenter, 1911–1937)
When she began her film career, Harlean Carpenter assumed her mother's maiden name, Jean Harlow. She appeared in numerous films as an extra and in Hal Roach comedy shorts. Her big break came in Howard Hughes's HELL'S ANGELS in 1930 in which she achieved immediate acclaim for her star quality, that intangible thing that can't be defined but if you have it—and Harlow had it—you don't need to describe it. Harlow was as hard as a diamond, swaggering before men, daring them to appraise her. She could vamp with the best of them, but not in a way that made her seem unapproachable. The platinum blonde beauty also proved to be a deft comedienne as she demonstrated in films like RED-HEADED WOMAN and BOMBSHELL. Her tragically short life has been nauseatingly detailed in many biographies and two poorly made movie biopics. Those who grew up with Marilyn Monroe, or the many inappropriate successors since, might find it enlightening and delightful to view some of Harlow's pictures and see what the original blonde bombshell had going for her. Her own assessment of her success was nicely put: "The men like me because I don't wear a brassiere. And the women like me because I don't look like a girl who would steal a husband. At least not for long."

KEY ROLES

Helen / HELL'S ANGELS, 1930, United Artists, d-Howard Hughes.
Harlow is a girl faithful only to herself, sharing the love of two brothers and others in this tale of pilots in the British Royal Flying Corps during World War I.

Gwen Allen / THE PUBLIC ENEMY, 1931, Warners, d-William A. Wellman.
Harlow is a girl who responds to bootlegger James Cagney only when he's about to give up on her. At least she doesn't share Cagney's end: dead, wrapped like a mummy, and dumped on his mom's doorsteps.

Anne Schuyler / PLATINUM BLONDE, 1931, Columbia, d-Frank Capra.
Harlow is a snobbish socialite married to a reporter (Robert Williams) who soon tires of Harlow's sterile world and longs for Loretta Young, another reporter. Williams carries most of the film, but he died shortly after its completion.

Lil Andrews / RED-HEADED WOMAN, 1932, MGM, d-Jack Conway.
Chester Morris becomes so infatuated with his employee (Harlow) that he divorces his wife to marry her. However, Harlow is rejected by Morris's society friends. To get her proper place Harlow compromises a wealthy businessman and forces him to get his socially prominent friends to accept her invitation to a party. But she makes a fool of herself. Morris goes back to his ex-wife and Harlow becomes the mistress of a nobleman. In this film Harlow has an affair with Charles Boyer, who unhappily was cast as her chauffeur. He was so outraged at this slight that he ever after refused to sign long-term contracts with any studio.

Vantine / RED DUST, 1932, MGM, d-Victor Fleming.
Harlow is a prostitute on the run from the police who takes refuge at a remote Indochina rubber plantation managed by Clark Gable. Indifferent to her initially, Gable later discovers that she is really sensitive and kind, and plans to stake her to a new start. Infatuated with Gable, she has to suffer through his attentions to Mary Astor, the wife of a young engineer. But before the film is over, Gable decides that Harlow is the girl for him.

Lola Burns / BOMBSHELL, 1933, MGM, d-Victor Fleming.
Weary of her movie roles as a sexpot, film star Harlow longs for a new image. Her plans to wed a marquis are ruined by a studio publicist (Lee Tracy). When she

tries to adopt a baby, her dad (Frank Morgan) and brother (Ted Healy) outrage adoption officials. When she meets Franchot Tone she believes that she's finally found what she has been looking for—a member of a cultured and respectable family. But his family rejects her. She finally realizes that being a film star is not so bad.

Kitty Packard / DINNER AT EIGHT, 1934, MGM, d-George Cukor.
In this all-star movie, Harlow is a hard-boiled tomato who is married to industrialist Wallace Beery and having an affair with physician Edmund Lowe. The star of the film is marvelous Marie Dressler. The film ends with guests going in to dinner, and Harlow and Dressler having the following classic conversation. Harlow: "I was reading a book the other day." Dressler, with a remarkable double-take: "Reading a book!" Harlow: "Yes. It's all about civilization or something—a nutty kind of a book. Do you know that the guy said that machinery is going to take the place of every profession?" Dressler: "Oh, my dear. That's something you need never worry about."

Dolly Portland "China Doll" / CHINA SEAS, 1935, MGM, d-Tay Garnett.
Clark Gable's discarded mistress (Harlow) joins him on his ship sailing for Singapore. Also aboard is Gable's English sweetheart (Rosalind Russell) and a trader (Wallace Beery) who is in love with Harlow. Beery is also in cahoots with pirates that attack the ship. After some exciting times, the ship reaches port and Gable plans to marry Harlow.

Suzy Trent / SUZY, 1936, MGM, d-George Fitzmaurice.
Harlow is an American showgirl in London in 1914 who is in love with inventor Franchot Tone. Because of him she finds herself involved with German spies and famous French flying ace Cary Grant.

Gladys Benton / LIBELED LADY, 1936, MGM, d-Jack Conway.
Harlow is the tough blonde fiancée of newspaper editor Spencer Tracy who has printed a libelous attack on society girl Myrna Loy and is now trying to sully the latter's reputation so she will lose her libel suit against him. Tracy's weapon is William Powell, whom he convinces Harlow to marry. The plan is then to have Powell get Loy to fall in love with him. When this is accomplished, Harlow can sue Loy for alienation of affection. Loy's suit against Tracy will be thrown out of court because he will have been proven correct when he branded her a home-wrecker. Powell and Harlow will then divorce and Tracy will marry Harlow. Somehow it works out just that way.

OTHER ROLES

1929: *Hazel* / THE SATURDAY NIGHT KID. **1931:** *Anne Courtland* / THE SECRET SIX; *Rose Mason* / THE IRON MAN; *Goldie* / GOLDIE. **1932:** *Cassie Barnes* / THREE WISE GIRLS; *Daisy* / THE BEAST OF THE CITY. **1933:** *Ruby Adams* / HOLD YOUR MAN. **1934:** *Eadie* / THE GIRL FROM MISSOURI. **1935:** *Mona Leslie* / RECKLESS. **1936:** *Hattie Miller* / RIFFRAFF; *Whitey Wilson* / WIFE VS. SECRETARY. **1937:** *Crystal Wetherby* / PERSONAL PROPERTY; *Carol Layton* / SARATOGA.

HARRIS, JULIE

(1925–)
Trained at the Yale Drama School and the Actor's Studio, Julie Harris made her screen debut at age 17, repeating her stage role as the 12-year-old Frankie in THE MEMBER OF THE WEDDING. Her work rated an Oscar nomination. She has made only sporadic appearances in films since, while her work on the stage has won her five Tony Awards. Slim and fragile-looking with a croaky voice, Harris's movie roles usually have been neurotic, anguished women. Her made-for-TV movies include THE HOUSE ON GREENAPPLE ROAD (1969), HOME FOR THE HOLIDAYS (1972), and BACKSTAIRS AT THE WHITE HOUSE (1979).

KEY ROLES

Frankie Addams / THE MEMBER OF THE WEDDING, 1952, Columbia, d-Fred Zinnemann.
Scrawny Julie Harris, who was 26, plays 12-year-old Frankie, who learns something about life in a small Georgia town one summer when her sister gets married and her little friend (Brandon De Wilde) dies.

Abra / EAST OF EDEN, 1955, Warners, d-Elia Kazan.
Harris is Dick Davalos's girl in California in 1917, but she is strangely attracted to his "bad" brother (James Dean). It's John Steinbeck's story of Cain and Abel.

Sally Bowles / I AM A CAMERA, 1955, Great Britain, Romulus, d-Henry Cornelius.
Harris plays an amoral and reckless young English girl who has a platonic relationship with a young British writer in Berlin in the early 1930s.

Grace Miller / REQUIEM FOR A HEAVYWEIGHT, 1962, Columbia, d-Ralph Nelson.
When heavyweight boxer Anthony Quinn is told he must never fight again or risk being killed, he tries to find something else he can do. Harris is a counselor who helps him.

Eleanor Vance / THE HAUNTING, 1963, Great Britain, MGM, d-Robert Wise.
Harris is one of two mediums who join Richard Johnson and Russ Tamblyn in spending a weekend in a haunted Boston mansion. She and Claire Bloom may have a lesbian interest in each other.

Alison Langdon / REFLECTIONS IN A GOLDEN EYE, 1967, Warners, d-John Huston.
In this Carson McCullers story, Harris plays a neurotic invalid who cuts off her nipples with garden shears. But as everyone in this movie is repressed and sexually mixed-up, her actions seem only moderately unusual.

OTHER ROLES

1958: *Helen Cooper* / THE TRUTH OUT WOMEN. **1960:** *Sally Hamil* / SALLY'S IRISH ROGUE. **1966:** *Betty Fraley* / HARPER; *Miss Thing* / YOU'RE A BIG BOY NOW. **1968:** *Gladys* / THE SPLIT. **1970:** *Gerri Mason* / THE PEOPLE NEXT DOOR. **1975:** *Betsie* / THE HIDING PLACE. **1976:** *Alice Feinchild* / VOYAGE OF THE DAMNED. **1979:** *Mrs. Greenwood* / THE BELL JAR.

HARRIS, RICHARD

(1932–)
Richard Harris's year of birth in Ireland has been given as early as 1930 and as late as 1932. His earliest successes were as macho, swaggering men with some hidden inner sensitivity as in his first major success in THIS SPORTING LIFE, for which he received an Academy Award nomination. He found parts in British "New Wave" movies and then went on to all-star productions. He has had some unexpected success as a singer, selling over five million copies of the song "MacArthur Park." Although some of his later performances, notably in A MAN CALLED HORSE, were inter-

esting, one must conclude that Harris has not lived up to his early promise, despite his insistence, "You can sum up my life and my acting in one sentence: I play all the strings in the bow, because I want to find out how many strings there are...."

KEY ROLES

John Mills / MUTINY ON THE BOUNTY, 1962, MGM / Arcola, d-Lewis Milestone.

Harris is one of the able-bodied seamen who put the idea of mutiny in the mind of Fletcher Christian (Marlon Brando).

Frank Machin / THIS SPORTING LIFE, 1963, Great Britain, Rank, d-Lindsay Anderson.

In probably his best role, Harris is a tough miner who becomes a successful rugby player. He was nominated for an Oscar for his performance as the sensitive workingman who finds himself between classes—a celebrity as a sports star, but only a piece of meat to the owners. His inner crudeness also prevents him from winning the love of widow Rachel Roberts.

Rafer Hoxworth / HAWAII, 1966, United Artists, d-George Roy Hill.

This New England sea captain takes it for granted that Julie Andrews will wait for him. He's more than a little annoyed when he discovers that she has wed dour, self-righteous missionary Max Von Sydow who has taken her with him to Hawaii. Harris keeps showing up over the years, hoping to get her back and show her what she passed up.

King Arthur / CAMELOT, 1967, Warners, d-Joshua Logan.

While not on a par with Richard Burton as the founder of the code of chivalry and the Knights of the Round Table, Harris has made a fine living portraying Arthur in this movie and on the stage. His singing is appropriate to the part.

James McParlan / THE MOLLY MAGUIRES, 1970, Paramount, d-Martin Ritt.

Harris is a plant, forced by the authorities and the company to infiltrate the miners in 1870 Pennsylvania to expose the leaders of an Irish secret society trying to improve the workers' lot through the use of violence.

John Morgan / A MAN CALLED HORSE, 1970, Cinema Center, d-Elliot Silverstein.

In 1825, English aristocrat Harris is captured by Indians, is treated like an animal, proves his ability to endure pain, and eventually becomes their leader.

Oliver Cromwell / CROMWELL, 1970, Great Britain, Columbia, d-Ken Hughes.

This is a rather dull biopic and Harris plays the English leader as a fairly boring person. Perhaps he was, but it doesn't make for interesting cinema or history.

Parker / TARZAN, THE APE MAN, 1981, MGM, d-John Derek.

Harris has the honor of playing Bo Derek's father in the newest and least interesting filming of an adventure of Edgar Rice Burroughs's hero.

OTHER ROLES

1958: *lover* / ALIVE AND KICKING. **1959:** *Terence O'Brien* / SHAKE HANDS WITH THE DEVIL; *Higgins* / THE WRECK OF THE MARY DEARE. **1960:** *Sean Reilly* / A TERRIBLE BEAUTY. **1961:** *Corporal Johnstone* / THE LONG AND THE SHORT AND THE TALL; *Barnsby* / THE GUNS OF NAVARONE. **1964:** *Corrado Zeller* / RED DESERT; *Robert* / I TRE VOLTI. **1965:** *Capt. Benjamin Tyreen* / MAJOR DUNDEE; *Knut Straud* / THE HEROES OF TELEMARK. **1966:** *Cain* / THE BIBLE; *Christopher White* / CAPRICE. **1970:** *Eitan* / BLOOMFIELD, (THE HERO). **1971:** *Zachary Bass* / MAN IN THE WILDERNESS. **1973:** *Kilpatrick* / THE DEADLY TRACKERS. **1974:** *Harry Crown* / 99 and 44/100% DEAD; *Fallon* / JUGGERNAUT. **1975:** *Richard I* / ROBIN AND MARIAN. **1976:** *John Morgan* / THE RETURN OF A MAN CALLED HORSE; *Eugene Striden* / ECHOES OF A SUMMER. **1977:** *Dr. Jonathan Chamberlain* / THE CASSANDRA CROSSING; *Captain Nolan* / ORCA—KILLER WHALE; *John Carter* / GOLDEN RENDEZVOUS. **1978:** *Rafer Janders* / THE WILD GEESE. **1979:** *Falk* / RAVAGERS; *Danny Travis* / THE LAST WORD. **1981:** *Gulliver* / GULLIVER'S TRAVELS. **1982:** *John Morgan* / TRIUMPHS OF A MAN CALLED HORSE. **1984:** *Martin Steckert* / MARTIN'S DAY.

HARRISON, REX

(Sir Reginald Carey, 1908–)

Rex Harrison's film career prior to World War II was rather ordinary and he usually found himself in the shadows of his leading ladies. Thereafter he established himself on the stage both in London and in New York. His film roles in the 1940s were those of suave, urbane, sophisticated Englishmen. In 1963 he was nominated for an Oscar for being the best thing in the overblown epic, CLEOPATRA. In 1964 he won a highly deserved Oscar for his recreation of his Broadway role as Prof. Henry Higgins in MY FAIR LADY. From then on his film career has been mainly disappointing as he has accepted well-paying roles that have not made much of his special talents. Harrison remembers all his roles fondly or so he says: "I have never regretted the choice of any parts I have done. Because you get involved in the part, you grow to love the character, and you can never regret something you love."

KEY ROLES

Frank Burden / STORM IN A TEACUP, 1937, Great Britain, London Films / United Artists, d-Victor Saville.

Harrison is a reporter, newly arrived in a small Scottish town, where the provost (Cecil Parker) orders a dog destroyed because its owner cannot pay the license fee. Harrison makes the case a national scandal, ruining Parker's chances of becoming a candidate for Parliament. Parker sues Harrison, but the former's daughter (Vivien Leigh), who has come to love Harrison, perjures herself to save him.

Doctor Lawford / THE CITADEL, 1938, Great Britain, MGM British, d-King Vidor.

Harrison plays one of Robert Donat's classmates at medical school in this story of how Donat, an idealistic young man, fights slum conditions in a Welsh mining community, only to leave it later to join Harrison in a lucrative London society practice. The death of another friend, though, sends him back to those who really need him.

Gus Bennett / NIGHT TRAIN TO MUNICH, 1940, Great Britain, 20th Century Productions / MGM, d-Carol Reed.

In this humorous thriller, Harrison is tricked by Nazi agent Paul Henreid who is after Margaret Lockwood's scientist father and his invention. But Harrison gains control of the situation, kills Henreid, flees with Lockwood and her father on a night train to Munich, then goes on to Switzerland by way of a funicular railway across a chasm.

Adolphus Cusins / MAJOR BARBARA, 1940, Great Britain, Pascal / General Films, d-Gabriel Pascal.

Harrison is a young professor who joins the Salvation Army to be near Wendy Hiller, and is soon engaged to the army's prettiest officer. When he meets her father, munitions manufacturer Robert Morley, the elder man's philosophy almost cripples the romance. But Harrison is eventually chosen to be Morley's successor and Hiller sees it as a chance to save more souls.

Charles Condomine / BLITHE SPIRIT, 1945, Great Britain, Two Cities / Cineguild, d-David Lean.
Harrison is superb in this delightful Noel Coward comedy about a married writer who finds that the spirit of his dead first wife has materialized after a seance and he can't get rid of it. Shortly thereafter, his second wife is also killed and stays around to participate in the haunting. It takes all of Margaret Rutherford's considerable skills to send the ladies on their way, but Harrison is soon to join them for eternity.

Vivian Kenway / THE RAKE'S PROGRESS, 1946, Great Britain, Eagle-Lion, d-Sidney Gilliat.
Harrison is a cad who, after having been sent down from Oxford, is found a position on a coffee plantation by his father. There he seduces the wife of his best friend, marries Lilli Palmer for her money, swindles her, drives her to attempt suicide because of his affair with his father's secretary, and then goes to an unheroic death in war.

King Mongkut / ANNA AND THE KING OF SIAM, 1946, 20th Century-Fox, d-John Cromwell.
Harrison portrays the King of Siam, a man who is trying to build bridges between his backward country and the modern world. He is assisted by an English governess brought to Bangkok to educate his many children. Harrison's portrayal pales next to that of Yul Brynner.

Ghost of Capt. Daniel Griggs / THE GHOST AND MRS. MUIR, 1947, 20th Century-Fox, d-Joseph L. Mankiewicz.
In this charming, sentimental fable, Harrison is the ghost of a sea captain who built the home now occupied by widow Gene Tierney and her children. It's delightful whimsy in which Harrison and Tierney fall in love. A touching scene at the end is when an elderly Tierney passes away and her ghost lover says, "And now you will never be tired again. Come, Lucia. Come, my dear." Then a young and beautiful Tierney rises from the corpse and follows Harrison to a new afterlife.

Stephen Fox / THE FOXES OF HARROW, 1947, 20th Century-Fox, d-John M. Stahl.
Harrison took over the role of a philanderer in the New Orleans of 1820 when Tyrone Power refused it. The film is a flat adaptation of Frank Yerby's steamy novel and Harrison's acting doesn't help matters much.

John / THE FOUR POSTER, 1952, Columbia, d-Irving Reis.
Harrison and his current real-life wife (Lilli Palmer) make this history of a marriage, told through a series of bedroom scenes, tolerable entertainment.

Julius Caesar / CLEOPATRA, 1963, 20th Century-Fox, d-Joseph L. Mankiewicz and others.
Of the various actors who have portrayed Julius Caesar—Warren William, Claude Rains, Louis Calhern, John Gielgud, etc.—Harrison is the one who seems to have it right. But his performance isn't enough to save the picture from being a monumental bore, especially as he is assassinated before the intermission.

Prof. Henry Higgins / MY FAIR LADY, 1964, CBS / Warners, d-George Cukor.
Harrison made the role of the elocution expert his on the stage and so his magnificent performance in the film was expected. He takes a dirty cockney flower girl (Audrey Hepburn) and teaches her to speak properly and pass as a lady. When she carries it off beautifully, he takes all the credit and, as usual, ignores her part in the triumph. That there will be no change in his attitude, he makes perfectly clear to the girl, promising, "If you come back to me, I shall treat you just as I have always treated you. I can't change my nature, and I don't intend to change my manners."

Pope Julius II / THE AGONY AND THE ECSTASY, 1965, 20th Century-Fox, d-Carol Reed.
This is just another of those cases in which Harrison rises above the limitations of the material and becomes the best thing in an otherwise boring film. He is the pope who commissions Michelangelo (Charlton Heston) to paint the ceiling of the Sistine Chapel, and proves to be a large pain for the artist.

Cecil Fox / THE HONEY POT, 1966, United Artists, d-Joseph L. Mankiewicz.
Harrison is a millionaire who pretends to be dying in order to trick three of his former mistresses (Susan Hayward, Maggie Smith, and Capucine) out of their money.

Dr. John Dolittle / DOCTOR DOLITTLE, 1967, 20th Century-Fox, d-Richard Fleischer.
This film, in which Harrison portrays a veterinarian who learns to talk to his patients, is among the biggest box-office failures of all time, despite having the Academy Award-winning song "Talk to the Animals" by Leslie Bricusse.

OTHER ROLES

1930: *George* / THE GREAT GAME; *bit* / THE SCHOOL FOR SCANDAL. **1934:** *Aubrey Bellingham* / ALL AT SEA; *Tom Jakes* / GET YOUR MAN. **1935:** *Ronnie* / LEAVE IT TO BLANCHE. **1936:** *Tommy Stapleton* / MEN ARE NOT GODS. **1937:** *Leonard Drummond* / SCHOOL FOR HUSBANDS. **1939:** *Dr. Freddie Jarvis* / OVER THE MOON; *Jacques Sauvin* / THE SILENT BATTLE; *Bob Stevens* / TEN DAYS IN PARIS. **1940:** *Harley Prentiss* / ST. MARTIN'S LANE, (SIDEWALKS OF LONDON). **1941:** *Bob Stevens* / MISSING TEN DAYS. **1945:** *Maj. David Bruce* / I LIVE IN GROSVENOR SQUARE; *guest* / JOURNEY TOGETHER. **1948:** *Sir Alfred de Carter* / UNFAITHFULLY YOURS; *Matt Denant* / ESCAPE. **1951:** *Arthur Groome* / THE LONG DARK HALL. **1953:** *guest* / MAIN STREET TO BROADWAY. **1954:** *Saladin* / KING RICHARD AND THE CRUSADERS. **1955:** *Charles Hathaway* / THE CONSTANT HUSBAND. **1958:** *Jimmy Broadbent* / THE RELUCTANT DEBUTANTE. **1960:** *Tony Preston* / MIDNIGHT LACE. **1962:** *Jimmy Bourne* / THE HAPPY THIEVES. **1964:** *Marquess of Frinton* / THE YELLOW ROLLS-ROYCE. **1968:** *Victor Chanebusse* / A FLEA IN HER EAR. **1969:** *Charles Dyer* / STAIRCASE. **1975:** *narrator* / THE GENTLEMAN TRAMP. **1977:** *Duke of Norfolk* / THE PRINCE AND THE PAUPER, (CROSSED SWORDS); *Colbert* / THE FIFTH MUSKETEER. **1978:** *Brian Walker* / ASHANTI; *Van Osten* / A TIME TO DIE; *Shalimar* / SHALIMAR.

HARVEY, LAURENCE

(Larushka M. Skikne, 1928–1973)
As a child, Laurence Harvey and his Jewish parents emigrated from Lithuania to South Africa, where at 14 he lied about his age and joined the navy, but was found out and sent home. He made his stage debut in 1947 and debuted in films the next year. Nothing much happened with his career until 1959 when he

appeared in ROOM AT THE TOP, for which he received a Best Actor Academy Award nomination. However, his best performance came three years later when he portrayed a brainwashed ex-POW in THE MANCHURIAN CANDIDATE. The unusual actor who said, "Some of my best moments are spent with me," died of cancer at 45.

KEY ROLES

Romeo Montague / ROMEO AND JULIET, 1954, Great Britain, Rank, d-Renato Castellani.

The film looks better than it plays and Harvey isn't any more poorly cast than others. If that's not faint praise, we don't know what is.

Sir Kenneth / KING RICHARD AND THE CRUSADERS, 1954, Warners, d-David Butler.

In this unintentionally campy tale of the dreaded Saladin, Richard the Lion-Hearted, and assorted other crusaders, Harvey passes for the young romantic lead. He must have felt that shouting was the way to show emotion—either that or he had discovered that Rex Harrison and George Sanders were deaf.

Joe Lampton / ROOM AT THE TOP, 1959, Great Britain, Remus, d-Jack Clayton.

Harvey is an ambitious, young clerk who gets the daughter of a rich man pregnant so he can marry her, and causes the death of his real love, Simone Signoret.

Johnny Jackson / EXPRESSO BONGO, 1959, Great Britain, British-Lion, d-Val Guest.

Harvey is an aspiring talent agent who spots teenage singer Cliff Richard in a coffeehouse and promotes him into an international star. He loses his hold on Richard when it is revealed that he is exploiting the lad and that his contract is invalid.

Col. William Travis / THE ALAMO, 1960, United Artists / Wayne, d-John Wayne.

Despite Wayne's direction and the apparent contest between the Duke, Harvey, and Richard Widmark to see who can do the worst job of acting, this action picture is passably exciting when, late in the movie, it finally gets around to some action.

Weston Liggett / BUTTERFIELD 8, 1960, MGM, d-Daniel Mann.

Harvey's involvement with call girl Elizabeth Taylor leads to tragedy for both of them. When Taylor is killed, he grieves to his wife (Dina Merrill): "I don't suppose anybody would think that she was a good person. Strangely enough, she was. On the surface, she was all sex and devil-may-care, yet everything in her was struggling toward respectability. She never gave up trying."

Raymond Shaw / THE MANCHURIAN CANDIDATE, 1962, United Artists, d-John Frankenheimer.

Harvey is a Korean War "hero" who comes home after being released by the North Koreans. He's a walking time bomb who has been brainwashed to carry out the will of a contact who will reveal herself to him with a deck of cards. She turns out to be his mother (Angela Lansbury) and the target for assassination is a presidential candidate.

Wilhelm Grimm / THE WONDERFUL WORLD OF THE BROTHERS GRIMM, 1962, MGM, d-Henry Levin.

Harvey and Karl Boehm portray the German fairy tale writers, and three of their stories—"The Dancing Princess," "The Cobbler and the Elves," and "The Singing Bone"—are dramatized in detail.

Miles Brand / DARLING, 1965, Great Britain, Anglo-Amalgamated, d-John Schlesinger.

Harvey is a wealthy company director who lures Julie Christie from her journalist lover (Dirk Bogarde) and exposes her to some of the more lurid sides of international society.

OTHER ROLES

1948: *Francis Merivale* / HOUSE OF DARKNESS; *Sergeant Lawson* / MAN ON THE RUN; *bit* / THE DANCING YEARS. **1949:** *John Matthews* / THE MAN FROM YESTERDAY; *Lieutenant Mourad* / CAIRO ROAD. **1950:** *Freddie* / THE SCARLET THREAD; *P / O Hooper* / LANDFALL; *Edmond* / THE BLACK ROSE. **1951:** *Mag Maguire* / THERE IS ANOTHER SUN; *Ned* / A KILLER WALKS. **1952:** *Jordie* / I BELIEVE IN YOU; *Jerry Nolan* / WOMAN OF TWILIGHT. **1953:** *François* / INNOCENTS IN PARIS. **1955:** *Miles Ravenscourt* / THE GOOD DIE YOUNG; *Christopher Isherwood* / I AM A CAMERA. **1956:** *John Durrance* / STORM OVER THE NILE. **1957:** *George* / THREE MEN IN A BOAT; *Walter de Frece* / AFTER THE BALL. **1958:** *Humphrey Tavistock* / THE TRUTH ABOUT WOMEN; *Lt. Lionel Crabb* / THE SILENT ENEMY; *narrator* / POWER AMONG MEN. **1961:** *Private Bamforth* / THE LONG AND THE SHORT AND THE TALL; *Paul Lathrope* / TWO LOVES; *John Buchanan* / SUMMER AND SMOKE. **1962:** *Dove Linkhorn* / A WALK ON THE WILD SIDE. **1963:** *Ivan Kalin* / A GIRL NAMED TAMIKO; *Rex Black* / THE RUNNING MAN. **1964:** *Sean McKenna* / THE CEREMONY; *Philip Carey* / OF HUMAN BONDAGE; *the husband* / THE OUTRAGE. **1965:** *Joe Lampton* / LIFE AT THE TOP. **1966:** *Dr. Francis Trevellyan* / THE SPY WITH A COLD NOSE. **1967:** *Alexander Eberlin* / A DANDY IN ASPIC. **1968:** *King Leontes* / THE WINTER'S TALE; *Cethegus* / KAMPF UM ROM, (FIGHT FOR ROME). **1969:** *Cethegus* / KAMPF UM ROM II. **1970:** *Hamlet* / THE MAGIC CHRISTIAN. **1971:** *Farley* / WUSA. **1972:** *Major Kirsanov* / ESCAPE TO THE SUN. **1973:** *John Wheeler* / NIGHT WATCH. **1975:** *cameo* / F FOR FAKE.

HAVER, JUNE

(June Stovenour, 1926–)

June Haver was groomed by MGM to succeed Betty Grable (she was referred to as "the pocket Grable"), but she never quite achieved the success of World War II's number one pinup. In 1953 she retired from films and entered a convent to become a nun. Illness forced her to leave a year later and, although she had planned to return to the convent when she recovered, she instead met Fred MacMurray, whose wife had just died after a long illness, and soon thereafter they were married. Haver never returned to films.

KEY ROLES

Rosie Dolly / THE DOLLY SISTERS, 1945, 20th Century-Fox, d-Irving Cummings.

When Alice Faye couldn't be persuaded to come out of retirement to team with Betty Grable as the Hungarian sisters, an act popular in vaudeville in the early part of the century, Darryl F. Zanuck brought in Haver who was being groomed to fill Grable's tights just as Grable had once stood by to take over for Faye. Haver's off-the-stage role in the movie isn't as large as Grable, and she has far fewer problems with her love life.

Katie / I WONDER WHO'S KISSING HER NOW, 1947, 20th Century-Fox, d-Lloyd Bacon.

In this fairly typical, fictionalized account of a songwriter, Haver is the girl composer Joe Howard is wondering about when he writes the title song. Seems they had a falling out, but he can't get her out of his mind. Other songs and musical numbers featuring Haver include "What's the Use of Dreaming?" "Hello, Ma Baby," and "Goodbye My Lady Love."

Marilyn Miller / LOOK FOR THE SILVER LINING, 1949, Warners, d-David Butler.

Haver isn't outstanding as Broadway star Marilyn Miller. In fact, she is constantly upstaged by Ray Bolger. Still, she gives it her best shot and looks sweet singing the title song by Buddy De Silva and Jerome Kern, and "Sunny" by Kern, Yip Harbach, and Oscar Hammerstein II.

Doris Fisher / OH, YOU BEAUTIFUL DOLL, 1949, 20th Century-Fox, d-John M. Stahl.

Haver portrays the daughter of composer Fred Fisher, lovingly played by S. Z. Sakall. He wants to write operas but a song plugger recognizes the potential of his melodies and adds lyrics. The songs performed by Haver and Mark Stevens (voice dubbed by Bill Shirley) include "There's a Broken Heart for Every Light on Broadway," "Peg O' My Heart," "Chicago," and "Come Josephine in My Flying Machine." Lyrics for the first tune were written by Howard Johnson; Alfred Bryan supplied them for the others.

Patricia O'Grady / THE DAUGHTER OF ROSIE O'GRADY, 1950, 20th Century-Fox, d-David Butler.

Heroine Haver falls in love with none other than showman Tony Pastor, a match not approved of by her alcoholic father. Besides the title song by Monty C. Brice and Walter Donaldson, the musical numbers include "Ma Blushin' Rosie" by Edgar Smith and John Stromberg, and "As We Are Today" by Ernesto Lecuona and Charles Tobias.

OTHER ROLES

1943: *Maybelle* / THE GANG'S ALL HERE. **1944:** *Cri-Cri* / HOME IN INDIANA; *Mary "Irish" O'Brien* / IRISH EYES ARE SMILING. **1945:** *Lucilla* / WHERE DO WE GO FROM HERE? **1946:** *Pam* / THREE LITTLE GIRLS IN BLUE; *Jenny* / WAKE UP AND DREAM. **1948:** *Rad McGill* / SCUDDA HOO! SCUDDA HAY! **1950:** *Liza Martin* / I'LL GET BY. **1951:** *Connie Scott* / LOVE NEST. **1953:** *Jeannie* / THE GIRL NEXT DOOR.

HAWN, GOLDIE

(1945–)

Rowan and Martin's bubble-headed, doll-faced, lovable scatterbrain, Goldie Hawn has proven that she's no dummy, winning a Best Supporting Actress Academy Award for her second film, CACTUS FLOWER. She was also nominated for an Oscar for PRIVATE BENJAMIN, which she produced herself. She's a charmer and has come a long way as a comedienne from her times as a great "kook." Daughter of a musician, Hawn took ballet and tap-dancing lessons as a child and, while studying drama at American University, she supported herself by running a dance school. She did some repertory work and made a brief appearance in THE ONE AND ONLY, GENUINE, ORIGINAL FAMILY BAND before bursting onto the national scene as the gyrating go-go dancer who usually blew her lines in a most delightful way on "Laugh-In."

KEY ROLES

Toni Simmons / CACTUS FLOWER, 1969, Columbia, d-Gene Saks.

To deceive his mistress (Hawn), dentist Walter Matthau talks his receptionist (Ingrid Bergman) into posing as his wife. Just about the time Matthau discovers Hawn making do with someone her own age, he decides to make his arrangement with Bergman permanent.

Jill / SHAMPOO, 1975, Columbia, d-Hal Ashby.

Hawn appears as the most vulnerable of the many women hairdresser Warren Beatty beds and bores in this not–altogether-likable sex comedy.

Amanda "Duchess" Quaid / THE DUCHESS AND THE DIRTWATER FOX, 1976, 20th Century-Fox, d-Melvin Frank.

In this western spoof, Hawn is a saloon singer who joins up with Barbary Coast con man George Segal in some rough adventures involving a band of outlaws, a group of traveling Mormons, and a Jewish wedding.

Judy Benjamin / PRIVATE BENJAMIN, 1980, Warners, d-Howard Zieff.

When her husband dies while making love to her on their wedding night, Hawn is at her wit's end and impulsively joins the army, for which her Jewish princess upbringing seems particularly unsuited. But, with the help of Eileen Brennan as a gung-ho officer, she learns.

Glenda / SEEMS LIKE OLD TIMES, 1980, Columbia, d-Jay Sandrich.

When her ex-husband (Chevy Chase) innocently gets involved in a bank robbery, he seeks help from Hawn, a lawyer now married to the district attorney. The farce has a number of good moments but is not as funny as it should have been.

Kay Walsh / SWING SHIFT, 1984, Warners, d-Jonathan Demme.

This is a nostalgic look at a World War II defense plant where Hawn works while her husband (Ed Harris) is in the service. She has an affair with fellow worker Kurt Russell and then must decide with whom she wishes to stay.

OTHER ROLES

1968: *giggly girl* / THE ONE AND ONLY, GENUINE, ORIGINAL FAMILY BAND. **1970:** *Marion* / THERE'S A GIRL IN MY SOUP. **1971:** *Dawn Divine* / $ (DOLLARS). **1972:** *Jill* / BUTTERFLIES ARE FREE. **1974:** *Lou Jean Poplin* / THE SUGARLAND EXPRESS; *Oktyabrina* / THE GIRL FROM PETROVKA. **1978:** *Gloria Mundy* / FOUL PLAY. **1980:** *Anita* / LOVERS AND LIARS. **1982:** *Paula McCullen* / BEST FRIENDS. **1984:** *Sunny* / PROTOCOL. **1985:** *Molly* / WILDCATS. **1987:** *Joanna Stayton / Anne* / OVERBOARD.

HAY, WILL

(1888–1949)

This British music-hall comedian made several wonderfully hilarious movies in the 1930s and 1940s, usually portraying shifty and often disreputable figures of tatty authority. Few Americans have had the special pleasure of seeing this master at work, and some may believe that this is because his brand of humor cannot be appreciated in the colonies. But in this ever smaller world, we can use all the laughs we can get and Hay, with the help of Graham Moffatt, Moore Marriott, and other peculiarly British comedians, has provided more than his share.

KEY ROLES

Dr. Benjamin Twist / GOOD MORNING, BOYS, 1937, Great Britain, Gainsborough, d-Marcel Varnel.

In this film, known as WHERE THERE'S A WILL in the United States, Hay portrays the headmaster at St. Michael's boys' school. Hay almost loses his position but his boys become involved in a theft of the Mona Lisa while on a trip to Paris and save his job for him. It's a very slick comedy.

William Porter / OH, MR. PORTER! 1937, Great Britain, Gainsborough, d-Marcel Varnel.

This story is about an incompetent railroad worker (Hay) who is made stationmaster at a run-down halt and, with the "help" of Moore Marriott and Graham Moffatt, deals with gun runners. If you are in the right frame of mind and tolerant of what has occurred over the years in movie comedy, you may just find this to be one of the funniest movies ever filmed.

Prof. Benjamin Tibbetts / OLD BONES OF THE RIVER, 1938, Great Britain, Gainsborough, d-Marcel Varnel.

Hay goes up the river in Africa to open a school for the natives. He is given the assignment of collecting the taxes as well and, with the help of Graham Moffatt and Moore Marriott, stirs up a full-scale revolt, barely escaping with his life. It's a spoof of SANDERS OF THE RIVER.

William Lamb / THE GHOST OF ST. MICHAEL'S, 1941, Great Britain, Ealing, d-Marcel Varnel.

Hay is a new master at St. Michael's and the butt of the boys' jokes. With the advent of World War II, the school is moved to a gloomy old castle where phantom pipes play when anyone is about to die. These pipes prophesy the deaths of two headmasters, but Hay and his friend Claude Hulbert discover that the murderer is the matron who signals to German subs.

William Fitch / MY LEARNED FRIEND, 1944, Great Britain, Ealing, d-Will Hay.

When Mervyn Jones is released from prison, he goes about the task of killing anyone responsible for his conviction. Last on his list is Hay, his incompetent barrister. It's a crazy farce with a chase across the face of Big Ben where Jones dies trying to kill Hay and his friend Claude Hulbert.

OTHER ROLES

1934: *Magistrate Brutus Poskett* / THOSE WERE THE DAYS; *Vicar Rev. Richard Jed* / DANDY DICK. **1935:** *William Garland* / RADIO PARADE OF 1935; *Dr. Alec Smart* / BOYS WILL BE BOYS. **1936:** *Benjamin Stubbins* / WHERE THERE'S A WILL; *Ben Cutlet* / WINDBAG THE SAILOR. **1938:** *Dr. Benjamin Twist* / CONVICT 99; *Benjamin Twist* / HEY! HEY! U.S.A. **1939:** *Sergeant Dudfoot* / ASK A POLICEMAN; *Captain Viking* / WHERE'S THAT FIRE? **1941:** *Professor Davis* / THE BLACK SHEEP OF WHITEHALL. **1942:** *skipper* / THE BIG BLOCKADE; *William Potts* / THE GOOSE STEPS OUT.

HAYDEN, STERLING

(Christian Walter, 1916–1986)

A solid, weathered-looking actor, Sterling Hayden was too busy being his own man to become a top star, but now and then he gave indications of how much talent he really had. Unfortunately, there were appearances that made one wonder if he could act at all, as he delivered lines as if he were reading them—and not that well. But who can forget his portrayal of the hooligan in THE ASPHALT JUNGLE or his mad air force colonel in DR. STRANGELOVE? This strong, silent actor, who was best playing semi-corrupt characters, appeared in numerous made-for-TV movies including A SOUND OF DIFFERENT DRUMMERS (1957), THE LONG MARCH (1958), and CAROL FOR ANOTHER CHRISTMAS (1964). His foreign language films are COBRA / LE SAUT DE L'ANGE (1971), LE GRAND DEPART (1972), CRY ONION (1975), and LEUCHTTURM DES CHAOS (1983). Hayden was a sailor who paid the bills by, now and then, making a movie.

KEY ROLES

Dix Handley / THE ASPHALT JUNGLE, 1950, MGM, d-John Huston.

Hayden has strong arms and a weak brain as a small-time crook whom criminal-mastermind Sam Jaffe needs in his plans for one last big robbery. Hayden is a hard man to kill when everything goes wrong with the caper, and he bleeds to death while trying to escape with his gal Jean Hagen.

Pervis DeJong / SO BIG, 1953, Warners, d-Robert Wise.

In this remake of the Pulitzer Prize-winning novel by Edna Ferber, Hayden is schoolteacher Jane Wyman's poor and backward-farmer husband. He dies from the strain of hard work, reducing his wife and son "So-Big" to abject poverty.

Johnny Guitar / JOHNNY GUITAR, 1954, Republic, d-Nicholas Ray.

Hayden is a loner who moseys into a gambling saloon managed by Joan Crawford in the wilds of Arizona. Crawford has built her place on a site where a railroad will soon be coming through, and her plans have earned her the hatred of Ward Bond and Mercedes McCambridge. Hayden goes gunless because he tends to be trigger-happy and he'd rather not kill anyone. He falls in love with Crawford, and the two are able to survive and overcome their enemies' desires to kill them.

Tod Shaw / SUDDENLY, 1954, United Artists, d-Lewis Allen.

In this minor suspense movie, Hayden is the sheriff in a sleepy California town through which the U.S. president is to pass. As the president is a target for hired killer Frank Sinatra, Hayden must prevent the assassination.

Johnny Clay / THE KILLING, 1956, United Artists, d-Stanley Kubrick.

In this first-class thriller, Hayden is an ex-con who organizes a $2 million racetrack heist. The events of the day are shown from the viewpoints of various characters.

Gen. Jack D. Ripper / DR. STRANGELOVE, 1963, Great Britain, Columbia, d-Stanley Kubrick.

Convinced that the Russians are draining America's vitality by adding chemicals to U.S. water, air force general Hayden launches a nuclear attack on the U.S.S.R. Attempts to recall the bombers fail and a doomsday machine is activated.

Police Captain McCluskey / THE GODFATHER, 1972, Paramount, d-Francis Ford Coppola.

Hayden is a corrupt police captain who conspires with other mobsters to kill the Godfather (Marlon Brando). They wound him but do not successfully put him away. Al Pacino is used as the instrument of revenge, blowing away both Hayden and his gangster boss.

OTHER ROLES

1941: *Norman Williams* / VIRGINIA; *Adrian* / BAHAMA PASSAGE. **1947:** *himself* / VARIETY GIRL; *Tad McDonald* / BLAZE OF NOON. **1949:** *Bert Donner* / EL PASO; *Joe Cooper* / MANHANDLED. **1951:** *John Burrows* / JOURNEY INTO LIGHT; *Tex McCloud* / FLAMING FEATHER. **1952:** *McCabe* / THE DENVER AND RIO GRANDE; *Kit Gerardo* / THE GOLDEN HAWK; *Dan Collier* / FLAT TOP; *Jim Johannson* / THE STAR. **1953:** *Will Hall* / TAKE ME TO TOWN; *John Nelson* / KANSAS PACIFIC; *Steve* / FIGHTER ATTACK. **1954:** *Detective Sergeant Sims* / CRIME WAVE; *Bart Laish* / ARROW IN THE DUST; *Sir Gawain* / PRINCE VALIANT; *Joseph Conroy* / NAKED

ALIBI. **1955:** *Tim Chipman* / TIMBERJACK; *Adm. John M. Hoskins* / THE ETERNAL SEA; *Clay* / SHOTGUN; *Capt. Russ Edwards* / BATTLE TAXI; *Jim Bowie* / THE LAST COMMAND; *Rick Martin* / TOP GUN. **1956:** *Dane Arnold* / THE COME-ON. **1957:** *John Emmett* / FIVE STEPS TO DANGER; *Bill Doyle* / CRIME OF PASSION; *Sheriff Galt* / THE IRON SHERIFF; *John Garth* / VALERIE; *Treleaven* / ZERO HOUR; *Turner* / GUN BATTLE AT MONTEREY. **1958:** *George Hansen* / TERROR IN A TEXAS TOWN; *Scotty* / TEN DAYS TO TULARA. **1969:** *Michael Carlson* / HARD CONTRACT. **1970:** *Lepridon* / LOVING. **1973:** *Roger Wade* / THE LONG GOODBYE; *Maj. Wrongway Lindbergh* / THE FINAL PROGRAMME. **1974:** *Malcolm Robarts* / DEADLY STRANGERS. **1976:** *Leo Dalco* / 1900. **1978:** *King Zharko Stepanowicz* / KING OF THE GYPSIES. **1979:** *grandfather* / THE OUTSIDER; *Z. K. Dawson* / WINTER KILLS. **1980:** *Tinsworthy* / 9 TO 5. **1981:** *Duke Stuyvesant* / GAS. **1982:** *Howard Anderson* / VENOM.

HAYES, HELEN

(Helen Hayes Brown, 1900–)

Helen Hayes is an actress who projects sincerity and warmth. Her appearances in the movies have been all too infrequent as she has spent so much time becoming "The First Lady of the American Stage." She won her first Oscar for THE SIN OF MADELON CLAUDET when she was 31 and her second for AIRPORT when she was 69. Since then she has spent most of her time in TV movies such as THE SNOOP SISTERS (1973), A FAMILY UPSIDE DOWN (1978), and A CARIBBEAN MYSTERY (1983). She compares the difference between theater and movie audiences, saying: "In the theater, you have a special audience; you can switch back and forth from 'good' people to 'bad' people and get away with it. On the screen, the public somehow wants to accept you the way they see you. You acquire a certain image for them."

KEY ROLES

Madelon Claudet / THE SIN OF MADELON CLAUDET, 1931, MGM, d-Edward Selwyn.

Helen Hayes won an Oscar for her performance in this sob story about a self-sacrificing mother who works as a streetwalker and cleaning woman to put her illegitimate son (Robert Young) through medical school.

Leora Tozer / ARROWSMITH, 1931, Goldwyn / United Artists, d-John Ford.

Hayes appears as the young bride of Ronald Colman, the dedicated medical researcher of Sinclair Lewis's Nobel Prize-winning novel. He loses her to the bubonic plague epidemic he's fighting.

Catherine Barkley / A FAREWELL TO ARMS, 1932, Paramount, d-Frank Borzage.

Hayes is an English nurse who falls in love with Gary Cooper during World War I. She is also loved by a doctor (Adolphe Menjou) who has her transferred to separate her from Cooper. When Cooper comes back from the front seriously wounded, Menjou saves his life with an operation and, regretting his actions, sends Cooper to Milan to recuperate with Hayes. After a blissful period, Cooper returns to the front and Hayes, discovering she is pregnant, crosses the border to Switzerland to have their baby. He arrives to find the baby has been born dead and Hayes is near death just as they learn the war is over.

Angela Chiaramonte / THE WHITE SISTER, 1933, MGM, d-Victor Fleming.

Flighty Hayes has a marriage arranged for her by her father, but she meets Clark Gable and a flirtation leads to love. They run away together but he is called to active service in war. She pledges to wait for him, but two years later she receives word that he has been killed. She enters a convent to become a nun, but Gable isn't dead, he's only a prisoner, and he finally escapes and comes looking for Hayes. When he finds her, it's too late—she has taken her final vows.

Lucille Jefferson / MY SON JOHN, 1952, Paramount, d-Leo McCarey.

Hayes and her husband Dean Jagger are devout Catholics who are horrified when they learn that their eldest son (Robert Walker) is a godless Communist.

Dowager Empress / ANASTASIA, 1956, 20th Century-Fox, d-Anatole Litvak.

Hayes is the litmus test to see if White Russians led by Yul Brynner have been successful in preparing Ingrid Bergman to pass herself off as the daughter of Russia's assassinated czar. Hayes is the ranking Russian aristocrat living in exile and she almost comes to believe that Bergman is really her executed granddaughter. But in the last lines of the movie, when she is asked what is to be said to the dignitaries who have gathered to meet the czar's daughter, she replies: "Say? Oh, I will say, 'The play is over. Go home.'"

Ada Quonsett / AIRPORT, 1970, Universal, d-George Seaton.

Hayes is a little old lady who makes a habit of riding airplanes without buying tickets. On one snowy night she finds herself sitting next to Van Heflin, who is carrying a bomb, and she is enlisted to help try and disarm him.

OTHER ROLES

1917: *the heroine* / THE WEAVERS OF LIFE. **1920:** *Babs* / BABS. **1933:** *Lien Wha* / THE SON-DAUGHTER; *Stella Hallam* / ANOTHER LANGUAGE; *Madame Fabian* / NIGHT FLIGHT. **1934:** *Maggie Wylie* / WHAT EVERY WOMAN KNOWS; *guest* / CRIME WITHOUT PASSION. **1935:** *Vanessa Ellis* / VANESSA, HER LOVE STORY. **1943:** *guest* / STAGE DOOR CANTEEN. **1953:** *guest* / MAIN STREET TO BROADWAY. **1959:** *guest* / THIRD MAN ON THE MOUNTAIN. **1973:** *Mrs. Steinmetz* / HERBIE RIDES AGAIN. **1975:** *Hettie* / ONE OF OUR DINOSAURS IS MISSING. **1977:** *Lady St. Edmund* / CANDLESHOE.

HAYMES, DICK

(1919–1980)

It must be admitted that Dick Haymes was a better singer than actor (some would go so far as to say "Thank, God!"). His Decca hits included "You'll Never Know," "Little White Lies," "Long Ago and Far Away," and "The Old Master Painter." Still, he appeared in some pleasant musicals of the 1940s in which his fine baritone voice was put to good use.

KEY ROLES

Ernest R. Ball / IRISH EYES ARE SMILING, 1944, 20th Century-Fox, d-Gregory Ratoff.

In this largely fictitious biopic Haymes appears as the real-life composer who collaborated on songs such as "Mother Machree," "Dear Little Boy of Mine," and "When Irish Eyes Are Smiling." June Haver stars as Mary "Irish" O'Brien, the woman who inspired the title tune.

William Frake / STATE FAIR, 1945, 20th Century-Fox, d-Walter Lang.

Crooner Haymes accompanies his farm family—sister Jeanne Crain, father Charles Winninger, and mother Fay Bainter—to the Iowa State Fair, where he finds romance with singer Vivian Blaine. Everyone gets into the act of singing Rodgers and Hammerstein's "It's a Grand Night for Singing."

John Pritchard / THE SHOCKING MISS PILGRIM, 1947, 20th Century-Fox, d-George Seaton.

Haymes co-stars with Betty Grable in this story about a woman typist fighting for a place in a male-dominated business world. He joins Grable in singing the movie's best song, "For You, for Me, for Evermore," a hitherto unpublished George Gershwin song reworked by Ira Gershwin and Kay Swift.

John Matthews / UP IN CENTRAL PARK, 1948, Universal-International, d-William A. Seiter.

Haymes, a *New York Times* reporter, helps Deanna Durbin uncover the crooked political activities of Boss Tweed and his organization. The film isn't much, nor are the songs by Sigmund Romberg and Dorothy Fields.

OTHER ROLES

1944: *Lt. Dick Ryan* / FOUR JILLS IN A JEEP. **1945:** *Joe Davis, Jr.* / BILLY ROSE'S DIAMOND HORSESHOE. **1946:** *Jimmy Hale* / DO YOU LOVE ME? **1947:** *Jeff Stephens* / CARNIVAL IN COSTA RICA. **1948:** *Joe* / ONE TOUCH OF VENUS. **1951:** *Benny* / ST. BENNY THE DIP. **1952:** *narrator* / HOLLYWOOD FUN FESTIVAL. **1953:** *Joe Carter* / ALL ASHORE; *Beauregard Clemment* / CRUISIN' DOWN THE RIVER. **1976:** *James Crawford* / WON TON TON, THE DOG WHO SAVED HOLLYWOOD.

HAYWARD, LOUIS

(Seafield Grant, 1909–1985)

Born in South Africa, Louis Hayward was raised in London where he began acting in films and on the stage. After his Broadway debut in 1935, he went to Hollywood where for 20 years he played debonair heroes, swashbucklers, and made an ideal Simon Templar, The Saint. By the end of the 1930s he was reduced to second-rate adventure pictures. Ida Lupino's first husband, Hayward never became a big star; there were too many other actors who did what he did and, according to those who mattered, did it better. Tyrone Power was more handsome, Errol Flynn was more swashbuckling, and both were better actors.

KEY ROLES

Simon Templar / THE SAINT IN NEW YORK, 1938, RKO, d-Ben Holmes.

Hayward was borrowed from Universal to play the popular detective created by Leslie Charteris. He was replaced by George Sanders for later films in the series. In this one, Hayward leaves South America for New York on a mission to halt the criminal activities of the Big Apple's criminal kingpin. The film is a winner; Hayward even captures a crook while disguised as a nun.

Stephen Earley / DUKE OF WEST POINT, 1938, United Artists, d-Alfred E. Green.

In this silly rah-rah story, Hayward is a skilled athlete fresh from Cambridge who is considered a bit too cocky for his own good at West Point. He redeems himself by winning the big hockey game. Joan Fontaine provides his romantic interest.

Louis XIV / Philippe / THE MAN IN THE IRON MASK, 1939, United Artists, d-James Whale.

In this pleasing swashbuckler, Hayward expertly plays both the nasty king of France and the brother he imprisons and forces to wear an iron mask to conceal his identity. As one would expect, the bad Hayward gets his comeuppance, and the good one gets the throne as well as Joan Bennett.

Oliver Essex / MY SON, MY SON, 1940, United Artists, d-Charles Vidor.

Hayward gets the opportunity to redeem himself for a spoiled and vicious life which bitterly disappoints his self-made father (Brian Aherne). After being given everything his father never had, Hayward repays dear old dad by ruining the daughter of the old man's closest friend and by becoming his father's rival for the affections of an artist. But Hayward dies a hero's death in World War I in Flanders. (In the novel the scamp is hanged.)

Philip Lombard / AND THEN THERE WERE NONE, 1945, Popular Pictures, d-Rene Clair.

In one of the finest mysteries ever filmed, Hayward is one of two who survive a weekend on a lonely island where the unknown host kills his guests one by one, using means suggested by the nursery rhyme "Ten Little Indians."

Richard Shelton / THE BLACK ARROW, 1948, Columbia, d-Gordon Douglas.

It's an improbable but still entertaining tale with Hayward as a knight who, during the War of the Roses, seeks the murderer of his father.

Peter Blood / CAPTAIN PIRATE, 1952, Columbia, d-Ralph Murphy.

In this sequel to Hayward's THE FORTUNES OF CAPTAIN BLOOD (1950), he's a reformed pirate who raises the skull and crossbones once again to find the real buccaneers when he's accused of sacking Cartagena.

Morey Bernstein / THE SEARCH FOR BRIDEY MURPHY, 1956, Paramount, d-Noel Langley.

Hayward is an amateur hypnotist who sends his neighbor (Teresa Wright) into a previous incarnation as an Irish peasant girl. But at the end he can't bring her back.

OTHER ROLES

1932: *Paul Geneste* / SELF-MADE LADY. **1933:** *David Fenner* / CHELSEA LIFE. **1934:** *Duncan* / SORRELL AND SON. **1935:** *Jack Kerry* / THE FLAME WITHIN; *Richard Orland* / A FEATHER IN HER HAT. **1936:** *Denis Moore* / ANTHONY ADVERSE; *Anthony McClellan* / THE LUCKIEST GIRL IN THE WORLD; *Gregory Bengard* / ABSOLUTE QUIET; *tart man* / TROUBLE FOR TWO. **1937:** *Barry Gilbert* / MIDNIGHT INTRUDER; *Lt. Jean Herbillion* / THE WOMAN I LOVE. **1938:** *Bill Duncan* / THE RAGE OF PARIS; *Philip Duncan* / CONDEMNED WOMAN. **1940:** *Count of Monte Cristo* / SON OF MONTE CRISTO; *Jimmy Harris* / DANCE, GIRL, DANCE. **1941:** *Albert Feather* / LADIES IN RETIREMENT. **1942:** *ballroom extra* / THE MAGNIFICENT AMBERSONS. **1946:** *Edmond Dantes* / RETURN OF MONTE CRISTO; *Jim Cameron* / YOUNG WIDOW; *Ephraim Poster* / THE STRANGE WOMAN. **1947:** *Barney Page* / REPEAT PERFORMANCE. **1948:** *Philip Grayson* / WALK A CROOKED MILE; *Vic Lambdin* / RUTHLESS. **1949:** *Captain Sirocco* / THE PIRATES OF CAPRI. **1950:** *Peter Blood* / THE FORTUNES OF CAPTAIN BLOOD; *Stephen Byrne* / THE HOUSE BY THE RIVER. **1951:** *Dr. Jekyll* / THE SON OF DR. JEKYLL; *Dick Turpin* / THE LADY AND THE BANDIT. **1952:** *D'Artagnan* / LADY IN THE IRON MASK. **1953:** *Denham* / THE ROYAL AFRICAN RIFLES; *Simon Templar* / THE SAINT'S RETURN. **1954:** *Edward Harper* / DUFFY OF SAN QUENTIN. **1967:** *Major Benson* / CHUKA; *Mike Culligan* / THE CHRISTMAS KID. **1969:** *himself* / THE PHYNX. **1973:** *Tim Fowley* / TERROR IN THE WAX MUSEUM.

HAYWARD, SUSAN

(Edythe Marrener, 1916–1975)

Susan Hayward was an aggressive, red-headed beauty who took a long time to become established as a star. She turned out to be ideal portraying women who wouldn't give in to the desires of men and received her first of five Oscar nominations for her role as a neglected, alcoholic wife in SMASH UP. She received a second nomination for portraying a woman who gets her husband to believe that her expected child is his when it's not in MY FOOLISH HEART. Her next nomination was for WITH A SONG IN MY HEART, as the crippled singer Jane Froman. This was followed by I'LL CRY TOMORROW, as alcoholic singer Lillian Roth. And she was finally a winner for portraying a woman sent to the gas chamber in I WANT TO LIVE. After this triumph her roles were mainly as overwrought women in forgettable melodramas.

KEY ROLES

Isobel Rivers / BEAU GESTE, 1939, Paramount, d-William A. Wellman.

As the foreword to the movie says, "The love of a man for a woman waxes and wanes like the moon, but the love of brother for brother is steadfast as the stars and endures like the word of the prophet...." For the love of his brothers, Ray Milland leaves behind his beloved Hayward to follow Gary Cooper and Robert Preston in joining the French Foreign Legion.

Drusilla Alston / REAP THE WILD WIND, 1942, Paramount, d-Cecil B. DeMille.

Hayward's beloved in this adventure yarn of salvaging ships off the southeastern United States coast is Robert Preston, who sometimes helps his brother (Raymond Massey) wreck ships to be salvaged. But he's really put out with Massey when he learns that Hayward has drowned on one such ship.

Estelle Masterson / I MARRIED A WITCH, 1942, United Artists, d-Rene Clair.

When Salem witch Veronica Lake comes back to haunt the descendant of the Puritan who had her burned at the stake, it's his poor fiancée Hayward who suffers the most.

Constance Chesley / THE FIGHTING SEABEES, 1944, Republic, d-Edward Ludwig.

This movie reputedly tells the story of the forming of the Seabees, a military unit of construction workers. Hayward is a reporter who falls out of love with naval officer Dennis O'Keefe when she falls in love with John Wayne, the boss of the workers.

Cherokee Lansing / TULSA, 1949, Eagle-Lion, d-Stuart Heisler.

Hayward, the daughter of a cattle rancher, builds an oil empire. The publicity pieces of the day read "Meet Cherokee Lansing...half wildcat...half angel...all woman."

Eloise Winters / MY FOOLISH HEART, 1949, Goldwyn, d-Mark Robson.

Hayward was nominated for an Oscar for her work in this very sentimental story of a World War II romance between her and soldier Dana Andrews, resulting in her being forced to convince her husband that the baby she is expecting is his. The theme song by Victor Young is quite lovely.

Irene Bennett / HOUSE OF STRANGERS, 1949, 20th Century-Fox, d-Joseph L. Mankiewicz.

In this dark drama, Hayward is Richard Conte's girlfriend. Conte turns his back on his outwardly close Italian family when he sees how his older brothers treat their father (Edward G. Robinson) after he gets out of prison for illegal banking activities.

Harriet Boyd / I CAN GET IT FOR YOU WHOLESALE, 1951, 20th Century-Fox, d-Michael Gordon.

Hayward is a New York model who works her way up in the garment business to become a dress designer with her own company. She almost lets her ambition destroy her relationship with her partners, but she's just not quite ruthless enough to carry through with her plans.

Bathsheba / DAVID AND BATHSHEBA, 1951, 20th Century-Fox, d-Henry King.

In another corny Bible movie, Gregory Peck as King David goes ape when he sees Hayward bathing and vows to have her. This leads him to neglect his duties almost to the point of sacrificing his kingdom. Some of his people feel that Hayward has earned the fate of an adulteress.

Jane Froman / WITH A SONG IN MY HEART, 1952, 20th Century-Fox, d-Walter Lang.

Jane Froman provides the singing voice for this biopic about her—a singer who survives the crash of an airplane while touring with the USO to various military camps during World War II. Hayward provides everything else, though, and very nicely. It's a winning performance by Hayward as the brave woman who refuses to allow herself to become a cripple.

Rachel Donaldson Robards Jackson / THE PRESIDENT'S LADY, 1953, 20th Century-Fox, d-Henry Levin.

This film about Andrew Jackson (Charlton Heston) and his wife Rachel (Hayward) concentrates on the scandal surrounding their marriage. Hayward is divorced by her first husband who accuses her of adultery. She and Heston marry and later learn her divorce was not legal. Even when they get everything straightened out, humiliation and scorn are things they must live with until her death shortly after he is elected president.

Leah Fuller / GARDEN OF EVIL, 1954, 20th Century-Fox, d-Henry Hathaway.

Three American adventurers (Gary Cooper, Richard Widmark, and Cameron Mitchell) agree to help Hayward rescue her husband who is injured and trapped in a gold mine. They have all kinds of trouble with their passions as well as with Indians.

Lillian Roth / I'LL CRY TOMORROW, 1955, MGM, d-Daniel Mann.

Hayward is excellent in this biopic about Broadway / Hollywood star Lillian Roth. She becomes an alcoholic and her degradation is graphically shown and should act as a deterrent for others.

Barbara Graham / I WANT TO LIVE, 1958, United Artists, d-Robert Wise.

Hayward gives a tough-nosed performance as a call girl who is ultimately executed for murder even though there is real doubt as to her guilt. The movie makes a strong case against capital punishment and won Hayward her Academy Award.

Helen Lawson / VALLEY OF THE DOLLS, 1967, 20th Century-Fox, d-Mark Robson.

In what many suspect was typecasting, Hayward portrays an aging star who is being replaced by a new, younger sensation. Of course the real story is about the use of drugs, but the scene in which Patty Duke snatches Hayward's wig and flushes it in a toilet, revealing Hayward as an old doll, is a pretty nasty one.

OTHER ROLES

1937: *starlet bit* / HOLLYWOOD HOTEL. **1938:** *bit* / THE AMAZING DR. CLITTERHOUSE; *telephone operator* / THE SISTERS; *amateur actress* / COMET OVER BROADWAY; *coed* / CAMPUS CINDERELLA; *Gloria Adams* / GIRLS ON PROBATION. **1939:** *Judith Schofield* / OUR LEADING CITIZEN; *Betty McGlen* / $1,000 A TOUCHDOWN. **1941:** *Hester Stoddard* / ADAM HAD FOUR SONS; *Carol Hopkins* / SIS HOPKINS; *Millie Pickens* / AMONG THE LIVING. **1942:** *Tana Mason* / THE FOREST RANGERS; *Genevieve* / STAR SPANGLED RHYTHM. **1943:** *Jill Wright* / CHANGE OF HEART, (HIT PARADE OF 1943); *Charmain Kitteridge* / JACK LONDON; *Kate Benson* / YOUNG AND WILLING. **1944:** *Janice Blair* / AND NOW TOMORROW; *Mildred Douglas* / THE HAIRY APE. **1945:** *Lucy Overmire* / CANYON PASSAGE. **1946:** *June Goth* / DEADLINE AT DAWN. **1947:** *Angie Evans* / SMASH-UP, THE STORY OF A WOMAN; *Verna Carlson* / THEY WON'T BELIEVE ME; *Tina Bordereau* / THE LOST MOMENT. **1948:** *Morna Dabney* / TAP ROOTS; *Janet Busch* / THE SAXON CHARM. **1950:** *Mary Elizabeth Eden Thompson* / I'D CLIMB THE HIGHEST MOUNTAIN. **1951:** *Vinnie Holt* / RAWHIDE. **1952:** *Louise Merritt* / THE LUSTY MEN; *Helen* / THE SNOWS OF KILIMANJARO. **1953:** *Ellen Burton* / WHITE WITCH DOCTOR. **1954:** *Messalina* / DEMETRIUS AND THE GLADIATORS. **1955:** *Katie O'Neill* / UNTAMED; *Jane Hoyt* / SOLDIER OF FORTUNE; *Borta* / THE CONQUEROR. **1957:** *Dottie Poole* / TOP SECRET AFFAIR. **1959:** *Mary Sharron* / A WOMAN OBSESSED; *Gabrielle Dauphin* / THUNDER IN THE SUN. **1960:** *Content Delville* / THE MARRIAGE-GO-ROUND. **1961:** *Ada Gillis* / ADA; *Rae Smith* / BACK STREET. **1963:** *Laura Pember* / STOLEN HOURS; *Christine Allison* / I THANK A FOOL. **1964:** *Valerie Hayden* / WHERE LOVE HAS GONE. **1967:** *Mrs. "Lone Star" Crockett Sheridan* / THE HONEY POT. **1972:** *Elizabeth Reilly* / THE REVENGERS.

HAYWORTH, RITA

(Margarita Carmen Cansino, 1918–1987)

For many movie fans, Rita Hayworth will be remembered in a black evening gown and elbow-length black gloves, seductively drawing on a cigarette. That was Hayworth as the title character in GILDA. She made such an observation about herself when she noted sadly, "Every man I knew had fallen in love with Gilda and wakened with me." Hayworth's life was a bigger melodrama than any picture she ever appeared in. The daughter of Spanish dancers, she danced with her parents from the age of 12. After Columbia Studios signed her to a contract and remade her image by raising her hairline, turning her into a redhead, and changing her name, she made a number of "B" pictures before returning to dancing with Fred Astaire in YOU'LL NEVER GET RICH and YOU WERE NEVER LOVELIER. This was followed by her years as a "love goddess," best exemplified by GILDA. Her marriages to Orson Welles, Prince Aly Khan, and Dick Haymes (her second, third, and fourth of five husbands) made as much news as any of her pictures. Hayworth continued to perform in the 1960s and 1970s but she developed Alzheimer's disease and was cared for by her daughter by Aly Khan, Yasmin, until her death. Shortly before she died a benefit was held by her daughter and friends to raise funds for research into the causes of and cures for the disease.

KEY ROLES

Judy McPherson / ONLY ANGELS HAVE WINGS, 1939, Columbia, d-Howard Hawks.

Hayworth is the ex-wife of Cary Grant, the owner of an airplane firm in South America who sends his pilots on almost suicidal night mail flights. She shows up with her new husband, a one-time ace flyer, and looks sultry, but Jean Arthur is the female star who gets the man.

Natalie Roguin / THE LADY IN QUESTION, 1940, Columbia, d-Charles Vidor.

Brian Aherne serves on a jury that acquits Hayworth of murder. He takes her into his home without informing his family of her past problems and becomes worried when his son (Glenn Ford) falls for her.

Virginia Brush / THE STRAWBERRY BLONDE, 1941, Warners, d-Raoul Walsh.

Correspondent school dentist James Cagney loses strawberry-blonde Hayworth to a chiseling Jack Carson and marries Olivia de Havilland on the rebound. Cagney spends five years in jail after being made Carson's fall guy for the latter's corrupt activities. He later considers killing Carson with gas while treating him but, after becoming reacquainted with Hayworth, he finally realizes that he married the right girl, after all.

Dona Sol des Muire / BLOOD AND SAND, 1941, 20th Century-Fox, d-Rouben Mamoulian.

Hayworth is a beautiful, heartless Spanish woman who chooses her latest lover based on who is at the peak of celebrity at the moment. In this account it is matador Tyrone Power, whom she dumps when he loses his touch.

Sally Elliott / MY GAL SAL, 1942, 20th Century-Fox, d-Irving Cummings.

In this dreary biopic about songwriter Paul Dresser, Hayworth appears as a Broadway singer who carries on a stormy romance with him.

Marcia Acuna / YOU WERE NEVER LOVELIER, 1942, Columbia, d-William A. Seiter.

Hayworth dances very nicely in this movie about a romance in Argentina that her father (Adolphe Menjou) promotes between her and song-and-dance-man Fred Astaire. Some experts believe that Hayworth was the best dancer who ever worked with Astaire, but not his best dancing partner.

Rusty Parker / Maribelle Hicks / COVER GIRL, 1944, Columbia, d-Charles Vidor.

This wartime musical about a girl who achieves fame when she becomes a cover girl, is usually rated higher than it deserves, but it's hard to ignore its role in making Hayworth the "love goddess" that *Life* magazine later named her.

Gilda Mundson / GILDA, 1948, Columbia, d-Charles Vidor.

Hayworth and Glenn Ford once were lovers. Now she is the new wife of his new boss, Buenos Aires casino owner George Macready. She makes a spectacle of herself in Macready's club by performing a striptease to the song "Put the Blame on Mame." She moves as if equipped with fluid motion, her body coming at the audience one wave at a time. Unfortunately, Ford puts an end to the entertainment by slapping her across the face in a shocking and memorable scene. The two become unwitting bigamists when they believe her husband is killed. When Macready shows up again, an aging janitor puts him away for good.

Elsa Bannister / THE LADY FROM SHANGHAI, 1948, Columbia, d-Orson Welles.

In this unusual film noir, Hayworth is married to crippled Everett Sloane. When she becomes involved with Irish seaman Orson Welles (her real-life husband at the time, although the marriage was at its end), she ends up in a gun battle with Sloane in a hall of mirrors at an amusement park.

Princess Salome / SALOME, 1953, Columbia, d-William Dieterle.
Hayworth's mother (Judith Anderson) gets her to dance the dance of the seven veils for Charles Laughton to excite the dirty old man so he will agree to give the head of John the Baptist to his wife.

Sadie Thompson / MISS SADIE THOMPSON, 1953, Columbia, d-Curtis Bernhardt.
Hayworth is a shady lady on the run from the law on a South Seas island during World War II. She is briefly converted by preacher José Ferrer, but reverts to her usual self when he proves to be like all the other men she's known.

Vera Simpson / PAL JOEY, 1957, Columbia, d-George Sidney.
Before marrying a wealthy man, Hayworth was a stripper called "Vanessa the Undressa." Now widowed, she becomes "bewitched, bothered and bewildered" by fast-talking heel Frank Sinatra. Her plans to financially back a nightclub featuring him are abandoned when she discovers that he loves Kim Novak.

Ann Shankland / SEPARATE TABLES, 1958, United Artists, d-Delbert Mann.
Hayworth plays Burt Lancaster's glamorous ex-wife. She wants him back, but finds that the manager (Wendy Hiller) of the English seaside guest house where he is staying is his mistress. Their story is intertwined with those of several others staying at the hotel.

OTHER ROLES

As Rita Cansino

1935: *Carmen* / UNDER THE PAMPAS MOON; *Nayda* / CHARLIE CHAN IN EGYPT; *specialty dancer* / DANTE'S INFERNO; *Tamara Petrovitch* / PADDY O'DAY. **1936:** *Carmen Zoro* / HUMAN CARGO; *Maria Maringola* / MEET NERO WOLFE; *Paula Castillo* / REBELLION. **1937:** *Carmen* / TROUBLE IN TEXAS; *Angela Gonzales* / OLD LOUISIANA; *Rita* / HIT THE SADDLE.

As Rita Hayworth

1937: *Rita* / CRIMINALS OF THE AIR; *Sue Collins* / GIRLS CAN PLAY; *Mary Gillespie* / THE SHADOW; *Betty Holland* / THE GAME THAT KILLS; *Betty Morgan* / PAID TO DANCE. **1938:** *Gail Preston* / WHO KILLED GAIL PRESTON?; *Mary* / THERE'S ALWAYS A WOMAN; *Jerry Wheeler* / CONVICTED; *Marcia Adams* / JUVENILE COURT. **1939:** *Judith Alvarez* / THE RENEGADE RANGER; *J. G. Bliss* / HOMICIDE BUREAU; *Karen* / THE LONE WOLF SPY HUNT; *Patricia Lane* / SPECIAL INSPECTOR. **1940:** *Patricia O'Malley* / MUSIC IN MY HEART; *Joan Forrester* / BLONDIE ON A BUDGET; *Leonora Stubbs* / SUSAN AND GOD; *Nina Barona* / ANGELS OVER BROADWAY. **1941:** *Irene Malcolm* / AFFECTIONATELY YOURS; *Sheila Winthrop* / YOU'LL NEVER GET RICH. **1942:** *Ethel Halloway* / TALES OF MANHATTAN. **1945:** *Rosalind "Roz" Bruce* / TONIGHT AND EVERY NIGHT. **1947:** *Terpsichore* / *Kitty Pendleton* / DOWN TO EARTH. **1948:** *Carmen* / THE LOVES OF CARMEN. **1952:** *Chris Emery* / AFFAIR IN TRINIDAD. **1957:** *Irena* / FIRE DOWN BELOW. **1959:** *Adelaide Geary* / THEY CAME TO CORDURA. **1960:** *Jo Morris* / THE STORY ON PAGE ONE. **1962:** *Eve Lewis* / THE HAPPY THIEVES. **1964:** *Lili Alfredo* / CIRCUS WORLD. **1966:** *Rosalie Kenny* / THE MONEY TRAP; *Monique* / THE POPPY IS ALSO A FLOWER. **1967:** *Aunt Caterina* / THE ROVER. **1969:** *Martha* / SONS OF SATAN. **1971:** *Mara* / ROAD TO SALINA; *Mrs. Golden* / THE NAKED ZOO. **1972:** *Señora de la Plata* / THE WRATH OF GOD.

HEFLIN, VAN

(Emmett Evan Heflin, 1910–1971)
Underrated as an actor, craggy-faced Van Heflin was best playing men of integrity, but not as the major character; he was most at home as the second male lead. He was nominated for an Oscar only once, winning for JOHNNY EAGER, but he could just as well have been nominated for his work in THE STRANGE LOVE OF MARTHA IVERS, THE PROWLER, SHANE, and 3:10 TO YUMA. He received outstanding reviews for his stage work, particularly for "A View from the Bridge" and "Patterns." This authentic-looking American concluded his film career in undistinguished and almost undistinguishable pictures in the 1960s, but fortunately we have his earlier work by which to remember him.

KEY ROLES

Rader / SANTA FE TRAIL, 1940, Warners, d-Michael Curtiz.
Heflin, a classmate of Jeb Stuart (Errol Flynn), joins up with abolitionist John Brown, not for noble reasons but for profit. When he later betrays Brown and his followers at Harper's Ferry, the old man kills him. No such character actually existed, but he made for a good villain.

Jeff Hartnett / JOHNNY EAGER, 1941, MGM, d-Mervyn LeRoy.
In this well-made gangster melodrama, Heflin plays a buddy of despicable gangster Robert Taylor. He knows his place, though, observing, "You keep me around because even Johnny Eager has to have one friend." Heflin won an Oscar for this role.

Andrew Johnson / TENNESSEE JOHNSON, 1942, MGM, d-William Dieterle.
Heflin gives a sincere performance as the first U.S. president to be impeached. The story is clearly sympathetic to Johnson and so his enemies come across as vengeful men rather than ones who questioned whether the uneducated, alcoholic ex-senator from Tennessee was fit to carry out the policies of Abraham Lincoln.

John Thornway / PRESENTING LILY MARS, 1943, MGM, d-Norman Taurog.
Heflin portrays a Broadway producer with whom ambitious young singer Judy Garland has an affair as she rises from small-town anonymity to Broadway stardom. The Booth Tarkington tale isn't much but the cast does a good job and it is pleasant.

Sam Masterson / THE STRANGE LOVE OF MARTHA IVERS, 1946, Paramount, d-Lewis Milestone.
Heflin knew Barbara Stanwyck and her weakling D.A. husband (Kirk Douglas) when they were children and she became wealthy by killing her aunt. Stanwyck and Douglas try numerous means to get Heflin out of town— Stanwyck comes on to him hot and heavy, and Douglas tries to interest him with Lizabeth Scott.

Timothy Haslam / GREEN DOLPHIN STREET, 1947, MGM, d-Victor Saville.
Set in New Zealand of the 19th century, the film features Heflin as the center of a family conflict with two sisters who are after the same man. The film also includes a Maori uprising, an earthquake, and a tidal wave. It's silly but somewhat fun if one doesn't expect too much.

Athos / THE THREE MUSKETEERS, 1948, MGM, d-George Sidney.

Heflin has the dubious distinction of having been married to the crafty and evil agent of Cardinal Richelieu, Milady de Winter (Lana Turner). Ultimately, he orders her beheaded for all the mischief she has caused him, D'Artagnan, and the other musketeers.

Charles Bovary / MADAME BOVARY, 1949, MGM, d-Vincente Minnelli.

Heflin is the dull husband who drives his wife (Jennifer Jones) into the arms of a lover (Louis Jourdan). Heflin isn't the only dull thing in this movie.

Webb Garwood / THE PROWLER, 1951, Horizon / United Artists, d-Joseph Losey.

Heflin is a bitter cop who meets Evelyn Keyes while he is checking on a prowler she thinks she's seen in her neighborhood. They become lovers and plot to kill her husband, a sterile disc jockey. After doing the deed, she is found to be pregnant, which makes people a mite suspicious. Finally she betrays Heflin to the police.

Stedman / MY SON JOHN, 1952, Paramount, d-Leo McCarey.

Heflin is a government agent investigating the activities of Robert Walker, an American Catholic who has become a Communist. It's a movie about a witch hunt in a time when nothing could be worse than being suspected of being a Commie.

Joe Starrett / SHANE, 1953, Paramount, d-George Stevens.

Heflin is one of the small-time farmers wanted off his land by a cattleman who thinks it's his. The cattleman brings in a gunfighter (Jack Palance) to enforce his point. On the side of the farmers rides Shane (Alan Ladd) hoping he can put away his guns. Together Heflin and Ladd fight off the efforts to dislodge the homesteaders.

Maj. Neal Benton / THE RAID, 1954, 20th Century-Fox, d-Hugo Fregonese.

During the American Civil War, six confederate soldiers led by Heflin escape from a union prison and, instead of heading south, set out for Canada carrying out a raid on a small Vermont village on their way.

Jerry / WOMAN'S WORLD, 1954, 20th Century-Fox, d-Jean Negulesco.

Heflin and his wife (Arlene Dahl) are one of three couples brought to New York by Clifton Webb so he may choose a new general manager. Dahl believes her wiles have gotten Heflin all of his promotions, but it's only when he dumps her that Webb chooses him for the job.

Fred Stables / PATTERNS, 1956, United Artists, d-Fielder Cook.

The tough boss of a New York corporation forces a showdown between a rising young executive (Heflin) and an older man who is Heflin's friend but whom the big boss hopes will resign.

Dan Evans / 3:10 TO YUMA, 1957, Columbia, d-Delmer Daves.

Heflin is a rancher who needs the money offered to get a notorious outlaw (Glenn Ford) to the 3:10 train to Yuma. Ford's gang intends to see that Heflin doesn't live to see his prisoner board the train. It's a most suspenseful western.

Emelyan Pugachov / TEMPEST, 1959, Italy / France / Yugoslavia, Paramount / Pathe / Bosnia, d-Alberto Lattuada.

Heflin proclaims that he is Grand Duke Peter of Russia from whom Catherine has usurped the throne and he plans to take it back.

D. O. Guerrero / AIRPORT, 1970, Universal, d-George Seaton.

Heflin is a desperate man who takes out a large insurance policy on himself with his wife (Maureen Stapleton) as benefactor and boards an airplane with a bomb. He succeeds in blowing himself away and almost takes a planeload of people with him.

OTHER ROLES

1936: *Gerald* / A WOMAN REBELS. **1937:** *Rev. Samuel Woods* / THE OUTCASTS OF POKER FLAT; *George Wilson* / FLIGHT FROM GLORY; *Val* / SATURDAY'S HEROES; *Clarke Parker* / ANNAPOLIS SALUTE. **1939:** *bit* / BACK DOOR TO HEAVEN. **1941:** *Elliott Morgan* / THE FEMININE TOUCH; *Bill King* / H. M. PULHAM, ESQ. **1942:** *Gordon McKay* / KID GLOVE KILLER; *Henry Taggart* / SEVEN SWEETHEARTS; *Rocky Custer* / GRAND CENTRAL MURDER. **1946:** *James I. Hessler* / TILL THE CLOUDS ROLL BY. **1947:** *David Sutton* / POSSESSED. **1948:** *Keith Alexander* / TAP ROOTS; *Frank R. Enley* / ACT OF VIOLENCE; *narrator* / THE SECRET LAND. **1949:** *Mark Dwyer* / EAST SIDE, WEST SIDE. **1951:** *Jim Bridger* / TOMAHAWK; *Brad Stubbs* / WEEKEND WITH FATHER. **1953:** *Irish Gallagher* / WINGS OF THE HAWK; *Nicholas Chapman* / SOUTH OF ALGIERS. **1954:** *John Gale* / TANGANYIKA; *Peter* / BLACK WIDOW. **1955:** *Luke Fargo* / COUNT THREE AND PRAY; *Colonel Huxley* / BATTLE CRY. **1958:** *Lee Hackett* / GUNMAN'S WALK. **1959:** *Sgt. John Chawk* / THEY CAME TO CORDURA. **1960:** *Velko* / FIVE BRANDED WOMEN; *Reger* / UNDER TEN FLAGS. **1963:** *Joe Trent* / CRY OF BATTLE. **1964:** *Duncan Bell* / THE WASTREL; *Joe Trent* / TO BE A MAN. **1965:** *Ben Amand* / THE GREATEST STORY EVER TOLD; *Mike Vido* / ONCE A THIEF. **1966:** *Curly* / STAGECOACH. **1967:** *Bill MacLean* / THE MAN OUTSIDE. **1968:** *Sam Cooper* / THE RUTHLESS FOUR. **1969:** *Sam Mirakian* / THE BIG BOUNCE.

HEMMINGS, DAVID

(1941–)

A former boy soprano, David Hemmings took up painting when his voice changed. After some stage and TV work, he appeared in films as bratty schoolboys and troubled teenagers, experiencing his greatest success and an almost cult following as the modish photographer in BLOWUP. Nothing followed to match this success, although he continued in leading roles for the next few years, before settling into more support-type roles in both films and on television. His made-for-TV movies include CHARLIE MUFFIN (1979), DR. JEKYLL AND MR. HYDE (1982), and CALAMITY JANE (1984). His foreign language films include NO ES NADA, MAMA and SOLO UN JUEGO (1974), PROFUNDO ROSSO (1976), and SQUADIA ANTITRUFFA (1977). Hemmings has also directed several films including RUNNING SCARED (1973), JUST A GIGOLO (1978), RACE FOR THE YANKEE ZEPHYR (1981), and COME THE DAY (1985).

KEY ROLES

Thomas / BLOWUP, 1966, Great Britain, MGM, d-Michelangelo Antonioni.

Hemmings is a London photographer who takes some pictures that may show a murder taking place, but the evidence is stolen, perhaps by Vanessa Redgrave, who has offered herself in trade for the negatives.

Mordred / CAMELOT, 1967, Warners, d-Joshua Logan.

Hemmings is Arthur's illegitimate son who has no use for chivalry and is responsible for Arthur finding proof of a more than chivalrous love existing between his queen Guenivere and dear friend Lancelot.

Captain Nolan / THE CHARGE OF THE LIGHT BRIGADE, 1968, Great Britain, United Artists / Woodfall, d-Tony Richardson.

Hemmings is less dashing and daring than Errol Flynn and more of a comic book hero in this inaccurate story of the circumstances leading up to the charge at Balaklava during the Crimean War, immortalized by Tennyson in his poem.

Alfred the Great / ALFRED THE GREAT, 1969, Great Britain, MGM, d-Clive Donner.

Hemmings takes the throne of England in 871 A.D. from his weakling brother. They apparently used a lot of four-letter words back then when they weren't hacking each other apart.

Hugh Hendron / THE PRINCE AND THE PAUPER, (CROSSED SWORDS), 1977, International Film Production, d-Richard Fleischer.

Hemmings is ranked seventh in the credits of this remake of Mark Twain's story about a London street urchin and young Edward VI changing places and of the dangers both face. At least his name appears above Charlton Heston's, who plays Henry VIII.

OTHER ROLES

1950: *bit* / NIGHT AND THE CITY. **1954:** *bit* / THE RAINBOW JACKET. **1957:** *Ken* / FIVE CLUES TO FORTUNE; *bit* / SAINT JOAN; *Danny Willard* / THE HEART WITHIN. **1959:** *schoolboy* / IN THE WAKE OF A STRANGER; *Ted* / MEN OF TOMORROW; *Kenny* / NO TREE IN THE STREET. **1960:** *Ginger* / THE WIND OF CHANGE. **1961:** *Brian* / TWO LEFT FEET. **1962:** *Bert* / SOME PEOPLE. **1963:** *Dave Martin* / BE MY GUEST. **1966:** *Christian* / EYE OF THE DEVIL. **1968:** *John* / THE LONG DAY'S DYING; *Bob* / ONLY WHEN I LARF; *Dildano* / BARBARELLA; *Walter Leybourne* / *Benjamin Oakes* / THE BEST HOUSE IN LONDON. **1969:** *Leigh Hartley* / THE WALKING STICK; *Tim Brett* / FRAGMENT OF FEAR. **1970:** *John Ebony* / UNMAN, WITTERING AND ZIGO. **1971:** *Jerry Nelson* / THE LOVE MACHINE. **1973:** *Robert* / VOICES. **1974:** *Charlie Braddock* / JUGGERNAUT. **1975:** *Richard Swiveller* / MR. QUILP. **1977:** *Keith* / THE SQUEEZE; *Eddy* / ISLANDS IN THE STREAM. **1978:** *Captain Kraft* / JUST A GIGOLO; *Col. Anthony Narriman* / POWER PLAY; *Edward* / THE DISAPPEARANCE; *Armstrong* / BLOOD RELATIVES. **1979:** *Inspector Foxborough* / MURDER BY DECREE. **1980:** *Inspector Hutton* / BEYOND REASONABLE DOUBT. **1982:** *Gavin Wilson* / MAN, WOMAN AND CHILD.

HENIE, SONJA

(1910–1969)

Born in Oslo, Norway, Sonja Henie was given her first ice skates when she was six. While improving her skating, Henie also took ballet lessons which later allowed her to combine the two talents on the ice and made her not only an Olympic figure skating champion in 1928, 1932, and 1936, but one of the world's highest-paid performers in the 1930s and 1940s for her movie work in lightweight but enjoyable romantic musicals. Her ice shows also remained popular into the 1950s. She once said that she wished to do for skating what Fred Astaire did for dancing and perhaps she did. She died in her sleep of leukemia on a flight taking her home to Oslo.

KEY ROLES

Greta Muller / ONE IN A MILLION, 1936, 20th Century-Fox, d-Sidney Lanfield.

While preparing for the Olympics, Henie is discovered in Switzerland by an American theatrical manager. He brings her to Madison Square Garden where she is a triumph on ice. Her love interest is Don Ameche.

Lili Heiser / THIN ICE, 1937, 20th Century-Fox, d-Sidney Lanfield.

This film was among the biggest moneymakers of the studio for the year. Henie, never an actress, just pleased audiences with her smiles and skating. In the film she is a Swiss hotel ski instructor who falls for Tyrone Power without knowing that he is a prince with plans to make her his princess.

Trudy Erickson / HAPPY ENDING, 1938, 20th Century-Fox, d-Roy Del Ruth.

Henie smiles and skates winningly in this empty story about an amorous bandleader and his manager who show up in Norway and put the rush on her. She returns to America where she becomes a sensational skating star.

Karen Benson / SUN VALLEY SERENADE, 1941, 20th Century-Fox, d-H. Bruce Humberstone.

Henie skates all over the famed Idaho ski resort. The plot has the pianist with the Glenn Miller band finding himself stuck with a Norwegian refugee he has sponsored, who turns out to be champion skater Henie. She stages an ice show when Miller's vocalist quits in a huff.

OTHER ROLES

1927: *bit* / SVY DAGER FOR ELIZABETH. **1938:** *Kristina Nielson* / MY LUCKY STAR. **1939:** *Trudi Hovland* / SECOND FIDDLE; *Louise Favers (Norden)* / EVERYTHING HAPPENS AT NIGHT. **1942:** *Katina Jonsdottir* / ICELAND. **1943:** *Nora* / WINTERTIME. **1945:** *Chris Linden* / IT'S A PLEASURE. **1948:** *Karen* / THE COUNTESS OF MONTE CRISTO. **1958:** *herself* / HELLO LONDON.

HENREID, PAUL

(Paul von Henreid, 1907–)

Austrian-born Paul Henreid began his career in his native land appearing in several films including BAROUD (1932), MORGENROT (1934), and LACHEN AM FREIBAD (1935). He fled to England where he made a few appearances in small parts, then moved on to Hollywood appearing as a romantic leading man in a number of "women's movies." These were followed by a few unconvincing appearances in swashbuckling adventure films. Henreid will always be remembered for two roles: that of the courageous freedom fighter in CASABLANCA who taunts the Nazis by having the musicians in Rick's Cafe play "La Marseilles," and as Bette Davis's married lover in NOW, VOYAGER who gave the world a new romantic gesture by lighting two cigarettes in his mouth before giving one to Davis.

KEY ROLES

Max Staefel / GOODBYE, MR. CHIPS, 1939, Great Britain, MGM, d-Sam Wood.

Using the name Paul von Henreid, he appears as the German friend of British schoolmaster Robert Donat. At the outbreak of World War I, he is forced to return to the fatherland.

Karl Marsen / NIGHT TRAIN TO MUNICH, 1940, Great Britain, 20th Century-Fox, d-Carol Reed.

Still as von Henreid, he is a Gestapo agent who uses Margaret Lockwood to get to her Czech industrialist father, but he is thwarted by Rex Harrison, Basil Radford, and Naunton Wayne.

Jerry Durrance / NOW, VOYAGER, 1942, Warners, d-Irving Rapper.

Henreid is the romantic architect whom New England spinster Bette Davis meets and falls in love with on a cruise after she blossoms from a repressed, dowdy woman to one of poise following psychiatric treatment. Their love is doomed to be incomplete as he is married and cannot divorce his wife. But as Davis reminds him in the classic final line, "Let's not ask for the moon when we have the stars."

Victor Laszlo / CASABLANCA, 1943, Warners, d-Michael Curtiz.

Henreid is superb as the impressive underground leader who arrives at Humphrey Bogart's cafe in Casablanca hoping to find a way to escape to Portugal. With him is his wife Ingrid Bergman who had had an affair with Bogart back in Paris when she thought Henreid dead. Having suffered at the hands of the Nazis and in constant danger of being sent back to a concentration camp by the Germans, Henreid is very understanding about the bond between Bergman and Bogart.

Arthur Nicholls / DEVOTION, 1946, Warners, d-Curtis Bernhardt.

This movie was made in 1943 but not released until 1946. In the story about the three Brontë sisters Henreid plays an Irish-born minister and the object of the affections of both Emily (Ida Lupino) and Charlotte (Olivia De Havilland). The romantic yearnings are fictitious so we don't know why Anne (Nancy Coleman) is unaffected.

Henry / BETWEEN TWO WORLDS, 1944, Warners, d-Edward A. Blatt.

Henreid and his wife (Eleanor Parker) commit suicide out of despair and find themselves on a strange ocean liner with a group of other people whom they know were killed in a bomb raid on London. In this remake of OUTWARD BOUND, Henreid gives a controlled if not very logical portrayal of a man who questions the wisdom of his suicide.

Richard Schumann / SONG OF LOVE, 1947, MGM, d-Clarence Brown.

It's a slightly absurd story of Richard and Clara Schumann and their friend Johann Brahms. It looks a great deal better than it is, and if Henreid does not distinguish himself by his acting, at least he looks the part of the composer.

Edri-al-Gadrian / PIRATES OF TRIPOLI, 1955, Columbia, d-Felix Feist.

Henreid is a pirate captain who comes to the aid of a lovely oriental princess (Patricia Medina). This is one of several swashbucklers made by the romantic lover and is the best of the lot, although it's definitely a "B" picture.

Cardinal / EXORCIST II: THE HERETIC, 1977, Warners, d-John Boorman.

In the disappointing sequel to THE EXORCIST, Cardinal Henreid sends in the new clerical troops to rid Linda Blair of her demons.

OTHER ROLES

1937: *bit* / VICTORIA THE GREAT. **1940:** *bit* / UNDER YOUR HAT; *Victor Brandt* / AN ENGLISHMAN'S HOME. **1942:** *Paul Lavallier* / JOAN OF PARIS. **1944:** *Count Stephen Orvid* / IN OUR TIME; *Vincent* / THE CONSPIRATORS; *guest* / HOLLYWOOD CANTEEN. **1945:** *Laurent Van Horn* / THE SPANISH MAIN. **1946:** *Philip Carey* / OF HUMAN BONDAGE; *Karel Novak* / DECEPTION. **1948:** *John Muler* / *Dr. Bartok* / HOLLOW TRIUMPH. **1949:** *Comm. Paul Vogel* / ROPE OF SAND. **1950:** *Dr. Jason* / SO YOUNG, SO BAD; *Jean Lafitte* / LAST OF THE BUCCANEERS. **1951:** *Paul Rencourt* / PARDON MY FRENCH. **1952:** *Dr. Stephen Brice* / FOR MEN ONLY; *Abu Andar* / THIEF OF DAMASCUS. **1953:** *Kazah* / SIREN OF BAGDAD; *Hugo Bishop* / MAN IN HIDING. **1954:** *Florenz Ziegfeld* / DEEP IN MY HEART; *Conrad Hegner* / KABARETT. **1956:** *guest* / MEET ME IN LAS VEGAS; *Capt. Henrique Monteros* / A WOMAN'S DEVOTION. **1957:** *Anton* / TEN THOUSAND BEDROOMS. **1959:** *Eduardo Barroso* / HOLIDAY FOR LOVERS; *Nikko Regas* / NEVER SO FEW. **1962:** *Etienne Laurier* / THE FOUR HORSEMEN OF THE APOCALYPSE. **1965:** *General Zeimann* / OPERATION CROSSBOW. **1967:** *narrator* / PEKING REMEMBERED. **1969:** *the general* / THE MADWOMAN OF CHAILLOT.

HEPBURN, AUDREY

(Edda van Hepburn-Ruston, 1929–)

Born in Holland, the slim, demure, and fragile-looking Audrey Hepburn was trained for the ballet. During World War II she and her parents became involved in the Resistance. In 1948, she won a ballet scholarship in London, where she also modelled and took acting lessons. She had a few small movie roles when French novelist Colette insisted that she play the title role of "Gigi" on Broadway. Her success in the play led to her being cast in ROMAN HOLIDAY, for which she was awarded an Oscar. Her elfin beauty and charm made her much in demand for the next 15 years. She received other Oscar nominations for SABRINA, THE NUN'S STORY, BREAKFAST AT TIFFANY'S, CHARADE, and WAIT UNTIL DARK. In 1964, Hepburn was cast as Eliza Doolittle in MY FAIR LADY and, although she was quite good, she was bucking the belief by most people that she was in a role that should have gone to Julie Andrews. In 1967, she left films and returned, perhaps unwisely, in 1976 with ROBIN AND MARIAN. She has made only two films since, neither worthy of her talents.

KEY ROLES

Princess Anne / ROMAN HOLIDAY, 1953, Paramount, d-William Wyler.

Hepburn is a princess on an official visit to Rome who slips away and, with the help of reporter Gregory Peck and photographer Eddie Albert, experiences some fun and love. The cute little pixie won an Academy Award for capturing the hearts of her audiences. She is so appealing when, drugged and settling down for the night in Gregory Peck's apartment, she innocently observes: "This is very unusual. I've never been alone with a man before—even with my dress on. With my dress off, it's most unusual."

Sabrina Fairchild / SABRINA, 1954, Paramount, d-Billy Wilder.

Hepburn is the daughter of the chauffeur for a family consisting of two brothers. One is William Holden, a playboy on whom she has a terrible crush; the other is Humphrey Bogart, a typical hard-working, serious businessman for whom she finally falls.

Natasha Rostov / WAR AND PEACE, 1956, Pontii / De Laurentiis, d-King Vidor and Mario Soldati.

Hepburn looks lovely in her Russian gowns in this production of Leo Tolstoy's story of one Russian family's adventures at the time of Napoleon's invasion. Henry Fonda, the illegitimate son of a count, falls in love with Hepburn, but is unable to declare his feelings because he considers himself unworthy. Both feel better about things when the count legitimizes Fonda's birth and leaves him his fortune.

Jo Stockton / FUNNY FACE, 1956, Paramount, d-Stanley Donen.

In this movie one realizes how thin Hepburn really is as she is transformed from a shy bookstore salesperson to a beautiful fashion model by photographer Fred Astaire. He makes her look as if she can dance.

Arianne Chavasse / LOVE IN THE AFTERNOON, 1957, Allied Artists, d-Billy Wilder.
Once again Hepburn is stuck with a co-star (Gary Cooper) who is clearly too old and too tired for her. He's a philanderer in Paris and she's the daughter of a private detective who warns Cooper that a jealous husband is out to shoot him.

Sister Luke (Gabrielle van der Mal) / THE NUN'S STORY, 1959, Warners, d-Fred Zinnemann.
Hepburn is a Belgian girl who joins a strict order of nuns and is sent to the Congo, where an agnostic doctor (Peter Finch) causes her such doubts about her faith that she ultimately "leaps over the wall."

Holly Golightly / BREAKFAST AT TIFFANY'S, 1961, Paramount, d-Blake Edwards.
As one of the characters in the movie says, Hepburn is a "real" phony. She's a slightly crazy girl in New York, looking for a rich man to give her the things she wants. But poor writer George Peppard spoils her plans when they fall in love.

Karen Wright / THE CHILDREN'S HOUR, 1962, United Artists, d-William Wyler.
Hepburn and fellow schoolmistress Shirley MacLaine have their lives and careers shattered by a vicious student who accuses them of being lesbian lovers.

Eliza Doolittle / MY FAIR LADY, 1964, CBS / Warners, d-George Cukor.
Hepburn is lovely as the cockney flower girl taught to speak correctly by arrogant elocutionist Rex Harrison. There was much controversy over the role going to her as many felt that Broadway star Julie Andrews should have recreated her stage triumph. At the Academy Awards, Rex Harrison, who played Henry Higgins on the stage with Andrews and on the screen with Hepburn, diplomatically spoke of his two "fair ladies."

Susy Hendrix / WAIT UNTIL DARK, 1967, Warners / Seven Arts, d-Terence Young.
Photographer Efrem Zimbalist, Jr., unwittingly smuggles a drug-filled doll into the country and three desperate men go to great lengths to recover it from his blind wife (Hepburn). It's a sharp and suspenseful movie with Hepburn impressive as the woman who must save herself from a murderer's plot.

OTHER ROLES

1948: *bit* / NEDERLAND IN 7 LESSONS. **1951:** *extra* / ONE WILD OAT; *cigarette girl* / LAUGHTER IN PARADISE; *Chiquita* / THE LAVENDER HILL MOB; *Eve Lester* / YOUNG WIVES' TALE. **1952:** *Melissa Walter* / NOUS IRONS A MONTE CARLO; *Linda Farrel* / MONTE CARLO BABY; *Nora Brent* / THE SECRET PEOPLE. **1959:** *Rima* / GREEN MANSIONS. **1960:** *Rachel Zachary* / THE UNFORGIVEN. **1963:** *Reggie Lampert Vass* / CHARADE. **1964:** *Gabrielle Simpson* / PARIS WHEN IT SIZZLES. **1966:** *Nicole Bonnet* / HOW TO STEAL A MILLION; *Joanna Wallace* / TWO FOR THE ROAD. **1976:** *Lady Marian* / ROBIN AND MARIAN. **1979:** *Elizabeth Roffe* / BLOODLINE. **1981:** *Angela Niotes* / THEY ALL LAUGHED.

HEPBURN, KATHARINE

(1907–)

"When I started out I didn't have any desire to be an actress or learn how to act. I just wanted to be famous." So said Kate Hepburn, who surely got her wish, as well as becoming one of the greatest movie actresses of all time. Certainly she has achieved what no other actress ever has: four Oscars—for MORNING GLORY, GUESS WHO'S COMING TO DINNER, THE LION IN WINTER, and ON GOLDEN POND—as well as eight other nominations—for ALICE ADAMS, THE PHILADELPHIA STORY, WOMAN OF THE YEAR, THE AFRICAN QUEEN, SUMMERTIME, THE RAINMAKER, SUDDENLY LAST SUMMER, and LONG DAY'S JOURNEY INTO NIGHT. It would be incorrect to believe that her Oscar winners were her best films or even that her nominated roles were all better than those for which she was overlooked by the nominating committee. Hepburn was always good, but sometimes the story, the director, or the other players didn't measure up to her example. She has also won acclaim for her TV movies, THE GLASS MENAGERIE (1973), LOVE AMONG THE RUINS (1975), and THE CORN IS GREEN (1979). Her career carries a message for young actresses—or, shall we say, brilliantly talented young actresses: don't let others decide what roles, stories, directors, or leading men are best for you. Hepburn refused to keep quiet on these and other matters. This slim, New England-bred beauty with the distinctive, crisp voice never played by the rules of Hollywood and, in fact, would have nothing to do with its society or, by her standards, ridiculous lifestyles. Her long-standing friendship with Spencer Tracy has been detailed all too often and requires no mention other than to observe how well they worked together in their movies. Hepburn is quite frankly a remarkable human being—a great treasure.

KEY ROLES

Sidney Fairfield / A BILL OF DIVORCEMENT, 1932, RKO, d-George Cukor.
Hepburn learns that insanity runs in her family when she meets her father (John Barrymore) for the first time after he escapes from an asylum. She sends her fiancé away, not wishing to risk having children who would be similarly afflicted.

Eva Lovelace / MORNING GLORY, 1933, RKO, d-Lowell Sherman.
Stagestruck Hepburn arrives in New York from Vermont, has an affair with theatrical manager Adolphe Menjou, falls in love with Douglas Fairbanks, Jr., and decides she doesn't need either after becoming a Broadway star. It's in the play within this movie that Hepburn says, "The calla lilies are in bloom again. Such a strange flower, suitable to any occasion. I carried them on my wedding day, and now I place them here in memory of something that has died."

Jo March / LITTLE WOMEN, 1933, RKO, d-George Cukor.
Hepburn is one of the four March sisters who live in Concord, Massachusetts, during the Civil War. She desperately wishes to write, but is afraid to leave her family until she meets a professor (Paul Lukas) who helps her develop her writing.

Alice Adams / ALICE ADAMS, 1935, RKO, d-George Stevens.
Eager for social recognition, klutzy Hepburn sets her cap for Fred MacMurray, and fabricates a false prominence for her family hoping to impress him. When she brings him home to meet the folks, she apologizes for her home by lying: "Here's the foolish little house where I live. It is a queer little place, but, you know, my father is so attached to it that the family has just about given up hope of getting him to build farther up. You know, he doesn't mind us being extravagant about anything else, but he won't let us change one

single thing about his precious little old house." At the dinner party where MacMurray meets her family, they show themselves for what they are—lowlifes.

Mary Stuart / MARY OF SCOTLAND, 1936, RKO, d-John Ford.

In the 16th century this Scottish queen is accused of treason by Elizabeth I and is sent to the block when she refuses to sign away her claim to the English throne.

Terry Randall / STAGE DOOR, 1937, RKO, d-Gregory La Cava.

Hepburn is a smug debutante who moves into New York's Footlight Club which houses girls bent on show business careers. When she is awarded a part that Andrea Leeds thought would be hers, the latter commits suicide. This has such an effect on Hepburn that she finds the emotional depths needed to make the play a hit, and gives credit to Leeds in her curtain speech: "I suppose that I should thank you on behalf of the company, and I know that I am grateful to you for your applause. But I must tell you that I don't deserve it. I'm not responsible for what happened on this stage tonight. The person you should be applauding died a few hours ago—a young and brilliant actress who could no longer find a spot in the theater. And it was for her more than for anyone else that I was able to go on. And I hope that, wherever she is, she knows and understands and forgives."

Susan Vance / BRINGING UP BABY, 1938, RKO, d-Howard Hawks.

Hepburn is delightful as a madcap girl who owns a pet leopard and falls for Cary Grant, a zoologist. He is trying to construct a dinosaur but loses a pivotal bone that is buried by a dog on the property of Hepburn's aunt. The scene in the nightclub where the lower part of the back of Hepburn's dress is torn away is classic.

Linda Seton / HOLIDAY, 1938, Columbia, d-George Cukor.

Hepburn is the unconventional sister of Doris Nolan who has brought her fiancé (Cary Grant) home to their elegant mansion. Before long Hepburn has fallen in love with impractical Grant and, by the end of the film, the two are off together to Europe to pursue his dream of seeing the world before starting a career.

Tracy Lord / THE PHILADELPHIA STORY, 1940, MGM, d-George Cukor.

Just before her marriage to a stuffy, self-made man, Hepburn's first husband (Cary Grant) reappears. Also arriving at her Philadelphia mansion are writer James Stewart and photographer Ruth Hussey who are allowed to cover the nuptials to prevent their magazine from printing a scandalous but true story about Hepburn's father and a showgirl. In the next 24 hours she learns what a prig she is, takes a drunken midnight swim with Stewart, and decides that Grant's the one for her.

Tess Harding / WOMAN OF THE YEAR, 1942, MGM, d-George Stevens.

Hepburn is an international affairs columnist who disparages baseball and finds herself the object of an attack by sports columnist Spencer Tracy. They become fast friends and although they have little in common, they get married. In this their first film together, Tracy walks out on Hepburn when he gets no domesticity from her. But after hearing the wedding vows taken by her father and his new bride, she determines to make a go of her marriage.

Mary Matthews / STATE OF THE UNION, 1948, MGM, d-Frank Capra.

When her husband (Spencer Tracy) sees himself as presidential timber, Hepburn sees it as a chance to outsmart the owner of a newspaper chain—and Tracy's mistress (Angela Lansbury). Better than that, she's able to get him to recognize that he has allowed himself to be used by politicians.

Amanda Bonner / ADAM'S RIB, 1949, MGM, d-George Cukor.

Hepburn is an attorney who defends Judy Holliday, a woman accused of trying to murder her husband and his "friend," Jean Hagen. The prosecuting attorney is hubby Spencer Tracy and Hepburn's means of getting her client off almost end their marriage.

Rose Sayer / THE AFRICAN QUEEN, 1951, Horizon / United Artists, d-John Huston.

Hepburn is masterful as the aging spinster who, during World War II, travels down an African river with gin-soaked Humphrey Bogart. They fall in love as they suffer the hardships of the trip. At the movie's end they plot to destroy a German gunboat that patrols the mouth of the river. When their initial go is unsuccessful, they are picked up by the gunboat and ordered hanged. But Bogart gets the captain to marry them before carrying out the sentence, and their old boat insures that they'll have time for a honeymoon.

Pat Pemberton / PAT AND MIKE, 1952, MGM, d-George Cukor.

Hepburn is a talented athlete whom sports promoter Spencer Tracy believes he can make into an all-around champion. Her only drawback is that she loses all her concentration when her fault-finding fiancé is present. This is resolved when Tracy takes the fiancé's place. Interestingly, in Hepburn's previous movie she appeared as a fragile, elderly woman and in this one she shows off a still very fine figure.

Jane Hudson / SUMMERTIME, 1955, Lopert / United Artists, d-David Lean.

Middle-aged spinster Hepburn arrives in Venice and encounters Rossano Brazzi, with whom she falls hopelessly in love. He feels the same but is married. They have a few lovely days together on the island of Burano. Then she leaves Venice, richer for the experience which brought her both happiness and sadness.

Lizzie Curry / THE RAINMAKER, 1956, Paramount, d-Joseph Anthony.

Once again Hepburn plays a plain spinster, this time on a drought-plagued farm in the Southwest. Into her world comes rainmaker Burt Lancaster, who not only delivers rain but also shows her that she is more of a woman than she knows.

Mrs. Violet Venable / SUDDENLY LAST SUMMER, 1959, Horizon / Columbia, d-Joseph L. Mankiewicz.

This New Orleans matriarch's mind, as well as her beauty, is fading. Her son died in North Africa the previous summer and Hepburn will stop at nothing to prevent her niece (Elizabeth Taylor) from recalling that Hepburn's homosexual son was torn apart by a pack of boys upon whom he had preyed.

Mary Tyrone / LONG DAY'S JOURNEY INTO NIGHT, 1962, Embassy, d-Sidney Lumet.

In this autobiographical Eugene O'Neill play, Hepburn is the drug-addicted mother married to a pompous actor whose one son suffers from tuberculosis while the other is an alcoholic.

Christina Drayton / GUESS WHO'S COMING TO DINNER, 1967, Columbia, d-Stanley Kramer.
The last picture made with Hepburn's dear Spencer Tracy, who died just after its completion, has been given more critical acclaim than it deserves because of its stars and the fact that it deals with an interracial love affair between Sidney Poitier and Hepburn's real-life niece, Katharine Houghton.

Eleanor of Aquitaine / THE LION IN WINTER, 1968, Avco Embassy, d-Anthony Harvey.
Hepburn is right at home as the strong-willed, estranged wife of King Henry II of England (Peter O'Toole) who is brought from her castle prison at Christmastime along with their three sons to argue over who will succeed Henry as king.

Ethel Thayer / ON GOLDEN POND, 1981, Universal, d-Mark Rydell.
Hepburn is the understanding wife of eighty-year-old Henry Fonda, and mother of Jane Fonda in this sweet story of their summer spent together at a New Hampshire vacation cottage.

OTHER ROLES

1933: *Lady Cynthia Darrington* / CHRISTOPHER STRONG. **1934:** *Trigger Hicks* / SPITFIRE; *Lady Babbie* / THE LITTLE MINISTER. **1935:** *Constance Dane* / BREAK OF HEARTS. **1936:** *Sylvia Scarlett* / SYLVIA SCARLETT; *Pamela Thistlewaite* / A WOMAN REBELS. **1937:** *Phoebe Throssel* / QUALITY STREET. **1942:** *Christine Forrest* / KEEPER OF THE FLAME. **1944:** *Jade* / DRAGON SEED. **1945:** *Jamie Rowan* / WITHOUT LOVE. **1946:** *Ann Hamilton* / UNDERCURRENT. **1947:** *Lutie Cameron* / THE SEA OF GRASS; *Clara Wieck Schumann* / SONG OF LOVE. **1956:** *Vinka Kovelenko* / THE IRON PETTICOAT. **1957:** *Bunny Watson* / DESK SET. **1969:** *Aurelia* / THE MADWOMAN OF CHAILLOT. **1971:** *Hecuba* / THE TROJAN WOMEN. **1973:** *Agnes* / A DELICATE BALANCE. **1975:** *Eula Goodnight* / ROOSTER COGBURN. **1978:** *Miss Pudd* / OLLY, OLLY, OXEN FREE. **1984:** *Grace Quigley* / THE ULTIMATE SOLUTION OF GRACE QUIGLEY.

HESTON, CHARLTON

(John C. Carter, 1923–   )
Assuming the surname of his stepfather when a child, Charlton Heston began acting at Northwestern University. He appeared in an amateur film in 1945 and made his Broadway debut in 1947 with Katharine Cornell in "Antony and Cleopatra." His professional film debut was in DARK CITY in 1950 and he came to the attention of the public with a bang as the circus boss in THE GREATEST SHOW ON EARTH in 1952. Throughout his career, Heston has seemed most at home in period pieces and epics such as THE TEN COMMANDMENTS and BEN HUR, for which he won the Best Actor award. He took notice of this, saying, "I don't seem to have a Twentieth Century face." This has led some critics to question his acting ability, reasoning that such movies substitute spectacle for emotion. In fact, Heston has proven to be a much more versatile actor than he is generally credited for as an examination of the following list of roles will bear out.

KEY ROLES

Brad / THE GREATEST SHOW ON EARTH, 1952, Paramount, d-Cecil B. DeMille.
Heston is the circus manager of Ringling Brothers-Barnum and Bailey Circus. He is loved by his top flyer (Betty Hutton), but when he imports top aerialist Cornel Wilde and gives him the center ring instead of giving it to Hutton, the romance becomes strained.

Andrew Jackson / THE PRESIDENT'S LADY, 1953, 20th Century-Fox, d-Henry Levin.
Heston looks the part of the Tennessee lawyer whose frail wife dies shortly after he is elected president. Much of the story is spent on the problems they have with the legitimacy of their marriage.

Maj. Bernard "Barney" Benson / THE PRIVATE WAR OF MAJOR BENSON, 1955, Universal, d-Jerry Hopper.
Heston's outspoken views win him the military assignment as commandant of a boys' military school run by an order of nuns. The martinet is softened by the experience.

Moses / THE TEN COMMANDMENTS, 1956, Paramount, d-Cecil B. DeMille.
The adult Moses, treated as a candidate to succeed Cedric Hardwicke as pharaoh, discovers that he is in fact the son of slave parents and had been taken in as a baby by the pharaoh's sister. He is judged a traitor and is banished to the desert from which he returns many years later as God's agent to get the new pharaoh (Yul Brynner) to free the Israelites. When this is accomplished after a series of plagues, including the death of the first-born son of every Egyptian, Heston leads his people to the Promised Land. But he himself is denied seeing it because, in anger, he broke the tablets which contained the ten commandments, given to him by God.

Steve Leech / THE BIG COUNTRY, 1958, United Artists, d-William Wyler.
Heston is superb as a vicious ranch foreman who quarrels with a retired sea captain (Gregory Peck) over Carroll Baker and the water rights that fuel the feud between two western families headed by Charles Bickford and Burl Ives.

Judah Ben-Hur / BEN HUR, 1959, MGM, d-William Wyler.
Heston is an aristocratic Jew who is sent to the Roman galleys as a slave, in part for his views such as: "Rome is an affront to God. Rome is strangling my people and my country and the whole earth," which he unwisely says to his boyhood friend (Stephen Boyd), a Roman officer. Heston saves the life of Jack Hawkins, a Roman general who, as a reward, adopts him as his son. This offers Heston the chance to take revenge on his old enemy Boyd, whom he defeats in a chariot race. Later he returns to Israel to find that his mother and sister have become lepers. But they are cured by a follower of Christ and all become Christians.

Maj. Matt Lewis / 55 DAYS AT PEKING, 1962, Allied Artists, d-Nicholas Ray.
Heston leads a detachment of U.S. marines which joins other military units in defending the diplomatic compound in Peking from attack by Boxers during the final days of the last Chinese empress's reign.

Michelangelo / THE AGONY AND THE ECSTASY, 1965, 20th Century-Fox, d-Carol Reed.
Heston, as the famous 16th-century painter and sculptor, clashes with Pope Julius II (Rex Harrison) on artistic matters when the latter employs him to paint the Sistine Chapel ceiling.

Maj. Amos Dundee / MAJOR DUNDEE, 1965, Columbia, d-Sam Peckinpah.
During the Civil War, Union cavalry officer Heston leads a group of misfits into Mexico to chase a band

of marauding Apaches who massacred everyone at a New Mexico outpost.

Gen. Charles "Chinese" Gordon / KHARTOUM, 1966, United Artists, d-Basil Dearden.

The fabled British colonial general makes a last desperate and unsuccessful defense of the ancient city of Khartoum against the followers of the religious leader called The Mahdi (Laurence Olivier).

Will Penny / WILL PENNY, 1967, Paramount, d-Tom Gries.

Heston, a middle-aged cowpuncher, runs into trouble with a family of maniacal cutthroats while courting a fetching, young widow.

George Taylor / PLANET OF THE APES, 1968, 20th Century-Fox, d-Franklin J. Schaffner.

Heston is an American astronaut who, with his crew, awakens from suspended animation while on a long intergalactic flight to find himself back on the earth of the future when apes rule and humans are their slaves.

Detective Thorn / SOYLENT GREEN, 1973, MGM, d-Richard Fleischer.

In 2022 the people of New York live in perpetual heat, eating synthetic foods. Police detective Heston, investigating a murder, discovers that the principal ingredient of their foods is made from human parts.

Cardinal Richelieu / THE THREE MUSKETEERS, 1973, 20th Century-Fox, d-Richard Lester.

Heston makes a very effective scheming, conniving prince of the church and prime minister of France who is thwarted by the Musketeers (Michael York, Alan Bates, Richard Chamberlain, and Frank Finlay) in his attempt to discredit the queen by proving that she is having an affair with Buckingham of England. He returns to the role in the sequel.

Bill Tyler / THE MOUNTAIN MEN, 1980, Columbia, d-Richard Lang.

Heston is a grizzled, aging fur trapper in Wyoming who battles with an Indian chief (Stephen Macht) and his warriors over the latter's wife (Victoria Racimo), who has run away and is offered protection by Heston. It's a violent, meaningless story written by Heston's son, which may explain how it came to be produced, but not why.

OTHER ROLES

1950: *Danny Haley* / DARK CITY. **1952:** *Boake Tackman* / RUBY GENTRY; *War Bonnet* / *Jim Ahern* / THE SAVAGE. **1953:** *Buffalo Bill Cody* / PONY EXPRESS; *Ed Bannon* / ARROWHEAD; *Dr. Tom Owen* / BAD FOR EACH OTHER; *Christopher Leiningen* / THE NAKED JUNGLE. **1954:** *Harry Steele* / SECRET OF THE INCAS. **1955:** *William Clark* / THE FAR HORIZONS; *Casey Cole* / LUCY GALLANT. **1956:** *Colt Saunders* / THREE VIOLENT PEOPLE. **1958:** *Ramon Miguel "Mike" Vargas* / TOUCH OF EVIL; *Andrew Jackson* / THE BUCCANEER. **1959:** *John Sands* / THE WRECK OF THE MARY DEARE. **1961:** *Rodrigo Diaz de Bivar* / *El Cid* / EL CID. **1962:** *Capt. Paul MacDougall* / THE PIGEON THAT TOOK ROME; *Richard "King" Howland* / DIAMOND HEAD. **1965:** *John the Baptist* / THE GREATEST STORY EVER TOLD; *Chrysagon* / THE WAR LORD. **1967:** *Lionel Evans* / COUNTERPOINT. **1968:** *Ron "Cat" Catlan* / NUMBER ONE. **1969:** *George Taylor* / BENEATH THE PLANET OF THE APES. **1970:** *Whip Hoxworth* / THE HAWAIIANS; *Marc Antony* / JULIUS CAESAR. **1971:** *Robert Neville* / THE OMEGA MAN. **1972:** *Capt. Hank O'Hara* / SKYJACKED; *John Thornton* / CALL OF THE WILD; *Marc Antony* / ANTONY AND CLEOPATRA. **1974:** *Cardinal Richelieu* / THE FOUR MUSKETEERS; *Alan Murdock* / AIRPORT 1975; *Stuart Graff* / EARTHQUAKE. **1976:** *Capt. Matt Garth* / MIDWAY; *Capt. Peter Holly* / TWO-MINUTE WARNING; *Sam Burgarde* / THE LAST HARD MAN. **1978:** *Henry VIII* / CROSSED SWORDS; *Capt. Peter Blanchard* / GRAY LADY DOWN. **1980:** *Matthew Corbeck* / THE AWAKENING. **1983:** *Silas and Ian McGee* / SEARCH FOR THE MOTHER LODE: THE LAST GREAT TREASURE.

HILLER, DAME WENDY

(1912–)

Wendy Hiller has made far too few movies, concentrating more on the British stage. Among her film appearances are several truly memorable performances. She was nominated for an Academy Award for Best Actress for PYGMALION, won an Oscar for Best Supporting Actress for SEPARATE TABLES, and also was nominated for A MAN FOR ALL SEASONS. She was honored with the title Dame in 1975.

KEY ROLES

Eliza Doolittle / PYGMALION, 1938, Great Britain, Pascal, d-Anthony Asquith.

Hiller is a wonderful cockney flower girl taught by Leslie Howard to speak English properly and thus be taken by all as a lady.

Barbara Undershaft / MAJOR BARBARA, 1940, Great Britain, Pascal, d-Gabriel Pascal, Harold French, and David Lean.

Hiller is an officer in the Salvation Army and Rex Harrison, who sees and falls in love with her at first sight, joins the army to be with her and they are soon engaged. She is the daughter of the world's biggest munitions manufacturer who shows up after a long absence. Her father's ability to buy respectability with the army doesn't set well with Hiller but she changes her mind about things when she discovers how well his workers live and that he plans to make Harrison his successor in the family business.

Joan Webster / I KNOW WHERE I'M GOING, 1945, Great Britain, GFD / The Archers, d-Michael Powell and Emeric Pressburger.

Hiller is a determined girl on her way to the Hebrides to marry a wealthy man when she becomes stranded on Mull and marries a young naval officer (Roger Livesey) instead. He is later revealed to be a Scottish lord and the owner of the small island where they met, so she doesn't lose much by settling for true love.

Pat Cooper / SEPARATE TABLES, 1958, United Artists, d-Delbert Mann.

Hiller received an Oscar for Best Supporting Actress as the proprietor of a British seaside guest house and mistress of Burt Lancaster in this genteel melodrama.

Gertrude Morel / SONS AND LOVERS, 1960, Great Britain, 20th Century-Fox / Company of Artists, d-Jack Cardiff.

Hiller is the mother in this story of a drunken Nottingham miner's family. Her son learns about life and love in a basically intelligent rendition of D. H. Lawrence's autobiographical novel.

Alice More / A MAN FOR ALL SEASONS, 1966, Great Britain, Columbia / Highland, d-Fred Zinnemann.

Hiller is the loyal, simple, and uneducated wife of Sir Thomas More (Paul Scofield), once Henry VIII's most respected minister. But when the king decides to break with the Catholic church, More tries to keep his head by keeping his tongue, but it doesn't work.

OTHER ROLES

1937: *Betty Lovejoy* / LANCASHIRE LUCK. **1951:** *Mrs. Almayer* / OUTCAST OF THE ISLANDS. **1952:** *Lucinda Bentley* / SINGLE

HANDED. **1957:** *Elizabeth* / SOMETHING OF VALUE; *Edith Clitterburn* / HOW TO MURDER A RICH UNCLE. **1963:** *Anna Berniers* / TOYS IN THE ATTIC. **1969:** *Mrs. Micawber* / DAVID COPPERFIELD. **1974:** *Princess Dragomiroff* / MURDER ON THE ORIENT EXPRESS. **1976:** *Rebecca Weiler* / VOYAGE OF THE DAMNED. **1977:** *Allison Crosby* / THE CAT AND THE CANARY. **1980:** *Mothershead* / THE ELEPHANT MAN. **1982:** *Winnie Bates* / MAKING LOVE. **1987:** *Aunt D'Arcy* / THE LONELY PASSION OF JUDITH HEARNE.

HOBART, ROSE

(Rose Kefer, 1906–)

Born in New York City, Rose Hobart was the daughter of well-known musician Paul Kefer. She made her New York stage debut in "Lullaby" in 1923 and, as a result of her work on the stage in "Death Takes a Holiday," she was invited to Hollywood where she made her screen debut in LILIOM in 1930. Her best roles followed in the early 1930s. She returned to the Broadway stage in the mid-1930s and, when she came back to films in the 1940s, her star status was downgraded to that of a featured player, often in "B" pictures. Her screen career ended in 1949 when she was named by the House Committee on Un-American Activities as a fellow traveler and was for all practical purposes blacklisted. Hobart appeared in a number of TV series from the 1950s on.

KEY ROLES

Julie / LILIOM, 1930, Fox Films, d-Frank Borzage.

Hobart is a servant girl who becomes enamored of a merry-go-round barker (Charles Farrell) at a Budapest amusement park. They marry, but he loses his job and she is forced to support them both. When he discovers that she is pregnant, he participates in a robbery and kills himself when the heist goes wrong. The chief magistrate in heaven gives him a chance to return to earth, but Hobart doesn't know him and resents his attempts to enter her garden. He returns to heaven where the magistrate convinces him he can only make his wife happy by leaving her with fond memories of him.

Linda Randolph / EAST OF BORNEO, 1931, Universal, d-George Melford.

Hobart braves all kinds of dangers while searching the jungles of Borneo for her doctor husband (Charles Bickford) who had run off when he felt betrayed by her. She finds him in excellent health acting as the personal physician of a prince in his jungle palace. The climax is a spectacular volcanic eruption.

Muriel Carew / DR. JEKYLL AND MR. HYDE, 1931, Paramount, d-Rouben Mamoulian.

Hobart has the thankless and easily forgettable role of Dr. Jekyll's society fiancée whom he leaves, in spirit at least, when he becomes Mr. Hyde to be with the far more interesting and sexy prostitute Ivy (Miriam Hopkins).

Babe Laval / CONVENTION GIRL, 1935, Flacon / First Division, d-Luther Reed.

Hobart is the proverbial tramp with a heart of gold who gets in trouble with a gangster boyfriend when she helps out a conventioneer from Philadelphia.

Dale Layden (Mary Jones) / I'LL SELL MY LIFE, 1941, Select, d-Elmer Clifton.

Hobart sacrifices her own life in order to get her brother out of the fix he's gotten into. It's a modest little thriller.

Katherine Mason / CONFLICT, 1945, Warners, d-Curtis Bernhardt.

Hobart is the wife of Humphrey Bogart, a successful architect who falls in love with her sister (Alexis Smith). He asks Hobart for a divorce but she refuses. He has an automobile accident and has a bad leg injury that leaves him immobile, but he heals faster than he lets on and, when Hobart goes off to a mountain retreat, he follows, strangles her, puts her in the car, and pushes it off a cliff. He hurries home to await being told of Hobart's death but it doesn't come, even when he reports her missing. He is haunted by his dead wife, thinking he smells her perfume or sees her. Finally he returns to the scene of the crime and, in doing so, gives himself away to the police who had set up an elaborate trap to trick him into revealing his guilt.

Virginia / THE FARMER'S DAUGHTER, 1947, RKO, d-H. C. Potter.

As Joseph Cotten's fiancée, Hobart rightly suspects that having a maid as pretty as Loretta Young living in the same home could cause her some trouble. Her snobbish attitude toward Young doesn't win her points with Cotten, however.

OTHER ROLES

1930: *Isabel Bravel* / A LADY SURRENDERS. **1931:** *Molly Prescott* / CHANCES; *Ann Brock* / COMPROMISED. **1932:** *Claire Strong* / SCANDAL FOR SALE. **1933:** *Ruth Hackett* / THE SHADOW LAUGHS. **1939:** *Anne Neville* / TOWER OF LONDON. **1940:** *Peggy Nolan* / WOLF OF NEW YORK; *Irene Burrows* / SUSAN AND GOD; *Ramona Lisa* / A NIGHT AT EARL CARROLL'S. **1941:** *Mrs. Merton* / ZIEGFELD GIRL; *Alice North* / SINGAPORE WOMAN; *Mrs. Carter Wardley* / LADY BE GOOD; *Mrs. Donnelly* / NOTHING BUT THE TRUTH; *Mrs. West* / NO HANDS ON THE CLOCK; *Carol Brent* / MR. AND MRS. NORTH. **1942:** *Claire Barrington* / A GENTLEMAN AT HEART; *Alma Pearce* / WHO IS HOPE SCHUYLER?; *Rosemary Walsh* / PRISON GIRL; *Mrs. Black* / DR. GILLESPIE'S NEW ASSISTANT. **1943:** *Mrs. Carson* / SALUTE TO THE MARINES; *Fraulein von Teufel* / THE ADVENTURES OF SMILIN' JACK; *Della* / THE MAD GHOUL; *Mrs. Burns* / CRIME DOCTOR'S STRANGEST CASE. **1944:** *Mrs. Powell* / SONG OF THE OPEN ROAD; *Lilyan Gregg* / THE SOUL OF A MONSTER. **1945:** *Dorothy* / THE BRIGHTON STRANGLER. **1946:** *Connie Palmer* / THE CAT CREEPS; *Marta Lestrade* / CANYON PASSAGE; *Edith Dexter* / CLAUDIA AND DAVID. **1947:** *Dean Agnes Meeler* / THE TROUBLE WITH WOMEN; *Diantha Marl* / CASS TIMBERLANE. **1948:** *Lydia Matthews* / MICKEY. **1949:** *Eleanora* / BRIDE OF VENGEANCE.

HOBSON, VALERIE

(1917–)

Valerie Hobson entered films when she was 16, shortly after beginning her professional acting career on the stage. After a brief and disappointing time in Hollywood she returned to Great Britain and became a popular, dependable leading lady for 15 years, retiring when she was only 37. Her characters were usually elegant, upper-class English ladies. She stood by her husband, politician John Profumo, during the famous Christine Keeler sex scandal in 1963, which toppled the British cabinet.

KEY ROLES

Elizabeth Frankenstein / BRIDE OF FRANKENSTEIN, 1935, Universal, d-James Whale.

Remember that Frankenstein is the name of the creator of the monster, not the monster itself. Thus, even though the title of this movie refers to the creation Frankenstein makes as a mate for the monster, Hobson appears as the wife of the good doctor and logically is the title character.

Helena Landless / THE MYSTERY OF EDWIN DROOD, 1935, Universal, d-Stuart Walker.

Hobson is fine in a supporting role in this filming of Dickens's unfinished novel about an opium-addicted choirmaster. The addict kills his nephew because of his love for a woman also desired by the nephew and then tries to frame the woman's real love for the killing.

Pat Drake / THIS MAN IS NEWS, 1938, Great Britain, Paramount / Pinebrook, d-David MacDonald.

Hobson is the wife of a reporter who, for a practical joke, tells his editor that he has just seen a murder. The story is printed and then comes true. The reporter is arrested but, with the help of Hobson, escapes and continues to make news. When the guilty are caught, Hobson and hubby get the glory.

Jill Blacklock / THE SPY IN BLACK, 1939, Great Britain, Harefield / Columbia, d-Michael Powell.

Hobson is a British spy posing as a German spy posing as a schoolteacher who catches a U-boat captain who is to contact the German spy. Follow that?

Draguisha / THE SILENT BATTLE, 1939, Great Britain, Paramount, d-Herbert Mason.

Hobson is a Bosnian girl who is persuaded by an armaments manufacturer that she can save her imprisoned father by assassinating the country's president.

Mrs. Sorensen / CONTRABAND, 1940, Great Britain, British National, d-Michael Powell.

Hobson's a British naval intelligence officer who falls into the hands of German spies operating out of a movie house before she turns the tables on them.

Estella / Estella's mother / GREAT EXPECTATIONS, 1946, Great Britain, Cineguild, d-David Lean.

Hobson not only appears as the daughter of the convict Pip befriended when he was a child, but as her mother as well. The daughter is a haughty beauty raised to ruin men, not love them, but the grown-up Pip's (John Mills) infatuation is too much for him to ever abandon her, especially when he discovers that her father is his benefactor, ex-convict Finlay Currie.

Blanche Fury / BLANCHE FURY, 1947, Great Britain, Cineguild, d-Marc Allegret.

Hobson takes the position of governess to the daughter of widower Michael Gough and agrees to marry Gough even though she is in love with Stewart Granger. Granger kills Gough but, when he decides to kill the daughter also, Hobson turns him in. He is hanged and she dies having his child.

Edith D'Ascoyne / KIND HEARTS AND CORONETS, 1949, Great Britain, Ealing, d-Robert Hamer.

Hobson is lovely and serene as the wife of Alec Guinness in his role as the last remaining obstacle in the way of Dennis Price's inheriting a title, as Price kills off his relatives one by one.

Countess of Chell / THE CARD, (THE PROMOTER), 1951, Great Britain, British Film Makers, d-Ronald Neame.

Hobson is a countess who has an interest in Alec Guinness, a man who prospers by his wits and becomes the youngest mayor of a British village.

OTHER ROLES

1933: *Rene* / EYES OF FATE. **1934:** *Susie* / TWO HEARTS IN WALTZ TIME; *Maria* / THE PATH OF GLORY; *Molly Butler* / BADGER'S GREEN; *Mauna* / STRANGE WIVES. **1935:** *Sandra Rogers* / RENDEZVOUS AT MIDNIGHT; *Lisa Glendon* / WEREWOLF OF LONDON; *Janet Baker* / CHINATOWN SQUAD; *Eleanor Dominey* / THE GREAT IMPERSONATION; *Susan* / OH, WHAT A NIGHT! **1936:** *Claire Barry* / AUGUST WEEKEND; *Tania* / THE SECRET OF STAMBOUL; *Laura Anstey* / NO ESCAPE. **1937:** *Glory Fane* / JUMP FOR GLORY. **1938:** *Mrs. Carruthers* / THE DRUM; *Kay Hammond* / Q PLANES. **1939:** *Pat Drake* / THIS MAN IN PARIS. **1941:** *Mary Ann Morison* / ATLANTIC FERRY. **1942:** *Carol Bennett* / UNPUBLISHED STORY. **1943:** *Maruschka Brunn* / THE ADVENTURES OF TARTU. **1946:** *Diana Wentworth* / THE YEARS BETWEEN. **1948:** *Eleanor Byrne* / THE SMALL VOICE. **1949:** *Stella* / TRAIN OF EVENTS; *Hester Grahame* / THE ROCKING HORSE WINNER; *Carol North* / INTERRUPTED JOURNEY. **1952:** *Alex Cornwall* / WHO GOES THERE?; *Stella Cartwright* / MEET ME TONIGHT. **1953:** *Alycia Roach* / THE VOICE OF MERRILL; *Barbie Lomax* / BACKGROUND. **1954:** *Catherine* / KNAVE OF HEARTS.

HODIAK, JOHN

(1914–1955)

John Hodiak began his career with radio acting assignments and, when World War II came along, his high blood pressure problem made him 4-F. The absence of so many young male actors during the war gave him his chance in the movies. After the war, despite his rather stiff acting style, he was given some interesting roles in which he didn't do much to distinguish himself. His movie career was going nowhere when he died at 41 of a coronary thrombosis.

KEY ROLES

Kovak / LIFEBOAT, 1944, 20th Century-Fox, d-Alfred Hitchcock.

Hodiak is an able-bodied seaman who is among a group of passengers and crew members of a ship torpedoed by a U-boat, which itself is sunk. They pick up the captain of the sub and it then becomes a battle of wills between the German and Hodiak, who also has a half-serious romance with Tallulah Bankhead.

Eric Moore / SUNDAY DINNER FOR A SOLDIER, 1944, 20th Century-Fox, d-Lloyd Bacon.

Hodiak is the soldier that a poor family living on a houseboat in Florida invites to a Sunday chicken dinner. He finds that Anne Baxter is also quite a dish.

Major Joppolo / A BELL FOR ADANO, 1945, 20th Century-Fox, d-Henry King.

Hodiak is the American major who, after his troops take over the Italian town of Adano, wins the affection of all when he arranges to replace the local bell, the town's one important possession.

Col. Edward Martin / COMMAND DECISION, 1948, MGM, d-Sam Wood.

Hodiak is the leader of the daylight bombing raid over Schweinhafen by American planes during World War II. The first run bombs the wrong target, but though the second attempt is successful, Hodiak and 50 bombers are lost.

Louis Barra / THE PEOPLE AGAINST O'HARA, 1951, MGM, d-John Sturges.

Hodiak is the district attorney in the case of an ex-alcoholic defense lawyer (Spencer Tracy) who sacrifices himself to prove his client's innocence. Try as he does, Hodiak can't prevent Tracy's death.

Cochise / CONQUEST OF COCHISE, 1953, Columbia, d-William Castle.

Don't expect Hodiak to be as good an actor as Jeff Chandler in the role of the great Apache chief who has a love affair with a Spanish aristocrat's daughter.

OTHER ROLES

1943: *Hart Ridges* / A STRANGER IN TOWN; *clerk* / SWING SHIFT MAISIE; *Roy Hartwood* / I DOOD IT; *Boris* / SONG OF RUSSIA. **1944:** *Flip Hennahan* / MAISIE GOES TO RENO; *Lt. Tom West* / MARRIAGE IS A PRIVATE AFFAIR. **1946:** *Ned Trent* / THE HARVEY GIRLS; *George Taylor* / SOMEWHERE IN THE NIGHT; *Ace Connors* / TWO SMART PEOPLE. **1947:** *Tony Arnelo* / THE ARNELO AFFAIR; *Eddie Bendix* / DESERT FURY; *Manuel Cortez* / LOVE FROM A STRANGER. **1948:** *Dr. Robert Sunday* / HOMECOMING. **1949:** *Tug Hintten* / THE BRIBE; *Jarvess* / BATTLEGROUND. **1950:** *Pete Karczag* / A LADY WITHOUT PASSPORT; *Spike Romway* / THE MINIVER STORY. **1951:** *Tom Lawry* / NIGHT INTO MORNING; *Brecan* / ACROSS THE WIDE MISSOURI; *Chick Johnson* / THE SELLOUT. **1952:** *Danny* / BATTLE ZONE. **1953:** *Capt. George Slocum* / MISSION OVER KOREA; *McCord* / AMBUSH AT TOMAHAWK GAP. **1954:** *Maj. Matthew Brady* / DRAGONFLY SQUADRON. **1955:** *John J. Armstrong* / TRIAL. **1956:** *Maj. Ward Thomas* / ON THE THRESHOLD OF SPACE.

HOFFMAN, DUSTIN

(1937–)

Dustin Hoffman admitted, "I always used to think I wanted to be an actor, when all along what I really wanted, deep down, was to be a movie star. It's something you just don't admit, even to yourself." Some would say that his movie star image is secondary to his reputation as a fine, versatile actor. Too short and unusual looking to be much of a romantic lead, he qualifies as a star character actor which allows him to have better roles than if he had become stuck in routine love stories. He received high praise for his work in off-Broadway roles, made his film debut in THE TIGER MAKES OUT, and became a superstar with THE GRADUATE, for which he received an Academy Award nomination. He was also nominated for his work in MIDNIGHT COWBOY, LENNY, and TOOTSIE, winning for KRAMER VS. KRAMER. He hasn't made very many movies recently but was spectacular as Willy Loman in "Death of a Salesman" on Broadway and in a made-for-TV movie.

KEY ROLES

Ben Braddock / THE GRADUATE, 1967, United Artists, d-Mike Nichols.

Shortly after graduating from college, Hoffman enters into an affair with Anne Bancroft, the wife of his father's business associate. Then he meets and falls in love with Bancroft's daughter (Katharine Ross) and finds what hellish fury is a woman scorned. The film said many important things to an entire generation, but they might be hard pressed now to say what precisely the message was.

Ratso Rizzo / MIDNIGHT COWBOY, 1969, United Artists, d-John Schlesinger.

Hoffman is a tubercular con man befriended by a dim-witted Texan (Jon Voight) who has come to New York to offer his services to the ladies as a stud for hire. The friends live in a deserted building and, when Hoffman realizes that another winter in New York will be the end of him, they get on a bus for Florida. But Hoffman dies as they reach the land of sunshine and warmth.

Jack Crabb / LITTLE BIG MAN, 1970, Stockbridge / Cinema Center, d-Arthur Penn.

Hoffman portrays a 121-year-old man who reminisces about cowboys, Indians, gunfighters, cavalry, good women and bad, from the time he and his sister survived an attack by one tribe of Indians and were rescued by another, until the battle of Little Big Horn. The film has no apparent point, and it's hard to say what sub-genre of western it is intended to be, but there are some enjoyable parts, even if the whole is nothing special.

David Summer / STRAW DOGS, 1971, Great Britain, Cinerama, d-Sam Peckinpah.

Hoffman is a mild-mannered American mathematician staying in a Cornish village, the home of his beautiful wife. She sort of encourages some of her old boyfriends and they and others lay seige to both her and their home, forcing Hoffman to become a violent defender of both.

Lenny Bruce / LENNY, 1974, United Artists, d-Bob Fosse.

Hoffman is superb portraying the comic whose act was always monitored by the police because of the topics he chose to joke about. His questioning humor is mild compared to what comedians use for material today.

Carl Bernstein / ALL THE PRESIDENT'S MEN, 1976, Warners, d-Alan J. Pakula.

Hoffman and Robert Redford portray the two *Washington Post* reporters who broke the story of the White House cover-up of the Watergate scandal.

Ted Kramer / KRAMER VS. KRAMER, 1980, Columbia, d-Robert Benton.

Hoffman won an Oscar for his portrayal of an advertising man who has so little time for his family that his wife (Meryl Streep) leaves him and their seven-year-old son. After the divorce, Hoffman becomes a caring father, even to the point of losing his job over the time he spends with his son. Later Streep shows up and takes him to court to get custody of the boy. She wins but allows the boy to stay with his dad as this seems the best thing for the lad.

Michael Dorsey / Dorothy Michaels / TOOTSIE, 1983, Columbia, d-Sydney Pollack.

Unable to find work as an actor, Hoffman dresses himself as a woman and wins a pivotal part on a soap opera. The problem is that he comes to love a co-star (Jessica Lange), and her dad has a crush on him.

OTHER ROLES

1967: *Hap* / THE TIGER MAKES OUT; *Jason Fisher* / MADIGAN'S MILLIONS. **1969:** *John* / JOHN AND MARY. **1971:** *Georgie Sacourey* / WHO IS HARRY KELLERMAN AND WHY IS HE SAYING THESE TERRIBLE THINGS ABOUT ME? **1972:** *Alfredo* / ALFREDO, ALFREDO. **1973:** *Louis Degas* / PAPILLON. **1976:** *Babe Levy* / MARATHON MAN. **1978:** *Max Dembo* / STRAIGHT TIME. **1979:** *Wally Stanton* / AGATHA. **1985:** *himself* / PRIVATE CONVERSATIONS (documentary). **1987:** *Chuck "Hawk" Clarke* / ISHTAR.

HOLDEN, WILLIAM

(William F. Beedle, Jr., 1918–1981)

Holden, who made his stage debut in 1938 and had a couple of brief movie appearances, got his big break when Barbara Stanwyck chose him to appear opposite her in GOLDEN BOY in 1939. He publicly expressed his appreciation to Stanwyck years later when they appeared together to present an Oscar at the Academy Awards. After his triumph as the young violinist, Holden found himself in a series of juvenile roles that, while pleasant, did not make great demands on his talent. It wasn't until SUNSET BOULEVARD in 1950 that the character Holden later played so often emerged. He seemed perfect as a man to be trusted but not always to do the right thing. When things went bad Holden's characters didn't cry over spilled milk but tried to make the best they could of things. Such a person was his survivor in STALAG 17, for which he won an Oscar. His roles in BORN YESTERDAY and NETWORK, which along with SUNSET BOULEVARD earned him Oscar nominations, also had a bit of the fatalist in them. Perhaps there was some of this in the real Holden whose problems with alcohol ultimately resulted in his death when he sustained what should have been a minor head wound that instead put him into an alcoholic coma. The craggy face and strong voice of his later years eloquently complemented the smiling and handsome boyish features of his young acting days.

KEY ROLES

Joe Bonaparte / GOLDEN BOY, 1939, Columbia, d-Rouben Mamoulian.

As a boy all Holden's character wanted was to play the violin. As an adult he finds other interests including prize fighting and sexy Barbara Stanwyck. This Clifford Odets play was tampered with to ensure a happy ending, despite the fact that Holden breaks his hand and kills a man in the ring.

George Gibbs / OUR TOWN, 1940, United Artists, d-Sam Wood.

In this very nice screen version of Thornton Wilder's play, Holden is the doctor's son in Grover's Corner who marries the girl next door and loses her to childbirth.

Andrew Long / THE REMARKABLE ANDREW, 1942, Paramount, d-Stuart Heisler.

This is certainly not a very good movie, but Holden scores as the small-town clerk framed by crooked politicians. He calls on and receives assistance from his namesake Andrew Jackson and the ghosts of other great American historical figures.

Lt. William Seacroft / DEAR RUTH, 1947, Paramount, d-William D. Russell.

In this lightweight family comedy, Holden arrives at the home of Joan Caulfield to meet in person the girl that he has been communicating with while stationed overseas. She doesn't know what he's talking about as it was her kid sister who did the writing, signing her sister's name and sending a picture of the elder girl. How does it work out? Well the sequel is called DEAR WIFE (1950).

Big Davey Harvey / RACHEL AND THE STRANGER, 1948, RKO, d-Norman Foster.

Holden is a backwoodsman who has lost his wife and is in need of someone to care for his son. He buys bondswoman Loretta Young and takes little note of her until Robert Mitchum comes courting and Holden realizes he has come to love Young.

Joe Gillis / SUNSET BOULEVARD, 1950, Paramount, d-Billy Wilder.

The story is told in flashback as Holden's corpse floats in a swimming pool and reminisces about how he came to be there. He takes up with an eccentric ex-silent screen star (Gloria Swanson) who is writing her memoirs and wants him to help her. She falls in love with him and keeps him in style until he thinks he can do better without her. He gets shot in the back as he walks out on her.

Lt. William Calhoun / UNION STATION, 1950, Paramount, d-Rudolph Mate.

Holden is a police detective who heads the manhunt for the kidnappers of a blind girl in a crowded metropolitan train station where the ransom is to be paid.

Paul Verall / BORN YESTERDAY, 1950, Columbia, d-George Cukor.

Holden is a writer hired by crooked junk tycoon Broderick Crawford to teach his dumb mistress (Judy Holliday) how to act and talk correctly. But she learns so much from her Pygmalion that she gets the upper hand on Crawford. Holden is a dedicated teacher on a crusade to make everyone smarter: "It's sort of a cause. I want everybody to be smart. I want 'em to be as smart as they can be. A world full of ignorant people is too dangerous to live in."

Sefton / STALAG 17, 1953, Paramount, d-Billy Wilder.

Holden has found a way to live a little better than his fellow POWs in a German Stalag during World War II. When it's learned that there's a traitor in the barracks, Holden is naturally suspected. He is able to unmask the real spy after taking a terrific beating and uses this as a diversion to escape, taking with him a pilot he's not too crazy about but who has information that must be protected. As he leaves his fellow prisoners he advises them, "Just one more word: if I ever run into any of you bums on a street corner, just let's pretend we never met before."

Bernie Dodd / THE COUNTRY GIRL, 1954, Paramount, d-George Seaton.

Holden is a Broadway director who is in constant conflict with Grace Kelly, the wife of an alcoholic singing star (Bing Crosby) who is attempting a comeback. Holden tells her, "There are two kinds of women: those who pay too much attention to themselves and those who don't pay enough." He doesn't tell Grace which he thinks she is but their bickering turns to love.

Mark Elliott / LOVE IS A MANY SPLENDORED THING, 1955, 20th Century-Fox, d-Henry King.

Holden is an American foreign correspondent in Hong Kong who falls in love with a Eurasian physician, but he can't marry her because his wife won't give him a divorce. He is killed when he goes to Korea to cover the war and his farewell to his girlfriend is: "Remember the blue beetle promised us a long and happy life."

Hal Carter / PICNIC, 1956, Columbia, d-Joshua Logan.

Holden drifts into a small mid-western town on the Fourth of July to look up an old college friend and put the bite on him, but he ends up stealing his buddy's girl (Kim Novak). Holden tells all he ever learned at his father's knee: "Son, the man of the house has got to have a pair of boots because he's got to do a lot of kicking."

Shears / THE BRIDGE ON THE RIVER KWAI, 1957, Columbia, d-David Lean.

Holden is an American sailor posing as an officer who escapes from a Japanese prison camp just as a new bunch of British prisoners are brought in. The British want him to guide them back to the camp so that they can blow up the bridge the Japanese are forcing the POWs to build. He returns but loses his life because the British commander (Alec Guinness) has become an unwitting collaborator for whom the bridge has become the only thing that keeps him going. Guinness tries to prevent the commandos from destroying it.

Maj. Hank Kendall / THE HORSE SOLDIERS, 1959, United Artists, d-John Ford.

Holden is the surgeon assigned to John Wayne's command of Union soldiers who make a raid deep in Confederate territory to destroy a railroad supply center. Holden and the Duke are constantly at odds. It seems Wayne lost his wife while she was under a surgeon's knife.

Eric Erickson / THE COUNTERFEIT TRAITOR, 1962, Paramount, d-George Seaton.

Holden is an American-born Swedish citizen who agrees to act as a British spy because he can move freely in Germany and has many friends in the Nazi country. He completes his mission but blows his cover and only barely makes it to safety.

Pike Bishop / THE WILD BUNCH, 1969, Warners-Seven Arts, d-Sam Peckinpah.

Holden is the leader of a gang of tough and cynical outlaws who are chased into Mexico in 1914 where they are hired by a rebel general to rob a munitions train. They end up in a bloody battle with their employer when he double-crosses them.

Max Schumacher / NETWORK, 1976, United Artists, d-Sidney Lumet.

Holden heads up the news division of a major network and leaves his wife to have an affair with Faye Dunaway, who is turning television news broadcasting into a circus. The theater of the absurd is headed by Holden's longtime friend, anchorman Peter Finch, who has gone bonkers. Aging Holden notes with resignation: "All of sudden, it's closer to the end than it is the beginning, and death is suddenly a perceptible thing for me—with definable features."

Tim Culley / S.O.B., 1981, Paramount, d-Blake Edwards.

Holden is a hard-drinking Hollywood movie director of a flop musical starring Julie Andrews. Her producer husband gets the brilliant idea of turning it into a soft-porn picture with Andrews baring her breasts.

OTHER ROLES

1938: *inmate* / PRISON FARM. **1939:** *graduating student* / MILLION DOLLAR LEGS; *Tim Taylor* / INVISIBLE STRIPES. **1940:** *P. J. "Petey" Simmons* / THOSE WERE THE DAYS. **1941:** *Peter Muncie* / ARIZONA; *Al Ludlow* / I WANTED WINGS; *Dan Thomas* / TEXAS. **1942:** *Casey Kirby* / THE FLEET'S IN; *Michael Stewart* / MEET THE STEWARTS. **1943:** *Norman Reese* / YOUNG AND WILLING. **1947:** *Colin McDonald* / BLAZE OF NOON; *guest* / VARIETY GIRL. **1948:** *Jason* / APARTMENT FOR PEGGY; *Al Walker* / THE DARK PAST. **1949:** *Capt. Del Stewart* / THE MAN FROM COLORADO; *Jim Dawkins* / STREETS OF LAREDO; *Dick Richmond* / MISS GRANT TAKES RICHMOND. **1950:** *Bill Seacroft* / DEAR WIFE; *Johnny Rutledge* / FATHER IS A BACHELOR. **1951:** *Peterson* / FORCE OF ARMS. **1952:** *Commander White* / SUBMARINE COMMAND; *Boots Malone* / BOOTS MALONE; *Jerry McKibbon* / THE TURNING POINT. **1953:** *Donald Gresham* / THE MOON IS BLUE; *Stanley Brown* / FOREVER FEMALE. **1954:** *Captain Roper* / ESCAPE FROM FORT BRAVO; *McDonald Walling* / EXECUTIVE SUITE; *David Larrabee* / SABRINA. **1955:** *Lt. Harry Brubaker* / THE BRIDGES AT TOKO-RI. **1956:** *Lt. Col. Colin Black* / THE PROUD AND THE PROFANE; *Maj. Lincoln Bond* / TOWARD THE UNKNOWN. **1958:** *David Ross* / THE KEY. **1960:** *Robert Lomax* / THE WORLD OF SUZIE WONG. **1962:** *Father O'Bannion* / SATAN NEVER SLEEPS; *Robert Hayward* / THE LION. **1964:** *Richard Benson* / PARIS WHEN IT SIZZLES; *Ferris* / THE SEVENTH DAWN. **1966:** *Alvarez Kelly* / ALVAREZ KELLY. **1967:** *Ransome* / CASINO ROYALE. **1968:** *Lt. Col. Robert Frederick* / THE DEVIL'S BRIGADE. **1969:** *Laurent* / THE CHRISTMAS TREE. **1971:** *Ross Bodine* / WILD ROVERS. **1972:** *John Benedict* / THE REVENGERS. **1973:** *Frank Harmon* / BREEZY. **1974:** *Wolkowski* / OPEN SEASON; *James Duncan* / THE TOWERING INFERNO. **1978:** *Richard Thorn* / DAMIEN—OMEN II; *Barry "Dutch" Detweiler* / FEDORA. **1979:** *Jim Sandell* / ASHANTI. **1980:** *Shelby Gilmore* / WHEN TIME RAN OUT. **1981:** *Patrick Foley* / THE EARTHLING.

HOLLIDAY, JUDY

(Judith Tuvim, 1922–1965)

On Broadway Judy Holliday created the role of the dumb but smart blonde in "Born Yesterday," a role she triumphantly repeated in the movie for which she received an Academy Award. This fine comedienne with the unusual shrieking voice had a fine sense of timing but a far too short career; she died of cancer at 42. A Rodgers and Hammerstein song from "South Pacific" best salutes her: "There's Nothing Like a Dame." Holliday recognized how important her peculiar speaking voice was to her career: "I seem to be blessed with fine pumice somewhere around my vocal chords."

KEY ROLES

Doris Attinger / ADAM'S RIB, 1949, MGM, d-George Cukor.

Holliday is very touching as the none-too-bright wife and mother who tries to defend the sanctity of her home by closing her eyes and shooting in the general direction of her philandering husband and his mistress. She's put on trial for attempted murder but her defense attorney (Katharine Hepburn) bests her screen husband, prosecuting attorney Spencer Tracy, in the trial.

Billie Dawn / BORN YESTERDAY, 1950, Columbia, d-George Cukor.

"Do me a favor, will ya, Harry? Drop dead!" With this statement beautiful-but-dumb blonde Holliday announces her independence from her boorish junk dealer lover Broderick Crawford. Crawford thought she was too dumb to move in the society his money is an entry to. He hires writer William Holden to give her some "class" and she learns her lessons well.

Nina Tracy / PHFFFT!, 1954, Columbia, d-Mark Robson.

The title refers to the sound of an expiring marriage between Holliday and Jack Lemmon who feel that they must be missing something. They are forced to re-evaluate their divorce.

Laura Partridge / THE SOLID GOLD CADILLAC, 1956, Columbia, d-Richard Quine.

Holliday owns a few shares of stock in a corporation whose founder is leaving his position as president to work for the government in Washington. The other officers of the company are little better than crooks and Holliday instinctively recognizes this. To get her off their backs they give her the do-nothing job of shareowner liaison officer. She becomes the darling of the small stockholders and, with the help of the former president (Paul Douglas), takes back control of the company.

Ella Peterson / BELLS ARE RINGING, 1960, MGM, d-Vincente Minnelli.

Holliday works for a telephone answering service, getting too much involved in the lives of her customers, particularly songwriter Dean Martin who isn't living up to his promise. The service is also being used as a front for a bookie. It's a musical with few decent tunes save Jules Styne's "The Party's Over" and Holliday's "I'm Goin' Back to the Bonjour Tristesse Brassiere Company."

OTHER ROLES

1938: *extra* / TOO MUCH JOHNSON. **1944:** *bit* / GREENWICH VILLAGE; *welder* / SOMETHING FOR THE BOYS; *Ruth Miller* / WINGED VICTORY. **1952:** *Florence Keefer* / THE MARRYING KIND. **1954:** *Gladys Glover* / IT SHOULD HAPPEN TO YOU. **1956:** *Emily Rocco* / FULL OF LIFE.

HOLM, CELESTE

(1919–)

Blonde, blue-eyed Celeste Holm studied acting at the University of Chicago, making her Broadway debut at age 19. After her success as Ado Annie in "Oklahoma" in 1943, she was signed by 20th Century-Fox. This intelligent, versatile actress won an Oscar for her third movie, GENTLEMAN'S AGREEMENT (1947), and was nominated twice more for COME TO THE STABLE (1949) and ALL ABOUT EVE (1950). Her views on her profession are summed up as follows: "Acting is controlled schizophrenia. That sounds neurotic but isn't. You are playing someone else while being yourself." She has appeared in numerous made-for-TV movies including COSTRA NOSTRA, ARCH ENEMY OF THE FBI (1966), THE DELPHI BUREAU (1972), THE UNDERGROUND MAN (1974), DEATH CRUISE (1974), CAPTAINS OF THE KINGS (1976), LOVE BOAT II (1978), and BACKSTAIRS AT THE WHITE HOUSE (1979).

KEY ROLES

Anne / GENTLEMAN'S AGREEMENT, 1947, 20th Century-Fox, d-Elia Kazan.

Holm is given some of the best lines in this story of magazine writer Gregory Peck posing as a Jew in order to get information on a series on anti-Semitism. She is something of a Greek chorus when she angrily points out the lack of commitment of Peck's fiancée (Dorothy McGuire): "...I'm intolerant of hypocrites... She'd rather let Dave lose that job than risk a fuss up there...She's afraid. The Kathys everywhere are afraid of getting the gate from their little groups of nice people. They make little clucking sounds of disapproval... But do they fight? Oh, no!"

Emily Hefferen / CHICKEN EVERY SUNDAY, 1948, 20th Century-Fox, d-George Seaton.

Holm is the practical wife of Dan Dailey, a man with many vague schemes that never quite work. When he loses the mortgage money on one of his investments, Holm has had enough, but friends of the couple reunite them.

Sister Scholastica / COME TO THE STABLE, 1949, 20th Century-Fox, d-Henry Koster.

Holm and Loretta Young are two French nuns who come to the United States with the object of building a hospital for children. They choose Bethlehem, Connecticut, where a painter allows them the use of her stable. From there they set out to raise the money that brings their dreams to fruition.

Karen Richards / ALL ABOUT EVE, 1950, 20th Century-Fox, d-Joseph L. Mankiewicz.

Like everyone else in the film, Holm, wife of playwright Hugh Marlowe and best friend of stage actress Bette Davis, is taken in by Anne Baxter, an aspiring actress who wants everything that Davis has. Holm even arranges for Davis to miss a performance so her understudy Baxter can go on and be acclaimed by audience and critics. But when Baxter makes a play for Holm's husband, enough is enough!

Sylvia Crewes / THE TENDER TRAP, 1955, MGM, d-Charles Walters.

Holm is a cellist and one of many girlfriends of bachelor Frank Sinatra. When David Wayne, an old friend, arrives for a visit with Sinatra, he thinks that Holm is just wonderful, but she sends him home to his wife and finds a single man who wants only her.

Liz Imbrie / HIGH SOCIETY, 1956, MGM, d-Charles Walters.

Holm is the photographer for a scandal magazine who, with writer Frank Sinatra, wins the right to cover Grace Kelly's wedding to her second husband. She's in love with Sinatra, but has to stand by patiently until Kelly decides that Old Blue Eyes isn't for her and goes back to her first hubby (Bing Crosby) instead.

OTHER ROLES

1946: *Miriam* / THREE LITTLE GIRLS IN BLUE. **1947:** *Celeste* / CARNIVAL IN COSTA RICA. **1948:** *Susie Smith* / ROAD HOUSE; *Grace* / THE SNAKE PIT. **1949:** *Doris Borland* / EVERYBODY DOES IT; *narrator* / A LETTER TO THREE WIVES. **1950:** *Flame O'Neil* / CHAMPAGNE FOR CAESAR. **1961:** *Helen* / BACHELOR FLAT. **1967:** *Louise Halloran* / DOCTOR, YOU'VE GOT TO BE KIDDING. **1973:** *Aunt Polly* / TOM SAWYER. **1976:** *Marian* / BITTERSWEET LOVE. **1978:** *Florence Hollister* / THE PRIVATE FILES OF J. EDGAR HOOVER. **1987:** *Jack's mother* / THREE MEN AND A BABY.

HOPE, BOB

(Leslie Townes Hope, 1903–)

Affectionately called "old ski nose" in honor of his rather pronounced turned-up snout, Bob Hope has been a favorite of radio, movies, and television for over 50 years. His tours overseas to entertain the troops, especially at Christmastime, cheer hundreds of thousands of lonely servicemen. Hope got his start in vaudeville in the 1920s where he perfected the character that has delighted audiences evermore—the none-too-bright, not too brave know-it-all who at the first sign of danger is likely to be found behind some woman's skirt whimpering like the coward he is. Some critics question the comic genius of Hope, insisting that all he has is good writers and good delivery of their lines. That may be so, but it's hard to argue with success as he has become one of the richest entertainers of all time. If you only know his late television work, you can be forgiven for believing he lacks originality; but his work on the radio in the 1930s and 1940s, and the movies of the same period, say otherwise.

KEY ROLES

Buzz Fielding / THE BIG BROADCAST OF 1938, 1938, Paramount, d-Mitchell Leisen.

Many are aware that in his film debut Hope sang Ralph Rainger and Leo Robin's Academy Award-winning "Thanks for the Memories" with Shirley Ross and it was so popular that he adopted it as his theme song. However, hearing Hope end one of his radio or TV shows with a few lines from the song fails to deliver the pleasure of the moving number heard in the movie, which was in every other way a nothing production. Hope is a radio announcer who, along with his three alimony-seeking ex-wives, is aboard an ocean liner competing in a race across the Atlantic.

Steve Merrick / THANKS FOR THE MEMORY, 1938, Paramount, d-George Archainbaud.

Fans so loved Shirley Ross and Hope in the previous movie that Paramount brought them back as newlyweds who agree that she should return to work as a model to support him in his efforts to become a successful author. They had another million dollar song hit with "Two Sleepy People" by Frank Loesser and Hoagy Carmichael.

Wallie Campbell / THE CAT AND THE CANARY, 1939, Paramount, d-Elliott Nugent.

To the question, "Don't big empty houses scare you?" Hope answers, "Not me. I used to be in vaudeville." This is typical of his character in this story about the gathering of prospective heirs at the bayou home of an eccentric millionaire ten years after his death. It gets pretty spooky and three people meet their maker.

Ace Lannigan / ROAD TO SINGAPORE, 1940, Paramount, d-Victor Schertzinger.

The first road picture with Bing Crosby, Dorothy Lamour, and Bob Hope is fairly controlled. The ad-libbing came later. In this one the boys escape to the South Seas to get away from the dangers of marriage-minded women. But in Singapore they encounter beautiful Lamour for whom they compete.

Larry Lawrence / GHOST BREAKERS, 1940, Paramount, d-George Marshall.

Hope's reaction to Richard Carlson's description of zombies—"It's worse than horrible because a zombie has no will of his own. You see them sometimes walking around blindly, with dead eyes, following orders, not knowing what they do, not caring"—is "You mean like Democrats." He's a radio commentator who becomes involved with Paulette Goddard and helps her rid her spooky Cuban island and castle of things that go bump in the night.

Fearless Hubert Frazier / ROAD TO ZANZIBAR, 1941, Paramount, d-Victor Schertzinger.

Two stranded girls, Dorothy Lamour and Una Merkel, con Hope and Crosby into taking them on a long safari in darkest Africa without letting the two romantically inclined shnooks know that they are taking Lamour to her rich fiancé.

Don Bolton / CAUGHT IN THE DRAFT, 1941, Paramount, d-David Butler.

Movie star Hope enlists in the army after unsuccessfully avoiding the draft and tries to impress Dorothy Lamour, daughter of the colonel. He proves to be a disaster as a soldier as do his agent and chauffeur who join up with him.

Larry Haines / MY FAVORITE BLONDE, 1942, Paramount, d-Sidney Lanfield.

Hope works second banana to a penguin and Madeleine Carroll is so desperate that she seeks his help in carrying instructions from the British government to an aviation company in Los Angeles. But they must deal with a bunch of Nazi agents before completing their mission.

Robert Kitteredge / THEY GOT ME COVERED, 1943, RKO, d-David Butler.

Hope is an incompetent foreign correspondent who always misses the big story. When he's fired he tries to get his job back by exposing Axis saboteurs. Naturally he bungles his way to success.

Ronnie Jackson / MY FAVORITE BRUNETTE, 1947, Paramount, d-Elliott Nugent.

Hope is just about to go to the gas chamber as he tells how he was a baby photographer who wanted to be a private detective like the guy next door (Alan Ladd). He became involved with a mystery woman and a bunch of sinister types, leading to his present predicament. As always Hope, through no fault of his own, not only survives but gets the girl.

Painless Peter Potter / THE PALEFACE, 1948, Paramount, d-Norman Z. McLeod.

Hope is a correspondent school dentist who moves west and meets Calamity Jane, who is seeking the scoundrel selling guns to the Indians. If she is successful she will be pardoned for past crimes. To avoid suspicion, she marries Hope, who becomes an unwilling hero, singing the Oscar-winning "Buttons and Bows" by Jay Livingston and Ray Evans.

Humphrey / FANCY PANTS, 1950, Paramount, d-George Marshall.

Hope is an incompetent actor who newly rich Lucille Ball and her mother believe is a British butler. They take him home to the Wild West, where he is mistaken for an English lord. It's a loose remake of RUGGLES OF RED GAP.

Peanuts White and Eric Augustine / MY FAVORITE SPY, 1951, Paramount, d-Norman Z. McLeod.

As a second-rate burlesque comic, Hope bears a striking resemblance to a notorious spy, also played by Hope. The former is forced into impersonating the latter in Tangiers where he runs into counterspy Hedy Lamarr. When the real spy shows up, Hope is in double trouble.

Eddie Foy / THE SEVEN LITTLE FOYS, 1955, Paramount, d-Melville Shavelson.

Although vaudevillian Eddie Foy swears he will always remain single, he falls in love with a ballet dancer, marries, and before he knows it has seven kids. She dies and after a while, not knowing what else to do with them, Hope works the kids into the act. He does a nice job dancing with James Cagney, once more playing George M. Cohan in a cameo. And Hope sings the Bert Williams classic "Nobody."

James J. Walker / BEAU JAMES, 1957, Paramount, d-Melville Shavelson.

Hope portrays the charming but essentially crooked mayor of New York City during the 1920s who, although Catholic and married, takes up with a showgirl while trying to run the city. He isn't allowed to keep his job, but not because of his infidelity.

Parker Ballantine / CRITIC'S CHOICE, 1963, Warners, d-Don Weis.

Hope is a Broadway critic who finds he must review a new play written by his wife. Will the marriage survive? Are you kidding?

OTHER ROLES

1938: *Bud Brady* / COLLEGE SWING; *Jim Brewster* / GIVE ME A SAILOR. **1939:** *John Kidley* / NEVER SAY DIE; *Nicky Nelson* / SOME LIKE IT HOT. **1941:** *Steve Bennet* / NOTHING BUT THE TRUTH; *Jim Taylor* / LOUISIANA PURCHASE. **1942:** *Orville "Turkey" Jackson* / ROAD TO MOROCCO; *guest* / STAR SPANGLED RHYTHM. **1943:** *Jerry Walker* / LET'S FACE IT. **1944:** *"Sylvester the Great" Crosby* / THE PRINCESS AND THE PIRATE. **1945:** *Chester Hooton* / ROAD TO UTOPIA. **1946:** *Monsieur Beaucaire* / MONSIEUR BEAUCAIRE. **1947:** *Michael Valentine* / WHERE THERE'S LIFE; *Hot Lips Barton* / ROAD TO RIO; *guest* / VARIETY GIRL. **1949:** *Sorrowful Jones* / SORROWFUL JONES; *Freddie Hunter* / THE GREAT LOVER. **1951:** *The Lemon Drop Kid* / THE LEMON DROP KID. **1952:** *Junior Potter* / SON OF PALEFACE; *Harold Gridley* / ROAD TO BALI; *cameo* / THE GREATEST SHOW ON EARTH. **1953:** *Wally Hogan* / OFF LIMITS; *Stanley Snodgrass* / HERE COME THE GIRLS; *cameo* / SCARED STIFF. **1954:** *Pippo Poppolin* / CASANOVA'S BIG NIGHT. **1956:** *Francis X. Dignan* / THAT CERTAIN FEELING; *Maj. Chuck Lock-*

wood / THE IRON PETTICOAT. **1958:** *Robert Leslie Hunter* / PARIS HOLIDAY. **1959:** *Milford Farnsworth* / ALIAS JESSE JAMES; *guest* / THE FIVE PENNIES. **1961:** *Adam J. Niles* / BACHELOR IN PARADISE. **1962:** *Chester Babcock* / THE ROAD TO HONG KONG. **1963:** *Matt Merriwether* / CALL ME BWANA. **1964:** *Frank Larrimore* / A GLOBAL AFFAIR. **1965:** *Bob Holcomb* / I'LL TAKE SWEDEN. **1966:** *Tom Meade* / BOY, DID I GET A WRONG NUMBER!; *cameo* / NOT WITH MY WIFE YOU DON'T!; *guest* / THE OSCAR. **1967:** *Henry Dimsdale* / EIGHT ON THE LAM. **1968:** *Sgt. Dan O'Farrell* / THE PRIVATE NAVY OF SGT. O'FARRELL. **1971:** *Frank Benson* / HOW TO COMMIT MARRIAGE. **1972:** *Dan Bartlett* / CANCEL MY RESERVATION. **1979:** *guest* / THE MUPPET MOVIE.

HOPKINS, ANTHONY

(1937–)

Anthony Hopkins, a stocky figure with a fine Welsh accent, has expressed disinterest in being the usual leading man. He prefers interesting character roles of men under stress which he plays in movies, on the stage, and on television. Interested in a career as a concert pianist, Hopkins went to the Welsh College of Music and Drama, where he showed promise as an actor. In 1965 he joined the Old Vic and made his first major appearance in "The Dance of Death" as understudy to Laurence Olivier. Hopkins has been most successful in various period pictures. His TV movies include VICTORY AT ENTEBBE (1976), THE LINDBERGH KIDNAPPING CASE (1976), MAYFLOWER: THE PILGRIM'S ADVENTURE (1979), THE BUNKER (1981), THE HUNCHBACK OF NOTRE DAME (1983), and GUILTY CONSCIENCE (1985).

KEY ROLES

Prince Richard the Lion-Hearted / THE LION IN WINTER, 1968, Great Britain, Haworth, d-Anthony Harvey.

Hopkins is one of three possible heirs to the throne of Henry II. The king and his estranged queen, Eleanor of Acquitaine, argue over whom to appoint as Henry's successor. Hopkins is the strongest of the three and is the eventual winner, but according to this story Henry was about to kill all of his sons because he trusted none of them. One also understands why, later, brother John will attempt to usurp the throne from Richard.

Siegfried Farnon / ALL CREATURES GREAT AND SMALL, 1974, Venedon / EMI, d-Claude Whatham.

The picture deals with the life and love of the pre-war Yorkshire country assistant veterinarian celebrated in James Herriot's books. It's a simple tale with a style of long ago.

Corky / Voice of Fats / MAGIC, 1978, 20th Century-Fox, d-Richard Attenborough.

Hopkins is a schizophrenic ventriloquist who is gradually losing grip with reality while his dummy is taking over. Hopkins provides the voice of Fats the dummy as well.

Frederick Treves / THE ELEPHANT MAN, 1980, Great Britain, Brooksfilms, d-David Lynch.

Hopkins is a British surgeon who treats a hideously deformed sideshow freak (John Hurt). With Hopkins's help, Hurt becomes a popular member of fashionable society.

Capt. William Bligh / THE BOUNTY, 1984, de Laurentiis, d-Roger Donaldson.

Hopkins is summoned before a court martial to explain the events leading up to the taking of his ship Bounty by Fletcher Christian (Mel Gibson). In this version, Christian and Bligh were "close" friends prior to the voyage.

OTHER ROLES

1967: *Brechtian* / THE WHITE BUS. **1969:** *Claudius* / HAMLET; *John Avery* / THE LOOKING GLASS WAR. **1971:** *Philip Calvert* / WHEN EIGHT BELLS TOLL. **1972:** *Lloyd George* / YOUNG WINSTON. **1973:** *Torvald Helmer* / A DOLL'S HOUSE. **1974:** *Kostya* / THE GIRL FROM PETROVKA; *Supt. John McCleod* / JUGGERNAUT. **1977:** *Elliot Hoover* / AUDREY ROSE; *Lt. Col. John Frost* / A BRIDGE TOO FAR. **1978:** *Captain Johnson* / INTERNATIONAL VELVET. **1980:** *Adam Evans* / A CHANGE OF SEASONS. **1986:** *Frank Doel* / 84 CHARING CROSS ROAD. **1987:** *Bill* / THE GOOD FATHER.

HOPKINS, MIRIAM

(Ellen Miriam Hopkins, 1902–1972)

This petite blonde was born in Georgia and retained a charming trace of a drawl throughout her career. After graduation from Syracuse University she went to New York to study ballet, but broke her ankle and was forced to look for other theater work. She starred in a number of Broadway shows and then began a career in films that lasted 35 years. Her leading roles in the 1930s made her one of the industry's top stars. Later she continued to make her mark in some superb matronly supporting roles. Her bitchiness in several fine women's movies delighted audiences, but she had a reputation of being very hard to work with.

KEY ROLES

Princess Anna / THE SMILING LIEUTENANT, 1931, Paramount, d-Ernst Lubitsch.

Hopkins appears as a dowdy visiting princess who falls for Viennese Guard officer Maurice Chevalier, who is then ordered to marry her. Chevalier's mistress, violinist Claudette Colbert, in a display of great good sportsmanship, shows Hopkins how to improve her appearance and be attractive to her reluctant fiancé.

Ivy Pearson / DR. JEKYLL AND MR. HYDE, 1932, Paramount, d-Rouben Mamoulian.

Hopkins is superb as the waterfront prostitute who is helped by good Dr. Jekyll, and who probably puts some not-so-pure thoughts in his mind. He acts on those thoughts when he becomes Mr. Hyde, ultimately killing Hopkins after brutalizing her over a period of time.

Lily Vantier / TROUBLE IN PARADISE, 1932, Paramount, d-Ernst Lubitsch.

Hopkins is quite a bit put out when her jewel thief partner (Herbert Marshall) falls in love with Kay Francis, their next intended victim. It's a wonderful movie with everyone in top form.

Temple Drake / THE STORY OF TEMPLE DRAKE, 1933, Paramount, d-Stephen Roberts.

Hopkins is stunning in the role of the southern belle who finds she likes rough treatment and degradation with a gangster and brothel owner. Even though it's tame compared to the novel *Sanctuary* by William Faulkner on which it is based, it sparked the creation of the Catholic Church's Legion of Decency censorship board the next year.

Becky Sharp / BECKY SHARP, 1935, RKO, d-Rouben Mamoulian.

In this first full-length production in three-color Technicolor, Hopkins portrays the antiheroine of Thackeray's *Vanity Fair*. She's an ambitious and frivolous girl who rises out of the mud of a battlefield to the foot of the throne during Regency England. The film is a milestone but not an interesting movie.

Martha Dobie / THESE THREE, 1936, Goldwyn / United Artists, d-William Wyler.
Hopkins and Merle Oberon turn an old run-down home into a school for girls, but one of their pupils (Bonita Granville) spitefully tells her grandmother that the two teachers and a doctor (Joel McCrea) have some kind of ménage à trois going on. The truth comes out but the school is finished and so is the close relationship between the two women.

Delia Lovell Ralston / THE OLD MAID, 1939, Warners, d-Edmund Goulding.
When her beau is killed in the Civil War, unwed Bette Davis lets cousin Hopkins raise her illegitimate child as her own. The battles between Davis and Hopkins are something to see.

Mrs. Leslie (Caroline) Carter / THE LADY WITH RED HAIR, 1941, Warners, d-Curtis Bernhardt.
This is the impressive biopic of celebrated stage actress Caroline Carter, telling of her association with impresario David Belasco.

Millie Drake / OLD ACQUAINTANCE, 1943, Warners, d-Vincent Sherman.
This movie presents the splendid lifelong battle of wits and meddling in each other's lives of two catty novelists (Hopkins and Bette Davis).

Lavinia Penniman / THE HEIRESS, 1949, Paramount, d-William Wyler.
No longer a leading lady, Hopkins portrays the silly old romantic aunt of plain Olivia de Havilland. She encourages her niece's romance with charming fortune hunter Montgomery Clift.

Lily Mortar / THE CHILDREN'S HOUR, 1962, United Artists, d-William Wyler.
In the second filming of the Lillian Hellman play, Hopkins plays the flighty and unreliable aunt of one of the two teachers accused by a malicious child of being lesbian lovers.

OTHER ROLES

1930: *Marion Lenox* / FAST AND LOOSE. **1931:** *Rosie Duggan* / TWENTY-FOUR HOURS. **1932:** *Emma Krull* / TWO KINDS OF WOMEN; *Gloria Bishop* / DANCERS IN THE DARK; *Maria Yaskaya* / THE WORLD AND THE FLESH. **1933:** *Gilda Farrell* / DESIGN FOR LIVING; *Louise Starr* / THE STRANGER'S RETURN. **1934:** *Lydia Darrow* / ALL OF ME; *Curly Flagg* / SHE LOVES ME NOT; *Dorothy Hunter* / THE RICHEST GIRL IN THE WORLD. **1935:** *Mary Rutledge* / BARBARY COAST; *Phyllis Manning Lorrimore* / SPLENDOR. **1937:** *Ann Williams* / MEN ARE NOT GODS; *Helene Maury* / THE WOMAN I LOVE; *Virginia Travis* / WOMAN CHASES MAN; *Susan Fletcher* / WISE GIRL. **1940:** *Julia Haynes* / VIRGINIA CITY. **1942:** *Flo Melton* / A GENTLEMAN AFTER DARK. **1951:** *Fran Carleton* / THE MATING SEASON. **1952:** *Julia Hartswood* / CARRIE; *The Duchess* / THE OUTCASTS OF POKER FLAT. **1965:** *Maude Brown* / FANNY HILL. **1966:** *Mrs. Reeves* / THE CHASE.

HORNE, LENA

(1917–)

This beautiful black singer and actress is a most remarkable lady in that both her looks and her voice seem to be getting better all the time. When she was young, though, Hollywood didn't know what to do with her and in most of her movies she was given only specialty numbers in which she thrilled audiences but which had little to do with the story of the movie. She also appeared in a number of shorts including HARLEM HOTSHOTS (1940), HARLEM ON PARADE (1942), BOOGIE WOOGIE DREAM (1942), and MANTAN MESSES UP (1946).

KEY ROLES

Georgia Brown / CABIN IN THE SKY, 1943, MGM, d-Vincente Minnelli.
Horne is a source of temptation for likable gambler Eddie "Rochester" Anderson, who can't resist temptation. In this all-black musical there's not only a tug of war between Horne and Anderson's wife (Ethel Waters) but also one between agents of heaven and hell for his soul. Horne doesn't have the best songs—those went to Waters—but she does nicely with "Honey in the Honeycomb" by John Latoche and Vernon Duke.

Selena Rogers / STORMY WEATHER, 1943, 20th Century-Fox, d-Andrew Stone.
This film traces the evolution of black music from 1911 to 1936. It is held together by the briefest of plots about a romance between Horne and Bill Robinson. The show stopper is Horne's singing the title number by Harold Arlen and Ted Koehler as Katherine Dunham and her troupe dance to the music. Other songs performed by Horne with Robinson or Cab Calloway include "I Can't Give You Anything But Love" and "There's No Two Ways About Love."

Guest / THOUSANDS CHEER, 1943, MGM, d-George Sidney.
Horne gives a memorable rendition of Andy Razaf and Fats Waller's "Honeysuckle Rose" in this MGM contribution to the war effort. The story is about a soldier and the colonel's beautiful daughter, with their growing love setting the stage for a big show with most of the studio's stars performing.

Guest / ZIEGFELD FOLLIES, 1946, MGM, d-Vincente Minnelli and others.
In this movie deceased Flo Ziegfeld wishes he could put on just one more show with stars then available. Horne gives a scorching performance singing "Love" by Hugh Martin and Ralph Blane.

Claire Quintana / DEATH OF A GUNFIGHTER, 1969, Universal, d-Robert Totten.
After a 12-year absence from the screen, the beautiful Horne appears as a madam and mistress to a small-town marshal who has fallen from favor with the powers that be. She eventually marries him but we only get one song from her: "Sweet Apple Wine" by Oliver Nelson and Carol Hall.

Glinda / THE WIZ, 1978, Universal, d-Sidney Lumet.
Horne sings a black pride number, "Believe in Yourself" by Charlie Smith, as she portrays the good witch in this all-black version of THE WIZARD OF OZ.

OTHER ROLES

1938: *Ethel* / THE DUKE IS TOPS. **1942:** *specialty number* / PANAMA HATTIE. **1943:** *specialty number* / I DOOD IT; *specialty number* / SPRING FEVER. **1944:** *Fernway de la Fer* / BROADWAY RHYTHM; *specialty number* / TWO GIRLS AND A SAILOR. **1946:** *Julie* / TILL THE CLOUDS ROLL BY. **1948:** *specialty act* / WORDS AND MUSIC. **1950:** *specialty act* / DUCHESS OF IDAHO. **1956:** *specialty act* / MEET ME IN LAS VEGAS.

HOWARD, LESLIE

(Leslie Stainer, 1890–1943)

Many will recall Leslie Howard most fondly for his role in GONE WITH THE WIND, as the only man Scarlett O'Hara really loved but the one she could not have.

Howard saw things differently, remarking, "I haven't the slightest intention of playing another weak, watery character such as Ashley Wilkes. I've played enough ineffectual characters already." And so he had, but so well that such roles seemed made for the distinguished British stage and screen actor. Born in London, he worked as a bank clerk until the outbreak of World War I when he joined the British army. After having been invalided out of service in 1918 he was determined to become an actor. He toured the provinces and made his London debut the same year. He went to the United States in 1920 to make his Broadway debut and, after numerous stage successes, made his first starring movie (OUTWARD BOUND) in 1930, having appeared in shorts and silents as early as 1914. Until his death he pleased audiences as actor, producer, and director of numerous fine movies. He lost his life when the airliner in which he was traveling was shot down over the Bay of Biscay by Nazis who reportedly believed that Prime Minister Churchill was aboard.

KEY ROLES

Tom Prior / OUTWARD BOUND, 1930, Warners, d-Robert Milton.

Howard is a high-strung alcoholic wastrel who is one of several passengers on a mysterious fog-shrouded ocean liner with apparently only one crewmember, a steward. Howard slowly comes to the realization that they are all dead and on their way to their judgment. What he doesn't know is that his mother, from whom he has long been separated, is also aboard.

John Carteret / SMILIN' THROUGH, 1932, MGM, d-Sidney Franklin.

In this third filming of Jane Cowl and Jane Murfin's well-loved romance, country squire Howard falls in love with Norma Shearer, who is coveted by half-crazed Fredric March. On the day of Howard and Shearer's wedding, March shoots at the former and kills the latter. As she dies in her intended's arms, she promises always to be near him and that they will one day be reunited. Through the years her spirit appears to him when needed and before they are united in death she convinces him not to stand in the way of his niece's love for the son of the man who had killed her.

Peter Standish / BERKELEY SQUARE, 1933, Fox Films, d-Frank Lloyd.

In this romantic fantasy, Howard lives in 1933 London in a Berkeley Square mansion and is obsessed with the notion that he can transport himself back to 1784, which marks the date that one of his ancestors arrived from the Americas. He succeeds and becomes that ancestor and falls in love with Heather Angel whom he knows he can never have since he must return to his own age.

Philip Carey / OF HUMAN BONDAGE, 1934, RKO, d-John Cromwell.

Although the film is clearly Bette Davis's, Howard is excellent as the quite in-control but helplessly infatuated medical student who feels bonded to the slatternly waitress / prostitute who really despises him.

Sir Percy Blakeney / THE SCARLET PIMPERNEL, 1935, Great Britain, London Films, d-Harold Young.

In this first-class adventure yarn, Howard is excellent as the dashing Englishman who poses as a fop to disguise his work as one who saves French aristocrats from the guillotine. He can't resist thumbing his nose at his adversaries by writing the doggerel, "We seek him here, we seek him there, those Frenchies seek him everywhere. Is he in heaven? Is he in hell? That demmed, elusive Pimpernel."

Alan Squier / THE PETRIFIED FOREST, 1936, Warners, d-Archie Mayo.

Most people wouldn't be pleased if they found themselves held hostage by a mad-dog killer and his gang, but wandering, despairing writer Howard welcomes it, saying, "Let there be killing. All this evening I've had a feeling of destiny closing in." The killer, Humphrey Bogart, obliges Howard, killing him so that Bette Davis can collect his insurance and fulfill her dream of going to Paris.

Prof. Henry Higgins / PYGMALION, 1938, Great Britain, Pascal, d-Anthony Asquith and Leslie Howard.

Long before Rex Harrison came along and made the role his in "My Fair Lady," Howard superbly played the phonetics professor who takes a cockney flower girl and trains her to speak the king's English so well that she passes for a duchess. Before his success he tells the girl (Wendy Hiller): "Yes, you squashed cabbage leaf, you disgrace to the noble architecture of these columns, you incarnate insult to the English language, I can pass you off as the queen of Sheba."

Ashley Wilkes / GONE WITH THE WIND, 1939, MGM / Selznick, d-Victor Fleming, George Cukor, and Sam Wood.

It occurs to us that had Howard spoken plainly to Vivien Leigh of his great love for Olivia de Havilland, she wouldn't have spent all of her life chasing after the unattainable and might have had a little less of a problem in her romantic life. But then that would have been a different story. But Clark Gable as Rhett Butler wonders the same thing, raging at Scarlett: "Of course, the comic figure in all this is the long-suffering Mr. Wilkes! Mr. Wilkes who can't be mentally faithful to his wife and won't be unfaithful to her technically. Why doesn't he make up his mind?"

Holger Brandt / INTERMEZZO, 1939, Selznick / United Artists, d-Gregory Ratoff.

In this film, which introduced the lovely Swedish actress Ingrid Bergman to the United States, Howard portrays a married violinist who has an affair with Bergman, his piano accompanist. He soon misses his family and Bergman sends him back.

Reginald Mitchell / THE FIRST OF THE FEW, (SPITFIRE), 1941, Great Britain, Melbourne / British Aviation, d-Leslie Howard.

In this impressive but low-key biopic, Howard portrays the man who saw World War II coming and developed the Spitfire fighter plane for the British Air Force.

Philip Armstrong Scott / FORTY-NINTH PARALLEL, (THE INVADERS), 1941, Great Britain, GFD / Ortus, d-Michael Powell.

Few Americans knew that the 49th parallel in the title referred to the boundary of Canada and the United States. Howard is just one of several fine actors—including Raymond Massey, Laurence Olivier, Anton Walbrook, and Eric Portmann—who impress in this effective propaganda piece about seven stranded U-boat men trying to reach neutral United States from Canada.

OTHER ROLES

1917: *Rollo* / THE HAPPY WARRIOR. **1919:** *Tony Dunciman* / THE LACKEY AND THE LADY. **1931:** *Dan Pritchard* / NEVER THE TWAIN

SHALL MEET; *Berry* / FIVE AND TEN; *Dwight Winthrop* / A FREE SOUL; *David Trent* / DEVOTION. **1932:** *Max Tracey* / RESERVED FOR LADIES; *Tom Collier* / THE ANIMAL KINGDOM. **1933:** *John Carlton* / SECRETS; *Capt. Fred Allison* / CAPTURED. **1934:** *Albert Latour* / THE LADY IS WILLING; *Stephen Locke* / BRITISH AGENT. **1936:** *Romeo Montague* / ROMEO AND JULIET. **1937:** *Basil Underwood* / IT'S LOVE I'M AFTER; *Atterbury Dodd* / STAND-IN. **1942:** *Prof. Horatio Smith* / PIMPERNEL SMITH; *voice* / IN WHICH WE SERVE.

HOWARD, TREVOR

(1916–1987)

Gravelly-voiced Trevor Howard worked on the stage prior to World War II when he joined the army. In 1943 he was wounded and returned to the theater, making his film debut in 1944. Looking at his career now, it is clear that his best roles were among his first films. The quality of the movies in which he appeared during his last dozen years is clearly inferior to his considerable talent for portraying believable characters about whom audiences care. Like many a fine actor past his peak, but still in demand, Howard made his share of cheap foreign movies, took the money, and ran. These include DIE REBELLION (1978) and THE DEVIL IMPOSTER (1983). His made-for-TV movies include CATHOLICS (1973), NIGHT FLIGHT (1978), STAYING ON (1980), INSIDE THE THIRD REICH (1982), and THE DEADLY GAME (1982).

KEY ROLES

Dr. Alec Harvey / BRIEF ENCOUNTER, 1946, Great Britain, Cineguild, d-David Lean.

In one of the sweetest love stories ever filmed, Howard is a British physician who helps take a cinder out of the eye of Celia Johnson as they both wait for a train. This innocent meeting leads to a once-a-week love affair between the two married, middle-class people, neither of whom are really dissatisfied with their mates. They agree not to meet again when he is offered a post overseas and their last moments together are ruined by a gabby woman friend of Johnson's.

Dr. Barney Barnes / GREEN FOR DANGER, 1946, Great Britain, Rank, d-Sidney Gilliat.

Howard is a surgeon who is among the suspects when murder takes place in the operating theater of a wartime emergency hospital. It's an excellent comedy-thriller, very popular in its day and still worth seeing.

Major Calloway / THE THIRD MAN, 1950, Great Britain, British Lion, d-Carol Reed.

Howard is the British officer in post-World War II Vienna who convinces Joseph Cotten that the latter's old friend (Orson Welles), believed dead, was an unfeeling black market profiteer who sold diluted medicine, which only worsened the conditions of dreadfully ill children. When Welles shows up alive, both Howard and Cotten pursue him.

Harry Scobie / THE HEART OF THE MATTER, 1953, Great Britain, British Lion, d-George More O'Ferrall.

In 1942 in an African colony, Howard has an affair while his wife is away. He is not ready to end things and ask forgiveness in the confessional, so this staunch Catholic police officer considers suicide, because he knows his wife will expect him to take communion with her at mass when she returns. If it occurs to the reader that there might be other solutions, the fault lies with the writers, not Howard.

Chris Ford / THE KEY, 1958, Great Britain, Columbia, d-Carol Reed.

Howard is a World War II tugboat skipper about to embark on a dangerous mission. He passes the key to an apartment and the girl who goes along with it (Sophia Loren) to younger tugboat captain William Holden, just as someone earlier had passed the key on to Howard before going to his death at sea.

Merel / THE ROOTS OF HEAVEN, 1958, 20th Century-Fox, d-John Huston.

This is the flawed but marvelous story of a man (Howard) who takes up the cause of the African elephant, finally banding together with a small group of like-minded men and women to fight the poachers and hunters who would destroy the great beasts. Howard, a charismatic Christ-like figure, converts too few to his cause to succeed, but he is willing to be crucified while trying.

Walter Morel / SONS AND LOVERS, 1960, Great Britain, 20th Century-Fox, d-Jack Cardiff.

Howard was nominated for an Academy Award for his moving portrayal of a Nottingham miner and family man. It is among the best work Howard ever did on the screen.

Capt. William Bligh / MUTINY ON THE BOUNTY, 1962, MGM, d-Lewis Milestone.

Howard makes a feisty no-nonsense Bligh who considers ordinary seaman as so much scum and isn't much impressed with foppish sounding officers like Fletcher Christian. Apparently, Howard didn't think much of his co-star Marlon Brando, either.

Maj. Frank Finchman / VON RYAN'S EXPRESS, 1965, 20th Century-Fox, d-Mark Robson.

Howard is the ranking British officer among POWs in an Italian camp. When American pilot Frank Sinatra is brought to the camp, career man Trevor finds himself out-ranked by a 90-day wonder. Reluctantly, Howard takes orders from Sinatra as the prisoners attempt to escape through German lines to Switzerland after Italy leaves the war.

Lord Cardigan / THE CHARGE OF THE LIGHT BRIGADE, 1968, Great Britain, United Artists / Woodfall, d-Tony Richardson.

As Lord Cardigan, Howard restlessly seeks military glory and so, along with other arrogant senior officers, plans to lead the British army into Crimea to protect the Ottoman Empire from the Russians. One outcome is the charge at Balaklava immortalized by Alfred, Lord Tennyson.

Father Collins / RYAN'S DAUGHTER, 1970, Great Britain, MGM / Faraway, d-David Lean.

As the village priest, Howard wields a lot of power but he can't prevent the townsfolk from shearing the head of the schoolteacher's wife, whom they believe has betrayed IRA members while having an affair with a sick British officer. Howard may have introduced the fad of wearing gloves with no fingers.

Clyde Massey / 11 HARROWHOUSE, 1974, Great Britain, 20th Century-Fox, d-Aram Avakian.

In a role typical of most of his parts from this point on, Howard has the undemanding task of playing a wealthy man who hires a diamond salesman to rob the vaults of the diamond exchange. This accomplished, Howard no longer feels there is any need for his employee. His days of carrying the action are about over.

OTHER ROLES

1944: *officer* / THE WAY AHEAD. **1945:** *Sil Carter* / THE WAY TO THE STARS. **1946:** *Lt. David Barnes* / I SEE A DARK STRANGER. **1947:** *Dr. Whiteside* / SO WELL REMEMBERED; *Clem Morgan* / THEY MADE ME A FUGITIVE. **1948:** *Steve Stratton* / THE PASSIONATE FRIENDS. **1949:** *David Redfern* / THE GOLDEN SALAMANDER. **1950:** *Capt. Peter Churchill* / ODETTE. **1951:** *David Somers* / THE CLOUDED YELLOW; *guest* / LADY GODIVA RIDES AGAIN. **1952:** *Peter Willems* / OUTCAST OF THE ISLANDS; *Lt. Col. Hugh Fraser* / THE GIFT HORSE. **1954:** *Inspector Lewis* / THE LOVERS OF LISBON; *Major Court* / THE STRANGER'S HAND; *narrator* / APRIL IN PORTUGAL. **1955:** *Captain Thompson* / THE COCKLESHELL HEROES. **1956:** *Fallentin* / AROUND THE WORLD IN 80 DAYS; *Browne* / RUN FOR THE SUN. **1957:** *Frank McNally* / INTERPOL; *James Prothero* / MANUELA. **1960:** *John Bain* / MOMENT OF DANGER. **1962:** *John Bullit* / THE LION. **1964:** *Major Kensington* / MAN IN THE MIDDLE; *Cmdr. Frank Houghton* / FATHER GOOSE. **1965:** *Professor Lindemann* / OPERATION CROSSBOW; *Colonel Statter* / MORITURI; *Colonel Mostyn* / THE LIQUIDATOR. **1966:** *Lincoln* / THE POPPY IS ALSO A FLOWER. **1967:** *Freddie Young* / TRIPLE CROSS. **1968:** *Robert Hook* / PRETTY POLLY. **1969:** *Air Vice Marshall Keith Park* / BATTLE OF BRITAIN; *grandfather* / TWINKY. **1971:** *The Inspector* / THE NIGHT VISITOR; *Sir Trevor Dawson* / CATCH ME A SPY; *Lord Advocate Grant* / KIDNAPPED. **1972:** *William Cecil* / MARY, QUEEN OF SCOTS; *Pope Leo* / POPE JOAN; *Richard Wagner* / LUDWIG; *Lieutenant Cartwright* / THE OFFENCE. **1973:** *Superintendent Bellamy* / CRAZE; *Dr. Rank* / A DOLL'S HOUSE. **1974:** *Paul Bellamy* / PERSECUTION; *Abbe Faria* / THE COUNT OF MONTE CRISTO; *Colonel Azarin* / WHO?; *narrator* / CAUSE FOR CONCERN. **1975:** *Col. Benjamin Strang* / CONDUCT UNBECOMING; *Commander Rice* / HENNESSY. **1976:** *Squire Western* / THE BAWDY ADVENTURES OF TOM JONES; *Capt. Foster Fyans* / ELIZA FRASER; *Lieutenant Colonel Silkin* / ACES HIGH. **1977:** *Sir Hector Geste* / THE LAST REMAKE OF BEAU GESTE; *the man* / STEVIE; *Alec Mackenzie* / SLAVERS; *Narrator* / BABEL YEMEN. **1978:** *first elder* / SUPERMAN; *narrator* / HOW TO SCORE A MOVIE. **1979:** *Father Malone* / HURRICANE; *Sir Michael Hughes* / METEOR. **1980:** *Jack Cartwright* / THE SEA WOLVES; *Windwalker* / WINDWALKER; *Sir Henry Rawlinson* / SIR HENRY AT RAWLINSON END. **1982:** *Judge Broomfield* / GANDHI; *Lord Ames* / THE MISSIONARY. **1983:** *Yoshka* / LIGHT YEARS AWAY. **1984:** *King Arthur* / SWORD OF THE VALIANT. **1985:** *Brigadier Crosshawe* / TIME AFTER TIME.

HUDSON, ROCK

(Roy Scherer Fitzgerald, 1925–1985)

When he came out of the navy in 1946, Hollywood took one look at Rock Hudson and saw another Victor Mature. They took off his shirt, gave him a tremendous build-up, and threw him in a series of not very good movies in which he was even worse. As the big, beefy, good-natured giant later said, "The only thing I can say in my defense is that I did the best I could. It was pretty rotten, I agree, but it was my best." Still, he was learning his craft and he surprised many with pretty fair performances in films such as GIANT and WRITTEN ON THE WIND. He found a comfortable niche in some silly sex comedies with Doris Day which seem even better now than when first released. Hudson, unlike many contract players before and since, survived the system and became a star even though he never developed into much of an actor. More than enough has been said about the cause of his death and his sexual preferences. The one good thing that came from his terrible end is that it seemed to get more people concerned about AIDS and finding a cure for this disease.

KEY ROLES

Frank Truscott / SCARLET ANGEL, 1952, Universal-International, d-Sidney Salkow.

Just when Yvonne de Carlo has succeeded in passing herself off as the bride of a deceased son of a wealthy San Francisco family, ex-lover Hudson shows up. She chooses him over wealth and position.

John Wesley Hardin / THE LAWLESS BREED, 1953, Universal, d-Raoul Walsh.

Hudson was top-starred for the first time, portraying a real-life gunman of the early West. As usual in such movies, Hudson kills his first man in self-defense and things just escalate from there.

Bob Merrick / MAGNIFICENT OBSESSION, 1954, Universal, d-Douglas Sirk.

In this remake of the Lloyd Douglas novel, Hudson, who had worked his way up through the weak westerns, got a chance to show what he had learned about acting. He didn't embarrass himself in this tearjerker about a playboy who is partially responsible for the blindness of a woman (Jane Wyman). He reforms, goes off to study to be a surgeon, operates on her, restores her sight, and wins her love.

Ron Kirby / ALL THAT HEAVEN ALLOWS, 1956, Universal, d-Douglas Sirk.

Enough fans liked the teaming of Hudson and Jane Wyman for the studio to bring them back in this story of a woman falling in love with her gardener who is 15 years younger. She ultimately lets her heart rule over the social pressures brought by her friends who oppose the liaison.

Mitch Wayne / WRITTEN ON THE WIND, 1956, Universal, d-Douglas Sirk.

Hudson is the lifelong buddy of dissolute Robert Stack, member of a Texas oil family. The younger members of the family have been ruined by too much money and no responsibilities. Hudson finds sexy, immoral Dorothy Malone too hot for him. All in all, they are no match for the Ewings when it comes to excesses.

Bick Benedict / GIANT, 1956, Warners, d-George Stevens.

Hudson is a Texas cattleman who goes back East to find a bride (Elizabeth Taylor). She's not happy being treated like "women folks" and demands that her macho husband treat her as a partner in their marriage. Besides the problems with his wife, Hudson has to put up with the fact that a once-worthless cowboy (James Dean) has become an oil tycoon because of a parcel of land left to him by Hudson's sister. One of Hudson's buddies (Chill Wills) says: "Bick, you should have shot that fella a long time ago. Now, he's too rich to kill."

Burle Devlin / THE TARNISHED ANGELS, 1957, Universal, d-Douglas Sirk.

Hudson is a reporter who joins up with an unhappy troupe of air aces who perform in the sky over circuses and fairs, risking their lives in planes constantly in need of repair.

Lt. Frederick Henry / A FAREWELL TO ARMS, 1957, 20th Century-Fox, d-Charles Vidor.

Hudson is merely adequate in this so-so remake of Ernest Hemingway's story of love between a French officer and an English nurse during World War I.

Brad Allen / PILLOW TALK, 1959, Universal, d-Michael Gordon.

Hudson is excellent as the songwriter with the same line and tune for every girl. He shares a party line with interior decorator Doris Day who doesn't appreciate his crooning tying up the line. He considers her interruptions the complaints of an old maid. But when he sees her he tries to add her to the bunch of notches on his bed. Now doesn't that sound like a match made in heaven? It's a delightfully funny movie.

Jerry Webster / LOVER COME BACK, 1962, Universal, d-Delbert Mann.

Hudson is an advertising man who uses questionable tactics, read "36-24-36," to win clients from competing agents, such as Doris Day, who attempt to earn customers the old-fashioned way. He's forced to come up with a product that an advertising campaign has made a big demand for and also "takes" Day in.

George Kimbell / SEND ME NO FLOWERS, 1964, Universal, d-Norman Jewison.

Hudson, a hypochondriac, overhears his doctor discussing another patient's fatal condition and believes his days are numbered. He decides he must find a good replacement for himself as husband to Doris Day. She believes his actions are motivated by his having an affair with another woman.

Antiochus Wilson / SECONDS, 1966, Paramount, d-John Frankenheimer.

Hudson is an old man who has undergone a special service for the rich that brings back their youth and vigor. He later learns that he is to be used as a corpse for others, the only way the rejuvenations can be accomplished.

Maj. Donald Craig / TOBRUK, 1967, Universal, d-Arthur Hiller.

Hudson is an American officer attached to a British column that, together with some German Jews, forms a special attack unit whose mission is to destroy Rommel's vital fuel supply at Tobruk.

Michael "Tiger" McDrew / PRETTY MAIDS ALL IN A ROW, 1971, MGM, d-Roger Vadim.

Hudson is a very with-it high school counselor who, besides sleeping with a dozen or so willing coeds, also finds time for his sexy wife and a new teacher (Angie Dickinson). Hudson does have one little shortcoming, though: when any of his lovers becomes a bit too possessive he kills them.

OTHER ROLES

1948: *a lieutenant* / FIGHTER SQUADRON. **1949:** *detective* / UNDERTOW. **1950:** *store detective* / I WAS A SHOPLIFTER; *truck driver* / ONE WAY STREET; *Young Bull* / WINCHESTER '73; *Johnny Higgins* / PEGGY. **1951:** *Captain Ras* / THE DESERT HAWK; *Burt Hanna* / TOMAHAWK; *upperclassman* / AIR CADET; *Roy Clark* / THE FAT MAN; *Speed O'Keefe* / IRON MAN; *Cpl. John Flagg* / BRIGHT VICTORY. **1952:** *Charley Jones* / HERE COME THE NELSONS; *Trey Wilson* / BEND OF THE RIVER; *Dan* / HAS ANYBODY SEEN MY GAL?; *Dan Hammond* / HORIZONS WEST. **1953:** *Lance Caldwell* / SEMINOLE; *Gilliatt* / SEA DEVILS; *Harun* / THE GOLDEN BLADE; *Peter Keith* / BACK TO GOD'S COUNTRY; *Ben Warren* / GUN FURY. **1954:** *Taza* / TAZA, SON OF COCHISE; *Capt. Jeffrey Claybourne* / BENGAL BRIGADE. **1955:** *Michael Martin* / CAPTAIN LIGHTFOOT; *Clint Saunders* / ONE DESIRE. **1956:** *Dr. Michael Parker* / NEVER SAY GOODBYE; *guest* / FOUR GIRLS IN TOWN. **1957:** *Col. Dean Hess* / BATTLE HYMN; *Peter McKenzie* / SOMETHING OF VALUE. **1958:** *David Bell* / TWILIGHT FOR THE GODS. **1959:** *John Rambeau* / THIS EARTH IS MINE. **1961:** *Dana Stribling* / THE LAST SUNSET; *Robert Talbot* / COME SEPTEMBER. **1962:** *Dr. Anton Drager* / THE SPIRAL ROAD. **1963:** *Jim Caldwell* / A GATHERING OF EAGLES; *narrator* / MARILYN. **1964:** *Roger Willoughby* / MAN'S FAVORITE SPORT?; *Carter Harrison* / STRANGE BEDFELLOWS. **1965:** *Paul Chadwick* / A VERY SPECIAL FAVOR. **1966:** *Dr. Bartholomew Snow* / BLINDFOLD. **1968:** *Comdr. James Ferraday* / ICE STATION ZEBRA. **1969:** *Capt. Mike Harmon* / A FINE PAIR; *Col. James Langdon* / THE UNDEFEATED. **1970:** *Maj. William Larrabee* / DARLING LILI; *Captain Turner* / HORNET'S NEST. **1973:** *Chuck Jarvis* / SHOWDOWN. **1976:** *Dr. Paul Holliston* / EMBRYO. **1978:** *David Shelby* / AVALANCHE. **1980:** *Jason Rudd* / THE MIRROR CRACK'D. **1984:** *Frank Stevenson* / THE AMBASSADOR.

HUNTER, JEFFREY

(Henry H. McKinnies, Jr., 1927–1969)

After navy service, Jeffrey Hunter enrolled at Northwestern University as a drama student, followed by graduate work at UCLA. He was offered a screen test by 20th Century-Fox after appearing in a college production of "All My Sons" and made his movie debut with a bit part in JULIUS CAESAR. Good-looking, virile Hunter was very popular with young fans for a few years, and made quite a stir when he was announced for the role of Jesus Christ in KING OF KINGS. After that his career was mostly downhill. Among his last films were forgettable foreign-made trash such as FROZEN DEAD (1967), SEXY SUSAN SINS AGAIN (1968), FIND A PLACE TO DIE (1969), and VIVA AMERICA (1970). He died after surgery for injuries sustained in a fall.

KEY ROLES

Andrew Brown / SAILOR OF THE KING, 1953, 20th Century-Fox, d-Ray Boulting.

In this remake of BROWN ON RESOLUTION, Hunter is the product of a World War I affair between a naval officer (Michael Rennie) and a girl (Wendy Hiller). The father has no knowledge of the son. During World War II Hunter is a sailor who survives the sinking of a cruiser and is the lone survivor on an island. With a rifle, this sharpshooter delays the departure of a German cruiser until the British fleet closes in and sinks it. Rennie is the captain of the British ship that picks up Hunter, but they still don't know of their relationship and never will.

Martin Pawley / THE SEARCHERS, 1956, Warners, d-John Ford.

Hunter is the foster son of John Wayne's brother. When the brother's family is slaughtered and their youngest daughter taken by the rampaging Indians, the Duke and Hunter trail them for seven years—Hunter to save the child, Wayne to kill her because she has been "used" by savages.

Gordon Grant / A KISS BEFORE DYING, 1956, United Artists, d-Gerd Oswald.

When a psychopathic college boy (Robert Wagner) murders his pregnant girlfriend (Joanne Woodward), Hunter helps his uncle, the sheriff, with the case which is first ruled a suicide. Woodward's sister shows up insisting it's murder. Wagner stays one step ahead of Hunter by supplying the police with a murderer whom Wagner kills, making it look as if the man took his own life. But even Hunter starts catching on when Wagner goes after the other sister, first as a lover and later as another victim.

Lt. Thomas Cantrell / SERGEANT RUTLEDGE, 1960, Warners, d-John Ford.

Hunter is the military defense attorney who is able to prove that black sergeant Woody Strode is innocent of rape and murder in the old West of 1881.

Jesus Christ / KING OF KINGS, 1961, MGM, d-Nicholas Ray.

Although the movie was dubbed "I Was a Teenage Jesus" by wags, Hunter isn't any worse than most performers who find themselves working in an epic—and no better, come to think of it.

OTHER ROLES

1950: *bit* / JULIUS CAESAR. **1951:** *Danny* / 14 HOURS; *The Kid* / CALL ME MISTER; *Chad Carnes* / TAKE CARE OF MY LITTLE GIRL; *Creighton* / THE FROGMEN. **1952:** *Ed Miller* / RED SKIES OF MONTANA; *Dr. Bob Grayson* / BELLES ON THEIR TOES; *Bill Ainslee* / DREAMBOAT; *Ben Tyler* / LURE OF THE WILDERNESS. **1954:** *Johnny Colt* / THREE YOUNG TEXANS; *Prince Haidi* / PRINCESS OF THE NILE. **1955:** *Owen Brown* / SEVEN ANGRY MEN; *Little Dog* / WHITE FEATHER; *Matuwir* / SEVEN CITIES OF GOLD. **1956:** *William A. Fuller* / THE GREAT LOCOMOTIVE CHASE; *Thad* / THE PROUD ONES. **1957:** *Bless Keough* / GUN FOR A COWARD; *Frank James* / THE TRUE STORY OF JESSE JAMES; *David Martin* / NO DOWN PAYMENT. **1958:** *Captain Ranson* / COUNT FIVE AND DIE; *Adam Caulfield* / THE LAST HURRAH; *Nico Kantaylis* / IN LOVE AND WAR; *guest* / MARDI GRAS. **1960:** *Guy Gabaldon* / HELL TO ETERNITY; *Fred Morrow* / KEY WITNESS. **1961:** *Matt Jameson* / MAN-TRAP. **1962:** *George Tweed* / NO MAN IS AN ISLAND; *Sergeant Fuller* / THE LONGEST DAY. **1963:** *Lacer* / GOLD FOR THE CAESARS. **1964:** *Timothy Higgins* / THE MAN FROM GALVESTON. **1965:** *Jim Grayam* / BRAINSTORM; *Joaquin Murieta* / MURIETA. **1966:** *Justin Power* / DIMENSION 5. **1967:** *Joe Novak* / THE CHRISTMAS KID; *Garver Logan* / A WITCH WITHOUT A BROOM; *Lieutenant Benteen* / CUSTER OF THE WEST; *cameo* / A GUIDE FOR THE MARRIED MAN. **1968:** *Lt. Lyman P. Jones* / THE PRIVATE NAVY OF SGT. O'FARRELL.

HUNTER, KIM

(Janet Cole, 1922–)

A stage actress since the age of 17, Kim Hunter has made only a few movies with her greatest success being the repeat of her Broadway role, Stella Kowalski in A STREETCAR NAMED DESIRE, for which she won an Academy Award. Shortly afterwards, because of the Red Scare, she was blacklisted for several years. Even though her movie career was damaged, she continued working on stage and TV. Her made-for-television movies include DIAL HOT LINE (1970), IN SEARCH OF AMERICA (1971), UNWED FATHER (1974), ELLERY QUEEN (1975), THE DARK SIDE OF INNOCENCE (1976), THE GOLDEN GATE MURDERS (1979), SKOKIE (1981), and PRIVATE SESSIONS (1985). Her advice on acting is: "Whatever the technique, your aim must always be to achieve command over your audience." More often than not, she did.

KEY ROLES

Mary Gibson / THE SEVENTH VICTIM, 1943, RKO, d-Mark Robson.

Hunter goes to New York to find her sister who is under the control of a band of Satanists.

June / A MATTER OF LIFE AND DEATH, (STAIRWAY TO HEAVEN), 1946, Great Britain, GFD / Archers, d-Michael Powell and Emeric Pressburger.

In this strange but enjoyable fantasy, Hunter is an American girl who falls in love with a brain-damaged pilot (David Niven) whose life and death is fought for by a surgeon—first on the operating table and then in a heavenly court where the absurd argument is made that no girl from an innocent country like the United States should be allowed to love a man from an old corrupt one such as England.

Stella Kowalski / A STREETCAR NAMED DESIRE, 1951, Feldman / Kazan, d-Elia Kazan.

Hunter, married to brutish Marlon Brando, is expecting a baby when she welcomes her sister (Vivien Leigh) into her small New Orleans apartment. The latter is only a step or two away from insanity. Hunter tries but is unsuccessful in getting her husband to treat Leigh gently. Leigh has delusions that she is still the popular young girl she once was. But while Hunter is having her baby, Brando rapes Leigh and pushes her over the edge.

Nora Hutchinson / DEADLINE U.S.A., 1952, 20th Century-Fox, d-Richard Brooks.

Hunter is the girlfriend of crusading newspaper editor Humphrey Bogart who, despite personal threats, goes ahead with a story about the crimes of a powerful mobster.

Dr. Zira / PLANET OF THE APES, 1968, 20th Century-Fox, d-Franklyn Schaffner.

Hunter portrays a kindly Simian scientist in this story about astronauts caught in a time warp, who land on earth in a time in the future when apes rule and humans are slaves. She appears in two of the four sequels in the same role.

OTHER ROLES

1943: *Doris* / TENDER COMRADE. **1944:** *Johnson's girl* / A CANTERBURY TALE; *Millie* / WHEN STRANGERS MARRY. **1945:** *Frances Hotchkiss* / YOU CAME ALONG. **1952:** *Helen Watson* / ANYTHING CAN HAPPEN. **1956:** *Martha Lockridge* / STORM CENTER; *Fran West* / BERMUDA AFFAIR. **1957:** *Helen Ditmar* / THE YOUNG STRANGER. **1958:** *Mary Kingman* / MONEY, WOMEN AND GUNS. **1964:** *Dr. Bea Brice* / LILITH. **1968:** *Betty Graham* / THE SWIMMER. **1970:** *Dr. Zira* / BENEATH THE PLANET OF THE APES. **1971:** *Dr. Zira* / ESCAPE FROM THE PLANET OF THE APES; *Walker's mother (cut)* / JENNIFER ON MY MIND. **1976:** *Good Witch* / DARK AUGUST. **1987:** *Amanda Hollins* / THE KINDRED.

HURT, WILLIAM

(1950–)

Stepson of Time-Life founder Henry Luce III, William Hurt was a theological student who gravitated to acting, which he studied at Juilliard. Tall, fair-haired, and softspoken, Hurt has only made seven movies at the time of this writing, but they are of such variety that it appears that if his sensitivity doesn't do him in, he should be a major force in movies for many years to come. He might be described as a hunk by his female fans, but more than that, he's an actor of rare talent, perfect at playing vulnerable characters.

KEY ROLES

Eddie Jessup / ALTERED STATES, 1979, Warners, d-Ken Russell.

Hurt, a research scientist and seeker of heightened forms of consciousness, tries Mexican hallucinogens and laboratory-based sensory deprivation tests to experience his altered states. He overdoses and makes something of a monkey of himself in a sort of reverse evolution.

Ned Racine / BODY HEAT, 1981, Ladd Company, d-Lawrence Kasdan.

In this film noir that must have escaped from a time warp, Hurt is an unsuccessful lawyer who has a tempestuous affair with married Kathleen Turner. She gets him to suggest that maybe they should do her husband in, but she's pulling all his strings and does a great Barbara Stanwyck to his Fred MacMurray, as in DOUBLE INDEMNITY.

Nick / THE BIG CHILL, 1983, Shambers, d-Lawrence Kasdan.

Hurt is a druggie who gathers with six other college radicals of the sixties and early seventies when their former leader commits suicide. It's a nostalgic look at a bunch of activism drop-outs who got away from the incubator of a college campus, lost their idealism, and became "me"-centered.

Luis Molina / KISS OF THE SPIDER WOMAN, 1985, U.S. / Brazil, Island Alive, d-Hector Babenco.

Hurt is a witty, vulnerable homosexual confined to prison for child molestation. His cellmate, Raul Julia, is a radical journalist. Hurt is offered parole if he can get Julia to disclose the information the officials can't get from him by torture. Ultimately Hurt and Julia make love and when Hurt is released he's killed trying to help the rebels. The title refers to the movie plot that Hurt relates to Julia in an attempt to kill boredom. Hurt won an Oscar for his performance.

James Leeds / CHILDREN OF A LESSER GOD, 1986, Paramount, d-Randa Haines.

Hurt portrays a sensitive teacher who falls in love with an idealistic young deaf woman (Marlee Matlin). His eloquent emoting is marvelous and the sexual chemistry between the two is memorable. For a while Hurt and Matlin had a love affair off the screen as well. Matlin won an Oscar for her performance.

Tom Grunick / BROADCAST NEWS, 1987, 20th Century-Fox, d-James Brooks.

Is Hurt portraying Dan Rather, Tom Brokaw, Peter Jennings, or perhaps a bit of each? In the film, he's a former TV sportscaster being groomed to become an anchorman. He's good-looking, charming, and not very bright. It is his personality, not his news ability, that his network is hoping to sell. And with producers like Holly Hunter and reporters like Albert Brooks to make him look good, what does it matter if he doesn't understand most of the stories he reads? It's a grand movie with excellent performances from the three principals. Hurt set a record with his third Best Actor Academy Award nomination in as many years.

OTHER ROLES

1980: *Darryl Deever* / EYEWITNESS. **1983:** *Arkady Renko* / GORKY PARK.

HUSSEY, RUTH

(Ruth Carol O'Rourke, 1914–)

A former Powers model, Ruth Hussey had her best go at movies during the 1940s, although she never was a big star. She had her greatest success on the stage in 1945 when she appeared opposite Ralph Bellamy on Broadway in "State of the Union." In her movies, Hussey was usually very lady-like and sophisticated, wearing expensive, stylish clothes—a woman a man could always be proud to be with. She was nominated for an Oscar for her role in THE PHILADELPHIA STORY.

KEY ROLES

Miss Watts / THE WOMEN, 1939, MGM, d-George Cukor.

Hussey is one of the 135 women who make up the cast of this story starring Norma Shearer as a woman who divorces in haste, allowing Joan Crawford to get her husband. But later Shearer goes back after him. Hussey has a few good lines in this memorable battle between "ladies."

Lily Cole / FAST AND FURIOUS, 1939, MGM, d-Busby Berkeley.

In this comedy / mystery, Hussey becomes involved with detective Franchot Tone, his wife (Ann Sothern), and murder at a seashore resort where a bathing beauty contest is being held.

Liz Imbrie / THE PHILADELPHIA STORY, 1940, MGM, d-George Cukor.

Hussey sums up her role fairly well with the observation, "I can't afford to hate anybody. I'm only a photographer." She arrives with the man she loves, writer Jimmy Stewart, at the home of Katharine Hepburn, to cover Hepburn's second wedding. She has to stand by and wait to see if Hepburn will throw Stewart back as he has become infatuated with the redhead.

Kay Motford / H.M. PULHAM, ESQ., 1941, MGM, d-King Vidor.

Hussey is the family-approved young woman whom Robert Young of Boston marries, despite being in love with New Yorker Hedy Lamarr. The couple live a hum-drum life together until late in life when Young, while writing a family biography, has a belated fling.

Pamela Fitzgerald / THE UNINVITED, 1944, Paramount, d-Lewis Allen.

Hussey and her composer brother (Ray Milland) buy a mansion high on a cliff overlooking the sea in rural England, despite the objections of the owner's granddaughter, Gail Russell. The house is haunted and very much a threat to Russell. Through seances and old medical records found in the attic of the local doctor, they learn the truth about the house and its ghostly inhabitants. When all is cleared up Milland gets the granddaughter and Hussey the local doctor.

Eve Meredith Curtis / I, JANE DOE, 1948, Republic, d-John H. Auer.

When a French girl comes to the United States seeking the flyer she married during World War II, she finds that he was already married to attorney Hussey. The French girl kills the philanderer, and his widow becomes her defense attorney when she discovers the girl is pregnant.

Jennie Sousa / STARS AND STRIPES FOREVER, 1952, 20th Century-Fox, d-Henry Koster.

Wives of famous men who are the subjects of movie biopics seldom have a chance to do much more than admire their spouses and forgive them for their idiosyncrasies. This story of the March King, John Philip Sousa, is no different.

OTHER ROLES

1937: *Annette* / MADAME X; *bit* / BIG CITY; *Jane* / MAN-PROOF. **1938:** *Margaret Lee* / JUDGE HARDY'S CHILDREN; *Madame Le Polignac* / MARIE ANTOINETTE; *Nadine Pierpont* / HOLD THAT KISS; *Joan Thayer* / RICH MAN, POOR GIRL; *Peggy Norton* / TIME OUT FOR MURDER; *Kate McKim* / SPRING MADNESS. **1939:** *Eve* / HONOLULU; *Mary Turner* / WITHIN THE LAW; *Sybil Ames* / MAISIE; *Dorothy Waters* / *Linda Mills* / ANOTHER THIN MAN; *Helen Ingram* / BLACKMAIL; *Elizabeth Browne* / NORTHWEST PASSAGE. **1940:** *Charlotte* / SUSAN AND GOD; *Lorna Gray* / FLIGHT COMMAND. **1941:** *Martha Gray* / FREE AND EASY; *Susan Drake* / OUR WIFE; *Norma Haven* / MARRIED BACHELOR. **1942:** *Daisy Denton* / PIERRE OF THE PLAINS; *Eliza McCardle* / TENNESSEE JOHNSON. **1943:** *Barbara* / TENDER COMRADE. **1944:** *Ellen Foster* / MARINE RAIDERS. **1945:** *Hedy Fredericks* / BEDSIDE MANNER. **1949:** *Jordan Baker* / THE GREAT GATSBY. **1950:** *Meg Norton* / LOUISA; *Lorna Marvis* / MR. MUSIC. **1951:** *Ann Jackson* / THAT'S MY BOY. **1952:** *Christine Powell* / WOMAN OF THE NORTH COUNTRY. **1953:** *Nora Conners* / THE LADY WANTS MINK. **1960:** *Mary Gilbert* / THE FACTS OF LIFE.

HUTTON, BETTY

(Elizabeth June Thornburg, 1921–)

A blonde, blue-eyed dynamo, Betty Hutton sadly admitted, "Nobody loved me unless I bought them, and so I bought everybody." This vivacious musical star hit her peak in the late 1940s and early 1950s and then was gone, no longer needed. Nicknamed "The Blonde Bombshell," her singing style was an ear-splitting shout and every part of her body shook in a dozen different directions. She made the mistake of demanding that her second husband, Charles O'Curran, direct all her future films, resulting in Paramount letting her go after THE GREATEST SHOW ON EARTH in 1952. Hutton made only one more movie. She appeared occasionally on stage but proved unreliable. Her fans were startled to read in the 1970s that she had been reduced to working as a cook and housekeeper at a Catholic rectory in Rhode Island and had spent five years undergoing psychiatric treatment in a mental hospital. Later she was given another chance to be part of the entertainment world when she appeared in "Annie" in 1980.

KEY ROLES

Bessie Dale / THE FLEET'S IN, 1942, Paramount, d-Victor Schertzinger.

Hutton, fresh from Broadway, sings the show's two best songs, "Build a Better Mousetrap" and "Arthur Murray Taught Me Dancing in a Hurry" by Johnny Mercer and Victor Schertzinger. The story centers around a painfully shy sailor who is the center of bets on whether he can get a kiss from nightclub singer Dorothy Lamour. The sailor's buddy ends up with Hutton.

Polly Judson / STAR SPANGLED RHYTHM, 1942, Paramount, d-George Marshall.

Hutton is a telephone operator at Paramount studios who eggs on gateman Victor Moore to pose as the head of the studio to impress the friends of his sailor son. It's then decided to put on a show for the servicemen. The Johnny Mercer and Harold Arlen songs, "That Old Black Magic" and "The Road to Dreamland," were big hits.

Trudy Kockenlocker / THE MIRACLE OF MORGAN'S CREEK, 1944, Paramount, d-Preston Sturges.

Hutton has a great time at a wartime party and finds herself pregnant but has no idea who's the father. She gets a dopey 4-F Eddie Bracken to take credit for the expected child. The miracle is the number of babies she delivers: five. Trying to convince Bracken to marry her she tells him, "I'm in terrible trouble, Norval. Somehow I just naturally turned to you. Like you said that night, you remember, you almost wished I'd be in terrible trouble so you could help me out of it? Well, you certainly got your wish." For its time it was amazingly brash, giving a bronx cheer to imagined American morals and ideals.

Texas Guinan / INCENDIARY BLONDE, 1945, Paramount, d-George Marshall.

Hutton portrays the vaudeville singer, cowgirl movie star, and cabaret singer who was a famous character of the crazy twenties. She makes customers at her club pay inflated prices and regularly greets them with "Hello, Sucker" and they love it. The best song is "It Had to Be You" by Gus Kahn and Isham Jones.

Pearl White / THE PERILS OF PAULINE, 1947, Paramount, d-George Marshall.

Hutton appears as the queen of the silent serials in this movie that features a lot of old-time players including villainous Paul Panzer, James Finlayson, Chester Conklin, and Creighton Hale. Songs include "Daddy Don't Preach to Me" and "I Wish I Didn't Love You So" by Frank Loesser.

Annie Oakley / ANNIE GET YOUR GUN, 1950, MGM, d-George Sydney.

Ethel Merman played the role on Broadway 1,159 times. Judy Garland was scheduled for the film version but couldn't make it and Hutton was brought in to play the backwoods sharpshooter who falls in love with her co-star, Howard Keel. The Irving Berlin songs sung by Hutton include "I've Got the Sun in the Morning," "You Can't Get a Man with a Gun," and "Doin' What Comes Naturally."

Blossom Seeley / SOMEBODY LOVES ME, 1952, Paramount, d-Irving Brecher.

Hutton portrays the vaudeville headliner of the early part of the century. The film depicts her trials and tribulations with her husband and partner Benny Fields (Ralph Meeker). Besides the title song, Hutton sings many old-time favorites including "Rose Room," "Way Down Yonder in New Orleans," and "I Cried for You."

Holly / THE GREATEST SHOW ON EARTH, 1952, Paramount, d-Cecil B. DeMille.

Hutton is a daredevil trapeze artist in love with circus manager Charlton Heston. She is outraged when he brings in another aerialist (Cornel Wilde) and hands him the center ring. Wilde hurts his arm and Hutton regains the big star role and she rallies the circus performers after a train wreck to ensure that the show goes on.

OTHER ROLES

1943: *Bubbles Hennessy* / HAPPY GO LUCKY; *Winnie Porter* / LET'S FACE IT. **1944:** *Bobby Angel* / AND THE ANGELS SING; *Susie and Rosemary Allison* / HERE COME THE WAVES. **1945:** *guest* / DUFFY'S TAVERN; *Judy Peabody* / THE STORK CLUB. **1946:** *Peggy Harper* / CROSS MY HEART. **1948:** *Georgina Allerton* / DREAM GIRL. **1949:** *Eleanor Collier* / RED HOT AND BLUE. **1950:** *Kitty McNeil* / LET'S DANCE. **1951:** *guest* / SAILOR BEWARE. **1957:** *Maggie Brewster* / SPRING REUNION.

IRELAND, JOHN

(1914–)

Rumor has it that John Ireland's career was nipped in the bud when director Howard Hawks kept cutting his role in RED RIVER because both were romantically interested in Joanne Dru. Ireland eventually married Dru, the second of three marriages, but even though he showed as much promise as the suffering Montgomery Clift in the classic western, he never became a major star. He has spent most of his long career in "B" movies as second-rung heroes or villains. Ireland has made numerous foreign films of dubious value including ODIO PER ODIO (1967), TRUSTING IS GOOD, SHOOTING IS BETTER (1967), FLIGHT OF THE HAWK (1967), UNA PISTOLA PER CENTO BARE (1968), CAXAMBU (1968), TUTTO PER TUTTO (1968), I KILL YOU AND COMMEND YOU TO GOD (1968), THE DAMNED HOT DAY OF FIRE (1968), CARNIVAL CIRCUIT (1969), THE STRANGLER OF VIENNA (1972), TEN WHITES KILLED ONE LITTLE INDIAN (1973), and LA FURIE DU DESIR (1975).

KEY ROLES

Billy Clanton / MY DARLING CLEMENTINE, 1946, 20th Century-Fox, d-John Ford.

In this superb black-and-white western, Ireland is the youngest son of Old Clanton who, with his gang, takes on the Earps and Doc Holliday at the OK Corral.

Cherry Valance / RED RIVER, 1948, Monterey, d-John Ford.

Ireland is a fast man with a gun who joins the cattle drive headed by John Wayne and his foster son Montgomery Clift, also handy with firearms. The obvious competition between Ireland and Clift makes it pretty clear that some showdown is to be expected, but it comes between Wayne and Clift.

Bob Ford / I SHOT JESSE JAMES, 1949, Lippert, d-Samuel Fuller.

Ireland portrays "the dirty little coward who shot Mr. Howard and laid poor Jesse in his grave." His motivation, according to this film, was to get the pardon that would allow him to marry his childhood sweetheart.

Jack Burden / ALL THE KING'S MEN, 1949, Columbia, d-Robert Rossen.

Ireland is a reporter who writes a story about an honest man (Broderick Crawford) from a small town who's trying to get elected to public office. Crawford fails on his first attempt but becomes a hero to the people when his predictions of what could happen if the crooks are returned to office come true. As he grows to a be powerful and corrupt political figure, he has Ireland around keeping a little book on people that contains information that can bring them into line. Ireland hangs on even when the politician goes for the former's childhood sweetheart.

Hurricane Smith / HURRICANE SMITH, 1952, Paramount, d-Jerry Hopper.

Ireland is a fugitive from justice who has stashed away a fortune but needs provisions for his boat to go after it. Along comes a scientist who wants to rent the boat, but it soon becomes obvious that his interests are not scientific and he's also after Ireland's loot.

Judson Prentiss / QUEEN BEE, 1955, Columbia, d-Randall MacDougall.

Ireland is the ex-lover of Joan Crawford, who is the ruthless wife of a southern mill owner. She prevents Ireland's marriage to a young woman who commits suicide when she learns of his relation with the queen bee. Guilt-ridden and thoroughly repelled by Crawford, he takes her out driving and deliberately crashes, killing them both.

Johnny Ringo / GUNFIGHT AT THE O.K. CORRAL, 1957, Paramount, d-John Sturges.

Ireland is back exchanging lead with the Earps and Doc Holliday at the O.K. Corral, but now as a gunfighter who teams up with the Clantons.

Crixus / SPARTACUS, 1960, Universal-International, d-Stanley Kubrick.

Ireland is a gladiator and one of Kirk Douglas's lieutenants when the latter leads a slave revolt against the Romans.

Sergeant Harry / 55 DAYS AT PEKING, 1962, Allied Artists, d-Nicholas Ray.

Ireland is the non-commissioned officer who is second-in-command to Charlton Heston, the commander of a group of American marines who, together with troops from several other nations, defend the international compound at Peking against the Boxer rebels who are operating with the tacit approval of China's last empress.

Steve Marak / I SAW WHAT YOU DID, 1965, Universal, d-William Castle.

When a couple of girls play a prank by telephoning people at random and saying "I saw what you did; I know who you are," they get John Ireland, who has killed his wife to satisfy his demanding lover. He thinks he knows who has called him and goes after them.

OTHER ROLES

1945: *Windy* / A WALK IN THE SUN. **1946:** *Detective Engelhofer* / BEHIND GREEN LIGHTS; *Bennie Smith* / IT SHOULDN'T HAPPEN TO A DOG; *Howard Williams* / WAKE UP AND DREAM; *voice* / SOMEWHERE IN THE NIGHT. **1947:** *Duke Martin* / RAILROADED; *Karty* / THE GANGSTER; *Reno* / I LOVE TROUBLE; *narrator* / REPEAT PERFORMANCE. **1948:** *Paul Lester* / OPEN SECRET; *Fantail* / RAW DEAL; *Capt. Jed Calbern* / A SOUTHERN YANKEE; *Saint Severe* / JOAN OF ARC. **1949:** *Lednov* / ROUGHSHOD; *Frazee* / THE WALKING HILLS; *Danny Johnson* / ANNA LUCASTA; *"Early" Byrd* / MR. SOFT TOUCH; *Bitter Creek* / THE DOOLINS OF OKLAHOMA; *narrator* / UNDERCOVER MAN. **1950:** *Steve Conway* / CARGO TO CAPETOWN; *Johnny* / THE RETURN OF JESSE JAMES. **1951:** *John Barrington* / THE SCARF; *Lt. John Haywood* / LITTLE BIG HORN; *Hub Fasken* / VENGEANCE VALLEY; *Pete Ferreday* / THE BASKETBALL FIX; *Quantrell* / RED MOUNTAIN; *Jeff Waring* / THE BUSHWHACKERS. **1953:** *Sergeant Fletcher* / COMBAT SQUAD; *John Williams* / THE 49TH MAN; *Rochelle* / HANNAH LEE. **1954:** *Ralph Payne* / SECURITY RISK; *Clint McDonald* / SOUTHWEST PASSAGE; *ringleader* / THE STEEL CAGE; *Frank Webster* / THE FAST AND THE FURIOUS; *Eddie* / THE GOOD DIE YOUNG. **1955:** *Pel* / THE GLASS TOMB; *bomber pilot* / HELL'S HORIZON. **1956:** *Cane Miro* / GUNSLINGER. **1957:** *Griff Parker* / STORMY CROSSING. **1958:** *Louis Canetto* / PARTY GIRL; *Jonas Bailey* / NO PLACE TO LAND. **1960:** *Max Hammond* / FACES IN THE DARK. **1961:** *Ray Reed* / RETURN OF A STRANGER; *Johnny Greco* / NO TIME TO KILL. **1963:** *prison warden* / THE CEREMONY. **1964:** *Ballomar* / THE FALL OF THE ROMAN EMPIRE. **1966:** *Sergeant Harmon* / DAY OF THE NIGHTMARE. **1967:** *Tom Horn* / FORT UTAH. **1968:** *Dan Shelby* / ARIZONA BUSHWHACKERS; *Captain O'Connor* / DIRTY HEROES; *Stuart* / EL "CHE" GUEVARA. **1970:** *detective* / ONE ON TOP OF THE OTHER; *Mr. Hadley* / THE ADVENTURERS. **1972:** *Jacob Kogan* / ESCAPE TO THE SUN. **1973:** *movie director* / THE HOUSE OF SEVEN CORPSES; *sheriff* / WELCOME TO ARROW BEACH. **1975:** *Lieutenant Nulty* / FAREWELL, MY LOVELY. **1976:** *McGowan* / THE SWISS CONSPIRACY. **1977:** *Tony Santore* / LOVE AND THE MIDNIGHT AUTO SUPPLY; *Clift* / MADAM KITTY. **1979:** *Senator Smedley* / THE SHAPE OF THINGS TO COME. **1980:** *David Cole* / GUYANA, CULT OF THE DAMNED. **1982:** *Hank Walden* / THE INCUBUS. **1984:** *Brewer* / MARTIN'S DAY. **1985:** *priest* / THE TREASURE OF THE AMAZON.

JACKSON, GLENDA

(1937–)

Twice an Academy Award winner for WOMEN IN LOVE and A TOUCH OF CLASS, British actress Glenda Jackson left school at age 16 to join an amateur theater group. She made her London stage debut in "All Kinds of Men" and her film debut in THIS SPORTING LIFE (1963) in a small role. She received critical acclaim for her work on stage in "Marat / Sade" as Charlotte Corday both in London and New York. She has an expressive voice and sharp confidence. Her appearance is not that of a great beauty but of an interesting person with an eroticism that almost surprises. Her own views on her looks are: "I've always thought that I'm not pretty enough to be thought beautiful, and not quite plain enough to be considered interesting." She received an additional Oscar nomination for her role in HEDDA. She is a remarkable actress with a tremendous talent, whose every appearance promises something possibly unique and great.

KEY ROLES

Charlotte Corday / MARAT / SADE, 1966, Great Britain, United Artists, d-Peter Brook.

The alternate title tells the whole story: "The Persecution and Assassination of Jean-Paul Marat as Performed by the Inmates of the Asylum of Charenton Under the Direction of the Marquis de Sade." Jackson is the French maid who kills Marat in his bath.

Gudrun Brangwen / WOMEN IN LOVE, 1969, Great Britain, Brandywine, d-Ken Russell.

Jackson and her sister, Jennie Linden, live in a Midlands mining town. She is attracted to Oliver Reed, the son of a mine owner, while her sister is attended by Alan Bates, a school inspector. While on vacation in the Alps, Reed tries to strangle Jackson because of her friendship with a bisexual, but he then walks away to die in the cold.

Alex Greville / SUNDAY, BLOODY SUNDAY, 1971, Great Britain, United Artists, d-John Schlesinger.

Jackson is a wealthy divorcee who shares the love of sculptor Murray Head with Harley Street physician Peter Finch. When Head walks out on both his lovers they are left to comfort each other.

Queen Elizabeth I / MARY, QUEEN OF SCOTS, 1971, Great Britain, Universal, d-Charles Jarrott.

Vanessa Redgrave as Mary Stuart refuses to waive her claim to the British throne. This leads Elizabeth I to order the former's imprisonment and execution. It's not the most dramatic presentation of a historical event, but the two stars make it interesting.

Vicki Allessio / A TOUCH OF CLASS, 1972, Great Britain, Avco / Brut, d-Melvin Frank.

Jackson is a dress designer who has a hectic affair with George Segal, a married American businessman. It's an amusing sex farce filmed at a frantic pace, but whether she performed at Oscar level is questionable.

Hedda Gabler / HEDDA, 1976, Great Britain, Brut, d-Trevor Nunn.

In Henrik Ibsen's drama, Jackson is a neurotic, strong-willed woman who finds herself pregnant. Bored with her husband, she entertains herself by taking revenge on an ex-lover but finds that her plan backfires.

Sarah Bernhardt / THE INCREDIBLE SARAH, 1976, Great Britain, Readers Digest, d-Richard Fleischer.

Jackson is impressive in this enjoyable biopic of the life of the great French actress up to the age of thirty-five.

Ann Atkinson / HOUSE CALLS, 1977, Universal, d-Howard Zeiff.

This is a fun comedy with Jackson playing a divorcee who interrupts widower doctor Walter Matthau's enjoyment of his refound sexual freedom and forces him to think about love and marriage again.

OTHER ROLES

1963: *bit* / THIS SPORTING LIFE. **1965:** *bit* / THE BENEFIT OF THE DOUBT. **1968:** *Vivien* / NEGATIVES; *guest* / TELL ME LIES. **1970:** *Nina Milyukova* / THE MUSIC LOVERS. **1971:** *guest* / THE BOY FRIEND. **1972:** *Alice* / TRIPLE ECHO. **1973:** *Emma Nelson* / A BEQUEST TO THE NATION; *Solange* / THE MAIDS. **1974:** *Sister Geraldine* / THE TEMPTER. **1975:** *Elizabeth Fielding* / THE ROMANTIC ENGLISHWOMAN. **1976:** *Alexandra* / NASTY HABITS. **1978:** *Conor MacMichael* / THE CLASS OF MISS MACMICHAEL; *Stevie Smith* / STEVIE. **1979:** *Tricia* / LOST AND FOUND. **1980:** *Isabelle Garnell* / HEALTH; *Isabel von Schmidt* / HOPSCOTCH. **1982:** *Margaret Grey* / RETURN OF THE SOLDIER. **1983:** *Sophie* / GIRO CITY. **1985:** *Neaera Duncan* / TURTLE DIARY. **1987:** *Charlotte* / BEYOND THERAPY.

JOHNS, GLYNIS

(1923–)

The daughter of Mervyn Johns, Glynis made her film debut at age 14 in SOUTH RIDING. Her attractive, husky voice and lovely, blue eyes served her well as she was growing up and she made a most impressive appearance as a voluptuous mermaid in MIRANDA. She has been especially adept in comedy roles, with her biggest Hollywood successes in the 1960s. She starred in the television series "Glynis" before going on to numerous Broadway appearances including "A Little Night Music." Johns claims being a star is not all it's made out to be: "I have not enjoyed being a star. It has made me ill, exhausted, and unhappy."

KEY ROLES

Dizzy Clayton / PERFECT STRANGERS, (VACATION FROM MARRIAGE), 1945, Great Britain, MGM-London Films, d-Alexander Korda.

Childish-voiced Johns teaches fellow Wren Deborah Kerr how to have a little fun while separated from her stuffy husband, who is in the Royal Navy.

Miranda / MIRANDA, 1948, Great Britain, GFD / Gainsborough, d-Ken Annakin.

Johns is a mermaid a doctor catches while on a fishing trip in Cornwall. He brings her back to London disguised as an invalid. The jokes are pretty much as would be expected and an unnecessary sequel (MAD ABOUT MEN) was made in 1954.

Ruth Earp / THE CARD, 1952, Great Britain, Rank, d-Ronald Neame.

Johns is a gold digger, one of several women out to snatch Alec Guinness, a bright young clerk who finds many ingenious ways of improving his fortune and place in society.

Maid Jean / THE COURT JESTER, 1955, Paramount, d-Norman Panama and Melvin Frank.

Johns provides a bit of romance for Danny Kaye who, posing as a court jester, is able to foil the plans of an evil baron to usurp the English crown.

Mrs. Firth / THE SUNDOWNERS, 1960, Great Britain / Australia, Warners, d-Fred Zinnemann.

Johns is the wife and mother of an Irish sheepdrover. She travels from job to job with him in the Australian bush in the twenties.

Teresa / THE CHAPMAN REPORT, 1962, Warners, d-George Cukor.

When a sex investigator interviews female suburbians on their sex lives, Johns decides it's time to put a little spice in her life by having an affair with a pro football player. But she finds that the lout has no finesse or concern for her pleasures.

Ambolyn Griffith / PAPA'S DELICATE CONDITION, 1963, Paramount, d-Franklin Schaffner.

At the turn of the century in a small Texas town, Johns must put up with the alcohol-inspired shenanigans of husband Jackie Gleason, who buys a drugstore so he can get a drink whenever he wants, and a circus to please his little girl.

OTHER ROLES

1937: *Midge Carne* / SOUTH RIDING. **1938:** *Marjorie Osborne* / MURDER IN THE FAMILY; *Nina* / PRISON WITHOUT BARS. **1939:** *Mary Carr* / ON THE NIGHT OF THE FIRE (THE FUGITIVE). **1940:** *Sheila Briggs* / THE BRIGGS FAMILY; *Winnie* / UNDER YOUR HAT. **1941:** *Miss Sheridan* / THE PRIME MINISTER; *Anna* / FORTY-NINTH PARALLEL. **1943:** *Paula Palacek* / ADVENTURES OF TARTU. **1944:** *Gwyneth* / THE HALFWAY HOUSE. **1946:** *Millie* / THIS MAN IS MINE. **1947:** *Judy Dawson* / FRIEDA; *Mabel Chiltern* / AN IDEAL HUSBAND. **1948:** *Joan* / THIRD TIME LUCKY. **1949:** *Mimi Warburton* / DEAR MR. PROHACK; *guest* / HELTER SKELTER. **1950:** *Lisa* / STATE SECRET. **1951:** *Katherine* / FLESH AND BLOOD; *Nicola Fallaize* / APPOINTMENT WITH VENUS; *Stella Cotman* / ENCORE; *May Jones* / THE MAGIC BOX. **1953:** *Mary Tudor* / THE SWORD AND THE ROSE; *Barbara Vining* / PERSONAL AFFAIR; *Helen Mary* / ROB ROY, THE HIGHLAND ROGUE; *Jean Raymond* / THE WEAK AND THE WICKED. **1954:** *Marion Southey* / THE SEEKERS; *Martha Jones* / THE BEACHCOMBER; *Miranda* / *Caroline* / MAD ABOUT MEN. **1955:** *Josephine Luton* / JOSEPHINE AND MEN. **1956:** *Cary* / LOSER TAKES ALL; *Mamie* / ALL MINE TO GIVE; *companion* / AROUND THE WORLD IN 80 DAYS. **1958:** *Kay Trevor* / ANOTHER TIME, ANOTHER PLACE. **1959:** *Kitty O'Brady* / SHAKE HANDS WITH THE DEVIL. **1960:** *Clarissa Hailsham-Brown* / THE SPIDER'S WEB. **1962:** *Jane* / THE CABINET OF CALIGARI. **1964:** *Mrs. Banks* / MARY POPPINS. **1965:** *Vina Leaf* / DEAR BRIGITTE. **1967:** *Sabine Manning* / DON'T JUST STAND THERE. **1969:** *Mrs. Squeezum* / LOCK UP YOUR DAUGHTERS. **1971:** *Myfanwy Price* / UNDER MILK WOOD. **1973:** *Eleanor* / VAULT OF HORROR.

JOHNSON, CELIA

(1908–1982)

Celia Johnson made only eleven films, her best three being for David Lean. Had she made no film other than BRIEF ENCOUNTER, she still would have merited inclusion in this book. A student at the Royal Academy of Dramatic Arts, she made her stage debut in "Major Barbara" and her first major appearance on the stage in the early 1930s. Recognized as one of the 16 most distinguished British stage actresses, Johnson made only occasional movie appearances. Her made-for-TV movies are LES MISERABLES (1978), STAYING ON (1979), and THE HOSTAGE TOWER (1980).

KEY ROLES

Alix Kinross / IN WHICH WE SERVE, 1942, Great Britain, Two Cities, d-Noel Coward and David Lean.

Johnson portrays the wife of Noel Coward, captain of a British destroyer that had been torpedoed once, towed back to port, and when back in action is dive-bombed and sunk. As the captain and others of his crew cling to a raft, they think of their loved ones back home. It was an effective World War II flag-waving picture.

Cynthia / DEAR OCTOPUS, 1942, Great Britain, Gainsborough, d-Harold French.

The octopus is the family of a couple who are celebrating their golden wedding anniversary. Three generations meet at the country home and Johnson, the couples' companion and unofficial secretary to the family, is coaxed away by an author relative.

Laura Jesson / BRIEF ENCOUNTER, 1946, Great Britain, Cineguild, d-David Lean.

Johnson is charming as the married housewife who meets an equally married doctor at the railway station. They meet again later by chance and the moment their friendship turns to love is very beautiful. In her home, watching her husband as he reads his paper, she thinks to herself: "This is my home. You're my husband. And my children are upstairs in bed. I'm a happily married woman—or, rather, I was until a few weeks ago. This is my whole world, and it's enough—or rather, it was until a few weeks ago. But, oh, Fred, I've been so foolish. I've fallen in love. I'm a lonely woman. I didn't think such violent things could happen to lonely people." She meets with her love (Trevor Howard) a few more times but they cannot bring themselves to consummate their love. They realize they have no future and when he is offered a post abroad, he accepts. Their last meeting is spoiled by the appearance of a gossipy friend of Johnson's.

Maud St. James / THE CAPTAIN'S PARADISE, 1953, Great Britain, London Films, d-Anthony Kimmins.

Alec Guinness has Johnson, a very proper, quiet, homebody as his wife in Gibraltar. This sea captain also has another wife, fiery party girl Yvonne de Carlo in Kalik, North Africa. Each month he travels back and forth between the two ports and spends the best of both worlds with his ladies. When the women learn of each other, they want to exchange lifestyles.

OTHER ROLES

1944: *Ethel Gibbons* / THIS HAPPY BREED. **1949:** *Barbara Faber* / THE ASTONISHED HEART. **1952:** *Matty* / I BELIEVE IN YOU. **1954:** *Jenny Gregory* / THE HOLLY AND THE IVY. **1956:** *Joanna* / A KID FOR TWO FARTHINGS. **1957:** *Miss Trant* / THE GOOD COMPANIONS. **1969:** *Miss MacKay* / THE PRIME OF MISS JEAN BRODIE.

JOHNSON, VAN

(Charles Van Johnson, 1916–)

A former chorus boy, Van Johnson became a star during World War II when all the established male actors were in the service. Still, Johnson has spent a great deal of his screen time in some military uniform. He became a teen idol with his baby face, red hair, freckles, and great smile which made him the movies' favorite boy-next-door. He wasn't a great actor but he pleased audiences at a time when they wanted to see good-looking young men in movies with basically happy endings. Like most actors who remained active in the late 1960s and 1970s, Johnson made his share of cheap foreign movies such as THE PRICE OF POWER (1969) and EYE OF THE SPIDER (1971). His TV movies include THE PIED PIPER OF HAMELIN (1957), THE DOOMSDAY FLIGHT (1966), COMPANY OF KILLERS (1970), CALL HER MOM (1972), THE GIRL ON THE LATE, LATE SHOW (1974), RICH MAN, POOR MAN (1976), GETTING MARRIED (1978), and THE KIDNAPPING OF THE PRESIDENT (1980).

KEY ROLES

Dr. Randall Adams / DR.GILLESPIE'S NEW ASSISTANT, 1942, MGM, d-Willis Goldbeck.

When Lew Ayres announced that he was a conscientious objector to the war, he was dropped from the Kildare series and Johnson was added to provide the romantic interest. The story is about an amnesia case.

Ted Randall / A GUY NAMED JOE, 1943, MGM, d-Victor Fleming.

In this wartime fantasy, no one is named Joe. Johnson is a young pilot who takes an interest in the girlfriend of the late Spencer Tracy. The latter's heavenly assignment is to serve as a pilot guardian angel for Johnson, and Tracy is not thrilled by the choice.

John Dyckman Brown III / TWO GIRLS AND A SAILOR, 1944, MGM, d-Richard Thorpe.

Johnson is a wealthy sailor who anonymously contributes to the entertainment plans that sisters June

Allyson and Gloria De Haven have for World War II servicemen.

Ted Lawson / THIRTY SECONDS OVER TOKYO, 1944, MGM, d-Mervyn LeRoy.
Johnson loses a leg in the Jimmy Doolittle bombing raid of Tokyo in 1942. At the time of the film it was a grand flag-raiser that reminded Americans of how shortly after Pearl Harbor we were able to invade Japanese airspace and strike a blow against their homeland.

Spike McManus / STATE OF THE UNION, 1948, MGM, d-Frank Capra.
Johnson is a public relations man working for Angela Lansbury, who is owner of a newspaper chain. She plans to make her lover (Spencer Tracy) president of the United States and Johnson will see to it that Tracy's good side is shown and his problems with his wife are not. The only thing is that Johnson prefers the wife to his boss. When Tracy regains his integrity and goes back to his wife (Katharine Hepburn), Johnson is happily fired.

Andy Larkin / IN THE GOOD OLD SUMMERTIME, 1949, MGM, d-Robert Z. Leonard.
In this musical remake of THE SHOP AROUND THE CORNER, Johnson is the head clerk of a music store who maintains a platonic mail correspondence with a young woman. He doesn't realize that this ideal woman friend is his fellow clerk (Judy Garland) with whom he is always fighting.

Holley / BATTLEGROUND, 1949, MGM, d-William A. Wellman.
Johnson is one of a squad of American foot soldiers trapped by the Germans at Bastogne in 1944, during the Battle of the Bulge. This excellent film was enormously successful, considering everyone predicted that no one wanted to see a war picture in 1949.

Lt. Steve Maryk / THE CAINE MUTINY, 1954, Columbia, d-Edward Dmytryk.
Johnson is the executive officer aboard the minesweeper Caine during World War II. When the new skipper arrives, he's war-weary Humphrey Bogart who goes to pieces during a storm. Johnson takes command of the ship and is tried for mutiny. Although his defense attorney is able to show that Bogie is mentally unbalanced, Johnson realizes that he and other officers let the skipper down because they didn't care for his "Mickey Mouse, by-the-book" ways.

Charles Wills / THE LAST TIME I SAW PARIS, 1954, MGM, d-Richard Brooks.
Johnson recalls his romance with wealthy Elizabeth Taylor in Paris. This updating of F. Scott Fitzgerald's *Babylon Revisited* is no great shakes, but the photography is lovely.

Pvt. Arthur Hugenon / MIRACLE IN THE RAIN, 1956, Warners, d-Rudolph Mate.
Plain Jane Wyman falls for soldier Johnson and, when he's killed in action, she keeps their appointment at the steps of a church with his ghost.

Al Yearling / DIVORCE, AMERICAN STYLE, 1967, Columbia, d-Bud Yorkin.
Johnson plays an automobile dealer who is selected to be the new husband for Debbie Reynolds so that her divorced husband (Dick Van Dyke) can get out of paying alimony. Though he later loses her to Van Dyke, who goes back to her, maybe he should stick around as Van Dyke and Reynolds don't solve the problems that split them the first time.

OTHER ROLES

1940: *bit* / TOO MANY GIRLS. **1942:** *Lt. Wade Wall* / SOMEWHERE I'LL FIND YOU; *Burt Bell* / MURDER IN THE BIG HOUSE; *Michael Fitzpatrick* / THE WAR AGAINST MRS. HADLEY. **1943:** *Dr. Randall Adams* / DR. GILLESPIE'S CRIMINAL CASE; *Marcus Macauley* / THE HUMAN COMEDY; *Everett Arnold* / PILOT NO. 5; *reporter* / MADAME CURIE. **1944:** *Sam Bennett* / THE WHITE CLIFFS OF DOVER; *Dr. Randall Adams* / THREE MEN IN WHITE; *Dr. Randall Adams* / BETWEEN TWO WOMEN. **1945:** *Maj. Thomas Milvaine* / THRILL OF A ROMANCE; *Capt. James Hollis* / WEEKEND AT THE WALDORF; *Bill Chandler* / EASY TO WED. **1946:** *guest* / ZIEGFELD FOLLIES; *bandleader* / TILL THE CLOUDS ROLL BY; *Sgt. Michael Hanlon* / NO LEAVE, NO LOVE; *Alec Brooke* / HIGH BARBAREE. **1947:** *Henry Carson* / THE ROMANCE OF ROSY RIDGE. **1948:** *Tech Sgt. Immanuel T. Evans* / COMMAND DECISION; *Greg Rawlings* / THE BRIDE GOES WILD. **1950:** *Dr. Lincoln Bartlett* / GROUNDS FOR MARRIAGE; *Dick Layn* / DUCHESS OF IDAHO. **1951:** *Eric Wainwright* / TOO YOUNG TO KISS; *Lt. Michael Grayson* / GO FOR BROKE; *Adam Burch* / IT'S A BIG COUNTRY; *Michael Lawrence* / THREE GUYS NAMED MIKE. **1952:** *Dan Pierce* / INVITATION; *Father John* / WHEN IN ROME; *Joseph T. Gresham* / WASHINGTON STORY; *John Alden* / PLYMOUTH ADVENTURE. **1953:** *Joe Bedloe* / CONFIDENTIALLY CONNIE; *Waldo Williams* / REMAINS TO BE SEEN; *Ray Lloyd* / EASY TO LOVE. **1954:** *Capt. James Farraday* / THE SEIGE AT RED RIVER; *Lt.(jg) Howard Thayer* / MEN OF THE FIGHTING LADY; *Jeff Douglas* / BRIGADOON. **1955:** *Maurice Bendrix* / THE END OF THE AFFAIR. **1956:** *Scott Ethan Martin* / SLANDER; *Donald Martin* / THE BOTTOM OF THE BOTTLE; *Phillip Hannon* / 23 PACES TO BAKER STREET. **1957:** *Len Carmody* / KELLY AND ME; *Carson* / ACTION OF THE TIGER. **1958:** *Sergeant Richardson* / *Kroner* / THE LAST BLITZKREIG. **1959:** *Paul Mathry* / WEB OF EVIDENCE; *Maj. Baxter Grant* / SUBWAY IN THE SKY. **1960:** *Lemaire* / THE ENEMY GENERAL. **1963:** *Bill Austin* / WIVES AND LOVERS. **1968:** *Warrant Off. Darrel Harrison* / YOURS, MINE AND OURS; *Father Chase* / WHERE ANGELS GO...TROUBLE FOLLOWS. **1969:** *Air Marshall George Taylor* / BATTLE SQUADRON. **1985:** *Larry* / PURPLE ROSE OF CAIRO.

JOLSON, AL

(Asa Yoelson, 1886–1950)
"The Jazz Singer," as Al Jolson was known, died shortly after returning from Korea where he was entertaining troops. His father was a Jewish cantor who hoped his son would follow in his footsteps, but as in Jolson's most famous movie role, Jolson had his heart set on a show business career. Applying burnt cork to his face, this minstrel invented the "Mammy" singer who often dismissed his show's company so he could entertain the audience for hours. Jolson made some silent shorts, but it didn't seem to make much sense to work in a medium where he couldn't do what he enjoyed most—sing for a live audience. As he would say so often, "Turn up the lights, I want to see their faces." Even though he ushered in the sound era, he was never as good on the screen as he was when he faced the crowds he loved and who loved him so.

KEY ROLES

Jakie Rabinowitz (Jack Robin) / THE JAZZ SINGER, 1927, Part Talkie, Warners, d-Alan Crosland.
When George Jessel wanted too much to repeat his Broadway success and Eddie Cantor turned it down fearing it might prove a failure, Jolson was given the assignment of appearing in the first feature length movie with singing and talking. Jolson, considered by many as the greatest American entertainer of the time, appears as the cantor's son who becomes alienated from his father when he chooses to become a jazz singer rather than follow the family's tradition. Everyone familiar with movies knows that this is the first film of feature length in which the characters both speak and sing. Actually it was Bobby Gordon

who played Jakie at 13 and not Jolson who was first heard singing in the film. But no one who saw the film when it was first released will ever forget Jolson yelling, "Wait a minute! Wait a minute! You ain't heard nothin' yet." His songs include "Toot Toot Tootsie Goodbye" by Gus Kahn, Dan Russo, and Ernie Erdman; "Mammy" by Sam Lewis, Joe Young, and Walter Donaldson; and Irving Berlin's "Blue Skies."

Al Stone / THE SINGING FOOL, 1928, Part Talkie, Warners, d-Lloyd Bacon.
In this musical tearjerker, Jolson not only loses his wife but his beloved little boy as well. He is comforted by cigarette girl Betty Bronson. His big number is the enormous hit "Sonny Boy" by Buddy De Sylva, Lew Brown, and Ray Henderson. Other songs include "I'm Sittin' on Top of the World" by Sam Lewis, Joe Young, and Ray Henderson, and "The Spaniard who Blighted My Heart" by Billy Merson.

Bumper / HALLELUJAH, I'M A BUM, 1933, Warners, d-Lewis Milestone.
Jolson is the self-proclaimed mayor of the Central Park hobos. He cleans up his image for Madge Evans, who has lost her memory, but goes back to his old ways when she regains it, and no longer needs him. Besides the Rodgers and Hart title song, which had to be changed to "Hallelujah, I'm a Tramp" in England, Jolson sings "You Are Too Beautiful" and "I've Got to Get Back to New York."

Al Howard / GO INTO YOUR DANCE, 1935, Warners, d-Archie Mayo.
In his only movie appearance with then wife Ruby Keeler, Jolson portrays an arrogant Broadway star whose bad behavior closes all employment doors to him. With the encouragement of nightclub dancer Keeler, Jolson opens a successful casino in New York. He sings "About a Quarter to Nine" and "A Latin from Manhattan" by Al Dubin and Harry Warren.

Ted Cotter / ROSE OF WASHINGTON SQUARE, 1939, 20th Century-Fox, d-Gregory Ratoff.
Jolson wasn't given top billing but he almost stole the show in this slightly disguised biopic of Fanny Brice. He delights with all-time favorites "My Mammy," "Toot Toot Tootsie, Goodbye," "Pretty Baby," "Rock-A-Bye Your Baby with a Dixie Melody," and "California Here I Come."

Al Jolson's Voice / THE JOLSON STORY, 1946, Columbia, d-Alfred E. Green.
This biopic, and the sequel JOLSON SINGS AGAIN, were blockbusters for the studio and Jolson's singing thrilled a whole new generation of fans. Larry Parks portrays Jolson, but it's Al's voice.

OTHER ROLES

1929: *guest* / SONNY BOY; *Joe Lane* / SAY IT WITH SONGS; *guest* / NEW YORK NIGHTS. **1930:** *Al Fuller* / MAMMY; *Gus* / BIG BOY; *guest* / SHOWGIRL IN HOLLYWOOD. **1934:** *Al Wonder* / WONDER BAR. **1936:** *Al Jackson* / THE SINGING KID. **1939:** *guest* / HOLLYWOOD CAVALCADE; *E. P. Christy* / SWANEE RIVER. **1945:** *guest* / RHAPSODY IN BLUE. **1949:** *Jolson's voice* / JOLSON SINGS AGAIN.

JONES, JENNIFER

(Phyllis Isley, 1919–)
While attending the American Academy of Dramatic Arts, Jennifer Jones met actor Robert Walker who later became her first husband. Both were brought to Hollywood in 1939 where she made her film debut in the DICK TRACY'S G-MEN serial. Her career was guided by David O. Selznik, who became her second husband. She won an Oscar for her second feature length film, THE SONG OF BERNADETTE. In the next few years her great beauty graced extremely different movies. She played a youngster experiencing first love in SINCE YOU WENT AWAY; a tragic, earthy half-breed in DUEL IN THE SUN; a melancholy spirit in PORTRAIT OF JENNIE; and literary ladies in MADAME BOVARY and CARRIE. She moved to Europe with Selznick in 1950 and her films in the next few years were disappointing. When she came back to Hollywood in 1955 she made a hit as a Eurasian doctor in the lovely tearjerker LOVE IS A MANY SPLENDORED THING. Jones only made a few more films before retiring in 1961, then reappeared in films every few years, the best being THE TOWERING INFERNO in which she falls for con man Fred Astaire. Jones must be credited for exploring various aspects of a woman's sexuality in several interesting if flawed movies, with her performances of mixed but provocative appeal.

KEY ROLES

Bernadette Soubirous / THE SONG OF BERNADETTE, 1943, 20th Century-Fox, d-Henry King.
The prologue to the movie says: "For those who believe in God, no explanation is necessary. For those who do not believe in God, no explanation is possible." Jones portrays the French peasant girl to whom the Virgin Mary appears at Lourdes. The film made Jones a star and won her an Oscar for her dignified portrayal.

Jane Hilton / SINCE YOU WENT AWAY, 1944, Selznick / United Artists, d-John Cromwell.
When the husband of Claudette Colbert and father of Jones and teenager Shirley Temple, goes off to war, this well-off family must simply cope. None are shy of male attention. Jones's attention comes from then husband Robert Walker, a GI who must also go away to war.

Singleton / LOVE LETTERS, 1945, Paramount, d-William Dieterle.
During World War II, Robert Sully has his buddy (Joseph Cotten) write love letters to Sully's girl (Jones) back home. Jones marries Sully but is disillusioned by the way he treats her. Her stepmother kills the drunken Sully while he is beating Jones and suffers a stroke that leaves her speechless. As for Jones, the shock causes her to become an amnesiac. She is tried for the killing and given a one-year jail term. About this time, Cotten shows up and immediately falls in love with Jones.

Pearl Chavez / DUEL IN THE SUN, 1946, Selznick, d-King Vidor and others.
When her southern gentleman gambler father is hanged for killing her unfaithful Indian mother, Jones is taken in by Lillian Gish to live on a large ranch owned by Lionel Barrymore. She causes trouble between two brothers—sensible Joseph Cotten and wild Gregory Peck. Peck and Jones end up killing each other despite the passion and love between them. As preacher Walter Huston puts it: "You call her a child, Laura Belle? Under that heathen blanket, there's a full-blossomed woman fit for the devil to drive men crazy."

Jennie Appleton / PORTRAIT OF JENNIE, 1948, Selznick, d-William Dieterle.
In this fantasy, painter Joseph Cotten meets a little girl (Jones) in Central Park. She speaks of strange

things, but he is taken by her beauty. Each time he runs into her thereafter she is older, "hurrying to catch up with him." When she is old enough he falls in love with her and paints her portrait, the best work of his career. He also learns that she had died in Cape Cod years ago when she was washed out to sea at a lighthouse by an unexpected storm. He goes to the spot on the anniversary of the event intent on saving her. She shows up but he is unable to alter her fate.

Emma Bovary / MADAME BOVARY, 1949, MGM, d-Vincente Minnelli.
Jones is better than the others in this rather dull production of the Flaubert classic about a passionate woman who marries a boring man, takes a lover, and commits suicide.

Carrie Meeber / CARRIE, 1952, Paramount, d-William Wyler.
Jones is superb as the country girl who comes to Chicago and goes through a series of lovers on her way to becoming a successful actress. This is a fine version of Theodore Dreiser's *Sister Carrie*.

Gwendolyn Chelm / BEAT THE DEVIL, 1954, Great Britain, Romulus, d-John Huston.
Jones displays a talent for comedy portraying a scatterbrained woman who is among the odd assortment of travelers on a boat bound for the African coast to acquire land known to contain uranium deposits. As an example of her reasoning, she warns her husband, "Harry, we must beware of these men. They're desperate characters. Not one of them looked at my legs."

Han Suyin / LOVE IS A MANY SPLENDORED THING, 1955, 20th Century-Fox, d-Henry King.
Jones was nominated for an Academy Award for her portrayal of a Eurasian physician in Hong Kong who falls in love with married reporter William Holden. The title song (which won an Oscar) makes their bittersweet and doomed love seem very beautiful.

Elizabeth Barrett / THE BARRETTS OF WIMPOLE STREET, 1957, MGM, d-Sidney Franklin.
Jones looks right for the part of the poetess who counts the ways she loves Robert Browning and survives her father's unnatural interest in her. But the film is inferior to the 1934 production.

Lisolette Mueller / THE TOWERING INFERNO, 1974, 20th Century-Fox, d-John Guillermin.
Jones has found some romance with charming con man Fred Astaire, but dies a heroine's death when the world's tallest building is destroyed by fire on the night of its formal opening.

OTHER ROLES

1939: *Celia Braddock* / THE NEW FRONTIER. **1946:** *Cluny Brown* / CLUNY BROWN. **1949:** *China Valdez* / WE WERE STRANGERS. **1951:** *Hazel Woodus* / GONE TO EARTH. **1952:** *Ruby Gentry* / RUBY GENTRY. **1954:** *Mary Forbes* / INDISCRETION OF AN AMERICAN WIFE. **1955:** *Miss Dove* / GOOD MORNING, MISS DOVE. **1956:** *Betsy Rath* / THE MAN IN THE GREY FLANNEL SUIT. **1958:** *Catherine Barkley* / A FAREWELL TO ARMS. **1961:** *Nicole Diver* / TENDER IS THE NIGHT. **1966:** *Carol* / THE IDOL. **1969:** *Astrid* / CULT OF THE DAMNED.

JONES, SHIRLEY

(1934–)

When producers conducted a nation-wide search for a girl to play Laurey in Rodgers and Hammerstein's OKLAHOMA, they came up with Shirley Jones, a youngster with a pleasant voice and sweet innocent looks. When, five years later, she won a Best Supporting Actress Award, she was no longer sweet. Instead she was a sexy woman who had been reduced to prostitution after being ruined by Elmer Gantry (played by Burt Lancaster). Despite the award, her movie career has not been much since, except for THE MUSIC MAN in 1962. Most of her work has been on TV as the mother on the successful "The Partridge Family" series, and made-for-TV movies including SILENT NIGHT, LONELY NIGHT (1969), BUT I DON'T WANT TO GET MARRIED (1970), THE GIRLS OF HUNTINGTON HOUSE (1973), WINNER TAKE ALL (1975), YESTERDAY'S CHILD (1977), WHO'LL SAVE THE CHILDREN? (1978), and A LAST CRY FOR HELP (1979).

KEY ROLES

Laurey Williams / OKLAHOMA! 1955, Magna, d-Fred Zinnemann.
Jones lives with her aunt on a farm and is courted by cowboy Gordon MacRae. To keep him in his place she encourages the attentions of a mean hired man (Rod Steiger) and it almost results in her and MacRae's deaths. She sings "Many a New Day" and, with MacRae, "People Will Say We're in Love" and "Surrey with the Fringe on Top."

Julie Jordon Bigelow / CAROUSEL, 1956, 20th Century-Fox, d-Henry King.
Jones is the sweet factory girl who is attracted to a loud-mouthed, bullying carousel barker (Gordon MacRae). They marry impulsively and he is fired from his job. He treats Jones badly and beats her, but when he learns she is going to have a baby, he participates in an unsuccessful robbery to get money for his family and is killed. When his daughter is graduating from school he is given the chance to come back for one day to see her. His temper as bad as ever, he slaps his daughter and disappears, then Jones explains how a slap could feel like a caress. Jones sings "What's the Use of Wonderin'" and, with MacRae, "If I Loved You."

Lulu Bains / ELMER GANTRY, 1960, United Artists, d-Richard Brooks.
Jones is the daughter of the head of the Bible College that evangelist Elmer Gantry attended. After he seduced her, she was thrown out by her father and became a whore. When Gantry and Sister Falconer (Jean Simmons) bring their revival to town, Jones sees a way to avenge herself and make some money in the bargain. She sets up Gantry to have pictures of him taken with her in compromising positions. When she releases them to the newspaper, Gantry is disgraced for a brief time.

Marian Pardoo / THE MUSIC MAN, 1962, Warners, d-Morton DaCosta.
As the unmarried librarian in a small town, who has been left all the books in the library by its donor, Jones is often talked about in an unflattering way by the ladies of River City, Iowa. However, she's the only one not completely bamboozled by a fast-talking salesman of boys' bands (Robert Preston) when he hits the town. Her songs include Meredith Willson's "Goodnight My Someone" and "Being in Love."

OTHER ROLES

1957: *Liz Templeton* / APRIL LOVE. **1959:** *Linda Cabot* / NEVER STEAL ANYTHING SMALL; *Betty Barnaby* / BOBBIKINS. **1960:** *Suzie Murphy* / PEPE. **1961:** *Marty Purcell* / TWO RODE TOGETHER. **1963:** *Amy Martin* / A TICKLISH AFFAIR. **1964:** *Janet Walker* / BEDTIME STORY; *Karen Williams* / DARK PURPOSE. **1965:** *Janice*

Claridge / FLUFFY; *Marigold Marado* / THE SECRET OF MY SUCCESS. **1970:** *Jenny* / THE CHEYENNE SOCIAL CLUB; *Flo* / THE HAPPY ENDING. **1979:** *Gina Rowe* / BEYOND THE POSEIDON ADVENTURE. **1984:** *LaDonna* / TANK.

JOURDAN, LOUIS

(Louis Gendre, 1919–)

This French leading man made numerous films in France during World War II including LE CORSAIR (not finished, 1939), LA COMEDIE DU BONHEUR (1940), PREMIER RENDEZVOUS (1941), L'ARLESIENNE, FELICIE NANTEURIL and LA VIE DE BOHEME (1942), LES PETITES DU QUAI AUX FLEURS, UNTEL PERE ET FILS (1943), and LA BELLE AVENTURE (1945). But Hollywood did not use Jourdan to his best advantage. He pleased audiences in a few melodramas and was excellent in GIGI, but generally one wishes that more challenges had been offered him since on several occasions he suggested that he might have been able to deliver if given better roles. During the 1970s he looked rather good in TV movies such as RUN A CROOKED MILE (1971), THE COUNT OF MONTE CRISTO (1976), and THE MAN IN THE IRON MASK (1977).

KEY ROLES

Andre Latour / THE PARADINE CASE, 1948, Selznick, d-Alfred Hitchcock.

Barrister Gregory Peck falls in love with his client (Alida Valli) who is on trial for the murder of her blind husband. Peck tries to prove what he hopes is true, that Jourdan has killed his employer because the latter was about to discharge him for making advances to his wife. The truth comes out after Jourdan commits suicide: Valli loved Jourdan and actually killed her husband.

Stefan Brand / LETTER FROM AN UNKNOWN WOMAN, 1948, Universal, d-Max Ophuls.

In a much-neglected, brilliant melodrama, Jourdan is a caddish musician who has been adored by Joan Fontaine since her childhood. When she is grown, they meet one night and become lovers. He goes away, promptly forgets Fontaine, and is unaware that she has his son. Later when she has wed an understanding man, she meets Jourdan again and her feelings are just as strong, but he has no recollection of her. Their son dies and she does also, but she sends Jourdan a letter telling him everything and he at last remembers her just before going to a duel (which he will no doubt lose) with Fontaine's husband.

Uncle Desmond Bonnard / THE HAPPY TIME, 1952, Columbia, d-Richard Fleischer.

Jourdan's brother's 13-year-old son falls in love with the new maid in a French-Canadian house during the twenties. Philandering Jourdan gets the blame when the boy sneaks into her room and kisses her, awakening her from sleep. It's a delightful little family comedy.

Prince Dino Di Cessi / THREE COINS IN THE FOUNTAIN, 1954, 20th Century-Fox, d-Jean Negulesco.

Of three American girls working in Rome who find romance, Maggie McNamara lands herself a prince—Jourdan.

Gaston Lachaille / GIGI, 1958, MGM, d-Vincente Minnelli.

Jourdan is a bored, rich Parisian who finds the only things of interest are the simple times he shares with a young girl (Leslie Caron) and her grandmother. Caron is being trained to follow the family tradition of being a kept woman. But when she blossoms into a lovely woman, Jourdan, who sings charmingly of the change in her in the Lerner and Loewe title song, decides he wants to marry her.

Philippe Forrestier / CAN-CAN, 1960, 20th Century-Fox, d-Walter Lang.

Jourdan is a French judge who tries to enforce the law against the lewd Can-Can dance performed by Shirley MacLaine and the girls of her club. But he falls for the dancer, then loses her to Frank Sinatra, a shady lawyer.

Mark Champselle / THE V.I.P.S, 1962, Great Britain, MGM, d-Anthony Asquith.

Jourdan is running away with Elizabeth Taylor, the wife of a man (Richard Burton) who neglects her. When the flight is delayed by bad weather, she has time to compare the two men in her life and goes back with her husband.

Kamal Khan / OCTOPUSSY, 1983, Great Britain, Eon / Danjaq, d-John Glen.

Jourdan is an evil Afghan prince who plans to plunder Czarist treasures from the U.S.S.R. He is up against James Bond (Roger Moore) and after he violently puts away various adversaries, 007 removes him from the list of active bad guys.

OTHER ROLES

1948: *Ottavio Quaglini* / NO MINOR VICES. **1949:** *Rodolphe Boulanger* / MADAME BOVARY. **1950:** *Andre Laurence* / BIRD OF PARADISE. **1951:** *Capt. Pierre Francois La Rochelle* / ANNE OF THE INDIES. **1952:** *Henri* / RUE DE L'ESTRAPADE. **1953:** *Boccaccio / Paganino / Guilio / Bertrando* / DECAMERON NIGHTS. **1956:** *Dr. Nicholas Agi* / THE SWAN; *Lyle Benton* / JULIE; *Michel* / THE BRIDE IS MUCH TOO BEAUTIFUL. **1957:** *Duc Beauvais* / DANGEROUS EXILE. **1959:** *David Savage* / THE BEST OF EVERYTHING. **1960:** *Paul* / LEVIATHAN. **1961:** *Edmond Dantes* / THE COUNT OF MONTE CRISTO. **1962:** *Drusco* / AMAZONS OF ROME; *Tom* / DISORDER; *Mathias Sandorf* / MATHIAS SANDORF. **1965:** *Marc Fontaine* / MADE IN PARIS. **1967:** *Charles Beaulieu* / PEAU D'ESPION. **1968:** *Henri Tournel* / A FLEA IN HER EAR; *Cardinal Acquaviva* / CERVANTES. **1977:** *Prince di Siracusa* / THE SILVER BEARS. **1982:** *Arcane* / SWAMP THING.

KAHN, MADELINE

(1942–)

Comedienne Madeline Kahn can be a bit much for those who like their humor just the least bit subtle. She hits you in the face almost as if she is throwing a custard pie. Her biggest successes have been with another over-active over-achiever, Mel Brooks. Still, she has her place in the comical scheme of things.

KEY ROLES

Eunice Burns / WHAT'S UP, DOC? 1972, Warners, d-Peter Bogdanovich.

Kahn's the fiancee of the dullest musicologist in the world (Ryan O'Neal), and since musicologists are the dullest people in the world, that will give you some idea of how bad off she is. Still she's luckier than Barbra Streisand, who ends up with O'Neal—a man who finds musical excitement in banging rocks together.

Trixie Delight / PAPER MOON, 1973, Paramount, d-Peter Bogdanovich.

Kahn is a good-time-had-by-all who latches on to Ryan O'Neal, a traveling con man. But O'Neal's real-life daughter (Tatum) effectively dumps Kahn by arranging for Ryan to catch her with the hotel clerk.

Elizabeth / YOUNG FRANKENSTEIN, 1974, 20th Century-Fox, d-Mel Brooks.

Kahn is the fiancée of young Frederick Fronk-ensteen who finds his grandfather's notebooks and creates a new monster. Kahn is impressed by the size of the monster's private parts and marries him, but Gene Wilder (as Frankenstein) has already made a medical exchange with his creation and now has what Kahn thought was the most important part of the born-again creature.

Victoria Brisbane / HIGH ANXIETY, 1977, 20th Century-Fox, d-Mel Brooks.

In his tribute to Alfred Hitchcock, Mel Brooks has Kahn appearing as a bizarre lady who encompasses all the Hitchcock heroines into one rather unusual person who is spellbound by what she sees in her rear window when her man gets vertigo.

Empress Nympho / HISTORY OF THE WORLD—PART ONE, 1981, Brooksfilm, d-Mel Brooks.

Kahn is an oversexed ruler in this sophomoric, tasteless tale of familiar episodes in history with concentration on the adolescent sexual urges of a bunch of idiots. This will delight any 7- to 12-year-old in the house.

OTHER ROLES

1974: *Lili Von Shtupp* / BLAZING SADDLES. **1975:** *Jenny* / THE ADVENTURE OF SHERLOCK HOLMES' SMARTER BROTHER; *Kitty O'Kelly* / AT LONG LAST LOVE. **1977:** *Estie Del Ruth* / WON TON TON, THE DOG WHO SAVED HOLLYWOOD. **1978:** *Mrs. Montenegro* / THE CHEAP DETECTIVE. **1979:** *guest* / THE MUPPET MOVIE. **1980:** *Mrs. Link* / FIRST FAMILY; *Bunny Weinberger* / HAPPY BIRTHDAY, GEMINI; *Cynthia* / SIMON; *sorceress* / WHOLLY MOSES. **1983:** *Betty* / YELLOWBEARD. **1985:** *Mrs. White* / CLUE.

KAYE, DANNY

(David Daniel Kaminsky, 1918–1987)

Danny Kaye, one of the world's most beloved comedians, shared only a bit of his unusual talents on the movie screen. He was first a sensation on the stage, to which he often returned in triumph. He also demonstrated his unique talent on television and, perhaps more importantly, in the many in-person appearances he made on behalf of the children of the world and the United Nations. He was blessed with a brilliant wife, Sylvia Fine, who created songs and clever routines that were some of the best things Kaye ever did. His ability to make sense with double-talk, tongue-twisters, and rhymes amazed and delighted audiences. In various Goldwyn productions Kaye played meek men who became unexpected heroes and were admired by beauties such as the statuesque Virginia Mayo. He was a kid who never quite grew up and we are all better for it.

KEY ROLES

Danny Weems / UP IN ARMS, 1944, Goldwyn, d-Elliott Nugent.

Kaye made a spectacular film debut described by one critic as the most exciting debut since Greta Garbo's. He plays a hypochondriac who, along with his roommate (Dana Andrews) and the two girls that will win them (Dinah Shore and Constance Dowling), finds himself in the service in the Pacific during World War II. The most memorable number in the film is the inspired "Manic-Depressive Picture Presents" written by the soon-to-be Mrs. Kaye, Sylvia Fine, for her talented man to perform.

Busby Bellew / Edwin Dingle / WONDER MAN, 1945, Goldwyn, d-Bruce Humberstone.

Kaye portrays twins—one a fast-talking entertainer who is a witness to a murder and is killed so he won't testify, and his long-lost brother, a mild-mannered Milquetoast who takes his brother's place and gets a lot of help from the deceased's ghost.

Walter Mitty / THE SECRET LIFE OF WALTER MITTY, 1947, Goldwyn, d-Norman Z. McLeod.

Kaye is an editor for a New York publishing company who is under his mother's thumb and the domination is about to be transferred to an equally in-charge fiancée. Kaye daydreams constantly of himself as heroic men, always with the same beautiful blonde admiring his derring-do. Then, all of a sudden, she appears for real as Virginia Mayo and Kaye must be a real hero and deal with foreign agents.

Hans Christian Andersen / HANS CHRISTIAN ANDERSEN, 1952, Goldwyn, d-Charles Vidor.

Kaye portrays the Danish fairy tale storyteller who writes a ballet for a prima donna with whom he falls in love, believing that she is brutalized by her director and husband. Kaye is a delight, the music is enjoyable, and the story is nonsense.

Jerry / KNOCK ON WOOD, 1953, Columbia, d-Norman Panama and Melvin Frank.

Kaye is a ventriloquist who innocently becomes involved with spies trying to smuggle stolen plans in his dummy.

Hawkins / THE COURT JESTER, 1956, Paramount, d-Norman Panama and Melvin Frank.

Many argue that this is Kaye's best film. He appears as a simple peasant posing as a court jester who thwarts Basil Rathbone's plans to rule England. For some the sequence of the "pellet with the poison's in the vessel with the pestle, the chalice from the palace has the brew that is true" is one of the funniest in movies.

Red (Ernest Loring) Nichols / THE FIVE PENNIES, 1959, Paramount, d-Melville Shavelson.

In this rag-to-riches biopic of cornetist Red Nichols, Kaye is excellent in a straight role as a musician whose loss of popularity is compounded by his young daughter's polio.

OTHER ROLES

1946: *Burleigh Sullivan* / THE KID FROM BROOKLYN. **1948:** *Prof. Hobart Frisbee* / A SONG IS BORN. **1949:** *Georgi* / THE INSPECTOR GENERAL; *guest* / IT'S A GREAT FEELING. **1951:** *Henri Duran* / *Jack Martin* / ON THE RIVIERA. **1954:** *Phil Davis* / WHITE CHRISTMAS. **1957:** *S. I. Jacobowsky* / ME AND THE COLONEL. **1958:** *Andrew Larabee* / MERRY ANDREW. **1961:** *Pfc. Ernie Williams* / *Gen. MacKenzie Smith* / ON THE DOUBLE. **1963:** *Ernie Klenk* / THE MAN FROM THE DINER'S CLUB. **1969:** *the ragpicker* / THE MADWOMAN OF CHAILLOT.

KEATON, DIANE

(Diane Hall, 1946–)

Even when a role calls for Diane Keaton to be unreasonable and petty, her innate vulnerability makes one want to assure her that things will be all right. She has proven to be both a skilled comedienne and an actress who can handle serious, even deep, material. She has been willing to take chances with her career and thus has not allowed the public to grow tired of her. Her long association with Woody Allen has long since left the lovers stage, but she seems more than happy to be a part of his repertory company and make small cameo appearances in his pictures.

KEY ROLES

Joan Vecchio / LOVERS AND OTHER STRANGERS, 1970, ABC Pictures, d-Cy Howard.

Keaton arrives at the wedding of her husband's brother having decided to get a divorce. Her in-laws want to know "what's the story," but she and her husband can no more tell why they are breaking up than can the older generation explain why they have stayed together.

Kay Corleone / THE GODFATHER, PART II, 1974, Paramount, d-Francis Ford Coppola.

Keaton played the same role in the original, but in the crush of characters her role wasn't much. In the sequel, she marries the new Don (Al Pacino) and finds herself relegated to the role of all wives of Mafiosa—ignorant of her husband's activities and expected to produce and raise children without any real closeness to the man she loves.

Annie Hall / ANNIE HALL, 1977, United Artists, d-Woody Allen.

In this semi-serious comedy based on the real-life relationship between Keaton and Allen, Keaton is a midwestern WASP who moves in with a death-obsessed, ultra-liberal, Jewish comedian. Keaton's mannish layered look became the fashion for a time and probably contributed to her winning an Oscar.

Theresa Dunn / LOOKING FOR MR. GOODBAR, 1977, Paramount, d-Richard Brooks.

By day Keaton is a teacher of deaf children. By night she prowls the bars, ready to be picked up for one-night stands. In the process she meets many men including a sadistic stud, one decent man, and ultimately, a bisexual psychopath who kills her.

Mary Wilke / MANHATTAN, 1979, United Artists, d-Woody Allen.

In Allen's black-and-white masterpiece, Allen first meets Keaton when she is having an affair with his married friend. Allen considers her shallow but finally has an affair with her himself. She can't be true, though, and returns to her married lover who leaves his wife for her.

Louise Bryant / REDS, 1981, Paramount, d-Warren Beatty.

Keaton was nominated for an Academy Award for her portrayal of the radical writer who has an ongoing romance with John Reed (Warren Beatty), the American writer who wrote *Ten Days that Shook the World*, the story of the Russian Revolution that led to the Communist takeover.

OTHER ROLES

1972: *Kay Corleone* / THE GODFATHER; *Linda Christie* / PLAY IT AGAIN, SAM. **1974:** *Luna* / SLEEPER. **1975:** *Sonja* / LOVE AND DEATH. **1976:** *Lissa Chestnut* / HARRY AND WALTER GO TO NEW YORK; *Katie Bingham* / I WILL, I WILL...FOR NOW. **1978:** *Renata* / INTERIORS. **1982:** *Faith Dunlap* / SHOOT THE MOON. **1984:** *Charlie* / THE LITTLE DRUMMER GIRL. **1985:** *Mrs. Soffel* / MRS. SOFFEL. **1986:** *Lenny McGrath* / CRIMES OF THE HEART. **1987:** *band-singer* / RADIO DAYS; *J. C. Wiatt* / BABY BOOM.

KEEL, HOWARD

(Harold Leek, 1917–)

Possessor of a fine baritone voice and an imposing physique, Howard Keel has been described as an actor who sings, rather than a singer who acts. This son of a coal miner started as a singing busboy in Los Angeles then moved on to appearances in a west coast stage production of "Carousel" in 1945. He made his film debut in 1948 in a forgettable British film while appearing in London in "Oklahoma." Two years later he became a star with his role in ANNIE GET YOUR GUN. He made several musicals before concentrating on straight acting roles. When these parts ran out, he appeared in nightclubs, often with his former co-star, Kathryn Grayson. He has come back strong as an actor and singer with his success on TV's "Dallas."

KEY ROLES

Frank Butler / ANNIE GET YOUR GUN, 1950, MGM, d-George Sidney.

Keel portrays the established sharpshooting star of a Wild West show that picks up a backhill's terror with a gun, Annie Oakley. She promptly falls in love with the handsome Mr. Butler, sings "You Can't Get a Man with a Gun," and cleans up her personal act until he finds her quite presentable and attractive. With Betty Hutton as Annie, Keel sings Irving Berlin's "They Say that Falling in Love Is Wonderful" and, by himself, "The Girl that I Marry."

Gaylord Ravenal / SHOW BOAT, 1951, MGM, d-George Sidney.

In this Technicolor remake of the Hammerstein and Kern musical of life and love aboard a Mississippi showboat, Keel is a manly Ravenal who, with Kathryn Grayson, sings "Make Believe" and "You Are Love." In this version the gambling man returns to his wife and daughter rather than stand aside and watch both become musical stars on Broadway. In other words, its not true to the Edna Ferber story.

"Stretch" Barnes / "Smoky" Callaway / CALLAWAY WENT THATAWAY, 1951, MGM, d-Melvin Frank and Norman Panama.

Suppose a Hopalong Cassidy-like actor, whose westerns have become a big hit on TV, no longer looks or acts like the Hoppy the kids see and love on the small screen. Suppose everyone is screaming for him to make public appearances and pick up a bundle of money. What would you do? The same thing that the backers of the cowboy actor in this flick do—find a look-alike.

Tony Naylor / LOVELY TO LOOK AT, 1952, RKO, d-Mervyn LeRoy.

In this Technicolor remake of the Jerome Kern and Dorothy Fields musical ROBERTA, Keel accompanies his friend (Red Skelton) to Paris when the latter inherits a dress salon. They discover that the salon, run by two sisters, is almost bankrupt. Romances blossom and everything works out okay in the end. Keel sings the title number and, with Kathryn Grayson, "You're Devastating."

Wild Bill Hickok / CALAMITY JANE, 1953, MGM, d-David Butler.

As the frontiersman Hickok, Keel takes second place to Doris Day as a cute Calamity Jane in buckskin, but he does justice to the Sammy Fain and Paul Francis Webster songs, particularly "I Can Do without You."

Fred Graham / Petruchio / KISS ME KATE, 1953, MGM, d-George Sidney.

The stormy backstage life of Keel and his ex-wife (Kathryn Grayson) parallels what is going on in front of the lights in a musical version of Shakespeare's "The Taming of the Shrew." Their songs together include "So in Love" and "Wunderbar," and all of the Cole Porter numbers are showstoppers.

Adam Pontabee / SEVEN BRIDES FOR SEVEN BROTHERS, 1954, MGM, d-Stanley Donen.

Even though this marvelous musical was one of the most dance-oriented ever made, and dancing was not Keel's strong point, he was at his best as the oldest of seven mountain men who goes to town to find a wife to take care of him and his loutish brothers. He finds a perfect woman in Jane Powell. When his siblings reckon they'd like brides too, he helps them kidnap six local beauties. Keel's best song is Gene DePaul and Johnny Mercer's "Bless Your Beautiful Hide."

Haj / KISMET, 1955, MGM, d-Vincente Minnelli.

Keel is a beggar-poet whose lovely daughter (Ann Blyth) becomes the beloved of the Caliph, Vic Damone. Keel himself ends up with Dolores Gray who is the wife of the evil Wazir who also longs for Blyth but is put to rest by Keel. Keel sings the Bob Wright, Chet Forrest, and Alexander Borodin numbers "Fate," "Gesticulate," and "The Olive Tree."

Simon Peter / THE BIG FISHERMAN, 1959, Centurion, d-Frank Borzage.

In a very flat production, Keel plays the follower of Christ who is the rock upon which Christ builds his church. But did the rock have to be so dull?

OTHER ROLES

1948: *Boke* / THE SMALL VOICE. **1950:** *Hazard Endicott* / PAGAN LOVE SONG. **1951:** *Mike Jamison* / THREE GUYS NAMED MIKE; *Slim Shelby* / TEXAS CARNIVAL. **1952:** *Vince Heldon* / DESPERATE SEARCH. **1953:** *Rick Grayton* / FAST COMPANY; *King Cameron* / RIDE, VAQUERO. **1954:** *Capt. Mike Malone* / ROSE MARIE. **1954:** *cameo* / DEEP IN MY HEART; *Hannibal* / JUPITER'S DARLING. **1958:** *Donavan* / FLOODS OF FEAR. **1961:** *Colonel Devlin* / ARMORED COMMAND. **1963:** *Bill Masen* / THE DAY OF THE TRIFFIDS. **1966:** *Waco* / WACO. **1967:** *Capt. Tom York* / RED TOMAHAWK; *Levi Walking Bear* / THE WAR WAGON. **1968:** *Lee Travis* / ARIZONA BUSHWHACKERS.

KEELER, RUBY

(Ethel Keeler, 1909–)

This Canadian-born song-and-dance woman realized that she wasn't very adept at either. She later acknowledged: "It's amazing. I couldn't act. I had that terrible singing voice, and now I can see I wasn't the greatest tap dancer in the world either." But for a brief period in the 1930s, this one-time wife of Al Jolson was very popular for her appearances with Dick Powell in light musical comedies that helped people briefly forget the Depression.

KEY ROLES

Peggy Sawyer / FORTY-SECOND STREET, 1933, Warners, d-Lloyd Bacon.

In the world's most beloved movie cliche, Keeler is the hick chorus girl who is picked by the director of a Broadway musical to go on in place of the star when the latter hurts herself the day before opening night. It is a delight to see Keeler pick them up and lay them down without too much grace in numbers like "Shuffle off to Buffalo" by Al Dubin and Harry Warren, staged by Busby Berkeley. She goes out a youngster but comes back a star.

Polly Parker / GOLD DIGGERS OF 1933, 1933, Warners, d-Mervyn LeRoy.

Keeler and her two showgirl roommates are out of work. They meet a young songwriter (Dick Powell) whom they believe is as broke as they are, but he's really filthy rich. He arranges to put on his show with a juicy part for Keeler and roles for the other girls. When his leading man can't go on, he takes the role himself, which brings his older brother and family lawyer running to protect him from gold diggers, but these two end up with the roommates. Keeler and Powell get together on stage with "Shadow Waltz" by Harry Warren and Al Dubin.

Barbara Hemingway / DAMES, 1934, Warners, d-Ray Enright.

A millionaire purity fanatic (Hugh Herbert) enlists the aid of his cousin (Guy Kibbee) to form a society to stamp out all theater, for which Kibbee will be rewarded with 10 million dollars. Naturally, Kibbee gets involved with a chorus girl who tries to blackmail him, and Keeler, Kibbee's own daughter, appears in a Broadway show the rich nut wants to shut down. Dick Powell and Keeler are featured in the production number "I Only Have Eyes for You" by Al Dubin and Harry Warren.

Kathleen "Kit" Fitts / FLIRTATION WALK, 1934, Warners, d-Frank Borzage.

Keeler's in love with West Point cadet Dick Powell. There's not much plot here, but the musical has some very agreeable numbers including the title song and "Mr. and Mrs. Is the Name" by Mort Dixon and Allie Wrubel.

Dorothy Wayne / GO INTO YOUR DANCE, 1935, Warners, d-Archie Mayo.

In the only movie made with then husband Al Jolson, Keeler plays an understanding dancer who helps a big-headed star recover after he loses his popularity.

OTHER ROLES

1933: *Bea Thorn* / FOOTLIGHT PARADE. **1935:** *June Blackburn* / SHIPMATES FOREVER. **1936:** *Colleen Riley* / COLLEEN. **1937:** *Jane Clarke* / READY, WILLING AND ABLE. **1938:** *Kitty Carey* / MOTHER CAREY'S CHICKENS. **1941:** *Betty Blake* / SWEETHEART OF THE CAMPUS. **1970:** *cameo* / THE PHYNX.

KELLY, GENE

(Eugene Curran Kelly, 1912–)

Gene Kelly has been referred to as "the second best dancer in movie history," but that's not quite right. The styles of Kelly and Fred Astaire were so different that comparison is bound to be unfair. Astaire was the smooth ballroom dancer who could make any partner, including a hat rack, look good. Kelly was all acrobatic and modern ballet. Kelly put it this way: "My style is strong, wide-open bravura. Fred's is intimate, cool, easy." In addition to his dancing, Kelly has often served as choreographer and director of movies. His movie appearances have not been limited to musicals though. He has made numerous forays into straight roles in dramas such as THE BLACK HAND and INHERIT THE WIND. His performance in ANCHORS AWEIGH won him his only Oscar nomination, however. While still in college he formed a song-and-dance act with his brother Fred and opened the Gene Kelly School of

Dance. Small parts in Broadway shows led to the lead role in "Pal Joey" in 1940 and his film debut in 1942.

KEY ROLES

Harry Palmer / FOR ME AND MY GAL, 1942, MGM, d-Busby Berkeley.

In his debut Kelly teams up with Judy Garland and George Murphy to form a vaudeville act in the early part of the century. There are romantic complications—Murphy loves Garland, Garland loves Kelly, and Kelly loves Kelly. Kelly dances to "Oh, Johnny, Oh," "They Go Wild, Simply Wild Over Me," and with Garland to "Oh, You Beautiful Doll."

Danny McGuire / COVER GIRL, 1944, Columbia, d-Charles Vidor.

This is the simple story of a Brooklyn nightclub dancer (Rita Hayworth) who deserts her lover (Kelly) to become a cover girl but learns that riches and notoriety aren't everything and returns to the man she loves. The best Kelly number is the "Alter Ego" routine in which he dances with his reflection in a shop window, then the reflection becomes flesh and blood and challenges Kelly to try new steps.

Joseph Brady / ANCHORS AWEIGH, 1945, MGM, d-George Sidney.

Kelly and Frank Sinatra are a couple of sailors on leave in Hollywood. In order to impress Kathryn Grayson, Kelly tells her he can get her an audition with Jose Iturbi. On this simple plot are hung some delightful musical numbers, including Kelly's famous dance with grumpy mouse Jerry from the Tom and Jerry cartoon series, a Mexican hat dance with a cute little girl, and a fantasy in which Kelly, dressed to the tees, displays all his athletic skill in a fandango-like routine.

Serafin / THE PIRATE, 1948, MGM, d-Vincente Minnelli.

Kelly, a strolling player in the Caribbean, is almost hanged as the notorious pirate "Mack the Black" because of his love for Judy Garland. Garland admires the exploits of the unknown buccaneer who in reality is the man to whom she is reluctantly engaged. Kelly and Garland dance and sing to "Be a Clown" while Kelly's work with the production number "Nina" is the highlight of the film.

D'Artagnan / THE THREE MUSKETEERS, 1948, MGM, d-George Sidney.

While this film is not a musical, Kelly's acrobatic skills and athletic prowess make his dueling movements seem very much like dancing. He portrays the Dumas hero who, with friends Athos, Porthos, and Aramis, saves the queen from a great deal of shame set up by nasty Cardinal Richelieu.

Dennis Ryan / TAKE ME OUT TO THE BALL GAME, 1949, MGM, d-Busby Berkeley.

The setting has Kelly and Frank Sinatra as two turn-of-the-century baseball players on a pro team owned by Esther Williams. They have to deal with the usual romantic nonsense and a plan to get them to throw a big game. Kelly's solo number is "The Hat My Father Wore on St. Patrick's Day." He joins in with Sinatra on the title song and joins Jules Munshin for "O'Brien to Ryan to Goldberg."

Gabey / ON THE TOWN, 1949, MGM, d-Gene Kelly and Stanley Donen.

Three sailors (Kelly, Sinatra, and Jules Munshin) have 24 hours of liberty in New York City and they plan to see everything and find romance—which they do. Kelly dances with Vera-Ellen to "Main Street" and with his two buddies to "New York, New York" by Leonard Bernstein, Betty Comden, and Adolph Green.

Jerry Mulligan / AN AMERICAN IN PARIS, 1951, MGM, d-Vincente Minnelli.

Kelly is an ex-GI painter who stays in Paris after the war. He finds a rich female sponsor who wants more than to carry his canvases, but he falls in love with lovely gamin Leslie Caron and they dance beautifully in a climactic ballet. Other George Gershwin songs are "I Got Rhythm," "S'Wonderful," and "Love Is Here to Stay."

Don Lockwood / SINGIN' IN THE RAIN, 1952, MGM, d-Gene Kelly and Stanley Donen.

Kelly is a silent film star who is able to make the adjustment to sound, but his co-star (Jean Hagen) has a voice to match her horrible personality. The solution to save the picture is to have Debbie Reynolds, Kelly's new girl-friend, dub Hagen's voice. In what may be the best Hollywood musical of all time, Kelly dances delightfully to the title song, clowns with Donald O'Connor on "Moses Supposes" and serenades Reynolds with "You Were Meant for Me."

Tommy Albright / BRIGADOON, 1954, MGM, d-Vincente Minnelli.

While grouse hunting in Scotland, bored Kelly and his drunken buddy Van Johnson come across a village that only appears for one day in each century. There Kelly finds and falls in love with Cyd Charisse and ultimately chooses to spend his life in the strange little town. The numbers featuring Kelly include "Almost Like Being in Love" and "The Heather on the Hill."

Himself / Pierrot / Sinbad / The Marine / INVITATION TO THE DANCE, 1956, MGM, d-Gene Kelly.

Kelly tells three stories in dance and mime, the first being "Circus" composed by Jacques Ibert. It is the story of lovesick Pierrot (Kelly) who falls to his death from a high wire while trying to impress the girl of his dreams. The second story, "Ring Around the Rosy" with music by André Previn, is a La Ronde-type tale that traces the ownership of a bracelet and Kelly dances with eight others in this sequence. Finally there is "Sinbad the Sailor" to Rimsky-Korsakov's "Scheherazade" that combines live action with cartoon figures featuring Kelly as Sinbad.

Noel Airman / MARJORIE MORNINGSTAR, 1958, Warners, d-Irving Rapper.

Kelly is the camp entertainment director in the Catskills who has all the girls falling in love with him, including Natalie Wood. They all believe that he has great musical talent but later we see that it's better for him to remain a big fish in a small pond as he can't make it away from his camp shows. His song is "A Very Special Love," the Academy Award-winning number by Sammy Fain and Paul Francis Webster.

E. K. Hornbeck / INHERIT THE WIND, 1960, United Artists, d-Stanley Kramer.

Kelly plays an H. L. Mencken-like character in this fictionalized account of the famous Scopes "Monkey Trial" of the 1920s when the Tennessee law against teaching the theory of evolution was tested. The following is an example of Kelly's cynical reporting, and particularly his pleasure in abusing Fredric March's William Jennings Bryan-like character: "As you know, for all last night and today, the legion of the unwashed and holy have been rivering out of the rustic backways to listen to their pop messiah coo and bellow. The high priest of mumbo-jumbo, Matthew Harrison Brady, has alternately been stuffing himself with fried chicken and belching platitudes since his arrival here two days ago."

OTHER ROLES

1943: *Vito S. Allesandro* / PILOT NO. 5; *Alec Howe* / *Black Arrow* / DUBARRY WAS A LADY; *Eddie Marsh* / THOUSANDS CHEER; *Victor* / THE CROSS OF LORRAINE. **1944:** *Robert Manette* / CHRISTMAS HOLIDAY. **1946:** *guest* / *Bromide* / ZIEGFELD FOLLIES. **1947:** *Leo Gogarty* / LIVING IN A BIG WAY. **1948:** *guest* / WORDS AND MUSIC. **1950:** *Johnny Columbo* / THE BLACK HAND; *Joe D. Ross* / SUMMER STOCK. **1951:** *Icarus Xenophon* / IT'S A BIG COUNTRY. **1952:** *Capt. Jeff Eliot* / THE DEVIL MAKES THREE; *guest* / LOVE IS BETTER THAN EVER. **1954:** *Lt. Bradville, USN* / CREST OF THE WAVE; *cameo* / DEEP IN MY HEART. **1955:** *Ted Riley* / IT'S ALWAYS FAIR WEATHER. **1956:** *Sinbad's voice* / THE MAGIC LAMP (ANIMATED). **1957:** *Mike Andrews* / THE HAPPY ROAD; *Barry Nichols* / LES GIRLS. **1960:** *guest* / LET'S MAKE LOVE. **1964:** *Jerry Benson* / WHAT A WAY TO GO! **1967:** *Andy Miller* / THE YOUNG GIRLS OF ROCHEFORT. **1973:** *Bill Boylan* / FORTY CARATS. **1974:** *host* / THAT'S ENTERTAINMENT!, **1976:** *host* / THAT'S ENTERTAINMENT!, PART 2. **1977:** *Will Atkins* / VIVA KNIEVEL!, **1980:** *Danny McGuire* / XANADU. **1981:** *guest* / REPORTERS.

KELLY, GRACE

(1928–1982)

When she married Prince Rainier of Monaco at the peak of her film career, Grace Kelly became "Her Serene Highness," a title that could have applied to the ice-cool blonde she played in less than a dozen movies. She was nominated for a Best Supporting Actress Academy Award for MOGAMBO and won the Best Actress Oscar for her performance in THE COUNTRY GIRL. She supported her acting studies by modeling and made her film debut in 1950, but wasn't really noticed until she played the too-young bride of Gary Cooper in HIGH NOON. Although she was delightful in each of her movies from then on, she was at her best and looked her best in the three movies she made for director Alfred Hitchcock.

KEY ROLES

Amy Kane / HIGH NOON, 1952, United Artists, d-Fred Zinnemann.

Kelly is the Quaker bride of retiring Marshal Gary Cooper. When he learns that a man who has sworn to kill him will be arriving on the noon train to be met by three of his henchmen, Cooper feels he has to face the four now or forever be running. Kelly informs him that if he insists in starting their marriage this way, she's leaving. But she stands by her man when it really counts.

Linda Nordley / MOGAMBO, 1953, MGM, d-John Ford.

In this Technicolor remake of RED DUST, Kelly plays the wife of a British anthropologist and goes for a great white hunter (Clark Gable), while her husband goes for gorillas. Fortunately for her, Gable decides that shady lady Ava Gardner is more his type.

Margot Wendice / DIAL M FOR MURDER, 1954, Warners, d-Alfred Hitchcock.

Kelly's tennis-playing husband (Ray Milland) has plans to have her murdered while she is home alone. When she kills her attacker, the hubby tries to make it seem that she killed the man because he was blackmailing her. She is almost executed for the crime.

Lisa Fremont / REAR WINDOW, 1954, Hitchcock, d-Alfred Hitchcock.

When her lover, news photographer Jimmy Stewart, is confined to his room with a broken leg, he suspects that one of the neighbors he's been spying on through his rear window has killed his wife. Kelly does his legwork for him and almost gets both of them killed.

Georgie Elgin / THE COUNTRY GIRL, 1954, Paramount, d-George Seaton.

When theatrical director Bill Holden attempts to star one of his idols (Bing Crosby) in a show despite the latter's alcohol problems, he is convinced that the biggest problem is Crosby's wife, Kelly. Holden asks Kelly: "Why is it that women always think they understand men better than men do?" Her reply: "Maybe because they live with them." Despite their constant sparring over Crosby, they do fall in love.

Frances Stevens / TO CATCH A THIEF, 1955, Paramount, d-Alfred Hitchcock.

Kelly is an American beauty who helps Cary Grant, formerly known as "The Cat" when he was an international jewel thief, prove that he's not up to his old tricks when a string of burglaries with his modus operandi occur on the Riviera.

Tracy Lord / HIGH SOCIETY, 1956, MGM, d-Charles Walters.

Kelly reprises Katharine Hepburn's role in THE PHILADELPHIA STORY as the unforgiving goddess whose second wedding plans are interrupted by her ex-husband, her philandering father, and a writer and photographer from a scandal magazine.

OTHER ROLES

1951: *Mrs. Fuller* / 14 HOURS. **1954:** *Catherine Knowland* / GREEN FIRE; *Nancy Brubaker* / THE BRIDGES AT TOKO-RI. **1956:** *Princess Alexander* / THE SWAN.

KENDALL, KAY

(Justine McCarthy, 1926–1959)

A former British chorus girl and music hall performer, Kay Kendall got her break when she was cast opposite Sid Field on stage in "London Town," but it wasn't until GENEVIEVE in 1953 that her work in films brought her any notice. After that her sparkling personality graced a number of enjoyable lightweight movies. Married to Rex Harrison in 1957, this luminous comedienne died two years later of leukemia.

KEY ROLES

Rosalind Peters / GENEVIEVE, 1952, Great Britain, Sirus / Rank, d-Henry Cornelius.

Kendall is the sophisticated girlfriend of Kenneth More who helps him compete in the annual "old crocks" rally with John Gregson and his wife Dinah Sheridan. Their entry in the classic car race from London to Brighton is a lovely 1904 auto called Genevieve.

Monica Hathaway / THE CONSTANT HUSBAND, 1954, Great Britain, Individual / London Films, d-Sidney Gilliat.

Kendall is the last of seven women whom Rex Harrison has married without divorcing, so perhaps it's not correct for her to have his last name. Harrison suffered from amnesia throughout his marrying jag and goes to jail to escape the seven wives. On his release, though, he's snatched up by the female barrister who represented him.

Laura Foster / SIMON AND LAURA, 1955, Great Britain, Group / Rank, d-Muriel Box.

Kendall and her warring stage husband (Peter Finch) stay together because of a successful television show that stars them. When the audiences start dropping off, the two explode on the air and the viewers love it. So they must stay on together fighting in front of the camera as well as away from it.

Lady Wren / LES GIRLS, 1957, MGM, d-George Cukor.

In this flashback movie, three ex-showgirls and their male partner all have different recollections of which girl loved the guy. These take place during a court suit brought by two of the girls (Tania Elg and Mitzi Gaynor) against the third (Kendall) over a memoir she has written.

Sheila Broadbent / THE RELUCTANT DEBUTANTE, 1958, MGM, d-Vincente Minnelli.

Kendall and Rex Harrison are an urbane, noble couple having a great many problems introducing their American educated daughter (Sandra Dee) to London society. Kendall was superb with her death only a year away. The seriousness of her illness was kept from her, but husband Harrison knew.

Dolly Fabian / ONCE MORE, WITH FEELING, 1959, Great Britain, Columbia, d-Stanley Donen.

In her final film appearance, this talented actress with so much potential is charming in a charmless movie as the dissatisfied wife of musical conductor Yul Brynner.

OTHER ROLES

1944: *bit* / FIDDLERS THREE; *bit* / DREAMING; *bit* / CHAMPAGNE CHARLIE. **1945:** *lady in waiting* / WALTZ TIME. **1946:** *Patsy* / LONDON TOWN. **1950:** *Doreen* / DANCE HALL. **1951:** *secretary* / HAPPY GO LOVELY; *Sylvia* / LADY GODIVA RIDES AGAIN. **1952:** *Alexia* / WINGS OF DANGER; *Sandra* / CURTAIN UP; *Lady Caroline* / IT STARTED IN PARADISE; *Vera* / MANTRAP. **1953:** *Barbara Gale* / STREET OF SHADOWS; *Eve Lewis* / THE SQUARE RING; *lonely hearts singer* / MEET MR. LUCIFER. **1954:** *Carol* / FAST AND LOOSE; *Isabel* / DOCTOR IN THE HOUSE. **1955:** *Isabel, Countess of Marcroy* / QUENTIN DURWARD. **1956:** *Ronnie* / ABDULLA THE GREAT.

KENNEDY, ARTHUR

(John Arthur Kennedy, 1914–)

Five times nominated for Best Supporting Actor for CHAMPION, BRIGHT VICTORY, TRIAL, PEYTON PLACE, and SOME CAME RUNNING, Arthur Kennedy proved his acting ability on Broadway as well, originating the roles of Chris Miller in "All My Sons," Biff in "Death of a Salesman," and John Proctor in "The Crucible." Never the leading star, Kennedy was something better: an actor who could be counted on to give good performances, film after film. His made-for-TV movies include THE MOVIE MURDERER (1970), A DEATH OF INNOCENCE (1971), THE PRESIDENT'S PLANE IS MISSING (1971), CRAWLSPACE (1972), and NAKIA (1974). Like most aging American actors Kennedy has made his share of foreign quickies such as FAMILY KILLER (1975), BRUTAL JUSTICE (1978), and ASSAULT WITH A DEADLY WEAPON U.S.A. (1982).

KEY ROLES

Eddie Kenny / CITY FOR CONQUEST, 1940, Warners, d-Anatole Litvak.

To support his composer brother Kennedy, New York truck driver James Cagney becomes a boxer who eventually is blinded. Kennedy acknowledges his brother in his curtain speech after performing his symphony: "Yes, my brother made music with his fists so that I might make a gentler music—the symphony that you have heard tonight. It is his as much as mine. And so, with deep pride and gratitude, I dedicate this music to my brother, known to most of you as Young Samson."

Ned Sharp / THEY DIED WITH THEIR BOOTS ON, 1941, Warners, d-Raoul Walsh.

The bad blood between Kennedy and Errol Flynn (as George Custer) goes back to their days at West Point. Kennedy sees a way to make a fortune in Indian land but, when Flynn discovers the plot, he forces Kennedy to accompany him to the Battle of Little Big Horn.

Bramwell Brontë / DEVOTION, 1946, Warners, d-Curtis Bernhardt.

Kennedy is the best thing in this absurd production of the lives and loves of the Brontë sisters—Charlotte, Emily, and Anne. He portrays their tormented brother.

Jack Waldron / BOOMERANG, 1947, 20th Century-Fox, d-Elia Kazan.

When a clergyman is shot dead in a New England town, stranger Kennedy is picked up and charged with the crime. But the DA isn't so sure and prevents a conviction of a man who may very well be innocent. It is based on fact and the killer has never been found.

Connie Kelly / CHAMPION, 1949, United Artists, d-Mark Robson.

Kennedy is the crippled brother of Kirk Douglas, a boxer who has no noticeable redeeming virtues. Kennedy doesn't know this at first, but when he catches on he tells Douglas, "You stink! You stink from corruption. You're worse than a murderer. You're a graverobber." Douglas sinks so low that he slugs his crippled brother.

Mr. Woodry / THE WINDOW, 1949, RKO, d-Ted Tetzlaff.

When Kennedy's son (Bobby Driscoll), who is in the habit of making up wild stories, sees Paul Stewart and Ruth Roman commit a murder through his tenement window, Kennedy thinks it's just another tall tale. But the killers believe the boy saw them. It's a taut thriller.

Tom Wingfield / THE GLASS MENAGERIE, 1950, Warners, d-Irving Rapper.

Kennedy is the brother of shy, crippled Jane Wyman who, at his mother's urging, brings home one of the men he works with (Kirk Douglas) so his sister will have a gentleman caller. This movie adaptation of the Tennessee Williams play is disappointing.

Larry Nevins / BRIGHT VICTORY, 1951, Universal, d-Mark Robson.

Blind war veteran Kennedy must come to grips with his affliction and adjust to civilian life. His performance is very moving and is well worth staying up late to see on a television screening.

Vern Haskell / RANCHO NOTORIOUS, 1952, RKO, d-Fritz Lang.

Kennedy trails the man who raped and killed his sweetheart to "Chuck-a-Luck," a hideout for outlaws run by Marlene Dietrich. Once there Kennedy, Dietrich, Mel Ferrer, and the others practice each and every one of the seven deadly sins in this curious western.

Vic Hansbro / THE MAN FROM LARAMIE, 1955, Columbia, d-Anthony Mann.

Kennedy is Donald Crisp's ambitious foreman and Crisp is in a range war with Aline MacMahon. She is aided by James Stewart who is hot on the trail of the man who gave it to his brother.

Barney Castle / TRIAL, 1955, MGM, d-Mark Robson.

Kennedy arranges for young inexperienced lawyer Glenn Ford to help defend a Mexican boy accused of rape and murder. Apparently, Kennedy wants to see the boy become a martyr rather than be acquitted in order to incite hatreds. Kennedy rages at black judge Juano Hernandez: "You ought to disqualify yourself for incompetence. You're a frightened little man, selling out his own people for a fancy title and a black gown. They may call you Judge to your face, but they got better words for you behind your back. You're a handkerchief head! You're an Uncle Tom!"

Lucas Cross / PEYTON PLACE, 1957, 20th Century-Fox, d-Mark Robson.

Kennedy is the disgusting drunken bum who abuses his family and rapes and impregnates his daughter. The daughter kills him, though, when it looks like a younger sister may suffer a similar fate.

Bart Hunter / A SUMMER PLACE, 1959, Warners, d-Delmer Daves.

In this soap opera, Kennedy's wife (Dorothy McGuire) has an affair with Richard Egan and the two ultimately marry. But when their children fall in love, things are very difficult for them, but not so much because of Kennedy as he is slowly dying and has other things on his mind.

Jim Lefferts / ELMER GANTRY, 1960, United Artists, d-Richard Brooks.

Kennedy is the honest and skeptical newspaperman who travels with the Sister Falconer-Elmer Gantry Revival Tour to cover it not as a religious movement but as a circus.

Jackson Bentley / LAWRENCE OF ARABIA, 1962, Great Britain, Columbia / Horizon, d-David Lean.

Kennedy is the Norman Thomas-like American newspaperman who publicizes Lawrence of Arabia's exploits, making him a celebrity throughout the world.

Dr. Duval / FANTASTIC VOYAGE, 1960, 20th Century-Fox, d-Richard Fleischer.

When a top scientist is shot and suffers brain damage, Kennedy is one of a team of surgeons and others who are miniaturized and injected into the man's bloodstream to operate on the patient from within. But one is there to see that they fail.

OTHER ROLES

1941: *Red Hattery* / HIGH SIERRA; *Joe Geary* / STRANGE ALIBI; *Johnny Rocket* / KNOCKOUT; *George Foster* / HIGHWAY WEST; *Jim Younger* / BAD MEN OF MISSOURI. **1942:** *Fl. Off. Jed Forrest* / DESPERATE JOURNEY. **1943:** *Lt. Tommy McMartin, Bombardier* / AIR FORCE. **1947:** *The Sundance Kid (Harry Longbaugh)* / CHEYENNE. **1949:** *Alan Palmer* / TOO LATE FOR TEARS; *Chalk* / THE WALKING HILLS; *Tommy Ditman* / CHICAGO DEADLINE. **1952:** *Lane Waldron* / RED MOUNTAIN; *Dr. Ben Barringer* / THE GIRL IN WHITE; *Emerson Cole* / BEND OF THE RIVER; *Wes Merritt* / THE LUSTY MEN. **1954:** *Alan Curtis* / IMPULSE. **1955:** *Santiago* / THE NAKED DAWN; *Jesse Bard* / THE DESPERATE HOURS; *Joe Quinn* / CRASHOUT. **1956:** *Rick Harper* / THE RAWHIDE YEARS. **1958:** *First Mate Ramsay* / TWILIGHT FOR THE GODS; *Frank Hirsch* / SOME CAME RUNNING. **1961:** *Willie O'Reilly* / HOME IS THE HERO; *Clyde Inglish* / CLAUDELLE INGLISH. **1962:** *Dr. Quimper* / MURDER, SHE SAID; *Doc Adams* / HEMINGWAY'S ADVENTURES OF A YOUNG MAN; *Pontius Pilate* / BARABBAS. **1963:** *Ferro Maria Ferri* / ITALIANO BRAVA GENTE. **1964:** *Doc John Holliday* / CHEYENNE AUTUMN. **1965:** *Patrick Brown* / JOY IN THE MORNING; *Captain Love* / MURIETA. **1966:** *Bill Bowdre* / NEVADA SMITH. **1967:** *American father* / MONDAY'S CHILD. **1968:** *General Lesly* / ANZIO; *Owen Forbes* / DAY OF THE EVIL GUN; *Roy Colby* / DEAD OR ALIVE. **1969:** *Albert Dixon* / HAIL, HERO! **1971:** *Walter Pell* / GLORY BOY. **1977:** *Monsignor Franchino* / THE SENTINEL. **1978:** *Bishop* / THE TEMPTER.

KERR, DEBORAH

(Deborah Kerr-Trimmer, 1921–)

"The camera always seems to find an innate gentility in me." So said lovely Scottish-born actress Deborah Kerr. She studied ballet and made her first stage appearance with the Sadler's Wells Ballet. Her first real film role was in MAJOR BARBARA and her U.S. debut was made in 1947 in THE HUCKSTERS. Never an Oscar winner, she was nominated six times for EDWARD, MY SON; FROM HERE TO ETERNITY; THE KING AND I; HEAVEN KNOWS, MR. ALLISON; SEPARATE TABLES; and THE SUNDOWNERS. She retired from films in 1969 and since then has appeared on both the London and New York stages. This ladylike, sincere-looking reddish-blonde had a quiet glamour and her acting ability was evident in both comedy and drama.

KEY ROLES

Sally Hardcastle / LOVE ON THE DOLE, 1941, Great Britain, British National, d-John Baxter.

Kerr is a Lancashire mill girl during the Depression who loves militant factory worker Clifford Evans. He refuses to marry her and live on the dole when he loses his job. When he loses his life in a scuffle with the police, she gives herself to a rich old admirer so her father and brothers will be given jobs.

Edith Hunter / Barbara Wynne / Johnny Cannon / THE LIFE AND DEATH OF COLONEL BLIMP, 1943, Great Britain, The Archers, d-Michael Powell and Emeric Pressburger.

In this story about a career British army officer, Kerr plays the three women Roger Livesey loves over the course of his life. The first is stolen from him by his friend Anton Walbrook, a German officer. He marries the second but she dies. And the last is his driver during World War II when he is an old man.

Sister Clodagh / BLACK NARCISSUS, 1946, Great Britain, The Archers, d-Michael Powell and Emeric Pressburger.

Kerr heads a group of five Episcopal nuns who open a school and hospital in an unused palace high in the Himalayas. After a nun treats a child who dies, the villagers desert the school and hospital. One nun throws herself at the local agent and, when he rejects her, she attacks Kerr but is killed in a fall. The others leave the place of their failure.

Kay Dorrence / THE HUCKSTERS, 1947, MGM, d-Jack Conway.

Kerr is the very ladylike woman convinced by Clark Gable to endorse his client's soap in a series of advertisements. She and Gable have a brief romance but he finds Ava Gardner more to his liking.

Evelyn Boult / EDWARD, MY SON, 1948, Great Britain, MGM-British, d-George Cukor.

When her husband becomes obsessed with his son's success, committing fraud and arson, Kerr drinks herself to death.

Lygia / QUO VADIS, 1951, MGM, d-Mervyn LeRoy.

Kerr is a Christian girl with whom Roman commander Robert Taylor falls in love. Jealous, Nero's wife Poppea sees that both are thrown to the lions.

Karen Holmes / FROM HERE TO ETERNITY, 1953, Columbia, d-Fred Zinnemann.

Kerr is the captain's wife who has an affair with her husband's very capable top sergeant (Burt Lancaster). She falls in love, but he spoils everything by wondering about all her other reported lovers at every base where her husband has been stationed. She acts the way she does because her husband's unfaithfulness caused her to lose the child she was carrying and she can never have another.

Anna Leonowens / THE KING AND I, 1956, 20th Century-Fox, d-Walter Lang.

Kerr's singing was dubbed by Marni Nixon, but her presence in this lovely musical version of ANNA AND THE KING OF SIAM is very much appreciated for the sensitivity and believability she brings to the role of the English governess brought to Siam by the king to educate his children. She finds herself advising the king as he tries to find ways to enter the modern age while maintaining some of his country's customs.

Laura Reynolds / TEA AND SYMPATHY, 1956, MGM, d-Vincente Minnelli.

The writer, director, and producer had to be very careful in bringing this play by Robert Anderson to the screen. It deals with a boy (John Kerr) whose life is made miserable by his classmates and Kerr's husband, a brutish schoolmaster. Sensitive John gets the treatment in part because he hasn't had any experience with girls and doesn't seek any. Deborah at the end, says to John as she begins to unbutton her blouse: "Years from now, when you talk about this—and you will—be kind."

Terry McKay / AN AFFAIR TO REMEMBER, 1957, 20th Century-Fox, d-Leo McCarey.

In this remake of LOVE AFFAIR, Kerr is an ex-nightclub singer who falls in love with wealthy Cary Grant aboard an ocean liner, but an accident prevents her from meeting him later at a prearranged time and place and he believes she had second thoughts about the romance.

Sibyl Railton-Bell / SEPARATE TABLES, 1958, United Artists, d-Delbert Mann.

Kerr portrays a plain spinster who, along with her domineering mother, is among those staying at an English seaside guest house. She is briefly attracted to David Niven who is posing as a retired English major, but he is forced to admit to her that not only is he a fraud but that he also molests women in cinemas.

Ida Carmody / THE SUNDOWNERS, 1960, Great Britain / Australia, Warners, d-Fred Zinnemann.

Kerr is married to a migrant sheep drover (Robert Mitchum) who makes a meager living in the Australian outback. They seem just too happy as they make do with very little and share what they have with whomever they meet.

Miss Giddens / THE INNOCENTS, 1961, Great Britain, 20th Century-Fox, d-Jack Clayton.

In this film version of the fantasy *The Turn of the Screw* by Henry James, Kerr is a governess to two orphans in a wealthy family who gradually comes to believe that her young charges are possessed by evil spirits of deceased servants.

Hannah Jelkes / THE NIGHT OF THE IGUANA, 1964, MGM / Seven Arts, d-John Huston.

In this steamy and exhausting film production of Tennessee Williams's play, Kerr is an artist wandering with her aged grandfather. She joins a group of travelers in Mexico, guided by a defrocked clergyman (Richard Burton), when they stop at a run-down hotel run by a middle-aged American woman. Everyone there has the hots for the ex-minister.

Prudence Hardcastle / PRUDENCE AND THE PILL, 1968, 20th Century-Fox, d-Fielder Cook.

Kerr's daughter borrows her mother's birth control pills, replacing them with aspirin which, as you might imagine, causes no end of complications.

OTHER ROLES

1939: *bit* / CONTRABAND. **1940:** *Jenny Hill* / MAJOR BARBARA. **1941:** *Mary Brodie* / HATTER'S CASTLE; *Guglielma Springett* / PENN OF PENNSYLVANIA. **1942:** *Kari Alstead* / THE AVENGERS. **1945:** *Catherine Wilson* / VACATION FROM MARRIAGE. **1946:** *Birdie Quilty* / THE ADVENTURESS, (I SEE A DARK STRANGER). **1947:** *Nona Tybar* / IF WINTER COMES. **1950:** *Alison Kirbe* / PLEASE BELIEVE ME; *Elizabeth Curtis* / KING SOLOMON'S MINES. **1952:** *Princess Flavia* / THE PRISONER OF ZENDA. **1953:** *Joan Willoughby* / THUNDER IN THE EAST; *Priscilla Effington* / DREAM WIFE; *Catherine Parr* / YOUNG BESS; *Portia* / JULIUS CAESAR. **1955:** *Sarah Miles* / THE END OF THE AFFAIR. **1956:** *Lee Ashley* / THE PROUD AND THE PROFANE. **1957:** *Sister Angela* / HEAVEN KNOWS, MR. ALLISON. **1958:** *Anne Larson* / BONJOUR TRISTESSE. **1959:** *Lady Diana Ashmore* / THE JOURNEY; *Grace Allingham* / COUNT YOUR BLESSINGS; *Sheila Graham* / BELOVED INFIDEL. **1960:** *Hilary Rhyall* / THE GRASS IS GREENER. **1961:** *Martha Radcliffe* / THE NAKED EDGE. **1964:** *Miss Madrigal* / THE CHALK GARDEN. **1965:** *Valerie Edwards* / MARRIAGE ON THE ROCKS. **1967:** *Agent Mimi* / *Lady Fiona McTarry* / CASINO ROYALE; *Catherine de Montfaucon* / EYE OF THE DEVIL. **1969:** *Elizabeth Brandon* / THE GYPSY MOTHS; *Florence Anderson* / THE ARRANGEMENT. **1985:** *Helen* / THE ASSAM GARDEN.

KEYES, EVELYN

(1919–)

Evelyn Keyes, a former dancer in nightclub choruses, was placed under personal contract to Cecil B. DeMille and, after a succession of supporting roles, moved to Columbia where she found success in a number of comedy roles over the next dozen years. Despite her speculating, "I have often wondered what would have happened to me if I had needed a size 38 bra instead of a modest 34," her frank autobiography, which caused a minor sensation, indicated that this measurement did not restrict her popularity away from the camera.

KEY ROLES

Suellen O'Hara / GONE WITH THE WIND, 1939, Selznick / MGM, d-Victor Fleming and others.

Keyes got the name of her autobiography, *Scarlett O'Hara's Younger Sister*, from this appearance, perhaps as revenge against Vivien Leigh who snatches Keyes's beau from her and marries him.

Bette Logan / HERE COMES MR. JORDAN, 1941, Columbia, d-Alexander Hall.

Keyes is the girl meant to love Robert Montgomery no matter what body he's wearing after he is killed prematurely in a plane crash and his body is cremated. He meets Keyes when he briefly inhabits the body of a wealthy man whose wife and lover are trying to kill him. When they finally succeed, he is given another body and when he runs into Keyes, they just know they've met before.

Lucy / LADIES IN RETIREMENT, 1941, Columbia, d-Charles Vidor.

Keyes was given praise for her performance as the maid in this strange house where companion-housekeeper Ida Lupino kills the mistress to prevent her half-crazed sisters from being sent to an institution.

The Genie / A THOUSAND AND ONE NIGHTS, 1945, Columbia, d-Alfred E. Green.

Keyes is a sexy redheaded genie who falls for Alladin (Cornel Wilde) and messes up his marriage plans to a princess (Adele Jergens).

Julie Benson / THE JOLSON STORY, 1946, Columbia, d-Alfred E. Green.

Keyes's character name in this biopic of the great entertainer and singer would have been Ruby Keeler, but the latter would not give her permission to use her name. Keeler needn't have worried. Keyes's role as Jolson's wife has her not only idolized by the great man but something of a saint as well.

Nancy Hobbs / JOHNNY O'CLOCK, 1947, Columbia, d-Robert Rossen.

In this film noir, Keyes helps clear a gambler (Dick Powell) of the murder of a crooked policeman and her sister. Along the way they have time to fall in love.

Kathy O'Fallan / MRS. MIKE, 1949, Nassour / Huntington Hartford, d-Louis King.

Keyes marries a Northwest Mounted Policeman and goes with him to his remote outpost where she endears herself to the Indians and others who live in the area.

Susan Gilvray / THE PROWLER, 1951, United Artists, d-Joseph Losey.

Keyes sees a prowler peering through her bathroom window and calls the police. Van Heflin answers the call and so starts the relationship which leads to their affair and Heflin's killing her husband. The latter was infertile, so Heflin takes Keyes to a desert town to have their baby so as not to arouse suspicion. It's too late, though. Other cops have figured out what happened and Heflin is killed in a wild mountain chase.

OTHER ROLES

1938: *bit* / ARTISTS AND MODELS ABROAD; *bit* / DANGEROUS TO KNOW; *bit* / PARIS HONEYMOON; *nurse* / MEN WITH WINGS; *Madeleine* / THE BUCCANEER; *Linda Lee* / SONS OF THE LEGION. **1939:** *Mrs. Calvin* / UNION PACIFIC; *Mary Patterson* / SUDDEN MONEY. **1940:** *Miss Vlissenger* / SLIGHTLY HONORABLE; *Martha Garth* / BEFORE I HANG; *Françoise Morestan* / THE LADY IN QUESTION. **1941:** *Helen Williams* / THE FACE BEHIND THE MASK; *Lynn Perry* / BEYOND THE SACRAMENTO. **1942:** *Ruth Morley* / THE ADVENTURES OF MARTIN EDEN; *Susie Thompson* / FLIGHT LIEUTENANT. **1943:** *Allison MacLeod* / THE DESPERADOES; *Jane Craig* / DANGEROUS BLONDES; *Carol Harkness* / THERE'S SOMETHING ABOUT A SOLDIER. **1944:** *Mary O'Ryan* / NINE GIRLS; *Jacqueline Harrison* / STRANGE AFFAIR. **1946:** *Hannah Brockway* / RENEGADES; *Vicki Dean* / THE THRILL OF BRAZIL. **1948:** *Millie McGonigle* / THE MATING OF MILLIE; *Grizel Dane* / ENCHANTMENT. **1949:** *Jenny Jones* / MR. SOFT TOUCH. **1950:** *Sheila Bennet* / THE KILLER THAT STALKED NEW YORK. **1951:** *Vivian Craig* / SMUGGLER'S ISLAND; *Rose Warren* / THE IRON MAN. **1952:** *Jean Harper* / ONE BIG AFFAIR. **1953:** *Cecily Taine* / SHOOT FIRST; *Linda James* / 99 RIVER STREET. **1954:** *Dona Williams* / HELL'S HALF ACRE. **1955:** *Virgie Rayne (Mrs. Gannon)* / TOP OF THE WORLD; *Helen Sherman* / THE SEVEN YEAR ITCH. **1957:** *flirt* / AROUND THE WORLD IN 80 DAYS.

KNOX, ALEXANDER

(1907–)

Although cast as a leading man in his first few films in the early 1940s, Alexander Knox wasn't the usual handsome beefcake actor that Hollywood tried to supply for the girls who were left behind during World War II. He was clearly an intellectual when stars were supposed to be instinctive hunks who acted first and thought later. His best role was as Woodrow Wilson, a surprisingly good biopic. Thereafter he was relegated to supporting roles of varying demands on his talents. He believed: "On the stage and on the screen there are two kinds of actors: actors who behave and actors who act."

KEY ROLES

Humphrey Van Weyden / THE SEA WOLF, 1940, Warners, d-Michael Curtiz.

Knox is among the passengers picked up by Capt. Wolf Larson of the freighter Sea Wolf when the ferry they were on crashed and sunk in San Francisco Bay. The psychopathic captain keeps them prisoner but likes to match his wits with the intellectual Knox.

Thomas Woodrow Wilson / WILSON, 1944, 20th Century-Fox, d-Henry King.

Knox appears as the U.S. president who was elected once because "he kept us out of war," who then led the country in the "war to end all wars." After World War I, he tried to single-handedly mold the post-war world in his own vision of peace and prosperity. Knox's performance is a remarkable combination of makeup and scholarly determination which surely would have pleased the dedicated ex-president of Princeton.

Dr. Aeneas McDonnell / SISTER KENNY, 1946, RKO, d-Dudley Nichols.

Knox helped script this biopic of the nurse who instigates a new treatment for polio. He plays a physician who comes to see that she is on the right track.

Judge Bailey / THE JUDGE STEPS OUT, 1948, RKO, d-Boris Ingster.

Knox is a Boston judge who grows tired of his selfish wife and routine life and disappears (like Judge Crater, we suppose). In the course of his wanderings he falls in love with the owner of a cafe where he takes a job washing dishes.

Salter / I'D CLIMB THE HIGHEST MOUNTAIN, 1951, 20th Century-Fox, d-Henry King.

Knox, now moving into supporting roles, injects charm into this story about a circuit-riding preacher (William Lundigan) who marries a city girl and brings her to a rural Georgia community. Knox is an agnostic, but that doesn't make him a bad man in Lundigan's eyes.

Walter Keyser / OPERATION AMSTERDAM, 1959, Great Britain, Rank, d-Michael McCarthy.

Diamond expert Knox is part of a team whose mission it is to rescue a million pounds worth of diamonds from a safe in Amsterdam right under the noses of the Germans in 1940.

Sir Evelyn Baring / KHARTOUM, 1966, Great Britain, United Artists, d-Basil Dearden.

Knox's role as a British government official is pretty typical of the parts he played for the next twenty years—brief, not terribly important, and forgettable. The story is about the last days of General "China" Gordon, played by Charlton Heston.

OTHER ROLES

1938: *Dr. Lomond* / THE GAUNT STRANGER. **1942:** *Rector* / THIS ABOVE ALL; *German captain* / THE COMMANDOS STRIKE AT DAWN. **1943:** *Wilhelm Grimm* / NONE SHALL ESCAPE. **1945:** *Max Wharton* / OVER 21. **1948:** *Mallory St. Aubyn* / THE SIGN OF THE RAM. **1951:** *Megroth* / SATURDAY'S HERO. **1952:** *Dr. Clifford Frazer* / PAULA. **1953:** *Dr. Clive Esmond* / THE SLEEPING TIGER. **1954:** *Chief Justice* / THE DIVIDED HEART; *George Girard* / THE GREATEST LOVE. **1956:** *Mr. Joyce* / REACH FOR THE SKY. **1957:** *Stephen MacKenzie* / HIGH TIDE AT NOON. **1958:** *Father Godwin* / THE VIKINGS. **1959:** *Petrie* / THE WRECK OF THE MARY DEARE. **1960:** *Sir Edgar Clarke* / THE TRIALS OF OSCAR WILDE. **1961:** *Bernard* / THE DAMNED. **1962:** *Sir Charles Eggerston* / CRACK IN THE MIRROR; *Maj. Gen. Walter Bedell Smith* / THE LONGEST DAY. **1965:** *Reverend Anderson* / MISTER MOSES. **1966:** *Frank Saville* / THE PSYCHOPATH; *college provost* / ACCIDENT; *minister* / MODESTY BLAISE. **1967:** *American general* / HOW I WON THE WAR. **1968:** *Madero* / VILLA RIDES; *Henry Clarke* / SHALAKO; *General Peronne* / FRAULEIN DOKTOR. **1969:** *Buffington* / SKULLDUGGERY. **1971:** *American Ambassador Root* / NICHOLAS AND ALEXANDRA; *Colonel De Graaf* / PUPPET ON A CHAIN. **1978:** *Meyer* / HOLOCAUST 2000. **1983:** *general* / GORKY PARK. **1985:** *Senator Hornby* / JOSHUA, THEN AND NOW.

LADD, ALAN

(1913–1964)

Asked to comment on his career, Alan Ladd replied, "My career? I was kept busy. Isn't that enough?" From 1936 to 1942 he was kept very busy in the movies. Unfortunately his parts rarely were identified in the credits nor did he have many lines. Twenty-six movies and probably not twenty-six minutes of screen time. But with number twenty-seven this five-foot-four blond with the deep voice became an overnight sensation as the killer in THIS GUN FOR HIRE. In it he was paired with a five-foot-two sexy blonde, Veronica Lake. Audiences liked the chemistry and they appeared together in six more pictures. Ladd's height was a problem for an actor usually featured as a tough guy. It called for a lot of short co-stars and shots that made him appear taller than he really was. In SHANE his fistfight with six-footer Ben Johnson was always shot uphill from Johnson's perspective and downward when seeing things Ladd's way. Unsmiling Ladd was not a charismatic actor; he just came along at the right time when audiences were interested in imperturbable antiheroes. He died in 1964 as a result of an overdose of sedatives and alcohol, perhaps intentionally.

KEY ROLES

Philip Raven / THIS GUN FOR HIRE, 1942, Paramount, d-Frank Tuttle.

Ladd plays a professional killer who is hired to do a job by fifth columnists during World War II. When he completes his assignment his employers double-cross him and he's out for revenge aided by Veronica Lake. Audiences found him very tough but writer Raymond Chandler disagreed: "Alan Ladd is hard, bitter, and occasionally charming, but he is, after all, a small boy's idea of a tough guy."

Ed Beaumont / THE GLASS KEY, 1942, Paramount, d-Stuart Heisler.

The pair of Ladd and Lake were rushed into production of this remake of the Dashiell Hammett murder mystery first filmed in 1935. Ladd is the right-hand man of a shady politician (Brian Donlevy) accused of murder. Ladd, once again with the help of enigmatic Lake, tracks down the real culprits and clears his boss.

Johnny Morrison / THE BLUE DAHLIA, 1946, Paramount, d-George Marshall.

Just back from the service, Ladd discovers that his wife hasn't been faithful and she's defiant about the fact. When she's murdered, Ladd and his shell-shocked buddy (William Bendix) are the number-one suspects. And one more time he gets involved with Veronica Lake, who helps him clear things up.

Charles Stewart / TWO YEARS BEFORE THE MAST, 1946, Paramount, d-John Farrow.

In this account of cruelty at sea by Richard Henry Dana, Ladd portrays a shipowner's son shanghaied to serve under sadistic Captain Howard da Silva. After insisting that they can't do this to him, Ladd learns that the skipper can and does. He's flogged so cruelly that he leads a mutiny that results in a trial and new laws to protect seamen.

Luke "Whispering" Smith / WHISPERING SMITH, 1948, Paramount, d-Leslie Fenton.

In his first western and first Technicolor picture, Ladd plays a railroad detective who is given the task of discovering who is behind a series of intentional train wrecks and lootings. To his regret, he discovers that an old friend married to a woman he once loved is involved.

Jay Gatsby / THE GREAT GATSBY, 1949, Paramount, d-Elliott Nugent.

Hollywood keeps attempting to successfully film F. Scott Fitzgerald's story of a southern belle and the young World War I officer whom she inspires to make a fortune so he'll be worthy of her. By the time he succeeds, he finds that she hasn't waited. She is now married to a wealthy man she doesn't really love and who has many affairs himself. Ladd handles the role a bit better than did Robert Redford in the 1974 production.

Jim Bowie / THE IRON MISTRESS, 1952, Warners, d-Gordon Douglas.

Ladd impersonates the western adventurer who designed the famous knife that bears his name. The film concentrates mostly on Bowie's life in New Orleans and his unhappy relationship with a proud beauty (Virginia Mayo). It ends before Bowie meets his end at the Alamo.

Shane / SHANE, 1953, Paramount, d-George Stevens.

In what is certainly among the best westerns ever made, Ladd portrays a weary gunfighter who is trying to escape his reputation, put away his guns, and find some peace. He feels he may have achieved his goal when he signs on with a family of homesteaders. But these people are in the way of the big ranching outfits who hire a gunman to get rid of them. Reluctantly, Ladd straps on his guns, wipes out the opposition, then rides away, with young Brandon De Wilde yelling for him to come back and stay.

Joseph C. "Mac" McConnell / THE MCCONNELL STORY, 1955, Warners, d-Gordon Douglas.

The film traces the career and death of a Korean War ace jet pilot portrayed by Ladd.

Nevada Smith / THE CARPETBAGGERS, 1964, Paramount, d-Edward Dmytryk.

In his final film appearance, Ladd portrays a former western outlaw who becomes a western film star. This is a thinly disguised story about Howard Hughes (George Peppard) and, at the end of the film, Ladd gets the opportunity to give Peppard the beating many wished they could have administered.

OTHER ROLES

1932: *bit* / ONCE IN A LIFETIME. **1936:** *bit* / PIGSKIN PARADE. **1937:** *bit* / LAST TRAIN FROM MADRID; *bit* / SOULS AT SEA; *bit* / HOLD 'EM NAVY; *student* / FRESHMAN YEAR. **1938:** *auditioning singer* / THE GOLDWYN FOLLIES; *bit* / COME ON, LEATHERNECKS. **1939:** *cadet* / BROTHER RAT AND A BABY; *Colin Farrell* / RULERS OF THE SEA; *Karl* / BEASTS OF BERLIN. **1940:** *Danny* / THE LIGHT OF WESTERN STARS; *bit* / GANGS OF CHICAGO; *Junior* / IN OLD MISSOURI; *bit* / THE HOWARDS OF VIRGINIA; *Rex Rearick* / THOSE WERE THE DAYS; *Newton* / CAPTAIN CAUTION; *bit* / WILDCAT BUS; *Johnny Williams* / MEET THE MISSUS. **1941:** *bit* / GREAT GUNS; *reporter* / CITIZEN KANE; *bit* / CADET GIRL; *Don Wilcox* / PETTICOAT POLITICS; *Richard Hartley* / THE BLACK CAT; *animator* / THE RELUCTANT DRAGON; *Jimmy Kelly* / PAPER BULLETS. **1942:** *Baby* / JOAN OF PARIS; *Lucky Jordan* / LUCKY JORDAN; *guest* / STAR SPANGLED RHYTHM. **1943:** *Mr. Jones* / CHINA. **1944:** *Dr. Merek Vance* / AND NOW TOMORROW. **1945:** *Salty O'Rourke* / SALTY O'ROURKE; *guest* / DUFFY'S TAVERN. **1946:** *John Martin* / O.S.S. **1947:** *Neale Gordon* / CALCUTTA; *guest* / VARIETY GIRL; *Joe Madigan* / WILD HARVEST; *unbilled private eye cameo* / MY FAVORITE BRUNETTE. **1948:** *Maj. Larry Briggs* / SAIGON; *Rocky Gilman* / BEYOND GLORY. **1949:** *Ed Adams* / CHICAGO DEADLINE. **1950:** *Webster Carey* / CAPTAIN CAREY, U.S.A. **1951:** *Choya* / BRANDED; *Al Goddard* / APPOINTMENT WITH DANGER. **1952:** *Brett Sherwood* / RED MOUNTAIN. **1953:** *Steve Gibbs* / THUNDER IN THE EAST; *Paul Lartal* / DESERT LEGION; *Hugh Tallant* / BOTANY BAY. **1954:** *Canada MacKendrick* / PARATROOPER; *Sgt. Thomas O'Rourke* / SASKATCHEWAN; *Duncan Craig* / HELL BELOW ZERO; *John* / THE BLACK KNIGHT; *Johnny McKay* / DRUM BEAT. **1955:** *Steve Rollins* / HELL ON FRISCO BAY. **1956:** *Cash Adams* / SANTIAGO. **1957:** *Chad Morgan* / THE BIG LAND; *Dr. James Calder* / BOY ON A DOLPHIN. **1958:** *Alec Austen* / THE DEEP SIX; *John Chandler* / THE PROUD REBEL; *Peter Van Hook* / THE BADLANDERS. **1959:** *John Hamilton* / THE MAN IN THE NET. **1960:** *Jim Hadley* / GUNS OF THE TIMBERLAND; *Kincaid* / ALL THE YOUNG MEN; *Mitch Barrett* / ONE FOOT IN HELL. **1961:** *Horatio* / DUEL OF CHAMPIONS. **1962:** *Walt Sherill* / 13 WEST STREET.

LAKE, VERONICA

(Constance Ockelman, 1919–1973)

Veronica Lake's first three movie appearances were as Constance Keane, but it was as Veronica Lake that she made her first major impact in I WANTED WINGS. More famous for her peekaboo hairdo than her acting ability, her teaming with Alan Ladd was quite the hit in the 1940s. Since so many women working in defense plants copied her hair style, she was asked for safety's sake to change her way of wearing her hair and to encourage her fans to do likewise. In 1948, when her contract expired, she left Hollywood, later explaining, "If I had stayed in Hollywood I would have ended up like Alan Ladd and Gail Russell—dead and buried." She made three more movies, including a Canadian cheapie, and had plenty of problems in those years including bankruptcy, public drunkenness, and being reduced to working as a barmaid in a second-rate New York hotel. Most of us prefer to remember the silky look of this petite, kitten-like woman.

KEY ROLES

Sally Vaughn / I WANTED WINGS, 1941, Paramount, d-Mitchell Leisen.

In this story about the training of air cadets, Wayne Morris, Ray Milland, and William Holden all are distracted from their work by seductive Lake with her peekaboo hairdo of long blonde curls hanging over one eye. Critics weren't impressed but audiences believed a new star had been born.

The Girl / SULLIVAN'S TRAVELS, 1941, Paramount, d-Preston Sturges.

When Joel McCrea, a director of lightweight comedies, decides his next work should be a serious look at the effects of poverty on the country, he leaves his luxurious life and crosses the country posing as a hobo. For most of the trip his companion is Lake dressed as a boy. He finds some romance, some insight into the misery many are suffering, the realization that people want to laugh, and how work serves a useful purpose. Lake is quite good in this grim but entertaining comedy.

Ellen Graham / THIS GUN FOR HIRE, 1942, Paramount, d-Frank Tuttle.

The FBI hire a nightclub singer / magician (Lake) to help trap the foreign agent who paid off a hired assassin with marked money. She agrees but only if her police detective boyfriend (Robert Preston) isn't told of her involvement. In carrying out her assignment, she runs into the hired killer (Alan Ladd) and a romance briefly flares.

Janet Henry / THE GLASS KEY, 1942, Paramount, d-Stuart Heisler.

Lake makes the most of her come-hither looks in this tale of a political boss (Brian Donlevy) who is cleared of a murder charge by his assistant (Alan Ladd). Lake is the daughter of a gubernatorial candidate. She first makes a play for Donlevy but ends up in the arms of Ladd.

Jennifer / I MARRIED A WITCH, 1942, Paramount, d-Rene Clair.

Lake is a 17th-century witch who, after being burned at the stake, had her spirit imprisoned in a tree until it was hit by lightening in 1942, freeing her to seek revenge on the descendant of the Puritan who sentenced her to death. She causes him to fall in love with her, upsetting both his fiancée and his political plans.

Lt. Olivia D'Arcy / SO PROUDLY WE HAIL, 1943, Paramount, d-Mark Sandrich.

Lake is lovely in her portrayal of an American nurse in World War II. The story details the terrible siege of Bataan and, although Lake and her co-stars (Claudette Colbert and Paulette Goddard) usually look as if they have just come from a complete overhaul at the beauty parlor, it makes for a grand patriotic show.

Nan Rogers / MISS SUSIE SLAGLE'S, 1945, Paramount, d-John Berry.

This film is better than was the opinion at the time of its initial release. It's star is Miss Lillian Gish as the title character. She is a woman who runs a Baltimore boarding house for students studying at Johns Hopkins medical school. Nevertheless, Lake is top billed as a student nurse whose romance with an intern ends tragically.

Joyce Harwood / THE BLUE DAHLIA, 1946, Paramount, d-George Marshall.

Ex-serviceman Alan Ladd's no-good wife is having an affair with Lake's no-good husband. When the "lady" in question is found murdered, naturally Ladd and Lake find they have something in common. Lake is quite appealing and the scenes between her and Ladd are sensitive and touching.

Susan Neaves / SAIGON, 1948, Paramount, d-Leslie Fenton.

In their final movie together, Ladd and Lake travel around the Orient. It's the story of an ex-fly boy who does a job for a crooked importer and finds himself involved in murder, danger, and intrigue. In the advertisements for the picture Lake was undervalued as "the half-million dollar blonde."

OTHER ROLES

1939: *bit* / ALL WOMEN HAVE SECRETS; *sorority girl* / SORORITY HOUSE. **1940:** *bit* / YOUNG AS YOU FEEL; *classmate* / FORTY LITTLE MOTHERS. **1942:** *guest* / STAR SPANGLED RHYTHM. **1944:** *Dora Brockmann* / THE HOUR BEFORE THE DAWN. **1945:** *Teddy Collins* / BRING ON THE GIRLS; *Dorothy Dudge* / OUT OF THIS WORLD; *guest* / DUFFY'S TAVERN; *Sally Martin* / HOLD THAT BLONDE. **1947:** *Connie Dickason* / RAMROD; *guest* / VARIETY GIRL. **1948:** *Letty Stanton* / THE SAINTED SISTERS; *Candy Cameron* / ISN'T IT ROMANTIC? **1949:** *Dolores Greaves* / SLATTERY'S HURRICANE. **1952:** *Mary Stevens* / STRONGHOLD. **1970:** *Dr. Elaine Frederick* / FLESH FEAST.

LAMARR, HEDY

(Hedwig Eva Maria Kiesler, 1914–)

Born in Vienna, Hedy Lamarr made her movie debut in GELD AUF DER STRASSE (MONEY ON THE STREET) in 1930 using the name Hedy Kiesler. She exploded onto the world scene in 1933 with SYMPHONIE DER LIEBE / EXTASE in which she not only became the first woman to appear naked in a non-blue feature film, but also was the first to simulate intercourse on the screen. The movie was more discussed than seen and it was severely cut for foreign distribution, arriving in a much abridged form in the U.S. in 1940. Lamarr felt the attention this appearance received was much ado about nothing, even when one of her husbands tried to buy up all the existing prints. She correctly observed, "If you use your imagination you can look at any actress and see her nude. I hope to make you use your imagination." When she moved to Hollywood, Louis B. Mayer changed her name to one inspired by silent screen star Barbara La Marr. Hedy would not experience the same kind of success that other European actresses like Garbo, Dietrich, and Bergman found when they moved to the United States, but she did glamorize several steamy pictures that called for a sexy brunette, such as ALGIERS, WHITE CARGO, and SAMSON AND DELILAH.

KEY ROLES

Eva / EXTASE, (ECSTASY), 1933, Czechoslovakia, Universal Elektra, d-Gustav Machaty.

Lamarr is a young, disillusioned bride of a much older man who is dull and void of any passion. She goes to the home of her father's estate and files for divorce. While swimming nude in a forest pool, the horse on which she has placed her clothes moseys off to visit another horse and, while chasing the animal, she stumbles across a young engineer who retrieves her clothes and makes no advances. Later she seeks him out in his cabin, and they make love. They plan to go away together but when her husband commits suicide she leaves her lover.

Gaby / ALGIERS, 1938, United Artists, d-John Cromwell.

In this remake of the French PEPE LE MOKO, Lamarr is the lovely mistress of a wealthy Parisian visiting Algiers. She meets and falls in love with thief Charles Boyer, who is safe only in the native quarters, the Casbah. Their love affair is the cause of his death as he leaves the Casbah to find her before she sails away. A former lover of Boyer's had told Lamarr that he had been killed by the police. The news was merely premature.

Johnny Jones (Johanna Janns) / COME LIVE WITH ME, 1941, MGM, d-Clarence Brown.

Lamarr is a refugee from Vienna who, in order to stay in the United States, makes a strictly platonic marriage with a struggling author (Jimmy Stewart). But, of course, they fall in love.

Dolores "Sweets" Ramirez / TORTILLA FLAT, 1942, MGM, d-Victor Fleming.

Lamarr is a sultry Portuguese worker in a cannery in California who is able to handle lazy half-breed Mexicans Spencer Tracy and John Garfield, who are both hot for her. The characters probably would be considered stereotypes by anyone of Portuguese or Mexican origin, but this was a time when our good neighbor policy did not include portraying them respectfully in movies.

Tondelayo / WHITE CARGO, 1942, MGM, d-Richard Thorpe.

"I am Tondelayo," seductive Lamarr introduces herself as she slinks her way through bamboo curtains at a British rubber plantation out there in the "Empire." She traps a young planter into marrying her and causes him to fall apart. When she tries to poison him, an old hand at dealing with "white cargo" and trash (Walter Pidgeon) sees how things are and forces her to drink the potion.

Delilah / SAMSON AND DELILAH, 1949, Paramount, d-Cecil B. DeMille.

In this DeMille sex and bible epic, Lamarr is the girl who gives strongman Victor Mature a haircut, sapping his strength and allowing him to be captured by the Philistines. He gets even when, blind and with his hair grown out again, he pulls down the temple in which he is chained, killing Lamarr and everyone else.

Lily Dalbray / MY FAVORITE SPY, 1951, Paramount, d-Norman Z. McLeod.

Lamarr is an international spy in Tangier playing in a three-way struggle for some microfilm. She ultimately teams up with vaudevillian Bob Hope, posing as a master spy who is his exact double, against the likes of sinister Francis L. Sullivan. She chooses Hope because his kisses cause runs in her nylons.

OTHER ROLES

1930: *young girl* / GELD AUF DER STRASSE. **1931:** *secretary* / DIE BLUMENFRAU VON LINDENAU, (THE FLOWER WOMAN OF LINDENAU); *Kathe Brandt* / HIS MAJESTY, KING BALLYHOO. **1932:** *Helene* / DIE KOFFER DES HERRN O.F., (THE TRUNKS OF MR. O.F.). **1939:** *Manon de Vargnes* / LADY OF THE TROPICS. **1940:** *Georgi Gragore* / I TAKE THIS WOMAN; *Karen Van Meer* / BOOM TOWN; *Theodora* / COMRADE X. **1941:** *Sandra Kolter* / ZIEGFELD GIRL; *Marvin Myles* / H. M. PULHAM, ESQ. **1942:** *Lucienne Talbot* / CROSSROADS. **1943:** *Vicky Whitley* / THE HEAVENLY BODY. **1944:** *Irene* / THE CONSPIRATORS; *Allida Bedereaux* / EXPERIMENT PERILOUS. **1945:** *Princess Veronica* / HER HIGHNESS AND THE BELLBOY. **1946:** *Jenny Hager* / THE STRANGE WOMAN. **1947:** *Madeleine Damien* / DISHONORED LADY. **1948:** *Dr. J. O. Loring* / LET'S LIVE A LITTLE. **1950:** *Marianne Lorress* / A LADY WITHOUT A PASSPORT; *Lisa Roselle* / COPPER CANYON. **1954:** *Hedy Windsor* / LOVES OF THREE QUEENS. **1957:** *Joan of Arc* / THE STORY OF MANKIND; *Vanessa Windsor* / THE FEMALE ANIMAL.

LAMOUR, DOROTHY

(Dorothy Kaumeyer, 1914–)

This former Miss New Orleans made the sarong famous—or did the sarong make her famous? Whatever, she looked great in the South Seas wraparound she wore in numerous films. Never a great actress, she was always a good sport about it. In addition to her South Seas roles, Lamour is fondly remembered as a delectable stooge for the looniness of Bob Hope and Bing Crosby in the seven Road pictures. Her singing was always pleasant even though she was seldom given good songs. As of 1987 she was still appearing in big band oldie shows.

KEY ROLES

Ulah / THE JUNGLE PRINCESS, 1936, Paramount, d-William Thiele.

In this unpretentious production, Lamour made her screen debut and first appearance in a sarong with the latter being more impressive than the former. She's a female Tarzan reared with a pet tiger by natives of a tropical island. She is wooed by a British hunter (Ray Milland) who shows up on her island.

Marama / THE HURRICANE, 1937, Samuel Goldwyn / United Artists, d-John Ford and Stuart Heisler.

Lamour is back in a sarong in this story about the innocence of Polynesian natives versus the cynicism and cruelty of their civilized masters. She is the wife of Jon Hall and they are happy until he is imprisoned for striking a white man. With each escape attempt his sentence is lengthened and when he kills a man, the orders are to take him dead or alive. He and Lamour are able to get away when they survive a great typhoon.

Mima / ROAD TO SINGAPORE, 1940, Paramount, d-Victor Schertzinger.

In the first of the Road pictures with Bing Crosby and Bob Hope, Lamour is a native Singapore girl who is rescued by the boys from a cabaret whipcracker (Anthony Quinn). It's pretty tame stuff compared with what was to come, but audiences loved it.

Arla Dean / MOON OVER BURMA, 1940, Paramount, d-Louis King.

Lamour is a singer stranded in Rangoon who arouses a rivalry between two lumberjacks (Preston Foster and Robert Preston). The three find themselves menaced by a forest fire.

Aloma / ALOMA OF THE SOUTH SEAS, 1941, Paramount, d-Alfred Santell.

Fans finally got to see Lamour wearing a sarong in Technicolor and she looked better than ever. The story has her in a romantic triangle on a South Seas island with Jon Hall and Katherine DeMille.

Christina Hill / THEY GOT ME COVERED, 1943, Samuel Goldwyn, d-David Butler.

Playing the perfect foil, Lamour is the fiancée of an incompetent foreign correspondent (Bob Hope) who almost single-handedly breaks up a spy ring in New York City.

Lolita Sierra / A MEDAL FOR BENNY, 1945, Paramount, d-Irving Pichel.

Without sarong or song, Lamour gives one of her best performances as a paisano in a southern California town that is aroused with posthumous adulation for a dead ne'er-do-well who apparently died a hero's death in battle. Lamour had been the sweetheart of the generally despised man.

Carlotta Montay / MY FAVORITE BRUNETTE, 1947, Paramount, d-Elliott Nugent.

Lamour is the mysterious woman, menaced by gangsters, who gets baby photographer Bob Hope, mistaken for a private eye, framed for murder. But a last-minute reprieve saves him from execution.

Phyllis / THE GREATEST SHOW ON EARTH, 1952, Paramount, d-Cecil B. DeMille.

Lamour is far down the list of credits as a dumb but voluptuous aerialist who makes her living with the circus by hanging from her teeth and spinning.

Lalah / ROAD TO BALI, 1952, Paramount, d-Hal Walker.

Technically this is the last of the road pictures to star Lamour, Hope, and Crosby, although she appeared in the United Artists production ROAD TO HONG KONG ten years later in a cameo appearance. In this one she still provides the female focal point of the romantic triangle as an island princess in danger from a jealous male relative who wants to succeed her as the ruler of their tribe.

OTHER ROLES

1937: *Anita Alvarez* / SWING HIGH, SWING LOW; *Carmelia Castillo* / THE LAST TRAIN FROM MADRID; *Molly Fuller* / HIGH, WIDE, AND HANDSOME; *specialty act* / THRILL OF A LIFETIME. **1938:** *Dorothy Williams* / THE BIG BROADCAST OF 1938; *Tura* / HER JUNGLE LOVE; *Nicky Duvall* / SPAWN OF THE NORTH; *Manuela* / TROPIC HOLIDAY. **1939:** *Norma Malone* / ST. LOUIS BLUES; *Diane Wilson* / MAN ABOUT TOWN; *Audrey Hilton* / DISPUTED PASSAGE. **1940:** *Lucky Dubarry* / JOHNNY APOLLO; *Dea* / TYPHOON; *Albany Yates (Lady Lillian)* / CHAD HANNA. **1941:** *Donna Latour* / ROAD TO ZANZIBAR; *Tony Fairbanks* / CAUGHT IN THE DRAFT. **1942:** *The Countess* / THE FLEET'S IN; *Tama* / BEYOND THE BLUE HORIZON; *Princess Shalimar* / ROAD TO MOROCCO; *guest* / STAR SPANGLED RHYTHM. **1943:** *Millie Cook* / DIXIE; *Ann Castle* / RIDING HIGH. **1944:** *Nancy Angel* / AND THE ANGELS SING; *Lona* / RAINBOW ISLAND. **1945:** *Sal Van Hoyden* / ROAD TO UTOPIA; *guest* / DUFFY'S TAVERN; *Angel O'Reilly* / MASQUERADE IN MEXICO. **1947:** *Lucia Maria De Andrade* / ROAD TO RIO; *Fay Rankin* / WILD HARVEST; *guest* / VARIETY GIRL. **1948:** *Gloria Manners* / ON OUR MERRY WAY; *Lulu Belle Davis* / LULU BELLE; *Carol Maynard* / THE GIRL FROM MANHATTAN; *Mary O'Leary* / SLIGHTLY FRENCH; *Meri Kramer* / MANHANDLED. **1949:** *Anna Maria St. Claire* / THE LUCKY STIFF. **1951:** *guest* / HERE COMES THE GROOM. **1962:** *herself* / THE ROAD TO HONG KONG. **1963:** *Fleur* / DONOVAN'S REEF. **1964:** *head sales lady* / PAJAMA PARTY. **1976:** *visiting film star* / WON TON TON, THE DOG WHO SAVED HOLLYWOOD. **1987:** *Martha Spruce* / CREEPSHOW 2.

LANCASTER, BURT

(Burton Stephen Lancaster, 1913–)

In his younger days, Burt Lancaster was a gymnast and acrobat touring with his small friend Nick Cravat, who later appeared with Lancaster in a couple of his swashbucklers. Muscular, and with a flashing smile and great set of teeth, Lancaster was called upon when producers needed a man of athletic prowess for action films. But his earliest movies had him as brooding men in film noirs like THE KILLERS, his debut film, BRUTE FORCE, and KISS THE BLOOD OFF MY HANDS. He was allowed to crack that great grin in THE CRIMSON PIRATE, THE RAINMAKER, and of course in his Oscar-winning performance in ELMER GANTRY. He was also nominated for Oscars for FROM HERE TO ETERNITY, BIRDMAN OF ALCATRAZ, and ATLANTIC CITY. Lancaster has such a powerful presence that he is worth seeing even in his poor films. After becoming a successful actor he formed a production company with agent Harold Hecht (who had discovered him) and producer James Hill. They produced Lancaster's films and others including the critically acclaimed MARTY. Lancaster has been one of the most successful actors for thirty years and he seems in no hurry to retire as evidenced by his fun role with old friend Kirk Douglas in TOUGH GUYS in 1986 at the age of 73.

KEY ROLES

Ole "Swede" (Pete Lunn) Anderson / THE KILLERS, 1946, Universal, d-Robert Siodmak.
Ex-boxer Lancaster waits in a dingy hotel room in a small town for two hired guns to arrive and kill him, making no effort to save himself. An insurance investigator (Edmond O'Brien) discovers why.

Joe Collins / BRUTE FORCE, 1947, Universal, d-Jules Dassin.
Lancaster is one of a group of convicts so brutalized by sadistic prison captain Hume Cronyn that they attempt a break with bloody and tragic results.

Bill Saunders / KISS THE BLOOD OFF MY HANDS, 1948, Universal, d-Norman Foster.
Lancaster, a bitter war vet, kills the proprietor of an English pub and takes refuge in the room of a nurse who falls in love with him. When she kills a blackmailer who recognizes Lancaster, he convinces her that they both should give themselves up to the police.

Dardo / THE FLAME AND THE ARROW, 1950, Warners, d-Jacques Tourneur.
In medieval Italy, Lancaster is a rebel swashbuckler who leads his followers against the tyrant of the city of Granezia. He's a happy Italian Robin Hood.

Jim Thorpe / JIM THORPE—ALL AMERICAN, 1951, Warners, d-Michael Curtiz.
The best movie athlete since Douglas Fairbanks portrays the man often named as the greatest athlete of all time, the American Indian who won Olympic medals in track and field, and was a star in both professional football and baseball.

Doc Delaney / COME BACK, LITTLE SHEBA, 1952, Paramount, d-Daniel Mann.
Lancaster is an alcoholic ex-chiropractor let down by his slovenly wife (Shirley Booth) and the girl (Terry Moore) whom he idolizes. It's Booth's film but Lancaster is in top form.

Sgt. Milton Warden / FROM HERE TO ETERNITY, 1953, Columbia, d-Fred Zinnemann.
Lancaster is the perfect top kick of an army company stationed at Schofield Barricks in Hawaii just prior to the Japanese attack of Pearl Harbor. He has an affair with his company commander's wife (Deborah Kerr), and looks the other way when the other noncoms give Montgomery Clift the treatment when he refuses to join the company's boxing team.

Joe Erin / VERA CRUZ, 1954, United Artists, d-Robert Aldrich.
Lancaster is one of several American mercenaries hired by Emperor Maximilian to transport a French countess from Mexico City to Vera Cruz. When they discover that they are also transporting a fortune in gold, there's a falling out among the boys with Lancaster and Gary Cooper having a shoot-out.

Mike Ribble / TRAPEZE, 1956, United Artists, d-Carol Reed.
Lancaster is a crippled ex-trapeze star who hopes to make a comeback by teaching young flyer Tony Curtis the triple somersault. His plan is threatened by the ambition of circus performer Gina Lollobrigida who will go with anyone willing to take her out of poverty. Lancaster tries to prove to Curtis how cheap she is, but falls for her instead.

Bill Starbuck / THE RAINMAKER, 1956, Paramount, d-Joseph Anthony.
Lancaster is a charming con man who promises rain to a drought-stricken Kansas farm community and not only delivers but also helps plain spinster Katharine Hepburn recognize her value. His con is very charming: "How do you know I'm a liar? How do you know I'm a fake? Maybe I can bring rain. Maybe when I was born, God whispered a special word in my ear. Maybe he said, 'Bill Starbuck, you ain't gonna have much in this world. You ain't gonna have no money, no fancy spurs, no white horse with a golden feather—but, Bill Starbuck, wherever you go, you'll bring rain.' Maybe that's my one and only blessing."

Wyatt Earp / GUNFIGHT AT THE O.K. CORRAL, 1957, Paramount, d-John Sturges.
With help from tubercular gambler and dentist Doc Holliday, Lancaster and his brothers take on the Clayton gang in a shoot-out at the O.K. Corral. He also reluctantly has a romance with lady gambler Rhonda Fleming.

J. J. Hunsecker / SWEET SMELL OF SUCCESS, 1957, United Artists, d-Alexander Mackendrick.
Lancaster is a ruthless Walter Winchell-like Broadway newspaper columnist who uses amoral press agent Tony Curtis to help break up the romance of his sister and a young jazz drummer. Lancaster is marvelously evil.

Anthony Anderson / THE DEVIL'S DISCIPLE, 1959, United Artists, d-Guy Hamilton.
Lancaster is a New England minister at the time of the American Revolution. He finds himself taking up arms against the British while his wife is found with Kirk Douglas, who acts like a Sidney Carton willing to be hanged by British general Laurence Olivier in the place of Lancaster. Both men survive in this adventure-comedy by George Bernard Shaw.

Elmer Gantry / ELMER GANTRY, 1960, United Artists, d-Richard Brooks.
"And what is love? Love is the morning and the evening star." So says Lancaster as the opportunistic Elmer Gantry who half believes the message he's preaching in Jean Simmons's revival crusade. But Lancaster is such a charming sinner that it's hard to be sure. Nevertheless, he's magnificent in the role and surely deserving of his Oscar. Listening to him sing out in the black church into which he wanders after his drunkenness and wenching leave him with no money, one just knows that here is an actor perfect for his part.

Robert Stroud / THE BIRDMAN OF ALCATRAZ, 1962, United Artists, d-John Frankenheimer.
Lancaster is a hardened murderer who spends almost his entire adult life in solitary confinement and becomes an expert on the diseases of birds. It's understandable as birds, animals, and flowers are preferable to many humans.

Gen. James M. Scott / SEVEN DAYS IN MAY, 1964, Paramount, d-John Frankenheimer.
Lancaster is the chairman of the Joint Chiefs of Staff who is planning a military takeover of the country when the president makes a treaty with the Russians. He is thwarted in part because of the actions of his second-in-command, Kirk Douglas.

Bill Dolworth / THE PROFESSIONALS, 1966, Columbia, d-Richard Brooks.
Lancaster is a dynamite expert and one of four men hired by Ralph Bellamy to bring back his wife, who was kidnapped by a Mexican revolutionary. They

discover, though, that she went willingly with her captor.

Ned Merrill / THE SWIMMER, 1968, Columbia, d-Frank Perry.

Middle-aged advertising man Lancaster decides to swim home through the backyard pools of all of his neighbors in the Gold Coast of Connecticut.

Lou / ATLANTIC CITY, 1981, Paramount, d-Louis Malle.

Lancaster is marvelous as an aging small-time mobster who finally gets his chance to prove himself both as a man and as a gangster. He helps young Susan Sarandon dispose of a cache of cocaine that her ex-husband stole from some Philly pushers and for which he is killed. Lancaster proudly beds Sarandon and kills the killers threatening her, before going back to the old dame he's been taking care of for years.

Felix Happer / LOCAL HERO, 1983, Warners, d-David Puttnam.

Lancaster is an eccentric Houston oil tycoon more interested in stars than oil. He sends a young man to a small village on the Scottish coast to buy the land to be used as a port for North Sea oil. Instead, Lancaster agrees to turn it into a fishland wildlife preserve.

OTHER ROLES

1947: *Tom Hanson* / DESERT FURY; *guest* / VARIETY GIRL. **1948:** *Frankie Madison* / I WALK ALONE; *Chris Keller* / ALL MY SONS; *Henry Stephenson* / SORRY, WRONG NUMBER. **1949:** *Steve Thompson* / CRISS CROSS; *Mike Davis* / ROPE OF SAND. **1950:** *Steve Buchanan* / MISTER 880. **1951:** *Owen Daybright* / VENGEANCE VALLEY; *Sgt. Mike Kincaid* / TEN TALL MEN. **1952:** *Vallo* / THE CRIMSON PIRATE. **1953:** *Sgt. James O'Hearn* / SOUTH SEA WOMAN; *guest* / THREE SAILORS AND A GIRL. **1954:** *Capt. David O'Keefe* / HIS MAJESTY O'KEEFE; *Massai* / APACHE. **1955:** *Big Eli* / THE KENTUCKIAN; *Alvaro Mangiacavallo* / THE ROSE TATTOO. **1958:** *Lt. Jim Bledsoe* / RUN SILENT, RUN DEEP; *John Malcolm* / SEPARATE TABLES. **1960:** *Ben Zachary* / THE UNFORGIVEN. **1961:** *Hank Bell* / THE YOUNG SAVAGES; *Ernest Janning* / JUDGMENT AT NUREMBERG. **1963:** *Dr. Matthew Clark* / A CHILD IS WAITING; *cameo* / THE LIST OF ADRIAN MESSENGER; *Prince Don Fabrino Salina* / THE LEOPARD. **1965:** *Labiche* / THE TRAIN; *Thaddeus Gearhart* / THE HALLELUJAH TRAIL. **1968:** *Joe Bass* / THE SCALPHUNTERS. **1969:** *Maj. Abraham Falconer* / CASTLE KEEP; *Mike Rettig* / THE GYPSY MOTHS. **1970:** *Mel Bakersfield* / AIRPORT. **1971:** *Bob Valdez* / VALDEZ IS COMING; *Jered Maddox* / LAWMAN. **1972:** *McIntosh* / ULZANA'S RAID. **1973:** *Cross* / SCORPIO. *Farrington* / EXECUTIVE ACTION. **1974:** *Jim Slade* / THE MIDNIGHT MAN. **1975:** *professor* / CONVERSATION PIECE. **1976:** *Moses* / MOSES; *Alfredo Berlinghieri* / 1900; *Ned Buntline* / BUFFALO BILL AND THE INDIANS, OR SITTING BULL'S HISTORY LESSON. **1977:** *MacKenzie* / THE CASSANDRA CROSSING. *Lawrence Dell* / TWILIGHT'S LAST GLEAMING; *Dr. Moreau* / THE ISLAND OF DR. MOREAU. **1978:** *Maj. Asa Barker* / GO TELL THE SPARTANS. **1979:** *Colonel Durnford* / ZULU DAWN. **1980:** *Bill Doolin* / CATTLE ANNIE AND LITTLE BRITCHES. **1981:** *Gen. Mark Clark* / LA PELLE, (THE SKIN). **1983:** *Maxwell Danforth* / THE OSTERMAN WEEKEND. **1985:** *Teschemacher* / LITTLE TREASURE. **1986:** *Harry Doyle* / TOUGH GUYS.

LANDIS, CAROLE

(Frances Lillian Ridste, 1919–1948)

This shapely blonde, winner of beauty contests from the age of 12 and married four times, never appeared in anything but routine movies. She allegedly committed suicide over her frustration in being unable to marry her lover Rex Harrison. Landis wasn't happy with her reputation as a multi-marriage failure. As she pointed out, "I was ex-wifed to death. It might be the husband's fault, you know." Perhaps Landis would have been more than just a beauty had she ever worked with a good director, but she was appreciated by a lot of World War II GIs not just for her pinups but also for all the USO tours she made to entertain them.

KEY ROLES

Loana / ONE MILLION B.C., 1940, Hal Roach / United Artists, d-Hal Roach, Hal Roach, Jr., and D. W. Griffith.

In this grunt and groan epic filled with anachronistic dinosaurs, Landis's body nicely fills the animal skins she seductively wraps herself in. It's a story of survival and she's a member of the Shell tribe who falls in love with Victor Mature of the Rock tribe.

Sally Willows / TURNABOUT, 1940, Hal Roach / United Artists, d-Hal Roach.

Landis is the wife of a man who works hard all day while she does nothing but loll about their well-appointed home. An oriental idol comes to life and gives them their wish to change roles. Next morning hubby wakes up with a falsetto voice and effeminate ways while Landis wakes with a deep voice, puts on trousers, and goes off to the office. The havoc all this causes makes for some good fun.

Barbara Latimer / MOON OVER MIAMI, 1941, 20th Century-Fox, d-Walter Lang.

Landis is Betty Grable's sister and together with their aunt they move from Texas to Miami intent on landing rich husbands. Grable poses as a wealthy woman with Landis serving as her secretary and the aunt as their maid. After some romantic mix-ups Landis ends up with wealthy playboy Robert Cummings.

Vicky Lynn / I WAKE UP SCREAMING, 1941, 20th Century-Fox, d-H. Bruce Humberstone.

Landis is murdered in this one, leaving her sister (Betty Grable) to demand action on solving the case. Grable falls in love with the chief suspect and discovers that the killer is the police detective assigned to the case. Apparently he had a thing for Landis that wasn't reciprocated.

Edna Fraser / MANILA CALLING, 1942, 20th Century-Fox, d-Herbert Leeds.

In this "B" war adventure, Landis is an entertainer who chooses to stay with the leader of a band of Americans who forms a guerrilla unit and fights on after the Japanese invasion of Mindanao in the Philippines.

Herself / FOUR JILLS IN A JEEP, 1944, 20th Century-Fox, d-William A. Seiter.

This is the story of the 1942-1943 USO tour of Landis, Martha Raye, Kay Francis, and Mitzi Mayfair. There's not much story but Landis looks stunning with her blonde hair blowing.

OTHER ROLES

1937: *extra* / A STAR IS BORN; *extra* / A DAY AT THE RACES; *bit* / BROADWAY MELODY OF 1938; *bit* / THE EMPEROR'S CANDLESTICKS; *bit* / VARSITY SHOW; *bit* / ADVENTUROUS BLONDE; *Carol* / BLONDES AT WORK. **1938:** *bit* / GOLD DIGGERS IN PARIS; *commissary cashier* / BOY MEETS GIRL; *June Cooper* / MEN ARE SUCH FOOLS; *bit* / OVER THE WALL; *secretary* / FOUR'S A CROWD; *bit* / WHEN WERE YOU BORN? **1939:** *Nancy Evans* / THREE TEXAS STEERS; *June* / COWBOYS FROM TEXAS. **1940:** *June McCarthy* / MYSTERY SEA RAIDER. **1941:** *Penguin Moore* / ROAD SHOW; *Ann Carrington* / TOPPER RETURNS; *Lily Brown* / DANCE HALL; *Gene Baxter* / CADET GIRL. **1942:** *Helen Mason* / A GENTLEMAN AT HEART; *Kathryn Baker* / IT HAPPENED IN FLATBUSH; *Mae Collins* / MY GAL SAL; *Natalie* / ORCHESTRA WIVES; *Kay Evans* / THE POWERS GIRL. **1943:** *Flossie Fouchere* / WINTERTIME. **1944:** *Jill McCann* / SECRET COMMAND.

1945: *Helene* / HAVING WONDERFUL CRIME. **1946:** *Janet Bradley* / BEHIND GREEN LIGHTS; *Julia Andrews* / IT SHOULDN'T HAPPEN TO A DOG; *Loretta* / SCANDAL IN PARIS. **1947:** *Mae Earthleigh* / OUT OF THE BLUE. **1948:** *Kay Sheldon* / THE BRASS MONKEY; *Linda Medbury* / THE SILK NOOSE.

LANE, PRISCILLA

(1917–)

Priscilla Lane was the prettiest of the three blonde Lane sisters who appeared in movies. The others were Lola and Rosemary. She also had her best roles away from her siblings with whom she appeared in FOUR DAUGHTERS, DAUGHTERS COURAGEOUS, FOUR WIVES, and FOUR MOTHERS. Her best solo work was in BLUES IN THE NIGHT and ARSENIC AND OLD LACE. Lane very nicely portrayed a series of daughters, girlfriends, and fiancées of some of Warner Brothers' top male stars, but she never became a major star in her own right.

KEY ROLES

Ann Lemp / FOUR DAUGHTERS, 1938, Warners, d-Michael Curtiz.

The picture belongs mostly to John Garfield, but Lane is the sister he loves and she works nicely with the indolent stranger who alters the lives of four sisters in a small-town American family. Lane repeated this role in two sequels—FOUR WIVES and FOUR MOTHERS, whose titles tell it all.

Ellen Murray / YES, MY DARLING DAUGHTER, 1939, Warners, d-William Keighley.

Lane shocks her family by announcing that she plans to spend a weekend with her fiancé. The censors snipped away most of the suggestive scenes but the film was still a winner at the box office. Actually, Lane's virtue was as safe as if she had spent the weekend on retreat at a convent.

Buff Masters / DAUGHTERS COURAGEOUS, 1939, Warners, d-Michael Curtiz.

Lane and her sisters are not pleased when their wandering father drops in just about the time that their mother has found a good man to marry. On the other hand, she doesn't seem to recognize the same wanderlust in John Garfield, the man she plans to take as a husband. Lucky for her and her mother, both men hit the road.

Ginger / BLUES IN THE NIGHT, 1941, Warners, d-Anatole Litvak.

In this serious musical, Lane is one of the gals tied to jazz musicians who spend their lives getting nowhere with one-night musical stands.

Patricia Martin / SABOTEUR, 1942, Universal, d-Alfred Hitchcock.

Lane is the pretty blonde who gets tangled up with a man on the run (Robert Cummings) trying to prove he's not the saboteur who fire-bombed the airplane factory where he worked. Naturally, at first, she wants to get away from him, believing the worst about him, but she comes to believe he's guiltless and helps him track down the real culprit and his fellow conspirators.

Elaine Harper / ARSENIC AND OLD LACE, 1944, Warners, d-Frank Capra.

Lane is the daughter of the minister who lives just across a church cemetery from Cary Grant's eccentric but lovable old aunts and his crazy brother who thinks he is Teddy Roosevelt. She and Grant have just married and are about to leave on their honeymoon when Cary discovers that his aunts have been poisoning lonely old men and his other brother, a mass murderer, has also come home to roost. Thinking that he's part of a family of loonies, he wants to call off his marriage so as not to bring any more nuts into the world. Lane thinks he's just scared of the responsibility of marriage.

OTHER ROLES

1937: *Betty Bradley* / VARSITY SHOW. **1938:** *Barbara Blake* / LOVE, HONOR AND BEHAVE; *Jane Hardy* / COWBOY FROM BROOKLYN; *Linda Lawrence* / MEN ARE SUCH FOOLS; *Joyce Winfree* / BROTHER RAT. **1939:** *Mabel* / DUST BE MY DESTINY; *Jean Sherman* / THE ROARING TWENTIES; *Ann Lemp Dietz* / FOUR WIVES. **1940:** *Maureen Casey* / THREE CHEERS FOR THE IRISH; *Joyce Winfree* / BROTHER RAT AND A BABY. **1941:** *Ann Lemp Dietz* / FOUR MOTHERS; *Pamela McAllister* / MILLION DOLLAR BABY. **1942:** *Coralie Adams* / SILVER QUEEN. **1943:** *Janie Brown* / THE MEANEST MAN IN THE WORLD. **1947:** *Nancy Crane* / FUN ON A WEEKEND. **1948:** *Doris Brewster* / BODYGUARD.

LANGE, HOPE

(1931–)

An attractive blonde, Hope Lange made her Broadway debut at the age of 12 in "The Patriots" in 1943. In 1956 she won praise for her first film appearance in BUS STOP and the next year she received an Oscar nomination for her role as the girl raped by her father in PEYTON PLACE. Most of her biggest acting successes have been on television with the series "The Ghost and Mrs. Muir" and "The New Dick Van Dyke Show." Her made-for-TV movies include CROWHAVEN FARM (1970) and THAT CERTAIN SUMMER (1972).

KEY ROLES

Elma / BUS STOP, 1956, 20th Century-Fox, d-Joshua Logan.

Lange is a young waitress who helps hide would-be singer and actress Marilyn Monroe from Don Murray, a cowboy who has come to the big city of Phoenix to take part in a rodeo and find himself a wife. He thinks Monroe will do just fine. Lange is impressed with Monroe's worldliness, even though the blonde bombshell is terribly naive and vulnerable.

Selena Cross / PEYTON PLACE, 1957, 20th Century-Fox, d-Mark Robson.

Lange lives on the wrong side of the tracks with her brutal, drunken father, world-weary mother, and an assortment of siblings. Her father sexually abuses her with regularity and she puts up with it until he threatens others and she kills him. She is acquitted at her trial, when the character of her victim is brought out.

Queenie Martin / POCKETFUL OF MIRACLES, 1961, United Artists, d-Frank Capra.

In this remake of LADY FOR A DAY, Lange is the girlfriend of a New York bootlegger (Glenn Ford) who helps transform an old apple seller (Bette Davis) into a regal dowager to impress her long-absent daughter, her daughter's fiancé, and his father before the two marry and settle down in Spain.

OTHER ROLES

1957: *Zee* / THE TRUE STORY OF JESSE JAMES. **1958:** *Hope Plowman* / THE YOUNG LIONS; *Andrea Lenaine* / IN LOVE AND WAR. **1959:** *Caroline Baker* / THE BEST OF EVERYTHING. **1961:** *Irene Sperry* / WILD IN THE COUNTRY. **1963:** *Millie Mehaffey* / LOVE IS

A BALL. **1974:** *Joanna Kersey* / DEATH WISH. **1985:** *Mrs. Walsh* / A NIGHTMARE ON ELM STREET 2: FREDDY'S REVENGE. **1986:** *Mrs. Williams* / BLUE VELVET.

LANGE, JESSICA

(1949–)

Jessica Lange got her start as a latter-day scream queen in the remake of KING KONG in 1976. No one took much note of her as an actress at that time but within six years critics had a different opinion of her talents. She was nominated for an Oscar for FRANCES (1982) and COUNTRY (1984), winning the Best Supporting Actress Award for TOOTSIE (1982). Lange reveals a tawdry sexuality in several of her movies, including THE POSTMAN ALWAYS RINGS TWICE and CRIMES OF THE HEART, which may suggest the way her roles will be going for a few years to come.

KEY ROLES

Dwan / KING KONG, 1976, Dino de Laurentiis, d-John Guillermin.

The problem with this remake of the 1933 classic is that the producer, director, and screenwriters couldn't make up their minds as to whether they were filming an updated version of the classic story of beauty and the beast or making a spoof of the genre. Lange surely looks good enough to arouse beasts or men in this strange tale of a giant ape that develops a romantic attachment to a blonde about one-tenth his size.

Frances Farmer / FRANCES, 1982, EMI / Brooksfilm, d-Graeme Clifford.

Lange looks remarkably like the tragic 1930s actress who spent a hellish period in mental institutions after her mother had her committed; she was repeatedly raped by guards and inmates alike. It's pretty strong stuff and, while Lange's acting is impeccable, such glum material seldom wins an actress the Oscar.

Julie / TOOTSIE, 1982, Columbia, d-Sydney Pollack.

Lange didn't walk away empty-handed in the 1982 Oscar sweepstakes, as she won the Best Supporting Actress Award for her role as the TV soap opera star who is loved by an actor (Dustin Hoffman) and befriended by the female actress he is posing as in the cast of the same show.

Jewell Ivy / COUNTRY, 1984, Far West Productions, d-Richard Pearce.

Lange and husband Sam Shepard find their life unraveling when the government attempts to foreclose on their land. Life is tough but they have the courage to go on fighting for the life and land they love.

OTHER ROLES

1979: *Angelique* / ALL THAT JAZZ. **1980:** *Louise* / HOW TO BEAT THE HIGH COST OF LIVING. **1981:** *Cora Papadakis* / THE POSTMAN ALWAYS RINGS TWICE. **1985:** *Patsy Cline* / SWEET DREAMS. **1986:** *Meg Magrath* / CRIMES OF THE HEART.

LANSBURY, ANGELA

(1925–)

Born in London, Angela Lansbury came from a political family and was evacuated to the United States at the beginning of World War II. She earned an Oscar nomination for her first motion picture (GASLIGHT) in which she portrayed the sexy maid who went for the master as he tried to drive her mistress mad. Throughout her years in movies Lansbury has shown great versatility, but is perhaps best remembered for being a hard-as-nails broad in STATE OF THE UNION and the Communist controller of her own son in THE MANCHURIAN CANDIDATE. She has enjoyed considerable success in Broadway shows such as "Mame" and "Sweeney Todd" and is currently enjoying a successful career as a youngish Miss Marple-like detective in the TV series "Murder, She Wrote."

KEY ROLES

Nancy Oliver / GASLIGHT, 1944, MGM, d-George Cukor.

Lansbury is the saucy young maid who unwittingly helps Charles Boyer in his attempts to convince his wife (Ingrid Bergman) that she is going mad. Lansbury is a flirt with the master and in no way disguises her dislike of her mistress.

Sibyl Vane / THE PICTURE OF DORIAN GRAY, 1945, MGM, d-Albert Lewin.

The man whose portrait ages while he stays forever young causes the death of a demure cabaret singer (Lansbury), but many years later, when her brother brings Dorian Gray up on charges, he drops them believing the youthful-looking Hurd Hatfield couldn't possibly be the culprit.

Kay Thorndyke / STATE OF THE UNION, 1948, MGM, d-Frank Capra.

Having inherited a newspaper empire from her father, hard-hearted, tough Lansbury plans to make her lover, industrialist Spencer Tracy, president of the United States, even though this requires that he get back with his estranged wife, crafty Katharine Hepburn.

Mavis Pruitt / THE DARK AT THE TOP OF THE STAIRS, 1960, Warners, d-Delbert Mann.

Lansbury is a hard-working widow in a small Oklahoma town whose way of life has the gossips' tongues wagging, particularly about her friendship with married Robert Preston. Although she wishes it could be more, both know theirs is just a friendship.

Raymond's mother (Mrs. Iselin) / THE MANCHURIAN CANDIDATE, 1962, United Artists, d-John Frankenheimer.

Lansbury's second husband is to be nominated for vice president on his party's ticket and her brainwashed son (Laurence Harvey) has been programmed to kill the presidential nominee when the two candidates come together at the convention podium.

Eglantine Price / BEDKNOBS AND BROOMSTICKS, 1971, Disney, d-Robert Stevenson.

Lansbury is a kindly witch who in 1940, with the help of three evacuee children, rides on her magic bedstead to prevent the invasion of England by the Germans.

Miss Jane Marple / THE MIRROR CRACK'D, 1980, EMI, d-Guy Hamilton.

While not on a par with Dame Margaret Rutherford, Lansbury is impressive enough in this minor Agatha Christie story about murder and movie stars.

OTHER ROLES

1944: *Edwina Brown* / NATIONAL VELVET. **1946:** *Em* / THE HARVEY GIRLS; *Dusty Willard* / THE HOODLUM SAINT; *guest* / TILL THE CLOUDS ROLL BY. **1947:** *Clotilde de Marelle* / THE PRIVATE AFFAIRS OF BEL AMI; *Mabel Sabre* / IF WINTER COMES. **1948:** *Susan Bratten* / TENTH AVENUE ANGEL; *Queen Anne* / THE THREE MUSKETEERS. **1949:** *Audrey Quail* / THE RED DANUBE; *Semadar* /

SAMSON AND DELILAH. **1951:** *Mrs. Edwards* / KIND LADY. **1952:** *Leslie* / MUTINY. **1953:** *Valeska Chauval* / REMAINS TO BE SEEN. **1954:** *Doris Hillman* / KEY MAN. **1955:** *Tally Dickson* / A LAWLESS STREET; *Madame Valentine* / THE PURPLE MASK. **1956:** *Princess Gwendolyn* / THE COURT JESTER; *Myra Leeds* / PLEASE MURDER ME. **1958:** *Minnie Littlejohn* / THE LONG, HOT SUMMER; *Mabel Claremont* / THE RELUCTANT DEBUTANTE. **1960:** *Countess Lina* / A BREATH OF SCANDAL. **1961:** *Pearl* / SEASON OF PASSION; *Sarah Lee Gates* / BLUE HAWAII. **1962:** *voice of Marguerite Laurier* / THE FOUR HORSEMEN OF THE APOCALYPSE; *Annabel Willart* / ALL FALL DOWN. **1963:** *Sibyl Logan* / IN THE COOL OF THE DAY. **1964:** *Isabel Boyd* / THE WORLD OF HENRY ORIENT; *Phyllis* / DEAR HEART. **1965:** *Claudia* / THE GREATEST STORY EVER TOLD; *Lady Blystone* / THE AMOROUS ADVENTURES OF MOLL FLANDERS; *Mama Jean Bello* / HARLOW. **1966:** *Gloria* / MISTER BUDDWING. **1970:** *Countess Herthe von Ornstein* / SOMETHING FOR EVERYONE. **1978:** *Mrs. Salome Otterbourne* / DEATH ON THE NILE. **1982:** *voice* / THE LAST UNICORN. **1983:** *Ruth* / THE PIRATES OF PENZANCE. **1984:** *Granny* / THE COMPANY OF WOLVES.

LANZA, MARIO

(Alfredo Cocozza, 1921–1959)

Mario Lanza sold 1.5 million copies of "Be My Love" and another million of "The Loveliest Night of the Year." Despite his success with records and movies, critics were divided on his voice. His biggest problem for movies was his weight. The man enjoyed putting it on but it became harder and harder to slim down sufficiently to be considered a romantic lead. For THE STUDENT PRINCE in 1954, he didn't make it and could supply only the singing voice for Edmond Purdom, who looked more the part of a young prince at Heidelberg finding romance with a beer-hall waitress. Lanza died of a heart attack brought on from the excesses of dieting.

KEY ROLES

Johnny Donnetti / THAT MIDNIGHT KISS, 1949, MGM, d-Norman Taurog.

MGM proclaimed Lanza a new Caruso in his film debut. He plays a singing truck driver who sweeps Philadelphia heiress Kathryn Grayson off her feet. The film is enjoyable schmaltz with Lanza singing "Celeste Aida," "Mama Mia Che Vo Sape," and with Grayson, "They Didn't Believe Me."

Pepe Abelland Duvalle / THE TOAST OF NEW ORLEANS, 1950, MGM, d-Norman Taurog.

In a role similar to that of his debut, Lanza is a singing New Orleans fisherman who is groomed for an operatic career by David Niven, manager of famous soprano Kathryn Grayson. Grayson and Lanza have a stormy relationship that apparently parallels the real feelings they had for each other away from the camera—they hated each other. Still they make beautiful music together, most notably in "Be My Love" by Nicholas Brodszky and Sammy Cahn.

Enrico Caruso / THE GREAT CARUSO, 1951, MGM, d-Richard Thorpe.

In this, the most successful box-office film in Lanza's short career, he portrays the great Italian tenor with enormous gusto even though the story is mostly fiction. Fortunately, the movie concentrates mostly on the music most associated with Caruso, such as "Vesti la Giubba," "Ave Maria," "Because," and "Mattinata." In addition, Lanza sings a new song by Irving Aaronson and Paul Francis Webster, "The Loveliest Night of the Year."

OTHER ROLES

1952: *Renaldo Rossano* / BECAUSE YOU'RE MINE. **1954:** *singing voice of Prince Karl* / THE STUDENT PRINCE. **1956:** *Damon Vincenti* / SERENADE. **1958:** *Marc Revere* / THE SEVEN HILLS OF ROME. **1959:** *Tonio Costa* / FOR THE FIRST TIME.

LAUGHTON, CHARLES

(1899–1962)

Speaking of himself, the great actor Charles Laughton joked, "I have a face like the behind of an elephant"—an overstatement surely. Laughton wasn't a handsome, dashing leading man, but with his marvelous voice and expressive face, no real cinema buff could ever mind. Laughton won an Academy Award for his portrayal of Henry in THE PRIVATE LIFE OF HENRY VIII and received nominations for MUTINY ON THE BOUNTY and WITNESS FOR THE PROSECUTION. But he could have just as well been given the distinction for many other movies, including THE SIGN OF THE CROSS, RUGGLES OF RED GAP, REMBRANDT, THE HUNCHBACK OF NOTRE DAME, and ADVISE AND CONSENT. Laughton had many doubts about his talent. He directed only one film and it was a box-office failure, but since its release THE NIGHT OF THE HUNTER has come to be respected as one of the most original and compelling thrillers ever filmed. With his doubts Laughton often overplayed, but even when he was a silly old ham he was superior to mere mortal actors. One wishes the opportunity to applaud his unique mastery just one more time.

KEY ROLES

Sir William Porterhouse / THE OLD DARK HOUSE, 1932, Universal, d-James Whale.

Laughton, with his Lancashire accent, tries to add some merriment to the occasion by getting everybody to talk about themselves in this horror tale about stranded travelers who take refuge in the house of a family of eccentrics.

Nero / THE SIGN OF THE CROSS, 1932, Paramount, d-Cecil B. DeMille.

Laughton looks as degenerate as he acts in the role of the crazy Roman emperor who fiddled while Rome burned. In this story he sends his favorite officer to the lions for falling in love with a Christian girl.

clerk / IF I HAD A MILLION, 1932, Paramount, d-James Cruze and others.

Laughton is the best thing in this multi-part comedy about an eccentric millionaire who gives various people a million dollars to test their reactions. Laughton plays a respectable clerk who takes the news calmly and, without saying a word, walks down a long line of desks to his boss's office, knocks, goes in, gives his superior a raspberry, and slams the door.

Henry VIII / THE PRIVATE LIFE OF HENRY VIII, 1933, Great Britain, London Films, d-Alexander Korda.

Laughton is marvelous as the king who divorces his first wife and beheads his second before acquiring and getting rid of four others in various ways.

Edward Moulton-Barrett / THE BARRETTS OF WIMPOLE STREET, 1934, MGM, d-Sidney Franklin.

Laughton is the tyrannical father of poetess Elizabeth Barrett whose opposition to her romance with Robert Browning is partially because of his own unnatural interest in her. The bluenoses tried their best to snip out any incestuous inferences but, as Laughton said, "...they can't censor the gleam in my eye."

Marmaduke Ruggles / RUGGLES OF RED GAP, 1935, Paramount, d-Leo McCarey.

In this charming film, Laughton is a British gentleman's gentleman who is won in a poker game by his employer's nouveau-riche cousin. When Laughton is taken back home to the Old West, his manner makes the locals believe he is a lord. But Laughton is a true democrat at heart and he leaves service and goes into the restaurant business after giving a drink-inspired recitation of the Gettysburg Address.

Inspector Javert / LES MISÉRABLES, 1935, 20th Century-Fox, d-Richard Boleslawski.

Laughton relentlessly pursues a prisoner (Frederic March) who escapes from the galleys and becomes a respectable citizen. Laughton's civil servant mentality is finally cracked when he lets his prey go free in the sewers of Paris. Laughton then kills himself because he has gone against his code of never deviating from a rule, no matter what his head and heart say.

Capt. William Bligh / MUTINY ON THE BOUNTY, 1935, MGM, d-Frank Lloyd.

Laughton's Bligh is a man who sees the captain of a merchant ship as the lord and master of all the seamen under his command. He may punish them at will and take their lives if he sees fit. By the time Clark Gable and others take over the ship, audiences really hate the smirking, evil-looking Bligh. Even though there is some admiration of his seamanship when he takes the long boat that he and other loyal crewmen were set adrift in by the mutineers, thousands of miles from safety, it isn't enough to forgive him for his cruelty.

Rembrandt van Rijn / REMBRANDT, 1936, Great Britain, London Films, d-Alexander Korda.

The story of 25 years in the life of the great Dutch painter is told with subtle dignity. After the death of his wife, he can no longer get commissions and sinks into poverty, his work no longer appreciated. He becomes entangled with his housekeeper, who drives him to distraction, and finds some happiness with the love of a serving maid.

Ginger Ted / VESSEL OF WRATH, (THE BEACHCOMBER), 1938, Great Britain, Mayflower, d-Erich Pommer.

Laughton is a beachcomber and scoundrel on a small Malay island where his drinking bouts and weakness for native girls get him in trouble with the controleur and a female missionary. When he accompanies the missionary to quell a jungle epidemic, they discover some good things about each other and eventually marry, then return to England to run a pub.

Quasimodo / THE HUNCHBACK OF NOTRE DAME, 1939, RKO, d-William Dieterle.

Laughton is the horribly deformed bell ringer of Notre Dame cathedral in Paris who repays the kindness of a gypsy girl—she had given him drink when he was publicly punished—by giving her sanctuary in the church when she is condemned to death for a murder that the bell ringer's master committed.

Sir Simon de Canterville / the ghost / THE CANTERVILLE GHOST, 1944, MGM, d-Jules Dassin.

When Margaret O'Brien inherits an English castle, she makes friends with the resident ghost (Laughton) who she in turn introduces to GIs billeted in the area.

Philip / THE SUSPECT, 1945, Universal, d-Robert Siodmak.

The story takes place in turn-of-the-century London with Laughton as a mild-mannered shopkeeper married to a shrewish, nagging wife. He meets a nice young girl, falls in love, and decides to kill his wife. He does so and convinces the police that she was killed in a fall. But two men doubt his story. One, a neighbor, attempts to blackmail Laughton and is killed for his trouble. The other, a detective, gets Laughton to confess when it appears that the neighbor's wife will be blamed for her husband's death.

Earl Janoth / THE BIG CLOCK, 1947, Paramount, d-John Farrow.

Laughton is a publishing magnate who murders his mistress in a rage. He then assigns one of his editors to find the man who had been seen with the dead woman the night of her murder because he may have seen Laughton arrive at her apartment. The editor is the man.

Soapy, the bum / O. HENRY'S FULL HOUSE, 1952, 20th Century-Fox, d-Henry Koster.

Laughton portrays the hobo who tries unsuccessfully to get himself arrested so he will have a warm place to spend the winter in this version of "The Cop and the Anthem."

Henry Hobson / HOBSON'S CHOICE, 1954, Great Britain, British-Lion, d-David Lean.

In the 1890s a tyrannical Lancashire bootmaker (Laughton) is outsmarted by his oldest daughter who marries his apprentice and pushes him to compete with her father and bring him to heel, so to speak.

Sir Wilfrid Robarts / WITNESS FOR THE PROSECUTION, 1957, United Artists, d-Billy Wilder.

Recovering from a heart attack, Laughton risks his health to take the case of a man charged with murdering an older woman who had named him her heir. He is puzzled by the behavior of the accused's wife, who ends up as a witness for the prosecution, perjures herself, and sees her husband acquitted.

Gracchus / SPARTACUS, 1960, Universal-International, d-Stanley Kubrick.

Laughton is a Roman senator who opposes Laurence Olivier's plans to have himself declared dictator at the time of a slave uprising led by a former gladiator. He entrusts Peter Ustinov with taking the leader's wife and child to safety, saying: "You and I have a tendency towards corpulence. Corpulence makes a man reasonable, pleasant and phlegmatic. Have you noticed that the nastiest of talents are invariably thin?"

Sen. Seabright Cooley / ADVISE AND CONSENT, 1962, Columbia, d-Otto Preminger.

In his final film, Laughton portrays a charming, rascally southern senator who cleverly opposes the president's nominee for secretary of state.

OTHER ROLES

1928: *policeman* / BLUEBOTTLES; *Rajah* / DAYDREAMS. **1929:** *visitor* / PICCADILLY. **1930:** *Job* / WOLVES; *himself* / COMETS; *Captain Grossman* / DOWN RIVER. **1932:** *Cmdr. Charles Storm* / DEVIL AND THE DEEP; *William Marble* / PAYMENT DEFERRED; *Dr. Moreau* / ISLAND OF LOST SOULS. **1933:** *Horace Prin* / WHITE WOMAN. **1937:** *Claudius* / I, CLAUDIUS (unfinished). **1938:** *Charles Saggers* / ST. MARTIN'S LANE. **1939:** *Sir Humphrey Pengallan* / JAMAICA INN. **1940:** *Tony Patucci* / THEY KNEW WHAT THEY WANTED. **1941:** *Jonathan Reynolds* / IT STARTED WITH EVE. **1942:** *Jonas Tuttle* / THE TUTTLES OF TAHITI; *Charles Smith* / TALES OF

MANHATTAN. **1943:** *Rr. Adm. Stephen Thomas* / STAND BY FOR ACTION; *cameo* / FOREVER AND A DAY; *Albert Lory* / THIS LAND IS MINE; *Jocko Wilson* / THE MAN FROM DOWN UNDER. **1945:** *Capt. William Kidd* / CAPTAIN KIDD. **1946:** *Sheridan* / BECAUSE OF HIM. **1948:** *Lord Horfield* / THE PARADINE CASE; *Haake* / ARCH OF TRIUMPH; *the bishop* / THE GIRL FROM MANHATTAN. **1949:** *A. J. Bealer* / THE BRIBE; *Insp. Jules Maigret* / THE MAN ON THE EIFFEL TOWER. **1951:** *Fred Begley* / THE BLUE VEIL; *Alan de Maletroit* / THE STRANGE DOOR. **1952:** *Capt. William Kidd* / ABBOTT AND COSTELLO MEET CAPTAIN KIDD. **1953:** *King Herod Antipas* / SALOME; *King Henry VIII* / YOUNG BESS. **1960:** *Admiral Russell* / UNDER TEN FLAGS.

LAUREL, STAN

(A. Stanley Jefferson, 1895–1965)

HARDY, OLIVER

(Oliver Norvel Hardy, 1892–1957)

There is no way to speak of Stan Laurel and Oliver Hardy separately. They go together like Damien and Phythias, Gilbert and Sullivan, and Sears and Roebuck. These two lovable comedians have achieved a cult status that is hard to explain. When they made their films they were appreciated, but hardly adored. But being called a cult hero is sometimes a disservice to an actor; instead of being evaluated for performances and contributions to motion picture history, he or she is declared magnificent and not to be analyzed or compared with others. Laurel and Hardy were not comical gods—they were men of tremendous talent and timing who tried many things, some that worked and some that didn't. They deserve to be remembered—for their special triumphs that can be savored forever—but not deified. Laurel and Hardy appeared in many movie productions separately before being teamed by Hal Roach, with most of these being silent shorts. Exceptions include three of Hardy's solo films: ZENOBIA (1939), THE FIGHTING KENTUCKIAN (1949), and RIDING HIGH (1950). In the movies that the boys made together, they almost always appeared as themselves, so the following listing differs from others in this book. The first list gives the titles of Laurel's solo films; the second those of Hardy; and the third their joint efforts with their key movies discussed as is the case with other artists.

KEY ROLES

Laurel's solo appearances

1917: NUTS IN MAY; THE EVOLUTION OF FASHION. **1918:** HOOT MON; HICKORY HIRAM; WHOSE ZOO; PHONEY PHOTOS; HUNS AND HYPHENS; JUST RAMBLING ALONG; NO PLACE LIKE JAIL; BEARS AND BAD MEN; FRAUDS AND FRENZIES; DO YOU LOVE YOUR WIFE?; LUCKY DOG; IT'S GREAT TO BE CRAZY. **1919:** MIXED NUTS; SCARS AND STRIPES; WHEN KNIGHTS WERE COLD; HUSTLING FOR HEALTH. **1920:** UNDER TWO JAGS; WILD BILL HICCUP; RUPERT OF HEE-HAW, (COLD SLAW). **1921:** THE SOILERS; ORANGES AND LEMONS; THE RENT COLLECTOR. **1922:** THE EGG; THE PEST; THE CARPENTER; THE BOOTLEGGER; THE GARDENER; THE MINER; WEAK END PARTY. **1923:** THE NOON WHISTLE; WHITE WINGS; PICK AND SHOVEL; KILL OR CURE; GAS AND AIR; MUD AND SAND; THE HANDY MAN; SHORT ORDERS; A MAN ABOUT TOWN; THE WHOLE TRUTH; SCORCHING SANDS; SAVE THE SHIP; ROUGHEST AFRICA; FROZEN HEARTS; MOTHER'S JOY; COLLARS AND CUFFS; A DARK HOUSE; COWBOYS CRY FOR IT. **1924:** ZEB VS. PAPRIKA; POSTAGE DUE; NEAR DUBLIN; BROTHERS UNDER THE CHIN; SHORT KILTS; MONSIEUR DON'T CARE; WEST OF HOT DOG; SMITHY. **1925:** MANDARIN MIX-UP; SOMEWHERE IN WRONG; PIE-EYED; THE SNOW HAWK; NAVY BLUE DAYS; TWINS; THE SLEUTH; DR. PYCKLE AND MR. PRYDE; HALF A MAN. **1926:** ATTA BOY; ON THE FRONT PAGE; NOW I'LL TELL ONE; SHOULD TALL MEN MARRY?; EVE'S LOVE LETTERS; GET 'EM YOUNG. **1927:** SEEING THE WORLD.

Hardy's solo appearances

1914: OUTWITTING DAD; BACK TO THE FARM; PINS ARE LUCKY; THE SOUBRETTE AND THE SIMP; THE SMUGGLER'S DAUGHTERS; THE FEMALE COP. **1915:** WHAT HE FORGOT; CUPID'S TARGET; SPAGHETTI AND LOTTERY; GUS AND THE ANARCHISTS; SHODDY THE TAILOR; THE PAPERHANGER'S HELPER; SPAGHETTI A LA MODE; CHARLEY'S AUNT; ARTISTS AND MODELS; THE TRAMPS; THE PRIZE BABY; AN EXPENSIVE VISIT; CLEANING TIME; MIXED FLATS; SAFETY WORST; TWIN SISTERS; BABY; WHO STOLE THE DOGGIES?; A LUCKY STRIKE; THE NEW BUTLER; MATILDA'S LEGACY; HER CHOICE; CANNIBAL KING; WHAT A CINCH; CLOTHES MAKE THE MAN; THE DEAD LETTER; AVENGING BILL; THE HAUNTED HAT; THE SIMP AND THE SOPHOMORES; BABE'S SCHOOL DAYS; ETHEL'S ROMEOS; THE NEW ADVENTURES OF J. RUFUS WALLINGFORD; SOMETHING IN HER EYE; A JANITOR'S JOYFUL JOB; FATTY'S FATAL FUN; UPS AND DOWNS; THIS WAY OUT. **1916:** CHICKENS; FRENZIED FINANCE; BUSTED HEARTS; A STICKY AFFAIR; BUNGLES' RAINY DAY; THE TRYOUT; BUNGLES ENFORCES THE LAW; BUNGLES' ELOPEMENT; BUNGLES LANDS A JOB; ONE TOO MANY; THE SERENADE; NERVE AND GASOLINE; THEIR VACATION; MAMMA'S BOYS; A BATTLE ROYAL; ALL FOR A GIRL; HIRED AND FIRED; WHAT'S SAUCE FOR THE GOOSE; THE BRAVE ONES; THE WATER CURE; THIRTY DAYS; BABY DOLL; THE SCHEMERS; SEA DOGS; HUNGRY HEARTS; EDISON BUGG'S INVENTION; NEVER AGAIN; BETTER HALVES; A DAY AT SCHOOL; A TERRIBLE TRAGEDY; SPAGHETTI; AUNT BILL; THE HEROES; IT HAPPENED IN PIKERSVILLE; HUMAN HOUNDS; DREAMY KNIGHTS; LIFE SAFERS; THEIR HONEYMOON; AN AERIEL JOYRIDE; SIDETRACKED; STRANDED; LOVE AND DUTY; ARTISTIC ATMOSPHERE; THE REFORMERS; ROYAL BLOOD; THE CANDY TRAIL; THE PRECIOUS PARCEL; A MAID TO ORDER; TWIN FLATS; A WARM RECEPTION; PIPE DREAMS; MOTHER'S CHILD; PRIZE WINNERS; AMBITIOUS ETHEL; THE GUILTY ONES. **1917:** HE WINKED AND WON; FAT AND FICKLE; THE BOYCOTTED BABY; WANTED—A BAD MAN; THE OTHER GIRL; THE LOVE BUGS; BACK STAGE; THE HERO; DOUGH-NUTS; CUPID'S RIVAL; THE VILLAIN; A MILLIONAIRE; A MIXUP IN HEARTS; THE GOAT; THE GENIUS; THE STRANGER; THE FLY COP; THE MODISTE; THE STAR BOARDER; THE CHIEF COOK; THE CANDY KID; THE STATION MASTER; THE HOBO; THE PEST; THE PROSECUTOR; THE BAND MASTER; THE SLAVE. **1918:** THE ARTIST; THE BARBER; KING SOLOMON; HIS DAY OUT; THE ORDERLY; THE ROGUE; THE SCHOLAR; THE MESSENGER; THE HANDY MAN; BRIGHT AND EARLY; THE STRAIGHT AND NARROW; PLAYMATES. **1919:** FRECKLED FISH; HOP THE BELLHOP; LIONS AND LADIES; MULES AND MORTGAGES; TOOTSIE AND TAMALES; HEALTHY AND HAPPY; FLIPS AND FLOPS; YAPS AND YOKELS; MATES AND MODELS; SQUABS AND SQUABBLES; BUNGS AND BUNGLERS; SWITCHES AND SWEETIES. **1920:** DAMES AND DENTISTS; MAIDS AND MUSLIN; SQUEAKS AND SQUAWKS; FISTS AND FODDER; PALS AND PUGS; HE LAUGHS LAST; SPRINGTIME; THE DECORATOR; HIS JONAH DAY; THE BACK YARD. **1921:** THE FALL GUY; THE SAWMILL. **1922:** GOLF; THE COUNTER JUMPER; FORTUNE'S MASK; THE LITTLE WILDCAT; ONE STOLEN NIGHT. **1923:** THE THREE AGES; REX, KING OF THE WILD HORSES. **1924:** THE GIRL IN THE LIMOUSINE; HER BOY FRIEND; KID SPEED; THE WIZARD OF OZ; THE PERFECT CLOWN. **1925:** IS MARRIAGE THE BUNK?; ISN'T LIFE TERRIBLE?; ENOUGH TO DO; WANDERING PAPAS; YES, YES, NANETTE; NAVY GRAVY; STICK AROUND; HOP TO IT; SHOULD SAILORS MARRY? **1926:** STOP, LOOK AND LISTEN; MADAME MYSTERY; LONG LIVE THE KING; THUNDERING FLEAS; ALONG CAME AUNTIE; CRAZY LIKE A FOX; BE YOUR AGE; SHOULD MEN WALK HOME?; THE NICKEL HOPPER; THE GENTLE CYCLONE; A BANKRUPT HONEYMOON; A SEA DOG'S TALE; CRAZY TO ACT; SAY IT WITH BABIES. **1927:** NO MAN'S LAW; FLUTTERING HEARTS; THE LIGHTER THAT FAILED; LOVE 'EM AND FEED 'EM; ASSISTANT WIVES; GALLOPING GHOSTS; BARNUM AND RINGLING INC.; WHY GIRLS SAY NO; THE HONORABLE MR. BUGGS. **1939:** *Dr. Tibbitt* / ZENOBIA. **1949:** *Willie Paine* / THE FIGHTING KENTUCKIAN. **1950:** *horse player* / RIDING HIGH.

Laurel and Hardy together

Stanilo and Olivero / FRA DIAVOLO, (THE DEVIL'S BROTHER), 1933, MGM, d-Hal Roach and Charles Rogers.

The boys play two wandering vagrants who decide to become hold-up men. Their first victim is Fra Diavolo who turns the tables on them and makes them his servants. They aid him in his plot to relieve a rich couple of their fortune.

Stan and Ollie / SONS OF THE DESERT, 1934, MGM, d-William A. Seiter.

Laurel and Hardy are sworn to attend the annual meeting of their fraternal order, but their wives have other ideas. Pretending illness, Ollie gets a doctor to prescribe an ocean voyage with Stan coming along. The wives buy it. Instead of taking the sea trip the boys go to their convention, but their ship is sunk with all aboard reported as lost. When their grief-stricken wives see the boys cavorting at the convention in the newsreel, they are ready when Stan and Ollie arrive home with an incredible story.

Stanley Dum and Ollie Dee / BABES IN TOYLAND, 1934, MGM, d-Gus Meins and Charles Rogers.
Evil and lecherous Barnaby tries to force Bo-Peep to become his wife. He takes over Toyland with an army of demons but is ultimately defeated by the toymaker's bumbling assistants (Laurel and Hardy) with the help of some giant-sized wooden soldiers.

themselves / OUR RELATIONS, 1936, MGM, d-Harry Lachman.
Laurel and Hardy are sailors who have been entrusted to deliver a diamond ring on shore. Aware of their weakness when on leave, they leave all their money with the captain. This particular port of call just happens to be the home of the boys' twin brothers. The four get mixed up, the diamond is lost, some gangsters and girls mess up their plans, but everything is brought to a satisfactory conclusion by the end of the sixth reel.

themselves / WAY OUT WEST, 1937, MGM, d-James Horne.
The boys are entrusted with delivering a gold mine deed to the daughter of their recently deceased partner, but they don't know what she looks like and are induced to give the deed to a girl who is passed off as the rightful heir. The rest of the film deals with the boys putting things right. They even sing "Tumblin' Tumbleweeds."

themselves / BLOCK-HEADS, 1938, MGM, d-John G. Blystone.
During the "Big Push" in World War I, Hardy goes over the top and Laurel is left behind to guard the trench. Twenty years later, and unaware of the armistice, Laurel is still at his post. Accidentally discovered, he is brought home to a hero's welcome and visits Hardy's home where the latter's wife makes it clear that Laurel is not welcome and she stalks out. Laurel's adjustment to civilian life is very difficult for both friends.

themselves / THE FLYING DEUCES, 1939, RKO, d-Edward Sutherland.
Jilted by his girl, Hardy plans suicide and Laurel is willing to help but not accompany him. They are talked out of the attempt by a legionnaire who convinces the boys to join the French Foreign Legion. They are so bad as soldiers that they are ordered shot by a firing squad but escape by plane, which crashes. Laurel is unhurt but Hardy is killed and is reincarnated as a horse.

themselves / A CHUMP AT OXFORD, 1940, United Artists, d-Alfred Goulding.
When these street cleaners foil a bank robbery, the president of the bank rewards them by sending them to Oxford University to get an education. While there, a blow to the head transforms Laurel into the school's most brilliant student, but he doesn't stay that way.

OTHER ROLES

Shorts

1917: LUCKY DOG. **1926:** 45 MINUTES FROM HOLLYWOOD. **1927:** DUCK SOUP; SLIPPING WIVES; LOVE 'EM AND WEEP; WHY GIRLS LOVE SAILORS; WITH LOVES AND HISSES; SUGAR DADDIES; SAILORS BEWARE; THE SECOND HUNDRED YEARS; CALL OF THE CUCKOOS; HATS OFF; DO DETECTIVES THINK?; PUTTING PANTS ON PHILIP; THE BATTLE OF THE CENTURY. **1928:** LEAVE 'EM LAUGHING; FLYING ELEPHANTS; THE FINISHING TOUCH; FROM SOUP TO NUTS; YOU'RE DARN TOOTIN'; THEIR PURPLE MOMENT; SHOULD MARRIED MEN GO HOME?; EARLY TO BED; TWO TARS; HABEAS CORPUS; WE FAW DOWN. **1929:** LIBERTY; WRONG AGAIN; THAT'S MY LIFE; BIG BUSINESS; DOUBLE WHOOPEE; BACON GRABBERS; ANGORA LOVE; UNACCUSTOMED AS WE ARE; BERTH MARKS; MEN O'WAR; PERFECT DAY; THEY GO BOOM; THE HOOSE-GOW. **1930:** NIGHT OWLS; BLOTTO; BRATS; BELOW ZERO; HOG WILD; THE LAUREL-HARDY MURDER CASE; ANOTHER FINE MESS. **1931:** BE BIG; CHICKENS COME HOME; LAUGHING GRAVY; OUR WIFE; COME CLEAN; ONE GOOD TURN; BEAU HUNKS. **1932:** HELPMATES; ANY OLD PORT; THE MUSIC BOX; THE CHIMP; COUNTRY HOSPITAL; SCRAM; THEIR FIRST MISTAKE; TOWED IN A HOLE. **1933:** TWICE TWO; ME AND MY PAL; THE MIDNIGHT PATROL; BUSY BODIES; DIRTY WORK. **1934:** OLIVER THE EIGHTH; GOING BYE BYE; THEM THAR HILLS; THE LIFE GHOST. **1935:** TIT FOR TAT; THE FIXER UPPERS; THICKER THAN WATER.

Feature Films

1929: THE HOLLYWOOD REVUE OF 1929. **1930:** THE ROGUE SONG. **1931:** PARDON US. **1932:** PACK UP YOUR TROUBLES. **1934:** HOLLYWOOD PARTY. **1935:** BONNIE SCOTLAND. **1936:** THE BOHEMIAN GIRL. **1937:** PICK A STAR. **1938:** SWISS MISS. **1940:** SAPS AT SEA. **1941:** GREAT GUNS. **1942:** A-HAUNTING WE WILL GO. **1943:** AIR RAID WARDENS; JITTERBUGS; THE DANCING MASTERS. **1944:** THE BIG NOISE. **1945:** THE BULLFIGHTERS; NOTHING BUT TROUBLE. **1951:** ATOLL K.

LAURIE, PIPER

(Rosetta Jacobs, 1932–)

Petite, red-headed Piper Laurie was so cute and had such a whistle-bait figure that no one at her studio, Universal, tried to find out if she could act. Years after her ingenue days were behind her, she proved that indeed she could as Paul Newman's crippled girlfriend in THE HUSTLER. The next year she retired to get married but made a grand comeback fifteen years later in CARRIE. She was nominated for Oscars for both of these movies.

KEY ROLES

Tina / THE PRINCE WHO WAS A THIEF, 1951, Universal, d-Rudolph Mate.
Laurie is a little thief whose ability to get her lithe body into small, tight places helps thief Tony Curtis regain his rightful place as a prince in 13th-century Tangiers.

Liz Fielding / JOHNNY DARK, 1954, Universal, d-George Sherman.
Laurie provides the romantic interest for Tony Curtis in this story of a Canada-to-Mexico road race.

Sarah Packard / THE HUSTLER, 1961, 20th Century-Fox, d-Robert Rossen.
Laurie's performance as the girl crippled in both mind and body who finds some brief happiness with pool hustler Paul Newman was all the more surprising because she had never been called on before to do anything other than look cute. She commits suicide after allowing George C. Scott to have her, which is just enough to make Newman break the chains that Scott has him in—perhaps what she had intended. In her showdown with Scott she wearily concedes: "And the way you're looking at me, is that the way you look at a man you've just beaten? As if you had just taken his money and now you want his pride?"

Margaret White / CARRIE, 1976, United Artists, d-Brian de Palma.

Apparently Laurie's daughter (Sissy Spacek), a repressed teenager, has inherited powerful telekinetic powers from her religious freak mother. After Spacek destroys all those at school who have ever tormented or befriended her, she goes home to mother and they have a mental knife-throwing contest that ends with both of them dead and their home in ruins.

OTHER ROLES

1950: *Cathy Norton* / LOUISA; *Chris Abbott* / THE MILKMAN. **1951:** *Frances Travers* / FRANCIS GOES TO THE RACES. **1952:** *Lee Kingshead* / NO ROOM FOR THE GROOM; *Millicent Blaisdell* / HAS ANYBODY SEEN MY GAL?; *Kiki* / SON OF ALI BABA. **1953:** *Angelique Duroux* / MISSISSIPPI GAMBLER; *Princess Khairuzan* / THE GOLDEN BLADE. **1954:** *Louise Graham* / DANGEROUS MISSION; *Rannah Hayes* / DAWN AT SOCORRO. **1955:** *Laura Evans* / SMOKE SIGNAL; *Sarah Hatfield* / AIN'T MISBEHAVIN'. **1957:** *Mina van Runkel* / KELLY AND ME; *Delia Leslie* / UNTIL THEY SAIL. **1977:** *Ruby Claire* / RUBY. **1981:** *Mary Horton* / TIM; **1985:** *Aunt Em* / RETURN TO OZ. **1987:** *Mrs. Norman* / CHILDREN OF A LESSER GOD.

LAWFORD, PETER

(1923–1984)

This British leading man married into the Kennedy clan and became a member of the Sinatra "Rat Pack," but Peter Lawford never impressed critics with his acting talents. On the other hand they didn't find him offensive, either. His own observation was, "I never did become the next Ronald Colman." He made his screen debut at the age of eight in the British film POOR OLD BILL. When he moved to the United States in 1942, he made many bit appearances before achieving a place as a light romantic interest through the late 1940s and 1950s before settling into mostly character roles from the 1960s on.

KEY ROLES

John Ashwood II / THE WHITE CLIFFS OF DOVER, 1944, MGM, d-Clarence Brown.

In this flag-waving tearjerker, Lawford portrays the son that Irene Dunne loses in World War II after having lost his father in World War I.

John S. Penrose / MY BROTHER TALKS TO HORSES, 1946, MGM, d-Fred Zinnemann.

Lawford takes second billing to Butch Jenkins whose ability to communicate with animals proves lucrative for Lawford when the nags give Jenkins tips on horse races.

Tommy Marlowe / GOOD NEWS, 1947, MGM, d-Charles Walters.

At MGM everyone appeared in musicals and Lawford acquits himself quite well in this story of a big man on campus who ultimately falls for the pretty brain (June Allyson) who is tutoring him. They make an enthusiastic team with the numbers "The French Lesson" and "The Varsity Drag" by DeSylva, Brown, and Henderson.

Jonathan Harrow III / EASTER PARADE, 1948, MGM, d-Charles Walters.

Lawford appears as dancer Fred Astaire's best friend in this musical tale about how the great dancer has to break in a new partner (Judy Garland) when Ann Miller leaves him for a better offer. Lawford shares an Irving Berlin number, "A Fella with an Umbrella," with Garland.

Laurie Laurence / LITTLE WOMEN, 1948, MGM, d-Mervyn LeRoy.

Lawford doesn't embarrass himself in this remake of the Louisa May Alcott classic and his portrayal is at least as good as that of Douglass Montgomery in the 1933 version. It's a picture for the female stars, though; men are about as important as the furniture.

Lord John Brindale / ROYAL WEDDING, 1950, MGM, d-Stanley Donen.

Lawford provides the romantic interest for Jane Powell when she accompanies her brother and partner (Fred Astaire) to London to entertain at the time of the wedding of Princess Elizabeth to Prince Philip.

Jimmy Foster / OCEAN'S ELEVEN, 1960, Warners, d-Lewis Milestone.

When Frank Sinatra and his Rat Pack decided to have some fun while "old blue eyes," Dean Martin, and Sammy Davis, Jr., were appearing in Las Vegas, they made this movie about a group of old wartime buddies who plan to rob several Vegas casinos at the same time. Lawford is Sinatra's best friend and it's his mother's latest husband, professional gangster Cesar Romero, who figures out what happened and ruins their big score.

Sen. Lafe Smith / ADVISE AND CONSENT, 1962, Columbia, d-Otto Preminger.

Lawford is a womanizing U.S. senator who votes whichever way the majority leader instructs him to, but stands on his own two feet when a friend and fellow senator is driven to suicide during the advise and consent proceedings on the president's nomination of a new secretary of state.

Christopher Pepper / SALT AND PEPPER, 1968, United Artists, d-Richard Donner.

When Lawford is reduced to appearing in a movie with Sammy Davis, Jr., in which the most clever thing is that the white man is called Pepper and the black man is Salt, you know that both are in trouble careerwise. The feeble story has them as the owners of a Soho nightclub who solve a murder in swinging London.

OTHER ROLES

1930: *bit* / POOR OLD BILL. **1938:** *cockney boy* / LORD JEFF. **1942:** *pilot* / MRS. MINIVER; *bit* / EAGLE SQUADRON; *bit* / THUNDER BIRDS; *Ronnie Kenvil* / A YANK AT ETON; *bit* / LONDON BLACKOUT MURDERS; *bit* / RANDOM HARVEST. **1943:** *bit* / GIRL CRAZY; *Roger* / THE PURPLE V; *bit* / THE IMMORTAL SERGEANT; *bit* / PILOT NO. 5; *bit* / ABOVE SUSPICION; *bit* / SOMEONE TO REMEMBER; *bit* / THE MAN FROM DOWN UNDER; *bit* / SHERLOCK HOLMES FACES DEATH; *bit* / THE SKY'S THE LIMIT; *bit* / PARIS AFTER DARK; *bit* / FLESH AND FANTASY; *bit* / ASSIGNMENT IN BRITTANY; *bit* / SAHARA; *bit* / WEST SIDE KID; *bit* / CORVETTE K-225. **1944:** *Anthony de Canterville* / THE CANTERVILLE GHOST; *Thornley* / MRS. PARKINGTON. **1945:** *Jow Carraclough* / SON OF LASSIE; *David Stone* / THE PICTURE OF DORIAN GRAY. **1946:** *Lawrence Patterson, Jr.* / TWO SISTERS FROM BOSTON; *Andrew Carmel* / CLUNY BROWN. **1947:** *Jamie Shellgrove* / IT HAPPENED IN BROOKLYN. **1948:** *Lt. Lawrence Kingalee* / ON AN ISLAND WITH YOU; *Ritchie Lorgan* / JULIA MISBEHAVES. **1949:** *Maj. John McPhimister* / THE RED DANUBE. **1950:** *Jeremy Taylor* / PLEASE BELIEVE ME. **1952:** *Mark MacLene* / JUST THIS ONCE; *Richard Connor* / KANGAROO; *Tony Brown* / YOU FOR ME; *Nicholas Revel* / THE HOUR OF 13; *Capt. Dion Lenbridge* / ROGUE'S MARCH. **1954:** *Evan Adams II* / IT SHOULD HAPPEN TO YOU. **1959:** *Capt. Grey Travis* / NEVER SO FEW. **1960:** *Major Caldwell* / EXODUS; *guest* / PEPE. **1962:** *Sgt. Larry Barrett* / SERGEANT'S THREE; *Lord Lovat* / THE LONGEST DAY. **1964:** *Tony Collins* / DEAD RINGER. **1965:** *Frederic Summers* / SYLVIA; *Paul Bern* / HARLOW. **1966:** *Steve Marks* / THE OSCAR; *Manny* / A MAN CALLED ADAM. **1968:** *Justin Young* / BUONA SERA, MRS. CAMPBELL; *the senator* / SKIDOO. **1969:** *Ted Gunther* / THE APRIL FOOLS. **1970:** *Chris Pepper* / *Lord Sydney Pepper* / ONE MORE TIME. **1971:** *Campbell* / THEY ONLY KILL THEIR MASTERS. **1974:** *Host* /

THAT'S ENTERTAINMENT! **1975:** *Lord Carter* / ROSEBUD. **1976:** *slapstick star* / WON TON TON, THE DOG WHO SAVED HOLLYWOOD.

LEIGH, JANET

(Jeanette Morrison, 1927–)

Janet Leigh, a personal discovery of Norma Shearer, was signed to an MGM contract in 1947. With her breathtaking figure and lovely face, she found herself playing nice girls in the early part of her career as well as secondary roles to her then husband Tony Curtis in a series of period and costume pictures. She looked good but had little to do. When she appeared in the Hitchcock thriller PSYCHO, fans realized that this studio-manufactured star actually could act. Her bloody death in the film earned her an Academy Award nomination. Unfortunately, this wasn't followed up with many additional chances to demonstrate her talent during the rest of her movie career. She has appeared in numerous made-for-TV movies including HONEYMOON WITH A STRANGER (1969), THE HOUSE ON GREENAPPLE ROAD (1970), MURDOCK'S GANG (1973), TELETHON (1977), and THE FALL GUY (1980). She has also taken some deserved satisfaction in the work of her actress daughter, Jamie Lee Curtis, who has demonstrated that she inherited her mother's eye-catching figure and lack of modesty in front of the camera.

KEY ROLES

Meg March / LITTLE WOMEN, 1948, MGM, d-Mervyn LeRoy.

Leigh plays the first of the March sisters to marry and is bitterly resented by Jo (June Allyson), who doesn't wish to see their sister act broken up. With Margaret O'Brien's death that break up is inevitable. As Meg, Leigh is slightly vain about her looks and with some justification.

June Forsyte / THAT FORSYTE WOMAN, 1949, MGM, d-Compton Bennett.

Leigh makes the mistake of introducing her fiancé (Robert Young) to Greer Garson, which leads to a love affair between Young the architect and the "modern" woman who rebels against her husband's (Errol Flynn) belief that he owns her. When Young dies, Garson leaves Flynn to marry Walter Pidgeon, the black sheep of the family and Leigh's daddy.

Aline de Gavrillac de Bourbon / SCARAMOUCHE, 1952, MGM, d-George Sidney.

Leigh is the beautiful young aristocrat with whom Stewart Granger falls in love. She then comes to believe she may be his sister in this tale set just before the French Revolution when Granger, a man without a legitimate name, becomes the clown Scaramouche and a swordsman who seeks revenge on Leigh's fiancé (Mel Ferrer) who is in fact his half-brother.

Lina Patch / THE NAKED SPUR, 1953, MGM, d-Anthony Mann.

Leigh is the feisty girlfriend of Robert Ryan, who is tracked and captured by three bounty hunters led by James Stewart. Killer Ryan and Leigh turn their captors against each other, playing on their greed and suspicion as they travel through Indian country back to civilization.

Bess Houdini / HOUDINI, 1953, Paramount, d-George Marshall.

The picture is Tony Curtis's as the famed escape artist and Leigh, who at the time was his real-life wife, plays the perfect spouse on the screen as well, looking on admiringly as her man performs his fabulous stunts.

Aleta / PRINCE VALIANT, 1954, 20th Century-Fox, d-Henry Hathaway.

Leigh is a princess who is loved by Viking prince Robert Wagner who was trained by Sir Gawain in the court of King Arthur. She is also sought by Sir Brack, who is eventually revealed to be the deadly Black Knight who is in league with usurpers who would overthrow Arthur. In this film based on the comic strip by Harold Foster, Prince Valiant takes care of things and gets Leigh as well.

Ivy Conrad / PETE KELLY'S BLUES, 1955, Warners, d-Jack Webb.

Leigh is a wealthy flapper who, during the 1920s, thinks jazz musician Jack Webb is the cat's pajamas. But he thinks she's too scatterbrained to take seriously, as Webb takes everything seriously. She changes his mind.

Eileen Sherwood / MY SISTER EILEEN, 1955, Columbia, d-Richard Quine.

Older sister Betty Garrett works overtime to prevent her yummy but not very astute sister (Leigh) from tumbling for every man she sees when the two girls move from Ohio to New York to make it to the top.

Susan Vargas / TOUCH OF EVIL, 1958, Universal-International, d-Orson Welles.

Leigh is on a honeymoon with her husband (Charlton Heston), a Mexican government official. They clash with a ruthless, twisted Texas cop (Orson Welles) who has framed a young man for murder. Leigh is also given a hellish time by a gang of narcotics racketeers.

Marion Crane / PSYCHO, 1960, Shamley / Hitchcock, d-Alfred Hitchcock.

When this film was released it was something of a shock to see Leigh in a revealing slip in a hotel room, obviously having just been in bed with her married lover for a "quickie" at lunch. It was even more shocking when the almost always good girl took off with $40,000 of her employer's money. But no one was prepared to have a star of her magnitude murdered so early in the film and in the way it happened. Who can forget?

Rosie De Leon / BYE BYE BIRDIE, 1962, Columbia, d-George Sidney.

In this fun musical, Leigh puts on a dark-haired wig and plays the long-time fiancée of Dick Van Dyke, a graduate chemist who is in the songwriting business to please his mother. Because of the old lady and the fact that he's a bust as a songwriter, it looks like they'll never get married. When Presley-like Conway Birdie gets drafted, Leigh comes up with a plan she hopes will solve her problems.

OTHER ROLES

1947: *Lissy Anne MacBean* / THE ROMANCE OF ROSY RIDGE; *Effie Bright* / IF WINTER COMES; *Margit Mitchell* / HILLS OF HOME. **1948:** *Dorothy Feiner Rodgers* / WORDS AND MUSIC; *Edith Enley* / ACT OF VIOLENCE. **1949:** *Evelyn Heldon* / THE DOCTOR AND THE GIRL; *Maria Buhlen* / THE RED DANUBE; *Connie* / HOLIDAY AFFAIR. **1951:** *Isabelle Dempsey* / STRICTLY DISHONORABLE; *Jennifer Paige* / ANGELS IN THE OUTFIELD; *Nancy Peterson* / TWO TICKETS TO BROADWAY; *Rose Szabo* / IT'S A BIG COUNTRY. **1952:** *Lucy Duncan* / JUST THIS ONCE; *Abby Ames* / FEARLESS FAGAN. **1953:** *Connie Bedloe* / CONFIDENTIALLY CONNIE. **1954:** *Chris Hall* / WALKING MY BABY BACK HOME; *Wally Cook* / LIVING IT UP; *Lady Anne* / THE BLACK SHIELD OF FALWORTH; *Karen Stephenson* / ROGUE COP. **1956:** *Linda Latham* / SAFARI. **1957:** *Anna* / JET

PILOT. **1958:** *Morgana* / THE VIKINGS; *Lt. Vicki Loren* / THE PERFECT FURLOUGH. **1960:** *Ann Wilson* / WHO WAS THAT LADY?; *guest* / PEPE. **1962:** *Rosie* / THE MANCHURIAN CANDIDATE. **1963:** *Bertie Austin* / WIVES AND LOVERS. **1966:** *Dr. Elizabeth Acord* / THREE ON A COUCH; *Susan Harper* / HARPER; *Nora* / KID RODELO; *Cherry McMahon* / AN AMERICAN DREAM. **1968:** *Vivian Miller* / HELLO DOWN THERE; *Mary Ann* / GRAND SLAM. **1972:** *Gert Meredith* / ONE IS A LONELY NUMBER. **1974:** *Gerry Bennett* / NIGHT OF THE LEPUS. **1979:** *Florence* / BOARDWALK. **1980:** *Kathy Williams* / THE FOG.

LEIGH, VIVIEN

(Vivian Mary Hartley, 1913–1967)

Everyone has heard the official story: GONE WITH THE WIND was already under way and the role of Scarlett O'Hara had not yet been cast, although half the actresses in Hollywood had tested for the part, when Myron Selznick introduced Vivien Leigh to his brother David who knew at once that he had found his Scarlett. Leigh had mixed feelings about the part that brought her a first Oscar: "I never liked Scarlett. I knew it was a marvelous part, but I never cared for her." She won her second Academy Award in 1951 for A STREETCAR NAMED DESIRE. Born in India, the dark-haired, blue-eyed Leigh made far too few films but maintained an active stage career despite her weakening health and her nervous distress which led to the breakup of her marriage to Laurence Olivier.

KEY ROLES

Madeleine Godard / DARK JOURNEY, 1937, Great Britain, London Films, d-Victor Saville.

Leigh runs a Stockholm dress shop and is a double agent working for the British. When she falls in love with Conrad Veidt, who's on the other side, she has a conflict of interest to resolve.

Elsa Craddock / A YANK AT OXFORD, 1937, Great Britain, MGM-British, d-Jack Conway.

Louis B. Mayer objected to Leigh being signed as the second female lead in this story of a brash American at Oxford University who is put in his place by all concerned. But the production chief of MGM-British wouldn't tolerate Mayer's interference and Leigh worked out just fine.

Scarlett O'Hara / GONE WITH THE WIND, 1939, Selznick / MGM, d-Victor Fleming and others.

Leigh is brilliant as the high-strung southern woman who doesn't care for the restrictions placed on the behavior of ladies in a male-dominated world, particularly when she knows and eventually proves that she can manage things very well. While Leslie Howard is her ideal notion of a husband, and she resists Clark Gable as much as she can, one might speculate that Scarlett sees herself as the strong person in a relationship.

Myra Lester / WATERLOO BRIDGE, 1940, MGM, d-Mervyn LeRoy.

Leigh meets a young officer (Robert Taylor) with whom she falls in love. His family is not pleased with their son's choice for a wife and, when he is reported missing-in-action, they will not help her. She sinks into prostitution, but he's not dead and they meet again.

Emma Hart, Lady Hamilton / LADY HAMILTON, (THAT HAMILTON WOMAN), 1941, Great Britain, London Films, d-Alexander Korda.

Leigh and her co-star Laurence Olivier had been married a year when they appeared together as the married wife of a British aristocrat and as Lord Nelson, the hero of Trafalgar, whose love affair scandalized all England. As neither can get free from her / his respective spouse, Emma and Nelson set up housekeeping. But she encourages him to go off to the wars, and soon learns that despite his victory he has paid for it with his life.

Cleopatra / CAESAR AND CLEOPATRA, 1946, Great Britain, Rank, d-Gabriel Pascal.

In this story by George Bernard Shaw, Caesar is a tired, aging man with no appetite for romance with such an inexperienced child as Leigh. He promises her that another will come who will teach her of love, referring to Mark Antony.

Anna Karenina / ANNA KARENINA, 1948, Great Britain, London Films, d-Julien Duvivier.

Leigh suffered by comparison to the Great Garbo in the role of the wife of a Russian aristocrat who has an affair with a dashing officer and loses everything, finally ending her suffering by throwing herself under the wheels of a train.

Blanche DuBois / A STREETCAR NAMED DESIRE, 1951, Feldman / Kazan, d-Elia Kazan.

Dear, mad Blanche is touchingly played by Leigh, who had many problems of the mind herself. She is too gentle to be around her sister's brutish husband, who not only treats her with contempt and refuses to let her live in her dreams, but pushes her over the brink when he rapes her. As she is led away she remarks, "Whoever you are, I have always depended on the kindness of strangers."

Karen Stone / THE ROMAN SPRING OF MRS. STONE, 1961, Warners, d-Jose Quintero.

Leigh is a middle-aged woman visiting Rome who allows herself to be picked up by gigolo Warren Beatty and briefly feels young, beautiful, and loved again—but it's only make-believe.

Mary Treadwell / SHIP OF FOOLS, 1965, Columbia, d-Stanley Kramer.

Leigh is among the passengers aboard a German ocean liner that in 1933 leaves Vera Cruz bound for Bremerhaven. Audiences are given the opportunity to examine the passengers' unhappinesses and weaknesses. Leigh looks particularly pitiful when she observes, "You are not young, Mrs. Treadwell. You have not been young for years. Behind these old eyes you hide a 16-year-old heart" as she scrutinizes herself in a mirror.

OTHER ROLES

1934: *schoolgirl* / THINGS ARE LOOKING UP. **1935:** *Rose Venables* / THE VILLAGE SQUIRE; *Phil Stanley* / GENTLEMAN'S AGREEMENT; *Marjorie Belfer* / LOOK UP AND LAUGH. **1937:** *Cynthia* / FIRE OVER ENGLAND; *Victoria Grow* / STORM IN A TEACUP. **1938:** *Libby* / ST. MARTIN'S LANE. **1939:** *Wanda* / 21 DAYS. **1955:** *Hester Collyer* / THE DEEP BLUE SEA.

LEIGHTON, MARGARET

(1922–1976)

Aristocratic, tall, elegant, and dignified, blonde British actress Margaret Leighton made an impressive screen debut in THE WINSLOW BOY in 1948. Nominated for Best Supporting Actress for THE GO-BETWEEN in 1970, her greatest successes were on the London and Broadway stages, winning Tonys for "Separate Tables" and "The Night of the Iguana." Whether on the boards or in front of the cameras, Leighton was best portraying highly vulnerable women whose calm exterior masked emotional chaos.

KEY ROLES

Catherine Winslow / THE WINSLOW BOY, 1948, Great Britain, London Films, d-Anthony Asquith.

When Leighton's family rallies around her young brother expelled from naval college for allegedly stealing a postal order, it ruins the health of her father and costs her a fiancé. She does seem to have a future with Robert Donat, a famous barrister who is brought in to exonerate the lad.

Flora MacDonald / BONNIE PRINCE CHARLIE, 1948, Great Britain, London Films, d-Anthony Kimmons.

Leighton helps Prince Charles Stuart (David Niven) evade capture by the British when he and his highlanders invade England.

Milly / UNDER CAPRICORN, 1949, Great Britain, Transatlantic / Warners, d-Alfred Hitchcock.

Leighton is a treacherous housekeeper in Australia who dominates a young woman (Ingrid Bergman), who follows Joseph Cotten from England when he is sent to Australia for killing his brother. Cotten becomes the colony's richest citizen and marries Bergman. Leighton, slowly poisoning her mistress, is exposed in time to save Bergman. There's a bit of THE PARADINE CASE and NOTORIOUS in this Hitchcock failure.

Caddy / THE SOUND AND THE FURY, 1959, 20th Century-Fox, d-Martin Ritt.

Leighton is a member of a once-proud southern family that has lost its financial base and the will to recover. It's a rather dull production of the William Faulkner novel and Leighton acts like a not quite mad Blanche DuBois, but her moral stature has crumpled considerably.

Emily Fitzjohn / WALTZ OF THE TOREADORS, 1962, Great Britain, Rank, d-John Guillermin.

Leighton is the ill and neglected wife of a lecherous retired general (Peter Sellers) who loses his young mistress to his aide and sadly realizes that his wife is his only female refuge.

Agatha Andrews / SEVEN WOMEN, 1966, MGM, d-John Ford.

Leighton is one of seven American women who in 1935 find their isolated Chinese mission overrun by bandits. All Ford has done is transport one of his westerns to China with Mongols taking the place of the Indians.

Mrs. Maudsley / THE GO-BETWEEN, 1970, Great Britain, MGM / EMI, d-Joseph Losey.

Leighton is superb as she hints at her growing suspicion of the deceitful Julie Christie, who uses a young boy to carry love letters between herself and a nearby farmer. As Christie is to be engaged to a Boer War veteran, the boy wishes to stop acting as a postal service when he learns the nature of the letters. But on his 13th birthday he and Leighton discover the farmer (Alan Bates) and Christie making passionate love in the farmer's hayloft. Leighton, who has been too genteel to express her suspicions before, explodes with terrible ferocity.

OTHER ROLES

1950: *Leonora Vail* / THE ASTONISHED HEART; *Marguerite Blakeney* / THE ELUSIVE PIMPERNEL. **1951:** *Sgt. Helen Smith* / CALLING BULLDOG DRUMMOND. **1952:** *Janet Preston* / HOME AT SEVEN; *Margaret Gregory* / THE HOLLY AND THE IVY. **1954:** *Eve Ravenscourt* / THE GOOD DIE YOUNG; *Helen Teckman* / THE TECKMAN MYSTERY; *Valerie Carrington* / CARRINGTON, V.C. **1955:** *Miss Chesterman* / THE CONSTANT HUSBAND. **1957:** *Judith Wynter* / *Leonie* / THE PASSIONATE STRANGER. **1964:** *Alice Russell* / THE BEST MAN. **1965:** *Mrs. Kenton* / THE LOVED ONE. **1969:** *Constance, the madwoman of Passy* / THE MADWOMAN OF CHAILLOT. **1971:** *Gladys* / ZEE AND CO. **1972:** *Lady Melbourne* / LADY CAROLINE LAMB. **1973:** *Lady Frances Nelson* / A BEQUEST TO THE NATION; *Madame Orloff* / FROM BEYOND THE GRAVE; *Lady* / FRANKENSTEIN: THE TRUE STORY. **1974:** *court lady* / GALILEO. **1976:** *Ma Gore* / TRIAL BY COMBAT.

LEMMON, JACK

(John Uhler Lemmon, 1925–)

Educated at Phillips Academy and Harvard University, Lemmon worked as a piano player in a New York saloon, appeared on radio in soap operas, and served as producer and actor on several early 1950s TV series including "That Wonderful Guy," "The Couple Next Door," and "Heaven for Betsy." He made his Broadway debut in 1953 and his first film for Columbia, IT SHOULD HAPPEN TO YOU, the next year. He received a Best Supporting Actor Oscar for MISTER ROBERTS, and nominations for SOME LIKE IT HOT, THE APARTMENT, THE DAYS OF WINE AND ROSES, THE CHINA SYNDROME, and TRIBUTE, winning again for an inferior role in SAVE THE TIGER. He has been equally skilled in comedy and drama, trying many different things in movies. He wishes he could have tried more, complaining, "Suddenly you find that you're only giving two performances a year. You're a success as an actor, but vast limitations have been placed on your work. If you defy the system—take a character role, as many fine actors in England do—then you're not a star any more, and the best pictures won't be offered to you."

KEY ROLES

Pete Sheppard / IT SHOULD HAPPEN TO YOU, 1954, Columbia, d-George Cukor.

Lemmon supports Judy Holliday in this daffy comedy about a model who wants to become famous so she rents a New York City billboard, puts her name on it, and naturally becomes a celebrity. Lemmon stands by as her puzzled boyfriend.

Ens. Frank Pulver / MISTER ROBERTS, 1955, Warners, d-John Ford and Mervyn LeRoy.

Lemmon is the number one goldbrick on a World War II cargo ship who is so successful in ducking work that, when he accidentally runs into the captain (James Cagney), the latter is surprised to hear how long this officer he doesn't recognize has been aboard. But when the executive officer is finally transferred to a fighting ship and can no longer buck the tyrannical and insensitive captain, Lemmon takes up the job.

Private Hogan / OPERATION MAD BALL, 1957, Columbia, d-Richard Quine.

Lemmon is a private in the post-World War II army but he has more going for him than Eisenhower. He decides to hold a party for the enlisted men and the many nurses, all of whom are officers. To do this he must outsmart officers like Ernie Kovacs and Arthur O'Connell but, naturally, that's a piece of cake.

Frank Harris / COWBOY, 1958, Columbia, d-Delmer Daves.

Lemmon is a desk clerk in a Chicago hotel who convinces cowman Glenn Ford, who needs money, to take him as a partner on a cattle drive. By the end of it, Lemmon is a full-blown cowboy.

Jerry / Daphne / SOME LIKE IT HOT, 1959, United Artists, d-Billy Wilder.

With friend Tony Curtis, musician Lemmon is a witness to the St. Valentine's Day Massacre in Chicago. To escape the mobsters responsible, they pose as female band players on their way to Florida for the winter season. Curtis is interested in the band's singer (Marilyn Monroe), but Lemmon ends up the fiancée of Joe E. Brown who, when Lemmon finally tells him that he can't marry him because he's a man, nonchalantly observes: "Well, nobody's perfect."

C. C. "Bud" Baxter / THE APARTMENT, 1960, United Artists, d-Billy Wilder.

Lemmon is an ambitious clerk with a large New York company who gets promotions by lending out his apartment to superiors for their trysts. His problems accelerate when he discovers that the elevator operator he admires (Shirley MacLaine) has been to his place with the big boss (Fred MacMurray).

Joe Clay / DAYS OF WINE AND ROSES, 1962, Warners, d-Blake Edwards.

Lemmon is a public relations man who marries Lee Remick and introduces her to his habit of drinking a lot. Before long they are both alcoholics. Later he is able to break the habit, but she doesn't want to.

Nestor Patou / IRMA LA DOUCE, 1963, United Artists, d-Billy Wilder.

Lemmon is a naive French policeman who falls for prostitute Shirley MacLaine and, when he becomes her pimp, takes on all kinds of extra jobs so he can be her only customer. But when he decides to get rid of this character he's almost executed for killing himself.

Professor Fate / Prince Hapnik / THE GREAT RACE, 1965, Warners, d-Blake Edwards.

As Professor Fate, Lemmon is the villain in the turn-of-the-century auto race from New York to Paris. As Hapnik, he's a prince in a mythical country who is in danger of losing his throne.

Felix Ungar / THE ODD COUPLE, 1968, Paramount, d-Gene Saks.

When his wife throws him out, hypochondriac TV writer Lemmon, who has a mania for neatness, moves in with slobbish sportswriter Walter Matthau, who is long divorced. They almost drive each other crazy.

Howard Brubaker / THE APRIL FOOLS, 1969, National General, d-Stuart Rosenberg.

Lemmon is a married stockbroker who meets the wife of his boss (Catherine Deneuve) at a party and a day later they run away to Paris.

Harry Stoner / SAVE THE TIGER, 1973, Paramount, d-John G. Avildsen.

Lemmon won the Oscar for his performance as a disillusioned dress manufacturer who arranges to have one of his factories torched for the insurance money he and his partner need to keep the business going. Lemmon is okay but not Academy Award caliber.

Jack Godell / THE CHINA SYNDROME, 1979, Columbia, d-James Bridges.

Lemmon is the chief engineer for a nuclear power plant in California who, when he discovers that his company is trying to cover up a radiation leak, takes over the control room and threatens to close down the plant if nothing is done about the potentially dangerous situation.

Scottie Templeton / TRIBUTE, 1980, 20th Century-Fox, d-Bob Clark.

Dying of cancer, Broadway press agent Lemmon tries to get to know his son who lives with Lemmon's ex-wife.

Ed Horman / MISSING, 1982, Universal, d-Costa-Gavras.

Lemmon is an American businessman whose son has disappeared in Chile during a right-wing coup. He joins his daughter-in-law (Sissy Spacek), whom he doesn't quite approve of, in searching for his son and discovers that being an American means nothing to authorities. By the time he learns that his son is dead, he has been radicalized.

OTHER ROLES

1954: *Robert Tracy* / PHFFFT! **1955:** *Marty Stewart* / THREE FOR THE SHOW; *Bob Baker* / MY SISTER EILEEN. **1956:** *Peter Warne* / YOU CAN'T RUN AWAY FROM IT. **1957:** *Tony* / FIRE DOWN BELOW. **1958:** *Nicky Holroyd* / BELL, BOOK AND CANDLE. **1959:** *George Denham* / IT HAPPENED TO JANE. **1960:** *guest* / PEPE. **1961:** *Lt. Rip Crandall* / THE WACKIEST SHIP IN THE ARMY. **1962:** *William Gridley* / THE NOTORIOUS LANDLADY. **1963:** *Hogan* / UNDER THE YUM YUM TREE. **1964:** *Sam Bissell* / GOOD NEIGHBOR SAM. **1965:** *Stanley Ford* / HOW TO MURDER YOUR WIFE. **1966:** *Harry Hinkle* / THE FORTUNE COOKIE. **1967:** *Harry Berlin* / LUV. **1970:** *George Kellerman* / THE OUT-OF-TOWNERS. **1971:** *cameo* / KOTCH. **1972:** *Peter Wilson* / THE WAR BETWEEN MEN AND WOMEN; *Wendell Armbruster* / AVANTI! **1974:** *Hildy Johnson* / THE FRONT PAGE. **1975:** *Mel* / THE PRISONER OF SECOND AVENUE. **1976:** *Alexander Main* / ALEX AND THE GYPSY. **1977:** *Don Gallagher* / AIRPORT '77. **1981:** *Victor Clooney* / BUDDY BUDDY. **1984:** *Father Farley* / MASS APPEAL. **1985:** *Robert Traven* / MACARONI. **1986:** *Harvey Fairchild* / THAT'S LIFE.

LESLIE, JOAN

(Joan Brodel, 1925–)

This child entertainer made her stage debut at age two and went on to perform in vaudeville with her two sisters. She was spotted by a talent scout for MGM and signed to play Robert Taylor's sister in CAMILLE in 1936. She continued to appear in child roles until 1941 when she changed her name from Joan Brodel to Joan Leslie and graduated to a series of goody-goody, next-door-type girls which kept her busy but brought her no distinction as an actress. Her career went into decline when she left Warner Brothers in 1946 and in the mid-1950s she retired from movies to become a successful dress designer.

KEY ROLES

Velma / HIGH SIERRA, 1941, Warners, d-Raoul Walsh.

Leslie is a crippled girl for whom "Mad Dog" Earle (Humphrey Bogart) arranges a corrective operation that has her up and dancing. She's grateful but makes it clear that she has no romantic interest in the aging outlaw.

Gracie William / SERGEANT YORK, 1941, Warners, d-Howard Hawks.

It is to win Leslie's hand that Gary Cooper gets religion, quits his hell-raising ways, and works doubly hard to get some farmland. But war comes along and he is forced to become a soldier and, despite his convictions that killing is wrong, he becomes the most decorated soldier in World War I and returns to Tennessee and Leslie to find that a grateful state has provided them with a farm.

Mary Cohan / YANKEE DOODLE DANDY, 1942, Warners, d-Michael Curtiz.
Leslie is the quiet, almost backwards girl who becomes the adoring wife of America's great flag-raising showman. As George M. Cohan was a man of big ego and James Cagney plays him that way, it's only right that Leslie is a retiring and rather boring wife.

Julie Adams / RHAPSODY IN BLUE, 1945, Warners, d-Irving Rapper.
Leslie's role in this biopic of composer George Gershwin is a figment of the screenwriter's imagination or perhaps she is meant to represent a number of women who passed Gershwin's way during his short lifetime.

Judy Jones / CINDERELLA JONES, 1946, Warners, d-Busby Berkeley.
Leslie is a girl who stands to inherit a fortune if she manages to marry a man of unusual intelligence by a certain date. After searching all over for Mr. Right, she discovers that her old boyfriend has the right grey matter.

Sally Maris / THE WOMAN THEY ALMOST LYNCHED, 1953, Republic, d-Allan Dwan.
As her career drew to a close Leslie found work at the cheaper studios, as in this case. She portrays the title character who just barely escapes execution for being a spy in the Old West.

OTHER ROLES

As Joan Brodel

1936: *Marie Jeanette* / CAMILLE. **1938:** *Patricia Falconer at 11* / MEN WITH WINGS. **1939:** *Wendy Conway* / TWO THOROUGHBREDS; *girl* / NANCY DREW—REPORTER; *Betsy Phillips* / WINTER CARNIVAL; *autograph seeker* / LOVE AFFAIR. **1940:** *Marjorie Blake* / MILITARY ACADEMY; *college girl* / STAR DUST; *girl* / YOUNG AS YOU FEEL; *party guest* / SUSAN AND GOD; *Shelley* / LADDIE; *Jones's sister* / FOREIGN CORRESPONDENT.

As Joan Leslie

1941: *Mary Mathews* / THIEVES FALL OUT; *Mary Coster* / THE WAGONS ROLL AT NIGHT; *Mary* / GREAT MR. NOBODY. **1942:** *Katherine Chernen* / THE HARD WAY; *Patricia Stanley* / THE MALE ANIMAL. **1943:** *Eileen Dibble* / THIS IS THE ARMY; *Cat Dixon* / THANK YOUR LUCKY STARS; *Joan Manion* / THE SKY'S THE LIMIT. **1944:** *herself* / HOLLYWOOD CANTEEN. **1945:** *Sally* / WHERE DO WE GO FROM HERE?; *Sally Sawyer* / TOO YOUNG TO KNOW. **1946:** *Janie Conway* / JANIE GETS MARRIED; *Connie Reed* / TWO GUYS FROM MILWAUKEE. **1947:** *Sheila Page* / REPEAT PERFORMANCE. **1948:** *Chris Johnson* / NORTHWEST STAMPEDE. **1950:** *Donna* / BORN TO BE BAD; *Daphne Lattimer* / THE SKIPPER SURPRISED HIS WIFE. **1951:** *Laurie Bidwell* / MAN IN THE SADDLE. **1952:** *Ellen Hanley* / HELLGATE; *Mary Kimber* / TOUGHEST MAN IN ARIZONA. **1953:** *Lt. Polly Davis* / FLIGHT NURSE; *Garnet Hale* / JUBILEE TRAIL. **1954:** *Sarah Moffit* / HELL'S OUTPOST. **1956:** *Annalea* / THE REVOLT OF MAMIE STOVER.

LEWIS, JERRY

(Joseph Levitch, 1926–)
"I appeal to children who know I get paid for doing what they get slapped for. I flout dignity and authority, and there's nobody alive who doesn't want to do the same thing." Thus does Jerry Lewis explain his success as a movie comedian, first with partner Dean Martin, and later on his own. He may be right in his assessment of his appeal. French critics in particular, far more than those in America, have praised him as a comical genius. But the French—they are so strange. Lewis with or without Martin portrayed juveniles of arrested mental development who some friend or foe took advantage of in some idiotic and improbable story, but in the long run the simpleton triumphed. After seeing Lewis's antics a couple of dozen times, one gets bored. Lewis has raised millions of dollars for charity but some feel that they would contribute more to his cause if he'd stay off television over Labor Day.

KEY ROLES

Seymour / MY FRIEND IRMA, 1949, Paramount, d-George Marshall.
The movie was meant to showcase Marie Wilson, but Lewis and partner Dean Martin steal the show with Lewis being even dumber than Irma.

Private First Class Korwin / AT WAR WITH THE ARMY, 1950, Paramount, d-Hal Walker.
With this film Dean Martin and Lewis became full-fledged movie stars. Lewis is your usual incompetent soldier who, despite having the IQ of a wall, bungles through to make all the problems he causes work out before the 93-minute film is over. Plot? What plot?

Harvey / THE CADDY, 1953, Paramount, d-Norman Taurog.
In this looney-tune film, Dean Martin is a golf pro and Lewis, too shy to play before people, becomes his caddy and gives him advice that makes him a success. They tear up the course so much that they are banned from the pro circuit and go into show business. Maybe they should have persisted at golf.

Wade Kingsley, Jr. / PARDNERS, 1956, Paramount, d-Norman Taurog.
Lewis is a tenderfoot from the East who helps ranch foreman Dean Martin foil rustlers and land grabbers.

Sidney Pythias / THE DELICATE DELINQUENT, 1957, Paramount, d-Don McGuire.
In his first movie sans Dean Martin, Lewis is a janitor who gets mistaken for a member of a street gang and is to be reformed by good cop Darren McGavin.

Stanley / THE BELLBOY, 1960, Paramount, d-Jerry Lewis.
Taking over as producer and director as well as star, Lewis forgot the need for writers in this plotless series of havoc-creating gags with Lewis as a bellboy in a Miami luxury hotel.

Prof. Julius Ferris Kulp / Buddy Love / THE NUTTY PROFESSOR, 1963, Paramount, d-Jerry Lewis.
Reaching for the classics, Lewis comes up with a comedy version of Dr. Jekyll and Mr. Hyde about a weird and eccentric chemistry professor who invents a potion that turns him into a debonair swinger.

Stanley Belt / THE PATSY, 1964, Paramount, d-Jerry Lewis.
When a major movie comedy star dies suddenly, the studio picks dumb Hollywood hotel bellboy Lewis to replace the deceased.

OTHER ROLES

1950: *Seymour* / MY FRIEND IRMA GOES WEST. **1951:** *Junior Jackson* / THAT'S MY BOY. **1952:** *Melvin Jones* / SAILOR BEWARE; *Hap Smith* / JUMPING JACKS; *guest* / ROAD TO BALI. **1953:** *Ted Rogers* / THE STOOGE; *Myron Mertz* / SCARED STIFF. **1954:** *Virgil Yokum* / MONEY FROM HOME; *Homer* / LIVING IT UP; *Jerry Hotchkiss* /

THREE RING CIRCUS; *Wilbur Hoolick* / YOU'RE NEVER TOO YOUNG. **1955:** *Eugene Fullstack* / ARTISTS AND MODELS. **1956:** *Malcolm Smith* / HOLLYWOOD OR BUST. **1957:** *Bixby* / THE SAD SACK. **1958:** *Clayton Poole* / ROCK-A-BYE BABY; *Gilbert Wooley* / THE GEISHA BOY. **1959:** *John Paul Steckler* / DON'T GIVE UP THE SHIP. **1960:** *Kreton* / VISIT TO A SMALL PLANET; *Cinderfella* / CINDERFELLA. **1961:** *Herbert H. Heebert* / THE LADIES' MAN; *Morty S. Tashman* / THE ERRAND BOY. **1962:** *Lester March* / IT'S ONLY MONEY; *guest* / IT'S A MAD, MAD, MAD, MAD WORLD. **1964:** *Raymond Phiffier* / WHO'S MINDING THE STORE?; *Jerome Littlefield* / THE DISORDERLY ORDERLY. **1965:** *Willard Woodward* / *Everett Peyton* / *James Peyton* / *Capt. Eddie Peyton* / *Julius Peyton* / *Bugs Peyton* / *Skylock Peyton* / THE FAMILY JEWELS; *Robert Reed* / BOEING BOEING. **1966:** *Christopher Pike* / *Warren* / *Ringo* / *Rutherford* / *Heather* / THREE ON A COUCH; *Peter Mattemore* / WAY...WAY OUT. **1967:** *Gerald Clamson* / THE BIG MOUTH. **1968:** *George Lester* / DON'T RAISE THE BRIDGE, LOWER THE RIVER. **1969:** *Peter Ingersoll* / *Fred Dobbs* / HOOK, LINE & SINKER. **1970:** *Brendan Byers III* / WHICH WAY TO THE FRONT? **1981:** *Bo Hooper* / HARDLY WORKING. **1983:** *Jerry Langford* / THE KING OF COMEDY; *himself* / SMORGASBORD. **1984:** *Wilbur* / *Caleb* / SLAPSTICK (OF ANOTHER KIND).

LOCKWOOD, MARGARET

(Margaret Day, 1916?-)

Born in Pakistan of British parents, Margaret Lockwood became a stage actress as a fairy in "A Midsummer Night's Dream" at the age of twelve and made her film debut in LORNA DOONE seven years later. She became a star with Alfred Hitchcock's THE LADY VANISHES in 1938. In the 1940s she became Britain's favorite villainess in several films in which her dark witch-like features and deep cleavage made her the center of attraction for fans even when critics were not impressed. She left films in the 1950s for television and the stage, making only occasional movie appearances.

KEY ROLES

Iris Henderson / THE LADY VANISHES, 1938, Great Britain, Gainsborough / MGM, d-Alfred Hitchcock.

Lockwood befriends Dame May Whitty on a transcontinental train and, when the latter disappears, finds that everyone on the train has his or her own reasons for denying ever having seen the woman. She is helped by Michael Redgrave, not so much because he believes her story, but because she is quite attractive.

Jenny Sunley / THE STARS LOOK DOWN, 1939, Great Britain, Grand National, d-Carol Reed.

Set in a coal-mining community in the north of England, the film features Lockwood as a shallow girl who marries Michael Redgrave, a university student and the son of the man who leads a strike against unsafe conditions in the mines. When Redgrave takes a teaching post, Lockwood renews her affair with the local bookie, which causes Redgrave to leave her and dedicate his life to improving the conditions in the mines that have taken the lives of his father and brother.

Vicky Standing / SUSANNAH OF THE MOUNTIES, 1939, 20th Century-Fox, d-William A. Seiter.

In this Shirley Temple vehicle, Lockwood is the daughter of the commandant of a troop of Northwest Mounted Police in Canada. Together with her sweetheart (Randolph Scott) she eventually makes a fine parent for the little orphan who is the sole survivor of an Indian attack.

Mary Shaw / RULERS OF THE SEA, 1939, Paramount, d-Frank Lloyd.

Lockwood provides the romantic interest for Douglas Fairbanks, Jr., in this story of the planning, building, and maiden voyage of the first steamship to cross the Atlantic Ocean.

Anne Bombach / NIGHT TRAIN TO MUNICH, 1940, Great Britain, 20th Century Productions, d-Carol Reed.

Lockwood meets a young German in a concentration camp and together they escape. But it's just a ruse to learn the whereabouts of her father, the inventor of a new weapon that the Germans are intent on stealing, and her friend (Paul Henreid) is a Nazi. It's a humorous thriller as British agent Rex Harrison and Lockwood must get her father and his plans back from the Nazis.

Janet Royd / QUIET WEDDING, 1941, Great Britain, Gainsborough, d-Ralph Smart.

Lockwood and her fiancé would like a quiet wedding but they have not counted on the plans of their families and friends that nearly end the marriage before it's started. Finally the groom-to-be kidnaps his bride and they leave all behind.

Heather Shaw / THE MAN IN GREY, 1943, Great Britain, Gainsborough, d-Leslie Arliss.

Lockwood is the former schoolmate of the miserably unhappy wife of a sadistic lord and is hired to be the governess of the unhappy couple's child. She soon becomes the master's mistress and schemes to become his wife. When she can't get rid of the wife in any other way she allows her rival to die from a severe cold for which the lord beats Lockwood to death with a horsewhip.

Penny Randolph / DEAR OCTOPUS, 1943, Great Britain, Gainsborough, d-Harold French.

Lockwood is among the three generations of a British family who have gathered to celebrate the golden wedding anniversary of the head of the family and his wife. The octopus of the title is the family itself in this talky but enjoyable drama.

Barbara Worth / THE WICKED LADY, 1945, Great Britain, Gainsborough, d-Leslie Arliss.

Self-centered Lockwood, a 17th-century adventuress, steals the wealthy fiancé of a friend and marries him, but soon becomes bored. She takes up the life of a highwaywoman and has a passionate affair with another of her newly chosen profession. But when he's not completely loyal she almost succeeds in getting him hanged. He escapes and the two shoot and kill each other.

Freda Jeffries / CAST A DARK SHADOW, 1955, Great Britain, Frobisher, d-Lewis Gilbert.

Lockwood is a widow from the working class who marries a man who has murdered his first wife and is more than willing to employ these means again when he becomes attracted to yet another woman.

OTHER ROLES

1935: *Annie Ridd* / LORNA DOONE; *Mildred Perry* / THE CASE OF GABRIEL PERRY; *Emily* / SOME DAY. **1935:** *Ann* / HONOURS EASY; *Vera* / MAN OF THE MOMENT; *Donna Agnes* / MIDSHIPMAN EASY. **1936:** *Betty Stanton* / JURY'S EVIDENCE; *Georgina Hunstanton* / THE AMATEUR GENTLEMAN; *Blanquette* / THE BELOVED VAGABOND; *Ellen O'Hare* / IRISH FOR LUCK. **1937:** *Jenny Green* / THE STREET SINGER; *Mimi* / WHO'S YOUR LADY FRIEND?; *Imogene* / DR. SYN; *Margaret Williams* / MELODY AND ROMANCE. **1938:** *Jeannie McAdam* / OWD BOB; *Catherine Lawrence* / BANK HOLIDAY. **1939:** *Leslie James* / A GIRL MUST LIVE. **1940:** *Anne Graham* / THE GIRL IN THE NEWS. **1942:** *Helene Ardouin* / ALIBI. **1944:** *Nina* / GIVE US THE MOON; *Lissa Campbell* / LOVE STORY. **1945:** *Annette*

Allenbury / A PLACE OF ONE'S OWN; *Edie Story* / I'LL BE YOUR SWEETHEART. **1946:** *Bedelia Carrington* / BEDELIA; *Fanny Rose* / HUNGRY HILL. **1947:** *Jassy Woodroffe* / JASSY; *Lucy* / THE WHITE UNICORN. **1948:** *Ann Markham* / LOOK BEFORE YOU LOVE. **1949:** *Nell Gwynne* / CARDBOARD CAVALIER; *Lydia Garth* / MADNESS OF THE HEART. **1950:** *Frances Gray* / HIGHLY DANGEROUS. **1952:** *Margaret Manderson* / TRENT'S LAST CASE. **1953:** *Annie Farrell* / LAUGHING ANNE. **1954:** *Marissa Mengues* / TROUBLE IN THE GLEN. **1976:** *stepmother* / THE SLIPPER AND THE ROSE.

LOMBARD, CAROLE

(Jane Alice Peters, 1908–1942)

At the age of seven, Carole Lombard appeared as the Queen of the May in a school pageant and her mother began planning a stage career for her lovely daughter. She started her film career with Fox Film Corporation but it wasn't until signing with Paramount that she became a star. Lombard co-starred with all the major male stars and her fame as a romantic comedienne mounted with films such as WE'RE NOT DRESSING, TWENTIETH CENTURY, MY MAN GODFREY, NOTHING SACRED, and MR. AND MRS. SMITH. In the early years of her career her beautiful face was badly cut in an automobile accident and she was told that she would always be disfigured, but a well-known Hollywood plastic surgeon took care of that problem. Lombard married William Powell in 1931 and divorced him two years later. In 1939 she married Clark Gable. When she was just about finished with her movie TO BE OR NOT TO BE, she and 21 others perished in the crash of a luxury airplane near Las Vegas, and movies lost a unique and sophisticated comical beauty. Lombard had a love-hate relationship with the Hollywood studio star system, noting: "I can't call my soul my own—I have no say about my own business. Lincoln freed the slaves, but he didn't hear about me at the time"; on another occasion she commented: "Hollywood is where they write the alibis before they write the story."

KEY ROLES

Connie Randall / NO MAN OF HER OWN, 1932, Paramount, d-Wesley Ruggles.

In this romantic comedy, Lombard, a small-town librarian, marries a big-time gambler (Clark Gable) who she naively believes is a Wall Street broker. She is unaware that he has gone through with the wedding to win a bet. However, he finds that he loves her and wants to keep her from the unsavory things about his life.

Helen Hathaway / BOLERO, 1934, Paramount, d-Wesley Ruggles.

Dancing in a clinging satin gown with George Raft, whose pants are so tight it's a wonder that he can dip, Lombard and the famous coin flipper are no competition for Astaire and Rogers. Lombard views the dance team as merely a business arrangement, but Raft has an idea that theirs should be a more personal pairing.

Doris Worthington / WE'RE NOT DRESSING, 1934, Paramount, d-Norman Taurog.

In this version of J. M. Barrie's "The Admirable Crichton," Lombard portrays the spoiled heiress who finds out what a man seaman Bing Crosby is. They end up on an island but it's not deserted because George Burns and Gracie Allen are naturalists who live there.

Lilly Garland (Mildred Plotka) / TWENTIETH CENTURY, 1934, Columbia, d-Howard Hawks.

This is the movie that established Lombard as a comedienne. Most of the action takes place on the Twentieth Century—a train between Chicago and New York, which at the time was the ultimate in speed and luxury. She's an actress who is tricked by a producer (John Barrymore), her former lover, into signing for his new play. When Barrymore, in a moment of desperation, suggests, "I could cut my throat," Lombard answers, "If you did, greasepaint would run out of it. That's the trouble with you, Oscar—with both of us. We're not people. We're lithographs. We don't know anything about love until it's written and rehearsed. We're only real in between curtains."

"Alabam" Georgia Lee / LADY BY CHOICE, 1934, Columbia, d-David Burton.

As a publicity stunt Lombard, a fan dancer, "adopts" old rummy May Robson on Mother's Day. It's not as good as LADY FOR A DAY, but it has its comical moments.

Diana Harrison / RUMBA, 1935, Paramount, d-Marion Gering.

Lombard is an heiress who meets dancer George Raft when they win a Cuban lottery with duplicated tickets. When his partner refuses to go on at their Broadway opening, Lombard steps in to dance the big number with him.

Irene Bullock / MY MAN GODFREY, 1936, Universal, d-Gregory La Cava.

In this screwball Depression comedy, scatterbrained Lombard finds a "forgotten man" (William Powell) at the city dump and brings him home as an item for a scavenger hunt. She installs him as the butler in her wealthy but eccentric family and as he takes control of the family she falls in love with him. It turns out that he's wealthier than they are. She finally gets him before a preacher and says: "Stand still, Godfrey. It'll all be over in a minute."

Hazel Flagg / NOTHING SACRED, 1937, United Artists, d-William Wellman.

When a doctor mistakenly diagnoses small-town Vermont girl Lombard as having only six months to live, a reporter for a New York paper brings her to the city and makes her a heroine. But it gets embarrassing for all concerned when she doesn't die. Lombard tries, really she does, saying: "Oh, let me alone. I wish I really could die, go someplace by myself and die alone, like an elephant."

Amy Peters / THEY KNEW WHAT THEY WANTED, 1940, RKO, d-Garson Kanin.

Lombard is a waitress who agrees to marry an Italian, California vineyard owner after a courtship through the mail. However, she is shocked to discover that he had sent the photograph of his handsome foreman because he was afraid she would never agree to the marriage otherwise. It's a lovely story that was later made into the musical opera "The Most Happy Fellow."

Ann Smith / MR. AND MRS. SMITH, 1941, RKO, d-Alfred Hitchcock.

Surprisingly, this amusing comedy about a much-married couple (Lombard and Robert Montgomery) who discover their marriage isn't legal was directed by the master of suspense, Alfred Hitchcock.

Maria Tura / TO BE OR NOT TO BE, 1942, United Artists, d-Ernst Lubitsch.

Lombard is a Polish actress married to a Shakespearean actor (Jack Benny) who, together with others in their troupe, must impersonate various Nazis including Hitler to escape Warsaw after the Germans take over the country in World War II.

OTHER ROLES

1921: *bit* / A PERFECT CRIME. **1925:** *Celia Hathaway* / MARRIAGE IN TRANSIT; *Sybil Estabrook* / HEARTS AND SPURS; *Ellen Boyd* / DURAND OF THE BADLANDS. **1928:** *Millie Claudert* / THE DIVINE SINNER; *another dame* / POWER; *Blonde Rosie* / ME, GANGSTER; *Cleo* / SHOW FOLKS; *Jennie* / NED MCCOBB'S DAUGHTER. **1929:** *Billie Davis* / HIGH VOLTAGE; *Marg Banks* / BIG NEWS. **1930:** *Rhoda Philbrook* / THE RACKETEER; *Virginia Hoyt* / THE ARIZONA KID; *Pauline* / SAFETY IN NUMBERS; *Alice O'Neil* / FAST AND LOOSE. **1931:** *Mary Grayson* / IT PAYS TO ADVERTISE; *Rachel Fendley* / LADIES' MAN; *Anne Merrick* / UP POPS THE DEVIL; *Kay Dowling* / I TAKE THIS WOMAN. **1932:** *Penelope Newbold* / NO ONE MAN; *Doris Blake* / SINNERS IN THE SUN; *Mae* / VIRTUE; *Anne Holt* / NO MORE ORCHIDS. **1933:** *Colly Tanner* / FROM HELL TO HEAVEN; *Roma Courtney* / SUPERNATURAL; *the beautiful lady* / THE EAGLE AND THE HAWK; *Abby Fane* / BRIEF MOMENT; *Judith Denning* / WHITE WOMAN. **1934:** *Toni Carstairs* / NOW AND FOREVER; *Mary Magiz* / THE GAY BRIDE. **1935:** *Regi Allen* / HANDS ACROSS THE TABLE. **1936:** *Kay Colby* / LOVE BEFORE BREAKFAST; *Princess Olga* / THE PRINCESS COMES ACROSS. **1937:** *Maggie King* / SWING HIGH, SWING LOW; *Helen Bartlett* / TRUE CONFESSION. **1938:** *Kay Winters* / FOOLS FOR SCANDAL. **1939:** *Jane Mason* / MADE FOR EACH OTHER; *Julie Eden* / IN NAME ONLY. **1940:** *Anne Lee* / VIGIL IN THE NIGHT.

LOY, MYRNA

(Myrna Williams, 1905–)

Myrna Loy started her professional career as a chorus girl at Grauman's Chinese Theatre at the age of 18. She later found herself being offered small parts as exotic, half-caste, mysterious sirens because of her slightly oriental appearance and her languid almond-shaped green eyes. She was stuck in such roles until she made her first of 13 films with William Powell, MANHATTAN MELODRAMA, which was followed by the first of the "Thin Man" series. From then on Loy, who was dubbed "The Queen of the Movies" when Clark Gable was named "King," became the perfect screen wife—witty, tolerant, beautiful, resourceful, loyal, sexy, and just looney enough to be really interesting. After World War II she appeared less frequently but usually as a sophisticated woman whose beauty was as great in middle-age as it had been when she was a femme fatale.

KEY ROLES

Queen Morgan Le Fay / A CONNECTICUT YANKEE, 1931, Fox Films, d-David Butler.

When 19th-century Connecticut blacksmith Will Rogers dreams himself back in the court of King Arthur his greatest enemies are Merlin and the beautiful but evil Morgan Le Fay (Loy).

Countess Valentine / LOVE ME TONIGHT, 1932, Paramount, d-Rouben Mamoulian.

In this comedy musical, Loy makes it perfectly clear that she is available for all male comers, but no one seems to be listening as all the men pass her up and fall all over themselves for the star of the piece, Jeanette MacDonald. When the latter faints, Loy is asked if she can go for a doctor. She replies, "Sure, send him in."

Fah Lo See / THE MASK OF FU MANCHU, 1932, MGM, d-Charles Brabin.

In one of her many roles as an Oriental, Loy portrays the evil daughter of Fu Manchu. She's a nymphomaniacal sadist but she makes her way of killing a man look like fun.

Cecilia Henry / THE ANIMAL KINGDOM, 1932, RKO, d-Edward H. Griffith.

For a change, Loy is the proper woman in the film. She is married to intellectual publisher Leslie Howard and she is mortified by some of his activities. Realizing the marriage is a mistake, he takes up again with Ann Harding, the artist he once loved, and tries to argue that a man should be allowed to have both a wife and a mistress.

Mary Howard / WHEN LADIES MEET, 1933, MGM, d-Harry Beaumont.

Loy and Ann Harding exchange roles in this smart comedy. This time Ann is the wife and Loy the novelist mistress of Harding's husband. The two clash nicely when, as the title suggests, they meet.

Nora Charles / THE THIN MAN, 1934, MGM, d-W. S. Van Dyke II.

Loy and William Powell first worked together in MANHATTAN MELODRAMA and fans sensed a fine chemistry. In this first of six teamings of them as Nick and Nora Charles, they established the easy relationship that made the series so successful. The mysteries they were called upon to solve, as in this case the disappearance of the title character, weren't what brought in the audiences, but rather the clever things the loving couple said to each other and others in the cast.

Evelyn Prentice / EVELYN PRENTICE, 1934, MGM, d-William K. Howard.

Appearing again with William Powell, Loy is the wife of a criminal lawyer. She has an affair with a man who then tries to blackmail her husband. When she kills him she finds it handy to have such a smart attorney husband.

Alice / BROADWAY BILL, 1934, Columbia, d-Frank Capra.

Loy is the independent sister-in-law of Warner Baxter, who has bolted the wealthy family he has married into to make a champ out of a racing horse named Broadway Bill. She helps him train the horse and win the big race, and the two fall in love.

Linda Stanhope / WIFE VS. SECRETARY, 1936, MGM, d-Clarence Brown.

Loy starts believing the rumors that her husband (Clark Gable) may be having an affair with his secretary (Jean Harlow). Of course there's not a word of truth to it.

Billie Burke / THE GREAT ZIEGFELD, 1936, MGM, d-Robert Z. Leonard.

Loy portrays the second wife of great showman Florenz Ziegfeld (portrayed by her favorite leading man, William Powell). As Flo is quite the lady's man, she has to be most understanding.

Margit Agnew / DOUBLE WEDDING, 1937, MGM, d-Richard Thorpe.

Once again Loy is teamed with William Powell in this zany comedy about a domineering sister (Loy) who also runs her sibling's fiancé. Enter Powell as an artist who encourages the young couple to revolt and, upon meeting Loy, falls in love with her on first sight and undertakes to tame this unapproachable woman.

Ann Barton / TEST PILOT, 1938, MGM, d-Victor Fleming.

Loy is married to pilot Clark Gable and she worries every time he takes his plane up to do his aerobatics as he tests advances in aviation. But it is their good friend, mechanic Spencer Tracy, who gets killed.

Lady Edwina Esketh / THE RAINS CAME, 1939, 20th Century-Fox, d-Clarence Brown.

Loy is an English lady who is romantically attracted to a young Indian aristocrat (Tyrone Power) who has recently returned from America to set up a medical practice among the needy people of Ranchipur. She and other useless British parasites prove their mettle after a gigantic flood and earthquake.

Susan Ireland / LOVE CRAZY, 1941, MGM, d-Jack Cummings.

When Loy threatens to divorce William Powell, he resorts to all kinds of tricks to keep her, including dressing as his own sister. It's a hilarious comedy with Loy and Powell in top form.

Millie Stephenson / THE BEST YEARS OF OUR LIVES, 1947, Goldwyn, d-William Wyler.

In one of the best movies ever made, Loy portrays the wife of Frederic March, one of three ex-servicemen whose adjustment to civilian life after coming home from World War II is examined with great intelligence and sensitivity.

Muriel Blandings / MR. BLANDINGS BUILDS HIS DREAM HOUSE, 1948, RKO, d-H. C. Potter.

This comedy is still enjoyable today although the prices that Cary Grant and wife Loy must pay to build their dream house in the Connecticut country seem like chicken feed. The interplay among Grant, Loy, and Melvyn Douglas as an ex-suitor who still very much admires Loy, is excellent.

Ann Gilbreth / CHEAPER BY THE DOZEN, 1950, 20th Century-Fox, d-Walter Lang.

Loy and her husband (Clifton Webb) are efficiency experts and need to be to raise their twelve children.

OTHER ROLES

1925: *bit* / PRETTY LADIES. **1926:** *bit* / BEN-HUR; *maid* / THE CAVE MAN; *Maja* / DON JUAN; *Roma* / ACROSS THE PACIFIC; *Sally Short* / WHY GIRLS GO BACK HOME; *living statue* / THE EXQUISITE SINNER; *the vamp* / FINGER PRINTS; *Irene Quartz* / THE GILDED HIGHWAY; *maid* / SO THIS IS PARIS. **1927:** *Countess Veya* / THE CLIMBERS; *Belinda White* / BITTER APPLES; *Claudette Ralston* / A SAILOR'S SWEETHEART; *Mary Carlton* / THE GIRL FROM CHICAGO; *Fifi* / HAM AND EGGS AT THE FRONT; *Mulatta* / THE HEART OF MARYLAND; *Edith Van* / SIMPLE SIS; *chorus girl* / THE JAZZ SINGER. **1928:** *vamp* / WHAT PRICE BEAUTY; *Tiza Torreon* / TURN BACK THE HOURS; *Onoto* / CRIMSON CITY; *Yvonne De Russo* / PAY AS YOU ENTER; *Joan Whitley* / IF I WERE SINGLE; *Juanita Sheldon* / BEWARE OF MARRIED MEN; *Isobel* / *State Street Sadie* / STATE STREET SADIE; *Gertie Fairfax* / THE MIDNIGHT TAXI. **1929:** *dancer* / *slave girl* / NOAH'S ARK; *Myrna* / FANCY BAGGAGE; *Azuri* / THE DESERT SONG; *Nubi* / THE SQUALL; *Yassmini* / BLACK WATCH; *Rose Duhamel* / HARDBOILED ROSE; *native girl* / EVIDENCE; *guest* / SHOW OF SHOWS. **1930:** *Manuella* / THE GREAT DIVIDE; *Mildred Vane* / THE JAZZ CINDERELLA; *Lea* / CAMEO KIRBY; *Moira* / ISLE OF ESCAPE; *Lolita Romero* / UNDER A TEXAS MOON; *Narita* / COCK O' THE WALK; *Sophie* / BRIDE OF THE REGIMENT; *Lola* / LAST OF THE DUANES; *Kara, the Firefly* / THE TRUTH ABOUT YOUTH; *Eleanore* / RENEGADES; *Carmita* / ROGUE OF THE RIO GRANDE; *Susan Hale* / THE DEVIL TO PAY. **1931:** *Linda Gregory* / THE NAUGHTY FLIRT; *Alice Lester* / BODY AND SOUL; *Flo Curtis* / HUSH MONEY; *Kay Graham* / TRANSATLANTIC; *Evie Lawrence* / REBOUND; *Paula Lambert* / SKYLINE; *Elaine* / CONSOLATION MARRIAGE; *Joyce Lanyon* / ARROWSMITH. **1932:** *Isabelle* / EMMA; *Eileen Pinchon* / THE WET PARADE; *Becky Sharp* / VANITY FAIR; *Sari Loder* / THE WOMAN IN ROOM 13; *Myra* / NEW MORALS FOR OLD; *Ursula Georgi* / THIRTEEN WOMEN. **1933:** *Coco* / TOPAZE; *Diana* / THE BARBARIAN; *Belle Morgan* / THE PRIZEFIGHTER AND THE LADY; *Gertie Waxted* / PENTHOUSE; *Brazilian pilot's wife* / NIGHT FLIGHT. **1934:** *Laura* / MEN IN WHITE; *Eleanor Packer* / MANHATTAN MELODRAMA; *Annemarie "Fraulein Doktor"* / STAMBOUL QUEST. **1935:** *Sheila Mason* / WINGS IN THE DARK; *Vivian Palmer* / WHIPSAW. **1936:** *Irene Campton* / PETTICOAT FEVER; *Mary Wallace* / TO MARY—WITH LOVE; *Connie Allenbury* / LIBELED LADY; *Nora Charles* / AFTER THE THIN MAN. **1937:** *Katie O'Shea* / PARNELL. **1938:** *Mimi Swift* / MAN-PROOF; *Wilma Harding* / TOO HOT TO HANDLE. **1939:** *Cora Jordan* / LUCKY NIGHT; *Margot Sherwood Merrick* / THIRD FINGER, LEFT HAND; *Nora Charles* / ANOTHER THIN MAN. **1940:** *Kay Wilson* / I LOVE YOU AGAIN. **1941:** *Nora Charles* / SHADOW OF THE THIN MAN. **1944:** *Nora Charles* / THE THIN MAN GOES HOME. **1946:** *Jane* / SO GOES MY LOVE. **1947:** *Margaret Turner* / THE BACHELOR AND THE BOBBY SOXER; *Nora Charles* / SONG OF THE THIN MAN; *Mrs. Ashton* / THE SENATOR WAS INDISCREET. **1949:** *Alice Tiflin* / THE RED PONY. **1952:** *Ann Gilbreth* / BELLES ON THEIR TOES. **1956:** *Mrs. Cartwright* / THE AMBASSADOR'S DAUGHTER. **1958:** *Florence Shrike* / LONELYHEARTS. **1960:** *Martha Eaton* / FROM THE TERRACE; *Aunt Bea* / MIDNIGHT LACE. **1969:** *Grace Greenlaw* / THE APRIL FOOLS. **1974:** *Mrs. Devaney* / AIRPORT 1975. **1979:** *Maureen Lawson* / THE END. **1980:** *Stella Liberti* / JUST TELL ME WHAT YOU WANT.

LUPINO, IDA

(1918–)

Ida Lupino's theatrical roots trace back to the 17th century and her parents were British actor Stanley Lupino and actress Connie Emerald. She made her stage debut at the age of twelve and was an extra in the films of British International Studios in the late 1920s. In her first real movie role she played the Lolita-like adulterous flapper in HER FIRST AFFAIR, a role her mother had auditioned for. She signed a contract with Paramount and after her success as the vulnerable and rage-filled prostitute model in THE LIGHT THAT FAILED, she signed with Warner Brothers where she appeared as dubious, hard women, frequently from the wrong side of the tracks. Lupino became an American citizen in 1948 and, unsatisfied with her career, referred to herself as "the poor man's Bette Davis," and turned to screenwriting, directing, and producing. She competently directed second features and, with Dick Powell, Charles Boyer, and David Niven, formed Four Star Productions to make shows for television. Lupino's female roles were often women on the verge of hysteria, or at least of great nervousness—humorless, frail, and tentative, racy but respectable.

KEY ROLES

Ann Brandon / THE ADVENTURES OF SHERLOCK HOLMES, 1939, 20th Century-Fox, d-Alfred Werker.

In order to carry out his plan to steal the British Crown Jewels, Professor Moriarity first performs two murders to keep Sherlock Holmes busy in other directions. One murder involves young Lupino who is menaced by a clubfooted gaucho.

Bessie Broke / THE LIGHT THAT FAILED, 1939, Paramount, d-William Wellman.

Lupino is the cockney model who, in a fit of jealousy, splashes the masterpiece of an almost blind artist (Ronald Colman) with turpentine. This film established Lupino as a dramatic star. Her desire for Colman is so intensely portrayed that audiences were stunned by her passion.

Lana Carson / THEY DRIVE BY NIGHT, 1940, Warners, d-Raoul Walsh.

Lupino is the scheming, murderous wife of a trucking baron who gets truck driver George Raft involved in her plot because he thinks she loves him. Her mad act while confessing that she caused the asphyxiation of husband Alan Hale is something to behold: "He was laughing. Yes, he—he was laughing. He kissed me when he was drunk. Yes, he kissed me when he was drunk. So I got a new car, and I bought some new clothes. Yes, pretty. And he—he used to tell terrible jokes, and he'd laugh at them. He was always laughing. Then I saw him lying there, drunk and I heard the motor running. Then I saw the doors, and I heard the motor. I saw the doors. The doors made me do it. Yes, the doors made me do it. The doors made me do it. The doors made me do it."

Marie Garson / HIGH SIERRA, 1941, Warners, d-Raoul Walsh.

When aging Humphrey Bogart, just out of prison, is given the assignment of pulling one last big job for his old boss, he discovers that his accomplices are two green kids who have brought along Lupino to their mountain hideout. She soon tires of being fought over and hit by the two hoods and is more than a little impressed with Bogart's criminal record. This respect turns to love and she's the only one who cries for him when he's hunted down and killed like a mad dog.

Ruth Webster / THE SEA WOLF, 1941, Warners, d-Michael Curtiz.

Lupino supplies the love interest for John Garfield's character in this story of a mentally disturbed captain of a bad ship ("Ghost") who picks up some victims of a ferryboat accident in San Francisco Bay and treats them as prisoners.

Ellen Creed / LADIES IN RETIREMENT, 1941, Columbia, d-Charles Vidor.

Lupino is the housekeeper for a wealthy elderly woman. She is allowed to bring her two strange sisters to live with them, but when they become more than the old lady can stand, she orders them out of the house. Rather than see her siblings in an institution, Lupino murders her employer and hides the fact. All goes well, until a blackmailing relative of the deceased shows up.

Helen Chernen / THE HARD WAY, 1942, Warners, d-Vincent Sherman.

The movie opens with Lupino about to commit suicide. Stopped by a policeman, she explains her decision and in flashbacks we learn how she tried to carve out a successful show business career for her sister (Joan Leslie) and ended up alienating everyone, including sis.

Emily Brontë / DEVOTION, 1946, Warners, d-Curtis Bernhardt.

In one of Hollywood's many absurd biopics of literary people, Lupino is adequate in the role of the author of *Jane Eyre*, but her life is nowhere as interesting as her heroine's.

Lily Stevens / ROAD HOUSE, 1948, 20th Century-Fox, d-Jean Negulesco.

Lupino does her own singing in this intriguing film noir and her rendition of "Again" is just right for this moody picture. She falls in love with Cornel Wilde, the manager of the road house where she works, but the owner (Richard Widmark) wants her for himself. He frames Wilde on a robbery charge and gets him released into his custody. He tries to get Wilde to run away so he can kill him, but Lupino ends up doing the honors to Widmark.

Mrs. Gordon / BEWARE, MY LOVELY, 1952, RKO, d-Harry Horner.

The handyman (Robert Ryan) whom Lupino hires turns out to be a mental defective who imprisons and threatens to rape and murder her and then forgets what he has planned to do, and asks her what jobs she wants him to do around the house.

Amelia Van Zandt / WOMEN'S PRISON, 1955, Columbia, d-Lewis Seiter.

Lupino is the villain of this study of conditions in women's prisons. She is the warden who is a borderline psychopath, who takes out her anger at the fact that she has never been able to hit it off with men, on her prison inmates.

Elvira Bonner / JUNIOR BONNER, 1972, ABC / Booth, d-Sam Peckinpah.

Lupino is the mother of aging rodeo star Steve McQueen and the estranged wife of Robert Preston, an old reprobate. Nothing important happens, but families often are like that.

OTHER ROLES

1933: *Anne* / HER FIRST AFFAIRE; *Jane* / MONEY FOR SPEED; *Jill* / HIGH FINANCE; *Mary Elton* / THE GHOST CAMERA. **1934:** *Ada Wallis* / I LIVED WITH YOU; *Princess* / PRINCE OF ARCADIA; *Barbara Hilton* / SEARCH FOR BEAUTY; *Esther Smith-Hamilton* / COME ON MARINES; *Marigold Tate* / READY FOR LOVE. **1935:** *Mignon de Charelle* / PARIS IN SPRING; *Pat Reynolds* / SMART GIRL; *Agnes* / PETER IBBETSON. **1936:** *Hope Harcourt* / ANYTHING GOES; *Monique Pelerin* / ONE RAINY AFTERNOON; *Gert Malloy* / YOURS FOR THE ASKING; *Jane* / THE GAY DESPERADO. **1937:** *Doris Malone* / SEA DEVILS; *Paula Quinn* / LET'S GET MARRIED; *Paula* / ARTISTS AND MODELS; *Marietta* / FIGHT FOR YOUR LADY. **1939:** *Val Carson* / THE LONE WOLF SPY HUNT; *Lila Thorne* / THE LADY AND THE MOB. **1941:** *Stella Goodwin* / OUT OF THE FOG. **1942:** *Anna* / MOONTIDE; *Kathi Thomas* / LIFE BEGINS AT EIGHT-THIRTY. **1943:** *Jenny* / FOREVER AND A DAY; *guest* / THANK YOUR LUCKY STARS. **1944:** *Jennifer Whittredge* / IN OUR TIME; *guest* / HOLLYWOOD CANTEEN. **1945:** *Jean Howard* / PILLOW TO POST. **1947:** *Petey Brown* / THE MAN I LOVE; *Libby* / DEEP VALLEY; *Gemma Smith* / ESCAPE ME NEVER. **1949:** *Julia Thomas* / LUST FOR GOLD. **1950:** *Deborah Chandler Clark* / WOMAN IN HIDING. **1951:** *Mary Malden* / ON DANGEROUS GROUND. **1953:** *Agnes Calley* / JENNIFER; *Phyllis Martin* / THE BIGAMIST. **1954:** *Lilli Marlowe* / PRIVATE HELL 36. **1955:** *Marion Castle* / THE BIG KNIFE. **1956:** *Mildred Donner* / WHILE THE CITY SLEEPS; *Alice* / STRANGE INTRUDER. **1974:** *herself* / DEADHEAD MILES. **1975:** *Mrs. Preston* / THE DEVIL'S RAIN. **1976:** *Mrs. Skinner* / FOOD OF THE GODS. **1978:** *mother* / MY BOYS ARE GOOD BOYS.

LYNN, DIANA

(Dolores Loehr, 1926–1971)

Diana Lynn was a musical child prodigy on the piano, playing with the Los Angeles Junior Symphony Orchestra. Her entry into films was by chance with her first two appearances featuring her musical talents, not her acting. With her pert, pretty looks, she made an appealing sassy younger sister to the star in several movies, but when she became an adult, her comedy ability and sweetness didn't get her anywhere. She retired from the screen in 1955, becoming a busy and successful TV performer.

KEY ROLES

Lucy Hill / THE MAJOR AND THE MINOR, 1942, Paramount, d-Billy Wilder.

Lynn has some good little sister lines in this story about Ginger Rogers, who dresses herself up as a 12-year-old so she can travel for half fare aboard a train. She is looked after by Ray Milland, the head of a military school for boys.

Emmy Kockenlocker / THE MIRACLE OF MORGAN'S CREEK, 1944, Paramount, d-Preston Sturges.

Lynn is the younger sister of Betty Hutton. Hutton finds herself pregnant and can't remember the name of the soldier with whom she was partying, so Lynn helps her convince Eddie Bracken to help her out by marrying her and being a father to the six sons that are on the way. Once again Lynn is given some of the best lines including, "Nobody believes good unless they have to, if they've got a chance to believe something bad."

Emily Kimbrough / OUR HEARTS WERE YOUNG AND GAY, 1944, Paramount, d-Lewis Allen.
This filming of the memoirs of actress Cornelia Otis Skinner and her friend Emily (Lynn) is innocent fun with no message and nothing of lasting importance except that two young girls had fun while visiting Paris in 1923.

Jane Stacy / MY FRIEND IRMA, 1949, Paramount, d-George Marshall.
Lynn plays straight woman to Marie Wilson's dumb blonde, but finds herself almost lost in the shuffle when Martin and Lewis, in their first movie, steal the show.

Jane / BEDTIME FOR BONZO, 1951, Universal-International, d-Frederick de Cordova.
Lynn co-stars with future president Ronald Reagan and the chimpanzee that professor Reagan intends to use to demonstrate that environment determines character by bringing the chimp up as a human baby. Lynn is a farmgirl who finds employment taking care of baby, and successfully breaks up Reagan's engagement to Lucille Barkley.

OTHER ROLES

As Dolly Loehr

1939: *girl at a piano* / THEY SHALL HAVE MUSIC. **1941:** *herself* / THERE'S MAGIC IN MUSIC. **1942:** *herself* / STAR SPANGLED RHYTHM.

As Diana Lynn

1943: *Phyllis Michael* / HENRY ALDRICH GETS GLAMOUR. **1944:** *Josie Angel* / AND THE ANGELS SING; *Phyllis Michael* / HENRY ALDRICH PLAYS CUPID. **1945:** *Betty Miller* / OUT OF THIS WORLD; *guest* / DUFFY'S TAVERN. **1946:** *Emily Kimbrough* / OUR HEARTS WERE GROWING UP; *Mary Lou Medford* / THE BRIDE WORE BOOTS. **1947:** *Connie Donovan* / EASY COME, EASY GO; *guest* / VARIETY GIRL. **1948:** *Martha Burnside* / *Mallory Flagg* / RUTHLESS; *Perry Dunklin* / TEXAS, BROOKLYN AND HEAVEN; *Julie Hudson* / EVERY GIRL SHOULD BE MARRIED. **1949:** *Nancy Langley* / PAID IN FULL. **1950:** *Jane Stacy* / MY FRIEND IRMA GOES WEST; *Lady Marianne* / ROGUES OF SHERWOOD FOREST; *Peggy Brookfield* / PEGGY. **1951:** *Ginny Curtayne* / THE PEOPLE AGAINST O'HARA. **1952:** *Zerelda Wing* / MEET ME AT THE FAIR. **1953:** *Julie Barnes* / PLUNDER OF THE SUN. **1954:** *Gwen Williams* / TRACK OF THE CAT. **1955:** *Peggy* / AN ANNAPOLIS STORY; *Susie* / THE KENTUCKIAN; *Nancy Collins* / YOU'RE NEVER TOO YOUNG.

MACDONALD, JEANETTE

(1901–1965)
While usually remembered for her teaming with Nelson Eddy, Jeanette MacDonald's best roles were opposite Maurice Chevalier and Clark Gable. She made her first stage appearance at the age of three. Nineteen years later the green-eyed, red-haired beauty made her film debut in a Lubitsch operetta, THE LOVE PARADE, opposite Chevalier. After three other films with the charming Frenchman, she signed with MGM. Shortly thereafter she was teamed with Eddy in several enjoyable if not very dramatic operettas in which the two sang their hearts out and tried to upstage each other. MacDonald, who insisted, "If ever I publish my memoirs they will be called,'The Iron Butterfly,'" usually won the battle.

KEY ROLES

Queen Louise of Sylvania / THE LOVE PARADE, 1929, Paramount, d-Ernst Lubitsch.
In her screen debut MacDonald plays a queen who, while waiting for her dream lover to come along, is informed of the sexual prowess of her foreign emissary (Maurice Chevalier) in Paris. She orders him home to prove himself and, satisfied with his lovemaking, she marries him. He's not pleased with his role and so she ups the ante by making him king. Her songs include "Dream Lover," "March of the Grenadiers," and, with Chevalier, "Anything to Please the Queen" and "My Love Parade," all by Victor Schertzinger and Clifford Grey.

Colette Bertier / ONE HOUR WITH YOU, 1932, Paramount, d-Ernst Lubitsch and George Cukor.
There's not much story here, except that two married couples go for each other's spouses, some more seriously than others. MacDonald's songs with Maurice Chevalier, by Oscar Strauss, Richard Whiting, and Leo Robin, include "We Will Always Be Sweethearts" and the title number.

Princess Jeanette / LOVE ME TONIGHT, 1932, Paramount, d-Rouben Mamoulian.
In this pure musical-comedy delight with songs by Richard Rodgers and Lorenz Hart, MacDonald is a French princess who suffers fainting spells because she needs to be made love to. Maurice Chevalier is a tailor introduced to her as a baron and she comes to realize he has the power to make her well. To ensure that she gets her man she chases a train while on horseback to prevent him from leaving her. Her songs include "Lover" and, with Chevalier, the title song.

Princess Marie (Marietta) / NAUGHTY MARIETTA, 1935, MGM, d-W. S. Van Dyke II.
MacDonald was Louis B. Mayer's favorite star and she repaid his admiration by teaming with Nelson Eddy to make this Victor Herbert picture a box-office success. She plays a French princess who finds love in Louisiana with a dashing mercenary. Her songs include "'Neath the Southern Moon," "Italian Street Song," and "Ah, Sweet Mystery of Life."

Marie de Flor / ROSE MARIE, 1936, MGM, d-W. S. Van Dyke II.
This version of the Rudolf Friml operetta is much different from that staged before and since with lyrics by Otto Harbach and Oscar Hammerstein II. In this version, MacDonald is a Canadian opera star who learns that her brother (James Stewart) is sought for murder. She sets out to find him in the northwest but runs into Mountie Nelson Eddy and a romance develops. Who will get to Stewart first? The songs include "Indian Love Call" and the title song.

Mary Blake / SAN FRANCISCO, 1936, MGM, d-W. S. Van Dyke II.
MacDonald takes a job singing in a Barbary Coast saloon run by Clark Gable. He puts her under personal contract and, when the Nob Hill swells find she has an operatic voice, Gable is at first unwilling to give her up. He eventually does, but after the earthquake of 1906 he is reunited with her, finally knowing how much she means to him. MacDonald gives stirring renditions of the title song by Bronislau Kaper,

enough to stay up late to hear her sing it in TV screenings of the picture.

Marcia Morney (Miss Morrison) / MAYTIME, 1937, MGM, d-Robert Z. Leonard.

Only "Will You Remember" remains from Sigmund Romberg's original score in this production with opera star MacDonald falling in love with a penniless singer (Nelson Eddy) who is shot and killed by her jealous impresario (John Barrymore). Other featured songs include "The Month of Maying" and "Love's Old Sweet Song."

Mary Robbins / SWEETHEARTS, 1938, MGM, d-W. S. Van Dyke II.

MacDonald and Nelson Eddy are placed in a contemporary setting for a change as a musical-comedy team in the sixth year of their hit Broadway show "Sweethearts" when an unscrupulous agent convinces them to leave it and go to Hollywood. That turns out badly for both their public and private lives. Their songs include the Victor Herbert title number, "Summer Serenade," and "Pretty as a Picture" by Herbert with lyrics by Bob Wright and Chet Forrest.

Marianne de Beaumanoir / NEW MOON, 1940, MGM, d-Robert Z. Leonard.

In a story very similar to that of NAUGHTY MARIETTA, MacDonald is a French aristocrat forced to flee to Louisiana where she falls for a pirate chief (Nelson Eddy). Their songs by Oscar Hammerstein II, Laurence Schwab, and Frank Mandel include "Lover Come Back to Me," "Softly as in a Morning Sunrise," "One Kiss," and "Wanting You."

Kathleen / Moonyean Clare / SMILIN' THROUGH, 1941, MGM, d-Frank Borzage.

MacDonald teams for the first time with her real-life husband Gene Raymond in this rather flat remake of the 1932 picture of three generations of problems caused when MacDonald is accidentally killed by a jealous suitor on her wedding day. Normally, something like that would take MacDonald out of the picture but not in this fantasy.

OTHER ROLES

1930: *Katherine de Vaucelles* / THE VAGABOND KING; *Countess Vera von Conti* / MONTE CARLO; *Joan Wood* / LET'S GO NATIVE; *Jenny Swanson* / THE LOTTERY BRIDE; *Carlotta Manson* / OH, FOR A MAN! **1931:** *Jeanne Drake* / DON'T BET ON WOMEN; *Annabelle Leigh* / ANNABELLE'S AFFAIRS. **1934:** *Shirley* / THE CAT AND THE FIDDLE; *Sonia* / THE MERRY WIDOW. **1937:** *Nina Maria Azara* / THE FIREFLY. **1938:** *Mary Robbins* / THE GIRL OF THE GOLDEN WEST. **1939:** *Mary Hale* / BROADWAY SERENADE. **1940:** *Sarah Millick* / BITTER SWEET. **1942:** *Anna Zador* / *Brigitta* / I MARRIED AN ANGEL; *Marcia Warren* / CAIRO. **1944:** *guest* / FOLLOW THE BOYS. **1948:** *Louise Rayton Morgan* / THREE DARING DAUGHTERS; *Helen Lorfield Winter* / THE SUN COMES UP.

MACLAINE, SHIRLEY

(Shirley Maclean Beaty, 1934–)

Shirley MacLaine's wide smile and pixieish face made her perfect for wholesome tomboys, or dumb, good-natured women in both comedies and dramas. Originally a dancer, she began in the chorus of "Oklahoma" and "Me and Juliet." In the best Hollywood tradition she got her chance when Carol Haney broke her leg. MacLaine went on in "The Pajama Game" and was signed soon thereafter by Hal Wallis who was in the audience. She made her film debut in a Hitchcock movie, THE TROUBLE WITH HARRY, in 1955 and has been nominated for Academy Awards for SOME CAME RUNNING, THE APARTMENT, IRMA LA DOUCE, and THE TURNING POINT, finally winning for a lesser performance in TERMS OF ENDEARMENT in 1983. Away from the screen, MacLaine has been outspoken and controversial in her political views and lately in her interest in reincarnation and out-of-body experiences. Speaking of her acting she has said: "In front of the cameras I have to be careful what I think because it all shows." MacLaine's brother is the talented actor and director Warren Beatty.

KEY ROLES

Jennifer Rogers / THE TROUBLE WITH HARRY, 1955, Paramount, d-Alfred Hitchcock.

In her film debut, MacLaine appears in this seldom seen Hitchcock comedy-thriller about a group of eccentrics, including MacLaine, that discovers a body—Harry—in a Vermont woods. They bury, disinter, and rebury it several times because they believe someone will think they had something to do with the death.

Princess Aouda / AROUND THE WORLD IN 80 DAYS, 1956, United Artists / Michael Todd, d-Michael Anderson.

MacLaine is an Indian princess whom Phineas Fogg has rescued from a funeral pyre on his eighty-day trip around the world. He takes her along for the rest of the journey.

Irene Molloy / THE MATCHMAKER, 1958, Paramount, d-Joseph Anthony.

MacLaine is the milliner that Yonkers businessman Paul Ford sees as his wife, but matchmaker Shirley Booth sees herself more suited for the role while fixing MacLaine up with Ford's clerk, Anthony Perkins.

Meg Wheeler / ASK ANY GIRL, 1959, MGM, d-Charles Walters.

In this predictable Cinderella story, receptionist MacLaine sets her cap for wealthy playboy Gig Young but settles for his more serious older brother, David Niven.

Simone Pistache / CAN-CAN, 1959, 20th Century-Fox, d-Walter Lang.

MacLaine is a Parisian nightclub owner and dancer whose performances of the outlawed can-can dance bring her to the attention of aristocratic judge Louis Jourdan. He wishes to take her away from all this, but she returns to her long-time lover (Frank Sinatra), a shady attorney.

Fran Kubelik / THE APARTMENT, 1960, United Artists, d-Billy Wilder.

When her affair with a married man (Fred MacMurray) goes bad, elevator girl MacLaine attempts suicide in the apartment of Jack Lemmon, a junior executive in the same company. He greatly admires MacLaine but his progress up the corporate ladder is greased by lending out his apartment to his superiors for their extramarital flings, and that includes the big boss, MacMurray, who uses it for his meetings with MacLaine.

Martha Dobie / THE CHILDREN'S HOUR, 1962, United Artists, d-William Wyler.

In this second filming of the play by Lillian Hellman, MacLaine and fellow teacher Audrey Hepburn find their lives in shambles when a vicious child spreads rumors that the two are lesbian lovers. MacLaine commits suicide because, even though nothing happened between the two women, she knows that on her part there is some truth to the accusation.

Irma La Douce / IRMA LA DOUCE, 1963, United Artists, d-Billy Wilder.

MacLaine is a Parisian prostitute, loved by a former gendarme (Jack Lemmon) who becomes her pimp. But because he hates sharing her with other men, he visits her in disguise as an English lord and becomes her only client. But this leads to other complications which almost cost Lemmon his head.

Charity Hope Valentine / SWEET CHARITY, 1968, Universal, d-Bob Fosse.

MacLaine gives a rousing performance as the New York taxi dancer who has a tough time finding true love. Unfortunately, only MacLaine, Paula Kelly, and Chita Rivera seem to know what to do with the material. The girls are great with the "Hey, Big Spender" number by Cy Coleman and Dorothy Fields.

Deedee Rodgers / THE TURNING POINT, 1977, 20th Century-Fox, d-Herbert Ross.

MacLaine is a retired ballet dancer who visits with her aging ex-colleague (Anne Bancroft) when The American Ballet Theatre comes to Oklahoma. MacLaine's daughter is a talented dancer looking for her break, which dancer Mikhail Baryshnikov supplies.

Eve Rand / BEING THERE, 1979, United Artists, d-Hal Ashby.

MacLaine is the young wife of an elderly financier (Melvyn Douglas) who insists on taking nonentity Peter Sellers to her mansion when her limousine slightly injures him. The illiterate, child-like Sellers is mistaken by everyone as a deep thinker and Douglas and MacLaine see him as her next husband when death comes to Douglas.

Aurora Greenway / TERMS OF ENDEARMENT, 1983, Paramount, d-James L. Brooks.

MacLaine won her Oscar for playing an eccentric widow who fights off various suitors, chooses to have an affair with a next door neighbor, retired astronaut Jack Nicholson, and fights with her beloved daughter (Debra Winger) whose marriage she continually interferes with. It ends tearfully when Winger dies of cancer.

OTHER ROLES

1956: *Bessie Sparrowbush* / ARTISTS AND MODELS. **1957:** *Virginia Duval* / HOT SPELL. **1958:** *Ginny Moorehead* / SOME CAME RUNNING; *Dell Payton* / THE SHEEPMAN. **1959:** *Sharon Kensington* / CAREER. **1960:** *tipsy girl cameo* / OCEAN'S ELEVEN. **1961:** *Katie Robbins* / ALL IN A NIGHT'S WORK; *Anna Vorontosov* / TWO LOVES. **1962:** *Lucy Dell (Yoko Mori)* / MY GEISHA. **1963:** *Gittel Mosca* / TWO FOR THE SEESAW. **1964:** *Louisa Foster* / WHAT A WAY TO GO! *Mae Jenkins* / THE YELLOW ROLLS ROYCE; *Jenny Ericson* / JOHN GOLDFARB, PLEASE COME HOME. **1966:** *Nicole Chang* / GAMBIT. **1967:** *Paulette / Maria Teresa / Linda / Edith / Eve Minou / Marie / Jeanne* / WOMAN TIMES SEVEN. **1968:** *Harriet Blossom* / THE BLISS OF MRS. BLOSSOM. **1969:** *Sister Sara* / TWO MULES FOR SISTER SARA. **1971:** *Sophie Brentwood* / DESPERATE CHARACTERS. **1972:** *Norah Benson* / THE POSSESSION OF JOEL DELANEY. **1973:** *guest* / THE YEAR OF THE WOMAN. **1980:** *Karen Evans* / A CHANGE OF SEASONS; *Evelyn* / LOVING COUPLES. **1984:** *Veronica* / CANNONBALL II.

MACMURRAY, FRED

(1908–)

Fred MacMurray began his show business career as a crooner and saxophone player with various bands. In 1934 he signed a contract with Paramount and had his first leading role with GRAND OLD GIRL in 1935. Good looking and versatile, this model for the comic book superhero Captain Marvel found himself playing lovable bumblers and romantic leads in numerous light farces and comedies in the 1930s and 1940s. His best dramatic roles were those in which he was a genial, spineless weakling exploited by others, with a voice that betrayed his lack of moral conviction. In the early 1960s he began the highly successful TV series "My Three Sons," which wasn't too demanding. He also found his movie career extended by the Disney studio, as he appeared in a series of family comedies in which he portrayed aging schlemiels. MacMurray never became a major star, but his 40 years of moviemaking helped him become one of Hollywood's most wealthy citizens. His first wife died in 1953 and a year later he married actress June Haver when she returned from a convent where she had gone to become a nun.

KEY ROLES

Peter Dawes / THE GILDED LILY, 1935, Paramount, d-Wesley Ruggles.

In his first of seven teamings with Claudette Colbert, MacMurray is a newspaper reporter and she's a stenographer. His favorite meeting place is a bench outside New York City's public library, where they have friendly arguments on many minor topics. He's in love with her, but she has ambitions to marry well. It seems she may get her wish when an English lord puts a rush on her, but she comes back to MacMurray.

Arthur Russell / ALICE ADAMS, 1935, RKO, d-George Stevens.

This version of the Booth Tarkington story about a social-climbing, small-time girl has a happy ending as MacMurray proposes to Katharine Hepburn despite her phoniness and the cloddish behavior of her family.

Jack Hale / TRAIL OF THE LONESOME PINE, 1936, Paramount, d-Henry Hathaway.

MacMurray portrays a stranger from the city who gets caught up in the lives of a primitive Kentucky mountain family that is feuding with a neighboring clan. He comes to love Sylvia Sidney, a member of the family he tries to educate.

Skid Johnson / SWING HIGH, SWING LOW, 1937, Paramount, d-Mitchell Leisen.

MacMurray trades his sax for a trumpet in this story of entertainers (MacMurray and Carole Lombard) stranded in Panama, who marry then split when he's offered a job on Broadway. Jealous of a singer, Lombard divorces him and he goes on the skids, then recovers and wins her back.

Kenneth Bartlett / TRUE CONFESSION, 1937, Paramount, d-Wesley Ruggles.

MacMurray portrays a struggling lawyer who becomes famous when he wins an acquittal for his wife (Carole Lombard), who has confessed to the murder of her boss. She has done nothing of the kind. She's just an uninhibited liar.

David Beebe / SING, YOU SINNERS, 1938, Paramount, d-Wesley Ruggles.

MacMurray is the hard-working brother of happy-go-lucky Bing Crosby, who loses all the money they make as a musical act with younger brother Donald O'Connor. They end up buying a horse that surprises all by winning a race.

Tom Verney / TAKE A LETTER, DARLING, 1942, Paramount, d-Mitchell Leisen.

MacMurray becomes a male secretary to advertising executive Rosalind Russell. The outcome is never in doubt, but the comedy along the way is quite entertaining.

Walter Neff / DOUBLE INDEMNITY, 1944, Paramount, d-Billy Wilder.

MacMurray is an insurance salesman whom Barbara Stanwyck seduces into murdering her older husband for the insurance he doesn't even know he has. Then she double-crosses him, having never really been interested in him as a lover. Her stepdaughter's boyfriend has that role. After MacMurray and Stanwyck shoot each other he has time to dictate his confession on a machine for his friend, claims investigator Edward G. Robinson.

Eddie Rickenbacker / CAPTAIN EDDIE, 1945, 20th Century-Fox, d-Lloyd Bacon.

MacMurray is passable in this rather flat biopic of World War I ace Eddie Rickenbacker who, while adrift on a life raft after his plane crashes in the Pacific, thinks back over his life in aviation.

Eddie York / Francis Pemberton / PARDON MY PAST, 1946, Columbia, d-Leslie Fenton.

In this fine comedy-drama, MacMurray plays dual roles: a man who unsuspectingly incurs the debts and problems of a famous but shady playboy, and the playboy himself.

Bob MacDonald / THE EGG AND I, 1947, Universal-International, d-Chester Erskine.

MacMurray convinces wife Claudette Colbert to abandon the city and take up life on a chicken farm. Neither know what they have let themselves in for, but with the help of Ma and Pa Kettle, they manage.

Mike Frye / CALLAWAY WENT THATAWAY, 1951, MGM, d-Melvin Frank and Norman Panama.

When an old-time cowboy star's films become a hit with a new generation of kids on television, promoter MacMurray must find someone to take the place of the now hopeless drunk.

Lt. Tom Keefer / THE CAINE MUTINY, 1954, Columbia, d-Edward Dmytryk.

Herman Wouk wrote the novel upon which the movie is based but, as José Ferrer toasts as he throws a glass of champagne in MacMurray's face, "Now, here's to the real author of 'The Caine Mutiny.' Here's to you, Mr. Keefer." MacMurray deserves the salute because as a pseudo-intellectual, he convinces mere simple folk like Van Johnson that the captain (Humphrey Bogart) is crazy and incompetent to run the ship. So, during a typhoon Johnson takes over command of the ship from Bogart. At Johnson's trial for mutiny, MacMurray's testimony is that he didn't know what was going on.

Paul Sheridan / PUSHOVER, 1954, Columbia, d-Richard Quine.

MacMurray is an honest cop who falls in love with a gangster's moll (Kim Novak) and finds himself involved with murder.

Wilson Daniels / THE SHAGGY DOG, 1959, Disney, d-Charles Barton.

MacMurray is the father of a boy who turns into a big shaggy dog and, although he's never liked dogs before, he doesn't seem to mind the change in his son.

J. D. Sheldrake / THE APARTMENT, 1960, United Artists, d-Billy Wilder.

MacMurray is the big boss of a New York company who uses the apartment of junior executive Jack Lemmon to meet with his lover (Shirley MacLaine) whom Lemmon also fancies. She sees her affair with MacMurray going nowhere and that's just the direction MacMurray wants it to go. He is undone, though, by a former lover who squeals on him to his wife.

Prof. Ned Brainard / THE ABSENT MINDED PROFESSOR, 1961, Disney, d-Robert Stevenson.

MacMurray invents a lighter-than-air substance he calls flubber. He applies it to the tires of his model-T and the car is able to fly, which comes in handy when he captures some spies.

OTHER ROLES

1929: *extra* / GIRLS GONE WILD; *rancher* / TIGER ROSE. **1935:** *Sandy* / GRAND OLD GIRL; *Ross Martin* / CAR 99; *Richard Hood* / *Richard "Dick" Grant* / MEN WITHOUT NAMES; *Theodore Drew III* / THE BRIDE COMES HOME. **1936:** *Jack Gordon* / THIRTEEN HOURS BY AIR; *King Mantell* / THE PRINCESS COMES ACROSS; *Jim Hawkins* / THE TEXAS RANGERS. **1937:** *Roger Coverman* / MAID OF SALEM; *Buzzy Bellew* / CHAMPAGNE WALTZ; *Ralph Houston* / EXCLUSIVE. **1938:** *Johnny Prentice* / COCOANUT GROVE; *Pat Falconer* / MEN WITH WINGS. **1939:** *Chick O'Bannion* / CAFE SOCIETY; *Albert "King" Cole* / INVITATION TO HAPPINESS; *Bill Burnett* / HONEYMOON IN BALI. **1940:** *John Sargent* / REMEMBER THE NIGHT; *Charles Browne* / LITTLE OLD NEW YORK; *Bill Cardew* / TOO MANY HUSBANDS; *Gil Farra* / RANGERS OF FORTUNE. **1941:** *Stonewall Elliott* / VIRGINIA; *Dwight Houston* / ONE NIGHT IN LISBON; *Victor Ballard* / NEW YORK TOWN; *Cmdr. Joe Blake* / DIVE BOMBER. **1942:** *Dr. Corey McBain* / THE LADY IS WILLING; *Don Stuart* / THE FOREST RANGERS; *cameo* / STAR SPANGLED RHYTHM. **1943:** *Randy Britton* / FLIGHT FOR FREEDOM; *Richard Myles* / ABOVE SUSPICION; *Jim Ryan* / NO TIME FOR LOVE. **1944:** *Lee Stevens* / STANDING ROOM ONLY; *Happy Morgan* / AND THE ANGELS SING; *Lt. Daniel Bellamy* / PRACTICALLY YOURS. **1945:** *Pete Marshall* / MURDER, HE SAYS; *Bill* / WHERE DO WE GO FROM HERE? **1946:** *Clint Barkley* / SMOKY. **1947:** *Peter Morley* / SUDDENLY IT'S SPRING; *Matt Gordon* / SINGAPORE. **1948:** *Al* / ON OUR MERRY WAY; *Bill Dunnigan* / THE MIRACLE OF THE BELLS; *Vincent Doane* / DON'T TRUST YOUR HUSBAND; *Grant Jordan* / FAMILY HONEYMOON. **1949:** *George Cooper* / FATHER WAS A FULLBACK. **1950:** *Johnny Macklin* / BORDERLINE; *Chris* / NEVER A DULL MOMENT. **1951:** *Peter Lockwood* / A MILLIONAIRE FOR CHRISTY. **1953:** *Captain Boll* / FAIR WIND TO JAVA. **1954:** *Sid* / WOMAN'S WORLD. **1955:** *Meriwether Lewis* / THE FAR HORIZONS; *Tom Ransome* / THE RAINS OF RANCHIPUR; *Jack Wright* / AT GUNPOINT. **1956:** *Clifford Groves* / THERE'S ALWAYS TOMORROW. **1957:** *Will Keough* / GUN FOR A COWARD; *Gentry* / *John Coventry* / QUANTEZ. **1958:** *Jim Scott* / DAY OF THE BAD MAN; *Ben Cutler* / GOOD DAY FOR A HANGING. **1959:** *Jim Larsen (Kincaid)* / FACE OF A FUGITIVE; *Neal Harris* / THE OREGON TRAIL. **1962:** *Harry Willard* / BON VOYAGE! **1963:** *Prof. Ned Brainard* / SON OF FLUBBER. **1964:** *Thad McCloud* / KISSES FOR MY PRESIDENT. **1966:** *Lemuel Siddons* / FOLLOW ME, BOYS! **1967:** *Anthony J. Drexel Biddle* / THE HAPPIEST MILLIONAIRE. **1973:** *Charley Appleby* / CHARLEY AND THE ANGEL. **1978:** *Clarence* / THE SWARM.

MACRAE, GORDON

(1921–1986)

Actor, singer, performer from childhood, and band vocalist in the 1940s, Gordon MacRae landed a singing lead on Broadway in 1949. He went to Hollywood and, after a non-singing debut, made his first movie musical, LOOK FOR THE SILVER LINING, in 1949. This was followed by a number of musicals co-starring Doris Day. Handsome and clean-cut, MacRae scored heavily with the musicals OKLAHOMA and CAROUSEL, but by 1956 the days of Hollywood musicals were over and he concentrated on a nightclub and stage singing career. His only film after 1956 was a low-budget picture directed by Cliff Robertson, THE PILOT (1979), that was released on a limited basis and seen by very few.

KEY ROLES

Frank Carter / LOOK FOR THE SILVER LINING, 1949, Warners, d-David Butler.

It was his first musical and MacRae's performance matches everyone else's in this dull biopic of Marilyn Miller, the famous musical star—inadequate. He portrays Miller's first husband and one can see why the two divorced.

William Sherman / ON MOONLIGHT BAY, 1951, Warners, d-Roy Del Ruth.

There is little magic in this version of the Penrod stories by Booth Tarkington, concentrating as it does on the dull romance of Doris Day and the boy next door (MacRae). With a little help from other members of the family, they sing the old songs "Pack Up Your Troubles," "Cuddle Up a Little Closer," "I'm Forever Blowing Bubbles," and the title number.

Curley / OKLAHOMA! 1955, Magna / Rodgers and Hammerstein, d-Fred Zinnemann.

MacRae is at his best as the likable bragging cowboy who wins farm girl Shirley Jones despite the menace of hired man Rod Steiger. His songs include "Oh, What a Beautiful Morning," and with Jones, "Surrey with the Fringe on Top," "People Will Say We're in Love," and a rousing version of the title song.

Billy Bigelow / CAROUSEL, 1956, 20th Century-Fox, d-Henry King.

MacRae is a carnival barker who marries Maine mill worker Shirley Jones, treats her badly, and when she announces that she is pregnant, decides he must get some money and is killed in an attempted robbery. Years later he is allowed to return to earth to redeem himself by helping his now grown-up daughter. MacRae does a nice job on Rodgers and Hammerstein's "Soliloquy" and with Jones in "If I Loved You."

OTHER ROLES

1948: *Johnny Grant* / THE BIG PUNCH. **1949:** *Bob Corey* / BACKFIRE. **1950:** *Tony Pastor* / THE DAUGHTER OF ROSIE O'GRADY; *Logan Barrett* / RETURN OF THE FRONTIERSMAN; *Jimmy Smith* / TEA FOR TWO; *Tom Fletcher* / WEST POINT STORY. **1951:** *guest* / STARLIFT. **1952:** *Tony Williams* / ABOUT FACE. **1953:** *William Sherman* / BY THE LIGHT OF THE SILVERY MOON; *choir boy Jones* / THREE SAILORS AND A GIRL; *Paul Bonnard (El Khobar)* / THE DESERT SONG. **1956:** *B. G. DeSylvia* / THE BEST THINGS IN LIFE ARE FREE.

MARCH, FREDRIC

(Frederick M. Bickel, 1897–1975)

Fredric March saw acting as hard work in which one's role is carefully studied and lines are learned early. This accomplished, March then grew into his character without any appeal to method acting, which he disdained. After serving as an artillery officer during World War I he became a stage actor, touring with the Theatre Guild Repertory Company. In 1928 Paramount hired him to make talking pictures with his first major role being a takeoff of John Barrymore in THE ROYAL FAMILY OF BROADWAY. After the expiration of his contract with Paramount he preferred to freelance in order to choose his own parts. Most of the time he chose wisely. March received Oscar nominations for THE ROYAL FAMILY OF BROADWAY, A STAR IS BORN, and DEATH OF A SALESMAN. He won the Academy Award for DR. JEKYLL AND MR. HYDE and THE BEST YEARS OF OUR LIVES. March was one of the few actors whose film and stage careers developed simultaneously, with his most notable stage triumph being "Long Day's Journey into Night." The length of his career matched his marriage to actress Florence Eldridge, whom he wed in 1927. As a young actor he played a wide variety of leading roles in various genres. In middle-age, he found a comfortable niche in character roles. When he retired, he joked, "Let me confirm that I have definitely retired. Not, however, as definitely as James Cagney." He was wrong. Cagney came back to films, but not so March.

KEY ROLES

Tony Cavendish / THE ROYAL FAMILY OF BROADWAY, 1930, Paramount, d-George Cukor.

March repeats the wicked impersonation of John Barrymore that won him a screen contract after his success on Broadway in this sophisticated comedy. It's about the off-stage escapades of a famous theatrical family. The Barrymores were not amused.

Dr. Henry Jekyll / Mr. Hyde / DR. JEKYLL AND MR. HYDE, 1931, Paramount, d-Rouben Mamoulian.

Handsome Dr. Jekyll (March) is transformed into grinning, ape-like Mr. Hyde by gradual camera exposures. March shared an Oscar with Wallace Beery (for THE CHAMP), who had one less vote for Best Actor, but the Academy called it a tie.

Kenneth Wayne / Jeremy Wayne / SMILIN' THROUGH, 1932, MGM, d-Sidney Franklin.

March plays both the jealous rejected suitor who kills Norma Shearer while aiming for Leslie Howard on the latter's wedding day, and a descendant years later who wishes to marry a Shearer look-alike, an arrangement that doesn't sit well with Howard. But he checks with the deceased Shearer's spirit, and she convinces him to give his blessing.

Marcus Superbus / THE SIGN OF THE CROSS, 1932, Paramount, d-Cecil B. DeMille.

Claudette Colbert is the wicked wife of Nero who lusts after March, a Roman officer, but he has fallen in love with Christian Elissa Landi, and for this affront he is allowed to join his beloved in an arena full of lions.

Prince Sirki / DEATH TAKES A HOLIDAY, 1934, Paramount, d-Mitchell Leisen.

March is the personification that death takes when it decides to investigate why humans fear it so. While death is away from business, not a living thing on earth dies, but when it returns to work, death takes a willing Evelyn Venable with it.

Robert Browning / THE BARRETTS OF WIMPOLE STREET, 1934, MGM, d-Sidney Franklin.

March's plans to marry Elizabeth Barrett are met with obstinate opposition from her father who has an unhealthy affection for her. As the great poet, March seems right at home and his acting is only slightly stilted seen today.

Jean Valjean / LES MISÉRABLES, 1935, 20th Century-Fox, d-Richard Boleslawski.

March is superb as the unjustly sentenced wretch who spends years as a galley slave for stealing a loaf of bread to feed his sister's starving family. When he escapes, he starts life anew and becomes a wealthy, prominent citizen but is hounded by cruel and relentless Inspector Javert.

Count Alexei Vronsky / ANNA KARENINA, 1935, MGM, d-Clarence Brown.

March observed, "Co-starring with Garbo hardly constitutes an introduction." But then again the picture is Garbo's with March only the handsome Russian officer for whose love she gives up everything, including at last, her life.

Anthony Adverse / ANTHONY ADVERSE, 1936, Warners, d-Mervyn LeRoy.

In this rousing spectacle, March portrays a 19th-century young man whose many adventures mature him. Most people felt the 136 minutes aged them a bit also.

Norman Maine / A STAR IS BORN, 1937, Selznick / United Artists, d-William A. Wellman.

March is the alcoholic movie star whose career goes downhill just as his wife's (Janet Gaynor) star is ascending. Thinking himself a burden to her, he commits suicide by walking into the ocean. When Lionel Stander, a studio employee who had grown weary of making excuses for March's antics, hears of the suicide, he mourns not, callously observing: "First drink of water he had in 20 years and then he had to get it by accident. Bud, how do you wire congratulations to the Pacific Ocean?"

Wally Cook / NOTHING SACRED, 1937, Selznick / United Artists, d-William A. Wellman.

When Carole Lombard, who has been incorrectly diagnosed as dying of radium poisoning, expresses a desire to see New York City before she dies, she is brought to the Big Apple by wisecracking reporter March who falls for her, even when she doesn't die. March's editor, Walter Connolly, rages at his star reporter: "I am sitting here, Mr. Cook, toying with the idea of removing your heart and stuffing it—like an olive."

William Spence / ONE FOOT IN HEAVEN, 1941, Warners, d-Irving Rapper.

March gives a pious portrayal of a Methodist minister who spends a very good life moving from one parish to another. It's not exciting, but if one is in the mood for a little sentimentality this can't be beat.

Wallace Wooley / I MARRIED A WITCH, 1942, United Artists, d-Rene Clair.

March plays the descendant of the man who condemned witch Veronica Lake to be burnt at the stake. Her spirit is released in the 1940s and she seeks her revenge by causing March to fall in love with her.

Samuel Clemens / Mark Twain / THE ADVENTURES OF MARK TWAIN, 1944, Warners, d-Irving Rapper.

While March makes a convincing Mark Twain, the producers' decision to cram as much of the life of the great American humorist into the 130-minute picture as they could results in the audience's learning very little about the man.

Al Stephenson / THE BEST YEARS OF OUR LIVES, 1946, Samuel Goldwyn, d-William Wyler.

March is an army sergeant who returns home after serving in World War II. He finds it difficult to return to business as usual in his job as a bank official, but even though he lets his feelings show on occasion, he doesn't walk away from his job or the people who don't seem to understand what the war was all about. Frustrated, March complains: "Last year, it was Kill Japs. This year, it's Make Money." This is the film of which Sam Goldwyn said: "I don't care if it doesn't make a nickel. I just want every man, woman, and child in America to see it."

Willy Loman / DEATH OF A SALESMAN, 1951, Columbia, d-Laslo Benedek.

March portrays an aging traveling salesman who recognizes the emptiness of his life and commits suicide. His wife (Mildred Dunnock) pleads with her uncaring sons as she sees the man she has loved so long slowly falling apart: "Attention must finally be paid to such a man. He's not to be allowed to fall into his grave like an old dog."

Loren Phineas Shaw / EXECUTIVE SUITE, 1954, MGM, d-Robert Wise.

When the president of a furniture manufacturing company dies, the board members meet to name a new CEO. March, the comptroller, wrings his hands like a cross between Uriah Heep and Pontius Pilate as he tries to make a deal with director Louis Calhern to get the job.

Don Hilward / THE DESPERATE HOURS, 1955, Paramount, d-William Wyler.

When three escaped convicts take his family hostage in his home, March has to find a way to save them. With a little help from the police, he does.

Jerry Kingsley / MIDDLE OF THE NIGHT, 1959, Columbia, d-Delbert Mann.

March is an elderly manufacturer who falls in love with young Kim Novak and shocks his family when he announces that he plans to take her as his wife.

Matthew Harrison Brady / INHERIT THE WIND, 1960, United Artists, d-Stanley Kramer.

One must admit that March overplays his William Jennings Bryan role in this fictionalized account of the famous "monkey trial" in Tennessee in the 1920s when a teacher was convicted of teaching the theory of evolution. March's battle with Spencer Tracy (as Clarence Darrow) is nevertheless a masterful interplay between two magnificent actors.

President Jordan Lyman / SEVEN DAYS IN MAY, 1964, Seven Arts, d-John Frankenheimer.

March is a president of the United States whose popularity is at an all time low. General Burt Lancaster is planning a military takeover because March has signed a treaty with the USSR, but with the help of Kirk Douglas, Lancaster's second-in-command, March is able to prevent the coup.

OTHER ROLES

1929: *Trumbell Meredith* / THE DUMMY; *Gil Gilmore* / THE WILD PARTY; *Richard Hardell* / THE STUDIO MURDER MYSTERY; *Jim Hutton* / PARIS BOUND; *Pierre* / JEALOUSY; *Gregory Pyne* / FOOTLIGHTS AND FOOLS; *Martin Boyne* / THE MARRIAGE PLAYGROUND. **1930:** *Howard Vanning* / SARAH AND SON; *Dwight Howell* / LADIES LOVE BRUTES; *guest* / PARAMOUNT ON PARADE; *Gunner McCoy* / TRUE TO THE NAVY; *Dan O'Bannion* / MANSLAUGHTER; *Paul Lockridge* / LAUGHTER. **1931:** *Jerry Stafford* / HONOR AMONG LOVERS; *Rudek Berken* / THE NIGHT ANGEL; *Dick Grady* / MY SIN. **1932:** *Buddy Drake* / *Arthur Drake* / STRANGERS IN LOVE; *Jerry Corbett* / MERRILY WE GO TO HELL; *guest* / MAKE ME A STAR. **1933:** *Sabien Pastal* / TONIGHT IS OURS; *Jerry Young* / THE EAGLE AND THE HAWK; *Tom Chambers* / DESIGN FOR LIVING. **1934:** *Don Ellis* / ALL OF ME; *Mace Townsley* / GOOD DAME; *Benvenuto Cellini* / THE AFFAIRS OF CELLINI; *Prince Dmitri Nekhlyudov* / WE LIVE AGAIN. **1935:** *Alan Trent* / THE DARK ANGEL. **1936:** *Lt. Michel Denet* / THE ROAD TO GLORY; *Earl of Bothwell* / MARY OF SCOTLAND. **1938:** *Jean Lafitte* / THE BUCCANEER; *Bill Spencer* / THERE GOES MY HEART; *Sam Wye* / TRADE WINDS. **1940:** *Barry Troxel* / SUSAN AND GOD; *Hendrick Heyst* / VICTORY. **1941:** *Josef Steiner* / SO ENDS OUR NIGHT; *Lucas Drake* / BEDTIME STORY; *cameo* / LAND OF LIBERTY. **1944:** *Mike Frame* / TOMORROW THE WORLD. **1948:** *Marcus Hubbard* / ANOTHER PART OF THE FOREST; *Judge Calvin Cooke* / LIVE TODAY AND TOMORROW. **1949:** *Christopher Columbus* / CHRISTOPHER COLUMBUS. **1951:** *Papa Esposito* / IT'S A BIG COUNTRY. **1953:** *Karel Cernik* / MAN ON A TIGHTROPE. **1954:** *Rr. Adm. George Tarrant* / THE BRIDGES AT TOKO-RI. **1956:** *Philip of Macedonia* / ALEXANDER THE GREAT; *Ralph Hopkins* / THE MAN IN THE GRAY FLANNEL SUIT. **1957:**

narrator / ALBERT SCHWEITZER. **1962:** *Dr. Joseph Pearson* / THE YOUNG DOCTORS. **1963:** *Gerlach* / THE CONDEMNED OF ALTONA. **1966:** *Alexander Faver* / HOMBRE. **1970:** *Mayor Jeff Parks* / TICK, TICK, TICK. **1973:** *Harry Hope* / THE ICEMAN COMETH.

MARSHALL, HERBERT

(1890–1966)

Reared in a theatrical family, suave Herbert Marshall apprenticed as an accountant before going on the stage in 1911. He served with the British forces in World War I and lost a leg, which went unnoticed in his acting career. After the war he became a leading man on both the London and Broadway stages. Late in his 30s he made his film debut in MUMSIE. Urbane, upper-class, and with a mellifluous voice, Marshall was on his way to a long, successful film career first playing debonair, mature leading men and later playing detached, unruffled, thoughtful characters. His sensitive, well-behaved, sober husbands and lovers served to highlight the glamorous stars with whom he appeared. His work was dependable, and his voice was a treat for the ears.

KEY ROLES

Sir John Menier / MURDER, 1930, Great Britain, British-International, d-Alfred Hitchcock.

Marshall is a juror who helps sentence a young actress to death for murder. He later becomes convinced of her innocence and traps the real murderer into giving himself away.

Michael Rowe / MICHAEL AND MARY, 1932, Great Britain, Gaumont, d-Victor Saville.

When her husband deserts her during the Boer War, Edna Best marries Marshall. Years later the missing husband shows up and threatens the couple with blackmail, but is killed in a fall. Marshall and Best confess all to their son and his fiancée and find their love all the stronger.

Gaston Monescu (La Valle) / TROUBLE IN PARADISE, 1932, Paramount, d-Ernst Lubitsch.

In this masterpiece of sophisticated comedy, Marshall and Miriam Hopkins are jewel thieves after the baubles of Kay Francis. But things are complicated when Marshall falls in love with Francis, which doesn't set well with Hopkins. To illustrate how debonair Marshall's characters are, here are his instructions to a waiter: "It must be a marvelous supper. We may not eat it, but it must be marvelous. And, waiter, you see that moon? I want to see that moon in the champagne."

Gerald Shannon / THE DARK ANGEL, 1935, Goldwyn / United Artists, d-Sidney Franklin.

Marshall plays a decent man in love with Merle Oberon, whose husband (Fredric March) is believed dead, killed in World War I. But March is alive and Marshall discovers this. Despite his love he brings Oberon to March who, though blind, has carefully arranged everything in his room so as to hide the fact. Not wanting to be a burden to his wife, he tries to convince her that his feelings for her have changed. Things look good for Marshall, but March innocently gives himself away and Oberon insists on continuing their marriage.

Sir Frederick Barker / ANGEL, 1937, Paramount, d-Ernst Lubitsch.

Marshall is a British diplomat whose neglect of his wife (Marlene Dietrich) almost results in her having an affair with an old friend. The butler and the valet (Edward Everett Horton and Ernest Cossart) have the best lines in this film that doesn't have enough of the "Lubitsch touch."

Stephen Fisher / FOREIGN CORRESPONDENT, 1940, United Artists, d-Alfred Hitchcock.

Marshall is ostensibly a man of peace, but he turns out to be a fifth columnist in this story of a young American reporter who becomes entangled with spies when he is a witness to the assassination of a Dutch statesman.

Robert Crosbie / THE LETTER, 1940, Warners, d-William Wyler.

Marshall played the lover in the 1929 version of this Somerset Maugham story about a rubber plantation owner's wife who kills a man in what at first seems to be self-defense. Later a letter is offered for sale to her lawyer that proves that she and the deceased were lovers. This time around, Marshall is the trusting husband, given the business by Bette Davis.

Horace Giddens / THE LITTLE FOXES, 1941, Goldwyn, d-William Wyler.

Marshall's tirade at his bitch of a wife (Bette Davis), who will let him die rather than fetch his medicine, sums up this Lillian Hellman story: "Maybe it's easy for the dying to be honest. I'm sick of you, sick of this house, sick of my unhappy life with you. I'm sick of your brothers and their dirty tricks to make a dime....You'll wreck this town, you and your brothers. You'll wreck this country, you and your kind, if they let you. But not me. I'll die my own way, and I'll do it without making the world any worse. I leave that to you."

Geoffrey Wolfe / THE MOON AND SIXPENCE, 1943, United Artists, d-Albert Lewin.

Marshall plays the Somerset Maugham-like narrator who tells the story of an English stockbroker who deserts his wife to become a painter. After having an affair with the wife of a Dutchman who had helped him, the painter (George Sanders) goes to Tahiti. It's based on Maugham's friendship with Paul Gauguin.

John Hillgave / THE ENCHANTED COTTAGE, 1944, RKO, d-John Cromwell.

Marshall portrays the blind friend of a disfigured man and a plain woman who, when alone in their cottage, appear beautiful to each other. Marshall is the only one of their friends or relatives who can share in and explain the transformation.

Somerset Maugham / THE RAZOR'S EDGE, 1946, 20th Century-Fox, d-Edmund Goulding.

Marshall acts as a link between the characters in this long and involved Maugham story of a man who, on his return from World War I, questions his values and seeks to find sources of wisdom.

Scott Chavez / DUEL IN THE SUN, 1946, Selznick, d-King Vidor.

Marshall is a gentleman from the Old South who has shamed his family by marrying an Indian and becoming a gambler while his wife dances and apparently sleeps with all comers. Finally, he can stand it no longer when he sees that their young daughter is in danger of following in her mother's footsteps. He kills his wife and her current lover and suggests at his trial that he be taken out and hanged, a sentence he receives. His last act is to send his daughter to live with a woman that he should have married.

OTHER ROLES

1927: *Colonel Armytage* / MUMSIE. **1929:** *Geoffrey Hammond* / THE LETTER. **1931:** *Gerry Anson* / THE CALENDAR; *Lord Danford* / SECRETS OF A SECRETARY. **1932:** *Waverly Ango* / THE FAITHFUL HEART; *Edward Faraday* / BLONDE VENUS; *Count von Dopental* / EVENINGS FOR SALE. **1933:** *Oliver Lane* / THE SOLITAIRE MAN; *Stephan* / I WAS A SPY. **1934:** *Arnold Ainger* / FOUR FRIGHTENED PEOPLE; *Napier Harpenden* / OUTCAST LADY; *Dr. Walter Fane* / THE PAINTED VEIL; *Lord Philip Rexford* / RIPTIDE. **1935:** *Dr. Max Sporum* / THE GOOD FAIRY; *Gordon Phillips* / THE FLAME WITHIN; *Steven Gaye* / ACCENT ON YOUTH; *Jim Buchanan* / IF YOU COULD ONLY COOK. **1936:** *Dr. Michael Talbot* / THE LADY CONSENTS; *Harry Ashton* / FORGOTTEN FACES; *Allan Barclay* / TILL WE MEET AGAIN; *Dr. Stephen Dominick* / GIRLS' DORMITORY; *Thomas Lane* / A WOMAN REBELS; *Christopher Drew* / MAKE WAY FOR A LADY. **1937:** *Jonathan Blair* / BREAKFAST FOR TWO. **1938:** *Richard Todd* / MAD ABOUT MUSIC; *Jim Howard* / ALWAYS GOODBYE; *Stephen Holland* / WOMAN AGAINST WOMAN. **1939:** *Dufresne* / ZAZA. **1940:** *Gray Meredith* / A BILL OF DIVORCEMENT. **1941:** *Roger Woodruff* / WHEN LADIES MEET; *John Davis* / KATHLEEN; *Sen. John Coleridge* / ADVENTURE IN WASHINGTON. **1943:** *Michael Kingsley* / YOUNG IDEAS; *guest* / FOREVER AND A DAY; *Paul Turner* / FLIGHT FOR FREEDOM. **1944:** *Dr. M. J. Standish* / ANDY HARDY'S BLONDE TROUBLE. **1945:** *Dr. Charles Evans* / THE UNSEEN. **1946:** *Traybin* / CRACK-UP. **1947:** *Willard I. Whitcombe* / HIGH WALL; *Miles Rushworth* / IVY. **1949:** *Archibald Craven* / THE SECRET GARDEN. **1950:** *Stanton* / THE UNDERWORLD STORY. **1951:** *Dr. Jameson* / ANNE OF THE INDIES; *Dr. James Curtis* / CAPTAIN BLACKJACK. **1953:** *Mr. Tremayne* / ANGEL FACE. **1954:** *Earl of Mackworth* / THE BLACK SHIELD OF FALWORTH; *Dr. Van Ness* / GOG; *Dr. Donald Stanton* / RIDERS TO THE STARS. **1955:** *Lord Leicester* / THE VIRGIN QUEEN. **1956:** *Stephen Collins* / WICKED AS THEY COME. **1957:** *Inspector Mackenzie* / THE WEAPON; *Robert Hedges* / STAGE STRUCK. **1958:** *Inspector Charas* / THE FLY. **1960:** *Charles Manning* / MIDNIGHT LACE; *Governor Thornwall* / A FEVER IN THE BLOOD; *Henry Addison* / COLLEGE CONFIDENTIAL. **1962:** *the prime minister* / FIVE WEEKS IN A BALLOON. **1963:** *Sir Wilfrid Lucas* / THE LIST OF ADRIAN MESSENGER; *Dr. Jubal Harrington* / THE CARETAKERS. **1965:** *Austin Parsons* / THE THIRD DAY.

MARTIN, DEAN

(Dino Crocetti, 1917–)

After high school, Dean Martin established himself as a nightclub singer and then was teamed with comic Jerry Lewis in many films. In the 1950s the duo became the highest-paid comedy stars in the country. After flourishing in nightclubs, they made their film debut in MY FRIEND IRMA, the first of sixteen films made together. Martin sang the songs, kissed the girls, and stood by while Lewis made an ass of himself. They broke up the act in 1956. Martin appeared in a series of spy spoofs, became a successful recording star, and started a long-running television variety show. He enjoyed playing a lazy, alcoholic lecher and the role worked much better for him than when he appeared in straight dramas where he was expected to act, rather than trot out his adopted persona. He joked: "The only reason I drink is because when I am sober I think I am Eddie Fisher."

KEY ROLES

Steve Laird / MY FRIEND IRMA, 1949, Paramount, d-George Marshall.

With partner Jerry Lewis, Martin has a supporting role in this story about a dumb blonde whose con man boyfriend lends her apartment to two soda jerks (Martin and Lewis) and they steal the show.

Sgt. Vic Puccinelli / AT WAR WITH THE ARMY, 1950, Paramount, d-Hal Walker.

The film is pure slapstick, but the public ate it up as Martin and Jerry Lewis play havoc with the army. Martin contributes by giving voice to the musical numbers "You and Your Beautiful Eyes" and "The Navy Gets the Gravy but the Army Gets the Beans" by Mack David and Jerry Livingston.

Slim Mosely, Jr. / PARDNERS, 1956, Paramount, d-Norman Taurog.

In this remake of Bing Crosby's RHYTHM ON THE RANGE, Martin and Jerry Lewis spoof westerns, missing more often than they hit, but the customers didn't seem to mind at the time.

Michael Whiteacre / THE YOUNG LIONS, 1958, 20th Century-Fox, d-Edward Dmytryk.

In probably his best straight role, Martin is a Broadway playboy whose girlfriend (Barbara Rush) has taken skiing lessons in Europe from Marlon Brando. When the war breaks out, both Martin and Brando enter the service of their countries. Martin becomes friends with a Jew (Montgomery Clift) and the remainder of this very intelligent war movie moves back and forth between the soldiers as it works its way up to the time their lives cross and one dies.

Dude / RIO BRAVO, 1959, Warners, d-Howard Hawks.

Martin is a once-proud lawman who has become a falling-down drunk; John Wayne is a sheriff who has a prisoner he's trying to hold in jail until the arrival of the U.S. marshal. The prisoner's friends are intent on freeing him, so the Duke has to sober Martin up to help him fight off the bad guys.

Jeffrey Moss / BELLS ARE RINGING, 1960, MGM, d-Vincente Minnelli.

Martin once again is straight man for a comedian, only this time the comic is Judy Holliday and neither she nor Martin can bring any magic to the story of a girl working for an answering service and her more than professional interest in a songwriter whose well has run dry. Martin's musical numbers include "Do It Yourself" and with Judy, "Better than a Dream" and "Just in Time."

Julian Berniers / TOYS IN THE ATTIC, 1963, United Artists, d-George Roy Hill.

In this screen version of the Lillian Hellman play about incest, infidelity, and imbecility, Martin is a ne'er-do-well who is looked after by his two aging spinster sisters in their shabby New Orleans home.

Matt Helm / THE SILENCERS, 1966, Columbia, d-Phil Karlson.

In this spoof of James Bond movies, Martin is an American agent who is licensed to kill and who beds down every woman that he meets. It's all done tongue-in-cheek and in very bad taste, but male chauvinist pigs enjoy how easily Martin scores with the underdressed women in this film and its three sequels.

Vernon Demerest / AIRPORT, 1970, Universal, d-George Seaton.

Just before taking off in a snow storm, married pilot Martin learns that his stewardess girlfriend is pregnant. It just isn't his day, because when in the air he's informed that there is a man with a bomb on board.

OTHER ROLES

1950: *Steve Laird* / MY FRIEND IRMA GOES WEST. **1951:** *Bill Baker* / THAT'S MY BOY; *Al Crowthers* / SAILOR BEWARE. **1952:** *Chick Allen* / JUMPING JACKS; *Bill Miller* / THE STOOGE; *guest* / ROAD TO BALI. **1953:** *Larry Todd* / SCARED STIFF; *Joe Anthony* / THE CADDY; *Honey Talk Nelson* / MONEY FROM HOME. **1954:** *Steve* / LIVING IT UP; *Pete Nelson* / THREE RING CIRCUS. **1955:** *Bob Miles* / YOU'RE NEVER TOO YOUNG; *Richard Todd* / ARTISTS AND MOD-

ELS. **1956:** *Steve Wiley* / HOLLYWOOD OR BUST. **1957:** *Ray Hunter* / TEN THOUSAND BEDROOMS. **1958:** *Bama Dillert* / SOME CAME RUNNING. **1959:** *Maudy Novak* / CAREER. **1960:** *Michael Haney* / WHO WAS THAT LADY?; *Sam Harmon* / OCEAN'S ELEVEN; *guest* / PEPE. **1961:** *Tony Ryder* / ALL IN A NIGHT'S WORK; *Bo Gillis* / ADA. **1962:** *Sgt. Chip Deal* / SERGEANTS 3; *Steve Flood* / WHO'S GOT THE ACTION?; *guest* / THE ROAD TO HONG KONG. **1963:** *Jason Steel* / WHO'S BEEN SLEEPING IN MY BED?; *the bum* / COME BLOW YOUR HORN. **1964:** *Joe Jarrett* / FOUR FOR TEXAS; *Leonard Crawley* / WHAT A WAY TO GO!; *Little John* / ROBIN AND THE SEVEN HOODS; *Dino* / KISS ME, STUPID. **1965:** *Tom Elder* / THE SONS OF KATIE ELDER; *Ernie Brewer* / MARRIAGE ON THE ROCKS; **1966:** *Sam Hollis* / TEXAS ACROSS THE RIVER. **1967:** *Matt Helm* / MURDERERS' ROW; *Alex Flood* / ROUGH NIGHT IN JERICHO; *Matt Helm* / THE AMBUSHERS. **1968:** *Dee Bishop* / BANDOLERO!; *David Sloane* / HOW TO SAVE A MARRIAGE; *Van Morgan* / FIVE CARD STUD; *Matt Helm* / WRECKING CREW. **1971:** *Joe Baker* / SOMETHING BIG. **1973:** *Billy Massey* / SHOWDOWN. **1975:** *Joe Ricco* / MR. RICCO. **1981:** *Jamie Blake* / THE CANNONBALL RUN. **1984:** *Jamie Blake* / CANNONBALL RUN II.

MARVIN, LEE

(1924–1987)

New York-born Lee Marvin quit school to join the marines and was wounded and spent 13 months in a hospital. He studied acting at The American Theatre Wing, made his film debut in YOU'RE IN THE NAVY NOW, and took a Broadway role in "Billy Budd." He made a living in films portraying cruel, sadistic hoodlums until he was signed to be on the side of the law in the TV series "M-Squad." Thereafter he became an unusual star, winning an Oscar for his dual comedy role in CAT BALLOU in 1965. In 1979 Marvin became involved in a landmark legal case in which it was decided that he pay "palimony" to Michelle Triola for the years they lived together. This may have inspired him to observe, "Love is a matter of degrees. I think of a gas tank with the empty and full positions." Marvin's characters generally were cold and often brutal. His pale hair, icy blue-grey eyes, and stony face contributed to the feeling that all of his characters could and would explode at the least provocation.

KEY ROLES

Chino / THE WILD ONE, 1953, Columbia, d-Laslo Benedek.

Marvin is the bad motorcycle punk leader as opposed to Marlon Brando, the good motorcycle punk leader, in this tale of the takeover of a small town by black-jacket hoods who arrive on their "hogs" like locusts.

Vince Stone / THE BIG HEAT, 1953, Columbia, d-Fritz Lang.

Marvin got a lot of attention for a new low in violent behavior by throwing scalding coffee in the face of Gloria Grahame, thus permanently disfiguring her. She gets her revenge with a little bit of help from undercover cop Glenn Ford.

Hector David / BAD DAY AT BLACK ROCK, 1954, MGM, d-John Sturges.

Marvin is a mean cowboy who tests the courage of one-armed Spencer Tracy when he arrives in a desert whistle stop in California. He has gone there to find out what happened to the parents of a Japanese-American soldier who had died in Europe while serving under Tracy's command.

Liberty Valance / THE MAN WHO SHOT LIBERTY VALANCE, 1961, Paramount, d-John Ford.

Marvin is a mean stagecoach robber who cruelly beats tenderfoot Jimmy Stewart and leaves him for dead. No one seems willing to stand up to him, but a shaken Stewart eventually does and is proclaimed a hero when Marvin is killed. But it was someone else who fired the fatal shot.

Charlie / THE KILLERS, 1963, Universal-International, d-Don Siegel.

In a movie called THE KILLERS, and at this point in his career, what else would Marvin be but one of the assassins who kill John Cassavetes.

Tim Strawn / Kid Sheleen / CAT BALLOU, 1965, Columbia, d-Eliot Silverstein.

With the help of a horse that appears as drunk as he is most of the time, Marvin won an Oscar for his dual role of a drunken gunfighter who sobers up long enough to kill his own brother (also played by Marvin), a gunfighter who had been hired to kill Jane Fonda's daddy.

Major Reisman / THE DIRTY DOZEN, 1966, MGM, d-Robert Aldrich.

Marvin is given the assignment of turning 12 psychopathic, condemned criminal soldiers into a fighting unit that will go behind enemy lines and kill a large number of German officers at a retreat where they are sent for "R and R" between battles.

Ben Rumson / PAINT YOUR WAGON, 1968, Paramount, d-Joshua Logan.

Marvin and his partner (Clint Eastwood) share a wife (Jean Seberg) during the California Gold Rush. Marvin even sings, having a hit with "Wanderin' Star."

Monte Walsh / MONTE WALSH, 1969, Cinema Center, d-William A. Fraker.

Marvin and fellow aging cowboy Jack Palance find life increasingly hopeless and when an old acquaintance kills Palance, Marvin evens the score.

Sam Longwood / THE GREAT SCOUT AND CATHOUSE THURSDAY, 1976, American International, d-Don Taylor.

In this peculiar western, Marvin seeks revenge on a partner who has absconded with their stake and ends up falling in love with young prostitute Kay Lenz.

OTHER ROLES

1951: *bit* / YOU'RE IN THE NAVY NOW; *Snively* / DOWN AMONG THE SHELTERING PALMS; *an M.P.* / DIPLOMATIC COURIER; *Tinhorn Burgess* / THE DUEL AT SILVER CREEK. **1952:** *Pinky* / WE'RE NOT MARRIED; *Ralph Bainter* / HANGMAN'S KNOT; *Sergeant Magruder* / SEMINOLE; *Corporal Bowman* / THE GLORY BRIGADE; *Mooney* / EIGHT IRON MEN. **1953:** *Blinky* / GUN FURY; *Dan Kurth* / THE STRANGER WON A GUN; *Meatball* / THE CAINE MUTINY; *Shaughnessy* / GORILLA AT LARGE. **1954:** *Lieutenant Keating* / THE RAID; *the murderer* / A LIFE IN THE BALANCE; *Brundage* / NOT AS A STRANGER. **1955:** *Dill* / VIOLENT SATURDAY; *Babe Kossuck* / I DIED A THOUSAND TIMES; *Al Gannaway* / PETE KELLY'S BLUES; *Slob the Cook* / SHACK OUT ON 101; *Sgt. Lloyd Carractart* / PILLARS OF THE SKY; *Bill Masters* / SEVEN MEN FROM NOW; *Capt. John Miller* / THE RACK. **1956:** *Colonel Bartlett* / ATTACK!; *Orville "Flash" Perkins* / RAINTREE COUNTY. **1957:** *Tobias Brown* / THE MISSOURI TRAVELER. **1961:** *Tully Crow* / THE COMANCHEROS. **1962:** *Boots Gilhooley* / DONOVAN'S REEF. **1963:** *Sergeant Ryker* / SERGEANT RYKER. **1964:** *Bill Tenny* / SHIP OF FOOLS. **1965:** *Henry Rico Fardan* / THE PROFESSIONALS. **1967:** *Walker* / POINT BLANK. **1968:** *the American* / HELL IN THE PACIFIC; *himself* / TONIGHT LET'S ALL MAKE LOVE IN LONDON. **1971:** *Leonard* / POCKET MONEY; *Nick Devlin* / PRIME CUT. **1972:** *"A" Number One* / EMPEROR OF THE NORTH POLE. **1973:** *Hickey* / THE ICEMAN COMETH; *Harry Spikes* / THE SPIKES GANG. **1974:** *Sheriff Bascomb* / THE KLANSMAN. **1975:** *Flynn O'Flynn* / SHOUT AT THE DEVIL. **1978:** *Col. Harry Wargrave* / AVALANCHE EXPRESS; *Sergeant Possum* / THE BIG RED ONE. **1980:** *Sgt. Edgar Millen* / DEATH

HUNT. **1982:** *Jack Osborne* / GORKY PARK. **1983:** *Jimmy Cobb* / CANICULE.

MARX, CHICO

(Leonard Marx, 1886–1961)

MARX, GROUCHO

(Julius Marx, 1890–1977)

MARX, HARPO

(Adolph Marx, 1888–1964)

MARX, ZEPPO

(Herbert Marx, 1901–1979)

The zany antics of the Marx Brothers, with their suggestive winks, leers, and wisecracks, broke up vaudeville fans for many years. While their films were more popular years after they were made than at their time of release, they established the Marx Brothers among the most popular movie comedy acts of all time. Zeppo appeared in only the first five movies and brother Gummo (Milton) left the act before they entered films. Cigar-chewing Groucho, with his painted-on mustache, was the star of the team, but Chico, with his pointed hat, seedy jacket, sly smile, deadpan face, and phony Italian accent, and Harpo the mute, with his battered plug hat atop frizzled mop hair and an idiotic grin on his innocent face, have each been praised as a comic genius. While Groucho and Chico delighted audiences with double-talk, Harpo was a master pantomimist who specialized in direct action, depending on a squeeze horn to punctuate his messages. The brothers made their Broadway debut in 1924 in a revue called "I'll Say She Is." In the early 1930s after several Broadway hits and the stock market crash, they turned to the movies. In each film Chico showed his artistry with a piano and Harpo with, naturally, a harp. After the team broke up, Groucho made occasional film appearances and delighted new audiences with his TV quiz show, "You Bet Your Life."

KEY ROLES

(The name given first is Groucho's; his brothers' characters' names are identified in the text.)

Hammer / THE COCOANUTS, 1929, Paramount, d-Robert Florey.

Groucho, the manager of a hotel in Florida, hopes to make money by auctioning off parcels of land on the property. He is aided and abetted, as well as undone, by Chico and Harpo, who are called by those names, and in a straight role, Zeppo plays Jamison.

Capt. Jeffrey Spaulding / ANIMAL CRACKERS, 1930, Paramount, d-Victor Heerman.

Groucho is a famous explorer in this film with a flimsy plot about the theft of a painting belonging to society woman Margaret Dumont. He sings the song that became his theme, "Hooray for Captain Spaulding," by Bert Kalmar and Harry Ruby. Harpo is the Professor, Chico is Signor Emmanuel Ravelli, and Zeppo is Horatio Jamison.

Prof. Quincey Adams Wagstaff / HORSE FEATHERS, 1932, Paramount, d-Norman Z. McLeod.

Groucho plays the crackpot president of Huxley College; his son is played by Zeppo; and Harpo and Chico are mistaken for football players Groucho hires to attend his college so the team can win the big game.

Rufus T. Firefly / DUCK SOUP, 1933, Paramount, d-Leo McCarey.

Groucho is the new president of the republic of Freedonia, whose entire budget is financed by Margaret Dumont. Harpo as Brownie and Chico as Chicolini jump back and forth as spies for Freedonia and for its archenemy, the neighboring country of Sylvania. Zeppo, in his last film appearance with his brothers, is Bob Rolland, one of Groucho's aides in his war with Sylvania.

Otis B. Driftwood / A NIGHT AT THE OPERA, 1935, MGM, d-Sam Wood.

Groucho is a fast-talking promoter who signs the wrong opera singer, who in the end turns out to be the right one, in the best of the Marx Brothers' films. Harpo is Tomasso and Chico is Florello in this wonderfully absurd assault on opera with some of the most memorable scenes in all motion picture comedy history. The ship stateroom sequence is only the most obvious.

Dr. Hugo Z. Hackenbush / A DAY AT THE RACES, 1937, MGM, d-Sam Wood.

Groucho is personal physician to wealthy Margaret Dumont. Too bad that he's really only a vet. He and Harpo as Stuffy, and Chico as Tony, help save a sanitarium run by Maureen O'Sullivan by winning a horse race.

OTHER ROLES

1931: *four stowaways* / MONKEY BUSINESS. **1938:** *Gordon Miller (Groucho), Faker Englund (Harpo), Harry Binelli (Chico)* / ROOM SERVICE. **1939:** *J. Cheever Loophole (Groucho), Punchy (Harpo), Antonio (Chico)* / AT THE CIRCUS. **1940:** *S. Quentin Quale (Groucho), Rusty Panello (Harpo), Joe Panello (Chico)* / GO WEST. **1941:** *Wolf J. Flywheel (Groucho), Wacky (Harpo), Ravelli (Chico)* / THE BIG STORE. **1946:** *Ronald Kornblow (Groucho), Rusty (Harpo), Corbaccio (Chico)* / A NIGHT IN CASABLANCA. **1949:** *Sam Grunion (Groucho), Harpo (Harpo), Faustino the Great (Chico)* / LOVE HAPPY.

Groucho's solo appearances

1947: *Lionel Q. Devereaux* / COPACABANA. **1950:** *guest* / MR. MUSIC. **1951:** *Emil J. Keech* / DOUBLE DYNAMITE. **1952:** *Benny Linn* / A GIRL IN EVERY PORT. **1957:** *Peter Minuit* / THE STORY OF MANKIND; *George Schmidlapp (cameo)* / WILL SUCCESS SPOIL ROCK HUNTER? **1969:** *"God"* / SKIDOO.

MASON, JAMES

(1909–1984)

James Mason, the son of a wealthy wool merchant, was educated at Cambridge with a degree in architecture, made his stage debut in 1933, and made his first film in 1935. Over the next few years he became Britain's most popular leading man. After World War II his criticism of British filmmaking made him unpopular in England and he moved to the United States. His career in the States was busy, although some of his roles were beneath his talents. As even he noted, "I'm tired of playing the lecherous, middle-aged chap who is forever vaulting the generation gap." With his rich, mellow voice and sardonic looks, Mason was excellent as a dignified romantic villain with more than a hint of cruelty just below the surface. Mason was talented, intelligent, versatile, and independent, and one of the world's most respected actors.

KEY ROLES

Mark Warren / I MET A MURDERER, 1939, Great Britain, Grand National, d-Roy Kellino.

Mason, a young farmer, is driven to desperation by his nagging wife and her drunken brother. When she deliberately kills his dog, he kills her and goes on the run. Before the police catch up with him he meets a girl with whom he spends a few happy days.

Stephen Deremid / THE NIGHT HAS EYES, 1942, Great Britain, Pathe, d-Leslie Arliss.

When two teachers go to Yorkshire where one of their friends had disappeared a year earlier, they encounter a reclusive, moody composer (Mason) whose housekeeper and her husband turn out to be the murderers of the missing woman.

Marquis de Rohan / THE MAN IN GREY, 1943, Great Britain, Gainsborough, d-Leslie Arliss.

Sadistic Mason has no love for his wife and he soon takes the latter's childhood friend, who has been employed as a governess, for his mistress. But when this one (Margaret Lockwood) schemes to become his wife and allows her rival to die from a severe cold, Mason beats her to death with a horsewhip.

Lord Manderstoke / FANNY BY GASLIGHT, 1944, Great Britain, Gainsborough, d-Anthony Asquith.

Phyllis Calvert, the illegitimate daughter of a cabinet minister, goes to live with him after her foster father is killed in a brawl with evil Mason. Her father's wife, who is Mason's mistress, threatens a scandal over the girl, so the minister commits suicide. His secretary (Stewart Granger) kills Mason in a duel and wins Calvert.

Nicholas / THE SEVENTH VEIL, 1945, Great Britain, Theatrecraft, d-Compton Bennett.

A psychiatrist helps Ann Todd strip away the veils of her traumatic life. She is a pianist who was so badly caned as a child that she was unable to play. She is then put in the care of a cruel guardian (Mason) who breaks up her romances. She finally realizes this is his way of showing his love and decides that he's the man she's always wanted.

Capt. Jerry Jackson / THE WICKED LADY, 1946, Great Britain, Gainsborough, d-Leslie Arliss.

Mason is a highwayman who meets up with Lady Skelton (Margaret Lockwood) who has taken up the same trade out of boredom. As a result of their affair he is almost hanged and, in the end, the two fatally wound each other.

Johnny McQueen / ODD MAN OUT, 1946, Great Britain, Two Cities, d-Carol Reed.

Mason is an IRA rebel recently escaped from prison, who is shot and wounded in an attempted raid. Deserted by his accomplices, he is pursued through Belfast by the police. Trying to reach the docks he is helped by his girl (Kathleen Ryan) and when the police close in on them, she shoots at them so that she and Mason will be killed together.

Hendrick van der Zee / PANDORA AND THE FLYING DUTCHMAN, 1951, Great Britain, Romulus, d-Albert Lewin.

Mason is the fabled Flying Dutchman doomed to roam the seas. Every seven years, though, he is given six months ashore to seek a girl willing to die for him and end his eternal suffering. The candidate this time round is a heartbreaker named Pandora.

Cicero (Elyesa Bazna) / FIVE FINGERS, 1952, 20th Century-Fox, d-Joseph L. Mankiewicz.

Mason, the valet to the British ambassador in Ankara, arranges to sell military secrets to the Germans, but because they don't quite trust him they don't make use of the information.

Brutus / JULIUS CAESAR, 1953, MGM, d-Joseph L. Mankiewicz.

Mason is excellent as one of the conspirators who assassinate Julius Caesar because they fear he will proclaim himself king of Rome. They are in turn routed by the forces of Mark Antony.

Captain Nemo / 20,000 LEAGUES UNDER THE SEA, 1954, Disney, d-Richard Fleischer.

Mason seems ideally suited to portray Jules Verne's mysterious captain who lives in a futuristic submarine and has found a way to live completely from the sea.

Norman Maine / A STAR IS BORN, 1954, Warners, d-George Cukor.

The fact that this remake of the 1937 film classic is so absorbing owes much to the rich performance of Mason as the drunken movie star whose career is on the skids just as that of his wife (Judy Garland) is taking off. Rather than be a burden to her he walks into the ocean. Mason gives Garland sound advice: "Listen to me, Esther, a career is a curious thing. Talent isn't always enough. You need a sense of timing—an eye for seeing the turning point or recognizing the big chance when it comes along and grabbing it. A career can rest on a trifle. Like—like us sitting here tonight. Or it can turn on somebody saying to you, 'You're better than that. You're better than you know.' Don't settle for the little dream. Go on to the big one."

Maxwell Fleury / ISLAND IN THE SUN, 1957, 20th Century-Fox, d-Robert Rossen.

In this tale of interracial love on a West Indian island, Mason, the head of a ruling family, murders a drifter whom he believes was having an affair with his wife. He is pursued by a police inspector who suspects him of the crime until finally Mason confesses.

Phillip Van Damm / NORTH BY NORTHWEST, 1959, MGM, d-Alfred Hitchcock.

Mason is the foreign spy who believes that Cary Grant is a U.S. agent who is after him. In reality the American agent is Eva Marie Saint, Mason's mistress, who falls for Grant, who innocently becomes involved.

Prof. Oliver Lindenbrook / JOURNEY TO THE CENTER OF THE EARTH, 1959, 20th Century-Fox, d-Henry Levin.

Back again in a Jules Verne story, Mason is an Edinburgh professor who leads an assortment of colleagues down an explorer's trail to the earth's center.

Paul Delville / THE MARRIAGE-GO-ROUND, 1961, 20th Century-Fox, d-Walter Lang.

Swedish knockout Julie Newmar decides that she and brilliant professor Mason would produce a perfect baby. His wife (Susan Hayward) prefers that he pass up the honor.

Humbert H. Humbert / LOLITA, 1962, MGM, d-Stanley Kubrick.

Mason is a middle-aged teacher who becomes sexually obsessed with a 14-year-old nymphet, even going so far as to marry the girl's widowed mother to be near her. When the mother runs in front of a car upon learning the truth, he and the girl become as man and wife. In the Nabokov novel the girl was only 12 and the difference of two years has an effect on the shock value.

Count von Klugermann / THE BLUE MAX, 1966, 20th Century-Fox, d-John Guillermin.

Mason is a German general in World War I who is very tolerant of his young wife's affairs, especially when she takes up with a young pilot whom Mason wishes to make a hero as a rallying point for the ordinary German citizen.

James Leamington / GEORGY GIRL, 1966, Great Britain, Columbia, d-Silvio Narizzano.

Mason is an aging lech who finally gets his wish to take his butler's rather plump and not too attractive daughter as his wife, when she turns down his offer to become his mistress.

Charles Dobbs / THE DEADLY AFFAIR, 1967, Great Britain, Columbia, d-Sidney Lumet.

Mason is a foreign office man who attempts to unravel the mystery surrounding the apparent suicide of a colleague. He uncovers a spy ring.

Dr. John Watson / MURDER BY DECREE, 1979, Great Britain / Canada, Avco, d-Bob Clark.

Mason helps Sherlock Holmes (Christopher Plummer) investigate the case of Jack the Ripper.

Sir Randolph Nettleby / THE SHOOTING PARTY, 1984, Great Britain, European Classics, d-Alan Bridges.

Mason plays an English nobleman on the eve of World War I who senses that things are changing and the way of life he has loved so long is just about over. His performance is a fitting farewell for an actor who had pleased so many in 50 years of making films.

OTHER ROLES

1935: *Jim Martin* / LATE EXTRA. **1936:** *Henry Hamilton* / TWICE BRANDED; *John Merriman* / TROUBLED WATERS; *Bunny Barnes* / PRISON BREAKER; *Stephen Nelville* / BLIND MAN'S BLUFF; *Larry* / THE SECRET OF STAMBOUL; *Hillary Vane* / FIRE OVER ENGLAND. **1937:** *Tom Tulliver* / THE MILL ON THE FLOSS; *Captain Haverall* / THE HIGH COMMAND; *Robert Leyland* / CATCH AS CATCH CAN. **1938:** *Jean Tallion* / THE RETURN OF THE SCARLET PIMPERNEL. **1941:** *Mike Cardby* / THIS MAN IS DANGEROUS. **1942:** *Dr. Renwick* / HATTER'S CASTLE; *Andre Laurent* / ALIBI; *Raoul de Carnot* / SECRET MISSION. **1943:** *Streeter* / THUNDER ROCK; *Ted Robbins* / THE BELLS GO DOWN; *Cmdr. Richard Heritage* / THEY MET IN THE DARK. **1944:** *Alan Thurston* / CANDLELIGHT IN ALGERIA; *Peter Vadassy* / HOTEL RESERVE. **1945:** *Mr. Smedhurst* / A PLACE OF ONE'S OWN; *Geoffrey* / THEY WERE SISTERS. **1947:** *Michael Joyce* / THE UPTURNED GLASS. **1949:** *Larry Quinada* / CAUGHT; *Gustave Flaubert* / MADAME BOVARY; *Marlon Donnelly* / THE RECKLESS MOMENT; *Brandon Bourne* / EAST SIDE, WEST SIDE. **1950:** *Doc Matson* / ONE-WAY STREET. **1952:** *Field Marshal Erwin Rommel* / THE DESERT FOX; *Del Palma* / LADY POSSESSED; *Rupert of Hentzau* / THE PRISONER OF ZENDA; *captain* / FACE TO FACE. **1953:** *Field Marshal Erwin Rommel* / THE DESERT RATS; *Charles Coudray* / THE STORY OF THREE LOVES; *Capt. Paul Gilbert* / BOTANY BAY; *Ivo Kern* / THE MAN BETWEEN; *the murderer* / *Major Linden* / *Jonah Watson* / CHARADE. **1954:** *Sir Brack* / PRINCE VALIANT. **1956:** *guardian angel* / FOREVER DARLING; *Ed Avery* / BIGGER THAN LIFE. **1958:** *Jim Molner* / CRY TERROR; *Capt. Edwin Rumill* / THE DECKS RAN RED. **1960:** *Cmdr. Max Easton* / A TOUCH OF LARCENY; *Sir Edward Carson* / THE TRIALS OF OSCAR WILDE. **1962:** *Jacob Webber* / THE LAND WE LOVE; *Johnson* / ESCAPE FROM ZAHRAIN; *Capt. Brett Aimsley* / TIARA TAHITI. **1964:** *Timonides* / THE FALL OF THE ROMAN EMPIRE; *Captain Blayne* / TORPEDO BAY; *Bob Conway* / THE PUMPKIN EATER. **1965:** *Gentleman Brown* / LORD JIM; *Regnier* / THE UNINHIBITED; *Kam Ling* / GENGHIS KHAN. **1967:** *John Sawyer* / STRANGER IN THE HOUSE; *narrator* / THE LONDON NOBODY KNOWS. **1968:** *Charles Calvert* / DUFFY; *Emperor Franz Josef* / MAYERLING. **1969:** *Bradley Monahan* / AGE OF CONSENT; *Trigorin* / THE SEA GULL. **1970:** *Rafe Crompton* / SPRING AND PORT WINE; *Alan* / KILL! KILL! KILL!; *Ross* / COLD SWEAT. **1971:** *Montero* / BAD MAN'S RIVER. **1972:** *Jerome Malley* / CHILD'S PLAY. **1973:** *Philip* / THE LAST OF SHEILA; *Sir George Wheeler* / THE MACKINTOSH MAN. **1974:** *Watts* / 11 HARROWHOUSE; *Brizard* / THE MARSEILLES CONTRACT. **1975:** *Maxwell* / MANDINGO; *Cyril Sahib* / AUTOBIOGRAPHY OF A PRINCESS. **1976:** *Remos* / VOYAGE OF THE DAMNED; *Ernst Furben* / INSIDE OUT. **1977:** *Colonel Brandt* / CROSS OF IRON. **1978:** *Edward Seibert* / THE BOYS FROM BRAZIL; *Grimes* / THE WATER BABIES; *Mr. Jordan* / HEAVEN CAN WAIT. **1979:** *Professor Bergson* / THE PASSAGE; *Sir Alec Nichols* / BLOODLINE. **1980:** *Admiral Brinsden* / NORTH SEA HIJACK. **1982:** *Odell Gardener* / EVIL UNDER THE SUN; *Ed Concannon* / THE VERDICT. **1983:** *Captain Hughes* / YELLOWBEARD. **1984:** *Bishop Nicolini* / THE ASSISI UNDERGROUND.

MASSEY, RAYMOND

(1896–1983)

Son of a prominent, wealthy Toronto family, Raymond Massey became an American citizen in 1944 after being wounded in the Canadian army in both wars. After World War I he moved to London to pursue a stage career. In 1931 he made his New York debut in "Hamlet" and his first film role as Sherlock Holmes in THE SPECKLED BAND. He created the title role in Robert Sherwood's "Abe Lincoln in Illinois" on the stage and in the film version. Massey was at his best portraying driven men who knew that their lives would change history. With his thundering voice and belligerent manner, tall, broad-shouldered Massey posed a smiling threat in many adventure movies. Brother of Canada's governor general, Massey has a son and daughter who are also actors.

KEY ROLES

Philip Waverton / THE OLD DARK HOUSE, 1932, Great Britain, Universal, d-James Whale.

Massey is among the travelers who must take refuge in the house of a family of eccentrics in this very fine horror comedy.

Chauvelin / THE SCARLET PIMPERNEL, 1934, Great Britain, London Films, d-Harold Young.

France sends Massey to England to uncover the Englishman who is saving French aristocrats from the guillotine. He is almost successful with the unwitting help of the man's wife, but in the end he fails and realizes this means his own death.

John and Oswald Cabal / THINGS TO COME, 1936, Great Britain, London Films, d-William Cameron Menzies.

Massey plays two roles in this expensive and impressive science fiction yarn: a man in England in 1940 at the beginning of a 30-year period of war and plague, and his descendant in 2036 when a massive revolt in a scientific city is unable to prevent the first couple from being sent to the moon.

Philip of Spain / FIRE OVER ENGLAND, 1936, Great Britain, Pendennis / United Artists, d-William Howard.

Massey is one of the villains of this story in which Laurence Olivier escapes the sea battle in which his father is captured and later burnt to death by the Inquisition. Olivier becomes a spy for Queen Elizabeth in Massey's court and brings back the plans of the invasion by the Armada.

Black Michael / THE PRISONER OF ZENDA, 1937, Selznick / United Artists, d-John Cromwell.

Once again Massey makes an excellent villain, this time as Ronald Colman's half-brother who schemes to win the latter's throne by kidnapping him and making him miss his coronation. He is thwarted when loyalists substitute a look-alike cousin for the missing monarch.

Abraham Lincoln / ABE LINCOLN IN ILLINOIS, 1940, RKO, d-John Cromwell.

Massey, a Canadian, seems so perfect portraying The Great Emancipator that he has ever after been fondly associated with the role of the rail-splitter from Illinois.

John Brown / SANTA FE TRAIL, 1940, Warners, d-Michael Curtiz.

Massey's booming voice and impressive curtain speech make him the best thing in this tale about a cavalry officer (Errol Flynn) whose path keeps crossing that of the bloody abolitionist, resulting in Massey's capture and hanging at Harper's Ferry.

King Cutler / REAP THE WILD WIND, 1942, Paramount, d-Cecil B. DeMille.

Massey is in the business of salvaging the cargoes of ships that pile up on the reefs off the Florida coast. However, he has an advantage over others in the business as he arranges for the ships to be scuttled.

Jonathan Brewster / ARSENIC AND OLD LACE, 1944, Warners, d-Frank Capra.

Mass murderer and criminally insane Massey feels he must compete with his two dotty old aunts who have poisoned a dozen homeless old men as a mercy. The tiebreaker as far as he is concerned will be his brother Cary Grant.

Gen. Claire Chennault / GOD IS MY CO-PILOT, 1945, Warners, d-Robert Florey.

Massey portrays the commander of the Flying Tigers, a group of American pilots who went to war for China against the Japanese before the United States got involved in the conflict.

Gail Wynard / THE FOUNTAINHEAD, 1949, Warners, d-King Vidor.

Massey is a wealthy newspaper publisher who hires an idealistic architect to design the perfect house for his wife. But, of course, a romance springs up between the architect and the wife, which is disastrous for all concerned.

John Brown / SEVEN ANGRY MEN, 1955, Allied Artists, d-Charles Marquis.

Massey repeats his role as the Kansas abolitionist who is determined to abolish slavery by violent means, prior to the American Civil War.

Adam Trask / EAST OF EDEN, 1955, Warners, d-Elia Kazan.

Massey is the stern, Bible-reading father of two extremely different sons in a California farming community in 1917. His wife is a madam in a neighboring town, though he has told the boys she is dead. One son can do no wrong in the old man's eyes; the other (James Dean) is considered to be as bad as the departed wife. Massey rejects Dean's birthday gift of money, saying: "If you want to give me a present give me a good life. That's something I can value."

OTHER ROLES

1931: *Sherlock Holmes* / THE SPECKLED BAND. **1937:** *Cardinal Richelieu* / UNDER THE RED ROBE; *Miguel del Vayo* / DREAMING LIPS; *Gov. Eugene De Laage* / THE HURRICANE. **1938:** *Prince Ghul* / DRUMS. **1939:** *Peter Charrington* / BLACK LIMELIGHT. **1941:** *Dr. Ingersoll* / DANGEROUSLY THEY LIVE. **1942:** *Andy Brock* / FORTY-NINTH PARALLEL; *Maj. Otto Baumeister* / DESPERATE JOURNEY. **1943:** *Capt. Steve Jarvis* / ACTION IN THE NORTH ATLANTIC. **1944:** *Frank Lalor* / THE WOMAN IN THE WINDOW. **1945:** *Arnim von Dahnwitz* / HOTEL BERLIN. **1946:** *Abraham Farlan* / A MATTER OF LIFE AND DEATH. **1947:** *Brig. Gen. Ezra Mannon* / MOURNING BECOMES ELECTRA; *Dean Graham* / POSSESSED. **1949:** *Old Randall McCoy* / ROSEANNA MCCOY; *Leland Willis* / CHAIN LIGHTNING. **1950:** *Wolf Larsen* / BARRICADE; *narrator* / CHALLENGE: SCIENCE AGAINST CANCER. **1951:** *Jacob Stint* / SUGARFOOT; *John Ives* / COME FILL THE CUP; *Nathan the Prophet* / DAVID AND BATHSHEBA. **1952:** *Big Jack Davis* / CARSON CITY. **1953:** *Yousseff* / THE DESERT SONG. **1955:** *General Snipes* / BATTLE CRY; *Junius Brutus Booth* / PRINCE OF PLAYERS. **1956:** *narrator* / THE TRUE STORY OF THE CIVIL WAR. **1957:** *the shah* / OMAR KHAYYAM; *narrator* / THE NAKED EYE. **1958:** *General Cummings* / THE NAKED AND THE DEAD. **1960:** *Abbott Donner* / THE GREAT IMPOSTOR. **1961:** *Willem* / THE FIERCEST HEART; *Captain Fellowes* / THE QUEEN'S GUARDS. **1962:** *narrator* / JACQUELINE KENNEDY'S ASIAN JOURNEY. **1963:** *Abe Lincoln* / HOW THE WEST WAS WON; *narrator* / REPORT ON CHINA. **1969:** *the preacher* / MACKENNA'S GOLD.

MATTHAU, WALTER

(Walter Matuschanskayasky, 1920–)

Walter Matthau has a lived-in look as he awkwardly moves around with a slouched posture, bloodhound face, and world-weary, grouchy voice. These characteristics, along with his sarcasm, wisecracks, and expert sense of timing have made him one of the top film comedians of our time. The son of a Russian orthodox priest who deserted his family when Matthau was little more than a baby, he worked as a child actor with the New York Yiddish Theatre and served in the air force during World War II before making his professional stage debut in 1946. After years of moving from bit parts to supporting roles, Matthau was signed to make movies. In his first picture, THE KENTUCKIAN, in 1955, he played the rather typical villain that was his screen persona until he scored a hit in Neil Simon's Broadway production of "The Odd Couple" in a part especially written by the playwright to fit his personality. After this triumph, Matthau was given more roles in comedies which led to his becoming a star. He won a Best Supporting Actor Oscar for THE FORTUNE COOKIE and has been nominated for KOTCH and THE SUNSHINE BOYS.

KEY ROLES

Mel Miller / A FACE IN THE CROWD, 1957, Warners, d-Elia Kazan.

Matthau is a cynical writer who helps create a media monster in Andy Griffith. In front of a TV audience Griffith is a down-home, Will Rogers-like country philosopher, but off-camera he is a power-crazy egomaniac.

Hamilton Bartholomew / CHARADE, 1963, Universal, d-Stanley Donen.

Cary Grant is not the only one different from whom he seems to be in this story. When Audrey Hepburn's husband is killed she finds four men after her. Matthau leads her to believe that he works for the U.S. government, but he's actually the killer.

Groeteschele / FAIL-SAFE, 1964, Columbia, d-Sidney Lumet.

Matthau is a civilian military adviser who is somewhat pleased when an American bomber is accidentally sent on its way to drop an atomic bomb on Moscow and can't be called back.

Ted Caselle / MIRAGE, 1965, Universal-International, d-Edward Dmytryk.

Matthau is a private detective hired by a man (Gregory Peck) who has lost the memory of his recent past and finds that he is being pursued by assassins. Matthau doesn't fare too well in this confusing "What is it?"

Willie Ginrich / THE FORTUNE COOKIE, 1966, United Artists, d-Billy Wilder.

Matthau won an Oscar for his portrayal of a crooked lawyer who forces his slightly injured client (Jack Lemmon) to sue a football player for causing his whiplash when the athlete ran him over on the sidelines of a football game. Matthau's ethics are nicely summed up in his counsel to another injured client: "Too bad it didn't happen further down the street—in front of the May Company. From them, you can collect! Couldn't you have dragged yourself another 20 feet?"

Paul Manning / A GUIDE FOR THE MARRIED MAN, 1967, 20th Century-Fox, d-Gene Kelly.

Although married to Inger Stevens, Matthau has a yearning for forbidden fruit and he is instructed in how to become a successful philanderer by Robert Morse, who has made a scientific study of unfaithfulness and has a story to illustrate every point.

Oscar Madison / THE ODD COUPLE, 1968, Paramount, d-Gene Saks.

Matthau is a divorced sportswriter who lives like a bum and he allows his fussy friend (Jack Lemmon) to move in with him when his wife throws him out. They couldn't be more different and nearly drive each other crazy. Offering refreshments to his poker buddies, Matthau announces: "I got brown sandwiches and green sandwiches...It's either very new cheese or very old meat."

Horace Vandergelder / HELLO, DOLLY! 1969, 20th Century-Fox, d-Gene Kelly.

In 1890, Matthau is a wealthy Yonkers grain merchant who hires widowed matchmaker Barbra Streisand to find him a young wife. She decides that she will meet his needs once she instructs him on what they are.

Dr. Julian Winston / CACTUS FLOWER, 1969, Columbia, d-Gene Saks.

To deceive his mistress (Goldie Hawn), dentist Matthau convinces his receptionist (Ingrid Bergman) to pose as his wife and later decides that he'd like to make the arrangement with Bergman permanent.

Joseph P. Kotcher / KOTCH, 1971, ABC / Kotch Company, d-Jack Lemmon.

Matthau plays an eccentric 72-year-old widower who has trouble with his family when he helps a pregnant babysitter.

Willy Clark / THE SUNSHINE BOYS, 1975, MGM, d-Herbert Ross.

In this film Matthau and George Burns had spent over forty years as a comedy team, but finally broke up, and Matthau has unpleasant recollections of his association with Burns. They have a chance to appear together again doing their old act on a TV program detailing the history of comedy. The confrontation between the two old men after so many years is quite delightful.

OTHER ROLES

1955: *Sam Bodine* / THE KENTUCKIAN; *Wes Todd* / THE INDIAN FIGHTER. **1956:** *Wally Gibbs* / BIGGER THAN LIFE. **1957:** *Al Dahlke* / SLAUGHTER ON TENTH AVENUE. **1958:** *Maxie Fields* / KING CREOLE; *Judge Kyle* / RIDE A CROOKED TRAIL; *Dr. Leon Karnes* / VOICE IN THE MIRROR; *Red Wildoe* / ONIONHEAD. **1960:** *Felix Andrews* / STRANGERS WHEN WE MEET; *Jack Martin* / GANGSTER STORY. **1962:** *Sheriff Johnson* / LONELY ARE THE BRAVE; *Tony Gagoots* / WHO'S GOT THE ACTION? **1963:** *Tony Dallas* / ISLAND OF LOVE. **1964:** *Doc* / ENSIGN PULVER; *Sir Leopold Sartori* / GOODBYE CHARLIE. **1968:** *Charlie the movie star* / THE SECRET LIFE OF AN AMERICAN WIFE; *General Smight* / CANDY. **1971:** *Henry Graham* / A NEW LEAF; *Sam Nash* / *Jesse Kiplinger* / *Roy Hubley* / PLAZA SUITE. **1972:** *Pete Seltzer* / PETE 'N' TILLIE. **1973:** *Charley Varrick* / CHARLEY VARRICK; *Jake Martin* / THE LAUGHING POLICEMAN. **1974:** *drunk* / EARTHQUAKE; *Lieutenant Garber* / THE TAKING OF PELHAM ONE TWO THREE. **1975:** *Walter Burns* / THE FRONT PAGE. **1976:** *Morris Buttermaker* / THE BAD NEWS BEARS. **1977:** *Lloyd Bourdell* / CASEY'S SHADOW. **1978:** *Marvin Michaels* / CALIFORNIA SUITE. **1980:** *Sorrowful Jones* / LITTLE MISS MARKER; *Miles Kendig* / HOPSCOTCH. **1981:** *Dan Snow* / FIRST MONDAY IN OCTOBER; *Trabucco* / BUDDY BUDDY. **1982:** *Herbert Tucker* / I OUGHT TO BE IN PICTURES. **1983:** *Sonny Paluso* / THE SURVIVORS. **1985:** *Joe Mulholland* / MOVERS AND SHAKERS. **1987:** *Becker* / THE COUCH TRIP.

MATTHEWS, JESSIE

(1907–1981)

A dark-haired British dancer and singer, Jessie Matthews, billed as "The Dancing Divinity," was one of eleven children born to a poor Soho family. In the 1930s she became Britain's most sought after star in a series of mediocre musical stories in which she appeared as stage-struck girls pretending to be someone else. But audiences did not come to see the stories. They wanted to be thrilled by the high kicks of the graceful, bright-eyed, sylphlike dancer who had no peer among the other female film dancers. Many times there was talk that she would be teamed with Fred Astaire, but unfortunately nothing came of it. Her theme song was "Over My Shoulder," which also was the title of her autobiography. By the 1940s she was no longer an audience favorite and found work on a popular British radio show and, for a time, ran a drama school in Australia.

KEY ROLES

Susie Dean / THE GOOD COMPANIONS, 1933, Great Britain, Gaumont, d-Victor Saville.

Matthews is the leading lady of the failing Dinky Doos pierrot troupe that is saved by a middle-aged spinster with a small legacy, a Yorkshire joiner, and a disillusioned music teacher. It was a phenomenally successful musical.

Rasi / WALTZES FROM VIENNA, 1934, Great Britain, Gaumont-British, d-Alfred Hitchcock.

In this untypical Hitchcock movie, Matthews is a pastry cook's daughter who loves Johann Strauss, Jr. Strauss is being aided in his musical career by a countess while at the same time feuding with his father.

Harriet Green / EVERGREEN, 1934, Great Britain, Gaumont-British, d-Victor Saville.

Matthews is as cute as a bug in this most famous British musical of the 1930s. She ascended to world stardom as a girl who poses as her own mother, a legendary music-hall star who falls for a publicity man.

Elizabeth / FIRST A GIRL, 1935, Great Britain, Gaumont-British, d-Victor Saville.

This is the original version of VICTOR / VICTORIA in which Matthews meets Sonnie Hale, a female impersonator, in a downpour. When he catches cold, she goes on in his place as a man impersonating a woman impersonating a man, and becomes the rage of Europe.

Elaine Bradford / IT'S LOVE AGAIN, 1936, Great Britain, Gaumont, d-Victor Saville.

In the most successful of her musicals, Matthews is a chorus girl who, to achieve her singing and dancing ambitions, impersonates an imaginary society woman just back from the East. But she eventually becomes a star on her own merits.

Kay Martin / SAILING ALONG, 1938, Great Britain, Gaumont-British, d-Sonnie Hale.

In the last of her musicals, Matthews dreams of becoming a stage star while the man she loves hopes to become a financial wheeler-dealer. When they are helped by an eccentric millionaire, she dances her way to stardom, and he makes his fortune. They give it all up to sail off together in his new boat.

OTHER ROLES

1923: *Pan* / THE BELOVED VAGABOND; *Edward, Prince of Wales* / THIS ENGLAND. **1924:** *extra* / STRAWS IN THE WIND. **1931:** *Tommy Tucker* / OUT OF THE BLUE. **1932:** *Annette Marquand* / THERE GOES THE BRIDE; *Celia Newbiggin* / THE MIDSHIPMAID. **1933:** *Leslie Farrar* / THE MAN FROM TORONTO; *Milly* / FRIDAY THE 13TH. **1937:** *Jeanne* / HEAD OVER HEELS IN LOVE; *Pat Wayne* / GANGWAY. **1939:** *Diane Castle* / CLIMBING HIGH. **1943:** *Mildred Trimble* / FOREVER AND A DAY. **1944:** *Dorothea Capper* / CANDLES AT NINE. **1947:** *herself* / LIFE IS NOTHING WITHOUT MUSIC. **1958:** *Anna* / TOM THUMB. **1978:** *Mrs. Tinsdale* / THE HOUND OF THE BASKERVILLES.

MATURE, VICTOR

(1915–)

Victor Mature made over fifty films but was seldom given much credit for being an actor. He didn't seem to mind, observing, "Actually, I am a golfer. That is my real occupation. I never was an actor, ask anybody, particularly the critics." Looking back at his film career, one must admit that he appeared in and contributed mightily to some very fine movies, but these go along with the true dogs he made that no one could have helped. With his sexy looks, open personality, broad smile, and impressive physique, "the gorgeous hunk," as he was nicknamed, was just perfect for costume pieces, and was equally good in some classic film noir roles. By the mid-1950s his career, which began in the early 1940s, was about at an end, although he later appeared in some spoofs of his own screen persona, such as AFTER THE FOX in 1966.

KEY ROLES

Tumak / ONE MILLION B.C., 1940, United Artists, d-Hal Roach, Hal Roach, Jr., and D. W. Griffith.

Mature is all beefcake in this grunt and groan story of two prehistoric tribes, the Rock people and the Shell people, who are constantly being attacked by large animals. Life is hard but Mature is always was clean-shaven.

Frankie Christopher (Botticelli) / I WAKE UP SCREAMING, 1941, 20th Century-Fox, d-H. Bruce Humberstone.

When a beautiful model is murdered, Mature is the chief suspect. But he convinces the dead girl's sister that he is innocent and together they track down the real killer.

Dr. Omar / THE SHANGHAI GESTURE, 1941, United Artists, d-Josef von Sternberg.

Wearing a fez, Mature is the philosophical Arab lover of the proprietress of a Shanghai gambling casino who taunts her ex-husband by showing him his daughter in a state of degradation.

Paul Dresser / MY GAL SAL, 1942, 20th Century-Fox, d-Irving Cummings.

In this biopic of songwriter Paul Dresser, who was the brother of author Theodore Dreiser, Mature is quite likable working with beautiful Rita Hayworth, who gives him inspiration and a certain amount of trouble.

Doc Holliday / MY DARLING CLEMENTINE, 1946, 20th Century-Fox, d-John Ford.

Mature gives a fiery portrayal of the consumptive dentist turned gambler and gunfighter who helps the Earp brothers in a shootout with the Clanton gang at the O.K. Corral.

Nick Bianco / KISS OF DEATH, 1947, 20th Century-Fox, d-Henry Hathaway.

In this spectacular film noir, Mature is a convict who is talked into informing on his own gang when they don't keep their word about caring for his family. He ends up having to face a psychopathic killer (Richard Widmark) out to take care of the squealer.

Samson / SAMSON AND DELILAH, 1949, Paramount, d-Cecil B. DeMille.

Mature is a religious strongman whose strength is related to his hair. When Philistine Delilah cuts his hair, Mature is taken prisoner by his enemies, blinded, and chained to pillars in their temple. But no one seems to notice that his hair has grown back and he pulls down the pillars and the temple on his enemies, Delilah, and himself. Earlier in the film, when he goes after a lion, Mature spurns the offer of a spear saying, "I won't need that. He's a young lion."

James Sullivan / MILLION DOLLAR MERMAID, 1952, MGM, d-Mervyn LeRoy.

Mature is the promoter who makes a fortune for Australian swimmer Annette Kellerman by involving her in all kinds of aquatic exploits.

Demetrius / THE ROBE, 1953, 20th Century-Fox, d-Henry Koster.

Mature is a Greek slave of a centurion (Richard Burton) who is put in charge of the crucifixion of Jesus Christ. It has quite an effect on both men. Burt Lancaster was the first choice for the role and Tyrone Power was supposed to get the Burton role.

Horemheb / THE EGYPTIAN, 1954, 20th Century-Fox, d-Michael Curtiz.

In this pretentious epic, Mature is an Egyptian warrior who ultimately takes over for the peace-loving pharaoh who is too gentle to be allowed to live and rule.

Tony Powell / AFTER THE FOX, 1966, United Artists, d-Vittorio de Sica.

When the Fox (Peter Sellers) escapes from jail to pull off a gold bullion heist, he uses the cover of making a movie with Mature as his star. Mature is splendid hamming it up in a parody of himself.

OTHER ROLES

1939: *Lefty* / THE HOUSEKEEPER'S DAUGHTER. **1940:** *Dan Marvin* / CAPTAIN CAUTION; *William* / NO, NO NANETTE. **1942:** *Jefferson Harper* / SONG OF THE ISLANDS; *Tommy Lundy* / FOOTLIGHT SERENADE; *Johnny Gray* / SEVEN DAYS' LEAVE. **1947:** *Michael Drego* / MOSS ROSE. **1948:** *Cash* / FURY AT FURNACE CREEK; *Lieutenant Candella* / CRY OF THE CITY. **1949:** *Danny James* / RED, HOT AND BLUE; *Pete Wilson* / EASY LIVING. **1950:** *Andy Clark* / WABASH AVENUE; *Jeff DeMarco* / STELLA; *Marc Fury* / GAMBLING HOUSE; *guest* / I'LL GET BY. **1952:** *Dave Andrews* / THE LAS VEGAS STORY;

captain / ANDROCLES AND THE LION; *Steve Bennett* / SOMETHING FOR THE BIRDS. **1953:** *Lt. Sam Prior* / THE GLORY BRIGADE; *Bill Blakely* / AFFAIR WITH A STRANGER; *Antar* / VEILS OF BAGDAD. **1954:** *Matt Hallett* / DANGEROUS MISSION; *Demetrius* / DEMETRIUS AND THE GLADIATORS; *"The Scarf"* / BETRAYED. **1955:** *Crazy Horse* / CHIEF CRAZY HORSE; *Shelley Martin* / VIOLENT SATURDAY; *Jed* / THE LAST FRONTIER. **1956:** *Ken Duffield* / SAFARI; *Ben Staves* / THE SHARKFIGHTERS. **1957:** *Zarak Khan* / ZARAK; *Charles Sturgis* / INTERPOL; *Harry Miller* / THE LONG HAUL; *Cliff Brandon* / CHINA DOLL. **1958:** *Sgt. David Thatcher* / NO TIME TO DIE. **1959:** *Ben Lassiter* / ESCORT WEST; *Hank Whirling* / THE BIG CIRCUS; *Mike Conway* / TIMBUKTU. **1960:** *Hannibal* / HANNIBAL; *Oleg* / THE TARTARS. **1968:** *Big Victor* / HEAD. **1972:** *Carmine Ganucci* / EVERY LITTLE CROOK AND NANNY. **1976:** *Nick* / WON TON TON, THE DOG WHO SAVED HOLLYWOOD. **1979:** *Harold Everett* / FIREPOWER.

MAYO, VIRGINIA

(Virginia Jones, 1920–)

Voluptuous blonde Virginia Mayo was a ballet dancer at the age of 17 with the St. Louis Opera Company and shortly thereafter played straightwoman to two men in a horse suit in vaudeville. After finding work in Eddie Cantor's "Banjo Eyes" on Broadway in 1941, she was signed to a contract with Samuel Goldwyn, who began grooming her to be a star. Her first leading role was with Bob Hope in THE PRINCESS AND THE PIRATE and she later teamed up with Danny Kaye in five movies, although in the first she had but a bit role. She proved she could score successfully in dramatic roles with THE BEST YEARS OF OUR LIVES. In her straight roles she was best when playing something of a slut, while in her musical parts she usually appeared as a demure young woman with just a hint of earthiness lurking below the surface for the right man to bring out. In her Technicolor extravaganzas no such man ever appeared. Her career was effectively over with the decline of the studio system, although she made movies now and then into the 1970s. She was married to actor Michael O'Shea until his death.

KEY ROLES

Princess Margaret / THE PRINCESS AND THE PIRATE, 1944, Goldwyn, d-David Butler.

Mayo looks as pretty as a princess in her pirate-like outfit in this lesser Bob Hope comedy. Hope has to protect her from Victor McLaglen and Walter Slezak, who have their own plans for her.

Ellen Shavley / WONDER MAN, 1945, Goldwyn, d-H. Bruce Humberstone.

Mayo lives in a flat above mild-mannered Danny Kaye, who is persuaded by the ghost of his murdered twin brother to find the killer. This takes him into show business and he finds that he's engaged to Vera-Ellen. But when he straightens everything out he returns to Mayo.

Marie Derry / THE BEST YEARS OF OUR LIVES, 1946, Goldwyn, d-William Wyler.

When she met Dana Andrews in his officer's uniform, Mayo found him exciting and they rushed into marriage. Once the war is over and he's trying to find work for which he's qualified, she wants to party and doesn't find him so appealing in civies.

Rosalind Van Hoorn / THE SECRET LIFE OF WALTER MITTY, 1947, Goldwyn, d-Norman Z. McLeod.

Whenever book editor and mama's boy Danny Kaye daydreams about his derring-do, the same beautiful blonde shows up. Ultimately, she shows up in real life in the lovely shape of Mayo and they get involved with spies.

Ruth Wilson / THE GIRL FROM JONES BEACH, 1949, Warners, d-Peter Godfrey.

Schoolteacher Mayo meets commercial artist Ronald Reagan, who finds her the real-life counterpart of his imaginary "perfect girl."

Verna Jarrett / WHITE HEAT, 1949, Warners, d-Raoul Walsh.

Mayo is the wife of violent James Cagney, a murdering gangster with a mother fixation. It's good for Mayo that Cagney never learns that she killed his ma with a shot in the back.

Lady Barbara Wellesley / CAPTAIN HORATIO HORNBLOWER, 1951, Great Britain, Warners, d-Raoul Walsh.

Mayo is a beautiful lady whom British captain Gregory Peck rescues from the Spaniards in the 19th century and nurses back to health when she becomes deathly ill. Love blossoms, but he's already married and she's promised to another. But they get together in the end.

Angela Gardner / Hot Garters Gertie / SHE'S WORKING HER WAY THROUGH COLLEGE, 1952, Warners, d-H. Bruce Humberstone.

Mayo is a burlesque queen who goes to college and teaches her English professor (Ronald Reagan) a thing or two.

Judalon de Bornay / THE IRON MISTRESS, 1952, Warners, d-Gordon Douglas.

Alan Ladd, as the inventor of the famous Bowie knife, has more trouble with Mayo than he did with the Mexicans at the Alamo. She's a high-spirited New Orleans girl and when she doesn't get what she wants, you can be sure somebody will get killed.

Helena / THE SILVER CHALICE, 1954, Warners, d-Victor Saville.

In this post-Biblical hokum, Mayo is an assistant to Jack Palance, a magician who believes that the cup Jesus used at the Last Supper will give him even greater magical powers. A slave (Paul Newman) has been commissioned to create a chalice for the cup and Mayo will use her charms to try and get it from him.

OTHER ROLES

1943: *model* / FOLLIES GIRL; *Mamie* / THE ADVENTURES OF JACK LONDON. **1944:** *nurse* / UP IN ARMS; *Carol* / SEVEN DAYS ASHORE. **1947:** *Polly Pringle* / THE KID FROM BROOKLYN; *Deborah Tyler* / OUT OF THE BLUE. **1948:** *Honey Swanson* / A SONG IS BORN; *Linda Vickers* / SMART GIRLS DON'T TALK. **1949:** *Flaxy Martin* / FLAXY MARTIN; *Colorado Carson* / COLORADO TERRITORY; *Carla North* / RED LIGHT; *Nancy Eagen* / ALWAYS LEAVE THEM LAUGHING. **1950:** *Julie Benson* / BACKFIRE; *Anne* / THE FLAME AND THE ARROW; *Eve Dillon* / WEST POINT STORY. **1951:** *Ann Keith* / ALONG THE GREAT DIVIDE; *Carol* / PAINTING THE CLOUDS WITH SUNSHINE; *herself* / STARLIFT. **1953:** *Catherine Terris* / SHE'S BACK ON BROADWAY; *Ginger Martin* / SOUTH SEA WOMAN; *Abby Nixon* / DEVIL'S CANYON. **1954:** *Lady Edith* / KING RICHARD AND THE CRUSADERS. **1955:** *Rita Delaine* / PEARL OF THE SOUTH PACIFIC. **1956:** *Ann Alaine* / GREAT DAY IN THE MORNING; *Sally* / THE PROUD ONES; *Louise Whitman* / CONGO CROSSING. **1957:** *Helen* / THE BIG LAND; *Cleopatra* / THE STORY OF MANKIND; *Ellen* / THE TALL STRANGER. **1958:** *Celia Gray* / FORT DOBBS. **1959:** *Norma Puntman* / WESTBOUND; *Jean Gruney* / JET OVER THE ATLANTIC. **1960:** *Duchess de Revalte* / THE REVOLT OF THE MERCENARIES. **1965:** *Sarah McCoy* / YOUNG FURY. **1966:** *Sable* / CASTLE OF EVIL. **1967:** *Linda Lee* / FORT UTAH. **1976:** *Miss Battley* / WON TON TON, THE DOG WHO SAVED HOLLYWOOD. **1977:** *Michelle* / HAUNTED. **1978:** *Countess Piazza* / *Ida* / FRENCH QUARTER.

MCCREA, JOEL

(1905–)

Joel McCrea never became as big a star as Gary Cooper, whom he physically resembled and had similar roles as in the early part of his career, because he just didn't care enough about it. This tall, rugged, handsome, reliable actor played a variety of roles in a wide range of movies that included comedies, straight dramas, and adventures, with the peak of his career being in the early 1940s. After World War II he was seen almost exclusively in westerns for fifteen years. Modest about his acting, he observed: "Acting? I never attempt it. A placid sort of fellow, that's me...so when I face the cameras, I just stay placid." However, McCrea was proud that he never appeared in a movie that lost money, an important achievement to the unpretentious cattleman whose wise investments made him one of the wealthiest American actors. He has been married to actress Frances Dee since 1933, another feat he should be proud of.

KEY ROLES

Johnny Baker / BIRD OF PARADISE, 1932, RKO, d-King Vidor.

McCrea is an adventurer who has an idyllic time with Dolores Del Rio on a South Seas island until she is needed to help her people and must throw herself into an active volcano to appease the gods.

Bob Whitney / THE MOST DANGEROUS GAME, 1932, RKO, d-Ernest B. Schoedsack and Irving Pichel.

McCrea is among the "guests" brought to the island home of Leslie Banks, a mad hunter whose prey this time is man.

Jim Carmichael / BARBARY COAST, 1935, Goldwyn, d-Howard Hawks.

In this juicy melodrama McCrea is the romantic interest for Miriam Hopkins, a lonely girl whom ruthless club owner Edward G. Robinson builds into a star during the gold rush days.

Dr. Joseph Cardin / THESE THREE, 1936, Goldwyn, d-William Wyler.

In this altered version of Lillian Hellman's "The Children's Hour," hateful schoolgirl Bonita Granville spreads the rumor of a heterosexual triangle involving McCrea, Merle Oberon, and Miriam Hopkins.

Dr. James Kildare / INTERNS CAN'T TAKE MONEY, 1937, Paramount, d-Alfred Santell.

The "Jeopardy" answer is "Joel McCrea." The question is "Who was the first Dr. Kildare in the movies?" The story here has nothing to do with the series that followed with Lew Ayres. In this one McCrea is a doctor who persuades a gangster friend to help Barbara Stanwyck find her missing child.

Dave Connell / DEAD END, 1937, Goldwyn, d-William Wyler.

McCrea lives in a New York slum on a dead end street just behind a luxury hotel. He ends up killing Humphrey Bogart, a notorious gangster who has returned to the neighborhood where he grew up.

Jeff Butler / UNION PACIFIC, 1939, Paramount, d-Cecil B. DeMille.

McCrea is a scout for a company building the Union Pacific railroad. He must deal with Indians, crooked gamblers, and a charming rascal (Robert Preston) who is his rival for Barbara Stanwyck.

Johnny Jones (Huntley Haverstock) / FOREIGN CORRESPONDENT, 1940, United Artists, d-Alfred Hitchcock.

McCrea is a jaunty reporter who is present when a Dutch official at a peace conference is assassinated. From then on he's involved in a series of thrilling adventures until it is discovered that a prominent man of peace is actually the one plugging for war. At the end McCrea makes an eloquent plea for the United States to oppose the Nazis in the coming war.

John L. Sullivan / SULLIVAN'S TRAVELS, 1941, Paramount, d-Preston Sturges.

McCrea is a director of comedy movies (somewhat like Sturges) who tires of having little to say of importance and so sets out to cross the country posing as a hobo to find what people are looking for. What he finds is that they want to laugh. Now aware that his pictures do have something important to say, he brags: "I'll tell you something else: there's a lot to be said for making people laugh. Did you know that's all some people have? It isn't much, but it's better than nothing in this cockeyed caravan."

Tom Jeffers / THE PALM BEACH STORY, 1942, Paramount, d-Preston Sturges.

This delightful comedy is seen all too infrequently nowadays. In it McCrea is an unsuccessful engineer whose wife (Claudette Colbert) leaves him to find a millionaire in Florida, even though she still loves him. When she finds a millionaire and his sister (Mary Astor), the only way things can work out is for McCrea and Colbert to have identical twins—and they do!

Joe Carter / THE MORE THE MERRIER, 1943, Columbia, d-George Stevens.

In crowded Washington during World War II, Jean Arthur is bamboozled into allowing Charles Coburn to share her apartment. He in turn sublets his half to Joel McCrea and then Coburn plays Cupid for the young people.

William F. Cody / BUFFALO BILL, 1944, 20th Century-Fox, d-William A. Wellman.

In this fictitious biopic of the famous frontiersman, McCrea fails to depict the wild West showman's philandering, although the film does make him out as crummy husband or father material. It's enjoyable without being accurate.

The Virginian / THE VIRGINIAN, 1946, Paramount, d-Stuart Gilmore.

McCrea repeats the 1929 Gary Cooper role about a man who is forced to hang his best friend for rustling, an action not understood by the girl they both courted. He must then go up against the real villain of the piece, in this case Brian Donlevy.

Ross McEwen / FOUR FACES WEST, 1948, United Artists, d-Alfred E. Green.

McCrea is a beleaguered outlaw torn between the need to fight and compassion for a helpless invalid as he is pursued by a relentless enemy.

Wyatt Earp / WICHITA, 1955, Allied Artists, d-Jacques Tourneur.

In this very fine minor western that is historically inaccurate, McCrea portrays Wyatt Earp as marshal of Wichita, Kansas, although Earp was never marshal anyplace.

Steve Judd / RIDE THE HIGH COUNTRY, 1962, MGM, d-Sam Peckinpah.

In this wonderful western, two old cowboy heroes (McCrea and Randolph Scott) team up to say a sort of so long to the genre. McCrea is an ex-lawman whose old colleague (Scott) has been reduced to earning a living in a sleazy sideshow carnival. When the two weary old-timers are hired to escort a gold shipment, McCrea wants them to take the gold for themselves but Scott is still a man of integrity.

OTHER ROLES

1927: *bit* / THE FAIR CO-ED; *bit* / THE ENEMY. **1929:** *Todd Sayles* / THE JAZZ AGE;*bit* / SO THIS IS COLLEGE; *Marco the Shark* / DYNAMITE; *Boyd Emerson* / THE SILVER HORDE. **1930:** *John Marvin* / LIGHTNIN'; *Thomas Mason* / ONCE A SINNER. **1931:** *Dick Brunton* / KEPT HUSBANDS; *John Neville, Jr.* / THE COMMON LAW; *Barry Craig* / BORN TO LOVE; *Jim Baker* / GIRLS ABOUT TOWN. **1932:** *Lawrence Ogle* / BUSINESS AND PLEASURE; *Red* / THE LOST SQUADRON; *Jacob Van Riker Pell* / ROCKABYE; *Sandy Baker* / THE SPORT PARADE. **1933:** *David Phelps* / THE SILVER CORD; *Dan Walters* / BED OF ROSES; *Jimmy Watts* / ONE MAN'S JOURNEY; *Blacky Gorman* / CHANCE AT HEAVEN. **1934:** *Garry Madison* / GAMBLING LADY; *John Adams* / HALF A SINNER; *Tony Travers* / THE RICHEST GIRL IN THE WORLD. **1935:** *Dr. Alex MacGregor* / PRIVATE WORLDS; *Dr. Donald Middleton* / OUR LITTLE GIRL; *Tony Baxter* / WOMAN WANTED; *Brighton Lorrimore* / SPLENDOR. **1936:** *Larry Stevens* / TWO IN A CROWD; *George Melville* / ADVENTURE IN MANHATTAN; *Richard Glasgow* / COME AND GET IT; *Ernie Holley* / BANJO ON MY KNEE. **1937:** *Ramsey MacKay* / WELLS FARGO; *Kenneth Nolan* / WOMAN CHASES MAN. **1938:** *Van Smith* / THREE BLIND MICE; *Joe Meadows* / YOUTH TAKES A FLING. **1939:** *Peter McCarthy* / THEY SHALL HAVE MUSIC; *Barry Corvall* / ESPIONAGE AGENT. **1940:** *T. H. Randall* / HE MARRIED HIS WIFE; *Ed Wallace* / THE PRIMROSE PATH. **1941:** *Russ Elliott* / REACHING FOR THE SUN; *cameo* / LAND OF LIBERTY. **1942:** *Ethan Hoyt* / THE GREAT MAN'S LADY. **1944:** *W. T. G. Morton* / THE GREAT MOMENT. **1945:** *David Fielding* / THE UNSEEN. **1947:** *Dave Nash* / RAMROD. **1949:** *Kip Davis* / SOUTH OF ST. LOUIS; *Wes McQueen* / COLORADO TERRITORY. **1950:** *Josiah Doziah Grey* / STARS IN MY CROWN; *Will Owens* / THE OUTRIDERS; *Chuck Conner* / SADDLE TRAMP; *Tom Banning* / FRENCHIE. **1951:** *Dan Mathews* / CATTLE DRIVE; *guest* / THE HOLLYWOOD STORY. **1952:** *Rick Nelson* / THE SAN FRANCISCO STORY. **1953:** *Zachary Hallock* / LONE HAND; *Lt. Col. Robert Tanie* / ROUGH SHOOT. **1954:** *Dee Rockwell* / BLACK HORSE CANYON; *Clete Mattson* / BORDER RIVER. **1955:** *Rick Thorne* / STRANGER ON HORSEBACK. **1956:** *Sam Houston* / THE FIRST TEXAN. **1957:** *Dr. John Brighton* / THE OKLAHOMAN; *Sergeant Hook* / TROOPER HOOK; *Mike Ryan* / GUNSIGHT RIDGE; *Ned Bannon* / THE TALL STRANGER. **1958:** *John Cord* / CATTLE EMPIRE; *Vinson* / FORT MASSACRE. **1959:** *Bat Masterson* / THE GUNFIGHT AT DODGE CITY. **1971:** *Pitcalin* / CRY BLOOD, APACHE. **1974:** *narrator* / THE GREAT AMERICAN COWBOY. **1976:** *Dan* / MUSTANG COUNTRY.

MCDOWALL, RODDY

(Roderick Andrew McDowall, 1928–)

Roddy McDowall made his acting debut at age nine in Great Britain. In 1940 he was evacuated to the United States, where his appearance in HOW GREEN WAS MY VALLEY (1941) brought him critical and public acclaim. Throughout the 1940s he was kept very busy, averaging two films a year. The youthful looks of this boyish star allowed him to play youngsters long after he was able to vote, but they also seriously limited his adult roles. During the 1950s he did a great deal of TV and stage work and when he returned to films, he found various roles in pictures of definitely mixed quality. He had one more hurrah with the PLANET OF THE APES series. The made-for-TV movies of this former major child star include NIGHT GALLERY (1969), TERROR IN THE SKY (1971), WHAT'S A NICE GIRL LIKE YOU...? (1972), THE ELEVATOR (1974), FLOOD (1976), THE THIEF OF BAGHDAD and SCAVENGER HUNT (1979), THE MEMORY OF EVA RYKER (1980), EVIL UNDER THE SUN (1982), THIS GUN FOR HIRE (1983), and THE ZANY ADVENTURES OF ROBIN HOOD (1984).

KEY ROLES

Huw Morgan / HOW GREEN WAS MY VALLEY, 1941, 20th Century-Fox, d-John Ford.

McDowall is excellent as the child who, as a man, fondly recalls his family's trials and tribulations in a small Welsh mining village. The story is so lovingly told that it could only have developed in the mind of a child who was loved and cherished by his sometimes gruff but always dependable parents and siblings.

Ronnie Cavanaugh / THE PIED PIPER, 1942, 20th Century-Fox, d-Irving Pichel.

McDowall is one of the children that elderly child-hater Monty Woolley finds himself smuggling out of occupied France during World War II.

Ken McLaughlin / MY FRIEND FLICKA, 1943, 20th Century-Fox, d-Harold Schuster.

In this beautifully photographed picture, McDowall yearns to own a colt. When his rancher father relents and allows the boy his dream, the former is not pleased with McDowall's choice. But the faith and love of the boy prove justified when the animal grows into a beautiful horse. By the way, Flicka means girl in Swedish.

Joe Carraclough / LASSIE COME HOME, 1943, MGM, d-Fred M. Wilcox.

As a member of a poor farming family, McDowall is heartbroken when they are forced to sell his collie. But the dog makes a remarkable journey to return to the boy. This was the beginning of a long career for Lassie.

Stanley Owen / HOLIDAY IN MEXICO, 1946, MGM, d-George Sidney.

As an aging adolescent, McDowall no longer rated star billing as he supported cute young Jane Powell in this story about the daughter of the American ambassador to Mexico falling for Jose Iturbi.

Malcolm / MACBETH, 1948, Republic, d-Orson Welles.

McDowall portrays the murdered King Duncan's son and rightful heir in this flawed but interesting low-budget quickie version of the famous Shakespeare play.

Bullwhip Griffin / THE ADVENTURES OF BULLWHIP GRIFFIN, 1967, Disney, d-James Neilson.

In this western spoof, McDowall is a very proper Boston butler who accompanies his master to the 1849 California gold rush where he learns to take care of himself among the rough and tough bullies of the wild, wild West.

Cornelius / PLANET OF THE APES, 1968, 20th Century-Fox, d-Franklin J. Schaffner.

Being made-up as a chimpanzee scientist proved steady work for McDowall as he appeared in four sequels and a TV series based on the film. It's the tale of an astronaut who winds up on Earth in an era when humans are the lower forms of life and apes are the rulers.

Ben Fischer / THE LEGEND OF HELL HOUSE, 1973, 20th Century-Fox, d-John Hough.

McDowall is a physical medium who joins three others in an investigation to determine if a house is really haunted. They encounter poltergeists and evil forces that possess them before they discover the house's secret.

OTHER ROLES

1937: *boy* / SCRUFFY; *Peter Osborne* / MURDER IN THE FAMILY; *boy* / I SEE ICE. **1938:** *boy* / JOHN HALIFAX—GENTLEMAN; *bit* / CONVICT 99; *boy* / HEY! HEY! U.S.A.; *bit* / SARAH SIDDONS; *boy* / HE OUTSIDER; *bit* / POISON PEN; *boy* / DEAD MAN'S SHOES. **1939:** *Ginger* / JUST WILLIAM; *boy* / HIS BROTHER'S KEEPER; *bit* / DIRT; *boy* / SALOON BOY. **1940:** *young Bob Slater* / YOU WILL REMEMBER; *Hugo* / THIS ENGLAND; *Vaner* / MAN HUNT. **1941:** *Albert Perkins* / CONFIRM OR DENY. **1942:** *young Benjamin Blake* / SON OF FURY; *Hugh Aylesworth* / ON THE SUNNY SIDE. **1944:** *John Ashwood II* / THE WHITE CLIFFS OF DOVER; *Francis Chisholm as a boy* / KEYS OF THE KINGDOM. **1945:** *Ken McLaughlin* / THUNDERHEAD, SON OF FLICKA; *Jimmy Graham* / MOLLY AND ME. **1948:** *David Balfour* / KIDNAPPED; *Roddy* / ROCKY. **1949:** *Alec* / TUNA CLIPPER; *Scott Jordan* / BLACK MIDNIGHT; *Ted* / KILLER SHARK. **1950:** *Jimmy* / BIG TIMBER. **1952:** *Erik* / THE STEEL FIST. **1960:** *Yuri Gilgoric* / THE SUBTERRANEANS; *Malcolm* / MIDNIGHT LACE. **1962:** *Private Morris* / THE LONGEST DAY. **1963:** *Octavian* / CLEOPATRA. **1964:** *Martin Ashley* / SHOCK TREATMENT. **1965:** *Matthew* / THE GREATEST STORY EVER TOLD; *Oliver Parsons* / THE THIRD DAY; *Gregory Benson* / THAT DARN CAT; *Dr. J., Jr.* / THE LOVED ONE. **1966:** *Allan "Mollymauk" Musgrave* / LORD LOVE A DUCK; *Walter Baines* / INSIDE DAISY CLOVER; *CIA agent Adam* / THE DEFECTOR. **1967:** *Tony Krum* / THE COOL ONES; *Arthur Pimms* / IT. **1968:** *Nate Ashbury* / HELLO DOWN THERE; *Nick Evers* / FIVE CARD STUD. **1969:** *Santoro* / ANGEL, ANGEL, DOWN WE GO; *Cornelius* / BENEATH THE PLANET OF THE APES. **1971:** *Cornelius* / ESCAPE FROM THE PLANET OF THE APES; *Mr. Jelk* / BEDKNOBS AND BROOMSTICKS; *Proffer* / PRETTY MAIDS ALL IN A ROW. **1972:** *Cornelius* / CONQUEST OF THE PLANET OF THE APES; *Acres* / THE POSEIDON ADVENTURE; *Frank Gass* / THE LIFE AND TIMES OF JUDGE ROY BEAN. **1973:** *Cornelius* / BATTLE FOR THE PLANET OF THE APES. **1974:** *Robert* / ARNOLD; *Stanton* / DIRTY MARY, CRAZY LARRY. **1975:** *Bobby Moore* / FUNNY LADY. **1976:** *Tony Da Vinci* / MEAN JOHNNY BARROWS; *Riley* / EMBRYO. **1978:** *Dr. Melton* / RABBIT TEST; *Stallwood* / THE CAT FROM OUTER SPACE. **1979:** *White Robe* / CIRCLE OF IRON; *Jenkins* / SCAVENGER HUNT. **1981:** *Gillespie* / CHARLIE CHAN AND THE CURSE OF THE DRAGON QUEEN. **1982:** *Rex Brewster* / EVIL UNDER THE SUN; *Terry Corrigan* / CLASS OF 1984. **1985:** *Peter Vincent* / FRIGHT NIGHT. **1987:** *Andrew* / OVERBOARD.

MCDOWELL, MALCOLM

(1943–)

Born to a Yorkshire working-class family, Malcolm McDowell joined a repertory theater on the Isle of Wight and later spent 18 months as a supernumerator with the Royal Shakespeare Company. He made his film debut in POOR COW in 1967 and became an international star with his appearance as the violent Teddy Boy in A CLOCKWORK ORANGE in 1971. Unfortunately for McDowell, he never had another role that was anywhere near as successful. This former coffee salesman has been most effective in brooding, angry roles and, as he gets older, he doesn't look right playing British rebels without causes.

KEY ROLES

Mick Travis / IF..., 1968, Great Britain, Memorial / Paramount, d-Lindsay Anderson.

McDowell is a nonconformist upperclassman at a British boarding school for boys who maintains that "violence and revolution are the only pure acts." By the end of the film, he and his rebellious friends set fire to an assembly hall on "Speech Day" and as the students, faculty, and guests flee the building, they open fire on them with weapons they have found hidden at the school.

Alex / A CLOCKWORK ORANGE, 1971, Great Britain, Warners, d-Stanley Kubrick.

McDowell is the leader of a gang of young hoodlums who rape and murder almost at will. When his mates turn on him, he is sent to prison where he is made a guinea pig for a new process that conditions him to become ill whenever he encounters violence or sex. He's released and becomes a victim of his new personality, although just at the end there are indications that he may suffer a relapse into old behavior.

Harry Flashman / ROYAL FLASH, 1975, Great Britain, 20th Century-Fox, d-Richard Lester.

McDowell is a 19th-century rogue forced by Bismarck to impersonate a Russian diplomat and marry a duchess. It's a fast-paced political satire.

H. G. Wells / TIME AFTER TIME, 1979, Great Britain, Warners, d-Nicholas Meyer.

As Wells, McDowell invents a time machine but Jack the Ripper uses it to escape into the future. McDowell must follow him to present-day San Francisco where Jack's about his usual mischief.

Caligula / CALIGULA, 1980, Italy, Penthouse Films, d-Tinto Brass (and others).

Producer Bob Guccione of *Penthouse* magazine presents much violence and hard-core sex in this tale of the decadence in the reign of the mad Roman emperor Caligula. It's sleazy and not for the weak-stomached.

OTHER ROLES

1967: *Billy* / POOR COW. **1970:** *Ansell* / FIGURES IN A LANDSCAPE. **1971:** *Bruce Pritchard* / THE RAGING MOON. **1973:** *Mick Travis* / O LUCKY MAN! **1976:** *Max Gunter* / VOYAGE OF THE DAMNED. **1977:** *Gresham* / ACES HIGH. **1979:** *Von Berkow* / THE PASSAGE. **1981:** *Mick Travis* / BRITANNIA HOSPITAL. **1982:** *narrator* / THE COMPLEAT BEATLES; *Paul Gallier* / CAT PEOPLE. **1983:** *Reggie* / GET CRAZY; *Colonel Cochrane* / BLUE THUNDER; *Maxwell Perkins* / CROSS CREEK. **1987:** *cameo* / SUNSET.

MCGUIRE, DOROTHY

(1919–)

Born in Omaha, charming Dorothy McGuire made her acting debut at the age of 13 opposite Henry Fonda at the local community playhouse. After moving to New York City she appeared in a radio soap opera and made her Broadway debut as Martha Scott's understudy in "Our Town." Her big chance came three years later when she starred in "Claudia" and repeated her success in the movie version. She stayed in Hollywood, winning wide acclaim for her roles as women who radiated kindness and warmth. Her leading ladies were usually gentle and loving but with a touch of toughness. When she moved into character roles she displayed these same admirable characteristics. Her roles were not glamorous but she projected an inner beauty that was terribly appealing. Her made-for-TV movies include SHE WAITS (1971), THE RUNAWAYS (1975), RICH MAN, POOR MAN (1976), THE INCREDIBLE JOURNEY OF DR. MEG LAUREL (1979), and GHOST DANCING (1983).

KEY ROLES

Claudia Naughton / CLAUDIA, 1943, 20th Century-Fox, d-Edmund Goulding.

McGuire is splendid recreating her Broadway role of a naive young bride for whom everything about marriage comes as a big surprise. She's a vague but essentially charming and loving child-woman whose tolerant husband helps her grow.

Katie Nolan / A TREE GROWS IN BROOKLYN, 1944, 20th Century-Fox, d-Elia Kazan.

McGuire is the strong but weary mother of a working-class family in Brooklyn in the early years of the century with a husband who is an alcoholic singing waiter. After he dies, it appears that she may have a more stable life when a policeman (Lloyd Nolan) comes courting.

Laura / THE ENCHANTED COTTAGE, 1945, RKO, d-John Cromwell.

McGuire is a plain girl whom a disfigured Robert Young marries because he believes she's all he deserves because of his appearance. But in their cottage, they appear attractive to each other and grow to love each other.

Helen Capel / THE SPIRAL STAIRCASE, 1945, RKO, d-Robert Siodmak.

In a small New England town in 1906, a psychopathic killer makes deformed girls his victims. McGuire realizes she may be next since she is a mute. Her only words in the picture are the last ones; after she has survived the killer's attempt on her life, she calls her doctor: "One. Eight. Nine. Dr. Parry? Come. This is Helen."

Kathy / GENTLEMAN'S AGREEMENT, 1947, 20th Century-Fox, d-Elia Kazan.

McGuire has the thankless role of supplying an example of a nice person who is tolerant of anti-Semitism when her non-Jewish love decides to pose as a Jew to gather material for a magazine series on anti-Semitism. She demonstrates her casualness about prejudice, saying: "It's detestable, but that's the way it is. It's even worse in New Canaan. There, nobody can sell or rent to a Jew. And even in Darien where Jane's house is and my house is, there's sort of a gentleman's agreement...."

Miss Francis / THREE COINS IN THE FOUNTAIN, 1954, 20th Century-Fox, d-Jean Negulesco.

McGuire is writer Clifton Webb's secretary in Rome. She loves him, but when he learns that an illness threatens his life he backs off on letting her know his true feelings. She pursues the matter, though, and they look forward to whatever time they have together.

Eliza Birdwell / FRIENDLY PERSUASION, 1956, Allied Artists, d-William Wyler.

As the mother in a family of Quakers, McGuire has a hard time keeping her husband and children in strict adherence to their convictions, particularly when the Civil War comes practically to their doorstep.

Sylvia Hunter / A SUMMER PLACE, 1960, Warners, d-Delmer Daves.

McGuire's summer affair on a Maine island with the father of her son's girlfriend causes much sexual confusion and anguish for all concerned, particularly when the two lovers divorce their respective spouses and marry.

Cora Flood / THE DARK AT THE TOP OF THE STAIRS, 1960, Warners, d-Delbert Mann.

When McGuire's traveling salesman husband loses his job during the 1920s in a small southwestern town, he keeps the news from her. When she complains about what they don't have compared to others it leads to a big fight and a breakup. But she's a good woman and he's a good man and they make things work out.

OTHER ROLES

1946: *Claudia Naughton* / CLAUDIA AND DAVID; *Pat Ruscomb* / TILL THE END OF TIME. **1950:** *Jane* / MOTHER DIDN'T TELL ME; *Ann Winslow* / MISTER 880; *Deborah Patterson* / CALLAWAY WENT THATAWAY. **1951:** *Nancy Greer* / I WANT YOU. **1952:** *Ellen Pierce* / INVITATION. **1953:** *Crystal Benson* / MAKE HASTE TO LIVE. **1955:** *Abbe Nyle* / TRIAL. **1957:** *Katie Coates* / OLD YELLER. **1959:** *Ma Pennypacker* / THE REMARKABLE MR. PENNYPACKER; *Martha Fairon* / THIS EARTH IS MINE. **1960:** *Mother Robinson* / SWISS FAMILY ROBINSON. **1961:** *Leah Slade* / SUSAN SLADE. **1963:** *Margaret Carey* / SUMMER MAGIC. **1965:** *The Virgin Mary* / THE GREATEST STORY EVER TOLD. **1971:** *Granny O'Flaherty* / FLIGHT OF THE DOVES.

MCQUEEN, STEVE

(Terence Steven McQueen, 1930–1980)

Abandoned by his father when he was an infant, Steve McQueen spent part of his childhood in a reform school. He joined the marines and, after leaving the service, had many jobs before making his stage debut with the Second Avenue Yiddish Theatre. He found work in television and had a small role in SOMEBODY UP THERE LIKES ME in 1956. His movie roles weren't much until after his TV series "Wanted Dead or Alive," and he established himself as a star with THE GREAT ESCAPE in 1963. This car and motorcycle enthusiast was not an actor—he dominated the screen by the force of his personality; his characters were usually intense and impassive at the same time. He was one of the most popular and highest paid actors of the 1960s and 1970s, even being nominated for an Academy Award for his portrayal in THE SAND PEBBLES in 1966. He once observed: "The world is as good as you are. You've got to learn to like yourself." He lost his battle with cancer in 1980.

KEY ROLES

Steve / THE BLOB, 1958, Tonylyn, d-Irwin S. Yeaworth, Jr.

In his first starring role McQueen is a teenager whose parents don't understand him and neither does a slimy space invader.

Vin / THE MAGNIFICENT SEVEN, 1960, United Artists, d-John Sturges.

McQueen is one of seven gunfighters hired by Mexican villagers to protect them from an army of bandits. He and two others survive and ride away after the job is done.

Buzz Rickson / THE WAR LOVER, 1962, Columbia, d-Philip Leacock.

McQueen is competing with Robert Wagner for Anne Field, but why this macho boob, who thinks war is great and girls are to be used, would be competition for any halfway decent guy is not made clear.

"Cooler King" Hilts / THE GREAT ESCAPE, 1963, United Artists, d-John Sturges.

McQueen's cool manner as a POW, and his ability with a motorcycle when he escapes, made him a star. He's among the very few Allied prisoners who survive; most of those recaptured are summarily executed. McQueen is defiantly put into solitary confinement once more when returned to the camp after his escape attempt.

Rocky Papasano / LOVE WITH THE PROPER STRANGER, 1963, Paramount, d-Robert Mulligan.

Musician McQueen tries to arrange an abortion for his pregnant girlfriend (Natalie Wood) but decides to get married instead. He proposes with a picket sign that reads: "Better Wed Than Dead."

The Cincinnati Kid / THE CINCINNATI KID, 1965, MGM, d-Norman Jewison.

Looking for the same kind of success with the game of poker that Paul Newman had with pool, McQueen portrays a card player in New Orleans in the late 1930s sitting in on a big-time stud poker game. But he's distracted by two women (Ann-Margret and Tuesday Weld).

Jake Holman / THE SAND PEBBLES, 1966, 20th Century-Fox, d-Robert Wise.

Why McQueen was nominated for an Academy Award for this movie is open to debate. His portrayal of a sailor aboard a gunboat patrolling the Yangtze River in China in 1926 shows no more emotion or acting ability than any of a dozen other of his portrayals.

Thomas Crown / THE THOMAS CROWN AFFAIR, 1968, United Artists, d-Norman Jewison.

McQueen is a bored tycoon who masterminds a bank heist and then plays with the beautiful insurance investigator (Faye Dunaway) who is sent to trip him up. The two have a sexy chess game.

Lt. Frank Bullitt / BULLITT, 1968, Warners, d-Peter Yates.

When an underworld witness in his charge is killed, McQueen hides the fact as he goes after the killers and searches for the evidence the witness had for the state's case against a major criminal.

Junior Bonner / JUNIOR BONNER, 1972, ABC / Booth-Gardner, d-Sam Peckinpah.

When his luck starts running out on the circuit, aging rodeo star McQueen returns to his hometown where his family is having problems. It's a decent slice-of-life picture and McQueen is rather appealing.

Henri Charrière, "Papillon" / PAPILLON, 1973, Corona / General Production Co., d-Franklin Schaffner.

In this film autobiography McQueen appears as the Devil's Island prisoner who is known as Papillon, meaning "butterfly," because of his many escapes and recaptures.

OTHER ROLES

1956: *Fidel* / SOMEBODY UP THERE LIKES ME. **1958:** *Martin Cabell* / NEVER LOVE A STRANGER. **1959:** *Bill Ringa* / NEVER SO FEW; *George Fowler* / THE GREAT ST. LOUIS BANK ROBBERY. **1961:** *Lt. Fergie Howard* / THE HONEYMOON MACHINE; *Reese* / HELL IS FOR HEROES. **1963:** *Sgt. Eustis Clay* / SOLDIER IN THE RAIN. **1965:** *Henry Thomas* / BABY, THE RAIN MUST FALL. **1966:** *Nevada Smith* / NEVADA SMITH. **1970:** *Boon Hoggenbeck* / THE REIVERS. **1971:** *guest* / ON ANY SUNDAY; *Michael Delaney* / LE MANS. **1972:** *Doc McCoy* / THE GETAWAY. **1974:** *Michael O'Hallorhan* / THE TOWERING INFERNO. **1976:** *Dr. Thomas Stockmann* / AN ENEMY OF THE PEOPLE. **1980:** *Tom Horn* / TOM HORN; *Pa Thorson* / THE HUNTER.

MENJOU, ADOLPHE

(1890–1963)

Considered one of the world's best-dressed men, the dapper and debonair Adolphe Menjou, with his waxed black mustache and impeccable wardrobe, made his film debut in 1914 and had his first starring role in 1923 after having served as a World War I captain in the ambulance corps. In 1929–1930 he worked in Paris on several French-language films. Motion picture sound suited this most sophisticated of boulevard actors in many elegant, cynical man-about-town roles and witty comedies. Trained as an engineer and educated at Cornell, Menjou spoke many languages. He was nominated for an Oscar for THE FRONT PAGE and became a friendly witness for the House Un-American Activities Committee in 1947. He was the cofounder in 1944 of the Motion Picture Alliance for the Preservation of American Ideals.

KEY ROLES

Pierre Revel / A WOMAN OF PARIS, 1923, Silent, United Artists, d-Charles Chaplin.

After a misunderstanding between a French country girl (Edna Purviance) and her lover (Carl Miller), an art student, Purviance becomes the mistress of a wealthy Parisian playboy (Menjou). Later she commissions the starving artist to do her portrait and they renew their affair, then again break off their relationship. The young man commits suicide and Purviance and Menjou never see each other again.

Prof. Josef Stock / THE MARRIAGE CIRCLE, 1924, Silent, Warners, d-James Flood.

Menjou sees his long-awaited chance to divorce his wife when she begins a flirtation with the husband of her best friend. The friend becomes interested in a business partner of her husbands who eventually turns his attention to Menjou's wife. Forbidden love is the sweetest in this picture.

Chancellor / FORBIDDEN PARADISE, 1924, Silent, Paramount, d-Ernst Lubitsch.

Menjou is the chancellor of a small European kingdom who puts down a revolt headed by the czarina's lover.

Albert Durant / THE GRAND DUCHESS AND THE WAITER, 1926, Silent, Paramount, d-Malcolm St. Clair.

Menjou is a millionaire who becomes infatuated with a Russian refugee in Paris (Florence Vidor). Unable to meet her, he disguises himself as a waiter and she hires him for her personal staff. But when she learns his true identity she flees and he runs after her to convince her of his love.

Prince Lucio de Rimanez / THE SORROWS OF SATAN, 1926, Silent, Paramount, d-D. W. Griffith.

Ricardo Cortez is a struggling writer who has completed a novel in which he rails at God and fate. He meets a mysterious nobleman (Menjou) who takes him to a fancy hotel where he is transfixed by the beauty of Lya De Putti. Menjou informs Cortez that he has inherited a large fortune and arranges the latter's marriage with De Putti. Married life proves a failure but when Cortez attempts to leave and return to his one true love, Menjou reveals his identity as Satan.

Le Bessier / MOROCCO, 1930, Paramount, d-Josef von Sternberg.

Menjou is a debonair man-of-the-world who clamors for the favors of cabaret singer Marlene Dietrich. But she prefers the love-'em-and-leave'-em treatment of legionnaire Gary Cooper. She turns down Menjou's promises of wealth and happiness and becomes a camp follower to be with the man she loves.

Walter Burns / THE FRONT PAGE, 1931, Hughes / United Artists, d-Lewis Milestone.

Menjou's performance as the fast-talking con man newspaper editor who tricks his retiring star reporter into covering one last story won him an Oscar nomination. The delivery of lines is so fast in this early talkie that any inattention will cost the hearer some great black comedy lines.

Major Rinaldi / A FAREWELL TO ARMS, 1932, Paramount, d-Frank Borzage.

Menjou is a surgeon during World War I who has his eyes on British nurse Helen Hayes and almost forgets his medical oath when he finds she prefers his friend, Gary Cooper.

Louis Easton / MORNING GLORY, 1933, RKO, d-Lowell Sherman.

Menjou is one of several men Katharine Hepburn finds she can do without after they help her achieve her goal of becoming a Broadway star.

Sorrowful Jones / LITTLE MISS MARKER, 1934, Paramount, d-Alexander Hall.

Debonair Menjou meets dimpled Shirley Temple when she is left as a marker for a bet and he finds he's stuck with her. It's an enjoyable Damon Runyon tale of gambling and gamblers.

Oliver Niles / A STAR IS BORN, 1937, Selznick / United Artists, d-William A. Wellman.

Menjou plays the studio head who comes up with a new name and a big build-up for Janet Gaynor, a cute and talented actress with whom an alcoholic star (Fredric March) has fallen in love.

John Cardwell / ONE HUNDRED MEN AND A GIRL, 1937, Universal, d-Henry Koster.

Menjou is the widowed father of a girl (Deanna Durbin) who hatches the plan of convincing Leopold Stokowski to form an orchestra of out-of-work musicians like her father. Menjou joyfully supports Durbin in this lovely fairy tale.

Deakon Maxwell / THE HOUSEKEEPER'S DAUGHTER, 1939, Roach / United Artists, d-Hal Roach.

In this zany crime farce, Menjou is a hard-drinking reporter who becomes involved with a sappy professor. Menjou falls in love with a gangster's moll and solves the murder of a showgirl.

Hilary Fairchild / A BILL OF DIVORCEMENT, 1940, RKO, d-John Farrow.

This is a virtual scene-for-scene remake of the 1932 version with Katharine Hepburn and John Barrymore. Menjou hangs tough and gives a performance to rival The Great Profile, as the father of strong-willed Maureen O'Hara, who arrives to meet her for the very first time after being released from a mental hospital.

Billy Flynn / ROXIE HART, 1942, 20th Century-Fox, d-William A. Wellman.

When brassy dancer Ginger Rogers is brought to trial for murder, she allows her trial to become a farce because she feels the publicity will be good for her career. Menjou is the wily lawyer who gets her acquitted, but that's not the end of it.

Wagner / STEP LIVELY, 1944, RKO, d-Tim Whelan.

Menjou contributes to the hijinks in this musical remake of the Marx Brothers' ROOM SERVICE. The stars of the piece are Frank Sinatra as a young playwright and George Murphy as a fast-talking Broadway producer.

Jim Conover / STATE OF THE UNION, 1948, MGM, d-Frank Capra.

Menjou is the savvy political pro brought in by newspaper tycoon Angela Lansbury to get the presidential nomination for her lover (Spencer Tracy). He wheels and deals with the cruds who show up in such campaigns, but his biggest headache is Katharine Hepburn, Tracy's estranged wife.

Lieutenant Kafka / THE SNIPER, 1952, Columbia, d-Edward Dmytryk.

In the last film in which he gets star billing, Menjou is the police officer who must track down a psychopath who kills a succession of blondes with a high-powered rifle.

General Broulard / PATHS OF GLORY, 1957, United Artists, d-Stanley Kubrick.

In this powerful anti-war film, Menjou is the general who orders a captain to fire on his own troops when some of them refuse an order to go over the top in World War I. The captain refuses and three soldiers are chosen at random to be executed as an object lesson. The French generals then hush up the incident. This is based on a true story and the film sticks pretty close to it.

OTHER ROLES

1914: *ringmaster* / THE MAN BEHIND THE DOOR. **1916:** *Julianai* / A PARISIAN ROMANCE; *baron* / NEARLY A KING; *society man* / THE HABIT OF HAPPINESS; *Howard Neal* / THE PRICE OF HAPPINESS; *Russian colonel* / THE CRUCIAL TEST; *a Capulet* / ROMEO AND JULIET; *bit* / THE SCARLET RUNNER; *bit* / MANHATTAN MADNESS; *bit* / THE DEVIL AT HIS ELBOW; *Pennington* / THE KISS; *Paul Dunston* / THE REWARD OF PATIENCE; *bit* / THE BLUE ENVELOPE MYSTERY. **1917:** *Joe Winder* / THE VALENTINE GIRL; *bit* / AN EVEN BREAK; *Count de Grivel* / THE AMAZONS; *the husband* / THE MOTH. **1920:** *reporter* / WHAT HAPPENED TO ROSA? **1921:** *Dr. Littlefield* / THE FAITH HEALER; *Bruce Ferguson* / COURAGE; *James Brewster* / THROUGH THE BACK DOOR; *Louis XIII* / THE THREE MUSKETEERS; *Count Michael* / QUEENIE; *Raoul de Saint Hubert* / THE SHEIK. **1922:** *Sterling* / HEAD OVER HEELS; *Dudley King* / IS MATRIMONY A FAILURE?; *Captain Fortine* / ARABIAN LOVE; *Duc de Langeais* / THE ETERNAL FLAME; *Cal Baldwin* / THE FAST MAIL; *Hubert Stem* / CLARENCE; *Louis Barney* / PINK GODS; *Bliss Gordon* / SINGED WINGS. **1923:** *Robert Townsend* / THE WORLD'S APPLAUSE; *Mr. Chepstow* / BELLA DONNA; *Count Rischenheim* / RUPERT OF HENTZAU; *Don Salluste* / THE SPANISH DANCER. **1924:** *Georges de Croy* / SHADOWS OF PARIS; *Bob Canfield* / THE MARRIAGE CHEAT; *Joseph Hudley* / FOR SALE; *Ralph Norton* / BROADWAY AFTER DARK; *Tommie Kemp* / BROKEN BARRIERS; *Arthur Merrill* / SINNERS IN SILK; *Edmond Durverne* / OPEN ALL NIGHT; *Ernest Steel* / THE FAST SET. **1925:** *Albert of Kersten-Rodenfels* / THE SWAN; *Walter Grenham* / A KISS IN THE DARK; *Mr. Hazlitt* / ARE PARENTS PEOPLE?; *Tony Hamilton* / LOST—A WIFE; *Serge IV, King of Molvania* / THE KING ON MAIN STREET.**1926:** *Max Haber* / A SOCIAL CELEBRITY; *guest* / FASCINATING YOUTH; *Chappel Maturin* / THE ACE OF CADS. **1927:** *Henri Martel* / BLONDE OR BRUNETTE; *Lucien D'Artois* / EVENING CLOTHES; *Albert Leroux* / SERVICE FOR LADIES; *Marquis de Marignan* / A GENTLEMAN OF PARIS; *Franz Rossi* / SERENADE. **1928:** *Captain Ferreol* / A NIGHT OF MYSTERY; *Henri* / HIS TIGER LADY; *Georges St. Germain* / HIS PRIVATE LIFE. **1929:** *Marquis D'Argenville* / MARQUIS PREFERRED; *Paul De Remy* / FASHIONS IN LOVE. **1930:** *Gerome* / THE PARISIAN; *M. Parkes* / L'ENIGMATIQUE MONSIEUR PARKES; *Gov. Boris Brusiloff* / NEW MOON. **1931:** *Bob Brown* / SOYONS GAI; *Walter Brockton* / THE EASIEST WAY; *Tony Minot* / MEN CALL IT LOVE; *Jean Paurel* / THE GREAT LOVER; *Captain Roberts* / FRIENDS AND LOVERS. **1932:** *Bob Grover* / FORBIDDEN; *Capt. Remy Baudoin* / PRESTIGE; *Andrew Hoyt* / BACHELOR'S AFFAIRS; *Thatcher Colt* / NIGHT CLUB LADY; *Maj. Carey Liston* / TWO WHITE ARMS; *Dan McQueen* / BLAME THE WOMAN. **1933:** *Thatcher Colt* / THE CIRCUS QUEEN MURDER; *Adolphe Ballou* / THE WORST WOMAN IN PARIS?; *T. R. Kent* / CONVENTION CITY. **1934:** *John Townsend* / EASY TO LOVE; *Pancho Gomez* / THE TRUMPET BLOWS; *Paul Molet* / JOURNAL OF A CRIME; *Stephen Karpath* / THE GREAT FLIRTATION; *Gregory Sheldon* / THE HUMAN SIDE; *Bailey Walsh* / THE MIGHTY BARNUM. **1935:** *Nicoleff* / GOLD DIGGERS OF 1935; *Professor De Vinci* / BROADWAY GONDOLIER. **1936:** *Gabby Sloan* / THE MILKY WAY; *Bruce Faraday* / SING, BABY, SING; *J. Hugh Ramsey* / WIVES NEVER KNOW. **1937:** *Ted Spencer* / ONE IN A MILLION; *Monsieur Victor* / CAFE METROPOLE; *Anthony Powell* / STAGE DOOR. **1938:** *Oliver Merlin* / THE GOLDWYN FOLLIES; *John Mannering* / LETTER OF INTRODUCTION; *J. B. Harcourt* / THANKS FOR EVERYTHING. **1939:** *Jim Mason* / KING OF THE TURF; *Tom Moody* / GOLDEN BOY; *Stanley Delmere* / THAT'S RIGHT—YOU'RE WRONG. **1940:** *Phil Manning* / TURNABOUT. **1941:** *Col. Carleton Carraway* / ROAD SHOW; *Frederic Osborne* / FATHER TAKES A WIFE. **1942:** *George Latimer* / SYNCOPATION; *Eduardo Acuna* / YOU WERE NEVER LOVELIER. **1943:** *Col. Hector Phyffe* / HI DIDDLE DIDDLE; *Thomas*

Moran / SWEET ROSIE O'GRADY. **1945:** *Kismet* / MAN ALIVE. **1946:** *ambassador* / HEARTBEAT; *Mr. Moody* / THE BACHELOR'S DAUGHTERS. **1947:** *J. Conrad Nelson* / I'LL BE YOURS; *Craig Warren* / MR. DISTRICT ATTORNEY; *Mr. Kimberly* / THE HUCKSTERS. **1949:** *Thomas Hutchins* / MY DREAM IS YOURS; *Grossman* / DANCING IN THE DARK. **1950:** *Gregg* / TO PLEASE A LADY. **1951:** *Caleb Jeffers* / THE TALL TARGET; *Pierre* / ACROSS THE WIDE MISSOURI. **1953:** *Fesker* / MAN ON A TIGHTROPE. **1955:** *Swiftwater Tilton* / TIMBERJACK. **1956:** *Senator Cartwright* / THE AMBASSADOR'S DAUGHTER; *Arthur Martin* / THE FUZZY PINK NIGHTGOWN. **1958:** *Frederick W. Sutton* / I MARRIED A WOMAN. **1960:** *Mr. Pendergast* / POLLYANNA.

MEREDITH, BURGESS

(George Burgess, 1908–)

A member of Eve Le Gallienne's Civic Repertory Theatre, Burgess Meredith had his first successful stage role in "Winterset" in 1935, then repeated the role on the screen the next year. He refused to be typecast, and was willing to take minor roles as well as starring roles, such as the protective George in OF MICE AND MEN. He has been nominated for Best Supporting Actor Awards for THE DAY OF THE LOCUST and ROCKY. He played many troubled nice guys as he became one of the most gifted and versatile performers of the American stage and screen. His third wife was Paulette Goddard who starred in DIARY OF A CHAMBERMAID which Meredith wrote and co-produced. As of late he has been in demand for elderly, eccentric characters. His thoughts on his craft include: "You have to act with joy, and not mislocate the center of the emotions, which is in the head, not in the stomach. The center of the emotions is right above the eyes."

KEY ROLES

Mio / WINTERSET, 1936, RKO, d-Albert Santell.

Meredith appears as the son of a man who had been executed 15 years earlier for a crime he did not commit. He is determined to clear his father's name. The story is a thinly disguised examination of the Sacco and Vanzetti case.

George / OF MICE AND MEN, 1939, Roach / United Artists, d-Lewis Milestone.

Meredith is forced to shoot his big, half-witted friend (Lon Chaney, Jr.) rather than let him be committed for killing the wife of the foreman's son. Chaney doesn't know his own strength and means no harm, but he once was kicked in the head by a horse. Meredith has promised that the two of them will have a little ranch someday where Chaney can mind the rabbits.

Sebastian / THAT UNCERTAIN FEELING, 1941, United Artists, d-Ernst Lubitsch.

Meredith is splendid as the zany self-proclaimed best pianist in the world whom Merle Oberon uses as an outlet for the frustrations of six years of marriage to boring Melvyn Douglas. Meredith insults everyone in the picture at least once.

Ernie Pyle / THE STORY OF G.I. JOE, 1945, United Artists, d-William A. Wellman.

Just as war correspondent Pyle reported on the dog soldiers rather than on the generals and their strategies, this movie concentrates on Pyle (Meredith) and a small group of infantrymen as they troop from North Africa to Italy.

Captain Mauger / DIARY OF A CHAMBERMAID, 1946, United Artists, d-Jean Renoir.

Meredith co-wrote and co-produced this film starring his wife of the time (Paulette Goddard) as a chambermaid who tires of her station in life. She vows to achieve wealth by choosing whichever man can give it to her. A valet murders an aging psychopath (Meredith) to get money so he can have the girl.

Felix Milne / MINE OWN EXECUTIONER, 1947, Great Britain, London Films, d-Anthony Kimmins.

Lay psychiatrist Meredith treats a schizophrenic ex-RAF officer who has tried to kill his wife. Meredith isn't getting along too well with his own spouse and has an affair with her friend. He also neglects his patient, who murders his wife and escapes to a high roof. Meredith climbs a ladder and tries to talk him down, but the man jumps to his death.

The Penguin / BATMAN, 1966, 20th Century-Fox, d-Leslie Martinson.

For those who think such things matter, Meredith looks just like the master criminal nemesis of the caped crusader who appeared in hundreds of comic books.

Judge Purcell / HURRY SUNDOWN, 1967, Paramount, d-Otto Preminger.

Reduced to small roles, not all very good, Meredith portrays the bigoted southern judge who will hear the claim of a black sharecropper against a white woman.

Mickey / ROCKY, 1976, United Artists, d-John G. Avildsen.

Meredith is an old-time fight manager who takes on the job of training an unranked 30-year-old boxer (Sylvester Stallone) who gets a crack at the heavyweight champ. Meredith helps Stallone prove he's not just "another bum."

OTHER ROLES

1937: *Dick Matthews* / THERE GOES THE GROOM. **1938:** *The Lippencott* / SPRING MADNESS. **1939:** *Quillery* / IDIOT'S DELIGHT. **1940:** *Steve Rockford* / CASTLE ON THE HUDSON; *Hank Taylor* / SECOND CHORUS. **1941:** *Johnny Barnes* / SAN FRANCISCO DOCKS; *Harry* / TOM, DICK AND HARRY. **1942:** *Frank Thompson* / STREET OF CHANCE. **1946:** *James Madison* / MAGNIFICENT DOLL. **1948:** *Oliver Pease* / ON OUR MERRY WAY. **1949:** *Heurtin* / THE MAN ON THE EIFFEL TOWER. **1953:** *Dick* / THE GAY ADVENTURE. **1957:** *Joe Butterfly* / JOE BUTTERFLY. **1962:** *Herbert Gelman* / ADVISE AND CONSENT. **1963:** *Fr. Ned Halley* / THE CARDINAL. **1965:** *Cmdr. Egan Powell* / IN HARM'S WAY. **1966:** *Doc Scully* / A BIG HAND FOR THE LITTLE LADY; *Dan Sullivan* / MADAME X; *Louis Halliburton* / THE KIDNAPPERS. **1967:** *Dr. Diablo* / TORTURE GARDEN. **1968:** *storekeeper* / MACKENNA'S GOLD; *Charlie Lightcloud* / STAY AWAY, JOE; *the warden* / SKIDOO. **1969:** *Ramsey* / HARD CONTRACT. **1970:** *Missouri Kid* / THERE WAS A CROOKED MAN. **1971:** *Bernard Kalman* / SUCH GOOD FRIENDS; *Captain Ned* / THE FATHER. **1972:** *Freedom Lovelace* / CLAY PIGEON; *Senator Watson* / THE MAN. **1974:** *Winters* / GOLDEN NEEDLES; *Harry Greener* / THE DAY OF THE LOCUST. **1976:** *Emilio Pajetta* / THE HINDENBURG; *brother* / BURNT OFFERINGS. **1977:** *Charles Chazen* / THE SENTINEL. **1978:** *Ben Greene* / MAGIC; *Hennessey* / FOUL PLAY; *Dr. Ernest Snow* / THE MANITOU; *Jack Stutz* / THE GREAT GEORGIA BANK HOAX. **1979:** *Mickey* / ROCKY II. **1980:** *Rene Valdez* / WHEN TIME RAN OUT... **1981:** *Fr. Seamus Fargo* / TRUE CONFESSIONS; *Captain Williams* / THE LAST CHASE; *Ammon* / THE CLASH OF THE TITANS. **1982:** *Mickey* / ROCKY III; *Zak* / FINAL ASSIGNMENT. **1985:** *ancient elf* / SANTA CLAUS.

MERMAN, ETHEL

(Ethel Zimmerman, 1909–1985)

Often called the "First Lady of American Musical Comedy," Ethel Merman had an untrained, exuberant voice that could be heard perfectly in any part of the theater no matter how large or what its acoustics.

After working in vaudeville and nightclubs, the big, brassy brunette stopped the show night after night with her rendition of "I Got Rhythm" in "Girl Crazy" on Broadway. She went on to triumph in over a dozen Broadway musicals including "Annie Get Your Gun," "Call Me Madam," and "Gypsy." Her movie appearances weren't as successful because she didn't need to belt out her songs with great power. Still, she had a few memorable screen moments that give a hint of her great talent.

KEY ROLES

Reno Sweeney / ANYTHING GOES, 1936, Paramount, d-Lewis Milestone.

Merman repeats the role she created on Broadway—one of two young girls the male stars of a musical comedy sign without knowing about the other. Everything is worked out aboard a transatlantic cruise. Merman sings Cole Porter's "You're the Top" and "I Get a Kick out of You" with great gusto.

Jerry Allen / ALEXANDER'S RAGTIME BAND, 1938, 20th Century-Fox, d-Henry King.

Merman's contributions to this salute to the music of Irving Berlin include "Blue Skies," "Heat Wave," "Everybody Step," and "My Walking Stick."

Mrs. Sally Adams / CALL ME MADAM, 1953, 20th Century-Fox, d-Walter Lang.

Merman is a Pearl Mesta-like Washington hostess who is named ambassadress to Lichtenberg. There she helps her assistant (Donald O'Connor) with his romance and finds love herself with the country's top general. As the "Hostess with the Mostest," she belts out Irving Berlin's "You're Just in Love" with O'Connor as well as "Can You Use Any Money Today?" and "The Best Thing for You."

Molly Donahue / THERE'S NO BUSINESS LIKE SHOW BUSINESS, 1954, 20th Century-Fox, d-Walter Lang.

This is the story of a vaudeville family with Merman and Dan Dailey as ma and pa, and Donald O'Connor, Janet Gaynor, and Johnny Ray as their musical children. Merman leads the troupe in a rousing rendition of the title number. Other Irving Berlin numbers include "Alexander's Ragtime Band," "Play a Simple Melody," and "Let's Have Another Cup of Coffee."

OTHER ROLES

1930: *Helen King* / FOLLOW THE LEADER. **1934:** *Edith* / WE'RE NOT DRESSING; *Dot Clark* / KID MILLIONS. **1936:** *Joyce Lennox* / STRIKE ME PINK. **1938:** *Flo Kelly* / HAPPY LANDING; *Linda* / STRAIGHT, PLACE AND SHOW. **1943:** *guest* / STAGE DOOR CANTEEN. **1963:** *Mrs. Marcus* / IT'S A MAD, MAD, MAD, MAD WORLD. **1965:** *Madame Coco La Fontaine* / THE ART OF LOVE. **1976:** *Hedda Parsons* / WON TON TON, THE DOG WHO SAVED HOLLYWOOD. **1980:** *cameo* / AIRPLANE!

MILES, SARAH

(1941–)

Dark-haired, willful-looking Sarah Miles was originally typed as slut material because of her sense of repressed sexuality smoldering just below the surface. As she noted, "There's a little bit of hooker in every woman. A little bit of hooker and a little bit of God." Once married to playwright Robert Bolt, to whom she is still very close, she won an Academy Award for Best Actress for her performance in RYAN'S DAUGHTER. But she has all too often been miscast or wasted in her movies.

KEY ROLES

Shirley Taylor / TERM OF TRIAL, 1962, Great Britain, Romulus / Warners, d-Peter Glenville.

Miles falls in love with her married teacher and tries to get him to sleep with her. When he refuses her tempting offer, she accuses him of attempted rape. He's tried and convicted but Miles breaks down and confesses that she lied because she felt humiliated by his refusal to make love to her.

Vera / THE SERVANT, 1963, Great Britain, Springbok Films, d-Joseph Losey.

Wealthy James Fox allows his manservant (Dirk Bogarde) to have more and more control over his life. Bogarde brings Miles in as maid, introducing her as his sister. She soon seduces Fox and the latter begins to ignore his fiancée, who has constantly complained about Bogarde's influence. One night Fox finds Bogarde and Miles making love and fires them both, but finds that he has become completely dependent on Bogarde and brings them back, this time with Bogarde as master.

Patricia Rawnsley / THOSE MAGNIFICENT MEN IN THEIR FLYING MACHINES, 1965, Great Britain, 20th Century-Fox, d-Ken Annakin.

Miles is responsible for talking her father, a British press lord, into sponsoring a London-to-Paris air race in 1910. She seems to be one of the prizes that an American entry (Stuart Whitman) wishes to claim.

Rosie Ryan / RYAN'S DAUGHTER, 1970, Great Britain, MGM, d-David Lean.

A young Irish woman (Miles) marries a dull schoolteacher (Robert Mitchum) and her boring life leads her into an affair with a shell-shocked British officer. The townspeople believe she gave information that resulted in the arrest of IRA soldiers and they shear her head and might have done her more harm had not the parish priest stepped in. She won an Oscar for her performance.

Lady Caroline Lamb / LADY CAROLINE LAMB, 1972, Great Britain, United Artists, d-Robert Bolt.

Miles stars as the wife of Jon Finch, a politician. When she has an affair with writer Lord Byron (Richard Chamberlain) it makes for a bloody scandal.

OTHER ROLES

1964: *Catherine* / THE CEREMONY. **1965:** *Cass* / I WAS HAPPY HERE. **1966:** *Patricia* / BLOWUP. **1973:** *Lady Franklin* / THE HIRELING; *Catherine Crocker* / THE MAN WHO LOVED CAT DANCING. **1976:** *Anne Osborne* / THE SAILOR WHO FELL FROM GRACE WITH THE SEA. **1978:** *Lash Canino* / THE BIG SLEEP. **1982:** *Dr. Marion Stowe* / VENOM. **1986:** *Sarah* / STEAMING. **1987:** *Grace Rohan* / HOPE AND GLORY; *Alice* / WHITE MISCHIEF.

MILLAND, RAY

(Reginald Truscott-Jones, 1905–1986)

After three years of service as a Royal Guardsman in London, Ray Milland entered British films in 1929 as Spike Milland. In 1930 he moved to Hollywood where for several years he played mostly second leads. In the mid-1930s, though, he graduated to roles of charming, suave, self-assured romantic leading men in drawing-room comedies and mysteries with a few adventure roles thrown in for good measure. Although Milland observed, "...good acting. It exhilarates me and robs me of sleep," few critics thought much of his acting ability until his Oscar-winning performance in THE LOST WEEKEND. Then, in revisionist movie history, it was decided that Milland's easy charm and smooth good looks had made everyone overlook his impressive body of work, his sensitive interpretations, and his performances of depth, vitality, and originality. Unfortunately, shortly thereafter he found work mostly in quickie horror movies and foreign trash including ROSE ROSSE PER IL FUHRER (1968), SLAVERS (1977), and LA RAGAZZA IN PIGIAMA GIALLO (1978). He has also appeared in numerous made-for-TV movies such as DAUGHTER OF THE MIND (1970), RIVER OF GOLD (1971), and LOOK WHAT'S HAPPENED TO ROSEMARY'S BABY (1976).

KEY ROLES

Christopher Powell / THE JUNGLE PRINCESS, 1936, Paramount, d-William A. Thiele.

Rising to stardom after three years as second and third male leads, Milland plays the handsome foreigner who arrives on the tropical isle where beautiful Dorothy Lamour has been raised along with her pet tiger. They fall in love and face the usual problems found in such stories—suspicious natives, unfriendly weather, erupting volcanoes, etc.

Bob Mitchell / HER JUNGLE LOVE, 1938, Paramount, d-George Archainbaud.

If one romantic island picture starring Milland and Dorothy Lamour was good, two would be even better, according to the studio. This time the studio added Technicolor and an earthquake to enhance the romance of skimpily clad Lamour and the handsome stranger who shows up on her island.

John Geste / BEAU GESTE, 1939, Paramount, d-William A. Wellman.

Of the three Geste boys—Gary Cooper, Robert Preston, and Milland—Milland is the only one allowed a romance in this all-action adventure story of three brothers in the French Foreign Legion, their sadistic sergeant, and attacking nomads. Milland makes it back to England and awaits Susan Hayward.

Alan Howard / FRENCH WITHOUT TEARS, 1940, Great Britain, Two Cities / Paramount, d-Anthony Asquith.

Milland is a young Englishman in France trying to learn about languages and sex. The latter is taught by Ellen Drew and Janine Darcy.

Tom Martin / ARISE, MY LOVE, 1940, Paramount, d-Mitchell Leisen.

Milland is an aviator whom Paris-based journalist Claudette Colbert helps out of some tough spots during the Spanish Civil War and World War II. The two are caught in a torpedo attack and the fall of Paris to the Germans.

Major Kirby / THE MAJOR AND THE MINOR, 1942, Paramount, d-Billy Wilder.

One wonders if Milland should have been taken from his boys' military school and given a real command in the army if he can't even tell that Ginger Rogers, despite the outlandish costume she wears to get on a train for half fare, is not a 12-year-old girl.

Stephen Tolliver / REAP THE WILD WIND, 1942, Paramount, d-Cecil B. DeMille.

Milland's talent for ventriloquism is only part of the charm Paulette Goddard ignores when her love (John Wayne) is around. Besides competing with Wayne for Goddard, Milland is out to catch those responsible for causing his company's ships to pile up on reefs, left to be salvaged by Raymond Massey and brother Robert Preston.

Roderick Fitzgerald / THE UNINVITED, 1944, Paramount, d-Lewis Allen.

In perhaps the most tingling and satisfying ghost story ever filmed, Milland and his sister buy an old English house high on a cliff and discover that it is haunted by one or more ghosts who wish to do harm to Gail Russell. Milland falls in love with Russell and saves her from her eerie fate.

Stephen Neale / MINISTRY OF FEAR, 1944, Paramount, d-Fritz Lang.

Milland gives a riveting performance as a man just released from a mental hospital who gets involved with Nazi spies when he mistakenly wins a cake at a village fair. He has a great deal more than sweets in his hands and the bad guys will stop at nothing to get it back.

Don Birnham / THE LOST WEEKEND, 1945, Paramount, d-Billy Wilder.

Milland's Academy Award-winning performance as a writer destroyed and degraded by drink was almost withheld from release because the preview cards were mostly negative. It was also reported that the liquor industry offered $5 million to suppress the film. Fortunately, audiences were given the opportunity to see this amazing portrayal of a man on a three-day bender who doesn't care if he lives or dies and has just about reached the point of preferring the latter. The stark realism of the picture is just as impressive today as on its first release and the film doesn't end on an upbeat. Milland ponders: "And out there in that great big concrete jungle, I wonder how many others there are like me—poor bedeviled guys on fire with thirst. Such comical figures to the rest of the world as they stagger blindly toward another binge, another bender, another spree."

Col. Ralph Denistoun / GOLDEN EARRINGS, 1947, Paramount, d-Mitchell Leisen.

In what should have been a first-rate love story with some adventure thrown in proved a weak film, probably because the stars (Milland and Marlene Dietrich) did not hit it off. He's a downed pilot behind German lines in World War II. She's a gypsy who disguises him as a gypsy, pierces his ears, and gives him the "golden earrings" of the title.

George Stroud / THE BIG CLOCK, 1948, Paramount, d-John Farrow.

In a surprisingly interesting thriller, Milland is the editor of a crime magazine that is part of the empire of publisher Charles Laughton. When Laughton kills his mistress, he realizes that there was a witness. He assigns Milland the job of uncovering the witness but Milland has his own reasons for not revealing that he was that witness.

Nick Beal / ALIAS NICK BEAL, 1949, Paramount, d-John Farrow.

In a first-rate Faust story, Milland is a modern devil who appears out of thin air to seek the soul of honest politician Thomas Mitchell. With a little help from Audrey Totter, sent in to seduce Mitchell, he almost succeeds.

Eric Yeager / RHUBARB, 1951, Paramount, d-Arthur Lubin.

Milland has the thankless task of being upstaged by a cat who wins the Best Animal Award of the year. In the story an eccentric millionaire leaves everything to his cat, including a baseball team. Milland is the team's publicist who makes the most of the unusual ownership, but the temperamental cat almost drives him crazy.

Alan Fields / THE THIEF, 1952, United Artists, d-Russel Rouse.

In this film without spoken dialogue, Milland is a nuclear scientist who passes secret information to foreign agents and is pursued by the FBI, which suspects what he's been doing.

Tony Wendice / DIAL M FOR MURDER, 1954, Warners, d-Alfred Hitchcock.

In an underrated and underappreciated performance, Milland is superb as a tennis bum who hires a man to kill his wife while his alibi is established by him being at a large banquet. When she gets the upper hand and kills her attacker in self-defense, Milland attempts to make it look premeditated and almost gets her hanged.

Guy Carrell / THE PREMATURE BURIAL, 1962, American International, d-Roger Corman.

Milland, who fears he will be buried alive, suffers just that fate, but comes back to take revenge against those responsible.

Dr. James Xavier / X—THE MAN WITH THE X-RAY EYES, 1963, American International, d-Roger Corman.

Milland is a scientist who develops X-ray vision, but it drives him mad. It's not a pleasant picture but Milland is very good.

Oliver Barrett III / LOVE STORY, 1970, Paramount, d-Arthur Hiller.

Milland plays Ryan O'Neal's wealthy father, who cuts off his son's cash flow when the latter marries below his station. Milland doesn't seem too broken up when the girl (Ali MacGraw) dies or when his son refuses to have anything to do with him. As one lady said when asked if she cried at the movie, "I sure did. Ray Milland is bald."

OTHER ROLES

1929: *Ian* / THE PLAYTHING; *Jim Edwards* / THE FLYING SCOTSMAN; *Tom Roberts* / THE LADY FROM THE SEA. **1930:** *bit* / THE INFORMER; *bit* / PASSION FLOWER; *bit* / GOODWIN SANDS; *ship's officer* / WAY FOR A SAILOR. **1931:** *Geoffrey Trent* / BACHELOR FATHER; *Freddie* / JUST A GIGOLO; *Charles Carter* / BOUGHT; *Lothar* / AMBASSADOR BILL; *Joe Reynolds* / BLONDE CRAZY; *rich young man* / POLLY OF THE CIRCUS. **1932:** *Eddie* / THE MAN WHO PLAYED GOD; *James Medland* / PAYMENT DEFERRED. **1933:** *Bob Travers* / THIS IS THE LIFE; *Dashwood* / ORDERS IS ORDERS. **1934:** *Lord Robert Coray* / BOLERO; *Prince Michael Stofani* / WE'RE NOT DRESSING; *Ted Lambert* / MANY HAPPY RETURNS; *Freddie Bastion* / MENACE; *Neil Howard* / CHARLIE CHAN IN LONDON. **1935:** *Charles Gray (Granville)* / THE GILDED LILY; *Tony St. John* / ONE HOUR LATE; *Carl* / FOUR HOURS TO KILL; *Taylor Henry* / THE GLASS KEY; *Peter Marshall* / ALIAS MARY DOW. **1936:** *Tommy Abbott* / NEXT TIME WE LOVE; *Jimmy Lawson* / THE RETURN OF SOPHIE LANG; *Bob Miller* / THE BIG BROADCAST OF 1937. **1937:** *Lord Michael Stuart* / THREE SMART GIRLS; *Lt. Samuel Gilchrist* / WINGS OVER HONOLULU; *John Ball, Jr.* / EASY LIVING; *Robert Herrick* / EBB TIDE; *John O'Halloran* / WISE GIRL; *Bulldog Drummond* / BULLDOG DRUMMOND ESCAPES. **1938:** *Ken Warren* / TROPIC HOLIDAY; *Scott Barnes* / MEN WITH WINGS; *Richard Carrington, Jr.* / SAY IT IN FRENCH. **1939:** *Lieutenant Nemassy* / HOTEL IMPERIAL; *Geoffrey Thompson* / EVERYTHING HAPPENS AT NIGHT. **1940:** *Don Marshall* / IRENE; *Dr. Timothy Sterling* / THE DOCTOR TAKES A WIFE; *Dr. William Crawford* / UNTAMED. **1941:** *Jeff Young* / I WANTED WINGS; *Tony Kenyon* / SKYLARK. **1942:** *Kenneth Harper* / THE LADY HAS PLANS; *George Cugat* / ARE HUSBANDS NECESSARY?; *guest* / STAR SPANGLED RHYTHM. **1943:** *Bill Trimble* / FOREVER AND A DAY; *Brad Cavanaugh* / THE CRYSTAL BALL. **1944:** *Charley Johnson* / LADY IN THE DARK; *John* / TILL WE MEET AGAIN. **1945:** *Sir Hugh Marcy* / KITTY. **1946:** *Lt. Dudley Briggs* / THE WELL-GROOMED BRIDE; *Jonathan Trumbo* / CALIFORNIA. **1947:** *Clive Loring* / THE IMPERFECT LADY; *Gilbert Sedley* / THE TROUBLE WITH WOMEN; *guest* / VARIETY GIRL. **1948:** *Mark Belles* / SO EVIL MY LOVE; *Maj. Robert Lawson* / SEALED VERDICT; *guest* / MISS TATLOCK'S MILLIONS. **1949:** *Vernon Simpson* / IT HAPPENS EVERY SPRING. **1950:** *Alec Stevenson* / A WOMAN OF DISTINCTION; *Steve Harleigh* / A LIFE OF HER OWN; *Johnny Carter* / COPPER CANYON. **1951:** *Clay Douglas* / CIRCLE OF DANGER; *Phillip Ainley* / NIGHT INTO MORNING. **1952:** *Brad Sheridan* / BUGLES IN THE AFTERNOON; *Kern Shaffer* / SOMETHING TO LIVE FOR. **1953:** *Patrick Fairlie* / JAMAICA RUN. **1955:** *Wes Steele* / A MAN ALONE; *Stanford White* / THE GIRL IN THE RED VELVET SWING. **1956:** *Capt. Robert John Evans* / LISBON. **1957:** *Joe di Marco* / THREE BRAVE MEN; *Nardo Denning* / THE RIVER'S EDGE. **1958:** *Colley Dawson* / THE SAFECRACKER; *Cmdr. David Rudge* / HIGH FLIGHT. **1962:** *Harry Baldwin* / PANIC IN THE YEAR ZERO. **1968:** *Simon Crawford* / HOSTILE WITNESS. **1972:** *the ambassador* / EMBASSY; *Dr. Maxwell Kirshner* / THE THING WITH TWO HEADS; *Jason Crockett* / FROGS; *Hunthin* / THE BIG GAME. **1973:** *Henry Flexner* / TERROR IN THE WAX MUSEUM; *Stewart Henderson* / THE HOUSE IN NIGHTMARE PARK. **1974:** *Hurry Hirschfield* / GOLD. **1975:** *Hurtil* / THE SWISS CONSPIRACY; *Jim Moss* / THE DEAD DON'T DIE. **1976:** *Aristotle Bolt* / ESCAPE TO WITCH MOUNTAIN; *Fleishacker* / THE LAST TYCOON; *Brigadier Whale* / ACES HIGH. **1977:** *Frank Richards* / THE UNCANNY; *head crook* / SURVIVAL RUN. **1978:** *Mr. Stafford* / BLACKOUT. **1979:** *Oliver Barrett III* / OLIVER'S STORY; *Colonel Brettle* / GAME FOR VULTURES. **1980:** *Wendell* / THE ATTIC.

MILLER, ANN

(Lucille Ann Collier, 1919–)

Vivacious, rosy-cheeked, darkhaired Ann Miller possessed one of the finest sets of gams ever seen on stage or screen. She was an exuberant dancer in a string of minor musicals in the late 1930s and 1940s. After signing a contract with MGM, she moved into better musicals with roles as sexy dancers in films like EASTER PARADE, in which she stopped the show with "Shakin' the Blues Away." She never achieved real star status, though, and all her acting talents were confined to her long legs and her fast, dazzling dancing. She was still impressive at the age of 60 when she appeared on Broadway with Mickey Rooney in "Sugar Babies."

KEY ROLES

Kitty Brown / TIME OUT FOR RHYTHM, 1941, Columbia, d-Sidney Salkow.

Miller dances her feet off in this dull musical with the numbers "Boogie Woogie Man," "Time out for Rhythm," and "Twiddlin' My Thumbs" by Sammy Cahn and Saul Chaplin. The silly story deals with two feuding theatrical agents.

Beverly Ross / REVEILLE WITH BEVERLY, 1943, Columbia, d-Charles Barton.

This is the insipid story of a girl who runs a wake-up service for soldiers at a military camp. Miller is great in numbers such as "Thumbs Up and V for Victory."

Eadie Allen / EADIE WAS A LADY, 1945, Columbia, d-Arthur Dreifuss.

Miller plays a gal with a double life—during the day she's a student in a straight-laced girls' school; at night she's the star of a burlesque show. Her numbers include "She's a Gypsy from Brooklyn" by L. Wolfe Gilbert and Ben Oakland, and the title song by Nacio Herb Brown, Buddy De Sylva, and Richard A. Whiting.

Claire Huddesen / ON THE TOWN, 1949, MGM, d-Gene Kelly and Stanley Donen.

In this simple but enjoyable picture about three sailors on 24-hour leave in New York City and the girls they meet, Miller is matched with Jules Munshin and provides some of the best dancing in the piece with her Adolph Green and Leonard Bernstein number "Prehistoric Man."

Bubbles Cassidy / LOVELY TO LOOK AT, 1952, MGM, d-Mervyn LeRoy.

In this remake of ROBERTA, Miller provides the torrid "I'll Be Hard to Handle." Her romantic interest is Red Skelton, who inherits half-interest in a Paris fashion salon run by Kathryn Grayson and Marge Champion. The Jerome Kern and Dorothy Fields music is delightful but the story is disappointing.

Lois Lane / Bianca / KISS ME KATE, 1953, MGM, d-George Sidney.

Photographed in 3-D, Miller is as delightful as ever in her musical numbers but acts like a duck out of water when called upon to emote as the girlfriend of both Howard Keel and Tommy Rall. Her numbers in this beguiling version of "The Taming of the Shrew" are "Too Darn Hot," "Tom, Dick and Harry," "Always True to You in My Fashion," and "Why Can't You Behave?"

Lisa Bellmount / SMALL TOWN GIRL, 1953, MGM, d-Busby Berkeley.

Berkeley proved he hadn't lost his magic, particularly in the number he designed for Miller. While she dances to "I've Got to Hear the Beat," the disembodied hands of over 50 musicians protrude from the floor, each holding a musical instrument.

OTHER ROLES

1937: *specialty number* / NEW FACES OF 1937; *Annie* / STAGE DOOR; *Betty* / THE LIFE OF THE PARTY. **1938:** *Billie Shaw* / RADIO CITY REVELS; *Hilda Manney* / ROOM SERVICE; *Essie Carmichael* / YOU CAN'T TAKE IT WITH YOU; *Violet McMaster* / TARNISHED ANGEL; *specialty number* / HAVING WONDERFUL TIME. **1940:** *Pepe* / TOO MANY GIRLS; *Annabella Potter* / HIT PARADE OF 1941; *Julie Shelton* / MELODY RANCH. **1941:** *Lola* / GO WEST, YOUNG LADY. **1942:** *Vicki Marlow* / TRUE TO THE ARMY; *Donna D'Arcy* / PRIORITIES ON PARADE. **1943:** *Ann Crawford* / WHAT'S BUZZIN' COUSIN? **1944:** *Terry Baxter* / JAM SESSION; *Winnie Clark* / HEY, ROOKIE; *Julie Carrer* / CAROLINA BLUES. **1945:** *Eve Porter* / EVE KNEW HER APPLES. **1946:** *Linda Lorens* / THE THRILL OF BRAZIL. **1948:** *Nadine Hale* / EASTER PARADE. **1950:** *Miss Lucky Vista* / WATCH THE BIRDIE. **1951:** *Sunshine Jackson* / TEXAS CARNIVAL; *Joyce Campbell* / TWO TICKETS TO BROADWAY. **1954:** *specialty number* / DEEP IN MY HEART. **1955:** *Ginger* / HIT THE DECK. **1956:** *Gloria Dell* / THE OPPOSITE SEX; *Mrs. Doris Patterson* / THE GREAT AMERICAN PASTIME. **1976:** *president's girl 2* / WON TON TON, THE DOG WHO SAVED HOLLYWOOD.

MILLS, JOHN

(1908–)

John Mills, son of a teacher, worked as a clerk before joining the music hall stage as a song and dance man. Modest and likable, he made his London stage debut in 1927 and his first screen appearance in 1932 in THE MIDSHIPMAID. His international reputation was made with his portrayal of Pip in GREAT EXPECTATIONS in 1946. Mills portrayed many military men in the 1940s, first as unflappable enlisted men who faced seemingly impossible odds with confidence, and later as officers who were equally in control. In the 1950s he gradually made the shift to character roles, even taking second billing to his daughter, Hayley. He has also appeared in movies with his other daughter, Juliet. He won an Oscar for playing the village idiot in RYAN'S DAUGHTER.

KEY ROLES

Bobby / THOSE WERE THE DAYS, 1934, Great Britain, British International, d-Thomas Bentley.

In this Pinero farce, Mills is a 20-year-old dressed by his mom to look much younger to fool her second husband (Will Hay), a stern magistrate to whom she has lied about her age.

Albert Brown / FOREVER ENGLAND, (BROWN ON RESOLUTION), 1935, Great Britain, Gaumont, d-Walter Forde.

In his first leading role, Mills is the result of a brief affair between his mother and a naval officer. He becomes a hero in World War I when he single-handedly keeps a German ship in port with his expert marksmanship and keeps it under fire until a British ship comes along and sinks it. But Mills is killed and the commander of the English ship discovers that the boy is his son as he is wearing the watch the officer had given to his love so long ago.

Peter Colley as a young man / GOODBYE, MR. CHIPS, 1939, Great Britain, MGM, d-Sam Wood.

Mills is one of Mr. Chipping's more interesting and noticeable students in the classic tale of an unpopular Latin teacher who is humanized by his wife and becomes headmaster.

Fl. Lt. George Perrey / COTTAGE TO LET, 1941, Great Britain, Gainsborough, d-Anthony Asquith.

A scientist (Leslie Banks) and his assistant (Michael Wilding) have invented a new bomb sight. Banks is kidnapped by agents acting for Mills, who plays a German posing as an RAF pilot. Then Mills is gunned down in a hall of mirrors by an MI5 agent (Alastair Sim).

Shorty Blake / IN WHICH WE SERVE, 1942, Great Britain, Two Cities, d-Noel Coward.

Mills is one of the enlisted men aboard a British destroyer that is torpedoed. Together with the others trying to stay alive until rescued, he clings to a raft and recalls his life at home.

Jim Colter / WATERLOO ROAD, 1944, Great Britain, Gainsborough, d-Sidney Gilliat.

When Mills learns that his wife is having a fling with a draft dodger (Stewart Granger) while Mills is in the army, he goes AWOL to find them and is the victor after a terrible fight during an air raid. He and his wife straighten out their differences and he goes back to camp.

Peter Penrose / THE WAY TO THE STARS, 1945, Great Britain, Two Cities, d-Anthony Asquith.

Mills is a new pilot assigned to a bomber station. He is befriended by Michael Redgrave who, shortly after his wife gives birth to a son, is killed in action. This makes Mills reluctant to commit himself to his own girl, but eventually they get back together with the help of Redgrave's widow.

Pip Pirrip / GREAT EXPECTATIONS, 1946, Great Britain, Cineguild, d-David Lean.

Anthony Wager (as Pip as a boy) has all the best scenes in this marvelous rendition of the Dickens classic. But Mills is quite good as the grown-up lad who has been made a young gentleman by an unknown benefactor who turns out to be an escaped convict Pip once fed. Mills also handles the love scenes with heartless Valerie Hobson with a certain crushed bewilderment.

Jim Ackland / THE OCTOBER MAN, 1947, Great Britain, Eagle Lion, d-Roy Baker.

After an accident in which a child is killed, Mills, who has sustained brain injuries, considers suicide. When a model at his hotel is found strangled, he really begins to crack up, helped along by the taunting of the real killer. The police finally get on the track of the right man, just as Mills is prevented from throwing himself under a train.

Robert Falcon Scott / SCOTT OF THE ANTARCTIC, 1948, Great Britain, Ealing, d-Charles Frend.

In this very impressive biopic, Mills plays the English explorer whose team is beaten to the South Pole by Amundsen. On their return from the Pole, Scott and his men freeze to death in a blizzard, dying only 11 miles from their main camp.

Alfred Polly / THE HISTORY OF MR. POLLY, 1949, Great Britain, Two Cities, d-Anthony Pelissier.

Miserable with his nagging wife, Mills, a draper, sets fire to his own store and sets off to find a new life. After battling with fearsome Finlay Currie, Mills settles down with Megs Jenkins, the plump woman who runs Potwell Inn.

Willie Mossop / HOBSON'S CHOICE, 1954, Great Britain, London Films, d-David Lean.

Mills, a talented but downtrodden bootmaker, works for tyrannical Charles Laughton who refuses to give dowries to his three daughters, although he could well afford to do so. He prefers to keep them as virtual slave labor for his comforts. The eldest, Brenda de Banzie, gets Mills to marry her and then sets him up in competition with her father. The combination brings Laughton to his knees.

Supt. Mike Halloran / TOWN ON TRIAL, 1957, Great Britain, Marksman / Columbia, d-John Guillermin.

When a local harlot is found strangled, Mills of Scotland Yard is called in and his brusque manner offends the locals. But in the end he captures the killer after a chase up a steeple.

Superintendent Graham / TIGER BAY, 1959, Great Britain, Independent Artists, d-J. Lee Thompson.

Mills takes second billing to daughter Hayley in this story of a 12-year-old tomboy who sees Horst Buchholz kill his unfaithful girlfriend. Buchholz kidnaps Hayley and a bond develops between them. Mills is the police officer who traps Hayley into giving Buchholz away.

Lt. Col. Basil Barrow / TUNES OF GLORY, 1960, Great Britain, United Artists / Knightsbridge, d-Ronald Neame.

As bagpipes play, martinet Mills arrives at a Highland regiment's peacetime headquarters to replace lax disciplinarian and hard-drinking Alec Guinness as commander. Their difference in approach sets up a popularity contest between the men that leads to Mills's suicide and Guinness's cracking up out of guilt and remorse.

Father Robinson / SWISS FAMILY ROBINSON, 1961, Great Britain, Disney, d-Ken Annakin.

When he and his family are shipwrecked on a deserted island, Mills must lead them into a new way of life. The kids are a bit older than in the Johann Wyss novel, and James MacArthur is along to supply some romantic interest for Janet Munro.

Masterman Finsbury / THE WRONG BOX, 1966, Great Britain, Columbia, d-Bryan Forbes.

Mills and Ralph Richardson are elderly Victorian brothers who are the last survivors of a tontine worth a hundred thousand pounds. In this black farce they try to murder each other but should also worry about two of their nephews.

Michael / RYAN'S DAUGHTER, 1971, Great Britain, Faraway / MGM / EMI, d-David Lean.

Mills won an Academy Award for Best Supporting Actor as the mute idiot in a 1916 Irish village along the coast where both the British and the IRA patrol. Mills sees and knows more than he is given credit for, but he's not bright enough to figure out what to do with his knowledge.

OTHER ROLES

1932: *Golightly* / THE MIDSHIPMAID. **1933:** *Ernest Elton* / THE GHOST CAMERA; *Fred* / BRITANNIA OF BILLINGSGATE. **1934:** *Peter Farrell* / RIVER WOLVES; *Tony Smithers* / A POLITICAL PARTY; *Anthony Haughton* / THE LASH; *Ralph Summers* / BLIND JUSTICE; *Ronnie Blake* / DOCTOR'S ORDERS. **1935:** *boy* / ROYAL CAVALCADE; *Tony* / CHARING CROSS ROAD; *Robert Miller* / CAR OF DREAMS. **1936:** *Johnnie Penrose* / FIRST OFFENCE; *Lord Guilford Dudley* / TUDOR ROSE, (NINE DAYS A QUEEN). **1937:** *Cpl. Bert Dawson* / OHMS; *Jim Connor* / THE GREEN COCKATOO, (FOUR DARK HOURS). **1940:** *Young Bill Busby* / OLD BILL AND SON. **1941:** *Bobby* / THE BLACK SHEEP OF WHITEHALL. **1942:** *Tom* / THE BIG BLOCKADE; *William Wilberforce* / THE YOUNG MR. PITT. **1943:** *Lt. Freddie Taylor* / WE DIVE AT DAWN. **1944:** *Billy Mitchell* / THIS HAPPY BREED. **1947:** *George Boswell* / SO WELL REMEMBERED. **1950:** *Bassett* / THE ROCKING HORSE WINNER; *Lieutenant Commander Armstrong* / MORNING DEPARTURE. **1951:** *Tom Denning* / MR. DENNING DRIVES NORTH. **1952:** *Terence Sullivan* / THE GENTLE GUNMAN; Davidson / THE LONG MEMORY. **1954:** *Pat Reid* / THE COLDITZ STORY; *Albert Parkis* / THE END OF THE AFFAIR. **1955:** *Commander Fraser* / ABOVE US THE WAVES; *John Hampden* / ESCAPADE. **1956:** *Mr. Dingle* / IT'S GREAT TO BE YOUNG; *Puncher Roberts* / THE BABY AND THE BATTLESHIP; *Platon Karatsev* / WAR AND PEACE; *cabbie* / AROUND THE WORLD IN 80 DAYS. **1957:** *Dr. Howard Latimer* / VICIOUS CIRCLE. **1958:** *Tubby Binns* / DUNKIRK; *Major Harvey* / I WAS MONTY'S DOUBLE; *Captain Anson* / ICE COLD IN ALEX. **1960:** *Barney* / SUMMER OF THE 17TH DOLL. **1961:** *Jacko Palmer* / FLAME IN THE STREETS; *Father Keogh* / THE SINGER NOT THE SONG. **1962:** *Captain Morgan* / THE VALIANT; *Lieutenant Colonel Clifford* / TIARA TAHITI. **1963:** *Maitland* / THE CHALK GARDEN. **1964:** *Tommy Tyler* / THE TRUTH ABOUT SPRING. **1965:** *General Boyd* / OPERATION CROSSBOW. **1966:** *Colonel Smedley-Taylor* / KING RAT; *Ezra Filton* / THE FAMILY WAY. **1967:** *Wing Cmdr. Howard Hayes* / AFRICA—TEXAS STYLE!; *Col. Stuart Valois* / CHUKA. **1969:** *Field Marshall Sir Douglas Haig* / OH! WHAT A LOVELY WAR; *the moorman* / RUN WILD, RUN FREE; *Sir William Hamilton* / LADY HAMILTON; *Insp. Franz Bulon* / A BLACK VEIL FOR LISA. **1970:** *Sir Philip* / ADAM'S WOMAN. **1971:** *Mr. Parker* / DULCIMA. **1972:** *Gen. Herbert Kitchner* / YOUNG WINSTON; *Canning* / LADY CAROLINE LAMB. **1973:** *Cleon Doyle* / OKLAHOMA CRUDE. **1976:** *Mike McCallister* / THE HUMAN FACTOR; *Bertie Cook* / TRIAL BY COMBAT. **1977:** *Blaise Meredith* / THE DEVIL'S ADVOCATE. **1978:** *Insp. Jim Carson* / THE BIG SLEEP. **1979:** *Sir Henry Bartle Frere* / ZULU DAWN. **1982:** *Lord Chelmsford* / GANDHI. **1984:** *Cambridge* / SAHARA. **1987:** *Montgomery Bell* / WHO'S THAT GIRL?

MINNELLI, LIZA

(1946–)

The daughter of Judy Garland and Vincente Minnelli, Liza made her film debut with her mother in IN THE GOOD OLD SUMMERTIME when she was three. She danced at the New York Palace Theater at age seven while Garland sang "Swanee." At 19 she became the youngest Best Actress Tony Award winner for the title role in "Flora the Red Menace." Recording and TV appearances, followed by nightclub tours, made her a top cabaret entertainer. Her screen career has been limited by the scarcity of vehicles to exploit her particular talents. Being cast as something of a kook in most of her movies has not helped. She was nominated for an Oscar for THE STERILE CUCKOO and won for CABARET. Although there's much about her mannerisms and even her voice that reminds one of Garland, Minnelli has her own special dynamism and magic which thus far seem more appropriate to the concert hall and stage than to the silver screen.

KEY ROLES

Pookie Adams / THE STERILE CUCKOO, 1969, Paramount, d-Alan J. Pakula.

Reviews are mixed on Minnelli as an insecure, talkative college girl who has her first sexual experience. Some critics believe Minnelli dug down deep into herself and exposed raw nerves. Then there are those who feel the comedy-drama was tiresome and routine. Judge for yourself.

Sally Bowles / CABARET, 1972, ABC Pictures, d-Bob Fosse.

There are some snobs who hold that musicals and stars of such should not be considered for Academy Awards. Perhaps they can make convincing arguments to support their position. But Minnelli, as the kooky cabaret singer in Berlin just before the Nazis take over, is a good counter argument. The dances and other musical numbers by John Kander and Fred Ebb are also a real plus.

Linda Marolla / ARTHUR, 1981, Warners / Orion, d-Steve Gordon.

Minnelli scores as the poor girlfriend of eccentric, wealthy Dudley Moore who is almost forced to marry the wrong girl to maintain his inheritance.

OTHER ROLES

1949: *cameo* / IN THE GOOD OLD SUMMERTIME. **1962:** *voice* / JOURNEY BACK TO OZ. **1967:** *Eliza* / CHARLIE BUBBLES. **1970:** *Junie Moon* / TELL ME THAT YOU LOVE ME, JUNIE MOON. **1974:** *host* / THAT'S ENTERTAINMENT! **1976:** *guest* / SILENT MOVIE; *Claire* / LUCKY LADY; *Nina* / A MATTER OF TIME. **1977:** *Francine Evans* / NEW YORK, NEW YORK. **1984:** *guest* / THE MUPPETS TAKE MANHATTAN. **1985:** *film clips* / THAT'S DANCING!

MIRANDA, CARMEN

(Maria da Cunha, 1909–1955)

"The South American Bombshell" was actually born in Lisbon, but her family moved to Brazil when she was a baby. She became one of Brazil's top entertainers with over 300 records, five films, and nine sold-out South American tours. Miranda made her U.S. film debut in DOWN ARGENTINE WAY in 1940 and, while never the romantic lead, was well paid for her extravagant dancing, singing, and flamboyant headgear (which compensated for her petite size of five-foot-two and 100 pounds). Besides her movies, "The Lady in the Tutti-Frutti Hat" also performed extensively in nightclubs and on television. It is rumored that she was fired by Fox when they discovered that she wore no panties under her garish swinging dresses. There is a rather famous still of her in a dance pose with Cesar Romero that appears to corroborate this contention. Whatever the truth, Miranda was certainly a unique talent in movies—volatile, tempestuous, and explosive. Who will ever forget her fruit basket hats and her frenetic, hippy dancing?

KEY ROLES

herself / DOWN ARGENTINE WAY, 1940, 20th Century-Fox, d-Irving Cummings.

Betty Grable is the star of this picture about an American heiress who falls in love with an Argentinian horsebreeder. However, Miranda, who has nothing to do with the plot, just about steals the movie with her rendition of "South American Way" by Al Dubin and Jimmy McHugh.

Rosita Rivas / WEEK-END IN HAVANA, 1941, 20th Century-Fox, d-Walter Lang.

Miranda has a crush on Cesar Romero in this film, but Alice Faye gets the man. Miranda is a blockbuster in the finale by Mack Gordon and Harry Warren, "The Nango."

Rosita / SPRINGTIME IN THE ROCKIES, 1942, 20th Century-Fox, d-Irving Cummings.

In this story about the on-again, off-again love affair of Broadway stars Betty Grable and John Payne, the latter begins a relationship with Miranda when Grable takes up with Cesar Romero. The pairing gets changed by the finale. Miranda performs "Tic Tac Do Meu Coracaco" and "Chattanooga Choo Choo."

Dorita / THE GANG'S ALL HERE, 1943, 20th Century-Fox, d-Busby Berkeley.

Second-billed Miranda makes her entrance wearing a huge headdress of fruit and pulled in a cart by two gold-painted oxen. As she sings "The Lady with the Tutti-Frutti Hat," 60 chorus girls dance around making many designs with the mammoth bananas they carry. The phallic overtones caused the number to be banned in Brazil. Once again Miranda has next to nothing to do with the plot about a soldier who has to choose between Alice Faye and Sheila Ryan.

Carmen Novarro / COPACABANA, 1947, United Artists, d-Alfred E. Green.

The only reason to mention this box-office flop is because it features two unique performers: Groucho Marx as an artists' agent and his sole client, Miranda. Her songs by Sam Coslow include "My Heart Was Doing a Bolero" and "Let's Do the Copacabana."

Marina Rodriguez / NANCY GOES TO RIO, 1950, MGM, d-Robert Z. Leonard.

In this remake of IT'S A DATE, Jane Powell and her mother (Ann Sothern) are both seeking the same acting role. Miranda contributes "Cha Bomm Pa Pa" by Ray Gilbert, and once again has nothing to do with the story.

OTHER ROLES

1941: *Carmen* / THAT NIGHT IN RIO. **1944:** *herself* / FOUR JILLS IN A JEEP; *Princess Querida* / GREENWICH VILLAGE; *Chiquita Hart* / SOMETHING FOR THE BOYS. **1946:** *Chita* / DOLL FACE; *Michele O'Toole* / IF I'M LUCKY. **1948:** *Rosita Cochellas* / A DATE WITH JUDY. **1953:** *Carmelita Castinha* / SCARED STIFF.

MITCHUM, ROBERT

(1917–)

Sleepy-looking, powerfully built Robert Mitchum, with his slow, distinctive speech and self-deprecating sense of humor, likes to give the impression that he doesn't take acting seriously, insisting, "Listen, I got three expressions: looking left, looking right, and looking straight ahead." This is deceptive. He has worked very hard to become the cool loner and anti-hero in numerous film noir and action movies. He always shows up on time for filming with his lines down pat. This ultimate tough guy has had one Oscar nomination, for THE STORY OF G.I. JOE. He broke into films as an extra and appeared in 19 movies his first year. While a conviction and jail sentence for smoking marijuana might have ended the career of any other actor, audiences felt it fit Mitchum's screen persona and were forgiving of his run-in with the law. Lately he has appeared in made-for-TV films such as THE WINDS OF WAR.

KEY ROLES

Pig Iron Matthews / GUNG HO! 1943, Universal, d-Ray Enright.
In this version of the real-life Makin Island raid in 1942, Mitchum impresses as a soldier with a throat wound that makes it impossible for him to speak. He throws his bayonet like a dagger when he is unable to shout out a warning to a buddy that a Japanese soldier is sneaking up behind him.

Lt. / Capt. Bill Walker / THE STORY OF G.I. JOE, 1945, United Artists, d-William A. Wellman.
Mitchum was nominated for an Oscar for his portrayal of the responsible officer who leads his group of infantrymen through the Italian campaign in World War II.

Jeb Rand / PURSUED, 1947, Warners, d-Raoul Walsh.
Mitchum is a Spanish-American War veteran who is bedeviled by disturbing events caused by an illicit love affair of long ago and accidentally brings tragedy to his adopted family.

Sgt. Peter Kelley / CROSSFIRE, 1947, RKO, d-Edward Dmytryk.
Mitchum is one of three soldiers who are suspected of killing a man in a New York hotel because he was Jewish. It's a taut thriller and Mitchum does himself proud as he helps to expose the real killer.

Jeff Bailey / OUT OF THE PAST, 1947, RKO, d-Jacques Tourneur.
Here's a film noir that deserves more attention. In his first starring role Mitchum plays a gas station owner in a small mountain town whose love for pretty Virginia Huston is ruined because of his past affair with evil Jane Greer. Mitchum is just right as the cynical, lazy-eyed anti-hero.

Lt. Duke Halliday / THE BIG STEAL, 1949, RKO, d-Don Siegel.
Mitchum, with the help of Jane Greer, pursues a man (Patric Knowles) who has snitched a $300,000 army payroll from him. Mitchum, in turn, is pursued by William Bendix. The chase takes place through Mexico at a high speed on some very primitive roads.

Frank Jessup / ANGEL FACE, 1952, RKO, d-Otto Preminger.
Mitchum is a rugged chauffeur whose affair with demented Jean Simmons, who murders her father and stepmother, ends when she backs the car they are in over a cliff, killing them both, because he refuses to marry her.

Matt Calder / RIVER OF NO RETURN, 1954, 20th Century-Fox, d-Otto Preminger.
When Mitchum rescues saloon singer Marilyn Monroe from gold camp toughs, she lets it be known that she has a gold claim. The two team up and, together with Mitchum's 10-year-old son, raft down the river of "no return" to hoped-for riches.

Curt Bridges / TRACK OF THE CAT, 1954, Warners, d-William A. Wellman.
In this highly symbolic but slow-moving film, Mitchum and his northern California backwoods family are menaced one winter by a marauding mountain lion.

Lucas Marsh / NOT AS A STRANGER, 1955, United Artists, d-Stanley Kramer.
When medical student Mitchum is in danger of having to leave school due to lack of funds, he romances and marries Olivia de Havilland, the head surgical nurse, even though he doesn't love her. Once in practice he has a tempestuous affair with Gloria Grahame.

Preacher Harry Powell / THE NIGHT OF THE HUNTER, 1955, United Artists, d-Charles Laughton.
This picture, the only film ever directed by Charles Laughton, is a superb, imaginative thriller with Mitchum as a psychopathic preacher. He is simply magnificent. He has married the widow of a man executed for stealing $10,000, and the money has never been recovered. But the deceased's two kids know where the loot is and Mitchum intends to get it from them. He is thwarted by wonderful Lillian Gish, who shelters the children after Mitchum kills their ma and is hard on their trail with more murder on his mind.

Mr. Allison / HEAVEN KNOWS, MR. ALLISON, 1957, 20th Century-Fox, d-John Huston.
This is the silly but enjoyable story of a marine (Mitchum) and a nun (Deborah Kerr) marooned together on a Japanese-controlled island during World War II. Although they are initially antagonistic toward each other, they eventually work together to outwit the enemy.

Captain Murrell / THE ENEMY BELOW, 1957, 20th Century-Fox, d-Dick Powell.
During World War II, Mitchum commands a destroyer that is tracked by a German submarine commanded by Curt Jurgens. Like two great chess masters, Mitchum and Jurgens make their moves in the cat-and-mouse-like game. Mitchum comes out on top, but the two commanders have grown to respect each other's military savvy.

Paddy Carmody / THE SUNDOWNERS, 1960, Great Britain / Australia, Warners, d-Fred Zinnemann.
Mitchum is an Irish sheepdrover who, with his wife and son, happily travels from job to job in the Australian bush during the 1920s. We see the indomitable spirit and the optimism of an ever-expanding family as more and more characters join Mitchum and wife Deborah Kerr on their travels.

Max Cady / CAPE FEAR, 1962, Universal, d-J. Lee Thompson.
Mitchum is an ex-con who blames Florida lawyer Gregory Peck for his imprisonment. He moves into town making not so veiled sexual threats against Peck's wife and teenage daughter. But the police can do nothing as he has committed no crime. Even when he savagely beats and rapes a girl, she refuses to testify against him out of fear. Ultimately Peck must take matters into his own hands and face Mitchum.

Sheriff J. B. Harrah / EL DORADO, 1967, Paramount, d-Howard Hawks.
Mitchum is a whiskey-soaked sheriff who joins forces with veteran gunfighter John Wayne to stand up against a cattle baron. If the picture looks familiar, it should. Back in 1959 director Hawks and star Wayne

made essentially the same movie (RIO BRAVO) with Dean Martin in the Mitchum role.

Charles Shaughnessy / RYAN'S DAUGHTER, 1970, Great Britain, MGM / Faraway, d-David Lean.

When Sarah Miles, one of schoolteacher Mitchum's former students, expresses her love for him, he marries her even though he sees potential problems with the difference in their ages and senses her desire to marry is motivated by boredom not love. When she has an affair with a young British officer, Mitchum is not too surprised. But he rallies to her support when she is treated as an informer by the locals who, as punishment, shear her head.

Eddie Coyle / THE FRIENDS OF EDDIE COYLE, 1973, Paramount, d-Peter Yates.

Mitchum is very good as the small-time Boston hoodlum who is forced to turn informer or face jail for life as a four-time loser. His underworld hoods get wind that he has turned squealer and eliminate him.

Philip Marlowe / FAREWELL, MY LOVELY, 1975, Avco Embassy, d-Dick Richards.

Mitchum is just about perfect as Raymond Chandler's private eye who is hired by ex-con Jack O'Halloran to find his missing girlfriend and finds himself wrapped up in homicide and smuggling in seedy post-World War II Los Angeles.

Philip Marlowe / THE BIG SLEEP, 1978, Great Britain, ITC, d-Michael Winner.

It might have been better if Mitchum had retired after playing Marlowe just once. His sleepy approach through this remake of the 1946 classic is weakened by moving the locale to London and trying too hard to make the loose ends come together.

OTHER ROLES

1943: *Rigney* / HOPPY SERVES A WRIT; *bit* / BORDER PATROL; *bit* / THE LEATHER BURNERS; *Tate Winters* / FOLLOW THE BAND; *henchman* / COLT COMRADES; *horse* / THE HUMAN COMEDY; *Panhandle Mitchell* / WE'VE NEVER BEEN LICKED; *Trigger Dolan* / BEYOND THE LAST FRONTIER; *Richard Adams* / BAR 20; *Ernie Jones* / DOUGHBOYS IN IRELAND; *Shepard* / CORVETTE K-225; *flyer* / AERIAL GUNNER; *Ben Slocum* / THE LONE STAR TRAIL; *Mickey* / THE DANCING MASTERS; *Rip Austin* / FALSE COLORS; *Drago* / RIDERS OF THE DEADLINE; *Chuck* / MINESWEEPER; *groaning man* / CRY HAVOC. **1944:** *CPO Jeff Daniels* / JOHNNY DOESN'T LIVE HERE ANY MORE; *Fred* / WHEN STRANGERS MARRY; *Bob Gray* / THIRTY SECONDS OVER TOKYO; *Jimmy Smith* / GIRL RUSH; *Jim Lacy (Nevada)* / NEVADA. **1945:** *Pecos Smith* / WEST OF THE PECOS. **1946:** *William Tabeshaw* / TILL THE END OF TIME; *Michael Garroway* / UNDERCURRENT; *Norman Clyde* / THE LOCKET. **1947:** *Paul Aubert* / DESIRE ME. **1948:** *Jim Fairways* / RACHEL AND THE STRANGER; *Jim Garry* / BLOOD ON THE MOON. **1949:** *Billy Buck* / THE RED PONY; *Steve* / HOLIDAY AFFAIR. **1950:** *Jeff Cameron* / WHERE DANGER LIVES. **1951:** *Dr. Mark Lucas* / MY FORBIDDEN PAST; *Dan Milner* / HIS KIND OF WOMAN; *Capt. Thomas McQuigg* / THE RACKET. **1952:** *Nick Cochran* / MACAO; *Col. Steve Janowski* / ONE MINUTE TO ZERO; *Jeff McCloud* / THE LUSTY MEN. **1953:** *Lonni Douglas* / WHITE WITCH DOCTOR; *Russ Lambert* / SECOND CHANCE. **1954:** *Doc* / SHE COULDN'T SAY NO. **1955:** *Clint Tollinger* / MAN WITH THE GUN. **1956:** *bishop* / FOREIGN INTRIGUE; *Wilson* / BANDIDO. **1957:** *Felix Bowers* / FIRE DOWN BELOW. **1958:** *Lucas "Luke" Doolin* / THUNDER ROAD; *Maj. Cleve Saville* / THE HUNTERS. **1959:** *Mike Morrison* / THE ANGRY HILLS; *Martin Brady* / THE WONDERFUL COUNTRY. **1960:** *Capt. Wade Hunnicutt* / HOME FROM THE HILL; *Dermot O'Neill* / THE NIGHT FIGHTERS. **1961:** *Archie Hall* / THE LAST TIME I SAW ARCHIE. **1962:** *Gen. Norman Cota* / THE LONGEST DAY; *Jerry Ryan* / TWO FOR THE SEESAW. **1963:** *Jim Slattery* / THE LIST OF ADRIAN MESSENGER; *Harry Stanton* / RAMPAGE. **1964:** *Lt. Col. Barney Adams* / MAN IN THE MIDDLE; *Rod Anderson* / WHAT A WAY TO GO! **1965:** *Joe Moses* / MISTER MOSES. **1967:** *Dick Summers* / THE WAY WEST. **1968:** *Dick Ennis* / ANZIO; *Lee Arnold* / VILLA RIDES; *Reverend Rudd* / FIVE CARD STUD; *Albert* / SECRET CEREMONY. **1969:** *Ben Kane* / YOUNG BILLY YOUNG; *Flagg* / THE GOOD GUYS AND THE BAD GUYS. **1971:** *Harry K. Graham* / GOING HOME. **1972:** *Van Horne* / THE WRATH OF GOD. **1975:** *Harry Kilmer* / THE YAKUZA. **1976:** *Pat Brady* / THE LAST TYCOON; *Adm. William F. Halsey* / MIDWAY. **1977:** *Quinlan* / THE AMSTERDAM KILL. **1978:** *Duke Parkhurst* / MATILDA; *Colonel Rogers* / BREAKTHROUGH. **1979:** *Donner* / NIGHTKILL. **1981:** *Ted* / AGENCY. **1982:** *Coach Delaney* / THAT CHAMPIONSHIP SEASON. **1984:** *Mr. Bibic* / MARIA'S LOVERS; *Peter Hacker* / THE AMBASSADOR.

MONROE, MARILYN

(Norma Jean Baker, 1926–1962)

Hollywood's most glamorous blonde sex symbol since Jean Harlow never seemed to find the happiness and joy she brought to her fans and admirers. There was always a sense of tragedy and doom surrounding this voluptuous star who seemed unable to find any personal happiness because she was never allowed to be anything other than her studio-created image. Her quotes reflect her yearning for a real personality: "It's nice to be included in people's fantasies, but you also like to be accepted for your own sake." And: "First, I'm trying to prove to myself that I'm a person. Then, maybe, I'll convince myself that I'm an actress." And she was an actress, really quite wonderful in light comedies such as SOME LIKE IT HOT. Three-times married—husband number two was Joe DiMaggio and number three was playwright Arthur Miller—Monroe was working on SOMETHING'S GOT TO GIVE when she died, apparently a suicide, at age 36. Although dead for more than 25 years, her legend is as alive as ever.

KEY ROLES

Angela Phinlay / THE ASPHALT JUNGLE, 1950, MGM, d-John Huston.

Monroe is the sexy mistress of financier Louis Calhern, who is bankrolling a jewel heist. After this film everyone wanted to know more about this spectacular beauty.

Miss Caswell / ALL ABOUT EVE, 1950, MGM, d-Joseph L. Mankiewicz.

Although far down the credits in this bitchy classic, starlet Monroe makes her presence felt at a party to which she was brought by George Sanders. She wonders why all producers look like "unhappy rabbits."

Nell / DON'T BOTHER TO KNOCK, 1952, 20th Century-Fox, d-Roy Baker.

Before gaining her reputation as a sex goddess, Monroe played a mentally disturbed young woman hired to babysit in a hotel. She is prevented by Richard Widmark from killing herself.

Rose Loomis / NIAGARA, 1953, 20th Century-Fox, d-Henry Hathaway.

Monroe's build-up really started when she played an unfaithful wife whose plan to kill her husband (Joseph Cotten) backfires in this film. Her walking away from the camera is a sight to be seen.

Lorelei Lee / GENTLEMEN PREFER BLONDES, 1953, 20th Century-Fox, d-Howard Hawks.

Monroe is on a transatlantic cruise with Jane Russell, out to find rich men and jewels. As she tells wealthy Charles Coburn: "I always say a kiss on the hand might feel very good, but a diamond tiara lasts forever." She discovers that the richest and most eligible bachelor aboard is George "Foghorn" Winslow, an 8-year-old.

Pola Debevoise / HOW TO MARRY A MILLIONAIRE, 1953, 20th Century-Fox, d-Jean Negulesco.

Monroe is blind as a bat without her glasses but doesn't let that put a crimp in her plans to find a rich husband. It even helps her meet David Wayne, who has a lot of money but can't get his hands on it because of problems with the IRS.

the girl / THE SEVEN YEAR ITCH, 1955, 20th Century-Fox, d-Billy Wilder.

Monroe is a model subletting an apartment upstairs from Tom Ewell, whose family is away for the summer. She's innocent and naive, but not as dumb as she seems. Ewell has a vivid imagination, fired by comments like Monroe's secret for summer comfort: "You know, when it's hot like this—you know what I do? I keep my undies in the icebox." Ewell fantasizes an affair when he invites her down to cool off in his air-conditioned apartment, but everything remains quite innocent. One of the most memorable scenes of the movie is Monroe's white skirt being blown above her head by the wind from a subway grating she is standing on.

Cherie / BUS STOP, 1956, 20th Century-Fox, d-Joshua Logan.

Monroe, a B-girl and horrible singer, finds herself the reluctant object of affection of lonely cowboy Don Murray. He wins her when he learns to show her some respect. Despite her outlandish costumes and miserable voice, she is very appealing and vulnerable.

Sugar Kane Kovalchick / SOME LIKE IT HOT, 1959, United Artists, d-Billy Wilder.

In perhaps her best role, Monroe is a none-too-bright, none-too-pure singer with an all-girl band in the 1920s who falls for Tony Curtis, a sax player posing as a girl in the band while hiding from mobsters. Life has not been easy for this spectacularly built but minimally talented gal. As she confesses: "I always get the fuzzy end of the lollipop." Her rendition of "Runnin' Wild" in a train aisle is a classic.

Rosalyn Tabor / THE MISFITS, 1961, United Artists, d-John Huston.

Monroe is an aimless divorcee who teams up with aimless cowboys Clark Gable and Montgomery Clift in this rather talky film written by Arthur Miller, Monroe's one-time husband. She tries to prevent the men from rounding up wild horses to be used for dog meat. It is fitting that she ended her film career with Gable because as a child she had a fantasy: "I was one of a family of many children, and Clark Gable was our father, and he liked me the best. Each night, when he came home, he'd swing me up onto his shoulder and tell me how pretty I was. Of all the children, he loved me best." In the film, Gable tells Monroe: "You're a real beautiful woman. It's almost kind of an honor sitting next to you. You just shine in my eyes. That's my true feeling, Rosalyn. What makes you so sad? I think you're the saddest girl I ever met."

OTHER ROLES

1948: *bit* / SCUDDA HOO! SCUDDA HAY!; *Evie* / DANGEROUS YEARS. **1949:** *Grunion's client* / LOVE HAPPY; *Peggy Martin* / LADIES OF THE CHORUS. **1950:** *blonde* / RIGHT CROSS; *Clara* / A TICKET TO TOMAHAWK; *Polly* / THE FIREBALL. **1951:** *Miss Martin* / HOME TOWN STORY; *Harriet* / AS YOUNG AS YOU FEEL; *Roberta Stevens* / LOVE NEST; *Joyce* / LET'S MAKE IT LEGAL. **1952:** *Peggy* / CLASH BY NIGHT; *Annabel Norris* / WE'RE NOT MARRIED; *Lois Laurel* / MONKEY BUSINESS; *a streetwalker* / O. HENRY'S FULL HOUSE. **1954:** *Kay Weston* / RIVER OF NO RETURN; *Vicky* / THERE'S NO BUSINESS LIKE SHOW BUSINESS. **1957:** *Elsie Marina* / THE PRINCE AND THE SHOWGIRL. **1960:** *Amanda Dell* / LET'S MAKE LOVE.

MONTEZ, MARIA

(Maria Africa Vidal de Santos Silas, 1920–1951)

Born in the Dominican Republic, the daughter of the Spanish consul to that country, exotic beauty Maria Montez was a triple threat—she couldn't act, couldn't sing, and couldn't dance—so Universal created a new movie genre to feature this strikingly attractive Latin actress. The studio's solution was to star Montez in costumed fantasies in storybook lands in which her lack of talent seemed almost a plus as her vibrant voice throbbed with promise as she sprawled seductively on some couch, clothed in revealing outfits. Montez was known affectionately as "The Queen of Technicolor" and "The Caribbean Cyclone." No one was more appreciative of her looks than Montez herself who observed, "Each time I look in the mirror, I want to scream. I am so beautiful." When she began to have some problems with her weight, she went to Europe with husband Jean-Pierre Aumont and appeared in a number of French and Italian movies. In 1951 she drowned in her bath, possibly after a heart attack.

KEY ROLES

Melahi / SOUTH OF TAHITI, 1941, Universal, d-George Waggner.

No one expects a beautiful native girl on a South Pacific island to act. It's enough that she looks like home cooking to four adventurers who drift ashore on her tropical paradise.

Sherazad / ARABIAN NIGHTS, 1943, Universal, d-John Rawlins.

This hokum is most entertaining with Montez as a dancer who helps the rightful Caliph of Baghdad (Jon Hall) to regain his throne which was usurped by his evil half-brother.

Princess Tahia / WHITE SAVAGE, 1943, Universal, d-Arthur Lubin.

Montez is the queen of a beautiful South Seas island who has trouble with shark hunters and crooks who are after her island's mineral rights.

Amara / ALI BABA AND THE FORTY THIEVES, 1944, Universal, d-Arthur Lubin.

This time Montez helps a deposed prince (Jon Hall) who has fallen in with the fabled forty thieves and their "Open Sesame" cave, win back his rightful place from marvelous villain Kurt Katch.

Tollea / Nadja / COBRA WOMAN, 1944, Universal-International, d-Robert Siodmak.

Audiences get twice as much of the lovely Montez to look at in this story of a South Seas girl who is kidnapped by snake worshipers ruled by her evil twin sister who needs a human sacrifice. Guess which sister feeds the vipers.

Rita / TANGIER, 1946, Universal-International, d-George Waggner.

In a nice change of pace for the exotic beauty, Montez plays a dancer hunting down the Nazi war criminal responsible for her father's death. In this one the Queen of Technicolor is reduced to appearing in monochrome.

OTHER ROLES

1941: *bathing beauty* / LUCKY DEVILS; *Marie* / THE INVISIBLE WOMAN; *Linda Calhoun* / BOSS OF BULLION CITY; *Inez* / THAT NIGHT IN RIO; *Zuleika* / RAIDERS OF THE DESERT; *Ilani* / MOONLIGHT IN HAWAII. **1942:** *Mrs. Sonya Dietrich Landers* / BOMBAY CLIPPER; *Marie Roget* / THE MYSTERY OF MARIE ROGET. **1944:** *guest* / FOLLOW THE BOYS; *Carla* / GYPSY WILDCAT; *Marina* / BOWERY TO BROADWAY. **1945:** *Naila* / SUDAN. **1947:** *the countess* / THE EXILE; *Marguerita* / PIRATES OF MONTEREY. **1948:** *Queen Antinea* / SIREN OF ATLANTIS. **1949:** *Dolores* / THE WICKED CITY; *Catherine* / PORTRAIT OF AN ASSASSIN. **1950:** *Tina* / THE THIEF OF VENICE.

MONTGOMERY, DOUGLASS

(Robert D. Montgomery, 1907–1966)

Fair-haired Douglass Montgomery began his career as Kent Douglass to avoid confusion with already popular Robert Montgomery. Most of his roles were in lackluster films unworthy of his talents. Of wholesome appearance, the six-footer had a steady if uneventful career in the 1930s and 1940s, mainly in second features. During World War II, he became popular on British radio and made a few British films before his career came to an end.

KEY ROLES

Roy Wetherby / WATERLOO BRIDGE, 1931, Universal, d-James Whale.

Still appearing as Kent Douglass, Montgomery is an army officer who marries a ballerina. When he is reported missing in action in World War I, his family ignores her and she becomes a prostitute to support herself. The couple meet again but it's too late—isn't it?

Laurie Laurence / LITTLE WOMEN, 1933, RKO, d-George Cukor.

In his first film as Douglass Montgomery he is Katharine Hepburn's co-star and initial love in this story of four sisters growing up around the time of the American Civil War.

Neville Landless / THE MYSTERY OF EDWIN DROOD, 1935, Universal, d-Stuart Walker.

Montgomery's acting is a bit too stagey in the Dickens tale of a drug-addicted choirmaster (Claude Rains) who is David Manners's rival for Heather Angel. Rains does in his competition and tries to lay the blame on Montgomery.

Stephen Foster / HARMONY LANE, 1935, Mascot, d-Joseph Santley.

This syrupy biopic of the composer of "Jeannie with the Light Brown Hair" and "Old Folks at Home" was meant for an audience of hicks at the time.

Charles Wilder / THE CAT AND THE CANARY, 1939, Paramount, d-Elliott Nugent.

Montgomery adds a great deal to the delight of this comedy-thriller about greedy relatives who have gathered in an old house to hear the reading of the will of an eccentric. The heir-apparent's (Paulette Goddard) life and sanity are threatened by clauses that would see the fortune go to others if she proved insane.

Johnny Hollis / THE WAY TO THE STARS, 1945, Great Britain, Two Cities / United Artists, d-Anthony Asquith.

Montgomery is an American flyer who arrives at a British bomber station in 1940. Along with many others he is killed defending Britain.

OTHER ROLES

As Kent Douglass

1930: *Bob Gilder* / PAID. **1931:** *Von Lear* / DAYBREAK; *Avery* / FIVE AND TEN; *Matt Law* / A HOUSE DIVIDED.

As Douglass Montgomery

1934: *David Perrin* / EIGHT GIRLS IN A BOAT; *Hand Pinneberg* / LITTLE MAN, WHAT NOW?; *Karl Roder* / MUSIC IN THE AIR; *guest* / THE GIFT OF GAB. **1935:** *Phil Ash-Orcutt* / LADY TUBBS. **1936:** *Hugh McGrath* / EVERYTHING IS THUNDER. **1937:** *Paul Maddox* / COUNSEL FOR CRIME; *Drake IV* / LIFE BEGINS WITH LOVE. **1946:** *David Anson* / WOMAN TO WOMAN. **1948:** *Jim Harding* / FORBIDDEN.

MONTGOMERY, ROBERT

(Henry Montgomery, 1904–1981)

Good-looking Robert Montgomery was unique in show business in that he achieved success as an actor and director in film, theater, radio, and television. He was also one of the first to realize that the day was fast approaching when the media would have a great influence on who is elected to political office and he became a media adviser to President Eisenhower. Perhaps he was thinking along these lines when he said, "My advice to you concerning applause is this: enjoy it but never quite believe it." He helped found the Screen Actors Guild and served as its president for four terms. He served in the PT boat service during World War II. The father of actress Elizabeth Montgomery, he was nominated for the Best Actor Academy Award in NIGHT MUST FALL and HERE COMES MR. JORDAN. He was at home playing arch comedians, dapper cads, breezy men-about-town, crazy killers, hard-boiled detectives, and noble war heroes.

KEY ROLES

Kent Marlowe / THE BIG HOUSE, 1930, MGM, d-George Hill.

Charged with manslaughter while driving under the influence of alcohol, Montgomery becomes the cellmate of Wallace Beery and Chester Morris. When Beery plans a break, Montgomery informs the warden and Morris quells the riot, winning a parole.

Lt. Thomas Knowlton / HELL BELOW, 1933, MGM, d-Jack Conway.

Montgomery appears as a submarine commander in this gripping adventure yarn that vividly shows the tension involved in living under the sea in cramped quarters.

Jimmy Lee / WHEN LADIES MEET, 1933, MGM, d-Harry Beaumont.

Montgomery is a publisher married to Ann Harding. When Myrna Loy, a successful novelist, falls in love with him, the two women clash nicely over Montgomery in this fine comedy.

Dill Todd / FORSAKING ALL OTHERS, 1934, MGM, d-W. S. Van Dyke.

Joan Crawford leaves Montgomery at the altar in the opening scene of the movie and walks out on him again at the end, deciding she'd rather stay with husband Clark Gable.

Lord Arthur Dilling / THE LAST OF MRS. CHEYNEY, 1937, MGM, d-Richard Boleslawski.

Director Boleslawski died just before this movie was finished. In it, con woman Joan Crawford ruins her career by falling in love with Montgomery while attempting to infiltrate British high society.

Danny / NIGHT MUST FALL, 1937, MGM, d-Richard Thorpe.

In a definite change of pace from his usual light comedy romantic leads, Montgomery plays a psychotic youth who has killed one woman and is now planning to do in Dame May Whitty. Poor May, she realizes too late his intentions and her last words are: "What a funny look on your face, dear. Smiling like that. You look so kind. So kind. What are you going to do with that...." Montgomery gives a spine-tingling performance.

John O'Hara / YELLOW JACK, 1938, MGM, d-George B. Seitz.

Montgomery is one of five U.S. soldiers who volunteer to serve as guinea pigs to help find the cause of yellow fever in Cuba in 1899.

Silky Kilmount / THE EARL OF CHICAGO, 1939, MGM, d-Richard Thorpe.

Again demonstrating his versa-tility, Montgomery portrays a Chicago mobster who inherits a British title, uneasily takes his place among the nobility, kills a man, and is sent to the gallows.

David Smith / MR. AND MRS. SMITH, 1941, RKO, d-Alfred Hitchcock.

In this quasi-screwball comedy, Montgomery and Carole Lombard learn that their marriage is void because of a shifting state line. The rest of the smartish comedy deals with when and how they will realize they should get back together.

Joe Pendleton / Leo Farnsworth / Tom Jarrett / HERE COMES MR. JORDAN, 1941, Columbia, d-Alexander Hall.

When an inexperienced angel takes boxer Montgomery out of a crashed plane, he's embarrassed to discover that Montgomery was supposed to survive. A superior, Mr. Jordan (Claude Rains), promises to find Montgomery a new body just as good as the one he had and he finally delivers, although Montgomery must endure dying in a body he temporarily inhabits.

Philip Marlowe / THE LADY IN THE LAKE, 1946, MGM, d-Robert Montgomery.

This is the first film to use the camera as the protagonist; what the audience sees is what Montgomery, as Raymond Chandler's private eye, sees. The only time Montgomery is visible is when we catch a glimpse of him in a mirror. Audiences didn't like the approach and so didn't warm to the story of him searching for a missing wife.

OTHER ROLES

1926: *bit* / COLLEGE DAYS. **1929:** *Biff* / SO THIS IS COLLEGE; *Andy McAllister* / UNTAMED; *William Foster (Spoofy)* / THREE LIVE GHOSTS; *Jack Marlett* / THEIR OWN DESIRE. **1930:** *Larry* / FREE AND EASY; *Don* / THE DIVORCEE; *Tony Jardine* / OUR BLUSHING BRIDES; *Nick Higgins* / SINS OF OUR CHILDREN; *Kelly* / LOVE IN THE ROUGH; *Wally* / WAR NURSE. **1931:** *Johnny Madison* / THE EASIEST WAY; *Steve* / STRANGERS MAY KISS; *Andre Martel* / INSPIRATION; *Jonesy* / SHIPMATES; *Raymond Dabney* / THE MAN IN POSSESSION; *Elyot Chase* / PRIVATE LIVES; *Willie Smith* / LOVERS COURAGEOUS. **1932:** *Max Clement* / BUT THE FLESH IS WEAK; *Hale Darrow* / LETTY LYNTON; *Larry Belmont* / BLONDIE OF THE FOLLIES; *William Wade* / FAITHLESS. **1933:** *Jeff Bidwell* / MADE ON BROADWAY; *Auguste Pellerin* / NIGHT FLIGHT; *Victor Hallam* / ANOTHER LANGUAGE. **1934:** *Paul Porter* / FUGITIVE LOVERS; *Tommy Treal* / RIPTIDE; *Nicholas Revel* / THE MYSTERY OF MR. X; *Lucky Wilson* / HIDE-OUT. **1935:** *Benjie* / VANESSA, HER LOVE STORY; *Kurt* / BIOGRAPHY OF A BACHELOR GIRL; *Sherry Warren* / NO MORE LADIES. **1936:** *Dascom Dinsmore* / PETTICOAT FEVER; *Prince Florizel* / TROUBLE FOR TWO; *Jim Crocker* / PICADILLY JIM. **1937:** *Freddy Matthews* / EVER SINCE EVE; *Bob Graham* / LIVE, LOVE AND LEARN; *David Conway* / THE FIRST HUNDRED YEARS. **1938:** *Malcolm Niles* / THREE LOVES HAS NANCY. **1939:** *Joel Sloane* / FAST AND LOOSE. **1940:** *Lord Peter Wimsey* / BUSMAN'S HONEYMOON. **1941:** *Philip Morrell* / RAGE IN HEAVEN; *Tommy Duncan* / UNFINISHED BUSINESS; *cameo* / LAND OF LIBERTY. **1945:** *Lt. John Brickley* / THEY WERE EXPENDABLE. **1947:** *Blackie Gagin* / RIDE THE PINK HORSE. **1948:** *Matt Saxon* / THE SAXON CHARM; *Casey Jackson* / JUNE BRIDE. **1949:** *Collier Laing* / ONCE MORE MY DARLING. **1950:** *Adam Heywood* / EYE WITNESS.

MOORE, DUDLEY

(1935–)

Tiny five-foot-two-and-a-half-inch British revue comedian Dudley Moore won an organ scholarship to Magdalen College, Oxford, and is recognized as a fine jazz pianist and composer of movie scores. He first came to the world's attention in 1960 with the revue "Beyond the Fringe." His work with tall Peter Cook included concerts and a successful British TV series, "Not Only, But Also." He became a movie star when Blake Edwards cast him in 10 in 1979. Since then he has made a specialty of finding humor in the human frailties of middle-aged men. Cuddly, pint-sized Moore has been married to Suzy Kendall and Tuesday Weld, and had a well-publicized romance with six-footer Susan Anton. Moore was nominated for an Academy Award for ARTHUR.

KEY ROLES

Stanley Moon / BEDAZZLED, 1967, Great Britain, 20th Century-Fox, d-Stanley Donen.

In this cult favorite, Moore, a short-order cook, is saved from suicide by Peter Cook, a very English devil who offers him seven wishes in exchange for his soul. Cook always gives Moore precisely what he asks for even though it's not really what he wants.

George Weber / 10, 1979, Warners / Orion, d-Blake Edwards.

Moore became an international superstar portraying the middle-aged composer who becomes infatuated with a woman (Bo Derek) 20 years younger than he, who fits his notion of the perfect woman. When he gets a chance to know and have sex with this goddess, he finds she's not so perfect after all. It's best to leave fantasies as fantasies.

Arthur Bach / ARTHUR! 1981, Warners / Orion, d-Steve Gordon.

Moore is a wealthy ne'er-do-well who can face the world only through a haze of alcohol. His grandmother threatens to cut off his money unless he marries his long-time society fiancée. But he meets kooky, poor Liza Minnelli and falls in love with her, as much as he's capable of, and finally gets up enough backbone to stand up to grandma (Geraldine Fitzgerald) and marry his choice.

Rob Salinger / MICKI AND MAUDE, 1984, Columbia, d-Blake Edwards.

It seems that Moore just loves babies. He becomes a bigamist and has two pregnant wives (Amy Irving and Ann Reinking) set to deliver on the same day at the same hospital at the same time. The message of the movie seems to be that there is hope for those with bigamist tendencies.

Claude Eastman / UNFAITHFULLY YOURS, 1984, 20th Century-Fox, d-Howard Zieff.

Moore is the conductor of a symphonic orchestra. By mistake he believes that his beautiful young wife (Nastassia Kinski) is having an affair with a soloist

(Armand Assante). During the concert, Moore reviews in his mind how he will take his revenge and how things will follow his careful plan. Of course nothing happens the way he imagines. It's a remake of a 1948 movie with the same title starring Rex Harrison.

OTHER ROLES

1964: *narrator* / THE HAT. **1965:** *John Finsbury* / THE WRONG BOX. **1968:** *Rupert Street* / 30 IS A DANGEROUS AGE, CYNTHIA. **1969:** *Lt. Kit Barrington* / MONTE CARLO OR BUST; *police sergeant* / THE BED-SITTING ROOM. **1972:** *dormouse* / ALICE'S ADVENTURES IN WONDERLAND. **1978:** *Stanley Tibbetts* / FOUL PLAY. **1980:** *Dr. John Watson* / THE HOUND OF THE BASKERVILLES; *Harvey / Herschel* / WHOLLY MOSES! **1982:** *Patrick Dalton* / SIX WEEKS. **1983:** *Jason* / ROMANTIC COMEDY; *Saul Benjamin* / LOVESICK. **1984:** *Wylie Cooper* / BEST DEFENSE. **1985:** *Patch* / SANTA CLAUS. **1987:** *Dr. Jack Hammond* / LIKE FATHER, LIKE SON.

MOORE, ROGER

(1927–)

"I replace everyone. I'll be replacing Mickey Mouse in about three years time." So Roger Moore jokes about his moving into the juicy role of James Bond in the sixth movie of the series when Sean Connery grew tired of the same old thing. Earlier, Moore had been brought into the "Maverick" TV series to fill in for James Garner when the latter left over a salary dispute. Moore has appeared in several other TV series including "The Alaskans" and "The Persuaders" but it was as the suave, edge-of-the-law crime-fighter Simon Templar in "The Saint" that the tall, handsome British actor made producers certain he would make a dandy 007. Unlike Connery, Moore played Bond for more low humor and physical tricks than pure macho strength. His antics must have kept an army of stunt men busy.

KEY ROLES

Capt. Michael Stuart / THE MIRACLE, 1959, Warners, d-Irving Rapper.

When young nun Carroll Baker breaks her vows and leaves the convent to follow British soldier Moore during the Peninsular War in Spain, a statue of the Virgin Mary steps down to take her place. It's incredible and not very well done. Those who thought it sacrilegious needn't have worried; not that many people risked scandal by seeing it.

James Bond / LIVE AND LET DIE, 1973, United Artists, d-Guy Hamilton.

In his first appearance as 007 Moore chases a master criminal (Yaphet Kotto) and becomes involved in West Indian voodoo. He seduces Jane Seymour and Lois Maxwell.

Ron Slater / GOLD, 1974, Great Britain, Hemdale / Avton, d-Peter Hunt.

Moore is a South African mining engineer who falls for Susannah York, the granddaughter of Ray Milland, and exposes a conspiracy in this old-fashioned picture with a fine ending.

James Bond / THE SPY WHO LOVED ME, 1977, United Artists / Eon, d-Lewis Gilbert.

The title character (Barbara Bach) is a glamorous Russian spy who ultimately succumbs to 007's charms, and joins forces with him to track down megalomaniac Curt Jurgens who oversees an undersea missile base.

Shawn Fynn / THE WILD GEESE, 1978, Great Britain, Rank, d-Andrew V. McLaglen.

Moore is one of four British mercenaries hired by British banker Stewart Granger to rescue the president of an emerging African nation. Being based on fact doesn't make this violent movie work any better.

Rufus Excaliber ffolkes / FFOLKES, (NORTH SEA HIJACK), 1979, Great Britain, Universal / Cinema Seven, d-Andrew V. McLaglen.

When a British oil rig in the North Sea is taken over by Anthony Perkins and a band of thugs to be held for ransom, woman-hating, cat-loving Moore is called in to deal with the baddies.

James Bond / OCTOPUSSY, 1983, Great Britain, Eon / Danjaq, d-John Glen.

The Bond movies with Moore get more unbelievable with each new picture. Here he takes on an evil Afghan prince (Louis Jourdan) who has arranged to steal czarist treasures from the Russians. He also beds lovely Maud Adams, who is the female villainess saved because her lust for Moore causes her to change allegiances.

OTHER ROLES

1945: *bit* / PERFECT STRANGERS; *bit* / CAESAR AND CLEOPATRA. **1946:** *bit* / GAIETY GEORGE; *bit* / PICCADILLY INCIDENT. **1949:** *bit* / PAPER ORCHID; *bit* / TROTTIE TRUE. **1954:** *Paul* / THE LAST TIME I SAW PARIS. **1955:** *Cyril Lawrence* / INTERRUPTED MELODY; *Jack* / THE KING'S THIEF. **1956:** *Prince Henri* / DIANE. **1961:** *Paul Wilton* / THE SINS OF RACHEL CADE; *Shaun Garrett* / GOLD OF THE SEVEN SAINTS; *Romulus* / RAPE OF THE SABINES. **1962:** *Enzo Prati* / NO MAN'S LAND. **1969:** *Gary Fenn* / CROSSPLOT. **1970:** *Harry Pelham* / THE MAN WHO HAUNTED HIMSELF. **1974:** *James Bond* / THE MAN WITH THE GOLDEN GUN. **1975:** *Michael Scott* / THAT LUCKY TOUCH. **1976:** *Sebastian Oldsmith* / SHOUT AT THE DEVIL; *Ulysses* / STREET PEOPLE; *Sherlock Holmes* / SHERLOCK HOLMES IN NEW YORK. **1979:** *James Bond* / MOONRAKER; *Maj. Otto Hecht* / ESCAPE TO ATHENA. **1980:** *Capt. Gavin Stewart* / THE SEA WOLVES. **1981:** *Harry* / AN ENGLISHMAN'S HOME; *Seymour* / THE CANNONBALL RUN; *James Bond* / FOR YOUR EYES ONLY. **1984:** *Dr. Judd Stevens* / THE NAKED FACE; *guest* / CURSE OF THE PINK PANTHER. **1985:** *James Bond* / A VIEW TO A KILL.

MORE, KENNETH

(1914–1982)

Square-faced and cheerful, Kenneth More made his film debut in 1935, but it wasn't until after World War II that he was a hit in supporting roles. When he appeared in GENEVIEVE in 1953, and with the success of DOCTOR IN THE HOUSE in 1954, he became a stalwart of British cinema. He was also a success on TV in "The Forsyte Saga" and the Father Brown series, projecting a no-nonsense good humor. More was able to show vulnerability and sensitivity when given the right material to work with, such as THE DEEP BLUE SEA with Vivien Leigh and REACH FOR THE SKY.

KEY ROLES

Lionel Fallaize / APPOINTMENT WITH VENUS, 1951, Great Britain, British Film Makers, d-Ralph Thomas.

More is among the large and entertaining cast in this story about the rescue of a pedigreed cow named Venus, left behind on the Channel island of Armorel that has been taken over by the Nazis during World War II.

Ambrose Clavenhouse / GENEVIEVE, 1953, Great Britain, General Film Distributors, d-Henry Cornelius.

More became a star after this movie in which he and his girl (Kay Kendall) are friendly rivals of John Gregson and his wife (Dinah Sheridan) in a race of vintage cars from London to Brighton. Things get interesting on the return trip with a wager as to which car will be the first over Westminster Bridge.

Richard Grimsdyke / DOCTOR IN THE HOUSE, 1954, Great Britain, General Film Distributors, d-Ralph Thomas.

The real star of this first of the "Doctor" series is Dirk Bogarde but More, Donald Sinden, and Donald Huston share in the hilarity of four medical students who get into an incredible number of bizarre situations as interns under the watchful and disapproving eye of head-of-staff James Robertson Justice.

Freddie Page / THE DEEP BLUE SEA, 1955, Great Britain, London Films, d-Anatole Litvak.

Vivien Leigh attempts suicide and is almost destroyed by her passionate love for charming ex-RAF pilot More, who doesn't feel as strongly about her. At last she finds the strength to save herself by breaking the relationship.

Douglas Bader / REACH FOR THE SKY, 1956, Great Britain, Rank, d-Lewis Gilbert.

In this biopic, More portrays an RAF pilot who loses his legs after a crash in 1931, but learns to walk again and leads five Battle of Britain squadrons before being taken prisoner by the Germans. He attempts to escape unsuccessfully on several occasions, but in 1945, after being rescued, he leads the victory air parade over London in a Spitfire.

William Crichton / THE ADMIRABLE CRICHTON, 1957, Great Britain, Modern Screenplays, d-Lewis Gilbert.

More is admirable as J. M. Barrie's perfect gentleman's gentleman who proves he is the better man when he and his employer and the latter's family are shipwrecked on a desert island. When a rescue ship shows up, though, he reverts to his very proper role.

Herbert Lightoller / A NIGHT TO REMEMBER, 1958, Great Britain, Rank, d-Roy Baker.

More is the second officer of the doomed Titanic on its maiden and only voyage. He represents the brave crew which tried desperately but to no avail to get all the passengers into the inadequate number of lifeboats. Even in the sea, his calm manner is responsible for saving lives. With such men, it is understandable that "there'll always be an England."

Capt. Jonathan Shepard / SINK THE BISMARCK! 1960, Great Britain, 20th Century-Fox, d-Lewis Gilbert.

In this fascinating, almost documentary account of the search for and destruction of the great German battleship Bismarck, More is a stern intelligence officer who directs a brilliant campaign from naval headquarters in London against the almost invincible ship.

OTHER ROLES

1935: *piano assistant* / LOOK UP AND LAUGH. **1938:** *part of a sketch* / WINDMILL REVELS; *part of a sketch* / CARRY ON LONDON. **1948:** *Lt. Teddy Evans* / SCOTT OF THE ANTARCTIC. **1949:** *Corporal Newman* / MAN ON THE RUN; *Spencer* / NOW BARABBAS WAS A ROBBER; *sergeant* / STOP PRESS GIRL. **1950:** *Lieutenant Commander James* / MORNING DEPARTURE; *Adam* / CHANCE OF A LIFETIME; *Willy* / THE CLOUDED YELLOW; *Stanley Peters* / THE FRANCHISE AFFAIR. **1951:** *Dobson* / NO HIGHWAY IN THE SKY. **1952:** *Tony Rackman* / BRANDY FOR THE PARSON; *Ted* / THE YELLOW BALLOON. **1953:** *Steve Quillan* / NEVER LET ME GO; *Patrick Plonkett* / OUR GIRL FRIDAY. **1954:** *Tony Kent* / RAISING A RIOT. **1958:** *David Webb* / NEXT TO NO TIME; *Jonathan Tibbs* / THE SHERIFF OF FRACTURED JAW. **1959:** *Richard Hannay* / THE 39 STEPS; *Captain Scott* / NORTHWEST FRONTIER. **1960:** *William Blood* / MAN IN THE MOON. **1961:** *Eliot* / THE GREENGAGE SUMMER. **1962:** *Capt. Colin Maud* / THE LONGEST DAY; *Chick Byrd* / THE COMEDY MAN; *Mr. Smith* / SOME PEOPLE; *Lieutenant Commander Badger* / WE JOINED THE NAVY. **1967:** *Dr. Reid* / THE MERCENARIES. **1969:** *Wilhelm II* / OH, WHAT A LOVELY WAR; *Colonel Foreman* / FRAULEIN DOKTOR; *Group Captain Baker* / BATTLE OF BRITAIN. **1970:** *Ghost of Christmas Present* / SCROOGE. **1976:** *Chamberlain* / THE SLIPPER AND THE ROSE. **1978:** *Sir Philip James* / LEOPARD IN THE SNOW. **1979:** *King Arthur* / THE SPACEMAN AND KING ARTHUR; *Professor Lindenbrook* / JOURNEY TO THE CENTER OF THE EARTH.

MORGAN, DENNIS

(Stanley Morner, 1910–)

In his first dozen films, fresh-faced Dennis Morgan was billed by his real name (which he never officially changed) or as Richard Stanley. This former announcer and lead singer in two operas made his film debut in the mid-1930s and, after being rechristened Dennis Morgan, was given leading roles in musicals and light comedies at Warners, often teamed with Jack Carson. He will be long remembered as the singer of "A Pretty Girl Is Like a Melody" in the mammoth production number in THE GREAT ZIEGFELD, even though his singing was dubbed by Alan Jones. While nothing in his film career merited raves, he was an agreeable personality and audiences enjoyed his work for what it was.

KEY ROLES

Wyn Strafford / KITTY FOYLE, 1940, RKO, d-Sam Wood.

Morgan provides more than adequate support for Ginger Rogers in her Academy Award-winning performance of a working girl who gets mixed up with one of the Philadelphia "main-liners" and suffers the snobbery of his family as well as losing their baby.

Johnny Dutton / CAPTAINS OF THE CLOUDS, 1942, Warners, d-Michael Curtiz.

Morgan is the well-disciplined Canadian pilot who can't teach rebellious and cocky James Cagney a thing when the latter enlists in the Royal Canadian Air Force. They are also rivals for the love of Brenda Marshall.

Tommy Randolph / THANK YOUR LUCKY STARS, 1943, Warners, d-David Butler.

Morgan is an unknown singer who teams with unknown songwriter Joan Leslie to put together an all-star charity show. He and Leslie team up for a rendition of "I'm Riding for a Fall" and "No Me, No You" by Arthur Schwartz and Frank Loesser.

Paul Hudson / THE DESERT SONG, 1944, Warners, d-Robert Florey.

In this Sigmund Romberg operetta, Morgan is an American who has fought in the Spanish Civil War and leads the Moroccan Riffs against the Nazis. His co-star is beautiful Irene Manning. Their songs include "The Riff Song," "One Alone," and "Romance."

Jack Norworth / SHINE ON, HARVEST MOON, 1944, Warners, d-David Butler.

In this fictitious biopic of the career of early 20th-century singer Nora Bayes (Ann Sheridan) and her songwriting husband (Morgan), they sing, with a bit of help from Irene Manning, the title number, "Take Me out to the Ball Game," "Time Waits for No One," and "I Go for You."

Jefferson Jones / CHRISTMAS IN CONNECTICUT, 1945, Warners, d-Peter Godfrey.

After being shipwrecked for months, Morgan is rescued and expresses the desire to have a meal prepared by cooking columnist Barbara Stanwyck in her Connecticut home which she shares with her husband and new baby. Her publisher accommodates. The only trouble is that she has no home in Connecticut, no husband, no baby, and she can't cook.

Prince Henry / TWO GUYS FROM MILWAUKEE, 1946, Warners, d-David Butler.

Morgan is a Balkan prince who, on a visit to the United States, befriends cab driver Jack Carson who helps him see the country from the eyes of a normal guy. He also finds some romance with Joan Leslie and Janis Paige.

Chauncey Olcott / MY WILD IRISH ROSE, 1947, Warners, d-David Butler.

Morgan has a very heavy Irish brogue as he plays songwriter and singer Olcott, but it doesn't prevent him from winning lovely redhead Arlene Dahl. Besides the title song, Morgan sings "Mother Machree" and "A Little Bit of Heaven."

Vince Nichols / PAINTING THE CLOUDS WITH SUNSHINE, 1951, Warners, d-David Butler.

There's not much to this story about three gold diggers out to marry wealth who settle for the next best thing, true love. The songs include the title number, "Tip-Toe through the Tulips," and "Birth of the Blues."

OTHER ROLES

As Stanley Morner

1936: *Tommy* / I CONQUER THE SEA; *Lieutenant Charbret* / SUZY; *singer* / THE GREAT ZIEGFELD; *bit* / PICCADILLY JIM; *bit* / DOWN THE STRETCH; *bit* / OLD HUTCH. **1937:** *Tommy* / SONG OF THE CITY; *Chuck Thompson* / MAMA STEPS OUT; *marine lieutenant* / NAVY BLUE AND GOLD. **1938:** *bit* / PERSONS IN HIDING; *Galton* / MEN WITH WINGS; *First Mate Rogers* / KING OF ALCATRAZ.

As Dennis Morgan

1939: *Jim Dolan* / WATERFRONT; *Michael Rhodes* / RETURN OF DR. X; *Joe Plummer* / NO PLACE TO GO. **1940:** *Angus Ferguson* / THREE CHEERS FOR THE IRISH; *Lieutenant Ames* / THE FIGHTING 69TH; *Tommy McCabe* / TEAR GAS SQUAD; *Chick* / FLIGHT ANGELS; *John Keith* / *Sergeant Conniston* / RIVER'S END. **1941:** *Richard "Rickey" Mayberry* / AFFECTIONATELY YOURS; *Cole Younger* / BAD MEN OF MISSOURI. **1942:** *Peter Kingsmill* / IN THIS OUR LIFE; *Corky Jones* / WINGS FOR THE EAGLE; *Paul Collins* / THE HARD WAY. **1944:** *Sgt. David Stewart* / THE VERY THOUGHT OF YOU; *guest* / HOLLYWOOD CANTEEN. **1945:** *Col. Robert L. Scott* / GOD IS MY CO-PILOT. **1946:** *Tom Collier* / ONE MORE TOMORROW; *Steven Ross* / THE TIME, THE PLACE AND THE GIRL. **1947:** *James Wylie* / CHEYENNE; *guest* / ALWAYS TOGETHER. **1948:** *Paul* / TO THE VICTOR; *Steve Carroll* / TWO GUYS FROM TEXAS; *Biff Grimes* / ONE SUNDAY AFTERNOON. **1949:** *guest* / IT'S A GREAT FEELING; *Bill Craig* / THE LADY TAKES A SAILOR. **1950:** *David Campbell* / PERFECT STRANGERS; *Sam Marley* / PRETTY BABY. **1951:** *Marc Challon* / RATON PASS. **1952:** *Dr. Ben Halleck* / THIS WOMAN IS DANGEROUS; *Mike McGann* / CATTLE TOWN. **1955:** *Dan Merrill* / PEARL OF THE SOUTH PACIFIC; *Jim Bridger* / THE GUN THAT WON THE WEST. **1956:** *Brad Collins* / URANIUM BOOM. **1976:** *tour guide* / WON TON TON, THE DOG WHO SAVED HOLLYWOOD.

MUNI, PAUL

(Muni Weisenfreund, 1896–1967)

During the 1930s Paul Muni was one of the most distinguished actors on stage or screen and was noted for his portrayals of historical characters. A perfectionist, he was very selective in the roles he agreed to play and then he required months of research and time to prepare for his performance. Audiences were delighted with the results of all of his preliminary work. He received Academy Award nominations for THE VALIANT, I AM A FUGITIVE FROM A CHAIN GANG, THE LIFE OF EMILE ZOLA, and THE LAST ANGRY MAN, winning for THE STORY OF LOUIS PASTEUR. By the 1940s his popularity had waned and few offers were made to him so he went on the stage and won a Tony for "Inherit the Wind." Muni and his wife had no time for Hollywood and he resented anyone who wasted his time. As he said, "If a man steals money or property from you that's one thing. But if he steals time, he steals a piece of your life."

KEY ROLES

Tony Camonte / SCARFACE: THE SHAME OF A NATION, 1932, Hughes / United Artists, d-Howard Hawks.

At the time of its release, this film, now considered a classic, was unfavorably reviewed and didn't attract large audiences. Muni, a mobster whose story is based on that of Chicago's Al Capone, is brutish, funny, and even at times touching. He has an incestuous interest in his sister (Ann Dvorak) which also caused trouble from the censors.

James Allen / Allen James / I AM A FUGITIVE FROM A CHAIN GANG, 1932, Warners, d-Mervyn LeRoy.

This film shattered audiences with its depiction of the cruel treatment Muni gets as he is unjustly sentenced to serve on a southern chain gang. He escapes and, like a modern-day Jean Valjean, makes something of himself. But Glenda Farrell, who knows his secret, forces him to marry her. When he finds someone (Helen Vinson) he really cares for, Farrell turns him in, and he is returned to finish out his sentence. He escapes again, but this time is forced to become a thief to live. When he meets briefly with Vinson before going on the run again, she asks him how he manages. Muni's simple and tragic answer is "I steal."

Joe Radek / BLACK FURY, 1935, Warners, d-Michael Curtiz.

Based on the real-life story of the murder of a Pennsylvania coal miner, this picture features Muni as a popular miner who is used by unscrupulous racketeers intent on controlling the Mineworkers Union.

Louis Pasteur / THE STORY OF LOUIS PASTEUR, 1936, Warners, d-William Dieterle.

Muni's dedicated Pasteur caught the imagination of audiences and won him his Academy Award. Muni struggles against ignorance and prejudice in his quest to find a cure for anthrax and hydrophobia. The photography by Tony Gaudio contributes greatly to the success of the picture. In the last lines of the picture Muni inspires future doctors with: "You young men—doctors and scientists of the future. Do not let yourselves be tainted by the barren skepticism, nor discouraged by the sadness of certain hours that creep over nations. Do not become angry at your opponents. For no scientific theory has ever been accepted without opposition. Live in a serene peace of libraries and laboratories. Say to yourselves first: 'What have I done for my instruction?' and as you gradually advance: 'What am I accomplishing?' until the time comes when you may have the immense happiness of thinking that you've contributed in some way to the welfare and progress of mankind."

Wang Lung / THE GOOD EARTH, 1937, MGM, d-Sidney Franklin.

This is a highly respected film with Muni portraying a Chinese farmer who works hard side by side with his obedient wife (Luise Rainer). When, after years of struggling, he becomes wealthy, he takes a second, younger wife. But when Rainer dies, he realizes how much she means to him and how great is his loss.

Emile Zola / THE LIFE OF EMILE ZOLA, 1937, Warners, d-William Dieterle.

This prestigious film was also successful financially as Muni gave an unforgettable performance as the French writer who champions the cause of unjustly imprisoned Captain Dreyfuss, sentenced to Devil's Island as a spy on flimsy evidence, but mainly because he is a Jew.

Benito Pablo Juarez / JUAREZ, 1939, Warners, d-William Dieterle.

This movie has many faults, not the least of which being the lousy Mexican accent of John Garfield. But no one can fault Muni who is most impressive as the ugly Indian president of the Republic of Mexico, intent on liberating his country from foreign rule and reestablishing democracy. His adversary in this struggle, whom he never meets, is the very decent but aristocratic Maximilian (Brian Aherne) set on the Mexican throne by Napoleon III of France.

Prof. Paul Elsner / A SONG TO REMEMBER, 1945, Columbia, d-Charles Vidor.

Muni is given top billing as the teacher and mentor of political activist musician Frederic Chopin (Cornel Wilde). There's a lot of fiction in the movie, but it did popularize Chopin in this country and Muni's performance as usual is top notch.

Dr. Sam Ableman / THE LAST ANGRY MAN, 1959, Columbia, d-Daniel Mann.

In his final screen appearance, Muni portrays a physician who works in the Brooklyn slums. TV producer David Wayne, desperate for an idea for a new show to save his job, convinces the powers-that-be to make a documentary about the commendable work being done by the dedicated and caring Dr. Ableman. Unfortunately, he doesn't know that Muni despises his poor patients and everything about the crummy neighborhood in which he works.

OTHER ROLES

1929: *James Dyke* / THE VALIANT; *Papa Chibou / Diablero / Willie Smith / Franz Schubert / Don Juan / Joe Gans / Napoleon* / SEVEN FACES. **1933:** *Orin Nordholm, Jr.* / THE WORLD CHANGES. **1934:** *Sam Bradshaw (Nellie Nelson)* / HI, NELLIE! **1935:** *Johnny Ramirez* / BORDERTOWN; *Dr. Lee Caldwell* / DR. SOCRATES. **1937:** *Lt. Claude Maury* / THE WOMAN I LOVE. **1939:** *Dr. David Newcombe* / WE ARE NOT ALONE. **1940:** *Pierre Esprit Radisson* / HUDSON'S BAY. **1942:** *Eric Toreson* / THE COMMANDOS STRIKE AT DAWN. **1945:** *Alexei Kulkov* / COUNTER-ATTACK. **1946:** *Eddie Kagle* / ANGEL ON MY SHOULDER. **1953:** *the man* / STRANGER ON THE PROWL.

MURPHY, GEORGE

(1902–)

Song-and-dance man George Murphy, a hoofer with years of Broadway experience before going to Hollywood, soon settled down as one of the second-rung stars. He was awarded a special Oscar in 1950 "for services in interpreting the film industry to the country at large." He served two terms as president of the Screen Actors Guild. In 1964 former Democrat Murphy, now a conservative Republican, defeated Pierre Salinger and won a U.S. Senate seat from California, but was unsuccessful in his bid for a second term partially because cancer had taken his voice.

KEY ROLES

Roger Wendling / LITTLE MISS BROADWAY, 1938, 20th Century-Fox, d-Irving Cummings.

Murphy dances with Shirley Temple in this story of Little Orphan Shirley who is adopted by the manager of a hotel catering to entertainers. Murphy's aunt, who owns the hotel, tries to send the child back to the orphanage but Murphy is able to change the old lady's mind.

Jerry Kelly / LITTLE NELLIE KELLY, 1940, MGM, d-Norman Taurog.

Murphy co-stars with Judy Garland in this film version of the old George M. Cohan starrer about the daughter of a New York cop who becomes a stage star. Garland portrays both Murphy's wife and his daughter in this nostalgic musical.

Tom / TOM, DICK AND HARRY, 1941, RKO, d-Garson Kanin.

Murphy is one of three suitors for small-town girl Ginger Rogers who can't decide which to marry. Murphy loses out to Burgess Meredith who makes bells ring for Rogers when he kisses her. It's a cream-puff piece, but suitable to the time of its release.

Jimmy K. Metcalfe / FOR ME AND MY GAL, 1942, MGM, d-Busby Berkeley.

In yet another nostalgic romp along show business's memory lane, Murphy is an entertainer teamed with Judy Garland, the girl he loves. Along comes heel Gene Kelly, who loves himself most, who steals Garland away. The picture is set in the time leading up to World War I.

Lt. Steve Bentley / BATAAN, 1943, MGM, d-Tay Garnett.

During World War II any able-bodied male actor too old to be drafted found himself in some war film meant to firm the resolve of the citizens of the country. In this one Murphy is an officer who is one of thirteen doomed men left to make a final defense against the invading Japanese on Bataan in the Philippines.

George Doane / SHOW BUSINESS, 1944, RKO, d-Edwin L. Marin.

This film's story, suggested by incidents in the career of Eddie Cantor, chronicles the fortunes of four friends in vaudeville from 1914 to 1929. One of the highlights of the film has the four—Cantor, Murphy, Constance Moore, and Joan Davis—in a very funny Grand Opera take-off.

Miller / STEP LIVELY, 1944, RKO, d-Tim Whelan.

Murphy is a fast-talking Broadway producer to whom Frank Sinatra, a young playwright, has lent money, and who now wants it back. Murphy has other plans for the dough, but everything works out for the best in this lightweight musical comedy.

OTHER ROLES

1934: *Jerry Lane* / KID MILLIONS; *Larry O'Roark* / JEALOUSY. **1935:** *Carl Brent* / I'LL LOVE YOU ALWAYS; *Jerry Davis* / AFTER THE DANCE; *Red Foster* / PUBLIC MENACE. **1936:** *Keat Shevlin* / WOMAN TRAP. **1937:** *Ted Lane* / TOP OF THE TOWN; *Bill Raeburn* / THE WOMEN MEN MARRY; *Michael Denis* / LONDON BY NIGHT; *Sonny Ledford* / BROADWAY MELODY OF 1938; *Hal Adams* / YOU'RE

A SWEETHEART. **1938:** *Barry Paige* / LETTER OF INTRODUCTION; *Rusty* / HOLD THAT CO-ED. **1939:** *Dan Clifford* / RISKY BUSINESS. **1940:** *King Shaw* / BROADWAY MELODY OF 1940; *Eddie Kerns* / TWO GIRLS ON BROADWAY; *Alan Blake* / PUBLIC DEB NO. 1. **1941:** *Coffee Cup* / A GIRL, A GUY AND A GOB; *Skeets Maguire* / RINGSIDE MAISIE; *Jimmy McGonigle* / RISE AND SHINE. **1942:** *Joe Jonathan* / THE MAYOR OF 44TH STREET; *Sands* / THE NAVY COMES THROUGH; *Jerry Hendricks* / THE POWERS GIRL. **1943:** *Jerry Jones* / THIS IS THE ARMY. **1944:** *Johnny Demming* / BROADWAY RHYTHM. **1945:** *Jake Justus* / HAVING WONDERFUL CRIME. **1946:** *Joseph Morton* / UP GOES MAISIE. **1947:** *Ted Parkinson* / THE ARNELO AFFAIR; *Larry Bishop* / CYNTHIA. **1948:** *Steve Abbott* / TENTH AVENUE ANGEL; *Patrick O'Donnell* / THE BIG CITY. **1949:** *Jack Bearnes* / BORDER INCIDENT; *"Pop" Ernest Stazak* / BATTLEGROUND. **1951:** *Insp. Matt Duggan* / NO QUESTIONS ASKED; *Mr. Callaghan* / IT'S A BIG COUNTRY. **1952:** *Inspector Belden* / WALK EAST ON BEACON; *Robert Fontaine Sr.* / TALK ABOUT A STRANGER.

MURRAY, DON

(1929–)

High-principled Don Murray has turned down roles because they offended his sense of morality and his career was interrupted when, during the Korean War, he declared himself a conscientious objector while playing on the Broadway stage. Quiet, self-effacing Murray has always given sincere, earnest, if not always interesting, performances, being nominated for an Oscar for his performance in BUS STOP. He was once married to Hope Lange and has directed the social message pictures THE CROSS AND THE SWITCHBLADE and DAMIEN. His many made-for-TV movies include THE BORGIA STICK (1967), DAUGHTER OF THE MIND (1969), A GIRL NAMED SOONER (1974), and THE FAR TURN (1979).

KEY ROLES

Bo / BUS STOP, 1956, 20th Century-Fox, d-Joshua Logan.

In his screen debut Murray is a brash cowboy unused to the big city or the people, for that matter, who come to town to compete in a rodeo. He sees pitifully untalented singer Marilyn Monroe, decides she should become his wife, and gives her nothing to say in the matter. But by the end of the movie she decides to accept his proposal.

Charlie Swanson / THE BACHELOR PARTY, 1957, United Artists, d-Delbert Mann.

Murray is one of five bookkeepers who throw a wedding eve party for one of their number in New York City. They do a round of tawdry bars, watch a blue movie, almost pick up a bar girl, and generally have a miserable time as their own personal despairs become known. Murray's is that he has just learned that his wife is going to have a baby and he doesn't know how they can afford it.

Johnny Pope / A HATFUL OF RAIN, 1957, 20th Century-Fox, d-Fred Zinnemann.

In one of Hollywood's first looks at drug addiction, Murray becomes hooked on drugs and tries to keep the news from his pregnant wife. His debts to his supplier push the situation beyond his control, but he makes a first step toward a cure by admitting to his wife that he has a problem.

Rev. Charles Dismas Clark / THE HOODLUM PRIEST, 1961, United Artists, d-Irvin Kershner.

In this dramatic but depressing picture, Murray portrays a Jesuit priest who tries to help young criminals, particularly Keir Dullea, a condemned murderer.

Sen. Brigham Anderson / ADVISE AND CONSENT, 1962, Columbia, d-Otto Preminger.

Murray is appointed by majority leader Walter Pidgeon to head up the U.S. Senate committee considering the president's nomination of ultra-liberal Henry Fonda to be secretary of state. The politics get so ugly that Murray's brief wartime homosexual affair may become public knowledge. As a result, he commits suicide.

OTHER ROLES

1958: *Tod Lohman* / FROM HELL TO TEXAS. **1959:** *Lat Evans* / THESE THOUSAND HILLS; *Kerry O'Shea* / SHAKE HANDS WITH THE DEVIL. **1960:** *Dan Keats* / ONE FOOT IN HELL. **1962:** *Kurt Schroeder* / ESCAPE FROM EAST BERLIN. **1964:** *Norman Vincent Peale* / ONE MAN'S WAY. **1965:** *Slim* / BABY, THE RAIN MUST FALL. **1966:** *Kid Rodelo* / KID RODELO; *Wild Bill Hickok* / THE PLAINSMAN. **1967:** *David Hillary* / SWEET LOVE, BITTER; *Justinian* / THE VIKING QUEEN; *Tom Harris* / TALE OF THE COCK. **1972:** *Breck* / CONQUEST OF THE PLANET OF THE APES; *Herb Shuttle* / HAPPY BIRTHDAY, WANDA JUNE. **1973:** *Cotter* / COTTER. **1976:** *Ed Lacy* / DEADLY HERO. **1981:** *Hugh* / ENDLESS LOVE. **1983:** *David* / I AM THE CHEESE. **1984:** *guest* / RADIOACTIVE DREAMS. **1986:** *Jack Keicher* / PEGGY SUE GOT MARRIED.

NEAGLE, ANNA

(Marjorie Robertson, 1904–1986)

Blonde British singer, dancer, and actress Anna Neagle rose from chorus girl to star of musicals and historical dramas and was made a dame of the British Empire in 1969. While never a great actress, she and her husband, director Herbert Wilcox, found the formula for box-office success. Neagle played every role from prostitute to queen, showgirl to spy. In Hollywood, she appeared mostly in routine musicals not helped by her modest singing voice. Back in England, she became the top box-office star of the 1940s. In the 1960s her career turned full circle when she returned to musicals on the London stage.

KEY ROLES

Sarah Linden / BITTER SWEET, 1933, Great Britain, British & Dominions, d-Herbert Wilcox.

In this weeper, Neagle marries her Vienna music teacher. To make ends meet, he must take a job with a cafe orchestra and she becomes a dancer. Her husband is killed in a duel with an amorous count. Years later, Neagle relates the story of her difficult but happy life to a young relative, which helps the latter decide whom she should love and wed.

Nell Gwyn / NELL GWYN, 1934, Great Britain, British & Dominions, d-Herbert Wilcox.

Neagle shows quite a lot of her ample bosom in her portrayal of "the Unofficial Queen of England"—the orange seller who becomes the mistress of King Charles II (Cedric Hardwicke). Neagle's mentor, Herbert Wilcox, had found the proper formula for his star—strongly independent women who could hold their own with men.

Peg Woffington / PEG OF OLD DRURY, 1935, Great Britain, British & Dominions, d-Herbert Wilcox.

Neagle gives a lively performance as the Irish actress who follows a man who jilted her from Dublin to London and, with the help of David Garrick (Cedric Hardwicke), becomes the foremost actress of her day.

Queen Victoria / VICTORIA THE GREAT, 1937, Great Britain, Imperator / RKO, d-Herbert Wilcox.

Neagle thrilled British audiences with her portrayal of the great British Queen and her 64-year reign. The film concentrates on her marriage to her consort, Prince Albert (Anton Walbrook).

Queen Victoria / SIXTY GLORIOUS YEARS, 1938, Great Britain, Imperator / RKO, d-Herbert Wilcox.
In trying to tell of the full life of Queen Victoria, one film just wasn't enough. So Wilcox brought Neagle back, this time in Technicolor, to show more events of the Queen's reign and life with her consort.

Edith Cavell / NURSE EDITH CAVELL, 1940, Great Britain, Imperator / RKO, d-Herbert Wilcox.
This is the touching, tragic story of the British nurse who was executed by the Germans in World War I as a spy.

Irene O'Dare / IRENE, 1940, RKO, d-Herbert Wilcox.
RKO had purchased the rights to this piece years earlier, hoping to team Fred Astaire and Ginger Rogers, but the studio ended up with Neagle and Ray Milland. It's a minor Cinderella story with Neagle giving out with a meager voice on the title song, "Alice Blue Gown," and "Castle of Dreams."

Nanette / NO, NO NANETTE, 1940, RKO, d-Herbert Wilcox.
In this Vincent Youmans musical Neagle attempts to pry her rich uncle away from gold diggers. The songs include the title number, "I Want to Be Happy," and "Tea for Two."

Amy Johnson / THEY FLEW ALONE, 1942, Great Britain, Imperator / RKO, d-Herbert Wilcox.
In this biopic of Britain's pioneer woman flyer, Neagle is married to dare-devil pilot Jim Molison (Robert Newton). While they establish many solo and joint flying records, their union goes up, up, and away.

Diana Fraser / PICCADILLY INCIDENT, 1946, Great Britain, Associated British / Pathe, d-Herbert Wilcox.
Neagle is a WREN who meets a royal marine officer during an air raid and they fall in love and marry. After the fall of Singapore, Neagle is reported lost at sea. Three years later her husband marries again. Neagle shows up and pretends she wants a divorce, but conveniently dies in another air raid.

Judy Howard / SPRING IN PARK LANE, 1948, Great Britain, British Lion, d-Herbert Wilcox.
Neagle is secretary for her wealthy art collector uncle when she recognizes his new footman as a nobleman on the run for having accepted a bad check for his family's art collection. The two fall in love and in storybook fashion the check turns out to be good after all.

Marie-Celine Sansom / ODETTE, 1950, Great Britain, British Lion, d-Herbert Wilcox.
By accident Neagle, a French girl married to an Englishman, accepts the dangerous assignment of agent for the British in Nazi-occupied France, with the code name Odette. She is captured and tortured but refuses to give information. She is sentenced to be executed but survives to be freed from a concentration camp in this story based on fact.

Florence Nightingale / THE LADY WITH A LAMP, 1951, Great Britain, British Lion, d-Herbert Wilcox.
This is a sincere, careful biopic of the gentlewoman who, with her angels of mercy, treats thousands of wounded soldiers in the Crimean War of the 1850s. She returns from the war championing hospital reform.

OTHER ROLES

1930: *bit* / THE SCHOOL FOR SCANDAL; *Muriel Ashton* / SHOULD A DOCTOR TELL? **1931:** *Charlotte* / THE CHINESE BUNGALOW. **1932:** *Viki* / GOODNIGHT VIENNA; *Hermione Wynne* / THE FLAG LIEUTENANT. **1933:** *Julie Alardy* / THE LITTLE DAMOZEL; *Queen Nadina* / THE QUEEN'S AFFAIR. **1936:** *Marjorie Kaye* / LIMELIGHT; *Pat* / THE THREE MAXIMS. **1937:** *Jacqueline* / LONDON MELODY. **1941:** *Sunny* / SUNNY; *cameo* / LAND OF LIBERTY. **1943:** *guest* / FOREVER AND A DAY; *Sally Maitland* / THE YELLOW CANARY. **1945:** *Lady Patricia Fairfax* / I LIVE IN GROSVENOR SQUARE. **1947:** *Catherine O'Halloran* / THE COURTNEYS OF CURZON STREET. **1949:** *Beth / Elizabeth / Betty / Liz* / ELIZABETH OF LADYMEAD; *Ellen Grahame* / MAYTIME IN MAYFAIR. **1952:** *Larry Forbes* / DERBY DAY. **1955:** *Carole Beaumont / Lilian Grey / Nell Gwyn / Queen Victoria* / LILACS IN THE SPRING; *Marla Karillos* / KING'S RHAPSODY. **1956:** *Valerie Carr* / MY TEENAGE DAUGHTER. **1957:** *Eleanor Hammond* / NO TIME FOR TEARS. **1958:** *Mary Randall Q.C.* / THE MAN WHO WOULDN'T TALK; *Frances Baring* / THE LADY IS A SQUARE.

NEAL, PATRICIA

(Patsy Neal, 1926–)

A drama student at Northwestern University and The Actors' Studio, Patricia Neal made her Broadway debut in "The Voice of the Turtle" in 1946 and her film debut in JOHN LOVES MARY in 1949. In that same year she attracted greater attention for her appearance in THE FOUNTAINHEAD. Her romance with co-star Gary Cooper was so publicized that she suffered a nervous breakdown. Neal projected intelligence and grace in her performances, even as the ever-tired housekeeper in HUD, for which she won an Oscar. She commanded much admiration for the dignified manner in which she bore and overcame a series of tragedies in her life, including a son who suffered severe brain damage, a daughter who died of measles, and her own near-fatal strokes which left her partially paralyzed, confined to a wheelchair, and incapable of articulate speech. She recovered enough to appear before the cameras again and was nominated for another Oscar for THE SUBJECT WAS ROSES. Since then she has made a few additional appearances in the United States and abroad and has also taken roles in made-for-TV movies such as THE HOMECOMING (1971), RUN, STRANGER, RUN (1974), TAIL GUNNER JOE (1977), and ALL QUIET ON THE WESTERN FRONT (1980).

KEY ROLES

Dominique Wynand / THE FOUNTAINHEAD, 1949, Warners, d-King Vidor.
While this attempt to make a major star of Neal was neither a financial nor a critical success, she definitely impressed both audiences and critics as the wife of a newspaper publisher (Raymond Massey). She has a tempestuous affair with architect Gary Cooper.

Sister Parker / THE HASTY HEART, 1949, Great Britain, Associated British, d-Vincent Sherman.
This is the story of a dour Scot (Richard Todd) who is sent to a World War II hospital ward in Burma. Everyone except him knows that he has only a few weeks to live and they try to become his friend, and he even falls in love with head nurse Neal before learning his fate and once again withdrawing into his shell. Neal explains Todd's sudden humility at one point saying, "He just swallowed his pride. It'll take him a moment or two to digest it."

Helen Benson / THE DAY THE EARTH STOOD STILL, 1951, 20th Century-Fox, d-Robert Wise.

In this science fiction classic, Michael Rennie, a visitor from another planet, lands on earth to encourage the search for world peace. He takes a room in a boarding house run by Neal. Her son introduces Rennie to an eminent mathematician who plans a meeting of the top scientists to hear Rennie's message. But by this time frightened citizens are intent on hunting down and destroying the alien. He is wounded, but through Neal manages to get a message to his eight-foot robot, Gort, not to destroy the world, a task of which he is apparently capable. Neal delivers the immortal words: "Gort! Klaatu barada nikto."

Marcia Jeffries / A FACE IN THE CROWD, 1957, Warners, d-Elia Kazan.
Neal is the woman who guides Andy Griffith, a power-mad hillbilly entertainer, to fame and fortune as a TV celebrity whose image as a clean-cut boy is all sham. Neal, who has become his secret lover, turns on his microphone when Griffith thinks it's off, and his audience hears him call them stupid slobs and suckers in his hands. And that's it for Griffith.

Alma Brown / HUD, 1963, Paramount, d-Martin Ritt.
Neal's performance as the weary housekeeper on the ranch run by Melvyn Douglas, his son Paul Newman, and grandson Brandon De Wilde, won her a much-deserved Academy Award. Even when she is raped by Newman, she resignedly accepts this as another chore in her "work-is-never-done" life.

Maggie Haynes / IN HARM'S WAY, 1965, Paramount, d-Otto Preminger.
Neal is a nurse who falls for big John Wayne in this all-star film that tells many stories, using Pearl Harbor and its aftermath as background.

Nettie Cleary / THE SUBJECT WAS ROSES, 1968, MGM, d-Ula Grosbard.
After her miraculous recovery from severe strokes, Neal returned to the big screen in this story about severe family tensions and earned an Oscar nomination. When husband Jack Albertson gifts her with roses, she reveals: "When you brought the roses, I felt something stir in me that I thought was dead forever."

OTHER ROLES

1949: *Mary McKinley* / JOHN LOVES MARY; *herself* / IT'S A GREAT FEELING. **1950:** *Margaret Jane Singleton* / BRIGHT LEAF; *Phyllis Horn* / THREE SECRETS; *Lenora Charles* / THE BREAKING POINT. **1951:** *Jean Bowen* / WEEKEND WITH FATHER; *Mary Stuart* / OPERATION PACIFIC; *Ann Challon* / RATON PASS. **1952:** *Anne Richards* / SOMETHING FOR THE BIRDS; *Joan Ross* / DIPLOMATIC COURIER; *Alice Kingsly* / WASHINGTON STORY. **1954:** *Susan North* / THE STRANGER FROM VENUS. **1961:** *2-E* / BREAKFAST AT TIFFANY'S. **1964:** *Allison Crawford* / PSYCHE 59. **1971:** *Maura Prince* / THE NIGHT DIGGER. **1972:** *Dr. Cara Clemm* / BAXTER. **1977:** *Lupe* / WIDOW'S NEST. **1979:** *Ariel Bergson* / THE PASSAGE. **1981:** *Stella* / GHOST STORY.

NEWMAN, PAUL

(1925–)

Born in Cleveland, Ohio, Paul Newman studied acting at the Yale School of Drama. He made his Broadway debut in "Picnic" and his first film appearance in a real stinker, THE SILVER CHALICE, in 1954. Fortunately for him, the death of James Dean got him the role of Rocky Graziano in SOMEBODY UP THERE LIKES ME, which started him on his way to superstar status. Newman, whose blue eyes and gorgeous looks have stirred desire in thousands of women over the years, has excelled at playing the antihero whose relationships with women are less than satisfactory. He has often chosen strange vehicles that have proven to be major disappointments, but when he has chosen roles wisely, he's as good as they come. Nominated for Oscars for his performances in CAT ON A HOT TIN ROOF, THE HUSTLER, HUD, COOL HAND LUKE, and THE VERDICT, Newman won for a good performance in a lesser movie, THE COLOR OF MONEY, in 1986, a sequel to THE HUSTLER. Married to Joanne Woodward, he has directed her in the pictures RACHEL, RACHEL; THE EFFECT OF GAMMA RAYS ON MAN-IN-THE-MOON MARIGOLDS; and THE GLASS MENAGERIE. The actor who has had a strange assortment of successes and failures, self-deprecatingly observed: "My own personality is so vapid and bland, I have to go steal the personality of other people to be effective on the screen."

KEY ROLES

Rocky Barbella (Graziano) / SOMEBODY UP THERE LIKES ME, 1956, MGM, d-Robert Wise.
It's rather difficult to visualize James Dean in the role of middleweight boxing champ Rocky Graziano, but he was scheduled for this role when he was killed in an automobile accident. Newman made the most of his opportunity and pleased audiences with his sensitive interpretation of the none-too-bright fighter.

Ben Quick / THE LONG HOT SUMMER, 1958, 20th Century-Fox, d-Martin Ritt.
Newman, a country handyman, has the reputation of setting fire to the barns and crops of those who treat him unkindly. He goes to work as a sharecropper for Mississippi landowner Orson Welles and takes a shine to the latter's outlandish daughter (Joanne Woodward).

Brick Pollitt / CAT ON A HOT TIN ROOF, 1958, MGM, d-Richard Brooks.
Newman received his first Oscar nomination for his role as a one-time football star who has been so dominated by his father, the dying "Big Daddy" (Burl Ives), that he is unsure of his own sexuality and is unable to make love with his wife (Elizabeth Taylor).

Ari Ben Canaan / EXODUS, 1960, United Artists, d-Otto Preminger.
Newman is one of the leaders of the Palestine-based Hagannah, a Jewish underground unit intent on making Palestine the home of the world's Jewish refugees after World War II.

Eddie Felson / THE HUSTLER, 1961, 20th Century-Fox, d-Robert Rossen.
Newman received his second Oscar nomination for his downbeat portrayal of antihero pool hustler "Fast" Eddie Felson who comes to New York to relieve Minnesota Fats (Jackie Gleason) of a big wad of money. His first effort is unsuccessful, but after meeting crippled Piper Laurie and falling under the sway of gambler George C. Scott, he gets a second chance to prove that he's no "loser." After Laurie commits suicide in Louisville because of Scott, Newman once again goes after Gleason and wins big, snapping at the hated Scott: "How can I lose? Because you were right. It's not enough that you just have talent. You gotta have character, too....Yeah, I sure got character now. I picked it up in a hotel room in Louisville."

Hud Bannion / HUD, 1963, Paramount, d-Martin Ritt.
In his third Academy Award-nominated portrayal, Newman is a hell-raising son of a modern-day Texas rancher, who is despised by his father (Melvyn Doug-

las), idolized by his nephew (Brandon De Wilde), and tolerated by the tired housekeeper (Patricia Neal). He doesn't improve in his father's eyes before the old man dies; his nephew becomes disgusted with him and leaves the ranch; and so does the housekeeper after Hud rapes her. At the end our antihero is all alone and has learned nothing.

Andrew Craig / THE PRIZE, 1963, MGM, d-Mark Robson.
Newman is an alcoholic American writer who, despite having lost his muse, is awarded the Nobel Prize for Literature. When he goes to Stockholm to receive his prize, he becomes involved in a plot to kidnap the physics prize winner.

Lew Harper / HARPER, 1966, Warners, d-Jack Smight.
Newman, a hard-boiled L.A. private eye, is hired by rich Lauren Bacall to find her missing husband. This leads him into the world of murderers and smugglers.

John Russell / HOMBRE, 1967, 20th Century-Fox, d-Martin Ritt.
Attempting to capitalize on his success with movies beginning with the letter "H" and his association with director Martin Ritt, Newman took on the unusual role of a despised half-caste who saves the passengers of a stagecoach from a gang of brutal robbers.

Luke Jackson / COOL HAND LUKE, 1967, Warners, d-Stuart Rosenberg.
Newman is a man going nowhere who is sentenced to work on a southern work gang where his refusal to buckle under to the system gets him beatings, chains, confinement to a hot box, and after one final escape attempt, death. Once again Newman was left at the altar in the Oscar sweepstakes. The best line in the picture is given by the very fine character actor Strother Martin as the head of the prison farm, who has just brutalized Newman: "What we've got here is failure to communicate."

Butch Cassidy (Robert Leroy Parker) / BUTCH CASSIDY AND THE SUNDANCE KID, 1969, 20th Century-Fox, d-George Roy Hill.
Newman demonstrates a fine talent for comedy in this tongue-in-cheek tale of the leader of the Hole-in-the-Wall Gang and his friend the Sundance Kid (Robert Redford). They find life in the Old West becoming less and less hospitable to bank and train robbers and so take their business to Bolivia where they are ultimately killed. Newman was originally intended for the Sundance Kid role, but director Hill convinced him that he could handle the comical aspects of Butch's character.

Judge Roy Bean / THE LIFE AND TIMES OF JUDGE ROY BEAN, 1972, National General, d-John Huston.
Newman portrays the Kentucky-born opportunist who, after moving to Texas, sets himself up as "The Law West of the Pecos." Most of those who come before his court of law end up losing all their possessions and are promptly hanged, no matter what their crime. Newman's only affection is for the actress Lily Langtry whom he has never seen, but adores as if she were a queen and goddess.

Henry Gondorff / THE STING, 1973, Universal, d-George Roy Hill.
Newman is a professional big-time con artist who, together with small-time con man Robert Redford, plans a "sting" of mobster Robert Shaw, who had ordered the murder of Redford's partner. While the teaming of Newman and Redford doesn't quite match their work in BUTCH CASSIDY AND THE SUNDANCE KID, it is an enjoyable picture with a number of clever switches and surprises.

Doug Roberts / THE TOWERING INFERNO, 1974, 20th Century-Fox, d-John Guillermin and Irwin Allen.
As the architect of the world's tallest building, Newman helps fire chief Steve McQueen find ways to save the guests at its gala opening party who are trapped in the penthouse when the structure catches fire. Cost-cutting devices made the supposedly fire-proof building go up in flames like kindling.

Murphy / FORT APACHE, THE BRONX, 1981, 20th Century-Fox, d-Daniel Petrie.
Newman is a veteran New York cop assigned to one of the city's most crime-plagued regions. He agonizes over turning in another policeman whom he suspects has killed a Puerto Rican suspect by flinging him off a rooftop.

Michael Gallagher / ABSENCE OF MALICE, 1981, Columbia, d-Sydney Pollack.
Hoping to learn about the disappearance of a union leader, Bob Balaban heads up an investigation that leads newspaper reporter Sally Field to believe that honest Miami liquor wholesaler Newman is a suspect because his uncle is a mobster. Her story in the paper almost destroys Newman and leads to the suicide of a girl he had befriended. Once more Newman was up for an Oscar, and once again he came away a loser.

Frank Galvin / THE VERDICT, 1982, 20th Century-Fox, d-Sidney Lumet.
Newman is an aging, alcoholic, and failing attorney who is unexpectedly handed a case of medical malpractice and successfully sues a Boston hospital run by the Catholic Archdiocese. Newman was nominated for an Oscar again but his wait was not yet over.

Eddie Felson / THE COLOR OF MONEY, 1986, Orion, d-Martin Scorsese.
Until this picture only Bing Crosby had ever been nominated twice for Academy Awards for the same character (he won as Father O'Malley in GOING MY WAY and was nominated for THE BELLS OF ST. MARY'S). Here Newman is a greying Eddie Felson, now a liquor salesman, who takes an interest in a young man (Tom Cruise) whom he sponsors as a pool hustler.

OTHER ROLES

1954: *Basil* / THE SILVER CHALICE. **1956:** *Capt. Edward W. Hall, Jr.* / THE RACK. **1957:** *Capt. Jack Harding* / UNTIL THEY SAIL; *Larry Maddux* / THE HELEN MORGAN STORY. **1958:** *Billy the Kid* / THE LEFT-HANDED GUN; *Harry Bannerman* / RALLY 'ROUND THE FLAG, BOYS! **1959:** *Tony Lawrence* / THE YOUNG PHILADELPHIANS. **1960:** *Alfred Eaton* / FROM THE TERRACE. **1961:** *Ram Bowen* / PARIS BLUES. **1962:** *Chance Wayne* / SWEET BIRD OF YOUTH; *Ad Francis* / HEMINGWAY'S ADVENTURES OF A YOUNG MAN. **1963:** *Steve Sherman* / A NEW KIND OF LOVE. **1964:** *Larry Flint* / WHAT A WAY TO GO!; *Juan Carrasco* / THE OUTRAGE. **1965:** *Armand* / LADY L. **1966:** *Prof. Michael Armstrong* / TORN CURTAIN. **1968:** *Pvt. Harry Frigg* / THE SECRET WAR OF HARRY FRIGG. **1969:** *Frank Capua* / WINNING. **1970:** *Rheinhardt* / WUSA. **1971:** *Hank Stamper* / SOMETIMES A GREAT NOTION. **1972:** *Jim Kane* / POCKET MONEY. **1973:** *Rearden* / THE MACKINTOSH MAN. **1975:** *Lew Harper* / THE DROWNING POOL. **1976:** *William F. Cody (Buffalo Bill)* / BUFFALO BILL AND THE INDIANS, OR SITTING BULL'S HISTORY LESSON; *guest* / SILENT MOVIE. **1977:** *Reggie Dunlop* / SLAP SHOT. **1979:** *Essex* / QUINTET. **1980:** *Hank Anderson* / WHEN TIME RAN OUT. **1984:** *Harry* / HARRY AND SON.

NICHOLSON, JACK

(1937–)

Jack Nicholson, a veteran of many low-budget quickie horror movies and biker films, got his big break when he replaced Rip Torn in EASY RIDER. Since then he has progressed to being among America's best actors; one who not only refuses to be typecast in any particular movie genre, but who actually takes on different appearances in his movies. He has won Oscars for ONE FLEW OVER THE CUCKOO'S NEST and TERMS OF ENDEARMENT, as well as being nominated for FIVE EASY PIECES, THE LAST DETAIL, CHINATOWN, PRIZZI'S HONOR, and IRONWEED. Besides acting, Nicholson has also written screenplays and, on occasion, has directed. He is droll, enigmatic, and dynamic. His dry voice and cynical smile, together with his intense personality, are as enjoyable in humorous roles as they are in dramatic ones. With obvious charisma and false modesty he explains his success: "I remember that someone once said that the whole thing is to keep working, and pretty soon they'll think you're good." This quixotic misfit, who rejects the status quo in a way that seems so attractive, may well be the best American actor at this time.

KEY ROLES

Wilbur Force / THE LITTLE SHOP OF HORRORS, 1960, Filmgroups, d-Roger Corman.

In this cult film about a nerd who develops a new plant that craves humans as the nourishment to make it grow, Nicholson is a young man who wears his hair parted down the middle and really gets turned on from the pain he experiences in a dental chair at the hands of a sadistic dentist.

Poet / HELL'S ANGELS ON WHEELS, 1967, U.S. Films, d-Richard Rush.

Nicholson is a gas station attendant who joins the Hell's Angels motorcycle gang. When he is jumped by four sailors at an amusement park, the head Angel comes to his assistance. But the friendship sours when Nicholson moves in on the former's girlfriend.

George Hanson / EASY RIDER, 1969, Columbia, d-Dennis Hopper.

Nicholson moves into the big time and an Academy Award nomination for his role as a drunken lawyer who joins Peter Fonda and Dennis Hopper on their travels across the country on motorcycles. He's killed by rednecks long before Fonda and Hopper are.

Robert Eroica Dupea / FIVE EASY PIECES, 1970, Columbia, d-Bob Rafelson.

Once again Nicholson is unwilling to grow up and accept responsibility for himself or anyone else, particularly not his very bright pregnant girlfriend (Karen Black). He briefly returns to his family of musicians and seduces his brother's fiancée but, even though she seems right for him, he hits the road, deserting her as well.

Jonathan / CARNAL KNOWLEDGE, 1971, Avco Embassy, d-Mike Nichols.

Nicholson is a man for whom sex is a competition, not an expression of love between a man and a woman. His sophomoric lustings carry well into middle age and reach a point where he cannot enjoy sex unless it is scripted.

David Staebler / THE KING OF MARVIN GARDENS, 1972, Columbia, d-Bob Rafelson.

Nicholson, an uncharismatic disc jockey, travels to Atlantic City and becomes embroiled in his brother Bruce Dern's numerous hair-brained schemes for making money.

Billy Buddusky / THE LAST DETAIL, 1973, Columbia, d-Hal Ashby.

Nicholson gives one of his finest performances as one of two career sailors who are assigned to escort a young sailor to military prison. They are given several days to make the delivery and attempt to make the prisoner's last days of freedom memorable.

J. J. Gittes / CHINATOWN, 1974, Paramount, d-Roman Polanski.

Set in the Los Angeles of the 1930s, the film features Nicholson as a private eye who specializes in getting pictures of unfaithful spouses for divorce proceedings. He's hired to check up on the water commissioner by a woman who says she is the man's wife. Nicholson gets the dirt and it's published but the real wife (Faye Dunaway) shows up and fires him. When the commissioner is killed, Nicholson begins to act like a hard-boiled detective and sets out to solve the murder and discover the secret of Dunaway and her father (John Huston).

Randle Patrick McMurphy / ONE FLEW OVER THE CUCKOO'S NEST, 1976, United Artists, d-Milos Forman.

Nicholson won his Academy Award for Best Actor as a prisoner who pretends to be insane so he can be transferred to an institution where he thinks he'll have an easier time. There he encounters a misguided head nurse (Louise Fletcher) who seems to take delight in preventing the patients from improving. Nicholson's disruption of the hospital's normal routine leads to tragic consequences, but his spirit is not broken even by shock treatment. He boasts: "They was giving me 10,000 watts a day, and you know, I'm hot to trot. The next woman takes me out is going to light up like a pinball machine and pay off in silver dollars."

Henry Moon / GOIN' SOUTH, 1978, Paramount, d-Jack Nicholson.

Director Nicholson gets a funny performance from actor Nicholson in this comedy-western. He is just about to be hanged as an outlaw when he's saved by a woman (Mary Steenburgen) who is willing to marry him because she needs help in her gold mine.

Jack Torrance / THE SHINING, 1980, Great Britain, Warners, d-Stanley Kubrick.

Nicholson, his wife, and small son serve as caretakers for a resort hotel closed for the season in a desolate location. Murders have occurred in the hotel, and that and the isolation make Nicholson go berserk and threaten his family.

Eugene O'Neill / REDS, 1981, Paramount, d-Warren Beatty.

Nicholson was nominated for Best Supporting Actor for his portrayal of the great American playwright who was a friend of John Reed, the radical writer of *Ten Days that Shook the World,* the story of the communist revolution in Russia in 1919.

Garrett Breedlove / TERMS OF ENDEARMENT, 1983, Paramount, d-James L. Brooks.

Nicholson won another Oscar for his portrayal of a womanizing astronaut who becomes the lover of an eccentric widow (Shirley MacLaine) who constantly interferes in her daughter's life and, in the end, in her death.

Charley Partana / PRIZZI'S HONOR, 1985, 20th Century-Fox, d-John Huston.

Nicholson is a top soldier in the Prizzi crime family. One of the old Don's sons buys a contract on him because he has "ruined" the other's daughter (Angelica Huston). The only problem is that the hit man is hit woman Kathleen Turner who has just married Nicholson. In the end, these two who love each other realize that they will have to kill each other to live. Nicholson wins out when his knife is faster than Turner's gun.

Francis Phelan / IRONWEED, 1987, Tri-Star, d-Hector Babenco.

Nicholson was nominated for an Oscar for his portrayal of a bum in Albany, New York, in 1938, and his performance is as good as has been seen on the screen in many a year. His work as the husband and father who dropped out of society twenty years earlier when he accidentally dropped and killed his 13-day-old son is unforgettable and awesome. His powerful portrayal causes us to reassess our assertion that he may be the best actor in the United States today. We must instead conclude that there is no doubt that he is the best actor in the United States today, and perhaps the best in the world.

OTHER ROLES

1958: *Jimmy* / THE CRY BABY KILLER. **1959:** *Buddy* / TOO SOON TO LOVE. **1961:** *Weary Reilly* / STUDS LONIGAN; *Johnny Varron* / THE WILD RIDE. **1962:** *Will Brocious* / THE BROKEN LAND. **1963:** *Rexford Bedlo* / THE RAVEN; *Andre Duvalier* / THE TERROR. **1964:** *Burnett* / BACK DOOR TO HELL. **1965:** *Jay Wickham* / FLIGHT TO FURY; *Dolan* / ENSIGN PULVER. **1966:** *Wes* / RIDE THE WHIRLWIND; *Billy Spear* / THE SHOOTING. **1968:** *Stoney* / PSYCH-OUT; *himself* / HEAD. **1970:** *Tad Pringle* / ON A CLEAR DAY YOU CAN SEE FOREVER. **1971:** *Mitch* / A SAFE PLACE. **1974:** *doctor, the specialist* / TOMMY; *David Locke* / THE PASSENGER. **1976:** *Oscar Sullivan* / THE FORTUNE; *Tom Logan* / THE MISSOURI BREAKS; *Brimmer* / THE LAST TYCOON. **1981:** *Frank Chambers* / THE POSTMAN ALWAYS RINGS TWICE. **1982:** *Charlie Smith* / THE BORDER. **1986:** *Mack* / HEARTBURN. **1987:** *David Van Horne* / THE WITCHES OF EASTWICK; *anchorman Bill Rorich* / BROADCAST NEWS.

NIVEN, DAVID

(James D. Nevins, 1909–1983)

David Niven continued to be one of the most popular actors for almost 50 years despite the fact that he appeared in very few outstanding movies. The suave Scottish-born actor was just so charming, and audiences were so taken with him, that they didn't mind that his vehicles were usually quite ordinary. Niven drifted into acting after being discharged from the British army in the 1930s, with his first good role being in THE DAWN PATROL in 1938. He demonstrated a flair for drawing room comedy but his career was interrupted for almost six years when, during World War II, he reenlisted in the British army and was discharged as a colonel. His sagging career was resurrected with AROUND THE WORLD IN 80 DAYS and he won an Academy Award for SEPARATE TABLES in 1958. His screen work from the 1960s on was very much a mixed bag, from charming appearances in light comedies to some very British types in action-adventure tales. Throughout his career Niven remained cheerful, writing two extremely interesting if not necessarily accurate autobiographies, *The Moon's a Balloon* and *Bring on the Empty Horses*. The gentleman rogue described his attitude toward himself thusly: "Print anything you like, and I'll swear I said it."

KEY ROLES

Bertie Wooster / THANK YOU, JEEVES, 1936, 20th Century-Fox, d-Arthur Greville.

Arthur Treacher is Niven's valet, Jeeves, who helps prevent Niven from becoming involved in a gun-running scheme.

Major Lockert / DODSWORTH, 1936, Goldwyn / United Artists, d-William Wyler.

Niven is one of five men Ruth Chatterton flirts with to prove she is still attractive in this Sinclair Lewis story about a man named Dodsworth (Walter Huston) who goes abroad with his wife (Chatterton) and finds a new set of values and a new love (Mary Astor).

Fritz von Tarlenheim / THE PRISONER OF ZENDA, 1937, Selznick / United Artists, d-John Cromwell.

Niven is the ever-loyal Fritz willing to sacrifice his life to ensure that the correct Ronald Colman ascends the throne of Ruritania.

Lt. Douglas Scott / THE DAWN PATROL, 1938, Warners, d-Edmund Goulding.

Niven and his buddy Errol Flynn have a happy-go-lucky attitude toward their dangerous work as World War I pilots, until Flynn is given command and is responsible for making decisions that send many young men, including Niven's inexperienced younger brother, to their deaths.

Edgar Linton / WUTHERING HEIGHTS, 1939, Goldwyn / United Artists, d-William Wyler.

Niven is able to marry Merle Oberon but he can't make her forget her lifelong love for the gypsy boy who has grown up (Laurence Olivier).

David Merlin / BACHELOR MOTHER, 1939, RKO, d-Garson Kanin.

When department store salesgirl Ginger Rogers finds an abandoned baby, Niven, the son of the store's owner, attempts to help her and everyone believes the two are really the child's parents. When the film came out it was one of the brightest comedies of the year.

A. J. Raffles / RAFFLES, 1939, Goldwyn / United Artists, d-Sam Wood.

Niven is a renowned cricketer and a compulsive and daring amateur thief. He is very charming as the gentleman who steals a valuable necklace from his hostess because his best friend, the brother of the girl he loves, desperately needs a thousand pounds.

Lt. Jim Perry / THE WAY AHEAD, 1944, Great Britain, Two Cities, d-Carol Reed.

Niven is an officer who trains seven unwilling civilian conscripts who, after a lot of sweating and grumbling, become part of the force invading North Africa. There they all face death as they move forward through a German smoke screen.

Squadron Leader Peter Carter / A MATTER OF LIFE AND DEATH, 1946, Great Britain, The Archers, d-Michael Powell and Emeric Pressburger.

Niven bails out of a blazing plane and is washed ashore apparently unharmed. He falls in love with American WAC Kim Hunter, with whom he was talking on the radio at the time of his plane crash. After he starts to have hallucinations in which he sees people from another world, he has a brain operation during which a battle goes on before a heavenly court as to whether he should be allowed to live or die. With the help of his surgeon and Hunter, the verdict is in his favor.

Aaron Burr / MAGNIFICENT DOLL, 1946, Universal, d-Frank Borzage.

In one of his rare villain roles, Niven is a former suitor of a woman (Ginger Rogers) who rejects him to marry John Madison (Burgess Meredith). Niven doesn't believe in democracy and wishes to take over the country by force with himself at its head.

Henry Brougham / THE BISHOP'S WIFE, 1947, Goldwyn / RKO, d-Henry Koster.

When Bishop Niven prays for help to construct a cathedral, angel Cary Grant shows up. But as is often the case, heaven acts in mysterious ways and Grant's attentions to Niven's wife (Loretta Young) are a source of great annoyance, until Niven understands that he is being shown what is really important in his roles as a spiritual leader and a man.

David Slater / THE MOON IS BLUE, 1953, United Artists, d-Otto Preminger.

Viewing this film today, one is bound to wonder what all the fuss was about when, at the time of its release, this film was denied the production code of approval and was condemned in sermons in most Catholic churches. In it Maggie McNamara is a virgin who refuses to be seduced by either middle-aged roué Niven or playboy architect William Holden.

Major Carrington, V.C. / CARRINGTON, V.C., 1955, Great Britain, British Lion, d-Anthony Asquith.

Desperate for money the army owes him, Niven warns his commanding officer that he'll take it from the company safe. When he does he is court-martialled, and his C.O. and shrewish wife refuse to tell the truth at his trial. He is kicked out of the service and is crushed, but is able to win an appeal when a telephone operator reveals that she overheard a conversation that supports his story.

Phileas Fogg / AROUND THE WORLD IN 80 DAYS, 1956, Todd / United Artists, d-Michael Anderson.

Niven is a Victorian gentleman who wagers that he can complete a trip around the world in 80 days. He leaves with his valet and on the way runs into almost everyone in Hollywood playing cameo roles.

Major Pollack / SEPARATE TABLES, 1958, United Artists, d-Delbert Mann.

Niven won an Academy Award for his touching portrayal of a phony retired British major who is not only a fraud but a molester of women at cinemas. It is the scene in which he confesses his deceit that won him the Oscar, as he pitifully says, "We all have our daydreams. Mine has just gone a step further than most people's. Sometimes—sometimes, I even manage to believe in the major myself."

Larry Mackey / PLEASE DON'T EAT THE DAISIES, 1960, MGM, d-Charles Walters.

Drama critic Niven becomes involved with a glamorous star to whom he gives an unfavorable review at the time his wife and children have moved into a home in the country. His review of this film couldn't have been very positive.

Corporal Miller / THE GUNS OF NAVARONE, 1961, Great Britain, Columbia, d-J. Lee Thompson.

In this exciting adventure film, Niven is an explosives expert reluctantly along on a mission to sabotage two giant German guns on a Turkish island during World War II.

Major Richardson / THE BEST OF ENEMIES, 1962, Columbia, d-Guy Hamilton.

During the Abyssinian campaign of 1941, British commander Niven and Italian captain Alberto Sordi take turns holding each other prisoner and, as the troops of the two countries cross the desert together, they learn mutual respect.

Sir Arthur Robertson / 55 DAYS AT PEKING, 1963, Allied Artists, d-Nicholas Ray.

Niven is the British Mission head at the time of the Boxer Rebellion in China. He assumes command of the defense of the international diplomatic quarter when the dowager empress of China encourages the Boxers to attack the "foreign devils."

Sir Charles Lytton / THE PINK PANTHER, 1964, United Artists, d-Blake Edwards.

Niven, alias "The Phantom," is an international jewel thief intent on stealing "The Pink Panther"—a priceless diamond owned by an Indian princess. His accomplice and mistress is the wife of bungling Inspector Clouseau (Peter Sellers) of the French police who has been tracking Niven for years.

Sir James Bond / CASINO ROYALE, 1967, Great Britain, Columbia, d-John Huston.

This Bond spoof, based on one of Ian Fleming's novels, has the heads of all the allied spy forces calling James Bond from retirement to fight SMERSH.

Gerald Hardcastle / PRUDENCE AND THE PILL, 1968, 20th Century-Fox, d-Fielder Cook.

Wealthy Niven has both a wife and a mistress and exchanges his wife's birth control pills for aspirins in the hope that she will become pregnant by her doctor lover and want a divorce. But a visiting niece also switches pills belonging to her mother. Before long, with all the switches, all the women become pregnant.

Dick Charleston / MURDER BY DEATH, 1976, Columbia, d-Robert Moore.

Niven and Maggie Smith are Nick and Nora Charles-like detectives who, along with several other fictional detectives, are invited to stay at the home of a wealthy recluse and the result is murder. But the laughs are too few and far between.

OTHER ROLES

1935: *sailor* / BARBARY COAST; *bit* / MUTINY ON THE BOUNTY; *Bill Gage* / WITHOUT REGRET; *Leo Cartwright* / A FEATHER IN HER HAT; *Clancy Lorrimore* / SPLENDOR. **1936:** *Teddy* / ROSE MARIE; *George Brittel* / PALM SPRINGS; *Capt. James Randall* / THE CHARGE OF THE LIGHT BRIGADE. **1937:** *Gerald Preston* / BELOVED ENEMY; *Paul de Brack* / DINNER AT THE RITZ; *Joe Gilling* / WE HAVE OUR MOMENTS. **1938:** *Christopher Leigh* / FOUR MEN AND A PRAYER; *Albert de Regnier* / BLUEBEARD'S EIGHTH WIFE; *Steve Harrington* / THREE BLIND MICE. **1939:** *Lieutenant McCool* / THE REAL GLORY; *Tony Halstead* / ETERNALLY YOURS. **1941:** *Geoffrey Crisp* / THE FIRST OF THE FEW. **1946:** *Dale Williams* / THE PERFECT MARRIAGE. **1947:** *Dr. Anthony Stanton* / THE OTHER LOVE; *Prince Charles* / BONNIE PRINCE CHARLIE. **1948:** *Gen. Sir Roland Dane* / ENCHANTMENT. **1949:** *Eric Phillips* / A KISS IN THE DARK; *Kenneth Marquis* / A KISS FOR CORLISS. **1950:** *Sir Peter Blackeney* / THE ELUSIVE PIMPERNEL; *Jacques Riboudeaux* / THE TOAST OF NEW ORLEANS. **1951:** *Captain Pindenny* / SOLDIERS THREE; *B. G. Bruno* / HAPPY GO LOVELY. **1952:** *Bill Shelby* / THE LADY SAYS NO; *Maj. Valentine Moreland* / APPOINTMENT WITH VENUS. **1954:** *Rex Allerton* / THE LOVE LOTTERY; *Jasper O'Leary* / HAPPY EVER AFTER. **1955:** *Duke of Brampton* / THE KING'S THIEF. **1956:** *Colonel Harris* / THE BIRDS AND THE BEES. **1957:** *Dr. Alan Coles* / OH, MEN! OH, WOMEN!; *Henry Brittingham-Brett* / THE LITTLE HUT; *Godfrey Smith* / MY MAN GODFREY; *Roger Tweakham* / THE SILKEN AFFAIR. **1958:** *Raymond* / BONJOUR TRISTESSE. **1959:** *Miles Doughton* / ASK ANY GIRL; *Chris Walters* / HAPPY ANNIVERSARY. **1962:** *Peter Whitefield* / THE CAPTIVE CITY; *Tom Jordan* / GUNS OF DARKNESS. **1963:** *guest* / THE ROAD TO HONG KONG. **1964:** *Lawrence Jamison* / BEDTIME STORY. **1965:** *Dr. Jason Love* /

WHERE THE SPIES ARE. **1966:** *Lord Dicky Lendale* / LADY L. **1967:** *Philippe de Montfaucon* / EYE OF THE DEVIL. **1968:** *Lieutenant Commander Finchhaven R.N.* / THE EXTRAORDINARY SEAMAN; *Johnathan Kingsley* / THE IMPOSSIBLE YEARS; *Maj. Giles Burnside* / BEFORE WINTER COMES. **1969:** *The Brain* / THE BRAIN. **1970:** *Alex Bolt* / THE STATUE. **1972:** *Charles Dreyer* / KING, QUEEN AND KNAVE. **1974:** *Count Dracula* / OLD DRACULA. **1975:** *Walter Bradbury* / PAPER TIGER. **1976:** *J. W. Osborne* / NO DEPOSIT, NO RETURN. **1977:** *Priory* / CANDLESHOE. **1978:** *Colonel Rice* / DEATH ON THE NILE. **1979:** *Professor Blake* / ESCAPE TO ATHENA; *Ivan (Bernard Drew)* / THE BIGGEST BANK ROBBERY. **1980:** *Chief Inspector Cyril Willis* / ROUGH CUT; *Col. W. H. Grice* / THE SEA WOLVES. **1982:** *Nick* / BETTER LATE THAN NEVER; *Sir Charles Lytton* / TRAIL OF THE PINK PANTHER. **1983:** *Sir Charles Lytton* / CURSE OF THE PINK PANTHER.

NOVAK, KIM

(Marilyn Pauline Novak, 1933–)

Chicago-born model Kim Novak was given a big build-up as a sex queen by Columbia when studio head Harry Cohn decided he needed a replacement for his rebellious reigning sex queen, Rita Hayworth. A lovely green-eyed blonde, Novak, with her beautiful shoulders and back and purring cat-like sexuality, projected too much vulnerability to be a convincing femme fatale. Hers was a standoffish coolness and earthy sensuality, and she was a much better actress than she has been given credit for, with her best performance being in Alfred Hitchcock's VERTIGO. Although not totally pleased with the role of sex symbol, she aided and abetted it as George Lait, a photographer, pointed out: "Kim has a cute habit of getting herself set for a still picture, and at the last moment, she unbuttons one more button on her cleavage."

KEY ROLES

Leona McLane / PUSHOVER, 1954, Columbia, d-Richard Quine.

Plainclothes cop Fred MacMurray is assigned to watch gun moll Novak in the hopes that she will lead him to her boyfriend, who's on the lam with $200,000. Instead she corrupts MacMurray and he kills the fugitive and takes the money for them. But the other cops figure out what happened so the scheme doesn't work.

Madge Owens / PICNIC, 1956, Columbia, d-Joshua Logan.

When wanderer William Holden comes to town over the Fourth of July, he accidentally steals his friend's beautiful girlfriend (Novak) who complains, "I get so tired of just being told I'm pretty." She's more than pretty; she's sensational looking—but a bit short in the brains department.

Molly / THE MAN WITH THE GOLDEN ARM, 1956, United Artists, d-Otto Preminger.

Novak helps professional gambler Frank Sinatra kick his drug habit cold-turkey. Sinatra is married to Eleanor Parker, a bitter, fake cripple. When Parker accidentally reveals she can walk, it looks like Novak is in Sinatra's future.

Jeanne Eagels / JEANNE EAGELS, 1957, Columbia, d-George Sidney.

Novak plays it fairly straight in this show business biopic weeper about a sideshow dancer who becomes a Broadway star but ruins her career because of her drug problems.

Linda English / PAL JOEY, 1957, Columbia, d-George Sidney.

Novak does a nice job singing Rodgers and Hart's "My Funny Valentine" in this story of a big-headed heel (Frank Sinatra) who ends up with nice girl Novak when he dumps rich bitch Rita Hayworth. The latter, because of Novak, goes back on her promise to supply the money to open Sinatra's very own nightclub in return for services rendered.

Madeleine Elster / Judy Barton / VERTIGO, 1958, Paramount, d-Alfred Hitchcock.

In her best performance, Novak portrays the wife of a man who asks retired cop Jimmy Stewart to protect her because he fears she is planning to commit suicide. Stewart, who has a dreadful phobia about heights, falls in love with her but can't prevent her from jumping from the top of a mission church because he can't climb the stairs. Devastated with his loss, he sees a girl who resembles the deceased and tries to remake her in the exact image of his lost love. But, as in most Hitchcock movies, all is not as it seems.

Gillian Holroyd / BELL, BOOK AND CANDLE, 1958, Columbia, d-Richard Quine.

Novak is a modern-day witch living in New York City who decides to make book publisher Jimmy Stewart fall in love with her. But she breaks a cardinal rule of witches and falls in love with him, thus losing all her powers.

Betty Preisser / MIDDLE OF THE NIGHT, 1959, Columbia, d-Delbert Mann.

When elderly widower garment manufacturer Fredric March falls in love with young Novak and makes plans to marry her, his family is outraged.

Moll Flanders / THE AMOROUS ADVENTURES OF MOLL FLANDERS, 1965, Great Britain, Paramount, d-Terence Young.

Although Novak looks the part of the servant girl who keeps losing her virtue to a series of noblemen though she prefers a highwayman, her acting seems wooden.

OTHER ROLES

1953: *model* / THE FRENCH LINE. **1954:** *Janis* / PHFFFT! **1955:** *Kay Greylek* / FIVE AGAINST THE HOUSE. **1956:** *Marjorie Oelrichs* / THE EDDY DUCHIN STORY. **1960:** *Maggie Gault* / STRANGERS WHEN WE MEET; *guest* / PEPE. **1962:** *Cathy* / BOY'S NIGHT OUT; *Carlyle Hardwicke* / THE NOTORIOUS LANDLADY. **1964:** *Mildred Rogers* / OF HUMAN BONDAGE; *Polly the Pistol* / KISS ME, STUPID. **1968:** *Lylah Clare* / THE LEGEND OF LYLAH CLARE. **1969:** *Lyda Kabanov* / THE GREAT BANK ROBBERY. **1973:** *Auriol Pageant* / TALES THAT WITNESS MADNESS. **1977:** *Poker Jenny* / THE WHITE BUFFALO. **1979:** *Helga* / JUST A GIGOLO. **1980:** *Lola Brewster* / THE MIRROR CRACK'D.

OBERON, MERLE

(Estelle M. O. Thompson, 1911–1979)

Born in Bombay, India, Merle Oberon arrived in London and succeeded in fabricating an exotic story of her origins, claiming that she had been born in Tasmania and that her Eurasian mother, who accompanied her, was her maid. She worked as a cafe hostess calling herself Queenie O'Brien before getting bit roles in movies, then was spotted by director-producer Alexander Korda who guided her to stardom and married her. When she arrived in Hollywood Samuel Goldwyn found her looks much too exotic and had her wipe off her makeup and adopt a "natural" look, sloe-eyes unadorned, looking like the British belle she played in several movies. She made several marvelous appearances, notably in WUTHERING

HEIGHTS and THE DARK ANGEL, the latter earning her an Oscar nomination. Earlier she had survived a near-fatal auto accident that was given as the reason for canceling a production of I, CLAUDIUS. Her dark beauty was successfully restored by facial surgery. Oberon, remembering her humble origins, said: "Without security it is difficult for a woman to look or feel beautiful."

KEY ROLES

Anne Boleyn / THE PRIVATE LIFE OF HENRY VIII, 1933, Great Britain, London Films, d-Alexander Korda.

Oberon's stay in the movie isn't long but she looks so lovely and brave when she goes to her execution that audiences sit up and take notice.

Marguerite Blakeney / THE SCARLET PIMPERNEL, 1934, Great Britain, London Films, d-Harold Young.

Oberon can't quite understand why her husband, British aristocrat Leslie Howard, has changed in his feelings for her and why he acts like such a twit. Seems he is actually the famed Scarlet Pimpernel who is saving French aristocrats from the guillotine and who believes that his wife had once betrayed a French relative to save herself. This isn't so, but she does almost deliver her husband to the French quite by accident.

Baroness Genevieve Cassini / FOLIES BERGERE, 1935, 20th Century-Fox, d-Roy Del Ruth.

Parisian millionaire Maurice Chevalier finds it necessary to be in two places at once and hires a Folies Bergère comedian, also Chevalier, to impersonate himself. The fun starts when wife Oberon and mistress Ann Sothern become involved in the deception.

Karen Wright / THESE THREE, 1936, Goldwyn / United Artists, d-William Wyler.

When Oberon inherits a large old house, she and her friend (Miriam Hopkins) convert it into a school for wealthy girls. Oberon falls in love with a local doctor (Joel McCrea) and problems arise when a lying, sadistic child (Bonita Granville) tells her grandmother that there is some three-way hanky-panky going on. This causes the school to close and the near ruination of the lives of all three adults.

Leslie Steel / THE DIVORCE OF LADY X, 1938, Great Britain, London Films, d-Tim Whelan.

Young divorce lawyer Laurence Olivier gives up his hotel room to Oberon. Shortly thereafter a peer employs Olivier to bring suit against his wife for staying with a man in the same hotel on the same night. For reasons of her own, Oberon lets Olivier believe that she is the wife. Later it is revealed that she is a widow and free to marry Olivier.

Catherine Earnshaw / WUTHERING HEIGHTS, 1939, United Artists, d-William Wyler.

As children, Cathy and her brother are raised with a wild gypsy boy and when they grow up, Cathy (Oberon) loves the gypsy Heathcliffe (Laurence Olivier). Her brother (Hugh Williams) hates Heathcliffe. When Oberon shows interest in neighboring squire David Niven and makes plans to marry him, Olivier runs away, only to return years later a very wealthy man who has taken over all of Williams's property and debts. He marries Niven's sister (Geraldine Fitzgerald) and makes her miserable because she is not Oberon. When Olivier learns that Oberon is dying, he hurries to her in time to hear her last words: "Heathcliffe, can you see the gray over there where our castle is? I'll wait for you until you come." Her wait is not long.

Lydia MacMillen / LYDIA, 1941, United Artists, d-Julien Duvivier.

Lydia (Oberon) is described as "like all women—wise and foolish, clever and absurd, good and bad." In flashback, the story tells of this lovely woman who was loved by four men, none of whom she wed because the one she really loved disappeared from her life. She spent her time productively over the next forty years devoting her efforts to helping endow homes for sightless children.

Kitty / THE LODGER, 1945, 20th Century-Fox, d-John Brahm.

In this psychological study of half-crazed Laird Cregar, Oberon is a dancer from a respectable family whose career is nearly cut short by the Jack-the-Ripper-like Cregar. Her savior is Scotland Yard's George Sanders.

George Sand / A SONG TO REMEMBER, 1945, Columbia, d-Charles Vidor.

In this biopic of Frederic Chopin, Franz Liszt introduces Chopin (Cornel Wilde) to feminist novelist George Sand (Oberon) and the two fall in love and have a tempestuous affair.

Empress Josephine / DESIREE, 1954, 20th Century-Fox, d-Henry Koster.

Still lovely, Oberon is not the female lead in this adaptation of a best-selling novel about Napoleon and the girl he didn't marry. That role goes to Jean Simmons who always seems to be around to provide a shoulder for Bonaparte (Marlon Brando) to lean on while Oberon is busy losing him.

OTHER ROLES

1930: *bit* / ALF'S BUTTON. **1931:** *bit* / NEVER TROUBLE TROUBLE; *bit* / FASCINATION. **1932:** *bit* / AREN'T WE ALL?; *bit* / FOR THE LOVE OF MIKE; *bit* / SERVICE FOR LADIES; *girl* / EBB TIDE; *Mrs. Hutchinson* / WEDDING REHEARSAL; *Ysobel d'Aunay* / EN OF TOMORROW. **1934:** *Marquise Yorisaka* / THE BATTLE; *Germaine* / THE BROKEN MELODY; *Antonia* / THE PRIVATE LIFE OF DON JUAN. **1935:** *Kitty Vane* / THE DARK ANGEL. **1936:** *Helen Drummond* / BELOVED ENEMY. **1937:** *Jane Benson* / OVER THE MOON. **1938:** *Mary Smith* / THE COWBOY AND THE LADY. **1939:** *Mrs. Richardson* / THE LION HAS WINGS. **1940:** *Joan Ames* / 'TIL WE MEET AGAIN. **1941:** *Jill Baker* / THAT UNCERTAIN FEELING; *Sue Mayberry* / AFFECTIONATELY YOURS. **1943:** *Marjorie* / FOREVER AND A DAY; *guest* / STAGE DOOR CANTEEN; *Nicole Larsen* / FIRST COMES COURAGE. **1944:** *Leslie Calvin* / DARK WATERS. **1945:** *Karin Touzac* / THIS LOVE OF OURS. **1946:** *Delarai* / A NIGHT IN PARADISE; *Ruby* / TEMPTATION. **1947:** *Cathy* / NIGHT SONG. **1948:** *Lucienne* / BERLIN EXPRESS. **1951:** *Elizabeth Rockwell* / PARDON MY FRENCH. **1952:** *Linda Venning* / 24 HOURS OF A WOMAN'S LIFE. **1954:** *Margaret Fobson* / ALL IS POSSIBLE IN GRANADA. **1954:** *Dorothy Donnelly* / DEEP IN MY HEART. **1956:** *Jessica Warren* / THE PRICE OF FEAR. **1963:** *Katherine Beckman* / OF LOVE AND DESIRE. **1966:** *herself* / THE OSCAR. **1967:** *The Duchess* / HOTEL. **1973:** *Serena Moore* / INTERVAL.

O'BRIEN, EDMOND

(1915–1985)

Heavy-cheeked, pudgy-fingered, hammy Edmond O'Brien played many screen roles with distinction, first in comedies, dramas, and thrillers, followed by leading roles in westerns before making the changeover to a character actor. He worked with Orson Welles's Mercury Theater Group before going to Hollywood with an RKO contract. O'Brien won an Academy Award for THE BAREFOOT CONTESSA and was nominated for SEVEN DAYS IN MAY. He starred in two TV series, "Sam Benedict" and "The Long Hot Summer."

KEY ROLES

Pierre Gringore / THE HUNCHBACK OF NOTRE DAME, 1939, RKO, d-William Dieterle.

O'Brien is the poet who is saved from death at the hands of the king of the Paris beggars when gypsy girl Maureen O'Hara agrees to marry him. Later he tries to use his words to save his bride from being executed as a suspected witch. He is reunited with her when she is pardoned by the king of France after being given sanctuary in the Notre Dame cathedral by the deformed bellringer (Charles Laughton).

Jim Reardon / THE KILLERS, 1946, Universal-International, d-Robert Siodmak.

O'Brien, an insurance investigator, uncovers the reason that Burt Lancaster made no attempt to get away from the two hired killers who had come to kill him.

Hank Fallon (Vic Pardo) / WHITE HEAT, 1949, Warners, d-Raoul Walsh.

O'Brien is a cop whose specialty is going undercover in penitentiaries to get evidence on cons. In this picture he's put in the same cell as violent psychopath James Cagney and is taken along when the latter breaks out.

Frank Bigelow / D.O.A., 1949, Cardinal Pictures, d-Rudolph Mate.

When businessman O'Brien discovers that he has been effectively murdered by a slow-acting poison, he uses the last few days of his life to find his own murderer, whom he kills.

Harry Graham / THE BIGAMIST, 1953, Independent Filmmakers, d-Ida Lupino.

O'Brien is a traveling salesman married to Joan Fontaine. While in San Francisco he picks up Ida Lupino and the next thing you know, she's carrying his baby. So he marries her without bothering to divorce Fontaine. Everything about his double life eventually unfolds and he's put on trial for bigamy with the judge saying he will render his decision next week. The picture ends leaving the audience to decide his fate.

Oscar Muldoon / THE BAREFOOT CONTESSA, 1954, United Artists, d-Joseph L. Mankiewicz.

O'Brien received an Oscar for telling off Howard Hughes-like producer Warren Stevens: "For four years, I've invited the guests and bought the favors and provided the entertainment and cleaned up the dirt and paid off the cops and paid off the guests, and now it's 'Good night, ladies, the party's over—I've had a lovely evening but I must be going.'" Up to that point he had been a high-paid public relations man and general errand boy for a man who had plans to make a major star of a barefooted Spanish dancer (Ava Gardner).

Winston Smith / 1984, 1956, Holiday, d-Michael Anderson.

Europe has become the fascist state of Oceana and O'Brien's job in the Ministry of Truth is to rewrite newspaper articles of the past so that they are in keeping with the prevailing views of unseen leaders. Love and sex are forbidden and, when he dares fall in love with Jan Sterling, both are captured and brainwashed.

The Voice / THE THIRD VOICE, 1960, 20th Century-Fox, d-Hubert Cornfield.

Laraine Day, the secretary / mistress of a wealthy American, is spurned by him when he decides to get married. So she arranges with O'Brien to kill the man and have O'Brien take his place until they get their hands on $250,000 of the dead man's money.

Sen. Raymond Clark / SEVEN DAYS IN MAY, 1964, Seven Arts, d-John Frankenheimer.

O'Brien is a boozy U.S. senator who has to keep dry long enough to help the president (Fredric March) deal with a military takeover of the country by Burt Lancaster and others in the joint chiefs of staff. O'Brien's performance rated an Academy Award nomination.

OTHER ROLES

1936: *prisoner* / PRISON BREAK. **1941:** *Stephen Herrick* / A GIRL, A GUY AND A GOB; *Bill Burke* / PARACHUTE BATTALION; *Red Reddy* / OBLIGING YOUNG LADY. **1942:** *Pennant* / POWDER TOWN. **1943:** *Tom Holliday* / THE AMAZING MRS. HOLLIDAY. **1944:** *Irving Miller* / WINGED VICTORY. **1947:** *Bob Regan* / THE WEB. **1948:** *Ben Hubbard* / ANOTHER PART OF THE FOREST; *Bill Friend* / A DOUBLE LIFE; *Lt. Tom Farrington* / FOR THE LOVE OF MARY; *Maj. Ed Hardin* / FIGHTER SQUADRON; *David Douglas* / AN ACT OF MURDER. **1950:** *Steve Connolly* / BACKFIRE; *Mal Granger* / 711 OCEAN DRIVE; *Jimmie Stevens* / THE ADMIRAL WAS A LADY; *Dan Purvis* / BETWEEN MIDNIGHT AND DAWN; *Dunn Jeffers* / THE REDHEAD AND THE COWBOY. **1951:** *John Vickers* / WARPATH; *Lefty Farrell* / TWO OF A KIND; *Larkin Moffatt* / SILVER CITY. **1952:** *John Conroy* / THE TURNING POINT; *guest* / THE GREATEST SHOW ON EARTH; *Jim Vesser* / THE DENVER AND THE RIO GRANDE. **1953:** *Ray Collins* / THE HITCH-HIKER; *Casca* / JULIUS CAESAR; *Ben Anthony* / COW COUNTRY; *Steve Rawley* / MAN IN THE DARK; *Capt. Matt Rearden* / CHINA VENTURE. **1954:** *Dr. Dan Maynard* / THE SHANGHAI STORY; *Barney Nolan* / SHIELD FOR MURDER. **1955:** *Fran McCarg* / PETE KELLY'S BLUES. **1956:** *Taggart* / A CRY IN THE NIGHT; *Colonel Timmer* / D-DAY, THE SIXTH OF JUNE; *Lt. Col. Frank Wasnick* / THE RACK; *Marty Murdock* / THE GIRL CAN'T HELP IT. **1957:** *Jagger* / THE BIG LAND. **1958:** *David Carson* / THE WORLD WAS HIS JURY; *Joseph Sharkey* / SING, BOY, SING. **1959:** *Stevenson* / UP PERISCOPE; *2nd Engineer Walsh* / THE LAST VOYAGE. **1961:** *Captain Glover* / THE GREAT IMPOSTOR. **1962:** *Tom Gaddis* / BIRDMAN OF ALCATRAZ; *McClosky* / MOON PILOT; *Gen. Raymond D. Barton* / THE LONGEST DAY. **1964:** *Col. Theron Pardee* / RIO CONCHOS. **1965:** *Oscar Stewart* / SYLVIA; *Chuck Dederich* / SYNANON. **1966:** *General Carter* / FANTASTIC VOYAGE. **1967:** *Ricco Barone* / THE VISCOUNT. **1969:** *Sykes* / THE WILD BUNCH; *Osborn Tremain* / THE LOVE GOD? **1974:** *Uncle Frank Kelly* / 99 AND 44 / 100% DEAD.

O'BRIEN, MARGARET

(Angela Maxine O'Brien, 1937–)

Margaret O'Brien was very possibly the best actress among all the child stars who ever appeared in movies. She wasn't as cute as Shirley Temple but dark-haired moppet O'Brien had a greater ability to sway the emotions of an audience. She was not a happy little trooper. Her characters seemed to have the burdens of the world on their little shoulders and even though she tended to be something of a whiner, she was really acting, not just appearing as a child. After making a movie with her, Lionel Barrymore observed, "If that child had been born in the Middle Ages, she'd have been burned as a witch." O'Brien certainly could turn on the tears when called on to do so. Seeking instructions, she once asked a director, "When I cry, do you want the tears to run all the way down, or should I stop them halfway down?" Unfortunately she was unable to make a successful transition to adult roles in films and since 1951 has worked mostly on stage and TV.

KEY ROLES

Margaret White / JOURNEY FOR MARGARET, 1942, MGM, d-W. S. Van Dyke.

Five-year-old O'Brien captured the hearts of audiences with her touching performance as an orphan of the London Blitz who is adopted and eventually brought to the United States by war correspondent Robert Young. The story is based on fact.

Alpha / LOST ANGEL, 1943, MGM, d-Roy Rowland.

In this one O'Brien is a foundling raised by scientists who are trying to make a child prodigy of her. Kindly reporter James Craig comes along, adopts her, and shows her what a normal childhood is like.

Lady Jessica de Canterville / THE CANTERVILLE GHOST, 1944, MGM, d-Jules Dassin.

O'Brien steals the picture from that old ham Charles Laughton. He portrays a 300-year-old ghost who needs a descendant to prove he's not a coward so he can get some rest. O'Brien comes up with just the man (Robert Young).

"Tootie" Smith / MEET ME IN ST. LOUIS, 1944, MGM, d-Vincente Minnelli.

As good as she is, Judy Garland has a lot of competition from O'Brien for acting honors in this wholesome story of a nice family in St. Louis at the turn of the century during the World's Fair. O'Brien is very appealing singing and dancing with Garland to "Under the Bamboo Tree."

Selma Jacobson / OUR VINES HAVE TENDER GRAPES, 1945, MGM, d-Roy Rowland.

Not much story here, but the charming incidents in a Wisconsin Norwegian farming family make for fine entertainment as a wise papa (Edward G. Robinson) dotes on his sweet little girl (O'Brien). When he wakes her up one night to take her to the fair grounds to give her a ride on an elephant, after having punished her by giving away her treasured roller skates, Robinson shows the kind of man he really is.

Beth March / LITTLE WOMEN, 1949, MGM, d-Mervyn LeRoy.

The film is too sticky sweet, but O'Brien proved she could still pull tears from audiences in this remake of Louisa May Alcott's classic story of four sisters growing up at the time of the U. S. Civil War. O'Brien gets to die, something all actresses love to do on screen.

Clarabel Tilbee / HELLER IN PINK TIGHTS, 1960, Paramount, d-George Cukor.

In her best film role as an adult, O'Brien adds some humorous support as a member of a dramatic company led by Anthony Quinn and Sophia Loren, that is touring the West in the 1880s.

OTHER ROLES

1941: *bit* / BABES ON BROADWAY. **1943:** *Margaret* / DR. GILLESPIE'S CRIMINAL CASE; *guest* / THOUSANDS CHEER; *Irene Curie at age five* / MADAME CURIE. **1944:** *Adele Varens* / JANE EYRE; *Mike* / MUSIC FOR MILLIONS. **1946:** *Emmy* / BAD BASCOMB; *Sheila O'Monahan* / THREE WISE FOOLS. **1947:** *Meg Merlin* / THE UNFINISHED DANCE; *Flavia Mills* / TENTH AVENUE ANGEL. **1948:** *Midge* / BIG CITY. **1949:** *Mary Lennox* / THE SECRET GARDEN. **1951:** *Betty Foster* / HER FIRST ROMANCE. **1956:** *Betty Foster* / GLORY. **1981:** *Hazel Johnson* / AMY.

O'BRIEN, PAT

(William P. O'Brien, 1899–1983)

Round-faced, solidly-built Pat O'Brien was just as Irish as Paddy's pig and he made the most of it in his long career as there was always the sweet hint of the lilting, soft Irish brogue in his voice. O'Brien chose acting instead of becoming a priest, but he was able to make up for resisting his vocation by appearing as the good Father in several movies. Making his Broadway debut in 1925 after serving in the navy during World War I, O'Brien became a well-known star in his film debut in THE FRONT PAGE. From then on he found himself in great demand as priests, fast-talking reporters, happy-go-lucky adventurers, and an occasional con man. By the 1940s he had moved into character roles. In the 1970s he appeared in numerous made-for-TV movies including THE OVER-THE-HILL GANG (1969), WELCOME HOME, JOHNNY BRISTOL (1971), THE ADVENTURES OF NICK CARTER and KISS ME, KILL ME (1976), and SCOUT'S HONOR (1980).

KEY ROLES

Hildy Johnson / THE FRONT PAGE, 1931, United Artists, d-Lewis Milestone.

O'Brien is a star reporter who is quitting the racket to get married. His editor (Adolphe Menjou) cons him into covering an execution as his last story. The condemned, an innocent man, is a political pawn. When the prisoner escapes, O'Brien helps hide him until his pardon comes through. It's a fast-paced, fast-talking black comedy.

Jack Lee / CEILING ZERO, 1935, Warners, d-Howard Hawks.

O'Brien plays the level-headed chief pilot of a civil aviation company who can't quite get his best pilot (Jimmy Cagney) to behave himself. The latter can't seem to play by the rules that O'Brien lays down and it costs the life of another pilot.

Click Wiley / PAGE MISS GLORY, 1935, Warners, d-Mervyn LeRoy.

Promoter O'Brien sends a composite photograph of a girl to a beauty contest, then has to find someone to match the picture when his entry wins. He comes up with Marion Davies. Davies had just moved to the Warners studio with the financial backing of William Randolph Hearst.

Patrick O'Malley / THE GREAT O'MALLEY, 1937, Warners, d-William Dieterle.

O'Brien is a tough Irish cop who has an ongoing feud with Humphrey Bogart, a man who experiences many catastrophes. O'Brien helps out because he's interested in Bogart's sister (Ann Sheridan).

Capt. Stephen Jameson / SAN QUENTIN, 1937, Warners, d-Lloyd Bacon.

O'Brien is a humane ex-army officer who becomes yard captain of San Quentin penitentiary. He takes an interest in con Humphrey Bogart because of an interest in Bogart's sister, nightclub singer Ann Sheridan. Wait a minute! Doesn't that sound familiar?

Fr. Jerry Connolly / ANGELS WITH DIRTY FACES, 1939, Warners, d-Ray Enright.

O'Brien convinces his boyhood friend (Jimmy Cagney) to go to the electric chair a coward in order to kill the hero worship of a group of young punks for the condemned mobster. When O'Brien and Cagney were kids they pulled off a robbery and were chased; O'Brien got away and Cagney was caught and sent to reform school. O'Brien became a priest and Cagney went through a series of crimes and prisons. At the end, talking to the boys, O'Brien tells them, "It's true boys and every word of it. He died like they said. All right, fellas, let's go and say a prayer for a boy who couldn't run as fast as I could."

Father Duffy / THE FIGHTING 69TH, 1940, Warners, d-William Keighley.

In this patriotic flag waver, O'Brien is the chaplain for the famous World War I Irish regiment. One of his hardest cases is an obnoxiously cocky young Irishman (James Cagney) whose cowardice in battle results in the death of several others. He is sentenced to death but, with a little encouragement from the good father, he goes to his death as a hero in battle.

Knute Rockne / KNUTE ROCKNE, ALL AMERICAN, 1940, Warners, d-Lloyd Bacon.

O'Brien was a big hit as the legendary University of Notre Dame football coach, even though he plays the Norwegian as an Irishman—no one seemed to mind. He is very effective giving the rousing half-time pep talks for which Rockne was famous.

Steve Case / TORRID ZONE, 1940, Warners, d-William Keighley.

O'Brien acts for the eighth time with friend Jimmy Cagney (they didn't appear together again until 1981 in RAGTIME) and plays a plantation owner somewhere in Central America with Cagney as his fiery foreman. The romantic interest is supplied by Ann Sheridan, who by then was affectionately known as "The Oomph Girl."

Frank Cavanaugh / THE IRON MAJOR, 1943, RKO, d-Ray Enright.

If the story of one football coach was a hit, what might one expect of a second story in which the coach is not only a winner at places like Dartmouth, Boston College, and Fordham, but is also a World War I hero? Not much beyond O'Brien's fine characterization of the man, unfortunately.

Father Dunne / FIGHTING FATHER DUNNE, 1948, RKO, d-Ted Tetzlaff.

O'Brien, with his collar turned once more, portrays a priest who in the early part of the 20th century struggles to found a home for underprivileged St. Louis newsboys.

John Gorman / THE LAST HURRAH, 1958, Columbia, d-John Ford.

O'Brien is the right-hand man to the Irish mayor of Boston (Spencer Tracy). Audiences are treated to a slew of fine old actors in bravado career curtain calls as Tracy and O'Brien go through one last political campaign. The other delightful old charmers include Basil Rathbone, Edward Brophy, Donald Crisp, James Gleason, John Carradine, Ricardo Cortez, Frank McHugh, and Wallace Ford. Holding up the distaff side is Jane Darwell, a most appealing mourner at an Irish wake.

OTHER ROLES

1921: *bit* / SHADOWS OF THE WEST. **1922:** *bit* / DETERMINATION. **1924:** *bit* / MARRY IN HASTE. **1929:** *Jim Kane* / THE FRECKLED RASCAL; *Jim Thayer* / FURY OF THE WILD. **1931:** *Steve* / CONSOLATION MARRIAGE; *Sport* / FLYING HIGH; *Conroy* / HONOR AMONG LOVERS; *Peter Shea* / PERSONAL MAID. **1932:** *Duke Talbot* / AIR MAIL; *Matt* / AMERICAN MADNESS; *Sam Bradshaw* / FINAL EDITION; *Kelly* / HELL'S HOUSE; *Jimmy Reed* / HOLLYWOOD SPEAKS; *Barney Slaney* / LAUGHTER IN HELL; *Waddell* / SCANDAL FOR SALE; *Frank Deane* / THE STRANGE CASE OF CLARA DEANE; *Jimmy* / VIRTUE. **1933:** *Brogan* / BOMBSHELL; *Butch Saunders* / BUREAU OF MISSING PERSONS; *Coach Gore* / COLLEGE COACH; *Matt Brennan* / DESTINATION UNKNOWN; *Andy Terrell* / THE WORLD GONE MAD. **1934:** *Ben Lear* / FLAMING GOLD; *Sergeant Thornhill* / FLIRTATION WALK; *Charley Lang* / GAMBLING LADY; *Biff Martin* / HERE COMES THE NAVY; *Spot Cash Cutler* / I SELL ANYTHING; *Terry* / I'VE GOT YOUR NUMBER; *Ritzy McCarthy* / THE PERSONALITY KID; *Rush Blake* / TWENTY MILLION SWEETHEARTS. **1935:** *Lt. William Brannigan* / DEVIL DOGS OF THE AIR; *Larry MacArthur* / IN CALIENTE; *Pat O'Hara* / THE IRISH IN US; *Stephen Chase* / OIL FOR THE LAMPS OF CHINA; *Babe Rivers* / OUTLAWED GUNS; *Al McGillevray* / STARS OVER BROADWAY. **1936:** *Dave Logan* / CHINA CLIPPER; *Dr. William Kennicott* / I MARRIED A DOCTOR; *Lee Laird* / PUBLIC ENEMY'S WIFE. **1937:** *Bill Morgan* / BACK IN CIRCULATION; *Red Blayd* / SLIM; *Butch Rogers* / SUBMARINE D-1. **1938:** *Frazier* / BAR 20 JUSTICE; *Bill Landin* / WOMEN ARE LIKE THAT. **1939:** *J. C. Benson* / BOY MEETS GIRL; *Roy Cadwick* / COWBOY FROM BROOKLYN; *John Quinn* / GARDEN OF THE MOON; *Joe Greet* / INDIANAPOLIS SPEEDWAY; *Bill Murphy* / THE KID FROM KOKOMO; *Dan O'Farrell* / THE NIGHT OF NIGHTS; *Thomas "Breezy" Elliott* / OFF THE RECORD. **1940:** *Warden Long* / CASTLE ON THE HUDSON; *Mike Farrough* / ESCAPE TO GLORY; *Hap O'Connor* / FLOWING GOLD; *John Webb* / SLIGHTLY HONORABLE; *Steve Burke* / 'TIL WE MEET AGAIN. **1942:** *Dan McCorn* / BROADWAY; *Sam Doyle* / FLIGHT LIEUTENANT; *Mallory* / THE NAVY COMES THROUGH; *Tim Reardon* / TWO YANKS IN TRINIDAD. **1943:** *Maj. Chick Davis* / BOMBARDIER; *Martin Carter* / HIS BUTLER'S SISTER. **1944:** *Maj. Steve Lockhard* / MARINE RAIDERS; *Sam Gallagher* / SECRET COMMAND. **1945:** *Michael Malone* / HAVING WONDERFUL CRIME; *Speed* / MAN ALIVE. **1946:** *George Steele* / CRACK-UP; *Patrick Nevil* / PERILOUS HOLIDAY. **1947:** *Dan* / RIFFRAFF. **1948:** *Gramp* / THE BOY WITH GREEN HAIR. **1949:** *Farley* / A DANGEROUS PROFESSION. **1950:** *Father O'Hara* / THE FIREBALL; *Martin Martin* / JOHNNY ONE-EYE. **1951:** *James Regan* / CRIMINAL LAWYER; *Vinnie Ricks* / THE PEOPLE AGAINST O'HARA. **1952:** *Lieutenant Commander Hale* / OKINAWA. **1954:** *Ernest "Texas" Conway* / JUBILEE TRAIL; *Frank Wallace* / RING OF FEAR. **1955:** *Gus Linden* / INSIDE DETROIT. **1957:** *Bart Crosbie* / KILL ME TOMORROW. **1959:** *Mulligan* / SOME LIKE IT HOT. **1965:** *Judge Murcott* / TOWN TAMER. **1970:** *guest* / THE PHYNX. **1978:** *Ben Dawson* / THE END. **1981:** *Delmas* / RAGTIME.

O'CONNOR, DONALD

(1925–)

The son of circus performers, Donald O'Connor moved into vaudeville with a family act, making him one of the last movie stars with vaudeville experience. O'Connor had leading roles in Universal movies with co-star Peggy Ryan. His other major co-star was Francis the talking mule in a series of films during the 1950s. Interspersed with these comedies, O'Connor worked in supporting roles in some of the biggest Hollywood musicals of the period, most notably his absolutely outstanding portrayal in SINGIN' IN THE RAIN. When the era of film musicals ended in the 1950s, he concentrated on a new career as a composer with his work, "Reflections d'un Comique," being performed under his direction by the Los Angeles Philharmonic Orchestra in 1956.

KEY ROLES

Mike Beebe / SING, YOU SINNERS, 1938, Paramount, d-Wesley Ruggles.

Young O'Connor holds his own with Fred MacMurray and Bing Crosby, who portray his older brothers and show-business partners in this minor musical.

Tom Sawyer / TOM SAWYER, DETECTIVE, 1938, Paramount, d-Louis King.

The title just about says it all. O'Connor as Tom Sawyer works with Billy Cook as Huckleberry Finn to solve a murder involving twin brothers.

Donald / MR. BIG, 1943, Universal, d-Charles W. Lamont.

O'Connor, Gloria Jean, and Peggy Ryan are among the youngsters who plan a jive show when the headmistress of their dramatic school is called away. There's not much going on except the spotlighting of these three talented kids. They perform to a number of oldies such as "Moonlight and Roses."

Donald Corrigan / CHIP OFF THE OLD BLOCK, 1944, Universal, d-Charles W. Lamont.

O'Connor once more carries the lead in a minor musical featuring young Universal stars, this time including Peggy Ryan and Ann Blyth. The very minor plot has O'Connor chasing Blyth while being pursued by Ryan. O'Connor's numbers include "Is It Good or Is It Bad?," "Mighty Nice to Have Met You," and "I Gotta Give My Feet a Break."

Pat Donahue, Jr. / PATRICK THE GREAT, 1945, Universal, d-Frank Ryan.

Peggy Ryan is once again teamed with O'Connor in this musical story of the conflict between O'Connor and his actor father when the former is offered a part in a Broadway show that the latter had sought. Songs include "For the First Time," "The Cubacha," and "When You Bump into Someone You Know."

Peter Stirling / FRANCIS, 1950, Universal-International, d-Arthur Lubin.

O'Connor returned five more times to the role of the only person to whom the talking mule, Francis, talks. O'Connor does a pretty good job of making it seem almost feasible. The stories in the series are simple-minded but agreeable and, taken for what they are, not bad.

Cosmo Brown / SINGIN' IN THE RAIN, 1952, MGM, d-Gene Kelly and Stanley Donen.

In what is arguably the best original Hollywood musical ever made, O'Connor gives without doubt his best performance playing silent screen star Gene Kelly's best friend and gofer. With his rendition of the Arthur Freed and Nacio Herb Brown number "Make 'Em Laugh," O'Connor created a classic which may very well be the best comical singing and dancing number ever seen on the screen.

Kenneth / CALL ME MADAM, 1953, 20th Century-Fox, d-Walter Lang.

O'Connor is the press attache to Ethel Merman, the Washington hostess who is made ambassador to Lichtenberg. There he falls for a princess (Vera-Ellen) and in the big hit "You're Just in Love" by Irving Berlin, O'Connor and Merman diagnose his ailment. He also sings "It's a Lovely Day Today."

Tim Donahue / THERE'S NO BUSINESS LIKE SHOW BUSINESS, 1954, 20th Century-Fox, d-Walter Lang.

O'Connor is the youngest of a family of vaudevillians headed up by Ethel Merman and Dan Dailey. When he gets too big for his britches, the family act breaks up but all are back together again at the end to sing Irving Berlin's title number.

Buster Keaton / THE BUSTER KEATON STORY, 1957, Paramount, d-Sidney Sheldon.

O'Connor's performance as the great silent screen comedian is admirable but the screenplay doesn't do justice to Keaton's career.

OTHER ROLES

1937: *bit* / MELODY FOR TWO. **1938:** *Butch Baker* / SONS OF THE LEGION; *Pat Falconer* / MEN WITH WINGS. **1939:** *Ted Streaver* / UNMARRIED; *Small Fry* / DEATH OF A CHAMPION; *Sticky Boone* / MILLION DOLLAR LEGS; *Butch Smiley* / NIGHT WORK; *Phil Dolan* / ON YOUR TOES; *young Beau Geste* / BEAU GESTE. **1942:** *Donny* / PRIVATE BUCKAROO; *Don* / GIVE OUT, SISTERS; *Jimmy Arnold* / GET HEP TO LOVE; *Frankie* / WHEN JOHNNIE COMES MARCHING HOME; *Tommy* / WHAT'S COOKIN'? **1943:** *Ricky* / IT COMES UP LOVE; *Don Warren* / TOP MAN. **1944:** *Jimmy Plum* / THIS IS THE LIFE; *guest* / FOLLOW THE BOYS; *Jimmy Monahan* / THE MERRY MONAHANS; *guest* / BOWERY TO BROADWAY. **1947:** *Charlie Read* / SOMETHING IN THE WIND. **1948:** *Milton Haskins* / ARE YOU WITH IT?; *Wilbur McMurty* / FEUDIN', FUSSIN' AND A-FIGHTIN'. **1949:** *William Waldo Winfield* / YES SIR, THAT'S MY BABY. **1950:** *Edward Timmons* / CURTAIN CALL AT CACTUS CREEK; *Roger Bradley* / THE MILKMAN; *Dave Crandall* / DOUBLE CROSSBONES. **1951:** *Peter Stirling* / FRANCIS GOES TO THE RACES. **1952:** *Peter Stirling* / FRANCIS GOES TO WEST POINT. **1953:** *Melvin Hoover* / I LOVE MELVIN; *Peter Stirling* / FRANCIS COVERS BIG TOWN; *Jigger Millard* / WALKING MY BABY BACK HOME. **1954:** *Peter Stirling* / FRANCIS JOINS THE WACS. **1955:** *Peter Stirling* / FRANCIS IN THE NAVY. **1956:** *Ted Adams* / ANYTHING GOES. **1961:** *Murray Prince* / CRY FOR HAPPY; *Aladdin* / THE WONDERS OF ALADDIN. **1974:** *Host* / THAT'S ENTERTAINMENT! **1981:** *dance teacher* / RAGTIME. **1982:** *cameo* / PANDEMONIUM.

O'HARA, MAUREEN

(Maureen FitzSimons, 1920–)

Beautiful, red-headed, Irish colleen Maureen O'Hara generally portrayed fiery women who stood up to their heroes through most of the film but, to the disgust of feminists, surrendered to him by the final frame. She appeared to believe the old saying: "Surrender for a woman is not defeat," but some might think John Wayne dragging her across the countryside in THE QUIET MAN or giving her a stiff spanking in MCLINTOCK was not the proper way to win a woman's heart, even though O'Hara seemed to thrive on such rough treatment. This spitfire had a brief career on the stage with Dublin's Abbey Players before moving to London and making her film debut in KICKING THE MOON AROUND in 1938. A Hollywood contract followed with 20th Century-Fox in 1939. Besides the John Ford westerns with Wayne, O'Hara also held her own in "easterns" and swash buckling adventure tales. Since the 1960s she made numerous TV appearances.

KEY ROLES

Esmerelda / THE HUNCHBACK OF NOTRE DAME, 1939, RKO, d-William Dieterle.

O'Hara is the gypsy girl who befriends the hunchback of Notre Dame (Charles Laughton), when the poor, dumb, deformed unfortunate is being publicly and unfairly punished. When later she is sentenced to death as a witch, he swings down from the cathedral and demands sanctuary for her within the church. When an army of beggers storms the cathedral to rescue her, the hunchback, misunderstanding their motives, pours hot metal and boulders down on them. She is ultimately saved and returned to her poet husband.

Angharad Morgan / HOW GREEN WAS MY VALLEY, 1941, 20th Century-Fox, d-John Ford.

Being the only daughter in the Morgan family, O'Hara shares with her mother the burden of caring for the many men of the mining family. She sets her cap for the new minister (Walter Pidgeon) but the marriage of the two is not to be and instead she weds the son of a mine owner.

Margaret Denby / THE BLACK SWAN, 1942, 20th Century-Fox, d-Henry King.

O'Hara is the beautiful daughter of the former governor of Jamaica who has been replaced by pirate Henry

Morgan, when he is given the task of routing his former associates. One of his staunchest allies (Tyrone Power) falls in love with O'Hara and decides to reform.

Julie / SENTIMENTAL JOURNEY, 1946, 20th Century-Fox, d-Walter Lang.

O'Hara is an actress married to a Broadway producer and they are unable to have a child. She finds a little orphan and they adopt her. Shortly after O'Hara dies of a heart attack and, at first, her husband can't relate to the child. But the youngster finally succeeds in filling the void in his life.

Doris Walker / MIRACLE ON 34TH STREET, 1947, 20th Century-Fox, d-George Seaton.

In this Christmas classic, O'Hara is an advertising executive with Macy's Department Store, who hires nice old Edmund Gwenn to play Santa Claus in the annual Thanksgiving Day Parade down 5th Avenue. He calls himself Kris Kringle and believes himself to be Santa Claus. But O'Hara is a hard-nosed woman who teaches her young daughter (Natalie Wood) to believe only in what she can see and understand. Later Gwenn is put on trial in a sanity hearing and the new love in O'Hara's life (John Payne) gets the court to declare Gwenn the real Santa Claus.

Tacey / SITTING PRETTY, 1948, 20th Century-Fox, d-Walter Lang.

O'Hara and her husband (Robert Young) employ self-declared genius Clifton Webb to play nanny to their three unruly children. He treats the parents, the children, and everyone else with the contempt he insists they deserve.

Kathleen Yorke / RIO GRANDE, 1950, Republic, d-John Ford.

O'Hara portrays the estranged wife of cavalry commander John Wayne. She shows up at his camp on the Mexican border in 1880 when their son, whom Wayne hasn't seen for years, joins his unit.

Mary Kate Danaher / THE QUIET MAN, 1952, Republic, d-John Ford.

When ex-boxer John Wayne goes back to his boyhood Irish home after having killed a man in the ring, he swears he will never fight again. This makes things rough for him when he falls in love with and marries O'Hara, only to find that she's ashamed of him because he won't fight her bullying brother (Victor McLaglen) who refuses to give her the dowry she believes she deserves. In the end, Wayne boots her and pulls her across the country before a big fight with McLaglen. She seems to love it.

Lady Godiva / LADY GODIVA, 1955, Universal-International, d-Arthur Lubin.

What more can be said? O'Hara portrays the wife of a Norman lord and rides naked through Coventry to prove her loyalty to her Saxon people who her husband is mistreating.

Beatrice Stevens / OUR MAN IN HAVANA, 1959, Great Britain, Columbia, d-Carol Reed.

O'Hara falls for vacuum cleaner salesman Alec Guinness who is recruited to spy for the British in Cuba. He manufactures phony reports, but this doesn't prevent him and O'Hara from getting in trouble with the local authorities.

Katherine McLintock / MCLINTOCK! 1963, United Artists, d-Andrew V. McLaglen.

In a western version of "The Taming of the Shrew," O'Hara gives husband John Wayne a bad time throughout the film and in the end he promises her a spanking. He chases her all over town to the cheers of everyone in the area, finally catches her, turns her over his knee, and paddles away. She becomes a docile loving wife once again. Do you believe it?

OTHER ROLES

1938: *secretary* / KICKING THE MOON AROUND; *Eileen O'Shea* / MY IRISH MOLLY. **1939:** *Mary Yelland* / JAMAICA INN. **1940:** *Sidney Fairchild* / A BILL OF DIVORCEMENT; *Judy* / DANCE, GIRL, DANCE. **1941:** *Lolita* / THEY MET IN ARGENTINA. **1942:** *2nd Lt. Mary Carter* / TO THE SHORES OF TRIPOLI; *Carolyn Bainbridge* / TEN GENTLEMEN FROM WEST POINT. **1943:** *Valentine* / THE IMMORTAL SERGEANT; *Louise Martin* / THIS LAND IS MINE; *Toni Donne* / THE FALLEN SPARROW. **1944:** *Louise Cody* / BUFFALO BILL. **1945:** *Francisca* / THE SPANISH MAIN. **1946:** *Katherine Hilliard* / DO YOU LOVE ME? **1947:** *Shireen* / SINBAD THE SAILOR; *Leslie Hale* / THE HOMESTRETCH; *Odalie D'Arceneaux* / THE FOXES OF HARROW. **1949:** *Adelaide Culver* / BRITANNIA MEWS; *Marian Washburn* / A WOMAN'S SECRET; *Elizabeth Cooper* / FATHER WAS A FULLBACK; *Princess Marjan* / BAGDAD. **1950:** *Katie* / COMANCHE TERRITORY; *Countess D'Arneau* / TRIPOLI. **1951:** *Princess Tanya* / FLAME OF ARABY. **1952:** *Claire* / AT SWORD'S POINT; *Dell McGuire* / KANGAROO; *Spitfire Stevens* / AGAINST ALL FLAGS; *Kate Maxwell* / THE REDHEAD FROM WYOMING. **1953:** *Elaine Corwin* / WAR ARROW. **1954:** *Joanna Dana* / FIRE OVER AFRICA. **1955:** *Mary O'Donnell* / THE LONG GRAY LINE; *Karen Harrison* / THE MAGNIFICENT MATADOR. **1956:** *Sylvia Merrill* / LISBON; *Joan Madison* / EVERYTHING BUT THE TRUTH. **1957:** *Min Wead* / THE WINGS OF EAGLES. **1961:** *Maggie McKendrick* / THE PARENT TRAP; *Kit Tilden* / THE DEADLY COMPANIONS. **1962:** *Peggy Hobbs* / MR. HOBBS TAKES A VACATION. **1963:** *Olivia Spencer* / SPENCER'S MOUNTAIN. **1965:** *Moira* / THE BATTLE OF THE VILLA FIORITA. **1966:** *Martha Evans* / THE RARE BREED. **1970:** *Elsie Waltz* / HOW DO I LOVE THEE? **1971:** *Martha McCandles* / BIG JAKE.

OLIVIER, SIR LAURENCE

(1907–1989)

Sir Laurence Olivier is generally regarded as the finest British actor of his generation. His career has spanned 70 years with his first love always being the stage. His first appearance on the boards was as Brutus in "Julius Caesar" in 1916. Dark, handsome, and very dashing, Olivier has won two special Oscars: one in 1944 for HENRY V and one in 1979 for career achievement. He won the Academy Award for HAMLET in 1948 and was nominated for awards for WUTHERING HEIGHTS, REBECCA, HENRY V, RICHARD III, THE ENTERTAINER, OTHELLO, SLEUTH, MARATHON MAN, and THE BOYS FROM BRAZIL. Knighted in 1947, Olivier became Lord Olivier in 1970. His three wives, all actresses, have been Jill Esmond, Vivien Leigh, and, since 1961, Joan Plowright. He has always been more highly praised for his stage work than his film work and in the last part of his film career he has substituted masks for acting in the various films in which he has appeared. Even though some of the masks have been interesting, the movies seldom were. Unlike his early days in movies his appearances lately have been as a great star rather than as an actor.

KEY ROLES

Orlando / AS YOU LIKE IT, 1936, Great Britain, Inter-Allied, d-Paul Czinner.

Elizabeth Bergner, looking good in men's clothes, is Rosalind, the daughter of a banished duke. She is in love with Orlando, played in a frenetic fashion by Olivier in this version of Shakespeare's play. The movie reviews were decidedly mixed.

Michael Ingolby / FIRE OVER ENGLAND, 1936, Great Britain, Pendennis / Mayflower, d-William K. Howard.
Olivier is very dashing as a man who infiltrates the Spanish court after his father has been burnt to death by the Inquisition. He takes the plans of the Spanish Armada to England and Queen Elizabeth.

Everard Logan / THE DIVORCE OF LADY X, 1938, Great Britain, London Films, d-Tim Whelan.
Olivier falls for lovely Merle Oberon when she lets him believe that she is the wife of a client who has hired Olivier to represent him in divorce proceedings. The man's complaint is that his wife spent the night in some unknown man's hotel room. Oberon had spent that night in that hotel in Olivier's room.

Heathcliffe / WUTHERING HEIGHTS, 1939, United Artists, d-William Wyler.
Olivier, grown from a gypsy lad to a man who has loved Merle Oberon all his life, loses her in life but is reunited with her in death. While still alive she sums up her feelings for him: "He's sunk so low—he seems to take pleasure in being mean and brutal—and yet he's more myself than I am. Whatever our souls are made of, his and mine are the same...my one thought in living is Heathcliffe. I am Heathcliffe. Everything he has suffered, I have suffered. The little happiness he's ever known, I had too. Oh, Ellen, if everything in the world died and Heathcliffe remained, life would still be full for me."

Maxim De Winter / REBECCA, 1940, Selznick International / United Artists, d-Alfred Hitchcock.
Olivier brings his new young bride to Manderley, his estate in Cornwall, where her life is made miserable by his moody indifference and the housekeeper who reveres the memory of the former wife, Rebecca. It comes out that the latter, far from being a paragon of virtue and the love of Olivier's life, was frequently unfaithful and, when she accidentally was killed, Olivier sank her body in a boat. In the novel by Daphne du Maurier, Maxim had actually murdered his first wife.

Mr. Darcy / PRIDE AND PREJUDICE, 1940, MGM, d-Robert Z. Leonard.
As was the case with REBECCA, Olivier wanted his new love, Vivien Leigh, to play opposite him in the film version of the Jane Austen novel, and once again he was disappointed. Instead Greer Garson has the role of one of five eligible daughters of a family Olivier considers beneath him. He says of her: "She looks tolerable enough, but I'm in no humor tonight to give consequence to the middle classes at play." Nevertheless, he develops sincere love for her.

Lord Horatio Nelson / THAT HAMILTON WOMAN, 1941, United Artists, d-Alexander Korda.
Olivier finally gets his wish to perform with Vivien Leigh in this romantic film about the affair between the British naval hero Lord Nelson and Emma, Lady Hamilton. While all England honors the Hero of Trafalgar, they seem to prefer gossiping about the two married lovers.

Johnnie / FORTY-NINTH PARALLEL, 1941, Great Britain, GFD / Ortus, d-Michael Powell.
The 49th Parallel is the boundary of the United States and Canada that seven stranded U-boat sailors are trying to reach before being apprehended by Canadian officials. In the film, the United States and Germany are not yet at war and if the men can cross the border, they will be safe. Olivier is a French-Canadian trapper taken captive by the Germans. He taunts his captors, and when he makes a break for it, he is shot and lies dying for two days.

Henry V / HENRY V, 1944, Great Britain, Two Cities, d-Laurence Olivier.
Besides acting and directing, Olivier also co-produced this magnificent production of the Shakespeare play about the coming of age and maturity of the British monarch. The movie opens on a miniature view of the London of Shakespeare's time and focuses on the stage of the Globe Theatre where the play begins and ends. In between, the plot is sometimes developed before painted backdrops and sometimes in real settings. Once again Olivier wished to cast his then-wife Vivien Leigh in the movie but she was under contract to David O. Selznick who would not agree to the casting.

Hamlet / HAMLET, 1948, Great Britain, Two Cities, d-Laurence Olivier.
Olivier won an Oscar for his portrayal of the moody Dane in a film that he also produced and directed. He also co-wrote with the Bard by reduction, eliminating what he considered excess baggage to bring the four-and-a-half-hour play down to a 155-minute movie. What remains is extremely enjoyable.

George Hurstwood / CARRIE, 1952, Paramount, d-William Wyler.
In this excellent production of Theodore Dreiser's first novel, *Sister Carrie*, Olivier is the second lover of the country girl who comes to Chicago to become a successful actress. Olivier, a wealthy restaurant manager, is brought to financial ruin by his infatuation for the girl.

Richard III / RICHARD III, 1955, Great Britain, London Films, d-Laurence Olivier.
Olivier is brilliant as the deformed monster who systematically eliminates the relatives who stand between him and the English throne. He treats the people in the film audience to numerous asides as he takes them into his confidence, letting them know of his plans or his observations as to what is happening in the play.

Gen. John Burgoyne / THE DEVIL'S DISCIPLE, 1959, Great Britain, United Artists, d-Guy Hamilton.
Olivier is a treat in this George Bernard Shaw view of the events leading up to the American Revolution. As England's general who has the assignment of routing the rebels, Olivier is gracious and charming as he sits in on the trial of Kirk Douglas.

Archie Rice / THE ENTERTAINER, 1960, Great Britain, Bryanston Films, d-Tony Richardson.
Olivier once described his performance as John Osborne's over-the-hill song-and-dance man as the one he was most proud of, as it was such a departure from his usual roles. There's little to admire about Archie Rice, but there's a great deal to admire about Olivier's portrayal.

Superintendent Newhouse / BUNNY LAKE IS MISSING, 1965, Great Britain, Columbia, d-Otto Preminger.
Olivier leads the search for the four-year-old illegitimate daughter of an American girl who has disappeared in London. But he can find no one who will admit the child even exists.

Othello / OTHELLO, 1965, Great Britain, British Home Entertainers / Eagle, d-Stuart Burge.
Olivier is outstanding as the jealous Moor who is goaded by his friend Iago into strangling his beloved and innocent wife, Desdemona.

The Mahdi / KHARTOUM, 1966, Great Britain, Blaustein / United Artists, d-Basil Dearden, Eliot Elisofon, and Yakima Canutt.

Having some dark makeup left over from OTHELLO, Olivier plays the fanatical religious leader who is determined to pray in every Mosque in cities occupied by the foreign white devils. This time he wants to say his prayers in Khartoum and Charlton Heston, as General "China" Gordon, is in his way.

Prime Minister Count Witte / NICHOLAS AND ALEXANDRA, 1971, Great Britain, Columbia, d-Franklin Schaffner.

Olivier is among the many fine actors and actresses who perform beautifully in this story about Czar Nicholas II of Russia from 1904 until the execution of his family in 1918.

Andrew Wyke / SLEUTH, 1972, Great Britain, Palomar, d-Joseph L. Mankiewicz.

In this very entertaining two-man show, Olivier is an eccentric mystery writer who invites his wife's lover into his remote home to discuss a way they both can profit from a robbery of jewels. He then reveals that he intends to kill the lover, but doesn't, as it was merely a trick to scare the poor man almost to death. But the latter, portrayed by Michael Caine, returns the compliment and things get really serious.

Dr. Szell / MARATHON MAN, 1976, Paramount, d-John Schlesinger.

Olivier is an ex-Nazi from Uruguay who has come to New York in search of diamonds that had been kept for him by his now-dead brother. He's outsmarted by Dustin Hoffman, who suffers plenty in a dentist's chair at the hands of Olivier.

Julius / A LITTLE ROMANCE, 1979, Warners, d-George Roy Hill.

Olivier is extremely hammy as the old con man who helps a pair of thirteen-year-olds, one a French boy and the other an American girl, get to Venice so they may kiss under the Bridge of Sighs at just the right time to make their love last forever. It's totally charming and just wouldn't work as well if not for Olivier.

Dr. Van Helsing / DRACULA, 1979, Great Britain, Universal, d-John Badham.

Olivier compares well with Edward Van Sloan as the man who recognizes the danger of Count Dracula and how to deal with him. This is a lush production of the horror classic. Frank Langella is better looking than Bela Lugosi, but the latter is more frightening.

OTHER ROLES

1930: *Peter Billie* / THE TEMPORARY WIDOW; *the man* / TOO MANY CROOKS. **1931:** *Julian Rolphe* / THE YELLOW TICKET; *Lieutenant Nichols* / FRIENDS AND LOVERS; *Straker* / POTIPHAR'S WIFE. **1932:** *Nick Allen* / WESTWARD PASSAGE. **1933:** *Nicholas Randall* / PERFECT UNDERSTANDING. **1934:** *Clive Dering* / NO FUNNY BUSINESS. **1935:** *Captain Ignatoff* / MOSCOW NIGHTS. **1936:** *Vincent Lunardi* / CONQUEST OF THE AIR. **1939:** *Larry Darrant* / 21 DAYS; *Tony McVane* / Q PLANES. **1943:** *Ivan Kouznetsoff* / THE DEMI-PARADISE. **1951:** *PC 94 B* / THE MAGIC BOX. **1952:** *Captain MacHeath* / THE BEGGAR'S OPERA. **1958:** *Grand Duke Charles* / THE PRINCE AND THE SHOWGIRL. **1960:** *Marcus Crassus* / SPARTACUS. **1962:** *Graham Weir* / TERM OF TRIAL. **1968:** *Premier Piotr Ilyich Kamenev* / THE SHOES OF THE FISHERMAN; *prologue speaker* / ROMEO AND JULIET. **1969:** *Sir John French* / OH! WHAT A LOVELY WAR; *Edgar* / THE DANCE OF DEATH; *Sir Hugh Dowding* / THE BATTLE OF BRITAIN; *Mr. Creakle* / DAVID COPPERFIELD. **1970:** *Dr. Chebutkin* / THREE SISTERS. **1972:** *Duke of Wellington* / LADY CAROLINE LAMB. **1976:** *Professor Moriarty* / THE SEVEN PERCENT SOLUTION. **1977:** *Dr. Spaander* / A BRIDGE TOO FAR. **1978:** *Loren Hardeman* / THE BETSY; *Ezra Lieberman* / THE BOYS FROM BRAZIL. **1981:** *Zeus* / CLASH OF THE TITANS; *Cantor Rabinowitz* / THE JAZZ SINGER; *Gen. Douglas MacArthur* / INCHON. **1983:** *Pfeufer* / WAGNER. **1984:** *Sir Gerald Scaith* / THE JIGSAW MAN; *Admiral Hood* / THE BOUNTY. **1985:** *Rudolf Hess* / WILD GEESE II.

O'NEAL, RYAN

(Patrick Ryan O'Neal, 1941–)

After showing little ambition in his early years for anything but swimming and surfing, Ryan O'Neal got his start in show business working as a stunt man on a TV show in Munich on which his screenwriter father and actress mother were working. Back in California he began working regularly on TV and got his break when he was chosen to play wealthy Rodney Harrington on TV's biggest soap opera, "Peyton Place." He made his screen debut in 1969 with a second feature, THE BIG BOUNCE, and became a star with LOVE STORY in 1970. His popularity was assured with his portrayal of an almost imbecilic absentminded Ph.D. musicologist in WHAT'S UP, DOC? in 1972, followed by the bible-selling con man shown up by real-life daughter Tatum in PAPER MOON. In 1975 he seemed to be overwhelmed by Thackeray's hero in the beautiful box-office failure, BARRY LYNDON. Since then none of his films have been much and he has become just another celebrity rather than an actor.

KEY ROLES

Oliver Barrett IV / LOVE STORY, 1970, Paramount, d-Arthur Hiller.

The movie is too campy to be criticized; it's sufficient to describe some of the soap opera cliches that screenwriter Erich Segal included in his tragic romance of two Harvard students. Ali MacGraw plays a girl from a poor but honest family and O'Neal the scion of an old rich family that cuts him off when he marries his Italian lover. She comes down with an incurable disease which is not named but fortunately doesn't show on her face or figure as it ravages her innards.

Howard Bannister / WHAT'S UP, DOC? 1972, Warners, d-Peter Bogdanovich.

O'Neal beautifully captures the nuances of an absentminded scholar who has concentrated so long on research, with findings of interest to a small handful of like-minded nerds, that he's incapable of keeping his mind on anything else and needs a keeper like Madeline Kahn to prevent him from hurting himself. What is hard to swallow in this madcap comedy is what a with-it sharpie like Barbra Streisand could possibly want with this boring musicologist? O'Neal looks attractive as an intellectual ass and pseudo-scholar who takes his work too seriously, undervaluing everything else.

Moses Pray / PAPER MOON, 1973, Paramount, d-Peter Bogdanovich.

It's tough being beaten out of acting honors by a kid and even more so when the kid is your own daughter, but such is the case in this movie. O'Neal is a con man with a bible-selling scheme who takes daughter Tatum along for the ride. No doubt O'Neal was a proud daddy when Tatum won an Oscar.

Barry Lyndon / BARRY LYNDON, 1975, Warners, d-Stanley Kubrick.

This movie looks much better than it is because the photography has been so lovingly used to give the same appearance as found in the great landscape and portrait paintings of the 18th century. O'Neal is an Irish adventurer who enlists in the British army, but deserts to marry a wealthy widow whom he treats badly. His downfall follows and, because of his egotism and his earlier unbridled ambition, no tears are shed for him.

Benson / PARTNERS, 1982, Titan, d-James Burrows.
O'Neal is the straight cop who teams with gay cop John Hurt to go undercover in an investigation of the murder of a homosexual in Los Angeles. It's an uneasy film, difficult to enjoy not because of the subject but because of the strange way it's handled.

OTHER ROLES

1968: *Scott Reynolds* / THE GAMES. **1969:** *Jack Ryan* / THE BIG BOUNCE. **1971:** *Frank Post* / WILD ROVERS. **1973:** *Webster* / THE THIEF WHO CAME TO DINNER. **1976:** *Leo Harrigan* / NICKELODEON. **1977:** *Brig. Gen. James A. Gavin* / A BRIDGE TOO FAR. **1978:** *the driver* / THE DRIVER. **1979:** *Oliver Barrett IV* / OLIVER'S STORY; *Eddie "Kid Natural" Scanlon* / THE MAIN EVENT. **1981:** *Bobby* / SO FINE. **1984:** *Albert Brodsky* / IRRECONCILABLE DIFFERENCES. **1987:** *Tim Madden* / TOUGH GUYS DON'T DANCE.

O'SULLIVAN, MAUREEN

(1911–)

A beautiful, demure brunette, Irish-born Maureen O'Sullivan is best remembered for playing Jane to Johnny Weissmuller's Tarzan in the 1930s. Educated at convent schools in Dublin and London and a finishing school in Paris, O'Sullivan was offered a part in SONG OF MY HEART opposite famous tenor John McCormack by director Frank Borzage when she was only 19. In 1932 she moved from Fox to MGM and made her first of six appearances as Jane in TARZAN, THE APE MAN. In 1942 she married director John Farrow and retired from films for six years to raise her growing family of seven children, including actresses Mia and Tisa Farrow. After the death of her husband in 1963, O'Sullivan carved out a new career on Broadway and was the co-host of TV's "Today" show for many months in 1965. Recently she has returned to the screen and is as appealing as ever.

KEY ROLES

Jane Parker / TARZAN, THE APE MAN, 1932, MGM, d-W. S. Van Dyke.
O'Sullivan's original jungle outfit was considered just too revealing and she was forced to cover more of her fine-looking thighs. She does, however, get away with teaching Tarzan to count on her toes which he fondles and mouths lovingly.

Dorothy Wynant / THE THIN MAN, 1934, MGM, d-W. S. Van Dyke.
O'Sullivan's inventor father is missing and she pleads with Nick Charles (William Powell) to help find him. Powell insists that he's retired from the detective business but he finally moves in on the case, only to discover the missing man has been murdered.

Henrietta Barrett / THE BARRETTS OF WIMPOLE STREET, 1934, MGM, d-Sidney Franklin.
O'Sullivan is the second daughter of Edward Moulten-Barrett and if he has designs for her like he does for her sister Elizabeth, the movie doesn't tell. But he does his best to dominate her totally and prevent her from finding happiness with the man she loves.

Dora / DAVID COPPERFIELD, 1934, MGM, d-George Cukor.
O'Sullivan is one of many actors who give splendid, almost cameo-like, performances in this beautiful film version of Dickens's story of a youngster who is badly treated by a cruel stepfather and grows up to become an author. The adult David marries O'Sullivan, but she becomes ill and dies, and David goes back to an old love.

Jane Bennet / PRIDE AND PREJUDICE, 1940, MGM, d-Robert Z. Leonard.
O'Sullivan is one of five daughters for whom the mother (Mary Boland) is determined to find good matches in this Jane Austen story of romance and social mores in early 19th-century England. Boland's methods often embarrass the girls and their father, but mama knows best as each finds the man of her dreams.

Edith Lambert / NEVER TOO LATE, 1965, Warners, d-Bud Yorkin.
O'Sullivan is a middle-aged woman who shares astonishment with her 60-year-old husband that she is going to have a baby. But the news is none too pleasing to her daughter and son-in-law who have tried just about everything to conceive with all efforts unsuccessful.

Norma / HANNAH AND HER SISTERS, 1986, Orion, d-Woody Allen.
O'Sullivan's role as Mia Farrow's mother (which, of course, she is) is small but effective. She's a former show business personality who on occasion drinks too much and has the same old argument with her husband (Lloyd Nolan) over and over about which one has been the most unfaithful.

OTHER ROLES

1930: *Eileen O'Brien* / SONG O' MY HEART; *Elinor Worthing* / SO THIS IS LONDON; *LN-18* / JUST IMAGINE; *Princess Louise* / THE PRINCESS AND THE PLUMBER. **1931:** *Alisande* / A CONNECTICUT YANKEE; *Kathleen Kearny* / SKYLINE. **1932:** *Miss Barton* / OKAY AMERICA; *Joyce Moore* / THE SILVER LINING; *Doris* / THE BIG SHOT; *Madeline* / STRANGE INTERLUDE; *Winnie Marble* / PAYMENT DEFERRED; *Lynn Harding* / SKYSCRAPER SOULS; *Sally* / THE FAST COMPANIONS. **1933:** *Helen* / ROBBERS' ROOST; *Mollie Kelly* / THE COHENS AND THE KELLYS IN TROUBLE; *Pat Severn* / TUGBOAT ANNIE; *Shirley Lorraine* / STAGE MOTHER. **1934:** *Jane Parker* / TARZAN AND HIS MATE; *Skip Carter* / WEST POINT OF THE AIR. **1935:** *Lenore* / CARDINAL RICHELIEU; *Linda Belton* / THE FLAME WITHIN; *Kitty* / ANNA KARENINA; *Ann* / WOMAN WANTED; *Hester* / THE BISHOP MISBEHAVES. **1936:** *Jane* / TARZAN ESCAPES; *Camden Terry* / THE VOICE OF BUGLE ANN; *Lorraine Lavond* / THE DEVIL DOLL. **1937:** *Judy Standish* / A DAY AT THE RACES; *Claire Donahue* / BETWEEN TWO WOMEN; *Maria* / THE EMPEROR'S CANDLESTICKS; *Martha Aldrich* / MY DEAR MISS ALDRICH. **1938:** *Molly Beaumont* / A YANK AT OXFORD; *June Evans* / HOLD THAT KISS; *Sheila Carson* / THE CROWD ROARS; *Madelon* / PORT OF SEVEN SEAS; *Alexander Benson* / SPRING MADNESS; *Mary Roberts* / LET US LIVE. **1939:** *Jane* / TARZAN FINDS A SON. **1940:** *Linda Lockwood* / SPORTING BLOOD. **1941:** *Abby Rawlston* / MAISIE WAS A LADY; *Jane* / TARZAN'S SECRET TREASURE; *Jane* / TARZAN'S NEW YORK ADVENTURE. **1948:** *Georgette Stroud* / THE BIG CLOCK. **1950:** *Julie* / WHERE DANGER LIVES. **1952:** *Marion Drew* / BONZO GOES TO COLLEGE. **1953:** *Sara Harper* / ALL I DESIRE; *Nancy Slocum* / MISSION OVER KOREA. **1954:** *Gladys Duffy* / DUFFY OF SAN QUENTIN. **1957:** *Doretta Mims* / THE TALL T. **1958:** *Emma Breslin* / WILD HERITAGE. **1969:** *cameo* / THE PHYNX. **1986:** *mother* / TOO SCARED TO SCREAM; *Elizabeth Alvorg* / PEGGY SUE GOT MARRIED. **1987:** *Grace Clark* / STRANDED.

O'TOOLE, PETER

(1932–)

Tall, fair-haired, and charismatic Irish actor Peter O'Toole trained at the Royal Academy of Dramatic Arts in the same class with Alan Bates and Albert Finney. He worked in repertory before winning critical acclaim for "The Long and the Short and the Tall," then burst on the world scene with LAWRENCE OF ARABIA, for which he received an Oscar nomination. Other nominations have come for BECKET, THE LION IN WINTER, GOODBYE, MR. CHIPS, THE RULING CLASS, and THE STUNT MAN. Although his self-indulgent acting is usually associated with his dramatic roles, he has a marvelous sense of comedy timing, best seen in the delightful film MY FAVORITE YEAR. His own assessment of his early success is: "I was sort of the Vanessa Redgrave of the fifties." Recently he has appeared in all too many inferior pictures and made-for-TV movies such as ROGUE MALE (1977), MASADA (1980), SVENGALI (1983), THE WORLD OF JAMES JOYCE (1983), and KIM.

KEY ROLES

T. E. Lawrence / LAWRENCE OF ARABIA, 1962, Great Britain, Columbia, d-David Lean.

O'Toole is magnificently mystical as the British adventurer who stands with the Arabs against the Turks and, annoyingly to his superiors, against British interests as well. His pale blue eyes on occasion stare maddeningly at the wide scenes of death and destruction before him. All sense of decency and pity has deserted him because of his almost religious zeal and dedication for his adopted cause. We gradually learn about him as he learns about himself, but in the end he is still a mystery to audiences and, we suspect, himself. Lawrence was a short exhibitionist who enjoyed dressing up in the flowing robes of the Arabs. Tall O'Toole hints at a certain madness in his character, brought on perhaps because of his doubts about his sexuality. At one point, he acknowledges that he is less than a god: "The truth is that I'm an ordinary man. You might have told me that, Brighton."

King Henry II / BECKET, 1964, Great Britain, Paramount, d-Peter Glenville.

As king, O'Toole knows that there are very few people he can trust or confide in. One person he is certain of is his friend Thomas à Becket (Richard Burton). O'Toole makes his boisterous Saxon friend first Chancellor of England and then, when he has trouble with the Catholic Church, Archbishop of Canterbury. But he does not count on Thomas taking the job seriously and soon finds that his problems with the church are greater than before. What hurts him most, though, is the loss of his close and trusted friend. Ultimately, O'Toole induces some of his barons to assassinate Becket in his cathedral, then accepts the punishment of a scourging.

Lord Jim / LORD JIM, 1965, Great Britain, Columbia, d-Richard Brooks.

O'Toole is a British merchant seaman who abandons his ship during a storm, leaving the passengers to drown. He is dismissed from service and becomes a wanderer in the Orient, looking for personal redemption. He becomes the champion of enslaved natives, is raped by a tribal chief, and ultimately must suffer death when the son of the chief is killed.

King Henry II / THE LION IN WINTER, 1968, Great Britain, d-Anthony Harvey.

Repeating his role in BECKET, O'Toole calls for his wife (Katharine Hepburn), who has long been banished from his court for her intrigues against him, to settle on his successor as king among his three sons, none of whom he trusts or cares for. He rages to Hepburn, "All my sons are bastards." While some of the verbal sparring is interesting, it goes on too long and becomes repetitive.

Arthur Chipping / GOODBYE, MR. CHIPS, 1969, Great Britain, MGM, d-Herbert Ross.

It takes a brave actor to recreate a role that most believe was handled definitively in an earlier movie. O'Toole does just that in his portrayal of the shy, unpopular schoolmaster who becomes more human to his young charges after he falls in love with and marries a singer. While he won't make anyone forget Robert Donat, O'Toole's portrayal, judged on its own merits, is quite fine and if the movie as a whole lacks the magic of the 1939 picture, it does have many pleasant moments.

Jack, 14th Earl of Gurney / THE RULING CLASS, 1971, Great Britain, Keep Films, d-Peter Medak.

O'Toole gets to play his mad act to a fare-thee-well in this tale of a British Lord who believes he is God and yearns for a good old-fashioned crucifixion.

Don Quixote de la Mancha / MAN OF LA MANCHA, 1972, United Artists, d-Arthur Hiller.

Someone must have forgotten to inform the makers of this movie that it was a musical. Choosing O'Toole, Sophia Loren, and James Coco for the three leading roles makes no sense, as the strength of the piece is the music by Mitch Leigh and Joe Darion and these three aren't singers. It looks good, but generally it seems to be a failed theater piece.

Eli Cross / THE STUNT MAN, 1978, Melvin Simon, d-Richard Rush.

When Vietnam veteran Steve Railsback, who is on the run from the police, stumbles onto a movie set and accidentally kills the stunt man, Christ-like director O'Toole offers to hide him from the police if he takes the dead man's place. It's a strange black comedy and somewhat hard to follow but well worth the effort.

Allan Swan / MY FAVORITE YEAR, 1982, MGM / United Artists, d-Richard Benjamin.

The time is the 1950s, the place is a Sid Caesar-like comedy show on television, and the guest is an Errol Flynn-like actor (O'Toole) who is a used-up alcoholic. Young writer Mark Linn-Baker is given the assignment of making certain his hero makes it to rehearsals and doesn't embarrass them too much with his drinking and wenching. It's a hilariously charming and touching movie and O'Toole is just marvelous. He was nominated for an Academy Award for his work.

OTHER ROLES

1959: *Robin MacGregor* / KIDNAPPED; *Captain Fitch* / THE DAY THEY ROBBED THE BANK OF ENGLAND. **1960:** *first trooper* / THE SAVAGE INNOCENTS. **1965:** *voice* / THE SANDPIPER; *Michael James* / WHAT'S NEW, PUSSYCAT? **1966:** *Simon Dermott* / HOW TO STEAL A MILLION; *General Tanz* / THE NIGHT OF THE GENERALS; *The Three Angels* / THE BIBLE; *guest* / CASINO ROYALE. **1967:** *Capt. Charles Edstaston* / GREAT CATHERINE. **1970:** *Sir Charles Henry Arbuthnot Pinkerton Ferguson* / COUNTRY DANCE; *Murphy* / MURPHY'S WAR. **1971:** *Captain Cat* / UNDER MILK WOOD. **1975:** *Larry Martin* / ROSEBUD; *Robinson Crusoe* / MAN FRIDAY; *Liviu* / FOXTROT. **1977:** *Tiberius* / CALIGULA. **1978:** *Lord Chelmsford* / ZULU DAWN. **1984:** *Zaltar* / SUPERGIRL. **1985:** *Harry* / CREATOR.

1986: *The British Governor* / CLUB PARADISE. **1987:** *Reginald Johnson (R.J.)* / THE LAST EMPEROR.

PACINO, AL

(Alfredo Pacino, 1939-)

"An actor becomes an emotional athlete. You work on yourself as an instrument." So says Al Pacino, one of the finest actors now working in the movie industry. Making very few films, he chooses his roles very carefully and has been rewarded by being nominated for Oscars for THE GODFATHER, SERPICO, THE GODFATHER, PART II, DOG DAY AFTERNOON, and ... AND JUSTICE FOR ALL, but as of yet has not come away a winner. Pacino usually appears as intense, brooding anti-heroes in very dramatic films. The small, dynamic actor of Sicilian descent attended the Lee Strasberg Actors Studio and won the Obie Award for his performance as a drunken psychotic in the off-Broadway play "The Indian Wants the Bronx" and in 1969 won his first Tony for "Does a Tiger Wear a Necktie?" In 1977, he won a second Tony for "The Basic Training of Pavlo Hummel."

KEY ROLES

Michael Corleone / THE GODFATHER, 1972, Paramount, d-Francis Ford Coppola.

Pacino is just back from World War II, looking very young at his sister's wedding. He's not supposed to go into the family business of importing olive oil, but when the competition gets rough, his father is gunned down and his brother needs a hit man, Pacino is ready. He blows away the opposition and goes into hiding in Italy for a few years, even taking a wife, but she's killed by a bomb meant for him. When he's called home he finds himself taking over the family business when his brother is killed and his father dies of a heart attack.

Frank Serpico / SERPICO, 1973, Paramount, d-Sidney Lumet.

Pacino is a New York cop who reveals police corruption and finds that his reward is he must leave the country. Pacino looks pretty scruffy but is the only memorable part of the movie.

Michael Corleone / THE GODFATHER, PART II, 1974, Paramount, d-Francis Ford Coppola.

Robert DeNiro won a deserved Oscar for his performance as the young Don Corleone in this film, but Pacino was just as deserving of one for his portrayal of the successor. Pacino completely dominates the action like no other actor ever has. His portrayal of a man who is able to adopt the selective morality of the professional mobster is fascinating to watch.

Sonny / DOG DAY AFTERNOON, 1975, Warners, d-Sidney Lumet.

Pacino and John Cazale pull a bank robbery in order to get money to pay for Pacino's homosexual lover's (Chris Sarandon) sex change operation. Everything goes wrong in this real-life drama and ends tragically. The transsexual who Sarandon's character is based on died recently.

Arthur Kirkland / ...AND JUSTICE FOR ALL, 1979, Columbia, d-Norman Jewison.

Pacino is a lawyer who has a lot of trouble with a nasty judge (John Forsythe) and then finds himself defending the arrogant jurist against a rape charge of which he is actually guilty.

Tony Montana / SCARFACE, 1983, Universal, d-Brian de Palma.

In this brutal version of the 1932 mobster classic starring Paul Muni, Pacino is just as mean as Al Capone but he's operating out of Miami in modern times. He's not even Italian—he's a Cuban émigré.

OTHER ROLES

1968: *Tony* / ME, NATALIE. **1971:** *Bobby* / THE PANIC IN NEEDLE PARK. **1973:** *Lion* / SCARECROW. **1977:** *Bobby Deerfield* / BOBBY DEERFIELD. **1980:** *Steve Burns* / CRUISING. **1982:** *Travalian* / AUTHOR! AUTHOR! **1985:** *Tom Dobb* / REVOLUTION.

PALMER, LILLI

(Lillie Marie Peiser, 1914–1986)

This beautiful, dark-haired German actress, the daughter of an actress and a surgeon, began her work in stock and cabarets. A Jew, she left Germany for France in 1933 and two years later made her film debut in Britain. Ten years later she moved to Hollywood. Slight and slim, her beauty wore well and she remained a leading lady late into her forties. Semi-retired in the 1970s, she became a best-selling author, a painter, and also continued her stage work. She made many non-English speaking pictures including HANS LE MARIN (1948), FEUERWERK (1953), MONTPARNASSE (1957), MÄDCHEN IN UNIFORM (1958), and LE TONNERRE DU DIEU (1965).

KEY ROLES

Natasha / CRIME UNLIMITED, 1934, Great Britain, Warners, d-Ralph Ince.

In a much-praised debut, Palmer is a Russian girl who helps a young police recruit with whom she falls in love unmask the mastermind behind a series of jewel thefts.

Melanie Kurtz / THUNDER ROCK, 1942, Great Britain, Charter Films, d-Roy Boulting.

Palmer is among the many ghosts of immigrants drowned on Lake Michigan who haunt a journalist who has retreated to a lighthouse on the lake because he is disgusted with the world of the 1930s.

Rikki Krausner / THE RAKE'S PROGRESS, 1946, Great Britain, Eagle-Lion, d-Sidney Gilliat.

Palmer is an Austrian who has the misfortune to fall in love with and marry a cad (Rex Harrison). He has married her for her money and drives her to the point of suicide because of his affair with his father's secretary.

Gina / CLOAK AND DAGGER, 1946, Warners, d-Fritz Lang.

In her U.S. debut, Palmer is an Italian partisan assigned to help physicist Gary Cooper locate and rescue an atomic scientist being held by the Nazis. While completing their mission, the two fall in love and Cooper promises to return to Palmer when the war is over.

Peg Born / BODY AND SOUL, 1947, Enterprise / United Artists, d-Robert Rossen.

Jewish boxer John Garfield falls for lovely artist Palmer but loses her when he gets tied up with a crooked promoter and a showgirl. After he gets some sense pounded into him he returns to Palmer.

Tisa Kepes / MY GIRL TISA, 1948, United States Pictures, d-Elliott Nugent.

Palmer is an immigrant in New York in the 1890s who falls for young politician Sam Wannamaker. She is threatened with deportation but is saved by the intervention of Teddy Roosevelt.

Abby / THE FOUR POSTER, 1952, Columbia, d-Irving Reis.

With husband Rex Harrison, Palmer relates the history of her marriage through a series of scenes that take place in their bedroom. This two-person story worked better on the stage than on the screen.

Katherine Doughtery / THE PLEASURE OF HIS COMPANY, 1961, Paramount, d-George Seaton.

When Palmer's ex-husband (Fred Astaire), an aging playboy, arrives unexpectedly in San Francisco for their daughter's wedding, the daughter (Debbie Reynolds) is delighted. But Palmer and her new husband (Gary Merrill) are not amused. Audiences, on the other hand, were.

Verena Podhajsky / MIRACLE OF THE WHITE STALLIONS, 1963, Disney, d-Arthur Hiller.

During World War II when the Nazis occupy Vienna, Palmer and her husband (Robert Taylor), who own the Spanish Riding School, seek help first from the Germans and later from the Americans to save their famed Lipizzan horses from extinction.

OTHER ROLES

1935: *Jeanette* / BAD BLOOD. **1936:** *Lilli* / SECRET AGENT. **1937:** *Lou* / THE GREAT BARRIER; *Gelda* / SUNSET IN VIENNA; *Yvette* / GOOD MORNING, BOYS; *Susan* / COMMAND PERFORMANCE. **1938:** *Baroness vòn Haltone* / THE MAN WITH 100 FACES; *Clytie Devine* / A GIRL MUST LIVE. **1940:** *Valerie* / BLIND FOLLY; *Judy Lansdowne* / THE DOOR WITH SEVEN LOCKS. **1943:** *Erna* / THE GENTLE SEX; *Brigid Knudsen* / ENGLISH WITHOUT TEARS. **1945:** *Baroness Edith de Kekesfaria* / BEWARE OF PITY. **1948:** *April Ashwell* / NO MINOR VICES. **1949:** *Brigid Knudsen* / HER MAN GILBEY. **1951:** *Mary Groome* / THE LONG DARK HALL. **1953:** *guest* / MAIN STREET TO BROADWAY. **1956:** *Anna Anderson* / IS ANNA ANDERSON ANASTASIA? **1959:** *Kathryn Ward* / BUT NOT FOR ME. **1960:** *Mother Katharine* / CONSPIRACY OF HEARTS. **1962:** *Marianne Mollendorf* / THE COUNTERFEIT TRAITOR. **1963:** *Julia Lambert* / ADORABLE JULIA. **1964:** *Lygia da Silva* / TORPEDO BAY; *Hilde Brenner* / OF WAYWARD LOVE. **1965:** *Freida* / OPERATION CROSSBOW; *Dutchy* / THE AMOROUS ADVENTURES OF MOLL FLANDERS. **1967:** *guest* / JACK OF DIAMONDS; *Elsa Shahn* / SEBASTIAN; *Jocasta* / OEDIPUS THE KING. **1968:** *Sheila Quentin* / NOBODY RUNS FOREVER; *Melanie* / DEVIL IN SILK. **1969:** *Madame de Montreiul* / DE SADE; *Adrianne* / HARD CONTRACT. **1971:** *Mrs. Charron* / MURDERS IN THE RUE MORGUE; *Dr. Viorne* / NIGHT HAIR CHILD; *Madame Fourneau* / THE HOUSE THAT SCREAMED. **1978:** *Esther Leiberman* / THE BOYS FROM BRAZIL. **1985:** *Althene Holcroft* / THE HOLCROFT COVENANT.

PARKER, ELEANOR

(1922–)

Eleanor Parker was a ravishing, red-gold-haired actress who was at her best portraying strong-willed women. She was nominated for Academy Awards for CAGED, DETECTIVE STORY, and INTERRUPTED MELODY. She had many fine leading roles during the period 1946 to 1957, but then went into a surprising decline. Spotted by a talent scout at the Pasadena Playhouse, she signed with Warners and worked in a series of bit parts and second leads in "B" movies before becoming a star with CAGED in 1950. Since the 1960s she has appeared mostly in supporting roles.

KEY ROLES

Ann / BETWEEN TWO WORLDS, 1944, Warners, d-Edward A. Blatt.

In this remake of OUTWARD BOUND, Parker and her husband (Paul Henreid) commit suicide then find themselves on a strange ship of the dead on its way to a meeting with "The Examiner" who will decide the passengers' fates. She and Henreid get another chance for life.

Mildred Rogers / OF HUMAN BONDAGE, 1946, Warners, d-Edmund Goulding.

In the second of three movie versions of Somerset Maugham's story of a crippled student who is almost ruined by a sluttish waitress with whom he is infatuated, neither Parker nor co-star Paul Henreid are up to the roles. It's a dull picture.

Sally Middleton / THE VOICE OF THE TURTLE, 1948, Warners, d-Irving Rapper.

Parker is an actress whose romance has just broken up. She shares her apartment with Ronald Reagan, a lonely soldier on leave, and of course they fall in love.

Marie Allen / CAGED, 1950, Warners, d-John Cromwell.

Parker won her acting spurs as a 19-year-old girl jailed for a crime committed by her husband. Having her baby in jail and the dehumanizing experience with guards and other prisoners hardens her by the time she is released.

Mary McLeod / DETECTIVE STORY, 1951, Paramount, d-William Wyler.

Parker is the wife of a New York police detective (Kirk Douglas) who hates crooks with a passion and a butchering abortionist in particular. He is destroyed when he learns that Parker was once the lover of a small-time mobster, became pregnant, and went to that same abortionist.

Mary Stuart Cherne / MANY RIVERS TO CROSS, 1954, MGM, d-Roy Rowland.

Parker demonstrates her talent for comedy in this story of a trapper (Robert Taylor) bound for Canada. He is helped by sharpshooting Parker, whom he saves in return from marauding Indians. He never does get to Canada.

Marjorie Lawrence / INTERRUPTED MELODY, 1955, MGM, d-Curtis Bernhardt.

Parker was nominated for an Academy Award for her portrayal of the Australian opera singer whose career is interrupted by polio. Actually it's a pretty ordinary movie.

Zosch Machine / THE MAN WITH THE GOLDEN ARM, 1956, United Artists, d-Otto Preminger.

Parker pretends she is unable to walk so she can shame her gambling drug dependent husband (Frank Sinatra) into staying with her. She gives herself away and—what do you know—he leaves her for Kim Novak.

Elizabeth Richmond / LIZZIE, 1957, MGM, d-Hugo Haas.

Parker tried hard to win an Oscar in this story of a girl who develops three new personalities after being raped and witnessing a murder. She was undone by the release of the far superior THREE FACES OF EVE the same year for which Joanne Woodward won the Oscar.

OTHER ROLES

1941: *bit (cut)* / THEY DIED WITH THEIR BOOTS ON. **1942:** *Norma* / BUSSES ROAR. **1943:** *Lefty Carstairs* / THE MYSTERIOUS DOCTOR; *Emlen Davies* / MISSION TO MOSCOW. **1944:** *Janet Wheeler* / THE VERY THOUGHT OF YOU; *Irene Carr* / CRIME BY NIGHT; *Kitty Kelly* / THE LAST RIDE; *guest* / HOLLYWOOD CANTEEN. **1945:** *Ruth Hartley* / PRIDE OF THE MARINES. **1946:** *Ellen Gayley* / NEVER SAY GOODBYE; *Fenella MacLean* / ESCAPE ME NEVER. **1948:** *Laura Fairle* / *Anne Catherické* / THE WOMAN IN WHITE. **1949:** *Jo Holloway* / CHAIN LIGHTNING; *guest* / IT'S A GREAT FEELING. **1950:** *Susan Chase* / THREE SECRETS. **1951:** *Joan Carlisle* / VALENTINO; *Christy Sloane* / A MILLIONAIRE FOR CHRISTY. **1952:** *Leonore* / SCARAMOUCHE; *Lucey Tibbetts* / ABOVE AND BEYOND. **1953:** *Carla Forester* / ESCAPE FROM FORT BRAVO. **1954:** *Joanna Leiningen* / THE NAKED JUNGLE; *Ann Mercedes* / VALLEY OF THE KINGS. **1956:** *Sabina* / THE KING AND FOUR QUEENS. **1957:** *Carol Carwin* / THE SEVENTH SIN. **1959:** *Eloise Rogers* / A HOLE IN THE HEAD. **1960:** *Hannah Hunnicutt* / HOME FROM THE HILL. **1961:** *Connie Rossi* / RETURN TO PEYTON PLACE. **1962:** *Anne Temaine* / MADISON AVENUE **1964:** *Louise Harris* / PANIC BUTTON. **1965:** *The Baroness* / THE SOUND OF MUSIC. **1966:** *Sophie Cantaro* / THE OSCAR; *Deborah Rojack* / AN AMERICAN DREAM; *Mrs. Doris Ruston* / WARNING SHOT. **1967:** *Esperia* / THE TIGER AND THE PUSSYCAT. **1969:** *Aunt Danny* / EYE OF THE CAT. **1979:** *Mrs. Thoren* / SUNBURN.

PAYNE, JOHN

(1912–)

Tough-looking John Payne started his movie career in light musicals with the likes of Alice Faye, Betty Grable, and Sonja Henie. When he grew a bit old for such carryings-on, he had a good run in a series of thrillers and action films. He starred in a TV series, "The Restless Gun," in the late 1950s, then returned to movies briefly in the 1960s. Virginia-born Payne, the son of an opera singer, studied acting at Columbia, then began as a vocalist working in stock before arriving in Hollywood in 1935 where he signed with Goldwyn. Nothing much happened with his career until the 1940s and then it wasn't all that much either.

KEY ROLES

Steve Nelson / KID NIGHTINGALE, 1939, Warners, d-George Amy.

Payne is an operatic tenor with an interest in the manly art of self-defense who falls in with a crooked promoter and sings as he knocks opponents out.

Skeets Harrigan / TIN PAN ALLEY, 1940, 20th Century-Fox, d-Walter Lang.

Songwriters Payne and Jack Oakie get the Blane sisters (Alice Faye and Betty Grable) to introduce their new song in this tuneful bit of entertainment with only one new song, "You Say the Sweetest Things, Baby," by Harry Warren and Mack Gordon. Payne and Faye have the usual problems but by the end of the picture they are in an embrace.

Rex Martin / THE GREAT AMERICAN BROADCAST, 1941, 20th Century-Fox, d-Archie Mayo.

Back together again, Payne and Jack Oakie try several businesses before going into radio broadcasting. Payne's wife (Alice Faye) goes to a former boyfriend for money to build up their radio station but Payne resents this and walks out on her. She goes on to become a big star before they get back together on a coast-to-coast broadcast.

Chris Winters / TO THE SHORES OF TRIPOLI, 1942, 20th Century-Fox, d-H. Bruce Humberstone.

Cocky young Payne joins the marines and has a run-in with a tough veteran sergeant (Randolph Scott) who teaches him some needed humility in this flag-waver. His change of attitude wins him the love of navy nurse Maureen O'Hara.

Johnnie Cornell / HELLO FRISCO, HELLO, 1943, 20th Century-Fox, d-H. Bruce Humberstone.

Payne runs a San Francisco Barbary Coast saloon and becomes a successful producer of a musical starring girlfriend Alice Faye. His success gives him access to the upper crust of the city's society and the attention of society woman Lynn Bari, whom he marries. Payne and Faye are reunited at the reopening of his old saloon after unhappy years apart, during which his marriage and fortunes had failed and Faye had become an international star.

Harry Fox / THE DOLLY SISTERS, 1945, 20th Century-Fox, d-Irving Cummings.

In this one, Betty Grable fills Alice Faye's usual role as the performer who loves the unworthy Payne. This time he tries to promote himself along with the fabled musical comedy stars Jenny and Rosie Dolly (the latter played by June Haver, who had moved up to the Betty Grable second girl role).

Fred Gailey / MIRACLE ON 34TH STREET, 1947, 20th Century-Fox, d-George Seaton.

Payne is a lawyer who falls in love with a Macy's executive (Maureen O'Hara) but almost loses the no-nonsense lady when he risks his career and reputation by representing Kris Kringle (Edmund Gwenn) in a sanity hearing. Gwenn maintains he is really and truly Santa Claus and Payne gets the court to agree. Piles of letters addressed to Santa Claus are delivered to his client by the U.S. Post Office, and Payne argues that this proves the U.S. government "...recognizes this man, Kris Kringle, to be the one and only Santa Claus."

Clay Fletcher / EL PASO, 1949, Paramount, d-Lewis R. Foster.

After the Civil War, lawyer Payne tames a western town by becoming faster with a gun than any of the local baddies.

Joe Rolfe / KANSAS CITY CONFIDENTIAL, 1952, United Artists, d-Phil Karlston.

After former police captain Preston Foster and three others hold-up a Kansas City bank, the police pick up Payne as their primary suspect. But he hunts down the gang in Guatemala where he falls for Foster's daughter, Colleen Gray.

Matt Brady / THE BOSS, 1956, United Artists, d-Bryon Haskin.

In a real change of pace, Payne portrays a ruthless and corrupt small-town political boss who maneuvers himself into a position of having virtually complete control of a midwestern state. In the end his associations with a crooked lawyer, a gangster, and the wrong girl bring him down.

OTHER ROLES

1936: *Harry* / DODSWORTH; *Jimmy Maxwell* / HATS OFF. **1937:** *Jim Preston* / FAIR WARNING. **1938:** *Bill Adams* / LOVE ON TOAST; *Martin Bates* / COLLEGE SWING; *Don Vincente* / GARDEN OF THE MOON. **1939:** *Jerry Harrington* / WINGS OF THE NAVY; *Eddie Green* / INDIANAPOLIS SPEEDWAY. **1940:** *Bud Borden* / STAR DUST; *Lee Danfield* / MARYLAND; *Richard Lansing* / THE GREAT PROFILE; *Slim* / KING OF THE LUMBERJACKS; *Bill Morrissey* / TEAR GAS SQUAD. **1941:** *Jay Williams* / WEEK-END IN HAVANA; *Dan Hopkins* / REMEMBER THE DAY; *Ted Scott* / SUN VALLEY SERENADE. **1942:**

Capt. James Murfin / ICELAND; *Dan* / SPRINGTIME IN THE ROCKIES; *Bill Smith* / FOOTLIGHT SERENADE. **1946:** *Bill* / SENTIMENTAL JOURNEY; *Gray Maturin* / THE RAZOR'S EDGE; *Jeff* / WAKE UP AND DREAM. **1948:** *Rick Mason* / LARCENY; *Eric Busch* / THE SAXON CHARM. **1949:** *Eddie Rice* / THE CROOKED WAY; *Captain China* / CAPTAIN CHINA. **1950:** *Todd Crayden* / THE EAGLE AND THE HAWK; *Lieutenant O'Bannion* / TRIPOLI. **1951:** *Pete Black* / PASSAGE WEST; *Steve Singleton* / CROSSWINDS. **1952:** *Dick Lindsay* / CARIBBEAN; *Kelly Hansen* / THE BLAZING FOREST. **1953:** *Barbarossa* / RAIDERS OF THE SEVEN SEAS; *Rock Grayson* / THE VANQUISHED; *Ernie Driscoll* / 99 RIVER STREET. **1954:** *Jefferson Harder* / RAILS INTO LARAMIE; *Dan Ballard* / SILVER LODE. **1955:** *Kirby Randolph* / SANTA FE PASSAGE; *Mike Cormack* / HELL'S ISLAND; *Bill Mayhew* / THE ROAD TO DENVER; *Tennessee* / TENNESSEE'S PARTNER. **1956:** *Ben Grace* / SLIGHTLY SCARLET; *John Willoughby* / REBEL IN TOWN; *MacKenzie* / HOLD BACK THE NIGHT. **1957:** *Maj. Paul Peterson* / BAILOUT AT 43,000; *Mike Brent* / HIDDEN BRENT. **1968:** *Oliver Drake (The Nobody)* / THEY RAN FOR THEIR LIVES.

PECK, GREGORY

(Elfred Gregory Peck, 1916–)

Tall, dark, and handsome, Gregory Peck graduated as a pre-med student from the University of California at Berkeley in 1939. He made an impressive stage debut in 1942 in "Morning Star" and the next year made his first film appearance in DAYS OF GLORY. He became a star with his next film, THE KEYS OF THE KINGDOM, for which he earned his first Oscar nomination. He was also nominated for GENTLEMAN'S AGREEMENT, THE YEARLING, and TWELVE O'CLOCK HIGH, winning for TO KILL A MOCKINGBIRD in 1963. This versatile actor often portrays responsible, committed men who possess both physical and moral strength, fundamentally good men who rise to the occasion when needed. He has proven likable in dramas, romantic comedies, adventures, and westerns, but only seldom allowing the dark side of his personality to come through in villainous or frail men. Active in charitable and political causes, he made the enemies list of President Nixon. His own industry recognized his positive contributions by giving him the Jean Hersholt Humanitarian Award in 1967.

KEY ROLES

Father Francis Chisholm / THE KEYS OF THE KINGDOM, 1944, 20th Century-Fox, d-John M. Stahl.

Peck portrays a priest whose first assignment is a mission in China, where he stays until he returns to Scotland as an elderly man. In China he suffers privation, civil wars, a small insincere flock, and unfriendly nuns, but as the years pass he sees the positive effect of his influence.

"J. B." (John Ballentine) / SPELLBOUND, 1945, United Artists, d-Alfred Hitchcock.

Peck arrives at a mental hospital where it is assumed he is the new director. However, it soon becomes clear that he is an amnesiac who may have murdered the man he is impersonating. Ingrid Bergman is a doctor who falls in love with him and, through psychoanalysis, slowly unravels the twin mysteries of who killed the new director and Peck's true identity.

Pa Baxter / THE YEARLING, 1946, MGM, d-Clarence Brown.

Peck is the hard-working loving father of a boy (Claude Jarman, Jr.) who desperately wishes to have a pet and a young deer seems to meet his needs. But the animal outlives its welcome by eating or destroying the poor backwards Florida family's crops and Peck must destroy the animal and also make his son understand why it is necessary.

Lewt McCandles / DUEL IN THE SUN, 1946, Selznick / Vanguard, d-King Vidor.

Peck is the wild son of rancher Lionel Barrymore. He sides with his Pa against good brother Joseph Cotten who has taken up the cause of small farmers. Peck also competes with his brother for the love of hot-blooded half-breed Jennifer Jones. The passion between the two destroys them.

Robert Wilson / THE MACOMBER AFFAIR, 1947, United Artists, d-Zoltan Korda.

Rugged, lean Peck is a great white hunter in Africa hired by wealthy Robert Preston to lead him on a safari. Preston is something of a coward and his beautiful wife (Joan Bennett) falls for their guide. Peck tries to give Preston courage, quoting a Somali proverb: "A brave man is afraid of a lion three times: when he first sees its track, when he first hears its roar, and when he first looks it in the eye." The story ends in tragedy.

Phil Green / GENTLEMAN'S AGREEMENT, 1947, 20th Century-Fox, d-Elia Kazan.

Peck is a magazine writer who pretends to be Jewish while researching and writing a series of articles about anti-Semitism in the United States. He finds that the worst offenders are the nice people who support the system with their "gentleman's agreements" about keeping Jews out of clubs, hotels, neighborhoods, and so forth.

Gen. Frank Savage / TWELVE O'CLOCK HIGH, 1949, 20th Century-Fox, d-Henry King.

Peck is a staff general who replaces his lifelong friend as commander of a bomber unit in England that sees itself as having bad luck. Peck feels there is no such thing as bad luck, just bad execution by men who are not properly dedicated to their job or led by their commander. He comes in, kicks a lot of butts, and after some problems at the beginning, puts some spirit in his group until they lose their designation as a jinxed unit. But the stress of sending so many men to their deaths proves too much for Peck and he suffers a nervous breakdown.

Jimmy Ringo / THE GUNFIGHTER, 1950, 20th Century-Fox, d-Henry King.

In the first of a series of realistic adult westerns, Peck portrays a gunfighter who is tired of being challenged by every fast-gun who recognizes him. He would very much like to retire and take up once again with his wife and boy. Just when it seems that he may get his wish, he is shot in the back by Skip Homeier. As he lies dying, Peck assures all that Homeier had been too fast for him, thus condemning him to the kind of life Peck had tried so hard to escape.

Joe Bradley / ROMAN HOLIDAY, 1953, Paramount, d-William Wyler.

In this charming picture, Peck is a newspaper writer in Rome who recognizes a princess (Audrey Hepburn) who has run away and is visiting the city hoping to have a little fun. He helps her find it and the affection that grows between them is real, but both realize that she must return to her responsibilities.

Tom Rath / THE MAN IN THE GRAY FLANNEL SUIT, 1956, 20th Century-Fox, d-Nunnally Johnson.

Advertising man Peck is shocked when World War II buddy Keenan Wynn shows up seeking help for the child Peck fathered in Italy when he had an extramarital affair with Marisa Pavan, now dead. When his wife (Jennifer Jones) learns of his infidelity, she is crushed and not the least bit understanding. Their marriage is in jeopardy but they finally think of the child's needs.

Captain Ahab / MOBY DICK, 1956, Warners, d-John Huston.

John Huston planned to star his father Walter as Ahab, but when he died, Peck was given the role. While one can speculate what wonderful things Walter Huston might have done with the whaling captain driven to find and take revenge against the great white whale which took more than his leg, Peck does not disappoint in this thrilling version of the Herman Melville classic.

James McKay / THE BIG COUNTRY, 1958, United Artists, d-William Wyler.

Peck co-produced this wonderful western about a retired sea captain (Peck) who goes west to marry Carroll Baker, heiress to the huge Terrill ranch. But she loses respect for him when he resists her encouragement to share her family's hatred for the rival ranching king, Burl Ives. Peck ultimately finds Jean Simmons more to his liking as the feud between the two patriarchs heats up and threatens to destroy both families.

Atticus Finch / TO KILL A MOCKINGBIRD, 1963, United Artists, d-Robert Mulligan.

Peck won a deserved Oscar for his role as the gentle southern widower with two young children. He is the lawyer assigned to defend a black man accused of raping a poor white trash girl. While he is able to prevent the lynching of his client and shows that the story of the girl is a lie, the black man is convicted and is killed trying to escape. It's a touching picture, with a great deal of credit going to the impressive work of Mary Badham as Peck's curious and lovable seven-year-old daughter.

Capt. Josiah Newman / CAPTAIN NEWMAN, M.D., 1963, Universal, d-David Miller.

During World War II, Peck is the head of the psychiatric unit of an army hospital. He struggles to help his patients while trying to convince the powers that be that battle fatigue is a real medical problem.

Robert Thorn / THE OMEN, 1976, 20th Century-Fox, d-Richard Donner.

Peck plays a man whose real son died in childbirth, so he arranged for another baby born at the same time to be presented to his wife as their child. When, at about five, the boy begins to show signs of demonic behavior, Peck's investigation convinces him that the child was fathered by the devil. After the child is responsible for the death of Peck's wife, Peck knows the evil one must be destroyed. But the little devil gets the upper hand and dispatches Peck, and gets ready to come back in two sequels.

Dr. Josef Mengele / THE BOYS FROM BRAZIL, 1978, 20th Century-Fox, d-Franklin J. Schaffner.

In a rare role as a villain, Peck portrays the evil medical doctor who used inmates of concentration camps as guinea pigs in thousands of grisly operations and horrible medical experiments. In this movie Nazi hunter Laurence Olivier learns that Peck has come up with a scheme to clone new Hitlers and sets out to thwart his plans of new world conquest.

OTHER ROLES

1943: *Vladimir* / DAYS OF GLORY. **1944:** *Paul Scott* / THE VALLEY OF DECISION. **1947:** *Anthony Keane* / THE PARADINE CASE. **1948:** *Stretch* / YELLOW SKY. **1949:** *Fedja (Feodor Dostoyevsky)* / THE GREAT SINNER. **1951:** *King David* / DAVID AND BATHSHEBA; *Capt. Horatio Hornblower* / CAPTAIN HORATIO HORNBLOWER. **1952:** *Capt. Richard Lane* / ONLY THE VALIANT; *Jonathan Clark* / THE WORLD IN HIS ARMS; *Harry* / THE SNOWS OF KILIMANJARO. **1954:** *Col. Steve Van Dyke* / NIGHT PEOPLE; *Henry Adams* / THE MILLION POUND NOTE. **1955:** *Forrester* / THE PURPLE PLAIN. **1957:** *Mike Hagen* / DESIGNING WOMAN. **1958:** *Jim Douglass* / THE BRAVADOS. **1959:** *Lt. Clemons* / PORK CHOP HILL; *F. Scott Fitzgerald* / BELOVED INFIDEL; *Dwight Towers* / ON THE BEACH. **1961:** *Capt. Keith Mallory* / THE GUNS OF NAVARONE. **1962:** *Sam Bowden* / CAPE FEAR; *Cleve Van Valen* / HOW THE WEST WAS WON. **1964:** *Manuel Artiguez* / BEHOLD A PALE HORSE. **1965:** *David Stilwell* / MIRAGE. **1966:** *David Pollock* / ARABESQUE; *narrator* / JOHN F. KENNEDY: YEARS OF LIGHTNING, DAY OF DRUMS. **1968:** *MacKenna* / MACKENNA'S GOLD. **1969:** *Sam Varner* / THE STALKING MOON; *Dr. John Hathaway* / THE MOST DANGEROUS MAN IN THE WORLD; *Charles Keith* / MAROONED. **1970:** *Sheriff Henry Tawes* / I WALK THE LINE. **1971:** *Clay Lomax* / SHOOTOUT. **1973:** *Deans* / BILLY TWO HATS. **1977:** *Gen. Douglas MacArthur* / MACARTHUR. **1980:** *Col. Lewis Pugh* / THE SEA WOLVES. **1987:** *the president* / AMAZING GRACE.

PEPPARD, GEORGE

(1929–)

George Peppard's career, with a few notable exceptions, has been a series of failed opportunities. He's a good-looking man but just isn't very interesting. He has gained more popularity working with Mr. T on the TV series "The A-Team" than from all of his movies. He never seemed able to gain any sympathy for his tough man roles from audiences. Usually he portrayed a man you wouldn't like to get to know better. He studied at the Actor's Studio but apparently didn't take the lesson on showing emotional depth. Before his screen debut in 1957 in THE STRANGE ONE, he appeared in TV dramas and on Broadway. After his film career hit the skids he returned to television with a series in the 1970s, "Banacek," and made-for-TV movies including THE BRAVOS (1971), ONE OF OUR OWN (1975), GUILTY OR INNOCENT: THE SAM SHEPPARD MURDER CASE (1975), TORN BETWEEN TWO LOVERS (1979), and CRISIS IN MID-AIR (1979).

KEY ROLES

Robert Marquales / THE STRANGE ONE, 1957, Columbia, d-Jack Garfein.

In this controversial movie about life at a southern military academy, Peppard plays a freshman who is instrumental in kicking the rotten, dominating Ben Gazzara out of the school for the good of the institution.

Paul Varjack / BREAKFAST AT TIFFANY'S, 1961, Paramount, d-Blake Edwards.

Peppard is a young writer who moves into an apartment building in New York and becomes involved in the life of a slightly crazy girl (Audrey Hepburn) with a strange and exotic life. They fall in love but she's looking for wealth.

Corporal Chase / THE VICTORS, 1963, Columbia, d-Carl Foreman.

In this crowded picture of the World War II adventures of an American infantry platoon, Peppard is one who is a little more experienced and a little less shocked by the horrors of how the civilians and the soldiers must and do live between battles.

Jason Cord / THE CARPETBAGGERS, 1964, Paramount, d-Edward Dmytryk.

In this *film à clef*, Peppard is a Howard Hughes-like playboy with no emotions who can make money, but not friends or lovers. People are to be used according to him, and this includes his wives and girlfriends. Through it all Peppard looks bored but that's how he is supposed to act.

Bruno Stachel / THE BLUE MAX, 1966, 20th Century-Fox, d-John Guillermin.

In Germany during World War I, Peppard is an ambitious pilot drawn from the lower classes who doesn't get along too well with his aristocratic fellow pilots, especially when he causes the death of one. But he has the support of a high-ranking officer and the latter's sexy young wife and he becomes an ace and a hero to the ordinary people. Once again, Peppard wears an unemotional mask.

Capt. Kurt Bergman / TOBRUK, 1967, Universal, d-Arthur Hiller.

Peppard is a German Jew in the British army who is part of an expedition assigned to blow up the Nazi fuel bunkers. It's an interesting adventure story with some spectacular moments but no great acting, except possibly from Nigel Green.

OTHER ROLES

1959: *Fedderson* / PORK CHOP HILL. **1960:** *Rafe Copley* / HOME FROM THE HILL; *Leo Percepied* / THE SUBTERRANEANS. **1962:** *Zeb Rawlings* / HOW THE WEST WAS WON. **1965:** *John Curtis* / OPERATION CROSSBOW; *Steve Mallory* / THE THIRD DAY. **1967:** *Dolan* / ROUGH NIGHT IN JERICHO. **1968:** *P. J. Detweiler* / P. J.; *Pete* / WHAT'S SO BAD ABOUT FEELING GOOD?; *Capt. Frank Matthews* / PENDULUM. **1969:** *Reno Davis* / HOUSE OF CARDS; *John Shay* / THE EXECUTIONER. **1970:** *Capt. Rod Douglas* / CANNON FOR CORDOBA; *Harker Fleet* / ONE MORE TRAIN TO ROB. **1972:** *Tuxan* / THE GROUNDSTAR CONSPIRACY. **1974:** *Vince Newman* / NEWMAN'S LAW. **1977:** *Denton* / DAMNATION ALLEY. **1978:** *T. M. Pryor* / FIVE DAYS FROM HOME. **1980:** *Cowboy* / BATTLE BEYOND THE STARS. **1984:** *Theo Brown* / TREASURE OF THE YANKEE ZEPHYR.

PERKINS, ANTHONY

(1932–)

Often a single movie is enough to ruin an actor's career but it is usually because the portrayal was so poor. Anthony Perkins's career has been harmed because he was so marvelous in PSYCHO. The son of stage and screen actor Osgood Perkins, Tony played several appealing parts as gawky and sensitive young men before his role as Norman Bates, but has not been allowed to develop as an actor since. No matter what his roles, audiences are waiting for him to go crazy and swing a knife. In the 1980s, he returned to his most famous role in two sequels and, although not as impressive as the original, they show that Perkins still has acting talent. Speaking of his technique, Perkins explained: "One of my stage directors taught me that the best acting is spare acting, the sparest, with the smallest gesture, the greatest economy. I've learned how to mete it out."

KEY ROLES

Fred Whitmarsh / THE ACTRESS, 1953, MGM, d-George Cukor.

Perkins is a shy young suitor who almost diverts Jean Simmons from leaving her home to make her mark as an actress.

Josh Birdwell / FRIENDLY PERSUASION, 1956, Allied Artists, d-William Wyler.

Perkins's performance as a young Quaker who finds it increasingly difficult to follow the tenets of his faith when the American Civil War comes to his doorstep, earned him an Oscar nomination.

Eben Cabot / DESIRE UNDER THE ELMS, 1957, Paramount, d-Delbert Mann.

In this film based on a play by Eugene O'Neill, the new bride (Sophia Loren) of New England farmer Burl Ives causes friction with his son (Perkins), who feels great lust for her.

Jimmy Piersall / FEAR STRIKES OUT, 1957, Paramount, d-Robert Mulligan.

Perkins portrays the Boston Red Sox outfielder who suffers nervous breakdowns and exhibits strange behavior both on and off the field. His problems are apparently the result of pressure placed on him by his father who wants him to be a major league baseball player no matter what the cost.

Cornelius / THE MATCHMAKER, 1958, Paramount, d-Joseph Anthony.

Perkins handles quite well the comedy of this Thornton Wilder story about a turn-of-the-century matchmaker and a Yonkers businessman. He shows some real charm as the one who gets Shirley MacLaine in the end and a promotion besides.

Norman Bates / PSYCHO, 1960, Shamley / Hitchcock, d-Alfred Hitchcock.

Perkins is perfect as the jittery motel manager who lives for his mother, even to the point of becoming her when necessary. Between times of playing his mother, he is fairly normal though pathetic, as he tries without much success to have a normal conversation with a woman (Janet Leigh) who stops at his motel while running towards her married lover and away from the crime of stealing $40,000 from her employer. She is killed in an unforgettable shower scene and Perkins becomes physically ill when he sees what his "mother" has done. But, like a good son, he cleans things up and gets rid of the body. As others investigate the disappearance of Leigh, Perkins is driven closer and closer to becoming his dominating mother until finally he has no existence of his own.

Joseph K. / THE TRIAL, 1962, France / Italy / West Germany, Paris / Europe / Ficit / Hisa, d-Orson Welles.

Perkins portrays Franz Kafka's victim of a nightmarish trial in which he is condemned for an unspecified crime.

Dennis Pitt / PRETTY POISON, 1968, 20th Century-Fox, d-Noel Black.

Perkins is a psychotic young man who meets a cute honor student (Tuesday Weld) and entertains her with tales of his being a spy. Despite her innocent appearance, she is a coldly manipulative horror who kills her mother and persuades Perkins to participate in a series of crimes. When the two are finally caught she once again becomes a sweet young thing and Perkins takes all the blame.

Kramer / NORTH SEA HIJACK, 1979, Great Britain, Universal / Cinema 7, d-Andrew V. McLaglen.

Called FFOLKES in the United States, this is the story of how Perkins and a band of killers take over a North Sea oil station and hold it for ransom. It is rescued by the derring-do of an eccentric man named ffolkes (Roger Moore).

Norman Bates / PSYCHO II, 1983, Universal, d-Richard Franklin.

Considering the general quality of sequels, this film is not too bad. When Norman Bates is released as a cured man from a mental institution, his victim's sister (Vera Miles) protests the release and keeps an eye on him. When murders begin again, it seems that maybe Perkins isn't as well as he seemed.

OTHER ROLES

1957: *Riley Wade* / THE LONELY MAN; *Ben Owens* / THE TIN STAR. **1958:** *Joseph Dufresne* / THIS ANGRY AGE; *Abel* / GREEN MANSIONS. **1959:** *Pete Holmes* / ON THE BEACH. **1960:** *Ray Blent* / TALL STORY. **1961:** *Philip Vander Besh* / GOODBYE AGAIN. **1962:** *Alexis* / PHAEDRA; *Robert Macklin* / FIVE MILES TO MIDNIGHT. **1964:** *Johnny* / TWO ARE GUILTY; *Milo Bogardus* / THE FOOL KILLER; *Harry Compton* / A RAVISHING IDIOT. **1966:** *Sergeant Warren* / IS PARIS BURNING? **1968:** *Christopher Balling* / THE CHAMPAGNE MURDERS. **1970:** *Chaplain Tappman* / CATCH-22; *Rainey* / WUSA. **1971:** *Charles Van Horn* / TEN DAYS WONDER; *Lionel Jeffries* / SOMEONE BEHIND THE DOOR. **1972:** *Reverend La Salle* / THE LIFE AND TIMES OF JUDGE ROY BEAN; *B. Z.* / PLAY IT AS IT LAYS. **1973:** *Gid* / LOVIN' MOLLY. **1974:** *Hector McQueen* / MURDER ON THE ORIENT EXPRESS. **1975:** *Sean* / MAHOGANY. **1978:** *Neil Curry* / REMEMBER MY NAME. **1979:** *John Ceruti* / WINTER KILLS; *Dr. Alex Durant* / THE BLACK HOLE; *Lawrence Miles* / DOUBLE NEGATIVE. **1980:** *Alfred* / TWICE A WOMAN. **1984:** *Rev. Peter Shayne* / CRIMES OF PASSION. **1986:** *Norman Bates* / PSYCHO III.

PETERS, JEAN

(1926–)

Dark-haired beauty Jean Peters became a star in her first film, CAPTAIN FROM CASTILE in 1947. This former Ohio State student and winner of a campus popularity contest was at her most appealing as spirited women in costume pieces. She had a sort of pouty look that passed for sexy. Her acting, while adequate for her roles, was nothing to get excited about. Her own view of actors was: "We need people to personify our dreams." She left movies when she married Howard Hughes, her second husband. She returned to acting on the stage 15 years later, after divorcing the celebrated recluse.

KEY ROLES

Catana Perez / CAPTAIN FROM CASTILE, 1947, 20th Century-Fox, d-Henry King.

Peters is a young peasant girl who, along with Spanish nobleman Tyrone Power, escapes the clutches of the Inquisition and joins the Conquistadors of Cortez in the new world. There she becomes Power's wife but their hopes for a new life are threatened when John Sutton, the officer who instigated the false charges against them, arrives. He's killed and Power is held responsible until cleared by an Indian prince.

Anne Bonney / ANNE OF THE INDIES, 1951, 20th Century-Fox, d-Jacques Tourneur.

Peters becomes a feared pirate captain on the Spanish Main. She is pursued by French officer Louis Jourdan who turns on the charm, but she sees through his trap. As revenge she captures Jourdan and his wife and leaves them on a desert island to die. Later she changes her mind and rescues them, then battles pirate rival Blackbeard to the death and is killed.

Laurie Harper / LURE OF THE WILDERNESS, 1952, 20th Century-Fox, d-Jean Negulesco.

In the early years of the century, Walter Brennan and his daughter (Peters) live in the Okefenokee Swamp of Georgia because he is a fugitive from justice. A young hunter (Jeffrey Hunter) comes across them and, by selling their pelts, is able to hire a good lawyer who clears the false charges against Brennan, allowing him and his daughter to leave the swamp. Peters then finds a new life with Hunter.

Polly Cutler / NIAGARA, 1953, 20th Century-Fox, d-Henry Hathaway.

While honeymooning with her husband (Casey Adams), Peters is taken hostage by Joseph Cotten after he has turned the tables on his unfaithful wife (Marilyn Monroe) and killed her. The boat they are in runs out of gas and smashes on the rocks. Cotten saves Peters by pushing her to safety and then is swept over the falls.

Anita / THREE COINS IN THE FOUNTAIN, 1954, 20th Century-Fox, d-Jean Negulesco.

While working in Rome, Peters and two other American girls find romance. The man in her life is Italian wolf Rossano Brazzi, but she brings out the good in him.

Catherine Marshall / A MAN CALLED PETER, 1955, 20th Century-Fox, d-Henry Koster.

Peters is the widow of the Scottish minister who wrote a bestselling book in which she told his story about becoming the chaplain of the U.S. Senate.

OTHER ROLES

1948: *Ann Freeman* / DEEP WATERS. **1949:** *Deborah Greenleaf* / IT HAPPENS EVERY SPRING. **1950:** *Ruth Manning* / LOVE THAT BRUTE. **1951:** *Dallas* / TAKE CARE OF MY LITTLE GIRL; *Alice Hodges* / AS YOUNG AS YOU FEEL. **1952:** *Josefa Zapata* / VIVA ZAPATA!; *Nellie Halper* / WAIT 'TIL THE SUN SHINES, NELLIE; *Susan* / O. HENRY'S FULL HOUSE. **1953:** *Candy* / PICKUP ON SOUTH STREET; *Lynne Cameron* / A BLUEPRINT FOR MURDER; *Vicki Lynn* / VICKI. **1954:** *Nalinle* / APACHE; *Barbara* / BROKEN LANCE.

PIDGEON, WALTER

(1897–1984)

Born in New Brunswick, Canada, Walter Pidgeon served in the Canadian army during World War I. He made his stage debut in 1922 and his first movie appearance in 1926. He specialized in distinguished and gentlemanly roles, and was most famous for his screen teamings with Greer Garson. Never a top star but always a top performer, he was nominated for Oscars for MRS. MINIVER and MADAME CURIE, but his best portrayal was probably in ADVISE AND CONSENT. His later stage roles were in "The Happiest Millionaire," "Take Me Along," "Take Her, She's Mine," and "Dinner at Eight." Speaking of how it was to be a movie actor, he noted, "I was like a kept woman during my twenty-one years at MGM. Hollywood was like an expensive, beautifully run club. You didn't need to carry money. Your face was your credit card all over the world."

KEY ROLES

Richard Marsden / THE THIRTEENTH JUROR, 1927, Silent, Universal, d-Edward Laemmle.

Pidgeon's wife is loved by a powerful and successful lawyer (Francis X. Bushman) whom a political machine hopes to ruin by spreading the word that he's having an affair with Pidgeon's wife. Bushman and his accuser struggle with the latter being killed. The police believe Pidgeon is the guilty party and the lawyer has a tough time convincing them that he is innocent.

Arthur Marsden / THE GORILLA, 1930, Warners, d-Bryan Foy.

Pidgeon is just one of a crew of actors who make monkeys out of themselves in this slapstick film about a couple of detectives who are employed by Pidgeon, the owner of a mansion, to track down the hairy beast who resides there and is causing a lot of fuss. Pidgeon had appeared in another role in the 1927 silent version.

Sam Bailey / THE SHOPWORN ANGEL, 1938, MGM, d-H. C. Potter.

Pidgeon is the man-about-town who is given the gate by Margaret Sullivan when she meets naive young soldier James Stewart.

Christopher Durant / SOCIETY LAWYER, 1939, MGM, d-Edwin L. Marin.

When lawyer Pidgeon outlives his usefulness to racketeer Eduardo Ciannelli, the latter frames him for murder, but Pidgeon beats the rap.

Nick Carter / **Robert Chalmers** / NICK CARTER—MASTER DETECTIVE, 1939, MGM, d-George B. Seitz.

In this first of a series, Pidgeon is the well-known sleuth who must deal with a killer on an airplane.

William Cantrill / DARK COMMAND, 1940, Republic, d-Raoul Walsh.

In pre-Civil War Kansas, ex-schoolteacher Pidgeon organizes a guerilla band to pillage the countryside, all in the name of working for the South. John Wayne puts an end to Pidgeon's extracurricular career.

Captain Thorndyke / MAN HUNT, 1941, 20th Century-Fox, d-Fritz Lang.

British sportsman and hunter Pidgeon, vacationing in Bavaria, goes to Adolf Hitler's home and gets him in his gun sights. But he is caught in the act and is beaten and left for dead by the Gestapo. He survives and returns to London where he finds himself tracked by German agents led by George Sanders. Trapped, he saves himself by killing Sanders.

Sam Gladney / BLOSSOMS IN THE DUST, 1941, MGM, d-Mervyn LeRoy.

Teamed with Greer Garson for the first time, Pidgeon has a thriving flour mill business in Texas when he marries a Wisconsin girl (Garson). They settle down and are delighted when they have a child, even though they are told they can have no others. When the boy dies a few years later, their marriage is almost ruined, but Garson finds comfort for her sorrow by starting a foundling home. Soon thereafter, Pidgeon suffers financial reverses and dies but Garson carries on.

Mr. Gruffydd / HOW GREEN WAS MY VALLEY, 1941, 20th Century-Fox, d-John Ford.

Pidgeon is a compassionate minister who befriends Roddy McDowall, the boy who will grow to be the narrator of this beautifully made film about a mining family in a small village in Wales. McDowall's sister (Maureen O'Hara) falls in love with Pidgeon but they are not able to marry.

Clem Miniver / MRS. MINIVER, 1942, MGM, d-William Wyler.

Pidgeon and his wife (Greer Garson) live in a country town outside of London. Their eldest son becomes engaged to a local girl on the night he is to be shipped out to the newly declared World War II. While Pidgeon and other men of the village are collecting all available boats to be used in the evacuation of Dunkirk, Garson finds a wounded German pilot in her garden and turns him over to the authorities. When their son and his girlfriend marry and return home from their honeymoon in time for the annual flower show, a German air raid interrupts the show and their new daughter-in-law is among those killed as the planes reduce the village to ruins. The vicar gathers his parishioners together in their shattered church where they reaffirm their faith in England's future.

Harry Witzel / WHITE CARGO, 1942, MGM, d-Richard Thorpe.

Pidgeon knows just how to handle sultry Hedy Lamarr, who drives men mad in this sex saga set on a rubber plantation. When he finds her trying to poison Richard Carlson, he forces her to drink the brew.

Pierre Curie / MADAME CURIE, 1943, MGM, d-Mervyn LeRoy.

Pidgeon is a notable scientist but, teamed with Greer Garson again, he takes a back seat to the charming redhead.

Chip Collyer / WEEKEND AT THE WALDORF, 1945, MGM, d-Robert Z. Leonard.

In this all-star modernized version of GRAND HOTEL, Pidgeon approximates the role played by John Barrymore and the public ate it up.

Maj. Gen. Roland Goodlaw Kane / COMMAND DECISION, 1948, MGM, d-Sam Wood.

Pidgeon is the commanding officer who believes in the importance of good press. He fears that Clark Gable's orders for daylight bombing runs over Germany, resulting in many casualties, can't be considered "good news."

Young Joslyn Forsyte / THAT FORSYTE WOMAN, 1949, MGM, d-Compton Bennett.

Pidgeon is the black sheep of the family who wins Greer Garson away from her husband (Errol Flynn) when the latter proves to be a cad and a bore.

Bulldog Drummond / CALLING BULLDOG DRUMMOND, 1951, Great Britan, MGM, d-Victor Saville.

Pidgeon moves into the long-running series about the exploits of the British adventurer. This time he goes undercover to catch a gang of thieves.

Frederick Alderson / EXECUTIVE SUITE, 1954, MGM, d-Robert Wise.

Pidgeon is among a group of trustees of a furniture company who maneuver and make deals as they prepare to select a replacement to the president of the company after the latter dies of a heart attack.

Dr. Morbius / FORBIDDEN PLANET, 1956, MGM, d-Fred Wilcox.

No one connected with this science-fiction film gave any credit for the story to William Shakespeare, but the whole plot of the latter's "The Tempest" was used. It was and remains an excellent movie in the genre with Pidgeon competing favorably with Robby the Robot for acting honors.

Sen. Bob Munson / ADVISE AND CONSENT, 1962, Columbia, d-Otto Preminger.

Loyal Senate majority leader Pidgeon is ready to pull out all the stops to gain the confirmation of President Franchot Tone's nomination for Secretary of State (Henry Fonda). But it's not going to be easy as Fonda has strong enemies and unscrupulous friends on both sides of the aisle.

Florenz Ziegfeld / FUNNY GIRL, 1968, Columbia, d-William Wyler.

When William Powell used up his copyright on the role of the famous showman, he turned it over to Pidgeon. He plays the man who was not always amused by the antics of the great Fanny Brice.

OTHER ROLES

1925: *Martin Innesbrook* / MANNEQUIN. **1926:** *Clyde Lord Geradine* / OLD LOVES AND NEW; *Basil Owen* / THE OUTSIDER; *Bravo* / MISS NOBODY; *Paul* / "MARRIAGE LICENSE?" **1927:** *Paul Sinclair* / THE GIRL FROM RIO; *Monte Carroll* / THE HEART OF SALOME; *Stevens* / THE GORILLA; *Arthur Wyatt* / THE GATEWAY OF THE MOON. **1928:** *Victor Trent* / CLOTHES MAKE THE WOMAN; *The U.S. consul* / WOMAN WISE; *Philip Drake* / TURN BACK THE HOURS; *Jack Clark* / MELODY OF LOVE. **1929:** *Tony Williams* / A MOST IMMORAL LADY; *Ned Thayer* / HER PRIVATE LIFE. **1930:** *Colonel Vultow* / BRIDE OF THE REGIMENT; *Lord Verney* / VIENNESE NIGHTS; *Paul de St. Cyr* / KISS ME AGAIN; *Ace Benton* / GOING WILD. **1931:** *Clay* / HOT HEIRESS. **1932:** *Commissioner Al Howard* / ROCKABYE. **1933:** *Bachelor* / THE KISS BEFORE THE MIRROR. **1934:** *Florestan, baritone* / JOURNAL OF A CRIME. **1936:** *Richard Morey* / BIG BROWN EYES; *David Roberts* / FATAL LADY. **1937:** *Paul Stacey* / GIRL OVERBOARD; *Hartley Madison* / SARATOGA; *"Micky" McGuire* / A GIRL WITH IDEAS; *Dr. Scott Logan* / SHE'S DANGEROUS; *Fraser James* / AS GOOD AS MARRIED; *Ken Morley* / MY DEAR MISS ALDRICH. **1938:** *Alan Wythe* / MAN-PROOF; *Sheriff Jack Rance* / THE GIRL OF THE GOLDEN WEST; *Bill Dennis* / TOO HOT TO HANDLE; *Richard Thurlow* / LISTEN, DARLING. **1939:** *Steve Donegan* / 6000 ENEMIES; *Tyler Flagg* / STRONGER THAN DESIRE. **1940:** *Tim Nolan* / THE HOUSE ACROSS THE BAY; *John Arlen* / IT'S A DATE; *Nick Carter* / PHANTOM RAIDERS; *Nick Carter* / SKY MURDER; *Sq. Cmdr. Bill Gary* / FLIGHT COMMAND. **1941:** *Jeff Sherman* / DESIGN FOR SCANDAL. **1943:** *guest* / THE YOUNGEST PROFESSION. **1944:** *Maj. August Parkington* / MRS. PARKINGTON. **1946:** *Jeffrey Evans* / HOLIDAY IN MEXICO, *Chris Matthews* / THE SECRET HEART. **1947:** *cameo* / CASS TIMBERLANE; *Mark Sabre* / IF WINTER COMES. **1948:** *William Sylvester Packett* / JULIA MISBEHAVES. **1949:** *Col. Michael "Jokey" Nicobar* / THE RED DANUBE. **1950:** *Clem Miniver* / THE MINIVER STORY. **1951:** *Colonel Brunswick* / SOLDIERS THREE; *Dwight Bradley Masen* / THE UNKNOWN MAN; *narrator* / QUO VADIS. **1952:** *Haven Allridge* / THE SELLOUT; *Prof. Frederick Kellerman* / THE MILLION DOLLAR MERMAID; *Harry Pebbel* / THE BAD AND THE BEAUTIFUL. **1953:** *Patrick J. McChesney* / SCANDAL AT SCOURIE; *Walter McBride* / DREAM WIFE. **1954:** *Cmdr. Kent Dowling* / MEN OF THE FIGHTING LADY; *James Ellswirth* / THE LAST TIME I SAW PARIS; *J. J. Shubert* / DEEP IN MY HEART. **1955:** *Rr. Adm. Daniel Xavier Smith* / HIT THE DECK; *narrator* / THE GLASS SLIPPER. **1956:** *James Rayburn* / THESE WILDER YEARS; *Col. Edward W. Hall, Sr.* / THE RACK. **1961:** *Admiral Nelson* / VOYAGE TO THE BOTTOM OF THE SEA. **1962:** *Col. Timothy Henderson* / THE TWO COLONELS; *James Haggin* / BIG RED. **1963:** *himself* / THE SHORTEST DAY. **1967:** *Orville Ames* / WARNING SHOT. **1969:** *narrator* / RASCAL; *the mastermind* / THE VATICAN AFFAIR. **1972:** *Dr. Larkin* / THE SCREAMING LADY; *Sen. Aren Lindner* / SKYJACKED. **1973:** *Dr. Samuel Andrews* / THE NEPTUNE FACTOR; *Casey* / HARRY IN YOUR POCKET. **1976:** *pickpocket* / TWO MINUTE WARNING; *Grayson's butler* / WON TON TON, THE DOG WHO SAVED HOLLYWOOD. **1977:** *the chairman* / SEXTETTE.

POITIER, SIDNEY

(1924–)

Born in Florida, Sidney Poitier was raised in the Bahamas, served in the U.S. army during World War II, and worked with the American Negro Theater. He made his Broadway debut in 1946 in an all-black production of "Lysistrata," his film debut in a Signal Corps documentary, FROM WHENCE COMETH MY HELP, in 1949, and his commercial movie debut in NO WAY OUT in 1950. Poitier was the first international black leading man. Nominated for an Oscar for THE DEFIANT ONES, he won for his performance in LILIES OF THE FIELD, becoming the first black to win the Best Actor award. In 1971 he directed his first film, BUCK AND THE PREACHER, and since then has directed eight other films, including UPTOWN SATURDAY NIGHT (1974), STIR CRAZY (1980), and HANKY PANKY (1982). Poitier has been the industry's Jackie Robinson, forever destroying the stereotype of black actors, although the number of black actors who have attained his position in films has been very few. He himself found it difficult to find good roles as he reached middle age, but at age sixty he seems to be making an acting comeback. He said about himself: "I'm an American first and foremost. Then I'm an actor. Finally, if you like, I'm a Negro."

KEY ROLES

Luther Brooks / NO WAY OUT, 1950, 20th Century-Fox, d-Joseph L. Mankiewicz.

Poitier is a graduate doctor working at a municipal hospital when two hoodlums are brought in. He operates on one because he believes there is a bigger problem than a mere gunshot wound. The man dies and his brother (Richard Widmark), who hates blacks, vows he will kill Poitier. It's an excellent indictment of prejudice.

Gregory Miller / THE BLACKBOARD JUNGLE, 1955, MGM, d-Richard Brooks.

Poitier is a student at Manual Trades High School in New York where dedicated first-year teacher Glenn Ford is trying to teach literature to a bunch of young punks. At first it seems that Poitier is just another troublemaker, but ultimately he proves that Ford has gotten to him despite one unfortunate racial slur.

Tommy Tyler / EDGE OF THE CITY, 1957, MGM, d-Martin Ritt.

In this tale of racial tensions in the New York railroad yards of the waterfronts, Poitier is a loader of freighters who becomes friends with an army deserter. This leads to Poitier's death in a brutal fight with a gang boss.

Noah Cullen / THE DEFIANT ONES, 1958, United Artists, d-Stanley Kramer.

Poitier is a convict on a southern chain gang who is chained to bigoted Tony Curtis. The two escape and fight with each other as they try to make their getaway. But eventually they learn they must put aside their racial feelings and pull together if they are to reach their goal of freedom.

Porgy / PORGY AND BESS, 1959, Goldwyn, d-Otto Preminger.

Poitier portrays the crippled Charleston, South Carolina, black man who falls in love with Bess, but has to compete with a strong Brock Peters for her love in this film version of the American folk opera by George Gershwin and DuBose Heyward.

Walter Lee Younger / A RAISIN IN THE SUN, 1961, Columbia, d-Daniel Petrie.

Poitier had appeared in the Broadway play about the life of a struggling black family in a cramped Chicago flat. They find themselves arguing over how to spend a $10,000 life insurance payment they have received.

Homer Smith / LILIES OF THE FIELD, 1963, United Artists, d-Ralph Nelson.

Poitier won an Oscar for his charming role as an itinerant black Baptist workman who helps a group of German nuns build a chapel in New Mexico. It's not a great movie but it is quite delightful even if its message is a bit too obvious.

Ben Munceford / THE BEDFORD INCIDENT, 1965, Columbia, d-James B. Harris.

The real significance of this film is that no mention is made of Poitier's color. He's a photographer aboard a nuclear destroyer that accidentally fires an atomic weapon at a Russian submarine that retaliates.

Gordon Ralfe / A PATCH OF BLUE, 1965, MGM, d-Guy Green.

Poitier helps a blind girl living in the slums who falls in love with him without knowing his color. The message is a bit obvious now but at the time of the film's release it had more to say. As a tearjerker too, it's not bad.

Virgil Tibbs / IN THE HEAT OF THE NIGHT, 1967, United Artists, d-Norman Jewison.

There's no mystery in this film as to who the real killer is. Even a redneck bigot could figure that out early in the movie. The real story of the film is the interplay between Rod Steiger, a southern sheriff not used to speaking respectfully to a black man, and black Philadelphia homicide detective Poitier who is asked to give Steiger a hand in solving a murder case. They begin to have some mutual respect reminiscent of THE DEFIANT ONES.

Dr. John Prentice / GUESS WHO'S COMING TO DINNER, 1967, Columbia, d-Stanley Kramer.

Looking at this film today, one sees it as embarrassing liberal claptrap, just about as condescending as the films that made us laugh at Stepin Fetchit. Look how enlightened Katharine Hepburn and Spencer Tracy are as they barely bat an eye when their daughter becomes engaged to one of the best-looking, brightest black doctors who ever existed. Give us a break. It's an overrated film and doesn't give Poitier a chance to demonstrate his talents as an actor. He needed and deserved more roles in which his acting could be judged and fewer where he played a black that whites could accept.

Jack Parks / FOR LOVE OF IVY, 1968, Cinemama, d-Daniel Mann.

When valuable maid Abby Lincoln gives notice, her family hires likable ne'er-do-well Poitier to romance her so that she will stay. Hollywood needed a black love affair at the time and this was the best it could do. Once again it might have worked better if they concentrated more on the love affair and less on the color of the participants.

Buck / BUCK AND THE PREACHER, 1972, Columbia, d-Sidney Poitier.

Poitier is an ex-Union soldier who becomes a wagonmaster for some former slaves headed west to homestead. They are bothered by nightriders but Poitier outsmarts them with a little help from a phony preacher con man (Harry Belafonte). It could be funnier.

OTHER ROLES

1952: *Reverend Maimangu* / CRY THE BELOVED COUNTRY; *Corp. Andrew Robertson* / RED BALL EXPRESS. **1954:** *Inman Jackson* / GO, MAN, GO! **1956:** *Gates Watson* / GOODBYE, MY LADY. **1957:** *Rau-Ru* / BAND OF ANGELS; *Kimani* / SOMETHING OF VALUE. **1958:** *Obam* / THE MARK OF THE HAWK; *Marcus* / VIRGIN ISLAND. **1960:** *Sgt. Towler* / ALL THE YOUNG MEN. **1961:** *Eddie Cook* / PARIS BLUES. **1962:** *doctor* / PRESSURE POINT. **1964:** *El Mansuh* / THE LONG SHIPS. **1965:** *Alan Newell* / THE SLENDER THREAD; *Simon of Cyrene* / THE GREATEST STORY EVER TOLD; *Toller* / DUEL AT DIABLO. **1967:** *Mark Thackeray* / TO SIR, WITH LOVE. **1969:** *Jason Higgs* / THE LOST MAN. **1970:** *Lt. Virgil Tibbs* / THEY CALL ME MR. TIBBS. **1971:** *Lt. Virgil Tibbs* / THE ORGANIZATION; *John Kane* / BROTHER JOHN. **1973:** *Matt Younger* / A WARM DECEMBER. **1974:** *Steve Jackson* / UPTOWN SATURDAY NIGHT. **1975:** *Shack Twala* / THE WILBY CONSPIRACY; *Clyde Williams* / LET'S DO IT AGAIN. **1977:** *Manny Durrell* / A PIECE OF THE ACTION.

POWELL, DICK

(1904–1963)

Born in Arkansas, Dick Powell sang in choirs as a boy and with local bands before organizing his own dance band. He worked in radio and vaudeville before being signed by Warners, where he became a star appearing in musicals with Ruby Keeler. By the early 1940s he had become obsolete as a juvenile in musicals and made a second career by moving into film noir pictures where he played tough private eyes or tough characters who were just on the edge of the law. He later proved to have executive ability, producing and directing TV shows for Four Stars Productions which he organized with David Niven, Ida Lupino, and Charles Boyer. Powell had charm, good looks, brains, and the courage to make changes in his career at just the right time. Powell, who died of cancer in 1963, was the director and producer of the 1956 movie THE CONQUEROR, filmed near Yucca Flat, Utah, where the U.S. government had exploded eleven atomic devices. More than ninety members of the 220-person cast and crew who worked on the picture on location developed cancer and more than forty-five died of their ailments. Statistically, this suggests more than a coincidence.

KEY ROLES

Billy Lawler / FORTY-SECOND STREET, 1933, Warners, d-Lloyd Bacon.

Powell is the juvenile in the Broadway musical directed by Warren Baxter during the Depression. He takes more than a professional interest in naive dancer Ruby Keeler, who replaces the incapacitated star on opening night. Powell croons "Young and Healthy" to blonde Toby Wing and a horde of chorus girls.

Brad Roberts (Robert Treat Bradford) / GOLD DIGGERS OF 1933, 1933, Warners, d-Mervyn LeRoy.

Songwriter Powell lives across the hall from three showgirls (Ruby Keeler, Joan Blondell, and Aline MacMahon). He's sweet on Keeler but he's not what he seems. He's actually from a very wealthy family that sends his brother and their lawyer to save him from the clutches of Keeler when he writes, produces, and stars in a show featuring the girls. Blondell and MacMahon pick off the brother and lawyer, respectively.

Scotty Blair / FOOTLIGHT PARADE, 1933, Warners, d-Lloyd Bacon.

Once again Powell discovers the charms of Ruby Keeler. In this picture Jimmy Cagney produces live prologues for New York movie theaters. Powell is a cocky gigolo who teams with Keeler in the production numbers "Honeymoon Hotel" and "By a Waterfall."

Jimmy Higgens / DAMES, 1934, Warners, d-Ray Enright.

Eccentric millionaire Hugh Herbert proposes to give Guy Kibbee ten million dollars since he is a moral man. Herbert hates the theater, so Kibbee must get rid of relative Powell who is associated with the theater. Then Kibbee's own daughter (Ruby Keeler) joins a show and the fun begins. Powell sings "I Only Have Eyes for You" to Keeler, who turns out to be his thirteenth cousin.

Dick "Canary" Dorcy / FLIRTATION WALK, 1934, Warners, d-Frank Borzage.

Powell is an army private stationed in Hawaii and Ruby Keeler is the general's daughter. When her fiancée catches the two in an embrace after a moonlight drive, Powell deserts so as not to create a scandal. Wishing to save him, Keeler tells him he means nothing to her. Determined to prove that he's just as good as her officer boyfriend, he enrolls at West Point just about the time Keeler's dad is made commandant. True love doesn't run smoothly but he graduates with honors and he and Keeler make plans to be wed. Keeler and Powell perform the title number and "Mr. and Mrs. Is the Name."

Lysander / A MIDSUMMER NIGHT'S DREAM, 1935, Warners, d-Max Reinhardt and William Dieterle.

As one of the lovers who find their lives mixed up by fairies in the woods of Athens at midnight, Powell looks as if he could use some help from Ruby Keeler.

Gary Blake / ON THE AVENUE, 1937, 20th Century-Fox, d-Roy Del Ruth.

Powell appears as a Broadway producer who stages a satire of an heiress (Madeleine Carroll). This enrages her but she later falls for Powell and everything works out okay. The Irving Berlin songs include "I've Got My Love to Keep Me Warm" and "The Girl on the Police Gazette."

Jimmy MacDonald / CHRISTMAS IN JULY, 1940, Paramount, d-Preston Sturges.

Powell shows a lively sense of humor as the clerk who incorrectly believes he has won $25,000 in a slogan contest and goes on a spending spree.

Larry Stevens / IT HAPPENED TOMORROW, 1944, United Artists, d-Rene Clair.

Reporter Powell meets an old man (John Philliber) who has the power to show him the next day's headlines. This helps him get scoops, until he reads of his death in tomorrow's paper.

Philip Marlowe / MURDER, MY SWEET, 1944, RKO, d-Edward Dmytryk.

Powell is the tough private eye who describes the beatings he suffers in a way that really makes one hurt: "I caught the blackjack right behind my ear. A black pool opened up at my feet. I dived in. It had no bottom." No longer the smiling song-and-dance man, Powell is hired by ex-con Mike Mazurki to locate the latter's missing girlfriend. While working on the case he encounters many dishonest people and crimes of very major natures.

Johnny O'Clock / JOHNNY O'CLOCK, 1947, Columbia, d-Robert Rossen.

Continuing with his new-found tough guy image, Powell is a gambler who appears to be mixed up in the death of a crooked cop, but he's able to clear himself with the help of Ellen Drew.

James Lee Bartlow / THE BAD AND THE BEAUTIFUL, 1952, MGM, d-Vincente Minnelli.

Powell is a novelist brought to Hollywood to write a screenplay for the movie to be made from his bestseller. Because of his wife (Gloria Grahame), he can't seem to get to work. So producer Kirk Douglas arranges for her to be escorted around by handsome actor Gilbert Roland. Powell finishes the screenplay but Grahame is killed in an automobile accident with Roland, and Powell holds Douglas responsible.

OTHER ROLES

1932: *Bunny Harmon* / BLESSED EVENT; *Dan* / TOO BUSY TO WORK. **1933:** *John Kent* / THE KING'S VACATION; *Phil Sargent* / COLLEGE COACH; *Jerry Ford* / CONVENTION CITY. **1934:** *Tommy* / WONDER BAR; *Buddy Clayton* / TWENTY MILLION SWEETHEARTS; *Bob Lane* / HAPPINESS AHEAD. **1935:** *Dick Curtis* / GOLD DIGGERS OF 1935; *Bingo Nelson* / PAGE MISS GLORY; *Richard Purcell* / BROADWAY GONDOLIER; *Richard John Melville III* / SHIPMATES FOREVER; *Eric Land* / THANKS A MILLION. **1936:** *Donald Ames* / COLLEEN; *Jerome Bonaparte* / HEARTS DIVIDED; *George Randall* / STAGE STRUCK. **1937:** *Rosmer Peck* / GOLD DIGGERS OF 1937; *Bob Brent* / THE SINGING MARINE; *Charles "Chuck" Daly* / VARSITY SHOW. **1938:** *Ronnie Bowers* / HOLLYWOOD HOTEL; *Elly Jordan* / COWBOY FROM BROOKLYN; *Bill Davis* / HARD TO GET; *Pete Mason* / GOING PLACES. **1939:** *Professor Hardwick* / NAUGHTY BUT NICE. **1940:** *Alan MacNally* / I WANT A DIVORCE. **1941:** *Fred Chambers* / MODEL WIFE; *Tommy Halstead* / *Russ Raymond* / IN THE NAVY. **1942:** *guest* / STAR SPANGLED RHYTHM; *Pete Hamilton* / HAPPY GO LUCKY. **1943:** *Link Ferris* / TRUE TO LIFE; *Steve Baird* / RIDING HIGH. **1944:** *William "Swanee" Swanson* / MEET THE PEOPLE. **1945:** *Gerard* / CORNERED. **1948:** *Michael Barrows* / TO THE ENDS OF THE EARTH; *John Forbes* / PITFALL; *Haven* / STATION WEST; *Whit Corbett* / ROGUE'S REGIMENT. **1949:** *Sgt. Mike Flannigan* / MRS. MIKE. **1950:** *Andrew Rockton Hale* / THE REFORMER AND THE REDHEAD; *Rick Garvey* / RIGHT CROSS. **1951:** *guest* / CALLAWAY WENT THATAWAY; *Rocky* / CRY DANGER; *John Kennedy* / THE TALL TARGET. **1951:** *Rex Shepherd* / YOU NEVER CAN TELL. **1954:** *Mark* / SUSAN SLEPT HERE.

POWELL, ELEANOR

(1910–1982)

The Dance Masters of America voted Eleanor Powell the world's greatest tap dancer. She incorporated the ballet moves she began to learn when only six in her routines as well as acrobatic moves that had to be seen to be believed. Her dancing emphasized high kicks, rapid chain turns, and gymnastics that would make Mary Lou Retton proud. The dark-haired musical star, married to Glenn Ford from 1943 to 1959, made her film debut in GEORGE WHITE'S SCANDALS in 1935. Not comfortable as an actress, Powell knew her movie career was over in the early 1940s. She became an ordained minister of the Unity Church and created and acted in the TV series "Faith of Our Children" from 1953 to 1956. Later she appeared in musical revues in Las Vegas and New York.

KEY ROLES

Nora Paige / BORN TO DANCE, 1936, MGM, d-Roy Del Ruth.

The plot of this musical is as silly as can be. Powell gets to go on in place of difficult star Virginia Bruce which pleases the sailor (James Stewart) with whom she has fallen in love. What counts is Powell dancing to songs and numbers such as "Rap-Rap-Tap on Wood" and the smash finale "Swingin' the Jinx Away" set on board a movie-musical battleship.

Sally Lee / BROADWAY MELODY OF 1938, 1937, MGM, d-Roy Del Ruth.

The plot of this musical about a theatrical boarding house in New York City is best remembered for Judy Garland's singing "You Made Me Love You" to a photo of Clark Gable. But Powell does her usual good work dancing to "Broadway Rhythm" and "I'm Feeling Like a Million."

Rosalie Romanikoff / ROSALIE, 1937, MGM, d-W. S. Van Dyke.

Powell is the Princess Rosalie of Romanza who, while attending college in the U.S., falls in love with football player Nelson Eddy. Enough of the ridiculous plot. The film gave her a chance to blow away audiences' minds with her dancing to the Cole Porter title number, which is one of the biggest production numbers ever seen in a movie. She also pleases with her tapping in "I've a Strange New Rhythm in My Heart."

Marilyn Marsh / LADY BE GOOD, 1941, MGM, d-Norman Z. McLeod.

As in Powell's other films, the less said about the plot the better. Tune in for the Gershwins' "Fascinating Rhythm" staged by Busby Berkeley in the finale where once again Powell successfully defends the title as Best on Taps. The other numbers include the Gershwins' title number and "You'll Never Know" by Roger Edens.

Herself / THOUSANDS CHEER, 1943, MGM, d-George Sidney.

Powell is one of the many guest artists in this wartime musical hit. In her specialty number she dances up a storm to a medley of songs including "The Gem of the Ocean" and "American Patrol."

OTHER ROLES

1935: *herself (specialty number)* / GEORGE WHITE'S SCANDALS; *Irene Foster / Madame Arlette* / BROADWAY MELODY OF 1936. **1939:** *Dorothy March / Brooks Mason* / HONOLULU. **1940:** *Clare Bennett (Brigit Callahan)* / BROADWAY MELODY OF 1940. **1942:** *Tallulah Winters* / SHIP AHOY. **1943:** *Constance Shaw* / I DOOD IT. **1944:** *Ginny Walker* / SENSATIONS OF 1945. **1950:** *herself (specialty number)* / THE DUCHESS OF IDAHO.

POWELL, JANE

(Suzanne Burce, 1929–)

Seen today Jane Powell is just as cute and appealing as she was when she was making all those fun MGM musicals of the 1940s and 1950s. Unfortunately, her film career ended when original Hollywood musicals lost their appeal. However, the petite, sweet-faced Powell was not daunted by this, noting, "I think now I've found my own happy ending without the help of a script," as she moved into TV and the theater. The vivacious blue-eyed blonde was meant to be another Deanna Durbin but Durbin had better material to work with. Powell looked like a teenager even as she approached the age of 30.

KEY ROLES

Judy Foster / A DATE WITH JUDY, 1948, MGM, d-Richard Thorpe.

In this bright musical, Powell and Elizabeth Taylor are rivals for the attentions of Robert Stack. This is just enough of a plot to get through to the songs which include Harold Adamson's "It's a Most Unusual Day" and "Strictly on the Corny Side" by Stella Unger and Alec Templeton.

Nancy Barklay / NANCY GOES TO RIO, 1950, MGM, d-Robert Z. Leonard.

Powell has the Deanna Durbin role in this musical remake of IT'S A DATE about a girl and her mother (Ann Sothern) who are both after the same part in a play and the same man (Barry Sullivan). Powell gets the part, Sothern gets Sullivan, and Powell sings "Time and Time Again" by Earl Brent and Fred Spielmans and joins with Sothern, Louis Calhern, and Carmen Miranda in a production of "Shine on Harvest Moon" by Jack Norworth and Nora Bayes.

Ellen Bowen / ROYAL WEDDING, 1951, MGM, d-Stanley Donen.

Powell got the role in which she is finally allowed to grow up because June Allyson got pregnant and her replacement, Judy Garland, got difficult. Powell and brother Fred Astaire are entertainers who go to London to work at the time that Princess Elizabeth is to marry Philip Mountbatten. They both find love—she with an English Lord (Peter Lawford) and Astaire with music hall dancer (Sarah Churchill)—and the two pairs marry on the same day as the royal couple. Powell and Astaire give out with "How Could You Believe Me When I Said I Love You When You Know I've Been a Liar All My Life?" She also sings the Alan Jay Lerner song "Too Late Now."

Cindy Kimbell / SMALL TOWN GIRL, 1953, MGM, d-Busby Berkeley.

Powell is the title character who so charms Farley Granger that by the time he finishes his 30-day sentence for speeding through town, he's ready to ditch his fiancée (Ann Miller) for her. Powell sings "Small Towns Are Smile Towns."

Milly Pontipee / SEVEN BRIDES FOR SEVEN BROTHERS, 1954, MGM, d-Stanley Donen.

In one of the most original and delightful movie musicals, Powell becomes the bride of Howard Keel, one of seven brothers who live a lonely life in the mountains of Oregon. When her brothers-in-law decide they want wives too, Keel encourages them to kidnap the girls of their choice. Powell forces the menfolk to wait out the winter in the barn while she stays in the house with the girls and an avalanche seals off the remote farm from angry relatives of the girls until spring. Everything works out when Powell delivers a baby and there are six quick but happy shot-gun weddings between the brothers and their choices. Powell sings "Goin' Courtin'," "June Bride," and "Wonderful, Wonderful Day" by Gene De Paul and Johnny Mercer.

OTHER ROLES

1944: *herself* / SONG OF THE OPEN ROAD. **1945:** *Cheryl Williams* / DELIGHTFULLY DANGEROUS. **1946:** *Christine Evans* / HOLIDAY IN MEXICO. **1948:** *Tess Morgan* / THREE DARING DAUGHTERS; *Polly Bradford* / LUXURY LINER. **1950:** *Patti Robinson* / TWO WEEKS WITH LOVE. **1951:** *Elizabeth Rogers* / RICH, YOUNG AND PRETTY. **1953:** *Penny Weston* / THREE SAILORS AND A GIRL. **1954:** *Athena Mulvain* / ATHENA; *guest* / DEEP IN MY HEART. **1955:** *Susan Smith* / HIT THE DECK. **1957:** *Dodie* / THE GIRL MOST LIKELY. **1958:** *Penny Windsor* / THE FEMALE ANIMAL; *Fayaway* / ENCHANTED ISLAND.

POWELL, WILLIAM

(1892–1984)

Born in Pittsburgh, the son of an accountant, suave, moustached William Powell became the film world's most urbane, cynical performer, at his best as a witty, sophisticated, man-about-town. He made his Broadway debut in 1912 in "The Ne'er-Do-Well" and his film debut in 1922 in SHERLOCK HOLMES. In his early films he most often portrayed villains or at least men who were not completely honorable. It was with THE THIN MAN and his teaming with Myrna Loy that he became recognized as the most charming, sophisticated leading man of the day. He was nominated for Academy Awards for THE THIN MAN, MY MAN GODFREY, and LIFE WITH FATHER. He chose to retire when still in demand after a masterful performance as Doc in MISTER ROBERTS in 1955.

KEY ROLES

Van Templeton / ALOMA OF THE SOUTH SEAS, 1926, Silent, Paramount, d-Maurice Tourneur.

Powell is something of a cad who takes advantage of beautiful native dancer Gilda Gray and in the end is drowned when the canoe carrying him and the man whom Gray loves capsizes during a storm.

Philo Vance / THE CANARY MURDER CASE, 1929, Paramount, d-Malcolm St. Clair.

When a blackmailing musical comedy star is found strangled in her apartment, four men become suspects, and whimsical society man and amateur detective Powell is called in on the case.

John B. Marsden ("Natural" David) / STREET OF CHANCE, 1930, Paramount, d-John Cromwell.

Powell is a powerful gambler devoted to his wife and younger brother. He wants to prevent the latter from taking up the life of a professional gambler so, to teach him a lesson, Powell cheats in a poker game in which his brother is a big winner. The other players catch him and Powell is shot and mortally wounded.

Dan Hardesty / ONE WAY PASSAGE, 1932, Warners, d-Tay Garnett.

While on an ocean voyage, dying Kay Francis meets and falls in love with Powell, a crook being taken home to begin a life sentence in prison. They keep their little secrets from each other and promise to meet again—but not in this world, it would seem.

Jim Wade / MANHATTAN MELODRAMA, 1934, MGM, d-W. S. Van Dyke.

Powell is the DA who has to prosecute his boyhood friend (Clark Gable) and at the same time win the latter's former mistress (Myrna Loy). The first teaming of Powell and Loy revitalized Powell's sagging career.

Nick Charles / THE THIN MAN, 1934, MGM, d-W. S. Van Dyke.

Powell and Myrna Loy seem so natural together, lovingly tossing insults and wisecracks at each other, that a large part of the movie-going public believed that they were married in real life. In this picture, the first of the Thin Man series, Powell is a retired private detective married to wealthy Loy. He is beseeched by Maureen O'Sullivan to locate her missing scientist father (Edward Ellis) the "thin man" of the title. The mystery's not much but it's the charming way the always slightly-tipsy couple solve it that matters.

Florenz Ziegfeld / THE GREAT ZIEGFELD, 1936, MGM, d-Robert Z. Leonard.

Powell portrays the great showman as a charming con man with an eye for the ladies as well as a sure instinct as to what the public wants to see on a stage. Ziegfeld's dazzling New York productions are nicely matched, and perhaps surpassed, by this spectacular movie.

Godfrey Smith / MY MAN GODFREY, 1936, Universal, d-Gregory La Cava.

Powell is a wealthy man who has given it all up to become a hobo. He's found as a "forgotten man" for a scavenger hunt by zany Carole Lombard, a member of a wealthy but eccentric family. He allows her to install him as the butler in her home and does his best to discourage her from falling in love with him, but this only has the opposite effect and by the end of this crazy, sophisticated comedy she has him fidgeting before a minister. In real life Powell and Lombard married in 1931, divorced in 1933, and remained good friends until her untimely death in 1942.

Bill Chandler / LIBELED LADY, 1936, MGM, d-Jack Conway.

When newspaper editor Spencer Tracy prints a story that heiress Myrna Loy is stealing another man's husband, she sues Tracy and the paper. Tracy has a brainstorm. He gets his old buddy (Powell) to marry his own fiancée (Jean Harlow) in name only and then Powell is to get Loy to fall in love with him so that Harlow can sue her for alienation of Powell's affections and her case against the paper will be lost. It's wacko!

Charles / THE LAST OF MRS. CHEYNEY, 1937, MGM, d-Richard Boleslawski.

Powell is the mastermind of a gang who back up Joan Crawford, posing as a wealthy Australian widow, so they can fleece members of British high society. But she messes things up when she falls in love.

Clarence Day / LIFE WITH FATHER, 1947, Warners, d-Michael Curtiz.

Powell is quite wonderful as the irascible turn-of-the-century husband and father who tries very hard to be an absolute tyrant in his home, but is defeated by his loving wife's insistence that he be baptized. He tries to give his son (James Lydon) some advice about women but it's a subject on which he's not an authority: "Women! They get stirred up, and then they try to get you stirred up, too. But don't you let them do it, Clarence. Don't you let them do it. Now if you can keep reason and logic in the argument—well a man can hold his own, of course—but if they switch you, pretty soon the argument's about whether you love them or not. I swear, I don't know how they do it. But don't you let them, Clarence. Don't you let them."

Sen. Melvin G. Ashton / THE SENATOR WAS INDISCREET, 1947, Universal-International, d-George S. Kaufman.

Powell is a foolish politician intent on getting nominated for and elected president. He hires a press agent, but that only makes things worse.

Mr. Peabody / MR. PEABODY AND THE MERMAID, 1948, Universal, d-Irving Pichel.

Perhaps the best thing about this story of an aging man who finds a mermaid (Ann Blyth) is this line (supplied by Nunnally Johnson): "Fifty—the old age of youth, the youth of old age."

J. D. Hanley / HOW TO MARRY A MILLIONAIRE, 1953, 20th Century-Fox, d-Jean Negulesco.

Powell is the elderly millionaire who meets Lauren Bacall's gold-digging needs exactly. First he decides he's too old for her and then she decides she would much rather marry a man she loves.

Doc / MISTER ROBERTS, 1955, Warners, d-John Ford and Mervyn LeRoy.

In his movie swan song, Powell proves he still has charm. He portrays a World War II cargo ship's medical officer and co-conspirator with carrying executive officer Henry Fonda and gold-bricking ensign Jack Lemmon against the insensitive captain (James Cagney).

OTHER ROLES

1922: *Foreman Wells* / SHERLOCK HOLMES; *DeValle* / OUTCAST; *Francis I* / WHEN KNIGHTHOOD WAS IN FLOWER. **1923:** *Gaspar de Vaca* / THE BRIGHT SHAWL. **1924:** *Tito Melema* / ROMOLA; *Duke of Orleans* / UNDER THE RED ROBE; *Prince Arnolfo da Pescia* / DANGEROUS MONEY. **1925:** *Julio* / TOO MANY KISSES; *Barnaby Powers* / FAINT PERFUME; *Nick Di Silva* / THE BEAUTIFUL CITY. **1926:** *Snake Landree* / DESERT GOLD; *Boldini* / BEAU GESTE; *Lorenzo Salvia* / SEA HORSES; *Jack Harrison* / THE RUNAWAY; *Scott Seldon* / THE LADY'S LIPS; *Tony Santelli* / TIN GODS; *George Wilson* / THE GREAT GATSBY; *Roddy Forrester* / WHITE MICE. **1927:** *Ramon Oliveros* / SENORITA; *Clan Dillon* / NEVADA; *Trent Regan*

/ NEW YORK; *Don Kendall* / LOVE'S GREATEST MISTAKE; *Harold Jones* / SPECIAL DELIVERY; *Prince Eric* / PAID TO LOVE; *Kada* / SHE'S A SHEIK. **1928:** *nemesis* / FEEL MY PULSE; *Leo Andreiev* / THE LAST COMMAND; *John Murdock* / THE VANISHING PIONEER; *Becque* / BEAU SABREUR; *Smith* / PARTNERS IN CRIME; *Dapper Frank Trent* / THE DRAGNET; *Froggy* / FORGOTTEN FACES. **1929:** *Philo Vance* / INTERFERENCE; *Philo Vance* / THE GREENE MURDER CASE; *Karl Kraley* / CHARMING SINNERS; *Captain Trench* / THE FOUR FEATHERS; *Robert Courtland* / POINTED HEELS. **1930:** *Philo Vance* / THE BENSON MURDER CASE; *Philo Vance* / PARAMOUNT ON PARADE; *John Nelson (Jim Montgomery)* / SHADOW OF THE LAW; *Gardoni* / BEHIND THE MAKEUP; *William Foster* / FOR THE DEFENSE. **1931:** *Michael Trevor* / MAN OF THE WORLD; *James Darricott* / LADIES' MAN; *Hugh Dawltry* / ROAD TO SINGAPORE. **1932:** *Gar Evans* / HIGH PRESSURE; *robber* / JEWEL ROBBERY; *Anton Adam* / LAWYER MAN. **1933:** *John Fletcher* / DOUBLE HARNESS; *Donald Free* / PRIVATE DETECTIVE 62; *Philo Vance* / THE KENNEL MURDER CASE. **1934:** *Sherwood Nash* / FASHIONS OF 1934; *Captain Tennant* / THE KEY; *John Prentice* / EVELYN PRENTICE. **1935:** *Ned Riley* / RECKLESS; *Clay Daizell* / STAR OF MIDNIGHT; *Fritz* / ESCAPADE; *Bill Gordon* / RENDEZVOUS. **1936:** *Dr. Bradford* / THE EX-MRS. BRADFORD; *Nick Charles* / AFTER THE THIN MAN. **1937:** *Baron Stephen Wolensky* / THE EMPEROR'S CANDLESTICKS; *Charles Lodge* / DOUBLE WEDDING. **1938:** *Johann Porok* / THE BARONESS AND THE BUTLER. **1939:** *Nick Charles* / ANOTHER THIN MAN. **1940:** *Larry Wilson* / *George Carey* / I LOVE YOU AGAIN. **1941:** *Steve Ireland* / LOVE CRAZY; *Nick Charles* / SHADOW OF THE THIN MAN. **1942:** *David Talbot* / CROSSROADS. **1943:** *guest* / THE YOUNGEST PROFESSION. **1944:** *William S. Whitley* / THE HEAVENLY BODY; *Nick Charles* / THE THIN MAN GOES HOME. **1946:** *Florenz Ziegfeld* / ZIEGFELD FOLLIES; *Terry Ellerton O'Neill* / THE HOODLUM SAINT. **1947:** *Nick Charles* / SONG OF THE THIN MAN. **1949:** *Prof. Andrew Gentling* / TAKE ONE FALSE STEP; *Emery Slade* / DANCING IN THE DARK. **1951:** *Doc Homer Brown* / THE TREASURE OF LOST CANYON; *professor* / IT'S A BIG COUNTRY. **1953:** *Steve Latimer* / THE GIRL WHO HAD EVERYTHING.

POWER, TYRONE

(Tyrone E. Power III, 1914–1958)

The son and grandson of actors, Tyrone Power was signed to a seven-year movie contract in 1936 based on his reputation as an actor on the Broadway stage. He had been given his start by Katharine Cornell as general understudy to the male leads in "Flower of the Forest" in 1935. A year later he appeared with Miss Cornell in "Romeo and Juliet" and "Saint Joan." After a few small movie roles his incredible success in LLOYDS OF LONDON established him as a popular, handsome leading man. During World War II, he was a transport pilot with the marines, and did four years of duty in the Pacific. He was a bit too solemn to be considered a great actor but his dark good looks and vibrantly deep voice made him a movie idol with the bobby-soxers of the 1940s. After leaving 20th Century-Fox, he formed an independent production company, then returned to Broadway in 1953 to join Judith Anderson and Raymond Massey in a concert reading of "John Brown's Body." He died of a heart attack after a dueling scene with George Sanders on the movie set of SOLOMON AND SHEBA at the age of 44.

KEY ROLES

Jonathan Blake / LLOYDS OF LONDON, 1936, 20th Century-Fox, d-Henry King.

In this quasi-historical tale, Power is a young Englishman who becomes the leading light of the great British insurance company in part because of his lifelong friendship with Lord Nelson.

Dion O'Leary / IN OLD CHICAGO, 1938, 20th Century-Fox, d-Henry King.

In one of the most expensive films of its time, Power is a charming rogue who competes for the love of singer Alice Faye with his brother (Don Ameche) who becomes the mayor of Chicago. It is their mother's cow that kicks over the lantern that starts the infamous fire of 1871.

Roger Grant (Alexander) / ALEXANDER'S RAGTIME BAND, 1938, 20th Century-Fox, d-Henry King.

In this glorification of ragtime, Power is a society kid who chooses pop music over serious music and becomes a big success. You would, too, if you had Irving Berlin providing the music for your band.

Jesse James / JESSE JAMES, 1939, 20th Century-Fox, d-Henry King.

When their mother is killed by a representative of a railroad cheating farmers out of their land, Power and his brother (Henry Fonda) become Robin Hood-like bandits in this highly romanticized but good-looking account of the two post-Civil War bank and train robbers. Power gets it in the back from John Carradine as he is straightening a picture on the wall of his home. "That dirty little coward shot Mr. Howard—and now poor Jesse is dead" (Carl Sandburg).

Bart Clinton / ROSE OF WASHINGTON SQUARE, 1939, 20th Century-Fox, d-Gregory Ratoff.

Power is the handsome scoundrel and lover of Ziegfield star Alice Faye whose love song "My Man" says it all. Fanny Brice thought the movie was about her and sued for an unauthorized use of her life story. She settled her claim out of court.

Don Diego Vega (Zorro) / THE MARK OF ZORRO, 1940, 20th Century-Fox, d-Rouben Mamoulian.

Power is very dashing as the son of a California Spanish nobleman around 1820 who returns home from Madrid to find that the state is under the rule of a dictator. At times he poses as an effeminate dandy in public, and at other times he becomes the masked avenger Zorro who disposes of the dictator and has a great duel to the death with Basil Rathbone.

Juan Gallardo / BLOOD AND SAND, 1941, 20th Century-Fox, d-Rouben Mamoulian.

Power recreates the role of a Spanish bullfighter which was one of Rudolph Valentino's biggest hits in 1922. He's a talented but naive toreador who is led astray by society woman Rita Hayworth, slighting his wife (Linda Darnell) in the process. The latter stands by him while the former deserts him and, in the end, he's gored and killed.

Jaime Waring / THE BLACK SWAN, 1942, 20th Century-Fox, d-Henry King.

Power is a swashbuckling pirate sailing and looting with Henry Morgan. When the British Crown hires a thief to catch a thief and makes Morgan governor of Jamaica, Power reforms and falls in love with Maureen O'Hara, the daughter of the former governor.

Larry Darrell / THE RAZOR'S EDGE, 1946, 20th Century-Fox, d-Edmund Goulding.

Power's first screen appearance after returning from World War II is in the Somerset Maugham story of a young man who returns from World War I not sure what he should believe. He loses his society girlfriend (Gene Tierney) when she marries another man. He later breaks up with Anne Baxter, an alcoholic who commits suicide. Tierney leaves her husband to return to Power but he rejects her and continues his search for truth and wisdom. He has things all figured out: "If I ever acquire wisdom, I suppose I'll be wise enough to know what to do with it."

Stan Carlisle / NIGHTMARE ALLEY, 1947, 20th Century-Fox, d-Edmund Goulding.

Power is an ambitious con man who teams up with an unscrupulous psychiatrist (Helen Walker) to fleece wealthy clients. He forces his wife (Colleen Gray) to be part of his crooked schemes but she panics during one of his fake spiritualism acts and he has to flee the cops. He takes to the bottle and ends up working as a geek in a carnival. Earlier, Power had wondered: "How do you get a guy to be a geek? Is that the only one? I mean, is a guy born that way?"

Pedro de Vargas / CAPTAIN FROM CASTILE, 1947, 20th Century-Fox, d-Henry King.

Sixteenth-century Spanish nobleman Power runs afoul of the Inquisition and his parents and sister die. In prison he gets the upper hand of John Sutton who had instigated the false charges against Power's family. He forces Sutton to renounce God and then thrusts him through with his sword, hoping not only to kill him but also send him to Hell. After escaping, Power joins Cortez as a Conquistador in the new world and is later shocked when Sutton shows up, having survived his wound. Later Sutton is put away for good and Power is held responsible, but is cleared by an Indian prince who did the deed.

Capt. Alan King / KING OF THE KHYBER RIFLES, 1953, 20th Century-Fox, d-Henry King.

Power is a captain in the Khyber Rifles but not socially acceptable because he is half-caste. When he falls in love with Terry Moore, daughter of his CO, he's quickly put in his place. But his bravery brings him the respect of his fellow officers and wins him the love of Moore.

Eddy Duchin / THE EDDY DUCHIN STORY, 1956, Columbia, d-George Sidney.

Power is a bit dull as the society bandleader and pianist of the 1930s and 1940s who had his share of tragedies.

Jake Barnes / THE SUN ALSO RISES, 1957, 20th Century-Fox, d-Henry King.

Power is an American newspaperman made impotent by an injury in World War I who becomes involved with Ava Gardner, a promiscuous titled woman who, with others of the "Lost Generation," moves around France and Spain looking for answers, but not solutions.

Leonard Vole / WITNESS FOR THE PROSECUTION, 1957, United Artists, d-Billy Wilder.

Likable Power is charged with the murder of an older woman whom he had befriended and who had named him her sole heir. He is defended by Charles Laughton, a barrister recovering from a heart attack. Power's wife (Marlene Dietrich) saves him by becoming a witness for the prosecution and is shown by Laughton to be giving perjured testimony.

OTHER ROLES

1932: *Donald Mackenzie* / TOM BROWN OF CULVER. **1934:** *West Point cadet* / FLIRTATION WALK. **1936:** *Count Vallais* / GIRLS' DORMITORY; *Karl Lanyi* / LADIES IN LOVE. **1937:** *Steve Layton* / LOVE IS NEWS; *Alexander Brown (Prince Alexis Panaieff)* / CAFE METROPOLE; *Prince Rudolph* / THIN ICE; *Raoul McLish* / SECOND HONEYMOON. **1938:** *Count Axel de Fersen* / MARIE ANTOINETTE; *Ferdinand de Lesseps* / SUEZ. **1939:** *Jimmy Sutton* / SECOND FIDDLE; *Maj. Rama Safti* / THE RAINS CAME; *Ken Norton* / DAY-TIME WIFE. **1940:** *Bob Cain (Johnny Apollo)* / JOHNNY APOLLO; *Jonathan Kent* / BRIGHAM YOUNG—FRONTIERSMAN. **1941:** *Tim Baker* / A YANK IN THE R.A.F. **1942:** *Benjamin Blake* / SON OF FURY; *Clive Briggs* / THIS ABOVE ALL. **1943:** *Lt. Ward Stewart* / CRASH DIVE. **1948:** *Stephen Fitzgerald* / THE LUCK OF THE IRISH; *Thomas Jefferson Tyler* / THAT WONDERFUL URGE. **1949:** *Andrea Orsini* / PRINCE OF FOXES. **1950:** *Walter of Gurnie* / THE BLACK ROSE; *Ensign Chuck Palmer* / AN AMERICAN GUERILLA IN THE PHILIPPINES. **1951:** *Tom Owens* / RAWHIDE; *Peter Standish* / I'LL NEVER FORGET YOU. **1952:** *Mike Kells* / DIPLOMATIC COURIER; *Duncan MacDonald* / PONY SOLDIER. **1953:** *Mark Fallon* / THE MISSISSIPPI GAMBLER. **1955:** *Marty Maher* / THE LONG GRAY LINE; *Paul Van Riebeck* / UNTAMED. **1957:** *Exec. Off. Alec Holmes* / ABANDON SHIP!; *presenter* / THE RISING OF THE MOON.

PRESLEY, ELVIS

(1935–1977)

Elvis Presley, a former truck driver born in Tupelo, Mississippi, made his first recording in 1954 and by 1956 had already laid claim to the title of King of Rock and Roll. He made his film debut in LOVE ME TENDER in 1956, followed by a series of box-office successes that did little to further the development of the motion picture industry. Presley had few good stories or top-notch directors but his fans didn't seem to mind as long as he got the chance to sing a few songs and romance a couple of good-looking girls. In 1969 he quit making movies and went back to performing in live concerts. In the last years of his life his increasing weight became an embarrassment, but his popularity remained legendary.

KEY ROLES

Clint Reno / LOVE ME TENDER, 1956, 20th Century-Fox, d-Robert D. Webb.

Presley appears as a Texas farm boy who, during the Civil War, marries the sweetheart of his brother when the latter's death is reported. But the brother isn't dead and on his return he resumes his friendship with his ex-sweetheart, which makes Presley quite jealous. Besides the title number, Presley sings "Poor Boy" and "We're Gonna Move."

Vincent Everett / JAILHOUSE ROCK, 1957, MGM, d-Richard Thorpe.

Presley is just out of jail and back on the trail. He becomes an unlikable pop star singing the big hit title song, as well as "Treat Me Nice" and "Young and Beautiful."

Danny Fisher / KING CREOLE, 1958, Paramount, d-Michael Curtiz.

In what may well have been his best performance, Presley is a New Orleans hustler out to make a fast buck. He rises from bus boy to Bourbon Street nightclub star singing tunes like "Dixieland Rock," "As Long As I Have You," and "Crawfish."

Chad Gates / BLUE HAWAII, 1961, Paramount, d-Norman Taurog.

Presley returns from Hawaii after army service to become a tour guide who shows pretty girls around the islands and sings songs such as "Almost Always True," "I Can't Help Falling in Love," "Hawaiian Wedding Song," and the title number.

Lucky Jackson / VIVA LAS VEGAS, 1964, MGM, d-George Sidney.

Presley is a singing race car driver who competes with Cesare Danova not only in fast cars but also with fast women like Ann-Margret. He sings the title number, plus "The Lady Loves Me," "What'd I Say?" and "The Climb."

Scott Heyward / CLAMBAKE, 1968, United Artists, d-Arthur Nadel.

A film that must have gotten Presley thinking about getting out of pictures is this loser in which a millionaire (Presley) changes places with a water-skiing instructor in an effort to see if he can find girls who like him for himself and not his money. His rather ordinary musical numbers include the title song and "A House That Has Everything."

OTHER ROLES

1957: *Deke Rivers* / LOVING YOU. **1960:** *Tulsa McCauley* / G.I. BLUES; *Pacer Burton* / FLAMING STAR. **1961:** *Glenn Tyler* / WILD IN THE COUNTRY. **1962:** *Toby Kwimper* / FOLLOW THAT DREAM; *Walter Gulick* / KID GALAHAD; *Ross Carpenter* / GIRLS! GIRLS! GIRLS! **1963:** *Mike Edwards* / IT HAPPENED AT THE WORLD'S FAIR; *Mike Windgren* / FUN IN ACAPULCO. **1964:** *Jodie Tatum and Lt. Josh Morgan* / KISSIN' COUSINS; *Charlie Rogers* / ROUSTABOUT. **1965:** *Rusty Wells* / GIRL HAPPY; *Lonnie Beale* / TICKLE ME; *Johnny Tyronne* / HARUM SCARUM. **1966:** *Rick Richards* / PARADISE HAWAIIAN STYLE; *Johnny* / FRANKIE AND JOHNNY; *Mike McCoy* / SPINOUT; *Ted Jackson* / EASY COME, EASY GO. **1967:** *Guy Lambert* / DOUBLE TROUBLE. **1968:** *Joe Lightcloud* / STAY AWAY, JOE; *Steve Grayson* / SPEEDWAY; *Greg Nolan* / LIVE A LITTLE, LOVE A LITTLE. **1969:** *Jess Wade* / CHARRO!; *Dr. John Carpenter* / CHANGE OF HABIT; *Walter Hale* / THE TROUBLE WITH GIRLS. **1970:** *himself* / ELVIS: THAT'S THE WAY IT IS. **1972:** *himself* / ELVIS ON TOUR.

PRESTON, ROBERT

(Robert Preston Meservey, 1917–1987)

Robert Preston was perhaps the most underrated actor ever to appear in a movie. Tall, rugged, and ever charming, Preston spent his early career as not-so-bad bad men who were more careless and unthinking than truly evil. After World War II he returned to Broadway, winning a Tony for his performance in "The Music Man," which he recreated for the screen. From then on he alternated between Broadway and Hollywood. His other stage triumphs included "I Do! I Do!," "Mack and Mabel," "The Male Animal," and "The Tender Trap." Although he never became a superstar, Preston, with his self-effacing style and subtle humor, was greatly appreciated in movies for nearly 40 years. He usually got the girl in his "B" movies, while in the "A"s he often died. Remarkably, Preston looked to be in his middle 30s when he started making movies and still did when in his 60s. He enjoyed his profession, observing: "Next to acting myself, watching other actors gives me my greatest joy."

KEY ROLES

Dick Allen / UNION PACIFIC, 1939, Paramount, d-Cecil B. DeMille.

Preston is a gambler who is saved from hanging for stealing the railroad payroll by Barbara Stanwyck, who marries him even though she really loves scout Joel McCrea. The three find themselves in a train wreck surrounded by hostile Indians. In the end, Preston conveniently gets killed so that McCrea and Stanwyck can get together.

Digby Geste / BEAU GESTE, 1939, Paramount, d-William A. Wellman.

Preston is the Geste brother who remembers his childhood promise to older brother Beau (Gary Cooper) to give him a Viking funeral when he dies, so he sets fire to the French Foreign Legion fort in which Cooper is killed. It serves as the funeral pyre and horrible sergeant Brian Donlevy is the cur to be burned at Cooper's feet. Then Preston heads for the desert where he joins his other brother (Ray Milland), the only one of the three Gestes to make it back to England alive.

Ronnie Logan / NORTHWEST MOUNTED POLICE, 1940, Paramount, d-Cecil B. DeMille.

Preston is a Northwest Mounted Policeman in love with the half-breed daughter (Paulette Goddard) of a man who is rousing the Indians against the British. He deserts his post to be with her, but is made into a hero by Gary Cooper, a Texas Ranger who has moved into Canada tracking the same villain. Of course, by this time, Preston is dead.

Dan Cutler / REAP THE WILD WIND, 1942, Paramount, d-Cecil B. DeMille.

Preston and his brother (Raymond Massey) not only salvage ships wrecked off the Atlantic coast, but make arrangements for the ships to pile up on shoals. When Susan Hayward, loved by Preston, is a victim of such a shipwreck, he turns on his brother and no longer cares if he lives or dies.

Michael Crane / THIS GUN FOR HIRE, 1942, Paramount, d-Frank Tuttle.

Preston is a police detective whose girlfriend (Virginia Mayo), unknown to him, is enlisted to help locate those behind a hired assassination. She takes up with the actual hit man (Alan Ladd) who, for a change in a Preston movie, is the one to die.

Joe Doyle / WAKE ISLAND, 1942, Paramount, d-John Farrow.

Preston is assumed killed in this first realistic movie about World War II as he and a group of doomed U.S. marines desperately try to hold Wake Island for as long as possible. Their eventual defeat is never in doubt but they die gloriously and stir up more hate for the Japanese.

Francis Macomber / THE MACOMBER AFFAIR, 1947, United Artists, d-Zoltan Korda.

Preston and his wife (Joan Bennett) arrive in Kenya for a safari which is their last attempt to hold their marriage together. Instead, Bennett makes a play for great white hunter Gregory Peck, whom she feels is much superior to her cowardly husband. Preston tries to prove himself to his wife in a wild buffalo hunt, but Bennett shoots him dead while attempting to save him from a stampeding buffalo. It's left in doubt whether she was aiming for the animal or for Preston.

Murray Sinclair / WHISPERING SMITH, 1948, Paramount, d-Leslie Fenton.

Railroad detective Alan Ladd fears that his good friend (Preston) is part of a gang of train wreckers. To complicate matters, Preston is married to Brenda Marshall, the woman Ladd loves. Sounds a bit like UNION PACIFIC, doesn't it? The solution is much the same.

Brad Brady / TULSA, 1949, Eagle-Lion, d-Stuart Heisler.

Preston is a two-fisted oil engineer whose belief in conserving Oklahoma's resources causes him conflict with Susan Hayward, the daughter of a cattle owner who plans to build an oil empire.

Rubin Flood / THE DARK AT THE TOP OF THE STAIRS, 1960, Warners, d-Delbert Mann.

In this marvelous domestic drama, Preston is a traveling salesman during the 1920s who loses his job. He doesn't tell his wife (Dorothy McGuire) and she chooses this time to complain about how little they have. She almost pushes him into the waiting arms of Angela Lansbury, but he loves McGuire and they work things out as he gets a new selling job. He's a battler, not a complainer, wisely noting: "Well, every man has his own sack of rocks to carry."

Harold Hill / THE MUSIC MAN, 1962, Warners, d-Morton DaCosta.

Preston repeats his Broadway triumph as the con man salesman who sells musical instruments to the parents of boys in a small Iowa town, claiming that he is a music professor. Shirley Jones, as the local librarian, is the only one not taken in by his claims of expertise, but she falls for his charms before everything is resolved. Meredith Willson songs sung by Preston include "Seventy-Six Trombones," "Marian the Librarian," "Trouble," and "The Sadder but Wiser Girl."

Jay Follett / ALL THE WAY HOME, 1963, Paramount, d-Alex Segal.

This deeply moving story by James Agee was adored by critics but movie fans stayed away. It's the story of how a family deals with the untimely death of a beloved husband and father. Preston is the father and his performance is superb, as is that of the rest of the outstanding cast.

Ace Bonner / JUNIOR BONNER, 1972, ABC / Booth-Gardner / Solar, d-Sam Peckinpah.

Preston just about steals the show in his role as the father of aging rodeo star Steve McQueen and husband of estranged wife Ida Lupino. It's hard to tell that it's a Peckinpah film as there is no violence.

Toddy / VICTOR / VICTORIA, 1982, Great Britain, MGM, d-Blake Edwards.

In his Oscar-nominated performance as an aging drag queen in 1934 Paris, Preston helps starving singer Julie Andrews become the sensation of the city as a female impersonator. Preston is the best thing in this enjoyable low sexual comedy.

OTHER ROLES

1938: *Robert MacArthur* / KING OF ALCATRAZ; *Bent Martin* / ILLEGAL TRAFFIC. **1939:** *Bradley Kent* / DISBARRED. **1940:** *Johnny Potter* / TYPHOON; *Chuck Lane* / MOON OVER BURMA. **1941:** *Steve* / THE LADY FROM CHEYENNE; *Donald Morse* / PARACHUTE BATTALION; *Paul Bryson, Jr.* / NEW YORK TOWN; *Steve Van Rungle* / THE NIGHT OF JANUARY 16TH. **1941:** *Robert Draper* / MIDNIGHT ANGEL. **1942:** *guest* / STAR SPANGLED RHYTHM. **1943:** *Capt. Nick Stanton* / NIGHT PLANE FROM CHUNGKING. **1947:** *Jim Davis* / WILD HARVEST; *cameo* / VARIETY GIRL. **1948:** *Reverend Andrews* / THE BIG CITY; *Jim Garry* / BLOOD ON THE MOON. **1949:** *David Boothe* / THE LADY GAMBLES. **1950:** *Kid Wichita* / THE SUNDOWNERS. **1951:** *Joe Warnder* / MY OUTLAW BROTHER; *Father Reed* / WHEN I GROW UP; *Matthew Fowler* / BEST OF THE BADMEN. **1952:** *John* / CLOUDBURST; *the sheriff* / FACE TO FACE. **1955:** *Col. Frank Marston* / THE LAST FRONTIER. **1962:** *Roger Morgan* / HOW THE WEST WAS WON. **1963:** *Steve Blair* / ISLAND OF LOVE. **1972:** *Joseph Dobbs* / CHILD'S PLAY. **1973:** *Beauregard Burnside* / MAME. **1977:** *Big Ed Bookman* / SEMI-TOUGH. **1981:** *Dr. Irving Finegarten* / S.O.B. **1984:** *Centauri* / THE LAST STARFIGHTER.

PRICE, VINCENT

(1911–)

Vincent Price, Master of the Macabre, was born in St. Louis, and made his stage debut in "Chicago" in London in 1930, then appeared in "Victoria Regina" in London and New York. He also gained experience with Orson Welles's Mercury Theater's production of "The Shoemakers Holiday." He made his film debut in SERVICE DE LUXE in 1938. The tall, handsome Price with his slight sneer, earned degrees in art history and English at Yale and in fine arts in London. He also became a cooking expert. In his early film career he didn't attain stardom, but when he turned his attention to the horror genre, he found his element. Price is a very fine actor but with THE HOUSE OF WAX he came into his own, giving sensitive portrayals of the eccentric, the slightly mad, and the all-out nuts in a series of truly enjoyable films. His acting was hammy, but delightfully so. He doesn't take his profession too seriously, noting: "One great actor of the past labeled himself and his fellow actors as sculptors in snow." He also is not thrilled by the tendency nowadays of actors looking like the people next door. "One of the deaths of Hollywood is that they tried to make everyone look normal. Some of the actresses who are around today look and sound like my niece in Scarsdale. I love my niece in Scarsdale but I wouldn't pay to see her act." No one will ever confuse Price with some normal guy from Scarsdale.

KEY ROLES

Duke of Clarence / TOWER OF LONDON, 1939, Universal, d-Rowland V. Lee.

Price stands between Richard Crookback (Basil Rathbone) and the throne of England, so Rathbone drowns Price in a vat of Price's favorite brew.

Clifford Pyncheon / THE HOUSE OF SEVEN GABLES, 1940, Universal, d-Joe May.

Price is very hammy as the Pyncheon accused by his brother (George Sanders) of murdering his father, resulting in a 20-year prison sentence. But Margaret Lindsay has inherited the house of the title and waits patiently for Price to come home so they may spend their remaining years together. The camera work catches the gloomy atmosphere of the Nathaniel Hawthorne classic.

Joseph Smith / BRIGHAM YOUNG—FRONTIERSMAN, 1940, 20th Century-Fox, d-Henry Hathaway.

Price doesn't last too long in this movie about the Mormons. The founder of the Church of Latter Day Saints is murdered by a lynch mob before Brigham Young leads his followers to the promised land near the Great Salt Lake in what is now Utah.

Shelby Carpenter / LAURA, 1944, 20th Century-Fox, d-Otto Preminger.

Price is a fussy playboy type who becomes one of the suspects in the attempted murder of a beautiful girl (Gene Tierney). This line best describes him: "I can afford a blemish on my character but not on my clothes."

Cardinal Richelieu / THE THREE MUSKETEERS, 1948, MGM, d-George Sidney.

Price makes a perfectly nasty sneering prince of the church and first minister of France who rules the king. But his plans to ruin the queen are thwarted by D'Artagnan and the Three Musketeers.

James Addison Reavis / THE BARON OF ARIZONA, 1950, Lippert, d-Samuel Fuller.

In a surprisingly enjoyable "B" picture, Price portrays a 19th-century clerk who forges claims to all the land in Arizona and tries to set up an independent country.

Prof. Henry Jarrod / HOUSE OF WAX, 1953, Warners, d-Andre de Toth.

In this 3-D movie, Price is a sculptor who is mutilated in a fire at his wax museum. He survives and opens a new one. The reason his creations look so lifelike is because underneath the wax are the bodies of real people. It is an enjoyable remake of THE MYSTERY OF THE WAX MUSEUM (1933) starring Lionel Atwill.

The Devil / THE STORY OF MANKIND, 1957, Warners, d-Irwin Allen.

As the devil, Price appears for the prosecution before a heavenly tribunal that is to decide whether mankind should be eliminated. The defense attorney in this totally silly film is the Spirit of Man, played by Ronald Colman. One may well wonder as to the point of such a movie.

Roderick Usher / HOUSE OF USHER, 1960, American International, d-Roger Corman.

In this minor horror masterpiece, Price, fearing for the sanity of his sister, buries her alive while she is in a cataleptic trance. The house of Usher falls as she comes back to enact revenge on her brother.

Nicholas Medina / THE PIT AND THE PENDULUM, 1961, American International, d-Roger Corman.

John Kerr arrives at a gloomy Spanish castle to inquire about his sister (Barbara Steele). He finds his agitated brother-in-law (Price), who informs him that his wife has died in the castle's torture chamber. The chamber had fascinated her ever since she learned that, as a boy, Price had seen his father entomb his mother alive after killing her lover. Now Price, hearing his wife's voice, fears that she has also been entombed alive.

Richard of Gloucester / TOWER OF LONDON, 1962, Admiral Pictures, d-Roger Corman.

Price moves up to the role of Crookback in this Poe-inspired black comedy remake of the 1939 film about Richard III's bloody ascent to the throne and his ultimate defeat at Bosworth Field.

Dr. Erasmus Craven / THE RAVEN, 1963, American International, d-Roger Corman.

This film has little to do with Poe's poem. Instead it has Price, Boris Karloff, and Peter Lorre as rival magicians. Karloff has stolen Price's wife and turned Lorre into a raven. It's a self-parody of the genre and really quite a lot of fun, with the trio in top form.

Duke Prospero / THE MASQUE OF THE RED DEATH, 1964, Great Britain, Anglo-Amalgamated, d-Roger Corman.

Price is a devil-worshipping prince in Italy during the 12th century. He practices his sadism in the safety of his castle while the plague rages outside. He and his guests practice all kinds of debauchery until at the great masque ball which is meant to be the culmination of the entertainment, Death enters and one by one his guests succumb to the plague.

Matthew Hopkins / THE WITCHFINDER GENERAL, 1969, Great Britain, Tigon, d-Michael Reeves.

Also known as THE CONQUEROR WORM, this is the tale of a cynical religious maniac (Price) at the time of the English Civil War. He roams the countryside instigating witchhunts for his personal profit and pleasure. While torturing a man and his wife, his victim escapes his bonds and proceeds to hack Price to death until a friend finishes Price off with a bullet to his bloody body.

Dr. Anton Phibes / THE ABOMINABLE DR. PHIBES, 1971, American International, d-Robert Fuest.

Price, hideously maimed in an automobile accident, is now only able to speak through an electronic gadget in his neck. He plots to kill the doctors who failed to save his wife's life in surgery after the accident and he models his revenge on the curses leveled on Egypt when Moses was trying to get Pharaoh to "let my people go."

OTHER ROLES

1938: *Robert Wade* / SERVICE DE LUXE. **1939:** *Sir Walter Raleigh* / THE PRIVATE LIVES OF ELIZABETH AND ESSEX. **1940:** *David Richardson* / GREEN HELL; *Geoffrey Radcliffe* / THE INVISIBLE MAN RETURNS. **1941:** *King Charles II* / HUDSON'S BAY; **1943:** *Dutour* / THE SONG OF BERNADETTE. **1944:** *William McAdoo* / WILSON; *Rev. Angus Mealey* / THE KEYS OF THE KINGDOM. **1945:** *Marquis de Fleury* / A ROYAL SCANDAL; *Russell Quinton* / LEAVE HER TO HEAVEN. **1946:** *Dr. Cross* / SHOCK; *Nicholas Van Ryn* / DRAGONWYCK. **1947:** *Inspector Clinner* / MOSS ROSE; *Maximilian* / THE LONG NIGHT; *Andrew Colby* / THE WEB. **1948:** *Boss Tweed* / UP IN CENTRAL PARK; *Mark Van Ratten* / ROGUE'S REGIMENT; *voice of Invisible Man* / ABBOTT AND COSTELLO MEET FRANKENSTEIN. **1949:** *Carwood* / THE BRIBE; *Pasha Al Nadim* / BAGDAD. **1950:** *Burnbridge Waters* / CHAMPAGNE FOR CAESAR; *Tracy Holland* / CURTAIN CALL AT CACTUS CREEK. **1951:** *George Brissac* / ADVENTURES OF CAPTAIN FABIAN; *Mark Cardigan* / HIS KIND OF WOMAN. **1952:** *Lloyd Rollins* / THE LAS VEGAS STORY. **1953:** *narrator* / PICTURA. **1954:** *Paul Adams* / DANGEROUS MISSION; *Gallico* / THE MAD MAGICIAN; *Casanova* / CASANOVA'S BIG NIGHT. **1955:** *Colonel Drake* / THE STORY OF COLONEL DRAKE; *Omar Khayyam* / SON OF SINBAD. **1956:** *Charles Winthrop* / SERENADE; *Walter Kyne, Jr.* / WHILE THE CITY SLEEPS; *Baka* / THE TEN COMMANDMENTS; *narrator* / THE VAGABOND KING. **1958:** *François* / THE FLY; *Frederick Loren* / HOUSE ON HAUNTED HILL. **1959:** *Hans Hagenfeld* / THE BIG CIRCUS; *Dr. Malcolm Wells* / THE BAT; *François* / THE RETURN OF THE FLY; *Dr. William Chapin* / THE TINGLER. **1961:** *Robur* / MASTER OF THE WORLD; *Benakon* / QUEEN OF THE NILE; *Romero* / THE RAGE OF THE BUCCANEERS; *narrator* / NAKED TERROR. **1962:** *Thomas De Quincey* / CONFESSIONS OF AN OPIUM EATER; *Carl Carmer* / CONVICTS FOUR; *Fortunato (Valdemar / Locke)* / TALES OF TERROR. **1963:** *narrator* / CHAGALL; *Alex Medbourne / Rappaccini / Gerald Pyncheon* / TWICE-TOLD TALES; *Simon Cordier* / DIARY OF A MADMAN; *W. Trumbull* / COMEDY OF TERRORS; *cameo* / BEACH PARTY. **1964:** *Charles Dexter Ward (Joseph Curwen)* / THE HAUNTED PALACE; *Robert Morgan* / THE LAST MAN ON EARTH. **1965:** *Verden Fell* / THE TOMB OF LIGEIA; *the captain* / CITY IN THE SEA; *narrator* / TABOOS OF THE WORLD; *Dr. Goldfoot* / DR. GOLDFOOT AND THE BIKINI MACHINE. **1966:** *Dr. Goldfoot* / DR. GOLDFOOT AND THE GIRL BOMBS. **1967:** *Felix Manderville* / HOUSE OF 1,000 DOLLS; *old prospector* / THE JACKALS. **1968:** *Dan Ruffalo* / MORE DEAD THAN ALIVE; *narrator* / SPIRITS OF THE DEAD. **1969:** *Mr. Morality* / THE TROUBLE WITH GIRLS; *Julian Markham* / THE OBLONG BOX. **1970:** *Lord Edward Whitman* / CRY OF THE BANSHEE; *Dr. Browning* / SCREAM AND SCREAM AGAIN. **1972:** *Dr. Anton Phibes* / DR. PHIBES RIDES AGAIN. **1973:** *Edward Lionheart* / THEATRE OF BLOOD. **1974:** *Paul Toombes* / MADHOUSE; *Stavos Mammonian* / PERCY'S PROGRESS; *Dervos* / JOURNEY INTO FEAR. **1976:** *narrator* / THE BUTTERFLY BALL. **1978:** *narrator* / DAYS OF FURY. **1980:** *Erasmus* / THE MONSTER CLUB. **1981:** *voice* / THE THIEF AND THE COBBLER. **1983:** *Lionel* / HOUSE OF THE LONG SHADOWS; *monk* / BLOODBATH AT THE HOUSE OF DEATH. **1984:** *narrator* / THRILLER. **1986:** *voice of Professor Ratigan* / THE GREAT MOUSE DETECTIVE. **1987:** *Mr. Maranov* / THE WHALES OF AUGUST.

QUINN, ANTHONY

(1915–)

Anthony Quinn claims to have appeared in over 200 films and he ought to know, but many of these must have been as an extra, for the list that follows includes only the English-speaking films for which he has been credited with appearances. Born in Mexico to an Irish fruit picker and a Mexican woman, he became a U.S. citizen in 1947. His early film career was limited to small sinister roles even after marrying Cecil B. DeMille's adopted daughter, Katharine. Quinn made an impression as the Mexican who was one of the three men unjustly lynched in THE OX-BOW INCIDENT. He won two Best Supporting Oscars for VIVA ZAPATA! and LUST FOR LIFE. Quinn also received Academy

Award nominations for WILD IS THE WIND and ZORBA THE GREEK, and the latter gained him international fame. But his best role was as the circus strongman in LA STRADA. Quinn has wasted his talent in far too many inferior movies in which he portrayed brutal, brooding, swaggering ethnic types including Mexicans, American Indians, Arabs, Italians, Cubans, Spaniards, etc. However, on occasion the results were spectacular. In characteristic fashion, Quinn complains: "In Europe, an actor is an artist. In Hollywood, if he isn't working, he's a bum."

KEY ROLES

Capt. Ricardo Alvarez / THE LAST TRAIN FROM MADRID, 1937, Paramount, d-James Hogan.

Quinn was far down the list of credits in this melodrama about the Spanish Civil War, but he was noticed.

Ramon / Francisco Maderos / THE GHOST BREAKERS, 1940, Paramount, d-George Marshall.

Quinn dies in New York City, but his twin brother shows up in Havana as Bob Hope and Paulette Goddard team up to claim her inheritance—a haunted castle on an island inhabited by zombies.

Manolo de Palma / BLOOD AND SAND, 1941, 20th Century-Fox, d-Rouben Mamoulian.

Quinn is part of toreador Tyrone Power's entourage when the latter is at the peak of his popularity and most successful in the bull ring. But Quinn leaves him to take his own turn with the cape, the sword, and Rita Hayworth when Power is on his way down.

Mullay Kasim / ROAD TO MOROCCO, 1942, Paramount, d-David Butler.

In this spoof of desert movies, Quinn is a villainous Bedouin leader who plans to marry Dorothy Lamour, a princess whose first husband is prophesized not to survive the wedding night. He plans to use either Bing Crosby or Bob Hope as a sacrificial lamb before becoming Lamour's second husband.

Juan Martines / THE OX-BOW INCIDENT, 1943, 20th Century-Fox, d-William A. Wellman.

Together with Dana Andrews and Francis Ford, Quinn is lynched by a posse that mistakenly believes that they are the ones who have killed the sheriff. When they find that the sheriff is not dead and they have hung innocent men, the leader of the mob kills himself.

Capt. Andres Bonifacio / BACK TO BATAAN, 1945, RKO, d-Edward Dmytryk.

Quinn, the grandson of a great Filipino patriot, is rescued from the Bataan Death March by John Wayne and his band of guerrillas to act as a rallying point for the people against the Japanese. He's not crazy about the idea, because his girl is making propaganda broadcasts for the Japs but, guess what, she's a double agent and when Quinn learns this, he's happy to be a symbolic leader of his people with Wayne the real head honcho.

Raul Fuentes / THE BRAVE BULLS, 1951, Columbia, d-Robert Rossen.

Once again Quinn plays second string toreador in a bullfighter story. This time it's Mel Ferrer who carries most of the tale, but Quinn looks impressively arrogant in the bull ring.

Eufemio Zapata / VIVA ZAPATA! 1952, 20th Century-Fox, d-Elia Kazan.

Quinn won an Oscar for his portrayal of the brother of the legendary Mexican revolutionary Emiliano Zapata (Marlon Brando). Quinn doesn't understand why conquering heroes aren't allowed the usual rights of rape and pillage as victors. He complains to his brother: "Look, I fought as long and as hard as you did. Every day you fought, I fought. I'm a general. Look, look here's my pay—a little dust. I can't even buy a bottle of tequila."

Zampano / LA STRADA, 1954, Italy, Ponti / de Laurentiis, d-Federico Fellini.

Simpleminded Giulietta Masina is sold to circus strongman Quinn whom she accompanies as he travels around the country giving exhibitions of his strength. She falls in love with the brute even though he constantly abuses her. When they meet acrobat Richard Basehart, he dramatically changes their lives. Quinn was never better.

Paul Gauguin / LUST FOR LIFE, 1956, MGM, d-Vincente Minnelli.

Quinn won another Best Supporting Actor Academy Award for his portrayal of the painter Gauguin in this biopic about Vincent Van Gogh (Kirk Douglas). The film should never have been made in Cinemascope.

Quasimodo / THE HUNCHBACK OF NOTRE DAME, 1957, France / Italy, Paris Films / Panitalia, d-Jean Delannoy.

As hard as he tries, Quinn doesn't make one forget Lon Chaney or Charles Laughton as the deformed bell-ringer who saves a gypsy girl, this time played by Gina Lollobrigida.

Craig Beldon / LAST TRAIN FROM GUN HILL, 1959, Paramount, d-John Sturges.

Sheriff Kirk Douglas is determined to take revenge on the man who raped and murdered his wife. Too bad that the villain turns out to be the son of his best friend, cattle king Quinn. Sparks fly in this excellent western.

Inuk / THE SAVAGE INNOCENTS, 1960, Great Britain / France / Italy, Magic / Playart / Gray, d-Nicholas Ray.

Quinn portrays an Eskimo who accidentally kills a Mountie and doesn't understand why he and his family are being pursued by those who wish to punish him. It's a well-meaning film but becomes a bit boring before the end.

Mountain Rivera / REQUIEM FOR A HEAVYWEIGHT, 1962, Columbia, d-Ralph Nelson.

Quinn is an aging heavyweight boxer who is told that his fighting days are over, but he's not trained to do anything else and no one who made money from him offers him much help.

Auda Abu Tayi / LAWRENCE OF ARABIA, 1962, Great Britain, Columbia, d-David Lean.

Quinn is a Bedouin chieftain who follows Lawrence of Arabia (Peter O'Toole) in the Arab battle with the Turks. He's as willing to fight the British as he is to fight other Arabs.

Alexis Zorba / ZORBA THE GREEK, 1964, 20th Century-Fox, d-Michael Cacoyannis.

When young English writer Alan Bates arrives in Crete, he meets lusty Greek Quinn who takes it upon himself to be Bates's mentor. He introduces Bates to a lovely widow (Irene Papas) who is coveted by all the men on the island but had by none. Their love results in her being killed by the locals for adultery. Zorba is a man who cannot be beaten down by life and Quinn portrays him superbly. He advises Bates: "Boss, life is trouble. Only death is not. To be alive is to undo your belt and look for trouble."

Kiril Lakota / THE SHOES OF THE FISHERMAN, 1968, MGM, d-Michael Anderson.

Quinn appears as a Russian bishop who has spent twenty years as a political prisoner and he is elected Pope of the Catholic Church. It's nothing much, religiously or dramatically.

Omar Mukhtar / LION OF THE DESERT, 1981, Falcon International, d-Moustapha Akkad.

Quinn portrays a patriarchal partisan who resists the Italians in Libya in 1929 and, after being captured, is hanged.

OTHER ROLES

1936: *Zingo Browning* / PAROLE!; *gangster bit* / SWORN ENEMY; *hood bit* / NIGHT WAITRESS; *Cheyenne Indian* / THE PLAINSMAN. **1937:** *the Don* / SWING HIGH, SWING LOW; *Kimo* / WAIKIKI WEDDING; *Nicholas Mazaney* / PARTNERS IN CRIME; *Harry Morgan* / DAUGHTER OF SHANGHAI. **1938:** *Beluche* / THE BUCCANEER; *Nicholas Kusnoff* / DANGEROUS TO KNOW; *Marty* / TIP-OFF GIRLS; *Legs* / HUNTED MEN; *Deane Fordline* / BULLDOG DRUMMOND IN AFRICA; *Lou Gedney* / KING OF ALCATRAZ. **1939:** *Mike Gordon* / KING OF CHINATOWN; *Jack Cordray* / UNION PACIFIC; *Chang Tai* / ISLAND OF LOST MEN; *Forbes* / TELEVISION SPY. **1940:** *Nick Buller* / EMERGENCY SQUAD; *Caesar* / ROAD TO SINGAPORE; *Francis Bradmore* / PAROLE FIXER; *Murray Burns* / CITY FOR CONQUEST; *Joe Yuma* / TEXAS RANGERS RIDE AGAIN. **1941:** *Trego* / KNOCKOUT; *Chic Collins* / THIEVES FALL OUT; *Crazy Horse* / THEY DIED WITH THEIR BOOTS ON; *Alex Moreno* / THE PERFECT SNOB. **1942:** *Leo Dexter* / LARCENY, INC.; *Wogan* / THE BLACK SWAN. **1944:** *Yellow Hand* / BUFFALO BILL; *George Carroll* / ROGER TOUHY, GANGSTER; *Michael Romanescue* / LADIES OF WASHINGTON; *Al Jackson* / IRISH EYES ARE SMILING. **1945:** *Indian chief* / WHERE DO WE GO FROM HERE?; *Chen Ta* / CHINA SKY. **1946:** *Don Luis Rivera y Hernandez* / CALIFORNIA. **1947:** *Emir* / SINBAD THE SAILOR; *Jose Martinez* / THE IMPERFECT LADY; *Charley Eagle* / BLACK GOLD; *Enrique Vargas* / TYCOON. **1951:** *Giovanni Larocca* / MASK OF THE AVENGER. **1952:** *Prince Ramon* / THE BRIGAND; *Portugee* / THE WORLD IN HIS ARMS; *Roc Brasiliano* / AGAINST ALL FLAGS. **1953:** *Tony Bartlett* / CITY BENEATH THE SEA; *Osceola* / SEMINOLE; *Jose Esqueda* / RIDE, VAQUERO; *Kiang* / EAST OF SUMATRA; *Ward Conway* / BLOWING WILD; *Antinous* / ULYSSES; *Alfio* / FATAL DESIRE; *Francesco* / FORBIDDEN WOMEN. **1954:** *Johnny McBride* / THE LONG WAIT; *Attila* / ATTILA. **1955:** *Luis Santos* / THE MAGNIFICENT MATADOR; *Phil Regal* / THE NAKED STREET; *Capt. Gaspar de Portola* / SEVEN CITIES OF GOLD. **1956:** *Dave Robles* / MAN FROM DEL RIO; *Big Tom Kupfen* / THE WILD PARTY. **1957:** *Ben Cameron* / THE RIVER'S EDGE; *Bob Kallen* / THE RIDE BACK; *Gino* / WILD IS THE WIND. **1958:** *Jack Duvall* / HOT SPELL. **1959:** *Frank Valentine* / THE BLACK ORCHID; *Tom Morgan* / WARLOCK. **1960:** *Tom Healy* / HELLER IN PINK TIGHTS; *Dr. David Rivera* / PORTRAIT IN BLACK. **1961:** *Col. Andrea Stavros* / THE GUNS OF NAVARONE. **1962:** *Barabbas* / BARABBAS. **1964:** *Captain Vinolas* / BEHOLD A PALE HORSE; *Serge Miller* / THE VISIT. **1965:** *Juan Chavez* / A HIGH WIND IN JAMAICA. **1966:** *Kublai Khan* / MARCO THE MAGNIFICENT; *Lieutenant Colonel Raspeguy* / LOST COMMAND. **1967:** *Johann Moritz* / THE 25TH HOUR; *Roc Delmonico* / THE HAPPENING; *Peyrol* / THE ROVER. **1968:** *Leon Alastray* / GUNS FOR SAN SEBASTIAN; *Maurice Conchis* / THE MAGUS. **1969:** *Italo Bombolini* / THE SECRET OF SANTA VITTORIA; *Matsoukas* / A DREAM OF KINGS. **1970:** *Will Cade* / A WALK IN THE SPRING RAIN; *Flapping Eagle* / FLAP; *Prof. F. W. J. "Paco" Perez* / R.P.M. **1971:** *narrator* / ARROZA. **1972:** *Capt. Frank Mattelli* / ACROSS 110TH STREET; *narrator* / THE VOICE OF LA RAZA. **1973:** *Deaf Smith* / DEAF SMITH AND JOHNNY EARS; *Don Angelo* / THE DON IS DEAD. **1974:** *Steve Ventura* / THE DESTRUCTORS. **1976:** *Gregorio Ferramonti* / THE INHERITANCE; *Hamza* / MOHAMMED, MESSENGER OF GOD. **1978:** *Theo Tomasis* / THE GREEK TYCOON; *Zulfigar* / CARAVANS; *Sanchez* / THE CHILDREN OF SANCHEZ. **1979:** *the Basque* / THE PASSAGE. **1981:** *Mariano* / HIGH RISK; *Bang* / THE CON ARTISTS; *Bruno Manzini* / THE SALAMANDER. **1983:** *Mosen Joaguin* / VALENTINA.

RAFT, GEORGE

(George Ranft, 1903–1980)

"What have I got to do to clear myself? I lead a quiet life. I don't ask for any trouble. I have never taken a drink. I don't get in any fights. If broads are an offense, then I plead guilty." So said George Raft. Brought up in New York's Hell's Kitchen, Raft worked his way up from a movie hoofer to a tough guy and gangster in many 1930s pictures, and was made famous by his coin-tossing hood in SCARFACE. In mid-career his supposed friendship with Mafia types began to get him unwanted publicity which cost him his Havana nightclub and got him banned from England. His film career began declining in the 1940s and by the end of the 1950s he was all but retired. Narrow-eyed, silky smooth Raft, with the dark slicked-down hair, became Hollywood's idea of what a mobster looked like. But unlike James Cagney and Humphrey Bogart he did not progress to a popular star in other roles. In fact, he rejected roles that made Bogart a major star such as THE MALTESE FALCON and HIGH SIERRA. It would be folly to suggest that had he taken these roles when offered, he would have experienced Bogie's success. Maybe he knew that they weren't the type of roles he could make work. Watching his old movies today, one notes a strong personality with little variety from film to film.

KEY ROLES

Guido Rinaldo / SCARFACE, 1932, Hughes / United Artists, d-Howard Hawks.

Before there was cool, Raft demonstrated it as a coin-flipping hood in this film à clef of notorious Chicago mobster Al Capone (Paul Muni). It was the most graphically violent movie of its day and had plenty of trouble with the censors.

Joe Anton / NIGHT AFTER NIGHT, 1932, Paramount, d-Archie Mayo.

Raft portrays an ex-boxer who runs a swanky nightclub and falls in love with a socialite. Mae West, in her first film, steals the picture from rising star Raft.

Steve Brodie / THE BOWERY, 1933, Fox Films, d-Raoul Walsh.

Raft portrays a man, who during the 1890s in New York, is a rival of Wallace Beery's, a notorious saloon keeper. To settle a bet, Raft jumps off the Brooklyn Bridge and survives—or did he jump?

Raoul de Baere / BOLERO, 1934, Paramount, d-Wesley Ruggles.

Yearning for a change from all his gangster roles, Raft was given the opportunity to show his dancing ability in this film about a perfectionist nightclub dancer. Raft insists on no romantic involvements with his female partners. He dumps one because she's unwilling to abide by this rule and replaces her with Carole Lombard. They become very successful, but when she is pursued by an English lord (Ray Milland), Raft forgets his own rule. Lombard leaves him to marry Milland. After World War I, Raft, now with a bad heart, unites with a new partner, but on opening night she's too drunk to go on and Lombard, who just happens to be in the audience, takes her place and dances to "Bolero." Raft dies before they can have an encore.

Joe Martin / RUMBA, 1935, Paramount, d-Marion Gering.

This clone of the very successful BOLERO, once again teamed Raft with Carole Lombard. She's an heiress who rescues dancer Raft when she steps in at the last moment to go on at the Broadway opening of his show when his partner walks out on him.

Ed Beaumont / THE GLASS KEY, 1935, Paramount, d-Frank Tuttle.

Raft plays the second-in-command to political boss Edward Arnold who becomes a primary suspect in the death of the son of a senator. Raft proves that the senator killed his own son in a rage.

Powdah / SOULS AT SEA, 1937, Paramount, d-Henry Hathaway.

Raft plays a loyal pal of Gary Cooper, an intelligence man whose mission in this 19th-century story is to get evidence against slave traders, even to the point of becoming one of them. Raft fares better than Cooper does in this popular action film.

Hood Stacey / EACH DAWN I DIE, 1939, Warners, d-William Keighley.

James Cagney, as a reporter framed for manslaughter by political crooks he is investigating, is the nominal star in this tough prison picture, but George Raft, in his only appearance with Cagney, steals the show. He plays a hardened con, saved by Cagney from death by an enemy. To pay back the favor, Raft escapes from jail, finds out who framed Cagney, returns to prison, and during a riot in which he is killed gets the finger man on Cagney to confess so the warden can hear.

Joe Fabrini / THEY DRIVE BY NIGHT, 1940, Warners, d-Raoul Walsh.

Truck driver Raft has an affair with the wife of a powerful truck company baron. She involves Raft in the killing of her husband. Raft is splendid, giving one of the best performances of his career.

Johnny Angelo / JOHNNY ANGEL, 1945, RKO, d-Edwin L. Marin.

This mystery thriller became a suprising box-office hit. Raft is a sea captain who sets out to track down mutineers who killed his father and stole gold bullion from the latter's ship. He is aided by Signe Hasso who was a witness to the murder.

Dan Beaumonte / ROGUE COP, 1954, MGM, d-Roy Rowland.

Raft is the head of a crime syndicate with police detective Robert Taylor on his payroll. Taylor turns on his employer when the latter disposes of Taylor's kid brother, an honest patrolman.

Spats Columbo / SOME LIKE IT HOT, 1959, United Artists, d-Billy Wilder.

In a spoof of his mobster roles, Raft plays a Chicago gangster who personally supervises the Saint Valentine's Day Massacre, which is witnessed by two musicians (Tony Curtis and Jack Lemmon). Raft finally catches up with Curtis and Lemmon in Florida where they are hiding out disguised as women in a girls' band. Raft and his henchmen are taken care of by other mobsters.

OTHER ROLES

1929: *gigolo* / QUEEN OF THE NIGHT CLUBS. **1931:** *Jimmy Kirk* / QUICK MILLIONS; *Maxie* / HUSH MONEY; *Joe-the-Frog* / PALMY DAYS; *William "Willie" Kenny* / TAXI. **1932:** *Louie Brooks* / DANCERS IN THE DARK; *Jack Houston* / MADAME RACKETEER; *Eddie Jackson* / IF I HAD A MILLION; *Nick Darrow* / UNDERCOVER MAN. **1933:** *Harry Glynn* / PICK-UP; *Nick Mason* / THE MIDNIGHT CLUB. **1934:** *Harvey Rogers* / ALL OF ME; *Manuel Montez* / THE TRUMPET BLOWS; *Harry Young* / LIMEHOUSE BLUES. **1935:** *Ray Angelo* / *Ray Ferraro* / STOLEN HARMONY; *Tops Cardona* / EVERY NIGHT AT EIGHT; *Spot Ricardi* / SHE COULDN'T TAKE IT. **1936:** *Enrico Scaffa* / IT HAD TO HAPPEN. **1938:** *Joe Dennis* / YOU AND ME; *Tyler Dawson* / SPAWN OF THE NORTH. **1939:** *Marty Black* / THE LADY'S FROM KENTUCKY; *Joe Lourik* / I STOLE A MILLION. **1940:** *Cliff Taylor* / INVISIBLE STRIPES; *Steve Larwitt* / THE HOUSE ACROSS THE BAY. **1941:** *Johnny Marshall* / MANPOWER; *cameo* / LAND OF LIBERTY. **1942:** *himself* / BROADWAY. **1943:** *guest* / STAGE DOOR CANTEEN; *Joe Barton* / BACKGROUND TO DANGER. **1944:** *Tony West* / FOLLOW THE BOYS. **1946:** *Joe Warne* / NOCTURNE; *Eddie Ace* / MR. ACE; *Kenny* / WHISTLE STOP. **1947:** *Mario Torio* / CHRISTMAS EVE; *Brad Durham* / INTRIGUE. **1948:** *Dan Gannin* / RACE STREET. **1949:** *Johnny Allegro* / JOHNNY ALLEGRO; *Kane* / A DANGEROUS PROFESSION; *Capt. Paul Gerard* / OUTPOST IN MOROCCO; *John Torno* / RED LIGHT. **1951:** *Nick Cain* / LUCKY NICK CAIN. **1952:** *Joe Gargen* / LOAN SHARK. **1953:** *Steve Rossi* / I'LL GET YOU; *Mike Conelli* / MAN FROM CAIRO. **1954:** *Detective Bruce* / BLACK WIDOW. **1955:** *Joe Victor* / A BULLET FOR JOEY. **1956:** *bouncer* / AROUND THE WORLD IN 80 DAYS. **1959:** *Stafford* / A JET OVER THE ATLANTIC. **1960:** *Jack Strager* / OCEAN'S ELEVEN. **1961:** *guest* / THE LADIES' MAN. **1964:** *detective* / FOR THOSE WHO THINK YOUNG; *guest* / THE PATSY. **1967:** *guest* / CASINO ROYALE; *Charles Binnaggio* / RIFIFI A PANAME; *Golden Dragon* / FIVE GOLDEN DRAGONS. **1968:** *Captain Garbaldo* / SKIDOO. **1969:** *elderly hood* / MADIGAN'S MILLIONS. **1972:** *Guido Scartucci* / HAMMERSMITH IS OUT; *cameo* / DEADHEAD MILES. **1977:** *himself* / SEXTETTE. **1978:** *Petey Cane* / THE MAN WITH BOGART'S FACE.

RAINER, LUISE

(1910–)

Vienna-born Luise Rainer won two Oscars in consecutive years for THE GREAT ZIEGFELD and THE GOOD EARTH, and a year later was dropped by MGM. No one was more cursed by winning the Oscar than her and there is much disagreement as to whether she deserved them in the first place. But as there is no objective judgment as to just what is an Oscar-worthy performance, the debate can never be resolved. Seeing Rainer in these two films, one can note the special appeal of the pretty, doll-like brunette as the vivacious Anna Helm and then in a complete change as the Chinese peasant wife, O-Lan. She began her movie career in the Austrian films JA, DER HIMMEL ÜBER WIEN (1930), SEHNSUCHT 202 (1931), and HEUT' KOMMT'S DRAUFT AN (1933).

KEY ROLES

Anna Held / THE GREAT ZIEGFELD, 1936, MGM, d-Robert Z. Leonard.

Everyone seems to be certain about precisely which scene won Rainer her Oscar for portraying the singing star and wife of the great showman Florenz Ziegfeld. In that scene she is speaking on the phone to William Powell, who portrays her ex-husband Ziegfeld, with whom she is clearly still in love. She tries gallantly to congratulate him on his marriage to Billie Burke. The audience sees her suffering, but Powell only hears her words. When she hangs up, she falls apart, sobbing in a way that can break the hardest heart.

O-Lan / THE GOOD EARTH, 1937, MGM, d-Sidney Franklin.

Dying is another good means of catching the attention of Academy Award voters and self-effacing Rainer, as a plain-looking Chinese peasant woman, dies well. Her husband (Paul Muni) tells her, "Don't leave me. I will sell the land." Always the good farm wife, she insists, "No, I will not allow that—for I must die sometime, but the land is there after me."

Poldi Vogelhuber / THE GREAT WALTZ, 1938, MGM, d-Julien Duvivier and Josef von Sternberg (uncredited).
Rainer portrays the long-suffering wife of Johann Strauss (Fernand Gravet) who pays more attention to coloratura Carla Donner (Miliza Korjus). It is a Viennese pastry which looks very good but is filled with whipped cream for a story.

OTHER ROLES

1935: *Leopoldine* / ESCAPADE. **1937:** *Anna Benton* / THE BIG CITY; *Countess Olga Muranova* / THE EMPEROR'S CANDLESTICKS. **1938:** *Gilberta Brigard (Frou Frou)* / THE TOY WIFE; *Louise* / DRAMATIC SCHOOL. **1943:** *Milada Pressinger* / HOSTAGES.

RAINES, ELLA

(Ella Wallace Raubes, 1921–)
Beautiful, green-eyed, strong-featured Ella Raines, with her distinctive mane of shoulder-length hair, was not used well by Hollywood. After a few interesting roles, she was only offered nice girl parts in mediocre movies. Her debut was as the only female in CORVETTE K-225, despite having no prior professional experience. Never frightened by facing a camera and not having the usual problems of typical starlets, she played resourceful heroines and bitchy mistresses in her first few years, before seeing her career slip away in the late 1940s and early 1950s.

KEY ROLES

Joyce Cartwright / CORVETTE K-225, 1943, Universal, d-Richard Rosson.
Raines reluctantly falls in love with Randolph Scott, the skipper of a Canadian corvette during World War II, because her older brother has been lost at sea. Then her younger brother is assigned to Scott's ship for his next crossing of the Atlantic to England.

Carol "Kansas" Richman / PHANTOM LADY, 1944, Universal, d-Robert Siodmak.
Raines's boss (Alan Curtis) is convicted on circumstantial evidence of the murder of his wife because he can't locate the unknown woman that he picked up at a bar on the fateful night who could provide him with an alibi. Raines sets out to find the gal, and discovers the real killer.

Libby / HAIL THE CONQUERING HERO, 1944, Paramount, d-Preston Sturges.
Sickly Eddie Bracken, son of a World War I hero who had sacrificed his life, attempts to enlist at the outbreak of World War II but is released from the marines as unfit. Rather than return home in disgrace, he takes a job at a shipyard and, through his marine friends, sends letters home to his mother, letting her believe he's still serving his country. He breaks off with Raines through the mail, claiming to have found a new girl. Some Guadalcanal marine heroes insist on taking him home and proclaim him a hero. He's showered with awards and Raines is back in his life. When he's offered the chance to run for mayor, he confesses his deception so movingly that all is forgiven and he and Raines plan to be married.

Mary / THE SUSPECT, 1945, Universal, d-Robert Siodmak.
Charles Laughton, a mild-mannered shopkeeper, is married to a shrewish, nagging wife. He meets Raines, a nice young woman, and when they fall in love he decides to kill his wife. He clubs her to death with a cane and persuades the police that she fell down the stairs. He's now free to marry Raines, but two people suspect the truth: a neighbor (Henry Daniell) whom Laughton is forced to kill to keep from being blackmailed, and a detective (Stanley Ridges) who doggedly persists in his investigation until Laughton confesses.

Marsha Peters / IMPACT, 1949, United Artists, d-Arthur Lubin.
Widow Raines falls in love with a man (Brian Donlevy) who is in hiding, allowing his cheating wife to stand trial for his murder. The actual deceased was the wife's lover. Raines convinces Donlevy to surrender to the police. He goes free and returns to Raines.

OTHER ROLES

1943: *Flo Norris* / CRY HAVOC. **1944:** *Arly Haroldav* / TALL IN THE SADDLE; *Stacie* / ENTER ARSENE LUPIN. **1945:** *Deborah Brown* / THE STRANGE AFFAIR OF UNCLE HARRY. **1946:** *Penelope Hampton* / THE RUNAROUND. **1947:** *Rissa Fortune* / TIME OUT OF MIND; *Noel Faraday* / THE WEB; *Cora* / BRUTE FORCE; *Poppy McNaughton* / THE SENATOR WAS INDISCREET. **1949:** *Chris Jackson* / THE WALKING HILLS; *Lucy* / A DANGEROUS PROFESSION; **1950:** *Phyllis Holmes* / THE SECOND FACE; *Nan Morgan* / SINGING GUNS. **1951:** *Louise Ryan* / THE FIGHTING COAST GUARD. **1952:** *Celia Evarts* / RIDE THE MAN DOWN. **1956:** *Rhona Ellison* / THE MAN IN THE ROAD.

RAINS, CLAUDE

(William Claude Rains, 1889–1967)
Born in London, the son of a well-known stage actor, Rains rose from a $2 a week page boy to become the first British stage and screen star to earn a million dollars for a single role—in 1946 in CAESAR AND CLEOPATRA. He failed his screen test for his first film in 1933, but got the part in THE INVISIBLE MAN anyway because of his voice. Rains's resonant, somewhat menacing voice remained his trademark. Although he began as a mad killer scientist, he is best remembered as suave, world-weary men. Never the winner of an Oscar, he was nominated four times for MR. SMITH GOES TO WASHINGTON, CASABLANCA, NOTORIOUS, and MR. SKEFFINGTON. Though only 5 feet, 7 inches tall, Rains projected a towering, dominant personality. He made his first stage appearance at the age of 11 in "Sweet Nell of Old Drury." He served with a Scottish regiment during World War I, then he became a U.S. citizen in 1938. Rains was a character actor who was given star roles. For 30 years he played many sympathetic parts and many villains, but even his villains were sympathetic as in the case of NOTORIOUS. The secret of his success was summed up succinctly as: "I learn the lines and pray to God."

KEY ROLES

Dr. Jack Griffin / THE INVISIBLE MAN, 1933, Universal, d-James Whale.
Rains makes his non-presence felt in this horror film in which he is invisible until the end, when he is dying. But his voice is so great that audiences have a strong feeling for his growing megalomania.

Paul Verin / THE MAN WHO RECLAIMED HIS HEAD, 1934, Universal, d-Edward Ludwig.
Rains is a writer of antiwar editorials, who is sent into war zones by his publisher (Lionel Atwill) to keep him out of the way while Atwill puts the make on Rains's wife (Joan Bennett). Rains arrives back in time to catch Atwill making unwelcome advances to Bennett and kills the cad.

D. A. Griffin / THEY WON'T FORGET, 1937, Warners, d-Mervyn LeRoy.

Rains portrays a ruthless, ambitious prosecuting attorney who, with the aid of yellow journalism, is elected governor after an innocent teacher is lynched for the murder-rape of a fifteen-year-old girl.

Prince John / THE ADVENTURES OF ROBIN HOOD, 1938, Warners, d-William Keighley and Michael Curtiz.

Rains gives a fine performance as the man who would usurp his brother Richard the Lion-Hearted's throne while the latter is away at the crusades. He is aided by Basil Rathbone and thwarted by Errol Flynn and the merry men of Sherwood Forest.

Sen. Joseph Payne / MR. SMITH GOES TO WASHINGTON, 1939, Columbia, d-Frank Capra.

Rains is the senior senator from the state which has just appointed naive Jimmy Stewart to fill the unexpired term of the deceased other senator. Rains is in the pocket of crooked political bosses, although he once was an honest man, and when Stewart appeals to his one-time sense of integrity and responsibility, Rains attempts suicide.

Mr. Jordan / HERE COMES MR. JORDAN, 1941, Columbia, d-Alexander Hall.

Rains is the heavenly agent who promises Robert Montgomery that he will have a body every bit as good as the one he lost when he was killed in a crashing plane, an accident he was supposed to survive.

Dr. Alexander Tower / KINGS ROW, 1942, Warners, d-Sam Wood.

Rains is a doctor in a small American town during the early years of the century who allows Robert Cummings to study medicine with him but not associate with his daughter, whom he sees is going crazy like her mother. Ultimately, he kills his daughter and then himself.

Dr. Jasquith / NOW, VOYAGER, 1942, Warners, d-Irving Rapper.

Rains is a psychiatrist who helps dowdy, repressed Bette Davis become an assured woman able to deal with a doomed love affair.

Capt. Louis Renault / CASABLANCA, 1943, Warners, d-Michael Curtiz.

In this very special wartime romance, Rains is the prefect of police in Casablanca. He makes a wager with Humphrey Bogart as to whether resistance hero Paul Henreid will escape the Nazis and make it to freedom in Portugal. When Bogie suggests 20,000 francs, Rains reveals his nature by replying, "Make it ten. I am only a poor corrupt official." Maybe so, but he's marvelous in his role.

Enrique Claudin (Eric) / THE PHANTOM OF THE OPERA, 1943, Universal, d-Arthur Lubin.

Musician Rains becomes disfigured when he kills a music publisher who has stolen his composition, and a pan of acid is thrown in Rains's face. He withdraws to the sewers beneath the Paris Opera House where he devotes himself to helping the career of a young singer (Susanna Foster) by killing off the singers for whom she is an understudy.

Job Skeffington / MR. SKEFFINGTON, 1944, Warners, d-Vincent Sherman.

Vain, irresponsible Bette Davis marries Rains simply because he loans her brother $25,000. She believes that since she is not in love with him, she need not be faithful to him. She loses her looks from illness and when he returns from a Nazi concentration camp, now blind, she finally returns his love. Before this, Rains had sought comfort away from Davis, explaining: "You mustn't think too harshly of my secretaries. They were kind and understanding when I came to the office after a hard day at home."

Julius Caesar / CAESAR AND CLEOPATRA, 1946, Great Britain, Eagle-Lion, d-Gabriel Pascal.

Egypt's young queen entrances the aging emperor (Rains) and, under his guidance, she shakes off those who dominate her and becomes a true ruler of her nation.

Alexander Sebastian / NOTORIOUS, 1946, RKO, d-Alfred Hitchcock.

Rains is such an excellent actor he draws sympathy from audiences even though he's one of a group of Nazis in Rio de Janeiro with plans of making a comeback. Ingrid Bergman is recruited to infiltrate his group of friends and report her findings to agent Cary Grant, with whom she's in love. She takes her job so seriously that she even marries Rains, but she blows her cover and the broken-hearted Rains confesses to his mother and co-conspirator: "I am married to an American agent."

Mr. Dryden / LAWRENCE OF ARABIA, 1962, Great Britain, Columbia, d-David Lean.

Rains is a British civil servant stationed in the Middle East at the time that Lawrence of Arabia rallies the Arabs against the Turks. The British have no intention of helping the Arabs become independent of British rule. Rains explains how things are to Lawrence (Peter O'Toole): "If we've told lies, you've told half-lies. And a man who tells lies—like me—merely hides the truth, but a man who tells half-lies has forgotten where he put it."

OTHER ROLES

1920: *Clarkis* / BUILD THY HOUSE. **1934:** *Lee Gentry* / CRIME WITHOUT PASSION. **1935:** *Maximus* / THE CLAIRVOYANT; *John Jasper* / THE MYSTERY OF EDWIN DROOD; *John Stevenson* / THE LAST OUTPOST. **1936:** *Don Luis* / ANTHONY ADVERSE; *Napoleon Bonaparte* / HEARTS DIVIDED; *Stefan Orloff* / STOLEN HOLIDAY. **1937:** *Earl of Hertford* / THE PRINCE AND THE PAUPER. **1938:** *Colonel Ferris* / GOLD IS WHERE YOU FIND IT; *Paul Ward* / WHITE BANNERS; *Adam Lemp* / FOUR DAUGHTERS. **1939:** *Det. Monty Phelan* / THEY MADE ME A CRIMINAL; *Napoleon III* / JUAREZ; *Haym Solomon* / SONS OF LIBERTY; *Jim Masters* / DAUGHTERS COURAGEOUS; *Adam Lemp* / FOUR WIVES. **1940:** *Mr. Halevy* / SATURDAY'S CHILDREN; *Don Jose Alvarez de Cordoba* / THE SEA HAWK; *David Belasco* / THE LADY WITH RED HAIR. **1941:** *Adam Lemp* / FOUR MOTHERS; *Sir John Talbot* / THE WOLF MAN. **1942:** *Nutsy* / MOONTIDE. **1943:** *Ambrose Pomfret* / FOREVER AND A DAY. **1944:** *Captain Freycinet* / PASSAGE TO MARSEILLES. **1945:** *Joseph Targel* / THIS LOVE OF OURS; *John Stephenson* / STRANGE HOLIDAY. **1946:** *The Devil* / ANGEL ON MY SHOULDER; *Alexander Hollenius* / DECEPTION. **1947:** *Victor Grandison* / THE UNSUSPECTED. **1948:** *Howard Justin* / THE PASSIONATE FRIENDS. **1949:** *Arthur Martingale* / THE ROPE OF SAND; *Elisha Hunt* / SONG OF SURRENDER. **1950:** *Paul DeLambre* / THE WHITE TOWER; *Frederic Lannington* / WHERE DANGER LIVES. **1951:** *Captain Skalder* / SEALED CARGO. **1953:** *Kees Popinga* / THE PARIS EXPRESS. **1956:** *Aristides Mavros* / LISBON. **1959:** *Phillipe Rambeau* / THIS EARTH IS MINE. **1960:** *Prof. George Edward Challenger* / THE LOST WORLD; *Professor Benson* / BATTLE OF THE WORLDS. **1961:** *mayor of Hamelin* / THE PIED PIPER OF HAMELIN. **1963:** *Art Harner* / TWILIGHT OF HONOR; *King Herod* / THE GREATEST STORY EVER TOLD.

RATHBONE, BASIL

(Philip Basil Rathbone, 1892–1967)

Basil Rathbone, son of a mining engineer in Johannesburg, just barely escaped death at the hands of the

Boers, so he was sent to England to be educated. When he was 18 he took a job selling insurance, but left to join a theatrical company managed by his cousins. During World War I, he won the Military Cross. After the war he moved to Hollywood where this suave, dark-haired, impeccably mannered actor spent most of his career as a contract player with MGM. In the 1930s he played sneering villains, then toward the end of the decade became the screen's most famous and best Sherlock Holmes. Oscar-nominated for ROMEO AND JULIET and IF I WERE KING, his stage work included "The Taming of the Shrew," "The Barretts of Wimpole Street," "The Heiress," "Julius Caesar," and "The Gioconda Smile." He ended his film career once again playing villains.

KEY ROLES

Philo Vance / THE BISHOP MURDER CASE, 1930, MGM, d-Nick Grinde.

In this early talkie, Rathbone is the amateur sleuth created by S. S. Van Dine, who unmasks a killer who sends warning notes in rhyme.

Mr. Murdstone / DAVID COPPERFIELD, 1934, MGM, d-George Cukor.

Rathbone is young David's hateful stepfather who enrages audiences by giving the boy an undeserved thrashing. When David's mother dies and the boy escapes to decent relatives, Rathbone's attempts to claim the boy are put to route by Edna May Oliver.

Alexei Karenin / ANNA KARENINA, 1935, MGM, d-Clarence Brown.

Rathbone's treatment of his wife (Greta Garbo) is such that the audience can understand and forgive her for risking all for an affair with Russian officer Fredric March. He doesn't win any points either when he denies her the privilege of seeing her son.

Tybalt / ROMEO AND JULIET, 1936, MGM, d-George Cukor.

Rathbone gives a memorable performance in this over-aged version of the romance of two Italian teenagers (would you believe Norma Shearer and Leslie Howard?) and the feud between their families which results in both their deaths.

Sir Guy de Gisbourne / THE ADVENTURES OF ROBIN HOOD, 1938, Warners, d-William Keighley and Michael Curtiz.

Not only does Rathbone oppose Errol Flynn as Robin Hood because he is supporting Claude Rains's plans to usurp his brother's throne, but he also fancies Maid Marian (Olivia de Havilland), who loves Flynn. Rathbone and Flynn have quite a sword fight in the climactic scene but, as the villain, Rathbone gets run through.

King Louis XI / IF I WERE KING, 1938, Paramount, d-Frank Lloyd.

Rathbone gives the performance of his career as the French king who matches wits with the 14th-century rascal poet François Villon (Ronald Colman). Rathbone is sly, wily, and forever plotting in this film blessed with a Preston Sturges script.

Major Brand / THE DAWN PATROL, 1938, Warners, d-Edmund Goulding.

In this story about the 59th Squadron of the British Royal Flying Corps in France during World War I, German aircraft are driving back the English. Rathbone is the squadron's commander who is constantly in conflict with the air ace Errol Flynn. Rathbone is pleased when he is promoted since Flynn takes over as commander of the squadron and will have to learn about the hell of sending young men to their deaths.

Baron Wolf von Frankenstein / SON OF FRANKENSTEIN, 1939, Universal, d-Rowland V. Lee.

Twenty-five years after his father's death, the new Baron von Frankenstein (Rathbone) returns to his ancestral home and takes up on his father's experiments. When he discovers that the monster is now in a coma, he brings it back to life with the usual results.

Sherlock Holmes / THE HOUND OF THE BASKERVILLES, 1939, 20th Century-Fox, d-Sidney Lanfield.

This is the first of fourteen films in which Rathbone portrays Sherlock Holmes and Nigel Bruce plays Dr. John Watson. In this one Holmes saves a Dartmoor baronet from death by a hound that specializes in eliminating the lords of the Baskervilles.

Richard III / TOWER OF LONDON, 1939, Universal, d-Rowland V. Lee.

With the help of his torturer (Boris Karloff), the Duke of Gloucester (Rathbone) murders his way to the British throne to become King Richard III.

Capt. Esteban Pasquale / THE MARK OF ZORRO, 1940, 20th Century-Fox, d-Rouben Mamoulian.

Rathbone is the icy villain in this elegant swashbuckler about young Tyrone Power who, upon returning from education in Spain, finds that California peasants are being oppressed by a dictator (J. Edward Bromberg) with Rathbone as his enforcer. There is a spectacular duel between Power and Rathbone which naturally Rathbone must lose.

Andre Trochard / WE'RE NO ANGELS, 1955, Paramount, d-Michael Curtiz.

Rathbone is a miserly old SOB who arrives on Devil's Island to check up on how his cousin is running his store. He's quite willing to dump the cousin but, before this can happen, he is bitten by a poisonous snake belonging to one of three convicts who are hiding out with the cousin and his family.

Norman Cass / THE LAST HURRAH, 1958, Columbia, d-John Ford.

Rathbone is an old patriarch of a WASP Boston family who hates the Irish Catholic mayor of the city (Spencer Tracy) and will do anything to defeat him, including backing a young Irish Catholic wimp.

OTHER ROLES

1921: *Amadis de Jocelyn* / INNOCENT; *Don Cesare Carelli* / THE FRUITFUL VINE. **1923:** *Joseph Surface* / THE SCHOOL FOR SCANDAL. **1924:** *Tony Winterslip* / TROUPING WITH ELLEN. **1925:** *Antoine* / THE MASKED BRIDE. **1926:** *Rizzio* / THE GREAT DECEPTION. **1929:** *Lord Arthur Dilling* / THE LAST OF MRS. CHEYNEY. **1930:** *Paul Gherardi* / A NOTORIOUS AFFAIR; *Edward* / THE LADY OF SCANDAL; *Paul* / THIS MAD WORLD; *Colonel Smith* / THE FLIRTING WIDOW; *Carl Vandry* / A LADY SURRENDERS; *Durant* / SIN TAKES A HOLIDAY. **1932:** *Capt. Alex Pastisch* / A WOMAN COMMANDS. **1933:** *Derek Nagel* / ONE PRECIOUS YEAR; *Ferdinand de Levis* / LOYALTIES. **1935:** *Pontius Pilate* / THE LAST DAYS OF POMPEII; *Captain Courtney* / A FEATHER IN HER HAT; *Marquis St. Evremonde* / A TALE OF TWO CITIES; *Captain Levasseur* / CAPTAIN BLOOD; *Henry Abbott* / KIND LADY. **1936:** *Wroxton* / PRIVATE NUMBER; *Count Anteoni* / THE GARDEN OF ALLAH. **1937:** *Michael Michailow* / CONFESSION; *Gerald Lovell* / LOVE FROM A STRANGER; *Selden* / MAKE A WISH; *Gorotchenko* / TOVARICH. **1938:** *Ahmed* / THE ADVENTURES OF MARCO POLO. **1939:** *Clive Randolph* / THE SUN NEVER SETS; *Sherlock Holmes* / THE ADVENTURES OF SHERLOCK HOLMES. **1940:** *Paul Reynard* / RIO; *Oliver Courtney* / RHYTHM ON THE RIVER. **1941:** *Dr. George Sebastian* / THE MAD DOCTOR;

Hartley / THE BLACK CAT; *Reggie Oliver* / INTERNATIONAL LADY; *Benoit* / PARIS CALLING. **1942:** *Dr. Santelle* / FINGERS AT THE WINDOW; *Henri Sarrou* / CROSSROADS; *Sherlock Holmes* / SHERLOCK HOLMES AND THE VOICE OF TERROR; *Sherlock Holmes* / SHERLOCK HOLMES AND THE SECRET WEAPON. **1943:** *Sherlock Holmes* / SHERLOCK HOLMES IN WASHINGTON; *Sig von Aschenhausen* / ABOVE SUSPICION; *Sherlock Holmes* / SHERLOCK HOLMES FACES DEATH; *guest* / CRAZY HOUSE. **1944:** *Sherlock Holmes* / SHERLOCK HOLMES AND THE SPIDER WOMAN; *Sherlock Holmes* / THE SCARLET CLAW; *George Adams* / BATHING BEAUTY; *Sherlock Holmes* / THE PEARL OF DEATH; *Lord Rockingham* / FRENCHMAN'S CREEK. **1945:** *Sherlock Holmes* / THE HOUSE OF FEAR; *Sherlock Holmes* / THE WOMAN IN GREEN; *Sherlock Holmes* / PURSUIT TO ALGIERS. **1946:** *Sherlock Holmes* / TERROR BY NIGHT; *Professor Aristide* / HEARTBEAT; *Sherlock Holmes* / DRESSED TO KILL. **1949:** *voice of Mr. Toad* / ICHABOD AND MR. TOAD. **1954:** *Lucio* / CASANOVA'S BIG NIGHT. **1956:** *Sir Ravenhurst* / THE COURT JESTER; *Sir Joel Cadman* / THE BLACK SLEEP. **1962:** *Lodac* / THE MAGIC SWORD; *Carmichael* / TALES OF TERROR; *narrator* / TWO BEFORE ZERO. **1963:** *John F. Black* / THE COMEDY OF TERRORS. **1964:** *Caiaphus* / PONTIUS PILATE. **1966:** *Dr. Faraday* / QUEEN OF BLOOD; *Reginald Ripper* / GHOST IN THE INVISIBLE BIKINI. **1967:** *Professor Hartman* / VOYAGE TO A PREHISTORIC PLANET; *Canuto Perez* / AUTOPSY OF A GHOST; *Gregor* / HILLBILLYS IN A HAUNTED HOUSE.

REAGAN, RONALD

(1911–)

When Jack L. Warner learned that Ronald Reagan was running for governor of California, he protested, "No, No! Jimmy Stewart for governor—Reagan for best friend." Warner had pretty much sized up the career of the good-looking pleasant actor who became president of the United States in 1980. He worked for Warners for 13 years in mostly easygoing parts that never made him a major star. "The Great Communicator" did have some good roles, though, a notable example being Drake in KINGS ROW, but it didn't lead to anything—his next movie was a piece of junk called JUKE GIRL. Reagan went to Hollywood in the 1930s after having found success in Midwest radio as an announcer. He appeared in over fifty movies, but most were of the "B" variety. He became politically active as a staunch liberal, was elected president of the Screen Actors Guild from 1947 to 1952 and again in 1959. He became a champion of conservatism after supporting Goldwater in the 1964 election. Formerly married to actress Jane Wyman, he married actress Nancy Davis in 1952, thus becoming the first divorced president of the United States.

KEY ROLES

Dan Crawford / BROTHER RAT, 1938, Warners, d-William Keighley.

This comedy about three cadets (Reagan, Wayne Morris, and Eddie Albert) is pleasant but Reagan comes in third in acting honors with Albert the most appealing.

Pat Remson / ANGELS WASH THEIR FACES, 1939, Warners, d-Ray Enright.

This is the Dead End Kids Show as they attempt to clear a kid thrown into jail for a fire he didn't start. Reagan is the a DA's son who wins the "oomph" girl, Ann Sheridan.

George Gipp / KNUTE ROCKNE—ALL AMERICAN, 1940, Warners, d-Lloyd Bacon.

Reagan portrays the great Notre Dame football player who dies in his senior year. On his deathbed he tells coach Rockne (Pat O'Brien) to ask the boys to "win one for the Gipper" when they are up against a tough opponent. Years later, Rockne does this and his undermanned team wins a game they aren't expected to win.

George Armstrong Custer / SANTA FE TRAIL, 1941, Warners, d-Michael Curtiz.

According to this picture, the young Custer competed with Jeb Stuart (Errol Flynn) for the affections of a girl who looks a lot like Olivia de Havilland. The two future Civil War generals have several run-ins with abolitionist John Brown.

Jimmy Grant / INTERNATIONAL SQUADRON, 1941, Warners, d-Lothar Mendes.

In this remake of CEILING ZERO, Reagan is an irresponsible flyer whose behavior results in the death of two comrades. After ferrying bombers to London, Reagan joins the Royal Air Force and redeems himself by going on a suicide mission.

Drake McHugh / KINGS ROW, 1942, Warners, d-Sam Wood.

Reagan gives the performance of his life as the best friend of a medical student (Robert Cummings) who has a special interest in the teachings of Sigmund Freud. Reagan falls victim to a cruel doctor (Charles Coburn) who likes to perform amputations without anesthetics; he amputates both of Reagan's legs unnecessarily. What Reagan says after finding his legs gone, "Where's the rest of me?," became the title of his autobiography.

Johnny Hammond / DESPERATE JOURNEY, 1942, Warners, d-Raoul Walsh.

In this improbable World War II story, Reagan is one of five men shot down over Nazi Germany who have many adventures and misadventures as they make their way back home to England. Reagan is an American, Erroll Flynn an Australian, Arthur Kennedy a Canadian, Alan Hale a World War I Scot, and Ronald Sinclair an Englishman.

Larry Hanrahan / STALLION ROAD, 1947, Warners, d-James Kern.

Reagan is a veterinary surgeon in a romantic triangle with a lady horsebreeder (Alexis Smith) and Zachary Scott, the other man to whom Smith turns when Reagan refuses to treat her ailing mare.

Tom Bates / THAT HAGEN GIRL, 1947, Warners, d-Peter Godfrey.

Reagan is a lawyer and war hero suspected of being illegitimate Shirley Temple's father, but he is actually the man with whom she is romantically involved. The romantic pairing was not easily accepted by fans of little Curly Top.

Sgt. Bill Page / THE VOICE OF THE TURTLE, 1948, Warners, d-Irving Rapper.

Reagan stars as a lonely soldier on furlough who woos and wins an actress (Eleanor Parker) who has shared her apartment with him. In this three-person play by John Van Druten, Eve Arden as Parker's wise-cracking friend completes the trio.

John Lawrence / JOHN LOVES MARY, 1949, Warners, d-David Butler.

American soldier Reagan agrees to a marriage of convenience to a British girl (Virginia Field) only to find the idea doesn't sit well with his fiancée (Patricia Neal) back home.

Yank / THE HASTY HEART, 1950, Great Britain, Warners, d-Vincent Sherman.

Reagan is a plain-speaking wounded American who shares a hospital ward in Burma with an arrogant

Scotsman (Michael Todd) who has only a short time to live.

Prof. Peter Boyd / BEDTIME FOR BONZO, 1951, Universal, d-Frederick de Cordova.

Reagan is a scientist who tries to raise a chimpanzee as a human baby with the help of pretty housekeeper Diana Lynn, to prove that environment determines character.

Grover Cleveland Alexander / THE WINNING TEAM, 1952, Warners, d-Lewis Seiler.

In this better than usual baseball biopic, Reagan plays one of the greatest pitchers of all time. He suffers from double vision and epilepsy, which is confused with alcoholism.

Cmdr. Casey Adams / HELLCATS OF THE NAVY, 1957, Columbia, d-Nathan Juran.

Reagan is a World War II sub commander assigned to determine why Japanese mines are resistant to sonar detectors. It's his only film with wife Nancy Davis.

OTHER ROLES

1937: *Andy McLeod* / LOVE IS ON THE AIR; *radio announcer* / HOLLYWOOD HOTEL. **1938:** *Jack Miller* / SWING YOUR LADY; *Pvt. Dennis Riley* / SERGEANT MURPHY; *Eric Gregg* / ACCIDENTS WILL HAPPEN; *Pat Dunn* / THE COWBOY FROM BROOKLYN; *announcer's voice* / THE AMAZING DR. CLITTERHOUSE; *announcer* / BOY MEETS GIRL; *Neil Dillon* / GIRLS ON PROBATION; *Jack Withering* / GOING PLACES. **1939:** *Lt. Brass Bancroft* / SECRET SERVICE OF THE AIR; *Alec Hamin* / DARK VICTORY; *Brass Bancroft* / CODE OF THE SECRET SERVICE; *Ed Clark* / NAUGHTY BUT NICE; *Jim* / HELL'S KITCHEN; *Brass Bancroft* / SMASHING THE MONEY RING. **1940:** *Dan Crawford* / BROTHER RAT AND A BABY; *Mr. Allen* / AN ANGEL FROM TEXAS; *Brass Bancroft* / MURDER IN THE AIR; *Eddie Kent* / TUGBOAT ANNIE SAILS AGAIN. **1941:** *Gil Jones* / THE BAD MAN; *Peter Rowan* / MILLION DOLLAR BABY; *Steve Talbot* / NINE LIVES ARE NOT ENOUGH. **1942:** *Steve Talbot* / JUKE GIRL. **1943:** *Johnny Jones* / THIS IS THE ARMY. **1949:** *John* / NIGHT UNTO NIGHT; *Bob Randolph (Robert Venerik)* / THE GIRL FROM JONES BEACH; *guest* / IT'S A GREAT FEELING. **1950:** *Hal Norton* / LOUISA; *Burt Rainey* / STORM WARNING. **1951:** *Vance Britten* / THE LAST OUTPOST; *Jeff Williams* / HONG KONG. **1952:** *John Palmer* / SHE'S WORKING HER WAY THROUGH COLLEGE. **1953:** *Dan McCloud* / TROPIC ZONE; *Frame Johnson* / LAW AND ORDER. **1954:** *Web Sloane* / PRISONER OF WAR; *Farrell* / CATTLE QUEEN OF MONTANA. **1955:** *cowpoke* / TENNESSEE'S PARTNER. **1961:** *narrator* / THE YOUNG DOCTORS. **1964:** *Browning* / THE KILLERS.

REDFORD, ROBERT

(Charles Robert Redford, Jr., 1937–)

Tall, blond, hawk-nosed Robert Redford has all-American good looks that have paid off at the box office. Fortunately for Redford, unlike several other handsome blond leading men of the past, he has acting ability. He made his film debut in WAR HUNT after years on TV and the stage. He has seldom attempted unsympathetic roles; even when he's not perfect, he looks just fine in comparison to those worse than him in films such as THE CHASE and DOWNHILL RACER. He was nominated for an Oscar for THE STING and won one as the director of ORDINARY PEOPLE. A producer, director, and actor, he's a man of intelligence and versatility, but his face remains his fortune.

KEY ROLES

Bubber Reeves / THE CHASE, 1966, Columbia, d-Arthur Penn.

There's no chase to speak of in this convoluted tale of young Texan Redford, who escapes from a prison where he has been sent for a crime he didn't commit. He heads for his home to confront his unfaithful wife and those who railroaded him, then is killed by a thug on the jailhouse steps as he is being brought in by the sheriff (Marlon Brando).

Paul Bratter / BAREFOOT IN THE PARK, 1967, Paramount, d-Gene Saks.

Young lawyer Redford and his brand new wife (Jane Fonda) move into their first home, a five-story walk-up with a broken sky light and a weird neighbor (Charles Boyer) who lives somewhere above them. They have some early marital problems, but both seem willing to compromise and their future looks promising.

The Sundance Kid (Harry Longbaugh) / BUTCH CASSIDY AND THE SUNDANCE KID, 1969, 20th Century-Fox, d-George Roy Hill.

Redford is the fast-gun sidekick of Butch Cassidy (Paul Newman), one of the last of the Old West's bank and train robbers. They find the climate not friendly to men in their profession so, with Etta Place, a schoolteacher played by Katharine Ross, they head for Bolivia where they hope to revive their career. But they find themselves facing federal soldiers in a shoot-out they can't win.

Bill McKay / THE CANDIDATE, 1972, Warners, d-Michael Ritchie.

Idealistic young lawyer Redford is talked into running for the U.S. Senate by Peter Boyle, who assures him that he can't beat the incumbent (Don Porter). As he campaigns he finds himself sometimes sacrificing his idealism, but he mainly stays the course and surprises himself by winning. Then he wonders what to do next.

Jeremiah Johnson / JEREMIAH JOHNSON, 1972, Warners, d-Sydney Pollack.

Ex-Mexican War soldier Redford, weary of civilization, learns to survive as a mountain man, living only on that which he can trap or hunt. He carries on a long feud with the Crow Indians as he becomes part of the wildlife with which he lives.

Hubbell Gardiner / THE WAY WE WERE, 1973, Columbia, d-Sydney Pollack.

Redford plays an All-American college student of the 1930s who is loved by campus radical Barbra Streisand. They meet again during World War II, and their affair leads to marriage. After the war, he gets a job in Hollywood as a screenwriter and later they realize that they are incompatible. They divorce and he finds a nice WASP girl for his next wife.

Johnny Hooker / THE STING, 1973, Universal, d-George Roy Hill.

When his partner and fellow con man is ordered killed by a Chicago mobster (Robert Shaw), Redford goes to Paul Newman, a more experienced con man, with the notion of pulling a sting on Shaw as revenge. They pull off the "Big Con" but not without some serious problems along the way.

Bob Woodward / ALL THE PRESIDENT'S MEN, 1976, Warners, d-Alan J. Pakula.

Working with Dustin Hoffman as Carl Bernstein, Washington Post reporter Redford breaks the story of the White House cover-up of the break-in at the Democratic National Headquarters in the Watergate complex in Washington.

Norman "Sonny" Steele / THE ELECTRIC HORSEMAN, 1979, Columbia / Universal, d-Sydney Pollack.

In this winsome yarn, Redford portrays a former rodeo star who unhappily is the spokesman for a breakfast cereal. He is dressed in an electrified costume and rides a very valuable horse. He concludes that at least the horse shouldn't be a captive and, with some help from reporter Jane Fonda, he sets the animal free.

Roy Hobbs / THE NATURAL, 1984, TriStar, d-Barry Levinson.

Redford is an exceptionally talented baseball player whose career and relationship with his childhood sweetheart are interrupted for many years when he takes up with the wrong kind of woman. But somehow he manages to make winning a baseball pennant equate with success as a human being, and the triumph of good over evil. He is finally reunited with his girl of long ago (Glenn Close) and the son he didn't know he had.

Denys Finch Hatton / OUT OF AFRICA, 1985, Universal, d-Sydney Pollack.

Redford is an African big game hunter who has a love affair with a Danish writer (Meryl Streep) living in Kenya. She is married but neither she nor her husband work at the marriage. Throughout the picture Redford keeps reappearing in Streep's life with their passion developing at an incredibly slow pace. He is killed in a plane crash, but she never forgets him.

OTHER ROLES

1962: *Pvt. Roy Loomis* / WAR HUNT. **1965:** *Hank* / SITUATION HOPELESS—BUT NOT SERIOUS; *Wade Lewis* / INSIDE DAISY CLOVER. **1966:** *Owen Legate* / THIS PROPERTY IS CONDEMNED. **1969:** *David Chappelet* / DOWNHILL RACER; *Christopher Cooper* / TELL THEM WILLIE BOY IS HERE. **1970:** *Halsy Knox* / LITTLE FAUSS AND BIG HALSY. **1972:** *John Archibald Dortmunder* / THE HOT ROCK. **1974:** *Jay Gatsby* / THE GREAT GATSBY. **1975:** *Waldo Pepper* / THE GREAT WALDO PEPPER; *Joe Turner* / THREE DAYS OF THE CONDOR. **1977:** *Maj. Julian Cook* / A BRIDGE TOO FAR. **1980:** *Henry Brubaker* / BRUBAKER. **1986:** *Tom Logan* / LEGAL EAGLES.

REDGRAVE, MICHAEL

(1908–1985)

Tall, scholarly-looking Michael Redgrave, a former journalist and schoolmaster, made his non-bit movie debut in a delightful way in 1939 in THE LADY VANISHES. The son of British actor Roy Redgrave, who starred in silent movies in Australia, Michael married actress Rachel Kempson and is the father of actresses Vanessa and Lynn, and son Corin. Knighted in 1959, Redgrave had many film successes, mostly in literary works. He demonstrated exceptional talent for bringing non-dramatic characters to life. He was nominated for a Best Actor Academy Award in 1947 for MOURNING BECOMES ELECTRA. The peak of his screen career was in the 1940s and early 1950s with his later roles being more like guest appearances.

KEY ROLES

Gilbert Redman / THE LADY VANISHES, 1938, Great Britain, Gainsborough, d-Alfred Hitchcock.

When Margaret Lockwood finds that elderly Dame May Whitty is missing from a fast-traveling, transcontinental train, no one but Redgrave is willing to believe Whitty even exists. Together they get to the bottom of the mystery and find themselves dealing with foreign spies.

David Fenwick / THE STARS LOOK DOWN, 1939, Great Britain, Grafton, d-Carol Reed.

In this grimly realistic movie, Redgrave is a young man from a mining town who wishes to better himself with a university education, but he is forced to leave the university to support his new self-centered wife. She hates the mining town and has an affair. After she leaves him, he turns all his energies to fighting with union officials over nationalization of mines. A flood in a mine claims the lives of Redgrave's father and younger brother, which makes him all the more determined to commit his life to improving working conditions for miners.

Arthur Kipps / KIPPS, 1941, Great Britain, 20th Century-Fox, d-Carol Reed.

Draper's assistant Redgrave inherits a fortune, then rejects an impoverished society girl to marry his childhood sweetheart. Their marriage is rocky because of conflicting ideas about how to live but things get better when they purchase a draper's store for themselves.

Stanley Smith / JEANNIE, 1941, Great Britain, Tansa Films, d-Harold French.

While at a trade fair to sell his new washing machine, Redgrave comes to the rescue of a Scots lass who has been left a bit of money from her skinflint father. She spends the money on a trip to Vienna and this leads to wedding plans with Redgrave when they are back in England.

David Charleston / THUNDER ROCK, 1942, Great Britain, Charter Films, d-Roy Boulting.

Author Redgrave despairs of the world and goes to live alone as lighthouse keeper at isolated Thunder Rock in Lake Michigan. He finds that he's visited by ghosts of people who were shipwrecked nearly a century earlier. They give him the strength to rejoin the world.

Flight Lt. David Archdale / THE WAY TO THE STARS, 1945, Great Britain, Two Cities, d-Anthony Asquith.

Redgrave is a veteran pilot who befriends a newly arrived pilot (John Mills), at a bomber station during World War II. Redgrave marries Rosamund John and shortly thereafter is killed. His death causes Mills to back out of his plans to marry until John intervenes and convinces him not to let the war make him to stop living.

Maxwell Frere / DEAD OF NIGHT, 1945, Great Britain, Ealing, d-Alberto Cavalcanti.

In this five-part movie consisting of five supernatural tales joined by a linking framework, Redgrave gives a brilliant performance as a deranged ventriloquist who finds himself trading places with his dummy Hugo. Eventually, Redgrave assumes the voice and personality of Hugo.

Hamer Radshaw / FAME IS THE SPUR, 1947, Great Britain, Two Cities, d-Roy Boulting.

Determined to fight for better conditions for miners of the north country, Redgrave becomes a Labor Party member of Parliament. He stirs the miners up against the owners, but over the years he changes, and disapproves of his wife when she becomes a suffragette. She is arrested and dies of TB when she is released. Redgrave later becomes a lord who is alone and friendless, a man who did not remain true to his ideals and principles.

Orin Mannon / MOURNING BECOMES ELECTRA, 1947, RKO, d-Dudley Nichols.

This three-hour version of Eugene O'Neill's six-hour play, based on the tragic story of Agamemnon, bombed at the box office, despite excellent performances by Redgrave, Rosalind Russell, Katina Paxinou, and Raymond Massey. Redgrave is Russell's weak brother who becomes inflamed by her sense of justice in this story of murder, doom, and gloom in a New England family after the Civil War.

Andrew Crocker-Harris / THE BROWNING VERSION, 1951, Great Britain, Javelin, d-Anthony Asquith.

Redgrave has taught at a public school for 20 years and now must retire due to ill health. This annoys his shrewish wife (Jean Kent) who is having an affair with one of the other masters. Redgrave has never been popular with his pupils, but one boy gives him a farewell present and this inspires him to give a passionate speech that draws loud applause. The he leaves his wife to find a new life.

Jack Worthing / THE IMPORTANCE OF BEING EARNEST, 1952, Great Britain, Two Cities, d-Anthony Asquith.

Men-about-town Redgrave and Michael Denison both pursue the loves of their life by claiming that their Christian names are Ernest, as the ladies will only consider marrying Ernests. They even plan to be rechristened but Redgrave is revealed to be honestly named Ernest. It's a jolly good show by Oscar Wilde.

Barnes Wallis / THE DAM BUSTERS, 1955, Great Britain, Associated British, d-Michael Anderson.

To breach the Ruhr dams during World War II, Redgrave invents five-ton mines that bounce along the water of the lake in front of the dams, imbed themselves in the dams, and destroy them. It takes a special squadron of bomber pilots who will have to fly very low to the water to deliver the mines along their way.

Fowler / THE QUIET AMERICAN, 1958, United Artists, d-Joseph L. Mankiewicz.

Redgrave is a cynical journalist in Saigon living with an Indochinese girl. Audie Murphy, known only as the American, falls in love with the girl and offers her marriage, something Redgrave never has. In the end Redgrave betrays Murphy to Communist rebels by telling them he was importing explosives to be used against them.

The Governor / THE LONELINESS OF THE LONG DISTANCE RUNNER, 1963, Great Britain, Woodfall Films, d-Tony Richardson.

Redgrave, the governor of a British reformatory, takes an interest in socially deprived Tom Courtenay when the latter proves to be a splendid long-distance runner. However, Courtenay doesn't reward Redgrave's faith in him.

The Older Leo Colston / THE GO-BETWEEN, 1971, Great Britain, MGM-EMI, d-Joseph Losey.

Redgrave is an elderly man who recalls a time fifty years earlier when he served as a go-between, delivering love letters from Julie Christie and a nearby farmer (Alan Bates). His innocent help leads to tragedy in this lovely version of the story by L. P. Hartley with a screenplay by Harold Pinter.

OTHER ROLES

1936: *bit* / SECRET AGENT (serial). **1938:** *Nicky Brooke* / CLIMBING HIGH. **1939:** *Alan McKenzie* / A STOLEN LIFE; *Peter* / A WINDOW IN LONDON. **1941:** *Charles MacIver* / ATLANTIC FERRY. **1942:** *Russian* / THE BIG BLOCKADE; *Peter* / LADY IN DISTRESS. **1946:** *Karel Hasek* / THE CAPTIVE HEART; *Michael Wentworth* / THE YEARS BETWEEN. **1947:** *Richard Carlyon* / THE MAN WITHIN. **1948:** *Mark Lamphere* / THE SECRET BEYOND THE DOOR. **1951:** *Mr. Lege* / THE MAGIC BOX. **1954:** *Air Commander Walty* / THE SEA SHALL NOT HAVE THEM; *Maître Deliot* / THE GREEN SCARF. **1955:** *Col. Eisenstein* / OH, ROSALINDA; *Burgomil Trebitsch* / CONFIDENTIAL REPORT. **1956:** *Gen. O'Connor* / 1984. **1957:** *David Graham* / TIME WITHOUT PITY. **1958:** *Percy Brand* / LAW AND DISORDER; *Sir Anthony Benson* / BEHIND THE MASK. **1959:** *general* / SHAKE HANDS WITH THE DEVIL; *Mr. Hyland* / THE WRECK OF THE MARY DEARE. **1960:** *Sir Matthew Carr* / NO MY DARLING DAUGHTER. **1961:** *the uncle* / THE INNOCENTS. **1964:** *W. B. Yeats* / YOUNG CASSIDY. **1965:** *medical officer* / THE HILL; *uncle* / THE HEROES OF TELEMARK. **1967:** *Harris* / ASSIGNMENT K. **1969:** *General Wilson* / OH! WHAT A LOVELY WAR; *headmaster* / GOODBYE, MR. CHIPS; *Air Vice Marshall Evill* / THE BATTLE OF BRITAIN; *Dan Peggotty* / DAVID COPPERFIELD; *James Wallraven* / CONNECTING ROOMS. **1970:** *James Harrington-Smith* / GOODBYE GEMINI. **1971:** *Grand Duke Sazonov* / NICHOLAS AND ALEXANDRA. **1972:** *Erik Fritsch* / THE LAST TARGET.

REDGRAVE, VANESSA

(1937–)

Daughter of Michael Redgrave and Rachel Kempson and sister of actress Lynn Redgrave, Vanessa has on occasion been the best actor in her distinguished family, but then she will disappoint by appearing in a vehicle that is beneath her talent. A gaunt, delicate beauty, her political views and convictions have frequently been criticized in the press, and they have probably not helped her box-office appeal. Yet she has been the darling of critics and has garnered her fair share of awards, including Best Actress nominations for MORGAN!, ISADORA, and MARY, QUEEN OF SCOTS, winning an Oscar for JULIA. Too tall for ballet, Redgrave turned to acting, making her stage debut in 1957 and her first movie appearance the next year. She has been married to and divorced from director Tony Richardson. Most successful in movies during the 1960s and early 1970s, her best role recently was in the made-for-TV picture PLAYING FOR TIME.

KEY ROLES

Leonie Delt / MORGAN! 1966, Great Britain, British Lion, d-Karel Reisz.

Redgrave has divorced her half-mad, talented artist husband (David Warner) and plans to marry her wealthy lover. But Warner, who has a fixation for gorillas and Karl Marx, kidnaps her and she becomes pregnant. She visits him at the mental institution to which he is committed at the end of the picture and it looks as if they are back together.

Jane / BLOWUP, 1966, Great Britain, MGM, d-Michelangelo Antonioni.

When London fashion photographer David Hemmings thinks he has taken a picture of a murder, a woman who is in the photograph (Redgrave) shows up and tries to seduce him to get the negatives. When this doesn't work, someone breaks in and steals the negatives and Hemmings loses interest in the whole thing.

Queen Guinevere / CAMELOT, 1967, Warners, d-Joshua Logan.

As Arthur's queen, Redgrave falls in love with her husband's most trusted friend and loyal knight, Lancelot. The two try to resist their feelings because of their love for Arthur but are found together and, in accordance with the laws set by Arthur, she must die. But the king is happy when Lancelot rescues her.

Isadora Duncan / ISADORA, 1968, Great Britain, Universal, d-Karel Reisz.

Told in episodic flashback, this biopic of Isadora Duncan is a tour-de-force for Redgrave. She is able to bring some of her ballet training to bear on her role as the eccentric, independent woman who was quite a bit like Redgrave herself.

Sister Jeanne / THE DEVILS, 1971, Great Britain, Warners, d-Ken Russell.

Redgrave is the mother superior of an order of French nuns in London during the 17th century. She is deranged and accuses cynical priest Oliver Reed of having taken on a diabolical form and seducing her and other nuns in the convent. Reed is tried as a witch and condemned to be burned alive.

Mary, Queen of Scots / MARY, QUEEN OF SCOTS, 1972, Great Britain, Universal, d-Charles Jarrott.

Redgrave, very regal as Mary, opposes Elizabeth I (Glenda Jackson) and is thrown into the Tower of London and executed.

Julia / JULIA, 1977, 20th Century-Fox, d-Fred Zinnemann.

Redgrave received her Oscar for her performance as Lillian Hellman's friend of wealthy circumstances who rejects her background to unselfishly devote herself to fighting Nazism. This results in her suffering bodily harm and eventually death.

OTHER ROLES

1958: *Pamela Gray* / BEHIND THE MASK. **1966:** *Jacky* / RED AND BLUE; *Anne Boleyn (uncredited bit)* / A MAN FOR ALL SEASONS. **1967:** *Sheila* / THE SAILOR FROM GIBRALTAR. **1968:** *Clarissa* / THE CHARGE OF THE LIGHT BRIGADE; *guest* / TONIGHT LET'S ALL MAKE LOVE IN LONDON. **1969:** *Immacolata* / VACATION; *Nina* / THE SEA GULL; *Sylvia Pankhurst* / OH! WHAT A LOVELY WAR; *Mary* / DROP OUT. **1971:** *Andromache* / THE TROJAN WOMEN. **1974:** *Mary Debenham* / MURDER ON THE ORIENT EXPRESS. **1975:** *Ann* / OUT OF SEASON. **1977:** *narrator* / THE PALESTINIAN. **1979:** *Agatha Christie* / AGATHA; *Helen* / YANKS; *Hedi Lindquist* / BEAR ISLAND. **1983:** *Cosima* / WAGNER. **1984:** *Olive Chancellor* / THE BOSTONIANS. **1985:** *Jean Travers* / WETHERBY; *Nancy* / STEAMING.

REED, DONNA

(Donna Mullenger, 1921–1986)

Iowa-born Donna Reed was so sweet looking it was hard for her to find roles that didn't type her as the girl next door or someone's cute sister. One time when she escaped such typecasting she won an Academy Award for Best Supporting Actress as a prostitute in FROM HERE TO ETERNITY, and even then she was a sweet well-mannered tart. Most fans will recall her more fondly as James Stewart's almost perfect wife in IT'S A WONDERFUL LIFE or a similar but more upfront role in her long-running TV series, "The Donna Reed Show."

KEY ROLES

Carol Halliday / SEE HERE, PRIVATE HARGROVE, 1944, MGM, d-Wesley Ruggles.

Reed was just the girl for shy, bumbling Robert Walker in this standard comedy about basic training of raw recruits during World War II. As usual she is pretty, vivacious, and wholesome—just the kind of girl any mom would wish her son to bring home.

Gladys Hallward / THE PICTURE OF DORIAN GRAY, 1945, MGM, d-Albert Lewin.

Long after Dorian Gray (Hurt Hatfield) had bartered his soul in exchange for eternal youth while his portrait, hidden in an attic, shows his true depravity and age, sweet, young Reed falls in love with him. He sweeps her aside as he does all women.

Mary Hatch Bailey / IT'S A WONDERFUL LIFE, 1946, RKO, d-Frank Capra.

For those who may not have noticed it before, Reed has a truly lovely face with eyes that tell so much about the depth of her love. In this classic picture, Jimmy Stewart is the lucky recipient of those looks and that love, which he finally learns to appreciate when an angel grants his wish that he had never been born, which gives him the opportunity to see how much he mattered in life.

Alma Lorene / FROM HERE TO ETERNITY, 1953, Columbia, d-Fred Zinnemann.

When this film was made, Hollywood was not allowed to call a whorehouse even a brothel, let alone admit that Reed is renting her body to all those Honolulu-based servicemen at the "club" where she acts as a "hostess." Montgomery Clift, who is being given the treatment back at the barracks, can find respite only with Reed. She won't let him forget what she is, and why she's not the marrying kind, noting, "I'm a girl you met at the New Congress Club. That's two steps up from the pavement." Such talk from "Little Miss Next-Door" so impressed the Academy voters that they gave her an Oscar.

Sacajawea / THE FAR HORIZONS, 1955, Paramount, d-Rudolph Mate.

In this picture, Reed is a sweet helpful Indian woman who makes life a lot easier for Lewis and Clark in their 1803 expedition west through the Louisiana Purchase territory.

Alice Hammond / THE BENNY GOODMAN STORY, 1956, Universal-International, d-Valentine Davies.

Reed is the girl who makes the music go round for the great jazz clarinetist (Steve Allen). In these biopics the actress posing as the wife either stands around looking proud of her man or gives him constant hell—Reed doesn't give Allen hell.

OTHER ROLES

As Donna Adams

1941: *secretary* / BABES ON BROADWAY; *Marie Theresa O'Reilly* / THE GETAWAY.

As Donna Reed

1941: *Molly Ford* / SHADOW OF THE THIN MAN; *Sally Hanson* / THE BUGLE SOUNDS. **1942:** *Marcia Bradburn* / CALLING DR. GILLESPIE; *Melodie Nesbit* / THE COURTSHIP OF ANDY HARDY; *Anthea Delano* / MOKEY; *Barbara Lawry* / EYES IN THE NIGHT; *Rosalia Martinez* / APACHE TRAIL. **1943:** *Bess Macauley* / THE HUMAN COMEDY; *Marcia Bradburn* / DR. GILLESPIE'S CRIMINAL CASE; *guest* / THOUSANDS CHEER; *Mary Wilson* / THE MAN FROM DOWN UNDER. **1944:** *Mary Lingen* / GENTLE ANNIE. **1945:** *2nd Lt. Sandy Davyss* / THEY WERE EXPENDABLE. **1946:** *Jean Kendrick* / FAITHFUL IN MY FASHION. **1947:** *Marguerite Patourel* / GREEN DOLPHIN STREET. **1948:** *Ann Daniels* / BEYOND GLORY. **1949:** *Rosita Jean D'Ur* / CHICAGO DEADLINE. **1951:** *Melissa* / SATURDAY'S HERO. **1952:** *Julie Allison* / SCANDAL SHEET; *Molly Hull* / HANGMAN'S KNOT. **1953:** *Alice Singleton* / TROUBLE ALONG THE WAY; *Alida* / RAIDERS OF THE SEVEN SEAS; *Kathy Taylor* / THE CADDY; *Jennifer Ballard* / GUN FURY. **1954:** *Laurie Mastin* / THREE HOURS TO KILL; *Laurie MacKaye* / THEY RODE WEST; *Marion Ellsworth* / THE LAST TIME I SAW PARIS. **1956:** *Edith Stannerd* / RANSOM; *Karyl Orton* / BACKLASH. **1957:** *Ann Wilson* / BEYOND MOMBASA. **1958:** *Carol Poulton* / THE WHOLE TRUTH. **1960:** *guest* / PEPE.

REED, OLIVER

(Robert Oliver Reed, 1938–)

A one-time nightclub bouncer and cab driver, the burly, powerful-looking Reed, a nephew of director Sir Carol Reed, made his film debut in THE ANGRY SILENCE in 1960. Early in his career he usually portrayed brooding, sullen, often vicious men. By the late 1960s he had moved into a variety of roles other than his menacing villain specialties. Although it was not expected of him, he became a leading man in strong, masculine roles. He has also shown a flair for lighthearted adventure stories. Reed is not modest about his value: "Do you know what I am? I'm successful. Destroy me and you destroy the British film industry. Keep me going and I'm the biggest star you've got. I'm Mr. England."

KEY ROLES

King / THE DAMNED, 1962, Great Britain, Hammer, d-Joseph Losey.

Also known as THESE ARE THE DAMNED, this picture tells the story of an American tourist (Macdonald Carey) who becomes involved with the sister of the leader (Reed) of a motorcycle gang. All three try to free a group of imprisoned radioactive children, but exposure to the children is fatal for all.

Tinker / THE SYSTEM, 1964, Great Britain, American International, d-Michael Winner.

Reed is a cynical beach photographer who makes contact with many young women with his camera. He takes advantage of each brief encounter then moves on to another girl, but when he meets a London fashion model the tables are turned and she deserts him after a brief fling.

Jean La Bete / THE TRAP, 1966, Canada / Great Britain, Parallel Productions, d-Sidney Hayers.

In 19th-century British Columbia, Reed returns after three years of trapping with a rich haul of fur. He's eager to find a wife and shows up at the once-a-year auction of castoff women offered for sale. He chooses mute Rita Tushingham and together they proceed by canoe to his remote cabin. She serves him well and even removes his gangrenous leg when it is crushed in one of his own traps. But she's not happy in the backwoods and leaves him, but he makes his way to her and they are reunited.

David Tremayne / THE JOKERS, 1966, Great Britain, Universal, d-Michael Winner.

Reed and his brother (Michael Crawford) concoct an elaborate and daring plan to "borrow" the crown jewels from the Tower of London after Reed is expelled from military school. They succeed but Reed decides against giving them back as planned.

Andrew Quint / I'LL NEVER FORGET WHAT'S 'IS NAME, 1968, Great Britain, Scimitar-Universal / Regional Films, d-Michael Winner.

Reed is a director of TV commercials who tires of the sham and superficiality of his life and tries to escape to work on a small literary magazine. But he finds that it's not the refuge of a simple life he had sought. He makes one final commercial which he intends to be a bitter attack, but it wins first prize at an annual commercial festival.

Bill Sykes / OLIVER! 1968, Great Britain, Romulus / Columbia, d-Carol Reed.

Reed is sufficiently black-hearted to satisfy any lover of the Dickens classic about Oliver Twist, a young orphan who falls in with a gang of pickpockets led by a man named Fagin. The youngster is forced to help cruel, brutal Reed in his burglaries. It's a musical but Reed's heart doesn't sing. His performance is very similar to that of Robert Newton, who had the part in the 1948 production.

Ivan Dragomiloff / THE ASSASSINATION BUREAU, 1968, Great Britain, Paramount, d-Basil Dearden.

Reed is the head of a bureau that provides assassinations for a fee. Aspiring reporter Diana Rigg gives him a commission to have the bureau assassinate him. He accepts the assignment then spends the rest of the film disposing of his old colleagues and wooing Rigg.

Gerald Crich / WOMEN IN LOVE, 1969, Great Britain, United Artists, d-Ken Russell.

In this film version of D. H. Lawrence's novel, Reed is a coal mine owner who meets independent-minded sculptor Glenda Jackson. Her sister marries Reed's friend, school inspector Alan Bates, and the four go on holiday in Switzerland, where Jackson, growing impatient with Reed, takes up with a bisexual German sculptor. Reed attacks both the bisexual and Jackson and then wanders off into the snow until he collapses, grieving for the inadequacy of love between a man and a woman.

Father Grandier / THE DEVILS, 1971, Great Britain, Warners, d-Ken Russell.

In one of Reed's strongest performances, he is a cynical priest who has fathered numerous illegitimate children. A hunchback nun (Vanessa Redgrave), whom he has not had, accuses him of witchcraft and demonic possession. He is brutally tortured and burned to death at the stake. This film, set in France during the 1630s, is surely one of the most shocking and weirdly interesting made in the 1970s.

Athos / THE THREE MUSKETEERS, 1974, 20th Century-Fox, d-Richard Lester.

In a slapstick production of the Dumas story, Reed is the former husband of Milady De Winter (Faye Dunaway). She's a wicked lady who acts as an agent of Cardinal Richelieu in his plot against the queen, while Reed helps young D'Artagnan (Michael York) protect her majesty's reputation.

Frank Hubbs / TOMMY, 1975, Great Britain, Columbia, d-Ken Russell.

In this bizarre film based on the rock opera by The Who, Reed plays the man who marries Ann-Margret, the mother of the title character, a young man who is deaf, dumb, and blind due to a childhood trauma. But he becomes a new messiah.

Gen. Rodolfo Grazianai / LION OF THE DESERT, 1981, Falcon International, d-Moustapha Akkad.

Reed portrays an Italian general who grows to respect his opponent, rebel leader Omar Mukhtar (Anthony Quinn), in Libya in 1929, and would spare him if he could, but Mussolini orders him hanged.

OTHER ROLES

1960: *bit* / THE LEAGUE OF GENTLEMEN; *sailor* / THE BULLDOG BREED; *bit* / THE REBEL; *bit* / THE TWO FACES OF DR. JEKYLL; *Plaid Shirt* / BEAT GIRL; *Melton* / SWORD OF SHERWOOD FOREST; *Mick* / THE ANGRY SILENCE. **1961:** *poet* / HIS AND HERS; *the guest* / NO LOVE FOR JOHNNIE; *Leon* / THE CURSE OF THE WEREWOLF. **1962:** *Harry Crabtree* / CAPTAIN CLEGG; *Brocaire* / THE PIRATES OF BLOOD RIVER. **1963:** *Simon Ashby* / PARANOIAC. **1964:** *Capt. Sylvester* / THE SCARLET BLADE; *Moise* / THE PARTY'S OVER. **1965:** *Eli Khan* / THE BRIGAND OF KANDAHAR. **1966:** *Ethan* / THE SHUTTERED ROOM. **1968:** *Hannibal Brooks* / HANNIBAL BROOKS. **1969:**

Patrick Standish / TAKE A GIRL LIKE YOU. **1970:** *Michael Caldwell* / THE LADY IN THE CAR WITH GLASSES AND A GUN. **1971:** *Frank Calder* / THE HUNTING PARTY. **1972:** *Russ McNeil* / Z.P.G.; *Harry Lomart* / SITTING TARGET; *sergeant* / TRIPLE ECHO; *Fabrizo* / DIRTY WEEKEND. **1973:** *sadistic landowner* / DAYS OF FURY. **1974:** *Athos* / THE FOUR MUSKETEERS; *Hugh Lombard* / TEN LITTLE INDIANS; *Otto von Bismarck* / ROYAL FLASH. **1975:** *Gabriel Lee* / THE SELLOUT. **1976:** *Joe Knox* / THE GREAT SCOUT AND CATHOUSE THURSDAY; *Ben* / BURNT OFFERINGS; *Vito Caprini* / BLOOD IN THE STREETS. **1977:** *Miles Henderson* / THE PRINCE AND THE PAUPER; *hit man* / MANIAC. **1978:** *Eddie Mars* / THE BIG SLEEP; *Wilson* / TOMORROW NEVER COMES; *Terrence Sutton* / THE CLASS OF MISS MACMICHAEL. **1979:** *Dr. Hal Raglan* / THE BROOD. **1981:** *Dr. Heckyl / Mr. Hype* / DR. HECKYL AND MR. HYPE; *Krokov* / CONDORMAN; *Dave* / VENOM. **1982:** *Doyle Lonnegan* / THE STING II; *U.S. millionaire* / SPASMS. **1983:** *Beasley* / TWO OF A KIND; *lawyer* / FANNY HILL. **1986:** *Gregory LeVay* / CAPTIVE.

REMICK, LEE

(1935–)

Lee Remick is a cool blonde with a strong erotic allure. Although born in Boston, she started her film career playing southern sexpots as in her debut as a majorette in A FACE IN THE CROWD. This talented, attractive leading lady, nominated for an Academy Award for her performance in DAYS OF WINE AND ROSES, has found it difficult to find good movie roles for mature beauties and has turned to the stage and television. Her made-for-TV movies and mini-series include QB VII and THE BLUE KNIGHT (1974), A GIRL NAMED SOONER, JENNIE, and HUSTLING (1975), IKE and TORN BETWEEN TWO LOVES (1979), THE WOMEN'S ROOM (1980), HAYWIRE (1981), THE LETTER (1982), THE GIFT OF LOVE: A CHRISTMAS STORY (1983), A GOOD SPORT and REARVIEW MIRROR (1984), and TOUGH LOVE (1985). Speaking of her self-image, she has remarked: "Everyone has a false image of himself. When I first saw myself on the screen, twenty-five feet tall, what I saw was so unexpected that I couldn't look at anyone else in the picture."

KEY ROLES

Betty Lou Fleckum / A FACE IN THE CROWD, 1957, Warners, d-Elia Kazan.

This story of a guitar-playing, homespun philosopher (Andy Griffith) who is a natural whenever he gets in front of a microphone is a first-rate movie, and Remick, in her debut as a sexy baton twirler, is a real plus to the film.

Eula Varner / THE LONG, HOT SUMMER, 1958, 20th Century-Fox, d-Martin Ritt.

Remick is the sexy wife of Tony Franciosa, the weak-kneed son of a man (Orson Welles) who runs a small Mississippi town. Welles has to worry when Paul Newman, who has a nasty habit of burning barns, comes to work for him and goes after Welles's strange daughter (Joanne Woodward). The boys hang around the old manse on warm summer nights and call for Remick to come out and play, which annoys Franciosa no end, but only amuses Remick.

Laura Manion / ANATOMY OF A MURDER, 1959, Columbia, d-Otto Preminger.

Playfully sexy Remick is allegedly raped and assaulted by the owner of an upper Michigan Peninsula bar. Her army officer husband (Ben Gazzara) goes to the bar and shoots and kills the assailant. Jimmy Stewart is hired to defend Gazzara against a murder charge and he has his hands full with Remick, who is promiscuous in spirit if not in practice.

Temple Drake / SANCTUARY, 1961, 20th Century-Fox, d-Tony Richardson.

The daughter of a southern governor, Remick is seduced by a bootlegger and likes it. From then on her life is one tragedy after another. This version of William Faulkner's unfilmable novel is more daring than the 1933 version, THE STORY OF TEMPLE DRAKE, but not as interesting.

Kirsten Arnesen (Clay) / DAYS OF WINE AND ROSES, 1962, Warners, d-Blake Edwards.

Public relations man Jack Lemmon becomes an alcoholic and little by little his wife (Remick) reaches the same point. He finally decides to get help but she's not ready to admit she has a problem. Instead she rationalizes that drinking makes the world a prettier place: "You see, the world looks so dirty to me when I'm not drinking. Joe, remember Fisherman's Wharf? The water when you looked close? That's the way the world looks to me when I'm not drinking."

Katherine Thorn / THE OMEN, 1976, 20th Century-Fox, d-Richard Donner.

When Remick's baby is born dead, dad Gregory Peck arranges for another baby born at the same time to take the dead child's place. A few years later, Peck discovers that his "son" has been fathered by the devil. Remick doesn't get the news because the little devil arranges for some accidents that kill her.

OTHER ROLES

1959: *Callie* / THESE THOUSAND HILLS. **1960:** *Carol Baldwin* / WILD RIVER. **1962:** *Kelly Sherwood* / EXPERIMENT IN TERROR. **1963:** *Molly Thatcher* / THE WHEELER DEALERS; *Stella Black* / THE RUNNING MAN. **1965:** *Georgette Thomas* / BABY, THE RAIN MUST FALL; *Cora Templeton Massingale* / THE HALLELUJAH TRAIL. **1968:** *Kate Palmer* / NO WAY TO TREAT A LADY; *Karen Leland* / THE DETECTIVE. **1970:** *Antonia Lynch-Gibson* / A SEVERED HEAD; *Fay* / LOOT. **1972:** *Viv Stamper* / SOMETIMES A GREAT NOTION. **1973:** *Julia* / A DELICATE BALANCE. **1975:** *Kate Brook* / HENNESSY. **1977:** *Barbara* / TELEFON; *Dr. Zonfeld* / THE MEDUSA TOUCH. **1979:** *Eugenia* / THE EUROPEANS. **1980:** *Greta Vandermann* / THE COMPETITION; *Maggie Stratton* / TRIBUTE.

REYNOLDS, BURT

(Burton Reynolds, 1936–)

Brought up in Florida, Burt Reynolds attended Florida State University on a football scholarship with a dream of playing in the National Football League. But his career was ended by a car accident. Given a contract by Universal, he became a regular in the series "Riverboat," "Gunsmoke," and "Hawk." He also achieved a lot of exposure by posing nude in a *Cosmopolitan* centerfold. Once married to Judy Carne, the "Sock it to Me" girl of "Laugh-In," his romances with Dinah Shore and Sally Field gained him as much publicity as some of his movies. Along with good ol' boy charm and a self-effacing sense of humor, his stud-like behavior made him a major film star in the 1970s. By 1980 he rivaled Clint Eastwood for most bankable male movie star. Most of his movies have been of the trivial, down-home variety or filled with gratuitous violence. Still his pictures are usually enjoyable because Reynolds is a natural comedian whom women find sexy and men imagine to be much like themselves.

KEY ROLES

Det. Steve Carella / FUZZ, 1972, United Artists, d-Richard A. Colla.

Doing anything for a laugh, Reynolds dresses as a nun while on stakeout in this farce about Boston cops out to catch a mysterious bomber (Yul Brynner). It has jokes and thrills but could use more of both at appropriate times.

Lewis / DELIVERANCE, 1972, Warners, d-John Boorman.

In one of his most macho roles, Reynolds and three other Atlanta businessmen take a weekend canoe trip down a dangerous river in Georgia's back-country. When Ned Beatty is raped by a mountain man, Reynolds kills the offender with his bow and arrow. While trying to complete their trip, they are trailed by another mountain man who shoots and kills Ronny Cox. Reynolds's leg is badly broken when he's thrown from a canoe and it's up to Jon Voight to seek out and kill their nemesis.

Paul Crewe / THE LONGEST YARD, 1974, Paramount, d-Robert Aldrich.

Reynolds is an ex-professional football player sent to a southern penitentiary where he's ordered by Warden Eddie Albert to get up a team of cons to play the guards and, by the way, to lose.

Bandit / SMOKEY AND THE BANDIT, 1977, Universal, d-Hal Needham.

Reynolds is a good ol' southern boy who is a whiz at driving anything on wheels. He can net a tidy sum of money by racing 1,800 miles from Georgia to Texas and back in 28 hours. On his trip he picks up a runaway bride (Sally Field) and they are pursued by her prospective father-in-law (Jackie Gleason), a redneck sheriff. It's not much but it grossed nearly $40 million.

Billy Clyde Puckett / SEMI-TOUGH, 1977, United Artists, d-Michael Ritchie.

Reynolds, a football player with a Miami pro team, shares an apartment with a teammate (Kris Kristofferson) and the daughter of the team's owner (Jill Clayburgh), as a platonic threesome. But both Reynolds and Kristofferson decide one should marry Clayburgh. It's an interesting satire, especially when it takes on an EST-like organization that charges its members large amounts of money, keeps them in discomfort, and with great brass tells them how stupid they are to take the treatment.

Sonny Hooper / HOOPER, 1978, Warners, d-Hal Needham.

In this salute to movie stunt men and women, Reynolds is one of the best in his field and has been for twenty years. But with all his scars and broken bones, he comes to the realization that even he can't keep it up forever. He has one last spectacular stunt he wishes to pull off before calling it quits—making a 450-foot jump in a jet-powered car over a collapsed bridge.

Phil Potter / STARTING OVER, 1979, Paramount, d-Alan J. Pakula.

We get a nice glimpse of Reynolds the sensitive man in this story of lonely men and women coping with divorce and trying to find someone new in their lives. He's a writer who falls for divorced schoolteacher Jill Clayburgh, but ex-wife Candice Bergen drops back into his life and briefly makes him forget why they divorced.

Sharky / SHARKY'S MACHINE, 1982, Warners, d-Burt Reynolds.

Reynolds is an Atlanta cop who has a beautiful, expensive hooker (Rachel Ward) under surveillance. As he watches her comings and goings, day by day, he falls in love with her (well, maybe in lust). He finds that she's involved with an underworld big shot and a crooked politician. Then she's killed—or is she?

David Fowler / THE MAN WHO LOVED WOMEN, 1983, Columbia, d-Blake Edwards.

In an interesting failure, Reynolds is perhaps miscast as a Los Angeles sculptor whose obsession for bedding down beautiful women is seriously interfering with his work. It's a remake of a very popular French film of a few years earlier.

Mike Murphy / CITY HEAT, 1984, Malpaso / Warners, d-Richard Benjamin.

There's not much plot in the picture, but the interplay between the two box-office kings—Reynolds as a wisecracking private eye and Clint Eastwood as a no-nonsense, tough cop—who team up in the 1930s to find a murderer is well worth the price of admission.

OTHER ROLES

1961: *Hoke Adams* / ANGEL BABY; *Skee* / ARMORED COMMAND. **1965:** *Mark Andrews* / OPERATION C.I.A. **1967:** *Navajo Joe* / NAVAJO JOE. **1968:** *Caine* / SHARK!; *Rob* / FADE-IN. **1969:** *Pat Morrison* / IMPASSE; *Sam Whiskey* / SAM WHISKEY; *Yaqui Joe* / 100 RIFLES. **1970:** *Douglas Temple* / SKULLDUGGERY. **1972:** *cameo* / EVERYTHING YOU ALWAYS WANTED TO KNOW ABOUT SEX (BUT WERE AFRAID TO ASK). **1973:** *Shamus McCoy* / SHAMUS; *Gator McKluskey* / WHITE LIGHTNING; *Jay Grobart* / THE MAN WHO LOVED CAT DANCING. **1975:** *W. W. Bright* / W. W. AND THE DIXIE DANCEKINGS; *Michael Oliver Pritchard* / AT LONG LAST LOVE; *Lt. Phil Gaines* / HUSTLE; *Walker* / LUCKY LADY. **1976:** *Gator McKluskey* / GATOR; *guest* / SILENT MOVIE; *Buck Greenway* / NICKELODEON. **1978:** *Sonny Lawson* / THE END. **1980:** *Jack Rhodes* / ROUGH CUT; *Bandit* / SMOKEY AND THE BANDIT II. **1981:** *J. J. McClure* / THE CANNONBALL RUN; *Buddy Evans* / PATERNITY. **1982:** *Sheriff Ed Earl Dodd* / THE BEST LITTLE WHOREHOUSE IN TEXAS; *Richard Babson* / BEST FRIENDS. **1983:** *Stroker Ace* / STROKER ACE; *cameo* / SMOKEY AND THE BANDIT 3. **1984:** *J. J. McClure* / CANNONBALL RUN II. **1985:** *Stick* / STICK. **1987:** *Malone* / MALONE; *Nick Escalande* / HEAT.

REYNOLDS, DEBBIE

(Mary Frances Reynolds, 1932–)

Texas-born, energetic, bouncy, and petite, Debbie Reynolds's popularity in movies was immediate, beginning with her first featured role in THE DAUGHTER OF ROSIE O'GRADY in 1950. This Miss Burbank of 1948 had all the appeal of a wholesome, cute cheerleader. While her singing and dancing were only average, her charm and enthusiasm made up for the lack of topnotch credentials for Hollywood musicals. She was a capable mimic who possessed a refreshing sense of humor. Her perfect marriage to singer Eddie Fisher ended when he provided comfort to Elizabeth Taylor after the death of her husband, Michael Todd, which led to a brief marriage for Fisher and Taylor. When the kind of films that could use an innocent girl-next-door type dried up, Reynolds moved into TV, nightclubs, and Broadway. She is the mother of actress Carrie Fisher, another woman having difficulty finding enough lightweight roles to keep a second generation girlish actress busy.

KEY ROLES

Helen Kane / THREE LITTLE WORDS, 1950, MGM, d-Richard Thorpe.

One of the best things about this decidedly ordinary biopic about the careers of songwriters Bert Kalmar and Harry Ruby is Reynolds's brief appearance as the "Boop Boop a Boop" girl.

Kathy Selden / SINGIN' IN THE RAIN, 1952, MGM, d-Gene Kelly and Stanley Donen.

In this movie about the trials and tribulations faced by the motion picture industry as it converts from silents to talkies, Reynolds is a singer and dancer who is hired to dub for nasty star Jean Hagen, who has a perfectly ghastly voice. It's among the best Hollywood musicals ever made and Reynolds's contribution is significant.

Susan / SUSAN SLEPT HERE, 1954, RKO, d-Frank Tashlin.

Reynolds is a 17-year-old left on her own in Hollywood just before Christmas. The cops bring her to the apartment of screenwriter Dick Powell as research material for a new movie (yes, it sounds suspicious to Reynolds as well), rather than make her spend the holidays in a detention center. Foolishly Powell marries the girl so she won't be put in some institution, with the idea of not consummating the marriage and getting a divorce later. Reynolds has other plans. When she begins eating her favorite treat, pickles and strawberries, Powell suspects that someone has taken advantage of her. But no—she's saved herself for Powell and counters all his arguments as to why they shouldn't go to bed and become really married.

Julie Gillis / THE TENDER TRAP, 1955, MGM, d-Charles Walters.

In this bit of fluff, Reynolds is a seemingly naive, young actress who nevertheless gets Casanova-like New York agent Frank Sinatra on her terms—or as the hit song says, "Love and marriage go together like a horse and carriage—you can't have one without the other."

Jane Hurley / THE CATERED AFFAIR, 1956, MGM, d-Richard Brooks.

Reynolds's forthcoming wedding is a source of much friction in her family when her mother (Bette Davis) insists on a bigger function than she and her New York taxi driver husband (Ernest Borgnine) can afford. Reynolds almost, just almost, hits the marriage bed before the ceremony.

Tammy Tyree / TAMMY AND THE BACHELOR, 1957, Universal-International, d-Joseph Pevney.

Reynolds is a backwoods tomboy who falls for a stranded flyer (Leslie Nielsen). The family appeal of this light entertainment is enhanced by Reynolds's rendition of the million-selling title song.

Lucretia Rogers / THE SECOND TIME AROUND, 1961, 20th Century-Fox, d-Vincent Sherman.

Young widow Reynolds and her two children arrive in an Arizona town in 1912 to start a new life. She has plenty of suitors in the wild boom town, but a few are put off when she becomes sheriff.

Molly Brown / THE UNSINKABLE MOLLY BROWN, 1964, MGM, d-Charles Walters.

Reynolds's only Oscar nomination was for her portrayal of an orphan who gains a fortune and ultimately her place in western society. In this musical version of the life of a remarkable real character, Reynolds survives, among other things, the sinking of the Titanic. She is especially bouncy but the music is nothing to get excited about.

Sister Ann / THE SINGING NUN, 1966, MGM, d-Henry Koster.

There was a singing nun who took her songs outside the convent and hit the charts, but it hardly seems the basis for a feature film. However, one should never underestimate Hollywood's unending need for ideas. Reynolds makes a cute, bouncy nun, habit and all.

Adelle Bruckner / WHAT'S THE MATTER WITH HELEN? 1971, Filmways, d-Curtis Harrington.

In this 1930s murder story, Reynolds and Shelley Winters run a dance school for Hollywood moppets hoping to make it in the movies. One of them is a killer.

OTHER ROLES

1948: *Boo's girlfriend* / JUNE BRIDE. **1950:** *Maureen O'Grady* / THE DAUGHTER OF ROSIE O'GRADY; *Melba Robinson* / TWO WEEKS WITH LOVE. **1951:** *Gwen* / MR. IMPERIUM. **1952:** *herself* / SKIRTS AHOY! **1953:** *Judy Leroy* / I LOVE MELVIN; *Pansy Hammer* / THE AFFAIRS OF DOBIE GILLIS; *Suzy Doolittle* / GIVE A GIRL A BREAK. **1954:** *Minerva Mulvain* / ATHENA. **1955:** *Carol Pace* / HIT THE DECK. **1956:** *Polly Parrish* / BUNDLE OF JOY. **1958:** *guest* / MEET ME IN LAS VEGAS; *Janet Blake* / THIS HAPPY FEELING. **1959:** *Marella Larkin* / THE MATING GAME; *Holly* / SAY ONE FOR ME; *Maggie Fitzpatrick* / IT STARTED WITH A KISS; *Nell Nash* / THE GAZEBO. **1960:** *Peggy Brown* / THE RAT RACE; *guest* / PEPE. **1961:** *Jessica Poole* / THE PLEASURE OF HIS COMPANY. **1962:** *Lilith Prescott* / HOW THE WEST WAS WON. **1963:** *Janice Courtney* / MY SIX LOVES; *Mary McKellaway* / MARY, MARY. **1964:** *Charlie Sorel / the woman* / GOODBYE CHARLIE. **1967:** *Barbara Harmon* / DIVORCE, AMERICAN STYLE. **1968:** *Jenny Henderson* / HOW SWEET IT IS. **1972:** *Charlotte's voice* / CHARLOTTE'S WEB. **1974:** *host* / THAT'S ENTERTAINMENT!

RICHARDSON, RALPH

(1902–1983)

When insurance clerk Ralph Richardson received a legacy, he decided to study fine art and then acting. How fortunate for all who have enjoyed his portrayals of well-bred, unassuming, intelligent characters and a few odd, well-mannered villains. Along with Laurence Olivier and John Gielgud, Richardson is rated as one of the three greatest actors of the century. His rich voice has pleased both film and stage audiences from the 1920s on. His peak as a movie actor was in the period from 1936 to 1952, from THINGS TO COME through THE SOUND BARRIER. From that time on his movie appearances have been mainly cameos, although some of these small character roles were outstandingly performed and made for a better movie than without him. He was already middle-aged when he made his U.S. debut in THE HEIRESS, for which he received a Best Supporting Actor nomination. He was knighted in 1947 and, when asked to comment on the art of acting, replied, "The art of acting consists of keeping people from coughing."

KEY ROLES

Morelle / BULLDOG JACK, 1935, Great Britain, Gaumont, d-Walter Forde.

Master criminal Richardson forces Fay Wray and her grandfather, both expert jewelers, to help him replace the gems in a statue in the British Museum with paste stones. He's foiled by Jack Hulbert standing in for an injured Bulldog Drummond.

The Boss / THINGS TO COME, 1936, Great Britain, London Films, d-William Cameron Menzies.

In this film adaptation of the H. G. Wells story, Richardson is a Hitler-Mussolini-like dictator in the year 2036. This isn't an actor's film. Its impact comes from a combination of predictions about the future and imaginative sets.

Robert Carne / SOUTH RIDING, 1937, Great Britain, London Films, d-Victor Saville.
Richardson is a country squire whose funds are rapidly being spent to keep his wife (Ann Todd) in an expensive nursing home. Initially Richardson opposes a housing scheme thought of by socialist John Clements, but finally comes to support it, even offering his own estate for the purpose at a bargain price on the condition that his mansion be turned into a school with Edna Best, whom he has come to love, as headmistress.

Maj. Charles Hammond / PLANES, 1939, Great Britain, Harefield / Columbia, d-Tim Whelan.
Richardson is a Scotland Yard inspector called in when bombers disappear in test flights. He discovers the inside man in the plot but his suspect is killed before he can get him to reveal the details of the scheme. With the help of test pilot Laurence Olivier, the gang behind the hijackings is captured.

Capt. John Durrance / THE FOUR FEATHERS, 1939, Great Britain, London Films, d-Zoltan Korda.
Richardson is one of three officers who give John Clements white feathers, the symbol of cowardice, when Clements resigns his commission on the eve of his regiment's departure for Sudan in 1898. Clements travels to Sudan and, disguised as a mute native, finds badly wounded Richardson blinded by the sun. Clements cares for his one-time friend and guides him to safety without Richardson knowing who has saved him. But Clements slips a white feather in Richardson's wallet to identify himself. He then leaves to redeem himself with the other ex-friends so he can return the other feathers, including one he had accepted from his fiancée.

Alexei Karenin / ANNA KARENINA, 1947, Great Britain, British Lion, d-Julien Duvivier.
Richardson is a civil servant in 1875 Moscow whose wife (Vivien Leigh) falls for officer Kieron Moore. The two become lovers and Richardson resolves to divorce Leigh, taking his son with him. Leigh's lover also leaves her and, now alone, she is killed by a train as she walks along the tracks.

Baines / THE FALLEN IDOL, 1948, Great Britain, British Lion, d-Carol Reed.
The eight-year-old son of a London-based ambassador is left alone for the weekend with kindly butler Richardson, whom the child (Bobby Henry) idolizes, and his harridan wife (Sonia Dresdel) whom he hates. Richardson is in love with an embassy typist (Michele Morgan). The boy overhears a conversation between the two lovers which he later is tricked into repeating for Dresdel and that night the boy hears Richardson and his wife in a violent argument. When Dresdel accidentally falls downstairs to her death, Henry, determined to protect his friend, withholds the precise evidence that will show Richardson innocent of his wife's death.

Dr. Austin Sloper / THE HEIRESS, 1949, Paramount, d-William Wyler.
Richardson gives a subtle and superb performance as the master of a Washington Square home who correctly deduces that Montgomery Clift, who is paying suit to his plain, sheltered, and naive daughter, is a fortune hunter. However, he seems less interested in protecting his daughter's feelings than he is in ensuring that his life is in no way disrupted. She ultimately turns her back on her dying father as punishment for treating her so cruelly.

John Richfield / THE SOUND BARRIER, 1952, Great Britain, London Films, d-David Lean.
Richardson, a ruthless aircraft factory owner, loses both his son and son-in-law in trying to break the sound barrier. His ambition alienates him from his daughter but when she finally sees some human traits in her father she returns to him with his fatherless grandson.

Rev. Martin Gregory / THE HOLLY AND THE IVY, 1953, Great Britain, London Films, d-George More O'Ferrall.
Richardson is a vicar who has recently lost his wife. He spends Christmas Eve with his three grown children and before the holiday is over, everyone tells some truth about himself. It's a witty comedy-drama.

Buckingham / RICHARD III, 1955, Great Britain, London Films, d-Laurence Olivier.
Richardson portrays the clever and scheming accomplice of the treacherous Duke of Gloucester (Laurence Olivier) as the latter plots and murders his way to the English throne. When he achieves his goal, Richardson's importance diminishes.

Sir Edward Carson / OSCAR WILDE, 1959, Great Britain, Vantage, d-Gregory Ratoff.
In this story about the trials of Oscar Wilde for his homosexual involvement with Lord Alfred Douglas in the 1890s, Richardson is memorable as the brilliant Queen's Counsel who mercilessly strips Wilde in court with his penetrating questions.

General Sutherland / EXODUS, 1960, United Artists, d-Otto Preminger.
Richardson is the British commander on Cyprus where Jewish refugees are kept in camps after World War II while some decision is made about what to do with them. Agents from Israel decide to take a shipload of them home to Israel and a stalemate develops, until Richardson's resignation forces his government to let the ship go to Israel.

James Tyrone, Sr. / LONG DAY'S JOURNEY INTO NIGHT, 1962, Landau, d-Sidney Lumet.
In 1912 Connecticut, Richardson is an aging actor who is married to a drug-addicted woman, and who has two sons—one an alcoholic and the other playwright Eugene O'Neill. His acting is superb as is that of Katharine Hepburn, Jason Robards, Jr., and Dean Stockwell.

Alexander Gromeko / DOCTOR ZHIVAGO, 1966, MGM, d-David Lean.
Richardson is the aristocratic father-in-law of Zhivago (Omar Sharif). When the revolution comes, Richardson finds his home taken over and travels with his starving family in the dead of winter to their summer home in the Urals. Later Richardson and his daughter are separated from Sharif and deported to France.

Joseph Finsbury / THE WRONG BOX, 1966, Great Britain, Columbia, d-Bryan Forbes.
Richardson and John Mills are two elderly brothers in Victorian London who are bonded together by a tontine—a financial arrangement whereby the last surviving family member inherits a fortune. They and their heirs try to kill each other.

The Devil / TALES FROM THE CRYPT, 1971, Great Britain, Metromedia, d-Freddie Francis.

Richardson is a sinister monk who shows the future to five people lost in catacombs. He turns out to be the devil.

Lord Greystoke / GREYSTOKE: THE LEGEND OF TARZAN, LORD OF THE APES, 1984, Great Britain, Warners, d-Hugh Hudson.

Richardson, the sixth Earl of Greystoke, is reunited with his grandson who has been raised from the time he was a baby by a band of apes in Africa. It's an absurd telling of the Tarzan story, but Richardson is not at fault.

OTHER ROLES

1933: *Nigel Hartley* / THE GHOUL; *Horace Dawes* / FRIDAY THE 13TH, (MILLIE THE NON-STOP VARIETY GIRL). **1934:** *Hugh Drummond* / THE RETURN OF BULLDOG DRUMMOND; *William Ammidon* / JAVA HEAD; *Paul Lebrun* / THE KING OF PARIS. **1936:** *Colonel Winstanley* / THE MAN WHO COULD WORK MIRACLES. **1937:** *Henry Manningdale* / THUNDER IN THE CITY. **1938:** *Lord Mere* / THE DIVORCE OF LADY X; *Dr. Denny* / THE CITADEL. **1939:** *Wing Commander Richardson* / THE LION HAS WINGS; *Will Kobling* / ON THE NIGHT OF THE FIRE, (THE FUGITIVE). **1942:** *Frank Lockwood* / THE DAY WILL DAWN. **1943:** *Jaap Van Leyden* / THE SILVER FLEET; *himself* / THE VOLUNTEER. **1946:** *Professor Heatherville* / SCHOOL FOR SECRETS. **1951:** *Captain Lingard* / OUTCAST OF THE ISLANDS. **1952:** *David Preston* / HOME AT SEVEN. **1957:** *Reverend Lambeth* / SMILEY; *Roger Wynter* / *Sir Clement* / THE PASSIONATE STRANGER. **1959:** *"C"* / OUR MAN IN HAVANA. **1962:** *Themistocles* / THE 300 SPARTANS. **1964:** *Charles Richmond* / WOMAN OF STRAW. **1967:** *William Gladstone* / KHARTOUM. **1969:** *Sir Edward Guy* / OH! WHAT A LOVELY WAR; *Henshaw* / MIDAS RUN; *Lord Fortnum of Alamein* / THE BED-SITTING ROOM; *Sir David* / BATTLE OF BRITAIN; *Leclerc* / THE LOOKING GLASS WAR; *Mr. Micawber* / DAVID COPPERFIELD. **1971:** *Sir Hudson Lowe* / EAGLE IN A CAGE; *Mr. Benton* / WHO SLEW AUNTIE ROO? **1972:** *King George IV* / LADY CAROLINE LAMB; *Caterpillar* / ALICE'S ADVENTURES IN WONDERLAND. **1973:** *Dr. Rank* / A DOLL'S HOUSE; *Monty, Sir James Burgess* / O LUCKY MAN! **1975:** *librarian* / ROLLERBALL. **1980:** *supreme being* / TIME BANDITS. **1981:** *Ulrich* / DRAGONSLAYER. **1983:** *Pfordten* / WAGNER; *Uncle Willie* / INVITATION TO A WEDDING. **1984:** *Jim* / GIVE MY REGARDS TO BROAD STREET. **1986:** *himself* / DIRECTED BY WILLIAM WYLER.

ROBARDS, JASON, JR.

(1922–)

The son of Jason Robards, Sr., who appeared in over 100 movies between 1921 and 1961, Jason Robards, Jr. made his first acting impression on the stage in various Eugene O'Neill productions such as "The Iceman Cometh" and "Long Day's Journey into Night." Especially effective in soul-searching roles, Robards admits that he has taken some inferior film roles because the money was good. However his good work has been recognized with Oscars for ALL THE PRESIDENT'S MEN (1976) and JULIA (1977) and a nomination for MELVIN AND HOWARD. His raspy voice and craggy expression do not make him the ideal romantic leading man, but in somewhat the same way as Humphrey Bogart, his less-than-handsome looks have become a plus. Another parallel with Bogart is that Robards was once married to Lauren Bacall, the third of his four wives.

KEY ROLES

Dick Diver / TENDER IS THE NIGHT, 1962, 20th Century-Fox, d-Henry King.

When Robards, an eminent psychiatrist, marries a wealthy neurotic patient (Jennifer Jones), they go to live on her Riviera estate and the easy life gradually dissipates his talents.

James Tyrone, Jr. / LONG DAY'S JOURNEY INTO NIGHT, 1962, Landau, d-Sidney Lumet.

Robards portrays the older, alcoholic brother of playwright Eugene O'Neill. The family must also deal with the drug addiction of the mother. It's a highly theatrical piece with excellent performances from Robards, Katharine Hepburn, Ralph Richardson, and Bradford Dillman.

Murray Burns / A THOUSAND CLOWNS, 1965, United Artists, d-Fred Coe.

Repeating his Broadway role as a hack TV gag writer, Robards shares his one-room apartment with his precocious 12-year-old nephew. As Robards is a nonconformist in this comedy, school and welfare authorities are concerned that the living conditions are not appropriate for the child.

John Cleves / ANY WEDNESDAY, 1966, Warners, d-Robert Ellis Miller.

Millionaire businessman Robards has set up his mistress (Jane Fonda) in an apartment belonging to his company and spends every Wednesday with her. Things blow up when a secretary gives Dean Jones the keys to the apartment to stay in while he's in town. Jones gets Fonda, and Robards goes back to his wife in this mildly amusing picture.

Doc Holliday / HOUR OF THE GUN, 1967, United Artists, d-John Sturges.

In this sequel to GUNFIGHT AT THE O.K. CORRAL, Robards is the drunken dentist turned gambler and gunfighter who ends up in a sanatorium with TB. This is much more violent than the earlier film.

Al Capone / THE ST. VALENTINE'S DAY MASSACRE, 1967, 20th Century-Fox, d-Roger Corman.

Robards portrays Capone as the violent, brutal monster that he really was as he orders the destruction of rival Bugs Moran. It's chilling when he tells a couple of his boys, who have betrayed him, to say their prayers as he waits to beat them to death with a baseball bat.

Raymond Paine / THE NIGHT THEY RAIDED MINSKY'S, 1968, United Artists, d-William Friedkin.

Robards portrays a burlesque slapstick comic who cruelly mistreats his partner (Norman Wisdom) and seduces an Amish girl (Britt Eklund). She's not shaken by the experiment as she goes on to accidentally invent striptease.

Cable Hogue / THE BALLAD OF CABLE HOGUE, 1970, Warners, d-Sam Peckinpah.

Robards, a prospector left to die in the desert by his partners, finds a water-hole that he turns into a successful business. He takes a lengthy and ineffectual revenge on those who had tried to kill him, and dies as he tries to be a hero.

Ben Bradlee / ALL THE PRESIDENT'S MEN, 1976, Warners, d-Alan J. Pakula.

Robards won the Best Supporting Actor Academy Award for his portrayal of *Washington Post* editor Ben Bradlee in this movie based on the investigation of reporters Woodward and Bernstein who broke the story of the White House link to the break-in of Democratic Headquarters at the Watergate complex.

Dashiell Hammett / JULIA, 1977, 20th Century-Fox, d-Fred Zinnemann.

Robards won his second Oscar for his portrayal of the mystery writer who was Lillian Hellman's lover. The story is about the anti-Nazi activities of Hellman's friend Julia.

Howard Hughes / MELVIN AND HOWARD, 1980, Universal, d-Jonathan Demme.

Robards was nominated for an Oscar for his portrayal of the legendary billionaire Howard Hughes. One of life's losers, Melvin Dummar (Paul Le Mat), encounters Robards on a Nevada highway and, believing him to be just a vagrant in need of help, agrees to give him a lift to Las Vegas. Robards tells Le Mat who he is but Le Mat doesn't believe him until he later learns that he has been left $156 million in Hughes's will.

Charles Halloway / SOMETHING WICKED THIS WAY COMES, 1983, Disney, d-Jack Clayton.

In this Ray Bradbury fantasy, Robards is the town's librarian who must save his family and friends from the sinister and evil temptations of a carnival's Master of Ceremonies, who can regulate age and time.

OTHER ROLES

1959: *Paul Kedes* / THE JOURNEY. **1961:** *Julius Penrose* / BY LOVE POSSESSED. **1963:** *George S. Kaufman* / ACT ONE. **1966:** *Henry Drummond* / A BIG HAND FOR THE LITTLE LADY. **1967:** *Nelson Downes* / DIVORCE, AMERICAN STYLE. **1968:** *Paris singer* / ISADORA. **1969:** *Cheyenne* / ONCE UPON A TIME IN THE WEST. **1970:** *Gen. Walter C. Scott* / TORA! TORA! TORA!; *Brutus* / JULIUS CAESAR; *Matthew South* / FOOLS. **1971:** *Cesar Charron* / MURDERS IN THE RUE MORGUE; *Joe's father* / JOHNNY GOT HIS GUN. **1972:** *Stephen Kozlenko* / THE WAR BETWEEN MEN AND WOMEN. **1973:** *Governor Wallace* / PAT GARRETT AND BILLY THE KID. **1975:** *John Gwilt* / MR. SYCAMORE. **1976:** *Lew Craddock* / A BOY AND HIS DOG. **1978:** *Ewing* / COMES A HORSEMAN. **1979:** *Capt. Bruckner* / HURRICANE. **1980:** *Adm. James Sandecker* / RAISE THE TITANIC! **1981:** *Gunther Berkdorff* / CABO BLANCO; *President U. S. Grant* / THE LEGEND OF THE LONE RANGER. **1983:** *Max Dugan* / MAX DUGAN RETURNS. **1987:** *Grandpa* / SQUARE DANCE.

ROBERTS, RACHEL

(1927–1980)

Not a beauty, Rachel Roberts was an expressive actress with an earthy appeal that served her well in roles of lower-to middle-class urban women for whom life had not been easy. The daughter of a Welsh Baptist minister, Roberts studied at the Royal Academy of Dramatic Arts, making her film debut in 1952 in VALLEY OF SONG and her London stage debut the next year in "The Buccaneer." Academy Award-nominated for THIS SPORTING LIFE, she was once wed to actor Rex Harrison of whom she said, "I used to be a very good actress. Then I married Rex Harrison and got lost...I couldn't live on one more yacht for one more day." She took her own life in 1980 after having spent the preceding few years on American television.

KEY ROLES

Brenda / SATURDAY NIGHT AND SUNDAY MORNING, 1961, Great Britain, Woodfall, d-Karel Reisz.

Roberts is the wife of a factory worker who works with 22-year-old Albert Finney. She and Finney spend Saturday nights together and, when she becomes pregnant, he hopes to procure an abortion for her, but without success. He offers to marry her, but she knows he doesn't love her and so decides to have the baby and suffer the consequences. Her husband and some chums beat Finney senseless when they learn what's what.

Mrs. Hammond / THIS SPORTING LIFE, 1963, Great Britain, Independent Artists, d-Lindsay Anderson.

Lonely widow Roberts rents a room to Richard Harris, a miner in northern England ambitious to find fame and fortune. In a small way he achieves his goals by playing rugby. Roberts initially rejects his romantic overtures but eventually they become lovers even though she still refuses to become emotionally involved with him. Later her guilt over their affair is more than she can stand and they separate after a series of rows. When he can stand the separation no longer he returns only to discover that she is dying in a hospital.

Suzanne / A FLEA IN HER EAR, 1968, 20th Century-Fox, d-Jacques Charon.

Roberts is persuaded by her childhood friend (Rosemary Harris) to write an anonymous note to the latter's husband asking to meet her at a hotel known as a house of assignation, because she wrongly suspects him of being unfaithful. The husband (Rex Harrison) passes the note on to Louis Jourdan, whom Harris finds quite attractive. Roberts's jealous South American husband sees the note and recognizes his wife's handwriting. It takes a lot of doing but ultimately everyone is back with who they should be with and no real harm has been done.

Joyce Eglington / THE RECKONING, 1970, Great Britain, Columbia, d-Jack Gold.

Nicol Williamson, a middle-level London executive of lower-class origins, is not adverse to using ruthless means to achieve his high ambitions. At a crucial point in his career he gets the news that his father back home in Liverpool has died and the cause has been listed as heart failure. But, as he later learns, his father really died in a pub fight with some local toughs. Roberts is the assistant to the doctor who falsified the cause of death for Williamson's father. She and Williamson make love with dear old dad laid out in the next room.

Mrs. Appleyard / PICNIC AT HANGING ROCK, 1976, Australia, Picnic Productions, d-Peter Weir.

In 1900 the girls of Appleyard College prepare for a picnic on Saint Valentine's Day. During the trip some of the girls disappear and are never found and headmistress Roberts jumps to her death from Hanging Rock, the site of the picnic.

OTHER ROLES

1952: *Bessie Lewis* / VALLEY OF SONG. **1953:** *barmaid* / THE LIMPING MAN. **1954:** *Pat* / THE WEAK AND THE WICKED; *Maggie* / THE CROWDED DAY. **1957:** *Elsie and Effie Longstaff* / THE GOOD COMPANIONS. **1962:** *Anne Howland* / GIRL ON APPROVAL. **1971:** *Della Randolph* / DOCTORS' WIVES; *Maybell* / WILD ROVERS. **1973:** *Gloria / Mme. Prillard* / O LUCKY MAN!; *Cathie* / THE BELSTONE FOX. **1974:** *Hildegarde Schmidt* / MURDER ON THE ORIENT EXPRESS; *Mrs. Garvey* / GREAT EXPECTATIONS. **1976:** *Nora Elliot* / ALPHA BETA. **1978:** *Gerda* / FOUL PLAY. **1979:** *Dr. Monk* / WHEN A STRANGER CALLS; *Mrs. Moreton* / YANKS. **1981:** *Mrs. Dangers* / CHARLIE CHAN AND THE CURSE OF THE DRAGON QUEEN.

ROBERTSON, CLIFF

(Clifford Parker Robertson, 1925–)

Personable, dark-haired Cliff Robertson made his movie debut in PICNIC, was personally picked by John F. Kennedy to play the President as a young man in PT-109, and won an Oscar for his role as a mentally retarded man who briefly becomes a genius in CHARLY. Never a major star, he was effectively blacklisted for a few years when he blew the whistle on Columbia Studios president David Begelman for embezzlement. He directed and starred in the movie J. W. COOP. His thoughts on the profession are summed up thusly: "This isn't exactly a stable business. It's like trying to stand up in a canoe with your pants down."

KEY ROLES

Alan Benson / PICNIC, 1955, Columbia, d-Joshua Logan.
In his debut Robertson is the son of a wealthy, small-town grain operator. Into his secure world comes William Holden, an ex-football player now down on his luck who steals Robertson's girlfriend (Kim Novak) at a Fourth of July picnic.

Lieutenant Hearn / THE NAKED AND THE DEAD, 1958, RKO, d-Jules Dassin.
Robertson may be the commanding officer in this story of an army platoon on a Pacific island during World War II, but Aldo Ray, the experienced, crafty top sergeant, is running the show. Robertson needs to worry because Ray doesn't feel officers are necessary.

John F. Kennedy / PT-109, 1963, Warners, d-Leslie H. Martinson.
Robertson portrays the President when he was a war hero on a PT-boat in the Pacific in World War II. It's an incredibly dull adventure story but Robertson looks presidential.

Joe Cantwell / THE BEST MAN, 1964, United Artists, d-Franklin Shaffner.
Robertson is a rather unsavory candidate for his party's nomination for president with his major opposition coming from liberal Henry Fonda. Fonda sacrifices his own ambitions to make certain Robertson doesn't get the nod.

William McFly / THE HONEY POT, 1967, United Artists, d-Joseph L. Mankiewicz.
Robertson is an actor hired by Rex Harrison, a millionaire living in isolation in Venice, to help him trick his three former mistresses by pretending he is on his deathbed. The updated version of Ben Johnson's "Volpone" isn't as good as it should be with the cast it has.

Charly Gordon / CHARLY, 1968, Selmur, d-Ralph Nelson.
Robertson is a 30-year-old man with the mind of a child but an intense desire to learn. His teacher brings him to a neurosurgeon who has successfully cured defective mice and is looking for a human subject. The operation is a success and Robertson soon reaches genius level. He falls in love with his teacher (Claire Bloom) and they spend an idyllic holiday together. But they discover that one by one the mice that had the operation are reverting to their former states and Robertson knows that his regression will soon follow. He won the Oscar for his performance but it wasn't a very good year for actors.

Cole Younger / THE GREAT NORTHFIELD MINNESOTA RAID, 1972, Universal, d-Philip Kaufman.
Robertson, as the leader of the Younger brothers, teams up with the James brothers to rob one of the biggest banks in the country. It's an interesting, moody western with Robertson leading the cast in interesting performances.

J. W. Coop / J. W. COOP, 1972, Columbia, d-Cliff Robertson.
After his release from prison, Robertson takes up the life of a rodeo cowboy and, through determination, becomes a minor star. Besides starring in and directing the film, Robertson was also the screenwriter and producer.

Hugh Hefner / STAR 80, 1983, Warners, d-Bob Fosse.
Robertson makes a convincing Hefner in this story about the brief life of Playboy centerfold Dorothy Stratton (Mariel Hemingway), who is brutally murdered by her hustler husband (Eric Roberts). It's an unappetizing story.

OTHER ROLES

1956: *Burt Hanson* / AUTUMN LEAVES. **1957:** *Pete* / THE GIRL MOST LIKELY. **1959:** *Kahoona* / GIDGET; *Lt. Cmdr. Jeff Conway* / BATTLE OF THE CORAL SEA. **1960:** *Clements* / AS THE SEA RAGES. **1961:** *Warren Kingsley* / ALL IN A NIGHT'S WORK; *Josef Everard* / THE BIG SHOW. **1962:** *Tolly Devlin* / UNDERWORLD, U.S.A.; *Dr. John Paul Otis* / THE INTERNS. **1963:** *Rev. Jim Larkin* / MY SIX LOVES; *Adam Tyler* / SUNDAY IN NEW YORK. **1964:** *Wing Cmdr. Roy Grant* / 633 SQUADRON. **1965:** *Sgt. Edward Baxter* / UP FROM THE BEACH; *Pete Jordan* / LOVE HAS MANY FACES; *David Frazer* / MASQUERADE. **1968:** *Maj. Alan Crown* / THE DEVIL'S BRIGADE. **1969:** *Lt. Sam Lawson* / TOO LATE THE HERO. **1973:** *Ace Eli* / ACE ELI AND RODGER OF THE SKIES. **1974:** *Lee Tucker* / MAN ON A SWING. **1975:** *Joe* / OUT OF SEASON. **1976:** *Higgins* / THREE DAYS OF THE CONDOR; *Maj. Rex Jeanette* / SHOOT; *Cmdr. Carl Jessup* / MIDWAY; *Michael Courtland* / OBSESSION; *Buzz Aldrin* / RETURN TO EARTH. **1977:** *narrator* / FRATERNITY ROW. **1978:** *David Ballard* / DOMINIQUE. **1980:** *pilot* / THE PILOT. **1983:** *Burroughs* / CLASS; *Alex Terson* / BRAINSTORM. **1985:** *daredevil driver* / SHAKER RUN. **1987:** *Delaney* / MALONE.

ROBINSON, EDWARD G.

(Emmanuel Goldenberg, 1893–1973)

"Some people have youth, some have beauty. I have menace." Thus did Robinson simplistically explain his success as a movie actor. He might have added that he also possessed considerable talent and played many roles where menace had nothing to do with the appreciation of his performance. Born in Rumania, he and his family fled the country to escape persecution. He arrived at Ellis Island at the age of 10. He soon mastered English and gave frequent speeches to his family and friends in preparation for his hoped-for career as a lawyer. While attending City College of New York, he decided to forgo a law career to become an actor. When he won a scholarship to the American Academy of Dramatic Arts he changed his name to Robinson. He played stock in Cincinnati and broke into legitimate theater in 1915, then joined the Theatre Guild and played a variety of roles. He experimented with silent pictures but it was with the coming of sound that his future in the medium was assured. After LITTLE CAESAR in 1931 he became an unlikely star. Stocky, squat, and craggy-faced, Robinson had a growl or a whine for a voice when playing a tough guy, but his tough, sinister film persona hid a gentle man with a love for fine art. He survived the McCarthy and House Un-American Activities Committee to appear in more than 100 films from 1929 to 1966.

KEY ROLES

Cesare Enrico Bandello (Rico) / LITTLE CAESAR, 1931, Warners, d-Mervyn LeRoy.
The film chronicles the rise and fall of an Italian gangster (Robinson) with the role clearly inspired by Al Capone. The movie is a masterpiece and established Robinson as a star and tough guy. His dying

words in the film, after being riddled with bullets, is the classic, "Mother of Mercy, is this the end of Rico?"

Joseph Randall / FIVE STAR FINAL, 1931, Warners, d-Mervyn LeRoy.

In this exposé of newspaper muckraking, Robinson is an editor who resurrects a 20-year-old unsolved murder case to attract readers and it results in the suicide of a woman because she fears exposure of her involvement in the case will ruin her daughter's chance for happiness. Her husband follows her in death upon finding her lifeless body. The daughter arrives at the newspaper office and threatens Robinson with a gun, but cannot bring herself to shoot, and Robinson realizes all too well what mischief his search for headlines has caused.

Arthur Ferguson Jones and Killer Mannion / THE WHOLE TOWN'S TALKING, 1935, Columbia, d-John Ford.

This is a comedy in which Robinson plays the dual roles of a meek clerk and the notorious gangster. The latter poses as his innocent double to escape the police.

Remy Marco / A SLIGHT CASE OF MURDER, 1938, Warners, d-Lloyd Bacon.

With the repeal of Prohibition, beer baron Robinson wants to go legitimate, only to discover his fortune dwindling because his beer, which he has never tasted, is undrinkable. He also finds himself the target of his former criminal associates.

Dr. Clitterhouse / THE AMAZING DR. CLITTERHOUSE, 1938, Warners, d-Anatole Litvak.

Robinson is a psychiatrist who, in order to study the criminal mind, becomes one himself and goes as far as to commit cold-blooded murder.

Ed Renard / CONFESSIONS OF A NAZI SPY, 1939, Warners, d-Anatole Litvak.

In the first major motion picture to deal with German espionage in the United States before World War II, Robinson heads a team of G-men who weed out Nazi spies and their American collaborators. The movie is presented in semi-documentary style.

Dr. Paul Ehrlich / DR. EHRLICH'S MAGIC BULLET, 1940, Warners, d-William Dieterle.

Robinson gives a restrained, brilliant performance as the scientist responsible for finding a cure for syphilis. The topic is sensitively but forthrightly handled.

Little John Sarto / BROTHER ORCHID, 1940, Warners, d-Lloyd Bacon.

In this spoof of gangster movies, Robinson is a big-time racketeer taken for a ride by some of his associates. He escapes and hides in a monastery where he becomes a peaceful monk who raises orchids.

Julius Reuters / A DISPATCH FROM REUTERS, 1940, Warners, d-William Dieterle.

This film is an interesting account of the problems faced by the German founder (Robinson) of the celebrated news-gathering bureau that still bears his name. His service was established when he scooped the world with news of the assassination of Abraham Lincoln.

Wolf Larsen / THE SEA WOLF, 1941, Warners, d-Michael Curtiz.

"My strength justifies me, Mr. Van Weyden—the fact that I can kill you or let you live as I choose, the fact that I control the destinies of all aboard the ship, the fact that it is my will and my will alone that rules here. That's justification enough." So says Robinson as the sadistic, psychopathic sea captain who torments not only the shipwrecks he has brought aboard his eerie ship "Ghost," but his crew as well.

Barton Keyes / DOUBLE INDEMNITY, 1944, Paramount, d-Billy Wilder.

In this classic film noir, Robinson is a claims adjuster for an insurance company for whom authorizing a settlement of a claim is like taking money from his own pocket. He hates cheats and his "Little Man" lets him know when something's not quite right. He rightfully suspects that a double indemnity claim on a man who allegedly fell from a train is a murder, but he doesn't reckon that his good friend, insurance agent Fred MacMurray, is the killer along with the deceased man's beautiful and deceitful wife (Barbara Stanwyck).

Prof. Richard Wanley / THE WOMAN IN THE WINDOW, 1944, RKO, d-Fritz Lang.

Respected family man Robinson stops to look in the window of an art gallery at the portrait of a beautiful woman and discovers she is standing next to him. He becomes involved with her and because of her commits an unpremeditated murder. Facing ruin, he decides to take his own life by drinking poison. But as he does so he wakes up in his club—it was all a dream.

Martinius Jacobson / OUR VINES HAVE TENDER GRAPES, 1945, MGM, d-Roy Rowland.

In this excellent depiction of farm and small-town life, Robinson is a Norwegian Wisconsin farmer who works hard for his family. His outwardly harsh behavior does not quite hide the fact that he is really a kindly man.

Christopher Cross / SCARLET STREET, 1946, Universal, d-Fritz Lang.

Amateur painter Robinson becomes involved with a beautiful prostitute who sells his paintings as her own. He kills her in a rage, but it's her pimp who is sent to the electric chair for the killing.

Joe Keller / ALL MY SONS, 1948, Universal, d-Irving Reis.

In this film based on the Arthur Miller play, Robinson portrays a small-town arms manufacturer who, during World War II, knowingly sold defective parts to the army air force which resulted in the deaths of 21 men. Then he allowed his innocent partner to take the rap and go to prison, where he died. Now, after the war, Robinson's son (Burt Lancaster) is learning the truth about his father.

Johnny Rocco / KEY LARGO, 1948, Warners, d-John Huston.

Robinson is a hood who has been deported from the United States and is planning his return as he and his hoods hold several people captive in a Key Largo hotel during a hurricane. One of the hostages (Humphrey Bogart) finally accepts the fact that he has to stop Robinson.

Gino Monzetti / HOUSE OF STRANGERS, 1949, 20th Century-Fox, d-Joseph L. Mankiewicz.

Robinson is an unscrupulous banker on New York's Lower East Side who employs his four sons at the lowest possible salaries and treats them like dirt. When he is arrested for illegal practices, his sons take over the bank and refuse him any access to it when he gets out of prison. When one son tries to help his father, his brothers have him jailed.

Lancey Howard / THE CINCINNATI KID, 1965, MGM, d-Norman Jewison.

In a film that attempts to do for the game of poker what THE HUSTLER did for pool, Robinson is the aging but suave champ of the game, challenged in 1930s New Orleans by Steve McQueen, the title character.

Sol Roth / SOYLENT GREEN, 1973, MGM, d-Richard Fleischer.

In his final screen appearance, fifty years after his debut, Robinson portrays an elderly philosopher in the year 2022 who, while sadly noting the horrendous effects of pollution and overpopulation, remembers the good old days before finally choosing legal euthanasia.

OTHER ROLES

1923: *Domingo Escobar* / THE BRIGHT SHAWL. **1929:** *"The Fox"* / THE HOLE IN THE WALL; *Tony Garotta* / NIGHT RIDE. **1930:** *Tony* / A LADY TO LOVE; *Cobra Collins* / OUTSIDE THE LAW; *Charlie Yong* / EAST IS WEST; *Dominic* / THE WIDOW FROM CHICAGO. **1931:** *Nick "The Barber" Venizelos* / SMART MONEY. **1932:** *Wong Low Get* / THE HATCHET MAN; *John Allen* / TWO SECONDS; *Mike Mascarena* / TIGER SHARK; *Yates Martin* / SILVER DOLLAR. **1933:** *James Francis "Bugs" Ahearn* / THE LITTLE GIANT; *John Hayden* / I LOVED A WOMAN. **1934:** *Jim "Buck" Turner* / DARK HAZARD; *Damon Welles* / THE MAN WITH TWO FACES. **1935:** *Louis Chamalis* / BARBARY COAST. **1936:** *Johnny Blake* / BULLETS OR BALLOTS. **1937:** *Dan Armstrong* / THUNDER IN THE CITY; *Nick Donati* / KID GALAHAD; *Joe Krozac* / THE LAST GANGSTER. **1938:** *John Lindsay* / I AM THE LAW. **1939:** *John Ingram* / BLACKMAIL. **1941:** *Hank McHenry* / MANPOWER; *Bruce Corey* / UNHOLY PARTNERS. **1942:** *Pressure Maxwell* / LARCENY, INC.; *Larry Browne* / TALES OF MANHATTAN. **1943:** *Steve Boleslavski* / DESTROYER; *Marshall Tyler* / FLESH AND FANTASY. **1944:** *Capt. Bart Manson* / TAMPICO; *Wilbert Winkle* / MR. WINKLE GOES TO WAR. **1946:** *Dean McWilliams* / JOURNEY TOGETHER; *Wilson* / THE STRANGER. **1947:** *Pete Morgan* / THE RED HOUSE. **1948:** *John Triton* / NIGHT HAS A THOUSAND EYES. **1949:** *guest* / IT'S A GREAT FEELING. **1950:** *George Constantin* / MY DAUGHTER JOY. **1952:** *Maurice Tillayou* / ACTORS AND SIN. **1953:** *Captain Barnaby* / VICE SQUAD; *John B. "Hans" Lobert* / BIG LEAGUER; *Henry Hayes* / THE GLASS WEB. **1954:** *Vincent Canelli* / BLACK TUESDAY. **1955:** *Lew Wilkison* / THE VIOLENT MEN; *Lloyd Hallett* / TIGHT SPOT; *Insp. Raoul Leduc* / A BULLET FOR JOEY; *Victor Scott* / ILLEGAL. **1956:** *Victor Amato* / HELL ON FRISCO BAY; *Rene Bressard* / NIGHTMARE; *Dathan* / THE TEN COMMANDMENTS. **1959:** *Tony Manetta* / A HOLE IN THE HEAD. **1960:** *Theo Wilkins* / SEVEN THIEVES; *guest* / PEPE. **1961:** *Sam Lewis* / MY GEISHA. **1962:** *Maurice Kruger* / TWO WEEKS IN ANOTHER TOWN. **1963:** *Dr. Max Stratman and Prof. Walter Stratman* / THE PRIZE. **1964:** *Simon Nurdlinger* / GOOD NEIGHBOR SAM; *Big Jim* / ROBIN AND THE SEVEN HOODS; *"Con Man"* / THE OUTRAGE; *Carl Schurz* / CHEYENNE AUTUMN. **1965:** *Cocky Wainwright* / A BOY TEN FEET TALL. **1968:** *Douglas* / THE BLONDE FROM PEKING; *Professor Samuels* / THE BIGGEST BUNDLE OF THEM ALL; *Prof. James Anders* / GRAND SLAM; *MacDowell* / IT'S YOUR MOVE; *Joe Ventura* / OPERATION ST. PETER'S; *Leo Joseph Smooth* / NEVER A DULL MOMENT. **1969:** *Old Adams* / MACKENNA'S GOLD. **1970:** *Krogstad* / SONG OF NORWAY.

ROGERS, GINGER

(Virginia Katherine McMath, 1911-)

Bright, vivacious Ginger Rogers made her stage debut with Eddie Foy's vaudeville troupe, touring the next few years as a dancer before moving on to Broadway and "Top Speed" in 1929. The next year she made her feature film debut in YOUNG MAN OF MANHATTAN. Her first film with Fred Astaire was in 1933 in FLYING DOWN TO RIO. The duo made nine more musicals together, all but one in the 1930s. Katharine Hepburn described the team like this: "She gave him sex, and he gave her class." Viewing those films today, it's still evident that their dancing together is as good as any that has ever been seen on the screen. Not a great beauty, Rogers depended on a wholesome appearance that could become glamorous when needed. She excelled at portraying self-reliant working girls who were wise, tough-minded, and humorous. But as she observed, "I wouldn't change places with Suzie Glutz who works in an office for anything." She won an Oscar for playing such a girl in KITTY FOYLE in 1940. She also made a successful transition from film to television and Broadway musicals such as "Mame" and "Hello Dolly."

KEY ROLES

Ann Lowell / FORTY-SECOND STREET, 1933, Warners, d-Lloyd Bacon.

Rogers gives a memorable performance as "Anytime Annie" who, as George E. Stone tells it, "only said 'no' once—and then she couldn't hear the question." Before Ruby Keeler is asked to replace star Bebe Daniels, "angel" Guy Kibbee thinks his new cutie, Rogers, might fill the bill. But she puts director Warner Baxter straight indicating Keeler's the girl for him.

Fay Fortune / GOLD DIGGERS OF 1933, 1933, Warners, d-Mervyn LeRoy.

Rogers's major contribution to this musical about show girls hunting for rich "sugar daddies" is being clad from head to toe in silver dollars singing "We're in the Money," including one verse in pig latin.

Honey Hale / FLYING DOWN TO RIO, 1933, RKO, d-Thorton Freeland.

The successful teaming of Fred Astaire and Ginger Rogers began with this film in which Rogers is a singer-dancer with an American band appearing in Rio de Janeiro. Their first big number is "The Carioca" in which the two are simply dazzling.

Mimi Glossop / THE GAY DIVORCEE, 1934, RKO, d-Mark Sandrich.

Astaire and Rogers prove that their first hit was no fluke when Rogers mistakes dancer Astaire for a professional correspondent hired by her lawyer to help provide grounds for divorce. Their dance numbers include "Night and Day" and the spectacular "The Continental."

Lizzie Gatz (aka Countess Tanka Scharwenka) / ROBERTA, 1935, RKO, d-William A. Seiter.

In this Jerome Kern and Otto Harbach musical, the story is definitely not the appeal. Rogers poses as a countess and rekindles her affair with old flame bandleader Astaire, who accompanied a friend to Paris when the latter inherited a chic dress salon. The musical numbers include "Smoke Gets in Your Eyes," "Yesterdays," "Lovely to Look At," and "I Won't Dance" by Kern, Oscar Hammerstein II, and Dorothy Fields.

Dale Tremont / TOP HAT, 1935, RKO, d-Mark Sandrich.

Astaire falls in love with Rogers and she with him but she resists because she believes he is the husband of a friend of hers. While getting this straightened out, they dance up a storm to "Cheek to Cheek," "Isn't this a Lovely Day," and "The Piccolino."

Sherry Martin / FOLLOW THE FLEET, 1936, RKO, d-Mark Sandrich.

Rogers, now singing in a San Francisco dance hall, teams up with her former partner (Astaire) to put on a fundraising show for the restoration of an old schooner. Their numbers include "Let's Face the Music and Dance," "Let Yourself Go," and "I'm Putting All My Eggs in One Basket."

Penelope "Penny" Carroll / SWING TIME, 1936, RKO, d-George Stevens.

Although the dancing duo's work together was always outstanding, their dancing in this film may be the best. At the very least it is the most effortless. As for the plot it hardly matters that Rogers is a New York dance teacher who falls for Astaire and teams up with him. Each of the Jerome Kern and Dorothy Fields numbers are perfect. They include "Pick Yourself Up," "The Way You Look Tonight," and "Never Gonna Dance."

Linda Keene / SHALL WE DANCE, 1937, RKO, d-Mark Sandrich.

In their next outing, Astaire and Rogers are two phonies who people believe are married. Ultimately, even they believe it's a good idea. Numbers include the Gershwin songs "Let's Call the Whole Thing Off," in which they tap dance while wearing roller skates, and "They All Laughed."

Jean Maitland / STAGE DOOR, 1937, RKO, d-Gregory La Cava.

Rogers portrays a witty, sarcastic, tough-as-nails broad who judges success purely by materialistic measures. She lives with several other aspiring actresses, singers, and dancers in a theatrical boarding house. She and others compete unsuccessfully with Katharine Hepburn for a lead in a Broadway show.

Polly Parrish / BACHELOR MOTHER, 1939, RKO, d-Garson Kanin.

Store clerk Rogers is mistaken for the mother of an abandoned baby. Her efforts to explain that the child is not hers are futile, so she finally accepts the proposal of the store owner's son (David Niven) so the kid will have a father.

Kitty Foyle / KITTY FOYLE, 1940, RKO, d-Sam Wood.

Rogers won an Oscar for her emotionally satisfying performance as a hard-working, white-collar Philadelphia girl who gets mixed up with a blueblood from the "Main Line," suffers the snobbery of his family, loses their baby, and ultimately finds the strength to leave her lover. It's a sudsy story and it's a bit hard to understand how Rogers beat out Katharine Hepburn in THE PHILADELPHIA STORY, Bette Davis in THE LETTER, Martha Scott in OUR TOWN, and Joan Fontaine in REBECCA, for the Best Actress Academy Award, but that's Oscar for you.

Roxie Hart / ROXIE HART, 1942, 20th Century-Fox, d-William A. Wellman.

Brassy dancer Rogers confesses to a murder committed by her hubby more in the hope that the publicity will help her career than through any concern for what happens to her husband. She is aided by clever attorney Walter Matthau who has his own reasons for wanting to turn the trial into a sideshow and farce. The action takes place at a delirious pace to match the snapping of Rogers's chewing gum.

Susan Applegate / THE MAJOR AND THE MINOR, 1942, Paramount, d-Billy Wilder.

Rogers poses as a 12-year-old in order to ride on a train for half-fare. Ray Milland, the head of a boys' military school, takes a fatherly interest in the child which soon changes when he takes her home and finds she's a bit older than he thought. This farce marks the directorial debut of Billy Wilder and although he had better films, this one is still fun.

Liza Elliott / LADY IN THE DARK, 1944, Paramount, d-Mitchell Leisen.

Rogers is the editor of a fashion magazine who is torn between three men. This and the tensions of the job are driving her over the edge, causing her chronic headaches and daydreams. She seeks a psychiatric cure and relives some of her dreams, including one circus extravaganza in which she sings "The Saga of Jenny." Nowadays the movie industry couldn't get away with Ray Milland's analysis of her problem: "She shouldn't try to be top man. She's not built for it. She's flying in the face of nature."

Dolly Payne / MAGNIFICENT DOLL, 1946, Universal, d-Frank Borzage.

This historical drama with Rogers as Dolly Madison and David Niven as Aaron Burr is pretty flat with just about everyone in the large cast wrong for their parts.

Edwina Fulton / MONKEY BUSINESS, 1952, 20th Century-Fox, d-Howard Hawks.

Rogers is married to scientist Cary Grant who is working on a formula to make people younger. He doesn't succeed, but one of his chimps does and puts it in the water cooler. Naturally Grant and Rogers quench their thirsts and revert to youngsters who enjoy squirting the well-rounded bottom of Marilyn Monroe with seltzer bottles.

Rosie Gilray / THE FIRST TRAVELING SALESLADY, 1956, RKO, d-Arthur Lubin.

Rogers and Carol Channing scratch through the screenplay of this movie for a few laughs and find mighty few. Rogers goes broke selling steel corset stays in 1897 and turns her hand to hawking barbed wire fencing to Texas ranchers, which is not considered fit work for a woman. The biggest cattle baron (David Brian), who has no use for fences, vows to stop Rogers or marry her, but she outwits him—no great chore since Brian's character is no great brain.

OTHER ROLES

1930: *Puff Randolph* / YOUNG MAN OF MANHATTAN; *Polly Rockwell* / QUEEN HIGH; *Ellen Saunders* / THE SAP FROM SYRACUSE; *Mary Brennan* / FOLLOW THE LEADER. **1931:** *Doris Blake* / HONOR AMONG LOVERS; *Baby Face* / THE TIP OFF; *Sally* / SUICIDE FLEET. **1932:** *Honey* / CARNIVAL BOAT; *Ruth* / THE TENDERFOOT; *Marie Morgan* / THE THIRTEENTH GUEST; *Jessie King* / HAT CHECK GIRL; *Alice Brandon* / YOU SAID A MOUTHFUL. **1933:** *Flip Daly* / BROADWAY BAD; *Glory Eden* / PROFESSIONAL SWEETHEART; *Patricia Morgan* / A SHRIEK IN THE NIGHT; *Molly Gilbert* / DON'T BET ON LOVE; *Dorothy* / SITTING PRETTY; *Marje Harris* / CHANCE AT HEAVEN. **1934:** *Mary Carroll* / RAFTER ROMANCE; *Cecilia "Pony" Ferris* / FINISHING SCHOOL; *Peggy* / TWENTY MILLION SWEETHEARTS; *Madge Roundtree* / CHANGE OF HEART; *Lilly Linder* / UPPER WORLD; *Sylvia Dennis* / ROMANCE IN MANHATTAN. **1935:** *Donna Martin* / STAR OF MIDNIGHT; *Carol Corliss (aka Clara Colfax)* / IN PERSON. **1938:** *Teddy Shaw* / HAVING WONDERFUL TIME; *Frances Brent (aka Francey La Roche)* / VIVACIOUS LADY; *Amanda Cooper* / CAREFREE. **1939:** *Irene Foote Castle* / THE STORY OF VERNON AND IRENE CASTLE; *Mary Gray* / FIFTH AVENUE GIRL. **1940:** *Ellie May Adams* / PRIMROSE PATH; *Jean Newton* / LUCKY PARTNERS. **1941:** *Janie* / TOM, DICK AND HARRY. **1942:** *Diane* / TALES OF MANHATTAN; *Katie O'Hara* / ONCE UPON A HONEYMOON. **1943:** *Jo* / TENDER COMRADE. **1944:** *Mary Marshall* / I'LL BE SEEING YOU. **1945:** *Irene Malvern* / WEEKEND AT THE WALDORF. **1946:** *Arlette* / HEARTBEAT. **1947:** *Victoria Stafford* / IT HAD TO BE YOU. **1949:** *Dinah Barkley* / THE BARKLEYS OF BROADWAY. **1950:** *Terry Scott* / PERFECT STRANGERS. **1951:** *Marsha Mitchell* / STORM WARNING; *Abigail Furnival* / THE GROOM WORE SPURS. **1952:** *Ramona Gladwyn* / WE'RE NOT MARRIED; *Gloria Marlowe* / DREAMBOAT. **1953:** *Beatrice Page* / FOREVER FEMALE. **1954:** *Lottie* / BLACK WIDOW; *"Johnny" Victor* / TWIST OF FATE. **1955:** *Sherry Conley* / TIGHT SPOT. **1956:** *Nancy Fallon* / TEENAGE REBEL. **1957:** *Mildred Turner* / OH, MEN! OH, WOMEN! **1965:** *Mama Jean Bello* / HARLOW; *Madame Rinaldi* / QUICK, LET'S GET MARRIED.

ROGERS, WILL

(William Penn Rogers, 1879-1935)

Drawling, straw-haired comedian Will Rogers, an entertainer with a sagging lower lip, won the hearts of the nation with his gentle jibes, jests, and home-spun philosophy. He made a number of silent features, shorts, and travelogues, but he was meant to be heard as well as seen and with talkies he became perhaps the most popular personality in the United States, just as he was once the reigning star of the Ziegfeld Follies. Rogers tickled the national funny bone with lines like: "There is only one thing that can kill the movies, and that is education." He was the gentle master of the wisecrack, but usually his targets laughed as hard as everyone else. As he noted, "I joked about every prominent man in my life, but I never met one I didn't like." He was killed in a plane crash near Point Barrow, Alaska, with master aviator Wiley Post.

KEY ROLES

Ichabod Crane / THE HEADLESS HORSEMAN, 1922, Silent, W. W. Hodkinson, d-Edward Venturini.

Rogers appears as Washington Irving's lanky schoolteacher who sees the advantage of marrying into the wealthy family of Sleepy Hollow's leading belle, Katrina Van Tassel. But his rival, Brom Bones, disguises himself as the region's phantom, the headless horseman, and scares the pedagogue away, never to return.

Pike Peters / THEY HAD TO SEE PARIS, 1929, Fox Films, d-Frank Borzage.

Rogers is an Oklahoma garage owner who strikes it rich in oil. His wife insists that the family go to Paris where she will try to marry off their daughter. But Rogers wants to go home and finally gets his wife to agree by pretending an interest in a singer.

Hank Martin / A CONNECTICUT YANKEE, 1931, Fox Films, d-David Butler.

Rogers is a Connecticut jack-of-all-trades with a great interest in the times of King Arthur. He dreams himself back to Camelot where he teaches the knights of the Middle Ages a thing or two about modern technology and Yankee shrewdness.

Abel Frake / STATE FAIR, 1933, Fox Films, d-Henry King.

In this slice-of-life film, Rogers is the father of a farm family for whom the state fair is the high point of the year. He's hoping his prize pig will win the blue ribbon and so it does.

David Harum / DAVID HARUM, 1934, Fox Films, d-James Cruze.

As is usual in Rogers's films, the plot plays second fiddle to the star's charm and horse sense. In this one he's a wily old rancher who plays cupid for some young people.

Andrew Yates / HANDY ANDY, 1934, Fox Films, d-David Butler.

Rogers is a small-town midwestern druggist whose wife has social aspirations which he neither shares nor helps. He does give out with more than a few crackerbarrel homilies, however.

Judge William "Billy" Priest / JUDGE PRIEST, 1934, Fox Films, d-John Ford.

The judge is quite a horse trader and his common sense approach to ensuring fair play in a criminal case becomes somewhat controversial. Forget it, the story doesn't count. People went to the theater to hear Rogers's latest wisecracks.

Kennesaw H. Clark / LIFE BEGINS AT FORTY, 1935, Fox Films, d-George Marshall.

Rogers is a delightful newspaper editor who goes about clearing the name of a man (Richard Cromwell) who was framed for a bank robbery years earlier.

Dr. John Pearly / STEAMBOAT ROUND THE BEND, 1935, 20th Century-Fox, d-John Ford.

In this star vehicle, Rogers is a Mississippi steamboat captain who defeats his rival and finds the evidence that clears his nephew of a murder charge.

OTHER ROLES

1918: *Bill Hyde* / LAUGHING BILL HYDE. **1919:** *Sam Lyman* / ALMOST A HUSBAND. **1920:** *Jubilo* / JUBILO; *Billy Fortune* / WATER, WATER, EVERYWHERE; *Jim* / JES' CALL ME JIM; *Sam Gardner* / THE STRANGE BOARDER; *Hutch* / HONEST HUTCH; *Alec Lloyd* / CUPID, THE COWPUNCHER. **1921:** *Hjalmar Maartens* / GUILE OF WOMEN; *Peep O'Day* / BOYS WILL BE BOYS; *Sam Cody* / DOUBLING FOR ROMEO; *Noah Vale* / A POOR RELATION. **1922:** *Ezra Botts* / ONE GLORIOUS DAY. **1923:** *himself* / HOLLYWOOD. **1927:** *Uncle Hen Kaye* / TIP TOES; *Maverick Brander* / A TEXAS STEER. **1929:** *himself* / HAPPY DAYS. **1930:** *Hiran Draper* / SO THIS IS LONDON; *"Lightnin'" Bill Jones* / LIGHTNIN'. **1931:** *Lemuel Morehouse* / YOUNG AS YOU FEEL; *the plutocrat* / THE PLUTOCRAT; *Bill Harper* / AMBASSADOR BILL. **1932:** *Earl Tinker* / BUSINESS AND PLEASURE; *Pike Peters* / DOWN TO EARTH; *Jubilo* / TOO BUSY TO WORK. **1933:** *Dr. Bull* / DR. BULL; *Mr. Skitch* / MR. SKITCH. **1935:** *Thomas Brown* / DOUBTING THOMAS; *Steve Tapley* / IN OLD KENTUCKY.

ROMAN, RUTH

(1924-)

Boston-born, dark-haired Ruth Roman became a Hollywood leading lady in the late 1940s but her somewhat cold looks kept her from becoming a major star. The daughter of a circus barker, Roman made regular appearances in the Queen of the Jungle series at Universal and had small parts in features throughout the 1940s. She got her break in the thriller THE WINDOW in 1949 and later that year in CHAMPION. Other than movies, Roman has appeared regularly on TV from the 1960s on in series such as "Dr. Kildare" and "Ironside."

KEY ROLES

Mrs. Kellerton / THE WINDOW, 1949, RKO, d-Ted Tetzlaff.

Roman gets her big break in this film noir about a murder of a seaman that she and her husband (Paul Stewart) commit, unaware that little Bobby Driscoll, who is trying to sleep on the fire escape, sees them. Frightened, he runs to tell his parents but, as he is a teller of tall tales, they don't believe him. However, Roman and Stewart find out he's seen their crime and they plan to do away with him.

Emma Bryce / CHAMPION, 1949, United Artists, d-Mark Robson.

Roman is the wife of a ruthlessly ambitious boxer (Kirk Douglas) who leaves her for blonde nightclub singer Marilyn Maxwell and later Lola Albright. She always hopes he will come back but he goes crazy and dies after his last fight.

Tonia Robles / DALLAS, 1950, Warners, d-Stuart Heisler.

Roman provides the romantic interest for Gary Cooper, an ex-Confederate guerrilla who pretends to be a marshal from the North when he arrives in a Texas frontier town and takes on a pair of no-good brothers (Raymond Massey and Steve Cochran). Roman handles her secondary role with style.

Anne Morton / STRANGERS ON A TRAIN, 1951, Warners, d-Alfred Hitchcock.

Roman is a U.S. senator's daughter in love with married tennis star Farley Granger, whose wife refuses to give him a divorce even though she doesn't want him and is repeatedly unfaithful. When she is killed, it turns out that the murder was committed by loony Robert Walker who believed he and Granger had a deal to exchange murders. Roman spends most of her time looking pained and hopeful.

Lily MacBeth / JOE MACBETH, 1956, Great Britain, Columbia, d-Ken Hughes.

Roman's husband is content being number two to an underworld boss, but she urges him to kill the mobster and become number one. The rest of the story parallels the MacBeth story, except that Joe (Edmond O'Brien) accidentally kills Roman before being gunned down by the boss's son Lennie.

OTHER ROLES

1943: *bit* / STAGE DOOR CANTEEN. **1944:** *bit* / LADIES COURAGEOUS; *envious girl* / SINCE YOU WENT AWAY; *checkroom girl* / STORM OVER LISBON. **1945:** *bit* / THE AFFAIRS OF SUSAN; *bit* / SEE MY LAWYER; *Gloria Revere* / YOU CAME ALONG; *woman* / INCENDIARY BLONDE. **1946:** *bit* / A NIGHT IN CASABLANCA. **1947:** *Ann Martin* / WHITE STALLION. **1948:** *bit* / THE BIG CLOCK; *bit* / NIGHT HAS A THOUSAND EYES; *Ruthie* / GOOD SAM; *Rose of Cimarron* / BELLE STARR'S DAUGHTER. **1949:** *Carol* / BEYOND THE FOREST; *Fay Washburn* / ALWAYS LEAVE THEM LAUGHING. **1950:** *Judith Burns* / BARRICADE; *Beth Donovan* / COLT .45; *Ann Lawrence* / THREE SECRETS. **1951:** *Shelley Carnes* / LIGHTNING STRIKES TWICE; *herself* / STARLIFT; *Catherine* / TOMORROW IS ANOTHER DAY. **1952:** *Maud Redwick* / INVITATION; *Stella* / MARA MARU; *Julie Webster* / YOUNG MAN WITH IDEAS. **1953:** *Sal* / BLOWING WILD. **1954:** *Peggy Merion* / TANGANYIKA; *Kate Martel* / DOWN THREE DARK STREETS; *Rita King* / THE SHANGHAI STORY. **1955:** *Ronda* / THE FAR COUNTRY. **1956:** *Nora Martin* / THE BOTTOM OF THE BOTTLE; *Boston Grant* / GREAT DAY IN THE MORNING; *Nora Willoughby* / REBEL IN TOWN. **1957:** *Ann Nicholson* / FIVE STEPS TO DANGER. **1958:** *Jane Brand* / BITTER VICTORY. **1959:** *the woman* / DESERT DESPERADOES. **1961:** *Jackie Fowler* / LOOK IN ANY WINDOW. **1965:** *Margot Eliot* / LOVE HAS MANY FACES. **1972:** *deranged mother* / THE BABY.

ROONEY, MICKEY

(Joe Yule, Jr., 1920-)

Mickey Rooney has done it all in show business—vaudeville, radio, films, legitimate theater, nightclubs, and television—and in every medium he has enjoyed unparalleled success. But he has been counted out more than once only to pop up again, surprising everyone by winning new audiences and awards. Bankrupt in 1962 after eight marriages—with actresses Ava Gardner and Martha Vickers among his spouses—Rooney was at one of the lowest points of his life. But he kept trying and learning and, in a spectacular comeback in the late 1970s and early 1980s, he was nominated for a Tony Award for Broadway's "Sugar Babies," an Oscar for his work in THE BLACK STALLION, and an Emmy for TV's "Bill." In 1982 he was given his second special Academy Award, this time for career achievement. Dynamic, pocket-sized Rooney made his stage debut with his parents at the age of two and appeared in a movie short posing as a midget when not quite six. The next few years he made 50 two-reel "Mickey McGuire" comedies in which he played a then-popular comic-strip character. He even became Mickey McGuire legally. In 1932 he changed his name to Mickey Rooney. He became the biggest box-office star in the country with the Andy Hardy series, BOYS TOWN, and the teen swing musicals with Judy Garland. Multi-talented Rooney was nominated for Oscars for THE HUMAN COMEDY, BABES IN ARMS, THE BOLD AND THE BRAVE, and THE BLACK STALLION. In 1938 the industry gave him a special Oscar "for bringing to the screen the spirit and personification of youth and for setting a high standard of ability and achievement." Brash, dynamic Rooney is a pint-sized sensation, equal parts of ability and ham.

KEY ROLES

Puck / A MIDSUMMER NIGHT'S DREAM, 1935, Warners, d-Max Reinhardt.

"What fools these mortals be." So says Rooney as a most delightful and nimble Puck in the Shakespeare tale of two pairs of lovers and the fairies that help them in the woods of Athens. Rooney broke his leg during filming and had to be wheeled around by unseen stagehands behind bushes on a bicycle.

Tommy Miller / AH, WILDERNESS, 1935, MGM, d-Clarence Brown.

Rooney appears as the young brother of a teenager who learns of both liquor and scarlet women on the same night. Rooney moved up to the teenager's role in 1948 in a film, titled SUMMER HOLIDAY.

Dan Troop / CAPTAINS COURAGEOUS, 1937, MGM, d-Victor Fleming.

Rooney isn't the number one youngster in this story of Portuguese fishermen. That honor goes to Freddie Bartholomew, but Rooney is more appealing.

Andy Hardy / A FAMILY AFFAIR, 1937, MGM, d-George B. Seitz.

Rooney appeared fourteen more times as Andy Hardy in this extremely popular series. In the course of it, for many, he defined "teenager"—a lad whose schemes and interest in girls always gets him into hot water, but who always has the good sense to go to his father for advice that usually clears things up.

Whitey Marsh / BOYS TOWN, 1938, MGM, d-Norman Taurog.

Rooney, a tough kid and brother of a hood sent to prison, is assigned to the care of Father Flanagan (Spencer Tracy) of Boys Town. Rooney wants nothing to do with the priest or the other kids as he hopes to become like his older brother. He causes a lot of trouble for everyone, himself included, until he gets wise and reforms.

Huckleberry Finn / THE ADVENTURES OF HUCKLEBERRY FINN, 1939, MGM, d-Richard Thorpe.

Rooney gives a fine performance as the Mark Twain character. His partnership with the excellent actor Rex Ingram as Jim works very well.

Mickey Moran / BABES IN ARMS, 1939, MGM, d-Busby Berkeley.

Rooney does everything but sell tickets in this superb piece of nonsense in which he teams with Judy Garland and says, "Hey kids, let's put on a show." The delightful musical numbers include "Where or When," "The Lady Is a Tramp," and the title song by Rodgers and Hart. In addition, the songs "I Cried for You" and "Good Morning" by producer Arthur Freed are handled well by the professional duo of Rooney and Garland.

Thomas Edison / YOUNG TOM EDISON, 1940, MGM, d-Norman Taurog.

In 1940 MGM covered the inventor's life completely with Rooney demonstrating his ingenuity as a youngster in this film and Spencer Tracy taking over in a separate movie, EDISON, THE MAN. In both cases, Edison is treated with a bit too much solemnity.

Jimmy Connors / STRIKE UP THE BAND, 1940, MGM, d-Busby Berkeley.

Rooney and Judy Garland are back together in this musical comedy designed to spotlight the remarkable talents of these two people. No matter what his size Rooney is larger than life as he carries the show and most of the musical numbers including the title song, a rousing finale by the Gershwins, "Sing, Sing, Sing," "The Sidewalks of New York," and "Drummer Boy."

Tommy Williams / BABES ON BROADWAY, 1942, MGM, d-Busby Berkeley.

Rooney, the number one box-office star for the third year in a row, again teams with Judy Garland as they take their idea of putting on a show to Broadway. The hits of the musical include "How About You," "Hoe Down," "Yankee Doodle Boy," "By the Light of the Silvery Moon," and the title number.

Timothy Dennis / A YANK AT ETON, 1942, MGM, d-Norman Taurog.

Freddie Bartholomew, now 18, is relegated to supporting now 20-year-old Rooney in this film that MGM hoped would experience the success of A YANK AT OXFORD. It didn't, but it wasn't because Rooney didn't try hard to play a young "ugly American" who wins the day when he learns to live by the traditions of the fine old English school.

Homer Macauley / THE HUMAN COMEDY, 1943, MGM, d-Clarence Brown.

Rooney portrays a Western Union boy who delivers those heartbreaking telegrams from the government during World War II which begin "We regret to inform you..." It's a sugary and overly sentimental attempt to show how good life is even with its tragedies.

Mi Taylor / NATIONAL VELVET, 1944, MGM, d-Clarence Brown.

In his last film appearance before army service, Rooney gives a restrained performance and lets Elizabeth Taylor's star be born in the story of a horse winning the Grand National with Taylor in the saddle and Rooney doing the training.

Richard Miller / SUMMER HOLIDAY, 1948, MGM, d-Rouben Mamoulian.

Rooney isn't alone in this musical remake of the Eugene O'Neill comedy "Ah, Wilderness," but he might as well have been as everyone else in the cast is present merely so that he can bounce his talent off them. The only one to give him any competition is "Butch" Jenkins who had Rooney's 1935 role.

Mike Forney / THE BRIDGES AT TOKO-RI, 1954, Paramount, d-Mark Robson.

Rooney is a helicopter pilot who rescues downed jet fighter pilots during the Korean War. He and William Holden both cash in on the same mission at the bridges of Toko-Ri.

Dooley / THE BOLD AND THE BRAVE, 1956, RKO, d-Lewis Foster.

This routine picture follows the adventures of three U.S. soldiers in the Italian campaign in 1944. Rooney is a pint-sized GI whose only ambition is to win enough in a floating crap game to open a restaurant in New Jersey after the war.

Baby Face Nelson (Lester Gillis) / BABY FACE NELSON, 1957, United Artists, d-Don Seigel.

Rooney gives a good account of himself as a gunman and killer who achieves the dubious distinction of "Public Enemy No. 1" before going down in a hail of bullets from the guns of the Feds.

Army / REQUIEM FOR A HEAVYWEIGHT, 1962, Columbia, d-Ralph Nelson.

Rooney is the trainer of an aging heavyweight (Anthony Quinn) who generally gets his brains beaten out. When the doctors tell him any more fighting will leave him blind and probably dead, his uncertainty of how he's going to make a living is shared by Rooney.

Cockeye / THE COMIC, 1969, Columbia, d-Carl Reiner.

Rooney portrays a Ben Turpin-like silent comic whose cross-eyes are his fortune. He gets to throw a custard pie in the face of a minister at the funeral of his old friend and colleague from the silent days, Dick Van Dyke.

Henry Dailey / THE BLACK STALLION, 1979, United Artists, d-Carroll Ballard.

The most beautiful part of this movie takes place after a 1946 shipwreck that leaves young Kelly Reno and a black stallion alone on an African shore. But Rooney received a deserved Academy Award nomination for his role as the old trainer who helps Reno, now rescued, ride the horse to victory at Santa Anita.

OTHER ROLES

1927: *bit* / ORCHIDS AND ERMINE. **1932:** *bit* / EMMA; *Mickey Fitzpatrick* / THE BEAST OF THE CITY; *boy* / SIN'S PAYDAY; *bit* / OFFICER 13; *Midge* / FAST COMPANIONS, (INFORMATION KID); *King Charles V* / MY PAL THE KING. **1933:** *Jimmy O'Hara* / THE BIG CAGE; *Freckles* / THE LIFE OF JIMMY DOLAN; *Ted the Third as a child* / BROADWAY TO HOLLYWOOD; *the kid* / THE BIG CHANCE; *Willie* / THE CHIEF. **1934:** *bit* / BELOVED; *messenger boy* / I LIKE IT THAT WAY; *Gladwyn Tootle* / LOVE BIRDS; *Blackie at 12* / MANHATTAN MELODRAMA; *boy swimmer* / CHAINED; *Willie* / HIDE-OUT; *Jerry* / UPPER WORLD; *Willie* / HALF A SINNER; *Freddie* / BLIND DATE; *Mickey* / DEATH OF THE DIAMOND. **1935:** *Freckles* / THE COUNTY CHAIRMAN; *crippled boy* / THE HEALER; *bit* / RECKLESS; *Jimmy* / RIFF-RAFF. **1936:** *Dick* / LITTLE LORD FAUNTLEROY; *Gig Stevens* / THE DEVIL IS A SISSY; *Snappy Sinclair* / DOWN THE STRETCH. **1937:** *Shockey* / THE HOOSIER SCHOOLBOY; *Swifty* / SLAVE SHIP; *Tim Donahue* / THOROUGHBREDS DON'T CRY; *Jerry Crump* / LIVE, LOVE AND LEARN. **1938:** *Mike* / LOVE IS A HEADACHE; *Andy Hardy* / JUDGE HARDY'S CHILDREN; *Andy Hardy* / YOU'RE ONLY YOUNG ONCE; *Chick Evans* / HOLD THAT KISS; *Terry O'Mulvaney* / LORD JEFF; *Andy Hardy* / LOVE FINDS ANDY HARDY; *Andy Hardy* / OUT WEST WITH THE HARDYS; *Mickey* / STABLEMATES. **1939:** *Andy Hardy* / THE HARDYS RIDE HIGH; *Andy Hardy* / ANDY HARDY GETS SPRING FEVER; *Andy Hardy* / JUDGE HARDY AND SON. **1940:** *Andy Hardy* / ANDY HARDY MEETS DEBUTANTE. **1941:** *Andy Hardy* / ANDY HARDY'S PRIVATE SECRETARY; *Whitey Marsh* / MEN OF BOYS TOWN; *Andy Hardy* / LIFE BEGINS FOR ANDY HARDY. **1942:** *Andy Hardy* / THE COURTSHIP OF ANDY HARDY; *Andy Hardy* / ANDY HARDY'S DOUBLE LIFE. **1943:** *guest* / THOUSANDS CHEER; *Danny Churchill, Jr.* / GIRL CRAZY. **1944:** *Andy Hardy* / ANDY HARDY'S BLONDE TROUBLE. **1946:** *Andy Hardy* / LOVE LAUGHS AT ANDY HARDY. **1947:** *Tommy McCoy* / KILLER MCCOY. **1948:** *Lorenz Hart* / WORDS AND MUSIC. **1949:** *Billy Coy* / THE BIG WHEEL. **1950:** *Dan Brady* / QUICKSAND; *Johnny Casar* / THE FIREBALL; *Freddie Frisby* / HE'S A COCKEYED WONDER. **1951:** *Denny O'More* / MY OUTLAW BROTHER; *Stanley Maxton* / THE STRIP. **1952:** *Mike Donnelly* / SOUND OFF. **1953:** *Herbert Tuttle* / OFF LIMITS; *Augustus "Geechy" Cheevers* / A SLIGHT CASE OF LARCENY; *Francis "Moby" Dickerson* / ALL ASHORE. **1954:** *Eddie Shannon* / DRIVE A CROOKED ROAD; *Blix Waterberry* / THE ATOMIC KID. **1955:** *Reverend Macklin* / THE TWINKLE IN GOD'S EYE. **1956:** *David Prescott* / FRANCIS IN THE HAUNTED HOUSE; *Frank Som-*

mers / MAGNIFICENT ROUGHNECKS. **1957:** *Yancey Skibo* / OPERATION MAD BALL. **1958:** *Andy Hardy* / ANDY HARDY COMES HOME; *Gus Harris* / A NICE LITTLE BANK THAT SHOULD BE ROBBED. **1959:** *Killer Mears* / THE LAST MILE; *Little Joe Braun* / THE BIG OPERATOR. **1960:** *Steven Conway* / PLATINUM HIGH SCHOOL; *Nick Lewis (Devil)* / THE PRIVATE LIVES OF ADAM AND EVE. **1961:** *Johnny Burke* / KING OF THE ROARING 20s; *Mr. Yunioshi* / BREAKFAST AT TIFFANY'S; *Beetle McKay* / EVERYTHING'S DUCKY. **1963:** *Ding Bell* / IT'S A MAD, MAD, MAD, MAD WORLD. **1964:** *Terrence Scanlon* / THE SECRET INVASION. **1965:** *Peachy Keane* / HOW TO STUFF A WILD BIKINI; *Norman Jones* / 24 HOURS TO KILL. **1966:** *Sgt. Ernest Wartell* / AMBUSH BAY. **1968:** *Cook 3rd Class W. J. Oglethorpe* / THE EXTRAORDINARY SEAMAN; *Adramalek* / THE DEVIL IN LOVE; *"Blue Chips" Packard* / SKIDOO. **1971:** *B. J. Lang* / B. J. LANG PRESENTS. **1972:** *guardian angel* / RICHARD. **1973:** *Preston Gilbert* / PULP. **1974:** *host* / THAT'S ENTERTAINMENT! **1977:** *Spiventa* / THE DOMINO PRINCIPLE; *Lampie* / PETE'S DRAGON. **1978:** *guest* / THE MAGIC OF LASSIE. **1979:** *Daad El Shur* / ARABIAN ADVENTURE. **1981:** *voice of Tod* / THE FOX AND THE HOUND. **1985:** *Mr. Cherigwood* / THE CARE BEARS MOVIE.

RUSSELL, GAIL

(1924–1961)

Hauntingly beautiful, Gail Russell entered motion pictures directly from Santa Monica High School with no previous acting experience. Dark-haired and limpid-eyed, she was an insecure introvert who was painfully shy. She was groomed for stardom and gave effective performances playing helpless women beset by problems. But her own problems were more tragic. She suffered from extreme stage fright throughout her career and her fear of the camera made her drink to get through her scenes. She became an alcoholic, found movie opportunities drying up, was divorced by husband Guy Madison, suffered through a romantic scandal involving John Wayne, and after her last film was completed she was found dead in her apartment surrounded by empty liquor bottles.

KEY ROLES

Stella Meredith / THE UNINVITED, 1944, Paramount, d-Lewis Allen.

Russell is the fragile beauty loved by a man (Ray Milland) who has bought her father's house. She is hated by Cornelia Otis Skinner, a nurse with a fixation for a dead woman, and has to deal with two very active ghosts, one who wants to drive her to suicide.

Cornelia Otis Skinner / OUR HEARTS WERE YOUNG AND GAY, 1944, Paramount, d-Lewis Allen.

After seeing Skinner's attitude toward Russell in the aforementioned movie, it's hard to imagine her the carefree young woman played by Russell. With her friend Emily Kimbrough (Diana Lynn), Russell finds fun and romance as a well-to-do flapper in Paris during the 1920s.

Barbara Brooks / SALTY O'ROURKE, 1945, Paramount, d-Raoul Walsh.

Russell is a schoolteacher girlfriend of Alan Ladd, the title character, who is a gambler involved in a crooked scheme to throw a horserace. She encourages him to seek a quieter, more honest life and when all his plans go haywire he sees the wisdom of her argument.

Penelope Worth / ANGEL AND THE BADMAN, 1947, Republic, d-James E. Grant.

The love of Quaker girl Russell saves a wounded gunslinger (John Wayne) from both the marshal who figures he'll have to shoot Wayne and some bad hombres who also have some bullets with his name on them.

Jean Courtland / NIGHT HAS A THOUSAND EYES, 1948, Paramount, d-John Farrow.

Vaudeville mentalist Edward G. Robinson makes predictions about the dangers in Russell's future and one by one they come true. His last vision is of her lying dead.

Angelique Desaix / WAKE OF THE RED WITCH, 1948, Republic, d-Edward Ludwig.

Told in flashback, this very good adventure story is about the rivalry of an East Indies-based sea captain (John Wayne) and a planter (Luther Adler) for Russell and pearls. Russell doesn't make it to the end of the film but the struggle between the two men continues.

OTHER ROLES

1943: *Virginia Lowry* / HENRY ALDRICH GETS GLAMOUR. **1944:** *Barbara, age 17* / LADY IN THE DARK. **1945:** *Elizabeth Howard* / THE UNSEEN; *guest* / DUFFY'S TAVERN. **1946:** *Cornelia Otis Skinner* / OUR HEARTS WERE GROWING UP; *Eileen* / THE BACHELOR'S DAUGHTERS. **1947:** *Virginia Moore* / CALCUTTA; *guest* / VARIETY GIRL. **1948:** *Gilly Johnson* / MOONRISE. **1949:** *Susan Jeffers* / EL PASO; *Princess Tara* / SONG OF INDIA; *Cissy Lathrop* / THE GREAT DAN PATCH; *Kim Mitchell* / CAPTAIN CHINA. **1950:** *Sunny Garcia* / THE LAWLESS. **1951:** *Janet Page* / AIR CADET. **1956:** *Annie Greer* / SEVEN MEN FROM NOW. **1957:** *Carol Morrow* / THE TATTERED DRESS. **1958:** *Lynn Dillon* / NO PLACE TO LAND. **1961:** *Flore Brancato* / THE SILENT CALL.

RUSSELL, JANE

(Ernestine Jane G. Russell, 1921–)

Brunette sex symbol Jane Russell was an image even before she became a star. Placed under personal contract to Howard Hughes, Russell's movie debut was delayed several years; the Legion of Decency was able to prevent the release of THE OUTLAW until 1946, even though it had been completed in 1943. Long before anyone saw the film, the country knew that her talented mentor had designed a special bra to enhance her more than ample breasts, and posters with her pouting face pronounced that she was "Mean, Moody and Magnificent." Russell remembered: "Sometimes the photographers would pose me in a low-necked nightgown and tell me to bend down and pick up the pails. They were not shooting the pails." It wasn't until Russell shifted to comedy that her real talent was discovered. She showed a delightfully self-deprecating humor about her erotic figure and her screen image as a too-hot-to-handle woman craved by all men. She was a smash in appearances opposite Bob Hope and his sexual ineffectiveness. She also was well cast with Robert Mitchum, something of a sex symbol himself. Once married to star pro football quarterback Bob Waterfield, Russell became the spokeswoman for Playtex and "full-figured women" after her film career was over.

KEY ROLES

Rio / THE OUTLAW, 1943 / 46, Hughes / United Artists, d-Howard Hughes.

This movie, despite all of its sexual hype, is, and was at the time of its delayed release and its wider distribution in 1950, a rather dull retelling of the Billy-the-Kid story. Russell's pouty looks make up a bit more than one side of a lust triangle with Jack Beutel and Walter Huston.

Calamity Jane / THE PALEFACE, 1948, Paramount, d-Norman Z. McLeod.

Russell goes undercover as she searches for some desperadoes. For her cover she hitches up with timid dentist Bob Hope, even to the point of marrying the clown. But each time it seems he may get some of the benefits of married life with the well-built beauty, someone, usually Russell herself, slugs him in the head with a gun. About as close as he gets to her is to sing the Academy Award winning song, "Buttons and Bows."

Dorothy Shaw / GENTLEMEN PREFER BLONDES, 1953, 20th Century-Fox, d-Howard Hawks.

Showing her excellent comedy ability, showgirl Russell and her equally well-built friend (Marilyn Monroe) are on an ocean liner headed for Paris, with the idea of finding rich husbands. Russell seems amused at how easy it is to twist men around her little finger when they get a glance at her super structure. Russell and Monroe team up on the Jule Styne and Leo Robin songs, "Two Little Girls from Little Rock" and "Bye Bye Baby" and she has a solo on "Ain't There Anyone Here for Love."

Mary Carson / THE FRENCH LINE, 1954, RKO, d-Lloyd Bacon.

In this film one gets to see Russell through the miracle of 3-D. Naturally the publicity phrase to hype the film suggests that "it'll knock both your eyes out." After all the film's hassle to get a Production Code, it proves to be a rather tame story of oil heiress Russell finding a husband while traveling to France.

Nella Turner / THE TALL MEN, 1955, 20th Century-Fox, d-Raoul Walsh.

Two Texan brothers (Clark Gable and Cameron Mitchell) head north to the Montana gold mines after the Civil War. Along the way they join up with a cattle drive and rescue Russell from Indians. Her presence with all those men is, as might be expected, troublesome, but an aging Gable ends up with her.

Mamie Stover / THE REVOLT OF MAMIE STOVER, 1956, 20th Century-Fox, d-Raoul Walsh.

This is the true story of prostitute Mamie Stover who makes a fortune in Honolulu catering to the servicemen on an assembly line-like basis. When she gets what she believes is enough money, she closes up shop and retires to her home in Mississippi.

OTHER ROLES

1947: *Joan Kenwood* / YOUNG WIDOW. **1950:** *Mildred Goodhue* / DOUBLE DYNAMITE. **1951:** *Julie Benson* / MACAO; *Belle Starr* / MONTANA BELLE; *Lenore Brent* / HIS KIND OF WOMAN. **1952:** *"Mike"* / SON OF PALEFACE; *Linda Rollins* / THE LAS VEGAS STORY; *guest* / ROAD TO BALI. **1955:** *Theresa* / UNDERWATER!; *Bonnie and Mimi Jones* / GENTLEMEN MARRY BRUNETTES; *Amanda Lawrence* / FOXFIRE. **1956:** *Annie Caldash* / HOT BLOOD. **1957:** *Laurel Stevens* / THE FUZZY PINK NIGHTGOWN. **1964:** *guest* / FATE IS THE HUNTER. **1966:** *Jill Stone* / WACO; *Nona Williams* / JOHNNY RENO. **1967:** *Mrs. Shorn* / BORN LOSERS. **1970:** *Alabama Tiger* / DARKER THAN AMBER.

RUSSELL, ROSALIND

(1908–1976)

A graduate of the American Academy of Dramatic Arts, Rosalind Russell made her Broadway debut in 1930 and four years later went to Hollywood with an MGM contract. For the next few years she played refined socialites and "other women" who were after the leading ladies' men. As she recalled, "I was always the threat, you see, to all the great women stars at Metro, and they certainly were legion." Her film debut was in EVELYN PRENTICE with her first leading role in RENDEZVOUS in 1935. She was typecast as a fast-talking career woman, playing some twenty-three such strong-willed ladies, and became a star portraying one in THE WOMEN. She reached her career peak in the 1940s moving into comedy in films such as HIS GIRL FRIDAY and MY SISTER EILEEN. After the war she returned to heavy dramas that won her praise but were disasters at the box office including MOURNING BECOMES ELECTRA, for which she received an Oscar nomination. She was also nominated for MY SISTER EILEEN, SISTER KENNY, and AUNTIE MAME. Russell returned to the stage in the 1950s and the film GYPSY was the only film she made late in life that was worthy of her talents. In 1972 she was given the Jean Hersholt Humanitarian Award for her charitable activities. Tall, slim, and intelligent, Russell had a fine career but will not be remembered as one of the major stars or as one of the outstanding actresses.

KEY ROLES

Sybil Barclay / CHINA SEAS, 1935, MGM, d-Tay Garnett.

Russell appears as an English lady who's a bit out of place with the likes of rough-and-ready ship captain Clark Gable, modern pirate Wallace Beery, and the proverbial "girl with a heart of gold," Jean Harlow. She doesn't get Gable but he'd have been all wrong for her anyway.

Harriet Craig / CRAIG'S WIFE, 1936, Columbia, d-Dorothy Arzner.

Russell is a middle-class wife who values her house and its furnishings more than she does her husband (John Boles). When he wises up, he leaves her with her true loves.

Olivia / NIGHT MUST FALL, 1937, MGM, d-Richard Thorpe.

Russell portrays a sensitive young woman who is fascinated by Robert Montgomery, a man who proves to be a real lady-killer—of rich old ladies.

Christine Manson / THE CITADEL, 1938, MGM, d-King Vidor.

Russell is the devoted and idealistic wife of a physician (Robert Donat) who, for a brief time, gives up his ideals for money. Her role in this highly successful production of the A. J. Cronin bestselling novel gave quite a boost to her career.

Sylvia Fowler / THE WOMEN, 1939, MGM, d-George Cukor.

In this all-female production of the play by Clare Boothe, Russell is a busybody who plots to have her friend (Norma Shearer) learn that her husband is having an affair with Joan Crawford. Shearer does learn it and heads for Reno and a divorce. Before long Russell arrives with the same intention because her husband is having an affair with Paulette Goddard. Russell changes allegiances from Shearer to Crawford when the latter marries the former's ex-husband. Both Crawford and Russell are in for some bad times before the picture is over.

Hildy Johnson / HIS GIRL FRIDAY, 1940, Columbia, d-Howard Hawks.

In this remake of THE FRONT PAGE, the Pat O'Brien role goes to Russell. She's a fast-talking newspaper reporter giving up her career to marry Ralph Bellamy. But her ex-husband and editor (Cary Grant) isn't willing to write off his star reporter without a fight.

So he talks Russell into covering an execution. It's a very funny black comedy.

Kendal Browning / HIRED WIFE, 1940, Universal, d-William A. Seiter.

Russell, a secretary who loves her boss (Brian Aherne), marries him to save his business by allowing him to put it in her name. Since the marriage was only to put off the IRS, Russell has to fight off a beautiful model (Virginia Bruce) to make the union permanent. It could be a lot funnier.

A. M. MacGregor / TAKE A LETTER, DARLING, 1942, Paramount, d-Mitchell Leisen.

Russell is an advertising executive who hires a tall, dark, and handsome male secretary (Fred MacMurray). While the outcome is predictable, there is fun getting there.

Ruth Sherwood / MY SISTER EILEEN, 1942, Columbia, d-Alexander Hall.

Russell and her sister (Janet Blair), two girls from Ohio, invade New York looking to make their mark. Russell, a writer, is kept very busy protecting her sexy, trusting sister from men. In the process she gets not only a job with a magazine but the editor (Brian Aherne) as well.

Tonie Carter / FLIGHT FOR FREEDOM, 1943, RKO, d-Lotha Mendes.

This highly fictionalized biopic of Amelia Earhart also contains some ingredients of the life of aviatrix Jacqueline Cochran. Russell is cast as a "Lady Lindbergh" who has more success at 10,000 feet than on the ground with the man in her life. The film suggests that Earhart's disappearance was due to a deliberate crash to give the United States the chance to photograph Japanese installations while searching for her.

Sister Elizabeth Kenny / SISTER KENNY, 1946, RKO, d-Dudley Nichols.

This film is a sincere, reverent salute to the fighting nurse who achieved fame with her treatment of polio. Russell's portrayal of the sacrificing woman makes her a trifle too saintly and the picture died at the box office.

Lavinia Mannon / MOURNING BECOMES ELECTRA, 1947, RKO, d-Dudley Nichols.

This Eugene O'Neill story was a movie failure with a then record-shattering loss of over $2 million. Still Russell gives a fine performance as the malignantly righteous Electra figure in this Freudian version of the return of Agamemnon after the victory of the Greeks over Troy, who finds his wife in love with a younger man. For this telling of the story the setting is the United States after the Civil War.

Susan Middlecott / A WOMAN OF DISTINCTION, 1950, Columbia, d-Edward Buzzell.

Russell, the dean of a New England woman's college, blames visiting astronomy professor Ray Milland when a malicious reporter spreads some nasty rumors about him. It's a so-so slapstick farce, with the best work coming from Edmund Gwenn as Russell's loving father who decides that it's way past time for Russell to put some romance in her life. He sees Milland as the man for the job.

Rosemary Sydney / PICNIC, 1956, Columbia, d-Joshua Logan.

Russell is an aging spinster schoolteacher who is jealous of the attention paid to Kim Novak at a Fourth of July picnic. Russell desperately wishes to marry Arthur O'Connell and says: "I'm no spring chicken either. Maybe I'm a little older than you think. My ways are formed too, but they can be changed. They gotta be changed. No good livin' like this, in rented rooms meetin' a bunch of old maids for supper every night, then comin' back home alone. Each year I keep tellin' myself is the last. Something'll happen. Nothing ever does—except I get a little crazier all the time."

Mame Dennis / AUNTIE MAME, 1958, Warners, d-Morton da Costa.

Russell is a wonder as the eccentric and volatile aunt who raises her brother's son, sharing all of her extravagant escapades with the lucky lad. As she insists to shy, scared Peggy Cass, "Life is a banquet, and most poor suckers are starving to death."

Rose Hovick / GYPSY, 1962, Warners, d-Mervyn LeRoy.

Russell gives an over-the-top performance as the world's most pushy stage mother. She keeps her two daughters, June and Louise, in show business, with the former becoming actress June Havoc and the latter becoming stripper Gypsy Rose Lee. But she never gets her own chance to star, which is her real ambition.

Mother Simplicia / THE TROUBLE WITH ANGELS, 1966, Columbia, d-Ida Lupino.

Russell is the mother superior of a school for teenage girls when two new students cause all kinds of trouble. It's innocent fun, but for those who remember how the "good sisters" squashed unruly children, seeing some nuns get theirs is a dream come true.

OTHER ROLES

1934: *Nancy Harrison* / EVELYN PRENTICE; *Sally Voorman* / THE PRESIDENT VANISHES. **1935:** *Dare* / WEST POINT OF THE AIR; *Doris* / THE CASINO MURDER CASE; *Josephine Mercer* / RECKLESS; *Joel Carter* / RENDEZVOUS; *Eleanor* / FORSAKING ALL OTHERS; *Countess Rafay* / THE NIGHT IS YOUNG. **1936:** *Beatrice Newnes* / IT HAD TO HAPPEN; *Lady Venetia* / UNDER TWO FLAGS; *Miss Vandeleur* / *Princess Brenda* / TROUBLE FOR TWO. **1937:** *Julie Stoddard* / LIVE, LOVE AND LEARN. **1938:** *Elizabeth Kent* / MAN-PROOF; *Jean Christy* / FOUR'S A CROWD. **1939:** *Garda Sloane* / FAST AND LOOSE. **1940:** *Linda Easterbrook* / NO TIME FOR COMEDY; *Ann Winters* / THIS THING CALLED LOVE. **1941:** *Anya Von Duren* / THEY MET IN BOMBAY; *Judge Cornelia Porter* / DESIGN FOR SCANDAL; *Julie Hathaway* / THE FEMININE TOUCH. **1943:** *Carole Kingsley* / WHAT A WOMAN. **1945:** *Louise Randall* / ROUGHLY SPEAKING; *Susan Lane* / SHE WOULDN'T SAY YES. **1947:** *Janet Ames* / THE GUILT OF JANET AMES. **1948:** *Valerie Stanton* / THE VELVET TOUCH. **1949:** *Marsha Meredith* / TELL IT TO THE JUDGE. **1952:** *Jo McBain* / NEVER WAVE AT A WAC. **1955:** *Kim Halliday* / THE GIRL RUSH. **1961:** *Mrs. Jacoby* / A MAJORITY OF ONE. **1962:** *Louise Harrington* / FIVE FINGER EXERCISE. **1967:** *Madame Rosepettle* / OH DAD, POOR DAD, MAMA'S HUNG YOU IN THE CLOSET AND I'M FEELING SO SAD. **1968:** *Mother Simplicia* / WHERE ANGELS GO, TROUBLE FOLLOWS; *Rosie Lord* / ROSIE. **1970:** *Mrs. Emily Pollifax* / MRS. POLLIFAX—SPY.

RYAN, ROBERT

(1909–1973)

A graduate of Dartmouth College, Robert Ryan was an undefeated intercollegiate boxing champion who went on to study at Max Reinhardt's acting studio in Los Angeles. He made his professional stage debut in 1938 in "Too Many Husbands" and in 1940 he signed a contract with Paramount and started his film career with GOLDEN GLOVES. In 1941 he moved to RKO before serving in the Marine Corps from 1944 to 1945. After the war he became a star with his role as a psychopathic anti-Semitic in CROSSFIRE. He did not become the usual leading man, though; instead he made a career of portraying tough guys with smooth surfaces and hell inside. Six-foot-three Ryan was at his best in villainous roles. Most of his career was spent in crime movies, melodramas, film noirs, and westerns, and the latter genre provided him with several great parts in which he gave outstanding performances. Ryan spent much of his life championing liberal causes. He fought for the abolishment of the House Un-American Activities Committee and was a founding member of the Committee on Sane Nuclear Policy. He died of cancer a year after his wife of 40 years died.

KEY ROLES

Joe Dunham / GANGWAY FOR TOMORROW, 1943, RKO, d-John H. Auer.

Ryan is a race car driver who is one of five people working side-by-side in a defense plant. They all ride to work together each day in the car of Charles Arnt, who has formed incorrect notions of each of his passengers. These are dispelled in flashbacks showing how each person has come to work for the war effort in his own way.

Lt. Scott Burnett / THE WOMAN ON THE BEACH, 1947, RKO, d-Jean Renoir.

In this film about a romantic triangle, Ryan is a coast guard lieutenant who has terrible nightmares about his combat service. He falls in love with bored Joan Bennett who is married to blind and bitter artist Charles Bickford. Audiences were not enthralled with the complex characterizations in the film. Those expecting a film noir were disappointed; those expecting a formula romance were even more disappointed.

Monty Montgomery / CROSSFIRE, 1947, RKO, d-Edward Dmytryk.

Ryan is chilling as the Jew-hater whose unprovoked murder of Sam Levene is ultimately exposed by GI Robert Mitchum and police captain Robert Young. The film made a star of Ryan, albeit a star villain.

Dr. Evans / THE BOY WITH GREEN HAIR, 1948, RKO, d-Joseph Losey.

War orphan Dean Stockwell, on a crusade against war, finds his hair changing to green. Ryan is a doctor who tries to understand the phenomenon which was clearly a message to everyone in the audience as to the cruelty of war.

Stoker Thompson / THE SET-UP, 1949, RKO, d-Robert Wise.

In this spectacular film noir, Ryan portrays a weary, inarticulate boxer who is betrayed by his manager and learns in the course of one of the most brutal movie fights ever that he's expected to go into the tank. He refuses, knocks out his opponent, and then must face the gamblers he has double-crossed.

Jeff Clanton / BEST OF THE BADMEN, 1951, RKO, d-William D. Russell.

Ryan, a Confederate officer, persuades a group of outlaws formerly with Quantrell's Raiders to surrender, take an oath to the Union, and get a new start in life. An unscrupulous detective (Robert Preston), hoping to collect rewards for the capture of the outlaws, frames Ryan for murder. But Ryan escapes and joins the outlaws now on the lam.

Earl Pfeiffer / CLASH BY NIGHT, 1952, RKO, d-Fritz Lang.

Barbara Stanwyck returns to her home village, after ten years of fruitless search for personal happiness, where she impulsively marries fisherman Paul Douglas, then succumbs to her attraction for Douglas's best friend, socialite Ryan. Things get very hot when Douglas discovers the infidelity.

Howard / BEWARE, MY LOVELY, 1952, RKO, d-Harry Horner.

In this chilling film noir, Ryan is a mental case with a persecution complex. Unaware of his mental state, widow Ida Lupino hires him to clean her old-fashioned house. He makes her a prisoner in her own home and threatens to rape and murder her. Fortunately for Lupino, Ryan's attention span is not long.

George Leslie / ABOUT MRS. LESLIE, 1954, Paramount, d-Daniel Mann.

Shirley Booth, an aging nightclub singer, has a platonic relationship with mysterious, wealthy Ryan. When he dies he leaves her enough money to buy a boarding house and she takes his name, even though they were never married.

Reno Smith / BAD DAY AT BLACK ROCK, 1954, MGM, d-John Sturges.

Ryan, the apparent leader of the residents of a small desert town, is hostile to a one-armed man (Spencer Tracy) who arrives in town trying to find out what happened to the parents of a Japanese-American soldier who had been in his command in Europe during World War II. Ryan and his cronies had allowed their patriotism after Pearl Harbor to get completely out of hand.

Ty Walden / GOD'S LITTLE ACRE, 1958, Security, d-Anthony Mann.

Ryan, a poor white trash farmer in Georgia, neglects his land in a fruitless search for gold. The picture is a bowdlerized version of the steamy Erskine Caldwell novel.

Earle Slater / ODDS AGAINST TOMORROW, 1959, United Artists, d-Robert Wise.

Former cop Ed Begley, nightclub singer Harry Belafonte, and ex-con Ryan plan to rob a bank but Ryan's racial prejudice leads to a bungled job.

John Claggart / BILLY BUDD, 1962, Great Britain, Anglo-Allied, d-Peter Ustinov.

In 1797 sadistic Master at Arms Ryan terrorizes the crew of a British warship and is killed by young, innocent, and naive Billy Budd who must hang for his unpremeditated crime.

Hans Ehrengard / THE PROFESSIONALS, 1966, Columbia, d-Richard Brooks.

Ryan is one of four men hired by Ralph Bellamy to rescue his wife (Claudia Cardinale) from a Mexican bandit (Jack Palance). But they find that the lady doesn't wish to be rescued.

Sergeant Mulligan / CUSTER OF THE WEST, 1967, Cinerama, d-Robert Siodmak.

Ryan plays a gold-hungry Irish deserter who is sentenced to death by Custer. He steals the picture in this far from historically accurate depiction of the events leading up to Custer's blunder at Little Big Horn.

Deke Thornton / THE WILD BUNCH, 1969, Warners, d-Sam Peckinpah.

Ryan is an ex-colleague of Texas bandits William Holden, Ernest Borgnine, and others. In 1914 he heads up a motley crew of gunmen sent to round up his old friends.

Captain Nemo / CAPTAIN NEMO AND THE UNDERWATER CITY, 1970, Great Britain, MGM, d-James Hill.

Ryan portrays Jules Verne's engaging commander of a mysterious submarine who picks up six shipwreck survivors and takes them to his undersea city.

OTHER ROLES

1940: *Pete Wells* / GOLDEN GLOVES; *Jim* / QUEEN OF THE MOB; *Constable Dumont* / NORTHWEST MOUNTED POLICE. **1941:** *Eddie* / TEXAS RANGERS RIDE AGAIN. **1943:** *Joe Connor* / BOMBARDIER; *Reg Fenton* / THE SKY'S THE LIMIT; *Lefty* / BEHIND THE RISING SUN; *Fr. Tim Donovan* / THE IRON MAJOR; *Chris* / TENDER COMRADE. **1944:** *Capt. Dan Craig* / MARINE RAIDERS. **1947:** *Allen Harper* / TRAIL STREET. **1948:** *Robert Lindley* / BERLIN EXPRESS; *Sundance Kid* / RETURN OF THE BADMEN; *Joe Parkson* / ACT OF VIOLENCE. **1949:** *Smith Ohlrig* / CAUGHT; *Brad Collins* / THE WOMAN ON PIER 13. **1950:** *David* / THE SECRET FURY; *Nick* / BORN TO BE BAD. **1951:** *Capt. Carl "Griff" Griffin* / FLYING LEATHERNECKS; *Nick Scanlon* / THE RACKET; *Jim Wilson* / ON DANGEROUS GROUND. **1952:** *Don Hammond* / HORIZONS WEST. **1953:** *Brad Carlton* / CITY BENEATH THE SEA; *Ben Vandergroat* / THE NAKED SPUR; *Carson* / INFERNO. **1954:** *Matt Kelly* / ALASKA SEAS; *Joe Hardgrave* / HER TWELVE MEN. **1955:** *Jim Brecan* / ESCAPE TO BURMA; *Sandy Dawson* / HOUSE OF BAMBOO; *Nathan Stark* / THE TALL MEN. **1956:** *Marshal Cass Silver* / THE PROUD ONES; *Bill* / BACK FROM ETERNITY. **1957:** *Lieutenant Benson* / MEN IN WAR. **1958:** *William Shrike* / LONELYHEARTS. **1959:** *Blaise Starrett* / DAY OF THE OUTLAW. **1960:** *Thor Storm* / ICE PALACE. **1961:** *Insp. William Gannon* / THE CANADIANS; *John the Baptist* / KING OF KINGS. **1962:** *Gen. James Gavin* / THE LONGEST DAY. **1965:** *General Grey* / BATTLE OF THE BULGE; *Richard Ashley* / THE CROOKED ROAD. **1966:** *General Bruce* / THE DIRTY GAME. **1967:** *Charley Barker* / THE BUSY BODY; *Col. Everett Dasher-Breed* / THE DIRTY DOZEN; *Ike Clanton* / HOUR OF THE GUN. **1968:** *Gov. Lem Carter* / A MINUTE TO PRAY, A SECOND TO DIE; *General Carson* / ANZIO. **1971:** *Marshal Cotton Ryan* / LAWMAN; *Gregory Austin* / THE LOVE MACHINE. **1972:** *Charley* / AND HOPE TO DIE. **1973:** *Pap Gutshall* / LOLLY MADONNA XXX; *Foster* / EXECUTIVE ACTION; *Mailer* / THE OUTFIT; *Larry Slade* / THE ICEMAN COMETH.

SAINT, EVA MARIE

(1924–)

Eva Marie Saint, a slender, wanly beautiful blonde, made her film debut at age 30 after years of work on stage and television. She won an Oscar for her first effort, ON THE WATERFRONT, but Hollywood didn't seem to know what to do with this intelligent actress who was not overly sexual or glamorous. She was most often cast as an outwardly fragile and vulnerable woman who possessed inner strength. Her way of paying attention to her male co-stars in scenes made many an actor look better than he was. Had she arrived on the scene some time later, she might have been offered roles that have gone to the likes of Jane Fonda and Meryl Streep, and no doubt she would have done wonders with them. Saint has returned to the stage and TV where she was once dubbed "the Helen Hayes of Television" to appear in made-for-TV movies such as THE MACAHANS (1976), A CHRISTMAS TO REMEMBER (1978), WHEN HELL WAS IN SEASON (1979), THE CURSE OF KING TUT'S TOMB (1980), SPLENDOR IN THE GRASS (1981), THE BEST LITTLE GIRL IN THE WORLD (1982), MALIBU and JANE DOE (1983), and FATAL VISION and LOVE LEADS THE WAY (1984).

KEY ROLES

Edie Doyle / ON THE WATERFRONT, 1954, Columbia, d-Elia Kazan.

After her brother is killed by crooked union officials on the waterfront, convent-trained Saint meets and falls in love with Marlon Brando, who had unwittingly fingered her brother. She gets under his skin to such a point that he agrees to give evidence against the corrupt union officials, one of whom is his own brother.

Celia Pope / A HATFUL OF RAIN, 1957, 20th Century-Fox, d-Fred Zinnemann.

In one of Hollywood's first major films on the subject of drug addiction, war veteran Don Murray gets hooked on narcotics and tries to keep it from Saint, his pregnant wife. When he finally admits he has a problem to himself and to her, she stands by him, but the effect on both is heart-rending.

Nell Gaither / RAINTREE COUNTY, 1957, MGM, d-Edward Dmytryk.

Elizabeth Taylor is the first female lead in this costly and ho-hum epic story of a belle who marries an Indiana schoolteacher and finds the life boring. But Saint outacts Taylor throughout this tediously long movie, playing the girl that Montgomery Clift should have married.

Eve Kendall / NORTH BY NORTHWEST, 1959, MGM, d-Alfred Hitchcock.

In the movie that shows Saint's multi-talents to best advantage, she portrays a U.S. agent and lover of James Mason, an enemy agent for some unspecified country. She falls in love with businessman Cary Grant when he is mistaken for an American agent and their scenes together on the train from New York to Chicago are deliciously titillating.

Kitty Fremont / EXODUS, 1960, United Artists, d-Otto Preminger.

Saint is a nurse who has lost her photographer husband in World War II and is on Cyprus trying to find a reason to live. Her answer comes when she meets a young Jewish girl refugee whom she wishes to take back to the United States. Instead, the girl accompanies other refugees to Palestine. Saint follows and meets Paul Newman, a nice young man born and raised on a kibbutz. When the United Nations accedes to partitioning Palestine in order to form the Jewish state of Israel, the Arabs pledge "Holy War" and one of the first casualties is the innocent young girl Saint has come to love. Saint joins up with Newman and the others to defend her new home.

Ann Hedler / 36 HOURS, 1964, MGM, d-George Seaton.

Saint is part of a plot by a German doctor (Rod Taylor) to convince James Garner, who knows the secret plans for invading Europe in 1944, that he is a victim of amnesia, that the war is many years over, and that he is back in the victorious U.S.A. He buys the story and gives Taylor the information he is seeking before escaping with Saint, who was forced to cooperate in the scheme. But the Nazi higher-ups don't believe the information is legitimate.

OTHER ROLES

1956: *Dunreath Henry* / THAT CERTAIN FEELING. **1962:** *Echo O'Brien* / ALL FALL DOWN. **1965:** *Claire Hewitt* / THE SANDPIPER. **1966:** *Elspeth Whittaker* / THE RUSSIANS ARE COMING, THE RUSSIANS ARE COMING; *Louise Frederickson* / GRAND PRIX. **1968:** *Sarah Carver* / THE STALKING MOON. **1970:** *Selma Wilson* / LOVING. **1972:** *Sheila Bartlett* / CANCEL MY RESERVATION. **1986:** *Lorraine Basner* / NOTHING IN COMMON.

SANDERS, GEORGE

(1906–1973)

Suave, civilized, and sneering, George Sanders was born in Russia to British parents and made his stage debut in the early 1930s and his first film in 1936, the same year he moved to Hollywood with a 20th Century-Fox contract. Displaying irresistible charm, Sanders made his first mark in "The Saint" and "The Falcon" series. During World War II he found himself portraying several nasty Nazis. While he did on occasion play a hero, he was at his best in morally ambiguous roles or as sophisticated heels who looked weary and indifferent. Without a doubt, his best appearance in this persona was as Addison De Witt in ALL ABOUT EVE, for which he won one of the most deserved Best Supporting Actor Academy Awards ever. His screen weariness and indifference carried over to real life. He observed, "Acting is like roller-skating. Once you know how to do it, it is neither stimulating nor exciting." When he could stand it no longer, he took his own life and left a suicide note that read: "Dear World, I am leaving because I am bored. I feel I have lived long enough. I am leaving you with your worries in this sweet cesspool—good luck."

KEY ROLES

Lt. Michael Bruce / LANCER SPY, 1937, 20th Century-Fox, d-Gregory Ratoff.

Sanders, an Englishman, is the exact double of a German officer. He goes to Germany posing as the escaped German and becomes a national hero though he secretly works for British intelligence.

Simon Templar / THE SAINT STRIKES BACK, 1939, RKO, d-John Farrow.

Sanders became the definitive Saint, taking over for Louis Hayward, in this story about the solutions to some ingenious homicides in San Francisco.

Schalger / CONFESSIONS OF A NAZI SPY, 1939, Warners, d-Anatole Litvak.

In this effective anti-Nazi propaganda piece, Sanders plays a preening, bullet-headed German officer and spy master who makes fun of the American notion of fair play.

Jack Flavell / REBECCA, 1940, David O. Selznick / United Artists, d-Alfred Hitchcock.

Sanders is a suave cad who attempts to blackmail Laurence Olivier over the death of the latter's first wife. Sanders was perfecting, in this film, his persona as a charming scoundrel who sneers condescendingly at everyone and everything he sees.

Scott ffolliott / FOREIGN CORRESPONDENT, 1940, Wagner / United Artists, d-Alfred Hitchcock.

Sanders and Robert Benchley are fellow reporters in London. They help another reporter (Joel McCrea) investigate the assassination of a Dutch statesman as the latter arrives at a peace conference. Near the end of the picture McCrea growls, "The German government will have to answer for this." Cynical Sanders replies: "Documents will undoubtedly be found, old boy, proving that it is a British trawler disguised as a German battleship, and the whole thing has been organized by the pirate, Churchill, to drag America into the war."

Maj. Quive-Smith / MAN HUNT, 1941, 20th Century-Fox, d-Fritz Lang.

Sanders makes a perfect Gestapo chief in this story of a hunter who gets Hitler in the sights of his rifle but is captured before he can decide whether to pull the trigger. Sanders plans to use the hunter (Walter Pidgeon) as part of an international intrigue.

Falcon (Gay Lawrence) / THE GAY FALCON, 1941, RKO, d-Irving Reis.

Leslie Charteris, creator of The Saint, sued over this film claiming that The Falcon was just his creation with a different name. Certainly as Sanders plays the hard-boiled detective, there could be little doubt that author Charteris knew of what he spoke. With Sanders in charge, the Falcon, who can't resist a pretty face or an interesting crime, solves a double murder and a diamond robbery. After two more appearances in the role, Sanders was bored with the character and turned it over to his real-life brother, Tom Conway.

Charles Strickland / THE MOON AND SIXPENCE, 1943, United Artists, d-Albert Lewin.

It would be difficult to find a man not suffering from mental illness who could behave more beastly to the people who care for and are kind to him than Sanders's character in this film à clef of painter Paul Gauguin.

Lord Henry Wotton / THE PICTURE OF DORIAN GRAY, 1945, MGM, d-Albert Lewin.

This Oscar Wilde story is about a man (Hurd Hatfield) who looks eternally young and handsome, while his portrait hidden in an attic shows the hideousness of his amoral, hedonistic life. Sanders disdainfully drops epigrams throughout the film including, "The only difference between a caprice and a lifelong passion is that the caprice lasts a little longer" and "Most people get by on a sort of creepy common sense and discover too late that the only thing one never regrets are one's mistakes."

Miles Fairley / THE GHOST AND MRS. MUIR, 1947, 20th Century-Fox, d-Joseph L. Mankiewicz.

Sanders is a romantic fraud who meets Gene Tierney when she brings the salty memoirs of the ghost of a sea captain in whose house she lives to a publisher. Tierney believes that Sanders's paying court to her means he plans to ask her to marry him, but then she meets Sanders's understanding wife.

Addison De Witt / ALL ABOUT EVE, 1950, 20th Century-Fox, d-Joseph L. Mankiewicz.

Sanders is superb as a New York drama critic in the story of a scheming, ambitious young actress who wants to replace an aging stage star in a playwright's new work. Sanders's great lines, marvelously delivered, include, "I have lived in the theater as a Trappist monk lives in his faith. In it I toil not, neither do I spin. I am a critic and a commentator. I am essential to the theater—as ants to a picnic, as the boll weevil to a cotton field"; "Look, closely, Eve. It's time you did. I am Addison De Witt. I am nobody's fool. Least of all yours;" and "Did I say killer? I meant champion. I get my boxing terms mixed." Some claim that his character was modeled on critic George Jean Nathan.

De Bois-Guilbert / IVANHOE, 1952, Great Britain, MGM, d-Richard Thorpe.

With his sharp tongue, villain Sanders doesn't need a sword to arm himself against Sir Walter Scott's medieval knight.

Clementi Sabourin / DEATH OF A SCOUNDREL, 1956, RKO, d-Charles Martin.

In this film à clef of the notorious financial manipulator and Lothario, Serge Rubenstein, Sanders lets all of his charming, caddish behavior hang out as a man who sells his soul to the highest bidder. The film has everything that makes life worthwhile: betrayal, suicide, murder, seduction, thievery, and a bit of comedy.

Landru / BLUEBEARD'S TEN HONEYMOONS, 1960, Great Britain, Anglo-Allied, d-W. Lee Wilder.

This story of the man who wooed, wed, and murdered ten women stars Sanders as a dangerous charmer. Such was not the case of the real Landru.

The Warlock / THE KREMLIN LETTER, 1970, 20th Century-Fox, d-John Huston.

Sanders is reduced to portraying an ugly transvestite and master spy in a story of American agents in Moscow trying to retrieve an arms treaty mistakenly signed.

OTHER ROLES

1936: *Curly Randall* / FIND THE LADY; *Roddy Burch* / STRANGE CARGO; *Indifference* / THE MAN WHO COULD WORK MIRACLES; *Lisle* / DISHONOR BRIGHT; *Lord Everett Stacy* / LLOYDS OF LONDON. **1937:** *Count Andre de Guyon* / LOVE IS NEWS; *Lefty* / SLAVE SHIP; *Rene Blanchard* / THE LADY ESCAPES. **1938:** *Del Forbes* / INTERNATIONAL SETTLEMENT; *Wyatt Leigh* / FOUR MEN AND A PRAYER. **1939:** *Eric Norvel* / MR. MOTO'S LAST WARNING; *Dr. de Reseke* / SO THIS IS LONDON; *Simon Templar* / THE SAINT IN LONDON; *Captain Swanson* / ALLEGHENY UPRISING; *Captain Heinrichs* / NURSE EDITH CAVELL. **1940:** *Anton Ragatzy* / THE OUTSIDER; *Forrester* / GREEN HELL; *Simon Templar* / *the boss* / THE SAINT'S DOUBLE TROUBLE; *Jaffrey Pyncheon* / THE HOUSE OF THE SEVEN GABLES; *Baron Von Tranisch* / BITTER SWEET; *Gurko Lanen* / THE SON OF MONTE CRISTO. **1941:** *Ward Andrews* / RAGE IN HEAVEN; *Simon Templar* / THE SAINT IN PALM SPRINGS; *The Falcon (Gay Lawrence)* / A DATE WITH THE FALCON; *Major Coombes* / SUNDOWN. **1942:** *Sir Arthur Blake* / SON OF FURY; *The Falcon (Gay Lawrence)* / THE FALCON TAKES OVER; *Tony Barling* / HER CARDBOARD LOVER; *Williams* / TALES OF MANHATTAN; *The Falcon (Gay Lawrence)* / THE FALCON'S BROTHER; *Capt. Billy Leech* / THE BLACK SWAN; *Fleg* / QUIET PLEASE, MURDER. **1943:** *George Lambert* / THIS LAND IS MINE; *Carl Steelman* / THEY CAME TO BLOW UP AMERICA; *Dr. Andre Marbel* / PARIS AFTER DARK. **1944:** *Gordon* / ACTION IN ARABIA; *John Warwick* / THE LODGER; *Fedor Michailovitch Petroff* / SUMMER STORM. **1945:** *Dr. Allan Middleton* / HANGOVER SQUARE; *John Quincy* / UNCLE HARRY. **1946:** *Vidocq* / A SCANDAL IN PARIS; *John Evered* / THE STRANGE WOMAN. **1947:** *George Duroy* / THE PRIVATE AFFAIRS OF BEL AMI; *Robert Fleming* / LURED; *King Charles II* / FOREVER AMBER. **1949:** *Lord Darlington* / THE FAN; *The Saran of Gaza* / SAMSON AND DELILAH. **1950:** *Mike Alexander* / CAPTAIN BLACKJACK. **1951:** *Noble* / I CAN GET IT FOR YOU WHOLESALE; *Felix Guignol* / THE LIGHT TOUCH. **1952:** *Nick Strang* / ASSIGNMENT—PARIS. **1953:** *Alexander Joyce* / JOURNEY TO ITALY; *Cosmo Constantine* / CALL ME MADAM. **1954:** *Albert Richter* / WITNESS TO MURDER; *Richard I* / KING RICHARD AND THE CRUSADERS; *Fabius Maximus* / JUPITER'S DARLING. **1955:** *Lord Ashwood* / MOONFLEET; *Dr. Jonathan Odell* / THE SCARLET COAT; *Charles II* / THE KING'S THIEF; *disc jockey* / NIGHT FREIGHT. **1956:** *Victor* / NEVER SAY GOODBYE; *Mark Loving* / WHILE THE CITY SLEEPS; *Larry Larkin* / THAT CERTAIN FEELING. **1957:** *Tim Waddington* / THE SEVENTH SIN. **1958:** *Carliss* / THE WHOLE TRUTH; *Stuyvesant Nicholl* / FROM THE EARTH TO THE MOON. **1959:** *the man* / THAT KIND OF WOMAN; *Adonijah* / SOLOMON AND SHEBA. **1960:** *Sir Charles Holland* / A TOUCH OF LARCENY; *Capt. Robert Adams* / THE LAST VOYAGE; *Gordon Zellaby* / VILLAGE OF THE DAMNED; *Sir Charles Brouard* / THE REBEL. **1961:** *Sir Arnold Hobbes* / CONE OF SILENCE; *Mr. Bing* / FIVE GOLDEN HOURS; *J. K.* / LE RENDEZ-VOUS. **1962:** *Major Hobson* / OPERATION SNATCH; *Thomas Ayerton* / IN SEARCH OF THE CASTAWAYS. **1963:** *Major Pickering* / CAIRO; *the guv'nor* / THE CRACKSMAN; *narrator* / ECCO. **1964:** *Raymond Fontaine* / DARK PURPOSE; *Benjamin Ballon* / A SHOT IN THE DARK; *Basil Palmer* / THE GOLDEN HEAD. **1965:** *the banker* / THE AMOROUS ADVENTURES OF MOLL FLANDERS. **1966:** *Gibbs* / THE QUILLER MEMORANDUM; *Professor Schlieben* / TRUNK TO CAIRO. **1967:** *Mr. Mordicus* / GOOD TIMES; *Calvin York* / WARNING SHOT. **1968:** *Captain Phillips* / ONE STEP TO HELL; *voice of Shere Khan, the tiger* / THE JUNGLE BOOK. **1969:** *Sidney Carter* / THE CANDY MAN; *Sir Francis Leybourne* / THE BEST HOUSE IN LONDON; *General Armstrong* / THE BODY STEALERS. **1970:** *follower of Su-Muru* / RIO 70. **1971:** *Lippincott* / ENDLESS NIGHT. **1972:** *the admiral* / DOOMWATCH; *Shadwell* / THE LIVING DEAD.

SARANDON, SUSAN

(Susan Tomalin, 1946–)

Susan Sarandon usually portrays a woman who is intelligent, sensual, vulnerable, and a bit off-beat. She appeared in a number of TV soap operas before finding film roles and, for a time, her only claim to fame was her appearance in the cult favorite THE ROCKY HORROR PICTURE SHOW. With her Oscar-nominated work in ATLANTIC CITY, she demonstrated that she's not just another kookie starlet but a serious actress. She will probably not become a major star, but that will be all right with her as she considers herself a character actress, first and foremost. Her talent and eroticism have been displayed, mostly on her terms, in a variety of roles that have added up to an appetizing "what might have been" rather than a satisfying career. Her made-for-TV movies include OWEN MARSHALL, COUNSELOR AT LAW (1971), THE HAUNTING OF ROSALIND (1973), F. SCOTT FITZGERALD AND THE LAST OF THE BELLES (1974), and ONE SUMMER LOVE (1976).

KEY ROLES

Melissa Compton / JOE, 1970, Cannon, d-John G. Avildsen.

Sarandon's debut is as a wayward teenager whose father kills her drug-addicted lover and in the end guns her down as well.

Janet Weiss / THE ROCKY HORROR PICTURE SHOW, 1975, Great Britain, 20th Century-Fox, d-Jim Sharman.

In this midnight movie cult favorite, Sarandon gives support to the claim made in many circles that her cleavage is the loveliest in movies today. In this outrageous version of the Frankenstein legend, she and her boyfriend (Barry Bostwick) seek shelter during a storm in a castle owned by a transvestite scientist (Tim Curry). Curry brings Rocky Horror, a handsome, muscular young man, to life to be used for the doctor's own sexual purposes. But Rocky prefers both Sarandon and her boyfriend.

Hattie / PRETTY BABY, 1978, Paramount, d-Louis Malle.

The movie is set in the Storyville section of New Orleans in 1917 and is told from the viewpoint of Brooke Shields, the 12-year-old daughter of prostitute Sarandon, who turns her child into a prostitute as well.

Sally / ATLANTIC CITY, 1981, Paramount, d-Louis Malle.

Sarandon works nights shucking clams at an Atlantic City seafood bar and, during the day, studies to become a blackjack dealer. Her flower child sister drops by with Sarandon's estranged husband and Sarandon couldn't care less. When this low-life is rubbed out by two mobsters anxious to get back the dope he stole from them, Sarandon is assisted by Burt Lancaster, an aging small-time hood who lives across the courtyard. He eagerly watches each night as she gets rid of the odor of seafood by washing herself with the juice of fresh lemons. He's got the drugs and he is able to live out his fantasies, by bedding Sarandon and blowing away the two killers, before letting her have the money he gets for the drugs.

Aretha / TEMPEST, 1982, Columbia, d-Paul Mazursky.

In this modern-day version of the Shakespeare play, Sarandon is John Cassavetes's mistress, living with him and his daughter on a lonely Aegean isle. In flashback we learn why he is there and how he met Sarandon.

OTHER ROLES

1972: *Sally* / LADY LIBERTY. **1974:** *Kate* / THE SATAN MURDERS; *Peggy Grant* / THE FRONT PAGE; *Mary Beth* / THE GREAT WALDO PEPPER; *Sarah* / LOVIN' MOLLY. **1977:** *Catherine Douglas* / THE OTHER SIDE OF MIDNIGHT. **1978:** *Rose* / KING OF THE GYPSIES; *jungle racer* / CHECKERED FLAG OR CRASH; *Ginny* / THE GREAT SMOKEY ROADBLOCK. **1979:** *Madeleine Ross* / SOMETHING SHORT OF PARADISE. **1980:** *Stephanie* / LOVING COUPLES. **1984:** *Sarah Roberts* / THE HUNGER; *Emily* / THE BUDDY SYSTEM. **1985:** *Judith Singer* / COMPROMISING POSITIONS. **1987:** *Jane Spofford* / THE WITCHES OF EASTWICK.

SCHEIDER, ROY

(1935–)

A member of the Lincoln Center Repertory Company in 1962, Roy Scheider made his stage debut in 1963 in "The Chinese Prime Minister." For awhile it appeared that Scheider would remain a talented supporting actor as with his role in THE FRENCH CONNECTION, for which he received an Oscar nomination, but with JAWS in 1975 he moved into the leading man category. He moved on to Academy Award-nominated work in ALL THAT JAZZ. Typically, Scheider portrays men of determination, only briefly slowed down by their very human flaws.

KEY ROLES

Buddy "Cloudy" Russo / THE FRENCH CONNECTION, 1971, 20th Century-Fox, d-William Freidkin.

Although he was in the shadow of Gene Hackman, Scheider's realistic portrayal of a gritty New York narcotics cop won much praise. He also didn't suffer the indignity Hackman did by appearing in the far inferior sequel.

Buddy Manucci / THE SEVEN-UPS, 1973, 20th Century-Fox, d-Philip D'Antoni.

Scheider gets first billing in this exciting police thriller about an unorthodox plainclothes detective who heads up a squad of cops who are just as brutal as the crooks they put away.

Martin Brody / JAWS, 1975, Universal, d-Steven Spielberg.

Scheider, the police chief of an East Coast resort island, sets out in a small boat with a determined fisherman (Robert Shaw) and a scientist (Richard Dreyfuss) to find the giant shark that has been attacking and killing residents. It's a taut thriller and Scheider came back in the sequel in 1978 without harming his career.

Joe Gideon / ALL THAT JAZZ, 1979, Columbia / 20th Century-Fox, d-Bob Fosse.

In this semi-autobiographical film, Scheider gives a brilliant performance as the Bob Fosse-like, self-destructive choreographer and director. The film alternates between reality and fantasy as we see Fosse's reaction to the heart attack that nearly killed him in 1974. In 1987 Fosse suffered a fatal heart attack.

Murphy / BLUE THUNDER, 1983, Columbia, d-John Badham.

As a policeman in Los Angeles, Scheider pilots a state-of-the-art helicopter. Haunted by memories of Vietnam, he goes berserk as he wages war against crime, battling combat jets above the crowded streets of the city.

OTHER ROLES

1964: *Philip Sinclair* / THE CURSE OF THE LIVING CORPSE. **1968:** *bit* / PAPER LION. **1969:** *Bennett* / STILETTO. **1970:** *Skip* / LOVING. **1971:** *Frank Ligourin* / KLUTE; *Mark* / PUZZLE OF A DOWNFALL CHILD. **1973:** *Lenny* / THE OUTSIDE MAN; *Howard* / THE FRENCH CONSPIRACY. **1975:** *Sam Stoneham* / SHEILA LEVINE IS DEAD AND LIVING IN NEW YORK. **1976:** *Doc Levy* / MARATHON MAN. **1977:** *Jackie Scanlon* / *"Juan Dominiguez"* / SORCERER. **1978:** *Martin Brody* / JAWS 2. **1979:** *Harry Hannon* / LAST EMBRACE. **1982:** *Sam Rice* / STILL OF THE NIGHT. **1983:** *Billy Young* / TIGER TOWN. **1984:** *guest* / IN OUR HANDS; *Heywood Floyd* / 2010. **1985:** *narrator* / MISHIMA. **1986:** *Harry Mitchell* / 52 PICK-UP; *Cavanaugh* / THE MEN'S CLUB.

SCHILDKRAUT, JOSEPH

(1895-1964)

Son of famous actor Rudolph Schildkraut, Joseph trained for the stage with his father's rival, Albert Basserman. In 1910 he came to the United States with his father and enrolled at the American Academy of Dramatic Arts before returning to Germany to star with Max Reinhardt's stage company. He returned to the United States in 1920 and within a year was a leading matinee idol on Broadway. His films in Germany and Austria included THE WANDERING JEW (1908), SCHLEMIEL (1914), and THE LIFE OF THEODORE HERZEL (1918). His U.S. film debut was in ORPHANS OF THE STORM in 1922. Schildkraut won the Best Supporting Actor Academy Award for his portrayal of Captain Dreyfuss in THE LIFE OF EMILE ZOLA. Despite his origins he was able to resist being typecast as a Middle European, but his acting talents seemed better suited to the stage than to the screen.

KEY ROLES

Judas Iscariot / KING OF KINGS, 1927, Silent, Pathe, d-Cecil B. DeMille.

Schildkraut takes full advantage of his villain role as the follower of Christ who betrays him for thirty pieces of silver and then hangs himself.

Gaylord Ravenal / SHOW BOAT, 1929, Part-talkie, Universal, d-Harry Pollard.

Schildkraut is a charming river gambler who marries a woman (Laura La Plante) raised on a showboat by her parents to be the star of their show. When her father is swept overboard during a storm, she and Schildkraut take their share of her inheritance and move to Chicago, where he loses their money and leaves his family. La Plante supports herself and her child by going on the stage singing Negro spirituals. When her mother dies, she and Schildkraut are reunited back on the showboat.

Herod / CLEOPATRA, 1934, Paramount, d-Cecil B. DeMille.

Schildkraut is a conniving, gossipy, Jewish king-to-be who conspires with Cleopatra to get the best possible terms for their respective countries from the conquering Romans.

Conrad, Marquis of Montferrat / THE CRUSADES, 1935, Paramount, d-Cecil B. DeMille.

Schildkraut, one of the leaders of the Third Crusade, has major disagreements with Richard the Lion Hearted (Henry Wilcoxon) about how best to deal with Saladin and the invasion of the Holy Land.

Batouch / THE GARDEN OF ALLAH, 1936, Selznick / United Artists, d-Richard Boleslawski.

Schildkraut is a flamboyant guide who takes Marlene Dietrich into the Algerian desert where she seeks rest and peace. Instead, after a fiery dance in a dancing den, a sultry performer starts a riot over the attention another woman is paying to Schildkraut's brother. Dietrich is rescued by Charles Boyer, a monk who has run away from a Trappist monastery in Tunis, and the two fall in love, are married, and go off in the desert for their honeymoon. But when a French officer recognizes Boyer, the jig is up. It's a ridiculous but interesting romance with all participants in high spirits.

Capt. Alfred Dreyfuss / THE LIFE OF EMILE ZOLA, 1937, Warners, d-William Dieterle.
French captain Schildkraut is unjustly accused of being a spy and is tried, found guilty, and sentenced to Devil's Island. It appears that his only crime is being Jewish and that he's being made a scapegoat by the military establishment for its own incompetence. Famed writer Emile Zola (Paul Muni) champions Schildkraut's cause and gets him released.

Duke of Orleans / MARIE ANTOINETTE, 1938, MGM, d-W. S. Van Dyke.
Schildkraut has a nice villainous role as the traitorous Duke of Orleans, the conniving, fastidious, scheming menace in the court at Versailles.

Fouquet / THE MAN IN THE IRON MASK, 1939, United Artists, d-James Whale.
Once again as a conniving man, Schildkraut coddles the wimpy king (Louis Hayward) who has imprisoned his own twin brother (also Louis Hayward) in a prison where he is forced to wear an iron mask. It's an enjoyable production of the Dumas adventure story.

Mr. Bannerjee / THE RAINS CAME, 1939, 20th Century-Fox, d-Clarence Brown.
Schildkraut is one of a number of high-class parasites in India during the Raj who come through in high style when the area is devastated by a flood.

Don Francisco / MONSIEUR BEAUCAIRE, 1946, Paramount, d-George Marshall.
Schildkraut is a haughty villain in this Bob Hope vehicle and Hope is a barber to the court of Louis XV in France. Hope is sentenced to the guillotine but is saved to impersonate the French ambassador to Spain. Hope and Schildkraut have a very comical sword duel.

Otto Frank / THE DIARY OF ANNE FRANK, 1959, 20th Century-Fox, d-George Stevens.
Schildkraut gives a most moving performance as the head of a Jewish-Dutch family that hides in an attic for three years before being discovered by the Nazis and sent to a concentration camp. The father is the only survivor.

OTHER ROLES

1922: *Chevalier de Vaudrey* / ORPHANS OF THE STORM. **1924:** *Raymond Valverde* / THE SONG OF LOVE. **1925:** *Kenneth Pauldon* / THE ROAD TO YESTERDAY. **1926:** *Larry O'Neil* / SHIPWRECKED; *King Stefan* / YOUNG APRIL; *Prince Nicholas Alexnon* / MEET THE PRINCE. **1927:** *Paul Kurt* / THE HEART THIEF; *Peter Olsen* / HIS DOG; *Jean La Coste* / THE FORBIDDEN WOMAN. **1928:** *Ludwig* / THE BLUE DANUBE; *Joe Ross* / TENTH AVENUE. **1929:** *Jack Morgan* / THE MISSISSIPPI GAMBLER. **1930:** *Carlos Lopez* / COCK O' THE WALK; *Joe Rooker* / NIGHT RIDE. **1931:** *Tony* / A LADY TO LOVE (German Version); *Count Andreas Scipio* / CARNIVAL. **1934:** *General Pascal* / VIVA VILLA!; *Zukowski* / SISTERS UNDER THE SKIN; *Sandor* / BLUE DANUBE. **1937:** *Danelo* / SLAVE SHIP; *Gaston de Bastonet* / SOULS AT SEA; *Prince Ferdi Zu Schwarzwald* / LANCER SPY; *Michael Andrews* / LADY BEHAVE. **1938:** *Baron Georg Marissey* / THE BARONESS AND THE BUTLER; *Vicomte Rene Latour* / SUEZ. **1939:** *Captain Kirvline* / IDIOT'S DELIGHT; *King Louis XIII* / THE THREE MUSKETEERS; *Hendrik Manderson* / MR. MOTO TAKES A VACATION; *Pierre Delaroch* / LADY OF THE TROPICS; *Hugo Ludwig* / PACK UP YOUR TROUBLES. **1940:** *Ferencz Vadas* / THE SHOP AROUND THE CORNER; *Al Taurez* / PHANTOM RAIDERS; *Lewis Rebstock* / RANGERS OF FORTUNE; *Leon Dumeray* / MEET THE WILDCAT. **1941:** *Bob Deming* / THE PARSON OF PANAMINT; *cameo* / LAND OF LIBERTY. **1945:** *Tito Morrell* / FLAME OF THE BARBARY COAST; *Mr. M* / THE CHEATERS. **1946:** *Peter Marquette* / THE PLAINSMAN AND THE LADY. **1947:** *Count Igor Savin* / NORTHWEST OUTPOST. **1948:** *Luis Savarin* / OLD LOS ANGELES; *Claude Faulkner* / GALLANT LEGION. **1960:** *Abraham Rothstein* / KING OF THE ROARING TWENTIES. **1965:** *Nicodemus* / THE GREATEST STORY EVER TOLD.

SCOTT, GEORGE C.

(1926–)

George Campbell Scott is one of the most powerful actors of the past 30 years. He plays unique characters who are often intense and sometimes angry. Scott made his stage debut in Joseph Papp's Shakespeare Festival's production of "Richard III," his film debut in THE HANGING TREE, and provided the best dramatic work of the TV season of 1963–64 with "East Side, West Side" playing a New York social worker. The program dealt with offbeat subjects in a realistic, gritty way and was doomed to cancellation. Those who saw Scott as Dancer in ANATOMY OF A MURDER recognized that someone wonderful had come to the movies. In the years to follow, Scott lived up to his potential, always professional and showing a disdain for show business. His thoughts on his art include: "The essence of art should be life and change—and that can't be where films are concerned. The film freezes your art forever. No matter how much better you become, there is no way to improve the performance you've done for the camera. It's locked. And there's a certain sad death in that." He received the Best Actor Academy Award for PATTON in 1980 but refused to accept it. He was also nominated for Best Actor for THE HOSPITAL (1972), and for Best Supporting Actor for ANATOMY OF A MURDER (1959) and THE HUSTLER (1961). With his raspy voice, broken nose, and craggy looks, he has given many superior character portrayals of highly individualistic men. He has also shown a talent for comedy and portrayals of sensitive men. He has made a number of appearances in made-for-TV movies and, during 1988, appeared in a comic TV series as the president of the United States.

KEY ROLES

Claude Dancer / ANATOMY OF A MURDER, 1959, Columbia, d-Otto Preminger.
Scott was nominated for an Academy Award for Best Supporting Actor, in only his second picture, for his stunning portrayal of the nasty city prosecuting attorney called to the Upper Peninsula of Michigan to help prosecute Ben Gazzara, an army officer who killed a man who may have raped his flirtatious wife (Lee Remick). Scott's performance is extraordinary.

Bert Gordon / THE HUSTLER, 1961, 20th Century-Fox, d-Richard Rossen.
As good as he was in ANATOMY OF A MURDER, Scott is even more brilliant as a gambler and manipulator of people in this gritty story of a pool hustler (Paul Newman). Scott owns Newman because, as he tells him when he loses all his money to Minnesota Fats

(Jackie Gleason), "Sure, you got drunk. That's the best excuse in the world for losing. No trouble losing when you got a good excuse. And winning! That can be heavy on your back, too. Like a monkey. You drop that load, too, when you got an excuse. All you gotta do is learn to feel sorry for yourself. One of the best indoor sports: feeling sorry for yourself—a sport enjoyed by all, especially the born losers."

Anthony Gethryn / THE LIST OF ADRIAN MESSENGER, 1963, Universal International, d-John Huston.
Versatile Scott portrays a retired British intelligence officer who traps mass murderer Kirk Douglas and saves the life of a youngster who stands in the way of Douglas inheriting a lordship.

Gen. "Buck" Turgidson / DR. STRANGELOVE, 1963, Great Britain, Columbia, d-Stanley Kubrick.
When a mad USAF general launches a nuclear attack on Russia, the chief of staff (Scott) tries to see the positive aspects of the situation in advising President Peter Sellers, "I don't say we wouldn't get our hair mussed, but I do say no more than ten to twenty million people killed." He proves in this film that he's adept at comedy as well as drama.

Mordecai Jones / THE FLIM FLAM MAN, 1967, 20th Century-Fox, d-Irvin Kershner.
Scott is so delightfully charming as an elderly con man and his victims are such deserving sheep to be fleeced that one can't help but root for him to escape from the police who are pursuing him.

Gen. George S. Patton, Jr. / PATTON, 1970, 20th Century-Fox, d-Franklin Schaffner.
Movie historians may very well conclude that this was the best film biography ever made and that Scott was the most successful actor in getting inside the bigger-than-life character being played. From the moment he first appears on the screen Scott is Patton, and that says a lot about a spectacular actor and a lot about a remarkable general. He is masterful as he addresses the unseen movie audience as if they are troops: "Be seated. Now I want you to remember that no bastard ever won a war by dying for his country. He won it by making the other poor dumb bastard die for his country."

Dr. Herbert Bock / THE HOSPITAL, 1972, United Artists, d-Arthur Hiller.
Scott gives another Oscar-nominated performance as a suicidal physician working in an inner city hospital. He has an affair with Diana Rigg, daughter of a crazy killer who uses the hospital's inefficiency to kill several doctors and nurses. Scott has found everything in life a major letdown, particularly his family: "We had a son, 23 years old. I threw him out of the house last year. Pietistic little humbug! He preached universal love, but he despised everyone. He had a blanket contempt for the middle class, even its decency. He detested my mother because she had a petty bourgeois pride in her son, the doctor. I cannot tell you how boorishly he ignored that rather good lady. When she died, he didn't even come to the funeral. He felt the chapel service was a hypocrisy. He told me his generation didn't live with lies. I said, 'Listen: everybody lives with lies.' I-I-I grabbed him by his poncho, and I dragged him the length of our seven-room, despicably affluent, middle-class apartment, and I flung him out. I haven't seen him since."

Dr. Jake Terrell / THE DAY OF THE DOLPHIN, 1973, Avco-Embassy, d-Mike Nichols.
Scott is a marine biologist who discovers that the dolphins he works with in his research are being used in a plot to blow up the yacht of the president of the United States.

Jake Van Dorn / HARDCORE, 1978, Columbia, d-Paul Schrader.
Scott is a religious man from Michigan who travels to the mean streets of Los Angeles in search of his daughter who has disappeared into the world of porno films, prostitution, live sex shows, massage parlors, and murderous perverts.

Gen. Harlan Bache / TAPS, 1981, 20th Century-Fox, d-Harold Becker.
Scott is the distinguished but slightly demented head of a military academy where the cadets go on strike when the school is sold for development. Led by Timothy Hutton, they take over the armory and show what they have learned when the new owners arrive with workers to raze the buildings.

OTHER ROLES

1958: *Dr. George Grubb* / THE HANGING TREE. **1964:** *Paolo Maltese* / THE YELLOW ROLLS-ROYCE. **1966:** *Abraham* / THE BIBLE; *Tank Martin* / NOT WITH MY WIFE YOU DON'T! **1969:** *Archie Bollen* / PETULIA. **1971:** *Justin Playfair* / THEY MIGHT BE GIANTS; *Harry Garmes* / THE LAST RUN. **1972:** *Sergeant Klivinsky* / THE NEW CENTURIONS. **1973:** *Noble "Mase" Mason* / OKLAHOMA CRUDE; *Dan Logan* / RAGE. **1974:** *John* / THE SAVAGE IS LOOSE. **1975:** *Walter Ballantine* / BANK SHOT; *Colonel Ritter* / THE HINDENBERG. **1977:** *Ruffler* / THE PRINCE AND THE PAUPER; *Thomas Hudson* / ISLANDS IN THE STREAM. **1978:** *Gloves Malloy* / *Spats Baxter* / MOVIE MOVIE. **1980:** *John Russell* / THE CHANGELING; *Barney Caine* / THE FORMULA. **1984:** *John Rainbird* / FIRESTARTER

SCOTT, LIZABETH

(Emma Matzo, 1922–)
Alluring, husky-voiced Lizabeth Scott, in the mold of Lauren Bacall and Veronica Lake, experienced modest success during the late 1940s and early 1950s. Initially billed as "The Threat" she never really became one, at least not for the major stars of the time. The sultry blonde usually played tough babes who pretty much got what they deserved. Never married, in 1955 she sued *Confidential* over the magazine's allegations regarding her sexual preferences. Her view of things was: "I'm in love with a wonderful life; a life of living alone." She quit movies shortly thereafter and has rarely been seen professionally since, although she has done off-screen narration for cat food commercials.

KEY ROLES

Ivy Hotchkiss / YOU CAME ALONG, 1945, Paramount, d-John Farrow.
Scott, a woman working for the Treasury Department, is assigned to conduct three GIs on a war bond tour. She falls in love with one whom she later learns is dying of leukemia. They marry anyway.

Toni Marachek / THE STRANGE LOVE OF MARTHA IVERS, 1946, Paramount, d-Lewis Milestone.
Scott is the woman that Kirk Douglas, an alcoholic district attorney, digs up to divert Van Heflin from his wife (Barbara Stanwyck). Heflin knows Stanwyck killed her autocratic aunt when still a teenager but both of them kept quiet about the matter, allowing an innocent man to be hanged for the crime. Scott is an

ex-convict but Heflin finds her hands cleaner than Stanwyck's.

Coral Chandler / DEAD RECKONING, 1947, Columbia, d-John Cromwell.
Humphrey Bogart and William Prince are two paratroopers on their way to Washington to be decorated. Along the way Prince disappears and Bogie sets out to find him. What he finds is Scott, the woman whose husband Prince supposedly killed. Actually she did the killing and in the end she gets her comeuppance, dying of injuries from a car crash.

Jane Palmer / TOO LATE FOR TEARS, 1949, United Artists, d-Bryon Haskin.
Scott is a lady Bluebeard who disposes of her husbands and a conspiring boyfriend. In the end this money-hungry conscienceless seductress slips from a balcony to her death, with her ill-gotten money falling like leaves around her.

Brady Kirby / TWO OF A KIND, 1951, Columbia, d-Henry Levin.
Scott is a glamorous woman who picks up Edmond O'Brien and gets him involved in an elaborate scheme to defraud an elderly couple by posing as their long-missing son.

OTHER ROLES

1947: *Paula Haller* / DESERT FURY; *Kay Lawrence* / I WALK ALONE; *guest* / VARIETY GIRL. **1948:** *Mona Stevens* / PITFALL. **1949:** *Liza Wilson* / EASY LIVING. **1950:** *Jane Langley* / PAID IN FULL; *Fran* / DARK CITY. **1951:** *Irene Hayes* / THE RACKET; *Joan* / THE COMPANY SHE KEEPS; *Chris* / RED MOUNTAIN. **1952:** *Alice Brent* / *Lilly* / A STOLEN FACE. **1953:** *Mary Carroll* / SCARED STIFF. **1954:** *Helen Curtis* / BAD FOR EACH OTHER; *Rose Evans* / SILVER LODE. **1957:** *Glenda Markle* / LOVING YOU; *Elsa Jenner* / THE WEAPON. **1972:** *Princess Betty Cippola* / PULP.

SCOTT, RANDOLPH

(George Randolph Scott, 1903–1987)
Known as the "Gentleman from Virginia," Randolph Scott is best remembered for his western roles in which he played men of solid integrity. Most notable was the so-called "Ranown" Cycle, a series of seven films directed by Budd Boetticher in which Scott played grim, resolute, aging cowboys. These began with SEVEN MEN FROM NOW in 1956 and ended with COMANCHE STATION in 1960. Scott's 35-year film career began in 1929 with THE FAR CALL. Early in his career he acted mostly in light romances and Paramount musicals. After World War II he became the western genre's noblest representative and, through wise investments, he became one of the industry's most wealthy men. He called it a career in 1962 with RIDE THE HIGH COUNTRY, a wonderful western in which he plays another highly moral, chivalrous man pursuing the simple-minded course of what he thinks is right.

KEY ROLES

John Kent / ROBERTA, 1935, RKO, d-William A. Seiter.
Some may forget that Irene Dunne was the main star of this musical and that her love affair with Scott was supposed to carry the romance, but with Astaire and Rogers in the show, Dunne and Scott didn't seem very important. To tell the truth, Scott was pretty wooden in the role of a man who inherits a Parisian fashion house run by Dunne.

Leo Vincey / SHE, 1935, RKO, d-Irving Pichel.
In H. Rider Haggard's classic fantasy about eternal youth, Scott limply plays a Cambridge professor who leads a team to a lost city ruled over by "She Who Must Be Obeyed," who cannot die until she falls in love. Guess who is one woman's poison.

Hawkeye / THE LAST OF THE MOHICANS, 1936, United Artists, d-George B. Seitz.
Scott is a solid and stolid frontier scout at the time of America's French and Indian War. He travels with Chingachgook and the latter's son Uncas, the last of the Mohicans, and they must deal with the stupidity of British officer Henry Wilcoxon, the treachery of Huron Bruce Cabot, and the beauty of Binnie Barnes and Heather Angel.

Anthony Kent / REBECCA OF SUNNYBROOK FARM, 1938, 20th Century-Fox, d-Allan Dwan.
Scott joins a long line of actors and actresses upstaged by cute little moppet Shirley Temple in this story of a Pollyanna-like singer whose dour aunt forbids her to have anything to do with show business people. But neighbor Scott just happens to be a talent scout for a radio show.

Vance Irby / VIRGINIA CITY, 1940, Warners, d-Michael Curtiz.
Southerner Scott tries to get a shipment of gold from Virginia City to the Confederacy for its war effort. He is aided by a dance hall girl (Miriam Hopkins) and a southern spy, and is thwarted by Errol Flynn, a damn Yankee.

Stephen Burkett / MY FAVORITE WIFE, 1940, RKO, d-Garson Kanin.
Just after having wife Irene Dunne declared legally dead and marrying Gail Patrick, Cary Grant is shocked to learn that Dunne and Scott have been rescued from a deserted island on which they have been shipwrecked for seven years. Besides trying to figure out who he is legally married to, Grant is suspicious of what went on back at the island between Scott and Dunne.

Sam Starr / WESTERN UNION, 1941, 20th Century-Fox, d-Fritz Lang.
Scott is chief scout for the telegraph company whose cables crooked politicians don't want laid. Things are complicated for him as his brother leads the gang hired to hamper the work.

Alexander McNamara / THE SPOILERS, 1942, Universal, d-Ray Enright.
In a rare villainous role, Scott and a phony judge steal mining claims from prospectors in the Yukon. He also has differences with John Wayne over saloon singer Marlene Dietrich and Scott and the Duke have one terrific fight at the climax.

Lieutenant Commander MacLain / CORVETTE K-225, 1943, Universal, d-Richard Rosson.
In this documentary-like film, Scott is a Canadian commander of the title ship who, while making an Atlantic crossing from Halifax to Britain, is attacked by both German subs and planes.

Colonel Thorwald / GUNG HO! 1943, Universal, d-Ray Enright.
In this story of the real-life Makin Island raid on August 17, 1942, Scott is the leader of 200 men who take back the island from the Japs. It's an effective propaganda piece that is still exciting today.

Steve Farrell / COLT .45, 1950, Warners, d-Edwin L. Marin.

A pair of Colt .45s, a new kind of gun, fall into the wrong hands—namely those of villain Zachary Scott—and the good Scott, Randolph, has to recover them.

Maj. Callicut / THE MAN BEHIND THE GUN, 1952, Warners, d-Felix Feist.

Scott, of course, is the man behind the gun who, while pretending to be a quiet schoolteacher, is in fact a U.S. cavalry officer out to put down a rebellion. He ends up helping to found Los Angeles.

Ben Stride / SEVEN MEN FROM NOW, 1956, Warners, d-Budd Boetticher.

In this better-than-average western, Scott is an ex-sheriff who exacts revenge from seven varmints responsible for his wife's death.

Gil Westrum / RIDE THE HIGH COUNTRY, 1962, MGM, d-Sam Peckinpah.

This film is both a loving tribute to the western genre and to two of its best proponents, Scott and Joel McCrea. These two aging ex-lawmen help transport gold from a mining camp to the bank, and rescue a woman from the tough miners. McCrea has ideas of how he could use the money, but Scott's integrity won't stand for any of that, even from a dear old friend.

OTHER ROLES

1928: *extra* / SHARPSHOOTER. **1929:** *extra* / DYNAMITE; *Helms* / THE FAR CALL; *rider* / THE VIRGINIAN; *bit* / THE BLACK WATCH. **1931:** *Steve Bradley* / WOMEN MEN MARRY. **1932:** *bit* / SKY BRIDE; *Larry* / A SUCCESSFUL CALAMITY; *Fadden* / HOT SATURDAY. **1933:** *bit* / ISLAND OF LOST SOULS; *Chane Weymer* / WILD HORSE MESA; *Hunt Blake* / HELLO, EVERYBODY; *Dr. Woodford* / MURDERS IN THE ZOO; *Jack Hare* / HERITAGE OF THE DESERT; *Grant Wilson* / SUPERNATURAL; *Jack Rock* / SUNSET PASS; *Randolph Morgan* / COCKTAIL HOUR; *Brett Dale* / MAN OF THE FOREST; *Lynn Hayden* / TO THE LAST MAN; *Dr. Robert Morley* / BROKEN DREAMS; *Tom Doan* / THE THUNDERING HERD. **1934:** *Jim Cleve* / LAST ROUND-UP; *Clint Belmet* / WAGON WHEELS. **1935:** *Larry Sutton* / ROCKY MOUNTAIN MYSTERY; *Tom Hartfield* / HOME ON THE RANGE; *Slaughter Somerville* / VILLAGE TALE; *Duncan Bedford* / SO RED THE ROSE. **1936:** *Bilge Smith* / FOLLOW THE FLEET; *Lt. James Knox* / AND SUDDEN DEATH; *Bud Norton* / GO WEST, YOUNG MAN. **1937:** *Peter Cortlandt* / HIGH, WIDE AND HANDSOME. **1938:** *Steve Fortness* / ROAD TO RENO; *Kirk Jordan* / THE TEXANS. **1939:** *Will Wright* / JESSE JAMES; *Insp. Angus "Monty" Montague* / SUSANNAH OF THE MOUNTIES; *Speed Bradshaw* / COAST GUARD; *Wyatt Earp* / FRONTIER MARSHAL; *Brad Reynolds* / 20,000 MEN A YEAR. **1940:** *Tom Jackson* / WHEN THE DALTONS RODE. **1941:** *Vance Shaw* / BELLE STARR; *Nick* / PARIS CALLING; *cameo* / LAND OF LIBERTY. **1942:** *Sgt. Dixie Smith* / TO THE SHORES OF TRIPOLI; *Cash Evans* / PITTSBURGH. **1943:** *Steve Upton* / THE DESPERADOES; *Capt. Buck Oliver* / BOMBARDIER. **1944:** *Honest John Calhoun* / BELLE OF THE YUKON; *guest* / FOLLOW THE BOYS. **1945:** *Dr. Gay Thompson* / CHINA SKY; *Adam Mercy* / CAPTAIN KIDD. **1946:** *Dan Mitchell* / ABILENE TOWN; *Mark Rowley* / BADMAN'S TERRITORY; *Bill Smith* / HOME, SWEET HOMICIDE. **1947:** *Bat Masterson* / TRAIL STREET; *Brazos Kane* / GUNFIGHTERS; *Jonathan* / CHRISTMAS EVE. **1948:** *Cole Armin* / ALBUQUERQUE; *Vance* / RETURN OF THE BADMEN; *Chris Denning* / CORONER CREEK. **1949:** *Tom Andrews* / CANADIAN PACIFIC; *Jim Carey* / THE WALKING HILLS; *Bill Doolin* / THE DOOLINS OF OKLAHOMA; *Jim Dancer* / FIGHTING MAN OF THE PLAINS. **1950:** *Andrew Barclay* / THE NEVADAN; *Jim Red Pern* / CARIBOO TRAIL. **1951:** *Jackson "Sugarfoot" Redan* / SUGARFOOT; *guest* / STARLIFT; *Britt Canfield* / SANTA FE; *Ned Britt* / FORT WORTH; *Owen Merritt* / MAN IN THE SADDLE. **1952:** *Silent Jeff* / CARSON CITY; *Matt Stewart* / HANGMAN'S KNOT. **1953:** *Jeff Travis* / THE STRANGER WORE A GUN; *Capt. David Porter* / THUNDER OVER THE PLAINS. **1954:** *Larry Delong* / RIDING SHOTGUN; *Jim Kipp* / THE BOUNTY HUNTER; *James Barlow* / RAGE AT DAWN. **1955:** *John Stewart* / TEN WANTED MEN; *Larry Madden* / TALL MAN RIDING; *Calem Ware* / A LAWLESS STREET. **1956:** *Capt. Tom Benson* / SEVENTH CAVALRY. **1957:** *Pat Brennan* / THE TALL T; *Cap Devlin* / SHOOT-OUT AT MEDICINE BEND; *Bart Allison* / DECISION AT SUNDOWN. **1958:** *Buchanan* / BUCHANAN RIDES ALONE; *John Hayes* / WESTBOUND. **1960:** *Jefferson Cody* / COMANCHE STATION.

SCOTT, ZACHARY

(1914–1965)

Texas-born Zachary Scott performed in repertory in England in his late teens. In 1943 he was signed by Warner Brothers and the next year made a sensational debut in THE MASK OF DIMITRIOS. After that, and for the better part of his career, the role as someone who could not be trusted was his stock in trade. He was the lecherous heel or a smooth scoundrel who always seemed to be avoiding the eyes of others. One notable exception to this casting was his role in THE SOUTHERNER as a most sympathetic farmer down on his luck. By the 1950s Scott's career was in sharp decline, and although he continued to make movies, none were memorable.

KEY ROLES

Dimitrios Makropoulous / THE MASK OF DIMITRIOS, 1944, Warners, d-Jean Negulesco.

Scott is a mysterious scoundrel whose exploits are traced by timid Dutch novelist Peter Lorre. The film, interrupted frequently with flashbacks to Scott, is more talk than action, but the work of Scott in his debut and that of Lorre and Sidney Greenstreet make this an enjoyable and interesting movie. Scott continually demonstrates the truth of his belief: "Ingenuity is never a substitute for intelligence."

Sam Tucker / THE SOUTHERNER, 1945, United Artists, d-Jean Renoir.

In probably his best role, Scott plays against the type that came to be associated with him. Here he appears as a hired hand who is tired of working for others. He finds a patch of wasteland, puts up a shack, and with his wife (Betty Field), old mother, and young son, tries to make a farm of the property. If it weren't for bad luck, he'd have no luck at all, as he puts up with the poor land, the weather, and a malicious neighbor. But hopefully he gives thanks to God: "Much obliged, Lord. Looks like the Tuckers are going to make it after all. Amen."

Monte Beragon / MILDRED PIERCE, 1945, Warners, d-Michael Curtiz.

In one of the best movie soap operas of all times, Scott is seen shot dead in the opening of the film. In the next hundred minutes, we find out why and by whom. He's a socialite with no money and no ambition who marries hard-working Joan Crawford, lives off her earnings from her various restaurants, and with Crawford's ungrateful daughter (Ann Blyth) looks down on Crawford's way of earning the money that is so lavished on them both.

Stephen Purcell / STALLION ROAD, 1947, Warners, d-James Kern.

Scott replaced Humphrey Bogart in the cast of this film a week before shooting started. He's part of a romantic triangle that includes veterinarian Ronald Reagan and lady horse breeder Alexis Smith. Bogie was smart to have nothing to do with this loser.

Horace Verdig / RUTHLESS, 1948, Eagle Lion, d-Edgar G. Ulmer.

Charming conniver Scott ruins several lives as he claws his way to where he wants to be. He's so good being so bad; he was just made to play heels.

Larry Pearce / ONE LAST FLING, 1949, Warners, d-Peter Godfrey.

Scott tries his hand at comedy in this story of a man whose wife (Alexis Smith), bored with being a housewife, returns to the job she had in her husband's music store. Things go badly when a former WAC girlfriend of Scott's shows up. Scott isn't a very funny cad.

Fielding Carlisle / FLAMINGO ROAD, 1949, Warners, d-Michael Curtiz.

Scott is a weak heel, under the thumb of small-town political boss Sidney Greenstreet, whose plans for his protege do not include carny girl Joan Crawford. Scott gets nothing for all his troubles in this one.

OTHER ROLES

1944: *guest* / HOLLYWOOD CANTEEN. **1945:** *Ronnie Mason* / *Marsh* / DANGER SIGNAL. **1946:** *Steve Maddux* / HER KIND OF MAN. **1947:** *Bob Hunter* / THE UNFAITHFUL; *Brad Criley* / CASS TIMBERLANE. **1948:** *Rex Durant* / WHIPLASH. **1949:** *Walter Colby* / FLAXY MARTIN; *Jason Brett* / COLT .45; *Charlie Burns* / SOUTH OF ST. LOUIS. **1950:** *Max Thursday* / GUILTY BYSTANDER; *David I. Starring* / SHADOW ON THE WALL; *Barry Holmes* / PRETTY BABY; *Curtis* / BORN TO BE BAD. **1951:** *Harvey Turner* / LIGHTNING STRIKES TWICE; *Greer* / THE SECRET OF CONVICT LAKE. **1952:** *Van* / WINGS OF DANGER; *Don Miguel Navarro* / STRONGHOLD. **1953:** *Harry Sheppard* / APPOINTMENT IN HONDURAS. **1955:** *Haney* / TREASURE OF RUBY HILLS; *Reb* / SHOTGUN; *Wade Evans* / FLAME OF THE ISLANDS. **1956:** *Kennedy* / BANDIDO. **1957:** *Max Brandt* / COUNTERFEIT PLAN; *John Sullivan* / MAN IN THE SHADOW. **1960:** *John A. Morrow* / NATCHEZ TRACE. **1961:** *Miller, game warden* / THE YOUNG ONE. **1962:** *Gregory De Witt* / IT'S ONLY MONEY.

SEGAL, GEORGE

(1934–)

Personable George Segal, with boyish charm, has had success both in dramatic roles and marital comedies. He is a natural playing neurotic but likable men who invite sympathy. An accomplished jazz musician, Segal broke into show business in New York clubs and the off-Broadway stage before landing TV work that led to his first film, THE YOUNG DOCTORS, in 1961. In the beginning he played arrogant characters but switched to comedies in the 1970s. In 1966 he was nominated for a Best Supporting Actor Oscar for WHO'S AFRAID OF VIRGINIA WOOLF? Segal's naturalistic acting style makes his potential losers rather charming. In the 1980s he has appeared in several made-for-TV movies including TRACKDOWN: FINDING THE GOODBAR KILLER (1983), ZANY ADVENTURES OF ROBIN HOOD (1984), and NOT MY KID (1985).

KEY ROLES

David / SHIP OF FOOLS, 1965, Columbia, d-Stanley Kramer.

Segal and Elizabeth Ashley play a married American couple on a German ocean liner bound for Bremerhaven from Vera Cruz in 1933. They quarrel because Segal, a painter, is unhappy living on her earnings.

Corporal King / KING RAT, 1965, Columbia, d-Bryan Forbes.

Segal is an opportunistic head of a black market operation in a Japanese POW camp on Singapore during World War II. He maintains his strength by raising rats which he sells to fellow prisoners as food.

Nick / WHO'S AFRAID OF VIRGINIA WOOLF? 1966, Warners, d-Mike Nichols.

Segal and his wife (Sandy Dennis) are new to the college where he teaches. They are invited to stop by the home of Richard Burton and Elizabeth Taylor; he's another professor and she's the daughter of the president of the college. The four spend the evening drinking and displaying all of their emotional warts. Segal was nominated for an Oscar.

Felix Sherman / THE OWL AND THE PUSSYCAT, 1970, Columbia, d-Herbert Ross.

Aspiring author and bookstore clerk Segal complains that neighbor Barbra Streisand is a prostitute (which she is) and gets her evicted. Then she invades his apartment and gets him evicted as well. Slowly but surely love develops between the two improbable characters.

Blume / BLUME IN LOVE, 1973, Warners, d-Paul Mazursky.

In this excellent comedy, Segal's wife (Susan Anspach) catches him in bed with his secretary and divorces him. Both seek psychiatric help and he goes through a period of recreational sex before he wins his wife back from Kris Kristofferson.

Steve Blackburn / A TOUCH OF CLASS, 1973, Great Britain, Avco Embassy, d-Melvin Frank.

Married American Segal living in London meets and falls in love with a divorced Englishwoman (Glenda Jackson). They take off for Spain, then continue their affair back in London, with Segal running back and forth between his wife and mistress.

Charlie Malloy / THE DUCHESS AND THE DIRTWATER FOX, 1976, 20th Century-Fox, d-Melvin Frank.

Segal is a gambler in the Old West who teams up with dance hall girl Goldie Hawn. It's a wild and woolly spoof that isn't as good as it is vulgar. Look for the sequence where Segal and Hawn pose as guests at a Jewish wedding.

Jeff Thompson / THE LAST MARRIED COUPLE IN AMERICA, 1980, Universal, d-Gilbert Cates.

Every Sunday Segal, his wife Natalie Wood, and their married friends get together for some touch football. The fun ends as one by one the couples break up and divorce until finally it's just Segal and Wood. He blows it when he can't resist an offer of sex with Valerie Harper and picks up a social disease that he passes on to his wife. This would seem to be the end for them but, after refusing to participate in a swinger's party in their house, they get back together.

OTHER ROLES

1961: *Dr. Howard* / THE YOUNG DOCTORS. **1962:** *1st commando up the cliff* / THE LONGEST DAY; *Lester Sweyd* / ACT ONE. **1964:** *Dr. Tony Parelli* / THE NEW INTERNS; *Matt Weaver* / INVITATION TO A GUNFIGHTER. **1965:** *Lt. Mahidi* / LOST COMMAND. **1966:** *Quiller* / THE QUILLER MEMORANDUM. **1967:** *Peter Gusenberg* / THE ST. VALENTINE'S DAY MASSACRE. **1968:** *Monroe Rieff* / BYE BYE BRAVERMAN; *Morris Brummel* / NO WAY TO TREAT A LADY. **1969:** *Dan Rockland* / THE SOUTHERN STAR; *Franco* / THE GIRL WHO COULDN'T SAY NO. **1970:** *Lt. Phil Hartman* / LOVING; *Gordon Hocheiser* / WHERE'S POPPA? **1972:** *Jay Jay* / BORN TO WIN; *Kelp* / THE HOT ROCK. **1974:** *Harry Benson* / THE TERMINAL MAN. **1975:** *Bill Denny* / CALIFORNIA SPLIT; *Sam Spade, Jr.* / THE BLACK BIRD. **1976:** *Col. Timothy Shaver* / RUSSIAN ROULETTE; **1977:** *Harry Calder* / ROLLERCOASTER; *Dick Harper* / FUN WITH DICK AND JANE. **1978:** *Robby* / WHO IS KILLING THE GREAT CHEFS OF EUROPE? **1979:** *Adam* / LOST AND FOUND. **1981:** *Walter Whitney* / CARBON COPY. **1985:** *Barry* / STICK.

SELLERS, PETER

(1925–1980)

Even Peter Sellers lost track of who he really was after playing so many exaggerated characters in a series of comedies, some of which were blessed with genius. Sellers got his start in show business as a child actor in a revue at age five. After serving in the Royal Air Force during World War II, he became entertainment director of a holiday camp, then a vaudeville comedian. He made his film debut in PENNY POINTS TO PARADISE in 1951. With the radio program "The Goon Show," his career began to accelerate; with I'M ALL RIGHT, JACK in 1959, he enjoyed wide popularity; with THE PINK PANTHER and his bungling Inspector Clouseau, he became an international star. He was nominated for an Oscar for his trio of roles in DR. STRANGELOVE and his simple-minded, misunderstood gardener in BEING THERE. Sellers was a moody perfectionist, a difficult man to work with, but his extraordinary talent for mimicry and his skill as a character actor served him well in a career filled with often outstanding comic performances. His numerous near-fatal heart attacks did not slow down the high living and over-work that finally took his life.

KEY ROLES

Percy Quill / THE SMALLEST SHOW ON EARTH, 1957, Great Britain, British Lion, d-Basil Dearden.

Sellers is the drunken projectionist at the fleabitten movie house inherited by Bill Travers and Virginia McKenna. Much fun is made from a small plot about a larger theater trying to buy the owners out and sabotaging the operation when their offer is rejected.

Sonny MacGregor / THE NAKED TRUTH, 1958, Great Britain, Rank, d-Mario Zampi.

In this black comedy, Sellers bands together with an entertainer, a novelist, and a peer after each has unsuccessfully attempted to kill the publisher of a scandal rag who threatens to expose their private lives.

Tully Bascombe / Grand Duchess Gloriana XII / Prime Minister Count Mountjoy / THE MOUSE THAT ROARED, 1959, Great Britain, Columbia, d-Jack Arnold.

Prime Minister Sellers advises the ruler of a bankrupt duchy (also played by Sellers) to invade America, lose, and be bailed out of financial difficulties by the United States. Sellers sends bowman Sellers (a third character) and a few stouthearted men on the invasion—and horrors, they win.

Fred Kite / I'M ALL RIGHT, JACK, 1959, Great Britain, British Lion, d-John Boulting.

In one of his best roles, Sellers appears as a shop steward who takes Ian Carmichael in as a roomer. The latter, aspiring to a career in industry, blunders so much that he causes a major confrontation between labor and management. Class-conscious Sellers has very set ideas about the amount and quality of work to be performed by members of his union, with of course no concern about the product being any good. The management team is equally uninterested in serving the needs of their consumers.

John Lewis / ONLY TWO CAN PLAY, 1962, Great Britain, British Lion, d-Sidney Gilliat.

Sellers works as a librarian in a Welsh town. Bored with his lowly position, his family, his small apartment, and his social life, he imagines affairs with beautiful women. Then one day Mai Zetterling comes along and is willing to make his dreams come true.

Claire Quilty / LOLITA, 1962, MGM, d-Stanley Kubrick.

James Mason has a fixation for pre-teen girls. He seeks out and shoots Sellers, who shares the fetish, when the latter steals away the girl of Mason's dreams (Sue Lyon).

Gen. Leo Fitzjohn / THE WALTZ OF THE TOREADORS, 1962, Great Britain, Continental, d-John Guillermin.

Sellers, a recently retired general, lives in an English manor house with his whining, bedridden wife. His only pleasure is the mistress of his mind (Dany Robin) with whom he fell in love 17 years earlier and, though they have never consummated their love, she has remained faithful to him. Unfortunately for Sellers his aide achieves in two days what Sellers could not accomplish in 17 years.

Pearly Gates / THE WRONG ARM OF THE LAW, 1963, Great Britain, Continental, d-Cliff Owen.

Sellers is the head of a London syndicate of thieves that uses a Bond Street dress salon as a front for its criminal activities. When Sellers is robbed by three Australians posing as policemen, a crime truce is called by all the gangs in the city so they can work cooperatively together to capture the foreigners.

Insp. Jacques Clouseau / THE PINK PANTHER, 1963, United Artists, d-Blake Edwards.

The Pink Panther is a priceless jewel belonging to a princess. David Niven, alias The Phantom, plans to steal the gem. Sellers has been chasing The Phantom for 15 years, never discovering that his own wife is Niven's lover and accomplice. All of these characters and others besides come together at a ski lodge for the very rich for some very comical shenanigans. The film started Sellers on a series that was unfortunately carried on even after he was dead.

Group Capt. Lionel Mandrake / Pres. Muffley / Dr. Strangelove / DR. STRANGELOVE OR: HOW I LEARNED TO STOP WORRYING AND LOVE THE BOMB, 1964, Great Britain, Columbia, d-Stanley Kubrick.

Sellers's three roles are a British adjutant to an Air Force general who unleashes a nuclear attack on Russia; the president of the United States who must attempt to explain this little boo-boo to the Soviet leader; and ex-Nazi scientist Dr. Strangelove, now an adviser to the president. The scientist figures that the top people in the government and a ten-to-one ratio of the most beautiful women could live comfortably in existing underground locations while the effects of the Soviet's doomsday machine wore off in a hundred years or so.

Henry Orient / THE WORLD OF HENRY ORIENT, 1964, United Artists, d-George Roy Hill.

Sellers plays a concert pianist whose plans for an affair with married Paula Prentiss are constantly foiled by two 14-year-old schoolgirls who are his fans.

Harold Fine / I LOVE YOU, ALICE B. TOKLAS, 1968, Warners, d-Hy Averback.

Sellers, an asthmatic Jewish attorney, is being pushed by his longtime fiancée to get married but he instead joins the flower people. It looks like the screenwriter was a little high when composing this strange story.

Sidney Wang / MURDER BY DEATH, 1976, Columbia, d-Robert Moore.

Sellers appears as a Charlie Chan-like detective who, along with an assortment of other fictional detectives, is invited to stay at the home of a wealthy recluse and solve his murder.

Chance the Gardener (Chauncy Gardner) / BEING THERE, 1979, Lorimar, d-Hal Ashby.

Illiterate gardener Sellers is taken for a philosopher and man of deep insight by wealthy kingmaker Melvyn Douglas and his young wife Shirley MacLaine. When Douglas dies, his influential pallbearers consider dumping Jack Warden as president and backing Sellers for the job.

OTHER ROLES

1951: *himself* / LONDON ENTERTAINS; *Groucho / Guiseppe / Cedric / Izzy / Gozzunk / Crystal Jollibottom* / LET'S GO CRAZY; *major / Arnold Fringe* / PENNY POINTS TO PARADISE. **1952:** *Major Bloodnock* / DOWN AMONG THE Z MEN. **1954:** *Private Goffin* / ORDERS ARE ORDERS. **1955:** *P. C. Diamond* / JOHN AND JULIE; *Harry* / THE LADYKILLERS. **1957:** *Hector Dimwiddle* / INSOMNIA IS GOOD FOR YOU. **1958:** *Tony* / TOM THUMB; *Chief Petty Officer Doherty* / UP THE CREEK; *prime minister* / CARLTON-BROWNE OF THE F.O. **1960:** *Mr. Martin* / THE BATTLE OF THE SEXES; *Dodger Lane* / TWO-WAY STRETCH. **1961:** *Lionel Meadows* / NEVER LET GO; *Dr. Ahmed el Kabir / Parega* / THE MILLIONAIRESS; *Auguste Topaze* / MR. TOPAZE; *cameo* / THE ROAD TO HONG KONG. **1963:** *Morgenhall / doctor* / THE DOCK BRIEF; *Rev. John Aspinall* / HEAVENS ABOVE. **1964:** *Insp. Jacques Clouseau* / A SHOT IN THE DARK. **1965:** *Fritz Fassbender* / WHAT'S NEW, PUSSYCAT? **1966:** *Dr. Pratt* / THE WRONG BOX; *Aldo Vanucci* / AFTER THE FOX. **1967:** *Evelyn Tremble* / CASINO ROYALE; *Juan Bautista* / THE BOBO; *Jean* / WOMAN TIMES SEVEN. **1968:** *Hrundi V. Bakshi* / THE PARTY. **1969:** *Sir Guy Grand* / THE MAGIC CHRISTIAN. **1970:** *Benjamin Hoffman* / HOFFMAN; *Robert Danvers* / THERE'S A GIRL IN MY SOUP. **1972:** *Albert T. Hopfnagel* / WHERE DOES IT HURT?; *the March Hare* / ALICE'S ADVENTURES IN WONDERLAND; *Sam* / THE OPTIMISTS OF NINE ELMS. **1973:** *Governor Latour / Maj. Robinson / Schroeder / Hitler / Prince Kyoto* / SOFT BEDS AND HARD BATTLES. **1974:** *Rouquet* / THE BLOCKHOUSE; *Queen Victoria* / THE GREAT MCGONAGALL. **1975:** *Insp. Clouseau* / THE RETURN OF THE PINK PANTHER. **1977:** *Insp. Clouseau* / THE PINK PANTHER STRIKES AGAIN. **1978:** *Insp. Clouseau* / REVENGE OF THE PINK PANTHER. **1979:** *Prince Rudolph / Syd Frewin* / THE PRISONER OF ZENDA; *Dr. Fu Manchu / Nayland Smith* / THE FIENDISH PLOT OF DR. FU MANCHU. **1982:** *Insp. Clouseau* / TRAIL OF THE PINK PANTHER.

SHAW, ROBERT

(1927–1978)

Robert Shaw studied at the Royal Academy of Dramatic Arts, then spent seven years in small roles at Stratford and the Old Vic. He made his first movie appearance in THE DAM BUSTERS in 1955, then made a name for himself in the British TV series "The Buccaneers." He spent a memorable career as a character actor and villain. Only late in his too-short life did this father of ten children from three wives have a few leads in U.S. movies. He was nominated for an Academy Award for A MAN FOR ALL SEASONS. He also wrote novels including *The Man in the Glass Booth* which was adapted for the stage and made into a movie. Talented, often troubled, Shaw died young of a heart attack.

KEY ROLES

Red Grant / FROM RUSSIA WITH LOVE, 1963, Great Britain, United Artists, d-Terence Young.

In what may be the best of the James Bond movies, Shaw is truly wonderful as an assassin working for a world crime organization whose target is none other than 007. Shaw almost succeeds, but Sean Connery as Bond sees through his cover just in time.

Ginger Coffey / THE LUCK OF GINGER COFFEY, 1964, Canada, Crawley, d-Irvin Kershner.

In this character study, Shaw nicely handles the role of a blarney-spouting Irish worker in Canada who finds it difficult to keep a job and take care of his family.

King Henry VIII / A MAN FOR ALL SEASONS, 1966, Great Britain, Columbia, d-Fred Zinnemann.

Shaw was nominated for an Oscar for his lusty portrayal of the king who deeply regrets the lost friendship and counsel of Thomas More when the two split over the king's decision to break with the Catholic Church so he can divorce his queen and marry Anne Boleyn. Nevertheless he sends More to the executioner's block.

George Armstrong Custer / CUSTER OF THE WEST, 1967, Cinerama, d-Robert Siodmak.

Shaw is credible portraying the arrogant, glory-seeking cavalry officer who leads his command to disaster at Little Big Horn. But he's out-acted by Robert Ryan in a small part.

Doyle Lonnegan / THE STING, 1973, Universal, d-George Roy Hill.

Shaw is hateful as a brutal big-time mobster who becomes the object of a big-time sting led by con men Paul Newman and Robert Redford. It's their way of taking revenge on Shaw for ordering the death of a fellow con artist.

Blue / THE TAKING OF PELHAM ONE TWO THREE, 1974, United Artists, d-Joseph Sargent.

Shaw is the cold-blooded leader of a gang of four desperate men who seize a New York subway car and hold its passengers hostage for a million dollars ransom. When the plan goes awry, Shaw commits suicide by touching the third rail and electrocuting himself.

Quint / JAWS, 1975, Universal, d-Steven Spielberg.

Shaw portrays a grizzled shark hunter who demands a large payment to locate and destroy the killer shark that is terrorizing an East Coast resort area. He's killed by his prey in the process.

Romer Treece / THE DEEP, 1977, Columbia, d-Peter Yates.

In this somewhat disappointing deep-sea story, Shaw, an experienced explorer of sea treasures, is sought out by Nick Nolte and Jacqueline Bisset who know the whereabouts of a rather modern sunken treasure also sought by criminal boss Lou Gossett.

OTHER ROLES

1955: *Sgt. Pulford* / THE DAM BUSTERS. **1956:** *Cpl. Hodge* / A HILL IN KOREA. **1959:** *Gorman* / SEA FURY. **1962:** *Lt. Field* / THE VALIANT. **1963:** *Marlow* / TOMORROW AT TEN; *Aston* / THE CARETAKER. **1965:** *Col. Hessler* / BATTLE OF THE BULGE. **1969:** *Squadron Leader Skipper* / BATTLE OF BRITAIN; *Francisco Pizarro* / THE ROYAL HUNT OF THE SUN. **1970:** *Stanley Weber* / THE BIRTHDAY PARTY. **1971:** *MacConnachie* / FIGURES IN A LANDSCAPE; *the priest* / A TOWN CALLED HELL; *Michael* / A REFLECTION OF FEAR. **1972:** *Lord Randolph Churchill* / YOUNG WINSTON. **1973:** *Leadbetter* / THE HIRELING. **1975:** *Richard Gastmann* / DER RICHTER UND SEIN HENKER. **1976:** *Sheriff of Nottingham* / ROBIN AND MARIAN; *Ned Lynch* / SWASHBUCKLER; *Charles / Earl Hodgson* / DIAMONDS. **1977:** *Kabalov* / BLACK SUNDAY. **1978:** *Mallory* / FORCE 10 FROM NAVARONE. **1979:** *Marenkov* / AVALANCHE EXPRESS.

SHEARER, NORMA

(Edith Norma Shearer, 1900–1983)

With the coming of sound and having played intelligent ingenues in silents, Norma Shearer moved into what became the typical Norma Shearer role: an emancipated woman, disillusioned by love or marriage, ambitious, poised, elegant, and a clotheshorse. Lovely Shearer was not a great actress but, married to producer Irving Thalberg, she was treated like she was, winning the Best Actress Award for THE DIVORCEE and nominated for THEIR OWN DESIRE, A FREE SOUL, THE BARRETTS OF WIMPOLE STREET, ROMEO AND JULIET, and MARIE ANTOINETTE. As Joan Crawford put it: "How can I compete with Norma when she sleeps with the boss?" Shearer's patrician profile, distinctive coiffure, and a wardrobe of gowns by Adrian made her the perfect sophisticated woman for a series of dramas about adultery. A hard-working actress who once was described by Lillian Hellman as having a face "unclouded by thought," Shearer retired after only a few movies in the 1940s.

KEY ROLES

Consuelo / HE WHO GETS SLAPPED, 1924, Silent, MGM, d-Victor Seastrom.

Shearer is a bareback rider with a circus who laughs when clown Lon Chaney confesses his love for her. But Chaney saves her from an arranged marriage to the man who stole both Chaney's invention and wife, allowing her to marry the man of her choice.

Ruth Lawrence / HIS SECRETARY, 1925, Silent, MGM, d-Hobart Henley.

Shearer, a plain girl, overhears the handsome junior partner she loves say he wouldn't kiss her for a thousand dollars. She goes to a beauty parlor and transforms herself into a knockout and ultimately gets her man.

Mary Dugan / THE TRIAL OF MARY DUGAN, 1929, MGM, d-Bayard Veiller.

Shearer is put on trial for the murder of her sugar daddy who was found shot dead in the apartment he kept for her. When her lawyer makes a very restrained attempt to cross-examine witnesses, her brother, also an attorney, takes over her defense, proving that her first lawyer is the actual murderer.

Fay Cheyney / THE LAST OF MRS. CHEYNEY, 1929, MGM, d-Sydney Franklin.

Shearer, an adventuress, poses as a wealthy Australian widow at a Monte Carlo hotel so she and her accomplices can steal a pearl necklace. She's caught in the act by Basil Rathbone who offers to let her get away with it if he can have his way with her; but she refuses and confesses all. She has a letter that would prove an embarrassment to all the guests, so they buy her off.

Jerry / THE DIVORCEE, 1930, MGM, d-Robert Z. Leonard.

Shearer marries newspaperman Chester Morris and on their third wedding anniversary she learns that he has been having an affair with another woman. She turns to Morris's friend (Robert Montgomery) for comfort. Morris refuses to accept her having affairs with other men so they get a divorce. After many affairs, she agrees to accompany Conrad Nagel to Japan as his wife, but his real wife pleads with her and, realizing she does not love Nagel, she backs out and soon is reunited with Morris. She won the Academy Award for her portrayal but one may wonder why.

Jan Ashe / A FREE SOUL, 1931, MGM, d-Clarence Brown.

One of the reasons that this picture was such a big success for Shearer was the presence of newcomer Clark Gable as her gangster lover. When Shearer is put on trial for Gable's murder, her father, attorney Lionel Barrymore, defends her and is so eloquent that he falls dead after his summation speech to the jury.

Amanda Chase Prynne / PRIVATE LIVES, 1931, MGM, d-Sidney Franklin.

In this Noel Coward comedy Shearer and Robert Montgomery, once husband and wife, find themselves honeymooning next door to each other with their new spouses (Reginald Denny and Una Merkel). Neither their fighting nor loving is quite over.

Kathleen Clare / Moonyean Clare / SMILIN' THROUGH, 1932, MGM, d-Sidney Franklin.

Shearer's reputation rested on sin and sophistication, but she shows her sugary sweet side in this romance in which she plays dual roles. First she is a woman killed on her wedding day by rejected suitor Frederic March, who was aiming for her bridegroom (Leslie Howard). Many years later she is a niece who wishes to marry March in a new guise as the murderer's descendant. Aging Leslie Howard, the girl's guardian, objects to the match until the spirit of his dead love visits him and intercedes for the young lovers.

Elizabeth Barrett / THE BARRETTS OF WIMPOLE STREET, 1934, MGM, d-Sidney Franklin.

Everyone is hammy in this production detailing the objections of Charles Laughton, as a tyrannical Moulton-Barrett, to the budding romance of his sickly daughter Elizabeth (Shearer) with writer Robert Browning (Fredric March).

Juliet Capulet / ROMEO AND JULIET, 1936, MGM, d-George Cukor.

Despite having no stage or Shakespearean experience and being a little long in the tooth for the teenage lover, Shearer's performance as Juliet is surprisingly good. Her months of study with Constance Collier paid off.

Marie Antoinette / MARIE ANTOINETTE, 1938, MGM, d-W. S. Van Dyke.

Absent from the screen for two years after the death of husband Irving Thalberg, Shearer was triumphant in the role he had planned for her since 1933. She plays the French queen who goes to her death at the guillotine after the French Revolution topples the monarchy.

Irene Fellara / IDIOT'S DELIGHT, 1938, MGM, d-Clarence Brown.

In this Robert E. Sherwood story, dancer Clark Gable, backed by an all-girl revue, meets old flame Shearer masquerading as a countess at a hotel on the Swiss border just at the outbreak of World War II. The blonde wig Shearer wears makes her look perfectly ridiculous.

Mary Haines / THE WOMEN, 1939, MGM, d-George Cukor.

After giving up her husband without a fight to showgirl Joan Crawford, Shearer has time to think about it. She decides to go after him because she still loves him and plans to fight fire with fire or, in the case of Crawford, cat with cat. As she explains to her mother,

"I've had two years to grow claws, Mother—jungle red."

OTHER ROLES

1920: *extra* / THE FLAPPER; *extra* / THE RESTLESS SEX; *extra* / WAY DOWN EAST; *Julie Martin* / THE STEALERS. **1921:** *bit* / THE SIGN ON THE DOOR; *bit* / TORCHY'S MILLIONS. **1922:** *bit* / THE LEATHER PUSHERS; *Jeanne Thornton* / THE MAN WHO PAID; *Helen Barnes* / THE BOOTLEGGERS; *Jess Driscoll* / CHANNING OF THE NORTHWEST. **1923:** *Marjorie Dare* / A CLOUDED NAME; *Dora Perkins* / MAN AND WIFE; *Jeanne* / THE DEVIL'S PARTNER; *Elinor Benton* / PLEASURE MAD; *Marjorie* / THE WANTERS; *Mimi Winship* / LUCRETIA LOMBARD. **1924:** *Jerry Vardon* / TRAIL OF THE LAW; *Elizabeth Gordon* / THE WOLF MAN; *Lillian Denton* / BLUE WATER; *Rose Dulane* / BROADWAY AFTER DARK; *Grace Durland* / BROKEN BARRIERS; *guest* / MARRIED FLIRTS; *Claire Endicott* / EMPTY HANDS; *Nancy Claxton* / THE SNOB. **1925:** *Marjorie Newton* / EXCUSE ME; *Molly* / *Florence Banning* / LADY OF THE NIGHT; *Mary Ellen Hope* / WAKING UP THE TOWN; *Katherine Emerson* / A SLAVE OF FASHIONS; *Frances White* / PRETTY LADIES; *Glory* / THE TOWER OF LIES. **1926:** *Mary* / THE DEVIL'S CIRCUS; *Nina Duane* / THE WANING SEX; *Dolly Haven* / UPSTAGE. **1927:** *Criquette* / THE DEMIBRIDE; *Mary Miller* / AFTER MIDNIGHT; *Kathie (Katchen)* / THE STUDENT PRINCE. **1928:** *Ann Dolan* / THE LATEST FROM PARIS; *Rose Trelawney* / THE ACTRESS; *Dolly* / A LADY OF CHANCE. **1929:** *guest* / THE HOLLYWOOD REVUE OF 1929; *Lally Marlett* / THEIR OWN DESIRE. **1930:** *Kitty Brown* / LET US BE GAY. **1931:** *Lisbeth Corbin* / STRANGERS MAY KISS. **1932:** *Nina Leeds* / STRANGE INTERLUDE. **1934:** *Lady Mary Rexford* / RIPTIDE. **1940:** *Countess Van Treck* / ESCAPE. **1941:** *Vicki Wilomirsky* / WE WERE DANCING. **1942:** *Consuelo Croyden* / HER CARDBOARD LOVER.

SHERIDAN, ANN

(Clara Lou Sheridan, 1915–1967)

Being described as "The Oomph Girl" during World War II and the popularity of her pin-up pictures with GIs made it hard for Ann Sheridan to be taken seriously as an actress but, truthfully, she was more than just a pretty face. Sheridan was accomplished portraying tough but optimistic and sometimes smoldering women; it's a pity she was saddled with so many inferior pictures. Charm was her trademark and her irresistible smile made her the hit of a number of comedies in the 1940s while her best dramatic role was in KINGS ROW. By the late 1940s her movie career was in decline and she became a freelance actress. In the 1960s she appeared in the daytime TV soap opera "Another World" followed by a not very successful TV series, "Pistols and Petticoats."

KEY ROLES

Betty Grogan / BLACK LEGION, 1936, Warners, d-Archie Mayo.

Sheridan gained some attention for her good looks in this story of factory worker Humphrey Bogart joining a secret pro-American clan when he loses a foreman's job to a foreign-born co-worker.

Laury Ferguson / ANGELS WITH DIRTY FACES, 1938, Warners, d-Michael Curtiz.

Sheridan provides some romance for heartless killer James Cagney in a story of slum kids whose admiration of Cagney is a major concern for priest Pat O'Brien. Sheridan is a tough cookie who doesn't take any guff.

Ruby Gilman / DODGE CITY, 1939, Warners, d-Michael Curtiz.

Sheridan is the second female lead behind Olivia de Havilland but neither have much to do in this adventure yarn featuring Errol Flynn as an Irish soldier of fortune who cleans up the small frontier town of the title.

Lee Donley / TORRID ZONE, 1940, Warners, d-William Keighley.

Sheridan moves into a starring role and steals the picture from James Cagney and Pat O'Brien. She is a gutsy nightclub singer who has a stormy romance with Cagney, the foreman of O'Brien's plantation somewhere in Central America. The wisecracks come fast and often in this entertaining escapist picture. She fires at O'Brien: "Mister, the stork that brought you must have been a vulture."

Cassie Hartley / THEY DRIVE BY NIGHT, 1940, Warners, d-Raoul Walsh.

Sheridan comes on strong as an understanding waitress in this story of brothers (George Raft and Humphrey Bogart) who are long distance truck drivers. Raft gets involved in a murder plot with Ida Lupino and Bogart loses an arm. When Raft first sees Sheridan he makes a play for her, saying: "I always have liked redheads." She snaps: "You shouldn't. Red means stop." He responds: "I'm color-blind."

Randy Monaghan / KINGS ROW, 1942, Warners, d-Sam Wood.

Sheridan plays the girl from the other side of the tracks in the small town of Kings Row, where murder, madness, and sadism make the community not a good place to live for her and two friends (Robert Cummings and Ronald Reagan) who grew up together. When Reagan has an accident, a cruel doctor (Charles Coburn) unnecessarily amputates both his legs. Despite Reagan's insistence that he has no intention of being a burden to her, Sheridan stands by her man.

Loraine Sheldon / THE MAN WHO CAME TO DINNER, 1942, Warners, d-William Keighley.

In this production of the George S. Kaufman-Moss Hart Broadway play, everyone is impersonating some famous friend or enemy of the writer and critic Alexander Wollcott, here played by Monty Woolley. Sheridan plays stage actress Gertrude Lawrence who competes for the attentions of a small-town newspaper publisher with Bette Davis, the great man's private secretary. Playing the role with all the theatrical skill she can muster, Sheridan is eliminated from the triangle when Woolley and Jimmy Durante conspire to ship her off in a mummy case.

Connie Fuller / GEORGE WASHINGTON SLEPT HERE, 1942, Warners, d-William Keighley.

In yet another Kaufman-Hart comedy, Sheridan persuades her unwilling husband (Jack Benny) to buy a converted farmhouse in Pennsylvania which, as the title suggests, once had a famous guest. That's about as clever as the picture gets.

Karen Stensgard / EDGE OF DARKNESS, 1943, Warners, d-Lewis Milestone.

Sheridan is a member of a Norwegian fishing village whose brave inhabitants fight the occupying Nazi forces in World War II. The fact that so many similar movies were being made at the time makes it surprising that this one seemed to break new ground and have a bit more to say.

Nora Bayes / SHINE ON HARVEST MOON, 1944, Warners, d-David Butler.

Sheridan was no Nora Bayes, but she tried valiantly to portray the early 1900s singing star in this ordinary backstage musical biopic.

Nora Prentiss / NORA PRENTISS, 1947, Warners, d-Vincent Sherman.

In this weeper, Sheridan is a nightclub singer who has an affair with a married doctor (Kent Smith) who breaks the law in his attempts to keep his wife from finding out about the affair.

Chris Hunter / THE UNFAITHFUL, 1947, Warners, d-Vincent Sherman.

In this loose remake of THE LETTER, Sheridan is a married woman who deeply regrets having been unfaithful to her husband while he was away at war. When he returns, she finds herself implicated in the murder of her former lover.

Lt. Catherine Gates / I WAS A MALE WAR BRIDE, 1949, 20th Century-Fox, d-Howard Hawks.

Sheridan, a WAC officer in Europe, has a very funny mission with French officer Cary Grant during which they fall in love and marry. To be able to accompany Sheridan back to the states, Grant overcomes bureaucratic red tape by putting on a skirt and wig and joining the group of war brides being shipped to the United States.

Bess Ballot / COME NEXT SPRING, 1956, Republic, d-R. G. Springsteen.

Sheridan and her husband (Steve Cochran) overcome his drunkenness and their neighbors to make a go of their Arkansas farm. It's quite ordinary.

OTHER ROLES

As Clara Lou Sheridan

1934: *beauty contestant* / SEARCH FOR BEAUTY; *bit* / BOLERO; *Shirley* / COME ON MARINES; *Lou* / MURDER AT THE VANITIES; *beauty operator* / KISS AND MAKE UP; *secretary* / SHOOT THE WORKS; *extra* / THE NOTORIOUS SOPHIE LANG; *Adele* / LADIES SHOULD LISTEN; *extra* / WAGON WHEELS; *girl* / MRS. WIGGS OF THE CABBAGE PATCH; *salesgirl* / COLLEGE RHYTHM; *bit* / YOU BELONG TO ME; *girl* / LIMEHOUSE BLUES; *bit* / ENTER MADAME. **1935:** *entertainer* / HOME ON THE RANGE; *dancer* / RHUMBA.

As Ann Sheridan

1935: *Mary White* / BEHOLD MY WIFE; *Mary Adams* / CAR 99; *Rita Balford* / ROCKY MOUNTAIN MYSTERY; *schoolgirl* / MISSISSIPPI; *nurse* / THE GLASS KEY; *Christian girl* / THE CRUSADES; *Beth Henry* / RED BLOOD OF COURAGE; *Carol Arlington* / FIGHTING YOUTH; *Lola Parker* / SING ME A LOVE SONG. **1937:** *Judy Nolan* / THE GREAT O'MALLEY; *May Kennedy* / SAN QUENTIN; *Valerie* / WINE, WOMEN AND HORSES; *Kay Allyn* / THE FOOTLOOSE HEIRESS; *Flo Allen* / ALCATRAZ ISLAND; *Margie Shannon* / SHE LOVED A FIREMAN. **1938:** *Sarah Keate* / THE PATIENT IN ROOM 18; *Sarah Keate* / MYSTERY HOUSE; *Maxine Chadwick* / COWBOY FROM BROOKLYN; *Madge Perry* / LITTLE MISS THOROUGHBRED; *Lydia Hoyt* / LETTER OF INTRODUCTION; *Fay Reynolds* / BROADWAY MUSKETEERS. **1939:** *Goldie* / THEY MADE ME A CRIMINAL; *Zelda Manion* / NAUGHTY BUT NICE; *Jill Baxter* / WINTER CARNIVAL; *Frankie Merrick* / INDIANAPOLIS SPEEDWAY; *Joy Ryan* / ANGELS WASH THEIR FACES. **1940:** *Kay* / CASTLE ON THE HUDSON; *Sarah Jane Ryan* / IT ALL CAME TRUE; *Peggy Nash* / CITY FOR CONQUEST. **1941:** *Anne Rogers* / HONEYMOON FOR THREE; *Margie Jordan* / NAVY BLUES. **1942:** *Lola Meers* / JUKE GIRL; *Roma Maple* / WINGS FOR THE EAGLE. **1943:** *guest* / THANK YOUR LUCKY STARS. **1944:** *Edna* / THE DOUGHGIRLS. **1946:** *Christie Sage* / ONE MORE TOMORROW. **1948:** *streetwalker cameo* / THE TREASURE OF THE SIERRA MADRE; *Georgia Moore* / SILVER RIVER; *Lu Clayton* / GOOD SAM. **1950:** *Stella* / STELLA; *Eleanor Johnson* / WOMAN ON THE RUN. **1952:** *"Red" McNamara* / STEEL TOWN; *Henrietta Smith* / JUST ACROSS THE STREET. **1953:** *Vermilion O'Toole* / TAKE ME TO TOWN; *Sylvia Sheppard* / APPOINTMENT IN HONDURAS. **1956:** *Amanda Penrose* / THE OPPOSITE SEX. **1957:** *one-third of a love triangle in Kenya* / WOMAN AND THE HUNTER. **1967:** *Henrietta "Hank" Hanks* / THE FAR OUT WEST.

SIDNEY, SYLVIA

(Sophia Kosow, 1910–)

Born in the Bronx, Sylvia Sidney had wide-eyed innocence and delicate features that made any man in the theater wish to protect her. The best part of her career was in the 1930s playing working-class girls who knew what suffering was all about. Petite and trim, Sidney had a heart-shaped face with deep, expressive, sad eyes and a joyous smile. Her superb emotional talent was aided by working with the best directors of the period. She left Broadway for Hollywood in 1930 when put under contract by Paramount then returned to the stage in the 1940s. In 1973 she returned to films and was nominated for an Oscar for her work in SUMMER WISHES, WINTER DREAMS. Her husbands were Bennett Cerf and Luther Adler. Speaking of her Hollywood years, Sidney said: "It was a dream world, a kind of Alice in Wonderland, with its kings and queens, princes and princesses, and our millions of loyal subjects. But it wasn't real, and it couldn't last."

KEY ROLES

Nan Cooley / CITY STREETS, 1931, Paramount, d-Rouben Mamoulian.

Sad-eyed Sidney became a star with her underacting as a mobster's daughter who is sent to jail for a murder she didn't commit. On her release from prison she is almost taken for a one-way ride.

Roberta Alden / AN AMERICAN TRAGEDY, 1931, Paramount, d-Josef von Sternberg.

Sidney's poignant performance as the young lover of Theodore Dreiser's tragic hero (Phillips Holmes) isn't enough to save the production. This so enraged Dreiser that he sued for damages.

Rose Maurrant / STREET SCENE, 1931, Goldwyn / United Artists, d-King Vidor.

Sidney is the studious daughter of a family living in a New York tenement building. At the climax her salesman father shoots his sluttish wife and the man he finds with her in their flat.

Jennie Gerhardt / JENNIE GERHARDT, 1933, Paramount, d-Marion Gering.

Sidney suffers beautifully as a poor, pregnant girl whose lover died in an accident before they could be married. She takes a position as a servant and falls in love with the son of the house but his family, learning of her background, won't hear of the match.

Nancy Lane / Princess Catterina / THIRTY DAY PRINCESS, 1934, Paramount, d-Marion Gering.

Sidney, an unemployed actress, is hired to impersonate a princess who gets the mumps while visiting New York hoping to get a loan for her country. Sidney succeeds at least with newspaper owner Cary Grant, who falls for her.

June Tolliver / TRAIL OF THE LONESOME PINE, 1936, Paramount, d-Henry Hathaway.

City stranger Fred MacMurray gets caught up in a feud between Kentucky mountain clans. He tries to educate Sidney, daughter of one of the families, and learns to love her.

Joan "Jo" Graham / YOU ONLY LIVE ONCE, 1937, United Artists, d-Fritz Lang.

Inspired by the Bonnie and Clyde legend, the film features Henry Fonda as a petty crook framed for murder. He and his faithful wife (Sidney) try to escape to Canada when he breaks out of prison. Sympathy is with these two as victims of society and the Depression.

Drina / DEAD END, 1937, Goldwyn / United Artists, d-William Wyler.
Sidney and her younger brother (Billy Halop) live on a slum street on the New York waterfront which faces the back of a luxury hotel. She tries to see that Halop grows up decently but conditions are such that the chances don't look good. Two role models arrive for Halop and the rest of the Dead End kids to consider emulating. One, Joel McCrea, has nothing and is also forced to live on the street, and the other is a killer from the neighborhood (Humphrey Bogart). When McCrea is forced to kill Bogart, things look more promising for McCrea, old flame Sidney, and brother Halop.

Mary Rogers / ONE THIRD OF A NATION, 1939, Federal Theatre, d-Dudley Murphy.
Sidney appears as a shopgirl who persuades a landlord to tear down his dangerous slums and replace them with decent housing for his tenants.

Iris Hilliard / BLOOD ON THE SUN, 1945, United Artists, d-Frank Lloyd.
In one of the few roles in which she is allowed to wear fashionable clothes and jewelry, Sidney is a Eurasian, pro-Chinese agent pretending to be working for the Japanese in Japan in the late 1930s. She and Jimmy Cagney, after a series of dangerous and violent adventures, are able to elude the Japanese Secret Police and make it to safety in the U.S. Consulate.

Fantine / LES MISERABLES, 1952, 20th Century-Fox, d-Lewis Milestone.
Sidney was meant to suffer in the Victor Hugo classic and suffer she does in this solemn remake of the brilliant 1935 Fox picture. She is a social pariah who Jean Valjean (Michael Rennie) intercedes for, much to the annoyance of police inspector Javert.

Mrs. Pritchett / SUMMER WISHES, WINTER DREAMS, 1973, Columbia, d-Gilbert Cates.
Middle-aged Joanne Woodward goes to pieces when her mother (Sidney) dies. The story is mighty thin, but Sidney's first film in 17 years won her an Oscar nomination.

OTHER ROLES

1929: *Valerie Briand* / THRU DIFFERENT EYES. **1931:** *Patricia* / CONFESSIONS OF A CO-ED. **1932:** *Kathleen Storm* / LADIES OF THE BIG HOUSE; *Helen Smith* / THE MIRACLE MAN; *guest* / MAKE ME A STAR; *Joan Prentice* / MERRILY WE GO TO HELL. **1933:** *Cho-Cho San* / MADAME BUTTERFLY; *Mary Richards* / PICK-UP. **1934:** *Lillie Taylor* / GOOD DAME; *Tonita Storm Cloud* / BEHOLD MY WIFE. **1935:** *Linda Brown* / ACCENT ON YOUTH; *Mary Burns* / MARY BURNS, FUGITIVE. **1936:** *Katherine Grant* / FURY. **1937:** *Sylvia Verloc* / THE WOMAN ALONE, (SABOTAGE); *Helen Dennis* / YOU AND ME. **1941:** *Flo Lorraine* / THE WAGONS ROLL AT NIGHT. **1946:** *Carrie Bowman* / THE SEARCHING WIND; *Margaret Wyndham Chase* / MR. ACE. **1947:** *Cecily Harrington* / LOVE FROM A STRANGER. **1955:** *Elsie* / VIOLENT SATURDAY. **1956:** *Hilda Carmichael* / BEHIND THE HIGH WALL. **1976:** *Elizabeth Mollin* / GOD TOLD ME TO. **1978:** *Aunt Marion* / DAMIEN—OMEN II. **1982:** *Donaldina Cameron* / HAMMETT. **1984:** *Margaret Smith* / CORRUPT.

SIMMONS, JEAN

(1929–)

Most Americans had their first glimpse of Jean Simmons in GREAT EXPECTATIONS in 1946 in which her captivating beauty as the young Estella was more than enough to forgive her for her nasty treatment of the young Pip. But actually Simmons had appeared in British movies for four years already, beginning her film career with GIVE US THE MOON in 1943. Simmons has always been able to combine an innocence and sweetness with sexuality and a naughty-but-nice persona. The demure brunette was nominated for a Best Supporting Actress Oscar for HAMLET despite being forced to wear a ridiculous blonde wig. She received a Best Actress nomination for THE HAPPY ENDING in 1969. The former child star grew up to be a vivacious woman with a stunning figure. Her characters have been touching, vulnerable, sensitive, selfish, manipulative, playful, sensual, cool, intense, and mad.

KEY ROLES

Estella as a girl / GREAT EXPECTATIONS, 1946, Great Britain, Cineguild, d-David Lean.
In one of the most satisfying filmings of a Charles Dickens story, Simmons is the haughty and proud teenager being trained by bitter, old Miss Haversham to manipulate men and young Pip in particular. Many a male seeing Simmons would have been more than willing to let her practice on them.

Kanchi / BLACK NARCISSUS, 1946, Great Britain, The Archers, d-Michael Powell and Emeric Pressburger.
Simmons is a beautiful Indian girl with whom Sabu, the young local ruler of a Himalayan village, runs off, deserting five Anglican nuns who run a school and a hospital near his palace.

Ophelia / HAMLET, 1948, Great Britain, Two Cities, d-Laurence Olivier.
Ophelia goes mad in this tale of the Danish prince Hamlet who learns from a ghost that his father was murdered by his uncle who then married the queen and set himself up as king. Simmons looks far gone from her first appearance in the film and her love for the melancholy Dane doesn't improve her mental health.

Vicky Barton / SO LONG AT THE FAIR, 1950, Great Britain, Gainsborough, d-Anthony Darnsborough.
Simmons and her brother (David Tomlinson) arrive in Paris to attend the Great Exhibition of 1889. After a night out, Simmons returns to the hotel and finds that Tomlinson has disappeared and that no one at the hotel will admit that he was ever there; his room is now a bathroom. Failing to get help from the police or the British consul, she turns to a painter (Dirk Bogarde) whom she and her brother met and he gets to the bottom of the mystery.

Diane Tremayne / ANGEL FACE, 1953, RKO, d-Otto Preminger.
Simmons portrays a beautiful but mentally disturbed young woman who plans to kill her rich stepmother. She succeeds but she hadn't counted on her father being in the car she fixed to lose its steering and go over a cliff. She had involved Robert Mitchum in her schemes and when he announces that he is leaving her, she abruptly throws the car they are driving into reverse, sending it and them over a cliff to their deaths.

Elizabeth I / YOUNG BESS, 1953, MGM, d-George Sidney.
In this overly long movie, Simmons portrays Elizabeth I in her early days before her reign was secure. The story bears little resemblance to the truth and in

this case, for sure, fact just has to be more interesting than fiction.

Diana / THE ROBE, 1953, 20th Century-Fox, d-Henry Koster.

Simmons portrays the childhood sweetheart of the centurion (Richard Burton) who supervises the crucifixion of Jesus Christ and is strangely affected by the event. Her love helps him find his salvation—but not on this earth as mad Emperor Caligula has both executed as Christians.

Ruth Gordon Jones / THE ACTRESS, 1953, MGM, d-George Cukor.

In a touching little drama, Simmons decides to become an actress and looks for the proper way to tell her stubborn, retired, seafaring father (Spencer Tracy).

Desiree Clary / DESIREE, 1954, 20th Century-Fox, d-Henry Koster.

In one of those romantic stories where one character seems to show up at every important historical event, Simmons is a fictional lover of Napoleon whom he never quite gets around to nor forgets.

Sarah Brown / GUYS AND DOLLS, 1955, MGM, d-Joseph L. Mankiewicz.

Simmons is a straight-arrow New York mission girl whom Frank Sinatra bets Marlon Brando can't get to take a trip to Havana with him. Brando succeeds but, because he has fallen in love with her, nobly denies it. Simmons is not bad in this musical with its Damon Runyon characters. She sings better than her co-star Brando, but that's faint praise, isn't it?

Julie Maragon / THE BIG COUNTRY, 1958, United Artists, d-William Wyler.

Simmons seems to be the only one who respects retired sea captain Gregory Peck's refusal to get into the middle of the feud between two western families. As such she proves to be a better match for him than his fiancée Carroll Baker.

Sister Sharon Falconer / ELMER GANTRY, 1960, United Artists, d-Richard Brooks.

Simmons is the lovely traveling evangelist of the 1920s who picks Burt Lancaster (as the title character) to become part of her band. He's crude and corrupt, but a spellbinder to the hicks in the tents and, on another level, to Simmons. They become lovers, but she is killed in a fire shortly after she comes to believe that she has a real calling from the Lord and can cure the sick.

Mary Follet / ALL THE WAY HOME, 1963, Paramount, d-Alex Segal.

This is the poignant story of a happy-go-lucky father (Robert Preston) and a strong, supportive mother (Simmons) who must learn to fill the great hole in her family's life when Preston dies. It's heart-rending, but in a sensitive, touching, and satisfying way.

OTHER ROLES

1943: *Heidi* / GIVE US THE MOON. **1944:** *bit* / MR. EMMANUEL; *Eva Watkins* / MEET SEXTON BLAKE; *bit* / SPORTS DAY; *Molly Dodd* / KISS THE BRIDE GOODBYE. **1945:** *singer* / THE WAY TO THE STARS; *handmaiden* / CAESAR AND CLEOPATRA; *Lady Brodrick* / HUNGRY HILL; *Joy Blake* / THE WOMAN IN THE HALL. **1947:** *Caroline Ruthyn* / UNCLE SILAS. **1948:** *Emmeline Foster* / THE BLUE LAGOON. **1949:** *Evelyne Wallace* / ADAM AND EVELYNE. **1950:** *Eve Bishop* / TRIO; *Judith Moray* / CAGE OF GOLD; *Sophie Malraux* / THE CLOUDED YELLOW. **1953:** *Lavina* / ANDROCLES AND THE LION; *Carolyn Parker* / AFFAIR WITH A STRANGER. **1954:** *Corby Lane* / SHE COULDN'T SAY NO; *Cally Canham* / A BULLET IS WAITING; *Merit* / THE EGYPTIAN. **1955:** *Lily Watkins* / FOOTSTEPS IN THE FOG. **1956:** *Hilda Crane* / HILDA CRANE. **1957:** *Anne Leeds* / THIS COULD BE THE NIGHT; *Barbara Leslie Forbes* / UNTIL THEY SAIL. **1958:** *Charlotte Brown* / HOME BEFORE DARK. **1960:** *Varinia* / SPARTACUS. **1961:** *Hattie Durrant* / THE GRASS IS GREENER. **1965:** *Susan Lampton* / LIFE AT THE TOP. **1966:** *the blonde* / MISTER BUDDWING. **1967:** *Molly Lang* / ROUGH NIGHT IN JERICHO; *Nancy Downes* / DIVORCE, AMERICAN STYLE. **1969:** *Mary Wilson* / THE HAPPY ENDING. **1971:** *woman* / SAY HELLO TO YESTERDAY. **1975:** *Estelle Benbow* / MR. SYCAMORE. **1979:** *Dominique Ballard* / DOMINIQUE.

SINATRA, FRANK

(Francis Albert Sinatra, 1915–   )

In the early 1940s slightly-built, dark-haired, Hoboken-born singer and actor Frank Sinatra was a romantic crooner, the idol of millions of screaming teenagers. He starred in a series of Hollywood musicals in the 1940s but by the end of the decade his movie career was in decline. His fine baritone voice and carefully phrased lyrics made him the most popular singer of the decade, but his singing career was threatened when his vocal chords hemorrhaged in 1952. He started an amazing comeback in 1953 when he won the role of Maggio in FROM HERE TO ETERNITY, for which he was happy to receive only $8,000. His estimation of the value of the role was correct as he won an Oscar as Best Supporting Actor. This led to other serious roles and a new career in the movies. He was also nominated for an Oscar for his performance as a drug addict in THE MAN WITH THE GOLDEN ARM. His voice also returned to top form and Sinatra became one of the biggest stars in show business. Sinatra has been dubbed many titles in his life; early he was "The Voice," then he became "Chairman of the Board," and affectionately "Ol' Blue Eyes." He is a magnanimous philanthropist for individuals and organizations but his longtime association with underworld figures has brought him much criticism. But as Sinatra said, "I'm for anything that gets you through the night, be it prayer, tranquilizers, or a bottle of Jack Daniels."

KEY ROLES

Clarence Doolittle / ANCHORS AWEIGH, 1945, MGM, d-George Sidney.

Thin and shy Sinatra is easily manipulated by fast-talking Gene Kelly, who to impress singer Kathryn Grayson, tells her that Sinatra personally knows Jose Iturbi, the artist for whom she wishes to audition. She gets her chance, no thanks to either Sinatra or Kelly. Sinatra's numbers are "The Charm of You," "What Makes the Sunset," and "I Fall in Love Too Easily."

Dennis Ryan / TAKE ME OUT TO THE BALL GAME, 1949, MGM, d-Busby Berkeley.

Sinatra is the second baseman on a turn-of-the-century baseball team owned by Esther Williams. His best friend (Gene Kelly) plays shortstop and makes a play for the boss. Sinatra on the other hand finds determined Betty Garrett more his style. His songs include "The Right Girl for Me" and with Garrett, "It's Fate Baby, It's Fate." With Kelly and Jules Munshin he sings "O'Brien to Ryan to Goldberg."

Chip / ON THE TOWN, 1949, MGM, d-Gene Kelly and Stanley Donen.

Sinatra, Gene Kelly, and Jules Munshin are three sailors with twenty-four hour leaves to spend in New York City. They each find the right girl; Sinatra's, once again, is Betty Garrett, a take charge taxi-driver.

He sings "Come Up to My Place" and "You're Awful" with Garrett, and "New York, New York" with Kelly and Munshin, and the title number with those two, Garrett, Vera-Ellen, and Ann Miller.

Angelo Maggio / FROM HERE TO ETERNITY, 1953, Columbia, d-Fred Zinnemann.
No one could seem more perfect for the role of the skinny, feisty soldier stationed in Hawaii just before the Japanese attack on Pearl Harbor. He gets into a fight with Ernest Borgnine, the sergeant in charge of the stockades, and as expected, he gets sent to the stockades and is beaten to death by Borgnine. Sinatra won a much deserved Oscar for this role and revitalized his career as well.

Nathan Detroit / GUYS AND DOLLS, 1955, MGM, d-Joseph L. Mankiewicz.
Strangely, Sinatra, the Damon Runyon character who runs "the oldest established, permanent floating crap game" in this movie version of the hit Frank Loesser musical, has only one solo number, "Adelaide." He does help out, however, on "Fugue for Tin Horns," "The Oldest Established," "Sue Me," and the title number.

Frankie Machine / THE MAN WITH THE GOLDEN ARM, 1955, United Artists, d-Otto Preminger.
Sinatra was nominated for an Academy Award for his painful performance of a gambler and drug addict who, with the help of Kim Novak, takes the cold-turkey cure. Sinatra is so convincing that the audience suffers right along with him.

Mike Connor / HIGH SOCIETY, 1956, MGM, d-Charles Walters.
In this remake of THE PHILADELPHIA STORY, Sinatra has the James Stewart role of a magazine writer assigned to cover Grace Kelly's marriage to husband number two while husband number one lives in the Newport mansion next door. Sinatra sings "Who Wants to Be a Millionaire" with Celeste Holm, "Well, Did You Evah" with Bing Crosby, and "Mind If I Make Love to You?" as a solo.

Joe E. Lewis / THE JOKER IS WILD, 1957, Paramount, d-Charles Vidor.
Sinatra portrays the singer who runs afoul of mobsters who cut his vocal chords. He regains his voice and becomes a nightclub comedian who makes a running joke about his drinking. His best song in the picture is "All The Way."

Joey Evans / PAL JOEY, 1957, Columbia, d-George Sidney.
In this Rogers and Hart musical Sinatra portrays a nightclub singer, heel, and womanizer. He acts as a gigolo for wealthy Rita Hayworth while putting the make on innocent Kim Novak. Hayworth plans to back the opening of a nightclub starring Sinatra, but she closes the joint when he pays too much attention to Novak. Sinatra is in fine voice singing "The Lady Is a Tramp," "I Could Write a Book," "There's a Small Hotel," and "I Didn't Know What Time It Was."

Bennett Marco / THE MANCHURIAN CANDIDATE, 1962, United Artists, d-John Frankenheimer.
Sinatra and Laurence Harvey are soldiers who, as prisoners during the Korean War, are brainwashed by the Reds and Harvey is programmed to assassinate a liberal presidential candidate. Sinatra finally catches on and tries to prevent the crime.

Col. Joseph Ryan / VON RYAN'S EXPRESS, 1965, 20th Century-Fox, d-Mark Robson.
American Air Force Officer Sinatra turns out to be the ranking officer in an Italian POW camp consisting mostly of British personnel. When Italy drops out of the war, the prisoners believe they are free but the Germans have other ideas. Led by Sinatra they hijack a train and head for Switzerland, but Sinatra doesn't reach the promised land.

Tony Rome / TONY ROME, 1967, 20th Century-Fox, d-Gordon Douglas.
Sinatra is a seedy Miami private detective who finds he's involved with murder when he's hired to keep an eye on a millionaire's daughter.

Joe Leland / THE DETECTIVE, 1968, 20th Century-Fox, d-Gordon Douglas.
Sinatra is a tough New York police detective whose wife (Lee Remick) is a nymphomaniac. When he's assigned to find the killer of a homosexual, he railroads the wrong man, getting him sent to the electric chair. Then Sinatra becomes disgusted when he finds that many in his department are corrupt.

OTHER ROLES

1941: *guest* / LAS VEGAS NIGHTS. **1942:** *guest* / SHIP AHOY. **1943:** *Frank* / HIGHER AND HIGHER; *guest* / REVEILLE WITH BEVERLY. **1944:** *Glen* / STEP LIVELY. **1946:** *guest* / TILL THE CLOUDS ROLL BY. **1947:** *Danny Webson Miller* / IT HAPPENED IN BROOKLYN. **1948:** *Father Paul* / THE MIRACLE OF THE BELLS; *Ricardo* / THE KISSING BANDIT. **1951:** *Johnny Dalton* / DOUBLE DYNAMITE; *Danny Wilson* / MEET DANNY WILSON. **1954:** *John Baron* / SUDDENLY. **1955:** *Barney Sloan* / YOUNG AT HEART; *Dr. Alfred Boone* / NOT AS A STRANGER; *Charlie Y. Reader* / THE TENDER TRAP. **1956:** *Johnny Concho* / JOHNNY CONCHO; *piano player* / AROUND THE WORLD IN 80 DAYS; *guest* / MEET ME IN LAS VEGAS. **1957:** *Miguel* / THE PRIDE AND THE PASSION. **1958:** *Lt. Sam Loggins* / KINGS GO FORTH; *Dave Hirsh* / SOME CAME RUNNING. **1959:** *Tony Manetta* / A HOLE IN THE HEAD; *Capt. Tom C. Reynolds* / NEVER SO FEW. **1960:** *Francois Durnais* / CAN-CAN; *Danny Ocean* / OCEAN'S ELEVEN; *guest* / PEPE. **1961:** *Harry* / THE DEVIL AT 4 O'CLOCK. **1962:** *1st Sgt. Mike Merry* / SERGEANTS 3; *guest* / THE ROAD TO HONG KONG. **1963:** *Alan Baker* / COME BLOW YOUR HORN; *gypsy stableman* / THE LIST OF ADRIAN MESSENGER; *Zack Thomas* / FOUR FOR TEXAS. **1964:** *Robbo* / ROBIN AND THE 7 HOODS; **1965:** *Chief Pharmacist's Mate Maloney* / NONE BUT THE BRAVE; *Dan Edwards* / MARRIAGE ON THE ROCKS. **1966:** *Vince Talmadge* / CAST A GIANT SHADOW; *Mark Brittain* / ASSAULT ON A QUEEN; *guest* / THE OSCAR. **1967:** *Sam Laker* / THE NAKED RUNNER. **1968:** *Tony Rome* / LADY IN CEMENT. **1970:** *Dingus Magee* / DIRTY DINGUS MAGEE. **1974:** *host* / THAT'S ENTERTAINMENT! **1980:** *Edward Delaney* / THE FIRST DEADLY SIN. **1984:** *himself* / CANNONBALL RUN II.

SMITH, ALEXIS

(Gladys Smith, 1921–)
Born in British Columbia, Alexis Smith was a ballet dancer in a production of "Carmen" when she was 13. She attended Hollywood High and studied drama at Los Angeles City College. This tall, stately actress with blue-green eyes and known as the "Ice Princess" confessed, "I typed myself—I played all my roles alike because I didn't know any better." She always got the roles that everyone else turned down. In 1959 she turned to TV and the stage but returned to the movies in the 1970s. She was at her best in roles supporting top male stars like Errol Flynn and Cary Grant. She has been married to actor Craig Stevens since 1944.

KEY ROLES

Victoria (Vicki) Ware / GENTLEMAN JIM, 1942, Warners, d-Raoul Walsh.
Smith provides the romantic interest for Errol Flynn, who is a charming Irish rogue and heavyweight box-

ing champion. As usual with Flynn's co-stars, Smith has little to do but look attractive.

Olivia Langdon Clemens / THE ADVENTURES OF MARK TWAIN, 1944, Warners, d-Irving Rapper.
Smith portrays Samuel Clemens's wife in this overly long biopic of the great American humorist. She supports Fredric March the best she can without demonstrating any particular acting style.

Christine Gilbert / RHAPSODY IN BLUE, 1945, Warners, d-Irving Rapper.
Smith was becoming quite adept at fading into the background when playing the love of some famous individual. In this case she loves George Gershwin (Robert Alda) but unselfishly gives him up.

Jeanne Starr / SAN ANTONIO, 1945, Warners, d-David Butler.
In this one Smith is back with Errol Flynn, who plays a Texas rustler in 1877 who tracks down a gang of cattle thieves. She's a handsome woman but once again she has nothing much to do.

Linda Lee Porter / NIGHT AND DAY, 1946, Warners, d-Michael Curtiz.
Here again Smith is stuck in a biopic, this time as the wife of composer Cole Porter (Cary Grant). At least she's no more miscast than Grant.

Cecily Latham / THE TWO MRS. CARROLLS, 1947, Warners, d-Peter Godfrey.
Smith is in line to be the next victim of a psychopathic artist (Humphrey Bogart) who paints his wives and then murders them with poisoned milk.

Winifred Stanley / HERE COMES THE GROOM, 1951, Paramount, d-Frank Capra.
Bing Crosby, a journalist who adopts a pair of war orphans, turns the cold, beautiful Smith into a hip-swinging glamour girl who goes after Franchot Tone, the man she's always loved. Smith gets into a fight with Jane Wyman and a wrestling match with Tone.

Allie Walker / BEAU JAMES, 1957, Paramount, d-Melville Shavelson.
Smith is the wife in name only of James J. Walker, the mayor of New York in the 1930s. He has a mistress (Vera Miles), but for his political career and because he's Catholic, he and Smith must maintain the fiction of their marriage.

OTHER ROLES

1940: *girl at wedding* / LADY WITH RED HAIR. **1941:** *bridesmaid* / AFFECTIONATELY YOURS; *bit* / SINGAPORE WOMAN; *bit* / THREE SONS O' GUNS; *gossip* / SHE COULDN'T SAY NO; *bit* / PASSAGE FROM HONG KONG; *bit* / FLIGHT FROM DESTINY; *Helen* / STEEL AGAINST THE SKY; *Elinor B. Fairchild* / THE SMILING GHOST; *Linda Fisher* / DIVE BOMBERS. **1943:** *dancer* / THANK YOUR LUCKY STARS; *Florence Creighton* / THE CONSTANT NYMPH. **1944:** *guest* / HOLLYWOOD CANTEEN; *Nan* / THE DOUGHGIRLS. **1945:** *Evelyn Turner* / CONFLICT; *Elizabeth* / THE HORN BLOWS AT MIDNIGHT. **1946:** *Cecilia Henry* / ONE MORE TOMORROW; *Nora Nesbitt* / OF HUMAN BONDAGE. **1947:** *Rory Teller* / STALLION ROAD; *guest* / ALWAYS TOGETHER. **1948:** *Marian Halcombe* / THE WOMAN IN WHITE; *Mrs. Blake* / THE DECISION OF CHRISTOPHER BLAKE; *Laurie Durant* / WHIPLASH. **1949:** *Rogue De Lisle* / SOUTH OF ST. LOUIS; *Lon Kyng* / ANY NUMBER CAN PLAY; *Olivia Pearce* / ONE LAST FLING. **1950:** *Maria Singleton* / MONTANA; *Mary Williams* / WYOMING MAIL; *Christine Miller (Sal Willis)* / UNDERCOVER GIRL. **1951:** *Liz Trent* / CAVE OF OUTLAWS. **1952:** *Amanda Waycross* / THE TURNING POINT. **1953:** *Ken Garven* / SPLIT SECOND. **1954:** *Glenda Esmond* / THE SLEEPING TIGER. **1955:** *Sue Hoskins* / THE ETERNAL SEA. **1958:** *Nita Hollaway* / THIS HAPPY FEELING. **1959:** *Carol Wharton* / THE YOUNG PHILADELPHIANS. **1975:** *Deidre Milford Granger* / ONCE IS NOT ENOUGH. **1977:** *Mrs. Hallet* / THE LITTLE GIRL THAT LIVES DOWN THE LANE. **1978:** *Sarah Blue* / CASEY'S SHADOW. **1981:** *Gloria* / THE TROUT. **1986:** *Belle* / TOUGH GUYS.

SMITH, MAGGIE

(1934–)
Red-haired Maggie Smith, a brilliant stage actress, has had very few film roles. However, she has had a high percentage of her performances honored by the Motion Picture Academy with Oscars for THE PRIME OF MISS JEAN BRODIE (1969) and CALIFORNIA SUITE (1978), and nominations for OTHELLO (1965) and TRAVELS WITH MY AUNT (1972). This daughter of an Oxford pathology professor has an excellent comedy sense and once remarked: "What I like about comedy is that it's very close to hysteria."

KEY ROLES

Miss Mead / THE V.I.P.S, 1963, MGM, d-Anthony Asquith.
Smith plays the faithful and adoring secretary of Rod Taylor, an Australian industrialist who faces ruin because the flight from London to New York has been canceled due to poor weather and he will be unable to make a meeting about a loan that might save him. Smith convinces Richard Burton to lend Taylor the money, thus saving the day.

Desdemona / OTHELLO, 1965, Great Britain, Warners, d-Stuart Burge.
This is a film version of the National Theatre of Great Britain stage production of the William Shakespeare play in which the Moor Othello (Laurence Olivier) is driven to murdering his wife Desdemona (Smith) because his erstwhile friend Iago (Frank Finlay) makes him believe she has been unfaithful.

Sarah Watkins / THE HONEY POT, 1967, United Artists, d-Joseph L. Mankiewicz.
Smith is a nurse / companion to wealthy hypochondriac Susan Hayward. When Hayward is murdered Smith discovers that the villain is their host (Rex Harrison) who had hoped to inherit Hayward's fortune. Instead, he commits suicide by throwing himself into one of the canals of Venice and Smith inherits the fortune.

Jean Brodie / THE PRIME OF MISS JEAN BRODIE, 1969, Great Britain, 20th Century-Fox, d-Ronald Neame.
Scottish middle-aged spinster Smith teaches at an exclusive school for girls in Edinburgh. She operates under the principle that her pupils are clean slates until she writes upon them. Her teaching philosophy is summarized like this: "Little girls, I am in the business of putting old heads on young shoulders, and all my pupils are the creme de la creme. Give me a girl of an impressionable age, and she is mine for life." Smith is a romantic devoted to art, music, and the fascist cause. She belittles anyone who dares disagree with her and she carries on an affair with an earthy painter who also takes up with Pamela Franklin, one of Smith's most attractive students. Ultimately, Smith's behavior both in and out of the classroom gets her fired. She won an Academy Award for her performance.

Aunt Augusta / TRAVELS WITH MY AUNT, 1972, Great Britain, MGM, d-George Cukor.
Smith is priceless as an eccentric Englishwoman who takes her bewildered nephew on a series of bizarre and comical adventures after her first meeting with him at his mother's funeral.

Diana Barrie / CALIFORNIA SUITE, 1978, Columbia, d-Herbert Ross.

In this West Coast version of Neil Simon's "Plaza Suite," Smith is in Hollywood to attend the Academy Awards. She is accompanied by her gay husband (Michael Caine). The two are quite good in a series of witty and sophisticated exchanges.

Charlotte Bartlett / A ROOM WITH A VIEW, 1985, Merchant, d-James Ivory.

Smith, the penniless aunt of Helena Bonham-Carter, acts as the young girl's chaperone when they travel to Italy. When they find themselves having been given rooms without views, Denholm Elliott insists that they take his and his son's rooms. The E. M. Forster story is about the young couple finding that they love each other, but its precious charm is in having many delightful characters such as Smith.

OTHER ROLES

1958: *Bridget Howard* / NOWHERE TO GO. **1962:** *Chantal* / GO TO BLAZES. **1964:** *Philpot* / THE PUMPKIN EATER. **1965:** *Nora* / YOUNG CASSIDY. **1968:** *Patty Terwilliger* / HOT MILLIONS. **1969:** *music hall star* / OH! WHAT A LOVELY WAR. **1973:** *Lila Fisher* / LOVE AND PAIN (AND THE WHOLE DAMN THING). **1976:** *Dora Charleston* / MURDER BY DEATH. **1978:** *Miss Bowers* / DEATH ON THE NILE. **1981:** *Thetis* / CLASH OF THE TITANS; *Lois Heidler* / QUARTET. **1982:** *Daphne Castle* / EVIL UNDER THE SUN; *Anderson* / BETTER LATE THAN NEVER. **1983:** *Lady Ames* / THE MISSIONARY. **1985:** *Joyce Chilvers* / A PRIVATE FUNCTION; *Lily Wynn* / LILY IN LOVE. **1987:** *Judith Hearne* / THE LONELY PASSION OF JUDITH HEARNE.

SOTHERN, ANN

(Harriette Lake, 1909–)

Doll-faced, blonde Ann Sothern made a first-rate sassy and high-spirited Maisie in a successful series of ten films as well as on a radio series. Her now sixty-year career on Broadway, movies, radio, and television has been enhanced by a wry, self-deprecating sense of humor and a fresh-faced beauty. While she is best known for playing self-confident chippies and hard-boiled gals who wisecrack their way through life, she has also been adept in character roles, and had a successful run in the TV series "Private Secretary" and "The Ann Sothern Show," in which she was a glamorous career woman. Although she has been plagued by ill health in recent years, she returned to the screen in 1987 in THE WHALES OF AUGUST and her performance among such old pros as Bette Davis, Lillian Gish, and Vincent Price earned her an Oscar nomination for Best Supporting Actress. The natural redhead who became a blonde has appeared in made-for-TV movies including THE OUTSIDER (1967), THE GREAT MAN'S WHISKERS (1971), THE WEEKEND NUN (1972), THE KILLING KIND (1973), CAPTAINS AND THE CLOUDS (1976), and A LETTER TO THREE WIVES (1985).

KEY ROLES

Jane Larrabee / KID MILLIONS, 1934, Goldwyn / United Artists, d-Roy Del Ruth.

In this tame Eddie Cantor star vehicle, Sothern and George Murphy, in his first screen role, play young lovers who are among the very few who are not trying to beat Cantor out of the fortune he has inherited, which is hidden somewhere in Egypt.

Connie Taylor / THERE GOES MY GIRL, 1937, RKO, d-Ben Holmes.

In a story reminiscent of THE FRONT PAGE and in anticipation of HIS GIRL FRIDAY, managing editor Richard Lane will try just about anything to prevent his star reporter (Sothern) from marrying a rival newspaperman, including faking a murder while the two are exchanging vows.

Maisie Ravier / MAISIE, 1939, MGM, d-Edwin L. Marin.

In this first installment of the enjoyable but forgettable series about the adventures of wisecracking, hard-boiled Brooklyn showgirl, Sothern solves the marital problems of Ian Hunter and puts her brand on ranch hand Robert Young.

Maisie Ravier / CONGO MAISIE, 1940, MGM, d-H. C. Potter.

What makes this second in the Maisie series worth mentioning is that it is a revision of RED DUST with Sothern's Jean Harlow to John Carroll's Clark Gable and Rita Johnson filling Mary Astor's shoes.

Dixie Donegan / LADY BE GOOD, 1941, MGM, d-Norman Z. McLeod.

There's not much plot to this revision of the Gershwin musical first filmed as a silent in 1928. Sothern is lovely to look at and the dancing of Eleanor Powell is, as usual, first-rate. Robert Young, John Carroll, and Red Skelton all have eyes for Sothern.

Hattie Maloney / PANAMA HATTIE, 1942, MGM, d-Norman Z. McLeod.

The 1940 Broadway hit doesn't survive the transplant to the screen. It wasn't Sothern's fault that the Cole Porter music was designed for the flamboyant style of Ethel Merman.

Rita Phipps / A LETTER TO THREE WIVES, 1949, 20th Century-Fox, d-Joseph L. Mankiewicz.

Sothern is one of three wives who is handed a letter from a woman named Addie saying that by the end of the day she will have left town with one of their husbands. All reflect in flashback on their less than happy unions.

Frances Elliot / NANCY GOES TO RIO, 1950, MGM, d-Robert Z. Leonard.

In this story of a mother and daughter, Sothern and Jane Powell are up for the same part in a play. Sothern settles for Barry Sullivan and leaves the show to her daughter.

OTHER ROLES

As Harriet Lake

1927: *bit* / BROADWAY NIGHTS. **1929:** *bit* / HEARTS IN EXILE; *bit* / SHOW OF SHOWS. **1930:** *bit* / WHOOPEE; *bit* / DOUGHBOYS; *bit* / HOLD EVERYTHING.

As Ann Sothern

1933: *dancer* / BROADWAY THROUGH A KEYHOLE. **1934:** *Jean* / LET'S FALL IN LOVE; *Jane Blodgett* / MELODY IN SPRING; *Ruth* / PARTY'S OVER; *Geraldine* / THE HELL CAT; *Kitty Taylor* / BLIND DATE. **1935:** *Mimi* / FOLIES BERGERE; *Marge Walker* / EIGHT BELLS; *Pat* / HOORAY FOR LOVE; *Linda* / THE GIRL FRIEND; *Adrienne Martin* / GRAND EXIT. **1936:** *Fay Stevens* / YOU MAY BE NEXT; *Mary* / HELLSHIP MORGAN; *Ann Edwards* / DON'T GAMBLE WITH LOVE; *Kit Bennett* / WALKING ON AIR; *Mary Cantillan* / MY AMERICAN WIFE; *Frances Cooke* / SMARTEST GIRL IN TOWN. **1937:** *Elinor* / DANGEROUS NUMBER; *Millicent Kendall* / FIFTY ROADS TO TOWN; *Mary Strand* / SUPER SLEUTH; *Toni Pemberton* / DANGER—LOVE AT WORK; *Betty Russell* / THERE GOES THE GROOM. **1938:** *Carol Rogers* / SHE'S GOT EVERYTHING; *Jean Livingstone* / TRADE WINDS. **1939:** *Garda Sloane* / FAST AND FURIOUS; *Eileen Connelly* / HOTEL FOR WOMEN; *Ethel Turp* / JOE AND ETHEL TURP CALL ON THE PRESIDENT. **1940:** *Flo Addams* / BROTHER ORCHID; *Maisie*

Ravier / GOLD RUSH MAISIE; *Dulcy Ward* / DULCY. **1941:** *Maisie Ravier* / MAISIE WAS A LADY; *Maisie Ravier* / RINGSIDE MAISIE. **1942:** *Maisie Ravier* / MAISIE GETS HER MAN. **1943:** *Julia Seabrook* / THREE HEARTS FOR JULIA; *Maisie Ravier* / SWING SHIFT MAISIE; *guest* / THOUSANDS CHEER; *Pat* / CRY HAVOC. **1944:** *Maisie Ravier* / MAISIE GOES TO RENO. **1946:** *Maisie Ravier* / UP GOES MAISIE. **1947:** *Maisie Ravier* / UNDERCOVER MAISIE. **1948:** *June Tyme* / APRIL SHOWERS; *Joyce Harmon* / WORDS AND MUSIC. **1949:** *Peggy* / THE JUDGE STEPS OUT. **1950:** *Dell Faring* / SHADOW ON THE WALL. **1953:** *Crystal Carpenter* / THE BLUE GARDENIA. **1964:** *Sade* / LADY IN A CAGE; *Mrs. Gamadge* / THE BEST MAN. **1965:** *Mrs. Argona* / SYLVIA. **1968:** *Angela* / CHUBASCO. **1974:** *Finzie* / GOLDEN NEEDLES. **1975:** *Sheba* / CRAZY MAMA. **1978:** *Mrs. Karmann* / THE MANITOU. **1980:** *Angel* / THE LITTLE DRAGONS. **1987:** *Tisha Doughty* / THE WHALES OF AUGUST.

SPACEK, SISSY

(Mary Elizabeth Spacek, 1950–)

Small, fair-haired, and freckled, Sissy Spacek appears much younger than her actual age. A former model, she studied with Lee Strasberg and broke into movies as an extra in the Andy Warhol movie TRASH in 1970. The cousin of actor Rip Torn, she had her first real film role in PRIME CUT and won national attention with BADLANDS. Spacek is versatile, accomplished, and willing to try a variety of roles. She has been rewarded with an Oscar for COAL MINER'S DAUGHTER and nominations for CARRIE, MISSING, and THE RIVER. Childlike Spacek is a very special actress and should have a long, productive career playing offbeat but interesting women who always have a bit of the little girl in them.

KEY ROLES

Holly Sargis / BADLANDS, 1973, Columbia, d-Terrence Malick.

In this black comedy loosely based on the killing spree of Charles Starkweather and Carol Fugate in the 1950s, Spacek is a teenage girl who isn't put out when young garbage collector Martin Sheen kills her father because he forbids them to see each other. She goes along with Sheen on a wandering murder spree across the country until he is caught and takes full responsibility for their crimes.

Carrie White / CARRIE, 1976, United Artists, d-Brian De Palma.

Spacek is a repressed teenager who lives with her very religious mother (Piper Laurie). The latter is so down on sex she doesn't even instruct the poor girl about menstruation and when Spacek has her first period in a shower at her high school she thinks she's bleeding to death. Later she has a bucket of pig's blood dumped on her while she's attending a prom. But woe to all who have tormented the child; she has telekinetic powers and brings death and destruction to all present at the prom, before returning home to have it out with mom. The ending is truly frightening.

Loretta Lynn / COAL MINER'S DAUGHTER, 1980, Universal, d-Michael Apted.

Spacek does her own singing in this excellent biopic of country singer Loretta Lynn who was wed at 13 and a mother at 14. Spacek won the Academy Award for her performance in a pretty standard story of slow advance toward show business success, the heartbreaks, alienation with loved ones, and finally reconciliation while maintaining her stardom.

Beth Horman / MISSING, 1982, Universal, d-Costantin Costa-Gavras.

When Spacek's journalist husband disappears in Chile, his father (Jack Lemmon) joins her in the search. Initially Lemmon believes his son and daughter-in-law caused their own problems by championing causes in a country where they had no business sticking their noses. But as he slowly learns that his son has been killed by the government, he becomes radicalized with Spacek's help.

Mae Garvey / THE RIVER, 1985, Universal, d-Mark Rydell.

Spacek gives a heartfelt performance as the Tennessee housewife who, along with her husband (Mel Gibson), must fight the river and those who wish to use it for their own selfish purposes, to keep their farm running.

Babe Magrath Botrelle / CRIMES OF THE HEART, 1986, De Laurentiis, d-Bruce Beresford.

Spacek is one of three eccentric sisters living in a small Mississippi town. She is accused of the attempted murder of her husband, explaining: "I didn't like his looks." While he's bleeding to death she offers him some lemonade, but he's not in the mood. She would like to commit suicide but she's just not good at killing.

OTHER ROLES

1970: *extra* / TRASH. **1971:** *Poppy* / PRIME CUT. **1973:** *Ginger* / GINGER IN THE MORNING. **1977:** *Pinky Rose* / 3 WOMEN; *Linda Murray* / WELCOME TO L.A. **1979:** *Carolyn Cassady* / HEART BEAT. **1981:** *Nita Longley* / RAGGEDY MAN. **1985:** *Marie Ragghianti* / MARIE. **1986:** *Gussie Sawyer* / VIOLETS ARE BLUE; *Jessie Cates* / 'NIGHT, MOTHER.

STALLONE, SYLVESTER

(Michael S. Stallone, 1946–)

Some might argue with a certain amount of conviction that "The Italian Stallion" is the only role ever played by Sylvester Stallone. All the others are merely aliases for Rocky Balboa. Perhaps, but Stallone has found a formula that works and his movies have been box-office smashes. Born in Hell's Kitchen, Stallone was sent to a school for children with learning and behavior problems in Switzerland, which proved to be an unhappy experience. Muscular and surly, he became a superstar by creating a character a lot of people like—the old-fashioned loser who becomes a winner. Even when Stallone is blowing away half the immediate world, this product of a scary childhood has an undeniable appeal.

KEY ROLES

Stanley Rosiello / THE LORDS OF FLATBUSH, 1974, Columbia, d-Martin Davidson.

This saga about a bunch of New York street toughs is notable only for seeing where Stallone and Henry Winkler got their starts. Some of the episodes are funny, though.

Frank Nitti / CAPONE, 1975, 20th Century-Fox, d-Robert D. Webb.

In this version of the oft-examined career of Chicago's brutal crime boss, Stallone plays the mobster who turns Capone into the Feds on income tax evasion and takes over the rackets while Al is in prison slowly losing his mind because of an untreated case of syphilis.

Rocky Balboa / ROCKY, 1976, United Artists, d-John G. Avildsen.

Not blessed with handsome or intelligent looks, Stallone took things in his own hands and created a role perfect for him that did not require him to appear very bright. Quite the contrary, he plays a small-time boxer who can withstand a lot of pain who gets a chance to fight the champ. This movie hit just the right chord with movie fans, earning over $54 million and making a wealthy man of Stallone, who had wisely cut himself in for a share of the profits in lieu of a large salary. The three sequels have been just as successful as Stallone is smart enough to give audiences what they want—a dumb hero who doesn't know enough to give up.

John Rambo / FIRST BLOOD, 1982, Carolco, d-Ted Kotcheff.

Stallone figured that if two men in a ring sweating and bleeding was a turn-on for the movie-going public, then more violence would make them even happier. His character, a former Green Beret, gets in trouble in a small California community and declares war. If you want action, you got action. In the first sequel, he returns to Vietnam to release some MIAs and maybe start the war again.

OTHER ROLES

1970: *bit* / PARTY AT KITTY AND STUDS. **1971:** *Mugger* / BANANAS. **1974:** *Jerry* / NO PLACE TO HIDE; *youth in park* / THE PRISONER OF SECOND AVENUE. **1975:** *Johnnie* / FAREWELL, MY LOVELY; *"Machine Gun" Joe Vitebo* / DEATH RACE 2000. **1978:** *Cosmo Carboni* / PARADISE ALLEY; *Johnny Kovak* / F.I.S.T. **1979:** *Rocky Balboa* / ROCKY II. **1981:** *Robert Hatch* / VICTORY; *Deke DaSilva* / NIGHTHAWKS. **1982:** *Rocky Balboa* / ROCKY III. **1984:** *Nick* / RHINESTONE. **1985:** *John Rambo* / RAMBO: FIRST BLOOD PART II; *Rocky Balboa* / ROCKY IV. **1987:** *Lincoln Hawk* / OVER THE TOP.

STANWYCK, BARBARA

(Ruby Stevens, 1907–)

Barbara Stanwyck is the best movie actress who has never won an Academy Award, although she was nominated for STELLA DALLAS; BALL OF FIRE; DOUBLE INDEMNITY; and SORRY, WRONG NUMBER, and could easily have been nominated for a dozen others. Her career has spanned 60 years in which she has excelled at playing good / bad girls, strong-willed, independent women, and sexy femme fatales. Husky-voiced Stanwyck in reality was just as tough as the characters she played and as confident of her impact on a movie as any woman who ever appeared before a camera, boasting, "Put me in the last fifteen minutes of a picture and I don't care what happened before. I don't even care if I was in the rest of the damn thing—I'll take it in those fifteen minutes." Her appeal has been best described, perhaps, by Herman Mankiewicz, who said: "Barbara Stanwyck is my favorite. My God, I could just sit and dream of being married to her, having a little cottage out in the hills, vines around the door. I'd come home from the office, tired, weary, and I'd be met by Barbara walking through the door holding an apple pie that she cooked herself. And wearing no drawers." Brassy but classy, Stanwyck is a one-of-a-kind actress who will never be replaced or surpassed.

KEY ROLES

Florence "Faith" Fallon / THE MIRACLE WOMAN, 1931, Columbia, d-Frank Capra.

There's nothing like a woman of God to make a lovely sinner. In this picture, Stanwyck portrays an Aimee Semple Macpherson-like evangelist whose miracle is how she can make the suckers pay.

Lora Hart / NIGHT NURSE, 1931, Warners, d-William A. Wellman.

Nurse Stanwyck is assigned to the case in which a drug addict and a chauffeur plan to starve two children in an extortion plot to grab their inheritance from their alcoholic mother. Stanwyck takes a right to the jaw from chauffeur Clark Gable, but she gets her revenge by sticking a bootlegger friend on him.

Selina Peake / SO BIG, 1932, Warners, d-William A. Wellman.

The director takes only 82 minutes to tell the involved tale of a woman (Stanwyck) who, after the death of her father, becomes a schoolteacher in a farming community, develops a friendship with a sculptor, marries a farmer who dies, and raises her son by herself. The boy grows up to be something of a disappointment, but Stanwyck finally finds happiness with the sculptor who has come back into her life.

Megan Davis / THE BITTER TEA OF GENERAL YEN, 1933, Columbia, d-Frank Capra.

During a Chinese civil war, Stanwyck and Gavin Gordon, who are about to be married, are separated when they rush out to help children during a bombing raid. Stanwyck regains consciousness aboard the private train of warlord Nils Asther, who treats her more as a guest than a prisoner, although they clash over their views of China. She unwittingly betrays him to his enemies but not before she accepts his challenge to die for her Christian beliefs. When the time for her to forfeit her life comes, he sets her free and returns her to her fiancée.

Lily Powers / BABY FACE, 1933, Warners, d-Alfred E. Green.

Stanwyck works her way up from working in a speakeasy to a New York society gal by spreading her favors around to various men in the company for which she works until a vice president sets her up in a swanky apartment. The plot isn't much, but the way Stanwyck looks and speaks to her conquests makes this worth seeing, even though it has a phony ending with her settling for true love.

Annie Oakley / ANNIE OAKLEY, 1935, RKO, d-George Stevens.

In this semi-western, Stanwyck is presented in a more or less historical account of "Little Miss Sure Shot" who has a passion for fellow sharpshooter Preston Foster. Besting him with a gun only slows the romance for a brief time.

Nora Clitheroe / THE PLOUGH AND THE STARS, 1937, RKO, d-John Ford.

During the "troubles" of 1916 Ireland, Stanwyck is determined to keep her husband (Preston Foster), a rebel officer, out of the fighting. The drama might be better were there more fighting and less rhetoric.

Janet Haley / INTERNES CAN'T TAKE MONEY, 1937, Paramount, d-Alfred Santell.

This picture introduces Max Brand's medical hero Dr. Kildare, but Joel McCrea isn't as good in the role as was Lew Ayres, who took it over and made a mint for MGM. In this story, the good doctor helps gangster's widow Stanwyck find her missing child.

Stella Martin Dallas / STELLA DALLAS, 1937, United Artists, d-King Vidor.

Stanwyck stands tall in this tearjerker about a sacrificing mother. She's a low-class girl who connives to marry well-born John Boles then loses him because she is uncouth and selfish. But she's also devoted to her daughter, wanting the child to have everything she hasn't had. When the girl is grown into a young woman, Stanwyck realizes that although she has not been able to rise above her origins, her daughter has. Stanwyck steps aside and allows the girl's father and his new wife to arrange the marriage of her daughter to a society man, then stands outside in the rain watching the wedding she can't attend.

Melsa Manton / THE MAD MISS MANTON, 1938, RKO, d-Leigh Jason.

Stanwyck is a zany socialite who involves her friends in solving a murder mystery. The blend of fun and mystery in the film is just right and her teaming with Henry Fonda was an inkling of good things to come.

Mollie Monahan / UNION PACIFIC, 1939, Paramount, d-Cecil B. DeMille.

Stanwyck is an Irish colleen who handles the mail for the builders of the great railroad in the 19th century. The temporary towns where the men stay while laying track attract a large number of gamblers and other unsavory characters, and Stanwyck gets caught in the middle between one of these (Robert Preston) and a scout for the company (Joel McCrea). She loves McCrea, but marries Preston in an attempt to prevent him for being hanged for a payroll robbery. Fortunately he gets killed and she gets together with McCrae.

Lorna Moon / GOLDEN BOY, 1939, Columbia, d-Rouben Mamoulian.

Stanwyck's role in the Clifford Odets play wasn't much, but it was built up for the film version. Still, Stanwyck was a star and Bill Holden was always grateful that she insisted he be cast as the poor boy torn between his two interests, prizefighting and the violin. Stanwyck provides just the right touch as the gal who complicates his choice. It was just another film for her but it made a star of Holden.

Jane / Eve Harrington / THE LADY EVE, 1941, Paramount, d-Preston Sturges.

In one of the most amusing and suggestive movies of its time, Stanwyck is a con woman working with her father (Charles Coburn) aboard a luxury liner. Their intended victim is simpleton Henry Fonda, whom Stanwyck literally makes fall for her. But somehow the fish gets off the hook and this makes her mad. She shows up at Fonda's mansion, looking just the same but claiming to be a different woman. Fonda buys the tale and ultimately marries her, but that doesn't end the fun.

Ann Mitchell / MEET JOHN DOE, 1941, Liberty Films, d-Frank Capra.

Stanwyck, a newspaper writer, creates a character named "John Doe" and has him write a letter to the paper protesting all the injustices suffered by the "little man." Reader response is so impressive that she and the editor begin a search for someone to play John Doe and serve as the author of a column called "I Protest" to be written by Stanwyck. Out-of-work ex-baseball pitcher Gary Cooper fills the bill. From this point on it's a race between the two falling in love and thwarting the presidential aspirations of a fascist newspaper publisher.

Sugarpuss O'Shea / BALL OF FIRE, 1941, Goldwyn, d-Howard Hawks.

In this farce inspired by "Snow White and the Seven Dwarfs," Stanwyck is a burlesque queen on the lam from the police who takes refuge with seven professors compiling a dictionary of slang. She teaches them some new lingo and latches on to Gary Cooper, who comes out of his shell long enough to take on some gangster friends of Stanwyck who have evil plans for her.

Dixie Daisy / LADY OF BURLESQUE, 1942, United Artists, d-William A. Wellman.

Stanwyck gets her big break on the bump-and-grind circuit when two showgirls are strangled with their own G-strings. The same fate almost befalls her.

Phyllis Dietrichson / DOUBLE INDEMNITY, 1944, Paramount, d-Billy Wilder.

In what may be the definitive film noir, Stanwyck, in a blonde wig, vamps insurance salesman Fred MacMurray and before he knows it, he's getting her older husband to unwittingly buy a policy that pays double for accidental death. Then with a little help from her, MacMurray arranges for the already-dead husband to "fall" to his death from a moving train. The two don't live happily ever after, however. Stanwyck was playing MacMurray for a chump, and had another man in the wings. The two end up fatally wounding each other while in an embrace.

Elizabeth Lane / CHRISTMAS IN CONNECTICUT, 1945, Warners, d-Peter Godfrey.

Stanwyck writes a column for Smart Housekeeping in which she tells of her lovely home in Connecticut, her husband, new baby, and the luscious meals she prepares. One of her constant readers is sailor Dennis Morgan, a national hero. When he asks to spend Christmas with Stanwyck and her family, her editor (Sydney Greenstreet) thinks it's a capital idea and plans to join the festivities himself. The problem is that Stanwyck lives in a flat in New York City, is unmarried, and has no child—and, oh yes, she can't cook. With this as a start, this smart movie only gets better.

Martha Ivers / THE STRANGE LOVE OF MARTHA IVERS, 1946, Paramount, d-Lewis Milestone.

As a teenager, Stanwyck's character had killed her autocratic aunt and allowed an innocent man to die for the crime. The young man with whom she had planned to elope kept quiet and ran away. Years later, he (Van Heflin) returns after Stanwyck has married alcoholic Kirk Douglas, the district attorney. Thinking that Heflin is back to blackmail her, she tries to rekindle the romance and holds out the possibility of killing her hubby; she's also willing to kill Heflin if that's necessary. But it's Stanwyck who ends up dead.

Leona Stevenson / SORRY, WRONG NUMBER, 1948, Paramount, d-Anatole Litvak.

Stanwyck is a neurotic invalid confined to her bed and dependent on her bedside telephone. Through a mix-up on the phone she overhears a plot to kill a woman and slowly realizes that she's the victim, that the murder was arranged by her husband, and that she is helpless to prevent it. It's a chilling story and a juicy role for Stanwyck.

Vance Jeffords / THE FURIES, 1950, Paramount, d-Anthony Mann.

Stanwyck goes over the top now and then in this powerful western drama about the conflict between a strong-willed daughter and an immovable cattle baron father (Walter Huston in his last screen appearance) before his death. It's a stimulating movie but the Freudian undertones often become overtones.

Julia O. Treadway / EXECUTIVE SUITE, 1954, MGM, d-Robert Wise.
As the daughter of the founder of a furniture company, Stanwyck is given special deference by the company's board members as they maneuver for control when the CEO dies unexpectedly of a heart attack.

Jo Courtney / WALK ON THE WILD SIDE, 1962, Columbia, d-Edward Dmytryk.
Stanwyck is the lesbian madam of the Doll's House, a New Orleans bordello where Laurence Harvey goes to retrieve his lost love Capucine, whom Stanwyck fancies for herself. She has Harvey beaten into unconsciousness by her bodyguard, who later shoots and kills Capucine by mistake.

OTHER ROLES

1927: *dancer* / BROADWAY NIGHTS. **1929:** *Ann Carter* / THE LOCKED DOOR; *Mexicali Rose* / MEXICALI ROSE. **1930:** *Kay Arnold* / LADIES OF LEISURE. **1931:** *Barbara O'Neil* / TEN CENTS A DANCE; *Anne Vincent* / ILLICIT. **1932:** *Lulu Smith* / FORBIDDEN; *Kitty Lane* / SHOPWORN; *Joan Gordon* / THE PURCHASE PRICE. **1933:** *Nan Taylor* / LADIES THEY TALK ABOUT; *Mary Archer* / EVER IN MY HEART. **1934:** *Marian Ormsby* / A LOST LADY; *Lady Lee* / GAMBLING LADY. **1935:** *Ruth Vincent* / THE SECRET BRIDE; *Shelby Barrett* / THE WOMAN IN RED; *Drue Van Allen* / RED SALUTE. **1936:** *Raphaelita Maderos* / A MESSAGE TO GARCIA; *Carolyn Martin* / THE BRIDE WALKS OUT; *Rita Wilson* / HIS BROTHER'S WIFE; *Pearl Holley* / BANJO ON MY KNEE. **1937:** *Lil Duryea* / THIS IS MY AFFAIR. **1938:** *Valentine Ransom* / BREAKFAST FOR TWO; *Margot Weston* / ALWAYS GOODBYE. **1940:** *Lee Leander* / REMEMBER THE NIGHT. **1941:** *Helen Hunt* / YOU BELONG TO ME. **1942:** *Hannah Sempler* / THE GREAT MAN'S LADY; *Fiona Gaylord* / THE GAY SISTERS. **1943:** *Joan Stanley* / FLESH AND FANTASY. **1944:** *guest* / HOLLYWOOD CANTEEN. **1945:** *Jessica Drummond* / MY REPUTATION. **1946:** *Sally Warren* / THE BRIDE WORE BOOTS; *Lily Bishop* / CALIFORNIA. **1947:** *Karen Duncan* / THE OTHER LOVE; *Sally Morton Carroll* / THE TWO MRS. CARROLLS; *Sandra Marshall* / CRY WOLF; *guest* / VARIETY GIRL. **1948:** *Polly Fulton* / B. F.'S DAUGHTER. **1949:** *Joan Boothe* / THE LADY GAMBLES; *Jessie Brown* / EAST SIDE, WEST SIDE. **1950:** *Thelma Jordan* / THELMA JORDAN; *Helen Ferguson* / NO MAN OF HER OWN; *Regina Forbes* / TO PLEASE A LADY. **1951:** *Lorna Bounty* / THE MAN WITH A CLOAK. **1952:** *Mae Doyle D'Amato* / CLASH BY NIGHT. **1953:** *Helen Stilwin* / JEOPARDY; *Julia Sturges* / TITANIC; *Naomi Murdock* / ALL I DESIRE; *Rela* / THE MOONLIGHTER; *Marina Conway* / BLOWING WILD. **1954:** *Cheryl Draper* / WITNESS TO MURDER; *Sierra Nevada Jones* / CATTLE QUEEN OF MONTANA. **1955:** *Martha Wilkinson* / THE VIOLENT MEN; *Gwen Moore* / ESCAPE TO BURMA. **1956:** *Norma Miller* / THERE'S ALWAYS TOMORROW; *Kit Banion* / THE MAVERICK QUEEN; *Ann Dempster* / THESE WILDER YEARS. **1957:** *Kathy Ferguson* / CRIME OF PASSION; *Cora Sutliff* / TROOPER HOOK; *Jessica Drummond* / FORTY GUNS. **1964:** *Maggie Morgan* / ROUSTABOUT. **1965:** *Irene Trent* / THE NIGHT WALKER.

STEIGER, ROD

(Rodney Stephen Steiger, 1925–)

Stocky, intense Rod Steiger is one of Hollywood's strongest proponents of Method acting which he learned at The Actor's Studio following five years in the Navy, which he joined at age 16. His first show business work was on the stage and in TV where he won acclaim for his portrayal of the title character in the original production of "Marty." After a small role in TERESA, he burst on the movie scene with his Oscar-nominated performance as Marlon Brando's brother in ON THE WATERFRONT. He was also nominated for his portrayal of a Jewish concentration camp survivor in THE PAWNBROKER for which he deserved to win, then walked off with the statuette for his stereotyped southern sheriff in IN THE HEAT OF THE NIGHT, which probably was not the best performance of the year. Since the 1970s realism has not been highly valued by moviemakers and goers, condemning Steiger to a string of mostly inferior roles in forgettable films.

KEY ROLES

Charlie Malloy / ON THE WATERFRONT, 1954, Columbia, d-Elia Kazan.
Steiger is the bright brother of Marlon Brando and has an in with crooked waterfront union official Lee J. Cobb. When he can't talk Brando out of telling what he knows about the crooked goings-on to a crime commission, he's murdered by his own buddies as a further warning to Brando.

Judd Fry / OKLAHOMA! 1955, Magna, d-Fred Zinnemann.
Steiger is the menacing hired hand on the farm of a young woman (Shirley Jones) and her aunt. When Jones agrees to have him take her to a box social to spite cowboy Gordon MacRae, Steiger takes this as a sign that she is to be his. When instead she marries MacRae, Steiger attempts to burn them alive on a haystack.

Al Capone / AL CAPONE, 1958, Allied Artists, d-Richard Wilson.
In this semi-documentary treatment of the career of the notorious gangland boss, Steiger only occasionally overplays the role.

Sol Nazerman / THE PAWNBROKER, 1965, Landau-Unger, d-Sidney Lumet.
In this engrossing character study Steiger gives an award-worthy performance of a Jewish pawnbroker in a New York slum who is haunted by memories of life in the Nazi concentration camps.

Komarovsky / DOCTOR ZHIVAGO, 1965, MGM, d-David Lean.
Steiger is the lover of dressmaker Adrienne Corri. He seduces her daughter (Julie Christie) who later shoots him at a party. Steiger, Christie, and Omar Shariff (as the title character) remain an intertwined triangle throughout the film.

Bill Gillespie / IN THE HEAT OF THE NIGHT, 1967, United Artists, d-Norman Jewison.
Steiger won an Oscar for his role as a somewhat stereotyped redneck southern sheriff who is forced to ask help of a black Philadelphia homicide officer (Sidney Poitier) in solving the murder of a wealthy industrialist in a small Mississippi town. Why he needs help is beyond us as the culprit is obvious to even the most naive and inexperienced moviegoer. The story and the mystery are not what makes this film work; rather it is the interplay between Steiger and Poitier as they grudgingly come to admire each other.

Christopher Gill / NO WAY TO TREAT A LADY, 1968, Paramount, d-Jack Smight.
Steiger is a psychotic killer who uses his talent for disguise and impersonation to trick lonely middle-aged women into letting him into their homes. After he strangles them, he paints a lipstick kiss on their foreheads.

Carl / THE ILLUSTRATED MAN, 1969, Warners, d-Jack Smight.
Former carnival roustabout Steiger seeks an old farmhouse and a mysterious woman (Claire Bloom)

whom he plans to kill. Twenty years earlier he had traded sex with her for the right to cover his body with tattoos, then "went back into the future." The one bare spot left on his body will show anyone who looks at it their future.

Napoleon Bonaparte / WATERLOO, 1970, Italy / USSR, Columbia, d-Sergei Bondarchuk.
Steiger plays the French emperor whose comeback is thwarted by Wellington at the Battle of Waterloo. The battle takes an hour of film time and is the best part of the picture.

W. C. Fields / W. C. FIELDS AND ME, 1976, Universal, d-Arthur Hiller.
Steiger captures some of the looks and mannerisms of the great comedian as he shows the one-time juggler's darker nature fueled by too much alcohol and encouraged by other drunks like John Barrymore.

OTHER ROLES

1951: *Frank* / TERESA. **1955:** *Stanley Hoff* / THE BIG KNIFE; *Maj. Allan Gullion* / THE COURT-MARTIAL OF BILLY MITCHELL. **1956:** *Pinky* / JUBAL; *Nick Benko* / THE HARDER THEY FALL; *Vasquez* / BACK FROM ETERNITY. **1957:** *O'Meara* / RUN OF THE ARROW; *Carl Schaffner* / ACROSS THE BRIDGE. **1958:** *Paul Hochen* / THE UNHOLY WIFE; *Paul Hoplin* / CRY TERROR. **1960:** *Paul Mason* / SEVEN THIEVES. **1961:** *Dr. Edmund McNally* / THE MARK; *Frank Morgan* / THE WORLD IN MY POCKET. **1962:** *Tiptoes* / CONVICTS FOUR; *destroyer commander* / THE LONGEST DAY; *Detective Sergeant Koleski* / 13 WEST STREET. **1963:** *Edoardo Nottola* / HANDS OVER THE CITY. **1964:** *Leo* / TIME OF INDIFFERENCE. **1965:** *Mr. Joyboy* / THE LOVED ONE; *the intermediary* / AND THERE CAME A MAN. **1967:** *the general* / THE GIRL AND THE GENERAL. **1968:** *Sgt. Albert Callan* / THE SERGEANT. **1969:** *Steve Howard* / THREE INTO TWO WON'T GO. **1971:** *Harold Ryan* / HAPPY BIRTHDAY, WANDA JUNE. **1972:** *Juan Miranda* / A FISTFUL OF DYNAMITE. **1973:** *Laban Feather* / THE LOLLY-MADONNA WAR; *Charles Siragusa* / LUCKY LUCIANO; *Hennessy* / HENNESSY. **1975:** *Louis* / DIRTY HANDS. **1977:** *Benito Mussolini* / MUSSOLINI ULTIMO ATTO. **1978:** *Senator Madison* / F.I.S.T. **1979:** *Father Delaney* / THE AMITYVILLE HORROR; *Joe Bomposa* / LOVE AND BULLETS; *General Webster* / BREAKTHROUGH. **1981:** *Benito Mussolini* / LION OF THE DESERT; *Tilghman* / CATTLE ANNIE AND LITTLE BRITCHES. **1982:** *Colonel Gluck* / LUCKY STAR; *Reb Saunders* / THE CHOSEN. **1984:** *Lieutenant McGreary* / THE NAKED FACE; *Max* / PORTRAIT OF A HITMAN.

STEWART, JAMES

(1908–)

Jimmy Stewart may be the most popular actor ever to have appeared in movies. The tall, gangling, long-faced star with the slow hesitant drawl projected sincerity, honesty, and trustworthiness. He was awarded a B.S. in architecture from Princeton but instead of designing stunning buildings, he was persuaded by classmate Joshua Logan to join the University Players at Falmouth, Massachusetts, where other players included Margaret Sullavan and Henry Fonda. He made his Broadway debut in the company's production of "Carrie Nation" in 1932. He made his feature film debut in MURDER MAN in 1935 and Margaret Sullavan helped him by insisting he appear in some of her films and they were excellent together. Stewart won an Academy Award in 1940 for THE PHILADELPHIA STORY and was nominated for MR. SMITH GOES TO WASHINGTON, IT'S A WONDERFUL LIFE, HARVEY, and ANATOMY OF A MURDER. During World War II Stewart was a bomber pilot who flew twenty missions over Germany. After the War, super-patriot and conservative Stewart stayed in the reserves and rose to the rank of brigadier general in 1959. He was best portraying ordinary men who learned to confront the system, often by themselves, and win. Before the war he appeared as the perfect Frank Capra populist hero and came back to the role in 1946 in his favorite part—George Bailey, the man who learned what it would be like had he never existed, in IT'S A WONDERFUL LIFE. Post-war Stewart became a western star and the hero of a number of suspense thrillers. Throughout his long career he seemed to understand how to make accommodations with life. As he said, "The secret of a happy life is to accept change gracefully." He has successfully appeared on the stage, notably in "Harvey" and starred in the TV series "The Jimmy Stewart Show" and "Hawkins." In 1980 Stewart was given a Life Achievement Award by the American Film Institute. Stewart made very few poor movies and all of his performances were interesting; because of this he probably is the movie actor with the most outstanding career achievement, and it's unlikely that anyone will ever rival him in this.

KEY ROLES

John de Flor / ROSE MARIE, 1936, MGM, d-W. S. Van Dyke.
Did you know that Jimmy Stewart could be a bad guy? In this version of the play by Otto A. Harbach and Oscar Hammerstein II, when Stewart escapes from prison and kills a man, his sister (Jeanette MacDonald) meets Mountie Nelson Eddy, who is out to get Stewart.

David Graham / AFTER THE THIN MAN, 1936, MGM, d-W. S. Van Dyke.
We hope readers will forgive us for revealing the ending of this more than fifty-year-old Nick and Nora Charles murder mystery, but good old Stewart is the murderer.

Chico / SEVENTH HEAVEN, 1937, 20th Century-Fox, d-Henry King.
In this remake of the 1927 silent romantic hit, Stewart has the Charles Farrell role of a Parisian sewer worker who has dreams of a beautiful wife and social position. Well, one out of two isn't bad, as Simone Simon surfaces in the Janet Gaynor role of a street waif whom Stewart rescues from the police and takes to his bleak seven-floor walk-up which they turn into an idyllic "seventh heaven."

Tony Kirby / YOU CAN'T TAKE IT WITH YOU, 1938, Columbia, d-Frank Capra.
Stewart is a member of the Kirby family, burdened down with concerns over money and social position. He falls in love with Jean Arthur of the Vanderhof family who live by Grandpa Lionel Barrymore's pet motto: "You can't take it with you! The only thing you can take with you is the love of your friends." Before this delightful social comedy is over the Kirbys have learned the lesson.

Jefferson Smith / MR. SMITH GOES TO WASHINGTON, 1939, Columbia, d-Frank Capra.
As he demonstrates in this picture, Stewart is a perfect Capra populist hero. He's naive, idealistic, and recently appointed to serve out the term of a dead senator from a state where all the politicians are controlled by corrupt boss Edward Arnold. Stewart finally wises up and tries to prevent their shenanigans by filibustering, but they are able to make him appear a crook until he gets through to the senior senator (Claude Rains) with, "I guess this is just

another lost cause, Mr. Paine. All you people don't know about lost causes. Mr. Paine does. He said once they were the only causes worth fighting for, and he fought for them once, for the only reason that any man ever fights for them. Because of just one plain, simple rule, 'love thy neighbor,' and, in this world today, full of hatred, a man who knows that one rule has a great trust. You know that rule, Mr. Paine, and I loved you for it, just as my father did. And you know that you fight for the lost causes harder than any others. Yes, you even die for them."

Tom Destry / DESTRY RIDES AGAIN, 1939, Universal, d-George Marshall.
When the murderers of the sheriff of Bottle Neck appoint the town drunk his replacement, he sobers up and sends for the son of a famous lawman who had cleaned up many western towns. The son (Stewart) arrives minus guns and doesn't seem the kind even to deal with hard-boiled dance hall girl Marlene Dietrich let alone the desperadoes, but looks are deceiving.

Alfred Kralik / THE SHOP AROUND THE CORNER, 1939, MGM, d-Ernst Lubitsch.
Stewart teams with Margaret Sullavan as two employees of a Budapest novelty shop who carry on an anonymous correspondence with each other, in which their friendship ripens, even though at work they don't seem to care for each other. This changes as they find they really have a lot in common when they tell each other their true feelings.

Macauley "Mike" Connor / THE PHILADELPHIA STORY, 1940, MGM, d-George Cukor.
As a sort of resident observer of the social scene, Stewart has the best lines in this almost perfect movie in which Katharine Hepburn learns a lot about love as she prepares to marry for the second time. After a tipsy flirtation with Stewart, she decides that her first husband (Cary Grant) was the right man after all. Among our hero's observations of how the rich live are: "The prettiest sight in this fine pretty world is the privileged class enjoying its privileges" and "I got it from a Spanish peasant's proverb: 'with the rich and mighty, always a little patience.' " Stewart won the Oscar, beating out pal Henry Fonda who was merely spectacular in THE GRAPES OF WRATH.

George Bailey / IT'S A WONDERFUL LIFE, 1947, RKO, d-Frank Capra.
Tell us that you don't shed happy tears when Todd Karns makes a toast to "My brother, George Bailey, the richest man I know" and we will know that you pull wings off butterflies, kick dogs, and take candy from babies. Viewing this most satisfyingly sentimental of Capra movies each Christmas season has become an enjoyable tradition. For those who have lived on a distant planet for years, it is the story of a very good man (Stewart) who is in trouble and wishes he had never been born. Henry Travers, an angel who has not yet won his wings, shows Stewart the consequences of his wish being granted.

McNeal / CALL NORTHSIDE 777, 1948, 20th Century-Fox, d-Henry Hathaway.
In this film based on a true story, Chicago newspaperman Stewart follows up on the story of a cleaning woman who offers the $5,000 she has earned over the past eleven years for information that will help her prove that her son is not guilty of killing a policeman a dozen years earlier. Stewart is at first unbelieving, but he finally gets the evidence that wins the convict his freedom.

Lin McAdam / WINCHESTER '73, 1950, Universal, d-Anthony Mann.
Stewart is a frontiersman who owns one of the new Winchester model 73 rifles, which he won in a Dodge City marksmanship contest. It is stolen by his own brother, (Stephen McNally), a murdering good-for-nothing. The gun passes from one person to another with Stewart always on its trail. But it finally gets back to McNally and he and Stewart have a showdown over the piece.

Tom Jeffords / BROKEN ARROW, 1950, 20th Century-Fox, d-Walter Lang.
This superb western accurately depicts the struggle between the Apaches and the white man in the 1870s. It focuses on two men, one of each race; Jeff Chandler as the great Apache chief Cochise, and Stewart as a veteran scout who attempts to make peace with the red man and marries one of their maidens (Debra Paget).

Elwood P. Dowd / HARVEY, 1950, Universal, d-Henry Koster.
Stewart is such a charming dipsomaniac and drop-out from the real world that he makes his life of total surrender to fantasy, lack of ambition, and a friendship with a six-foot invisible rabbit seem eminently appealing. The secret of his gentle madness is summed up in his advice: "When I was young, I was told that in this world you had to be very, very smart, or very, very kind. I recommend kindness."

Buttons / THE GREATEST SHOW ON EARTH, 1952, Paramount, d-Cecil B. DeMille.
Stewart plays a doctor sought for the mercy killing of his wife. He's become a clown with the circus and is never seen without his makeup. He gives himself away to a detective trailing him when he tends to the injured after a wreck of the circus train.

Glenn Miller / THE GLENN MILLER STORY, 1954, Universal, d-Anthony Mann.
Stewart facially resembles the great swing bandleader and the music is certainly memorable but the love story between Stewart and June Allyson is the typical swill one finds in these types of biopics.

L. B. "Jeff" Jeffries / REAR WINDOW, 1954, Paramount, d-Alfred Hitchcock.
Photographer Stewart is laid up with a broken leg and nothing more to do to pass the time than spy on his neighbors from his rear window which looks across a court into a number of apartments. Soon he begins to suspect that one neighbor has killed and dismembered his wife and with the help of girlfriend (Grace Kelly) he proves it.

Will Lockhart / THE MAN FROM LARAMIE, 1955, Columbia, d-Anthony Mann.
In this taut action thriller, Stewart is a cowboy who travels from Laramie, Wyoming, to New Mexico searching for those who killed his brother. It's a tried and true western formula, but the acting of Stewart and others makes it seem fresh.

Charles A. Lindbergh / THE SPIRIT OF ST. LOUIS, 1957, Warners, d-Billy Wilder.
This is a long but absorbing story with Stewart as "Lucky Lindy," the man who made the first solo nonstop flight across the Atlantic from New York to Paris in 1927. Stewart is excellent as aviation's great hero.

John "Scottie" Ferguson / VERTIGO, 1958, Paramount, d-Alfred Hitchcock.

A man uses Stewart's fear of heights in a plot to kill his wife. He hires private investigator Stewart to follow Kim Novak, who he claims is his wife because he believes she plans to kill herself. In the course of trailing her, Stewart pulls her out of the water at Golden Gate Park, and takes her home with him, and they fall in love. Yet when she runs up the stairs of a mission church with the intention of jumping, his vertigo makes it impossible for him to save her. Later he sees a girl that reminds him of his lost love and he tries to make her over in the image of the dead woman, which of course is who she really is.

Paul Biegler / ANATOMY OF A MURDER, 1959, Columbia, d-Otto Preminger.

Stewart takes the case of an army officer accused of murdering a man his wife swears raped her. Neither the officer (Ben Gazzara) nor his wife (Lee Remick) are ideal clients; Gazzara is an arrogant jealous man with a history of violence toward both his wife and men who pay too much attention to her, and Remick is a sexy flirt who seems just the type to be unfaithful. Despite the problems, Stewart gets Gazzara acquitted although the latter stiffs him for his fee.

Ranse Stoddard / THE MAN WHO SHOT LIBERTY VALANCE, 1962, Paramount, d-John Ford.

Lawyer Stewart goes west as a tenderfoot and is brutally beaten and left for dead by villain Lee Marvin. He is befriended by John Wayne, and when Stewart stands up to Marvin with a shaky gun, he is proclaimed a hero when Marvin falls dead. But it comes out later that the Duke fired the fatal shot.

Charlie Anderson / SHENANDOAH, 1965, Universal, d-Andrew V. McLaglen.

Stewart is a widower with six sons and a daughter living in Virginia at the time of the Civil War. He refuses to take sides in the conflict until one of his sons is mistaken for a Confederate soldier and is taken prisoner by Union troops.

Frank Towns / THE FLIGHT OF THE PHOENIX, 1965, 20th Century-Fox, d-Robert Aldrich.

The plane carrying a group of oil men is forced down in the Sahara desert and, after a few days and no rescue in sight, the men work to redesign the plane so that it can take off again. The man with the plan (Hardy Kruger) is a designer of model racing airplanes. Stewart is the pilot and, remarkably, they pull it off. Sadly, in making the picture veteran stuntman and pilot Paul Mantz was killed.

OTHER ROLES

1935: *Shorty* / THE MURDER MAN. **1936:** *Christopher Tyler* / NEXT TIME WE LOVE; *Dave* / WIFE VS. SECRETARY; *Elmer* / SMALL TOWN GIRL; *Terry Martin* / SPEED; *"Rowdy" Dow* / THE GORGEOUS HUSSY; *Ted Barker* / BORN TO DANCE. **1937:** *Paul North* / THE LAST GANGSTER; *"Truck" Cross* / NAVY BLUE AND GOLD. **1938:** *Jason Wilkins* / OF HUMAN HEARTS; *Peter Morgan* / VIVACIOUS LADY; *Pvt. Bill Pettigrew* / THE SHOPWORN ANGEL. **1939:** *John Mason* / MADE FOR EACH OTHER; *Larry Hall* / ICE FOLLIES OF 1939; *Guy Johnson* / IT'S A WONDERFUL WORLD. **1940:** *Martin Breitner* / THE MORTAL STORM; *Gaylord Esterbrook* / NO TIME FOR COMEDY. **1941:** *Bill Smith* / COME LIVE WITH ME; *Jimmy Haskel* / POT O'GOLD; *Gilbert Young* / ZIEGFELD GIRL. **1947:** *Rip Smith* / MAGIC TOWN. **1948:** *Slim* / ON OUR MERRY WAY; *Rupert Cadell* / ROPE. **1949:** *Marvin Payne* / YOU GOTTA STAY HAPPY; *Monty Stratton* / THE STRATTON STORY. **1950:** *John Royer* / MALAYA; *Bill Lawrence* / THE JACKPOT. **1951:** *Theodore Honey* / NO HIGHWAY IN THE SKY. **1952:** *Glyn McLyntock* / BEND OF THE RIVER; *Marsh Williams* / CARBINE WILLIAMS. **1953:** *Howard Kemp* / THE NAKED SPUR; *Steve Martin* / THUNDER BAY. **1955:** *Jeff Webster* / THE FAR COUNTRY; *Robert Holland* / STRATEGIC AIR COMMAND. **1956:** *Ben McKenna* / THE MAN WHO KNEW TOO MUCH. **1957:** *Grant McLaine* / NIGHT PASSAGE. **1958:** *Shepherd Henderson* / BELL, BOOK AND CANDLE. **1959:** *Chip Hardesty* / THE FBI STORY. **1960:** *Major Baldwin* / THE MOUNTAIN ROAD. **1961:** *Guthrie McCabe* / TWO RODE TOGETHER. **1962:** *Roger Hobbs* / MR. HOBBS TAKES A VACATION. **1963:** *Linus Rawlings* / HOW THE WEST WAS WON; *Frank Michaelson* / TAKE HER, SHE'S MINE. **1964:** *Wyatt Earp* / CHEYENNE AUTUMN. **1965:** *Robert Leaf* / DEAR BRIGITTE. **1966:** *Sam Burnett* / THE RARE BREED. **1968:** *Johnny Cobb* / FIRECREEK; *Mace Bishop* / BANDOLERO! **1970:** *John O'Hanlan* / THE CHEYENNE SOCIAL CLUB. **1971:** *Mattie Appleyard* / FOOLS' PARADE. **1974:** *host* / THAT'S ENTERTAINMENT! **1976:** *Dr. Hostetler* / THE SHOOTIST. **1977:** *Phillip Stevens* / AIRPORT '77. **1978:** *General Sternwood* / THE BIG SLEEP. **1978:** *Clovis Mitchell* / THE MAGIC OF LASSIE.

STREEP, MERYL

(Mary Louise Streep, 1951–)

Meryl Streep is perhaps the best actress now working in movies; each new performance is likely to be considered for an Academy Award and though she'll probably lose to an actress whose performance didn't match hers it'll be because voters will decide that she has had her share of recognition. Streep has impeccable academic credentials having studied her craft as an undergraduate at Vassar, then at Dartmouth, followed by three years at the Yale School of Drama where she appeared in 40 plays. Fair-haired, freckled-faced Streep is not a classical beauty, but as her performance in a movie progresses she becomes beautiful. Winner of a Best Supporting Actress Oscar for KRAMER VS. KRAMER and the Best Actress award for SOPHIE'S CHOICE, Streep has also been nominated for THE DEER HUNTER, THE FRENCH LIEUTENANT'S WOMAN, SILKWOOD, OUT OF AFRICA, and IRONWEED. Streep is always a class act and movie buffs can only look forward in thrilled anticipation to what is yet to come from this versatile and brilliant actress.

KEY ROLES

Linda / THE DEER HUNTER, 1978, Universal, d-Michael Cimino.

Streep was nominated for an Oscar for her role as Christopher Walken's girlfriend who turns to Robert De Niro for comfort when Walken doesn't choose to return from Vietnam after his fighting ends.

Karen Traynor / THE SEDUCTION OF JOE TYNAN, 1979, Universal, d-Jerry Schatzberg.

While still priming for star status Streep plays a southern, liberal political worker who has a brief but hungry affair with a Ted Kennedy-like U.S. Senator (Alan Alda) despite the fact that both are supposedly happily married.

Joanna Kramer / KRAMER VS. KRAMER, 1979, Columbia, d-Robert Benton.

In this excellent drama about a divorced couple who go to court over the custody of their son, there are no real villains. The husband's concentration on his career instead of the family leads to the split in the first place and the wife (Streep) at first willingly gives up her son so she can find herself. Both Dustin Hoffman as the father and Streep make strong appeals for their son in the court.

Sarah / Anne / THE FRENCH LIEUTENANT'S WOMAN, 1981, Great Britain, United Artists, d-Karel Reisz.

The decision to film the John Fowles novel about an 1867 British gentleman who abandons his fiancée for the former mistress of a long-gone French officer with the parallel story of the actors and actresses making the film seems an unnecessarily intrusive and unsuccessful device. Streep is superior as the Fowles character and as the actress who plays her.

Sophie Zawistowska / SOPHIE'S CHOICE, 1982, Universal, d-Alan J. Pakula.

Streep won the Best Actress Academy Award for her magnificent portrayal of a Polish woman who has survived a German concentration camp, only to find that her past still haunts her years later in Brooklyn. The title refers to the cruel choice she was forced to make in the concentration camp: which of her two children was to be sent to the gas chambers and which was to live. In the end, she lost both.

Karen Silkwood / SILKWOOD, 1983, ABC, d-Mike Nichols.

Another picture, another Oscar nomination. This time it was for Streep's meritorious portrayal of a nuclear processing plant worker who blows the whistle on safety problems and is mysteriously killed in an automobile accident on her way to tell her story to a reporter.

Karen Blixen / OUT OF AFRICA, 1985, Universal, d-Sydney Pollack.

Based on the writings of Baroness Karen Blixen, this love story about Streep and an African big-game hunter (Robert Redford) moves as slowly as does their passion, but that seems to be all right. She is married, but it's for convenience, not love. She doesn't seem unduly concerned about conventions and in this part of Africa at about the time of World War I the Europeans are a high-living bunch. Still she and Redford don't settle down to live happily ever after or even happily for a short time; he's always coming and going, and in the end is killed in an airplane crash.

Helen Marie Archer / IRONWEED, 1987, Tri-Star, d-Hector Babenco.

Streep is touching as the female tramp in the 1930s who, along with her man (Jack Nicholson), aimlessly moves through the days with no goal more pressing than finding a place to sleep at night. Her acting is almost enough to break one's heart. When she sings "He's My Pal" she briefly thinks its being received with great enthusiasm by the patrons of a crowded bar, but actually no one is paying much attention, and that rather sums up both her hope and hopelessness. With her Academy Award nomination Streep has set a record: seven nominations in 14 movies.

OTHER ROLES

1977: *Anne Marie* / JULIA. **1979:** *Jill* / MANHATTAN. **1982:** *Brooke Reynolds* / STILL OF THE NIGHT. **1984:** *Molly Gilmore* / FALLING IN LOVE. **1985:** *Susan Traherne* / PLENTY. **1986:** *Rachel* / HEARTBURN.

STREISAND, BARBRA

(1942–)

Barbra Streisand is not so much an actress as she is a superstar whose movies are events. She has never played second fiddle to any of her co-stars and, in fact, none of the performers who have appeared in movies with her—with the possible exception of Robert Redford—could even be considered a co-star. A magnificent singer, Streisand was awarded a Tony in 1970 merely for being the "Best Actress of the Decade." She is a woman of unusual looks but she has made everyone look harder and decide that she is truly beautiful. She won an Oscar for her first role in FUNNY GIRL, sharing the award with Katharine Hepburn, which many considered almost sacreligious. Many thought Streisand won the award not so much because of her performance as Fanny Brice but because of her singing popularity. Streisand has been considered a pain by her co-workers because of her rumored megalomania. Walter Matthau was moved to observe on the set of her one flop, HELLO, DOLLY!: "I have more talent in one of my farts than she has in her whole body." No doubt an exaggeration. Until her latest movie NUTS, Streisand has steered away from pictures in which she is not a likable character, even if she is portraying a kook. Besides her acting awards, she has won an Oscar for the song "Evergreen" which she wrote with Paul Williams. With YENTL she showed her versatile talent as producer, writer, director, composer, and star. It will be interesting to see what this former switchboard operator, nightclub singer, and Broadway star will do next.

KEY ROLES

Fanny Brice / FUNNY GIRL, 1968, Columbia, d-William Wyler.

In her debut and Academy Award-tying performance, Streisand is a delight portraying with both poignancy and good humor a very funny girl indeed. (The same can not be said of the sequel which is a mish-mash of an unstylish soap opera story line desperately missing wit, music, and romance.) While Streisand sounds great belting out the Jule Styne songs, it's hard to beat her singing Brice's torch song, "My Man."

Dolly Levi / HELLO, DOLLY! 1969, 20th Century-Fox, d-Gene Kelly.

Many things contributed to the failure of this Broadway hit to make it as a movie, but many probably stayed away when they learned that Streisand was coming on like a cross between Mae West and Harvey Korman. It didn't help, either, that Walter Matthau disliked his miscast co-star so much. Everything about the production was in excess. The best thing about the movie was the work of Michael Crawford and Marianne McAndrew, who at least seemed to be enjoying themselves.

Doris / THE OWL AND THE PUSSYCAT, 1970, Columbia, d-Herbert Ross.

Streisand dresses up as an outrageous prostitute living next door to book clerk George Segal. When he complains to the landlord, she's thrown out on the street and then walks over him as she moves into his apartment. These two opposites, extrovert and introvert, of course find some reason to fall in love.

Judy Maxwell / WHAT'S UP, DOC? 1972, Warners, d-Peter Bogdanovich.

Kooky Streisand, for reasons never made clear, takes one look at absent-minded, wimpy musicologist Ryan O'Neal and decides he's the boy for her. She moves in on him so quickly that he doesn't know what's hit him, and she pushes aside his equally unappealing fiancée (Madeline Kahn), bats those big eyes over her lovely crooked nose, and lands her fish.

Katie Morosky Gardiner / THE WAY WE WERE, 1973, Columbia, d-Sydney Pollack.

Streisand is a 1930s campus left-wing activist who falls in love with waspy Robert Redford, but doesn't get him until during the war when their paths cross again and he crashes in her bed. They eventually marry; he becomes a successful screenwriter and she mixes with the types that get called before the House Un-American Activities Committee. They finally split, not so much over her continuing radicalism but because he starts sleeping around. The Academy Award-winning title song is well on its way to becoming a standard classic.

Esther Hoffman / A STAR IS BORN, 1976, Warners, d-Frank R. Pierson.
This seems an unnecessary remake of the story of a rising and falling star, so well done twice before (first with Janet Gaynor and Fredric March, then with Judy Garland and James Mason); moving everything to the Rock arena is not exactly the same as injecting new life into the story. It's been reported that co-star Kris Kristofferson kept himself constantly soused to survive the experience of working with Streisand.

Yentl / YENTL, 1983, Great Britain, MGM / United Artists, d-Barbra Streisand.
Streisand does everything but play the role of Mandy Patinkin, the man she loves, in this tale of a Jewish girl in Poland many years ago who poses as a boy in order to get an education. As a man she marries Amy Irving whom she must constantly put off when Irving can't understand why they don't consummate their marriage.

Claudia Faith Draper / NUTS, 1987, Warners, d-Martin Ritt.
Streisand gives a memorable performance as a call girl who is different, unlikable, and even violent when pushed, but one who isn't crazy. At least that's what her court appointed counsel (Richard Dreyfuss) in a sanity hearing hopes to prove. She doesn't help her case much with her behavior as she directs a lot of anger at her mother and stepfather (Maureen Stapleton and Karl Malden). If she wins her sanity hearing she must face a murder trial for killing a customer who got too rough with her. When she describes what she does for her "Johns" to states attorney Robert Webber, she's explicit and deliberately exciting. It once was that such a role and performance was a sure-fire Oscar nominee, but then Streisand is not very popular with the Hollywood set.

OTHER ROLES

1970: *Daisy Gamble* / ON A CLEAR DAY YOU CAN SEE FOREVER. **1972:** *Margaret Reynolds* / UP THE SANDBOX. **1974:** *Henrietta (Henry)* / FOR PETE'S SAKE. **1975:** *Fanny Brice* / FUNNY LADY. **1979:** *Hillary Kramer* / THE MAIN EVENT. **1981:** *Cheryl Gibbons* / ALL NIGHT LONG.

SULLAVAN, MARGARET

(1911–1960)

Some consider Margaret Sullavan the June Allyson of the 1930s; the two did share petite figures, deceptive beauty, and unique, indescribable, distinctive voices. Others would argue that Sullavan was a far superior actress. This is being kind to the sad actress who suffered brightly and died magnificently in her Oscar-nominated part in THREE COMRADES. In seventeen years she made only sixteen movies and few of these were great melodramas, but her performances as vulnerable women with other-worldly qualities are fondly remembered by the many fans who loved her fey beauty and shy intelligence. Married four times—to actor Henry Fonda, director William Wyler, agent Leland Hayward, and Kenneth Wagg—she committed suicide in the Taft Hotel in New Haven during the tryout of "Sweet Love Remember'd." Sullavan had been fighting deafness for years and was terrified of missing her cues.

KEY ROLES

Mary Lane / ONLY YESTERDAY, 1933, Universal, d-John M. Stahl.
In her screen debut, Sullavan spends the night with an army officer (John Boles) and becomes pregnant. When Boles returns from World War I, he has no recollection of ever having met her. Some twelve years later he seduces her again, still not remembering her. It's really quite ridiculous, but Sullavan suffers so sweetly that it's rather precious.

Luisa Ginglebusher / THE GOOD FAIRY, 1935, Universal, d-William Wyler.
Sullavan is the helpless type who seems to attract men like flowers do bees. The film focuses on three admirers: an eccentric waiter (Reginald Owen), a millionaire (Frank Morgan) who promises to make her husband a wealthy man, and a lawyer (Herbert Marshall) whose name Sullavan picks out of the phone book.

Chessy Chester / THE MOON'S OUR HOME, 1936, Paramount, d-William A. Seiter.
In this comedy Sullavan is a headstrong actress who impulsively marries author-explorer Henry Fonda and then discovers that their temperaments clash. Fonda and Sullavan had married in real life in 1931 and divorced in 1933 and had just about the same problems as plagued the characters in this picture.

Pat Hollman / THREE COMRADES, 1938, MGM, d-Frank Borzage.
The story is from the novel by Erich Maria Remarque with a screenplay by F. Scott Fitzgerald. In it Sullavan is a lovely young woman who is dying of tuberculosis whose great spirit gives joy to three friends in post World War I Germany. In the final scene the two surviving comrades are joined in a church-yard by the ghosts of Sullavan and the other friend, who was killed in a riot. It's very effective and deeply moving.

Daisy Heath / THE SHOPWORN ANGEL, 1938, MGM, d-H. C. Potter.
Showgirl Sullavan meets and falls in love with a naive young soldier (James Stewart) who goes AWOL to be with her and she gives up her wealthy man-about-town for him.

Klara Novak / THE SHOP AROUND THE CORNER, 1939, MGM, d-Ernst Lubitsch.
In this charming story Sullavan works in the same novelty shop in Budapest as does Jimmy Stewart and they don't get along. Her spirits soar however when she receives letters from her anonymous pen pal. The two decide to meet and make arrangements so they will recognize each other, and her dear friend turns out to be, of course, Stewart, who arrives without her seeing him and departs. Sullavan looks beautifully resigned to the sadness of being stood up, but Stewart ultimately reveals his identity and it looks like there's happiness ahead for them.

Freya Rath / THE MORTAL STORM, 1940, MGM, d-Frank Borzage.
Calling Germany "somewhere in Europe," this picture was the first in which Hollywood took a crack at the Nazis. It depicts a family and their friends torn apart over Nazism and it caused Joseph Goebbels to ban all MGM productions from Germany.

Ray Smith / BACK STREET, 1941, Universal, d-Robert Stevenson.

Because of anti-German sentiments, Sullavan's character's name was changed from Schmidt of the 1932 production to Smith. It tells the sad story of a woman who remains her lover's back street mistress for some twenty years, because he has no intention of divorcing his wife and hurting his family and career. Charles Boyer is the man and, despite his rather shabby attitude, Sullavan finds reasons to love him.

OTHER ROLES

1934: *Lammchen Pinneberg* / LITTLE MAN, WHAT NOW? **1935:** *Vallette Bedford* / SO RED THE ROSE. **1936:** *Cicely Tyler* / NEXT TIME WE LOVE. **1939:** *Judy Linden* / THE SHINING HOUR. **1940:** *Ruth Holland* / SO ENDS OUR NIGHT. **1941:** *Jane Alexander* / APPOINTMENT FOR LOVE. **1942:** *cameo* / LAND OF LIBERTY. **1943:** *Lieutenant Smith* / CRY HAVOC. **1950:** *Mary Scott* / NO SAD SONGS FOR ME.

SUTHERLAND, DONALD

(1934–)

This tall, six-foot-four-inch, Canadian-born actor began acting while in college. He went to England to study at the London Academy of Music and Dramatic Art and spent a long time on British TV before landing a series of small movie roles. He belatedly became a star with roles in KLUTE and M*A*S*H. Aloof, gaunt, and hollow-eyed, Sutherland can seem idiotic or menacing without much change of expression. His own formula for his work is: "An actor is successful when he can create a character with the minimum of gesture and words. That is what I strive for."

KEY ROLES

Vernon Pinkley / THE DIRTY DOZEN, 1967, MGM, d-Robert Aldrich.

Sutherland is one of twelve GIs condemned either to death or long prison terms, who are recruited for special training for a suicide-like mission against a behind-the-lines retreat for high-ranking German officers during World War II. While in training this weak-minded, grinning psychopath impersonates a general and reviews troops with all the required pomp and circumstance. But he is among the first killed.

Hawkeye Pierce / M*A*S*H, 1970, 20th Century-Fox, d-Robert Altman.

The movies's humor is much more black than that of the TV series. Showing a hatred of war and an understandable desire to get out of Korea, Sutherland and his fellow doctors and nurses at a Mobile Army Surgical Hospital Unit are an amoral bunch, willing to try any cruel joke to pass the time.

Alex / ALEX IN WONDERLAND, 1971, MGM, d-Paul Mazursky.

This film is supposedly based loosely on director Mazursky's own experiences after the making of his smash hit, BOB AND CAROL AND TED AND ALICE, and Sutherland plays a hot young director who can't seem to duplicate the success of his first film.

John Klute / KLUTE, 1971, Warners, d-Alan J. Pakula.

Sutherland is a small town cop who goes to New York to seek a missing friend. His only clue is that the man somehow got hooked up with call girl Jane Fonda. Sutherland takes up with Fonda and barely saves her from the sadist who killed his friend as well as several prostitutes.

John Baxter / DON'T LOOK NOW, 1973, Great Britain, Paramount, d-Nicolas Roeg.

After his daughter drowns, an event he had sensed before it happened, Sutherland and his wife (Julie Christie) travel to Venice to try and forget their loss. There they meet two sisters, one a blind clairvoyant, who tells them that their daughter is trying to contact them, and so, it seems, she is.

Homer Simpson / THE DAY OF THE LOCUST, 1975, Paramount, d-John Schlesinger.

In this flawed but unforgettable look at the losers and misfits that descend upon Hollywood like locusts in the hopes of finding fame and fortune, Sutherland is a retired introvert so taunted by a bubble-headed extra (Karen Black) that he has a brainstorm that triggers a riot at a movie premier at Grauman's Chinese Theater.

Matthew Bennel / INVASION OF THE BODY SNATCHERS, 1978, United Artists, d-Philip Kaufman.

In this excellent remake of the 1956 science fiction classic, Sutherland is the protagonist who tells the remarkable and horrific tale of the "pods," which are organisms that grow human bodies to replace humans when they go to sleep.

Calvin / ORDINARY PEOPLE, 1980, Paramount, d-Robert Redford.

In the film that won the Oscar for Best Picture of the Year and another for Robert Redford in his directorial debut, Sutherland and Mary Tyler Moore are an upper-middle-class couple who, on the surface, seem happy but who have serious problems as a family. Their younger son (Timothy Hutton) breaks down filled with guilt about the accidental death of his brother, and before he has been able to pull things together with the help of a psychiatrist (Judd Hirsch), the break-up of his parents is inevitable.

OTHER ROLES

1964: *witch* / *sergeant* / CASTLE OF THE LIVING DEAD. **1965:** *Nevney* / THE BEDFORD INCIDENT; *Bob Carroll* / DR. TERROR'S HOUSE OF HORRORS. **1966:** *baby's father* / PROMISE HER ANYTHING. **1968:** *Joseph* / FANATIC; *Lord Peter Sanderson* / JOANNA; *Dave Negli* / THE SPLIT; *chorus leader* / OEDIPUS THE KING; *American* / SEBASTIAN. **1969:** *Charles Coupe* / *Pierre DeSisi* / START THE REVOLUTION WITHOUT ME. **1970:** *Fr. Michael Ferrier* / ACT OF THE HEART; *Oddball* / KELLY'S HEROES; *"Christ"* / JOHNNY GOT HIS GUN. **1971:** *the minister* / LITTLE MURDERS. **1972:** *himself* / F.T.A. **1973:** *Jesse Veldini* / STEELYARD BLUES; *Andy Hammond* / LADY ICE. **1974:** *Brulard* / S*P*Y*S. **1975:** *corpse* / END OF THE GAME; *Dan Candy* / ALIEN THUNDER. **1976:** *Attila* / 1900; *Casanova* / FELLINI'S CASANOVA; *Liam Devlin* / THE EAGLE HAS LANDED. **1977:** *Clumsy* / THE KENTUCKY FRIED MOVIE; *himself* / THE CINEMA ACCORDING TO BERTOLUCCI; *Carella* / BLOOD RELATIVES. **1978:** *Dave Jennings* / NATIONAL LAMPOON'S ANIMAL HOUSE. **1979:** *Agar* / THE GREAT TRAIN ROBBERY; *Robert Lees* / MURDER BY DECREE; *Reese* / A VERY BIG WITHDRAWAL; *Frank Lansing* / BEAR ISLAND. **1980:** *Prof. Roger Kelly* / NOTHING PERSONAL. **1981:** *Nick the Noz* / GAS; *Henry Faber* / EYE OF THE NEEDLE; *Jay Mallory* / THE DISAPPEARANCE; *Dr. Thomas Vrain* / THRESHOLD. **1982:** *Brian Costello* / MAX DUGAN RETURNS. **1984:** *Weslake* / CRACKERS. **1985:** *Brother Thaddeus* / HEAVEN HELP US; *Sergeant Major Peasy* / REVOLUTION. **1987:** *Fr. Bob Koesler* / THE ROSARY MURDERS; *Paul Gauguin* / THE WOLF AT THE DOOR.

TAYLOR, ELIZABETH

(1932–)

Elizabeth Taylor's spectacular beauty from childhood to the present has been such that her talent as an actress is often overlooked—even by the actress herself. Born in London of American parents, she was brought to Los Angeles just before the outbreak of World War II. In 1943 she signed a long-term contract with MGM that tied her to the studio until well into the 1960s. The raven-haired beauty made her film debut in THERE'S ONE BORN EVERY MINUTE in 1942. She became a star with NATIONAL VELVET in 1944 and blossomed from an adorable child-star into a beautiful woman in romantic leads without ever going through adolescence. Her best work, playing strong, shrewish women, sarcastic with men who tried unsuccessfully to dominate them, was in the mid-1950s and early 1960s. She won Oscars for BUTTERFIELD 8 and WHO'S AFRAID OF VIRGINIA WOOLF? and nominations for CAT ON A HOT TIN ROOF, RAINTREE COUNTY, and SUDDENLY LAST SUMMER. The public has been as fascinated with the violet-eyed beauty's not-so-private life and seven marriages as with her movies. Her first marriage was to hotel heir Nicky Hilton, followed by actor Michael Wilding, producer Michael Todd—who was killed in an airplane crash—and singer Eddie Fisher—stolen from his wife Debbie Reynolds, or so thought a large number of disapproving fans. Fisher didn't last long, being replaced by Richard Burton with whom Liz had a tempestuous affair on and off the set of CLEOPATRA. Taylor married Burton twice, but their teaming in films was very much a mixed bag, with both wasting their considerable talents in films they were well paid for but in which they didn't deliver much. Taylor's latest husband was politician John Warner. Her explanation for her many entries in the marriage sweepstakes is: "What do you expect me to do? Sleep alone?" Taylor, who has had persistent weight problems, recently brought her once spectacular figure back to a point any woman would be proud of, not just a 55-year-old woman. She has made some telling observations about herself, including, "I have the face and body of a woman and the mind of a child"; "I'm Mother Courage. I'll be dragging my sable coat behind me into old age"; and "When people say, 'She's got everything,' I've got only one answer: 'I haven't had tomorrow.' "

KEY ROLES

Velvet Brown / NATIONAL VELVET, 1944, MGM, d-Clarence Brown.
Originally RKO executives had Katharine Hepburn in mind to star in this story but they let it lapse and MGM picked it up. Although Taylor even then didn't look like a jockey, she won the hearts of audiences with her beautiful looks and indomitable spirit as a girl who, with the help of Mickey Rooney, trains and rides the horse that wins the Grand National.

Mary Skinner / LIFE WITH FATHER, 1947, Warners, d-Michael Curtiz.
Taylor's name is far down the list of credits in this story of the Day family, but her presence is felt as the pretty visitor who develops an adolescent romance with the oldest son of the family (Jimmy Lydon).

Amy March / LITTLE WOMEN, 1948, MGM, d-Mervyn LeRoy.
Looking lovely in her long curls, Taylor is the spoiled, flighty March sister in this remake of the 1933 classic film production of Louisa May Alcott's story of four sisters growing up during the Civil War. She weds Peter Lawford, the beau given up by her sister (June Allyson).

Kay Banks / FATHER OF THE BRIDE, 1950, MGM, d-Vincente Minnelli.
At about the time of this movie Taylor married in real life. But it's hoped that her character in this film and its sequel, FATHER'S LITTLE DIVIDEND, had a happier union than that of Taylor and playboy Nicky Hilton. She makes an adorable bride in this funny and touching look at the chaos an impending wedding has on the family of the bride.

Angela Vickers / A PLACE IN THE SUN, 1951, Paramount, d-George Stevens.
Taylor at 19 was so breathtakingly desirable that males in the audience felt more sympathy for Montgomery Clift and his problems with his pregnant girlfriend (Shelley Winters) than had some ordinarily beautiful actress played the society girl for whom Clift commits murder. Clift is executed for Winter's death. The decision by director George Stevens to play a love scene between Taylor and Clift in tight facial close-ups was inspired. She looks at Clift with such love as she says over and over: "Tell Mama. Tell Mama all."

Rebecca / IVANHOE, 1952, MGM, d-Richard Thorpe.
In this exciting production of Sir Walter Scott's novel of the Saxon knight Ivanhoe (Robert Taylor), he is treated by beautiful Jewish Taylor when he is injured defending her. She loves him but loses out to Joan Fontaine.

Leslie Lynnton Benedict / GIANT, 1956, Warners, d-George Stevens.
Taylor is the strong-willed woman from the East who marries Texas cattleman Rock Hudson and is unwilling to be relegated to only "women's interests." She befriends ranch hand James Dean who, when he is left a bit of land by Hudson's sister, becomes an oil baron. Taylor is the best thing in this overly-long version of the Edna Ferber novel.

Susanna Drake / RAINTREE COUNTY, 1957, MGM, d-Edward Dmytryk.
The production of this film was delayed two months when co-star Montgomery Clift suffered severe facial injuries in a car crash. Taylor is a southern belle who marries an Indiana schoolteacher during the Civil War era after telling him she's pregnant. She's not and she discovers that she's made a mistake, finding her married life boring. She develops the symptoms of insanity that killed her mother and finds herself in a medieval-like madhouse—more a prisoner than a patient.

Maggie "The Cat" Pollitt / CAT ON A HOT TIN ROOF, 1958, MGM, d-Richard Brooks.
The top moneymaker of the year was the highly charged conflict between Taylor and Paul Newman over his refusal to have sex with her. Instead he tries to forget his sexual identity crisis by staying drunk most of the time. Taylor demonstrates great dramatic ability as well as doing as much for a slip as any woman ever has.

Catherine Holly / SUDDENLY, LAST SUMMER, 1959, Columbia, d-Joseph L. Mankiewicz.
Taylor's domineering aunt (Katharine Hepburn) has her committed to an insane asylum where she is scheduled for an operation that will permanently erase the memory of the grisly way her homosexual cousin died.

Gloria Wandrous / BUTTERFIELD 8, 1960, MGM, d-Daniel Mann.
Taylor won an Oscar for her performance as an over-sexed model and call girl who has a stormy love affair with married Manhattan socialite Laurence Harvey.

Her off-screen antics gained her more news space; she almost died of pneumonia and she married Eddie Fisher. The first won her sympathy and perhaps the Oscar and the second made her a nasty home-wrecker in the eyes of many fans.

Cleopatra / CLEOPATRA, 1963, 20th Century-Fox, d-Joseph L. Mankiewicz.

Once again, Taylor's off-screen antics were of more interest than her performance in a movie, even when it was this over-blown, overly-long, boring story of the Queen of the Nile, Julius Caesar, and Mark Antony (played by her new lover Richard Burton).

Martha / WHO'S AFRAID OF VIRGINIA WOOLF? 1966, Warners, d-Mike Nichols.

Taylor is the bitchy, ball-busting wife of a college professor (Richard Burton) who has lost all ambition or hope of amounting to anything. He and Taylor entertain a young academic couple (George Segal and Sandy Dennis) who are new to the college in a long night of drinking and opening wounds. Taylor won her second Oscar for her powerful and absorbing performance as the dowdy, aging sexpot.

Leonora Penderton / REFLECTIONS IN A GOLDEN EYE, 1967, Warners, d-John Huston.

In this idiotic film, Taylor is the wife of a major in the peacetime army (Marlon Brando). She has an affair with a neighboring officer whose wife has cut off her nipples with garden shears, and her husband has the hots for a young soldier who rides nude on horseback through the woods.

OTHER ROLES

1942: *Gloria Twine* / THERE'S ONE BORN EVERY MINUTE. **1943:** *Priscilla* / LASSIE COME HOME. **1944:** *Helen Burns* / JANE EYRE; *Betsy, age 10* / THE WHITE CLIFFS OF DOVER. **1946:** *Kathie Merrick* / COURAGE OF LASSIE. **1947:** *Cynthia Bishop* / CYNTHIA. **1948:** *Carol Pringle* / A DATE WITH JUDY; *Susan Packett* / JULIA MISBEHAVES. **1950:** *Melinda Greyton* / CONSPIRATOR; *Mary Belney* / THE BIG HANGOVER. **1951:** *Kay Banks Dunstan* / FATHER'S LITTLE DIVIDEND; *guest* / CALLAWAY WENT THATAWAY. **1952:** *Anastasia Macaboy* / LOVE IS BETTER THAN EVER. **1953:** *Jean Latimer* / THE GIRL WHO HAD EVERYTHING. **1954:** *Louise Durant* / RHAPSODY; *Ruth Wiley* / ELEPHANT WALK; *Lady Patricia* / BEAU BRUMMEL; *Helen Ellswirth* / THE LAST TIME I SAW PARIS. **1960:** *the real Sally Kennedy* / SCENT OF MYSTERY. **1963:** *Frances Andros* / THE V.I.P.S. **1965:** *Laura Reynolds* / THE SANDPIPER; *guest* / WHAT'S NEW, PUSSYCAT? **1967:** *Katharina (Kate)* / THE TAMING OF THE SHREW; *Helen of Troy* / DR. FAUSTUS; *Martha Pineda* / THE COMEDIANS. **1968:** *Flora "Sissy" Goforth* / BOOM!; *Leonora* / SECRET CEREMONY. **1969:** *cameo* / ANNE OF THE THOUSAND DAYS. **1970:** *Fran Walker* / THE ONLY GAME IN TOWN. **1971:** *Rosie Probert* / UNDER MILK WOOD. **1972:** *Zee Blakeley* / X, Y AND ZEE; *Jimmie Jean Jackson* / HAMMERSMITH IS OUT. **1973:** *Ellen Wheeler* / NIGHT WATCH; *Barbara Sawyer* / ASH WEDNESDAY. **1974:** *Lise* / THE DRIVER'S SEAT; *host* / THAT'S ENTERTAINMENT! **1976:** *Queen of Light / Mother / Witch / Maternal Love* / THE BLUE BIRD. **1977:** *Desiree Armfeldt* / A LITTLE NIGHT MUSIC; *guest* / WINTER KILLS. **1980:** *Marina Rudd* / THE MIRROR CRACK'D.

TAYLOR, ROBERT

(Spangler Arlington Brugh, 1911–1969)

The son of a Nebraska country doctor, Robert Taylor majored in music in college, playing the cello. He won a screen test and a long-term contract with MGM in 1934, where he was dubbed "The Man with the Perfect Profile." With a new name Taylor was handsome to the point of prettiness, so he grew a moustache to counter this "pretty-boy" image. He made his film debut in HANDY ANDY in 1934 and for the next 30 years remained a major star. Not really a great actor, Taylor was a hard-working professional appreciated for his cooperation and understanding by directors and co-workers. Prior to World War II, in which he served as a flight instructor with the navy, Taylor played a series of romantic leads; after the war he moved into roles of mature, sometimes even flawed and corrupt men. Still extremely popular in the 1960s, he starred in the TV series "Death Valley Days" and "The Detectives" before dying in 1969 of lung cancer.

KEY ROLES

Bobby Merrick / MAGNIFICENT OBSESSION, 1935, Universal, d-John M. Stahl.

Taylor, a playboy in part responsible for the death of Irene Dunne's husband and her blindness, gets serious, becomes a surgeon, and restores the sight of the woman he has come to love.

Armand Duvall / CAMILLE, 1936, MGM, d-George Cukor.

Taylor makes a passionate lover for cynical courtesan Greta Garbo in one of the most praised films of all time. She dies beautifully in Taylor's arms. They make a beautiful pair.

Lee Sheridan / A YANK AT OXFORD, 1937, MGM, d-Jack Conway.

Taylor is a brash American college sports hero who has difficulty adjusting to the customs and traditions of the English when he attends Oxford on a scholarship. He rubs people the wrong way but ultimately proves his worth.

Erich Lohkamp / THREE COMRADES, 1938, MGM, d-Frank Borzage.

Taylor is one of three friends who find life hard in Germany after World War I. To make things worse, his optimistic wife (Margaret Sullavan) dies of tuberculosis and one of his comrades is killed in a riot.

Roy Cronin / WATERLOO BRIDGE, 1940, MGM, d-Mervyn LeRoy.

In one of the year's major successes, Taylor is a British officer who has an affair with ballerina Vivien Leigh. When she is led to believe he has been killed in the war, she becomes a streetwalker. Although they meet again, things don't work out for them.

William Bonney / BILLY THE KID, 1941, MGM, d-David Miller.

Reportedly, Billy the Kid was an imbecilic-looking, cold-blooded killer who was gunned down by the time he was twenty-one. Taylor was one of the most handsome and intelligent-looking actors of the period and in 1941 he was thirty. As Taylor plays him, the Kid tries to reform but that just isn't in the cards; he must have his date with destiny and Pat Garrett.

Johnny Eager / JOHNNY EAGER, 1941, MGM, d-Mervyn LeRoy.

Taylor, an unscrupulous mobster, is gunned down by some associates after he backs out of framing the daughter of the D.A. with a fake murder charge because he has fallen in love with her. Van Heflin gives the following eulogy for his friend: "This guy could have climbed the highest mountain in the world—if he just started up the right one."

Marcus Vinicius / QUO VADIS? 1951, MGM, d-Mervyn LeRoy.

Taylor is a Roman commander who falls in love with Christian girl Deborah Kerr, which incurs the disfavor of Emperor Nero (played as a mad ham by Peter Ustinov). It's a spectacular epic but the acting is over-the-top to match the grand scale of the story. The film had been started in 1949 with Gregory Peck and Elizabeth Taylor but the production was halted.

Ivanhoe / IVANHOE, 1952, MGM, d-Richard Thorpe.
Taylor is a Saxon knight who has sworn to help ransom King Richard the Lion Hearted, captured and held prisoner on his way back from the Crusades. He's loved by two women—lovely Jewess Liz Taylor and blonde Joan Fontaine, whom he chooses.

Sir Lancelot / KNIGHTS OF THE ROUND TABLE, 1953, MGM, d-Richard Thorpe.
Taylor is the heroic knight who falls in love with Guinevere (Ava Gardner), the queen of his friend and king, Arthur of England (Mel Ferrer). It is a blockbuster adventure story with acceptable performances from the three principals.

Christopher Kelvaney / ROGUE COP, 1954, MGM, d-Roy Rowland.
Taylor, the corrupt cop of the title, works for an underworld boss (George Raft) but turns in his resignation and seeks revenge when the mob kills his younger brother, an honest beat patrolman.

Bushrod Gentry / MANY RIVERS TO CROSS, 1954, MGM, d-Roy Rowland.
In a very amusing western, Taylor is a trapper on his way to Canada passing through a Kentucky settlement in 1798 who encounters a local beauty (Eleanor Parker) who has marriage on her mind. She's a sharpshooter who needs his quick-loading ability in a very funny sequence in which a group of Indians take turns charging them while Taylor works frantically to load and fire his flintlock rifle.

Jake Wade / THE LAW AND JAKE WADE, 1958, MGM, d-John Sturges.
When Taylor, the hero, Richard Widmark, the villain, and Patricia Owens, the love interest, seek loot buried in a ghost town, their search is interrupted by an Indian raid. It's a most enjoyable western.

Col. Alois Podhajsky / MIRACLE OF THE WHITE STALLIONS, 1963, Buena Vista, d-Arthur Hiller.
Taylor portrays the owner of the Vienna Spanish Riding School who rescues the school's prize Lippizaner horses during the waning days of World War II.

OTHER ROLES

1934: *Lloyd Burmeister* / HANDY ANDY; *Arthur White* / THERE'S ALWAYS TOMORROW; *Bill Renton* / A WICKED WOMAN. **1935:** *Dr. Ellis* / SOCIETY DOCTOR; *Steve Gordon* / TIMES SQUARE LADY; *Jaskerelli* / WEST POINT OF THE AIR; *Lt. Tom Randolph* / MURDER IN THE FLEET; *Bob Gordon* / BROADWAY MELODY OF 1936. **1936:** *Bob Dakin* / SMALL TOWN GIRL; *Richard Winfield* / PRIVATE NUMBER; *Chris* / HIS BROTHER'S WIFE; *Bow Timberlake* / THE GORGEOUS HUSSY. **1937:** *Raymond Dabney* / PERSONAL PROPERTY; *Lt. Richard Perry* / THIS IS MY AFFAIR; *Steve Raleigh* / BROADWAY MELODY OF 1938; *Tommy "Killer" McCoy* / THE CROWD ROARS. **1939:** *Blake Cantrell* / STAND UP AND FIGHT; *Bill Overton* / LUCKY NIGHT; *Bill Carey* / LADY OF THE TROPICS; *Jeff Holland* / REMEMBER? **1940:** *Ens. Alan Drake* / FLIGHT COMMAND; *Mark Preysing* / ESCAPE. **1941:** *Jimmy Lee* / WHEN LADIES MEET. **1942:** *Terry Trindale* / HER CARDBOARD LOVER. **1943:** *Lt. Gregg Masterson* / STAND BY FOR ACTION; *Sgt. Bill Dane* / BATAAN; *guest* / THE YOUNGEST PROFESSION. **1944:** *John Meredith* / SONG OF RUSSIA. **1946:** *Alan Garroway* / UNDERCURRENT. **1947:** *Steven Kenet* / HIGH WALL. **1949:** *Rigby* / THE BRIBE. **1950:** *Ward Kinsman* / AMBUSH; *Michael Curragh* / CONSPIRATOR; *Lance Poole* / DEVIL'S DOORWAY. **1951:** *Buck Wyatt* / WESTWARD THE WOMEN. **1953:** *Col. Paul Tibbets* / ABOVE AND BEYOND; *Rio* / RIDE, VAQUERO; *Joel Shore* / ALL THE BROTHERS WERE VALIANT; *guest* / I LOVE MELVIN. **1954:** *Mark Brandon* / VALLEY OF THE KINGS. **1955:** *Quentin Durward* / QUENTIN DURWARD. **1956:** *Charles Gilson* / THE LAST HUNT; *Brad Parker* / D-DAY THE SIXTH OF JUNE; *Cliff Barton* / THE POWER AND THE PRIZE. **1957:** *Lloyd Tredman* / TIP ON A DEAD JOCKEY. **1958:** *Steve Sinclair* / SADDLE THE WIND; *Thomas Farrell* / PARTY GIRL. **1959:** *MacKenzie Bovard* / THE HANGMAN; *John Nordley* / THE HOUSE OF THE SEVEN HAWKS. **1960:** *Robert Adamson* / KILLERS OF KILIMANJARO. **1963:** *Sam Brassfield* / CATTLE KING. **1964:** *Frank Costigan* / A HOUSE IS NOT A HOME. **1965:** *Barry Morland* / THE NIGHT WALKER. **1966:** *George Dean* / JOHNNY TIGER. **1967:** *Captain Martin* / SAVAGE PAMPAS. **1968:** *Prof. Karl Nichols* / THE GLASS SPHINX; *Mr. Farraday* / WHERE ANGELS GO, TROUBLE FOLLOWS; *Anderson, chief of American CIA* / THE DAY THE HOT LINE GOT HOT.

TEMPLE, SHIRLEY

(1928–)

Shirley Temple, the darling of the Depression, gave hope to adults that things would work out as they always did for her; even though she had some bleak experiences in most of her movies, through it all, she kept smiling. She could sing and dance a bit, but her star came not from her musical talents; it was her spirit that was infectious. At four Temple was picked from a dancing class by talent scout Charles Lamont to appear in comedies called Baby Burlesks, take-offs on adult movies. After a couple of small parts her star ascended in STAND UP AND CHEER as she did her little dance in her cute polka dot dress as James Dunn sang "Baby, Take a Bow." Temple was given a special miniature Oscar in 1935 for cheering up a Depression-weary nation; she was the number one box office attraction in 1936, 1937, and 1938. There was never a child-star like her, but like many others before and since, she was not able to make a successful transition to adult roles and in 1949 she walked away from films. For a time she appeared on TV, then became active in conservative politics, was appointed to the U.S. United Nations delegation, and in 1974 became ambassador to Ghana.

KEY ROLES

Shirley Dugan / STAND UP AND CHEER, 1934, Fox Films, d-Hamilton McFadden.
In this naive anti-Depression musical Temple became a star. Little more than a baby in the dearest little dress, she dances a simple time step, smiles, curtsies holding the hem of her dress, and wins the hearts of a nation. The rest of the picture, with its story about the Secretary of Entertainment (Warner Baxter) and his attempts to shake the nation's Depression blues, has long been forgotten by all but the most confirmed movie buffs.

Marty Jane / LITTLE MISS MARKER, 1934, Paramount, d-Alexander Hall.
Now four years old and a darling of the screen, Temple, though fourth-billed, is clearly the star of this Damon Runyan story of a man who puts up his daughter as a marker in a bet and then is killed. The gambler (Adolphe Menjou) is stuck with her, but like the rest of the world, he comes to love her.

Lloyd Sherman / THE LITTLE COLONEL, 1935, Fox Films, d-David Butler.
Temple ends a family feud in a southern household after the Civil War, plays Cupid for her sister, and wins over her grouchy old grandfather. There was no doubt this time who was the star; it was Temple's picture plain and simple.

Betsy Blair / CURLY TOP, 1935, 20th Century-Fox, d-Irving Cummings.

In this retread of DADDY LONG LEGS, Temple introduces the hit "Animal Crackers" by Ted Koehler, Irving Caesar, and Ray Henderson. She also does a hula and a tap dance on top of a grand piano while John Boles plays; he's the picture's Daddy Long Legs. He marries Temple's sister (Rochelle Hudson) and sings the title number.

Star / CAPTAIN JANUARY, 1936, 20th Century-Fox, d-David Butler.

Temple, a survivor of a shipwreck, is rescued by Guy Kibbee and his pal Slim Summerville and they raise her until an unfriendly sheriff arrives intent on sending her to an orphanage. While this is being worked out, Temple dances with Buddy Ebsen and sings a version of the sextet from "Lucia di Lammermoor" with Kibbee and Summerville. She also does an imitation basso profundo.

Sylvia Dolores / DIMPLES, 1936, 20th Century-Fox, d-William A. Seiter.

Temple lives with her charming con man grandfather in the mid-19th century and earns pennies as a street entertainer. When her grandfather steals from a wealthy woman (Helen Westley), Temple takes the blame; but Westley understands, adopts her, and helps her make it onto the legitimate stage in a performance of "Uncle Tom's Cabin." Temple does her tap dancing bit and even sings the Negro spirituals "Get on Board" and "Swing Low Sweet Chariot."

Priscilla Williams / WEE WILLIE WINKLE, 1937, 20th Century-Fox, d-John Ford.

Kipling's boy hero was transformed into a little girl to accommodate Temple. She lives at a British army base in India, wins over her crusty old grandfather (C. Aubrey Smith), and is captured by rebels, but manages to talk their leader (Cesar Romero) into calling off his attack on her grandfather's troops.

Heidi / HEIDI, 1937, 20th Century-Fox, d-Allan Dwan.

Temple is an orphan who warms up her bitter grandfather (Jean Hersholt), who has not spoken since his son ran away with a girl. He goes after Temple when a cruel aunt sells her as a servant.

Rebecca Winstead / REBECCA OF SUNNYBROOK FARM, 1938, 20th Century-Fox, d-Allan Dwan.

Temple was such a star that a medley of her past hits is included in this tale of a singing child. She is in the care of an uncle who dumps her on the farm of an aunt when he can't get a singing contract for her. Her next door neighbor is an agent for a radio show and arranges for her to make a broadcast and, what do you know, she becomes a star.

Sara Crewe / THE LITTLE PRINCESS, 1939, 20th Century-Fox, d-Walter Lang.

In her first Technicolor film Temple is placed in a boarding school when her widower father is reported killed in the Boer War. The mean headmistress makes her a servant until her shell-shocked father returns. She has several musical numbers with none other than Arthur Treacher.

Mytyl Tyl / THE BLUE BIRD, 1940, 20th Century-Fox, d-Walter Lang.

Eleven-year-old Temple gets a lot of competition for cuteness from Johnny Russell, who plays her brother in this visually beautiful fantasy and the first flop of Temple's career. The public didn't want allegories or the search for the bluebird of happiness.

Bridget "Brig" Hilton / SINCE YOU WENT AWAY, 1944, Selznick / United Artists, d-John Cromwell.

Temple's a teenager in this story of a well-to-do family of three women—Temple, her sister (Jennifer Jones), and mother (Claudette Colbert)—who must learn to cope when the man of the house is away at war.

Corliss Archer / KISS AND TELL, 1945, Columbia, d-Richard Wallace.

To protect another girl in this good-humored comedy, Temple pretends to be pregnant. She wasn't the nation's darling any more.

Susan Turner / THE BACHELOR AND THE BOBBY-SOXER, 1947, RKO, d-Irving Reis.

In this light family comedy, Temple develops a crush on Cary Grant who, to get her out of his hair, pretends to have an interest in her; but it's her sister, judge Myrna Loy, who really gets his attention.

Philadelphia Thursday / FORT APACHE, 1948, RKO, d-John Ford.

Temple is the daughter of the new commander of Fort Apache, a martinet who won't pay attention to his more experienced second-in-command. She is romanced by a young lieutenant (John Agar) whom she later married in real life.

OTHER ROLES

1932: *Gloria* / THE RED-HAIRED ALIBI. **1933:** *Mary Standing* / TO THE LAST MAN; *a child* / OUT ALL NIGHT. **1934:** *girl* / CAROLINA; *Betty Shaw* / MANDALAY; *Mary Golden* / NOW I'LL TELL YOU; *Shirley* / CHANGE OF HEART; *Shirley* / BABY TAKE A BOW; *Penelope Day* / NOW AND FOREVER; *Shirley Blake* / BRIGHT EYES. **1935:** *Molly Middleton* / OUR LITTLE GIRL; *Virgie Cary* / THE LITTLEST REBEL. **1936:** *Barbara Barry* / POOR LITTLE RICH GIRL; *Ching-Ching* / STOWAWAY. **1938:** *Betsy Brown* / LITTLE MISS BROADWAY; *Penny Hale* / JUST AROUND THE CORNER. **1939:** *Susannah Sheldon* / SUSANNAH OF THE MOUNTIES. **1940:** *Wendy* / YOUNG PEOPLE. **1941:** *Kathleen Davis* / KATHLEEN. **1942:** *Annie Rooney* / MISS ANNIE ROONEY. **1944:** *Barbara Marshall* / I'LL BE SEEING YOU. **1947:** *Barbara Olmstead* / HONEYMOON; *Mary Hagen* / THAT HAGEN GIRL. **1949:** *Ellen Baker* / MR. BELVEDERE GOES TO COLLEGE; *Dinah Sheldon* / ADVENTURE IN BALTIMORE; *Margaret O'Hara* / THE STORY OF SEABISCUIT; *Corliss Archer* / A KISS FOR CORLISS.

TIERNEY, GENE

(1920–)

Daughter of a prospectus stockbroker, Gene Tierney received her education in private schools in Connecticut and Switzerland. Her exquisitely modeled features and etched cheekbones made her perhaps the most strikingly beautiful actress ever to appear on the screen. A contract player with 20th Century-Fox, her best roles were as placid beauties whose looks hinted of mystery. She is best remembered for the radiantly beautiful Laura in the movie of that name, but her only Academy Award nomination was for her complex role in LEAVE HER TO HEAVEN. All good things in her life seemed to fade after the 1940s, though, leading to a nervous breakdown and a declining career in which she no longer was a star.

KEY ROLES

Ellie May Lester / TOBACCO ROAD, 1941, 20th Century-Fox, d-John Ford.

Tierney supplies some earthy sexiness in this cleaned up version of the Erskine Caldwell novel about "poor white trash" in Georgia.

Belle Starr / BELLE STARR, 1941, 20th Century-Fox, d-Irving Cummings.

Tierney wears a gun fetchingly on her hip in this highly romanticized account of the infamous Missouri bandit who fights the exploiters of the defeated Confederacy after the Civil War, until she is shot as she rides to warn her husband of a trap.

Poppy Charteris / THE SHANGHAI GESTURE, 1942, United Artists, d-Josef von Sternberg.

Tierney is the daughter of a man (Walter Huston) who wishes to close down the casino run by Ona Munson, a crafty oriental who looks like the Dragon Queen. Tierney complicates matters by becoming a big loser addicted to gambling. In the end she is shot by Munson when the latter discovers that Tierney is her own daughter. It's all lovely decadence and depravity.

Martha Van Cleve / HEAVEN CAN WAIT, 1943, 20th Century-Fox, d-Ernst Lubitsch.

Tierney portrays Don Ameche's wife in this story of family life in the late 19th century. Ameche is something of a minor Casanova even after landing the beautiful Tierney.

Laura Hunt / LAURA, 1944, 20th Century-Fox, d-Otto Preminger.

When this stylish murder mystery begins it appears that Tierney has been murdered by persons unknown. Various suspects surface for police detective Dana Andrews to interview as he and the audience learn something of the beauty whose portrait still hangs in her apartment. Just when Andrews falls in love with the deceased she shows up. It seems the body with a gunshot-obliterated face is that of a model who had been staying with Tierney. Now Andrews has the pleasure of solving a "murder" and has the girl as well.

Ellen Berent / LEAVE HER TO HEAVEN, 1945, 20th Century-Fox, d-John M. Stahl.

Tierney is a selfish and jealous woman who murders in order to keep the man she loves (Cornel Wilde). In addition, she allows her crippled brother to drown and deliberately causes her own miscarriage so she will not have to share Wilde's love with a child. Not surprisingly she loses him anyway and commits suicide, trying to make it seem that her sister murdered her. The decision to film this old-fashioned melodrama in Technicolor seems a mistake.

Isobel Bradley / THE RAZOR'S EDGE, 1946, 20th Century-Fox, d-Edmund Goulding.

Tierney is a society girl loved by Tyrone Power who, on his return from World War I, questions his values and goes off in search of wisdom. Tierney is spoiled and doesn't want to wait around while he's into heavy personal inquiry so she marries another. Later she offers to leave her husband and return to Power but he declines.

Lucy Muir / THE GHOST AND MRS. MUIR, 1947, 20th Century-Fox, d-Joseph L. Mankiewicz.

In this romantic fantasy, Tierney falls in love with the ghost of a deceased sea captain (Rex Harrison) in whose home she now lives with her two children. When her funds run out, he dictates his memoirs to her and she has them published. This leads her to meet charming author George Sanders whom she believes may propose marriage, but it seems he's already married.

Morgan Taylor / WHERE THE SIDEWALK ENDS, 1950, 20th Century-Fox, d-Otto Preminger.

In this far-fetched film noir, Tierney is the daughter of a taxi driver accused of murder. She is assisted in defending her father by Dana Andrews, a police detective who, because he was the son of a criminal, hates all crooks and in fact murdered the man Tierney's father is accused of killing.

Anne Scott / THE LEFT HAND OF GOD, 1955, 20th Century-Fox, d-Edward Dmytryk.

Tierney is a nurse loved by an American pilot (Humphrey Bogart) who had been working for a Chinese warlord. Disgusted with how he's making a living, Bogart escapes his Oriental employer disguised as a priest arriving at a mission. It's a contrived story with both Bogart and Tierney looking as if they didn't believe the day's script.

OTHER ROLES

1940: *Eleanor Stone* / THE RETURN OF FRANK JAMES; *Barbara Hall* / HUDSON'S BAY. **1941:** *Zia* / SUNDOWN. **1942:** *Eve* / SON OF FURY; *Susan Miller (Linda Washington)* / RINGS ON HER FINGERS; *Kay Saunders* / THUNDER BIRDS; *Miss Young* / CHINA GIRL. **1945:** *Tina* / A BELL FOR ADANO. **1946:** *Miranda Wells* / DRAGONWYCK. **1948:** *Anna Gouzenko* / THE IRON CURTAIN; *Sara Farley* / THAT WONDERFUL URGE; *Ann Sutton* / WHIRLPOOL. **1950:** *Mary Bristol* / NIGHT AND THE CITY. **1951:** *Maggie Carleton* / THE MATING SEASON; *Lilli Duran* / ON THE RIVIERA; *Marcia Stoddard* / THE SECRET OF CONVICT LAKE; *Midge Sheridan* / CLOSE TO MY HEART; *Teresa* / WAY OF A GAUCHO. **1952:** *Dorothy Bradford* / PLYMOUTH ADVENTURE. **1953:** *Marya Lamarkina* / NEVER LET ME GO; *Kay Barlow* / PERSONAL AFFAIR. **1954:** *Iris* / BLACK WIDOW; *Baketamon* / THE EGYPTIAN. **1962:** *Dolly Harrison* / ADVISE AND CONSENT. **1963:** *Albertine Prine* / TOYS IN THE ATTIC. **1964:** *Jane Barton* / THE PLEASURE SEEKERS.

TODD, ANN

(1909–)

A porcelain-featured, blonde British actress, Ann Todd is best remembered for her role in THE SEVENTH VEIL in which she needed the psychiatric cure to realize that she was in love with her seemingly cruel guardian. Working on the British stage since 1928, she entered the movies in the early 1930s and became an international star in the 1940s. Her third husband was director David Lean and she appeared in several of his movies. In the 1960s she turned to producing, writing, and directing several critically praised documentaries.

KEY ROLES

Madge Crane / SOUTH RIDING, 1938, Great Britain, London Films, d-Victor Saville.

Todd is the wife of a country squire (Ralph Richardson) who sees his fortune being drained to keep her in an expensive nursing home. In her absence he falls in love with Edna Best, the local schoolmistress.

Elena / PERFECT STRANGERS, 1945, Great Britain, London Films, d-Alexander Korda.

In the United States this film is titled VACATION FROM MARRIAGE, that being what Robert Donat does to escape his dull union with Deborah Kerr. He has a brief and satisfying affair with a widowed nurse (Todd). After the war Donat and Kerr, long separated, anticipate getting a divorce but they both have changed so much for the better that these "perfect strangers" fall in love.

Francesca Cunningham / THE SEVENTH VEIL, 1945, Great Britain, Ortus / Theatrecraft, d-Compton Bennett.

In her most famous role Todd is a talented concert pianist who, in flashback, helps her doctor (Herbert Lom) discover why she has made a suicide attempt.

He lifts the "veils" from her subconscious revealing an unhappy childhood in which a sadistic schoolmistress caned her hands. When orphaned she was put into the care of a stern, crippled bachelor (James Mason) who drove her to develop her musical talents. His guidance extended beyond her professional life as he constantly interfered with her romantic relationships. With Lom's help, Todd regains confidence in her artistry and also understands the depth of her feelings for Mason.

Olivia Harwood / SO EVIL MY LOVE, 1947, Great Britain, Paramount British, d-Lewis Allen.
In Victorian London Todd is a widow who, upon her return to the city, falls in love with an immoral artist (Ray Milland) who involves her in a plot to kill the husband of one of her old school chums.

Mary Justin / THE PASSIONATE FRIENDS, 1948, Great Britain, Cineguild, d-David Lean.
Before she married Claude Rains, Todd and Trevor Howard had been lovers. Five years later they renew the affair briefly, but she is forgiven by Rains on the condition that she does not see Howard again. Nine years later Todd and Howard meet by accident and spend an innocent day together; Rains finds out and says he will get a divorce. Todd tries to commit suicide by throwing herself under a train, but Howard saves her.

OTHER ROLES

1931: *Millicent* / KEEPERS OF YOUTH; *Pamela Crawford* / THESE CHARMING PEOPLE; *Peggy Murdock* / THE GHOST TRAIN; *Jane Bell* / THE WATER GYPSIES. **1934:** *Phyllis Drummond* / THE RETURN OF BULLDOG DRUMMOND. **1936:** *Mary Gordon* / THINGS TO COME. **1937:** *Carol Stedman* / THE SQUEAKER; *Ann Daviot* / ACTION FOR SLANDER. **1939:** *Ann Rider* / POISON PEN. **1941:** *Jane Kaye* / DANNY BOY. **1941:** *Kay Gordon* / SHIPS WITH WINGS; *Kate Hill* / REMEMBER THE DAY. **1946:** *Kathryn Davis* / GAIETY GEORGE. **1947:** *Frankie* / DAYBREAK. **1948:** *Gay Keane* / THE PARADINE CASE. **1949:** *Madeleine Smith* / MADELEINE. **1952:** *Susan Garthwaite* / THE SOUND BARRIER. **1954:** *Solange Vauthier* / THE GREEN SCARF. **1957:** *Honor Stanford* / TIME WITHOUT PITY. **1961:** *Jane Appleby* / TASTE OF FEAR. **1962:** *Arabella Blood* / THE SON OF CAPTAIN BLOOD. **1965:** *Mrs. Kurka* / NINETY DEGREES IN THE SHADE. **1971:** *Birdie Wemyss* / THE FIEND. **1979:** *Mrs. Castle* / THE HUMAN FACTOR.

TODD, RICHARD

(1919–)

Irish-born leading man Richard Todd first appeared on the British stage in 1937 and was a founding member of the Dundee Repertory Theatre in 1939. He served with distinction in World War II with the King's Own Light Infantry and the Parachute Regiment. After the war he briefly returned to the stage before becoming a major British film star with his role as the dying Scot in THE HASTY HEART. He contributed a number of fine characterizations in films in both England and the United States in the 1950s and early 1960s but his standing slipped and before long he was back in repertory while making a few film appearances in movies of questionable quality.

KEY ROLES

Cpl. Lachlan "Lachie" McLachlan / THE HASTY HEART, 1949, Great Britain, Associated British, d-Vincent Sherman.
Todd is brilliant as the embittered Scot in a Burma hospital who rejects the friendship of fellow patients who all know what he doesn't—that he is dying. He mistakes the pity of nurse Patricia Neal for love and, when he learns her true feelings, retreats even further into his shell. But before the end he learns the meaning of friendship.

Robin Hood / THE STORY OF ROBIN HOOD AND HIS MERRIE MEN, 1952, Great Britain, Disney / RKO, d-Ken Annakin.
It's the familiar story of the outlawed earl (Todd) who, with the aid of his bandits of Sherwood Forest and Maid Marian, opposes Prince John, who wants to usurp the throne of his brother while the latter is away on the Crusades.

Rob Roy MacGregor / ROB ROY, THE HIGHLAND ROGUE, 1954, Great Britain, Disney / RKO, d-Harold French.
In 1715 Scottish rebel leader Todd twice escapes from the British and, when he captures an important stronghold, is able to dictate his own terms for going to London to make peace.

Peter Marshall / A MAN CALLED PETER, 1955, 20th Century-Fox, d-Henry Koster.
Todd is quite good as the Scottish clergyman who becomes chaplain to the United States Senate. Truthfully it's a rather dreary biopic.

Guy Gibson / THE DAM BUSTERS, 1955, Great Britain, Associated British, d-Michael Anderson.
Todd is the wing commander of a hand-picked squadron that will fly suicidally close to the water to launch special bombs. The bombs will bounce along the lake leading up to the Ruhr dams, blowing them up and crippling the Nazi industrial strength.

Geoffrey Lawrence / THE VERY EDGE, 1963, Great Britain, British Lion, d-Cyril Frankel.
Todd's ex-model wife is pregnant but miscarries after being attacked by a rapist. She becomes frigid and Todd must try to help her.

Insp. Harry Sanders / DEATH DRUMS ALONG THE RIVER, 1963, Great Britain, Big Ben / Planet, d-Lawrence Huntington.
SANDERS OF THE RIVER, produced in 1935, had a sort of racist charm with Paul Robeson portraying a "good" native who helped the local civil servant rule his people. This remake has Todd investigating a murder in an African hospital and finding a hidden diamond mine.

OTHER ROLES

1948: *Herb Logan* / FOR THEM THAT TRESPASS. **1950:** *Jonathan Cooper* / STAGE FRIGHT. **1951:** *Richard Trevelyan* / LIGHTNING STRIKES TWICE. **1953:** *Edward Mercer* / VENETIAN BIRD; *the boy* / AFFAIR IN MONTE CARLO. **1954:** *Charles Brandon* / THE SWORD AND THE ROSE. **1955:** *Sir Walter Raleigh* / THE VIRGIN QUEEN. **1956:** *Lieutenant Commander Kerans* / YANGTSE INCIDENT. **1957:** *Ward Prescott* / CHASE A CROOKED SHADOW; *Dunois* / SAINT JOAN. **1958:** *Lt. Col. David Baird M.C.* / DANGER WITHIN. **1959:** *Sergeant Mitchem* / THE LONG AND THE SHORT AND THE TALL. **1960:** *Sam Hargis* / THE HELLIONS. **1961:** *John Cummings* / NEVER LET GO. **1962:** *Maj. John Howard* / THE LONGEST DAY; *Victor Webster* / THE BOYS. **1965:** *Wing Commander Kendall* / OPERATION CROSSBOW; *Darrell* / BATTLE OF THE VILLA FIORITA; *Insp. Harry Sanders* / COAST OF SKELETONS. **1969:** *Col. Victor Redmayne* / SUBTERFUGE. **1970:** *Basil Hallward* / DORIAN GRAY. **1972:** *Walter* / ASYLUM; *Barker* / THE BIG SLEEP. **1979:** *Geoffrey Steele* / HOME BEFORE MIDNIGHT. **1983:** *Sam Allyson* / HOUSE OF THE LONG SHADOWS.

TONE, FRANCHOT

(Stanislas Franchot Tone, 1905–1968)

Unfortunately for Franchot Tone his smooth, callow looks typed him as a shallow socialite or a slightly weak-willed friend of the real hero of the picture. He usually didn't get the girl but never seemed crushed by the turn of events. As he got older he was given more interesting character roles which he handled very nicely. He was nominated for a Best Actor Academy Award for his most impressive early career performance in MUTINY ON THE BOUNTY and might have won an Oscar for the role had there been a Best Supporting category that year. In the 1930s Tone showed up in both romances and comedies, playing second leads in the best of them. His screen career came to an end in the early 1950s and he returned to the stage. He also co-starred in the "Ben Casey" TV series in 1965-66. Tone was married and divorced four times; his first wife was Joan Crawford. He made headlines when he was beaten up by actor Tom Neal over Tone's third wife, Barbara Payton.

KEY ROLES

Tod Newton / DANCING LADY, 1933, MGM, d-Robert Z. Leonard.

Tone plays a socialite who finds small-time dancer Joan Crawford and helps her career by putting her into a show he is backing over the objections of director Clark Gable. The deal is if she fails, she marries Tone. When Gable discovers that she has talent and is willing to work very hard, he falls for her and Tone loses the leading lady to a more prominent star, as he did so often.

Lieutenant Fortesque / THE LIVES OF A BENGAL LANCER, 1935, Paramount, d-Henry Hathaway.

Tone, Gary Cooper, and Richard Cromwell are three officers with the Bengal Lancers on the Northwest Frontier who are captured, tortured, and become heroes during a tribal uprising.

Roger Byam / MUTINY ON THE BOUNTY, 1935, MGM, d-Frank Lloyd.

In easily his best role, Tone is a young midshipman who tries to prevent Fletcher Christian (Clark Gable) from taking command of the Bounty from the cruel Captain Bligh (Charles Laughton). He is knocked unconscious and cannot join Laughton and the other loyal seamen in the long boat in which they are set adrift. Because of his friendship with Gable while on the ship and on the islands, Laughton names him as a mutineer. He is later recaptured, thrown in irons, and put on trial back in England.

John Eaton / THE GORGEOUS HUSSY, 1936, MGM, d-Clarence Brown.

Tone is a cabinet member in the administration of Andrew Jackson. Because of the low origins of his wife (Joan Crawford) the other cabinet members' wives shun her. But President Jackson, whose own wife had been snubbed because of questions about the legality of their marriage, becomes her champion.

Jimmy Davis / THEY GAVE HIM A GUN, 1937, MGM, d-W. S. Van Dyke.

Before World War I Tone was a meek clerk, but after the war he becomes a hardened gangster despite the efforts of circus barker Spencer Tracy to set him on the straight and narrow path.

Otto Koster / THREE COMRADES, 1938, MGM, d-Frank Borzage.

Tone is one of three German veterans of World War I who try to adjust to post-war conditions and who are united in their love for Margaret Sullavan who is dying of tuberculosis. At this time the producers were unwilling to offend Germany so no mention of Nazi-Jewish problems was made.

Joel Sloane / FAST AND FURIOUS, 1939, MGM, d-Busby Berkeley.

MGM made three whodunnit films meant to be Nick and Nora Charles clones; but with each film they kept the husband and wife characters but changed the performers who portrayed them. This time it is Tone and Ann Sothern who look into a murder at a beauty contest.

John J. Bramble / FIVE GRAVES TO CAIRO, 1943, Paramount, d-Billy Wilder.

In this superb spy melodrama Tone is a British agent trying to learn all he can from Field Marshall Rommel (Erich von Stroheim) when the latter is the star guest of a Sahara oasis hotel where Tone has taken a job. In one of his best performances Tone is again upstaged by a co-star, this time the charismatic Stroheim.

The President / ADVISE AND CONSENT, 1962, Columbia, d-Otto Preminger.

Tone portrays a dying president of the United States who has sent the very controversial name of Henry Fonda to the Senate for approval as his new Secretary of State, because he has no faith in his vice president to run the country when he dies. After a lot of heartache for various senators he almost gets his way, but dies before the vice president must cast the tie-breaking vote, which he doesn't choose to do when he gets the message that Tone has died.

OTHER ROLES

1932: *bit* / THE WISER SEX. **1933:** *Hartley Beekman* / GABRIEL OVER THE WHITE HOUSE; *Ronnie Boyce-Smith* / TODAY WE LIVE; *Warren Foster* / STAGE MOTHER; *Gifford Middleton* / BOMBSHELL; *Guy Crane* / THE STRANGER'S RETURN. **1934:** *Tom Mannering* / MIDNIGHT MARY; *Douglas Hall* / MOULIN ROUGE; *Richard Girard* / THE WORLD MOVES ON; *Benny Horowitz* / STRAIGHT IS THE WAY; *Bob Bailey* / GENTLEMEN ARE BORN; *Tom Paige* / THE GIRL FROM MISSOURI; *Michael Alderson* / SADIE MCKEE. **1935:** *Bob Harrison* / RECKLESS; *Jim Salston* / NO MORE LADIES. **1936:** *Don Bellows* / DANGEROUS; *Foxhall* / ONE NEW YORK NIGHT; *Dick Barton* / EXCLUSIVE STORY; *Franz Josef* / THE KING STEPS OUT; *Sir Allan Deardon* / THE UNGUARDED HOUR; *Terry Moore* / SUZY; *Barnabas Pells* / LOVE ON THE RUN. **1937:** *Allan Meighan* / BETWEEN TWO WOMEN; *Giullo* / THE BRIDE WORE RED; *Dr. Valentine Brown* / QUALITY STREET. **1938:** *Peter Lawrence* / LOVE IS A HEADACHE; *Jimmy Kilmartin* / MAN-PROOF; *Paul Wagner* / THE GIRL DOWNSTAIRS. **1940:** *Kansas (Tim Mason)* / TRAIL OF THE VIGILANTES. **1941:** *Richard Calvert* / NICE GIRL?; *Mark Willows* / SHE KNEW ALL THE ANSWERS; *Robert Stevens* / THIS WOMAN IS MINE; *Christopher Reynolds* / THE WIFE TAKES A FLYER. **1942:** *guest* / STAR SPANGLED RHYTHM. **1943:** *Charles Gerard* / HIS BUTLER'S SISTER. **1944:** *Jim Hetherton* / THE HOUR BEFORE THE DAWN; *Jack Marlow* / PHANTOM LADY; *Dr. George Grover* / DARK WATERS. **1947:** *William Weldon* / HER HUSBAND'S AFFAIR. **1948:** *Robert Sanford* / EVERY GIRL SHOULD BE MARRIED; *Stuart Bailey* / I LOVE TROUBLE. **1949:** *Howard Mallort* / JIGSAW; *Radek* / THE MAN ON THE EIFFEL TOWER. **1951:** *Wilbur Stanley* / HERE COMES THE GROOM. **1958:** *Dr. Mikhail Lvovich Astroff* / UNCLE VANYA. **1964:** *Montasi Jr.* / LA BONNE SOUPE. **1965:** *CINCPAC I Admiral* / IN HARM'S WAY; *Rudy Lopp* / MICKEY ONE. **1968:** *Ambassador Townsend* / NOBODY RUNS FOREVER, (THE HIGH COMMISSIONER).

TRACY, SPENCER

(1900–1967)

Educated at a Jesuit prep school, Spencer Tracy had intended to become a priest but instead quit school in 1917 to join the navy. Following World War I he attended Ripon College in Wisconsin where he decided to become an actor. He attended the American Academy of Dramatic Arts in New York and made his stage debut in Theatre Guild's production of "R.U.R." in 1922. He made his feature film debut in 1930 in UP THE RIVER. One of the few actors never to experience a down period in his career, Tracy was an actor's actor, a thorough professional who, although he made light of what it took to be an actor in movies, was proud of his craft and impatient with others who delayed production of his films. He married Louise Treadwell in 1928. Years later his film partnership with Katharine Hepburn extended beyond the screen and the seven films in which they co-starred, but he remained married. Tracy's characters usually displayed rugged self-confidence and manly charm; his down-to-earth appeal made him a bigger-than-life star. He won Oscars for CAPTAINS COURAGEOUS and BOYS TOWN and was nominated for his performances in SAN FRANCISCO, FATHER OF THE BRIDE, BAD DAY AT BLACK ROCK, THE OLD MAN AND THE SEA, INHERIT THE WIND, JUDGMENT AT NUREMBERG, and GUESS WHO'S COMING TO DINNER. Tracy's views on his profession included, "Why do actors think they're so goddam important? They're not. Acting is not an important job in the scheme of things. Plumbing is." And, "Well, it's taken me forty years of doing it for a living to learn the secret. I don't know if I want to give it away. Okay, I'll tell you. The secret of acting is—learn your lines!" But there was more to his secret as Humphrey Bogart observed: "Spence is the best we have, because you don't see the mechanism working."

KEY ROLES

Tom Connors / 20,000 YEARS IN SING SING, 1932, Warners, d-Michael Curtiz.

When sent to prison Tracy refuses to play by the rules and he ends up in solitary. This changes him and he passes up a chance to be part of a break. A model prisoner, he is given a 24-hour leave to see his girl (Bette Davis) who is injured in an automobile accident. When Davis shoots the crooked lawyer responsible for Tracy being in prison, Tracy takes the blame and returns to face the electric chair.

Tom Gardner / THE POWER AND THE GLORY, 1933, Fox Films, d-William K. Howard.

Tracy starts as a track walker for a railroad, then moves up through an assortment of jobs until he becomes the railroad's president. Always too busy becoming a success, he neglects his son and is destroyed when he learns that the young man has fallen in love with Tracy's second wife.

Bill / A MAN'S CASTLE, 1933, Columbia, d-Frank Borzage.

Living in a Depression camp, Tracy takes in a hungry and desperate waif (Loretta Young) and he works at any job he can to keep them in his hovel. When he meets showgirl Glenda Farrell she offers to support him, but he learns that Young is going to have a baby. When a robbery attempt of his fails, he and Young hop a freight hoping to find a new life for them and their child.

Jim Carter / DANTE'S INFERNO, 1935, Fox Films, d-Harry Lachman.

After being fired as a ship's stoker Tracy wanders onto a carnival midway where he meets Henry B. Walthall and Claire Trevor who run a sideshow that recreates images from Dante's *Inferno*. He talks himself into a job as their barker and makes the concession pay, but in doing so is indirectly responsible for the deaths of several people in a crash of the unsafe pier on which the show stands. The building inspector whom he bribed to give the site the OK commits suicide. Tracy is cleared of all charges with the help of Trevor, who is now his wife, but she can no longer live with him and leaves, taking their son with her.

Joe Wilson / FURY, 1936, MGM, d-Joseph L. Mankiewicz.

While passing through a town on the way to meeting Sylvia Sidney, whom he is going to marry, Tracy is picked up as a suspect in a kidnapping. A lynch mob is formed and the jail is burned down as the newsreel cameras record all that is happening. Tracy is believed killed, but in reality he escapes. The leaders of the lynch mob, identified through the newsreel, are put on trial for Tracy's murder, and Tracy, scarred by the fire, bitterly follows the trial with hatred. Finally, Sidney learns that he's alive and she softens his heart so much so that he appears in the courtroom and all the murder charges are dropped. But as he tells the judge, "They're murderers. I know the law says they're not because I'm still alive, but that's not their fault."

Father Tim Mullin / SAN FRANCISCO, 1936, MGM, d-W. S. Van Dyke.

Tracy is a rugged San Francisco mission chaplain and longtime buddy of Barbary Coast saloon owner Clark Gable. Tracy befriends singer Jeanette MacDonald who has taken a job with Gable but has ambitions to sing opera for the swells on Nob Hill. With Tracy's help she gets her chance before the great earthquake of 1906, then afterwards the good priest reunites her with Gable as they have come to love each other.

Warren Haggerty / LIBELED LADY, 1936, MGM, d-Jack Conway.

Newspaper editor Tracy talks the paper's lawyer (William Powell) into marrying his own fiancée (Jean Harlow) so Powell can then get millionairess Myrna Loy to fall in love with him and be forced to drop her $5 million lawsuit against the paper that called her a homewrecker. Farfetched but fun.

Manuel / CAPTAINS COURAGEOUS, 1937, MGM, d-Victor Fleming.

Tracy, a Portuguese fisherman, rescues spoiled, bratty, and cheating Freddie Bartholomew who has fallen overboard an ocean liner sailing for Europe. Tracy teaches the boy about kindness and consideration for others, but in a race with another ship, Tracy falls into the sea and is drowned. He won an Oscar for his performance.

Father Edward J. Flanagan / BOYS TOWN, 1938, MGM, d-Norman Taurog.

Tracy got his second Oscar for his portrayal of the priest who, after hearing a condemned killer complain that if he had been helped as a boy he would not have become a murderer, puts all his efforts into forming Boy's Town, a place where boys in trouble can live and become useful citizens. Mickey Rooney, the brother of a convict, is used to test the priest's assertion that "there is no such thing as a bad boy."

Henry M. Stanley / STANLEY AND LIVINGSTONE, 1939, 20th Century-Fox, d-Henry King.

Tracy portrays the reporter for a New York newspaper who goes into unexplored areas of Africa in search of medical missionary Dr. David Livingstone. When he returns claiming to have found the long-missing man, he is not believed and is branded a fraud in English scientific circles. But in time he is able to prove that he did indeed find the lost shepherd and that he did recite the immortal line "Dr. Livingstone, I presume."

Maj. Robert Rogers / NORTHWEST PASSAGE, 1940, MGM, d-King Vidor.

During the 1759 French and Indian War Tracy is the rugged leader of a troop of rangers who make a strenuous forced march to destroy marauding Indians. It's a heroic adventure story even though its portrayal of Indians is terribly racist.

Thomas Alva Edison / EDISON, THE MAN, 1940, MGM, d-Clarence Brown.

In a respectful script, Tracy gives a fine portrayal of the man of 1% genius and 99% perspiration whose curiosity and dedication lead him to the invention of the incandescent lamp. Along with Mickey Rooney's portrayal in YOUNG TOM EDISON, this is MGM's tribute to the "Wizard of Menlo Park."

"Square John" Sand / BOOM TOWN, 1940, MGM, d-Jack Conway.

In this rather long picture oil wildcatters Tracy and Clark Gable make and lose fortunes, fight over Claudette Colbert and Hedy Lamarr, and in general have a hell of a good time. So does the audience.

Dr. Harry Jekyll / Mr. Hyde / DR. JEKYLL AND MR. HYDE, 1941, MGM, d-Victor Fleming.

Tracy tries hard but cannot match the performance of Fredric March in portraying the very good scientist and his alter ego, the murdering Mr. Hyde. His transformation is done by facial contortions, not make-up, and that seems a mistake.

Sam Craig / WOMAN OF THE YEAR, 1942, MGM, d-George Stevens.

Sportswriter Tracy takes exception to the remarks made by Katharine Hepburn in her column for the paper. This leads to a feud in print. When they get together they discover an overwhelming attraction for each other and before they know it, they marry. Wedded life is not smooth as Hepburn is not the homemaker type and he's not exactly the intellectual she's been used to; but all works out by the end of this first collaboration of Tracy and Hepburn. (The billing was always in that order in the credits; Tracy insisted.)

George Heisler / THE SEVENTH CROSS, 1944, MGM, d-Fred Zinnemann.

When Tracy and six others escape from a concentration camp in Nazi Germany in 1936, the commandant puts up seven crosses. The Gestapo tracks the men down one by one, returns them to the camp, and immediately puts them to death on a cross. With the help of some good people Tracy makes it to Holland and the seventh cross remains unused.

Grant Matthews / STATE OF THE UNION, 1948, MGM, d-Frank Capra.

Angela Lansbury, the unscrupulous head of a newspaper empire and mistress of industrialist Tracy, convinces him that he can become the Republican nominee for President of the United States. But this requires that Katharine Hepburn be at his side as his loving wife. Ultimately, with Hepburn's help, Tracy realizes that he still loves her and that in trying to get the nomination he has sacrificed all his ideals. He pulls out of the race and goes home with her.

Adam Bonner / ADAM'S RIB, 1949, MGM, d-George Cukor.

Defense attorney Tracy finds himself opposed in an attempted murder case by his lawyer wife (Katharine Hepburn). He objects to her courtroom tactics for winning the acquittal of Judy Holliday, who is accused of shooting at her philandering husband (Tom Ewell) and his lady friend (Jean Hagen). The case almost ends the marriage of Tracy and Hepburn, but his ability to shed some tears saves things.

Stanley T. Banks / FATHER OF THE BRIDE, 1950, MGM, d-Vincente Minnelli.

When his beautiful daughter (Elizabeth Taylor) announces that she is engaged to marry, Tracy can't place the name of the intended with any of the many beaus he has met. This is the least of his problems as he learns how disruptive a wedding of a daughter can be—and how expensive. It's a fun comedy with a number of very touching moments.

Mike Conovan / PAT AND MIKE, 1952, MGM, d-George Cukor.

Tracy is a sports promoter who has plans to make a champion of P.E. instructor Kate Hepburn. The only problem is that she loses her confidence whenever her fault-finding fiancé is around. Tracy solves this problem by replacing the other guy in her affections.

Clinton Jones / THE ACTRESS, 1953, MGM, d-George Cukor.

Tracy is a retired seagoing man whose daughter (Jean Simmons) is afraid to tell him of her plans to become an actress. But he proves to be a loving and understanding father after all.

Matt Devereaux / BROKEN LANCE, 1954, 20th Century-Fox, d-Edward Dmytryk.

Tracy is a cattle baron who forces his four sons to be his ranch hands. He never has anything good to say about them nor does he give them any credit for their contributions to his success. In this western version of HOUSE OF STRANGERS, Tracy is forced to put his land in the names of his sons, three of whom rebel against him, causing his death. Only his fourth son remains loyal.

John J. Macreedy / BAD DAY AT BLACK ROCK, 1955, MGM, d-John Sturges.

When the Santa Fe train pulls to a halt at whistle-stop Black Rock, California, one-armed Tracy steps off. He is there to discover what happened to the parents of a Japanese-American soldier who fought under his command in Germany during World War II, but he's met with suspicion and threats by a group of cowpokes led by Robert Ryan. Tracy learns that after Pearl Harbor these brave men got drunk, went to the farm of the Japanese couple, lit a fire that got out of control, and killed the man and wife. The victims were then buried, leaving Ryan and the others to keep their horrible deed secret ever since. Tracy has to kill or be killed.

The Old Man / THE OLD MAN AND THE SEA, 1958, Warners, d-John Sturges.

Tracy is an old Cuban fisherman who hasn't caught a fish for three months. Only a little boy has any faith in him as they set out to sea where Tracy struggles to catch a huge marlin, only to have it devoured by sharks before he can tow it to shore.

Frank Skeffington / THE LAST HURRAH, 1958, Columbia, d-John Ford.

An Irish political boss and mayor of Boston, Tracy plans one last campaign and wants his nephew (Jeffrey Hunter) along to see how old-time politics works. To everyone's surprise the old warrior loses to a wimpy newcomer and has a heart attack and dies, but not before audiences are royally entertained by an enchanting group of old-time performers headed by Tracy himself.

Henry Drummond / INHERIT THE WIND, 1960, United Artists, d-Stanley Kramer.

In this splendid production of the famous Tennessee "Monkey" trial of 1925, Tracy portrays the Clarence Darrow character in battle against the bible-thumping William Jennings Bryan character (Fredric March). Tracy is superb as the man of reason who expects laws to be reasonable. He challenges March with, "Then why did God plague us with the power to think, Mr. Brady? Why do you deny the one faculty of man that raises him above the other creatures on earth, the power of his brain to reason?"

Judge Dan Haywood / JUDGMENT AT NUREMBERG, 1961, United Artists, d-Stanley Kramer.

A retired Maine judge (Tracy) is appointed the American jurist to hear the war-crime trials of four former German judges. He and his fellow judges find the defendants guilty and give them life sentences, knowing full well that all will probably be free in seven years.

Matt Drayton / GUESS WHO'S COMING TO DINNER, 1967, Columbia, d-Stanley Kramer.

Tracy was sick and dying when he made his last screen appearance in this film in which he and Katharine Hepburn have their very liberal views put to the test when their daughter comes home announcing she is engaged to a black man—a handsome, well-spoken doctor.

OTHER ROLES

1930: *Saint Louis* / UP THE RIVER. **1931:** *Daniel J. "Bugs" Raymond* / QUICK MILLIONS; *William Donroy* / SIX CYLINDER LOVE; *Bill* / GOLDIE. **1932:** *William Kelley* / SHE WANTED A MILLIONAIRE; *Wilkie* / SKY DEVILS; *Dick Fay* / DISORDERLY CONDUCT; *Jack Doray* / YOUNG AMERICA; *Briscoe* / SOCIETY GIRL; *Tom Brian* / PAINTED WOMAN; *Dan Dolan* / ME AND MY GAL. **1933:** *Joe Buck* / FACE IN THE SKY; *Pat Jackson* / SHANGHAI MADNESS; *Edward Carson* / THE MAD GAME. **1934:** *Joe Graham* / LOOKING FOR TROUBLE; *Aubrey Piper* / THE SHOW-OFF; *Smoothie King* / BOTTOMS UP; *Murray Golden* / NOW I'LL TELL; *Crawbett* / MARIE GALANTE. **1935:** *Bill Shevlin* / IT'S A SMALL WORLD; *Steve Gray* / THE MURDER MAN; *Ross McBride* / WHIPSAW. **1936:** *Dutch Miller* / RIFF-RAFF. **1937:** *Fred Willis* / THEY GAVE HIM A GUN; *Joe Benton* / BIG CITY. **1938:** *John Hennessy* / MANNEQUIN; *Gunner Sloane* / TEST PILOT. **1940:** *Karl Decker* / I TAKE THIS WOMAN. **1941:** *Father Edward J. Flanagan* / MEN OF BOYS TOWN. **1942:** *Pilon* / TORTILLA FLAT; *Steven O'Malley* / KEEPER OF THE FLAME. **1943:** *Pete Sandidge* / A GUY NAMED JOE. **1944:** *Lt. Col. James H. Doolittle* / THIRTY SECONDS OVER TOKYO. **1945:** *Pat Jamieson* / WITHOUT LOVE. **1947:** *Col. James Brewton* / THE SEA OF GRASS; *Cass Timberlane* / CASS TIMBERLANE. **1949:** *Arnold Boult* / EDWARD, MY SON. **1950:** *Carnahan* / MALAYA. **1951:** *Stanley T. Banks* / FATHER'S LITTLE DIVIDEND; *James P. Curtayne* / THE PEOPLE AGAINST O'HARA. **1952:** *Capt. Christopher Jones* / PLYMOUTH ADVENTURE. **1956:** *Zachary Teller* / THE MOUNTAIN. **1957:** *Richard Sumner* / DESK SET. **1961:** *Father Matthew Doonon* / THE DEVIL AT 4 O'CLOCK. **1963:** *Capt. C. G. Culpepper* / IT'S A MAD, MAD, MAD, MAD WORLD.

TREVOR, CLAIRE

(Claire Wemlinger, 1909–)

Claire Trevor was typecast as a tough broad and often found herself playing a gun moll, saloon gal, kept woman, or worse. Born on Long Island, she attended Columbia University and studied at the American Academy of Theatre Arts in New York City. She made her professional stage debut in 1929 and the next year signed a movie contract with Warners. Never a big star, which she admitted was fine with her, Trevor was able to concentrate on some very fine performances like the one in STAGECOACH, and the ones for which she received Academy Award nominations for Best Supporting Actress: DEAD END, KEY LARGO, and THE HIGH AND THE MIGHTY. She won for the last two.

KEY ROLES

Betty McWade / DANTE'S INFERNO, 1935, 20th Century-Fox, d-Harry Lachman.

Trevor plays the daughter of the owner of a sideshow (Henry B. Walthall) depicting scenes from Dante's *Inferno*, and the wife of the show's barker, ruthless Spencer Tracy. When the latter's drive to make money results in many people's deaths, including her father's, Trevor stays long enough to help Tracy beat the rap and then takes their son and leaves him.

Bonnie Brewster / HUMAN CARGO, 1936, 20th Century-Fox, d-Allan Dwan.

Trevor and Brian Donlevy, reporters for rival newspapers, board a ship in Vancouver to expose a gang that smuggles illegal aliens into the country. They survive being discovered by the mobsters and the fourth estate triumphs.

Francie / DEAD END, 1937, United Artists, d-William Wyler.

When Humphrey Bogart, a wanted killer returns to his old neighborhood in a New York slum, he looks up his old girlfriend (Trevor) who has become a streetwalker. He does not catch on until she tells him, "I'm tired. I'm sick. Can you see it? Look at me good. You've been looking at me like I used to be." Her part is not very big, but her performance is memorable.

Dallas / STAGECOACH, 1939, United Artists, d-John Ford.

Trevor is superb as the lady of easy virtue with a heart of gold who is chased out of town. While traveling by stagecoach she finds her own knight in shining armor (John Wayne), who doesn't care about her past because he's not lily white himself.

"Gold Dust" Nelson / HONKY TONK, 1941, MGM, d-Jack Conway.

In this western Clark Gable is a con man who survives tar and feathering and almost ends up owning a gold-mining town. Trevor "entertains" in his saloon and gambling house, yearning for the boss; but Gable goes for Lana Turner, the daughter of another con man (Frank Morgan).

Velma / Mrs. Grayle / MURDER, MY SWEET, 1944, RKO, d-Edward Dmytryk.

In the best film version of any of Raymond Chandler's stories (according to the author himself), Trevor is a two-timing woman who has come a long way since she was the girlfriend of an ex-con (Mike Mazurki). Mazurki has hired private eye Dick Powell to locate his Velma. The mission is accomplished but there's no happy ending for Mazurki and Trevor.

Gaye Dawn / KEY LARGO, 1948, Warners, d-John Huston.

Trevor is extremely touching as the pitiful mistress of brutal gangster Edward G. Robinson. He taunts her about her drinking and forces her to sing "Moanin' Low" in her broken voice to earn another drink. She reminds him, "You gave me my first drink, Johnny." Ultimately the poor creature sides with Humphrey Bogart and Lauren Bacall against Robinson and his henchmen. Her Oscar was very much deserved.

May Holst / THE HIGH AND THE MIGHTY, 1954, Warners, d-William A. Wellman.

In this early filming of a near-fatal air disaster, Trevor portrays a world-weary woman who no longer cares about her own life. "There oughta be a home for dames like me. Yep, they shoulda organized. You know, a house somewhere with—with no mirror in it, far away where we'd never have to look at the young girls. They have homes for unmarried mothers, but everybody forgets about the girls who—who never quite managed to make things legal. I think I could start one. Yeah, I think I could call it May Holst's Home for Broken-Down Broads."

OTHER ROLES

1933: *the girl* / LIFE IN THE RAW; *newspaper woman* / THE LAST TRAIL; *Jane Lee* / THE MAD GAME; *Sally Johnson* / JIMMY AND SALLY. **1934:** *Tony Bellamy* / HOLD THAT GIRL; *Jerry Jordan* / WILD GOLD; *Kay Ellison* / BABY TAKE A BOW; *Elinor Norton* / ELINOR NORTON. **1935:** *Betty Ingals* / SPRING TONIC; *Janette Foster* / BLACK SHEEP; *Vicky Blake* / NAVY WIFE. **1936:** *Carol Barton* / MY MARRIAGE; *Julie Carroll* / THE SONG AND DANCE MAN; *Kitty Brant* / TO MARY WITH LOVE; *Nina Lind* / STAY FOR A NIGHT; *Jane Martin* / 15 MAIDEN LANE; *Carroll Aiken* / CAREER WOMAN. **1937:** *Barbara Blanchard* / TIME OUT FOR ROMANCE; *Dixie* / KING OF GAMBLERS; *Lucy "Tex" Warren* / ONE MILE FROM HEAVEN; *Marcia* / SECOND HONEYMOON; *Fay Loring* / BIG TOWN GIRL. **1938:** *Joan Bradley* / WALKING DOWN BROADWAY; *Christine Nelson* / FIVE OF A KIND; *Jo Keller* / THE AMAZING DR. CLITTERHOUSE; *Lee Roberts* / VALLEY OF THE GIANTS. **1939:** *Laura Benson* / I STOLE A MILLION; *Janie* / ALLEGHENY UPRISING. **1940:** *Mary McCloud* / DARK COMMAND. **1941:** *"Mike" King* / TEXAS. **1942:** *Connie Dawson* / THE ADVENTURES OF MARTIN EDEN; *Michele Allaine* / CROSSROADS; *Ruth Dillon* / STREET OF CHANCE. **1943:** *Countess Maletta* / THE DESPERADOES; *Ruth Jones* / GOOD LUCK, MR. YATES; *Dora Hand* / WOMAN OF THE TOWN. **1945:** *Lilah Gustafson* / JOHNNY ANGEL. **1946:** *Terry Cordeau* / CRACK-UP; *Cynthia* / THE BACHELOR'S DAUGHTERS. **1947:** *Helen Trent* / BORN TO KILL. **1948:** *Pat* / RAW DEAL; *Marion Webster* / THE VELVET TOUCH; *Clair Hodgson Ruth* / THE BABE RUTH STORY. **1949:** *Marguerite Seaton* / THE LUCKY STIFF. **1950:** *Madeleine Haley* / BORDERLINE. **1951:** *Lily Fowler* / BEST OF THE BADMEN; *Milly Farley* / HARD, FAST AND BEAUTIFUL. **1952:** *Connie Williams* / HOODLUM EMPIRE; *Louise Hawkson* / MY MAN AND I; *Nora Marko* / STOP, YOU'RE KILLING ME. **1953:** *Josie Sullivan* / THE STRANGER WORE A GUN. **1955:** *Idonee* / MAN WITHOUT A STAR; *Lady MacBeth* / LUCY GALLANT. **1956:** *Marie* / THE MOUNTAIN. **1958:** *Rose Morgenstern* / MARJORIE MORNINGSTAR. **1962:** *Clara Kruger* / TWO WEEKS IN ANOTHER TOWN. **1963:** *Helen Baird* / THE STRIPPER. **1965:** *Edna Lampson* / HOW TO MURDER YOUR WIFE. **1967:** *Moe* / THE CAPE TOWN AFFAIR. **1982:** *Charlotte Banning* / KISS ME GOODBYE.

TURNER, KATHLEEN

(1954–)

Kathleen Turner may be the film find of the 1980s. Sexy, funny, and a fine actress, Turner has already supplied considerable evidence that this tall, tawny beauty with the smooth-as-silk voice will be a star of importance for years to come. She sizzles in her sensuous roles and snaps, crackles, and pops in her comedy appearances.

KEY ROLES

Matty Walker / BODY HEAT, 1981, Warners, d-Lawrence Kasdan.

In a film reminiscent of the great DOUBLE INDEMNITY, Turner enlists an unwitting and apparently none-too-bright William Hurt in a plot to knock off her wealthy husband. The passion between Hurt and Turner is very hot, but kill a man just for sex? Makes one think of another Turner and a guy named Garfield.

Joan Wilder / ROMANCING THE STONE, 1984, 20th Century-Fox, d-Robert Zemeckis.

Turner, a plain and shy writer of romantic adventure novels, learns that her sister has been kidnapped in Columbia. She gets to live out one of her adventures with the help of Michael Douglas and is harassed by villains Zack Norman, Alfonso Arau, and a marvelously funny Danny DeVito. The trio of Turner, Douglas, and DeVito were reunited in a sort of sequel, THE JEWEL OF THE NILE, in 1985.

Irene Walker / PRIZZI'S HONOR, 1985, ABC, d-John Huston.

Turner is a mob hit woman who falls in love with top mobster Jack Nicholson, then helps him pull off a mob kidnapping during which a police captain's wife is killed. When the Don says she has to go she realizes that Nicholson will put his family allegiance above his wedding vows. She prepares to waste him but his knife is a bit faster than her revolver.

Peggy Sue Kelser / PEGGY SUE GOT MARRIED, 1986, Tri-Star, d-Francis Ford Coppola.

Turner passes out from excitement after being crowned queen of her 25th high school reunion and wakes up in 1960, her senior year. This gains her the chance to see if she wants to do things exactly the same as the first time; in particular, does she wish to marry her soon-to-be philandering husband (Nicolas Cage). Cage looks too young for this beauty in 1985 and in 1960. It's all Turner's show and she runs away with this very entertaining movie.

OTHER ROLES

1983: *Dolores Benedict Hfuhruhurr* / THE MAN WITH TWO BRAINS. **1984:** *China Blue* / *Joanna* / CRIMES OF PASSION. **1985:** *Joan Wilder* / JEWEL OF THE NILE. **1987:** *Julia* / JULIA AND JULIA.

TURNER, LANA

(Julia Turner, 1920–)

Known as "The Sweater Girl" for obvious reasons, Lana Turner had a raw, smoldering sex appeal. Her blonde good looks made her the definitive starlet of the 1930s and a major star in the 1940s. Never much of an actress, she nevertheless was nominated for an Oscar for PEYTON PLACE in 1957. Probably her most memorable role was in THE POSTMAN ALWAYS RINGS TWICE in which she encouraged drifter James Garfield to kill her husband and have her all to himself. In addition to her seven marriages, Turner had numerous highly publicized affairs; one with small-time mobster Johnny Stompanato lead to his death at the hands of Turner's daughter who was trying to protect her mother from Stompanato's beating. Turner's reaction to the troubles in her far-from-private life was, "Whenever I do something it seems so right. And turns out so wrong."

KEY ROLES

Cynthia Potter / LOVE FINDS ANDY HARDY, 1938, MGM, d-George B. Seitz.

Before her emergence as the number one pin-up of World War II, Turner usually played nice, quiet, refined girls. In this Andy Hardy story Turner is merely a cute teenager for whom Mickey Rooney makes a fool of himself.

Beatrix Emery / DR. JEKYLL AND MR. HYDE, 1941, MGM, d-Victor Fleming.

Turner has the unattractive role of Spencer Tracy's sensible and dull fiancée. She should have held out for the role of the prostitute that Ingrid Bergman wisely grabbed.

Elizabeth Cotten / HONKY TONK, 1941, MGM, d-Jack Conway.

Once again Turner plays a good girl. This time she's the daughter of con man Frank Morgan who is less than thrilled when Clark Gable, another shady character, marries his innocent little flower.

Lisbeth Bard / JOHNNY EAGER, 1941, MGM, d-Mervyn LeRoy.

Turner and Robert Taylor (as the title character), an unscrupulous underworld figure, have a fiery romance before he gets his in a hail of bullets when one of the few decent things he's ever done riles some associates.

Paula Lane / SOMEWHERE I'LL FIND YOU, 1942, MGM, d-Wesley Ruggles.

This teaming of Turner and Clark Gable was the highest grossing picture in the studio's history to that point. In it Gable and brother Robert Sterling are two war correspondents who make a play for Turner. Today viewers may well wonder why anyone would get excited about this ordinary wartime love story.

Bunny Smith / WEEKEND AT THE WALDORF, 1945, MGM, d-Robert Z. Leonard.

Somehow this remake of GRAND HOTEL doesn't have the zing of the original. Turner more or less reprises the role played by Joan Crawford. Her Wallace Beery is Edward Arnold in one of his nasty roles. But audiences seemed to like the film and it made big profits.

Cora Smith / THE POSTMAN ALWAYS RINGS TWICE, 1946, MGM, d-Tay Garnett.

An indelible image in this movie, at least for male viewers, is Turner's appearance the first time drifter John Garfield sees her—she's all in white, wearing a turban, a form-fitting blouse, and short, short shorts. Garfield is hooked by this cool-looking beauty and Cecil Kellaway, as her older husband, is a goner—it's just a matter of when and how. Typical of this kind of film noir, Turner and Garfield have a falling out after the deed and they both get their just deserts, even though they beat the rap of killing Kellaway.

Marianne Patourel / GREEN DOLPHIN STREET, 1947, MGM, d-Victor Saville.

This is the tedious story of two sisters (Turner and Donna Reed) who are after the same man (Richard Hart) in 19th-century New Zealand. The producers tried to include too much of the novel by Elizabeth Groudge and ended up with a mish-mash of incomplete plot-lines.

Virginia Marshland / CASS TIMBERLANE, 1947, MGM, d-George Sidney.

In this interesting but unexciting story, Turner is a poor girl who marries a wealthy judge (Spencer Tracy) who has some trouble keeping up with his young bride.

Milady de Winter / THE THREE MUSKETEERS, 1948, MGM, d-George Sidney.

Turner is nicely evil as the agent of Cardinal Richelieu who nearly succeeds in ruining the Queen's reputation. She cheats and kills while not seducing all the men that can prove useful to her. But in the end she is given over to an executioner to have her head removed from her shoulders.

Crystal Radek / THE MERRY WIDOW, 1952, MGM, d-Curtis Bernhardt.

The only thing memorable about this poorly produced musical is how well Turner looks in her black lingerie. Fernando Lamas is ordered to make love to the wealthy widow in hopes of saving the economy of a small country.

Georgia Lorrison / THE BAD AND THE BEAUTIFUL, 1952, MGM, d-Vincente Minnelli.

Turner is one of the victims of a manipulative movie producer (Kirk Douglas). She prospers in films after he almost forcibly pulls her up from being a drunken tramp and makes her a star by making her fall in love with him. But she discovers after her triumph on the screen that he doesn't want her.

Constance MacKenzie / PEYTON PLACE, 1957, 20th Century-Fox, d-Mark Robson.

The film version of Grace Metalious's sizzling bestseller is only medium warm and Turner is downright cold until Lee Philips, the new high school principal, comes along and takes her out in the moonlight to find some heat. Turner was nominated for an Oscar but it's difficult to figure out why.

Lora Meredith / IMITATION OF LIFE, 1959, Universal-International, d-Douglas Sirk.

Turner just wasn't in the class of other actresses who made a success of playing in "women's pictures." In this one she recreates the Claudette Colbert role of a woman who becomes rich marketing the pancake recipe of her black servant. The servant's life is tragic also because her daughter turns her back on her in an attempt to pass for white.

Holly Parker / MADAME X, 1966, Universal, d-David Lowell Rich.

In the third film production of the weepy play by Alexandre Bisson, Turner portrays a wealthy woman whose fortunes disappear as she goes down in the world. Years later she is accused of murder and is defended by her son whom she had to give up long before. He doesn't know it's his mother who sits on the witness stand.

OTHER ROLES

1937: *extra* / A STAR IS BORN; *Mary Clay* / THEY WON'T FORGET; *Auber* / THE GREAT GARRICK. **1938:** *bit* / FOUR'S A CROWD; *Miss Rutherford* / THE CHASER; *Nazama's maid* / THE ADVENTURES OF MARCO POLO; *Mado* / DRAMATIC SCHOOL. **1939:** *Rosalie* / CALLING DR. KILDARE; *Helen Thayer* / RICH MAN, POOR GIRL; *Jane Thomas* / THESE GLAMOUR GIRLS; *Patty Marlow* / DANCING CO-ED. **1940:** *Pat Mahoney* / TWO GIRLS ON BROADWAY; *Margy Brooks* / WE WHO ARE YOUNG. **1941:** *Sheila Regan* / ZIEGFELD GIRL. **1943:** *Peggy Evans* / *Carol Burden* / SLIGHTLY DANGEROUS; *guest* / THE YOUNGEST PROFESSION; *guest* / DUBARRY WAS A LADY. **1944:** *Theo Scofield West* / MARRIAGE IS A PRIVATE AFFAIR; *Valerie Parks* / KEEP YOUR POWDER DRY. **1948:** *Lt. Jane "Snapshot" McCall* / HOMECOMING. **1950:** *Lily Brannel James* / A LIFE OF HER OWN. **1951:** *Fredda Barlo* / MR. IMPERIUM. **1953:** *Nora Taylor* / LATIN LOVERS. **1954:** *Madeline* / THE FLAME AND THE FLESH. **1955:** *Carla Van Owen* / BETRAYED; *Samarra* / THE PRODIGAL; *Edwina*

Esketh / THE RAINS OF RANCHIPUR; *Elsa Keller* / THE SEA CHASE. **1956:** *Diane de Poitiers* / DIANE. **1957:** *Sara Scott* / ANOTHER TIME, ANOTHER PLACE. **1958:** *Maggie Colby* / THE LADY TAKES A FLYER. **1960:** *Sheila Cabot* / PORTRAIT IN BLACK. **1961:** *Marjorie Penrose* / BY LOVE POSSESSED. **1962:** *Rosemary Howard* / BACHELOR IN PARADISE. **1963:** *Melanie Flood* / WHO'S GOT THE ACTION? **1965:** *Kit Jordan* / LOVE HAS MANY FACES. **1969:** *Adriana Roman* / THE BIG CUBE. **1971:** *Tracy Carlyle Hastings* / THE LAST OF THE POWERSEEKERS. **1974:** *Carrie Masters* / PERSECUTION. **1976:** *Claire* / BITTERSWEET LOVE.

TUSHINGHAM, RITA

(1940–)

Plain, wide-eyed Rita Tushingham fit into the British realist school of non-heroines and won the British Academy Award, the New York Film Critics Award, and the Cannes Festival Award among others for her performance in her debut film in 1962, A TASTE OF HONEY. Since then she has made very few films and only a couple that are on a par with her first effort.

KEY ROLES

Jo / A TASTE OF HONEY, 1962, Great Britain, Woodfall Films, d-Tony Richardson.

There is much to admire about the acting in this film. Dora Bryan's single-minded selfishness as Tushingham's mother is most impressive; in addition, Murray Melvin's penniless homosexual who befriends Tushingham when she becomes pregnant by a black sailor who has gone back to the sea, is such a gentle creature, eager to act as the father of the expectant child. But it is Tushingham with her big, trusting, frightened eyes that makes this film the extraordinary piece of work it is. Life among the lower classes of England is something one is born to and it would seem few escape.

Kate Brady / THE GIRL WITH GREEN EYES, 1964, Great Britain, Woodfall Films, d-Desmond Davis.

Tushingham leaves her father's farm in Ireland to work in a grocery store and shares an apartment with a girl who went to convent school with her. She falls in love with a much older writer and he with her, but her conscience prevents her from having sex with him, even though they live together in his apartment. Her father gets wind of the living arrangement and, with some drunken cronies, lays siege to the home of the writer. They are routed by the man's housekeeper and an ancient shotgun. Tushingham surrenders herself to the writer but as they have nothing in common other than their love and passion, the affair does not last.

Nancy Jones / THE KNACK...AND HOW TO GET IT, 1965, Great Britain, Woodfall Films, d-Richard Lester.

A sex-starved young teacher (Michael Crawford) hopes to learn from his more experienced friend (Ray Brooks) how to be successful with girls. Instead, Crawford meets an innocent girl from the North (Tushingham) who prefers him to his fast-talking, sexist buddy.

OTHER ROLES

1963: *Dot* / THE LEATHER BOYS; *Catherine ("Cat")* / A PLACE TO GO. **1965:** *the girl* / DR. ZHIVAGO. **1966:** *Eve* / THE TRAP. **1967:** *Brenda* / SMASHING TIME. **1968:** *Bridget Rafferty* / DIAMONDS FOR BREAKFAST. **1969:** *Jenny* / THE GURU; *Penelope* / THE BED-SITTING ROOM. **1972:** *Brenda Thompson* / STRAIGHT ON TILL MORNING. **1975:** *Janice* / THE HUMAN FACTOR.

USTINOV, PETER

(1921–)

A screen and stage actor, film and stage director, playwright, novelist, screenwriter, and raconteur, Peter Ustinov has found success in each of these endeavors. Born in London of French and Russian descent, Ustinov is heavily-built with a mellifluous voice. He made his film debut in the 1940 short HULLO, FAME, served in the Royal Sussex Regiment, made World War II propaganda movies, directed his first film, THE SCHOOL FOR SECRETS, in 1946 and appeared in his own plays in 1951, 1956, 1967, 1968, and 1983, winning Tonys for "Romanoff and Juliet" for Best Play and Best Performance. He directed an opera at Covent Garden in 1962; was awarded a Grammy for his narration of the album "Peter and the Wolf"; received Oscar nominations for QUO VADIS? SPARTACUS, and TOPKAPI, winning for the last two; and received an Emmy for his portrayal of Dr. Johnson in "The Life of Samuel Johnson." He is also fluent in five or six languages and wrote a bestselling memoir, *Dear Me*. And on the seventh day he rested.

KEY ROLES

Private Angelo / PRIVATE ANGELO, 1949, Great Britain, Associated British-Pathe, d-Peter Ustinov.

Ustinov wrote the screenplay for this story of an Italian private who during World War II tries to escape the fighting and get back to his hometown where his girlfriend is waiting. After the war they marry, with the British corporal who is the father of her son as best man.

Nero / QUO VADIS? 1951, MGM, d-Mervyn LeRoy.

Ustinov received an Academy Award nomination for his mad act as the Roman emperor who burned the city of Rome and tried to blame the destruction on the Christians. While he's at it he sends the leads in the picture, (Robert Taylor as a Roman commander and Deborah Kerr as a Christian girl he loves) to the lions.

Emad / HOTEL SAHARA, 1951, Great Britain, Tower / GFD, d-Ken Annakin.

Ustinov is the proprietor of a World War II desert hotel in No Man's Land, which is at various times inhabited by British, Italian, Free French, and German troops. He and his mistress change the decor and their allegiances to suit each new group. Things seem to be back to normal when the Americans arrive.

Prince of Wales / BEAU BRUMMEL, 1954, Great Britain, MGM, d-Curtis Bernhardt.

Elegant Stewart Granger (as the title character) becomes a great favorite of the Prince of Wales' (Ustinov), but when they have a falling-out, Granger is forced to flee to France to escape his creditors. On his deathbed in France he is reconciled with Ustinov, who is now King George IV.

Jules / WE'RE NO ANGELS, 1954, Paramount, d-Michael Curtiz.

A gentlemanly safecracker (Ustinov) a counterfeiter / embezzler (Humphrey Bogart), and a murderer (Aldo Ray) escape from their Devil's Island prison and hide out at the store of a very incompetent manager, his wife, and daughter. Before returning to prison they make things right in the household they have briefly entered at Christmastime.

Batiatus / SPARTACUS, 1960, Universal-International, d-Stanley Kubrick.

Kirk Douglas (as the title character) begins the slave revolt in ancient Rome in Ustinov's gladiator school. Ustinov won an Oscar for playing a clever fellow who always finds a way to turn a profit, even when the cruel Roman commander (Laurence Olivier) crucifies all the defeated slaves along the Appian Way.

Rupert Vennecker / THE SUNDOWNERS, 1960, Great Britain / Australia, Warners, d-Fred Zinnemann.

Flamboyant Ustinov is easily the best thing in this amusing and leisurely-developed story of an Irish shepherd (Robert Mitchum), his wife (Deborah Kerr), their teenage son, and the people they meet as they travel from job to job in the Australian outback during the twenties.

The General / ROMANOFF AND JULIET, 1961, Universal-International, d-Peter Ustinov.

Ustinov is the General of Concordia, a minuscule republic wooed by both the Americans and Russians as both want its critical UN vote. Ustinov encourages the romance and marriage of the son of the Russian ambassador and the daughter of the American ambassador. Ustinov is superb; it's the rest of the cast that drag this comedy down.

Arthur Simpson / TOPKAPI, 1964, United Artists, d-Jules Dassin.

Ustinov received his second Oscar for his role as a shabby con man used by the police to spy on a gang of thieves who plan to steal a priceless jewel-encrusted dagger from a museum in Istanbul.

Marcus Pendleton / HOT MILLIONS, 1968, MGM, d-Eric Till.

In this very funny comedy Ustinov is an embezzler who has just finished a jail sentence. He had been caught by a computer, so while sitting in prison he studies them and becomes a whiz. Out of prison he takes the place of a known computer genius who is leaving the country and wins a position with a huge corporation headed by Karl Malden, then uses his knowledge of computers to have checks issued to fictitious companies he has established in cities all over Europe. He marries his secretary (Maggie Smith) who invests his ill-gotten gains and makes a fortune. It becomes possible to return all the embezzled money to Malden, who chooses not to prosecute, so Ustinov gets away with his biggest swindle of all time.

Gen. Maximilian Rodrigues de Santos / VIVA MAX! 1969, Commonwealth United, d-Jerry Paris.

Ustinov, a Mexican general, marches his troops into San Antonio, Texas, and takes over the Alamo. It should be much funnier.

Hercule Poirot / DEATH ON THE NILE, 1978, Great Britain, EMI, d-John Guillermin.

Ustinov makes a more than adequate Poirot in this Agatha Christie story about a spoiled heiress who is killed on a steamer cruising down the Nile.

OTHER ROLES

1940: *bit* / MEIN KAMPF—MY CRIMES. **1941:** *bit* / LET THE PEOPLE SING. **1942:** *Krauss* / THE GOOSE STEPS OUT; *priest* / ONE OF OUR AIRCRAFT IS MISSING; *Rispoli* / THE WAY AHEAD. **1950:** *Arnaud* / ODETTE. **1951:** *industry man* / THE MAGIC BOX. **1954:** *Kaptah* / THE EGYPTIAN; *narrator* / HOUSE OF PLEASURE. **1955:** *ringmaster* / LOLA MONTES. **1956:** *Don Alfonso* / THE WANDERERS. **1957:** *Mr. Bossi* / AN ANGEL OVER BROOKLYN; *Michael Kiminsky* / THE SPIES. **1959:** *voice* / ADVENTURES OF MR. WONDERFUL. **1962:** *Captain Vere* / BILLY BUDD. **1964:** *narrator* / THE PEACHES; *King Fawz* / JOHN GOLDFARB, PLEASE COME HOME. **1965:** *Prince Otto of Bavaria* / LADY L. **1967:** *Ambassador Pineda* / THE COMEDIANS. **1972:** *the doctor* / HAMMERSMITH IS OUT. **1976:** *Dr. Snodgrass* / TREASURE OF MATECUMBE; *Hnup Wan* / ONE OF OUR DINOSAURS IS MISSING; *old man* / LOGAN'S RUN; *voice* / ROBIN HOOD. **1977:** *Taubleman* / THE PURPLE TAXI. **1978:** *Sergeant Markov* / THE LAST REMAKE OF BEAU GESTE; *narrator* / THE MOUSE AND HIS CHILD; *Harry Hellman* / DOUBLE MURDERS; *narrator* / TARKA THE OTTER; *narrator* / WINDS OF CHANGE. **1979:** *Suleiman* / ASHANTI. **1981:** *Charlie Chan* / CHARLIE CHAN AND THE CURSE OF THE DRAGON QUEEN; *truck driver* / THE GREAT MUPPET CAPER; *Hercule Poirot* / EVIL UNDER THE SUN; *voice* / GRENDEL, GRENDEL, GRENDEL. **1984:** *Abdi Aga* / MEMED MY HAWK.

VELEZ, LUPE

(Maria Guadalupe Velez de Villalobos, 1909–1944)

Mexican-born Lupe Velez was stuck with the stereotyped roles Hollywood believed to represent Latin senoritas of less-than-refined backgrounds. Whether life imitated art or the other way around is difficult to say, but her not-so-private life was as volatile and explosive as her characterizations on screen. Her many affairs with actors like John Gilbert, Gary Cooper, and Randolph Scott were common knowledge and her tempestuous marriage to Johnny Weissmuller made all the papers. Tiny and dark-haired, Velez was signed in 1926 to play in Hal Roach comedy shorts. Her first big break was when Douglas Fairbanks spotted her and cast her opposite him in THE GAUCHO in 1928. With the coming of sound her heavy accent condemned her to what can be considered self-parodies, ending in the late 1930s and early 1940s with "The Mexican Spitfire" "B" movies with Leon Errol. In 1944, pregnant, unmarried, heavily in debt, and her career all but over, Velez took her own life after decorating her bedroom with flowers and having sessions with her hairdresser and makeup man.

KEY ROLES

The Mountain Girl / THE GAUCHO, 1928, Silent, United Artists, d-F. Richard Jones.

Gaucho leader Douglas Fairbanks is loved by mountain girl Velez who becomes jealous of the interest shown Fairbanks by Geraine Greear, "the girl of the shrine." Velez turns Fairbanks in to the authorities but he escapes in time to rescue Greear from being executed by his followers.

Lola Salazar / WOLF SONG, 1929, Silent, Paramount, d-Victor Fleming.

Velez, the daughter of a don, elopes with Kentucky trapper Gary Cooper and they live in a settlement until Cooper decides he's had it with civilization and returns to the Canadian wilderness. Velez returns to her family in California. But Cooper finds the nights too long and lonely and heads home, only to be shot by Indians. Somehow he makes it to the hacienda of his bride where she nurses him back to health.

Ming Toy / EAST IS WEST, 1930, Universal, d-Monta Bell.

Velez, the oldest of several children of a poor Chinese family, is rescued from the auction block by Lew Ayres and is sent to the U.S. where she attracts the attention of powerful Chinatown figure Edward G. Robinson. When the latter demands her hand, Ayres shows up in time to reveal that, as a baby, Velez was kidnapped from American parents. This kills Robinson's interest, leaving Ayres and Velez to marry.

Nenita / THE CUBAN LOVE SONG, 1931, MGM, d-W. S. Van Dyke.

In a story similar to that of "Madame Butterfly," Lawrence Tibbett is an American marine who fathers a son by Velez in Cuba then returns to his socialite girlfriend in San Francisco. Years later he returns to pick up his son and finds that Velez is dead.

Juanita Morales / HIGH FLYERS, 1937, RKO, d-Edward Cline.

In the final teaming of Bert Wheeler and Robert Woolsey, Velez has all the best of a rather dim comedy, impersonating Dolores Del Rio, Simone Simon, Shirley Temple, and also herself.

Carmelita Lindsay / THE GIRL FROM MEXICO, 1939, RKO, d-Leslie Goodwins.

In the first of eight films in the series, Velez plays a fiery Latin entertainer who goes after and captures Donald Woods, who is no match for her temperamental ways. She's egged on by Leon Errol who portrays Woods's accident-prone uncle.

OTHER ROLES

1927: *bit* / WHAT WOMEN DID FOR ME; *bit* / SAILORS BEWARE. **1928:** *Jania* / STAND AND DELIVER. **1929:** *Nanon Del Rayon* / LADY OF THE PAVEMENTS; *Toyo* / WHERE EAST IS EAST; *Rose* / TIGER ROSE. **1930:** *Anita Morgan* / HELL HARBOR; *Manette Fachard* / THE STORM. **1931:** *Katerina Maslova* / RESURRECTION; *Naturich* / THE SQUAW MAN. **1932:** *Lolita* / THE BROKEN WING; *Julia Cavanaugh* / MEN IN HER LIFE (Spanish language version); *Tula* / KONGO; *Tersita* / THE HALF-NAKED TRUTH. **1933:** *Pepper* / HOT PEPPER; *guest* / MR. BROADWAY. **1934:** *Slim Girl* / LAUGHING BOY; *Nina Madero* / PALOOKA; *herself* / HOLLYWOOD PARTY; *Vera* / STRICTLY DYNAMITE. **1935:** *Carlotta* / THE MORALS OF MARCUS. **1936:** *Mila* / GYPSY MELODY. **1938:** *Lupe* / LA ZANDUNGA; *Carla De Huelva* / MAD ABOUT MONEY. **1939:** *Carmelita Lindsay* / MEXICAN SPITFIRE. **1940:** *Carmelita Lindsay* / MEXICAN SPITFIRE OUT WEST. **1941:** *Carmelita Lindsay* / MEXICAN SPITFIRE'S BABY; *Carmelita Lindsay* / MEXICAN SPITFIRE AT SEA; *Madame La Zonga* / SIX LESSONS FROM MADAME LA ZONGA. **1942:** *Carmelita Lindsay* / MEXICAN SPITFIRE SEES A GHOST; *Carmelita Lindsay* / MEXICAN SPITFIRE'S ELEPHANT. **1943:** *Carmelita Lindsay* / MEXICAN SPITFIRE'S BLESSED EVENT; *Rita and Elaine Manners* / REDHEAD FROM MANHATTAN. **1944:** *Nana* / NANA.

VERA-ELLEN

(Vera-Ellen W. Rohe, 1920–1981)

A pert, slim-bodied dancer, Vera-Ellen had an engaging smile that lit up the screen during the 1940s and 1950s. Her partners included Fred Astaire, Gene Kelly, and Donald O'Connor. A former Radio City Music Hall Rockette and dancer at Billy Rose's Diamond Horseshoe, she made her screen debut at 19 with Danny Kaye in WONDER MAN. Often playing the little girl from the country who was able to hold off the wolves while realizing her dream to become a star, Vera-Ellen retired in 1956 when interest in Hollywood musicals waned.

KEY ROLES

Midge Mallon / WONDER MAN, 1945, Goldwyn / RKO, d-Bruce Humberstone.

In her debut Vera-Ellen is third-billed playing the longtime fiancée of nightclub comedian Danny Kaye—the Kaye who is bumped off and thrown in a lagoon in Prospect Park, Brooklyn, before he can testify against Steve Cochran in a murder trial. The other Kaye, twin brother of the deceased, is possessed by the ghost of his sibling until he can prove who murdered Kaye number 1. Kaye number 2's romantic interest is Virginia Mayo. Vera-Ellen performs "Bali Boogie" with Kaye and the Goldwyn Girls and "So in Love" with her singing dubbed by June Hutton.

Ivy Smith / ON THE TOWN, 1949, MGM, d-Gene Kelly and Stanley Donen.

When three sailors (Gene Kelly, Frank Sinatra, and Jules Munshin) arrive in Manhattan on a twenty-four-hour pass looking for love, Kelly falls for a poster of Miss Turnstiles (Vera-Ellen), whom he reckons must be a well-known celebrity. He sets out to meet and woo her and, as such things are possible in movie musicals, he achieves his objectives. Vera-Ellen dances to the "Miss Turnstiles Ballet" and joins with Kelly for "Main Street."

Jessie Brown Kalmar / THREE LITTLE WORDS, 1950, MGM, d-Richard Thorpe.

In one of the many biopics of pop music composers made in the 1950s, Vera-Ellen becomes the wife of lyricist Bert Kalmar (Fred Astaire). With the help of the wife of Harry Ruby she gets the two songwriters back together after a career split. She dances with Astaire to "Mr. and Mrs. Hoofer at Home" and "Thinking of You."

Princess Maria / CALL ME MADAM, 1953, 20th Century-Fox, d-Walter Lang.

When Ethel Merman is appointed ambassador to Lichtenberg, her press attache (Donald O'Connor) falls for the tiny nation's princess (Vera-Ellen). While the show really belongs to Merman, Vera-Ellen and O'Connor dance superbly to "It's a Lovely Day Today" and "Something to Dance About."

OTHER ROLES

1946: *Susie Sullivan* / THE KID FROM BROOKLYN; *Myra* / THREE LITTLE GIRLS IN BLUE. **1947:** *Luisa Molina* / CARNIVAL IN COSTA RICA. **1948:** *herself* / WORDS AND MUSIC. **1949:** *Maggie Phillips* / LOVE HAPPY. **1951:** *Janet Jones* / HAPPY GO LOVELY. **1952:** *Angela Bonfils* / THE BELLE OF NEW YORK. **1953:** *Christy* / THE BIG LEAGUER. **1954:** *Judy Lane* / WHITE CHRISTMAS. **1956:** *Jeanne MacLean* / LET'S BE HAPPY.

VOIGHT, JON

(1938–)

Blond, blue-eyed Jon Voight has worked so hard resisting typecasting that he has made very few movies in a 20-year film career and some of his choices for parts have been unfortunate. Nevertheless, he can take satisfaction for a few truly outstanding performances, including his Oscar-nominated work in MIDNIGHT COWBOY and his Oscar-winning work in COMING HOME; he was also nominated for an Oscar for RUNAWAY TRAIN. He is at home in sentimental melodramas in which his sometimes hidden vulnerability and sensitivity can be best exhibited. Voight is most interested in what he considers relevant character roles. He is a committed pacifist who was active in the anti-Vietnam War movement. His views on what should be our major concern are summarized as follows: "The only thing that should be taken seriously is a reverence for humanity, crazy humanity."

KEY ROLES

Joe Buck / MIDNIGHT COWBOY, 1969, United Artists, d-John Schlesinger.

Voight portrays a would-be stud in New York City. He's a likable dummy who, after being flim-flammed by a greasy bum with a game leg (Dustin Hoffman), befriends the tubercular little rat and takes him to Florida to escape the cold of the winter; but Hoffman dies just as they reach their destination. Voight's performance is spectacular and it's a tribute to his determination that he wasn't immediately cast in similar roles.

Ed / DELIVERANCE, 1972, Warners, d-John Boorman.
The contrast between the macho man Burt Reynolds and the gentle civilized Voight is a brilliant dramatic ploy in this excellent story of four men who spend a long weekend canoeing down a dangerous river where they find death. It's the quiet Voight, not the swaggering Reynolds, who must find a strength he didn't know he had to save himself and his companions.

Luke Martin / COMING HOME, 1978, United Artists, d-Hal Ashby.
Voight won his Academy Award for his portrayal of a Vietnam vet, paralyzed from the waist down, who becomes Jane Fonda's lover. She is married to gung-ho marine officer Bruce Dern who's in Vietnam doing battle with the Commies. It's not a film that will age well; you had to be there at the time to enjoy it and even then it's was a bit too cloyingly weepy for many tastes.

Billy / THE CHAMP, 1979, United Artists / MGM, d-Franco Zeffirelli.
In this remake of the Wallace Beery / Jackie Cooper weeper, Voight is a drunken gambler who dreams of a comeback in the ring while his young son (Ricky Schroder) keeps an eye on him. His ex-wife (Faye Dunaway) wants custody of the boy. The film gets too sentimental before the end and the extra 36 minutes it takes doesn't improve on the original.

Manny / RUNAWAY TRAIN, 1985, Cannon, d-Andrei Konchalovsky.
Wildman Voight is one of two convicts who escape from a prison and, accompanied by hostage Rebecca DeMornay, hop a train headed for disaster. It's an intense adventure movie based on a screenplay by Japanese director Akira Kurosawa, but it's a bit too serious and allegorical for its own good.

OTHER ROLES

1967: *Frank / False Frank* / FRANK'S GREATEST ADVENTURE; *Curly Bill Brocius* / HOUR OF THE GUN. **1969:** *Russ* / OUT OF IT. **1970:** *A* / THE REVOLUTIONARY; *Milo Minderbinder* / CATCH-22. **1973:** *Vic Bealer* / THE ALL-AMERICAN BOY. **1974:** *Pat Conroy* / CONRACK; *Peter Miller* / THE ODESSA FILE. **1975:** *Walter Tschanz* / END OF THE GAME. **1982:** *Alec Kovac* / LOOKIN' TO GET OUT. **1983:** *J. P. Tannen* / TABLE FOR FIVE. **1986:** *Jack* / DESERT BLOOM.

WAGNER, ROBERT

(1930–)

The son of a wealthy Pittsburgh steel executive, Robert Wagner appears to have been too good-looking to ever be taken seriously as an actor. He was quickly typecast as a pretty boy with no great ambitions or prospects of doing anything worthwhile and was only rarely allowed to deviate from his lightweight persona. In the late 1960s Wagner made a decision to move to TV where he has enjoyed great popularity in lightweight comical adventure and detective shows including "It Takes a Thief," "Switch," and "Hart to Hart." Married to and divorced from actress Natalie Wood, they remarried and were together at the time of her tragic drowning death.

KEY ROLES

Prince Valiant / PRINCE VALIANT, 1954, 20th Century-Fox, d-Henry Hathaway.
Give Wagner credit—he is able to keep a straight face while wearing the absurd-looking Prince Valiant wig throughout this adventure yarn about the son of the exiled king of Scandia who seeks King Arthur's help to overturn the usurper. He even gets both Debra Paget and Janet Leigh to show interest in him.

Joe Devereaux / BROKEN LANCE, 1954, 20th Century-Fox, d-Edward Dmytryk.
In this western version of HOUSE OF STRANGERS, Wagner is the only son of a powerful cattle baron (Spencer Tracy) who has any affection for the autocratic old man. The others look forward to his death so they can take over control of the ranch. Wagner takes the blame for a raid arranged by his father and goes to prison and, while he's away, his father loses the ranch to the remaining three sons and dies.

Bud Corliss / A KISS BEFORE DYING, 1956, United Artists, d-Gerd Oswald.
Even as a cold-blooded killer Wagner doesn't lose his boyish charm. When girlfriend Joanne Woodward insists they get married because she's pregnant, he first tries to cause an abortion by giving her pills he tells her are to keep her healthy. They make her ill but she doesn't take enough to do the job, so he then disposes of the problem by pushing her off the roof of the county courthouse. He later forces a student to sign a confession saying that he killed Woodward, then murders him and makes the death look like suicide. He's ultimately caught, of course.

Jesse James / THE TRUE STORY OF JESSE JAMES, 1957, 20th Century-Fox, d-Nicholas Ray.
With a title like that you've got to figure that the story is pure fiction. According to this film Jesse and Frank (Wagner and Jeffrey Hunter) chose a life of crime because they were on the losing side of the Civil War and it was their only way of fighting the carpetbaggers.

Werner Gerlach / THE CONDEMNED OF ALTONA, 1963, Italy / France, 20th Century-Fox, d-Vittorio De Sica.
Wagner is the decent-minded son of a Krupp-like German munitions manufacturer (Fredric March) and brother to demented Maximilian Schell in this pretentious story that won little critical acclaim or box-office support.

George Litton / THE PINK PANTHER, 1964, United Artists, d-Blake Edwards.
Wagner is the good-for-nothing nephew of David Niven, the infamous jewel thief called the Phantom. He makes a play for Niven's mistress (Capucine), who is also the wife of bumbling Peter Sellers, the French police inspector who has been on Niven's trail for years.

Dan Bigelow / THE TOWERING INFERNO, 1974, 20th Century-Fox, d-John Guillermin.
When a 138-story San Francisco skyscraper catches fire because the builder and subcontractor have cut corners, Wagner and his secretary-lover are trapped and killed in his office.

OTHER ROLES

1950: *bit* / THE HAPPY YEARS; *Coffman* / HALLS OF MONTEZUMA. **1951:** *Lieutenant (jg) Franklin* / THE FROGMEN; *Jerry Denham* / LET'S MAKE IT LEGAL. **1952:** *G.I. Paratrooper* / WITH A SONG IN MY HEART; *Willie* / STARS AND STRIPES FOREVER; *Lewisohn* / WHAT

PRICE GLORY. **1953:** *Jess Harker* / THE SILVER WHIP; *Giff Rogers* / TITANIC; *Tony Petrakis* / BENEATH THE 12 MILE REEF. **1955:** *Josh Tanner* / WHITE FEATHER. **1956:** *Chris Teller* / THE MOUNTAIN; *Sam Gifford* / BETWEEN HEAVEN AND HELL. **1957:** *Mark Fannon* / STOPOVER TOKYO. **1958:** *Lt. Ed Pell* / THE HUNTERS; *guest* / MARDI GRAS; *Frankie O'Neill* / IN LOVE AND WAR. **1959:** *Tony Vincent* / SAY ONE FOR ME. **1960:** *Chad Bixby* / ALL THE FINE YOUNG CANNIBALS. **1961:** *Gilbert Barrows* / SAIL A CROOKED SHIP. **1962:** *U.S. Ranger* / THE LONGEST DAY; *Ed Bohand* / THE WAR LOVER. **1966:** *Alan Traggert* / HARPER. **1967:** *Mike Banning* / BANNING. **1968:** *Harry* / THE BIGGEST BUNDLE OF THEM ALL; *Lawrence Colby* / DON'T JUST STAND THERE. **1969:** *Luther Erding* / WINNING. **1976:** *Lt. Cmdr. Ernest Blake* / MIDWAY.

WALKER, ROBERT

(1914–1951)

Born in Salt Lake City, Robert Walker attended the Academy of Dramatic Arts in New York then became a radio actor for Mutual and met his wife-to-be Jennifer Jones, who also worked in radio. The union produced Robert Walker, Jr., an actor who looked very much like his father but never amounted to much on the screen. Walker moved to Hollywood in 1939 and made his screen debut in WINTER CARNIVAL. After a few small roles he returned to radio working on soaps from 1940-1942. His first substantial role was in BATAAN in 1943 and the next year he got his big break with SEE HERE PRIVATE HARGROVE. Early in his career he was typed as sincere and likable, but after losing his wife to David O. Selznick his personal life deteriorated, although he married John Ford's daughter in 1948. He later developed a drinking problem and died of respiratory failure after a dose of sedatives. His premature death came just as it seemed he was making an important career shift with his superb villainous roles in his last two movies, STRANGERS ON A TRAIN and MY SON JOHN.

KEY ROLES

Leonard Purckett / BATAAN, 1943, MGM, d-Leslie Martinson.

In this stark and compelling war drama Walker is a kid sailor who finds himself with a group of soldiers expected to fight to the death on Bataan to buy time for MacArthur and the Allied forces. He's a very appealing kid and his death, although obviously coming, is a shock.

Marion Hargrove / SEE HERE, PRIVATE HARGROVE, 1944, MGM, d-Wesley Ruggles.

Walker is just right as the inept but likable recruit who is perpetually in and out of trouble in basic training. Sure enough, he turns out to be a first-rate soldier who gets a lot of encouragement from lovely Donna Reed.

William G. Smollett II / SINCE YOU WENT AWAY, 1944, United Artists, d-John Cromwell.

Walker plays opposite his wife (Jennifer Jones) in this picture produced by David O. Selznick, but the "man of a million memos" soon forced a divorce. The story tells about what happens during 1943 to the inhabitants of a typical American family (Claudette Colbert, Jennifer Jones, and Shirley Temple) when the man of the home is away at war. Jones falls in love with Walker.

Cpl. Joe Allen / THE CLOCK, 1945, MGM, d-Vincente Minnelli.

Walker and Judy Garland are very appealing as a soldier and a girl who meet under the big clock at Penn station in New York City, fall in love, and marry in a 48-hour period. Such things happened during World War II and it all rings true.

Jerome Kern / TILL THE CLOUDS ROLL BY, 1946, MGM, d-Richard Whorf.

In this better-than-average biopic of composer Jerome Kern, the usual cliches don't seem so offensive because the Kern music is performed by so many fine MGM contract players and because Walker gives a pleasant performance as usual.

Johannes Brahms / SONG OF LOVE, 1947, MGM, d-Clarence Brown.

At least the music in this biopic of composer Brahms and his friends the Robert Schumanns is beautiful. But whenever Hollywood takes on serious music the writers and directors become too reverent and make the characters seem bloodless.

Bruno Antony / STRANGERS ON A TRAIN, 1951, Warners, d-Alfred Hitchcock.

Walker had been hospitalized for alcohol abuse almost a year before returning to the screen and giving the performance of his life as the fey, memorable, and even charming maniac who proposes exchanging murders with Farley Granger as the two travel on a train. Thinking Granger has agreed to the plan, Walker carries out his part of the bargain, killing Granger's wife who refuses to give him a divorce. Then Walker expects Granger to kill Walker's father. When he refuses, Walker plots to frame him for the murder of his wife.

John Jefferson / MY SON JOHN, 1952, Paramount, d-Leo McCarey.

Walker was dead before the completion of this movie about an American Catholic family that is horrified when they learn that son John is a Communist. The film was part of Hollywood's witchhunt period, but Walker is brilliant as a son who bitterly disappoints his parents (Helen Hayes and Dean Jagger). Some of Walker's last scenes had to be faked and shots were borrowed from his other films.

OTHER ROLES

1939: *undergraduate* / WINTER CARNIVAL; *bit* / THESE GLAMOUR GIRLS; *bit* / DANCING CO-EDS. **1943:** *David LeGros* / MADAME CURIE. **1944:** *David Thatcher* / THIRTY SECONDS OVER TOKYO. **1945:** *Jimmy Dobson* / HER HIGHNESS AND THE BELLBOY; *Marion Hargrove* / WHAT NEXT, CORPORAL HARGROVE?; *John* / THE SAILOR TAKES A WIFE. **1947:** *Brock Brewton* / THE SEA OF GRASS; *Col. Jeff Nixon* / THE BEGINNING OR THE END. **1948:** *Eddie Hatch* / ONE TOUCH OF VENUS. **1950:** *Terence Keath* / PLEASE BELIEVE ME; *Commander W. Lattimer* / THE SKIPPER SURPRISED HIS WIFE; **1951:** *Lee Strobie* / VENGEANCE VALLEY.

WAYNE, JOHN

(Marion Michael Morrison, 1907–1979)

Somewhere in his career John Wayne became a legend and was to many the personification of an American ideal representing loyalty, integrity, honesty, and self-reliance. He was a giant of a man and a giant presence. Many others admired his screen persona but were turned off by his far-right political views. Wayne could never understand why his on-screen defense of American ideals was so lauded and his political stance away from films so roundly condemned by liberals. There are no doubt complex answers but one over-simplification is that, on the screen, Wayne was the brave and dedicated man he portrayed, but away from the screen he was just another wealthy movie star, no better than the rest of us. Iowa-born Wayne played football at the University of Southern California until an injury gave him time to find more extra work at the movie studios. By the time he made STAGECOACH in 1939, which is credited with making him a star, he had already appeared in more than 60 films, mostly quickie westerns for Monogram and Republic. Perhaps it was the large number of minor films in which he appeared that caused such a long time to pass before people began to realize that he could really act, even if he was usually asked to portray John Wayne in later years. He won an Oscar for his performance as an aging, one-eyed, fat bounty hunter in TRUE GRIT, but he also did fine work in the various films he made with John Ford. The Duke suggested his own epitaph: "I would like to be remembered—well the Mexicans have an expression, 'feo, fuerte y formal,' which means: He was ugly, was strong and had dignity." So be it.

KEY ROLES

Breck Coleman / THE BIG TRAIL, 1930, Fox Films, d-Raoul Walsh.
Had this western been better or Wayne's performance a bit more polished he might have become a big star nine years earlier. As it is this overblown epic has Wayne as a scout who leads a wagon train through every conceivable hazard from Missouri to Oregon.

Sandy Saunders (Singin' Sandy) / RIDERS OF DESTINY, 1933, Monogram, d-Robert N. Bradbury.
Sure enough, Wayne went through the phase when all cowboy heroes were expected to sing. Neither Gene Autry nor Roy Rogers needed to worry about competition from the Duke.

Stony Brooke / PALS OF THE SADDLE, 1938, Republic, d-George Sherman.
Wayne is the most prominent alumnus of the many actors who at one time or another made up one of "The Three Mesquiteers," a not-too-subtle western take-off on the exploits of the Three Musketeers. His partners in this one, and most of the other seven films, are Ray Corrigan and Max Terhune.

Johnny Ringo (The Ringo Kid) / STAGECOACH, 1939, United Artists, d-John Ford.
Wayne's first appearance in this classic western is dramatically delayed until all the other passengers riding the stagecoach to Lordsburg have been met and pigeonholed; then almost out of the blue Wayne appears along the route, twirling his rifle as he hitches a ride. He's fresh out of jail and back on the trail of the gang that murdered his father and brother. In the coach he finds a kindred spirit in Claire Trevor, a saloon girl who has been run out of town. By the time they reach their destination after surviving Indian attacks, Wayne and Trevor are in love and making long-range plans if he survives his showdown with the Plummer boys.

Ole Olsen / THE LONG VOYAGE HOME, 1940, United Artists, d-John Ford.
Wayne, a good-natured merchant seaman, is the only member of the crew of a rusty tramp steamer carrying high explosives on a voyage from the West Indies to Great Britain to get home safely after his ship is attacked by German planes.

Lt. Bruce Whitney / SEVEN SINNERS, 1940, Universal, d-Tay Garnett.
Marlene Dietrich, a singer at the Seven Sinners Cafe on the South Sea island of Boni-Komba, meets handsome naval officer Wayne who is so captivated by her that he's willing to give up everything, including his career, to marry her. But seeing that she's no good for him she skips town, but not before a good old-fashioned brawl reduces the cafe to rubble.

Capt. Jack Stuart / REAP THE WILD WIND, 1942, Paramount, d-Cecil B. DeMille.
Wayne, a sea captain off the Florida Keys in the 1840s, has competition for Paulette Goddard from Ray Milland, and his hands full from unscrupulous scavengers of wrecked ships whose demise they arrange. He loses both Goddard and his life when he explores a sunken ship in a diving suit looking for evidence that Susan Hayward had been aboard.

Wedge Donovan / THE FIGHTING SEABEES, 1944, Republic, d-Howard Lydecker and Edward Ludwig.
This adventure yarn supposedly tells the story of how the Seabees, armed and militarily trained construction workers, are formed during World War II when tough construction boss Wayne gets mad when he sees his workers picked off by the Japanese without having the means to fight back.

Capt. Kirby York / FORT APACHE, 1948, RKO, d-John Ford.
When military martinet Henry Fonda takes over command of the cavalry unit at Fort Apache, Arizona, his quest for glory concerns seasoned Indian fighter Wayne, his second in command. Because Fonda will not follow the Duke's advice for dealing with the Apaches, much of the troop is wiped out in an ambush, including Fonda. As is often the case, the facts get mixed up and Fonda is believed a hero—a myth Wayne, now in command, will not challenge.

Tom Dunston / RED RIVER, 1948, United Artists, d-Howard Hawks.
Macho cattle rancher Wayne and his adopted son (Montgomery Clift) are forced to drive their Texas herd north to Missouri in hopes of finding buyers. Wayne is a wagon train Captain Bligh to Clift's Fletcher Christian and ultimately Clift takes charge with the Duke swearing to get even: "You shoulda let 'em kill me 'cause I'm gonna kill you. I'll catch up with you. I don't know when, but I'll catch up. And every time you turn around, expect to see me, because one time you'll turn around and I'll be there. I'll kill you, Matt." When Wayne does catch up the two battle with fists but, with the help of Jeanne Crain, they make up.

Robert Marmaduke "Bob" Hightower / THREE GODFATHERS, 1948, MGM, d-John Ford.
Wayne and two other fugitives from the law encounter a dying woman and her baby while crossing a desert and they promise to save the child. In the end a weary Wayne staggers into New Jerusalem, Arizona, on Christmas Eve carrying the child.

Captain Ralls / WAKE OF THE RED WITCH, 1948, Republic, d-Edward Ludwig.
Wayne is a sea captain whose feud with a ruthless East Indies trader (Luther Adler) over the love of now deceased Gail Russell climaxes when Wayne is forced to dive for a fortune in pearls guarded by a giant octopus.

Capt. Nathan Brittles / SHE WORE A YELLOW RIBBON, 1949, RKO, d-John Ford.

Shot in Monument Valley, the movie has Wayne as a cavalry officer forced to retire just when his vast experience of warring with the Indians is most needed. He takes advantage of the very last moments of his enlistment to prevent a massacre.

Sgt. John M. Stryker / SANDS OF IWO JIMA, 1949, Republic, d-Allan Dwan.
Wayne was nominated for an Oscar for his portrayal of a battle-hardened marine sergeant who bullies a group of new recruits in training so much that they hate him, but they are also prepared to enter combat. He is shot down by a sniper when the bloody battle of Iwo Jima seems over and after the famous flag-raising ceremony had taken place. A letter home reveals to his men that there was more to this man than a kick-ass marine.

Sean Thornton / THE QUIET MAN, 1952, Republic, d-John Ford.
After having killed a man in the ring, prize-fighter Wayne quits the business and goes home to his boyhood village in Ireland. There he falls in love with fiery Maureen O'Hara and they marry. But when her big dumb brother (Victor McLaglen) refuses to part with her dowry and Wayne won't fight him for it, she believes he's a coward and tries to leave him. Wayne drags her back and has a donnybrook with McLaglen which leaves them great friends.

Dan Roman / THE HIGH AND THE MIGHTY, 1954, Warners, d-William A. Wellman.
When a passenger ship loses an engine on a flight from Honolulu to San Francisco, aging copilot Wayne, considered an "ancient pelican" by his boss, takes over from jittery pilot Robert Stack and insists there's a chance of reaching Frisco safely.

Ethan Edwards / THE SEARCHERS, 1956, Warners, d-John Ford.
When his brother's family is wiped out and his two nieces kidnapped by a band of raiding Indians, Wayne and half-breed Jeffrey Hunter spend five years searching for the surviving girl (Natalie Wood). At some point Hunter comes to the realization that Wayne means to kill the girl because by this time her captors have had her. But at the last moment Wayne changes his mind and spares the innocent girl.

Col. Davy Crockett / THE ALAMO, 1960, United Artists, d-John Wayne.
Wayne produced, directed, and starred in this initially slow-moving story about the attack on the Alamo by the 7,000 troops of Santa Anna in 1836. Wayne and the 180 other defenders die bravely in the exciting climax, but Wayne the director almost puts his audience to sleep for the greater part of the picture with talk and bickering involving Wayne, Richard Widmark as Jim Bowie, and Laurence Harvey as Col. William Travis.

George Washington McLintock / MCLINTOCK! 1963, United Artists, d-Andrew V. McLaglen.
This sexist western comedy teaches the lesson that uppity women are just looking for a masterful man to take them across his lap and give their fannies a warming. Wayne has borrowed some of his story from Shakespeare's "The Taming of the Shrew." He's a rancher whose wife (Maureen O'Hara) has not been living with him but who returns to town when their daughter returns home from school in the East. Wayne's real-life son Patrick tames the daughter (Stefanie Powers), while dad exerts some strong-arm charm on mom. One of the best sequences in the picture is a hilarious brawl involving everyone but the Indians.

Capt. Micheal Kirby / THE GREEN BERETS, 1968, Warners, d-John Wayne and Ray Kellogg.
In making this movie Wayne didn't win any converts to his jingoistic attitudes toward America's involvement in the Vietnam war. Instead he alienated himself from a large segment of a divided public bothered by a very unpopular war.

Reuben J. "Rooster" Cogburn / TRUE GRIT, 1969, Paramount, d-Henry Hathaway.
Whatever harm he did to his popular appeal with his stand on the Vietnam War, Wayne won many fans back to the fold with his truly enjoyable Oscar-winning parody of John Wayne as the peace officer who accompanies Kim Darby into the Badlands to track down her father's killer. What he finds is a gang led by Robert Duvall, whom he faces on a field of battle. He challenges Duvall and his three henchmen with, "Fill your hands, you son of a bitch."

John Simpson Chisum / CHISUM, 1970, Warners, d-Andrew V. McLaglen.
In this action-packed western Wayne is a ranching king who fights the land-grabbing schemes of villain Forrest Tucker. It's loosely based on the bloody Lincoln County cattle war of the 1870s.

Will Anderson / THE COWBOYS, 1972, Warners, d-Mark Rydell.
When his regular wranglers desert him, rancher Wayne hires eleven boys aged 9 to 15 to help him get his cattle to market. The boys come to manhood during the grueling 400-mile cattle drive that Wayne doesn't survive.

Det. Lt. Lon McQ / MCQ, 1974, Warners, d-John Sturges.
He's dressed in a suit and carries a police lieutenant's badge, but Wayne is just a western hero who once again takes the law in his own hands as he sets out to avenge the murder of a cop buddy. In the process, he exposes corruption in the Seattle police department.

John Bernard "J. B." Books / THE SHOOTIST, 1976, Paramount, d-Don Siegel.
Wayne made his last picture one of his best. As was the case with Wayne in real life, his character is suffering from cancer. Rather than go slowly from the disease, the aging legendary gunfighter goes out with guns blazing as he clears out villains in Carson City in 1901.

OTHER ROLES

1926: *extra* / BROWN OF HARVARD. **1927:** *football player* / THE DROP KICK. **1928:** *extra* / MOTHER MACHREE; *horse race spectator* / HANGMAN'S HOUSE. **1929:** *football player* / SALUTE; *Pete Donahue* / WORDS AND MUSIC (appeared as Duke Morrison). **1930:** *crew member* / MEN WITHOUT WOMEN; *bit* / ROUGH ROMANCE; *bit* / CHEER UP AND SMILE. **1931:** *Gordon Wales* / THREE GIRLS LOST; *Peter Brooks* / GIRLS DEMAND EXCITEMENT; *Lt. Bob Denton* / MEN ARE LIKE THAT; *Clint Turner* / RANGE FEUD; *Dusty* / MAKER OF MEN. **1932:** *Craig McCoy* / SHADOW OF THE EAGLE; *Steve Pickett* / TEXAS CYCLONE; *Duke* / TWO-FISTED LAW; *Buzz Kinney* / LADY AND GENT; *Larry Baker* / THE HURRICANE EXPRESS; *John Drury* / RIDE HIM COWBOY; *John Steele* / THE BIG STAMPEDE; *John Mason* / HAUNTED GOLD. **1933:** *John Trent* / THE TELEGRAPH TRAIL; *Tom Wayne* / THE THREE MUSKETEERS; *swarthy man* / CENTRAL AIRPORT; *John Bishop* / SOMEWHERE IN SONORA; *Dick Wallace* / HIS PRIVATE SECRETARY; *Smith* / THE LIFE OF JIMMY DOLAN; *Jimmy McCoy* / BABY FACE; *Capt. John Holmes* / THE MAN FROM MONTEREY; *Westerman* / COLLEGE COACH; *John Brant* / SAGEBRUSH

TRAIL. **1934:** *Jerry Mason* / THE LUCKY TEXAN; *Ted Hayden* / WEST OF THE DIVIDE; *John Carruthers* / BLUE STEEL; *John Weston* / THE MAN FROM UTAH; *Randy Bowers* / RANDY RIDES ALONE; *John Travers* / THE STAR PACKER; *Rod Drew* / THE TRAIL BEYOND; *John Tobin* / THE LAWLESS FRONTIER; *Chris Morrell* / 'NEATH ARIZONA SKIES. **1935:** *John Higgins* / TEXAS TERROR; *John Martin* / RAINBOW VALLEY; *John Scott* / THE DESERT TRAIL; *John Mason* / THE DAWN RIDER; *John Wyatt* / PARADISE CANYON; *John Wyatt* / WESTWARD HO; *John Dawson* / THE NEW FRONTIER; *John Middleton* / THE LAWLESS RANGE. **1936:** *Capt. John Delmont* / THE OREGON TRAIL; *John Tipton* / THE LAWLESS NINETIES; *John Clayborn* / KING OF THE PECOS; *John* / THE LONELY TRAIL; *John Blair* / WINDS OF THE WASTELAND; *Bob Randall* / THE SEA SPOILERS; *Pat* / CONFLICT. **1937:** *Biff Smith* / CALIFORNIA STRAIGHT AHEAD; *Bob Adams* / I COVER THE WAR; *Johnny Hanson* / IDOL OF THE CROWDS; *Duke Slade* / ADVENTURE'S END; *Dave Rudd* / BORN TO THE WEST. **1938:** *Stony Brooke* / OVERLAND STAGE RAIDERS; *Stony Brooke* / SANTE FE STAMPEDE; *Stony Brooke* / RED RIVER RANGE; **1939:** *Stony Brooke* / THE NIGHT RIDERS; *Stony Brooke* / THREE TEXAS STEERS; *Stony Brooke* / WYOMING OUTLAW; *Stony Brooke* / NEW FRONTIER; *Jim Smith* / ALLEGHENY UPRISING. **1940:** *Bob Seton* / DARK COMMAND; *John Philips* / THREE FACES WEST. **1941:** *Lynn Hollister* / A MAN BETRAYED; *John Reynolds* / LADY FROM LOUISIANA; *Matt Matthews* / THE SHEPHERD OF THE HILLS. **1942:** *Jack Morgan* / LADY FOR A NIGHT; *Roy Glennister* / THE SPOILERS; *Tom Craig* / IN OLD CALIFORNIA; *Jim Gordon* / FLYING TIGERS; *Pat Talbot* / REUNION IN FRANCE; *Charles "Pittsburgh" Markham* / PITTSBURGH. **1943:** *Duke Hudkins* / A LADY TAKES A CHANCE; *Dan Somers* / IN OLD OKLAHOMA. **1944:** *Rocklin* / TALL IN THE SADDLE. **1945:** *Duke Fergus* / FLAME OF THE BARBARY COAST; *Col. Joseph Madden* / BACK TO BATAAN; *Lt. Rusty Ryan* / THEY WERE EXPENDABLE; *John Devlin* / DAKOTA. **1946:** *Rusty Thomas* / WITHOUT RESERVATIONS. **1947:** *Quirt Evans* / ANGEL AND THE BADMAN; *Johnny Munroe* / TYCOON. **1949:** *John Breen* / THE FIGHTING KENTUCKIAN. **1950:** *Lt. Col. Kirby Yorke* / RIO GRANDE. **1951:** *"Duke" Gifford* / OPERATION PACIFIC; *Maj. Dan Kirby* / FLYING LEATHERNECKS. **1952:** *Big Jim McLain* / BIG JIM MCLAIN. **1953:** *Steve Williams* / TROUBLE ALONG THE WAY; *Captain Dooley* / ISLAND IN THE SKY; *Hondo Lane* / HONDO. **1955:** *Capt. Karl Ehrlich* / THE SEA CHASE; *Captain Wilder* / BLOOD ALLEY. **1956:** *Temujin (Genghis Khan)* / THE CONQUEROR. **1957:** *Frank W. "Sprig" Wead* / THE WINGS OF EAGLES; *Colonel Shannon* / JET PILOT; *Joe January* / LEGEND OF THE LOST. **1958:** *himself* / I MARRIED A WOMAN; *Townsend Harris* / THE BARBARIAN AND THE GEISHA. **1959:** *John T. Chance* / RIO BRAVO; *Col. John Marlowe* / THE HORSE SOLDIERS. **1960:** *Sam McCord* / NORTH TO ALASKA. **1961:** *Jake Cutter* / THE COMANCHEROS. **1962:** *Tom Doniphon* / THE MAN WHO SHOT LIBERTY VALANCE; *Sean Mercer* / HATARI!; *Gen. William T. Sherman* / HOW THE WEST WAS WON. **1963:** *Michael Patrick Donovan* / DONOVAN'S REEF; *Lt. Col. Benjamin Vandervoort* / THE LONGEST DAY. **1964:** *Matt Masters* / CIRCUS WORLD. **1965:** *the centurian* / THE GREATEST STORY EVER TOLD; *Capt. Rockwell Torrey* / IN HARM'S WAY; *John Elder* / THE SONS OF KATIE ELDER. **1966:** *Gen. Mike Randolph* / CAST A GIANT SHADOW. **1967:** *Taw Jackson* / THE WAR WAGON; *Cole Thornton* / EL DORADO. **1969:** *Chance Buckham* / HELLFIGHTERS; *Col. John Henry Thomas* / THE UNDEFEATED. **1970:** *Cord McNally* / RIO LOBO. **1971:** *Jacob McCandless* / BIG JAKE. **1972:** *guest* / CANCEL MY RESERVATION. **1973:** *Lane* / THE TRAIN ROBBERS; *J. D. Cahill* / CAHILL—UNITED STATES MARSHALL. **1975:** *Jim Brannigan* / BRANNIGAN; *Rooster Cogburn* / ROOSTER COGBURN.

WEBB, CLIFTON

(Webb Parmalee Hollenbeck, 1891–1966)

A seasoned performer from the age of ten, Clifton Webb was a well-known ballroom dancer by 19. He appeared regularly on the stage in light comedies and musicals but, although he had some small parts in silent movies, it wasn't until 1944 when his friend Otto Preminger cast him as the cultivated but cold villain of LAURA that he gave serious thought to a film career. His performance earned him an Oscar nomination as did his work in THE RAZOR'S EDGE, but he is certainly best remembered for his role as the pompous, self-proclaimed genius in SITTING PRETTY. Although he came late to films, his portrayals of sharp, self-centered, older gentlemen were greatly appreciated by fans and critics alike.

KEY ROLES

Waldo Lydecker / LAURA, 1944, 20th Century-Fox, d-Otto Preminger.

Webb is a bitchy intellectual who so loves Gene Tierney that he can't stand the thought of any other man having her; so he kills her but it isn't really her, just an unlucky girl staying with her. When Tierney reappears alive, well, and falling in love with the police detective assigned to the case (Dana Andrews), Webb makes a second attempt, crazily threatening her with a shotgun as he tells her, "The best part of myself, that's what you are. Do you think I'm going to leave it to the vulgar pawing of a second-rate detective who thinks you're a dame? Do you think I could bear the thought of him holding you in his arms, kissing you, loving you?"

Elliott Templeton / THE RAZOR'S EDGE, 1946, 20th Century-Fox, d-Edmund Goulding.

In this Somerset Maugham story of a man looking for truth and wisdom, Webb beautifully portrays a dilettante rich uncle, the last word in snobbery, who even on his deathbed is not at peace until he learns that his nephew has received a desirable social invitation from a princess and the bishop himself comes to give him the last rites.

Lynn Belvedere / SITTING PRETTY, 1948, 20th Century-Fox, d-Walter Lang.

In order to write a book on his experiences and to test some of his theories of child-rearing, fussy, precise, and insulting Webb takes the job of live-in babysitter for the unmanageable kids of Robert Young and Maureen O'Hara. Webb takes command and caustically turns the kids into model children. In his interview for the job, he is asked by O'Hara: "And may I ask what your profession is?" His matter-of-fact answer is: "Certainly, I am a genius." Parents who have ever dealt with a crying toddler at feeding time applaud Webb when he pours porridge over the kid's head. Webb repeated the role in two less successful sequels.

Frank Gilbreth / CHEAPER BY THE DOZEN, 1950, 20th Century-Fox, d-Walter Lang.

Webb portrays an efficiency expert who, with his wife (Myrna Loy), raises twelve children with utmost precision at the turn-of-the-century. His death is a great blow to the family.

John Philip Sousa / STARS AND STRIPES FOREVER, 1952, 20th Century-Fox, d-Henry Koster.

This is the story of John Philip Sousa from the time he left the marine band to form his own, until he became known as the "March King." Webb portrays the composer with military precision and audiences are entertained by the marvelous music.

Robert Sturges / TITANIC, 1953, 20th Century-Fox, d-Jean Negulesco.

In this dramatic account of the sinking of the "unsinkable" ship on its maiden voyage, Webb is an elegant snob who, during a fight with his wife (Barbara Stanwyck), learns that the son he loves so dearly is not his. From then on Webb shuns the boy, until the ship hits the iceberg and Webb discovers that blood is not the only thing that makes a father and son.

Shadwell / THREE COINS IN THE FOUNTAIN, 1954, 20th Century-Fox, d-Jean Negulesco.

In this story of three American girls (Dorothy McGuire, Maggie McNamara, and Jean Peters) working in Rome and hoping for romance, McGuire finally catches her boss (Webb) after making him understand that his declining health will not make him a burden for her.

OTHER ROLES

1920: *bit* / POLLY WITH A PAST. **1924:** *bit* / LET NOT MAN PUT ASUNDER. **1925:** *Maxim* / THE HEART OF A SIREN; *Tom Lawrence* / NEW TOYS. **1946:** *Hardy Cathcart* / THE DARK CORNER. **1949:** *Lynn Belvedere* / MR. BELVEDERE GOES TO COLLEGE. **1950:** *Charles* / FOR HEAVEN'S SAKE. **1951:** *Lynn Belvedere* / *Oliver Erwenter* / MR. BELVEDERE RINGS THE BELL; *Howard Osborne* / ELOPEMENT. **1952:** *Thornton Sayre* / DREAMBOAT. **1953:** *Robert Jordan* / MR. SCOUTMASTER. **1954:** *Gifford* / WOMAN'S WORLD. **1956:** *Cmdr. Ewen Montagu* / THE MAN WHO NEVER WAS. **1957:** *Victor Parmalee* / BOY ON A DOLPHIN. **1959:** *Pa Pennypacker* / THE REMARKABLE MR. PENNYPACKER; *Robert Dean* / HOLIDAY FOR LOVERS. **1962:** *Father Bovard* / SATAN NEVER SLEEPS.

WEISSMULLER, JOHNNY

(Peter John Weissmuller, 1904–1984)

"Me Tarzan, You Jane"; there isn't much more to say about the former gold medal-winning Olympic swimmer, except that he made a hell of a Tarzan and when his gut got too much for a mere loin cloth he put on a shirt, expanded his vocabulary slightly, and walked back into the brush as Jungle Jim. Married six times, most notably to his third wife Lupe Velez, he explained the secret of his movie success by saying: "The main thing is not to let go of the rope."

KEY ROLES

Tarzan / TARZAN, THE APE MAN, 1932, MGM, d-W. S. Van Dyke.

Had it not been for a broken shoulder, Herman Brix (aka Bruce Bennett) would have been cast as Tarzan in 1932 instead of Weissmuller. (Brix took up the role in a competing series in 1935.) To get Weissmuller for the role, the studio had to negotiate with BVD underwear, which had him under exclusive contract; Metro agreed to have all of their contract players photographed wearing BVD swimsuits for an ad campaign. The film ignores the story of the origin of the ape man, concentrating instead on the romance of Tarzan with English girl Maureen O'Sullivan. To clear matters up, Weissmuller never said, "Me Tarzan, you Jane"; instead, he alternates the words "Tarzan" and "Jane" as he taps first himself and then O'Hara to show he is getting the idea.

Tarzan / TARZAN AND HIS MATE, 1934, MGM, d-Cedric Gibbons.

After the tremendous success of their first Tarzan movie, MGM was beaten to the punch in releasing another ape man picture; Principal Pictures brought out TARZAN THE FEARLESS with Buster Crabbe in 1933. But Metro made a superior production, taking great care to provide Weissmuller and O'Sullivan with plenty of eyepopping adventures in the jungle. Censors did insist that their attire was too revealing and must be modified so as not to offend anyone.

Tarzan / TARZAN FINDS A SON, 1939, MGM, d-Richard Thorpe.

Although other studios continued to produce Tarzan movies with various actors in the title role, real fans eagerly awaited the more infrequent but higher quality films with Weissmuller in the lead. In this one he introduces Johnny Sheffield, whom he personally chose to be "Boy," his adopted son. Weissmuller really loved the kid and the affection was reciprocated and came through in their films together.

Johnny Duval / SWAMP FIRE, 1946, Paramount, d-William Pine.

Finally escaping the Tarzan role, Weissmuller gave evidence that he should head back to the jungle with his stiff portrayal of a bar pilot in the treacherous mouth of the Mississippi in the bayous of Louisiana. He goes to war and comes home with his nerves shot, but he gets them back. He looks best doing what he does best, swimming a river, killing an alligator, and rescuing his girl from a swamp fire; it's only when he has to say something that he has a problem.

Jungle Jim / JUNGLE JIM, 1948, Columbia, d-William Berke.

His middle-age spread forced Weissmuller to cover up his once magnificent physique, but he continued his Tarzan-like derring-do as Jungle Jim. Like Tarzan, he is a widely respected inhabitant of the jungle who makes a bad enemy to anyone who messes around in the darkest parts of Africa.

OTHER ROLES

1936: *Tarzan* / TARZAN ESCAPES. **1941:** *Tarzan* / TARZAN'S SECRET TREASURE. **1942:** *Tarzan* / TARZAN'S NEW YORK ADVENTURE. **1943:** *himself* / STAGE DOOR CANTEEN; *Tarzan* / TARZAN TRIUMPHS; *Tarzan* / TARZAN'S DESERT MYSTERY. **1945:** *Tarzan* / TARZAN AND THE AMAZONS. **1946:** *Tarzan* / TARZAN AND THE LEOPARD WOMAN. **1947:** *Tarzan* / TARZAN AND THE HUNTRESS. **1948:** *Tarzan* / TARZAN AND THE MERMAIDS. **1949:** *Jungle Jim* / THE LOST TRIBE. **1950:** *Jungle Jim* / MARK OF THE GORILLA. **1951:** *Jungle Jim* / PYGMY ISLAND; *Jungle Jim* / FURY OF THE CONGO; *Jungle Jim* / JUNGLE MANHUNT. **1952:** *Jungle Jim* / JUNGLE JIM IN THE FORBIDDEN LAND; *Jungle Jim* / VOODOO TIGER. **1953:** *Jungle Jim* / SAVAGE MUTINY. **1953:** *Jungle Jim* / KILLER APE. **1954:** *himself* / CANNIBAL ATTACK. **1955:** *himself* / JUNGLE MOON MEN; *Jungle Jim* / DEVIL GODDESS. **1970:** *guest* / THE PHYNX. **1975:** *stagehand* / WON TON TON, THE DOG WHO SAVED HOLLYWOOD.

WELCH, RAQUEL

(Raquel Tejada, 1940–)

A former TV weatherperson, model, and cocktail waitress, Raquel Welch has made a series of undistinguished films that concentrate more on her physical attributes than on her acting talents. This is unfortunate as Welch is not your typical, dumb sex-symbol, but rather an intelligent beauty who has shown she can handle comedy. As she ages her mature beauty may finally be appropriately exploited. She won excellent reviews for her work in Broadway's "Woman of the Year" in 1982. Concerning all the fuss over her curves, Welch wisely observed, "The mind can also be an erogenous zone."

KEY ROLES

Cora Peterson / FANTASTIC VOYAGE, 1966, 20th Century-Fox, d-Richard Fleischer.

Welch is one of a team of scientists who are miniaturized, placed in a tiny capsule, and injected into the body of a scientist whose blood clot they will try to relieve from the inside.

Loana / ONE MILLION YEARS B.C., 1966, Great Britain, Hammer, d-Don Chaffey.

This remake of the 1940 Hal Roach production starring Victor Mature and Carole Landis gives Welch the opportunity to cavort in strategically-torn animal skins. It's the same old story of warring prehistoric tribes joining forces to learn from each other and combat the monster animals that threaten them.

Fathom Harvill / FATHOM, 1967, 20th Century-Fox, d-Leslie Martinson.
In this spy spoof Welch skydives into Spain to retrieve an H-bomb triggering device lost when dropped in the Mediterranean Sea. Her sometime antagonistic, sometime romantic link is Tony Franciosa, who seems at first to be working for the Red Chinese, but in reality is a private detective working on the same side as Welch.

Lillian Lust / BEDAZZLED, 1967, Great Britain, 20th Century-Fox, d-Stanley Donen.
Welch's cameo role is as one of the seven deadly sins in this cult movie about a short-order cook (Dudley Moore) who is given his wishes very literally by a very proper British devil (Peter Cook).

Sarita / 100 RIFLES, 1969, 20th Century-Fox, d-Tom Gries.
Welch, a beautiful Yaqui Indian, teams up with black sheriff Jim Brown and the outlaw (Burt Reynolds) he pursues, to fight the military regime of a Mexican (Fernando Lamas) who had her father hanged. It's a stinker, but Welch looks good.

Myra Breckinridge / MYRA BRECKINRIDGE, 1970, 20th Century-Fox, d-Michael Sarne.
In the first 20th Century-Fox film to receive an "X" rating, Rex Reed undergoes a sex change and reappears as Welch in the Hollywood of the 1940s. She moves in on his uncle's talent school and fights to make herself a success. The film has little to recommend it unless lack of taste is your bag.

Constance Bonacieux / THE THREE MUSKETEERS, 1973, Panama, Film Trust, d-Richard Lester.
In this film Welch is given an opportunity to use her physical attributes as part of a fine comical performance rather than just scenery. She portrays a seamstress to the queen and mistress to D'Artagnan (Michael York) in this first half of a jokey version of the Dumas classic adventure yarn. In the sequel, THE FOUR MUSKETEERS, villainess Faye Dunaway strangles Welch with a string of pearls.

OTHER ROLES

1964: *bit* / ROUSTABOUT; *prostitute* / A HOUSE IS NOT A HOME. **1965:** *bit* / DO NOT DISTURB; *Jeri* / A SWINGIN' SUMMER. **1966:** *Juliana* / THE BIGGEST BUNDLE OF THEM ALL; *Tania Mottini* / SHOOT LOUD, LOUDER...I DON'T UNDERSTAND. **1967:** *Queen Elena* / THE QUEENS. **1968:** *Maria* / BANDOLERO!; *Nini* / THE OLDEST PROFESSION; *Elena* / THE BELOVED; *Kit Forrest* / LADY IN CEMENT. **1970:** *Michele* / FLAREUP; *slave driver* / THE MAGIC CHRISTIAN. **1971:** *Hannie Caulder* / HANNIE CAULDER. **1972:** *K. C. Carr* / KANSAS CITY BOMBER; *Eileen McHenry* / FUZZ; *Magdalena* / BLUEBEARD. **1973:** *Alice* / THE LAST OF SHEILA. **1974:** *Constance Bonacieux* / THE FOUR MUSKETEERS. **1975:** *Queenie* / THE WILD PARTY. **1976:** *Jugs* / MOTHER, JUGS AND SPEED. **1977:** *Lady Edith* / THE PRINCE AND THE PAUPER; *Jane* / L'ANIMAL. **1982:** *Walks Far Woman* / THE LEGEND OF WALKS FAR WOMAN.

WELD, TUESDAY

(Susan Ker Weld, 1943–)

Quite a little sexpot on TV's "The Many Loves of Dobie Gillis," Tuesday Weld has had, with a few exceptions, a forgettable career; she had the poor judgment to turn down leading roles in LOLITA, BONNIE AND CLYDE, and TRUE GRIT. Her private life has been extremely difficult; she was the support of her family as a child model when only three, had a nervous breakdown at nine, was an alcoholic at ten, and tried to commit suicide at twelve. The adorable blonde appeared in a number of nonsense films as a teenager but became more interesting in the 1960s with fine performances in THE CINCINNATI KID and PRETTY POISON. She continues to make big screen appearances but is more often found in made-for-TV movies such as REFLECTIONS ON MURDER (1974), F. SCOTT FITZGERALD IN HOLLYWOOD (1976), MOTHER AND DAUGHTER—THE LOVING WAR and A QUESTION OF GUILT (1980), MADAME X (1981), THE WINTER OF OUR DISCONTENT (1983), and SCORNED AND SWINDLED (1984).

KEY ROLES

Comfort Goodpasture / RALLY 'ROUND THE FLAG, BOYS! 1958, 20th Century-Fox, d-Leo McCarey.
Weld is a nubile teenager who can't get over how it feels to notice boys noticing her in this Max Schulman comedy about a small suburban community protesting a missile site to be built in the area.

Joy Elder / HIGH TIME, 1960, 20th Century-Fox, d-Blake Edwards.
When millionaire widower Bing Crosby decides to get the education he never received and enrolls in college, Weld is one of the coeds charmed by "Der Bingle." But he's not into chasing young girls; instead he finds faculty member Nicole Maurey more his speed.

Christian / THE CINCINNATI KID, 1965, MGM, d-Norman Jewison.
Weld portrays the wife of poker player Steve McQueen who strays to the bed of Ann-Margret between deals of a big stud-poker game in New Orleans in the 1930s. Weld's vulnerability is touchingly shown, winning her a great deal of audience sympathy.

Sue Ann Stepanek / PRETTY POISON, 1968, 20th Century-Fox, d-Noel Black.
Weld, a cute model high school student, meets Anthony Perkins, a psychotic who has served a jail term for his part in a death. He amuses her by making up stories about his life so he may appear more interesting and dangerous. She turns out to be, appearances notwithstanding, a vicious, coldly manipulative girl who kills her mother and then talks Perkins into a series of other crimes. When they are caught she reverts to her pose as a sweet innocent and Perkins takes all the blame.

Marge / WHO'LL STOP THE RAIN? 1978, United Artists, d-Karel Reisz.
When war correspondent Michael Moriarty tries to ship heroin from Vietnam to the U.S. with the help of his wife (Weld) and buddy (Nick Nolte), these two get involved with a crooked narcotics agent and sadistic gangsters.

OTHER ROLES

1956: *Dori* / ROCK, ROCK, ROCK. **1959:** *Dorothy Nichols* / THE FIVE PENNIES. **1960:** *Anne* / BECAUSE THEY'RE YOUNG; *Jody* / SEX KITTENS GO TO COLLEGE. **1961:** *Vangie Harper* / THE PRIVATE LIVES OF ADAM AND EVE; *Selena Cross* / RETURN TO PEYTON PLACE; *Noreen* / WILD IN THE COUNTRY; *Libby Bushmill* / BACHELOR FLAT. **1963:** *Bobby Jo Pepperdine* / SOLDIER IN THE RAIN. **1965:** *Jojo Holcomb* / I'LL TAKE SWEDEN. **1966:** *Barbara Ann Greene* / LORD LOVE A DUCK. **1970:** *Alma McCain* / I WALK THE LINE. **1971:** *Susan* / *Noah* / A SAFE PLACE. **1972:** *Maria Wyeth* / PLAY IT AS IT LAYS. **1977:** *Katherine Dunn* / LOOKING FOR MR. GOODBAR.

1980: *Kate* / SERIAL. **1981:** *Jessie* / THIEF. **1982:** *Gloria* / AUTHOR! AUTHOR! **1984:** *Carol* / ONCE UPON A TIME IN AMERICA.

WELLES, ORSON

(1915–1985)

The "Boy Genius," Orson Welles began his acting career at 16 with the Gate Theatre in Dublin and before 20 was acting on Broadway. In 1937 he founded with John Houseman the Mercury Theatre for which he acted, produced, and wrote some of the most original work of the period. It was his Mercury Theatre radio production of "The War of the Worlds" that scared thousands on the east coast one Halloween; he had them actually believing that Martians had landed in New Jersey. In 1939 Welles took his many talents and magnificent voice to Hollywood where he expanded on the ideas of Herman Mankiewicz, with whom he wrote the screenplay for the most distinguished American movie ever produced, CITIZEN KANE, starring and directed by Welles. A change of management at RKO took control from him of his second production, THE MAGNIFICENT AMBERSONS, which Welles always believed was ruined by others' editing. It might have been better if Welles had been able to complete it his own way, but it was still a "magnificent" movie. Welles spent the rest of his life trying to find enough funds so he could produce films the way he wished. This meant that he often wasted his talent on inferior pictures, making little pretense that he was in them for anything other than the money. The waste of this man's talents was appalling, but it would seem that he lived life the way he pleased and not to compromise was more important to him than a long list of outstanding efforts. He understood what was happening to him, saying: "I began at the top and I've been working my way down ever since"; and in 1960: "I've been given the use of my tools exactly eight times in twenty years."

KEY ROLES

Charles Foster Kane / CITIZEN KANE, 1941, RKO, d-Orson Welles.

Volumes have been written on the subject of the uniqueness and influence of this splendid cinematic experience. We can only add our own esteem for the film and the brilliant performances, not only of Welles, but of the many actors he brought with him from Mercury Theatre who contributed so much to the pleasure of the movie. Their work and that of Welles makes it possible for one who encounters the picture without knowing of its international reputation to thoroughly enjoy it without any need to feel reverent.

Colonel Haki / JOURNEY INTO FEAR, 1942, RKO, d-Norman Foster.

Welles produced and wrote this story about an engineer (Joseph Cotten) who, while in Istanbul with his wife, is pursued by Nazi executioners. Cotten is assisted in escaping by Welles who plays a Turkish intelligence officer. It's brilliant, tense and suspense-filled with Welles providing a nice character performance.

Edward Rochester / JANE EYRE, 1943, 20th Century-Fox, d-Robert Stevenson.

When Joan Fontaine takes the position of governess to Welles's ward, an attraction grows between employer and employee. He plans to marry her, but at the ceremony a stranger protests that Welles is already married; he confesses that his wife is a raving lunatic imprisoned in the attic of the mansion. Fontaine leaves but returns later to find Welles, now blind, sitting among the ruins of his estate; his wife had set a fire and perished in the blaze. Somehow Welles as a romantic hero just doesn't seem right.

Franz Kindler / Prof. Charles Rankin / THE STRANGER, 1946, RKO, d-Orson Welles.

Welles is an escaped Nazi war criminal who has successfully assumed a new identity as a college professor in a New England village. He is tracked by a suspicious investigator (Edward G. Robinson) just as he marries a local belle (Loretta Young). To escape, Welles is willing to kill her and anyone else who gets in his way.

Michael O'Hara / THE LADY FROM SHANGHAI, 1947, Columbia, d-Orson Welles.

When Welles comes to the aid of beautiful Rita Hayworth, who is being mugged, they have a brief flirtatious conversation, but she vanishes into the night. Soon thereafter he's hired as a crew member for a pleasure cruise on a yacht owned by Everett Sloane, who turns out to be the husband of the mysterious Hayworth. The two want Welles aboard to frame him for a planned murder of Sloane's associate. Welles is cleared when the couple have a showdown, gunning each other in a hall of mirrors in an abandoned amusement park. Some believe that director Welles's way of portraying Hayworth's character was his way of saying goodbye to the wife he was in the process of divorcing.

MacBeth / MACBETH, 1948, Republic, d-Orson Welles.

Welles was hampered by a lack of funds for his production of the Shakespeare play and it shows in the sets and props, but he tries very hard and there are a few memorable moments in this 21-day wonder.

Cagliostro / BLACK MAGIC, 1949, United Artists, d-Gregory Ratoff.

Welles portrays the legendary 18th-century self-proclaimed Count and charlatan who plots to substitute a double of Marie Antoinette for the wife of the Dauphin in order to control France. Things don't work out and he is killed in a rooftop duel.

Harry Lime / THE THIRD MAN, 1949, Great Britain, British Lion, d-Carol Reed.

Welles is a post-World War II black market gangster believed killed in an accident—but it seems he's alive and kicking. Yet as he says to friend Joseph Cotten, who wants him to help his mistress (Alida Valli): "What can I do, old man? I'm dead, aren't I?" Well, not then but with a little help from Cotten, just a little later.

Othello / OTHELLO, 1951, Mercury / Films Marceau, d-Orson Welles.

This is another of Welles's cheaply-made Shakespeare plays with poor technical quality and acting of questionable competence.

Father Mapple / MOBY DICK, 1956, Warners, d-John Huston.

In one of his controlled cameo performances Welles delivers a profound sermon to the sailors of New Bedford before they set sail for a long whaling voyage.

Hank Quinlan / TOUCH OF EVIL, 1958, Universal-International, d-Orson Welles.

Welles, who also wrote the screenplay, is a ruthless, twisted Texas police chief in a Mexican border town who, after framing a young man for murder, clashes with a Mexican narcotics investigator (Charlton Heston) who is on a honeymoon with his wife (Janet Leigh). The film reminds us of Welles's talent even though it's not on a par with his best work, despite the claims of its cult followers.

Will Varner / THE LONG, HOT SUMMER, 1958, 20th Century-Fox, d-Martin Ritt.

Welles is a Big Daddy-like southern tycoon whose family consists of his rebellious daughter (Joanne Woodward), his weakling son (Anthony Franciosa) and the latter's giddy wife (Lee Remick). It looks like he's about to add barn-burner Paul Newman to the bickering group when Newman develops an interest in Woodward.

Jonathan Wilk / COMPULSION, 1959, 20th Century-Fox, d-Richard Fleischer.

In one of his most controlled performances, Welles appears as the Clarence Darrow-like lawyer who defends rich, brilliant, but sick Chicago students Dean Stockwell and Bradford Dillman, the Leopold and Loeb-like killers of a young boy.

Hastler / THE TRIAL, 1962, France / Italy / West Germany, Paris / Europe / Ficit / Hisa, d-Orson Welles.

This is a gripping but muddled version of the Kafka story of Joseph K (Anthony Perkins) who is tried and condemned for an unspecified crime. Welles made a film that's not for everyone.

Cardinal Thomas Wolsey / A MAN FOR ALL SEASONS, 1966, Columbia, d-Fred Zinnemann.

Welles appears briefly as the prince of the Catholic Church who fears as he dies that he should have served his God as well as he had Henry VIII.

General Dreedle / CATCH-22, 1970, Paramount, d-Mike Nichols.

Welles is just one of the mad characters in this black comedy by Joseph Heller about the men of a U.S. air force base in the Mediterranean during World War II.

Long John Silver / TREASURE ISLAND, 1972, Great Britain, Massfilms, d-John Hough.

Massive Welles appears as the one-legged, old pirate befriended by Jack Hawkins in this spiritless international production.

OTHER ROLES

1940: *narrator* / SWISS FAMILY ROBINSON. **1942:** *narrator* / THE MAGNIFICENT AMBERSONS. **1944:** *guest* / FOLLOW THE BOYS; *John MacDonald (Kessler)* / TOMORROW IS FOREVER. **1946:** *narrator* / DUEL IN THE SUN. **1949:** *Cesare Borgia* / PRINCE OF FOXES. **1950:** *Bayan* / THE BLACK ROSE. **1951:** *himself* / RETURN TO GLENNASCAUL. **1953:** *Sigsbee Manderson* / TRENT'S LAST CASE; *Sanin Cejadory Mengues* / TROUBLE IN THE GLEN; *Ben Franklin* / SI VERSAILLES M'ETAIT CONTE; *narrator* / THE LITTLE WORLD OF DON CAMILLO. **1954:** *Hudson Lowe* / NAPOLEON. **1955:** *Lord Mountdrago* / THREE CASES OF MURDER; *Gregory Arkadin* / CONFIDENTIAL REPORT. **1957:** *Virgil Renchler* / MAN IN THE SHADOW. **1958:** *Cy Sedgewick* / THE ROOTS OF HEAVEN; *Captain Hart* / FERRY TO HONG KONG. **1959:** *narrator* / HIGH JOURNEY; *narrator* / SOUTH SEAS ADVENTURE; *King Saul* / DAVID AND GOLIATH. **1960:** *narrator* / MASTERS OF THE CONGO JUNGLE; *Hagolin / Lamoricière* / CRACK IN THE MIRROR; *Burandai* / THE TARTARS. **1961:** *Benjamin Franklin* / LAFAYETTE. **1963:** *Max Suda* / THE V.I.P.S; *the director* / ROGOPAG. **1964:** *narrator* / THE FINEST HOURS. **1966:** *Sir John Falstaff* / CHIMES AT MIDNIGHT; *Nordling* / IS PARIS BURNING?; *Ackermann* / MARCO THE MAGNIFICENT. **1967:** *Jonathan Lute* / I'LL NEVER FORGET WHAT'S 'IS NAME; *Le Chiffre* / CASINO ROYALE; *Louis of Mozambique* / THE SAILOR FROM GIBRALTAR; *Tiresias* / OEDIPUS THE KING. **1968:** *Charles Leschenhaut* / HOUSE OF CARDS; *Mr. Clay* / *narrator* / THE IMMORTAL STORY. **1969:** *narrator* / START THE REVOLUTION WITHOUT ME; *Plankett* / THE SOUTHERN STAR. **1970:** *Bresnavitch* / THE KREMLIN LETTER; *senator* / THE BATTLE OF NERETVA; *Louis XVIII* / WATERLOO. **1971:** *the magician* / A SAFE PLACE; *guest* / DIRECTED BY JOHN FORD. **1972:** *Old Seadog* / MALPERTIUS; *Mr. Cato* / NECROMANCY; *Theo Van Horn* / TEN DAYS WONDER. **1973:** *guest* / F FOR FAKE; *Mr. Delasandro* / GET TO KNOW YOUR RABBIT. **1975:** *narrator* / BUGS BUNNY SUPERSTAR. **1976:** *Estedes* / VOYAGE OF THE DAMNED. **1979:** *guest* / THE MUPPET MOVIE. **1981:** *narrator* / THE MAN WHO SAW TOMORROW; *narrator* / HISTORY OF THE WORLD, PART I. **1984:** *guest* / IN OUR HANDS; *alien father* / SLAPSTICK OF ANOTHER KIND.

WEST, MAE

(1892-1980)

Mae West's humorous but telling philosophy can be found in her wisecracks, including: "Sex is an emotion in motion," "I used to be Snow White, but I drifted," "When I'm good, I'm very good. When I'm bad, I'm better," "It's not the men in my life that counts—it's the life in my men," "I'm a fast movin' girl that likes 'em slow," "It takes two to make trouble for one," "When they make a better man than George Raft, I'll make him too," "Thanks, I enjoyed every inch of it," and "I'm the only antique in the movie industry—and you know how much antiques cost." West, always a rather plump, not especially attractive ex-vaudevillian, made a very special mark in the movie business by flagrantly and with great pleasure vulgarizing sex. While her talk and actions shocked blue-noses, they delighted others who found her openness about her sexual preferences both exciting and refreshing. She was not able to make many pictures, but she'll never be forgotten as long as there are female impersonators around. Her line, "Why don't you come up sometime and see me? I'm home every evening," will be forever misquoted as "Why don't you come up and see me sometime?"

KEY ROLES

Lady Lou / SHE DONE HIM WRONG, 1933, Paramount, d-Lowell Sherman.

Variety in 1912 described West as a "muscle dancer" who makes interesting movements in a seated position. In this film, based on her play "Diamond Lil," West runs an 1890s saloon owned by a crooked politician who keeps it and her. She makes her move on Cary Grant, who runs the next door rescue mission, and she delights audiences with little ditties like "I like a guy what takes his time" and "I wonder where my easy rider's gone."

Tira (Sister Honky Tonk) / I'M NO ANGEL, 1933, Paramount, d-Wesley Ruggles.

Carnival entertainer West has plans to move up the social ladder "wrong by wrong." She survives a murder charge and has wealthy Kent Taylor at her beck and call; and when even more wealthy Cary Grant tries to untangle his friend from this gold digger, he gets caught up in her web himself. He refuses to marry her, so she slaps him with a breach of promise suit; but during the trial she lets him off the hook. Her one-liners added fuel to the fire that censor groups like the Legion of Decency were lighting under the Hollywood moguls to clean up their act.

Ruby Carter / BELLE OF THE NINETIES, 1934, Paramount, d-Leo McCarey.

West wrote the weak script for this picture and the Hays office snipped out some of her best lines, even demanding a change of title from IT AIN'T NO SIN. In it West is a St. Louis saloon singer of songs like "My Old Flame" who in the 1890s heads for New Orleans, where among her many admirers is a boxer (John Mack Brown).

Frisco Dolly (Rose Carlton) / KLONDIKE ANNIE, 1936, Paramount, d-Raoul Walsh.

Back in the brawling 1890s West, once described as "the greatest female impersonator of all time," is a torch singer on the Barbary Coast of San Francisco who heads north for the Yukon to escape a murder charge and arrives disguised as evangelist Sister Annie. Her songs include "I'm an Occidental Woman in an Oriental Mood for Love."

Flower Belle Lee / MY LITTLE CHICKADEE, 1940, Universal, d-Edward Cline.

In the only pairing of West with W. C. Fields, the two stars wrote their own parts and made certain they got the lion's share of each episode. Since such an arrangement cannot possibly work when the two are in the same scene, the expected blockbuster is only a modest comedy. West is drummed out of a Western town when she becomes the object of a masked man's affection. On the train she meets fake medicine man Fields, promotes a phony marriage with him, helps him become the new sheriff of the next town, and shares her charms with all comers until Fields moves on.

Letitia Van Allen / MYRA BRECKINRIDGE, 1970, 20th Century-Fox, d-Michael Sarne.

Seventy-eight-year-old West is a talent agent, specializing in young virile men who have the kind of talents she's looking for, even if the movies aren't. If we can believe West, her part is art imitating life.

OTHER ROLES

1932: *Maudie Triplett* / NIGHT AFTER NIGHT. **1934:** *Cleo Burden* / GOIN' TO TOWN. **1937:** *Mavis Arden* / GO WEST, YOUNG MAN. **1938:** *Peaches O'Dea (Madame Fifi)* / EVERY DAY'S A HOLIDAY. **1943:** *Fay Lawrence* / THE HEAT'S ON. **1977:** *Marlo Manners* / SEXTETTE.

WIDMARK, RICHARD

(1914–)

A longtime radio actor on shows such as "Stella Dallas," "Pepper Young's Family," "March of Time," and "Inner Sanctum," Richard Widmark made a stunning screen debut as the maniacal Tommy Udo in 1947 in KISS OF DEATH. Although he made many films playing the lead and despite being a better actor than many who were considered matinee idols, his looks were not what was expected of a romantic player, so he never became a major star. Widmark did his best work in the 1950s and 1960s, but his only Oscar nomination was for that very first appearance. He has starred in the TV series "Madigan" and his made-for-TV movies include A TALENT FOR LOVING (1969), BROCK'S LAST CASE and VANISHED (1971), THE LAST DAY (1975), MR. HORN (1978), ALL GOD'S CHILDREN (1980), A WHALE FOR THE KILLING (1981), and BLACKOUT (1984).

KEY ROLES

Tommy Udo / KISS OF DEATH, 1947, 20th Century-Fox, d-Henry Hathaway.

Widmark shaved off his eyebrows to make himself look more maniacal for his part as a psychopathic killer who brutalizes and murders while giving out with a mad cackle of laughter. He happily pushes an old lady confined to a wheelchair down a flight of stairs to her death. When ex-con Victor Mature squeals on Widmark—watch out!

Jefty Robbins / ROAD HOUSE, 1948, 20th Century-Fox, d-Jean Negulesco.

Widmark owns a roadhouse near the Canadian border and his best friend (Cornel Wilde) is his manager. Things become more than a little strained when Ida Lupino is hired as a singer; Widmark goes wild for her but she prefers Wilde. Widmark frames Wilde for stealing and gets him released into his custody. He torments Wilde, trying to get him to make a break for the border so Widmark can kill him; instead, Lupino kills Widmark.

Alec Stiles / THE STREET WITH NO NAME, 1948, 20th Century-Fox, d-William Keighley.

In this semi-documentary crime melodrama, Widmark is a smart gang leader who uncovers the fact that Mark Stevens, a new member of the mob, is actually an FBI agent sent to infiltrate his organization. In the end the FBI proves too much for Widmark.

Dr. Clinton Reed / PANIC IN THE STREETS, 1950, 20th Century-Fox, d-Elia Kazan.

Widmark, a public health naval officer, and police captain Paul Douglas work together to find a fugitive murderer who is carrying plague germs before panic engulfs the city of New Orleans.

John Kernan / O. HENRY'S FULL HOUSE, 1952, 20th Century-Fox, d-Henry Hathaway.

In this grouping of five of O. Henry's stories, Widmark reprises his Johnny Udo character in "The Clarion Call." He is a killer caught by an old detective friend who used to sing in a quartet with him.

Jed Towers / DON'T BOTHER TO KNOCK, 1952, 20th Century-Fox, d-Roy Baker.

When his girlfriend (Anne Bancroft) gives him the brush-off, hotel guest Widmark flirts with Marilyn Monroe and she invites him to the room where she is babysitting a child. Their lovemaking is disturbed when the tot wakes up and Monroe displays homicidal tendencies. Widmark finds out that she has just been released from an asylum and he is able to prevent her from killing the child and committing suicide.

Skip McCoy / PICKUP ON SOUTH STREET, 1953, 20th Century-Fox, d-Samuel Fuller.

Widmark is a small-time crook who picks the purse of Jean Peters and comes away with vital military information that she unwittingly plans to turn over to the Communists. Before the movie is over, patriotism will win out over Widmark's greed.

Sgt. Thorne Ryan / TAKE THE HIGH GROUND, 1953, MGM, d-Richard Brooks.

In this routine war film, Widmark is a tough sergeant who puts recruits through hell to get them trained to fight in Korea.

Ben Devereaux / BROKEN LANCE, 1954, 20th Century-Fox, d-Edward Dmytryk.

The oldest of four sons of cattle baron Spencer Tracy, Widmark most hates his father for treating him merely as another hand on the ranch. When he has the opportunity to turn the tables on his father he does so gleefully.

Johnny Gannon / WARLOCK, 1959, 20th Century-Fox, d-Edward Dmytryk.

Former outlaw Widmark, now a deputy, is finally backed by the inhabitants of the western town of Warlock against the lawless elements, including strutting marshal Henry Fonda and his neurotic sidekick (Anthony Quinn).

Jim Bowie / THE ALAMO, 1960, United Artists, d-John Wayne.

Widmark is way over the top in his boisterous, whining portrayal of the famous inventor of a knife that bears his name, frontiersman, and defender of the Alamo.

Col. Tad Lawson / JUDGMENT AT NUREMBERG, 1961, United Artists, d-Stanley Kramer.

Widmark appears as the prosecuting attorney in the war crime trials of four former Nazi jurists. He effectively counters the arguments that there are no laws under which they can be tried.

Capt. Thomas Archer / CHEYENNE AUTUMN, 1964, Warners, d-John Ford.

Widmark leads the troops who move Cheyenne Indians to a new reservation in the 1860s, but once there the Indians attempt to make the 1,600-mile trek back home. It is director Ford's attempt to show the Indians in a sympathetic light after all the times he represented them as bloodthirsty savages; he's only partially successful.

Capt. Eric Finlander / THE BEDFORD INCIDENT, 1965, Great Britain, Columbia, d-James B. Harris.

Widmark is a ruthless, machine-like U.S. destroyer commander who pursues a Russian submarine in Arctic waters and accidentally fires an atomic weapon.

Daniel Madigan / MADIGAN, 1968, Universal, d-Don Siegel.

In this cop melodrama, Widmark is a tough New York detective who is out to bring in a dangerous criminal. It's an excellent, realistic look at the inner workings of police procedures and Widmark is ideally cast as the weary cop who puts his life on the line to do his job.

Marshal Frank Patch / DEATH OF A GUNFIGHTER, 1969, Universal, d-Allen Smithee.

When a western town wants to remove its marshal and he won't be removed, the townsfolk conclude that the only thing to do is have him killed. With Widmark as the marshal that isn't as easy as it seems.

Ratchett / MURDER ON THE ORIENT EXPRESS, 1974, Great Britain, EMI / GW Films, d-Sidney Lumet.

About the only one who doesn't participate in the killing of the despicable Widmark character in this Agatha Christie story is detective Hercule Poirot.

OTHER ROLES

1949: *Dude* / YELLOW SKY; *First Mate Dan Lunceford* / DOWN TO THE SEA IN SHIPS; *Will Slattery* / SLATTERY'S HURRICANE. **1950:** *Harry Fabian* / NIGHT AND THE CITY; *Ray Biddle* / NO WAY OUT; *Lt. Anderson* / HALLS OF MONTEZUMA. **1951:** *Lt. Cmdr. John Lawrence* / THE FROGMEN. **1952:** *Cliff Mason* / RED SKIES OF MONTANA; *Dave Jennings* / MY PAL GUS. **1953:** *CPO Sam McHale* / DESTINATION GOBI. **1954:** *Adam Jones* / HELL AND HIGH WATER; *Fiske* / GARDEN OF EVIL. **1955:** *Dr. Stewart McIver* / THE COBWEB; *Sgt. Joe Lawrence* / A PRIZE OF GOLD. **1956:** *Jim Slater* / BACKLASH; *Mike Latimer* / RUN FOR THE SUN; *Comanche Todd* / THE LAST WAGON. **1957:** *Dauphin of France* / SAINT JOAN; *Col. William Edwards* / TIME LIMIT. **1958:** *Clint Hollister* / THE LAW AND JAKE WADE; *Angie Poole* / THE TUNNEL OF LOVE. **1959:** *Ralph Anderson* / THE TRAP. **1961:** *Michael Reynolds* / THE SECRET WAYS; *Lt. Gary* / TWO RODE TOGETHER. **1963:** *Mike King* / HOW THE WEST WAS WON. **1964:** *Col. Glenn Stevenson* / FLIGHT FROM ASHIYA; *Rolfe* / THE LONG SHIPS. **1966:** *Col. Tom Rossiter* / ALVAREZ KELLY. **1967:** *Lije Evans* / THE WAY WEST. **1970:** *Dr. Taulbee* / THE MOONSHINE WAR. **1972:** *Red Dillon* / WHEN THE LEGENDS DIE. **1976:** *Sam Lucas* / THE SELLOUT; *Martin MacKenzie* / TWILIGHT'S LAST GLEAMING; *John Verney* / TO THE DEVIL IS A DAUGHTER. **1977:** *Agent Hoyt* / ROLLERCOASTER; *Tagge* / THE DOMINO PRINCIPLE. **1978:** *Dr. George A. Harris* / COMA; *General Slater* / THE SWARM. **1979:** *Otto Gerran* / BEAR ISLAND. **1980:** *Laszlo Szaba* / MADE IN THE USA. **1982:** *secretary of state* / THE FINAL OPTION; *Ransom* / HANKY PANKY; *L.A. cop* / NATIONAL LAMPOON'S MOVIE MADNESS. **1984:** *Ben Caxton* / AGAINST ALL ODDS.

WILDE, CORNEL

(Cornelius Louis Wilde, 1915–)

Cornel Wilde's acting abilities have always been suspect despite an Academy Award nomination for A SONG TO REMEMBER; he is better remembered as a competent lead or second lead in a series of adventure and costume pieces. When Hollywood had no further use for him, he formed his own production company and made several films starring himself and his second wife, Jean Wallace. A couple of these were better than most of the things he did when under contract to 20th Century-Fox and Warners.

KEY ROLES

Frédéric Chopin / A SONG TO REMEMBER, 1945, Columbia, d-Charles Vidor.

In this highly romanticized version of the great composer's life, Wilde plays him as a revolutionary espousing the cause of his native Poland against Czarist Russia. He goes to Paris to gain fame and money to support his political friends; instead, he meets and falls in love with feminist writer George Sand (Merle Oberon) and goes off with her to Marjorca where he becomes ill, quarrels with his love, exhausts himself with a concert tour, and dies. At least the wonderful Chopin music is credible.

Robert of Nottingham / THE BANDIT OF SHERWOOD FOREST, 1946, Columbia, d-George Sherman and Henry Levin.

As the son of Robin Hood, Wilde frustrates the plans of the regent (Henry Daniell) who plans to usurp the throne from the boy king of England. Thwarting usurpers runs in the family it would seem.

Bruce Carlton / FOREVER AMBER, 1947, 20th Century-Fox, d-Otto Preminger.

In this gargantuan historical romance set during the reign of Charles II of England, Wilde is a titled officer who takes a London courtesan (Linda Darnell) as his lover. She bears his child but falls on hard times when he goes abroad; she moves bed by bed up the social ladder until she becomes the favorite of the king. But she never forgets Wilde, her one true love, even though he leaves for America with their child.

Pete Morgan / ROAD HOUSE, 1948, 20th Century-Fox, d-Jean Negulesco.

Richard Widmark, the owner of a roadhouse near the Canadian border, becomes insanely jealous when singer Ida Lupino falls in love with his manager (Wilde). So he frames Wilde on a robbery charge and then has him released in his custody. To flaunt his control over Wilde, Widmark takes him and Lupino to his hunting lodge, where he is knocked unconscious during a drunken attack on Wilde. The two lovers try to escape to Canada, but Widmark comes to and pursues them, forcing Lupino to kill him to save Wilde.

The Great Sebastian / THE GREATEST SHOW ON EARTH, 1952, Paramount, d-Cecil B. DeMille.

When circus manager Charlton Heston brings in aerialist Wilde and puts him in the center ring, replacing Heston's sometime girlfriend (Betty Hutton), she decides to outshine her rival and challenges him to a contest in the air. Wilde is able to prove his talent and she comes to admire him. When he is injured it seems his days high above the circus crowds are over, but slowly he starts to get feeling back in his arm.

Bill Baxter / WOMAN'S WORLD, 1954, 20th Century-Fox, d-Jean Negulesco.
Wilde is one of three top field executives brought to New York by automobile manufacturer Clifton Webb so he may observe them and their wives before deciding who he should choose as his new general manager. Wilde and wife (June Allyson) would rather not be picked.

Omar Khayyam / OMAR KHAYYAM, 1957, Paramount, d-William Dieterle.
Wilde is adequate to the challenge of portraying the 11th-century Persian poet-philosopher who defends his Shah against the plots of assassins, but don't expect too much.

Sir Lancelot / LANCELOT AND GUINEVERE, 1962, Great Britain, Emblem, d-Cornel Wilde.
Now producing and directing his own films, Wilde is a fine Lancelot ably supported by his wife (Jean Wallace) as the fair Guinevere and Brian Aherne as an understanding but sorrowful King Arthur.

The Man / THE NAKED PREY, 1966, Paramount, d-Cornel Wilde.
Wilde is excellent in all of his movie-making capacities—acting, writing, and directing—in this harrowing movie of a white hunter (Wilde) in 1840 Africa whose safari is attacked by natives and killed horribly one by one, all save Wilde. For sport the natives strip Wilde and offer him freedom if he can outrun three warriors who will chase him day and night through the wilderness.

OTHER ROLES

1940: *Mr. Williams* / LADY WITH RED HAIR. **1941:** *Chet Oakley* / KISSES FOR BREAKFAST; *Louis Mendoza* / HIGH SIERRA; *Tom Rossi* / RIGHT TO THE HEART. **1942:** *Mike Lord* / THE PERFECT SNOB; *Robert* / LIFE BEGINS AT 8:30; *Jeff Bailey* / MANILA CALLING. **1943:** *Freddie Austin* / WINTERTIME. **1945:** *Aladdin* / A THOUSAND AND ONE NIGHTS; *Richard Harland* / LEAVE HER TO HEAVEN. **1946:** *Philippe Lascalles* / CENTENNIAL SUMMER. **1947:** *Jock Wallace* / THE HOMESTRETCH; *George* / *Johnny Blaine* / IT HAD TO BE YOU. **1948:** *Dave Connors* / THE WALLS OF JERICHO. **1949:** *Griff Marat* / SHOCKPROOF. **1950:** *Stanley Robin* / FOUR DAYS LEAVE; *Capt. Mark Bradford* / TWO FLAGS WEST. **1952:** *D'Artagnan* / AT SWORD'S POINT; *Don Arturo Bordega* / CALIFORNIA CONQUEST. **1953:** *Jean-Paul* / TREASURE OF THE GOLDEN CONDOR; *himself* / MAIN STREET TO BROADWAY; *Si Lahssen* / SAADIA; *Pierre St. Laurent* / STAR OF INDIA. **1954:** *Jean Obregon* / PASSION. **1955:** *Maj. John Boulton* / THE SCARLET COAT; *Charlie* / STORM FEAR; *Leonard Diamond* / THE BIG COMBO. **1956:** *Stephen Turino* / HOT BLOOD. **1957:** *Nick Jargin* / THE DEVIL'S HAIRPIN; *Matt Campbell* / BEYOND MOMBASA. **1958:** *Vic Scott* / MARACAIBO. **1959:** *Lee Martin* / EDGE OF ETERNITY. **1962:** *Constantine* / CONSTANTINE AND THE CROSS. **1967:** *Captain MacDonald* / BEACH RED. **1969:** *Frank Powers* / THE COMIC. **1971:** *narrator* / NO BLADE OF GRASS. **1975:** *Jim* / SHARK'S TREASURE. **1978:** *D'Artagnan* / THE FIFTH MUSKETEER; *Ragnar* / THE NORSEMAN.

WILDER, GENE

(Jerome Silberman, 1935–)

Gene Wilder is an unusual movie star. His early comic successes were as nebbishes, then he became popular for his unusual performances in a couple of Mel Brooks films, including an Oscar-nominated delight in THE PRODUCERS. His work with Richard Pryor moved him high up the list of popular actors in the 1970s and early 1980s, but he hasn't had much going for him the last few years.

KEY ROLES

Eugene Grizzard / BONNIE AND CLYDE, 1967, Warners, d-Arthur Penn.
Wilder makes an impressive film debut as an undertaker who gives chase when Bonnie Parker and Clyde Barrow steal his car, not knowing he is pursuing the famous bank robbers. They turn the tables on him, chase and capture him, and take him for a friendly ride until he makes the wrong kind of comment and is put out of the car far from town.

Leo Bloom / THE PRODUCERS, 1968, MGM, d-Mel Brooks.
Wilder is a great comical find as the bookkeeper who needs his blue blankee for support. He casually tells floundering Broadway producer Zero Mostel that a dishonest man could make money with a flop. Well, Mostel's a dishonest man. Together Wilder and Mostel put on a musical called "Springtime for Hitler" and sell some 2000% of the show to various little old ladies; they are sure it will close before the first performance is over. Instead it becomes a camp hit and they land in jail. As Mostel complains: "How could this happen? I was so careful. I picked the wrong play, the wrong director, the wrong cast. Where did I go right?"

Jim / BLAZING SADDLES, 1974, Warners, d-Mel Brooks.
In this crazy western parody, Wilder is a gunman so fast that no one ever sees his hands touch his six-guns. It's a chaotic film with as many misses as hits in a sophomoric plot filled with low comedy and tasteless jokes.

Dr. Frederick Frankenstein / YOUNG FRANKENSTEIN, 1974, 20th Century-Fox, d-Mel Brooks.
In Brooks's amusing spoof of the Frankenstein story, Wilder plays the grandson of the Baron who meddles where he shouldn't, as did his ancestor, and brings forth a monster, but a sensitive one.

George Caldwell / SILVER STREAK, 1976, 20th Century-Fox, d-Arthur Hiller.
While taking a train cross country, young publisher Wilder spends a blissful night with Jill Clayburgh. During their lovemaking he sees a murdered man dangling in front of their compartment window and finds himself in the middle of a murder and switch plot. He is thrown from the moving train several times, but reboards each time and, with the help of small-time crook Richard Pryor, Wilder foils mastermind Patrick McGoohan.

Skip Donahue / STIR CRAZY, 1980, Columbia, d-Sidney Poitier.
Wilder teams with Richard Pryor again in this adolescent farce about two New Yorkers heading for California who are wrongly accused of bank robbery. They are thrown into prison and plan their escape. The film has every prison gag ever filmed, and they aren't all funny.

OTHER ROLES

1970: *Quackser Fortune* / QUACKSER FORTUNE HAS A COUSIN IN THE BRONX; *Claude Coupe* / *Philippe DeSisi* / START THE REVO-

LUTION WITHOUT ME. **1971:** *Willy Wonka* / WILLY WONKA AND THE CHOCOLATE FACTORY. **1972:** *Dr. Ross* / EVERYTHING YOU ALWAYS WANTED TO KNOW ABOUT SEX (BUT WERE AFRAID TO ASK). **1974:** *the fox* / THE LITTLE PRINCE; *Stanley* / RHINOCEROS. **1975:** *Sigerson Holmes* / THE ADVENTURE OF SHERLOCK HOLMES' SMARTER BROTHER. **1977:** *Rudy Valentine* / THE WORLD'S GREATEST LOVER. **1979:** *Avram Belinsky* / THE FRISCO KID. **1981:** *Skippy* / SUNDAY LOVERS. **1982:** *Michael Jordan* / HANKY PANKY. **1984:** *Teddy Pierce* / THE WOMAN IN RED.

WILLIAM, WARREN

(Warren W. Krech, 1895–1948)

Warren William worked briefly as a newspaper reporter but after World War I went on the stage, training at the American Academy of Dramatic Arts in the 1920s. He was successful on Broadway and appeared in a few silent movies including the PERILS OF PAULINE serials and a few shorts such as HOW I PLAY GOLF—THE SPOON. In 1931, when John Barrymore broke with Warners, the studio frantically sought a matinee idol replacement and settled on William. Throughout the 1930s he co-starred with all the major actresses in films now mostly forgotten; exceptions are GOLD DIGGERS OF 1933 and CLEOPATRA, in which he played Julius Caesar. He also made several appearances as Perry Mason and was Sam Spade in a rather feeble early film version of Dashiell Hammett's *The Maltese Falcon* called SATAN MET A LADY. By the 1940s he was reduced to "B" movies, often in supporting roles.

KEY ROLES

Vincent Day / THE MOUTHPIECE, 1932, Warners, d-James Flood and Elliott Nugent.

The film opens with William, the prosecutor, summing up his case against an innocent boy in a murder trial. His eloquence is such that a guilty verdict is reached and the accused is sent to the chair, but a moment before the execution he is proven innocent. This turns William sour on prosecuting so he becomes the "mouthpiece" for mobsters and guilty criminals and uses exceptional means to get them off. Later, to help a woman, he double-crosses his criminal masters and is machine-gunned as he stands reading a newspaper.

Paul Kroll / THE MATCH KING, 1932, Warners, d-Howard Bretherton.

The film is based on the career of Ivar Kreuger (William) who believes that the best way to get money is to borrow it, then borrow more to pay back the first loan, and so on. This leads his business ventures to involve murder, forgery, and blackmail. This story of the problems of a dishonest match manufacturer who gets his comeuppance when he stoops to crime is highly entertaining.

J. Lawrence Bradford / GOLD DIGGERS OF 1933, 1933, Warners, d-Mervyn LeRoy.

William portrays the older, more sensible brother of a wealthy man (Dick Powell) who seeks a career as a musical comedy writer and the heart of a showgirl (Ruby Keeler). His family sends William and lawyer Guy Kibbee to protect Powell from gold diggers, but these two get picked off by showgirls Joan Blondell and Aline MacMahon.

Dave the Dude / LADY FOR A DAY, 1933, Columbia, d-Frank Capra.

William and other Damon Runyon characters conspire to pass off poor old Apple Annie as a wealthy society woman for one day in order to fool her daughter and the latter's South American fiancé's family. It's sentimental but it's rated the best transition of Runyon to the screen.

Perry Mason / THE CASE OF THE HOWLING DOG, 1934, Warners, d-Alan Crosland.

William, who had also played detective Philo Vance, keeps us wondering throughout the film if his co-star (Mary Astor) is a murderer. One unusual feature in the movie is the complete lack of background music.

Stephen Archer / IMITATION OF LIFE, 1934, Universal, d-John Stahl.

In melodramas like this one, leading men are indispensable but not important. It's the story of two women who raise their daughters alone. The two brave souls (Claudette Colbert and Louise Beavers) both suffer beautifully—Colbert because she and her now-grown daughter (Rochelle Hudson) both love the same man (William). But Colbert sends William away.

Julius Caesar / CLEOPATRA, 1934, Paramount, d-Cecil B. DeMille.

When the queen of the Nile (Claudette Colbert) is delivered to him wrapped in a rug, weary Caesar (William) doesn't know whether to make love to her or spank her. He chooses the former and takes her back to Rome with him with the intention of making her his wife, despite already having one. He is killed on the Ides of March and Cleopatra beats it back to Egypt to await the arrival of Mark Antony.

Ted Shayne / SATAN MET A LADY, 1936, Warners, d-William Dieterle.

The decision to play *The Maltese Falcon* for laughs did not prove to be a happy decision. Not only were there far too few real amusing moments, but Bette Davis didn't want to be in the film and it showed. The bejeweled falcon was changed to a ram's horn filled with gems; villain Caspar Guttman was made a woman played by Alison Skipworth; and William's character's name changed from Spade to Shayne.

Bernard Fleuriot / MADAME X, 1937, MGM, d-Sam Wood.

This vale of tears gave Gladys George a vehicle for her fine portrayal of a woman more sinned against than sinner. William portrays her hard-hearted husband who refuses to forgive her indiscretions and sets her on a long downward ride in life that is climaxed when she is defended against a murder charge by her now-grown son who doesn't know her.

Michael Lanyard / THE LONE WOLF SPY HUNT, 1939, Columbia, d-Peter Godfrey.

Brought out of retirement after a long period of inactivity, the Lone Wolf (William) goes about the task of smashing an enemy spy ring in Washington. Touched by the great success of the Thin Man series, William has to play the role at least in part for laughs.

D'Artagnan / THE MAN IN THE IRON MASK, 1939, United Artists, d-James Whale.

In this tale of the twin heirs to the throne of France, both are played by Louis Hayward. As the bad brother he imprisons the good one in a dungeon in the Bastille, fitting the unfortunate sibling with an iron mask to hide his identity even from his jailers. The good heir escapes with the help of William and the other musketeers, (Alan Hale, Miles Mander, and Bert Roach) and they fit the evil brother with the devilish face piece.

OTHER ROLES

1922: *Eban the carpenter* / THE TOWN THAT FORGOT GOD. **1927:** *bit* / TWELVE MILES OUT. **1930:** *bit* / LET US BE GAY. **1931:** *Neil Hartley* / EXPENSIVE WOMEN; *Captain Boris* / HONOR OF THE FAMILY. **1932:** *Lieutenant D'Ortelles* / THE WOMAN FROM MONTE CARLO; *Baron von Ullrich* / BEAUTY AND THE BOSS; *Hal Blake* / DARK HORSE; *Howard Raymond* / UNDER EIGHTEEN; *David Dwight* / SKYSCRAPER SOULS; *Henry Kirkwood* / THREE ON A MATCH. **1933:** *Chandra Chandler* / THE MIND READER; *Kurt Anderson* / EMPLOYEE'S ENTRANCE; *Kenneth Bixby* / GOODBYE AGAIN. **1934:** *Tony Wallace* / SMARTY; *Alexander Stream* / UPPER WORLD; *Robert Sheldon* / THE SECRET BRIDE; *Louis* / BEDSIDE; *John Braden* / DOCTOR MONICA; *Philo Vance* / THE DRAGON MURDER CASE. **1935:** *Walter Pritcham* / LIVING ON VELVET; *Perry Mason* / THE CASE OF THE CURIOUS BRIDE; *Perry Mason* / THE CASE OF THE LUCKY LEGS; *"Odds" Owen* / DON'T BET ON BLONDES. **1936:** *Chepstow* / THE WIDOW FROM MONTE CARLO; *Perry Mason* / THE CASE OF THE VELVET CLAWS; *Fred Harris* / STAGE STRUCK; *Vic Arnold* / TIMES SQUARE PLAYBOY; *Morgan* / GO WEST, YOUNG MAN. **1937:** *Dr. Phillip Jones* / OUTCAST; *Blackie Denbo* / MIDNIGHT MADONNA; *Colonel De Rougemont* / THE FIREFLY. **1938:** *Steve Emerson* / ARSENE LUPIN RETURNS; *Harry Borden* / THE FIRST HUNDRED YEARS; *Jim Stowell* / WIVES UNDER SUSPICION. **1939:** *Philo Vance* / THE GRACIE ALLEN MURDER CASE; *Bernard Dexter* / DAY-TIME WIFE. **1940:** *Jessie Lewisohn* / LILLIAN RUSSELL; *Michael Lanyard* / THE LONE WOLF STRIKES; *Jefferson Carteret* / ARIZONA; *Mark Dawson* / TRAIL OF THE VIGILANTES; *Michael Lanyard* / THE LONE WOLF MEETS A LADY. **1941:** *Michael Lanyard* / THE LONE WOLF TAKES A CHANCE; *Dr. Lloyd* / THE WOLF MAN; *Blackie* / WILD GEESE CALLING; *Michael Lanyard* / THE LONE WOLF KEEPS A DATE; *Michael Lanyard* / SECRETS OF THE LONE WOLF. **1942:** *Michael Lanyard* / COUNTER ESPIONAGE; *Harry Farrel* / WILD BILL HICKOK. **1943:** *Michael Lanyard* / ONE DANGEROUS NIGHT; *Michael Lanyard* / PASSPORT TO SUEZ. **1945:** *Brett Curtis* / STRANGE ILLUSION. **1946:** *Captain Burke* / FEAR. **1947:** *Laroche-Mathieu* / THE PRIVATE AFFAIRS OF BEL AMI.

WILLIAMS, ESTHER

(1923–)

Esther Williams was Hollywood's mermaid of the 1940s and 1950s when her spectacular build, winning smile, and swimming ability made her a star if never much of an actress; her spectacular water ballet sequences in several MGM musicals more than made up for any shortcomings in the thespian department. Williams was a swimming champ at 15 and modelled swimsuits for a department store while attending Los Angeles City College. At 18 she joined Billy Rose's Aquacade where she was spotted by an MGM talent scout. She appeared in a number of minor roles including her debut in an Andy Hardy picture before it was noted how good she looked in Technicolor. Her role in the Red Skelton vehicle "Sing or Swim" was built up and the title changed to BATHING BEAUTY. From then on Williams was a star. But as she later remarked, "All they ever did for me at MGM was to change my leading men and the water in the pool." Whether she could have succeeded in nonaquatic roles is almost moot because she was given very few chances to see what she could do on dry land. By the end of the 1950s audiences felt waterlogged spending so much time underwater with Williams, so the star who swam herself to the world's box-office top ten, retired.

KEY ROLES

Caroline Brooks / BATHING BEAUTY, 1944, MGM, d-George Sidney.

The plot of this styleless musical is of no great import; songwriter Red Skelton enrolls in a women's college to be near his swimming instructor wife (Williams). The highlight of the film is the John Murray Anderson-staged finale as Williams and several dozen aquatic chorines perform a water ballet to Strauss's "Blue Danube Waltz."

Maria Morales / FIESTA, 1947, MGM, d-Richard Thorpe.

Williams appears as the twin of Mexican heartthrob Ricardo Montalban in his American screen debut. When Montalban disgraces the family by refusing to become a matador because he would rather compose music, Williams dresses up in a torero's costume and enters the ring in his behalf, proving herself as good as any man. When the masquerade is ended Montalban is allowed to follow his heart and Williams has her share of male admirers.

K. C. Higgins / TAKE ME OUT TO THE BALL GAME, 1949, MGM, d-Busby Berkeley.

Williams is the new owner of a turn-of-the-century baseball team whose players include Frank Sinatra and Gene Kelly. While both of the boys have eyes for the comely Williams, she's too much woman for "old blue eyes" at this point in his film career. Kelly, an arrogant sort whose intentions aren't the noblest, finally wins the girl.

Eve Bennett / NEPTUNE'S DAUGHTER, 1949, MGM, d-Edward Buzzell.

Probably the best thing about this musical is the singing of Frank Loesser's "Baby, It's Cold Outside" by Williams, Ricardo Montalban, Red Skelton, and Betty Garrett. The plot—what there is of one—deals with swimsuit designer Williams rejecting the advances of Latin American polo player Montalban. Of course, there is an elaborate water ballet featuring Williams.

Annette Kellerman / MILLION DOLLAR MERMAID, 1952, MGM, d-Mervyn LeRoy.

Williams portrays the famous Australian swimming champion who found fame and fortune in the 1920s in aquatic shows at the New York Hippodrome and notoriety as the girl who first introduced the daring and even shocking one-piece bathing suit. What they don't show in this movie is that Annette Kellerman also was the first star to appear semi-nude in a film. The movie also features many spectacular Busby Berkeley-staged numbers with Williams.

Katy Higgins / DANGEROUS WHEN WET, 1953, MGM, d-Charles Walters.

The thin plot has Williams as a girl in training to swim the English Channel. She also swims in a sequence with the animated Tom and Jerry.

OTHER ROLES

1942: *Sheila Brooks* / ANDY HARDY'S DOUBLE LIFE. **1943:** *Ellen Bright* / A GUY NAMED JOE. **1945:** *Cynthia Glenn* / THRILL OF A ROMANCE. **1946:** *Kay Lorrison* / THE HOODLUM SAINT; *guest* / ZIEGFELD FOLLIES; *Connie Allenbury* / EASY TO WED; *herself* / TILL THE CLOUDS ROLL BY. **1947:** *Nora Cambaretta* / THIS TIME FOR KEEPS. **1948:** *Rosalind Reynolds* / ON AN ISLAND WITH YOU. **1950:** *Christine Riverton Duncan* / DUCHESS OF IDAHO; *Mimi Bennett* / PAGAN LOVE SONG. **1951:** *Debbie Telford* / TEXAS CARNIVAL; *guest* / CALLAWAY WENT THATAWAY. **1952:** *Whitney Young* / SKIRTS AHOY! **1954:** *Julie Hallerton* / EASY TO LOVE. **1955:** *Amytis* / JUPITER'S DAUGHTER. **1956:** *Lois Conway* / THE UNGUARDED MOMENT. **1958:** *Laura* / RAW WIND IN EDEN. **1961:** *Hillary Allen* / THE BIG SHOW.

WINGER, DEBRA

(1955–)

Small, dark, and feisty, Debra Winger appears capable of playing almost any role and playing it well. She has proven that when she's before the camera, audiences pay more attention to her than her macho leading men or even a great scene stealer like Shirley MacLaine. Nominated for Oscars for AN OFFICER AND A GENTLEMAN and TERMS OF ENDEARMENT, she has made only limited appearances because of a severe back injury. Linked by newspaper and magazine gossips with many eligible leading men including a governor, Winger married actor Timothy Hutton in 1986. Bette Davis has said that Winger is the new actress most like herself.

KEY ROLES

Sissy / URBAN COWBOY, 1980, Paramount, d-James Bridges.

Sexy, sluttish, and spunky, Winger is attracted to John Travolta, a Texas farm boy in Houston for an oil refinery job. They meet at Gilley's roadhouse where the guests party as if they are westerners of years gone by. The main attraction is a nasty mechanical bull that generates sexual tension not only in those who try to ride it but for the spectators as well. Travolta and Winger marry, separate, and move in with other people, but get together again when Travolta shows his prowess on the bull.

Paula Pokrifki / AN OFFICER AND A GENTLEMAN, 1982, Paramount, d-Taylor Hackford.

Moving right along, Winger proves more than a match for expressionless Richard Gere in this story of a brash young recruit who is given hell in training camp by drill instructor Lou Gossett, Jr., and between the sheets by Winger. He falls for this local woman who is looking to latch onto a future naval officer and escape her boring existence.

Emma Horton / TERMS OF ENDEARMENT, 1983, Paramount, d-James Brooks.

Winger, the daughter of a most interfering and argumentative mother (Shirley MacLaine), moves away from Houston with her husband (Jeff Daniels), a college professor. When he has an affair with one of his students, she takes up with married John Lithgow but stays with Daniels. They move once again, but hubby seems to have the same girl student. Just as divorce seems imminent, Winger is diagnosed as having cancer. Through it all, Winger shows remarkable range in making her performance seem real and very natural.

Laura Kelly / LEGAL EAGLES, 1986, Universal, d-Ivan Reitman.

In this lighthearted mystery thriller, Winger is a tireless and imaginative lawyer who joins forces with former assistant D.A. Robert Redford to defend Darryl Hannah against the charges of stealing a valuable painting done by her father and of murder. Winger would prefer that Redford not sleep with their client anymore.

Alexandra / BLACK WIDOW, 1987, 20th Century-Fox, d-Bob Rafelson.

Winger, an investigator for the Justice Department, is lonely and self-deprecating, everyone's pal but nobody's sweetheart. In this film she is contrasted with Theresa Russell, a beautiful, confident woman who marries older wealthy men, loves them for awhile, then painlessly kills them. The two women become acquaintances and share many things, including a man.

OTHER ROLES

1976: *Debbie* / SLUMBER PARTY. **1978:** *Jennifer* / THANK GOD IT'S FRIDAY. **1979:** *Melanie* / FRENCH POSTCARDS. **1982:** *voice* / E.T. THE EXTRA-TERRESTRIAL; *Suzy* / CANNERY ROW. **1984:** *Betty Parrish* / MIKE'S MURDER.

WINTERS, SHELLEY

(Shirley Schrift, 1922–)

Although Shelley Winters, like so many starlets, started her career as a sexpot, her looks were neither sultry nor passionate; in fact, she looked a bit common. That's probably why she was given the opportunity to become an actress and not just a sex symbol. She won Academy Awards for her excellent character performances in THE DIARY OF ANNE FRANK and A PATCH OF BLUE, with further nominations for A PLACE IN THE SUN and THE POSEIDON ADVENTURE. Winters studied acting at the New Theatre School in New York with Charles Laughton. She worked as a dress model, in the chorus of the La Congo nightclub in New York, and in summer stock before making her film debut in 1943 in WHAT A WOMAN! She won critical acclaim for her work in A DOUBLE LIFE with Ronald Colman after which she signed a contract with Universal and began studying at the Actors Studio in 1951. She has worked steadily in films to this day, finding even more work as she grows older. A woman with a fine sense of humor who was married three times, she observed: "In Hollywood all marriages are happy. It's trying to live together afterward that causes the problems."

KEY ROLES

Pat Kroll / A DOUBLE LIFE, 1948, Universal-International, d-George Cukor.

Sexy, curvy Winters portrays a waitress who has an affair with lonely Shakespearean actor Ronald Colman. She's not too bright but is fascinated by the actor. She later becomes afraid of him when, suffering from dementia, he finds it more and more difficult to differentiate between real life and his role as Othello. On stage he actually kills his ex-wife who is playing Desdemona.

Alice Tripp / A PLACE IN THE SUN, 1951, Paramount, d-George Stevens.

Winters works in the factory where Montgomery Clift is learning the ropes. They spend a night together and she later tells him: "George, I'm in trouble—real trouble, I think." Yes, indeed, she's pregnant and she demands that Clift marry her; he agrees but puts off doing so because he has met and fallen in love with society girl Elizabeth Taylor. Winters's whining demands become more frequent and Clift considers killing her. They go to a small town to get married and while waiting for the justice of the peace's office to open they take a ride in a rowboat; it capsizes and Winters drowns. Clift is charged with murder, convicted, and executed.

Fran Davis / PLAYGIRL, 1954, Universal-International, d-Joseph Pevney.

While still in her sexpot phase, Winters appears as a singer and roommate of a small-town girl (Colleen Miller) who almost overnight finds herself on the cover of *Glitter* magazine. Winters is jealous of all the attention her boyfriend (Barry Sullivan), the publisher of the magazine, is paying Miller and accidentally shoots him in a jealous scuffle.

Willa Harper / THE NIGHT OF THE HUNTER, 1955, United Artists, d-Charles Laughton.

In this spectacularly suspenseful film, Winters is the widow of a man executed for stealing $10,000, which he hid in his little girl's doll, telling her and her older brother not to tell Winters where the money is. Along comes self-ordained minister Robert Mitchum who served some time in the same cell with the deceased. He comes courting Winters and easily wins her, then murders her, ties her body to the seat of an automobile, and sinks it in the river. He then takes off after the fleeing kids.

Dixie Evans / THE BIG KNIFE, 1955, United Artists, d-Robert Aldrich.

Winters plays a blackmailing Hollywood floozy in this hard-hitting story of an actor (Jack Palance) who wants to break his contract with producer Rod Steiger so that he can make better pictures.

Mrs. Van Daan / THE DIARY OF ANNE FRANK, 1959, 20th Century-Fox, d-George Stevens.

Winters won her first Best Supporting Actress Academy Award for her role as a simple woman of meager resources who can barely cope with the confinement of her family and that of the Frank's in an attic during the German occupation of Amsterdam. The two families spend two years in hiding before they are discovered by the Gestapo. In real life, but not shown in the film, they were taken away to concentration camps in which only Anne Frank's father survived.

Sarah Garnell / THE CHAPMAN REPORT, 1962, Warners, d-George Cukor.

Winters gladly tells of her extramarital affair with Ray Danton to an anonymous researcher for a female sexual behavior study, but she discovers what a good husband she has in Harold J. Stone when Danton gives her the brush-off.

Polly Adler / A HOUSE IS NOT A HOME, 1964, Paramount, d-Russell Rouse.

Winters scores in this cheaply made and laundered account of the life and career of one of New York's most famous madams.

Rose-Ann D'Arcey / A PATCH OF BLUE, 1965, MGM, d-Guy Green.

Thirteen years before the time in which the movie is set, Winters accidentally blinded her five-year-old daughter in a family quarrel. Since that time the girl (Elizabeth Hartmann) has lived in a shabby tenement with her prostitute mother and alcoholic grandfather. Winters wants to start a whorehouse with Hartmann as a special attraction, but when Hartmann meets and falls in love with Sidney Poitier without knowing his color, mom's plans are ruined. Winters earned another Oscar for her performance.

Kate "Ma" Barker / BLOODY MAMA, 1970, American International, d-Roger Corman.

The producer, director, screenwriter, and Winters did their best to portray outlaw Kate Barker as the most sexually depraved and inhuman mother and murderer who ever existed. Winters is way over the top in this violent gangster story.

Helen Hill / WHAT'S THE MATTER WITH HELEN? 1971, Filmways, d-Curtis Harrington.

Winters and Debbie Reynolds, two middle-aged women sans men in their lives, find a certain fame when their sons are convicted of murder in the 1930s. Seeking anonymity they move from the Midwest to Hollywood where they open a dance studio for prospective Shirley Temples. But it seems that Winters's son came by his murderous nature naturally as mama becomes more and more strange.

Belle Rosen / THE POSEIDON ADVENTURE, 1972, 20th Century-Fox, d-Ronald Neame.

With her massive shape Winters can barely make the journey from the top of the Poseidon to the bottom in search of a way off the capsized boat. But when it comes to swimming underwater to save others, this woman is in her element, even though the exertion is too much for her heart.

OTHER ROLES

1943: *girl actress* / WHAT A WOMAN!; *bit* / THE BEAUTIFUL CHEAT; *bit* / THE RACKET MAN. **1944:** *bit* / TWO-MAN SUBMARINE; *"Tennessee" Collingwood* / NINE GIRLS; *Silver Rankin* / SHE'S A SOLDIER TOO; *Gloria Flynn* / SAILOR'S HOLIDAY; *Ulda Tienhoven* / KNICKERBOCKER HOLIDAY; *girl* / COVER GIRL. **1945:** *Bubbles* / TONIGHT AND EVERY NIGHT; *handmaiden* / A THOUSAND AND ONE NIGHTS. **1947:** *Hazel* / THE GANGSTER; *bit* / LIVING IN A BIG WAY. **1948:** *Tory* / LARCENY; *dance hall girl* / RED RIVER; *Brenda* / CRY OF THE CITY. **1949:** *Catherine Sykes* / TAKE ONE FALSE STEP; *Myrtle Wilson* / THE GREAT GATSBY; *Terry* / JOHNNY STOOL PIGEON. **1950:** *Coral* / SOUTH SEA SINNER; *Lola Manners* / WINCHESTER '73; *Frenchie Fontaine* / FRENCHIE. **1951:** *Peg Dobbs* / HE RAN ALL THE WAY; *Kate Denny* / BEHAVE YOURSELF; *Connie Thatcher* / THE RAGING TIDE; *Joy Carroll* / MEET DANNY WILSON. **1952:** *Binky Gay* / PHONE CALL FROM A STRANGER; *Jane Stevens* / UNTAMED FRONTIER; *Nancy* / MY MAN AND I. **1954:** *Grace Markey* / SASKATCHEWAN; *Sarah Wurble* / TENNESSEE CHAMP; *Myrtle La Mar* / TO DOROTHY, A SON; *Eva Bardeman* / EXECUTIVE SUITE. **1955:** *Toni Salerno* / MAMBO; *Natalia Landauer* / I AM A CAMERA; *Marie Gibson* / I DIED A THOUSAND TIMES; *Ruth Harris* / THE TREASURE OF PANCHO VILLA. **1959:** *Lorry* / ODDS AGAINST TOMORROW. **1960:** *Nellie Romano* / LET NO MAN WRITE MY EPITAPH. **1961:** *Mary Di Pace* / THE YOUNG SAVAGES. **1962:** *Charlotte Haze* / LOLITA. **1963:** *Madame Irma* / THE BALCONY; *Fran Cabrell* / WIVES AND LOVERS; *Lisa* / TIME OF INDIFFERENCE. **1965:** *woman of no name* / THE GREATEST STORY EVER TOLD. **1966:** *Fay Estabrook* / HARPER; *Ruby* / ALFIE. **1967:** *Mrs. Kolowitz* / ENTER LAUGHING. **1968:** *Kate* / THE SCALPHUNTERS; *Shirley Newman* / BUONA SERA, MRS. CAMPBELL; *Mrs. Flatow* / WILD IN THE STREETS. **1969:** *Mrs. Armstrong* / THE MAD ROOM. **1970:** *Lena Mervin* / HOW DO I LOVE THEE? **1971:** *Rosie Forrest* / WHO SLEW AUNTIE ROO?; *Dorothy Bluebell* / FLAP. **1972:** *Gabriella* / SOMETHING TO HIDE. **1973:** *Mrs. Cramer* / BLUME IN LOVE; *Mommy* / CLEOPATRA JONES. **1974:** *Mrs. Mathews* / JOURNEY INTO FEAR. **1975:** *Zelda Shapiro* / DIAMONDS; *Diana Steedeman* / THAT LUCKY TOUCH. **1976:** *Mrs. Lapinsky* / NEXT STOP, GREENWICH VILLAGE; *the concierge* / THE TENANT. **1977:** *Lean Gogan* / PETE'S DRAGON; *Tillie Turner* / TENTACLES; *Natalya* / THE THREE SISTERS. **1978:** *Queen Rachel* / KING OF THE GYPSIES; *Elvis's mother* / ELVIS. **1979:** *Nurse Andrea Harper* / CITY ON FIRE; *Elizabeta* / THE MAGICIAN OF LUBLIN; *Jane Phillips* / THE VISITOR. **1981:** *Eva Brown* / S.O.B. **1984:** *Becky Sherman* / OVER THE BROOKLYN BRIDGE. **1985:** *Bertha* / POOR PRETTY EDDIE; *Olga Nabakov* / DEJA VU. **1986:** *Galina* / VERY CLOSE QUARTERS.

WOOD, NATALIE

(Natasha Gurdin, 1938–1981)

Natalie Wood's death by drowning in 1981 ended a fruitful Hollywood career that began when she was only five. She matured from a cute child into a beautiful young woman who, at the time of her death, had become a fine example of how reaching the age of 40 in no way means a woman or actress is over the hill. She never looked lovelier than in her last few films. Harry Kunitz once noted, "Natalie Wood is built like a brick dollhouse." Not only was she a beautiful child and woman, she was a talented actress who received Academy Award nominations for REBEL WITHOUT A CAUSE, SPLENDOR IN THE GRASS, and LOVE WITH A PROPER STRANGER. She was adept at comedy as well as drama. While her roles as a young adult actress were as put upon, vulnerable women, it appeared in her last few roles that she was comfortably moving toward mature women who knew what they wanted and how to get it.

KEY ROLES

Susan Walker / MIRACLE ON 34TH STREET, 1947, 20th Century-Fox, d-George Seaton.
Raised by her mother (Maureen O'Hara) to believe in only what can be explained, Wood becomes a test case for Edmund Gwenn who claims to be the real Santa Claus. He is declared so by the State of New York in a sanity hearing and perhaps he really is.

Judy / REBEL WITHOUT A CAUSE, 1955, Warners, d-Nicholas Ray.
Now almost grown, teenager Wood doesn't get the attention her father once gave her. She runs with a fast crowd at her high school but develops a crush on a sensitive, weird new kid in town (James Dean). It's hell being a teenager.

Debbie Edwards / THE SEARCHERS, 1956, Warners, d-John Ford.
Wood is the niece that John Wayne has been searching for with half-breed Jeffrey Hunter ever since she was abducted by Indians who killed her parents and older sister five years earlier. Wayne plans to kill the poor girl because he knows that by now the Indian leader has claimed her as his squaw, but on seeing her he takes her in his arms and gently carries her to safety.

Marjorie Morgenstern / MARJORIE MORNINGSTAR, 1958, Warners, d-Irving Rapper.
Wood is a Jewish New Yorker whose great ambition is to become a Broadway star and marry Gene Kelly, a songwriter she deeply admires. Instead she ends up a suburban housewife married to Martin Milner, who is always there but whom she hardly ever notices.

Salome Davis / ALL THE FINE YOUNG CANNIBALS, 1960, MGM, d-Michael Anderson.
In one of many films about restless youth produced around this time, Wood, the daughter of a clergyman, falls in love with Robert Wagner, the son of a clergyman. But life in New York City is quite a shock for these two from such decent backgrounds; sex and drugs become problems.

Wilma Dean Loomis / SPLENDOR IN THE GRASS, 1961, Warners, d-Elia Kazan.
In a small Kansas town during the 1920s, Wood and Warren Beatty fall in love. They are frightened by their physical desires but are unwilling to have a sexual relationship. They wish to marry but their well-meaning parents only make their confusion and frustration worse. Her mother boasts of her aversion to men and lectures that nice girls don't have sexual feelings. His father, a self-made millionaire, advises Beatty to forget about marriage until he has completed Yale. The youngsters end their relationship when Wood suffers a nervous breakdown and Beatty becomes promiscuous.

Maria / WEST SIDE STORY, 1961, United Artists, d-Robert Wise and Jerome Robbins.
Wood makes a lovely Puerto Rican Juliet to Richard Beymer's Romeo in this Leonard Bernstein and Stephen Sondheim musical. In this version the warring families are two New York street gangs. Wood survives but Beymer doesn't. Her songs (dubbed by Marni Nixon) include "I Feel Pretty" and with Beymer (dubbed by Jimmy Bryant) "One Hand, One Heart." She also joins Rita Moreno in "A Boy Like That" and "I Have a Love."

Louise Hovick / Gypsy Rose Lee / GYPSY, 1962, Warners, d-Mervyn LeRoy.
Wood never looked lovelier than when transformed from a little child into the stripper who puts the "tease" in striptease. The musical drags in many parts but if one is not in a hurry to get anywhere there is enough in this Jule Styne and Stephen Sondheim work to enjoy.

Angie Rossini / LOVE WITH THE PROPER STRANGER, 1964, Paramount, d-Robert Mulligan.
Wood is a Manhattan sales clerk who meets and goes to bed with a musician (Steve McQueen) on their first date and gets pregnant. He prizes independence too much for marriage, so he tries to arrange an abortion for her. But when she flees from the appointment, he decides to marry her after all. All in all it's a well-handled presentation of an all-too-familiar problem with both Wood and McQueen very charming.

Maggie DuBois / THE GREAT RACE, 1965, Warners, d-Blake Edwards.
In this very long spoof of just about everything, Wood is a female newspaper reporter who is assigned to cover a 1908 car race from New York to Paris. She also wins the clean-cut hero (Tony Curtis) and helps thwart the dastardly villain (Jack Lemmon).

Carol Sanders / BOB & CAROL & TED & ALICE, 1969, Columbia, d-Paul Mazursky.
Wood and her husband (Robert Culp) seriously consider swapping mates with friends Elliott Gould and Dyan Cannon, but they call it off before it goes too far.

Mari Thompson / THE LAST MARRIED COUPLE IN AMERICA, 1980, Universal, d-Gilbert Cates.
One by one the friends of Wood and George Segal get divorced and take up with new partners, until Wood and Segal are about the only married couple left. They almost go by the board as well when he makes love to one of her friends, picks up a social disease, and passes it on to Wood.

OTHER ROLES

As Natasha Gurdin

1943: *bit* / HAPPY LAND.

As Natalie Wood

1946: *Margaret Hamilton* / TOMORROW IS FOREVER; *Carol Warren* / THE BRIDE WORE BOOTS. **1947:** *Anna Muir as a child* / THE GHOST AND MRS. MUIR; *Jenny* / DRIFTWOOD. **1948:** *Bean McGill* / SCUDDA HOO! SCUDDA HAY!; *Ruth* / CHICKEN EVERY SUNDAY. **1949:** *Susan Matthews* / THE GREEN PROMISE; *Ellen Cooper* / FATHER WAS A FULLBACK. **1950:** *Penny* / OUR VERY OWN; *Polly Scott* / NO SAD SONGS FOR ME; *Phyllis Lawrence* / THE JACKPOT; *Nan* / NEVER A DULL MOMENT. **1951:** *Pauline* / DEAR BRAT; *Stephanie Rawlins* / THE BLUE VEIL. **1952:** *Barbara Blake* / JUST FOR YOU; *Sally Burke* / THE ROSE BOWL STORY. **1953:** *Gretchen* / THE STAR. **1954:** *Helen as a child* / THE SILVER CHALICE. **1955:** *Seely* / ONE DESIRE. **1956:** *Maria Colton* / THE BURNING HILLS; *Liz* / A CRY IN THE NIGHT; *Susan Daniels* / THE GIRL HE LEFT BEHIND. **1957:** *Lois Brennan* / BOMBERS B-52. **1958:** *Monique Blair* / KINGS GO FORTH. **1959:** *Lory Austen* / CASH MCCALL. **1964:** *Helen Gurley Brown* / SEX AND THE SINGLE GIRL. **1966:** *Daisy Clover* / INSIDE DAISY

CLOVER; *Alva Starr* / THIS PROPERTY IS CONDEMNED; *Penelope Elcott* / PENELOPE. **1974:** *Ellen Prendergast* / PEEPER. **1979:** *Tatiana Nikolaevna Donskaya* / METEOR. **1980:** *guest* / WILLIE AND PHIL. **1983:** *Karen Brace* / BRAINSTORM.

WOODWARD, JOANNE

(1930–)

Educated at Louisiana State University, Joanne Woodward moved to New York to study at the Neighborhood Playhouse. She understudied in the Broadway production of "Picnic" and in 1955 was given a contract with 20th Century-Fox to make her debut in COUNT THREE AND PRAY. Her 1957 role in THE THREE FACES OF EVE won her national recognition and an Academy Award. She was also nominated for Oscars for RACHEL, RACHEL and SUMMER WISHES, WINTER DREAMS. Married to actor Paul Newman since 1958, she has been directed by him in RACHEL, RACHEL, THE EFFECT OF GAMMA RAYS ON MAN-IN-THE-MOON MARIGOLDS, HARRY AND SON, and THE GLASS MENAGERIE. Woodward is recognized as a near-great actress somewhat difficult to cast. She is a private person not well known by movie fans because, away from the camera and the stage, she doesn't live a public or glamorous life. Woodward hasn't done much to help herself become known, asserting, "The real me is all the parts I've played."

KEY ROLES

Dorothy Kingship / A KISS BEFORE DYING, 1956, United Artists, d-Gerd Oswald.

In her second movie Woodward is the pregnant girlfriend of Robert Wagner, who fakes a suicide note for her and gives her poison which he tells her are vitamins. When this doesn't work, he pushes her off the courthouse roof. Later he kills one of her male friends after forcing him to sign a confession saying that he killed Woodward. Woodward's sister becomes involved with Wagner too, but she is luckier than Joanne; Wagner is found to be the murderer before he strikes again.

Eve / THE THREE FACES OF EVE, 1957, 20th Century-Fox, d-Nunnally Johnson.

Woodward won an Oscar for her extraordinary portrayal of a young Georgia woman with multiple personalities. The film is based on a real story about an ordinary housewife who begins to have blackouts and becomes two completely different kinds of women—one is a saucy, sexy lady, the other an intelligent, well-balanced woman. With the help of a psychiatrist Woodward is able to discard her unfavorable personalities and emerge a mentally healthy human being.

Leola Boone / NO DOWN PAYMENT, 1957, 20th Century-Fox, d-Martin Ritt.

In this story of young couples living in an upper-class, suburban housing development, Woodward is married to tyrannical Cameron Mitchell who develops a yen for a neighbor's wife (Patricia Owens) and finally rapes her. But he is killed in a fight with his victim's husband.

Quentin Compton / THE SOUND AND THE FURY, 1959, 20th Century-Fox, d-Martin Ritt.

Faulkner's work reads better than it looks in this dreary movie in which Woodward is the illegitimate daughter of promiscuous Margaret Leighton. Both are under the thumb of Yul Brynner, her grandfather's stepson, who is the only one in this once-proud southern family capable of making enough money to support the others. Woodward resents him and in rebellion she takes up with a crude mechanic traveling with a carnival. Brynner won't hear of the relationship and emerges as not so much the household tyrant but someone concerned about her well-being; he may even have more tender feelings for her.

Lila Green / THE STRIPPER, 1963, 20th Century-Fox, d-Franklin Schaffner.

Woodward, a would-be actress, moves in with an old friend (Claire Trevor) whose son (Richard Beymer) falls in love with her. He encourages her to look for better things but the only work she can find is as a stripper at a stag show. Beymer is at the show and at first he is repelled by seeing the woman he loves being watched by lecherous men. Still he asks her to marry him but she wisely refuses.

Mary Meredith / A BIG HAND FOR THE LITTLE LADY, 1966, Warners, d-Fielder Cook.

Woodward is splendid as the meek little farmer's wife who is forced to play out her husband's (Henry Fonda) hand in the year's biggest poker game when he has bet their life's savings and suffers a heart attack. It's a delightfully suspenseful piece with an ending that could use more punch.

Rachel Cameron / RACHEL, RACHEL, 1968, Warners, d-Paul Newman.

Paul Newman was aided in his directorial debut by a stunning performance from wife Woodward as one of two middle-aged, sexually frustrated schoolteacher spinsters in a small New England town.

Dr. Mildred Watson / THEY MIGHT BE GIANTS, 1971, Universal, d-Anthony Harvey.

When George C. Scott develops delusions that he is Sherlock Holmes, his brother wants him committed and hires psychiatrist Woodward to examine him. Her name just happens to be Watson and the game is afoot.

Beatrice / THE EFFECT OF GAMMA RAYS ON MAN-IN-THE-MOON MARIGOLDS, 1972, 20th Century-Fox, d-Paul Newman.

An embittered mother and widow, Woodward tries to bring up her two extremely dissimilar daughters; one (Roberta Wallach) is outgoing and high-strung, the other (Nell Potts) is shy, retiring, and the winner of a science award at school for the project described in the movie's title. It's a touching story of an ordinary family's life together.

Rita Waldren / SUMMER WISHES, WINTER DREAMS, 1973, Columbia, d-Gilbert Cates.

Woodward is a neurotic New York housewife who goes to pieces when her mother (Sylvia Sidney) dies. Her husband (Martin Balsam) tries to calm her: "What the hell are you talking about a tumor? You don't have enough to occupy your brain so you put a tumor there to fill up the space." She improves when she accompanies Balsam to Bastogne where he served during World War II. It's a talky piece with excellent performances all around.

OTHER ROLES

1955: *Lissy* / COUNT THREE AND PRAY. **1958:** *Clara Varner* / THE LONG HOT SUMMER; *Grace Bannerman* / RALLY 'ROUND THE FLAG, BOYS! **1959:** *Carol Cutere* / THE FUGITIVE KIND. **1960:** *Mary St. John* / FROM THE TERRACE. **1961:** *Lillian Corning* / PARIS BLUES. **1963:** *Samantha Blake* / A NEW KIND OF LOVE. **1964:** *Molly Thomas* / SIGNPOST TO MURDER. **1966:** *Rhoda Shillitoe* / A FINE MADNESS. **1969:** *Elora Capua* / WINNING. **1970:** *Geraldine* / WUSA. **1975:** *Iris Devereaux* / THE DROWNING POOL. **1978:** *Jessica*

/ THE END. **1984:** *Lily* / HARRY AND SON. **1987:** *Amanda Wingfield* / THE GLASS MENAGERIE.

WRAY, FAY

(Vina Fay Wray, 1907–)

Fay Wray will forever be remembered as the object of King Kong's affections in the 1933 movie of that name, but this great scream queen made many movies before and after that role. Born in Canada, Wray was a reddish-brown-haired beauty with lovely almond eyes. An extremely photogenic and expressive actress, she learned her craft in silent films starting as a Wampas Baby Star in 1926, then moving from westerns to the big time in Erich von Stroheim's THE WEDDING MARCH, followed by the good / bad girl in Josef von Sternberg's THUNDERBOLT. For the next few years she was much in demand and made some memorable horror movies in which her piercing screams cut through the sexual tension as well as the fear. After KING KONG her career was on a down-slide and she made a series of "B" movies. In 1942 she left the screen for more than ten years before returning for several character roles in pictures of the 1950s.

KEY ROLES

Mitzi Schrammell / THE WEDDING MARCH, 1927, Silent, Paramount, d-Erich von Stroheim.

Wray, a crippled harpist, works in a wine garden in Vienna in 1914. Aristocratic and slightly jaded Prince Nicki (George Fawcett) starts a flirtation with her that turns to love. Despite their feelings, Nicki is forced to become engaged to the daughter of a wealthy commoner. A jealous butcher who wants Wray, no matter what the cost, threatens to kill the prince on his wedding day unless Wray marries him. She is able to prevent this and watches sadly as her true love leaves with his new bride.

Ethne Eustace / THE FOUR FEATHERS, 1929, Silent, Paramount, d-Merian C. Cooper and Ernest B. Schoedsack.

When British officer Richard Arlen leaves the service to marry Wray just as his regiment is sent to battle in the Sudan, everyone including Wray believes he is a coward; three of his friends send him a white feather symbolizing this. Arlen leaves England for the Sudan where, disguised as a native, he becomes a hero and is able to return the white feathers, including one for Wray.

Lora Nixon / POINTED HEELS, 1929, Paramount, d-A. Edward Sutherland.

Wray, a showgirl, leaves the business to marry a composer (Phillips Holmes). His wealthy family stops his allowance, forcing them to live in a modest flat while he works on a symphony. Wray goes back to the chorus and Holmes is taunted by her brother into writing a pop song. A producer long in love with Wray convinces Holmes that he is standing in the way of her career. Holmes is about to give her a divorce when the song becomes a hit and they are reunited.

Joan Xavier / DOCTOR X, 1931, Warners, d-Michael Curtiz.

Wray gets to demonstrate her lung power in this whodunit horror story featuring a one-armed doctor who adds an arm of synthetic flesh and a scary face.

Eve Trowbridge / THE MOST DANGEROUS GAME, 1932, RKO, d-Ernest B. Schoedsack and Irving Pichel.

Wray and Joel McCrea are shipwrecked and swim to the nearest island, which turns out to be owned by a big game hunter (Leslie Banks) whose favorite prey is humans.

Charlotte Duncan / MYSTERY OF THE WAX MUSEUM, 1933, Warners, d-Michael Curtiz.

Unfortunately for Wray, she reminds sculptor Lionel Atwell of his favorite creation in his old wax museum that was destroyed by fire, leaving him terribly disfigured and insane. Wearing a mask that makes him appear normal, he devises a way to create new wax figures by covering real corpses with wax.

Ann Darrow / KING KONG, 1933, RKO, d-Merian C. Cooper and Ernest B. Schoedsack.

In perhaps the most famous of all the horror pictures, Wray is a starving woman picked up by movie producer Robert Armstrong to accompany him and his ship to some undisclosed location where she is to become the star of his next picture. Instead, she is chosen by the natives of the island destination to become the bride of the gigantic ape, Kong. There is no doubt that the great beast has some sexual thoughts, no matter how impractical, and Wray senses his intentions and screams her heart out. Kong is captured and brought back to New York, but escapes when he believes that Wray is in danger. He is shot down from the Empire State building by airplanes after first setting Wray down safely. As producer Armstrong noted, "'Twas Beauty killed the Beast."

Lucy Calhoun / THE BOWERY, 1933, 20th Century-Fox, d-Raoul Walsh.

Among the many things that two Bowery characters (George Raft and Wallace Beery) of the 1890s fight over is Fay Wray. She is homeless and poverty-stricken and Beery befriends her, but Raft wins her heart. Furious Beery dares Raft to jump off the Brooklyn Bridge to prove his manhood and impress Wray; Raft agrees and survives the plunge.

Janet Krueger / THE COUNTESS OF MONTE CRISTO, 1934, Universal, d-Karl Freund.

In this comedy Wray is a bit player in a musical who convinces her friend (Patsy Kelly) to go with her to a fancy resort. There Wray wears the clothes from the show and convinces everyone that she is a countess.

Teresa / VIVA VILLA!, 1934, MGM, d-Jack Conway.

Wray portrays a Mexican aristocrat who is sympathetic to the cause of Pancho Villa (Wallace Beery), but his excesses force her to refuse him her continued support. Outraged, Beery orders her flogged. Later a stray bullet fired by one of Beery's men kills her.

Angela / THE AFFAIRS OF CELLINI, 1934, Fox / United Artists, d-Gregory La Cava.

Wray is the beautiful model and mistress of the Florentine rascal and rake Benvenuto Cellini (Fredric March). He leaves her when he catches the eye of the Duchess of Florence (Constance Bennett). In turn, the latter's husband takes a fancy to Wray.

Rene / THE CLAIRVOYANT, 1935, Great Britain, Gaumont, d-Maurice Elvey.

Wray is the wife of a fraudulent mind reader (Claude Rains) who is as surprised as anyone when his predictions start coming true.

Mrs. Brent / TAMMY AND THE BACHELOR, 1957, Universal-International, d-Joseph Pevney.

Wray portrays the mother of the bachelor (Leslie Nielsen) who is saved from a plane crash by backwoods girl Tammy (Debbie Reynolds). Wray spends all her time trying to turn her plantation into something out of *Gone with the Wind* but Reynolds straightens her out.

OTHER ROLES

1925: *Beth Slocum* / THE COAST PATROL. **1926:** *Lila Rogers* / LAZY LIGHTNING; *Pauline Stewart* / THE MAN IN THE SADDLE; *Jessie Hayden* / THE WILD HORSE STAMPEDE. **1927:** *Molly Vernon* / LOCO LUCK; *Roberts* / A ONE MAN GAME; *Mildred Orth* / SPURS AND SADDLES. **1928:** *Anna Lee* / THE FIRST KISS; *Christine Charteris* / LEGION OF THE CONDEMNED; *Elizabeth* / THE STREET OF SIN. **1929:** *Ritzy* / THUNDERBOLT. **1930:** *Marie Gardoni* / BEHIND THE MAKEUP; *"dream girl"* / PARAMOUNT ON PARADE; *Consuelo* / THE TEXAN; *Joan Randall* / THE BORDER LEGION; *Daisy* / THE SEA GOD. **1931:** *Marcia Collins* / THE FINGER POINTS; *Tasie Lockhart* / THE CONQUERING HORDE; *Lee Carleton* / NOT EXACTLY GENTLEMEN, (THREE ROGUES); *Helen* / DIRIGIBLE; *Ynez Dominguez* / CAPTAIN THUNDER; *Kay Roberts* / THE LAWYER'S SECRET; *Camile de Jonghe* / THE UNHOLY GARDEN. **1932:** *Fay* / STOWAWAY. **1933:** *Ruth Bertin* / THE VAMPIRE BAT; *Diane Templeton* / BELOW THE SEA; *Ann Carver* / ANN CARVER'S PROFESSION; *Vida Carew* / THE WOMAN I STOLE; *Cynthia Glennon* / THE BIG BRAIN; *Virginia Brush* / ONE SUNDAY AFTERNOON; *Wildeth Christie* / SHANGHAI MADNESS; *Kay Walling* / MASTER OF MEN. **1934:** *Marie Franck* / "B-24" / MADAME SPY; *Mary Fanshane* / ONCE TO EVERY WOMAN; *Gail* / BLACK MOON; *Nan Brockton* / CHEATING CHEATERS; *Louise Lorimer* / WOMAN IN THE DARK; *Joan Mitchell* / WHITE LIES. **1935:** *Ann Manders* / BULLDOG JACK; *Hilda Beach-Howard* / COME OUT OF THE PANTRY; *Jean* / MILLS OF THE GODS. **1936:** *Joyce Reid* / ROAMING LADY; *Lady Rowena* / WHEN KNIGHTS WERE BOLD; *Mary* / THEY MET IN A TAXI. **1937:** *Gloria Gay* / IT HAPPENED IN HOLLYWOOD (ONCE A HERO); *Kay Cabot* / MURDER IN GREENWICH VILLAGE. **1938:** *Linda Ware* / THE JURY'S SECRET; *Eleanor Dunlap* / SMASHING THE SPY RING. **1939:** *Carol* / NAVY SECRETS. **1940:** *Ted Dawson* / WILDCAT BUS. **1941:** *Molly* / ADAM HAD FOUR SONS. **1941:** *Mary Stanley* / MELODY FOR THREE. **1953:** *Mrs. Kimbell* / SMALL TOWN GIRL; *Marquise* / TREASURE OF THE GOLDEN CONDOR. **1955:** *Edna Devanel* / THE COBWEB; *Sue McLinnon* / QUEEN BEE; *Kay Stanley* / HELL ON FRISCO BAY. **1957:** *Beth Daley* / ROCK, PRETTY BABY; *Alice Pope* / CRIME OF PASSION. **1958:** *Beth Daley* / SUMMER LOVE; *Mrs. Martin* / DRAGSTRIP RIOT.

WRIGHT, TERESA

(Muriel Teresa Wright, 1918–)

Starting with her Oscar-nominated debut in THE LITTLE FOXES, brown-haired Teresa Wright had a wonderful decade of movies with another Academy Award nomination for THE PRIDE OF THE YANKEES and a win for MRS. MINIVER. But in the 1950s the good leading roles dried up and most of her notable work since then has been on television performing in such classic plays as "The Dark at the Top of the Stairs," "Tea and Sympathy," "Death of a Salesman," "Ah, Wilderness," and "Mornings at Seven."

KEY ROLES

Alexandra Giddens / THE LITTLE FOXES, 1941, Goldwyn / RKO, d-William Wyler.

Nominated for an Academy Award for her first picture, Wright plays Bette Davis's naive daughter who comes to understand how hateful her mother really is. She knows that Davis is responsible for the death of Wright's father (Herbert Marshall).

Carol Beldon / MRS. MINIVER, 1942, MGM, d-William Wyler.

Wright is the granddaughter of the local matriarch in a small English village who marries the son of Greer Garson and Walter Pidgeon, pilot Richard Ney. He survives his runs over occupied Europe but she is killed in a German raid. For her sweet and touching performance she won the Best Supporting Actress Award.

Eleanor Gehrig / THE PRIDE OF THE YANKEES, 1942, Goldwyn / RKO, d-Sam Wood.

Wright was nominated both for Best Actress for this picture and Best Supporting Actress for MRS. MINIVER in the same year. As was the case with Fay Bainter before her and later Jessica Lange, who also received both nominations in a single year, Wright won only for the Best Supporting work. At any rate, Wright is part of the reason that this admittedly sentimental film is the best baseball biopic ever made.

Young Charlie Newton / SHADOW OF A DOUBT, 1943, Universal, d-Alfred Hitchcock.

Wright, named for her mother's younger brother (Joseph Cotten), is delighted when Cotten comes for a visit, but soon her elation turns to fear as she begins to suspect that he is the infamous "Merry Widow" murderer. He confirms it when he tries to kill her but he's the one who falls from one train into the path of another.

Peggy Stephenson / THE BEST YEARS OF OUR LIVES, 1946, Goldwyn / RKO, d-William Wyler.

Wright, the daughter of returning World War II sergeant Fredric March, finds herself attracted to Dana Andrews, a former pilot who arrived home at the same time as her father. Unfortunately, he is married to Virginia Mayo, a party girl who wed him because he looked good in a uniform. Mayo isn't ready to settle down by a long shot and true love prevails when Andrews gets Wright, promising her in the last lines of the film: "You know what it will be, don't you, Peggy? It may take us years to get anywhere. Not enough money, no decent place to live. We have to work and sweat and get kicked around...." It sounds like heaven to Wright.

Ellen Wilozek / THE MEN, 1950, United Artists, d-Fred Zinnemann.

Wright gives one of the finest performances of her career as the understanding fiancée and, later, wife of a bitter paraplegic (Marlon Brando). The picture thoughtfully depicts the adjustment period of the young couple.

Annie Jones / THE ACTRESS, 1953, MGM, d-George Cukor.

It would seem that Wright moved too quickly into playing mothers with grown daughters, as is the case in this film. Ruth Gordon (Jean Simmons) remembers how it was in her family when, at seventeen, she decided to become an actress. Her mother (Wright) is a sweetheart about it, but how will father Spencer Tracy take the news?

Ruth Simmons / THE SEARCH FOR BRIDEY MURPHY, 1956, Paramount, d-Noel Langley.

An amateur hypnotist (Louis Hayward) throws Wright, an American housewife, into a previous incarnation as a long-dead Irish peasant girl called Bridey Murphy. At the climax Hayward can't bring Wright back to the present.

OTHER ROLES

1944: *Isabel Drury* / CASANOVA BROWN. **1947:** *Thor Callum* / PURSUED; *Millicent Hopkins* / THE IMPERFECT LADY; *Kate Farrell* / THE TROUBLE WITH WOMEN. **1948:** *Lark Ingoldsby* / ENCHANTMENT. **1950:** *Ellen Vanner* / THE CAPTURE. **1952:** *Edna Miller* / SOMETHING TO LIVE FOR; *Jillie Lawrence* / CALIFORNIA CONQUEST; *Laurie Osborne* / THE STEEL TRAP. **1953:** *Ellen Braden* / COUNT

THE HOURS. **1954:** *Grace Bridges* / TRACK OF THE CAT. **1957:** *Mary Saunders* / ESCAPADE IN JAPAN. **1958:** *Elizabeth Grant* / THE RESTLESS YEARS. **1969:** *Mrs. Spencer* / THE HAPPY ENDING. **1977:** *May* / ROSELAND. **1980:** *Laura Roberts* / SOMEWHERE IN TIME.

WYATT, JANE

(1912–)

Daughter of an investment broker and a drama critic, Jane Wyatt made her Broadway debut at 19 as an understudy, then moved into a series of leading roles on the stage. Arriving in Hollywood in 1934, she appeared in over 30 movies during the next 30 years. She co-starred with Robert Young in the long-running TV series "Father Knows Best," winning Emmys three straight years. Her made-for-TV movies include SEE HOW THEY RUN (1964), WEEKEND OF TERROR (1970), YOU'LL NEVER SEE ME AGAIN (1973), TOM SAWYER (1975), AMELIA EARHART (1976), A LOVE AFFAIR: THE ELEANOR AND LOU GEHRIG STORY (1977), SUPERDOME (1978), and MISSING CHILDREN: A MOTHER'S STORY (1986). In 1976 she returned to the big screen after an absence of eleven years.

KEY ROLES

Estella / GREAT EXPECTATIONS, 1934, Universal, d-Stuart Walker.

In the first sound version of the Dickens tale about a young English boy who becomes the recipient of a handsome allowance from a mysterious benefactor, Wyatt is the haughty beauty who has been trained from childhood by Miss Havisham to enslave men and ruin them. Interestingly, Valerie Hobson was originally intended to play the role but was instead given the part of Biddy and had all her scenes deleted. In the 1947 version, Hobson played the adult Estella.

Pat Duncan / THE LUCKIEST GIRL IN THE WORLD, 1936, Universal, d-Edward Buzzell.

When Wyatt proposes to marry Louis Hayward, a man of no means, her father tries to prevent the match; he will give his consent only if she lives on $150 for one month to prove she can stand being married to a poor man.

Sondra / LOST HORIZON, 1937, Columbia, d-Frank Capra.

Unlike poor Margo, Wyatt is what she seems to be to Ronald Colman when he and others are brought to Shangri-la, that is, a young, beautiful, and intelligent girl who could make his stay there as the new High Lama truly paradisaical. He has to leave for awhile with his brother and the old-young Margo, but eventually fights his way back over the mountains to Wyatt.

Angie Hunter / NONE BUT THE LONELY HEART, 1944, RKO, d-Clifford Odets.

Wyatt, a young cellist, lives in the same slum as shiftless cockney Cary Grant. Grant is not his usual urbane self in this movie; instead he treats Wyatt, who loves him, almost as badly as he does his mother (Ethel Barrymore). Grant dumps Wyatt for June Duprez, the divorced wife of a London mobster. As for his ma, he forces her to fend for herself in the shop she runs beneath their dingy home until he learns that she is dying of cancer in a prison hospital. She had been arrested for acting as a fence so she could have some money to leave her no-good son.

Madge Harvey / BOOMERANG, 1947, 20th Century-Fox, d-Elia Kazan.

Wyatt portrays the loyal and helpful wife of a Bridgeport, Connecticut, state's attorney (Dana Andrews) who prevents a vagrant (Arthur Kennedy) from being railroaded for the murder of a popular clergyman in a case unsolved to this day.

Mary Morgan / TASK FORCE, 1949, Warners, d-Delmer Daves.

In another prepping for her forthcoming role of Marian Anderson in TV's "Father Knows Best," Wyatt plays the undemanding role of the wife of a naval officer (Gary Cooper) who fights long and hard to promote the cause of aircraft carriers.

OTHER ROLES

1934: *Dinny Cherrell* / ONE MORE RIVER. **1936:** *Sally Rogers* / WE'RE ONLY HUMAN. **1940:** *Anne Webster* / GIRL FROM GOD'S COUNTRY. **1941:** *Joan Wyatt* / HURRICANE SMITH; *Ellen Craig* / WEEKEND FOR THREE; *Laura Anders* / KISSES FOR BREAKFAST. **1942:** *Myra* / THE NAVY COMES THROUGH; *Beth Ainsley* / ARMY SURGEON. **1943:** *Vinnie Marr* / BUCKSKIN FRONTIER; *Eleanor Sager* / THE KANSAN. **1946:** *Dr. Mary Palmer* / STRANGE CONQUEST; *Marta* / THE BACHELOR'S DAUGHTERS. **1947:** *Jane* / GENTLEMAN'S AGREEMENT. **1948:** *Sue Forbes* / PITFALL; *Miss Darlington* / NO MINOR VICES. **1949:** *Mrs. Marshall Brown* / BAD BOY; *Dr. Edith Cabot* / CANADIAN PACIFIC. **1950:** *Lois Macaulay* / OUR VERY OWN; *Marjorie Byrne* / HOUSE BY THE RIVER; *Janet Pringle* / MY BLUE HEAVEN; *Lois Frazer* / THE MAN WHO CHEATED HIMSELF. **1951:** *Maggie Powell* / CRIMINAL LAWYER. **1957:** *Prue Stubbins* / INTERLUDE. **1961:** *Anne Davis* / THE TWO LITTLE BEARS. **1965:** *Grace Kimbrough* / NEVER TOO LATE. **1976:** *Aunt Effie* / TREASURE OF MATECUMBE. **1986:** *Amanda, Spock's mother* / STAR TREK IV: THE VOYAGE HOME.

WYMAN, JANE

(Sarah Jane Fulks, 1914–)

Starting out as a blonde, Jane Wyman first appeared in films using her real name in bit parts in the early 1930s beginning with THE KID FROM SPAIN. She was featured in many "B" movies as a wisecracking friend of the lead but it wasn't until 1945 that the studios discovered that Wyman had acting ability (and brown hair). She was nominated for a Best Actress Academy Award for THE YEARLING and two years later won an Oscar for her touchingly sensitive performance as the deaf-mute in JOHNNY BELINDA. She also received nominations for THE BLUE VEIL and MAGNIFICENT OBSESSION. Finally considered a first-rate dramatic actress, Wyman appeared in a wide variety of roles in her long career, including musical comedies; but her reputation is based on her work in melodramas. Her second of three husbands from 1940 to 1948 was Ronald Reagan. Today Wyman stars in the prime-time soap opera "Falcon Crest."

KEY ROLES

Claire Adams / BROTHER RAT, 1938, Warners, d-William Keighley.

It's fun and games at a military academy with Wayne Morris, Ronald Reagan, and Eddie Albert as the main cadets, and Priscilla Lane, Wyman, and Jane Bryan as their respective girls.

Bliss Dobson / YOU'RE IN THE ARMY NOW, 1941, Warners, d-Lewis Seiler.

In this real stinker Wyman looks good compared to the likes of Jimmy Durante and Phil Silvers, two vacuum cleaner salesmen who are drafted into the army.

Susan Courtney / MAKE YOUR OWN BED, 1944, Warners, d-Peter Godfrey.

Still struggling for some decent roles, Wyman plays opposite Jack Carson as romantically linked private detectives who enter domestic service in the home of Alan Hale because he needs protection from Nazi agents.

Helen St. James / THE LOST WEEKEND, 1945, Paramount, d-Billy Wilder.

Although the picture belongs to Ray Milland for his brilliant performance as an alcoholic writer who spends a weekend trying to destroy himself with drink, Wyman in this film gets closer to the dramatic roles that will make her a star. She plays Milland's fiancée who argues against his taking his own life, saying, "It's just that I'd rather have you drunk than dead."

Gracie Harris / NIGHT AND DAY, 1946, Warners, d-Michael Curtiz.

In this poorly presented biopic of Cole Porter with Cary Grant hopelessly miscast in the lead role, Wyman is a fun-loving singer of some of the composer's early hits who later disappears from the film.

Ma Baxter / THE YEARLING, 1946, MGM, d-Clarence Brown.

Hard work on a poor, backwoods Florida farm makes Wyman tough and not very sensitive to her son's (Claude Jarman, Jr.) dream of having a pet, and certainly not the deer that Pa (Gregory Peck) decides the boy may raise. Mother knows best because when the animal becomes a yearling it eats the family's crops. Wyman was nominated for an Oscar for her splendid work in this film.

Belinda McDonald / JOHNNY BELINDA, 1948, Warners, d-Jean Negulesco.

If she had never done another film Wyman's reputation as a great actress would be established by her brilliant performance as the Cape Breton, Nova Scotia, deaf-mute girl who is befriended by a sympathetic doctor (Lew Ayres). When she is brutally raped by Steve McNally she blocks the incident out of her mind but cannot forget the child she is carrying. When the child is born, it is assumed that Ayres is the father; but McNally accidentally gives himself away to Wyman's father (Charles Bickford) who is killed in a struggle with McNally. When his wife (Jan Sterling) is unable to conceive, McNally decides that he wants his child. But when he goes to Wyman offering to adopt the baby he so frightens her that she kills him. She is put on trial until Sterling, realizing what her dead husband has done, comes to her defense. Wyman makes not a sound throughout the film, but no one's face has ever been more expressive.

Laura Wingfield / THE GLASS MENAGERIE, 1950, Warners, d-Irving Rapper.

In Tennessee Williams's beautiful play, shy, crippled Wyman has a gentleman caller (Kirk Douglas) arranged for her by her mother (Gertrude Lawrence) and brother (Arthur Kennedy).

Louise Mason / THE BLUE VEIL, 1951, RKO, d-Curtis Bernhardt.

Widowed by World War I, nurse Wyman decides to devote her life to children after losing her only child. She moves from one home to another taking care of other people's children and refusing to have a life of her own. Throughout her life she is self-sacrificing and uncomplaining even when, too old to be a nursemaid, she is reduced to working as a janitor in a school. With many other actresses the movie could have been sentimental slop, but in Wyman's capable hands it is very touching and a great love story.

Selina Dejong / SO BIG, 1953, Warners, d-Robert Wise.

Wyman, a schoolteacher, marries a farmer, raises their son alone when her husband dies, finds the boy has not grown into an admirable human being, and finally finds some belated happiness with a sculptor.

Helen Phillips / MAGNIFICENT OBSESSION, 1954, Universal, d-Douglas Sirk.

Even for an actress of Wyman's stature, this Lloyd C. Douglas story is a bit much. It's about a playboy who is partly responsible for the death of Wyman's husband and for her blindness. But he reforms, goes to medical school, and becomes a talented surgeon who restores her sight and replaces her husband as a love object. She was nominated for an Oscar for her role.

Cary Scott / ALL THAT HEAVEN ALLOWS, 1956, Universal-International, d-Douglas Sirk.

Audiences enjoyed the teaming of Wyman with Rock Hudson in MAGNIFICENT OBSESSION, so the studio brought the duo together again in this film. Middle-aged widow Wyman, living in a small town, hires a young gardener (Hudson). They are attracted to each other but she can think of plenty of reasons why she should put him out of her mind—the difference in their ages being the most obvious. Ultimately, she decides to marry him despite local prejudices and enjoys "all that heaven allows."

OTHER ROLES

As Sarah Jane Fulks

1932: *Goldwyn girl* / THE KID FROM SPAIN. **1933:** *bit* / ELMER THE GREAT. **1934:** *bit* / COLLEGE RHYTHM. **1935:** *bit* / RUMBA; *bit* / ALL THE KING'S HORSES; *girl* / STOLEN HARMONY. **1936:** *girl* / KING OF BURLESQUE; *bit* / ANYTHING GOES; *bit* / CAIN AND MABEL; *bit* / POLO JOE.

As Jane Wyman

1936: *bit* / GOLD DIGGERS OF 1937; *girl at party* / MY MAN GODFREY; *Dixie* / SMART BLONDE; *Bessie Fuffnick* / STAGE STRUCK. **1937:** *Babette* / THE KING AND THE CHORUS GIRL; *Dot* / READY, WILLING AND ABLE; *Stumpy's girlfriend* / SLIM; *Joan* / THE SINGING MARINE; *Flip Lane* / PUBLIC WEDDING; *Marjorie Day* / MR. DODD TAKES THE AIR. **1938:** *Elaine Burdette* / THE SPY RING, (SOMEWHERE IN PARIS); *Violet Coney* / HE COULDN'T SAY NO; *Betty Martin* / WIDE OPEN FACES; *Vivian* / THE CROWD ROARS. **1939:** *Alabama* / TAIL SPIN; *Myrna Winslow* / PRIVATE DETECTIVE; *Marian Bronson* / THE KID FROM KOKOMO; *Torchy Blane* / TORCHY PLAYS WITH DYNAMITE; *Judy Craig* / KID NIGHTINGALE. **1940:** *Claire Ramm* / BROTHER RAT AND A BABY; *Marge Allen* / AN ANGEL FROM TEXAS; *Nan Hudson* / FLIGHT ANGELS; *Joy O'Keefe* / MY LOVE CAME BACK; *Peggy Armstrong* / TUGBOAT ANNIE SAILS AGAIN; *Laura Ogden* / GAMBLING ON THE HIGH SEAS. **1941:** *Elizabeth Clochesay* / HONEYMOON FOR THREE; *Mary Hathaway* / BAD MEN OF MISSOURI; *Lynn Shotesbury* / THE BODY DISAPPEARS. **1942:** *Denny Costello* / LARCENY, INC.; *Connie* / MY FAVORITE SPY; *Flo La Verne* / FOOTLIGHT SERENADE. **1943:** *Jean* / PRINCESS O'ROURKE. **1944:** *Robbie Vance* / CRIME BY NIGHT; *Vivian* / THE DOUGHGIRLS; *herself* / HOLLYWOOD CANTEEN. **1946:** *Fran Connors* / ONE MORE TOMORROW. **1947:** *Ann Kincaid* / CHEYENNE; *Mary Peterman* / MAGIC TOWN. **1949:** *Polly Haines* / A KISS IN THE DARK; *Jennifer Smith* / THE LADY TAKES A SAILOR; *herself* / IT'S A GREAT FEELING. **1950:** *Eve Gill* / STAGE FRIGHT. **1951:** *Mary Lewis* / THREE GUYS NAMED MIKE; *Emmadel Jones* / HERE COMES THE GROOM; *herself* / STARLIFT. **1952:** *Betty Rogers* / THE STORY OF WILL ROGERS; *Carolina Hill* / JUST FOR YOU. **1953:** *Constance Stuart* / LET'S DO IT AGAIN. **1955:** *Lucy Gallant* / LUCY GALLANT. **1956:** *Ruth Wood* / MIRACLE IN THE RAIN. **1959:** *Mary Dean* / HOLIDAY FOR LOVERS. **1960:** *Aunt Polly* / POLLYANNA. **1962:** *Katie*

Willard / BON VOYAGE. **1969:** *Elaine Benson* / HOW TO COMMIT MARRIAGE.

WYNYARD, DIANA

(Dorothy Isobel Cox, 1906–1964)

Stately and gracious, British actress Diana Wynyard made her London stage debut in 1925 with a small role; seven years later she had a long run on Broadway with Basil Rathbone in "The Devil Passes." She made her screen debut with the three Barrymores in RASPUTIN AND THE EMPRESS and received an Oscar nomination for CAVALCADE. Perhaps her best performance was in the British production of GASLIGHT as the wife being terrorized by her murderous husband. The fair-haired actress was married to director Carol Reed from 1943 to 1947. Most of her career, from 1941 until her death of a kidney ailment in 1964, was spent on the stage.

KEY ROLES

Jane Marryot / CAVALCADE, 1933, Fox Films, d-Frank Lloyd.

Wynyard and Clive Brook toast the beginning of the 20th century as this Noel Coward story follows the family and its servants, their pain, sorrows, and triumphs for three decades from the Boer War through World War I. Pauline Kael called it an "orgy of British self-congratulation"; *Variety* described Wynyard as exceptional.

Alice Overton / LET'S TRY AGAIN, 1934, RKO, d-Vincent Lawrence.

Clive Brook is a busy physician who neglects his wife (Wynyard) who decides that she loves her niece's fiancé. The niece witnesses their one bit of lovemaking and tells the doctor; he's surprised to learn that he really doesn't care and arranges to divorce Wynyard so she may marry her lover. But as the niece is knitting little booties, so her fiancé sticks with her and the old married folks resume their marriage.

Bella Mallen / GASLIGHT, (ANGEL STREET), 1940, Great Britain, d-Thorold Dickinson.

In 1880 London, Anton Walbrook and his wife (Wynyard) buy a house where a widow was murdered 15 years earlier. Walbrook begins a campaign to drive his wife mad and her mind begins to crumble, but policeman Frank Pettingell shows her that not only is her husband behind her mental problems but that he also killed her aunt in the house and returned to search for the jewels he couldn't find at the time of the murder. When the story was remade in the U.S. in 1944, MGM bought the rights to this marvelous version, changed its name to ANGEL STREET, and made certain that it has seldom been seen since.

Helen Walshingham / KIPPS, 1941, Great Britain, 20th Century-Fox, d-Carol Reed.

Draper's assistant Michael Redgrave comes into a fortune and rejects an impoverished society girl (Wynyard) to marry his childhood sweetheart (Phyllis Calvert).

Mrs. Arnold / TOM BROWN'S SCHOOLDAYS, 1951, Great Britain, Renown, d-Gordon Parry.

Wynyard is headmaster Robert Newton's helpmate who acts as a confidant to the title character (John Howard Davies) during his days at Rugby Public School.

OTHER ROLES

1932: *Natasha* / RASPUTIN AND THE EMPRESS. **1933:** *Laura Seward* / MEN MUST FIGHT; *Elena* / REUNION IN VIENNA. **1934:** *Anne* / WHERE SINNERS MEET; *Clare Corven* / ONE MORE RIVER. **1939:** *Kit Kobling* / ON THE NIGHT OF THE FIRE. **1940:** *Irene Roder* / FREEDOM RADIO; *Mary Anne Wyndham-Lewis* / THE PRIME MINISTER. **1947:** *Lady Chiltern* / AN IDEAL HUSBAND. **1956:** *the matron* / THE FEMININE TOUCH. **1957:** *Mrs. Fleury* / ISLAND IN THE SUN.

YORK, MICHAEL

(1942–)

Oxford-educated, Michael York's gentle, refined, and almost boyish looks somewhat typed him as callow youths in adaptations of Shakespeare, Dickens, Dumas, Durrell, Pinter, Greene, and Wells, but they also made him a much-in-demand actor in the 1970s. His appeal seems to have waned and whether he can successfully move into starring character roles may depend upon how his looks mature.

KEY ROLES

William / ACCIDENT, 1967, Great Britain, Lippet, d-Joseph Losey.

York is an English nobleman killed in an automobile accident at the beginning of this film. His girlfriend (Jacqueline Sassard) is found in shock by Dirk Bogarde, an Oxford Don who had both the young people as students. He recalls how York had taken advantage of the girl, and when she regains consciousness, he seduces her.

Tom Pickle / THE GURU, 1969, 20th Century-Fox, d-James Ivory.

York is a popular British rock star in India, studying the sitar with famed musician Utpal Dutt. Among the guru's other devoted disciples is hippie Rita Tushingham. The two find little enlightenment in India, but they do fall in love and return to England to marry.

Darley / JUSTINE, 1969, 20th Century-Fox, d-George Cukor.

York is the narrator of this story, told in flashback, of an Alexandrian Jewess (Anouk Aimee) and her Christian millionaire husband (John Vernon). They plan to send arms to Palestine so the Jews can overcome the Moslems. Among Aimee's friends is schoolmaster York, who takes up with a consumptive belly dancer from Greece. It's a rather muddled attempt to film Lawrence Durrell's Alexandra Quartet in one picture.

Brian Roberts / CABARET, 1972, ABC / Allied Artists, d-Bob Fosse.

York is a British writer whose character is based on Christopher Isherwood, author of the stories on which this musical is based. He is in Berlin just before the Nazis take power and has affairs with eccentric, amoral Sally Bowles (Liza Minnelli) and also with a bisexual German baron (Helmut Griem). He also helps a Jewish couple (Marisa Berenson and Fritz Wepper) find that they are right for each other.

George Conway / LOST HORIZON, 1973, Columbia, d-Charles Jarrott.

York gets the role of the brother of the designated new High Lama of Shangri-la (Peter Finch) in this musical mishmash. York doesn't consider the place a paradise and wants to return to England; they do, but it's disastrous and Finch has to make his way back to his Himalayan love (Liv Ullman) by himself.

D'Artagnan / THE THREE MUSKETEERS, 1973, 20th Century-Fox, d-Richard Lester.

York portrays the Dumas hero as a lusty, acrobatic lad from the provinces who is handy with a sword and, at least as far as Faye Dunaway, Raquel Welch, and one or two other women will attest, adept in the bedroom as well. It's all done tongue-in-cheek, but an awful lot of people end up dead in this picture as in the sequel, THE FOUR MUSKETEERS.

Logan / LOGAN'S RUN, 1976, United Artists, d-Michael Anderson.

In this science fiction adventure yarn set in the year 2274, inhabitants are eliminated when they reach the age of 30. York is a cop whose job it is to track down those who have reached the magic age but who have gone on the run, which is precisely what York does when he reaches the magic number. He also discovers that there are some who have survived and have set up a separate society.

OTHER ROLES

1967: *Lucentio* / THE TAMING OF THE SHREW; *acrobat* / RED AND BLUE; *Tom Wabe* / SMASHING TIME. **1968:** *Tybalt* / ROMEO AND JULIET; *Peter Strange* / THE STRANGE AFFAIR. **1969:** *Guthrum* / ALFRED THE GREAT. **1970:** *Conrad Ludwig* / SOMETHING FOR EVERYONE. **1971:** *Geoffrey Richter-Douglas* / ZEPPELIN. **1972:** *Anthony Farrant* / ENGLAND MADE ME. **1974:** *D'Artagnan* / THE FOUR MUSKETEERS; *Count Andrenyi* / MURDER ON THE ORIENT EXPRESS. **1975:** *Lt. Arthur Drake* / CONDUCT UNBECOMING; *Pip Pirrip* / GREAT EXPECTATIONS. **1977:** *Beau Geste* / THE LAST REMAKE OF BEAU GESTE; *Prince George* / SEVEN NIGHTS IN JAPAN; *Andrew Braddock* / THE ISLAND OF DR. MOREAU. **1978:** *himself* / FEDORA. **1979:** *Charles Carruthers* / THE RIDDLE OF THE SANDS. **1980:** *naturalist* / THE WHITE LIONS; *Lyosha Petrov* / FINAL ASSIGNMENT. **1983:** *Rollo* / THE WEATHER IN THE STREETS. **1984:** *Alex Rodak* / SUCCESS IS THE BEST REVENGE.

YORK, SUSANNAH

(Susannah Y. Fletcher, 1941–)

London-born Susannah York was raised in a remote Scottish village but graduated from the Royal Academy of Dramatic Arts and began her career on the provincial stage. Her delicate, blue-eyed, blonde beauty carries an aura of sexuality which first attracted attention when she was a teenager on the brink of womanhood in THE GREENGAGE SUMMER. Her work in TOM JONES won her international praise and she received an Oscar nomination for THEY SHOOT HORSES, DON'T THEY? One of her best-known roles was as the young lesbian in the controversial THE KILLING OF SISTER GEORGE. In the early 1970s she scored a success with her children's fantasy book, *In Search of Unicorns*, which was quoted at length in her 1972 film, IMAGES.

KEY ROLES

Morag Sinclair / TUNES OF GLORY, 1960, Great Britain, Knightsbridge, d-Ronald Neame.

In her screen debut York is the daughter of a crude Scottish colonel (Alec Guinness) relieved of command because he is a lax disciplinarian and something of a drinker. Guinness gets into serious trouble when he strikes a corporal who is paying court to York. Guinness pleads with the new commandant (John Mills) to spare him a court-martial; Mills does but is then branded a weakling and kills himself.

Joss Grey / LOSS OF INNOCENCE, (THE GREENGAGE SUMMER), 1961, Great Britain, Columbia, d-Lewis Gilbert.

In this story of a girl becoming a woman, York at 16 is the oldest of four English children stranded in the champagne country of France. They are taken in at a chateau-hotel on the River Marne by the proprietor and her lover and before long, the proprietor has reason to be jealous of the fast-maturing York.

Cecily Koertner / FREUD, 1962, Universal, d-John Huston.

In this over-long, miscast biopic of the eminent Vienna doctor, York, as a composite patient, has every neurosis that the good doctor would ultimately name. Among other things she has a thing for her father, is sexually repressed, and is hysterical a good part of the time.

Sophie Western / TOM JONES, 1963, Great Britain, Woodfall, d-Tony Richardson.

Squire Western (Hugh Griffith) enjoys drinking and wenching with Tom Jones (Albert Finney) but he doesn't relish having the rascally bastard as the husband of his daughter (York). When Tom's parentage gets cleared up the squire gives the young couple his blessing.

Margaret More / A MAN FOR ALL SEASONS, 1966, Great Britain, Columbia, d-Fred Zinnemann.

York is the educated daughter of Sir Thomas More (Paul Scofield), who loses his post as Chancellor of England and his head because he will not say that he approves of Henry VIII's move to divorce his first wife, marry Anne Boleyn, and make himself head of the church of England. York and her mother (Wendy Hiller) are forced into exile.

Alice "Childie" McNaught / THE KILLING OF SISTER GEORGE, 1968, Great Britain, Cinerama, d-Robert Aldrich.

Aging actress Beryl Reid plays kindly nurse Sister George on a popular BBC soap opera. In reality she's an acid-tongued lesbian who constantly fights with her lover (York). Reid's behavior gets her written out of the show and she loses York to another woman willing to offer York her "protection."

Alice LeBlanc / THEY SHOOT HORSES, DON'T THEY? 1969, Cinerama, d-Sydney Pollack.

York is an aspiring actress competing in a dance marathon at the sleazy Aragon Ballroom during the Depression. Her partner (Robert Fields) is an impoverished farm worker. When her alternate gown is stolen, she moves on to other partners, and when Red Buttons dies from a heart attack, she has a mental breakdown in a shower.

Cathryn / IMAGES, 1972, Ireland, Columbia, d-Robert Altman.

York is a schizophrenic housewife writing a children's book called *In Search of Unicorns* (a book actually written and published by York). She becomes semi-hysterical when she is confronted by images of her former lovers and she cannot tell reality from fantasy. It's all very pretentious and overly long.

Lara / SUPERMAN, 1978, Warners, d-Richard Donner.

In a not very demanding role, but no doubt lucrative, York portrays Marlon Brando's wife on the doomed planet Krypton. She and her hubby send their son out in space, headed for earth, where he will become Superman. York shows up now and then in the series when Superman uses one of his green crystals to bring up images from a faraway galaxy.

OTHER ROLES

1960: *Ellen* / THERE WAS A CROOKED MAN. **1964:** *Candace Trumpey* / THE SEVENTH DAWN; *the actress* / SCENE NUN, TAKE ONE; *Susan* / SCRUGGS. **1965:** *Grace Moncton* / SANDS OF THE KALAHARI. **1966:** *Angel McGinnis* / KALEIDOSCOPE. **1967:** *Becky Howard* / SEBASTIAN. **1968:** *Segolene* / DUFFY. **1969:** *Eleanor* / OH! WHAT A LOVELY WAR; *Maggie Harvey* / THE BATTLE OF BRITAIN; *Hilaret* / LOCK UP YOUR DAUGHTERS. **1970:** *Hilary Dow* / COUNTRY DANCE; *Jane Eyre* / JANE EYRE. **1971:** *Stella* / X, Y & ZEE; *Penelope Ryan* / HAPPY BIRTHDAY, WANDA JUNE. **1974:** *Terry Steyner* / GOLD. **1975:** *Mrs. Marjorie Scarlett* / CONDUCT UNBECOMING; *Julia Richardson* / THAT LUCKY TOUCH. **1976:** *Ellen Bracken* / SKY RIDERS; *Eliza Frazer* / ADVENTURES OF ELIZA FRAZER. **1979:** *Julie Carver* / THE SILENT PARTNER; *Rachel Fielding* / THE SHOUT. **1980:** *Sue Lewis* / FALLING IN LOVE AGAIN; *Lara* / SUPERMAN II; *Jane Turner* / THE AWAKENING; *actress* / LONG SHOT. **1981:** *Dinah Booker* / LOOPHOLE. **1983:** *Lady Churchill* / YELLOWBEARD.

YOUNG, GIG

(Bryon Ellsworth Barr, 1913–1978)

Gig Young started his film career playing under the names Bryon Barr and Bryant Fleming. He was playing a character named Gig Young in THE GAY SISTERS when he learned that another actor was using the name Bryon Barr, so he became Gig Young. He deserved better than he got in terms of roles, as he usually played slightly ridiculous but sardonic characters who weren't substantial enough characters to get the girl and, like Rodney Dangerfield, didn't get any respect. Young was nominated for Academy Awards for COME FILL THE CUP and TEACHER'S PET, and won for THEY SHOOT HORSES, DON'T THEY? Late in his career he was stuck with a few quickie thrillers and horror movies. Married five times, he and his last wife committed suicide together.

KEY ROLES

Gig Young / THE GAY SISTERS, 1942, Warners, d-Irving Rapper.

In this story of three poor little rich girls (Barbara Stanwyck, Geraldine Fitzgerald, and Nancy Coleman), Coleman winds up marrying Young.

Sam Rosen / WAKE OF THE RED WITCH, 1948, Republic, d-Edward Ludwig.

Young, a seaman, is told the reason why hatred exists between John Wayne and Luther Adler as he sits at Adler's table on an East Indian Island. Young very much admires Adler's ward (Adele Mara), who looks something like the deceased Gail Russell who was the reason for the dispute between the two bitter enemies.

Boyd Copeland / COME FILL THE CUP, 1951, Warners, d-Gordon Douglas.

In one of his many portrayals of weak men, Young is the alcoholic nephew of publisher Raymond Massey, who assigns the task of reforming the young man to his editor (James Cagney), a former lush. Seems that Young is married to Cagney's ex-girlfriend, but is ignoring her while taking up with the moll of a mean and nasty gangster.

Mike Cutler / DESK SET, 1957, 20th Century-Fox, d-Walter Lang.

Young is something of a charming louse who takes advantage of Katharine Hepburn's brains and availability as he advances his own career in a large New York broadcasting company. As fellow worker Joan Blondell puts it to Hepburn: "Available? You're like an old coat that's hanging in his closet. Every time he reaches in there you are. Don't be there once." When efficiency expert Spencer Tracy shows up, Young belatedly gets jealous.

Dr. Hugo Pine / TEACHER'S PET, 1958, Paramount, d-George Seaton.

Young is a multi-talented professor and successful author who has a relationship with journalism professor Doris Day, until she gets a whiff of Clark Gable, a tough city editor who doesn't believe in journalism schools and enrolls in her class to show her up.

Roger / THAT TOUCH OF MINK, 1962, Universal-International, d-Delbert Mann.

Young is a would-be rebellious financial adviser to Cary Grant, who sends Young to apologize to Doris Day when his limousine splashes her with mud. Day is outraged and visits Grant personally to express her anger, and is encouraged all the way by Young, who wishes he had the nerve to tell off Grant himself. Instead, Day and Grant are attracted to each other and he proposes a romantic trip. She accepts but, as is the case in pictures of this era, she keeps her honor until, with the assistance of Young, she marries Grant.

Rocky / THEY SHOOT HORSES, DON'T THEY? 1969, Cinerama, d-Sydney Pollack.

Young won an Academy Award for his work as the cruel and cynical host of a Depression-period dance marathon. Throughout the ordeal for the exhausted and abused participants, Young brandishes bromides like, "There can only be one winner, folks, but isn't that the American way?" As he waves one poor soul off the dance floor he says, "We're going to miss you, Shirley. Isn't that right, folks? So long Shirl. But don't despair. Every heart in this room is with you, and that's what really counts. It's hard on all of us after we've lived all these hours and weeks together to see one of these wonderful, courageous kids fall out. But life goes on. And so does the marathon."

Hal Henderson / LOVERS AND OTHER STRANGERS, 1970, Cinerama, d-Cy Howard.

Looking old and weary, Young is marvelous as the father of the bride. When told by his son-in-law-to-be that he and the bride-to-be have been living together for over a year, Young assures him that he understands, insisting there are no generation gaps as far as he is concerned. This is surely in part due to the fact that he has a long-standing affair going on with Anne Jackson. Whenever she pressures him to get a divorce from Cloris Leachman, Young patiently explains, "You, Bernice, and I are, three of us, in a boat. Now, it's my boat, and it's your lake, but Bernice has the oars."

OTHER ROLES

As Bryon Barr or Bryant Fleming

1940: *floor walker* / MISBEHAVING HUSBANDS. **1941:** *Lieutenant Roberts* / THEY DIED WITH THEIR BOOTS ON; *pilot* / DIVE BOMBER; *sailor* / NAVY BLUES; *groom* / ONE FOOT IN HEAVEN; *soldier* / SERGEANT YORK; *soldier* / YOU'RE IN THE ARMY NOW; *bit* / THE MAN WHO CAME TO DINNER. **1942:** *student* / THE MALE ANIMAL; *student pilot* / CAPTAINS OF THE CLOUDS.

As Gig Young

1943: *Lt. Bill Williams* / AIR FORCE; *Rudd Kendall* / OLD ACQUAINTANCE. **1946:** *Caryl Dubrok* / ESCAPE ME NEVER. **1947:** *Walter Hartright* / THE WOMAN IN WHITE. **1949:** *Pete Thomas* / LUST FOR GOLD; *Alexander Darvac* / TELL IT TO THE JUDGE; *Porthos* / THE THREE MUSKETEERS. **1950:** *Paul* / HUNT THE MAN

DOWN. **1951:** *Captain Reiner* / TARGET UNKNOWN; *Lt. William Holloway* / ONLY THE VALIANT; *Vaughn* / SLAUGHTER TRAIL; *John Tirsen* / TOO YOUNG TO KISS. **1952:** *Jason Kent* / HOLIDAY FOR SINNERS; *Dr. Jeff Chadwick* / YOU FOR ME. **1953:** *Vance Court* / THE GIRL WHO HAD EVERYTHING; *Bob Danvers* / ARENA; *Cliff Willard* / TORCH SONG. **1954:** *Johnny Kelly* / CITY THAT NEVER SLEEPS. **1955:** *Alex Burke* / YOUNG AT HEART; *Chuck* / THE DESPERATE HOURS. **1958:** *Dick Pepper* / THE TUNNEL OF LOVE. **1959:** *Larry Ellis* / THE STORY ON PAGE ONE; *Evan Doughton* / ASK ANY GIRL. **1962:** *Willy Grogan* / KID GALLAHAD. **1963:** *Sonny Smith* / FOR LOVE OR MONEY; *David Barnes* / FIVE MILES TO MIDNIGHT. **1964:** *Cmdr. Key Weedon* / A TICKLISH AFFAIR. **1965:** *Richard Bramwell* / STRANGE BEDFELLOWS. **1967:** *Mike Kelton* / THE SHUTTERED ROOM. **1973:** *Charlie Mcready* / A SON-IN-LAW FOR CHARLIE MCREADY. **1974:** *Quill* / BRING ME THE HEAD OF ALFREDO GARCIA. **1975:** *Edward Douglas* / THE HINDENBERG; *Laurence Weyburn* / THE KILLER ELITE. **1976:** *Mortimer McGrew* / SHERLOCK HOLMES IN NEW YORK. **1979:** *Jim Marshall* / THE GAME OF DEATH.

YOUNG, LORETTA

(Gretchen Young, 1913–)

Loretta Young was only four when she began appearing as a child extra in movies as did her sisters Polly Ann and Elizabeth Jane. (The latter appeared in movies as Sally Blane.) Young, a blonde in some of her earlier movies, was a blue-eyed, brown-haired beauty who remained a top star for more than twenty years, although very few of her pictures were great films. One exception was THE FARMER'S DAUGHTER, for which she won an Academy Award; she was also nominated for COME TO THE STABLE. She retired from the screen in 1953 and began a second successful career on television with "The Loretta Young Show"; she played the leads in about half the dramas of her TV series. Since 1960 Young has devoted most of her time to Catholic charities.

KEY ROLES

Dorothy Hope / THE DEVIL TO PAY, 1930, United Artists, d-George Fitzmaurice.

Young, a high-society beauty with a boyfriend who is a Grand Duke, correctly suspects that Ronald Colman, who pays her court, is a professional gigolo. She falls for him when she discovers that the only reason he took money from her was to pay off the penniless duke and be rid of him.

Toya San / THE HATCHET MAN, 1932, Warners, d-William A. Wellman.

It seems that during this period every pretty actress was pressed into playing a Chinese girl at least once. In this one Young marries Edward G. Robinson, the hatchet man who has honorably killed her father. She has an affair with another man and Robinson sends her away. Later he finds that her lover has her in almost total bondage, so he gets out his trusty hatchet, cuts up the villain, and takes Young back again.

Eve / ZOO IN BUDAPEST, 1933, Fox Films, d-Rowland V. Lee.

This long-lost "classic" has Young as an orphan reaching the age when she will be bound out as an apprentice and will have to work years before attaining legal adulthood and can call her life her own. She plans to make a break for freedom when the orphanage takes its weekly outing to the Budapest zoo. An animal handler at the zoo (Gene Raymond) who is always in trouble because of his love of animals, helps the girl hide. The two suffer a series of ordeals, but by the end of the picture they have fallen in love and they seem to have a future when he obtains a position as a trainer and gamekeeper on an estate.

Trinia / A MAN'S CASTLE, 1933, Columbia, d-Frank Borzage.

Young is a starving but beautiful waif whom out-of-work Spencer Tracy takes to live in his hovel in a Depression shantytown on the banks of New York's East River. They become lovers but he has a chance to get out when a showgirl offers to keep him. When he finds that Young is going to have a baby, he takes her and leaves the camp to look for a better place to live.

Julie Rothschild / THE HOUSE OF ROTHSCHILD, 1934, Fox Films, d-Alfred Werker.

George Arliss is the star of this marvelous biopic of the European Jewish banking family, and Young, looking as lovely as anyone ever seen on screen, is his daughter. She and Robert Young provide the required secondary romantic story usually found in Arliss's later films.

Claire Blake / CALL OF THE WILD, 1935, 20th Century-Fox, d-William A. Wellman.

While Jack London's story is mostly about the dog Buck, the producers here stress the romance of Young and Clark Gable, which many gossips insist was not limited to in front of the cameras. In the movie Young, believing she is a widow, falls in love with Yukon prospector Gable, but surprise, surprise, her hubby is alive and well, at least temporarily.

Berengaria, Princess of Navarre / THE CRUSADES, 1935, Paramount, d-Cecil B. DeMille.

In what is probably DeMille's least appreciated epic, Young has a romance with Richard the Lion-Hearted (Henry Wilcoxon) during the Third Crusade. DeMille had said that Young's part called for the acting ability of Helen Hayes and the vivacity of Miriam Hopkins, which didn't exactly describe Young, but at least she was more animated than the wooden Wilcoxon.

Ramona / RAMONA, 1936, 20th Century-Fox, d-Henry King.

In the first 20th Century-Fox film in full Technicolor, Young portrays a beautiful half-breed who is brought up by a wealthy family. The son of the house (Kent Taylor) falls in love with her, but his parents won't hear of a mixed marriage. She marries Indian Don Ameche who provides her with happiness before tragedy befalls their union.

Laura Ridgeway / CAFE METROPOLE, 1937, 20th Century-Fox, d-Edward H. Griffith.

Young, a wealthy princess in Paris, is courted by Tyrone Power, who is under orders from Adolphe Menjou, to whom Power is deeply in debt. The idea is that Power will marry Young and Menjou will gain control of her fortune. True love conquers all, of course.

Ina Lewis / WIFE, DOCTOR AND NURSE, 1937, 20th Century-Fox, d-Walter Lang.

Young is a social butterfly in this entertaining piece of fluff. Both Young and Virginia Bruce, her Park Avenue physician-husband's nurse, love the doctor (Warner Baxter). When Young objects to Bruce, Baxter sends her packing, but he has become so dependent on her that his work suffers and he also neglects Young. The only solution is to bring Bruce back and make the best of the triangle.

Pamela Charters / THREE BLIND MICE, 1938, 20th Century-Fox, d-William A. Seiter.

Three sisters (Young, Pauline Moore, and Marjorie Weaver) arrive in California from Kansas, out to land rich husbands. Young poses as a rich socialite with her sisters pretending to be part of her staff—the idea is to take care of the oldest first. Their prey (Joel McCrea) isn't rich like they think, but when all is said and done he's the one that Young loves.

Doris Borland / WIFE, HUSBAND AND FRIEND, 1939, 20th Century-Fox, d-Gregory Ratoff.

Young, married to businessman Warner Baxter, has dreams of becoming a great singer while Baxter is encouraged to try his hand at opera by professional singer Binnie Barnes. She flops when she appears on stage and he makes a fool of himself, so they decide to reclaim their amateur status.

Nancy Troy / A NIGHT TO REMEMBER, 1942, Columbia, d-Richard Wallace.

This is a sparkling, zany comedy featuring a mystery writer (Brian Aherne) and his wife (Young) who work together to solve a murder in Greenwich Village.

Katrin Holstrom / THE FARMER'S DAUGHTER, 1947, RKO, d-H. C. Potter.

Young's portrayal of a girl of Scandinavian extract who takes a domestic position in the home of congressman Joseph Cotten and his politically powerful mother (Ethel Barrymore) won her an Oscar. She's a bright, enterprising woman who finds herself running for office herself and winning—both the seat and Cotten.

Julia Brougham / THE BISHOP'S WIFE, 1947, Goldwyn / RKO, d-Henry Koster.

Ever since David Niven was made a bishop, he has neglected his wife (Young) in an effort to get rich old Gladys Cooper to put up the money for a cathedral. When Niven prays for help, an angel in the person of Cary Grant shows up and pays more attention to Young than he does to getting the cathedral built. When Niven wonders how he can fight an angel for the affection of his wife, he is well on his way to regaining his perspective and no longer needs an angel.

Wilma Tuttle / THE ACCUSED, 1949, Paramount, d-William Dieterle.

In this film noir, psychology professor Young is cleverly enticed by a student (Douglas Dick) to a remote beach where he tries to seduce her. When she resists, he becomes more ardent and, frightened, she strikes him with a steel bar, killing him. She then drags his body to the water's edge and draws water into his lungs by giving him reverse artificial respiration to make it appear that he drowned. She doesn't get away with it but she is acquitted on the grounds of self-defense.

Sister Margaret / COME TO THE STABLE, 1949, 20th Century-Fox, d-Henry Koster.

Young and Celeste Holm are French nuns who arrive in a Connecticut town called Bethlehem where they intend to establish a children's hospital. Their great faith that the Lord will provide doesn't stop them from prodding some locals into helping the cause and God's work.

OTHER ROLES

1919: *child on operating table* / THE ONLY WAY; *child* / SIRENS OF THE SEA. **1921:** *Arab child* / THE SON OF THE SHEIK. **1927:** *bit* / NAUGHTY BUT NICE; *Denise Laverne* / THE MAGNIFICENT FLIRT; *Simonetta* / LAUGH, CLOWN, LAUGH. **1928:** *bit* / HER WILD OAT; *the girl* / THE WHIP WOMAN; *Carol Watts* / THE HEAD MAN. **1929:** *Gladys Cosgrove* / THE GIRL IN THE GLASS CAGE; *Patricia Carlyle* / THE FORWARD PASS; *Irma* / THE SQUALL; *Muriel* / THE CARELESS AGE; *Patricia Mason Stratton* / FAST LIFE; *herself* / SHOW OF SHOWS. **1930:** *Ann Harper* / LOOSE ANKLES; *Margery Seaton* / THE MAN FROM BLANKLEY'S; *Marion Ferguson* / THE SECOND FLOOR MYSTERY; *Mary Brennan* / *Margaret Waring* / ROAD TO PARADISE; *Marsinah* / KISMET; *Phyllis Ericson* / THE TRUTH ABOUT YOUTH. **1931:** *Isobel Brandon* / BEAU IDEAL; *Rosalie Evantural* / THE RIGHT OF WAY; *Noreen McMann* / THREE GIRLS LOST; *Elaine Bumpstead* / TOO YOUNG TO MARRY; *Claire McIntyre* / BIG BUSINESS GIRL; *Larry O'Brien* / I LIKE YOUR NERVE; *Gallagher* / PLATINUM BLONDE; *Gloria Bannister* / THE RULING VOICE. **1932:** *Sue Riley* / TAXI; *Buster* / PLAY GIRL; *Lola Davis* / WEEK-END MARRIAGE; *Grace Sutton* / LIFE BEGINS; *Marion Cullen* / THEY CALL IT SIN. **1933:** *Madeline* / EMPLOYEES ENTRANCE; *Marcia Stanislavsky* / GRAND SLAM; *Peggy* / THE LIFE OF JIMMY DOLAN; *Mary Martin* / MIDNIGHT MARY; *Ruth* / HEROES FOR SALE; *Margot* / THE DEVIL'S IN LOVE; *Florence Denny* / SHE HAD TO SAY YES. **1934:** *Lola Field* / BULLDOG DRUMMOND STRIKES BACK; *Letty Strong* / BORN TO BE BAD; *Countess Wilma* / CARAVAN; *June Arden* / THE WHITE PARADE. **1935:** *Margaret Maskelyne* / CLIVE OF INDIA; *Barbara Howard* / SHANGHAI. **1936:** *Lady Helen Dearden* / THE UNGUARDED HOUR; *Ellen Neal* / PRIVATE NUMBER; *Susie Schmidt* / LADIES IN LOVE. **1937:** *Tony Gateson* / LOVE IS NEWS; *Myra Cooper* / LOVE UNDER FIRE; *Vicki McLish Benton* / SECOND HONEYMOON. **1938:** *Lynn Cherrington* / FOUR MEN AND A PRAYER; *Empress Eugenie de Montigo* / SUEZ; *Sally Goodwin* / KENTUCKY. **1939:** *Mrs. Bell* / THE STORY OF ALEXANDER GRAHAM BELL; *Anita Halstead* / ETERNALLY YOURS. **1940:** *June Cameron* / THE DOCTOR TAKES A WIFE; *Marianna Duval* / HE STAYED FOR BREAKFAST. **1941:** *Annie* / THE LADY FROM CHEYENNE; *Lina Varsavina* / THE MEN IN HER LIFE; *Jane Drake* / BEDTIME STORY; *cameo* / LAND OF LIBERTY. **1943:** *Carolyn Grant* / CHINA. **1944:** *Roberta Harper* / LADIES COURAGEOUS; *Emily Blair* / AND NOW TOMORROW. **1945:** *Cherry de Longpre* / ALONG CAME JONES. **1946:** *Mary Longstreet* / THE STRANGER; *Maggie Williams* / THE PERFECT MARRIAGE. **1948:** *Rachel Harvey* / RACHEL AND THE STRANGER. **1949:** *Abby Abbott* / MOTHER IS A FRESHMAN. **1950:** *Clarissa Standish* / KEY TO THE CITY. **1951:** *Ellen Jones* / CAUSE FOR ALARM; *Nora* / HALF ANGEL. **1952:** *Paula Rogers* / PAULA; *Christine Carroll* / BECAUSE OF YOU. **1953:** *Jane McAvoy* / IT HAPPENS EVERY THURSDAY.

YOUNG, ROBERT

(1907–)

Robert Young has had a long, successful, and generally undistinguished career. His greatest success was not on the big screen but rather on TV in "Father Knows Best," "The Window on Main Street," and "Marcus Welby, M.D." Young's screen roles were generally lighthearted and bland but not offensively so. He was always prepared for his scenes and brought both intelligence and enthusiasm to the many roles of amicable young men that he played. Quiet-spoken, hard-working, dark-haired, and genial, Young averaged six movies a year in the 1930s. Most of these have long been forgotten, but not all entertainment has to be timeless to be of value.

KEY ROLES

Ricardo / THE KID FROM SPAIN, 1932, Goldwyn / United Artists, d-Leo McCarey.

Young and Eddie Cantor are college roommates tossed out of school after being caught in the girls' dorm. Young is from Mexico and he invites Cantor home where the latter is mistaken for a famous bullfighter from Spain. This helps both Cantor and Young get the girls of their dreams.

Alec Brennan / TUGBOAT ANNIE, 1933, MGM, d-Mervyn LeRoy.
In this slapstick hokum, Young is the son of elderly waterfront couple Marie Dressler and Wallace Beery. They not only encourage Young's love for Maureen O'Sullivan, but help him with his ship too.

Captain Fitzroy / THE HOUSE OF ROTHSCHILD, 1934, Fox Films, d-Alfred Werker.
Young provides the romantic interest for George Arliss's daughter (Loretta Young) in this superb story about the rise of the banking house of Rothschild in Europe at the time of the Napoleonic wars.

Tony Milburn / REMEMBER LAST NIGHT? 1935, Universal, d-James Whale.
In this murder mystery farce, Young is among a group of hard-drinking socialites who, after a wild night, find themselves involved in a murder they can't remember. All in all the film boasts four murders and two suicides.

Peter Carlton / IT'S LOVE AGAIN, 1936, Great Britain, Gaumont, d-Victor Saville.
Moving over to England, Young plays a journalist who makes up stories for his paper so he may compete with rival Jessie Matthews. When he makes up a female tiger hunter from India, Matthews impersonates this fiction and then the fun is supposed to begin—but only barely.

Gene Anders / I MET HIM IN PARIS, 1937, Paramount, d-Wesley Ruggles.
Young, a secretly married playboy in Paris, takes up with Claudette Colbert who is kicking up her heels after dumping boring fiancé Lee Bowman. She's attracted to the sincere-acting Young but explodes when she learns of his marital status. After spending some hilarious moments with Young and fellow suitor Melvyn Douglas in Switzerland, she ends up with Douglas and sends Young on his way.

Langdon Towne / NORTHWEST PASSAGE, 1940, MGM, d-King Vidor.
When the family of Ruth Hussey blocks his wedding plans, artist Young joins an expedition against hostile Indians with Rogers' Rangers and nearly loses his life. But he is able to return to and marry Hussey.

Fritz Marlberg / THE MORTAL STORM, 1940, MGM, d-Frank Borzage.
In a rare casting against type, Young appears as a fanatic Nazi in this story about the tragedy visited on the home of a non-Aryan German professor. While Young and his brothers were once students and friends of the professor and his daughter (Margaret Sullavan), they are in the end partially responsible for the professor being sent to a concentration camp, and Sullavan's death as she tries to escape the country with anti-Nazi friend Jimmy Stewart.

Richard Blake / WESTERN UNION, 1941, 20th Century-Fox, d-Fritz Lang.
Young is a tenderfoot whose quickness with a gun almost gets him and others in trouble with Indians while laying cross-country cables for Western Union.

Harry Pulham / H. M. PULHAM, ESQ., 1941, MGM, d-King Vidor.
While writing his memoirs, successful Boston businessman Young reflects over the rather boring years of his life, fondly remembering only a brief love affair with Hedy Lamarr. She didn't want to live his type of life and he didn't have the nerve to buck his father (Charles Coburn) so he married Ruth Hussey, a socially acceptable girl. Now Lamarr comes back into his life, but they realize their affair has no future; they separate and he returns home to the waiting arms of understanding and forgiving Hussey.

David Naughton / CLAUDIA, 1943, 20th Century-Fox, d-Edmund Goulding.
Young is especially tolerant of his childlike bride (Dorothy McGuire) in this charming story of new marriage and the adjustments both parties must make. It's a pleasantly humorous little picture with the sentimentality well under control.

Oliver / THE ENCHANTED COTTAGE, 1945, RKO, d-John Cromwell.
In this touching film, Young is an embittered, disfigured World War I veteran who breaks his engagement with his fiancée and marries exceedingly plain Dorothy McGuire. They move into a small cottage on his estate and the only person they will see is blind Herbert Marshall who is able to explain the miracle they undergo. Slowly, as they live together, Young's scars disappear and McGuire appears beautiful. When relatives come to see them, they make it painfully clear that the couple's ugliness has not left them. But once alone in their home, they are again transformed into a handsome couple.

Captain Finlay / CROSSFIRE, 1947, RKO, d-Edward Dmytryk.
Young portrays the clever police captain who discovers which of several soldiers killed Sam Levene solely because he was Jewish. All of the performances are first-rate in this film and Young proves he can handle some heat.

Harry / SITTING PRETTY, 1948, 20th Century-Fox, d-Walter Lang.
Young takes most of the verbal abuse from Clifton Webb when he and his wife (Maureen O'Hara) hire the self-proclaimed genius to become a live-in babysitter for their three uncontrollable kids. When O'Hara notes that her husband is modest about his accomplishments, Webb assures her, "Your husband has a great deal to be modest about."

OTHER ROLES

1931: *Jimmy Bradshaw* / BLACK CAMEL; *Dr. Jacques Claudet* / THE SIN OF MADELON CLAUDET; *Young Marco* / THE GUILTY GENERATION; *young officer* / HELL DIVERS. **1932:** *Kip Tarleton* / THE WET PARADE; *Gordon* / STRANGE INTERLUDE; *Ralph Thomas* / NEW MORALS FOR OLD; *Dick Ogden* / UNASHAMED. **1933:** *Claude* / TODAY WE LIVE; *Lt. Brick Walters* / HELL BELOW; *Geoffrey* / MEN MUST FIGHT; *Jim Fowler* / SATURDAY'S MILLIONS; *Bob Preble* / RIGHT TO ROMANCE. **1934:** *Will Connelly* / CAROLINA; *Bill Drexel* / LAZY RIVER; *John Stafford* / SPITFIRE; *Jack Forrester* / WHOM THE GODS DESTROY; *Pat Wells* / PARIS INTERLUDE; *Larry Kelly* / DEATH ON THE DIAMOND; *Tony Ferrera* / THE BAND PLAYS ON. **1935:** *Little Mike* / WEST POINT OF THE AIR; *Tony Spear* / VAGABOND LADY; *Pat* / CALM YOURSELF; *Jeff* / RED SALUTE; *Jack Bristow* / THE BRIDE COMES HOME. **1936:** *Charley Phelps* / THE LONGEST NIGHT; *Robert Marvin* / SECRET AGENT; *Joe Hatcher* / THE THREE WISE GUYS; *Hank Sherman* / SWORN ENEMY; *Hugh MacKenzie* / THE BRIDE WALKS OUT; *Tommy Randall* / STOWAWAY. **1937:** *Hank Medhill* / DANGEROUS NUMBER; *Grand Duke Peter* / THE EMPEROR'S CANDLESTICKS; *Tom Wakerfield* / MARRIED BEFORE BREAKFAST; *Rudi Pal* / THE BRIDE WORE RED; *Roger Ash* / NAVY BLUE AND GOLD. **1938:** *Fritz Hagedorn* / PARADISE FOR THREE; *Pierre Brossard* / JOSETTE; *Andre Vallane* / THE TOY WIFE; *Gottfried Lenz* / THREE COMRADES; *Bill Harrison* / RICH

MAN, POOR GIRL; *David Linden* / THE SHINING HOUR. **1939:** *George Smith* / *Joe Duffy* / HONOLULU; *Neil McGill* / BRIDAL SUITE; *Slim Martin* / MAISIE; *Michael Morgan* / MIRACLES FOR SALE. **1940:** *Anton* / FLORIAN; *Myles Vanders* / SPORTING BLOOD; *Douglas Lamont* / DR. KILDARE'S CRISIS. **1941:** *Jimmy Blake* / THE TRIAL OF MARY DUGAN; *Eddie Crane* / LADY BE GOOD; *Randolph Haven* / MARRIED BACHELOR. **1942:** *Joe Smith* / JOE SMITH, AMERICAN; *Homer Smith* / CAIRO; *John Davis* / JOURNEY FOR MARGARET. **1943:** *Bob Stuart* / SLIGHTLY DANGEROUS; *Sam Mackeever* / SWEET ROSIE O'GRADY. **1944:** *Cuffy Williams* / THE CANTERVILLE GHOST. **1945:** *Hank* / THOSE ENDEARING YOUNG CHARMS. **1946:** *Alex Hazen* / THE SEARCHING WIND; *Scott* / LADY LUCK; *David Naughton* / CLAUDIA AND DAVID. **1947:** *Larry Ballentine* / THEY WON'T BELIEVE ME. **1948:** *Nick Buckley* / RELENTLESS. **1949:** *Dr. Sheldon* / ADVENTURE IN BALTIMORE; *Steve Adams* / BRIDE FOR SALE. **1950:** *Philip Bosinney* / THAT FORSYTE WOMAN; *Vernon Walsh* / AND BABY MAKES THREE. **1951:** *James Merrill* / GOODBYE, MY FANCY; *Jeff Cohalan* / THE SECOND WOMAN. **1952:** *Dan Craig* / THE HALF-BREED. **1954:** *Stanley Moorehead* / SECRET OF THE INCAS.

Robert Anthony Nowlan, Jr., is a professor of mathematics at Southern Connecticut State University. Gwendolyn Wright Nowlan is the chairperson and professor of the School of Library Science and Instructional Technology at Southern Connecticut State University. Other books written by the Nowlans include *An Encyclopedia of Film Festivals* (JAI Press, 1988), *Cinema Sequels and Remakes* (McFarland, 1989), and *A Dictionary of Motion Picture Title Characters* (Neal-Schuman, 1990).